SECOND EDITION

Probation, Parole, and Community Corrections

DEAN J. CHAMPION

Minot State University

PRENTICE HALL
UPPER SADDLE RIVER, NEW JERSEY 07458

Library of Congress Cataloging-in-Publication Data

Champion, Dean J.
　　Probation, parole, and community corrections / Dean J. Champion. —
　　2nd ed.
　　　　p.　cm.
　　Rev. ed. of: Probation and parole in the United States. c1990.
　　Includes bibliographical references and index.
　　ISBN 0-02-320592-X
　　1. Probation—United States.　　2. Parole—United States.
　I. Champion, Dean J.　Probation and parole in the United States.
　II. Title
　　HV9304.C463　1996
　　364.6′3—dc20
　　　　　　　　　　　　　　　　　　　95-42246
　　　　　　　　　　　　　　　　　　　CIP

Acquisitions editor: Robin Baliszewski
Editorial assistant: Rose Mary Florio
Editorial/production supervision: Linda Pawelchak
Cover design: Wendy Alling Judy
Manufacturing buyer: Ed O'Dougherty

For Frank and Erma Champion

 © 1996, 1990 by Prentice-Hall, Inc.
Simon & Schuster/A Viacom Company
Upper Saddle River, New Jersey 07458

Previously published as *Probation and Parole in the United States*

Printed in the United States of America
10　9　8　7　6　5　4　3　2　1

ISBN 0-02-320592-X

Prentice-Hall International (UK) Limited, *London*
Prentice-Hall of Australia Pty. Limited, *Sydney*
Prentice-Hall Canada Inc., *Toronto*
Prentice-Hall Hispanoamericana, S.A., *Mexico*
Prentice-Hall of India Private Limited, *New Delhi*
Prentice-Hall of Japan, Inc., *Tokyo*
Simon & Schuster Asia Pte. Ltd., *Singapore*
Editora Prentice-Hall do Brasil, Ltda., *Rio de Janeiro*

Contents

Preface   xv

PART I
PROBATION: ORIGINS, FUNCTIONS, AND CONTEMPORARY DEVELOPMENTS

1
The Criminal Justice System: Components, Offenders, Programs, and Issues   1

Introduction   1

The game of Monopoly and crime.   Chapter objectives.

An Overview of the Criminal Justice System   4

Types of Offenses   7

Misdemeanors and felonies.   Violent and property crimes.   The Uniform Crime Reports *and the* National Crime Survey.

Classifying Offenders   10

> *Traditional offender categorizations.*

Criminal Justice System Components: Locating Probation, Parole, and Community Corrections   12

> *Law enforcement.   Prosecutorial decision making. Courts and judges.   Corrections.*

The Sentencing Process: Types of Sentencing and Sentencing Issues   20

> *Functions of sentencing.   Types of sentencing.   Sentencing issues.*

Key Terms.   Questions for Review.

2

Probation and Probationers: History, Philosophy, Goals, and Functions   30

Introduction   30

Probation Defined   32

Probation Distinguished from Parole   33

The History of Probation in the United States   33

> *Judicial reprieves and releases on an offender's recognizance.   John Augustus, the father of probation in the United States.   The ideal-real dilemma: Philosophies in conflict.   Public reaction to probation.*

The Philosophy of Probation   38

Models for Dealing with Criminal Offenders   42

> *The treatment or medical model.   The rehabilitation model.   The justice or due process model.   The "just-deserts" model.   The community model.*

Functions of Probation   48

> *Crime control.   Community reintegration.   Rehabilitation.   Punishment. Deterrence.*

A Profile of Probationers   52

First-Offenders and Recidivists   60

Probation Trends   61

Key Terms.   Questions for Review.

3

The Presentence Investigation Report: Background, Preparation, and Functions   65

Introduction   65

The Role of Probation Officers in Sentencing   66

Presentence Investigation (PSI)   68

The confidentiality of PSIs.   The preparation of PSIs.   Functions and uses of PSIs.   The defendant's sentencing memorandum.   The inclusion of victim impact statements.   Privatizing PSI preparation.   PSIs and presumptive sentencing systems.

The Sentencing Hearing   77

Aggravating and Mitigating Circumstances   78

Aggravating circumstances.   Mitigating circumstances.

Changing Responsibilities of Probation Officers Resulting from Sentencing Reforms   79

Probation and Public Risk: Predicting Dangerousness   81

Assessing offender risk: A brief history.   Classification and its functions.   Types of risk-assessment instruments.   False positives and false negatives.   The effectiveness of risk-assessment devices.   Some applications of risk/needs measures.   Selective incapacitation.

The Probation Decision and Sentencing Trends   96

Key Terms.   Questions for Review.

4

Diversion and Probation Options: From Alternative Dispute Resolution to Boot Camps and Shock Probation   113

Introduction   113

Civil Mechanisms in Lieu of Diversion and Probation   115

Alternative dispute resolution.   Victim-offender reconciliation projects.

Pretrial Diversion   118

Unconditional and conditional diversion.   The history and philosophy of diversion.   Functions of diversion.   Factors influencing pretrial diversion.   Criticisms of diversion.

Standard Probation   124

Intensive Supervised Probation (ISP)   126

The Georgia Intensive Supervised Probation program.   The New Jersey Intensive Supervised Probation program.   The Idaho Intensive Supervised Probation program.   The South Carolina Intensive Supervised Probation program.   Criticisms of the Georgia, New Jersey, Idaho, and South Carolina ISP programs.

Shock Probation and Split Sentencing   138

Split sentencing distinguished from shock probation.   The philosophy and objectives of shock probation.   The effectiveness of shock probation.

Boot Camps   142

Boot camp defined.   Goals of boot camps.   A profile of boot camp clientele. Boot camp programs.   Jail boot camps.   The effectiveness of boot camps. Boot camp costs compared with traditional incarceration.

Key Terms.   Questions for Review.

PART II
PAROLE: ORIGINS, FUNCTIONS, AND CONTEMPORARY DEVELOPMENTS

5
Jails and Prisons: Inmate Profiles and Contemporary Issues   155

Introduction   155

Jails and Jail Characteristics   156

Workhouses.   The Walnut Street Jail.   Subsequent jail developments. The number of jails in the United States.

The Functions of Jails   161

A Profile of Jail Inmates   164

Prisons and Prison Characteristics   169

The Functions of Prisons   173

Inmate Classification Systems   174

A Profile of Prisoners in U.S. Prisons   178

Some Jail and Prison Contrasts   181

Selected Jail and Prison Issues   182

Jail and prison overcrowding.   Violence and inmate discipline.   Jail and prison design and control.   Vocational-technical and educational programs in jails and prisons.   Jail and prison privatization.

The Role of Jails and Prisons in Probation and Parole
Decision Making   191

Key Terms.   Questions for Review.

6

Parole and Parolees: History, Philosophy, Goals, and Functions   196

Introduction   196

Parole Defined   197

The Historical Context of Parole   197

Parole and Alternative Sentencing Systems   200

Indeterminate sentencing and parole.   Pros and cons of indeterminate sentencing in relation to parole.   The shift to determinate sentencing.

The Philosophy of Parole   209

The Functions of Parole   209

Offender reintegration.   Crime deterrence and control.   Decreasing prison and jail overcrowding.   Compensating for sentencing disparities.   Public safety and protection.

A Profile of Parolees in the United States   213

Parole Trends   220

Key Terms.   Questions for Review.

7

Judges and Parole Boards: Probation and Parole Revocation Actions   228

Introduction   228

Judicial Discretion in Granting Probation   231

Parole Boards and Early-Release Decision Making   232

Parole board composition and diversity.   Functions of parole boards. Parole board decision making and inmate control.   Parole board orientations. Developing and implementing objective parole criteria.   Salient factor scores.

Types of Parole and an Overview of Parole Programs   257

Prerelease.   Standard parole with conditions.   Intensive supervised parole.

Furloughs.   Work release and study release.   Shock probation and shock parole.   Halfway houses.

Probation and Parole Revocation: Some Common Elements
and Landmark Cases   260

Mempa v. Rhay (1967).   Morrissey v. Brewer (1972).   Gagnon v. Scarpelli (1973).   Bearden v. Georgia (1983).   Black v. Romano (1985).

Cataloging the Rights of Probationers and Parolees   266

Probationer and parolee rights generally.

Key Terms.   Questions for Review.

PART III
COMMUNITY CORRECTIONS:
CREATIVE ALTERNATIVES TO INCARCERATION

8

An Overview of Community Corrections: Types, Goals, and Functions   275

Introduction   275

What Is Community Corrections?   277

The Community Corrections Act   278

The Philosophy of Community Corrections   279

The History of Community Corrections   282

Characteristics of Community Corrections Programs   283

Goals of Community Corrections   283

Facilitating offender reintegration.   Fostering offender rehabilitation. Providing an alternative range of offender punishments.   Heightening offender accountability.

Functions of Community Corrections   286

Client monitoring and supervision to ensure program compliance.   Ensuring public safety.   Employment assistance.   Individual and group counseling. Educational training and literacy services.   Networking with other community agencies and businesses.   Reducing jail and prison overcrowding.

Selected Issues in Community Corrections   293

Public resistance to locating community programs in communities (The NIMBY Syndrome: "Not in my back yard").   Punishment versus rehabilitation

*and reintegration.   Offender needs and public safety.   Net widening.
Privatization.   Services delivery.   Education and training of staff.
Coping with special needs offenders.*

Key Terms.   Questions for Review.

9

Home Confinement and Electronic Monitoring   306

Introduction   307

About Intermediate Punishments   308

Home Confinement Programs   309

Home confinement defined.   The early uses of home confinement.

The Goals of Home Confinement Programs   314

A Profile of Home Confinement Clients   315

Selected Issues in Home Confinement   316

*Home confinement may not be much of a punishment.   The constitutionality
of home confinement.   Public safety versus offender needs for community
reintegration.   Home confinement may not be much of a crime deterrent.*

Electronic Monitoring   320

Early Uses of Electronic Monitoring   320

Types of Electronic Monitoring Systems   321

*Continuous signaling devices.   Programmed contact devices.   Cellular
telephone devices.   Continuous signaling transmitters.*

Electronic Monitoring with Home Confinement   322

A Profile of Electronic Monitoring Clients   327

Selected Issues in Electronic Monitoring   329

*The ethics of electronic monitoring.   The constitutionality of electronic
monitoring and client rights.   Punishment versus rehabilitation
and reintegration.   The public safety issue.   The deterrence issue.
Privatization. Net widening.*

The Future of Home Confinement and Electronic Monitoring   336

Key Terms.   Questions for Review.

10

Work or Study Release and Furlough Programs   338

Introduction   338

Prerelease Programs   340

Work Release   340

*The goals of work release programs.   The functions of work release.
A profile of work releasees.   Determining inmate eligibility for work release
programs.   Weaknesses and strengths of work release programs.*

Study Release Programs   350

*Determining inmate eligibility for study release.   Advantages and disadvantages
of study release programs.*

Furlough Programs   352

*The goals of furlough programs.   The functions of furlough programs.
Determining inmate eligibility for furlough program involvement.
Weaknesses and strengths of furlough programs.*

Preparole Release Programs and Day Reporting Centers   357

Key Terms.   Questions for Review.

11

Halfway Houses and Community Residential Centers   361

Introduction   361

Halfway Houses   362

*The philosophy and characteristics of halfway houses. The functions of halfway
houses.   A profile of halfway house clients. Weaknesses and strengths of halfway
house programs.*

Community Residential Centers and Day Reporting/Treatment Programs   376

*Community residential centers.   The philosophy and goals of community
residential centers.   Day reporting centers.*

Other Programs and Sanctions   378

*Fines.   Day fines.   Community service orders and options.   Forms of
community service and restitution.   The effectiveness of community service and
restitution.   Restitution programs.*

Key Terms.   Questions for Review.

PART IV
PERSONNEL AND CLIENTS

12

Probation and Parole Officer Training, Retention, and Caseloads: Rewards and Hazards of PO Work 389

Introduction 389

Probation, Parole, and Corrections Officers: A Distinction 390

The Organization and Operation of Probation and Parole Programs 391

Selected criticisms of probation and parole programs. Probation and parole officers: A profile.

Selection Requirements, Education, and Training for POs 403

Recruiting women and minorities. Assessment centers and staff effectiveness. The Florida Assessment Center. The use of firearms in probation and parole work. Establishing negligence in training, job performance, and retention.

Probation and Parole Officer Caseloads 437

Ideal caseloads. Changing caseloads and officer effectiveness. Caseload assignment and management models.

Officer-Client Interactions 442

The Changing Probation and Parole Officer Role 444

Probation and Parole Officer Labor Turnover 445

Stress and Burnout in Probation and Parole Officer Role Performance 446

Stress. Burnout. Sources of stress. Mitigating factors that alleviate stress and burnout.

Key Terms. Questions for Review.

13

Utilizing Volunteers and Paraprofessionals in Intermediate Punishment Programs 460

Introduction 460

The Role of Volunteers in Corrections 461

Criticisms of Volunteers in Correctional Work 468

On the ethics of using volunteers. Economic considerations versus inadequate training. The legal liabilities of volunteers and agencies using them.

Paraprofessionals in Community Corrections   475

The education and training of paraprofessionals.   The roles of paraprofessionals.   Legal liabilities of paraprofessionals.

Key Terms.   Questions for Review.

14

Supervising Women and Special Needs Offenders: Officer-Client Interactions   483

Introduction   483

Female Probationers and Parolees: A Profile   484

Special Programs and Services for Female Offenders   486

Other Special Needs Offenders   496

Drug- and alcohol-dependent offenders.   Mentally ill offenders.   Sex offenders and child sexual abusers.   Offenders with physical handicaps and disabilities. AIDS: A growing problem in probation, parole, and community corrections.

Community Programs for Special Needs Offenders   503

Networking among agencies to maximize services delivery.   Individualizing offender needs.   Domestic violence prevention programs.   Supervising dangerous offenders.   Parent education and early childhood intervention services.

Key Terms.   Questions for Review.

15

Probation and Parole in the Juvenile Justice System   510

Introduction   510

Juveniles and Juvenile Delinquency   511

Delinquency and juvenile delinquents.   Status offenders.

An Overview of the Juvenile Justice System   513

The origins and purposes of juvenile courts.   Major differences between criminal and juvenile courts.   Parens Patriae.   Arrests and other options.   Intake screenings and detention hearings.   Petitions and adjudicatory proceedings. Transfers, waivers, and certifications.

Juvenile Rights   524

Landmark cases in juvenile justice.

Offense Seriousness and Dispositions: Aggravating and Mitigating Factors   528

Judicial dispositional options.   Nominal and conditional sanctions.   Custodial sanctions.   Nonsecure facilities.   Secure facilities.

Juvenile POs and Predispositional Reports 535

Juvenile Probation and Parole Programs 536

Unconditional and conditional probation. Intensive Supervised Probation (ISP) programs. The Ohio experience. The Allegheny Academy. Boston Offender Project (BOP). Other juvenile probation and parole programs.

Revoking Juvenile Probation and Parole 548

Recidivism and probation or parole revocation. Juvenile case law on probation revocations. Juvenile case law on parole revocations.

Key Terms. Questions for Review.

16

Evaluating Programs: Balancing Service Delivery and Recidivism Considerations 558

Introduction 558

Program Evaluation: How Do We Know Programs Are Effective? 559
Some recommended outcome measures.

Balancing Program Objectives and Offender Needs 565

Recidivism Defined 568

Rearrests. Reconvictions. Revocations of parole or probation. Reincarcerations. Technical program violations.

Recidivist Offenders and Their Characteristics 578

Avertable and nonavertable recidivists. Public policy and recidivism.

Probationers, Parolees, and Recidivism 581

Probationers and parolees compared. Prison versus probation. Curbing recidivism.

A View from Probationers and Parolees 585

Key Terms. Questions for Review.

Glossary 589

Bibliography 619

Cases Cited 662

Author Index 665

Subject Index 678

Preface

Probation, Parole, and Community Corrections is about adults and juveniles who have been convicted of criminal offenses or adjudicated as delinquent and punished. Judges may sentence offenders to incarceration in prison or jail for a definite period or they may suspend the sentence, subject to the offender's compliance with certain conditions. Judges may also sentence offenders to incarceration for a fixed period of years, but offenders may serve only a portion of that time. Parole boards, the court, or others may authorize the early release of offenders, again subject to certain conditions.

Some adult and juvenile offenders are permitted by the courts to remain free in their communities, provided that they comply with the imposed rules and regulations. Other offenders are granted early release from incarceration under similar provisions. These offenders will be supervised by officers and agencies as provided by law. This book is also about the agencies and personnel who monitor these offenders.

Besides describing probation and parole programs, various classes of offenders are portrayed. Additionally, several problems associated with the selection and training of probation and parole officers are highlighted, including their relationships with offender-clients.

Juvenile offenders pose special problems for those assigned to supervise them. A profile of juvenile offenders is presented, together with a discussion of several controversial issues associated with processing juveniles. The juvenile justice system is gradually acquiring several characteristics that are minimizing its distinctiveness from the criminal justice system. Larger numbers of juveniles are being processed as adult offenders, either through statutes or recommendations from prosecutors and juvenile judges. Since 1966, juveniles have been granted certain constitutional rights equivalent to those of adult offenders. Some of these rights are described, as well as the influence of these rights on juvenile probation and parole programs.

One premise of this book is that all components of the criminal juvenile justice systems are interrelated to varying degrees. While experts contend that these systems are better described as loosely related processes, each component has an impact on each of the other components. Police discretion influences the disposition of adult and juvenile offenders. In turn, the courts influence police discretion and affect prisons and jails through particular sentencing practices. Prison and jail problems such as overcrowding often overburden probation and parole officers with excessive offender caseloads. Varying offender caseloads influence the quality of officer-offender interaction and the ultimate effectiveness of probation and parole programs. Ineffective probation and parole programs may increase the number of repeat offenders who come to the attention of police when they commit new crimes. Thus, probation and parole programs do not exist in a vacuum, unaffected by other agencies and organizations.

Probation and parole policy decisions are sometimes politically motivated. However, economic considerations and limited human resources also play important parts in shaping correctional priorities. The influence of political and economic considerations on probation and parole programs as well as officer effectiveness is discussed.

Some of the pedagogical features of this book include highlighted key terms, a comprehensive glossary, and questions at the end of chapters to emphasize important points. Throughout the book, there are boxes that contain interesting vignettes taken from case law about probation and parole and various community corrections programs. These boxes are intended to supplement text material by providing examples of actual cases or situations and how they were resolved. Finally, a comprehensive bibliography is included to assist those interested in doing research in one or more areas of probation and parole.

The author wishes to acknowledge the following reviewers whose constructive criticisms increased the book's value as a teaching tool and resource: JoAnne M. Lecci, Nassau Community College; and Lois Wims, Salve Regina University.

PART I

Probation: Origins, Functions, and Contemporary Developments

1

The Criminal Justice System
Components, Offenders, Programs, and Issues

Introduction
An Overview of the Criminal Justice System
Types of Offenses
Classifying Offenders
Criminal Justice System Components:
  Locating Probation, Parole,
  and Community Corrections

The Sentencing Process:
  Types of Sentencing
  and Sentencing Issues
Key Terms
Questions for Review

INTRODUCTION

Some people don't get the point!

- Kriner (*Kriner v. State*, 1990) was convicted in an Alaska court for writing bad checks totalling $27,000. The court suspended imposition of the sentence and, because Kriner had no prior criminal record, placed him on probation. Two years later, while Kriner was still on probation, he was convicted of embezzling $4,000 from a charitable organization for which he worked. He was sentenced to a consecutive two-year term, of which one year was suspended. He was placed on probation again, with the special condition that he could not have a checking account or access to one. However, it was learned about a year later that he *had* a checking account and had recently written at least two *bad* checks. His probation was revoked and he was sentenced to 18 months in prison. He appealed, arguing that his sentence was "excessive."

- Lanford (*Lanford v. State*, 1990) was convicted in an Arkansas court for possessing a controlled substance and was sentenced to probation for five years. About two years later, Lanford was charged with selling cocaine and confined in the county jail. While there, he filed a lawsuit in federal court alleging unconstitutional conditions at the county jail. His defense attorney and the prosecutor worked out a deal whereby Lanford would plead guilty to cocaine possession, accept a five-year incarcerative term, and drop his lawsuit against the county pending in federal court. The presiding judge generally approved but added that he believed Lanford should serve a probationary term following his five-year imprisonment. Lanford expressed some reluctance over this judicial opinion, at which point the judge decided to impose his own sentence on Lanford of 20 years in the Arkansas Department of Corrections to run consecutively with any other sentence rendered at the time of sentencing. Lanford appealed, contending that the 20-year sentence was "excessive."

- Turner (*Turner v. U.S. Parole Commission*, 1991) was paroled from a 15-year sentence in 1983. While on parole, he was supposed to obey the law and report any subsequent arrests to his parole officer. Technically, reports of new arrests must be reported within two days following those arrests. During the term of his parole, Turner allegedly committed a new crime and was arrested by state police. Turner failed to report the new arrest to his probation officer. Despite this technical violation, the U.S. Parole Commission reinstated him in his parole program. Subsequently, Turner was convicted in the state court for the new crime. This time, the U.S. Parole Commission revoked Turner's parole for cause and a detainer warrant was issued in order to return him to federal prison to serve the remainder of his 15-year sentence. Turner appealed, filing a *habeas corpus* petition for relief and alleging that his new sentence was "excessive."

- Williams (*United States v. Williams*, 1990) was convicted of shoplifting from a federal post exchange and sentenced to an incarcerative term of 10 months, followed by a one-year term of supervised release. The supervised release period contained conditions, including submission to urinalysis testing and participation in a drug treatment and rehabilitation program. Subsequently, her supervised release was revoked because of her illegal use of a controlled substance, failure to report to her probation officer for urinalysis, and failure to participate in a drug treatment program. A U.S. magistrate revoked her supervised release and sentenced her to a one-year term of imprisonment, with no credit for time served while on supervised release. Williams appealed, contending among other things that the one-year term was "excessive."

The point is that probation and parole are, respectively, conditional sentences and releases from incarceration, either immediately following conviction for a crime or after a period of incarceration in a prison or jail. The conditions imposed have to do with behavioral requirements and involve agreements between the state and probationers and parolees that are based on mutual trust. The reward for probationers and parolees is freedom, limited or completely unrestricted. The penalties for violating this trust are more restricted freedom or complete loss of it. This book is about all types of programs involving convicted offenders and the various conditions of supervised release such programs involve. These programs are most often operated within the community and are designed to monitor offender behaviors more or less intensely. They are broadly labeled probation, parole, intermediate punishments, or community corrections.

The Game of Monopoly and Crime

In the game of *Monopoly,* players compete to acquire property and force their opponents into bankruptcy. Different cards and squares entitle players to certain advantages and rewards, such as bonuses or dividends. Other cards and spaces specify punishments, including fines and taxes. One card says "Go to Jail. Go Directly to Jail. Do Not Pass 'Go.' Do Not Collect $200." Players drawing that card have to go to a "Jail" square and stay there a period of time. Eventually, they get out of Jail and are allowed to continue to play the game. Players may draw another card that says "Get Out of Jail Free." They can save this card until they need it, if they happen to land in jail. This book is about people who commit crimes, get caught, and are punished. As in *Monopoly,* some people must serve some time in jail or prison. Others are fortunate enough to avoid confinement. Also, as in *Monopoly,* most of those who spend time in jail or prison are eventually released to continue their lives in communities.

The *Monopoly* analogy ends here. Crime is not a game for most people. Those who commit crimes risk getting caught and processed, to one degree or another, by the **criminal justice system**. This system consists of a complex network of agencies, bureaus, and organizations designed to process criminal offenders (Samaha, 1988:6). Those who have been arrested by police, charged with a criminal offense, prosecuted in court, found guilty, sentenced, and incarcerated in a jail or prison for a fixed period or allowed to remain free subject to several stringent behavioral conditions have been "processed" by the criminal justice system at all stages.

Chapter Objectives

This chapter provides an overview of the criminal justice system. Its general purpose is to locate probation and parole in relation to various components of this system. The first section of the chapter defines crime, distinguishes between several types of crime, and indicates different offense categories according to which offenders are classified. Two types of crime information sources are described, including the *Uniform Crime Reports* and the *National Crime Survey*. Additional material is presented depicting both traditional offender categorizations as well as selected special offender categories. These classifications include first-offenders and recidivists, drug/alcohol dependent offenders, offenders who are mentally and physically challenged, and those offenders with AIDS and other communicable diseases.

The next section of this chapter describes different components of the criminal justice system, including law enforcement, prosecutorial decision making, courts and court processing, sentencing, and corrections, and the interrelatedness of these components. When a crime is committed and someone is charged with committing it, the criminal justice system processes the offender through a series of established stages. The sentencing stage is crucial to convicted offenders.

Sentencing is a major concern of those who advocate justice reforms (Benekos, 1992; National Council on Crime and Delinquency, 1992). The federal government and most states have passed new sentencing legislation in response to criticisms that present sentencing practices are discriminatory according to gender, race or ethnic background, and/or socioeconomic status (*Corrections Compendium*, 1991b; Grimes, 1992; Johnson, 1992; McDonald and Carlson, 1992; Minnesota Sentencing Guidelines Commission, 1991; Sweeney and Haney, 1992; U.S. Sentencing Commission, 1991). Four different types of sentencing schemes are described, including indeterminate, determinate, presumptive or guidelines-based, and mandatory sentencing. Following this discussion are several important sentencing issues. The chapter concludes with a discussion of various forms of supervised release programs, including probation, parole, and community corrections. This discussion sets the stage for subsequent chapters that detail various aspects of supervised release programs, those who operate them, and the clientele served.

AN OVERVIEW OF THE CRIMINAL JUSTICE SYSTEM

The criminal justice system consists of the **law enforcement,** the **courts,** and **corrections.** The police serve the public by attempting to control crime and apprehend criminals. The courts determine a defendant's guilt or innocence and sentence convicted offenders. Corrections *punishes* or *rehabilitates* those who have been sentenced. In actual practice, however, events don't always turn out this way. The criminal justice system is seriously flawed in various respects.

Many criminals are never caught. Many of those criminals who are apprehended never go to trial. Some criminals who do go to trial are found innocent by judges or juries even though they are guilty. Not all criminals found guilty are incarcerated. And, criminals sentenced to imprisonment for "correction" and/or "rehabilitation" are not typically corrected or rehabilitated. Thus, in one way or another, all components of the criminal justice process are flawed to some degree.

This statement also applies to the programs described in this book: **probation, parole,** and **community corrections.**

Before presenting an in-depth discussion of probation, parole, and community corrections, it is important to understand where these programs fit into the criminal justice system. Figure 1.1 is a diagram of the criminal justice system. Entry into the criminal justice system begins with the commission of a crime, followed by the arrest of one or more suspected perpetrators of that crime. Assuming offenders have been identified and apprehended, their movement through the criminal justice system is similar for both the state and federal processing.

Alleged offenders are arrested, booked, and charged with one or more crimes. These crimes are either minor or major. Assuming a successful prosecution, offenders are found guilty and sentenced by judges. As illustrated in Figure 1.1, sentencing is coupled with corrections and leads to either probation or incarceration. Following the line in the diagram representing incarceration only for the felony category, one offender option after incarceration in a prison or penitentiary is parole.

This book describes what happens to offenders who are either sentenced to probation or paroled after serving a portion of their sentence in prison. In both instances, these offenders must comply with several restrictive conditions. Otherwise, their probation or parole may be revoked or canceled. This means that parolees may be returned to prison for some or all of the remainder of their original sentences. For probationers, this may mean incarceration for some or all of the originally prescribed sentence. Enforcing the conditions of probation and parole required of offenders are **probation** and **parole officers (POs).** Offenders are required to report to their POs regularly and to comply with other rules and regulations. Thus, a second major goal of this book is to describe the personnel and programs that manage probationers and parolees.

Following the juvenile offender path in Figure 1.1, the sentencing and corrections dispositions include warnings, probation, or commitment to either nonsecure or secure juvenile detention facilities. Releasing juveniles from any juvenile holding facility short of their original sentences may be equated with parole for adults and is called **aftercare.** Again, conditions are imposed that are associated with both probation and parole alternatives. Violations of these conditions may lead to revocation of probation or parole. The incarcerative penalties for juveniles who violate the conditions of their probation and aftercare are similar to procedures followed in adult cases in that juvenile offenders may have their parole revoked. However, juveniles are detained in special juvenile institutions. As with adults, juvenile probationers and parolees are assigned to POs who supervise them during the term of their probation or parole.

There is a significant omission in Figure 1.1. During the "prosecution and pretrial services" period, offenders (either adults or juveniles) may be diverted temporarily from the justice system by a recommendation from the prosecutor and with court approval. Offenders granted diversion are not prosecuted, brought to trial, sentenced, or incarcerated. Diversion of criminal defendants or juvenile offenders usually occurs prior to prosecution or adjudication. For all practical pur-

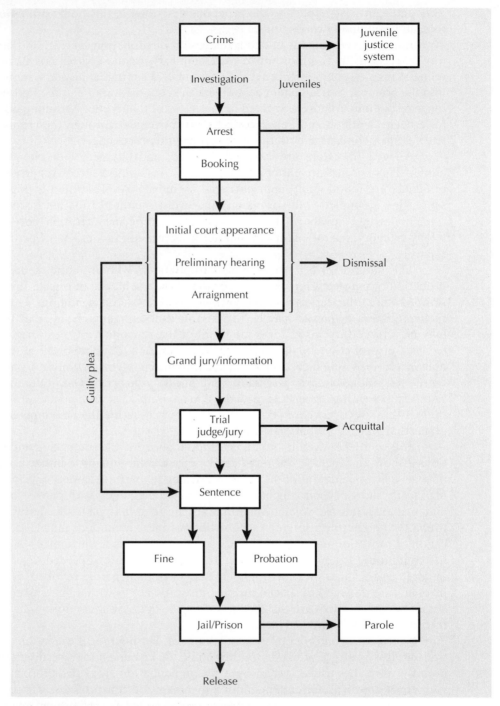

FIGURE 1.1 An overview of the criminal justice process.

poses, it is the equivalent of probation (Black, 1990:477). Like probation, diversion involves compliance with several conditions and restrictions for a fixed time period. The major difference between diversion and probation, however, is that upon successful completion of diversion, the offender's record (i.e., arrest record and other damaging information) may be expunged or the charges may be reduced to less serious ones. Another possible consequence is that the charges against the divertee may be dismissed.

Offenders granted diversion are usually supervised by POs. It is important to note that in some states, POs may have dual responsibilities in that they must supervise both probationers and parolees. In other states, however, sharp lines of responsibility are drawn—probation officers supervise only probationers while parole officers supervise only parolees. Thus, while the PO designation is used here to depict either probation or parole officers, jurisdictional differences may mandate separate or overlapping roles for these officers. There are other differences as well. In California, for example, probationers are supervised by county probation officers, while parolees from San Quentin and other state penal facilities are supervised by state parole officers through the Department of Corrections, Parole and Community Services Division (American Correctional Association, 1988:29). Thus, depending on the jurisdiction, POs may be assigned to (1) supervise adult probationers and/or parolees; (2) supervise juvenile probationers and/or parolees; (3) supervise offenders granted diversion; and (4) screen prospective probationers for the purpose of determining their degree of public risk or dangerousness. While these officers perform many other duties, their primary responsibility is the management of nonincarcerated offenders.

Corrections is the aggregate of programs, services, facilities, and organizations responsible for the management of people who have been accused or convicted of criminal offenses (Clear and Cole, 1986:537). This book focuses on the *nonincarcerative* dimension of corrections only. It does *not* describe the inner workings or subcultures of people-processing institutions such as jails or prisons, although parolees have been granted early release from these types of facilities.

TYPES OF OFFENSES

Crimes are violations of the law by people held accountable by the law. Two general categories of crime are misdemeanors and felonies.

Misdemeanors and Felonies

Crimes are divided into two general categories: (1) misdemeanors and (2) felonies.

Misdemeanors.   **Misdemeanors** are minor or petty offenses. These offenses carry less severe penalties compared with major crimes or felonies. Misdemeanor offenses may result in fines and/or incarceration for less than one year. **Misde-**

meanants are those who commit misdemeanors and usually spend their period of incarceration in a local jail. Examples of misdemeanors include making a false financial statement to obtain credit, engaging in prostitution, shoplifting, and trespassing.

Felonies.   **Felonies** are major crimes that carry more severe penalties. Usually, statutory penalties associated with felonies are fines and/or incarceration in a state or federal prison for one or more years. Felonies include arson, murder, rape, burglary, robbery, vehicular theft, and aggravated assault. Both misdemeanor and felony convictions create criminal records for offenders. In some jurisdictions, there is a third class of crimes known as **summary offenses.** These are petty crimes and ordinarily carry penalties of fines only. Also, convictions for these petty offenses will not result in a criminal record. Examples of summary offenses are speeding or dumping litter from an automobile on a public highway.

Each state has its own set of criminal statutes. Acts defined as crimes in one state may not be considered crimes in other states. Because of these interstate differences, it is sometimes difficult to apply standardized or umbella criteria suitable for defining misdemeanor and felony offenses applicable to all states at all times. Furthermore, felony offenders often enter guilty pleas to less serious felonies or even misdemeanors in exchange for leniency or some other prosecutorial concession (U.S. General Accounting Office, 1986). Thus, portrayals of serious crime in the United States will be flawed by this and other technical inaccuracies.

Violent and Property Crimes

A **violent crime** (crime of violence) is one characterized by extreme physical force, including murder or homicide, forcible rape, child sexual abuse, assault and battery by means of a dangerous weapon, robbery, and arson (Black, 1990:371). Sometimes these offenses are referred to as crimes of violence or **crimes against the person** because persons are directly involved as victims and are affected emotionally and physically as a result of the crime's commission. Nonviolent offenses include burglary, vehicular theft, embezzlement, fraud, forgery, and larceny. These are often referred to as **crimes against property**, and, although persons are indirectly victimized or affected by such offenses, their lives and physical well-being are not directly jeopardized by such acts. Two sources that report crime in the United States are the *Uniform Crime Reports (UCR)* and the *National Crime Survey*.

The Uniform Crime Reports and the National Crime Survey

The Uniform Crime Reports (UCR).   *The Uniform Crime Reports (UCR)* is published annually by the Federal Bureau of Investigation (FBI). This publication includes statistics about the number and kinds of crimes reported in the United

States annually by over 15,000 law enforcement agencies. The *UCR* is the major sourcebook of crime statistics in the United States. The *UCR* is compiled by gathering information on 29 types of crime from participating law enforcement agencies. Crime information is requested from all rural and urban law enforcement agencies and reported to the FBI. The FBI has established a **crime classification index. Index offenses** include eight serious types of crime used by the FBI to measure crime trends. Information is also compiled about 21 less serious offenses ranging from forgery and counterfeiting to curfew violations and runaways. Index offense information is presented in the *UCR* for each state, city, county, and township that has submitted crime information during the most recent year.

***Criticisms of the* UCR.**   Even though the *UCR* publishes the most current crime figures from reporting law enforcement agencies, many experts believe crime clocks are inaccurate in several respects. First, when criminals have been questioned about other crimes they have committed, the results show discrepancies between *UCR* figures and "self-report" information. In short, criminals escape detection or capture for many crimes they commit. Thus, it is generally accepted that there is more crime committed each year than official estimates such as the *UCR* disclose. Second, not all law enforcement agencies report crimes in a uniform manner. Third, police "crackdowns" in some jurisdictions may lead to numerous arrests, although there will be few resulting convictions. A fourth criticism is that not all law enforcement agencies report their crime figures on a consistent basis. A fifth criticism is that many crimes are committed that are never reported to the police. Sixth, when a crime report is submitted to the *UCR*, only the most serious offense is often reported. Generally, experts believe that the *UCR* is a gross underestimate of the amount of crime in the United States.

The* National Crime Survey (NCS).**   The limitations of the *UCR* and other official documents measuring the amount of crime have led some experts to draw comparisons between the *UCR* and the ***National Crime Survey (NCS), which is conducted annually in cooperation with the United States Bureau of the Census. The *NCS* is a random survey of approximately 60,000 dwellings, about 127,000 persons age 12 and over, and approximately 50,000 businesses. Smaller samples of persons from these original figures form the data base from which crime figures are compiled. Carefully worded questions lead people to report incidents that can be classified as crimes. This material is statistically manipulated in such a way as to make it comparable with *UCR* statistics. This material is usually referred to as **victimization data.**

The *NCS* distinguishes between a victimization and an incident. A **victimization** is the basic measure of the occurrence of a crime and is a specific criminal act that affects a single victim. An **incident** is a specific criminal act involving one or more victims.

Like the *UCR*, the *NCS* has certain persistent problems. Some crime victims cannot remember when or where the offense occurred. Other victims are reluctant to report a rape, particularly if the rapist is known to them, such as a family member or close friend. Nonreporting is also related to victim fear, feelings of helplessness or apathy, the perceived powerlessness of police, and fear of the authorities themselves. The poor are especially reluctant to report crime because they fear reprisals from the criminals who are often known to them. And, police may detect evidence of other crimes or statutory violations such as health code infractions, illegal aliens, and overcrowded apartment dwellings.

Despite the limitations of the *UCR* and the *NCS*, however, there are definite theoretical and research benefits accruing from these official crime sources (Blumstein, Cohen, and Rosenfeld, 1991; McDowall and Loftin, 1992). Other investigators use these sources for hypothesis tests involving the relation between crime trends over time and the influence of changing political administrations (Steffensmeier and Harer, 1991).

CLASSIFYING OFFENDERS

Classifying offenders is a complex activity. Objectively classifying criminals according to their crimes is one obvious way of differentiating between offenders. Felons are in one category; misdemeanants are placed in another category. Further simplified breakdowns are possible according to the *UCR*'s index offenses, such as robbery, larceny, aggravated assault, arson, or burglary. Classification schemes are used by prison and jail authorities to decide which **level of custody** is most appropriate for particular prisoners. In recent years, the incidence of AIDS (Acquired Immune Deficiency Syndrome) among prisoners has increased. One way of transmitting AIDS is receiving blood from others who have AIDS. Anal intercourse among prisoners is often linked with the transmission of this deadly virus. Semen contains the AIDS virus as well, and oral-genital contact may result in new AIDS victims among inmates. Thus, those diagnosed as having AIDS are often segregated from those who do not test positive for this virus (Moran et al., 1989; Olivero, 1990; Wilber, 1992).

Corrections officials also want to know which offenders should be placed in maximum-security custody and which should be confined in minimum-security facilities (Alexander and Austin, 1992; Austin and Chan, 1989; Berecochea and Gibbs, 1991; Cooper and Werner, 1990; Von Cleve, Jemelka, and Trupin, 1991). Certain prisoners pose a physical threat to other prisoners and should be isolated from them (Fraboni et al., 1990; Gibbs, 1991; Grande and Oseroff, 1991; MacKenzie and Buchanan, 1990). Sometimes prisoners can endanger themselves and are potential suicide risks (Ivanoff, 1992; Lester and Danto, 1993; Palermo, Liska, and Smith, 1991). Other prisoners are low risk and cost less to supervise, often requiring only minimal supervision by one or two correctional officers (Baird and Neuenfeldt, 1990).

Probation agencies and parole boards have a common interest in classifying offenders as well (Baird, 1992b). Different probation programs are designed with particular types of offenders in mind (U.S. Bureau of Justice Assistance, 1988). Some offenders may be impaired mentally or physically. Some may have personality disorders or poor self-concepts. Yet other offenders may have serious chemical dependencies (McGaha, 1991; Walker, 1992). Thus, particular treatment programs are specifically designed to meet certain offender needs (Bowker and Schweid, 1992; Wertleib and Greenberg, 1989). Below are various categorizations of offenders according to traditional and special or exceptional criteria.

Traditional Offender Categorizations

Besides violent and property offenders, two additional classifications include (1) first-offenders and (2) recidivists and career criminals.

First-Offenders.   **First-offenders** are those who commit one or more crimes but have no previous history of criminal behavior. There is nothing especially unique about first-offenders. They may commit violent crimes or property crimes. They may be male or female. They may be old or young. They may or may not have records as juvenile delinquents. No useful blanket generalizations can be made about first-offenders other than the fact they have no previous criminal history. However, even this statement may be inaccurate. For example, a first-offender in Colorado may have a prior record in Utah or California. Additionally, first-offenders may have committed previous crimes and escaped arrest. Depending on the sophistication of the police administration in the jurisdiction where offenders are arrested, computer checks with other jurisdictions may or may not disclose whether any offender has a prior criminal history.

First-offenders who commit only the offense for which they were apprehended and prosecuted and are unlikely to commit future crimes are called **situational offenders** (Haskell and Yablonsky, 1974). Situational offenders may commit serious crimes or petty offenses. The situation itself creates the unique conditions leading to the criminal act. An argument between husband and wife over something trivial may lead to the death of one of the spouses. An argument between a convenience store clerk and a customer may lead to a serious altercation, even death. Serious financial pressures or setbacks may prompt situational offenders to commit robbery or theft.

Situational offenders seldom need rehabilitation or counseling. They respond favorably to authorities whether on probation or incarcerated. Precisely because of the uniqueness of their act and the absence of a prior record, it is difficult to prescribe specific treatments for them. Jail and prison officials often consider some of these situational offenders good candidates for early release or parole and believe that they contribute unnecessarily to overcrowding.

Recidivists.   Besides first-offenders and situational criminals, some offenders, known as **recidivists**, continue to commit new offenses. Even after they have been apprehended, prosecuted, and incarcerated, a fairly large number of offenders continue their criminal activity when released. Petersilia (1985c, 1986b) and others report recidivism rates as high as 70 percent among those who have been granted early release from incarceration. Although there are disagreements among experts about how this phenomenon ought to be defined, **recidivism** is "the reversion of an individual to criminal behavior after he or she has been convicted of a prior offense, sentenced, and (presumably) corrected" (Maltz, 1984:1).

Career Criminals.   Career criminals are those offenders who earn their living through crime (Reckless, 1961). They go about their criminal activity in much the same way workers or professional individuals engage in their daily work activities. Career criminals often consider their work as a "craft," since they acquire considerable technical skills and competence in the performance of crimes. Reckless (1961) suggests that career criminals expect to get arrested and convicted occasionally as one of the risks of their criminal behavior. Career criminals have been epitomized by Edwin H. Sutherland's description of the professional thief (1972), although there are numerous contemporary versions of these types of offenders (Green, 1993; Greenberg, 1991; Keckeisen, 1993; McShane and Noonan, 1993). Sutherland suggests that differential association theory may explain why some criminals acquire their characteristics of persistent offending and adopt crime as a career. **Differential association theory** posits that criminal behavior is a function of four factors operating more or less simultaneously. These factors include frequency, priority, duration, and intensity. An example might be a person who prioritizes his or her associations with other criminals, giving them more attention and significance than law-abiding associations. And, this person's contacts with law-breakers are frequent, of fairly lengthy duration, and intense. This is not simply "guilt by association" or a "good apple" going bad simply because it is placed in close proximity with "bad apples." Rather, there are psychological and social factors impinging on certain persons that create influential conditions that contribute or lead to criminal behavior. Career criminals are those who have reached a stage of criminality from which they view crime as an occupation or profession.

CRIMINAL JUSTICE SYSTEM COMPONENTS: LOCATING PROBATION, PAROLE, AND COMMUNITY CORRECTIONS

The primary components of the criminal justice system include (1) law enforcement, (2) prosecutorial decision making, (3) courts and judges, and (4) corrections.

Law Enforcement

All law enforcement agencies give their officers arrest powers. Police officers have the authority to make arrests whenever law violations occur within their jurisdictions. These arrest powers include apprehending those suspected of committing crimes. Offenses justifying arrests may range from traffic violations such as driving recklessly to first-degree murder, forcible rape, or kidnapping. Law enforcement officers are empowered to enforce the laws and statutes of their jurisdictions. Primarily an investigative body, the FBI has arrest powers covering violations of over

200 federal laws and statutes. FBI agents observe all appropriate jurisdictional boundaries associated with their position. These agents do not issue traffic citations or monitor speeders on interstate highways. Accordingly, state troopers do not ordinarily investigate and arrest counterfeiters or conspirators in interstate gambling.

Arrest and Booking. In the criminal justice system, those with arrest powers investigate and apprehend persons suspected of criminal activity. An **arrest** involves taking law violators into custody. Ordinarily, police officers make arrests of criminal suspects. Once defendants have been taken into custody, they are usually booked. **Booking** is an administrative procedure designed to furnish personal background information to a bonding company and law enforcement officials. Booking includes compiling a file for a defendant, including his or her name, address, telephone number, age, place of work, relatives, and other personal data. The extensiveness of the booking procedure varies among jurisdictions. In some jurisdictions, the suspect may be photographed and fingerprinted; in others, defendants may answer a few personal, descriptive questions.

Bail. When defendants are arrested, a determination is made concerning whether they will be brought to trial. If a trial occurs, most defendants can obtain temporary release from detention. They may be **released on their own recognizance (ROR).** Bail is available only to those entitled to it. Those not entitled to bail include suspects likely to flee the jurisdiction if released temporarily, as well as those who pose a danger to others or themselves. **Bail** is a surety to procure the release of those under arrest and to assure that they will appear later to face criminal charges in court. Bail is ordinarily specified at the time criminal suspects are brought before a judge or magistrate in an initial appearance. An **initial appearance** is a preliminary specification of criminal charges against the defendant. Presiding judges can specify bail at that time or they may order certain defendants held until a preliminary hearing can be convened for the purpose of establishing probable cause. At the conclusion of preliminary hearings, bail may be ordered or suspects may be released on their own recognizance (ROR).

Prosecutorial Decision Making

After suspects have been arrested and booked for alleged violations of the law, prosecutors will examine their cases and the evidence against them and determine whether they should be prosecuted. Not all arrests for serious crimes result in prosecutions. Furthermore, not all prosecutions result in convictions. A **prosecution** is the carrying forth of criminal proceedings against a person culminating in a trial or other final disposition, such as a guilty plea in lieu of trial. Many factors influence a prosecutor's decision to prosecute suspects. This decision rests with the district attorney and involves a consideration of factors such as the sufficiency of evidence against the accused, the seriousness of the crime, the availability of witnesses, and the general circumstances associated with the arrest (Cole, 1970).

The criminal justice system begins with the arrest of criminal suspects.
(Paul Conklin/Monkmeyer Press)

Screening Cases.   The prosecuting attorney screens cases and determines which ones have the highest probability for conviction. The prosecutor also determines the priority given particular kinds of cases such as child sexual abuse or petty theft. In some instances, especially those involving petty crimes or minor offending, prosecutors may defer prosecution by placing suspects into diversionary programs. **Diversion** is a temporary suspension of a prosecution whereby suspects are required to remain law-abiding for specified periods and obey the law. After fulfilling the requirements of diversion in many jurisdictions, suspects may have their charges dropped by prosecutors. In the case of serious crimes alleged, however, prosecutors will move forward with prosecutions against these suspects.

Establishing Prosecutorial Priorities.   With the exception of Alaska and several other jurisdictions that have banned plea bargaining, prosecutors act as negotiators between defendants, their attorneys, and judges. Prosecutors attempt to work out mutually advantageous arrangements between the state and defendants. The role of the defense attorneys is to secure for their clients the best possible outcome, preferably an acquittal. The stage is set for negotiations. Prosecutors want guilty pleas from defendants. Defendants, who may or may not be guilty of the offense, weigh the alternatives. Considering the strength of the evidence and other factors, defendants, after consulting with their attorneys, may decide to plead guilty, provided the government makes adequate concessions (Champion, 1987c). In more than a few instances, sentences resulting from trial convictions are more severe than those imposed as the result of plea bargained convictions for the same offenses (Champion, 1988b; Kaplan and Skolnick, 1987:486).

Plea Bargaining.   Over 90 percent of all felony convictions in the United States are obtained prior to trial through plea bargaining (Alschuler, 1979a, 1979b; McDonald, 1985). **Plea bargaining** is a preconviction agreement between the defendant and the state whereby the defendant pleads guilty with the expectation of either a reduction in the charges, a promise of sentencing leniency, or some other governmental concession short of the maximum penalties that could be imposed under the law (McDonald, 1985:5–6).

Four Types of Plea Bargaining.   The first type is **implicit plea bargaining,** whereby defendants plead guilty with the expectation that they will receive more lenient sentences. The second is **sentencing recommendation plea bargaining,** whereby the prosecutor proposes a sentence in exchange for a guilty plea. The third is **charge reduction bargaining,** whereby the prosecutor downgrades charges in exchange for a guilty plea (some experts call this "overcharging"). The fourth type of plea bargaining is **judicial plea bargaining,** whereby the judge offers a specific guilty plea sentence (Padgett, 1985). Sentence recommendation plea bargaining and charge reduction plea bargaining are probably the most frequently used in plea negotiating (Maynard, 1984).

It should be noted that prosecutors have no authority to grant probation to any criminal defendant in exchange for a guilty plea. Prosecutors can only *recommend*. Judges have the final say to approve or disappove any plea agreement. The plea bargaining process is important to any criminal defendant entering into negotiations with government prosecutors. Several constitutional rights are waived by defendants, and they acquire a criminal record. In the present context, plea bargaining is described because it may include an offer of probation or a recommendation for leniency in sentencing in exchange for a guilty plea from a defendant.

Courts and Judges

Criminal Prosecutions.   If prosecutors persist in a prosecution against a particular suspect, the suspect becomes a **defendant** in the subsequent criminal proceeding. Prosecutors file **informations,** or formal criminal charges against specific defendants. In about half of all states, **grand juries** convene and issue indictments or presentments against criminal suspects. Indictments and presentments are also charges stemming from grand jury consideration of evidence against the accused. **Indictments** are charges against criminal suspects brought by the grand jury at the request of prosecutors. **Presentments** are criminal charges against the accused whereby the grand jury has acted on its own authority. These actions simply specify that sufficient evidence exists to establish probable cause that a crime has been committed and the accused committed it. **True bills** indicate that the grand jury has found sufficient evidence to establish probable cause that the accused committed a crime. **No true bills** issue from grand jury action and indicate that insufficient evidence exists to establish probable cause. When no true bills are issued, suspects are usually free from further criminal justice action against them.

It is important to note that grand juries do not determine one's guilt or innocence. Rather, they merely determine the fact of probable cause against the accused. This function is left to trial juries, known as **petit juries**. Thus, the grand jury function is similar to a preliminary hearing or preliminary examination, which resolves the same issue, probable cause. Again, depending on the jurisdiction within which a crime has been committed, a defendant will eventually appear in a courtroom to face formal criminal charges (Marshall et al., 1985). Trials are ordinarily preceded by arraignments. **Arraignments** are formal proceedings during which the finalized list of charges is furnished criminal defendants. Arraignments also are held for the purposes of entering a plea (e.g., guilty, not guilty, guilty but mentally ill), and determining a trial date. When criminal defendants plead not guilty to the charges against them, a trial date is established, and a trial will eventually be held to determine the guilt or innocence of the accused.

Court Dockets and Judicial Workloads. In many federal district courts as well as in state criminal courts, court calendars are glutted with cases. A majority of these are civil cases, but they consume much valuable court time. The courtroom is the place where the defendant's guilt or innocence is ultimately determined. It functions as a public forum for the airing of all relevant information in the case. The government presents its evidence against the accused, and the defense presents its side. Witnesses are called to testify both for and against the accused, and defendants have the right to cross-examine their accusers and to offer testimony and evidence in their own behalf. The courtroom is also the place where the sufficiency of evidence against the accused is tested. The prosecution carries the burden of proof against the accused and must establish guilt beyond a reasonable doubt.

Speedy Trials and Case Processing. All defendants are entitled to a **jury trial** in any criminal proceeding as a matter of right, if the charges are serious and could result in incarceration for a period of six months or more. This applies to either misdemeanors or felonies. A jury is an objective, impartial body of persons who convene to hear the case against the accused and make a determination of guilt or innocence on the basis of the factual evidence presented. Despite speedy trial measures, streamlined case processing, and other court reforms, most state and federal judges are overworked and their dockets are glutted with case backlogs. Therefore, judges encourage prosecutors to work out arrangements with defendants, if possible, so that the number of trials can be minimized.

Sentencing and Implications for Convicted Offenders. Defendants who are found not guilty are acquitted and freed from the criminal justice system. They cannot be tried again on the same charges, since this would be **double jeopardy.** Double jeopardy is guarded against by the Fifth Amendment: Persons cannot be tried again on the same charge or charges if they have been earlier acquitted in a trial where those same charges were litigated. However, if defendants are found guilty, an appeals process exists at both the state and local levels whereby these defendants may appeal the verdict and request a new trial. In the meantime, convicted offenders are sentenced.

Several options are available to judges in **sentencing** criminal defendants. For example, first-offenders may receive light sentences and not be incarcerated. However, convicted offenders with prior records will probably receive harsher sentences. Judges may sentence offenders to incarceration in a local jail or regional prison for a specified period of time. If the judge sentences convicted offenders to some nonincarcerative punishment, defendants may be placed on probation for a prescribed period. **Probation** is a sentence involving a conditional suspension of incarceration, usually with several behavioral provisions or conditions. These conditions are often prescribed by law. Although this is not an exhaustive list, these conditions include (1) not associating with other known criminals, (2) refraining from committing future criminal acts, (3) obtaining and maintaining employment, and/or (4) participating in appropriate medical or counseling programs and therapy. Also, in many cases, judges must sentence convicted offenders to prison according to prescribed statutes that bind judges and restrict their discretionary powers. Generally, however, convicted offenders collectively fall under the supervision of corrections.

Corrections

The last component of the criminal justice system is corrections. **Corrections** includes all of the agencies, organizations, and personnel who deal with convicted offenders after court processing and convictions. Typically, corrections are associated with jails and prisons. **Jails** are typically short-term confinement facilities operated by cities and county governments. They are usually used for persons enduring short-term confinement for misdemeanor offenses or for persons charged with more serious offenses who are awaiting trial. **Prisons** are long-term facilities that are more self-contained and house inmates serving sentences of one or more years. Even though prisons and jails are important features of the corrections system, they are hardly the dominant components of it. By mid 1993, for instance, 3.5 million adults were on probation or parole in the United States. This is over twice the combined number of inmates in United States prisons and jails. In mid-year 1993, the prison population consisted of about 909,185 inmates, while the jail population consisted of 455,081 inmates (Beck, Bonczar, and Gilliard, 1993:1).

Prison and Jail Overcrowding.   Frequently, there is little room in many prisons and jails to house new convicted offenders. In 1988, for instance, nearly 40 states were under court order to decrease their prison inmate populations to comply with health and safety standards as well as other factors. Among other states, Texas, Tennessee, and Louisiana have been targeted for rehabilitative reforms by the

BOX 1.1
If You Don't Like The Sentence, Shoot The Judge

The Case of Judge Howard Broadman

Being a judge these days is risky business. Sentence the wrong offender to the wrong punishment, in the offender's opinion, and you are liable to become marked for death. If you are Judge Howard Broadman, you stand an even greater likelihood of being victimized by those upset with your sentencing behavior.

Judge Howard Broadman is the presiding judge of the Tulare County, California Superior Court, located in Visalia. The judge is also a maverick, unlike a lot of other judges. In one case, for instance, Broadman became a subject of controversy when he sentenced a man who had stolen two six-packs of beer to the maximum sentence of four years in prison unless he agreed to wear a T-shirt with a message on the front reading *"I AM ON FELONY PROBATION FOR THEFT."* The offender decided to wear the shirt instead of doing four years in a California prison. Judge Broadman thought it would deter the offender from committing new crimes. It didn't. One offender, Russell Hacker, was a petty thief who was sentenced to wear a T-shirt proclaiming his crime instead of doing time. A coin collection was reported stolen a short time later. When police asked the victims if they could describe the man, they said, "Sure! He was wearing a T-Shirt saying 'I am on felony probation for theft,' " and the police officers had a pretty good idea of where to look. Hacker was subsequently arrested and the coin collection was recovered.

Among other unusual sentences imposed by Broadman are

- A man convicted of drunk driving was made to come to court each day and swallow a tablet of Antabuse, a drug producing violent nausea in persons who consume alcohol.
- A woman on welfare was sentenced to get a high school diploma.
- A woman was offered a choice of receiving a contraceptive implant and wearing it for three years, doing a year in the county jail, or doing a year in state prison. She opted for wearing the contraceptive device.

This last case was the straw that broke the camel's back. It involved Darlene Johnson, a mother of four who was charged with and convicted of abusing two of her children. When convicted, she was expecting a fifth child. The judge said, "I had a philosophical dilemma. Invading a human being's body is a big step. But locking somebody up in prison is also a big step. Clearly, I could just have locked her up for four years, but I thought it would be better to try to keep the family together, to see if she could get her act together. I thought that not having more children for the next three years would help in her potential rehabilitation."

What happened was that someone who didn't even know Darlene Johnson burst into Judge Broadman's courtroom shortly after her sentencing and fired a gun at him, missing Broadman's head by only three inches. Apparently, the man was a pro-life proponent who thought that killing Judge Broadman would somehow "save lives."

Even after this life-threatening ordeal,

Judge Broadman is not ready to throw in the towel. He believes that his sentences are just and that they offer a meaningful alternative to a criminal justice system in disarray. Judge Broadman believes in accountability: "If I can introduce some accountability into the individual, then maybe we can get accountability into the system as well," says Broadman. He added, "Society expects two things from me. It wants to be protected from criminals, and it wants me to produce crime-free individuals."

Should judges be permitted to impose exotic sentences such as those imposed by Judge Broadman? How important is accountability when sentencing offenders? Should sentences act as deterrents to further criminality, or should we view them largely as punitive and "just deserts"?

Source: Adapted from Michael Ryan, "Did the Judge Go Too Far?" *Parade*, September 1, 1991:8.

courts. Prison overcrowding is primarily responsible for the large increase in the number of nonincarcerated offenders currently under some form of correctional supervision (Champion, 1990).

Judicial Discretion in Sentencing Offenders. In 1984, Congress passed the **Sentencing Reform Act.** This Act has given federal judges considerable latitude in their sentencing of criminal offenders. The Act encourages judges to consider seriously various alternative sentences in lieu of incarceration, such as community service, restitution, and even probation. At the end of 1990, there was a noticable increase in both the federal and state probationer and parolee populations. The parolee population increased by 16.3 percent between 1989 and 1990, while the probationer population increased by 5.9 percent during the same period (Jankowski, 1991:1, 3).

Among the factors to be considered by the trial judge are the (1) nature and circumstances of the offense and the history and characteristics of the defendant; (2) need for the sentence imposed to reflect the seriousness of the offense, to promote respect for the law, to afford adequate deterrence to criminal conduct, and to protect the public from further crimes of the defendant; (3) kinds of educational or training services, medical care, or other correctional treatment that might be appropriate for any particular defendant; (4) kinds of sentences available; and (5) need to avoid unwarranted sentence disparities among defendants with similar records who have been found guilty of similar conduct (18 U.S.C., Sec. 3553, 1994:265).

The Availability of Community Services and Facilities. A prevailing view of sentencing equates punishment and control with incarceration (U.S. Sentencing Commission, 1991). In recent years, however, several proposals have been advanced and adopted in some jurisdictions that favor various **alternative sentencing**

forms or **creative sentencing** (Klein, 1988; McDonald and Carlson, 1992; Minnesota Sentencing Guidelines Commission, 1991). Alternative sentencing offers offenders, especially those who have committed relatively minor or nonviolent offenses, an opportunity to serve their sentences outside of the prison setting. Usually, alternative sentencing involves some form of community service, some degree of restitution to victims of crimes, becoming actively involved in educational or vocational training programs, or becoming affiliated with some other "good works" activity (Czajkoski and Wollan, 1986).

The primary goals of alternative sentencing are twofold. First, it is aimed at helping certain types of offenders avoid imprisonment. Imprisonment means associating with other criminals, and labeling theorists consider imprisonment as an important factor in contributing to one's self-concept as a criminal. Second, alternative sentencing is designed as a way of providing needed services and therapy while remaining relatively free within the community. Another goal is that alternative sentencing tends to reduce jail and prison overcrowding and reduce certain correctional operating costs (Klein, 1988; Wallace and Clarke, 1986:1).

THE SENTENCING PROCESS: TYPES OF SENTENCING AND SENTENCING ISSUES

Functions of Sentencing

The Sentencing Reform Act of 1984 restated a number of sentencing objectives that have guided sentencing judges in their leniency or harshness toward convicted defendants. Some of these objectives have been made explicit by various states and local jurisdictions in past years, while others have been implicitly incorporated into prevailing sentencing guidelines.

Some of the more important functions of sentencing are discussed below.

To Promote Respect for the Law.   A logical function of sentencing is to promote respect for the law by showing offenders what can happen to them when criminal laws are violated. But if current recidivism rates are a measure of the respect for the law acquired by convicted offenders, then our sentencing practices are not successfully fulfilling this particular objective. An examination of recidivism rates for 153,465 state prison inmates nationally reveals, for example, that 29 percent of these will return to prison for committing new crimes within one year of their release; 48 percent will return with two years of their release; and 60 percent will return within three years of their release (Greenfeld, 1985:3).

To Reflect the Seriousness of the Offense.   One objective of sentencing is to juxtapose the sentence with the seriousness of the offense. In federal district courts as well as many state courts, offenses are classified according to Class A, B, C, D, and E felonies, and Class A, B, and C misdemeanors. Each of these classifications carries with it a minimum and maximum term of years for the convict's imprisonment.

For example, if the crime is a Class A felony, then the maximum term of punishment is either life imprisonment or death, depending on the state. If the crime is a Class A misdemeanor, then the maximum term of imprisonment is less than one year but more than six months.

To Provide Just Punishment for the Offense.   In recent years, sentencing policies in most jurisdictions in the United States have shifted to reflect the justice model, which is a legitimatization of the power of the state to administer sanctions (Cavender, 1984; Fogel, 1979; Tonry and Zimring, 1983). The **justice model** is a philosophy that emphasizes punishment as a primary objective of sentencing, an abolition of parole, an abandonment of the rehabilitative ideal, and determinate sentencing.

To Deter Future Criminal Conduct.   Not only is sentencing designed as a punishment to fit the crime, but it is also designed to function as a deterrent to future criminal offending. We have seen that many jurisdictions either cannot or will not exercise sentencing practices that actually deter offenders from recidivism. Ideally, sentencing should deter criminals from contemplating future criminality. However, recidivism rates suggest that the system doesn't work as it is ideally conceived to work. Most states have **habitual offender statutes** that require the imposition of greater sentences on dangerous, multiple, or persistent offenders. But few state jurisdictions are enforcing such statutes (Hunzeker and Conger, 1985). In a survey of all state corrections departments in 1985, for example, Hunzeker and Conger (1985) found that three states reported no inmates serving time under these statutes, and that 17 other states reported fewer than 3 percent of their inmate populations consisting of these types of offenders. This would mean that although statutory mechanisms are in place in most states for incarcerating recidivists for prolonged periods, most jurisdictions refrain from doing so. A likely explanation for a state's reluctance to pursue habitual offender charges against any particular offender is prison overcrowding and the mandatory imprisonment provisions associated with an habitual offender conviction.

To Protect the Public from the Convicted Offender.   Incapacitating felons by imprisonment or hospitalization effectively isolates them from the public. Judges are currently concerned with the potential public risk posed by the felons to be sentenced appearing before them. Judges would like to be able to turn to specific social and personal background criteria for each convicted defendant and determine with some high measure of certainty the convict's potential for "staying clean" and not committing additional criminal acts. The criteria most often used by judges are frequently found to be unrelated to a convicted defendant's prospects for recidivism, however. Record-keeping practices of various jurisdictions are often so unsophisticated that the same defendant may go through the justice system several times as a first offender in different parts of the state. Also, persons convicted and punished for crimes in one state may commit additional crimes in other states. Again, faulty record-keeping or a quick check of state records will fail to disclose that the person has been convicted elsewhere for serious crimes and should be treated differently in sentencing. In short, it is not always an easy matter to identify recidivists.

To Provide Education and Vocational Training and/or Other Rehabilitative Relief. This is the rehabilitative function of sentencing. Some critics have observed that the rehabilitative ideal has declined over the years as a viable correctional goal (Cavender, 1984). Alternatives to incarceration, or alternative sentencing, currently include restitution to victims, community service, or educational or vocational training (Klein, 1988).

Types of Sentencing

During the last several decades, sentencing practices in most states have undergone transformation. Experts disagree about the number and types of sentencing systems currently used by the states (Koppel, 1984:2). Furthermore, new sentencing schemes continue to be proposed in contrast to existing ones (DeLuca, Miller, and Wiedemann, 1991). The following categorization is based on four sentencing types defined by the New York State Division of Criminal Justice Services (Frederick, Guider, and Monti, 1984): (1) indeterminate sentencing, (2) determinate sentencing, (3) presumptive sentencing, and (4) mandatory sentencing.

Indeterminate Sentencing. By far the most widely used sentencing practice for many years was indeterminate sentencing. In **indeterminate sentencing,** the court sets either explicit (according to statute) or implicit upper and lower bounds on the time to be served by the offender, and the actual release date from prison is determined by a parole board. The judge may sentence the offender to "one to ten years," or "not more than five years," and a parole board determines when the offender may be released within the limits of those time boundaries (Koppel, 1984:2).

Determinate Sentencing. An increasingly popular sentencing form, **determinate sentencing** is a fixed term of incarceration that must be served in full, less any "good time" earned while in prison. **Good time** is the reduction in the amount of time incarcerated amounting to a certain number of days per month for each month served. If inmates obey the rules and stay out of trouble, they accumulate good time credit that accelerates their release from incarceration. In states using determinate sentencing, there is no parole board discretion concerning a convict's early release (Neithercutt, Carmichael, and Mullen, 1990). However, a positive consequence of determinate sentencing has been to increase prisoner certainty about specific release dates (Neuhoff, 1987:3). Ideally, this type of sentencing shift should cause significant changes in both sentencing patterns among the states and federal government as well as the average length of time served by convicted offenders.

Presumptive Sentencing.   **Presumptive sentencing,** or **guidelines-based sentencing,** is a specific sentence, usually expressed as a range of months, for each and every offense or offense class. The sentence must be imposed in all unexceptional cases, but when there are mitigating or aggravating circumstances, judges are permitted some latitude in shortening or lengthening sentences within specific boundaries (Parnas et al., 1992). In October 1987, the U.S. Sentencing Commission implemented new federal guidelines similar to those used by various states, such as Minnesota. These guidelines were subsequently challenged as unconstitutional (see Box 1.2), but the U.S. Supreme Court upheld their constitutionality. An example of the sentencing grids used by states with guidelines-based or presumptive sentencing schemes is from Minnesota and is shown in Figure 1.2.

Presumptive sentencing has the following aims: (1) to establish penalties commensurate with harm caused by the criminal activity; (2) to produce a fairer system of justice; (3) to reduce the typical severity of penalties; (4) to incarcerate only the most serious offenders; (5) to reduce discretionary power of judges and parole authorities; (6) to allow special sentences for offenders for circumstances that are clearly exceptional; (7) to eliminate early release procedures for inmates; and (8) to make participation in treatment or rehabilitative programs completely voluntary by inmates with no effect on their terms of incarceration (Jensen et al., 1991; von Hirsch, 1976).

By 1985, 65 percent of the states had reformed their sentencing laws so that an offender's parole eligibility was either eliminated or made more difficult (some of these states shifted to determinate sentencing, thus eliminating parole board discretion). But at the same time, some interesting adjustments occurred in over half of the states adopting determinate sentencing. One important change was to increase the amount of "good time" and the way such time is calculated. Therefore, although the certainty of incarceration has increased under determinate sentencing, the sentences served are often shorter compared with what they might have been under indeterminate sentencing. Table 1.1 shows a distribution of states using predominantly indeterminate or determinate sentencing as of 1992.

Mandatory Sentencing.   **Mandatory sentencing** is the imposition of an incarcerative sentence of a specified length, for certain crimes or certain categories of offenders, where no option of probation, suspended sentence, or immediate parole elgibility exists (Koppel, 1984:2; Tonry, 1993). California, Hawaii, Illinois, Kentucky, and Michigan are a few of the many states that have enacted mandatory sentencing provisions for certain offenses. Michigan imposes an additional two-year sentence of "flat time" (whereby offenders must serve the full two years without relief from parole) if they use a dangerous weapon during the commission of a felony. In Kentucky, those convicted of being habitual offenders are sentenced to life without parole in prison for violating Kentucky's Habitual Offender Statute. Usually, mandatory sentences are prescribed for those who use dangerous weapons during the commission of a crime, for habitual offenders with three or more prior felony convictions, and for major drug dealers. But some critics question whether

BOX 1.2
Are Judges Too Lenient in Their Sentencing? Are They Biased Against Certain Convicted Offenders? What Can Be Done about It?

The Case of the U.S. Sentencing Commission and John Mistretta

In 1984, the U.S. Congress established the U.S. Sentencing Commission to examine and revise the existing U.S. criminal code, including the definitions of criminal conduct and accompanying punishments. This Commission was the product of continuing allegations that the federal judiciary was perpetuating a pattern of sentencing disparity among the numerous federal courts. Sentencing disparity exists in various forms. It occurs whenever offenders with similar criminal histories and convicted of identical crimes receive widely disparate or different sentences from the same judge or from different judges in the same judicial district. Disparities in sentencing are most frequently attributable to age, race, ethnicity, gender, and social class. These extralegal factors should have no prominent place in any courtroom, especially the federal courtroom. In November 1987, the U.S. Sentencing Commission set forth sentencing guidelines as a part of a general presumptive sentencing scheme. Some of the members of the U.S. Sentencing Commission were federal court judges. Besides *standardizing* sentencing, the Commission also scheduled parole for abolition in November 1992. Parole would be abandoned in favor of a new scheme called *supervised release* following one's incarceration. Sounds like parole.

Immediately following the adoption of these new sentencing guidelines, the federal judiciary was deluged with lawsuits from convicted offenders, alleging various constitutional violations. The leading violation alleged was that the guidelines were created, in part, by judges (on the U.S. Sentencing Commission) and that this was a violation of the "separation of powers" doctrine, whereby the judicial branch cannot pass laws similar to those passed by Congress. A leading case involved John Mistretta, who was convicted of cocaine dealing in a federal district court in Kansas City, Missouri. Mistretta was sentenced to 18 months as the *presumptive* or middle-range sentence from a range of 15 to 21 months associated with the possible incarcerative punishment for the cocaine offense. Mistretta's lawyers alleged that the new sentencing system violated the Constitution by "blurring" the separation of powers among the branches of the government. However, the U.S. Supreme Court upheld the constitutionality of the new sentencing guidelines by a vote of 8 to 1, contending that "the framers [of the Constitution] did not require ... the notion that the three branches must be entirely separate ... rather, there is a 'twilight area' in which the activities of the separate branches merge," according to Justice Harry A. Blackmun. Lawyers for many interest groups, including the ACLU and the Public Citizen Litigation Group, suggest that the *Mistretta* case is only the "opening shot" in a lengthy campaign to contest the constitutionality of these sentencing guidelines (*Mistretta v. United States*, 109 S.Ct. 647, 1989).

Sources: Adapted from Richard N. Ostling, "Let Punishment Fit the Crime: A Controversial Sentencing Scheme Gets a Go-Ahead," *Time*, January 30, 1989:63; and from Tamar Jacoby, *Newsweek*, January 30, 1989:76.

Presumptive Sentence Lengths in Months

Italicized numbers within the grid denote the range within which a judge may sentence without the sentence being deemed a departure.

Offenders with nonimprisonment felony sentences are subject to jail time according to law.

CRIMINAL HISTORY SCORE

SEVERITY LEVELS OF CONVICTION OFFENSE		0	1	2	3	4	5	6 or more
Sale of a Simulated Controlled Substance	I	12*	12*	12*	13	15	17	19 *18–20*
Theft-Related Crimes ($2500 or less) Check Forgery ($200–$2500)	II	12*	12*	13	15	17	19	21 *20–22*
Theft Crimes ($2500 or less)	III	12*	13	15	17	19 *18–20*	22 *21–23*	25 *24–26*
Nonresidential Burglary Theft Crimes (over $2500)	IV	12*	15	18	21	25 *24–26*	32 *30–34*	41 *37–45*
Residential Burglary Simple Robbery	V	18	23	27	30 *29–31*	38 *36–40*	46 *43–49*	54 *50–58*
Criminal Sexual Conduct 2nd Degree (a) & (b)	VI	21	26	30	34 *33–35*	44 *42–46*	54 *50–58*	65 *60–70*
Aggravated Robbery	VII	48 *44–52*	58 *54–62*	68 *64–72*	78 *74–82*	88 *84–92*	98 *94–102*	108 *104–112*
Criminal Sexual Conduct, 1st Degree Assault, 1st Degree	VIII	86 *81–91*	98 *93–103*	110 *105–115*	122 *117–127*	134 *129–139*	146 *141–151*	158 *153–163*
Murder, 3rd Degree Murder, 2nd Degree (felony murder)	IX	150 *144–156*	165 *159–171*	180 *174–186*	195 *189–201*	210 *204–216*	225 *219–231*	240 *234–246*
Murder, 2nd Degree (with intent)	X	306 *299–313*	326 *319–333*	346 *339–353*	366 *359–373*	386 *379–393*	406 *399–413*	426 *419–433*

First-degree murder is excluded from the guidelines by law and continues to have a mandatory life sentence. At the discretion of the judge, up to a year in jail and/or other nonjail sanctions can be imposed as conditions of probation.

FIGURE 1.2 Minnesota Sentencing Guidelines Grid.

(*Source:* Howard Abadinsky, *Probation and Parole: Theory & Practice*, 5th ed. Englewood Cliffs, NJ: Prentice Hall 1994.)

TABLE 1.1 Use of Indeterminate and Determinate Sentencing Forms by All States and the District of Columbia for 1992[a]

States Emphasizing Indeterminate Sentencing (Includes Some Presumptive and Mandatory Sentencing Provisions for Some States)

Alabama, Alaska, Arkansas, Delaware, District of Columbia, Florida, Georgia, Hawaii, Idaho, Iowa, Kansas, Kentucky, Louisiana, Maryland, Massachusetts, Michigan, Mississippi, Missouri, Nebraska, Nevada, New Hampshire, New York, North Dakota, Oklahoma, Oregon, Rhode Island, South Carolina, South Dakota, Texas, Utah, Vermont, Virginia, Washington, West Virginia, Wisconsin, and Wyoming.

States Emphasizing Determinate Sentencing (Includes Some Presumptive and Mandatory Sentencing Provisions)

Arizona, California, Colorado, Connecticut, Illinois, Indiana, Maine, Minnesota, New Jersey, New Mexico, North Carolina, Ohio, Pennsylvania, Tennessee, and Washington.

[a]Several states have adopted a hybrid sentencing policy that incorporates elements of all sentencing forms. Some states with parole boards provide mandatory and presumptive sentencing for specific offenses, and judges are extended greater discretionary powers in certain states operating principally under a determinate sentencing scheme.

Sources: Langan and Dawson, 1993; Maguire, Pastore, and Flanagan, 1993.

any significant deterrent value is obtained from such mandatory sentencing laws, since attorneys and judges find numerous ways to circumvent them to suit their own purposes (Tonry, 1993).

Sentencing Issues

This section examines briefly some of the major sentencing issues that continue to plague most jurisdictions. *Issues* are usually questions that need to be addressed and are not, as yet, resolved. They also involve factors that must be considered when sentencing offenders. Whereas a discussion of all sentencing issues that might be included here is beyond the scope of this book, several important issues have been selected here. These are (1) whether convicted offenders should be placed on probation or incarcerated; (2) the fact of jail and prison overcrowding; (3) the ineffectiveness of rehabilitation; and (4) offender needs and public safety.

Probation or Incarceration?   Should offenders be placed on probation or in jail or prison? This is often a difficult judicial decision. Probation officers might recommend probation to judges when filing a Presentence Investigation Report for some convicted offender, although the court may disregard this recommendation. The "just-deserts" philosophy is a dominant theme in American corrections today, and judges appear to be influenced by this philosophy as reflected in the sentences they impose. Generally, their intent is to impose sentences that are equated with the seriousness of the conviction offense. However, some evidence suggests that they are influenced by other factors as well, such as gender and/or ethnicity (Kempf and Austin, 1986; Meeker, Jesilow, and Aranda, 1992; Petersilia, 1983).

A sentencing hearing is conducted to determine appropriate punishments for offenders. (Stock Boston)

Jail and Prison Overcrowding. Jail and prison overcrowding conditions influence judicial discretion in sentencing offenders (Price et al., 1983). Although there is no consensus among state trial judges about the nature of judicial involvement in solving jail and prison overcrowding problems, a 1982–1983 survey of judges in 31 states showed that half of them said overcrowding of jail/prison facilities in their jurisdictions had been a factor in their sentencing decisions (Finn, 1984b). They also said that the overcrowding issue had caused them to consider more carefully various alternatives to prison or jail.

The Ineffectiveness of Rehabilitation. The failure of incarceration or various nonincarcerative alternatives to rehabilitate large numbers of offenders for long periods may not necessarily be the fault of those particular programs but rather the nature of clients served by those programs (Chaiken and Chaiken, 1984). It is generally acknowledged that jail and prison do not rehabilitate. While most prisons and some jails have one or more programs designed to assist inmates to develop new vocational skills and to counsel them, the effectiveness of these programs is questionable. Understaffing is a chronic problem often attributable to the lack of funding for such programs. Also, the equipment used in prison technical education programs is often outdated. If inmates earn an educational certificate, it often bears the name of the prison facility where the degree or accomplishment was acknowledged. Thus, employers are deterred from hiring such persons with prison records. Further, many of these institutions are principally concerned with the custody and control of their inmate populations, and rehabilitation is a remote consideration for them.

Offender Needs and Public Safety.   As the courts move voluntarily or involuntarily toward the greater use of felony probation, judicial concern is increasingly focused on determining which offenders should be incarcerated and which should not. Therefore, in recent years several investigators have attempted to devise prediction schemes that would permit judges and other officials to predict a convicted defendant's **dangerousness**. Obviously, this concern is directed toward the preservation of public safety and minimizing public risks possibly arising from placing violent and dangerous offenders on probation rather than imprisoning them. (A detailed discussion of predicting dangerousness, risk, and offender needs is provided in Chapter 3.)

KEY TERMS

Aftercare	"Good time"
Alternative sentencing	Grand jury
Arraignment	Guidelines-based sentencing
Arrest	Habitual offender statute
Bail	Implicit plea bargaining
Booking	Incident
Career criminal	Indeterminate sentencing
Charge reduction bargaining	Index offense
Child sexual abusers	Indictment
Community corrections	Information
Corrections	Initial appearance
Courts	Jail
Creative sentencing	Judicial plea bargaining
Crime classification index	Jury trial
Crime against property	Justice model
Crime against the person	Law enforcement
Criminal justice system	Level of custody
Dangerousness	Mandatory sentencing
Defendant	Misdemeanant
Determinate sentencing	Misdemeanor
Differential association theory	*National Crime Survey (NCS)*
Diversion	No true bill
Double jeopardy	Parole
Felony	Parole officers (POs)
First-offender	Petit jury
First-time offender	Plea bargaining

Presumptive sentencing
Presentment
Prison
Probation
Probation officers (POs)
Prosecution
Recidivism
Recidivist
Released on own recognizance (ROR)
Sentence recommendation plea bargaining

Sentencing
Sentencing Reform Act of 1984
Situational offender
Summary offense
True bill
Uniform Crime Reports (UCR)
Victimization data
Victimization
Violent crime

QUESTIONS FOR REVIEW

1. At the beginning of this chapter, several different legal cases involving probation and parole revocations were presented. What were some problems shared by each of the principal individuals in these cases?

2. What is the *Uniform Crime Reports (UCR)?* What kinds of information does it report? What can you say about its accuracy relative to general crime and crime trends in the United States?

3. What is the *National Crime Survey (NCS)?* How does it differ from the *UCR?* Explain. Do you believe it is more accurate as a reflection of the amount of crime in the United States? Why or why not?

4. What are the major components of the criminal justice system? Which part of the system deals with convicted offenders? Explain briefly the functions of this component relative to convicted offenders.

5. What is meant by *diversion?* Relate diversion to career criminals and first offenders meaningfully.

6. What is a *crime?* Distinguish between two general categories of crime. Explain how each is treated in terms of punishment. Your answer can include both the location where offenders might be housed as well as the sentence lengths judges might commonly impose.

7. What are *index offenses?* What is their usefulness regarding crime in the United States and crime trends?

8. Differentiate between a *victimization* and an *incident.*

9. Who are *situational offenders?* What can you speculate about their amount of expected recidivism in the future? Explain.

10. How do offenders with drug or alcohol dependencies pose problems for law enforcement and corrections officials? Explain.

2

Probation and Probationers

History, Philosophy, Goals, and Functions

Introduction

Probation Defined

Probation Distinguished from Parole

The History of Probation in the United
   States

The Philosophy of Probation

Models for Dealing with Criminal Offenders

Functions of Probation

A Profile of Probationers

First-Offenders and Recidivists

Probation Trends

Key Terms

Questions for Review

INTRODUCTION

• Seventy-nine-year-old Mildred Kaitz of Monticello, New York, didn't think anything about the 10-foot high plant growing in her yard beside her front porch. Curious neighbors wondered what it was. They asked Mildred, "What is that?" pointing at the large plant. "Marijuana," said Mildred. For many months, Mildred escaped police scrutiny until a neighborhood teenager who knew what the plant really was reported it to authorities. Mildred was promptly arrested and her plant was confiscated. In court later, Mildred told the judge that she was growing the marijuana to give to her son who was suffering from multiple sclerosis. It seems that the marijuana was alleviating the racking pain and nausea associated with the disease. Regardless of Mildred's altruistic motives and love for her son, the judge placed Mildred on probation for six months, with no fine and no time. Mildred said, "I don't feel guilty. I didn't grow it to sell it. I did it for my son." (*People,* January 10, 1994:94.)

• In May 1988, the U.S. Coast Guard stopped a $2.5 million, 133-foot yacht, *The Ark Royal,* in international waters between Cuba and Mexico. They boarded the vessel and conducted a thorough search, yielding one-tenth of one ounce of marijuana. The owner of the vessel was not on board, only the captain and a few crewmen. They were arrested and charged with marijuana possession, and the boat was seized by the government as being an instrument used to convey illegal substances. After much pressure from civil libertarians, the boat was returned to its rightful owner, only after the owner paid $1,600 in fines and fees. (*Time,* May 23, 1988:55.)

• In New York City in January 1990, Tony Freyre, 25, was arrested and charged with selling cocaine. In a five-minute proceeding a few months later, Freyre was sentenced to five years' probation. (*U.S. News & World Report,* April 9, 1990:24–27.)

• No probation for Quinones! Liwy Quinones, 19, was sentenced to 10 years in prison for "guarding" someone else's cocaine stash and accepting $200 for it. In New York City, a federal sting operation turned up numerous drug traffickers. Among those arrested were persons simply willing to sit on one's drugs temporarily for safe-keeping. Quinones's 10-year sentence is the result of recently implemented federal sentencing guidelines that specify a 10-year penalty for persons in possession of certain quantities of illegal drugs, despite the conspicuous absence of a prior criminal record. (*U.S. News & World Report,* April 9, 1990:24–27.)

It is clear from these various scenarios that the laws about the possession and/or distribution of illegal substances are unclear and inconsistent. It is also clear that a sentence of probation may or may not be applied according to judicial discretion or statute, depending on where offenders live.

This chapter is about probation in the United States. The first section defines probation and places it in a historical context. Probation is unique to the United States and its origins date to the 1830s. In addition to describing the historical antecedents of probation and its emergence throughout the nation, the philosophy of probation will be presented.

PROBATION DEFINED

Probation refers to the release of convicted offenders into the community under a conditional suspended sentence, avoiding imprisonment, showing good behavior, under the supervision of a probation officer (Black, 1990:1202). The word *probation* derives from the Latin term *probatio,* which means a period of proving or trial and forgiveness. Thus, offenders who prove themselves during the trial period by complying with the conditions of their probation are forgiven and released from further involvement with the criminal justice system. Their criminal records may not be expunged or forgotten, but at the very least, they avoid incarceration. Some states such as California allow expungement of records under certain conditions after probation has been served satisfactorily.

Because probation is applied in seemingly unusual situations, is not applied in other situations that seem vaguely identical, and is inconsistently applied in the same jurisdiction when logic says otherwise, we must consider the importance of variation among state as well as federal statutes. Every state or federal criminal statute carries statutory sanctions. These sanctions always provide for the possibility of incarceration and/or a fine, depending on the seriousness of the offense. In Tennessee, for instance, a convicted shoplifter is punished by "a fine of not more than three hundred dollars ($300) or imprisonment for not more than six (6) months, or both" (T.C.A., 39-3-1124, 1994). A conviction for violating a federal criminal law such as the willful destruction of U.S. government property not exceeding the sum of $100 is punishable by "a fine of not more than $1,000 or by imprisonment for not more than one year, or both" (18 U.S.C. Sec. 1361, 1995). If U.S. government property damage exceeds $100, the punishment escalates to "a fine of not more than $10,000 or imprisonment for not more than ten years, or both" (18 U.S.C., Sec. 1361, 1995).

The important phrase in these statutes is *not more than.* Judges have the discretionary power and authority to sentence offenders to the maximum penalties provided by law (i.e., as outlined in the criminal statutes). Or, judges may do nothing. A third option is that they might impose a portion of the maximum sentence prescribed by statute. Sometimes, a judge may say, "You are hereby sentenced to six months in the county jail and ordered to pay a $500 fine—the six-month sentence is to be suspended upon payment of the $500 fine plus court costs." Or, the judge may say, "You are sentenced to four years in prison, but I suspend this sentence and order you placed on probation for the four-year period." Most judges have a wide variety of sentencing options. Different types of sentencing systems were described in Chapter 1. Some states have sentencing systems that severely narrow judicial sentencing options.

The public seems ambivalent about probation and who receives it. Popular opinion views probation as a nonsentence, "getting off," or as a measure of leniency (Allen et al., 1985; Gray, 1986:26). Even experts disagree about how probation ought to be used. The word *probation* is sometimes used to indicate a legal disposition, a measure of leniency, a punitive measure, an administrative process, and a treatment method (Gray, 1986:26). A generally accepted definition of *probation* is the supervised release of offenders into the community in lieu of incarceration subject to conditions (Allen et al., 1985). With minor modifications, this definition is similar to the legal definition provided above by Black (1990:1202).

PROBATION DISTINGUISHED FROM PAROLE

Probation might be considered a "front-end" sentence, whereby judges impose conditional sentences in lieu of incarceration. In most cases, probationers are those who do not serve time in either jail or prison. Rather, they must conform to a more or less extensive list of conditions as specified in their probation orders from the court. There are some special types of probation, such as *shock probation* and *split sentencing,* whereby offenders might receive some short-term incarceration and then be placed into the community to serve the duration of their sentences on probation. These forms of probation are discussed at length in Chapter 4. Another distinguishing feature of probation is that offenders remain within the jurisdiction of sentencing judges while on probation. Thus, if probationers violate one or more conditions of their probation orders, judges normally decide whether to revoke or rescind their probation. Probation revocation is discussed together with parole revocation in Chapter 7. This is because both types of revocation actions involve common landmark U.S. Supreme Court cases, and it would be redundant to discuss probation revocation in one chapter and parole revocation in another. Other reasons exist for treating revocations in a single chapter. These are also treated in Chapter 7.

In contrast, *parole* is a conditional early release from incarceration, usually from a prison or penitentiary, by a parole board. Most states have parole boards that convene to decide whether offenders should be released short of serving their full sentences. We know that jails and prisons are chronically overcrowded. Thus, any measure that might reduce such overcrowding is used to alleviate these adverse conditions. Parole is one such measure, although alleviating prison overcrowding is only one of several important functions of parole. Parole differs from probation in that parolees have spent time, usually considerable time, in a prison setting. All parolees have in common the fact that they have been inmates of some state or federal facility in the past. Another distinguishing feature of parole is that *parole boards* have jurisdiction over parolees and control whether they are released early or short of serving their full terms of incarceration. Both judicial and parole board jurisdictions relative to probationers and parolees are discussed at length in Chapter 7. Another difference between probation and parole is that they have distinctly different histories. Below is a brief history of probation in the United States.

THE HISTORY OF PROBATION IN THE UNITED STATES

Many American laws and judicial procedures in the United States have been influenced by early British common law and judicial customs. Also, evidence shows a distinct British influence on United States prison architecture and design as well as other corrections-related phenomena (American Correctional Association, 1983; Evans, 1982).

Judicial Reprieves and Releases on an Offender's Recognizance

During the late 1700s and early 1800s, English judges increasingly exercised their discretion in numerous criminal cases by granting convicted offenders judicial reprieves. Under English common law, a **judicial reprieve** was the suspension of an incarcerative sentence of a convicted offender. A reprieval was a demonstration of judicial leniency, especially in those cases in which offenders had no prior records and had committed minor offenses and the punishments were deemed excessive by the courts. Judges believed that in certain cases, incarceration would serve no useful purpose. Although no accurate records are available about how many convicted offenders actually received judicial reprieves in English courts during this period, the practice of granting judicial reprieves was adopted by some judges in the United States.

Judges in Massachusetts courts during the early 1800s typically used their discretionary powers to suspend incarcerative sentences of particular offenders. Jail and prison overcrowding no doubt influenced their interest in devising options to incarceration. One of the more innovative judges of that period was Boston Municipal Judge Peter Oxenbridge Thatcher. Judge Thatcher used judicial leniency when sentencing offenders. He also sentenced some offenders to be released on their own recognizance (ROR), either before or after their criminal charges had been adjudicated. Thatcher's decision to release convicted offenders on their own recognizance amounted to an indefinite suspension of their incarcerative sentences. Thatcher believed that such sentences would encourage convicted offenders to practice good behavior and refrain from committing new crimes.

Judicial reprieves and suspensions of incarcerative sentences for indefinite periods continued throughout the nineteenth century, but the U.S. Supreme Court declared this practice unconstitutional in 1916. The Supreme Court believed that such discretion among judges infringed on the "separation of powers" principle by contravening the powers of the legislative and executive branches to write laws and ensure their enforcement. However, during the 1830s, when releases on an offender's own recognizance and judicial reprieves flourished, the stage was set for the work of another Boston correctional pioneer.

John Augustus, the Father of Probation in the United States

A substantial number of other court practices in the United States have been inherited from England, but there are many exceptions. In corrections, probation is one of those exceptions. Probation in the United States was conceived in 1841 by the successful cobbler or shoemaker and philanthropist, **John Augustus,** although historical references to this phenomenon may be found in writings as early as 422–437 B.C. Of course, the actions of Judge Thatcher may be interpreted by some scholars as probation, since he sentenced convicted offenders to release on their own recognizance in lieu of incarceration. However, John Augustus is most frequently credited with implementing probation on a fairly large scale, even though no local or state statutes were in effect at the time to condone it.

Strongly influenced by the temperance movement of the period, Augustus made a concerted effort to rehabilitate alcoholics and to assist those arrested for intoxication-related offenses. Appearing in a Boston municipal court one morning to observe offenders charged and sentenced for various crimes, Augustus intervened on behalf of a man charged with being a "common drunkard" (Augustus, 1852). As an alternative to having the convicted offender placed in the **Boston House of Corrections,** Augustus offered to supervise the man's behavior for a three-week period and guaranteed his subsequent reappearance in court. Knowing Augustus's reputation for philanthropy and trusting his motives, the judge agreed. When Augustus returned three weeks later with the "reformed" drunkard, the judge was so impressed that he fined the offender only one cent and court costs (which amounted to less than $4!) and suspended the usual sentence of incarceration (which was sometimes six months or more). Between 1841 and 1859, the year Augustus died, it is estimated that he saved nearly 2,000 men and women from incarceration by bailing them out and supervising them for a fixed probationary period.

During that same period, Augustus attracted several philanthropic volunteers to perform similar probation services. These volunteers worked with juvenile offenders as well as with adults. However, since few records were kept about the dispositions of juveniles because of their status, the precise number of those assisted by Augustus's volunteers is unknown. Estimates are that thousands of youths benefited as the result of these voluntary services.

John Augustus (1785–1859) was a Boston shoemaker who invented probation in 1841 and became the first "unofficial" probation officer.

The Ideal-Real Dilemma: Philosophies in Conflict

While probation is common in the United States today, especially for those offenders convicted of petty or less serious crimes, it was a true correctional innovation in 1841. Prior to the pioneering work of Augustus, offenders convicted of criminal offenses anticipated either fines, imprisonment, or both. Between 1790 and 1817, sentences in United States courts had to be served in their entirety (Bottomley, 1984). The number of federal prisoners increased beyond the government's capacity to confine them, and overcrowding became a critical correctional issue. Today jail and prison overcrowding is the most prominent problem correctional officials must confront. After 1817, prison systems began releasing some prisoners early before serving their full terms. These **early release** decisions were often made informally by prison administrators, with court approval. Thus, the informal use of parole in the United States technically preceded the informal use of probation by several decades. The history of parole in the United States is discussed at length in Chapter 6.

At present, the "get-tough" movement in the United States is pressing for a return to those sentencing policies practiced in the early 1800s, when convicted offenders had to serve their incarcerative sentences in their entirety. (The "get-tough" movement is not so much a matter of persons banding together to create harsher punitive public policies against criminal offenders. Rather, the term is used to characterize a general philosophy whose proponents seek tougher criminal laws, longer terms of incarceration for convicted offenders, larger fines for crimes, and closer supervision of offenders on probation or parole.) But prison and jail overcrowding continue to defeat efforts by judges and others to incarcerate larger numbers of convicted offenders for their full sentence duration. Court-ordered prison and jail inmate population reductions abbreviate the actual amount of time inmates serve. Logistical considerations involving where convicted offenders may be housed often conflict with philosophical concerns about "just deserts" and deserved punishment. Furthermore, the constitutional rights of inmates must be preserved. These include the right to prison and jail environments that enhance inmate health and safety. Although no constitutional provisions exist that obligate prison and jail administrators to provide *comfortable* quarters for inmates, penal authorities are obligated to ensure that their incarcerative environments are not "cruel and unusual" and in violation of the Eighth Amendment.

Public Reaction to Probation

Not everyone liked probation as an alternative to incarceration. Many citizens believed that probation was a form of coddling offenders and would cause them to not take their punishment seriously (Blauner and Migliore, 1992:21). Augustus himself was criticized by the press, politicians, and, especially, jailers. The livelihood of jailers was based on the cost of care and inmate accommodations, including provisions for food and clothing. Jailer income was based on jail occupancy.

The greater the occupancy, the greater the jailer's income. Under such a system of jailer rewards, some jailers embezzled funds intended for inmate food and clothing. Although it is unknown how much embezzlement occurred among county jailers, it is known that at least some jailers profited from large inmate populations.

Augustus's philanthropy directly decreased profiteering among those jailers embezzling funds allocated for inmate care. The lack of an effective system of accountability for these funds explains why the Boston House of Corrections (as well as other Massachusetts jails of that period) was described as "a rat-infested hellhole to be avoided if at all possible" (Lindner and Savarese, 1984; Probation Association, 1939).

But Augustus could not save everyone from incarceration. In fact, that was not his intention. He wanted to rescue only those he believed worthy of rehabilitation. Therefore, he screened offenders by asking them questions and engaging in informal background checks of their acquaintances and personal habits. Particularly, he limited his generosity to first offenders or those never before convicted of a criminal offense. By his own account, only one offender out of nearly 2,000 ever violated his trust (Probation Association, 1939). Pre-sentence investigations (PSIs) are now routinely conducted in all United States courts in which defendants have been convicted of felonies or less serious crimes for which they may be incarcerated. Presentence investigations are described in detail in Chapter 3.

When Augustus died in 1859, probation did not die with him. Various prisoner's and children's aid societies, many religion-based, continued to volunteer their services to courts in the supervision of convicted offenders on a probationary basis (Krajick, 1980; Task Force on Corrections, 1966). Another philanthropist, **Rufus Cook,** continued Augustus's work as well, particularly assisting juvenile offenders through the Boston Children's Aid Society in 1860 (Timasheff, 1941:10). **Benjamin C. Clark,** a philanthropist and volunteer "probation officer," assisted in probation work with court permission throughout the 1860s.

Considering probation's origins, it was fitting that Massachusetts became the first state to pass a probation statute in 1878. This statute authorized the mayor of Boston to hire the first probation officer, Captain Savage, a former police officer. He was supervised by the superintendent of police. Thus, probation was given official recognition, although it was based on political patronage. Several other states passed similar statutes before 1900. In 1901, New York enacted a statutory probation provision similar to that in Massachusetts. Between 1886 and 1900, a number of "settlements" were established, primarily in impoverished parts of cities, for the purposes of assisting the poor and improving the lot of the disadvantaged. These settlements were "experimental efforts to aid in the solution of the social and industrial problems . . . engendered by the modern conditions of life in a great city," and they were to figure prominently in the development and use of probation during that period (Lindner and Savarese, 1984).

In 1893, **James Bronson Reynolds,** an early prison reformer, was appointed headworker of the **University Settlement,** a private facility in New York operated to provide assistance and job referral services to community residents. When New York passed the probation statute in 1901, Reynolds seized this opportunity to involve the University Settlement in probation work. Interestingly, the statute itself prohibited compensation for persons performing "probation officer" chores. Probation work was to be simply another facet of the full-time work they did. For example, many early probation officers worked as police officers, deputies, or clerks in district attorneys' offices. The statute also provided that "private citizens would serve as probation officers without cost to the city or county" (Lindner and Savarese, 1984:7). Thus, the voluntary and privately operated University Settlement project was ideally suited to experiments with future probationers.

By 1922, 22 states had provided for probation in their corrections systems. During the late 1800s and early 1900s, federal district judges were also releasing certain offenders on their own recognizance following the pattern of Massachusetts and other states, often utilizing the services of various state probation officers to supervise offenders. The federal government implemented probation formally through a bill sponsored by the Judicial Committee of the House of Representatives on March 4, 1925. The United States Attorney General was given control of probation officers through another bill in 1930. The Federal Juvenile Delinquency Act was passed on June 16, 1938, so that probation could apply to juveniles as well as to adults, although "general probation" for both juveniles and adults had already been created technically through the 1925 and 1930 acts (Timasheff, 1941:64–66). Thus, all states had juvenile probation programs by 1927, and, by 1957, all states had statutes authorizing the use probation as a sanction for adults where appropriate (Coffey et al., 1974). Figure 2.1 summarizes the major developments influencing the evolution of probation in the United States.

The contemporary view of probation in the United States is quite different from the way it was originally conceived in 1841. In fact, even in recent years, dramatic changes have occurred in the forms of probation used and approved by the court. As will be seen, technological developments have generated several monitoring alternatives to the traditional probation officer–client relation. Chapter 4 examines several probation styles favored by various states. Chapters 9 through 11 and Chapter 16 describe present and future probationer and parolee monitoring systems and programs.

THE PHILOSOPHY OF PROBATION

Probation, especially during the 1970s and 1980s, has undergone significant changes in its general conception and implementation (Cunniff, 1986). At present, there are diverse opinions among experts about how probation should be reconceptualized and reorganized (Evans, 1993a, 1993b; McAnany, Thomson, and Fogel, 1984; Wilcenski, Disney, and Miklosey, 1993). One observer suggests that the reason for these disagreements and confusion is a general lack of understanding about what probation does and for whom. Even though the probation system supervises two-thirds of all convicted felons in the United States, it receives little publicity or financial support (Petersilia, 1988b:168–169).

Year	Event
1791	Passage of the Bill of Rights
1817	New York passes first good time statute
1824	New York House of Refuge is founded
1830	Judge Oxenbridge Thatcher in Boston introduces release on one's own recognizance
1836	Massachusetts passes first recognizance with monetary sureties law
1841	John Augustus introduces probation in the United States in Boston
1863	Gaylord Hubbell, warden of the State Correctional Facility at Ossining, N. Y. (Sing Sing), visits Ireland and is influenced by Walter Crofton's ticket of leave or mark system; later led to good time credits earned by prisoners for early release
1869	Elmira Reformatory established in New York where early release dates were set by the board of managers
1870	Establishment of the National Prison Association (later the American Correctional Association), emphasizing indeterminate sentencing and early release
1876	Zebulon Brockway releases inmates on parole from Elmira Reformatory
1878	First probation law passed by Massachusetts
1899	Illinois passes first juvenile court act, creating special juvenile courts
1906	Work release originates in Vermont through informal sheriff action
1913	Huber Law or first work release statute originates in Wisconsin
1916	U. S. Supreme Court declares that sentences cannot be indefinitely suspended by courts; rather, this was a legislative right
1918	Furlough program begun in Mississippi
1932	44 states have parole mechanisms
1954	All states and the federal government have probation and parole systems
1965	Prisoner Rehabilitation Act passed by Congress applicable to federal prisoners
1976	Maine abolishes parole

FIGURE 2.1 Major Events in the Development of Probation and Parole in the United States.

The ideas of "proving," or "trial," or "forgiveness" implicit in probation say much about its underlying philosophy. The primary aim of probation is to provide criminal offenders with the opportunity of proving themselves capable of refraining from further criminal activity. The incentive to refrain from committing other crimes, of course, is avoiding confinement behind bars in a jail or prison.

A prevailing belief is that incarceration is ineffective as a deterrent to crime. Locking up offenders only makes matters worse, according to some experts (Walker, 1989). However, new prison and jail construction is costly. Higher taxes are required to fund this construction. A less expensive alternative is probation. Some forms of probation such as electronic monitoring and home confinement are both effective and cheap. However, incarceration is advocated as a means whereby society may impose justice for those who have violated criminal laws. If incarceration is the "just" and deserved punishment, then it is the right thing for society to do, regardless of the cost of incarceration. Such thinking minimizes the importance and relevance of rehabilitation as an incarcerative aim. Offender punishment, containment, and control should be the priorities of incarceration. Rehabilitation may occur among some offenders, but this is an unintended fringe benefit (Champion, 1988c; Fichter, Hirschburg, and McGaha, 1986, 1987; Whitehead, 1991).

For guidance about the general philosophy of probation, we can examine the original intent of its pioneer, John Augustus. Augustus wanted to reform offenders. He wanted to rehabilitate the common drunk or petty thief. Thus, **rehabilitation** was and continues to be a strong philosophical aim of probation. But somewhere over the years, probation has changed from how Augustus originally conceived it. Let's look at how Augustus supervised his probationers. First, he stood their bail in the Boston Municipal Court. Second, he took them to his home or other place of shelter, fed them, and generally looked after them. He may have even provided them with job leads and other services through his many friendships as well as his political and philanthropic connections. In short, he provided his probationers with fairly intensive supervision and personalized assistance, financial and otherwise.

He supervised approximately 100 probationers per year between 1841 and 1859. We know that he kept detailed records of their progress. In this respect, he compiled what are now called presentence investigations, although he usually made extensive notes about offenders and their progress after they had been convicted. He showed intense interest in their progress, and no doubt many of these probationers were emotionally affected by his kindness and generosity. According to his own assessment of his performance, rehabilitation and reformation were occurring at a significant rate among his clients, and his own efforts were largely responsible.

But this oversimplifies the philosophy of probation. For example, John Augustus's probational goal was **behavioral reform.** Much of his philanthropy was directed toward those offenders with drinking problems. He believed that some offenders would change their set of "bad" behaviors (drunkenness and intemperance) to a set of "good" ones (sobriety and honesty), if they could avoid the taint of imprisonment. Several religious principles guided his belief, as did the views of the Temperance Society to which he belonged.

Present-day probation has become streamlined and bureaucratic. Although there are exceptions, relatively few probation officers feed and clothe their clients and look after their other personal needs. No probation officers sit in municipal courtrooms waiting for the right kinds of offenders who will be responsive to personalized attention and care. No probation officers eagerly approach judges with bail bonds and assume personal responsibility for a probationer's conduct, even if for brief periods.

Today, probation officers assess their work in terms of client caseloads and officer-client ratios. Extensive paperwork is required for each case, and this consumes enormous amounts of time. If we have strayed far afield from Augustus's original meaning of what probation supervision is and how it should be conducted, it has probably been largely the result of bureaucratic expediency. There are too many probationers and too few probation officers. It is hardly unexpected that the public has gradually become disenchanted with the rehabilitative ideal probation originally promised.

The rehabilitative aim of probation has not been rejected. Rather, it has been rearranged in a rapidly growing list of correctional priorities. One dominant, contemporary philosophical aim of probation is **offender control.** If we can't rehabilitate offenders, at least we can devise more effective strategies for controlling their behavior while on probation. Thus, this priority shift in the probation system's philosophical underpinnings has prompted the development of a string of nonincarcerative intermediate punishments, each connected directly with increased offender control by one means or another. Experts generally agree that the future of probation is closely aligned with the effectiveness of intermediate punishments. And, virtually every intermediate punishment established thus far contains one or more provisions for controlling offender behavior.

According to authorities, probation serves several purposes.

1. *Probation keeps those convicted of petty crimes from the "criminogenic environment of jails and prisons"* (Walker, 1989). Prisons are viewed as colleges of crime where inmates are not rehabilitated but rather learn more effective criminal techniques (Walker, 1989).

2. *Probation helps offenders avoid the stigma of the criminal label* (Walker, 1985:172). Some authorities believe that once offenders have been labeled as delinquent or criminal, they will act out these roles by committing subsequent offenses (Walker, 1985:172). Although probationers are criminals and their convictions are a matter of public record, they are less obtrusive in their communities compared with ex-convicts who have served time in prison. They often remain in their present jobs as a probation requirement, and they carry on otherwise normal lives. Petersilia (1985a) indicates that 1 percent of the entire population of California is currently on probation. Unless offenders disclose their probationary status to their neighbors, it is difficult to differentiate former offenders from nonoffenders.

3. *Probation allows offenders to integrate more easily with noncriminals.* Offenders may hold jobs, earn a living for their families and themselves, and develop more positive self-concepts and conforming behaviors not likely acquired if incarcerated. In this respect, "probation is the one correctional treatment program that seems to work" (Walker, 1985:175).

4. *Probation is a practical means by which to ease the problems of prison and jail overcrowding.* Larger numbers of sentences of probation are **front-end solutions** to overcrowding, meaning that steps are taken to divert certain offenders away from jails and prisons before they can become a part of and exacerbate the existing overcrowded conditions. Thus, probation serves the purely logistical function of enabling correctional institutions to more effectively manage smaller inmate populations. In a sense, this logistical consideration may be associated with an **economic philosophy** or numbers management, where the goal is to maximize **probation officer caseloads** or increasing the numbers of those supervised while minimizing supervisory costs, time expenditures, and probationer-client criminality.

It is interesting that some writers have been critical of the cost of probation relative to the cost of incarceration. Gray et al. (1991) conducted an extensive evaluation of studies that compared the cost of operating probation programs with the cost of incarceration. Although their study revealed many conflicting statements about the true cost of probation, these authors conclude that the long-term rehabilitative benefits of probation far outweigh the costs associated with incarcerating the same offenders. However, it should be noted that an underlying assumption of the Gray et al. (1991) research is the general endorsement of selective incapacitation, whereby the most likely recidivists are incapacitated. We have already examined some of the subjectivity and unfairness inherent in selective incapacitation as a crime control strategy. Nevertheless, from this point of view, selectively applied probation would be more cost-effective than incarceration.

MODELS FOR DEALING WITH CRIMINAL OFFENDERS

The Treatment or Medical Model

Despite the religious, moral, and philanthropic interests that influenced the early practice of probation, its current rehabilitative nature derives from the **treatment model** of treating criminals. Also known as the **medical model,** the treatment model considers criminal behavior as an illness to be remedied. The custodial approach of incarcerating criminals does not treat the illness; rather, it separates the ill from the well. When released from incarceration, the ill continue to be ill and are likely to commit further crimes.

The nonincarcerative alternative, probation, permits rehabilitation to occur, through treatment programs and therapeutic services not otherwise available to offenders under conditions of confinement. [Of course, rehabilitative measures within prison and jail settings have been attempted through the creation and use of vocational-technical, educational, and counseling programs as parallels to the treatment received by nonincarcerated probationers. Some writers have developed a cynical attitude toward prison rehabilitation programs and have labeled them "coerced rehabilitation" (Conrad, 1981:13–14).]

Some experts claim the fundamental flaw of the treatment model is that offenders are treated as objects (Finkelman, 1992; Harris, 1984:19; Mann, 1993). But selectively applying probation to some offenders and not to others leads to more fundamental criticisms justifiably associated with inequitable treatment on the basis of gender, race or ethnic status, socioeconomic differences, and other factors (Crew, 1991; Shichor, 1985; Spohn and Cederblom, 1991; Zatz, 1987). These **sentencing disparities** were examined briefly in Chapter 1.

The 1960s and 1970s have been regarded as the **progressive era,** when rehabilitation was stressed by liberals for both incarcerated and nonincarcerated offenders. However, rising crime rates and the recidivism of probationers and parolees stimulated a public backlash against social reform programs. Studies conducted in the 1970s disclosed the apparent lack of success of rehabilitation programs, including probation (Sechrest, White, and Brown, 1979; von Hirsch, 1976). While some critics contend that these studies are inconclusive and misleading, one result was the general condemnation of rehabilitation and specific probation alternatives (Cullen and Gilbert, 1982; Walker, 1985:167–169). Despite these criticisms, rehabilitation continues to be a strong correctional goal (Cunniff, Sechrest, and Cushman, 1992; Haddock and Beto, 1990).

The Rehabilitation Model

Closely related to the treatment or medical model is the **rehabilitation model.** This model stresses rehabilitation and reform. Although rehabilitation may be traced to William Penn's work in correctional reform, the most significant support for the rehabilitation orientation came from Zebulon Brockway's Elmira Reformatory in 1876. Eventually, federal recognition of rehabilitation as a major correctional objective occurred when the Federal Bureau of Prisons was established on May 14, 1930. Although the first federal penitentiary was built in 1895 in Leavenworth, Kansas, it took 35 more years for an official federal prison policy to be devised. The original mandate of the Bureau of Prisons called for rehabilitating federal prisoners through vocational and educational training, as well as the traditional individualized psychological counseling that was associated with the treatment model. In later years, encounter groups, group therapy, and other strategies were incorporated into federal prison operations and policy as alternative rehabilitative methods.

Between 1950 and 1966, over 100 prison riots occurred in federal facilities. These incidents were sufficient for officials to reconsider the rehabilitation model and define it as ineffective for reforming prisoners. There were other weaknesses of this model as well. Similar to the treatment model that preceded it, the rehabilitation model stresses "individual" treatment or reform, and as a result, inmate sanctions have often been individualized. This means that those who have committed similar offenses of equal severity might receive radically different rehabilitation or punishment. The inequity of this individualized system is apparent, and in many jurisdictions, such inequities in the application of sanctions have been associated with race, ethnicity, gender, or socioeconomic status (Zatz, 1987).

The Justice or Due Process Model

Although the rehabilitation ideal has not been abandoned, it has been supplemented by an alternative known as the **justice** or **due process model** (Ellsworth, 1990a, 1990b, 1990c; Fogel, 1975; Fogel and Hudson, 1981). The justice model is not intended to replace the rehabilitative model, but rather to enhance it (Fogel and Hudson, 1981:viii; Humphries, 1984; von Hirsch, 1983).

Probation practices in the United States have been influenced by the justice model in recent years through the imposition of more equitable sentences (Harlow, 1984). Sentencing reforms have been undertaken to eliminate sentencing disparities attributable to race, ethnic background, gender, or socioeconomic status (see Chapter 1). The justice model applied to probation stresses fair and equitable treatment (as well as punishment to fit the offenses). Probably the most important reason citizens currently object to probation is that they do not define it as a form of punishment. In response to this criticism, several justice-oriented writers (McAnany, 1984; McAnany and Thomson, 1982; Thomson and Fogel, 1980; von Hirsch, 1992) have proposed the following:

1. Probation is a penal sanction whose main characteristic is punitive.
2. Probation should be a sentence, not a substitute for a real sentence threatened after future offenses.
3. Probation should be a part of a single, graduated range of penal sanctions available for all levels of crime except for the most serious felonies.
4. The severity of the probation sentence should be determined by the quality and quantity of conditions (e.g., restitution or community service).
5. Neither the length of term nor any condition should be subject to change during the sentence, unless the conditions are violated.
6. Conditions should be justified in terms of seriousness of offense.
7. Where conditions are violated, courts should assess additive penalties through "show cause" hearings."

Despite these justice-oriented propositions to remedy certain defects in current probation practices, probation is not about to be abolished. In fact, it is increasingly being used at the state and federal levels (Champion, 1988c; Petersilia, 1985c). And, probation is not applied exclusively to low-risk property offenders or to those lacking prior records. Convicted murderers, rapists, arsonists, and robbers are receiving probation more often as well. This event has prompted greater interest in the development of instruments that attempt to forecast public risk or future dangerousness of offenders (Champion, 1994). Such instruments are described in Chapter 3.

The due process model rejects rehabilitation as the major objective of punishment, although it doesn't abandon it. By the same token, sentencing disparities for offenders convicted of similar crimes are opposed. Due process emphasizes one's constitutional right to a fair trial and consistent treatment under the law. The "equal protection" clause of the Fourteenth Amendment is also stressed. Sentencing disparities attributable to race, ethnic origin, gender, or socioeconomic status should not be tolerated.

Fogel (1975) has endorsed the principle of justice as fairness. Sentencing for crimes should be scaled proportionately according to the crime's seriousness. Coinciding with the general shift away from the rehabilitation model is the trend toward the development of sentencing guidelines (Shane-DuBow, Brown, and Olsen, 1985; Tonry and Zimring, 1983). Minnesota, California, and several other states have devised guidelines in recent years that are considered fair and impartial standards by which to gauge penalties for various offenses. The federal government has also devised presumptive sentencing guidelines, which went into effect November 1, 1987. These guidelines provide ranges of penalties that permit judges some discretion, although fairly strict adherence to these guidelines is encouraged. The intent of these general sentencing reforms is to achieve "just" criminal sanctions consistent with the doctrine espoused earlier by Beccaria and others (Tonry and Zimring, 1983).

BOX 2.1
Can Judges Require Probationers to Do Unusual Things?

The Case of Unusual and Unconstitutional Probation Conditions

Judges have a lot of sentencing power. They can legally incarcerate any defendant convicted of a crime. They can also place these offenders on probation. Furthermore, they can require their probationers to do different things and comply with various conditions while on probation. Some of these conditions are reasonable and expected. Some are downright unreasonable and unexpected. For instance, it would be entirely proper for a judge to sentence a convicted child molester to a community counseling program or to have a psychiatric examination. Also, it would not be unusual to require these individuals to make themselves available for on-the-spot visits from their probation officers or submit to random drug or alcohol checks. But it might be unreasonable for a judge to order a sex offender to be sterilized or castrated.

This Is Reasonable

The Minnesota Supreme Court has ruled that persons convicted of trespassing at a Planned Parenthood Clinic to protest abortions can legally be required, *as a condition of probation*, to stay 500 feet away from the clinic. (*State v. Friberg*, 44 CrL 2391 [Minn. SupCt.], 1989.)

This Is Unreasonable

A Vermont federal court ruled that probationers cannot be forced to incriminate themselves while participating in therapy as a part of a probation program. During his required "complete" sexual therapy program *while on probation,* a probationer who had been previously convicted of lewd and lascivious conduct with his stepdaughter was drawn into admitting during therapy that he had had oral sex with the girl but not intercourse. This admission was communicated to the court by the therapist and the probationer's probation program was immediately revoked on the grounds that this constituted a failure to complete the therapy program. The federal court declared that the probationer had a Fifth Amendment right against self-incrimination, especially when a subsequent admission would have been grounds for a sexual assault charge and prosecution. The court said, "If the state wishes to carry out rehabilitative goals in probation by compelling offenders to disclose their criminal conduct, they must grant them immunity from [further] criminal prosecution." (*Mace v. Amestoy*, 49 CrL 1254 [DC Vt.], 1991.)

This Is Unreasonable

A woman in Kansas was convicted of child endangerment. She was placed on probation by the judge but ordered to "refrain from becoming pregnant" *as a part of her probation program*. The Kansas Supreme Court declared this condition unconstitutional, noting that "such a condition could force the woman to choose between concealing her pregnancy and thus deny her child adequate medical care, abortion, or incarceration. Putting her in such a position was unreasonable" according to the court. (*State v. Mosburg,* 44 CrL 2391 [Kan. SupCt.], 1989.)

This Is Unreasonable

Gary Mills is a used-car salesman who owns his own business. He was convicted of turning back odometers on used cars he sold to customers and placed on probation. *As a condition of his probation,* Mills was ordered (1) not to own or operate a new or used car business during the term of his probation, (2) to seek employment in an occupation other than auto sales, and (3) to close his current auto business. The federal Fifth Circuit Court of Appeals heard his case and determined that although the occupational restriction provision was justified, his obligation to sell his business was not. The court said, "the scope of the occupational restriction exceeded what was reasonably necessary to protect the public. Requiring Mills to close and sell his business went beyond what was necessary. It was sufficient to ban Mills from all personal participation in the operations of his or any other car businesses during the term of his supervised release, but requiring him to sell his business amounted to punishment and was not permitted." (*United States v. Mills,* 51 CrL 1146 [5th Cir.], 1992.)

This Is Unreasonable

Grady was convicted of a crime and sentenced to probation. Among other conditions imposed by the court, Grady was required to "visit no bars, restaurants, or any place where alcoholic beverages are served without written permission from the probation officer" and "not to be within three blocks of known high drug areas as determined by the probation officer." The Florida District Court of Criminal Appeals declared these *conditions of probation* unconstitutional and "improper." (*Grady v. State,* 604 So.2d 1255 [Fla.Dist.App.], 1992.)

This Is Reasonable

Applewhite was convicted of two counts of second-degree burglary. He was sentenced to a consecutive prison term of five to fifteen years on each count, but the sentence was suspended and he was placed on probation for a period of five years. One *condition of probation* imposed by the judge was that Applewhite was required to enter and complete a well-known drug treatment program in his area known as the Second Genesis. Applewhite entered but failed to complete this program and his probation was subsequently revoked. He appealed, contending that this condition of probation was "excessive." The appeals court disagreed. The court noted that the probationer was a noted drug user and that the drug rehabilitation program was a reasonable and necessary part of his probation orders. (*Applewhite v. United States,* 614 A.2d 888 [D.C.App.], 1992.)

The justice model also contains the fundamental concept that sanctions should be influenced by past, proven criminal behavior rather than by predictions of future illegal acts. In this respect, the justice model requires a backward-looking perspective in applying sanctions (McAnany, Thomson, and Fogel, 1984:30). Sanctions should be clear, explicit, and highly predictable. This would overcome the indefiniteness associated with rehabilitation-oriented and individually based sentencing schemes currently used by judges in a majority of jurisdictions.

The "Just-Deserts" Model

The **"just-deserts"** or **deserts model** emphasizes equating punishment with the severity of the crime. In this respect, Beccaria's ideas are evident in the development of just-deserts as a punishment orientation. Therefore, retribution is an important component. Just-deserts dismisses rehabilitation as a major correctional aim. It alleges that offenders ought to receive punishments equivalent to the seriousness of their crimes. If rehabilitation occurs during the punishment process, this is not undesirable, but it is also not essential (Fogel, 1981).

Applying the "just-deserts" philosophy, offenders sentenced to prison would be placed in custody levels fitting the seriousness of their crimes. Petty offenders who commit theft or burglary might be sentenced to minimum-security facilities or "honor farms" with few guards and fences. Accordingly, robbers, rapists, and murderers would be placed in maximum-security prisons under close supervision. If offenders are sentenced to probation, their level of supervision would be adjusted to fit the seriousness of their offenses. The more serious the offense, the more intensive the supervision.

The just-deserts model has emerged in recent years as a popular alternative to the rehabilitation model that influenced correctional programs for many decades (Ellsworth, 1990a, 1990b, 1990c). Penal and sentencing reforms among jurisdictions are currently consistent with the just-deserts approach. Public pressure for applying the just-deserts orientation in judicial sentencing, including greater severity of penalties imposed, has stimulated the "get tough on crime" movement.

The Community Model

The **community model** is a relatively new concept based on the correctional goal of offender reintegration into the community (Byrne and Brewster, 1993; Clear, 1993). (See Chapter 8 for a discussion of intermediate punishments emphasizing community-based services that rely on the community correctional model.) Sometimes called the *reintegration model,* the community model stresses offender adaptation to the community by participating in one or more programs that are a part of **community-based corrections** (American Correctional Association, 1989b). More judges are using community-based corrections because they are in place within the community and because they offer a front-end solution to prison and jail overcrowding (Evans, 1993a, 1993b; Harland, 1993). Often, offenders are accommodated in large homes where curfews and other rules are imposed. Food, clothing, and employment assistance are provided. Sometimes, counselors and psychiatrists are on call to assist their clients with serious adjustment or coping problems if they occur (Larivee et al., 1990).

The primary strengths of the community model are that offenders are able to reestablish associations with their families and that they have the opportunity to work at jobs from which a portion of wages earned can be used for victim restitution, payment of fines, and defrayment of program maintenance costs. Furthermore, offenders may participate in psychological therapy or educational and vocational programs designed to improve their work and/or social skills (Cunniff, Sechrest, and Cushman, 1992). POs often function as brokers, locating important and necessary community services for their offender/clients. POs also provide a means whereby offenders can obtain employment.

The community correctional model also encourages citizen involvement in offender reintegration (American Correctional Association, 1993b; Lawrence, 1985, 1990; Shilton, 1992). Often, paraprofessionals may assist probation officers in their paperwork. Community volunteers assist offenders by performing cleaning and kitchen work. Occasionally, important community officials may be members of boards of directors of these community-based services, further integrating the community with the correctional program. However, the presence of community celebrities is sometimes purely symbolic, for example, when they are figureheads exclusively and seldom become actively involved in these programs. Nevertheless, these healthy liaisons with community residents generally increase community acceptance of offenders and offender programs. With such community support, offenders have a better chance of adapting to community life. In recent years, operators of community-based offender programs have been keenly aware of the importance of cultivating links with the community, especially with community leaders (American Correctional Association, 1993b; Lauen, 1990a, 1990b, 1990c; McCarthy and McCarthy, 1984).

FUNCTIONS OF PROBATION

The functions of probation are closely connected with its underlying philosophy. Within the rehabilitation context, the primary functions of probation are (1) crime control, (2) community reintegration, (3) rehabilitation, (4) punishment, and (5) deterrence.

Crime Control

The notion of **crime control** as a probation function stems directly from the fact that probationers are often supervised more or less closely by their POs. Jurisdictions with large numbers of probationers have difficulty supervising these offenders closely. This is because there simply aren't enough POs to do the job of supervision properly. In many cases, probationers mail a form to the probation office weekly or monthly. This form is usually a checklist that offenders use to report any law infractions, their most recent employment record, and other factual information. They may also pay preestablished fees to defray a portion of their probation costs and maintenance (Parent, 1989a). Of course, much of this information is self-reported and subjective. It is difficult, if not impossible, to verify the veracity of these self-report statements without some alternative supervisory scheme. Most of the time, probation agencies simply do not have the resources to conduct checks of this self-reported information. Only if offenders are rearrested within the jurisdiction supervising them do they come to the attention of probation offices again.

BOX 2.2
Automated Drive-In Windows for Probationers?

The Case of the New York City Probation Department

The technology has finally arrived. We are definitely in the electronic age. New York City has more than its fair share of probationers. The New York City Probation Department also has a problem typical of most other probation agencies—not enough money to run its department properly. There aren't enough probation officers to go around. And, there are lots of probationers. Some of these probationers are dangerous while others aren't. What, if anything, can be done to assist the probation department and free up its limited probation officer staff to work primarily with the more dangerous probationers?

In 1994, New York City implemented a new automated program in which terminals similar to automated bank machines were placed in kiosks in key locations throughout the city. These machines will enable low-risk probationers, about 60,000 of them annually, to check in on regular bases and answer a serious of questions relative to their current behavior and possible criminal conduct. The machines are equipped to conduct thumb print analyses and verifications, palm print and voice print analyses and identifications, or retina scans. Those offenders requiring special help or referrals to various agencies or human resources will receive such referral information from these machines, based on their answers to questions asked.

Especially for low-risk probationers, this tactic seems workable as a supervisory tool. In Los Angeles, California, for example, caseloads of probation officers might be as high as 2,000 clients per officer. There is no way officers can meet face-to-face with all of their probationer-clients on a monthly or even semimonthly basis. Many officers in Los Angeles tell their probationer-clients to call in once in a while. That is the extent of the supervision they will receive. Is it any wonder that the recidivism rate among these probationers is as high as 65 or 70 percent?

Commissioner Michael Jacobson, head of the New York City Probation Department, says that the new system is not a passing fancy or fad. In fact, it is his expectation that the automated check-in devices will only get better and more sophisticated in future years.

Should probationers be required to have face-to-face visits with their probation officers regularly? Are we spending enough money on our probation service? Do such check-in devices violate any of our constitutional rights? Should machines be vested with referral authority?

Source: *Corrections Digest*, "Automation Reporting for New York City's Low-Risk Offenders," *Corrections Compendium*, **18**, October 1993.

Precisely how much crime control occurs as the result of probation is unknown. When offenders are outside the immediate presence of probation officers, they may or may not engage in undetected criminal activity. Standard probation offers little by way of true crime control, since there is minimal contact between offenders and their probation officers. Various probation programs examined in Chapter 4 offer greater promise for taking a bite out of crime through greater offender monitoring. However, it is believed that even standard probation offers some measure of crime control by extending to probationers a degree of trust as well as minimal behavioral restrictions (Byrne and Brewster, 1993; Clear, 1993). It would be misleading to believe that no monitoring occurs under standard probation supervision. Probation officers are obligated to make periodic checks of workplaces and conversations with an offender's employer disclose much about how offenders are managing their time. But again, limited probation department resources confine these checks to so much cursory and superficial activity.

Community Reintegration

One obvious benefit for offenders receiving probation is that they avoid the **criminogenic environment** of incarceration (Walker, 1989). Offenders on probation usually maintain jobs, live with and support their families, engage in vocational or technical training or other educational programs, receive counseling, and lead otherwise normal lives (Lovell, 1985). Although minimum-security prisons and some jails do afford prisoners opportunities to learn skills and participate in programs designed to rehabilitate them, there is nothing about prisons and jails that comes close to the therapeutic value of remaining free within the community.

The effectiveness of probation under intensive supervision is illustrated by a New Jersey experiment. New Jersey Intensive Supervision Program officials accepted 226 convicted felons from 18,000 applicants for program participation (Pearson, 1985). Offenders maintained regular contact with probation officers during a 14-month period (1983–1984), either by telephone or face-to-face contact. Only 29 out of the original 226 clients were returned to prison, and only one of these was incarcerated for a new felony conviction. Similar patterns have been observed in other communities as well (American Correctional Association, 1993b; Champion, 1988c; Petersilia, 1985c, 1987a; Petersilia, Turner, and Peterson, 1986; Petersilia et al., 1985).

Rehabilitation

One benefit of probation is that it permits offenders to remain in their communities, work at jobs, support their families, make restitution to victims, and perform other useful services. In addition, offenders avoid the criminogenic influence of jail or prison environments (Walker, 1989). It is most difficult to make the transformation from prison life to community living, especially if an inmate has been incarcerated for several years. Prison life is highly regulated, and the nature of confinement bears no relation to life on the outside. The community reintegration function of probation is most closely associated with its rehabilitative aim (American Correctional Association, 1986a, 1993c; Dickey and Wagner, 1990; Ellsworth, 1990a, 1990b, 1990c).

Punishment

What can possibly pass for punishment under standard probation? First, there is always the sanctioning option of the probation officer to revoke an offender's probation for violating one or more probation conditions. Filing a late monthly report is a technical violation. Being absent from work without a legitimate excuse might also be a violation of an offender's probation terms. Other sanctions may be imposed as a part of standard probation, although they do not involve direct or frequent contact with the probation officer. For example, the judge may order the convicted offender to make restitution to victims or to pay for damages and medical bills sustained through whatever crime was committed. Public service of a particular type may be required, and others may be asked to report on the offender's work quality in the service performed. And, of course, the offender may be fined. A portion of an offender's wages may be garnished by the court regularly during the term of probation as payment toward the fine assessed. Obviously, the offender must sustain regular employment in order to meet these court-imposed fine obligations. These are punishments, although they are not particularly severe.

Deterrence

The deterrent value of probation is measured most often by recidivism figures among those placed on probation. Because of the low degree of offender control associated with standard probation supervision, which is tantamount to little or no supervision at all, recidivism rates are proportionately higher than those of offenders in more intensively supervised intermediate punishment programs. Experts disagree about the level of **deterrence** that probation yields. Does probation decrease an offender's likelihood of committing future crimes? Almost all studies of probation and its effects cite some program failures. This has caused skeptics to take a dim view of probation—even to consider it unworkable as a rehabilitative strategy (Martinson, 1974). However, others have pointed to "probation as the one correctional treatment program that seems to work" (Walker, 1989). When recidivism rates or the rates of new crimes committed by convicted offenders are compared for probationers and those who have been incarcerated, probationers have consistently lower crime rates. Therefore, one important factor is the cost-effectiveness of different available correctional options as measured by the amount of new crime.

Generally, probation programs are less costly than incarceration. They also exhibit less recidivism among their clients compared with ex-convicts released from prisons. Viewed from this perspective, probation functions as a deterrent. Some critics say that if probation and parole were done away with today, the crime rate in America would probably go up only about *2 percent.* This 2 percent would be probation and parole administrators and line staff who turned to crime only because they could find no other suitable employment for themselves (Callanan, 1987:16). This remark underscores the current lack of consensus about how probation functions in relation to courts and criminal defendants.

A PROFILE OF PROBATIONERS

The profile of probationers in the United States is changing annually. Each year, the probation population includes increasing numbers of felony offenders (Champion, 1988c; Gottfredson and Gottfredson, 1988). A general breakdown of the estimated number of felony convictions in state courts for 1990 is informative and presented in Table 2.1. Nearly 18 percent of all 829,344 convictions were for violent crimes, while property and drug offenses each accounted for about one-third of all convictions.

Which of these offenders were most likely to receive probation? First, an investigation of the sentences imposed for all convicted felony offenders in state courts for 1990 showed that of all 829,344 felons sentenced, about 29 percent were

TABLE 2.1 Number of Felony Convictions in State and Federal Courts, 1990

Most Serious Conviction Offense	Felony Convictions			Federal Felony Convictions as Percentage of Total
	Total	State	Federal	
All offenses	866,028	829,344	36,684	4.2%
Violent offenses	149,925	147,766	2,159	1.4%
Murder/manslaughter[a]	11,028	10,895	133	1.2
Rape	18,165	18,024	141	.8
Robbery	48,780	47,446	1,334	2.7
Aggravated assault	54,178	53,861	317	.6
Other violent[b]	17,774	17,540	234	1.3
Property offenses	290,860	280,748	10,112	3.5%
Burglary	109,846	109,750	96	.1
Larceny[c]	114,923	113,094	1,829	1.6
Motor vehicle theft	21,333	21,065	268	1.3
Other theft	93,590	92,029	1,561	1.7
Fraud/forgery[d]	66,091	57,904	8,187	12.4
Fraud[d]	34,341	26,877	7,464	21.7
Forgery	31,750	31,027	723	2.3
Drug offenses	289,737	274,613	15,124	5.2%
Possession	106,379	106,253	126	.1
Trafficking	183,358	168,360	14,998	8.2
Weapons offenses	23,089	20,733	2,356	10.2%
Other offenses[e]	112,417	105,484	6,933	6.2%

[a]Does not include negligent manslaughter.
[b]Includes offenses such as negligent manslaughter, sexual assault, and kidnapping.
[c]Includes motor vehicle theft.
[d]Includes embezzlement.
[e]Composed of nonviolent offenses such as receiving stolen property and immigration offenses.
Source: Langan, Parkins, and Chaiken 1994:2.

sentenced to probation terms averaging 42 months (Langan and Dawson, 1993:1–3). These figures are shown in Table 2.2.

Table 2.2 also shows a percentage breakdown of these offenders according to various offense categories, including violence offenses (murder, rape, robbery, aggravated assault, and "other" violence), property offenses (burglary, larceny, and fraud), drug offenses, weapons offenses, and "other" (Langan and Dawson, 1993:3). As can be seen from Table 2.2, 20 percent of all convicted violent offenders received probation. Weapons and property offenses were the two largest major felony categories for which probation was used as a punishment (38 percent and 34 percent respectively). Interestingly, those convicted of drug possession were less likely to go to prison, compared with those convicted of burglary and larceny. If these figures are typical of state and federal jurisdictions generally, no crime category is excluded from consideration for probation. Nearly 600 convicted murderers and over 2,500 convicted rapists received probation.

TABLE 2.2 Types of Felony Sentences Imposed by State Courts, 1990

Most Serious Conviction Offense	Total	Percentage of Felons Sentenced to Incarceration			
		Total	Prison	Jail	Probation
All offenses	100%	71%	46%	25%	29%
Violent offenses	100%	80%	59%	21%	20%
Murder[a]	100	95	91	4	5
Rape	100	86	67	19	14
Robbery	100	90	73	17	10
Aggravated assault	100	72	45	27	28
Other violent[b]	100	67	42	25	33
Property offenses	100%	66%	44%	22%	34%
Burglary	100	75	54	21	25
Larceny[c]	100	65	40	25	35
Fraud[d]	100	53	33	20	47
Drug offenses	100%	72%	43%	29%	28%
Possession	100	64	35	29	36
Trafficking	100	77	49	28	23
Weapons offenses	100%	62%	38%	24%	38%
Other offenses[e]	100%	66%	37%	29%	34%

Note: For persons receiving a combination of sentences, the sentence designation came from the most severe penalty imposed—prison being the most severe, followed by jail, then probation. Data on sentence type were available for 99.4% of the estimated total.

[a]Includes nonnegligent manslaughter.

[b]Includes offenses such as negligent manslaughter, sexual assault, and kidnapping.

[c]Includes motor vehicle theft.

[d]Includes forgery and embezzlement.

[e]Composed of nonviolent offenses such as receiving stolen property and driving while intoxicated.

Source: Langan and Dawson, 1993:2.

Probationers are often required to have face-to-face visits with their probation officers as a part of the probation program. (Cathy Cheney/Stock Boston)

Ordinarily, first-offenders, low-risk offenders, property offenders, and nonviolent offenders are prime candidates for probation of some form. Who gets probation and who gets jail or prison often depends on the jurisdiction under investigation. Those states without serious jail and prison overcrowding problems are able to accommodate more offenders who commit serious crimes. However, in states such as California, Texas, Louisiana, and Tennessee, serious overcrowding problems force judges and others to consider several alternatives to incarceration. Before we look at the profile of probationers in the United States, it is helpful for comparative purposes to consider the demographic characteristics of the population of convicted felons for 1990. This demographic information is shown in Table 2.3.

Table 2.3 shows that in 1990, 86 percent of all convicted felons were male and 47 percent were black. In 1990, women accounted for 16 percent of all drug offense felony convictions. The largest offense categories involving women were, respectively, fraud (38 percent), larceny (18 percent), drug possession (17 percent), drug trafficking (15 percent), and murder (10 percent) (Langan and Dawson, 1993:5). Nearly half of all offenders were in the 20–29 age category (48 percent). White and black violent offenders were fairly evenly divided (50 percent and 48 percent, respectively), whereas white property offenders were disproportionately represented compared with blacks (57 percent compared with 42 percent). In contrast, blacks

TABLE 2.3 Demographic Characteristics of Persons Convicted of Felonies by State Courts, 1990

Percentage of Convicted Felons

Most Serious Conviction Offense	Total	Sex		Race			Age					
		Male	Female	White	Black	Other	13–19	20–29	30–39	40–49	50–59	60+
All offenses	100%	86%	14%	52%	47%	1%	10%	48%	30%	9%	2%	1%
Violent offenses	100%	93%	7%	50%	48%	2%	11%	47%	27%	10%	3%	2%
Murder[a]	100	90	10	42	56	2	13	45	24	11	5	2
Rape	100	99	1	65	33	2	8	37	31	14	6	4
Robbery	100	94	6	36	63	1	16	55	23	5	1	—
Aggravated assault	100	91	9	53	44	3	9	47	29	10	3	2
Other violent[b]	100	94	6	72	24	4	7	38	32	15	5	3
Property offenses	100%	83%	17%	57%	42%	1%	12%	50%	27%	8%	2%	1%
Burglary	100	95	5	57	42	1	16	54	24	5	1	—
Larceny[c]	100	82	18	57	42	1	13	48	28	8	2	1
Fraud[d]	100	62	38	58	41	1	4	46	34	12	3	1
Drug offenses	100%	84%	16%	43%	56%	1%	7%	48%	33%	9%	2%	1%
Possession	100	83	17	45	54	1	6	46	35	10	2	1
Trafficking	100	85	15	42	57	1	7	50	31	9	2	1
Weapons offenses	100%	95%	5%	42%	57%	1%	12%	48%	26%	10%	3%	1%
Other offenses[e]	100%	90%	10%	65%	33%	2%	7%	44%	31%	12%	4%	2%

Note: Data on sex were available for 88% of estimated total; on race, 65%, on age, 80%.
— Less than 0.5%.

[a]Includes nonnegligent manslaughter.

[b]Includes offenses such as negligent manslaughter, sexual assault, and kidnapping.

[c]Includes motor vehicle theft.

[d]Includes forgery and embezzlement.

[e]Composed of nonviolent offenses such as receiving stolen property and driving while intoxicated.

Source: Langan and Dawson, 1993:5.

were disproportionately represented in the drug offense category compared with whites (56 percent compared with 43 percent).

What types of criminals are on probation in the United States? By the beginning of 1991, the United States adult probation population grew to a record 2,670,234 offenders serving a sentence of probation supervision in the community (Jankowski, 1991:1). This is a 19 percent increase in the probationer population of 2,242,053 reported for 1988 (Hester, 1988:1). Compared with the number of probationers in the United States in 1981, 1,335,359, the 1991 figure represents an increase of 100 percent. This is particularly significant because the general population grew by only 7 percent during the same period (U.S. Bureau of Census, 1994). One interpretation is that the probationer population in the United States is growing at a rate about 14 times faster than the general population. Table 2.4 shows the number of adult offenders on probation at year end, 1990.

TABLE 2.4 Adults on Probation, 1990

Region and Jurisdiction	Probation Population, 1/1/90	1990 Entries	1990 Exits	Probation Population, 12/31/90	Percentage Change in Probation Population during 1990	Number on Probation on 12/31/90 per 100,000 Adult Residents
U.S. Total	2,521,525	1,637,557	1,489,448	2,670,234	5.9%	1,443
Federal	59,106	20,388	21,272	58,222	–1.5%	31
State	2,462,419	1,617,169	1,468,176	2,612,012	6.1	1,411
Northeast	449,418	219,442	202,854	466,006	3.7%	1,198
Connecticut	42,842	28,738	24,940	46,640	8.9	1,838
Maine	6,851	4,698	4,000	7,549	10.2	821
Massachusetts	88,529	44,486	60,556	72,459	–18.2	1,554
New Hampshire	2,991	1,775	1,620	3,146	5.2	379
New Jersey	64,398	33,540	25,597	72,341	12.3	1,220
New York	136,686	47,656	39,076	145,266	6.3	1,058
Pennsylvania	89,491	46,111	38,275	97,327	8.8	1,071
Rhode Island	12,231	9,294	6,159	15,366	25.6	1,975
Vermont	5,399	3,144	2,631	5,912	9.5	1,408
Midwest	538,394	392,972	364,127	567,839	5.5%	1,289
Illinois	93,944	58,870	57,115	95,699	1.9	1,128
Indiana	61,177	65,388	58,482	68,683	12.3	1,680
Iowa	13,722	346	173	13,895	1.3	675
Kansas	21,675	12,683	12,175	22,183	2.3	1,222
Michigan	122,459	100,151	89,171	133,439	9.0	1,952
Minnesota	58,648	31,394	30,719	59,323	1.2	1,849
Missouri	44,158	25,000	26,836	42,322	–4.2	1,113
Nebraska	12,627	17,767	15,740	14,654	16.1	1,275
North Dakota	1,644	523	436	1,731	5.3	374
Ohio	78,299	59,049	53,968	83,380	6.5	1,036
South Dakota	2,757	3,995	3,592	3,160	14.6	635
Wisconsin	27,284	17,806	15,720	29,370	7.6	815

TABLE 2.4 (*Continued*)

Region and Jurisdiction	Probation Population, 1/1/90	1990		Probation Population, 12/31/90	Percentage Change in Probation Population during 1990	Number on Probation on 12/31/90 per 100,000 Adult Residents
		Entries	Exits			
South	984,909	695,398	638,295	1,042,012	5.8%	1,643
Alabama	25,519	14,251	12,084	27,686	8.5	928
Arkansas	15,552	3,531	3,100	15,983	2.8	924
Delaware	9,701	6,393	3,871	12,223	26.0	2,430
District of Columbia	10,132	8,070	8,460	9,742	−3.8	1,988
Florida	192,731	266,244	248,194	210,781	9.4	2,093
Georgia	125,147	76,042	66,349	134,840	7.7	2,838
Kentucky	8,062	3,030	3,610	7,482	−7.2	274
Lousiana	32,295	13,310	15,414	30,191	−6.5	1,009
Maryland	84,456	44,435	45,993	82,898	−1.8	2,291
Mississippi	7,333	3,138	2,250	8,221	12.1	450
North Carolina	72,325	41,981	36,477	77,829	7.6	1,550
Oklahoma	24,240	12,565	12,394	24,411	.7	1,057
South Carolina	31,623	14,405	13,741	32,287	2.1	1,258
Tennessee	30,906	21,925	20,112	32,719	5.9	894
Texas	291,156	151,767	134,566	308,357	5.9	2,538
Virginia	19,085	11,951	9,733	21,303	11.6	455
West Virginia	4,646	2,360	1,947	5,059	8.9	375
West	489,698	309,357	262,900	536,155	9.5%	1,385
Alaska	3,335	1,993	1,729	3,599	7.9	952
Arizona	27,340	11,978	8,921	30,397	11.2	1,133
California	284,437	173,883	152,620	305,700	7.5	1,389
Colorado	28,037	22,310	19,236	31,111	11.0	1,279
Hawaii	10,960	6,442	5,735	11,667	6.5	1,409
Idaho	4,025	2,024	1,672	4,377	8.7	627
Montana	3,459	1,873	1,280	4,052	17.1	702
Nevada	7,065	3,518	2,883	7,700	9.0	851
New Mexico	5,660	9,650	9,016	6,294	11.2	589
Oregon	31,878	15,742	9,989	37,631	18.0	1,777
Utah	5,524	3,596	3,290	5,830	5.5	532
Washington	74,918	54,791	44,892	84,817	13.2	2,353
Wyoming	3,060	1,557	1,637	2,980	−2.6	937

Note: Seven states estimated numbers in one or more categories. See the detailed probation notes for further information.

Source: Jankowski, 1991:2.

By the beginning of 1991, about 1.4 percent of the total United States population was on probation (Jankowski, 1991:1). This exceeds the proportionate representation of all adults on probation in California (Petersilia, 1985c). About 12 percent of all probationers were women (Bureau of Justice Statistics, 1992). The trend in probation, parole, and incarceration has been described for the years 1975 through 1983 (Petersilia, 1985c). Compared with the growth of prison and parole populations, the probation population grew considerably faster during that period. Between 1974 and 1983, the population of probationers grew by 63 percent, compared with a 48 percent increase in the prison population and a 38 percent increase in the population of parolees (Petersilia, 1985c:2).

Another description of probationers has been provided by the Bureau of Justice Statistics according to maximum time to be served. In 1990, offenders were tracked in all states from arrest to final disposition (Langan and Dawson, 1993). About 829,000 convictions and dispositions were involved in the final survey and examination of **Offender-Based Transactions Statistics (OBTS).** OBTS is defined as a system developed to collect data elements on defendants as they flow through the criminal justice system and to present summarized data for intelligent decision making in the criminal justice system (Honolulu Police Department, 1982:1). Table 2.5 shows the mean and median sentence lengths for these offenders according to different conviction offense categories.

For all 829,000 offenders, the average sentence length was 52 months. Since averages or means are very sensitive to very long or very short sentence lengths, Langan and Dawson (1993) used the median as a more stable and consistent measure of the overall average sentence length. The median is another type of average that is less sensitive to large or small sentence lengths. Note the difference in Table 2.5. While the overall *mean* sentence length is 52 months, the overall *median* sentence length is two years. Thus, the impact of life sentences or death sentences is offset by using the median value. Both the mean and median numbers of months are designated as sentence lengths for different offense categories. Notice in Table 2.5 that median probation sentences overall are about 36 months or 3 years. Within different crime categories, however, the median probation length for murderers and rapists placed on probation is 60 months, or about 5 years. Those convicted of robbery but placed on probation have a median sentence length of 4 years, or 48 months. The shortest probation sentence length is 24 months for weapons offenses. Table 2.5 is also to compare probationers to those incarcerated in either prisons or jails. Thus, we can see the average length of time murderers and others spend in prisons or jails compared with those convicted of similar offenses but sentenced to probation instead.

Probation decisions are made on the basis of several factors. One method of determining who receives a sentence of probation is to examine those criteria associated with a high likelihood of incarceration. Joan Petersilia (1985b:4) has reported a high statistical correlation between prison sentences and the following offender characteristics:

1. having two or more current convictions
2. having two or more adult prior convictions
3. being on parole or probation when arrested
4. being a drug addict
5. being armed
6. using a weapon
7. seriously injuring the victim

TABLE 2.5 Mean and Median Sentence Lengths for Felony Sentences Imposed by State Courts, 1990

Most Serious Conviction Offense	Maximum Sentence Length for Felons Sentenced to Incarceration			Probation
	Total	Prison	Jail	
Mean sentence				
All offenses	52 mo	75 mo	8 mo	42 mo
Violent offenses	91 mo	119 mo	10 mo	46 mo
Murder[a]	233	243	37	67
Rape	128	160	11	61
Robbery	97	115	12	50
Aggravated assault	52	78	9	43
Other violent[b]	57	85	7	45
Property offenses	47 mo	65 mo	8 mo	44 mo
Burglary	61	80	9	48
Larceny[c]	33	49	7	41
Fraud[d]	40	58	6	43
Drug offenses	44 mo	66 mo	9 mo	42 mo
Possession	30	49	6	39
Trafficking	52	74	10	44
Weapons offenses	34 mo	50 mo	7 mo	34 mo
Other offenses[e]	29 mo	44 mo	9 mo	39 mo
Median sentence				
All offenses	24 mo	48 mo	5 mo	36 mo
Violent offenses	54 mo	72 mo	6mo	36 mo
Murder[a]	240	240	12	60
Rape	72	120	6	60
Robbery	60	72	11	48
Aggravated assault	24	51	6	36
Other violent[b]	27	60	4	36
Property offenses	24 mo	48 mo	5 mo	36 mo
Burglary	36	54	6	36
Larceny[c]	23	36	4	36
Fraud[d]	24	36	3	36
Drug offenses	24 mo	48 mo	5 mo	36 mo
Possession	12	30	3	36
Trafficking	36	48	6	36
Weapons offenses	18 mo	36 mo	3 mo	24 mo
Other offenses[e]	13 mo	30 mo	4 mo	36 mo

Note: See note of Table 2.2. Means exclude sentences to death or to life in prison. Sentence length data were available for 97% of incarceration sentences and 97% of probation sentences.

[a]Includes nonnegligent manslaughter.

[b]Includes offenses such as negligent manslaughter, sexual assault, and kidnapping.

[c]Includes motor vehicle theft.

[d]Includes forgery and embezzlement.

[e]Composed of nonviolent offenses such as receiving stolen property and driving while intoxicated.

Source: Langan and Dawson, 1993:3.

It would seem, therefore, that those most likely to receive probation and not prison or jail sentences would be those without prior criminal records, those not addicted to drugs or alcohol, those committing offenses not involving any injury to victims, and those not using weapons during the commission of their offenses. At extreme ends of a continuum of offender seriousness or risk might be first-offenders and recidivists.

FIRST-OFFENDERS AND RECIDIVISTS

The most likely convicted felons to receive either diversion or probation are first-offenders. First-offenders do not have prior criminal records. First-time offenders commit a variety of crimes. Considering the seriousness of the offense, first-offenders committing violent crimes compared with nonviolent property offenses are less likely to be placed on probation.

The list of factors that influence a probation decision is not exhaustive, but it outlines some of what are referred to as aggravating circumstances considered by judges in sentencing decisions. **Aggravating circumstances** are any circumstances accompanying the commission of a crime that increase the enormity of the offense or add to its injurious consequences for victims (Black, 1990:65). Thus, using a weapon when committing a crime or seriously injuring victims will be viewed by the court as aggravating circumstances.

Mitigating circumstances are those factors that lessen the harshness of the sentence imposed. If those awaiting sentencing are first-time offenders, extremely old, mentally ill or retarded, or caused no harm to victims, then these factors are considered mitigating circumstances. Also, offenders may cooperate with the police in apprehending others who were involved in the crime. Judges will consider these factors in their sentencing decisions. Convictions in which one or more mitigating circumstances are present and no aggravating circumstances exist are most likely to result in probationary sentences or shorter incarcerative terms. Both aggravating and mitigating circumstances are described and discussed at length relative to PSI report preparation and sentencing hearings in Chapter 3.

Recidivism is an aggravating circumstance as well. Recidivists are criminal repeaters or habitual offenders (Black, 1990:1269). Sometimes, recidivism is measured in terms of whether offenders are rearrested or are sent to prison (Clarke and Crum, 1985; Delaware Executive Department, 1984; Oregon Crime Analysis Center, 1984). A rearrest does not mean that the arrestee has actually committed a new crime. Also, being taken to prison does not mean that further crimes have been committed. Probationers may be rearrested on suspicion, and some of these offenders may be placed in prison because of probation violations that are not necessarily criminal offenses (e.g., leaving the state without permission from a probation officer, excessive use of alcoholic beverages, or violating curfew).

Those offenders with extensive records of prior criminal convictions are in the high-risk category for being incarcerated. One objective of probation is to rehabilitate offenders and to reintegrate them into the community. Committing additional crimes is evidence that rehabilitation and reintegration have not occurred. Judges are less sympathetic in their decisions about those with prior records, especially where those records include convictions for violent offenses (Champion, 1988c).

PROBATION TRENDS

One response to the liberal, rehabilitative correctional philosophy of the 1960s and 1970s has been a greater emphasis upon just-deserts and the justice model as a correctional alternative. Despite this emphasis among correctional critics and others, many probation and parole officers and their agencies continue to operate within the framework of rehabilitation. Rehabilitation is not dead. Rather, other correctional themes are currently being promoted (Cullen and Gilbert, 1982). By attempting to predict the future of probation, however, the efforts of experts may serve to confuse more than to clarify probation's aims and accomplishments (Travisano et al., 1986).

Is the use of probation in the United States increasing? Yes. However, there are variations among the states about specific trends reported for different time periods. For the nation generally, the trend in the use of probation as a sentence has been reported in several sources. Table 2.6 shows the *actual numbers* of probationers across the years 1985 through 1990. Furthermore, Table 2.6 shows the *changing numbers* of the adult population on probation for those same years.

In 1985, there were 1,968,712 probationers in the United States, representing 1.12 percent of the total U.S. adult population. By 1990, there were 2,670,234 probationers, representing about 1.44 percent of the total U.S. adult population (Jankowski, 1991:5). Not only was there a direct and consistent increase in the actual numbers of probationers across these years, but the percentage of the total U.S. adult population on probation also increased systematically during that same period. Between 1989 and 1990, independent sources indicate that the numbers of probationers in the United States increased from 1,369 per 100,000 adults to 1,443 per 100,000 adults (Maguire, Pastore, and Flanagan, 1993:566). Indications are that the rate of probation use in the United States will increase well into the 1990s.

A broadening of get tough on crime policies is occurring as a part of general correctional reform, although this concern varies among selected jurisdictions (Cullen and Travis, 1984; Cullen, Clark, and Wozniak, 1985). One result of get-tough policies has been a decrease in decision-making power of judges when sentencing offenders. The federal government as well as some states, including California, Michigan, Indiana, and Arizona, currently have mandatory sentencing provisions for offenders who use firearms during the commission of crimes. Judges are required by state and federal statutes to add one or two years to any sentence of incarceration imposed as the mandatory penalty for firearms use. The intent of these mandatory sentencing provisions is to discourage criminals from using

TABLE 2.6 Correctional Populations: Percent of Adult Population under Sanction and Percent Change, 1985–90

Year	Total Estimated Correctional Population		Probation		Jail[a]		Prison		Parole	
	Number	Percent of Adult Population	Number	Percent of Adult Population	Number	Percent of Adult Population	Number	Percent of Adult Population	Number	Percent of Adult Population
1985	3,011,000	1.7%	1,968,712	1.12%	254,986	.15%	487,593	.28%	300,203	.17%
1986	3,240,000	1.8	2,144,621	1.19	272,736	.15	526,436	.30	325,638	.18
1987	3,460,000	1.9	2,247,158	1.25	294,092	.16	562,814	.31	355,505	.20
1988	3,713,000	2.0	2,356,483	1.30	341,893	.19	606,810	.33	407,977	.22
1989	4,055,000	2.2	2,521,525	1.37	393,303	.21	683,382	.37	456,803	.25
1990	4,350,000	2.4	2,670,234	1.44	403,019	.22	745,157	.40	531,407	.29
Percent change, 1985–90	44%		35.6%		36.6%		52.8%		77.0%	

Note: The following are estimates of the U.S. resident population age 18 or older on July 1: 1985—175,727,000; 1986—177,807,000; 1987—179,856,000; 1988—181,963,000; and 1989—184,157,000. The 1990 Decennial Census counted 185,105,000 on April 1, 1990. Population counts for probation, parole, and prison custody are for December 31, and jail counts are for June 30 in 1985–89 and June 29, 1990. Every year some states update their report; this table uses the corrected counts. Because some persons may have multiple statuses, the sum of the number of persons on probation, on parole, in jail, and in prison will provide an overestimate of the total correctional population.

[a]Estimates of jail populations include convicted and unconvicted adult inmates.

Source: Jankowski, 1991:5.

weapons that may endanger lives. It is doubtful that these mandatory penalties are having their intended effect, however.

Probation programs in general offer nonincarcerative alternatives to offenders. The avoidance of a jail or prison environment and its stigma are considered significant as deterrents to future criminal activity. Of course, no program is perfect, and there will always be recidivism among ex-offenders. Thus, it is unrealistic to expect that probation alone will function as the major means of crime control (Conrad, 1984). The major question is how much recidivism must occur before a program is declared ineffective. Programs that include intensive offender supervision are those most likely to have lower recidivism rates, although in some instances, these differences are not particularly significant (Travis, 1984). This is explained in part by the fact that probation officers spend as much as 70 percent of their time filling out paperwork associated with presentence reports rather than spending more time with offenders on a one-to-one basis (Davis, 1984; Steppe, 1986).

Despite the excessive paperwork and time allocations of probation officers, these programs offer much regarding offender rehabilitation and reintegration (F. Smith, 1984). One front-end problem associated with probation programs is the appropriate classification of offenders initially regarding program assignment (Clear and Gallagher, 1985). This classification is considerably more complicated than it appears (Champion, 1994). Often, a link exists between improper offender classification and program failure, suggesting that effective classification would at least decrease the negative image certain programs have displayed thus far.

In California and other similar jurisdictions, probation has been criticized as conducive to high rates of recidivism compared with other programs, such as intensive supervised probation (Petersilia, 1985c). As many as 65 percent of those felons granted probation are rearrested and/or commit new offenses, although other jurisdictions have reported significantly lower rates of recidivism, regardless of how this evaluation measure is conceptualized (Travis, Latessa, and Vito, 1987).

One explanation for California's high recidivism rate among probationers in later years may be the curtailing of the state's probation subsidy program in 1978. Between 1965 and 1978, correctional leadership in California was virtually unbridled by political and economic constraints. Numerous community-based programs were established, and innovative leadership and guidance were significant in assisting many probationers to "stay clean." In later years, however, jail and prison overcrowding reached epidemic proportions in California and other states, thus leading to decisions about probation programs based on other, more logistic considerations. The emphasis has shifted from offender rehabilitation to ways of alleviating the overcrowding problem. As one consequence, less attention is given individual offenders, while much interest is focused on practical solutions to space limitations in correctional institutions. In Chapter 4, intensive supervision programs are examined. These programs are some of the answers corrections officials have to the growing offender population nationwide. And, not unexpectedly, several of these programs demonstrate considerable promise for curbing recidivism and controlling crime.

KEY TERMS

Aggravating circumstances
John Augustus
Behavioral reform
Boston House of Corrections
Benjamin C. Clark
Community-based corrections
Community model
Rufus B. Cook
Crime control
Criminogenic environment
Deterrence
Due process model
Early release
Economic philosophy
Front-end solution
Judicial reprieve

Just-deserts model
Justice model
Medical Model
Mitigating circumstances
Offender-based transaction statistics
  (OBTS)
Offender control
Probation officer caseloads
Progressive Era
Rehabilitation
Rehabilitation model
Sentencing disparities
Standard probation programs
James Bronson Reynolds
Treatment model
University Settlement

QUESTIONS FOR REVIEW

1. Differentiate between probation and parole. What type of people are most likely to receive probation?
2. When was probation conceived? Briefly describe the early use of probation in the United States.
3. What are some of the more important functions of probation?
4. Compare and contrast the rehabilitative, treatment-oriented correctional philosophy with the justice model. Give some arguments favoring either perspective.
5. What is meant by a *front-end solution* to jail and prison overcrowding as applied to probation? Explain.
6. What is a judicial reprieve? What does it mean when a judge engages in ROR?
7. Why is it difficult to identify a general philosophy of probation?
8. What do you see as the relative merits of probation as an alternative to incarceration? Do you think everyone is in favor of probation? Why or why not? Explain.
9. How does probation assist offenders in avoiding the criminal label? Explain. Why is this important?
10. Identify three individuals associated with the early use of probation in the United States. What was the University Settlement? Was it successful? Why or why not?

3

The Presentence Investigation Report
Background, Preparation, and Functions

Introduction

The Role of Probation Officers in Sentencing

Presentence Investigation Reports (PSI)

The Sentencing Hearing

Aggravating and Mitigating Circumstances

Changing Responsibilities of Probation Officers Resulting from Sentencing Reforms

Probation and Public Risk: Predicting Dangerousness

The Probation Decision and Sentencing Trends

Key Terms

Questions for Review

Appendix: Sample Federal Presentence Investigation Report

INTRODUCTION

In most major felony cases and in some minor misdemeanor cases, judges will request probation officers to prepare reports about convicted offenders who are about to be sentenced. These reports are called *presentence investigation reports,* or *PSIs.* This chapter is about PSIs, their preparation, and their functions.

THE ROLE OF PROBATION OFFICERS IN SENTENCING

1. *Probation officers prepare presentence investigation reports at the request of judges.* Probation officers play a fundamental role in sentencing. At the request of judges, probation officers prepare presentence investigation reports or PSIs for various convicted offenders. A more comprehensive definition will be provided in the following section; it is sufficient for now to know that PSIs are more or less extensive compilations of situational and personal details about offenders, their crimes, crime victims, and any other relevant information yielded during the investigative process (Clear, Clear, and Burrell, 1989:2).

2. *Probation officers classify and categorize offenders.* Before sentences are imposed or sentence lengths are contemplated, probation officers do some preliminary categorizing of their offender-clients. The term *offender-client* is used because those who are sentenced to probation and become probationers are considered the clients of their supervising probation officers. The same term is applied to parolees as *parolee-clients.* The classification scheme devised by POs is largely an individual matter.

3. *Probation officers recommend sentences for convicted offenders.* Besides preparing PSIs, POs also make recommendations to judges about the sentences they believe are warranted under the circumstances associated with given offenses. In several states, POs are guided by presumptive sentencing guidelines or guidelines-based sentencing schemes. Using a numerical system, they can weigh various factors and generate a score (Petersilia, 1987a; Petersilia and Turner, 1987). Usually associated with this score are various incarcerative lengths, expressed in either years or months. The power of PO sentence recommendations should not be underestimated. Researchers have found fairly consistent and very high correlations between the sentence recommendations made by POs and the actual sentences subsequently imposed by judges, even though judges are not obligated to follow these recommendations (Rosecrance, 1988a:235).

Although we do not know for certain, it is reasonable to assume that POs either look for information in their investigations of offenders that confirms or justifies their sentence recommendations or for information that might lead to a modification or rejection of their recommendations. Their own work dispositions determine which investigative mode they tend to follow (Rosecrance, 1987a:40). Defendant types described by some probation officers in various jurisdictions include those that should receive (a) prison; (b) straight probation; (c) probation with some jail time; (d) plea bargain; or (e) diversion (Rosecrance, 1987a:44–45).

4. *Probation officers work closely with courts to determine the best supervisory arrangement for probationer-clients.* When offenders are sentenced to probation, POs may or may not supervise them closely. Usually, the greater the likelihood that an offender will recidivate, the more supervision will be directed toward that offender. Intensive supervised probation, discussed at length in Chapter 4, is partic-

Probation officers prepare PSI reports at the direction of judges prior to sentencing offenders. These reports include background information about the convicted offender as well as the offender's version of events. (Magnum Photos, Inc.)

ularly suited for more dangerous and chronic offenders with patterns of prior criminal behavior. Again, because of the likelihood of the existence of prior plea bargain agreements, the PO role in sentencing may be compromised or minimized. Some experts believe that PSIs seldom influence judicial sentencing, but rather, they serve to maintain the prevalent myth that criminal courts dispense individualized justice (Rosecrance, 1988a:236–237).

5. *Probation officers are a resource for information about any extralegal factors that might impact either positively or adversely on the sentencing decision.* Thus, judges may rely heavily on probation officer reports whether certain offenders are socially situated so that they can comply with different probation conditions. If judges want to impose restitution in particular cases, will offenders be able to repay the victims for damages inflicted? The PO has a fairly good sense of whether certain offenders will be able to comply with this and other probation conditions. Probation officers are not able to include every single factor in their reports that might be useful information for judges when imposing sentences (Drass and Spencer, 1987; Rosecrance, 1987a).

PRESENTENCE INVESTIGATION (PSI)

Whether a conviction is obtained through plea bargaining or a trial, a presentence investigation is often conducted on instructions from the court. This **presentence investigation** is sometimes waived in the case of negotiated guilty pleas, because an agreement has been reached between all parties concerning the case disposition and nature of sentence to be imposed.

When requested by federal district judges, these investigations are usually conducted within a 60-day period from the time judges make their requests. While there is no standard format among states, most investigations contain similar information. A **presentence investigation report** (**PSI**) is a document prepared, usually by a probation agency or officer, that provides background information on the convicted offender including name, age, present address, occupation (if any), potential for employment, the crime(s) involved, relevant circumstances associated with the crime, family data, evidence of prior record (if any), marital status, and other relevant data. Although it was much more informally prepared contrasted with contemporary PSIs, John Augustus has been credited with drafting the first one in 1841. It has been estimated that over 1 million PSIs are prepared by probation officers annually in the United States (Rosecrance, 1988a:235).

PSIs are written summaries of information obtained by the probation officer through interviews with the defendant and an investigation of the defendant's background (Drass and Spencer, 1987:280). An alternative definition is that PSIs are narrative summaries of an offender's criminal and noncriminal history, used to aid a judge in determining the most appropriate decision as to the offender's sentence for a crime (Clear, Clear, and Burrell, 1989:2). These documents are often partially structured in that they require probation officers to fill in standard information about defendants. PSIs also contain summaries or accounts in narrative form highlighting certain information about defendants and containing sentencing recommendations from probation officers (Drass and Spencer, 1987:280). In some instances, space is available for the defendant's personal account of the crime and why it was committed.

In all felony convictions in local, state, and federal trial courts, a presentence investigation is conducted. The purpose of this investigation is to assist the judge in determining the most appropriate punishment or sentence for the convicted defendant. This investigation is usually made by a probation officer attached to the court and consists of a check of all relevant background information about a convicted defendant. Similar investigations are conducted for all juvenile offenders as well.

A presentence investigation report is prepared from the facts revealed from the investigation. This report varies considerably in focus and scope from jurisdiction to jurisdiction, but it should contain at least the following items:

1. a complete description of the situation surrounding the criminal activity;
2. the offender's educational background;
3. the offender's employment history;
4. the offender's social history;
5. the residence history of the offender;
6. the offender's medical history;
7. information about the environment to which the offender will return;
8. information about any resources available to assist the offender;
9. the probation officer's view of the offenders' motivations and ambitions;
10. a full description of the defendant's criminal record; and
11. a recommendation from the probation officer as to the sentence disposition (Black, 1990:1184).

An informal component of many PSIs is the **narrative** prepared by the probation officer. In many instances, judges are persuaded to deal more leniently or harshly with offenders, depending upon how these narratives have been prepared. Probation officers exercise considerable discretion to influence the favorableness or unfavorableness of these reports for offenders. One important factor is the probation officer's judgment of the degree of public risk posed by the offender if placed on probation. Thus, probation officers must attempt to predict an offender's future behavior. This is one of the most difficult tasks associated with probation work. Assessments of offender risk to the public will be examined later in this chapter. An example of a PSI appears in this chapter's appendix.

The Administrative Office of the United States Courts uses standardized PSIs that include five core categories that must be addressed in the body of the report:

1. The offense, including the prosecution version, the defendant's version, statements of witnesses, codefendant information, and a victim impact statement
2. Prior record, including juvenile adjudications and adult offenses
3. Personal and family data, including parents and siblings, marital status, education, health, physical and mental condition, and financial assets and liabilities
4. Evaluation, including the probation officer's assessment, parole guideline data, sentencing data, and any special sentencing provisions
5. Recommendation, including the rationale for the recommendation and voluntary surrender or whether the offender should be transported to the correctional institution on his or her own or should be transported by U.S. Marshals.

Under existing federal sentencing guidelines implemented in November 1987, PSIs have not been eliminated. Rather, they now include material besides that listed above regarding an offender's **acceptance of responsibility** for the crime. Judges select sentences for offenders from a sentencing table and may lessen or enhance the severity of their sentences, based on probation officer recommendations, offender acknowledgment of wrongdoing or acceptance of responsibility, or other criteria.

Judges frequently treat the PSI in a way similar to the way they treat plea bargain agreements. They may concur with probation officer sentencing recommendations, or they may ignore the recommendations made in these reports. However, since most convictions occur through plea bargaining, the only connection a judge usually has with the defendant before sentencing is through the PSI. In federal district courts, judges may decide not to order PSIs if they believe there is sufficient information about the convicted offender to "enable the meaningful exercise of sentencing discretion, and the court explains this finding on the record" (18 U.S.C., Rule 32[c][1], 1995). If the defendant wishes, the PSI may be waived, with court permission.

The Confidentiality of PSIs

The general public is usually excluded from seeing the contents of PSIs. It is imperative that confidentiality be maintained concerning these reports. Often they contain the results of tests or examinations, psychiatric or otherwise. Probation officers contact former employers and work associates and include a summary of interview information as a part of the narrative. Ordinarily, only those court officials and others working closely on a particular case have a right to examine the contents of these reports.

The federal government requires the disclosure of the contents of PSIs to convicted offenders, their attorneys, and to attorneys for the government at least 10 days prior to actual sentencing (18 U.S.C., Sec. 3552[d], 1995). At state and local levels, this practice varies, and the PSI report may or may not be disclosed to the offender. Under 18 U.S.C., Fed. R. Cr. Proc. 32(c)(3)(B) (1995), some information in the PSI may be withheld from the defendant. The report may contain confidential information such as a psychiatric evaluation or a sentencing recommendation. The presiding judge determines those portions of the PSI to be disclosed to offenders and their counsels. Anything disclosed to defendants must also be made available to the prosecutors. Some federal courts have interpreted these provisions to mean that convicted offenders should have greatly restricted access to these PSI reports. Indeed, many federal prisoners have filed petitions under the **Freedom of Information Act** (**FOIA**) in order to read their own PSIs in some judicial districts (Shockley, 1988). This Act makes it possible for private citizens to examine certain public documents containing information about them, including IRS information or information compiled by any other government agency, criminal or otherwise. This is a drastic way of gaining access to a document that may or may not contain erroneous information about the offender, the circumstances of the offense, and other relevant information. Some experts believe that the postsentence disclosure of PSIs to prisoners ought to be converted into a routine function rather than a right to be enjoyed only after exhausting the provisions of the FOIA.

At least one state, California, permits an examination by the public of any

PSI filed by any state probation office for up to 10 days following its filing with the court. Under exceptional circumstances, however, even California courts may bar certain information from public scrutiny if a proper argument can be made for its exclusion. Usually, a good argument would be potential danger to one or more persons who have made statements or declarations in the report. Further, some witnesses or information givers do so only under the condition that they will remain anonymous. This anonymity guarantee must be protected by the court. But as has been previously indicated, most jurisdictions maintain a high level of confidentiality regarding PSI documents and their contents.

The Preparation of PSIs

Most PSIs are prepared by probation officers at the direction of criminal court judges. Clear, Clear, and Burrell (1989:173–175) note that there are three legal approaches to PSI preparation. In at least 23 states, PSI preparation is *mandatory* for all felony offense convictions (Clear, Clear, and Burrell, 1989:175). These authors note that other factors may initiate PSI preparation in these jurisdictions, such as when incarceration of a year or longer is a possible sentence; when the offender is under 21 or 18 years of age; and when the defendant is a first offender. In nine states, statutes provide for mandatory PSI preparation in *any* felony case in which probation is a possible consideration. When probation is *not* a consideration, the PSI preparation is optional or at the judge's discretion (North Carolina Administrative Office of the Courts, 1988). Finally, in 17 states, a PSI is totally discretionary with the presiding judge. Clear, Clear, and Burrell indicate an example of various state policies about the preparation of PSI reports:

> *New Jersey:* PSI is required in all felony cases; suggested in misdemeanor cases involving one or more years incarceration.
> *Connecticut:* PSI is mandatory for any case in which incarceration is to be one or more years.
> *Pennsylvania:* PSI is mandatory for any case in which incarceration is to be one or more years.
> *District of Columbia:* PSI is required unless offenders waive their right to one with court permission.
> *California:* PSI is mandatory for all felony convictions; discretionary for misdemeanor cases.
> *Arizona:* PSI is mandatory for anyone who must be incarcerated one year or more; may be ordered in other cases.
> *Texas:* PSI is totally at judge's discretion. (Clear, Clear, and Burrell, 1989:174)

Functions and Uses of PSIs

Although no standard format exists among the states for PSI preparation, many PSIs are patterned after those used by the Administrative Office of the United States Courts. The PSI was adopted formally by the Administrative Office of the

United States Courts in 1943. Since then, it has been revised several times. The 1984 version reflects changes in correctional law that have occurred in recent decades. Prior to 1943, informal reports about offenders were often prepared for judges by court personnel. Although the U.S. Probation Office represents federal interests and not necessarily those of individual states, their PSI functions have much in common with the general functions of PSI reports among the states.

A Summary of PSI Functions among the States. One function of the PSI is to provide the sentencing judge with an adequate analysis of the offender's background and prospects for rehabilitation. Ideally, this enables judges to be fairer in the sentencing process. A reasonably complete PSI assists the judge in dispensing more equitable sentences consistent with the justice model. Logically, with more factual and background information about offenses and offenders, judges can make more informed sentencing decisions, and sentencing disparities can be minimized among offenders convicted of similar offenses (Brantingham, 1985).

If offenders are placed on probation, the PSI permits probation officers to determine offender needs more clearly and to be more helpful in assisting offenders in locating jobs or completing applications for vocational/educational training. Thus, a second function of PSIs is to assist probation officers in their officer-client planning. Such planning may involve community service, restitution to crime victims, assignment to community-based corrections agencies, house arrest/**electronic monitoring,** or some other nonincarcerative alternative.

Probation officers are expected to assess the offender's dangerousness and public risk (Drass and Spencer, 1987:290). This assessment is a vital part of the narrative and the recommendation prepared by these officers. Probation officers have considerable influence in the sentencing disposition of offenders (Callanan, 1986:78). Thus, a third function of PSIs is to classify and categorize offenders into various risk categories. These risk assessments frequently determine the level of custody or supervision imposed by judges in sentencing. Offenders considered extremely dangerous to the public are seldom granted probation. Rather, they are committed to medium- and maximum-security prisons or other facilities, and for longer periods of incarceration. Their offenses and prior records are also primary determinants of length and severity of the sentence imposed.

For those incarcerated offenders, a PSI is of value to parole boards in determining one's early release and the conditions accompanying the granting of parole (Weintraub, 1987:26). This fact underscores both the short-term and the long-term relevance and importance of PSIs for influencing an offender's chances at securing freedom from the criminal justice system. Offenders may be prison inmates for many years. When they appear before parole boards 15, 20, or even 30 years after they have been incarcerated for their crimes, the parole boards refer to the PSI that was originally prepared at the time of their sentencing. This "ancient" document contains important information about the offender's earlier circumstances. Even though much of this material is badly dated, parole boards consider it in their early-release decision making.

A fourth function of PSIs is to permit probation officers or other supervisory authorities greater monitoring capability over offenders sentenced to some form of probation. The report contains background information, personal habits, and names of acquaintances of the offender. Should it become necessary to apprehend probationers for any probation violation or new crime alleged, the PSI also functions as a locating device. A fifth function is to provide research material for scholars to conduct investigations of crime patterns, parole board decision making, judicial sentencing trends, and other related phenomena. This function is unrelated to offender sentencing decisions, and it is closely tied to academic interests in the criminal justice process.

Criticisms of PSI Preparation.   PSIs have been criticized in recent years because of the subjectivity inherent in their preparation. Probation officers consider both factual background information as well as their personal impressions of offenders (Spica, 1987). Some probation officers rely heavily on statistical data about offenders when making recommendations about possible public risks offenders may pose. "Overpredicting" antisocial behavior has occurred, when misinterpretations of technical terminology have been made by probation officers. In some jurisdictions, PO supervisors encourage them not to oversimplify the background of offenders when preparing PSI reports. This is especially difficult when officers have heavy caseloads and time limitations.

Investigations of probation officer behaviors in PSI preparation have disclosed diverse perspectives ranging from rehabilitative to legalistic (Drass and Spencer, 1987; Rosecrance, 1985). A dilemma exists for many probation officers when preparing PSIs. They must balance quantitative data (e.g., arrest reports, probation records, juvenile adjudications) with qualitative data (e.g., alcohol adjustment, social history, substance abuse) (Spica, 1987:194). Spica suggests that a basic requirement for probation officers is that they possess a "sophisticated understanding of human nature" in their report preparations (1987:194–195). Spica notes that many officers lapse into "computerized thinking" about offenders, and they are inclined to rely on group norms for making decisions about individual offenders. Thus, it is difficult to avoid subjective decision making that may have adverse consequences for convicted offenders, both at the time of sentencing and later when parole boards consider them for early release.

Not all PSIs contain officer assessments of an offender's risk. Those reports that do contain such assessments are founded on many different criteria that are peculiar to each probation officer (Drass and Spencer, 1987:290–291). Currently, in federal district courts as well as in those states (e.g., Minnesota, Florida, Arizona, California, Washington) that have adopted sentencing guidelines, PSIs are declining in their importance and relevance, since sentencing decisions by judges are increasingly perfunctory as sentencing tables are consulted. Their value continues, however, as evidence of mitigating or aggravating circumstances about the offense and offender that may decrease or increase the harshness of sentences imposed, provided sentencing ranges exist.

The Defendant's Sentencing Memorandum

The Administrative Office of the United States Courts (Probation Division) has recommended the inclusion of a core concept of the PSI that reflects the offender's version of the offense (Weintraub, 1987:26). Although not specifically required under the 1987 federal sentencing guidelines, it is important that if such a statement is prepared, it should be prepared with assistance of defense counsel and attached to the PSI filed by the probation officer. Often, these memorandums contain material judges regard as mitigating, and the sentence imposed may be reduced in severity accordingly. Again, these memorandums are not required by law, although the offender's acceptance of responsibility weighs heavily in affecting the sentence federal judges impose.

Whether a PSI contains the defendant's version of the offense should be determined on the basis of the best interests of the offender. This is why the assistance of counsel is important. If offenders decide to appeal the conviction later, a written statement prepared by them about their version of the offense could be used by the court to impeach them and cause the appeal to fail. Thus, as some critics have said, there are "countervailing reasons why [defense] counsel often advises against submitting a 'defendant's version of the offense' following a conviction after trial" (Weintraub, 1987:26).

The Inclusion of Victim Impact Statements

In some jurisdictions, victims of crimes are required to submit their own versions of the offense as a victim impact statement (McCleod, 1986). The **victim impact statement** is a statement made by the victim and addressed to the judge for consideration in sentencing. It includes a description of the harm inflicted on the victim in terms of financial, social, psychological, and physical consequences of the crime. It also includes a statement concerning the victim's feelings about the crime, the offender, and a proposed sentence (Erez and Tontodonato, 1990:452–453). Although the federal government and states have no statutes currently requiring victims to file such statements with the court prior to sentencing, proponents of victim compensation regard victim impact statements as an increasingly important part of the sentencing process (Stephens, 1986). This is seen as a form of victim participation in sentencing, and a victim impact statement is given similar weight as the offender's version of events. Usually, these victim impact statements are not required. They pertain exclusively to the direct effects of the crime and are regarded as aggravating circumstances just as the offender's sentencing memorandum serves as a basis for mitigating circumstances. Whereas victim participation in sentencing raises certain ethical, moral, and legal questions, indications are that victim impact statements are used with increasing frequency and appended to PSIs in various jurisdictions (McCleod, 1986).

Victim impact statements usually take two forms. One is as an attachment to a PSI. The victim or victims create a written account of how the crime and offender

BOX 3.1.

Should First-Degree Murderers Be Allowed to Plea Bargain Their Cases to Short Prison Sentences and/or Probation?

The Case of Francis Malinosky

It happened in the fall of 1979. A Vermont school teacher had fallen in love with her supervisor two years earlier. Judith Leo-Coneys, 32, a Burlington, Vermont, special education teacher, became deeply involved with her boss, the assistant director of special education with the Burlington School District, Francis Malinosky. For over two years, they dated and made marriage plans. She moved some of her personal belongings into Malinosky's home and spent considerable time there. Malinosky had also fallen in love with Judith, a summer romance in full bloom. Even so, for unknown reasons, Judith Leo-Coneys decided to end her relationship with Malinosky. Malinosky was very distraught and tried to talk her out of breaking up with him. She was last seen going to Malinosky's home on November 5, 1979, to retrieve her personal belongings and effects.

Judith's friends became concerned about her sudden disappearance. Police quickly became involved and suspected foul play. They interviewed Francis Malinosky at great length, considering him a key suspect in her disappearance. Malinosky denied any knowledge of Leo-Coneys's whereabouts and considered the police investigation of him nothing more than a "small-town witch hunt." But police persistence made Malinosky increasingly uncomfortable. In December 1979, he also disappeared from Burlington. Police were never able to establish a clear connection between Malinosky and the disappearance of Judith Leo-Coneys and were unable to follow through with an arrest. They simply had no evidence. However, Malinosky's disappearance certainly gave them a new reason to suspect him.

Malinosky was not seen again until April 1990. He was arrested in Los Angeles after it had been determined that he had been staying in a motel under an alias. At this point, police had an 11-year-old unsolved case of a woman's disappearance. Every clue suggested that she had been murdered, but no body had ever been found. Malinosky decided to bargain with Burlington, Vermont, prosecutors. His offer to them: "I'll show you where her body is if you reduce your charge against me from first degree murder to voluntary manslaughter and give me a sentence of five years or less." The prosecution accepted. Shortly thereafter, Malinosky escorted Vermont detectives to a remote logging road in Cabot, Vermont. They retrieved Judith Leo-Coneys's badly decomposed body, which had been wrapped in a plastic shroud.

The judge was more than a little perturbed. "The penalty contemplated in the [plea] agreement simply doesn't fit the offense," he said. But he decided to accept the plea bargain because "it accomplished important goals that could not have been accomplished in any other way. It resolved what happened 11 years ago." Chittenden County, Vermont, State's Attorney William Sorrell added, "There was enough uncertainty about what might happen at the hands of a court or the hands of a jury that it made sense on both sides to try to reach an agreement."

What input, if any, should the relatives and loved ones of Judith Leo-Coneys have in Malinosky's sentencing hearing? Should Malinosky have been allowed to plea-bargain in this first-degree murder situation? How does the justice system suffer or benefit as the result of Malinosky's plea bargain arrangement?

Source: Adapted from Associated Press, "Guilty Plea-Bargain Ends 11-Year-Old Murder Case: Administrator Leads Police to Buried Victim," *Long Beach Press-Telegram,* November 27, 1990:A8.

influenced them, usually adversely. The second is in the form of a speech or verbal declaration. This is ordinarily a prepared document read by one or more victims at the time offenders are sentenced (Erez and Tontodonato, 1990:453). The admission of victim impact statements in either written or verbal form at the time of sentencing or in PSIs is controversial. Some experts believe that these statements are inflammatory and detract from objective sentencing considerations. Obviously prejudicial, victim impact statements may intensify sentencing disparities in certain jurisdictions with sentencing schemes that rely more heavily on subjective judicial impressions compared with those jurisdictions in which more objective sentencing criteria are used, such as mandatory sentencing procedures or guidelines-based sentencing schemes (Ranish and Shichor, 1985; *Booth v. Maryland,* 1987). Proponents of victim impact statements believe that such statements personalize the sentencing process by showing that actual persons were harmed by certain offender conduct. Also, victim's rights advocates contend that victims have a moral right to influence one's punishment (Rubel, 1986; Young, 1987). Even though this controversy continues, it is increasingly the case that victims are exerting greater influence and have growing input in sentencing decisions in most jurisdictions.

Privatizing PSI Preparation

The Private Preparation of PSIs.   Sometimes PSIs are prepared by private corporations or individuals. Criminological Diagnostic Consultants, Inc., of Riverside, California, founded by brothers William and Robert Bosic, is a corporation that prepares privately commissioned PSIs for defense attorneys and others (Kulis, 1983:11). William Bosic is a former prison counselor and probation officer, and his brother, Robert, is a retired police officer. Their claim is, "we don't do anything different than the probation department; we just do it better." The average cost of a government-prepared PSI averages about $250; privately prepared PSIs cost from $200 to $2,000 or more. The cost depends on the PSI contents and whether psychiatric evaluations of offenders are made. The amount of investigative detail required in particular cases influences preparation costs as well. Increasing numbers of PSIs are being prepared privately, often by ex-probation officers or others closely related to corrections. The quality of private PSI preparation varies greatly.

Some private agencies prepare quite elaborate and sophisticated reports for clients able to afford them.

Many jurisdictions now accept privately prepared sentencing memorandums to accompany the official PSI. These private-sector PSIs are often prepared by former probation officers or criminal justice consultants (Kulis, 1983; Weintraub, 1987:27). Defendant's sentencing memorandums contain similar PSI information, especially the defendant's version of what happened, and any mitigating factors that would lessen sentencing severity (Weintraub, 1987:26). This independently prepared report serves to make the official PSI more objective and to clarify or resolve facts that may be in dispute (Weintraub, 1987:26).

PSIs and Presumptive Sentencing Systems

Federal probation officers and those POs in states in which guidelines-based or presumptive sentencing schemes are used to determine the length of one's incarceration and/or probation have far less latitude in influencing one's sentencing severity compared with their PO counterparts in states that have an indeterminate or determinate type of sentencing scheme in effect. U.S. Probation Officer Harry Jaffe gives us an interesting "before-after" glimpse of how federal sentencing guidelines have modified the PO role in PSI preparation through greater bureaucratization of the position:

> At one time, the probation officer as a presentence writer could function adequately as a dull cataloguer of data: collecting education records here, verifying employment there, gathering medical records here, talking to family there. With guideline sentencing, however, these bits of social data bear not one iota on the calculation of sentence; so, such anecdotal material as what the defendant's mother's neighbor's best friend says about a defendant has no place in today's presentence report. . . . [Now] . . . guideline sentencing, with its numerical quantification of such abstractions as relevant conduct, obstructionism, and degrees of culpability, demands of the presentence writer sophisticated reasoning powers. Analyses must be made, inferences must be drawn, and options must be selected—all within the confines of a somewhat complex instructional manual whose text ranges from the translucent to the opaque. To be really good, therefore, at this task of presentence writing, the probation officer will need to employ a new kind of reasoning—syllogistic—heretofore foreign to probation work. (Jaffe, 1989:12)

THE SENTENCING HEARING

Under Rule 32 of the Federal Rules of Criminal Procedure (18 U.S.C., 1995), the contents of a PSI must be disclosed to defendants and their counsels, although some information is exempt from disclosure. Mental or psychological reports, interviews with family members or a personalized account of the defendant's marital problems, and certain personal observations by the probation officer and court are potentially excludable from PSIs.

In most jurisdictions, a **sentencing hearing** is held, during which defendants and their attorneys can respond to the contents of the PSI report. Also, an increasing number of jurisdictions are permitting crime victims to attend sentencing hearings and provide victim impact statements either orally, in writing, or both. Evidence suggests a general increase in citizen involvement at other stages of the criminal justice process as well (Rubin, 1985a, 1985b). Of course, many jurisdictions do not allow victims to participate in the sentencing process. The nature of victim participation varies among jurisdictions, although their participation often consists of an objective delineation of the personal and psychological effects of the crime and the financial costs incurred (McCleod, 1986).

Sentencing hearings also permit offenders and their attorneys to comment on the PSI report and append to it additional informational material that may mitigate the circumstances of the conviction offense. The role of defense attorneys is important particularly at this stage because they can work with the probation officer who prepared the report as well as the victims, and they can make timely legal attacks on erroneous information presented to the judge (Carroll, 1986).

In addition to considering the contents of a PSI, the oral and written reports furnished by victims and the offenders themselves, and attorney arguments from both the prosecution and defense, judges use their best judgment in arriving at the most equitable sentence for offenders. Judges consider mitigating and aggravating circumstances surrounding the offense, the age, psychological and physical condition, and social and educational background of the offender, and the minimum and maximum statutory penalties of incarceration and/or fines accompanying the crime in arriving at a decision. Judges also take into account both aggravating and mitigating circumstances.

AGGRAVATING AND MITIGATING CIRCUMSTANCES

Aggravating Circumstances

Aggravating circumstances are those that may intensify the severity of punishment. Some of the factors considered by judges to be "aggravating" include:

1. Whether the crime involved death or serious bodily injury to one or more victims;
2. Whether the crime was committed while the offender was out on bail facing other criminal charges;
3. Whether the offender was on probation, parole, or work release at the time the crime was committed;
4. Whether the offender was a recidivist and had committed several previous offenses for which he/she had been punished;
5. Whether the offender was the leader in the commission of the offense involving two or more offenders;
6. Whether the offense involved more than one victim and/or was a violent or nonviolent crime;
7. Whether the offender treated the victim(s) with extreme cruelty during the commission of the offense; and
8. Whether the offender used a dangerous weapon in the commission of the crime and the risk to human life was high.

If the convicted defendant has one or more aggravating circumstances accompanying the crime committed, the judge is likely to intensify the punishment prescribed. In simple terms, this means a longer sentence, incarceration in lieu of probation, or a sentence to be served in a maximum security prison rather than a minimum- or medium-security prison facility. Mitigating circumstances may cause the judge to be lenient with the defendant and prescribe probation rather than confinement in a jail or prison. A sentence of a year or less may be imposed rather than a five-year term.

Mitigating Circumstances

Mitigating factors are those circumstances considered by the sentencing judge to lessen the crime's severity. Some of the more frequently cited mitigating factors in the commission of crimes might be the following:

1. The offender did not cause serious bodily injury by his/her conduct during the commission of the crime;
2. The convicted defendant did not contemplate that his/her criminal conduct would inflict serious bodily injury on anyone;
3. The offender acted under duress or extreme provocation;
4. The offender's conduct was possibly justified under the circumstances;
5. The offender was suffering from mental incapacitation or physical condition that significantly reduced his/her culpability in the offense;
6. The offender cooperated with authorities in apprehending other participants in the crime or in making restitution to the victims for losses suffered;
7. The offender committed the crime through motivation to provide necessities for himself/herself or his/her family; and
8. The offender did not have a previous criminal record.

If a convicted defendant has one or more mitigating circumstances associated with the crime committed, the sentencing judge may lessen the severity of the sentence imposed. In view of the current trend toward greater use of felony probation, first offenders and nonviolent criminals are likely to be considered prime candidates for alternative sentencing that does not involve incarceration. But recidivists, especially those who have committed a number of violent acts and show every likelihood of continuing their criminal behavior, are likely candidates for punishment enhancement (e.g., longer, more severe sentences and/or fines). These circumstances are usually outlined in PSIs.

CHANGING RESPONSIBILITIES OF PROBATION OFFICERS RESULTING FROM SENTENCING REFORMS

We have already seen how the probation officer role has changed somewhat as the result of changing from one type of sentencing scheme to another. Under the previous indeterminate sentencing scheme used by the federal district courts, for example, the U.S. Probation Office used to have its probation officers collect diverse information about prospective probationers and present this information in a subsequent sentencing hearing. Probation officers frequently embellished their reports with personal observations and judgments. They also recommended sentences to federal district court judges, based on their own impressions of each case. However, the U.S. sentencing guidelines caused considerable changes in the PO role. Now, probation officers must learn to add and subtract points from an **offense seriousness score** according to whether a drug transaction occurred within a specified distance of a school, whether the offender used a dangerous weapon during the commission of the crime, and/or whether offenders accepted responsibility for their actions. In drug cases, amounts of drugs must be factored into an increasingly complex formula to determine where an offender's case might be categorized.

Ellen Steury (1989:95–96) illustrates the complexity of score determination under the new federal sentencing guidelines with a hypothetical example. She suggests the following:

> A hypothetical offense situation might be helpful in portraying the mechanics of the guidelines. Consider the case of a defendant convicted of armed robbery, where the facts are as follows: (1) the robbery offense; (2) was carefully planned; (3) $23,000 was stolen; (4) the robber pointed a gun at the teller; (5) no injuries occurred; (6) the offender had three previous felony convictions, of which two carried terms of imprisonment longer than 13 months and one carried a term of probation; (7) the offender had been out of prison six months at the time of committing the instant offense, but was not under legal sentence at the time of the offense; (8) had no other currently pending charges; (9) confessed to the crime, wholly cooperated with law enforcement authorities, and offered restitution. In the ordinary case, this fact situation would require the court to sentence the offender to a term of imprisonment between 57 months (4 years, 9 months) and 71 months (5 years, 11 months). In the hypothetical situation detailed above, each of the items would carry the following values:
>
> 1. The robbery itself carries a base level score of 18.
> 2. The "more than minimal planning" does not affect the sentence in the case of robbery, but it does (inexplicably) in other offenses such as burglary, property damage or destruction, embezzlement, and aggravated assault.
> 3. The amount of money taken increases the base level by two points.
> 4. Brandishing a firearm increases the base level by another three points.
> 5. The fact that no victim injuries occurred avoids other possible level increases, which would otherwise be calculated on the basis of the degree of the injury.
> 6. The criminal history score totals nine points, comprised of three points for each sentence of imprisonment longer than thirteen months, and one point for the sentence of probation; while the recency of the latest imprisonment incurs two additional points.
> 7. The absence of other pending charges avoids a possible score increase.
> 8. The confession, coupled with the cooperation and the volunteered restitution, might persuade the court to conclude that the offender had 'accepted responsibility' for the crime, which could result in decreasing the offense level score by two points.

In the above example, the offense points sum to 21, and the criminal history points sum to 9. The sentencing range associated with offense level 21 and the criminal history score of 9 (Category IV) is 57 to 71 months. Defendants so sentenced, or the government, could appeal by claiming that the guidelines had been incorrectly applied (18 U.S.C., Sec. 3742(a)(2) and Sec. 3742(b)(2), 1995). An appellate court would review the case.

If the sentencing court in its wisdom believed that the offender deserved less than 57 months or more than 71 months, a departure from the guidelines would be allowable, provided a written justification from the judge accompanied the departure. In such cases, defendants (if the sentence were longer than the maximum specified by the guidelines) or the government (if the sentence were shorter than the minimum specified by the guidelines) could appeal for a review of the stated reasons given by the judge for the departure (18 U.S.C., Sec. 3742(a)(3)(A) and Sec. 3742(b)(3)(A), 1995). (Steury, 1989:95–96)

It is clear from the Steury account that the sentencing of federal criminals has grown increasingly complex. In fact, computer programs have since been written to simplify the task of computing one's final score (Champion, 1994).

Frank Marshall, a probation officer with the U.S. Probation Office in Philadelphia, has observed several significant changes in PO work as the result of the federal sentencing guidelines that went into effect in November 1987. He notes that the U.S. Parole Commission was to be modified in 1992, that all parolees would be placed under the supervision of the U.S. Probation Office, and that a new term, *supervised release,* would replace terms such as *parole* and *special parole* in future years. Marshall also indicates that POs will acquire more sentencing responsibilities with the sentencing change. Federal district court judges will increasingly rely on PO work for determining appropriate sentences of offenders. At the same time, fewer convicted offenders will be eligible for probation or diversion (Marshall, 1989:153–164). In the few years following the sentencing guidelines, for example, federal sentencing patterns shifted so that probation as a sentence was imposed about 10 to 12 percent of the time in the postguidelines period, compared with 60 to 65 percent probation sentences in the preguidelines period (Champion, 1994). In short, the federal sentencing guidelines have drastically reduced the number of persons eligible for and receiving probation. The work of federal POs is not substantially reduced, however, since they now supervise parolees under supervised release and their PSI preparation has become more complex.

PROBATION AND PUBLIC RISK: PREDICTING DANGEROUSNESS

Assessing Offender Risk: A Brief History

Many risk-assessment measures have been devised and are used largely for the purpose of determining probabilities that offender-clients will engage in dangerous or maladjusted behaviors (Champion, 1994; Joyce, 1985:78). These probabilities are subsequently used for placement, program, and security decision making (Joyce, 1985:78). Needs measures and instruments enable corrections personnel and administrative staffs to highlight client weaknesses or problems that may have led to their convictions or initial difficulties. Once problem areas have been targeted, specific services or treatments might be scheduled and provided. Various Christian Reform movements have been credited with establishing early prisoner classification systems in the eighteenth century (American Correctional Association, 1983:194). Behavioral scientists, especially psychiatrists and psychologists, conducted research during the period between 1910 and 1920 and found that custody-level placements of inmates as well as other program assignments could be made by using certain psychological characteristics as predictors (American Correctional Association, 1983:196).

Criminologists and criminal justice scholars have become increasingly involved in devising risk-assessment inventories and needs indices, using combinations of psychological, social, socioeconomic, and demographic factors and related criteria to make dangerousness forecasts and behavioral predictions. Formal, paper-pencil risk and needs instruments began to proliferate during the 1960s (Spieker and Pierson, 1989:6). Some of this instrumentation was used with juvenile offenders. Later, numerous behavioral and psychological instruments were devised and used for the purpose of assessing client risk or inmate dangerousness. The Minnesota Multiphasic Personality Inventory (MMPI), consisting of 550 true-false items, was originally used in departments of corrections for personality assessments. Although this instrument is still used for personality assessment in many correctional settings, some researchers, such as Edwin Megargee, have extracted certain items from the MMPI for use as predictors of inmate violence and adjustment (Megargee and Carbonell, 1985). Classifications such as Megargee's are often designated as *MMPI-based assessments or classifications.* Applications of scales such as Megargee's have received mixed results and evaluations. In at least some studies, such scales have demonstrably low reliability (Johnson, Simmons, and Gordon, 1983; Megargee and Carbonell, 1985).

Herbert Quay's work preceded the work of Megargee (Quay and Parsons, 1971). Quay devised a relatively simple typology of delinquent behavior, classifying delinquents into four categories: Undersocialized Aggression, Socialized Aggression, Attention Deficit, and Anxiety-Withdrawal-Dysphoria. Juveniles would complete a self-administered questionnaire and their personality scores would be quickly tabulated. Depending on how particular juveniles were depicted and classified, different treatments would be administered to help them. Later, Quay devised a scale that he called *AIMS,* or the *Adult Internal Management System* (Quay, 1984). Again, Quay used self-administered inventories, the Correctional Adjustment Checklist and the Correctional Adjustment Life History (Sechrest, 1987:302–303). His adult typology consisted of five types of inmates: Aggressive Psychopathic, Manipulative, Situational, Inadequate-Dependent, and Neurotic-Anxious. Sechrest (1987:303) and others (Spieker and Pierson, 1989) consider AIMS more of an inmate management tool than a rehabilitative or treatment-centered one, however.

Another system is the *I-Level Classification,* which refers to the *Interpersonal Maturity Level Classification System.* This system was originally devised by Sullivan, Grant, and Grant (1957). It is based on a mixture of developmental and psychoanalytic theories and is administered by psychologists or psychiatrists in lengthy

BOX 3.2
Can You Get Probation for a Murder Conviction?

The Case of Robert Lee Perkins

Would you believe that a man could commit murder and get probation? It happened to Robert Lee Perkins, a 48-year-old from Los Angeles, California. Perkins was 28 years old when he shot and killed 37-year-old Rupert Davis in an argument over a woman on December 11, 1973. Perkins fled the Los Angeles area thereafter and became a fugitive from justice. He moved to Alabama where he worked under an assumed name for the next 20 years.

The story is even more interesting because Perkins stayed out of trouble with the law during that period, married, raised a family, and got an education. Being on the run or sought by police for murder plays havoc with one's conscience, however. Although Perkins believes there were extenuating circumstances, he decided after 20 years to make his peace with the state of California. He contacted a lawyer to be his defense attorney of

record. The defense attorney contacted the Los Angeles District Attorney's Office. After some negotiations, a plea bargain agreement was worked out whereby Perkins would plead guilty to murder, but he would receive a sentence of probation for five years. In addition, he must perform 250 hours of community service. When contacted by the press, the District Attorney's Office of Los Angeles County acknowledged that after two decades, the evidence needed to convict Perkins was scarce. Only one unreliable eyewitness was available, and that witness suffered from memory problems.

Should murderers be allowed to receive probation instead of incarceration? There is no statute of limitations on murder. Should it make any difference to courts if the murder occurred yesterday or 20 years ago? What should Perkins's penalty be for the murder he committed in 1973? Is probation and community service adequate punishment in this case?

Source: Adapted from Associated Press, "Man Gets Probation After Confessing to Murdering a Man 20 Years Ago," *Minot (ND) Daily News,* January 12, 1994:A-2.

clinical interviews (Spieker and Pierson, 1989). Clients are classified as being at particular "I-Levels," such as I-1, I-2, and so on, up to I-7. Each I-level is a developmental stage that reflects one's ability to cope with complex personal and interpersonal problems. The higher the I-level, the better-adjusted the client, according to its proponents. In recent years, several jurisdictions have devised special risk-assessment devices for females (Spieker and Pierson, 1989:7–8). For instance, Illinois developed and implemented a female initial classification instrument in January 1984 (Illinois Department of Corrections, 1988). Actually, the instrument devised for female offender classification is very similar to the one used to classify male offenders in Illinois, with minor variations.

It was not until the 1980s, however, that state corrections departments began to create and apply risk-assessment schemes with some regularity and in correctional areas beyond the institutional setting. For example, Arizona created its first Offender Classification System manual in 1986 (Arizona Department of Corrections, 1991). Instrumentation for risk assessment was established in Illinois in the mid-1980s (Illinois Department of Corrections, 1988). Tennessee sought requests for proposals in 1987 to devise risk measures for its inmate population. Missouri introduced a variation of AIMS for use in its Department of Corrections in 1988 (Spieker and Pierson, 1989). Iowa's Risk/Needs Classification System was implemented in December 1983 and revised extensively in 1992 (Iowa Department of Correctional Services, 1992). Many jurisdictions are currently revising or have recently revised their risk and needs instruments (Champion, 1994).

Classification and Its Functions

1. **Classification** assists in determining one's custody level if confined in either prisons or jails.
2. Classification helps to adjust one's custody level during confinement, considering behavioral improvement and evidence of rehabilitation.
3. While confined, inmates may be targeted for particular services and/or programs to meet their needs.
4. Classification may be used for offender management and deterrence relative to program or prison rules and requirements.
5. Classification may enable authorities to determine whether selective incapacitation is desirable for particular offenders or offender groupings.
6. **Classification systems** enable authorities to make decisions about appropriate offender program placements.
7. Classification systems help to identify one's needs and the provision of effective services in specialized treatment programs.
8. Classification schemes are useful for policy decision making and administrative planning relevant for jail and prison construction, the nature and number of facilities required, and the types of services to be made available within such facilities.
9. Classification systems enable parole boards to make better early-release decisions about eligible offenders.
10. Community corrections agencies can utilize classification schemes to determine those parolees who qualify for participation.
11. Classification systems enable assessments of risk and dangerousness to be made generally in anticipation of the type of supervision best suited for particular offenders.
12. Classification schemes assist in decision making relevant for community crime control, the nature of penalties to be imposed, and the determination of punishment.

The terms *dangerousness* and **risk** are often used interchangeably. They both convey propensities to cause harm to others or oneself, and, therefore, **risk assessment** becomes of paramount importance. What is the likelihood that any particular offender will be violent toward others? Does an offender pose any risk to public safety? What is the likelihood that any particular offender will commit suicide or attempt it? **Risk** (or dangerousness) **assessment instruments** are screening devices intended to distinguish between different types of offenders for purposes of determining initial institutional classification, security placement and inmate management, early release eligibility, and the level of supervision required under conditions of probation or parole. Most state jurisdictions and the federal government refer to these measures as risk assessment instruments rather than dangerousness instruments (Illinois has a dangerousness designation; Illinois Department of Corrections, 1988). There is considerable variance among states regarding the format and content of such measures. An example of a risk-assessment instrument (one used by the State of Minnesota) is shown in Figure 3.1.

Additionally, **needs-assessment** instruments are devices that measure an offender's personal/social skills, health well-being and emotional stability, educational level and vocational strengths and weaknesses, alcohol or drug dependencies, mental ability, and other relevant life factors, and which highlight those areas for which services are available and could or should be provided. A needs-assessment instrument devised by the Alaska Department of Corrections is shown in Figure 3.2. Needs-assessment instruments, measures, scales, or inventories identify the types of services offenders might require if incarcerated. If some offenders are illiterate, they may be placed, either voluntarily or involuntarily, into an educational program at some level, depending on the amount of remedial work deemed necessary (Oberst, 1988). Psychologically disturbed or mentally ill offenders may require some type of counseling or therapy. Some offenders may require particular medications for illnesses or other maladies.

Risk and needs assessments may also be referred to jointly and contained in a longer inventory or measure, labeled a **risk/needs instrument.** An inspection of these devices and the individual items included within them will indicate which factors seem to have the greatest priority and predictive utility. The offender needs-assessment inventory shown in Figure 3.2 also assigns greater or lesser weights to different items that focus on various dimensions of one's life. Those areas having the largest number of points potentially assigned include employment, emotional stability, and alcohol usage. These items have possible high scores of "5," "6," and "5" respectively. All other items, including academic/vocational skills, financial status, other substance abuse, mental ability, health, living arrangements, sexual behavior, and the officer's impression of a client's needs have a highest weight of "4" or less. Again, on the basis of one's cumulative score or raw point total, interpretive tables are consulted to determine the *level of needs* and *types of needs* that should be addressed with one or more services. These services might include alcohol or drug abuse treatment programs, vocational/educational training, employment counseling, or individual/group therapy (Robins et al., 1986). Those areas most indicative of one's greatest weaknesses or needs are typically those with the highest score weights.

Because of various flaws inherent in such instruments, there are grounds for some skepticism. Sechrest (1987) has found that classification schemes that match certain offenders with specific treatment programs often lack theoretical coherence. Thus, while classifications of offenders result in separate categorizations destined to receive certain treatments and services, considerable variation exists

Client Name Last First Middle	OID Number
Date-of Review (Day, Month, Year) Agent Last Name Agent Number	Conviction Offense(s)

```
                                              SCORE
Number of address changes during last 12 months client
was in community ..................................... 0   None
                                                      2   One
                                                      3   Two or more        _____
Age at first conviction (or juvenile adjudication) ....... 0   24 or older
                                                      2   20-23
                                                      4   19 or younger      _____
Number of prior probation/parole adjudicated violations
(adult or juvenile) .................................. 0   None
                                                      4   One or more        _____
Number of prior felony convictions (or juvenile
adjudications) ....................................... 0   None
                                                      2   One
                                                      4   Two or more        _____
Convictions or juvenile adjudications for:
(select applicable and add for score--do not exceed a
total of 5--include current offense)
   Burglary, theft, auto theft or robbery................ 2
   Worthless checks or forgery......................... 3
                                                      0   N/A                _____
Percentage of time employed during last 12 months
client was in community .............................. 0   60%
                                                      1   40%-59%
                                                      2   Under 40%
                                                      0   N/A                _____
Alcohol usage problems (last 12 months in community)
   No interference with functioning..................... 0
   Some interference with functioning................... 2
   Serious interference with functioning................ 4                   _____
Other drug usage problems (last 12 months in community)
   No interference with functioning..................... 0
   Some interference with functioning................... 1
   Serious interference with functioning................ 2                   _____
Attitude:
   Motivated to change; receptive to assistance.......... 0
   Dependent or unwilling to accept responsibility........ 3
   Negative; rationalizes/justifies behavior or not
   motivated to change................................ 5                      _____
Number of prior supervised periods of probation/parole
(adult or juvenile) .................................. 0   None
                                                      4   One or more        _____
Conviction or juvenile adjudication of any crime
against a person (felony, gross misdemeanor or mis-
demeanor) within the last five years ................... 15  Yes
                                                      0   No
                                                             TOTAL           _____
```

FIGURE 3.1. Minnesota Department of Corrections Assessment of Client Risk.

OFFENDER NEED ASSESSMENT

Client's Name _____ Officer's _____

Select the appropriate answer and enter the associated weight in the score column.
Total all scores to arrive at the need assessment score.

SCORE

1. ACADEMIC/VOCATIONAL SKILLS:
   a. High school or above skill level....................................0   [   ]
   b. Has vocational training; additional not needed....................1   [   ]
   c. Has some skills; additional needed................................2   [   ]
   d. No skills; training needed..3   [   ]
2. EMPLOYMENT:
   a. Satisfactory employment for 1 year or longer......................0
   b. Employed; no difficulties reported; or homemaker, student, retired
      or disabled and unable to work....................................2   [   ]
   c. Part-time, seasonal, unstable employment or needs additional
      employment; unemployed, but has a skill...........................3   [   ]
   d. Unemployed & virtually unemployable; needs training...............5   [   ]
3. FINANCIAL STATUS:
   a. Longstanding pattern of self-sufficiency..........................0   [   ]
   b. No current difficulties...1   [   ]
   c. Situational or minor difficulties.................................2   [   ]
   d. Severe difficulties...4   [   ]
4. LIVING ARRANGEMENTS (Within last six months):
   a. Stable and supportive relationships with family or others in
      living group 0
   b. Client lives alone or independently within another household......1
   c. Client experiencing occasional, moderate interpersonal problems
      within living group...2
   d. Client experiencing frequent and serious interpersonal problems
      within living group...4   [   ]
5. EMOTIONAL STABILITY:
   a. No symptoms of instability..0
   b. Symptoms limit, but do not prohibit adequate functioning..........3
   c. Symptoms prohibit adequate functioning............................5   [   ]
6. ALCOHOL USAGE (Current):
   a. No interference with functioning..................................0
   b. Occasional abuse; some disruption of functioning..................3
   c. Frequent abuse; serious disruption; needs treatment...............6   [   ]
7. OTHER SUBSTANCE USAGE (Current):
   a. No interference with functioning..................................0   [   ]
   b. Occasional substance abuse; some disruption of functioning; may
      need treatment..3
   c. Frequent substance abuse; serious disruption; needs treatment.....5   [   ]
8. MENTAL ABILITY:
   a. Able to function independently....................................0
   b. Some need for assistance; potential for adequate adjustment;
      mild retardation..2
   c. Deficiencies suggest limited ability to function independently;
      moderate retardation..3   [   ]
9. HEALTH:
   a. Sound physical health; seldom ill.................................0
   b. Handicap or illness interferes with functioning on a recurring
      basis...1
   c. Serious handicap or chronic illness; needs frequent medical care...3   [   ]
10. SEXUAL BEHAVIOR:
    a. No apparent dysfunction...0
    b. Real or perceived situational or minor problems...................2
    c. Real or perceived chronic or severe problems......................3   [   ]
11. OFFICER'S IMPRESSION OF CLIENT NEEDS:
    a. None..0
    b. Low...1
    c. Moderate..2
    d. High..4   [   ]

TOTAL SCORES 1 THROUGH 11   [   ]

FIGURE 3.2. Alaska Department of Corrections Offender Need Assessment Scale.

among individual offenders within each category. Therefore, there are frequent mismatches between classification systems and the treatment programs prescribed. For example, one or two points in either direction can make a great deal of difference to offenders.

Types of Risk-Assessment Instruments

Three basic categories of risk classifications have been identified (Morris and Miller, 1985:13–14):

1. Anamnestic prediction predicts offender behavior according to past circumstances. If circumstances are similar now, it is likely the offender will behave in the same way. For example, a presentence investigation report may show that an offender was alcohol- and drug-dependent, unemployed, inclined toward violence because of previous assault incidents, and poorly educated. Recidivists may be involved in circumstances similar to those that prevailed when they were convicted of their earlier offense. Thus, judges and others might rely heavily on the situational similarity of past and present circumstances to measure offender risk. However, if some offenders have made a significant effort between convictions to obtain additional education or training for better job performance, or if they are no longer alcohol- or drug-dependent, other types of behavioral forecasts will have to be made because different circumstances exist now compared with previous ones.

2. Actuarial prediction is based on the characteristics of a class of offenders similar to those being considered for probation, parole, or inmate classification. It is likely that those persons who exhibit similar characteristics to the general class of offenders will behave in ways similar to that particular class. In effect, this is an aggregate predictive tool. For instance, assume we have targeted and tracked a large sample of persons placed on probation for a two-year period. We determine that 65 percent of these probationers did not complete their probationary periods satisfactorily. We describe these "failures" as follows: They are predominantly young, unemployed, or underemployed; lack a high school education; were victims of child abuse; and are drug-dependent. Now, whenever young, unemployed, less educated, drug-dependent, former child-abuse victims are considered for probation, parole, inmate classification, or some intermediate sanctioning option, their chances of being placed in one program or another, or of being classified one way or another, may be influenced greatly by the general characteristics of previous program failures. Interestingly, it seems that program "failures" are more often described and used to structure risk instruments than are program "successes."

3. Clinical prediction is based on the predictor's professional training and experience working directly with the offender. Based on extensive diagnostic examinations, the belief is that the offender will behave in a certain way. The subjectivity inherent in clinical prediction is apparent. The skills of the assessor are important.

However, such prediction is more expensive, since each clinical prediction is individualized. Anamnestic and actuarial prediction utilize situational factors and general characteristics of offenders in forecasting their future risk. Interestingly, the highest degrees of validity are associated with actuarial and anamnestic predictions (for instance, those currently used by parole boards), and they are considered very reliable. In contrast, clinical prediction is most accurately described as an art and rests on the past successes of the predictor (Floud and Young, 1981:29, 1982). Clinical predictors are usually psychiatrists or psychologists with extensive clinical training and experience with deviant conduct and criminal behavior.

Any prediction tools that are used, and any claims about their validity and reliability, and/or the recommendations concerning their applicability to specific offender situations, are subject to certain limitations. For instance, Morris and Miller (1985:35–37) have suggested three guiding principles for parole boards to consider when making early release decisions.

1. Punishment should not be imposed, nor the term of punishment extended, by virtue of a prediction of dangerousness, beyond that which would be justified as a deserved punishment independently of that prediction.
2. Provided this limitation is respected, predictions of dangerousness may properly influence sentencing decisions and other decisions under criminal law.
3. The base expectancy rate of violence for the criminal predicted as dangerous must be shown by reliable evidence to be substantially higher than the base expectancy rate of another criminal with a closely similar criminal record and convicted of a closely similar crime but not predicted as unusually dangerous, before the greater dangerousness of the former may be relied on to intensify or extend his/her punishment.

One interest of social scientists is the prediction of behavior, generally for the purpose of acquiring a better understanding of it. Thus, much research is reported involving "experiments" in which social conditions are changed and participants are closely observed. In the work setting, supervisory styles are deliberately modified and worker reactions recorded. Later, a connection between supervisory style and worker reaction is developed. Perhaps supervisory policies will be implemented that are believed to elicit desirable employee reaction such as "greater loyalty" or "greater job satisfaction" or "greater productivity."

Judges and especially probation officers are interested in behavioral prediction as well. The PSI prepared for any offender sometimes contains a recommendation for some form of probation or incarceration. This recommendation is based on the probation officer's belief that the offender will be either a good risk or a poor risk for probation. This is behavioral prediction. **Prediction** means an assessment of some expected future behavior of a person including criminal acts, arrests or convictions (Gottfredson and Tonry, 1987:2). Predictions of future criminal behavior date back to biblical times, although our concern here is with contemporary developments and the current state-of-the-art prediction and assessment devices. In the United States, early systematic scientifically based research designed to forecast risk occurred in the 1920s (von Hirsch, 1983).

False Positives and False Negatives

Logistically, it is impossible to incarcerate all convicted criminals. There is no room in all U.S. prisons and jails to house them. And, corrections experts debate whether certain offenders should be incarcerated anyway (Rosecrance, 1986; Walker, 1985:65). Therefore, since many offenders will be returned to the community instead of incarcerated, predictions of dangerousness and public risk are integral features of a probation officer's role. Parole boards perform similar tasks. Assessments of convicted offenders and their expected future behavior involve prediction criteria such as age, prior record, gender, type and seriousness of offense, offender attitudes, and psychological factors among other things. Usually, classification schemes are devised that enable probation officers and the court to rely on scores and other numerical information to impose "just" penalties or appropriate punishments. Unfortunately, we have no foolproof prediction devices presently used in sentencing or early release decisions or probation officer recommendations. But we do have many prediction devices and schemes.

The Problems of False Positives and False Negatives.   Before examining the prediction and classification of offenders in greater detail, a simple prediction table is helpful to see what sorts of predictions are attempted and some of the problematic outcomes of these predictions. Table 3.1 shows the results of a study conducted by the National Council on Crime and Delinquency in 1972 (Wenck, Robison, and Smith, 1972).

In the 1972 study of a sample of 4,146 delinquent youths under the control of the California Youth Authority, an attempt was made by researchers to predict violence and nonviolence among the juvenile offenders. Four categories were created. The objective of the study was to predict true positives and true negatives. *True positives* are persons predicted to be violent and who subsequently commit a new violent offense. *True negatives* are those offenders predicted to be nonviolent who do not commit further offenses.

Error cells in Table 3.1 include **false positives,** or delinquents predicted to commit new violent offenses who don't, and **false negatives,** those offenders predicted to be nonviolent but do commit new violent offenses. Ideally, true positives require close supervision or monitoring, even incarceration, while true negatives

TABLE 3.1 Positive and Negative Predictions of Violence, National Council on Crime and Delinquency, 1972

	Predicted Violent	Predicted Nonviolent
	N	N
Actual Violent	"True Positives" (52)	"False Negatives" (52)
Actual Nonviolent	"False Positives" (404)	"True Negatives" (3,638)

Source: Wenck, Robison, and Smith, 1972:393–402.

may be placed on probation or diverted from the justice system. False positives (404 persons in the study results presented in Table 3.1) are those offenders who are needlessly incarcerated (Walker, 1985:57). False negatives are those of most concern to juvenile authorities.

In the general case, false positives and false negatives have been generalized to both adult and juvenile offenders. The task of an effective prediction scheme is to maximize the prediction and classification of true positives and negatives and minimize the numbers of offenders falling into the false positive or false negative category.

The Effectiveness of Risk-Assessment Devices

Present efforts to develop classification schemes to predict offender future behavior remain at best an unstable business (Wright, Clear, and Dickson, 1984). Risk-assessment devices developed and used in one state are often not applicable to offenders in other states (Wright et al., 1984). In some states such as Massachusetts, risk-assessment instruments are used by probation officers to decide which probationers should be supervised with varying frequency (Brown and Cochran, 1984). Results were favorable (i.e., lower recidivism rates were observed) when certain high-risk offenders received greater supervision by probation officers, compared with high-risk offenders who did not receive greater supervision.

A fairly comprehensive compilation of prediction and classification data in the 1980s has resulted in conclusions and recommendations that socioeconomic data and records of arrests and/or indictments should be systematically excluded as relevant sentencing criteria (Gottfredson and Tonry, 1987:408–409). Yet, many risk-assessment instruments currently use these and related criteria for sentencing, community supervision, and early release parole decisions (Petersilia and Turner, 1987:158). The hesitancy among certain professionals to use such instruments is based on the fact that socioeconomic information is inherently discriminatory. Those offenders who are unemployed, uneducated, or who have low incomes are at a disadvantage in the sentencing process compared with those who are employed, are more highly educated, and have good incomes. Often, they cannot afford the best legal aid available. Furthermore, indictments are charges of crime rather than certain evidence of criminal activity. Also, arrests do not mean convictions. Many charges against suspects are dropped by police or prosecutors later, although this information remains as a part of their records. Gottfredson and Tonry (1987) believe that offenders should not be penalized because of their socioeconomic status and unsubstantiated charges against them.

An examination of sentencing practices and other corrections decisions in a majority of the states has led to the development of a list of factors considered relevant to such decisions, which is shown in Table 3.2 (Petersilia and Turner, 1987:158).

Two important questions in designing any instrument to predict future criminal conduct are (1) which factors are most relevant in such predictions and (2) what weight should be given each of these factors?

One recurring criticism of prediction studies and the development of risk as-

TABLE 3.2 Factors Included in Formal Guidelines or Classification Instruments

Factor	Sentencing	Community Supervision	Parole Release
Criminal Record			
No. of parole/probation revocations	b	a	a
No. of adult and juvenile arrests	—	b	c
Age at first arrest	—	—	—
Nature of arrest crimes	—	—	—
No. of adult and juvenile convictions	a	b	a
Age at first conviction	—	a	c
Nature of prior convictions	a	b	a
Repeat of conviction types	c	—	c
No. of previous felony sentences	—	b	—
No. of previous probation sentences	—	b	—
No. of juvenile incarcerations	—	—	b
No. of jail terms served	—	—	b
No. of prison terms served	—	—	a
No. of incarcerations served	b	—	a
Age at first incarceration	—	—	b
Length of current term	—	—	c
Total years incarcerated	—	—	c
Commitment-free period evidenced	c	b	b
On probation/parole at arrest	b	b	b
Nature of current crime			
Multiple conviction crimes	b	—	—
Involves violence	a	—	a
Is property crime	—	—	c
Weapon involved	c	—	c
Victim injured	a	—	b
Victim/offender forcible contact	—	—	c
Social factors			
Current age	—	c	c
Educational level	—	c	c
Employment history	—	b	c
Mental health status	—	c	—
Family relationships	—	c	—
Living arrangements	—	c	c
Drug use	—	a	b
Juvenile use/abuse	—	b	—
Alcohol use/abuse	—	b	c
Companions	—	c	—
Address change in last year	b	—	—
Attitude	b	—	—
Financial status	c	—	—

sessment instruments is that much work is needed on the definition and measurement of criteria (Gottfredson and Gottfredson, 1990). This does not mean that all of the instruments presently developed are worthless as predictors of success on probation or parole. But it does suggest these measures are imperfect. Therefore, it may be premature to rely exclusively on instrument scores to decide who goes to

TABLE 3.2 (continued)

Factor	Sentencing	Community Supervision	Parole Release
Prison behavior			
Infractions	—	—	b
Program participation	—	—	c
Release plan formulated	—	—	c
Escape history	—	—	c

[a]75 percent or more of those instruments identified used this factor.
[b]50–74 percent of those instruments identified used this factor.
[c]25–49 percent of those instruments identified used this factor.

Source: Joan Petersilia and Susan Turner, "Guidelines-Based Justice: Prediction and Racial Minorities," in *Prediction and Classification: Criminal Justice Decision Making,* Don M. Gottfredson and Michael Tonry (eds.). Chicago: University of Chicago Press, 1987.

prison and who receives probation. But in many jurisdictions, risk-assessment scores are used precisely for this purpose.

Some Applications of Risk/Needs Measures

We have already discussed several of the many potential applications of risk/needs instruments and measures. One convenient way of highlighting the most common applications of these instruments by the different states is to examine their own utilization criteria and objectives. The following state utilization criteria are not intended to represent all other states or to typify them. Rather, they have been highlighted because of their diversity of objectives. For example, Iowa's Classification Risk-Assessment Scale is used for the following purposes:

1. Program planning;
2. Budgeting and deployment of resources;
3. Evaluating services, programs, procedures, and performances;
4. Measuring the potential impact of legislative and policy changes;
5. Enhancing accountability through standardization;
6. Equitably distributing the workload; and
7. Improving service delivery to clients. (Iowa Department of Correctional Services, 1992:6)

These goals are couched in the context of initial placement decisions and are closely related to management objectives, including allocating scarce resources most profitably in view of system constraints. Theoretically, if the system's procedural features are optimized, offender management is also. Presumably, the quality of services available to offender-clients would also be improved. But as we have seen, risk-assessments serve many purposes. For instance, the Ohio Parole Board uses a guideline system for determining early releases of certain offenders through parole or furlough. This guideline system incorporates a risk-assessment instrument and has the following objectives:

1. To provide for public protection by not releasing those inmates who represent a high risk of repeating violent or other serious crimes;
2. To provide an appropriate continuum of sanctions for crime;
3. To cooperate with correctional management in providing safe, secure, and humane conditions in state correctional institutions;
4. To recognize the achievement of those inmates with special identifiable problems relating to their criminal behavior who have participated in institutional programs designed to alleviate their problems; and
5. To make the decision-making process of the Adult Parole Authority more open, equitable, and understandable both to the public and to the inmate. (Ohio Parole Board, 1992:2).

In Ohio, the parole board guideline system objectives differ substantially from those in Iowa. The Ohio risk-assessment objectives are more offender-oriented, with emphases on the appropriateness of sanctions and identifying offender-client needs that may be met by particular services. There are also greater concerns for public safety and greater community comprehension of the parole decision-making process. Most states distinguish between offender evaluations for the purpose of determining their *institutional risk* and their *public risk*. Again, the device contents are often identical or very similar. An examination of the utilization criteria for other state risk assessment devices yields similar diversity of instrument goals.

Selective Incapacitation

The term *selective incapacitation* has become increasingly common in criminal justice literature in recent years. **Selective incapacitation** is incarcerating certain offenders deemed high risks to public safety and not incarcerating other offenders determined to be low risks, given similar offenses. Selective incapacitation applies to certain high-risk offenders and is designed to reduce the crime rate by incarcerating only those most likely to recidivate. Obviously, selective incapacitation is discriminatory in its application, and the ethics and fairness of predictive sentencing are frequently called into question (von Hirsch, 1984). Mental health professionals, psychiatrists and professionals who deal with violent persons on a regular basis also question the accuracy of dangerousness indices, especially when such devices are used for justifying **preventive confinement** (Monahan, 1984).

A conservative view is that much additional work is needed to validate not only the Rand instruments but other measures that purportedly measure an offender's risk and dangerousness (Blumstein, 1983). And, the U.S. Supreme Court is likely to be critical of any discriminatory scheme that incarcerates some and not others committing the same offenses within the due process and cruel and unusual punishment contexts of the Fourteenth and Eighth Amendments. These issues remain unresolved.

Probationers may become suspects and are subject to stops, interrogations, and searches by police officers whenever crimes are committed in neighborhoods where they reside. (The Image Works)

In those cases in which PSIs are ordered by the court, it is incumbent on the probation officer to include a sentencing recommendation. It is here that the probation officer uses his or her background information, regardless of its reliability or unreliability, to make a prediction and a recommendation consistent with that prediction. After all, even though most judges approve plea agreements, they are not required by law to approve them. And, offenders are advised when entering guilty pleas that the judge may or may not go along with the prosecutor's recommendation (18 U.S.C., Fed. Rule of Cr. Proc. 11, 1995). The judge has the option of increasing or decreasing the penalties set forth in the original plea agreement.

One of the better commentaries on dangerousness and risk-assessment instruments and how they ought to be used by probation officers and judges has been provided by Norval Morris (1984). He suggests several useful principles to be applied in tandem with judicial sentencing and probation officer PSI recommendations:

1. Clinical predictions of dangerousness should not be relied on other than for short-term intervention.
2. Decisions to restrict offender autonomy should be made by considering the actual extent of harm that may occur and how much individual autonomy of offenders ought to be limited.
3. Predictions of dangerousness are "present condition," not predictions of particular results.
4. Sufficiency of proof of dangerousness should not be confused with proof beyond a reasonable doubt, clear and convincing evidence, or on a balance of probability.
5. Punishment should not be imposed or extended, by virtue of a dangerousness prediction, beyond that justified as "deserved" punishment independent of that prediction.
6. Provided the previous limitation is respected, dangerousness predictions may properly influence sentencing decisions.
7. The base expectancy rate of criminal violence for the criminal predicted as dangerous should be shown by reliable evidence to be "substantially higher" than the rate for another criminal, with a closely similar crime, but not predicted as unusually dangerous, before greater dangerousness of the former may be relied on to intensify or extend the punishment. (Morris, 1984)

Regardless of the quality of predictability associated with risk-assessment instruments used by probation officers and others for classifying offenders and making sentencing recommendations, what does seem to work as a deterrent to future crime is intensive supervised probation, particularly considering its cost-effectiveness compared with incarceration (Latessa, 1986:70–71). Intensive supervised probation programs are discussed at length in Chapter 4. One continuing dilemma, however, is selecting those offenders best suited for higher levels of supervision (Latessa, 1986:70).

THE PROBATION DECISION AND SENTENCING TRENDS

In recent years, several articles about probation have begun with the eye-catching phrase, "Probation is in trouble!" Each article then justifies the phrase by citing mixed, confusing probation objectives and an absence of "mission," recidivism rates among probationers, the withdrawal of judicial and public support from probation services, and the lack of purposefulness of actions of probation officers themselves (Fitzharris, 1984; Rosecrance, 1986). While not advocating an abolition of probation, one of the more drastic proposals is eliminating the supervision of offender-clients by probation officers, with the monitoring function performed by clerical personnel appointed by the court (Rosecrance, 1986:26).

One critic has listed several reasons for probation's current state of "vulnerability":

1. An unclear mission;
2. Overstated, unspecified, and unmeasurable objectives;
3. Undemonstrated expertise and inadequate standards and training;
4. Unsubstantiated results;
5. A history of inadequate funding;
6. Isolation from the public (noninvolvement) and a lack of public awareness;
7. Lack of strategic planning and effective management techniques; and
8. A weak constituency. (Fitzharris, 1984:388)

Most of these criticisms are logistical, organizational, financial, and/or political. Nothing in this listing says that the "idea" of probation as an alternative to incarceration is bad. With better staffing through better funding, with better planning from administration including specific forms of probation for particular offenders, and with greater communication with the public about existing probation programs and aims, most of these reasons for probation's vulnerability would disappear. Another corrections expert has said that we should do away with terminology that implies that courts are not tough enough in dealing with offenders. Instead of granting probation, the judge should sentence convicted offenders to some form of community control (Barkdull, 1987:53). As understood by the public, probation is perceived as ineffective for offender improvement or for the society (Barkdull, 1987:51).

One major problem with probation seems to be inadequate public relations stemming from state and federal probation agencies. One suggestion is that "the challenge for probation in America in the 1980s is to develop community-based corrections programs that the community can both *understand and accept,* while furthering the pursuit of justice" (McAnany, Thomson, and Fogel, 1984, emphasis mine).

If probation practitioners were to be surveyed, it is likely that much consensus would be found about probation's goals. There is no mystery surrounding probation's objectives and philosophies. The apparent confusion about the manifest goals of probation is probably attributable to the diverse probation alternatives that are currently available to probationers (e.g., split-sentencing, community-based corrections, electronic monitoring, house arrest, intensive supervised probation, halfway-in houses, outreach services, diversion, group therapy and individualized counseling, restitution, community service, payment of fines, and many other activities).

The general trend in sentencing is toward greater use of determinate and mandatory provisions in state criminal statutes. Although this may mean greater certainty of incarceration for offenders convicted of certain crimes, periods of incarceration are not necessarily longer than incarcerative periods served under indeterminate sentencing. A majority of states currently have indeterminate sentencing. Even in those states where mandatory incarceration has been established for specific offenses, plea bargaining practices have successfully circumvented these new policies, which otherwise would result in greater numbers of offenders incarcerated for longer periods.

However, states such as Washington, Pennsylvania, and Minnesota report no significant increases in their prison populations as the result of their shift to determinate sentencing (Minnesota Sentencing Guidelines Commission, 1984; Washington State Sentencing Guidelines Commission, 1985). But there is a noticeable shift in sentencing and correctional policies at the state and federal levels designed to increase sentencing severity and the certainty of incarceration as deterrents to offenders (Abt Associates, Inc., 1987). Under federal and state provisions, high-risk, violent offenders are increasingly likely to be incapacitated, and for longer periods of confinement. By the same token, penalties for nonviolent and first offenders have generally decreased, and greater use of probation is occurring.

KEY TERMS

Acceptance of responsibility	Prediction
Actuarial prediction	Presentence investigation
Anamnestic prediction	Presentence investigation report (PSI)
Classification	Preventive Confinement
Classification system	Risk
Clinical Prediction	Risk assessment
False negative	Risk-assessment instrument
False positive	Risk/needs instrument
Freedom of Information Act (FOIA)	Selective incapacitation
Narrative	Sentencing hearing
Needs-assessment instrument	Victim impact statements
Offense seriousness score	

QUESTIONS FOR REVIEW

1. What are some general functions performed by probation officers? How do their functions relate to offender sentencing? Explain.
2. Distinguish between aggravating and mitigating circumstances. Give some examples of each. At what point in offender processing are such circumstances considered important?
3. What is a presentence investigation? Who prepares the PSI? Are such reports always prepared for all offenders? Under what circumstances would PSIs be prepared?
4. What are three kinds of risk prediction devices? Give an example of each. What is the general predictive value of such devices, as viewed by professionals?
5. What are some general functions of offender classification? Do you think these functions are realized in probation work? Why or why not?
6. Are offenders permitted to see PSIs? What is a defendant's sentencing memorandum? What is its purpose?
7. How do victims participate in sentencing? What method can victims use to inform judges about aggravating circumstances of the offense prior to the sentencing decision?

8. What is a victim impact statement? Is it required by law?
9. What are risk assessment measures? How are they used?
10. What information is usually provided in a PSI? What functions do PSIs serve?

APPENDIX: SAMPLE PSI REPORT

IN THE UNITED STATES DISTRICT COURT FOR THE NORTHERN
DISTRICT OF OHIO

```
UNITED STATES OF AMERICA  )§
                          )§
     v.                    )§    Docket No. 95-00014-01
                          )§
Molly McDougall            )§
```

PRESENTENCE REPORT

Prepared for: The Honorable Robert L.
                           Taylor
                           United States District Judge

Prepared by: John W. Phillips
                           United States Probation
                           Officer
                           (216) 633-6226

Sentencing Date: September 26, 1995 at
                           9:00 a.m.

Offense: 18 U.S.C. 656, Misapplication
                           of Funds by Bank Employee, a
                           class D Felony

Release Status: $1,000 Personal Surety Bond
                           (no presentence custodial
                           credit)

Identifying Data:

Date of Birth: February 2, 1973
Social Security Number: 881-22-4444
Address: 24 Apple Street
                           Cleveland, Ohio 44114

<u>Detainers</u>:   None.

<u>Codefendants</u>:   None.

<u>Assistant U.S. Attorney</u>   <u>Defense Counsel</u>

Michael Haynes   Jimmie Baxter
U.S. Courthouse   113 Main Street
Cleveland, Ohio 44114   Cleveland, Ohio 44114
(216) 333-3333   (216) 444-4444

Date report prepared: September 2, 1995

Revised September 12, 1995

PART A. THE OFFENSE

<u>Charge(s) and Conviction(s)</u>

1. Molly McDougall, the defendant, was indicted by a Northern District of Ohio grand jury on June 15, 1995. The indictment alleged that on May 2, 1995 while she was employed
by the Bank of Ohio in Cleveland, Ohio, the defendant misap-
plied bank funds, in violation of 18 U.S.C. 656. On July 25,
McDougall pled guilty to the charge.

2. Since the offense took place after November 1, 1987, the
Sentencing Reform Act of 1984 is applicable.

<u>The Offense Conduct</u>

4. The defendant McDougall began working at Bank of Ohio,
2100 Main Street, Cleveland, Ohio, in mid-January, 1995. On
April 30, 1995, she went to a local furniture store to purchase some bedroom furniture. The furniture she wanted to
buy cost $5,000, and McDougall asked the salesman whether
she could finance the purchase. The salesman advised Mc-
Dougall that because she had not established a credit rating, she could finance only one-half of the purchase price
and could pay the remainder of the purchase price, $2,500,
by check. McDougall did not have sufficient funds in her
checking account to cover a check in that amount, but
thought she would have it as soon as she could contact her
boyfriend, who was going to lend her the necessary funds.
Believing that her boyfriend would give her the funds before
her check to the furniture company could clear, McDougall
wrote the company a check for $2,500. The check was pre-
sented for payment before she could make a deposit to cover

it, and the bank, as a courtesy to an employee, paid it.
When her boyfriend failed to advance her any funds to cover
the overdraft, McDougall became desperate.

5. On May 2, 1995, McDougall devised a solution to her
problem. On that day, Victor Garcia came to her teller's
window and asked McDougall to deposit an $11,000 check to
his savings account. McDougall deposited the money to her
checking account, instead.

6. On May 17, 1995, Garcia advised the bank that his account did not contain the $11,000 he had deposited on May 2.
The bank immediately began an audit and soon discovered what
McDougall had done. When the Audit Manager confronted
McDougall with his discovery, McDougall admitted that she
had placed Garcia's deposit in her account. She stated that
when she diverted the check she was desperate, being fearful
that she would lose her job for having overdrawn her checking account. McDougall asserts that she intended to return
the money to Garcia's account but had not been able to obtain the $2,500 that she had spent when the auditor discov-
ered the misapplication of the money. She had planned to
replace the full $11,000 in one deposit entry to Mr. Gar-
cia's account.

7. According to bank records, on June 3, 1995, McDougall
paid the bank $8,550 of the funds she diverted. She still
owes the bank the remaining $2,450. The bank has not filed a
claim with its bonding company, which insured McDougall's fi-
delity, because McDougall has agreed to pay the $2,450 bal-
ance of the embezzlement.

Adjustment for Obstruction of Justice

8. The probation officer has no information suggesting that
the defendant impeded or obstructed justice.

Adjustment for Acceptance of Responsibility

9. During the interview with the probation officer, McDougall
was distraught and tearful regarding the offense, stating repeatedly that she is ashamed and embarrassed. When confronted
by bank officials, McDougall readily admitted that she committed the offense. Four days later, she made an $8,550 payment
toward restitution. She is clearly remorseful.

Offense Level Computation

10. Base Offense Level: The guideline for an 18 U.S.S. 656 offense is found in Section 2B1.1(a) of the Guidelines. The base offense level is 4.   4

11. Specific Offense Characteristics: Section 2B1.1(b) provides that if the value of the property taken is between $10,001 and $20,000, 5 levels are added. The instant offense entailed a loss of $11,000.   5

12. Adjustment for Role in the Offense: None   0

13. Victim-Related Adjustment: None   0

14. Adjustment for Obstruction of Justice: None   0

15. Adjustment for Acceptance of Responsibility: Based on the defendant's admission of guilt, her payment of restitution, and her remorse, pursuant to Section 3E1.1(a), two levels are subtracted.   −2

16. Total Offense Level: 7

PART B. THE DEFENDANT'S CRIMINAL HISTORY

Juvenile Adjudications

17. None

Criminal Convictions

18. None

Criminal History Computation

19. The defendant has no criminal convictions. Therefore, she has zero criminal history points and a criminal history category of I.

Other Criminal Conduct

20. None

PART C. SENTENCING OPTIONS

Custody

21. Statutory Provisions: The maximum term of imprisonment is 5 years. 18 U.S.C. 656.

22. Guideline Provisions: Based upon a total offense level of 7 and a criminal history category of I, the guideline imprisonment range is 1 to 7 months.

Supervised Release

23. Statutory Provisions: If a term of imprisonment is imposed, the court may impose a term of supervised release of not more than 2 years pursuant to 18 U.S.C. 3583(b)(2).

24. Guideline Provisions: If a sentence of imprisonment is imposed within the guideline range, a term of supervised release is not required but is optional. If more than one year imprisonment is imposed on the basis of a departure, supervised release is required. According to Section 5D3.2, the term of supervised release for a class D felony is 2 years.

Probation

25. Statutory Provisions: The defendant is eligible for probation by statute. Because the offense is a felony, 18 U.S.C. 3563(a)(2) requires that one of the following be imposed as a condition of probation: a fine, restitution or community service. For a felony, the authorized term of probation is not less than one year nor more than five years. 18 U.S.C. 3561(b)(1).

26. Guideline Provisions: The defendant is eligible for probation provided that the court impose a condition requiring intermittent confinement or community confinement for at least one month. Section 5B1.1(a)(2). Currently there are no facilities in the Cleveland area for intermittent confinement.
    However, there is currently bedspace available at the New Hope Halfway House at 500 Broadway Avenue in Cleveland. This facility appears to be a suitable facility if the de-

fendant were ordered to serve a sentence of community confinement.

27. If the court were to impose probation, the term must be at least one year but no more than five years. Section 5B1.2(a)(1).

PART D. OFFENDER CHARACTERISTICS

Family Ties, Family Responsibilities, and Community Ties

28. Molly McDougall was born on February 2, 1973, the fourth of seven children born to John and Ann McDougall. McDougall grew up in Fargo, North Dakota and moved to Cleveland with her family at the age of 15, when her father obtained employment as a cook at a Cleveland hotel.

29. McDougall is single. She resides with her parents and younger siblings at 24 Apple Street, Cleveland. The defendant states that she has not told her parents about the criminal charges against her, as she is exceedingly embarrassed and feels that she cannot discuss the matter with them. Marcus McDougall, the defendant's older brother, verified background information about the defendant. He reported that prior to this offense, McDougall never posed any serious problems for the family.

Mental and Emotional Health

30. According to the defendant, she has never suffered from any mental or emotional problems that would require professional intervention. It was obvious to the probation officer during the interview with Ms. McDougall that she is extremely remorseful about the outcome of this case. Her brother confirmed that McDougall has no history of mental or emotional problems but recently has been very anxious about the instant case.

Physical Condition, Including Drug Dependence and Alcohol Abuse

31. Molly McDougall reports that she is in good health and has never suffered from any serious illnesses or injuries. She states that she has never used illicit drugs and does not consume alcohol.

Education and Vocational Skills

32. A transcript from Monroe High School of Cleveland indicates that Molly McDougall was graduated in June, 1991 with
a grade point average of 2.5.

   She attended the Bank Training Institute in Cleveland in
1994, completing a five-week training course. The probation
officer verified this by examining Institute records. It was
the training from this vocational school that qualified Mc-
Dougall to be hired by Bank of Ohio.

Employment Record

33. At the present time, McDougall is employed as a recep-
tionist at Video Reproductions Incorporated on Third Street
in Cleveland. Her duties include answering telephones and
processing invoices. Her supervisor, Howard Allen, verified
that McDougall does not handle money. She has been employed
at this company since July 5, 1995, and according to Allen,
she has been a responsible employee. Allen is aware of the
charges pending against Ms. McDougall.

34. On May 30, 1995, when McDougall was discharged from
Bank of Ohio for the misapplication of the check, she had
been working as a teller since January 29, 1995. From December 1992 until March 1994, McDougall was employed by Macy's
department store in Cleveland as a salesclerk. She quit this
job to attend the Bank Training Institute.

PART E. FINES AND RESTITUTION

Statutory Provisions

35. The maximum fine is $250,000. 18 U.S.C. 3571(b).

36. A special assessment of $50 is mandatory. 18 U.S.C.
3013.

37. Restitution is owed to Bank of Ohio in the amount of
$2,450 and is payable to the following address:

> Bank of Ohio Collections
> Security Division
> 113 Grape Avenue
> Cleveland, Ohio 44114
> Attention: Mr. Young

Guideline Provisions About Fines

38. The fine range for this offense is from $2,450 less any restitution ordered with a minimum of $500 (Section 5E4.2(c)(1)(B) to $33,000 (Section 5E4.2(c)(2)(C).

39. Subject to the defendant's ability to pay, the court shall impose an additional fine amount that is at least sufficient to pay the costs to the government of any imprisonment, probation, or supervised release. Section 5e4.2(i).

    The most recent advisory from the Administrative Office of the United States Courts, dated March 15, 1995, suggests that a monthly cost of $_____ be used for imprisonment and a monthly cost of $_____ for supervision.

Defendant's Ability to Pay

40. Based upon a financial statement submitted by McDougall, a review of her bank records and a credit bureau check, the defendant's financial condition is as follows:

Assets

Cash

Cash on hand	$ 47
Checking account	130
U.S. Savings Bond	75

Unencumbered Assets

Stereo system	$ 500

Equity in Other Assets

1994 Toyota Corolla	$2,000	(equity based on Blue Book value)
TOTAL ASSETS	$2,752	

Unsecured Debts

Loan from brother	$ 300
Attorney fees balance	1,500
TOTAL UNSECURED DEBTS	$1,899

<u>Net Worth</u>	$ 952

<u>Monthly Cash Flow</u>

<u>Income</u>

Net salary	<u>$ 752</u>
TOTAL INCOME	$ 752

<u>Necessary Living Expenses</u>

Room and board	$ 150
Installment payment	
(car loan)	242
Gas and auto costs	50
Attorney fees	100
Clothing	<u>50</u>
TOTAL EXPENSES	$ 592

<u>Net Monthly Cash Flow</u>	$ 160

41. Based upon McDougall's financial profile, it appears that she has the ability to remit restitution if she makes monthly installments. However, her income is rather modest, and it does not appear that she could also pay a fine.

PART F. FACTORS THAT MAY WARRANT DEPARTURE

42. The probation officer has not identified any information that would warrant a departure from the guidelines.

Respectfully submitted,

FRANK D. GILBERT
CHIEF PROBATION OFFICER

By

_____

John W. Phillips
U.S. Probation Officer

Reviewed and Approved:

_____

WILLIAM HACKETT
SUPERVISOR

ADDENDUM TO THE PRESENTENCE REPORT

The probation officer certifies that the presentence report,
including any revision thereof, has been disclosed to the
defendant, her attorney, and counsel for the Government, and
that the content of the Addendum has been communicated to
counsel. The Addendum fairly states any objections they have
made.

OBJECTIONS

By the Government

The Government has no objections.

By the Defendant

The defense attorney maintains that the defendant's youth,
lack of a prior record, and her remorse are characteristics
that should be considered for a departure from the guidelines. He will present argument at the sentencing hearing
that community confinement is not necessary in this case and
that the court should depart by a sentence of probation with
restitution.
     The probation officer does not believe that a departure
is warranted. Remorse and lack of a prior record are factored into the guidelines. The Sentencing Commission policy
statement on age (Section 5H1.1) suggests that youth is not
a valid reason for departure.

CERTIFIED BY

FRANK D. GILBERT
CHIEF PROBATION OFFICER

By

_____

John W. Phillips
U.S. Probation Officer

Reviewed and Approved

_____

WILLIAM HACKETT
SUPERVISOR

SENTENCING RECOMMENDATION

United States v. Molly McDougall, Dkt No. 95-00014-01,
U.S. District Court, District of Northern Ohio

CUSTODY

<u>Statutory maximum</u>:   5 years

<u>Guideline range</u>:   1 to 7 months

<u>Recommendation</u>:   1 month community confinement

<u>Justification:</u>

According to the Guidelines, the defendant is eligible for probation provided that she serve at least one month of intermittent or community confinement. McDougall is a good candidate for probation because she has no prior record, is willing to make restitution to the victim, and is gainfully employed. A prison sentence does not appear to be necessary in this case since the defendant does not need to be incapacitated to deter her from further crime and other sanctions will provide sufficient punishment.

FINE

<u>Statutory maximum</u>:	$250,000
<u>Guideline range</u>:	$2,450 (or $500 if restitution is ordered) to $33,000 plus the cost of incarceration and/or supervision.
<u>Recommendation</u>:	$0

<u>Justification</u>:

Restitution to the victim bank is recommended as a condition of probation. The defendant's modest income will necessitate that the restitution be paid in monthly installments. At this point, McDougall does not have the ability to pay both restitution and a fine.

PROBATION

<u>Statutory term</u>:	Minimum of 1 year and a maximum of 5 years
<u>Guideline term</u>:	Minimum of 1 year and a maximum of 5 years
<u>Recommended term</u>:	4 years

<u>Recommended conditions</u>:

1. That the defendant not commit any crimes, federal, state, or local.
2. That the defendant abide by the standard conditions of probation recommended by the Sentencing Commission.
3. That the defendant by confined in a community treatment center or halfway house for 30 days, during which she will be allowed to maintain employment.
4. That the defendant pay restitution to Bank of Ohio in the amount of $2,450 in monthly installments of $55 per month.
5. That the defendant be prohibited from incurring new credit charges or opening additional lines of credit without the approval of the probation officer unless the defendant is in compliance with the payment schedule.
6. That the defendant provide the probation officer with access to any requested financial information.

7. That if the defendant should hold a fiduciary position in her employment, she be required to inform her employer of the instant conviction.

Justification:

A sentence of probation contingent upon 30 days' confinement in a halfway house and the payment of restitution will provide sufficient punishment for McDougall as well as a general deterrence to others. The guidelines require intermittent or community confinement as a condition of probation. Placement in a halfway house for the minimum sentence of 30 days is recommended so that McDougall can continue to work and pay restitution to the victim bank. Since she has a modest income and a substantial amount of restitution to pay, a four-year term of probation is recommended with the requirement that she pay no less than $55 per month toward restitution. Conditions of supervision requiring financial disclosure to the probation officer and a provision against incurring new credit debts are suggested in order to monitor the defendant's payments. Because the instant offense is a form of embezzlement, McDougall will be considered a third-party risk to an employer if she were to handle money. It is therefore suggested that while under supervision, she be required to inform any employer of the instant conviction if she holds a fiduciary position.

SPECIAL ASSESSMENT   **$50**

VOLUNTARY SURRENDER

If the court imposes a custodial sentence, McDougall appears to be a good candidate for a voluntary surrender.

Respectfully submitted,

FRANK D. GILBERT
CHIEF PROBATION OFFICER

By

_____

John W. Phillips
U.S. Probation Officer

Reviewed and Approved:

_____

WILLIAM HACKETT
SUPERVISOR

Date: September 12, 1995

4

Diversion and Probation Options
From Alternative Dispute Resolution to Boot Camps and Shock Probation

Introduction
Civil Mechanisms in Lieu of Diversion
   and Probation
Pretrial Diversion
Standard Probation

Intensive Supervised Probation (ISP)
Shock Probation and Split Sentencing
Boot Camps
Key Terms
Questions for Review

INTRODUCTION

- "O.K. You're the one who shoved me, grabbed my purse, pushed me down to the pavement, caused me to break my arm in three places and bruised my legs and back. You got $4.00 from my purse and threw the purse away in a trash can as you ran off. Luckily, you ran around a corner into the arms of two police officers. You got caught. Look at me! Look at my broken arm. I'm 80 years old. You're 19. It cost me probably four months of healing. My medical bills alone are over $6,000. I've got insurance to cover most of it. But I live on Social Security and some small investments. I'll get by. What about you? You *were* looking at five years for robbery. The cops found a knife on you. That mistake *might* have cost you another two years of mandatory time. But they found that you don't have much of a record. Just getting started, huh? We don't want you to get a criminal record yet, do we? You want to pay me for my pain and suffering and medical bills? How much is pain worth? How do you measure suffering? You got $4.00 out of it. Was it worth it? They say if you pay me for my expenses and do some community service, they aren't going to put you through a criminal trial. I don't agree with that. But you seem like a nice kid. Now that I am talking with you here, face-to-face. The D.A. says they aren't going to press charges if you and I can work something out. They say they want to divert you from criminal prosecution. What if we do work something out? Are you going out on the streets again and ripping off another old lady?"

- "Mr. and Mrs. Saunders? This is Louis Ruiz. His friend, here, is Eric Davis. Louis is 29 and Eric is 25. They're the ones who stole your pickup truck, Mr. Saunders. Left it in a ditch with flat tires, a bent frame, and bashed-in grill. They say they were drunk, just got laid off from the sawmill down the road. Saw your truck. Say you left your keys in it. Anyway, they're the ones who took it and wrecked it. If we wanted to, we could prosecute them for vehicular theft. They might do three years in the penitentiary. But neither one of them has a record. They both done bad and they know it. They told that to Detective Schyler here, and she said the guys were pretty upset. But Schyler and I don't know that prison's going to help 'em. We don't *know* for a fact that they were drunk, since we didn't catch 'em until two days later, and so DUI is up in the air. They probably were drunk. Eyewitnesses pointed them out to us. But if you're agreeable, they say they want to pay for your truck, maybe work out an arrangement to make payments to you from their pay from other work they're going to be doing. What we will do is divert them from the system. Not prosecute them. If you don't want to bring charges against them, they will see to it that your truck is as good as new. We'll make sure they follow through on these payments. What do you think?"

What do you think? These are two hypothetical examples of alternative dispute resolution in action. This is not an especially new way of dealing with some criminal offenders. But it is a strategy that seems to be increasingly employed. Above we have a mugger/robber and two auto thieves. There is no question that they have committed these crimes. Maybe among all three, they would be looking at 10 to 15 years in the state prison. But with diversion through alternative dispute resolution, they will not get a criminal record, and the victims will be compensated for their losses, as much as money can replace. Part of this chapter is about alternative dispute resolution and diversion, who qualifies for it, and how it is applied. These are two of several nonincarcerative alternative punishments the criminal justice system can impose.

CIVIL MECHANISMS IN LIEU OF DIVERSION AND PROBATION

Civil procedure and criminal procedure involve two separate systems. The most familiar portrayal of civil procedure is Judge Wapner's *People's Court* on television. This popular program resolves disputes between parties within certain monetary limits, with Judge Wapner acting as the impartial arbiter. Civil wrongs, or **torts,** are commonly settled in civil actions. In all civil actions, damages are sought, not criminal convictions. If someone backs out of a driveway and over a neighbor's garden and plants, the neighbor may sue to recover damages to the garden and plants. Damages might be eventually awarded in some monetary amount. This money would settle the case, since the neighbor could replant or replace the garden or damaged plants in it. In criminal actions, convictions are sought. Monetary penalties may be sought also in the form of fines. But these are not "damages" in the civil sense. Rather, they are additional penalties incurred besides possible incarceration. And, offenders are convicted and acquire criminal records.

Any "victim" can seek damages in a civil court as a remedy for being victimized. In an increasing number of cases, however, those who allegedly offend against victims may be prosecuted as criminals in the criminal justice system. But in numerous instances, the offenses alleged are petty or minor. Even though the criminal justice system might define certain conduct as criminal, that conduct might be redefined as a civil wrong. If conduct that could be defined as criminal is actually reinterpreted as a civil wrong or a tort, then civil mechanisms can be brought into action to resolve or mediate disputes between victims and offenders. Besides pursuing cases against offenders in civil actions, victims can seek compensation through other means, such as alternative dispute resolution.

Alternative Dispute Resolution

In cases involving minor criminal offenses, an option increasingly used by the prosecution is alternative dispute resolution. **Alternative dispute resolution (ADR)** is a community-based, informal dispute settlement between offenders and their victims (Marshall et al., 1985). Most often targeted for participation in these programs are misdemeanants (Alaska Judicial Council, 1992; Royse and Buck, 1991). A growing number of ADR programs are being implemented throughout the nation (Bass, 1987; Selva and Bohm, 1987). Some persons have begun to refer to ADR as a "movement" (Kaufman, 1990). A tavern brawl may result in arrests of brawlers and criminal charges of aggravated assault. These cases could consume valuable court time if a trial were held. However, if the offenders and victims agree, ADR can sometimes be used to dispose of these cases quickly and informally, mutually satisfying the parties involved (Lieberman and Henry, 1986). With early roots in the Midwest, victim-offender mediation or ADR programs now exist in more than 100 U.S. jurisdictions, 54 in Norway, 40 in France, 25 in Canada, 25 in Germany, 18 in England, 20 in Finland, and 8 in Belgium (Umbreit, 1991:165).

Victim-offender meetings often result in noncriminal solutions of problems through alternative dispute resolution. (Bob Daemmerich/Stock Boston)

In growing circles, ADR is also known as **restorative justice** (Umbreit, 1991:164). ADR involves the direct participation of the victim and offender, with the aim of mutual accommodation for both parties. ADR emphasizes restitution rather than punishment. There are smaller costs associated with it compared with trials, and criminal stigmatization is avoided (Marshall et al., 1985). However, it is sometimes difficult to decide which cases are best arbitrated through ADR and which should be formally resolved through trial. This should not be interpreted as meaning that juveniles are excluded from ADR. There are specific programs in various jurisdictions especially tailored for juvenile offenders (Bush, 1991). In short, ADR is a decriminalization procedure whereby satisfaction may be obtained by victims against offenders, particularly in those instances where property damage or theft has occurred and restitution is likely (Edwards, 1986). Restitution also makes such programs easier for victims to accept.

The Case of Sunshine Mediation Center.   Morrill and McKee (1993:450) describe the Sunshine Mediation Center (SMC), a pseudonym for an urban mediation program founded in 1981 in a southwestern city. Between 1985 and 1991, SMC handled between 800 to 1,100 cases per year. The typical range of problems and disputes handled by the SMC includes barking dog nuisances, landlord-tenant disputes, spouse and child abuse, broken financial obligations, and unpaid private and small commercial debts, as well as various misdemeanor cases. Government agencies were the largest referral source for cases. The basic premises of SMC included

1. Delivery of dispute settlement services
2. Personal growth
3. Community improvement

SMC was designed as an alternative to congested criminal and civil courts. Vital to the functioning of SMC was the use of volunteers as mediators. Usually, volunteers would arrive at a tentative case settlement over the telephone with both the victim and the offender. Then an evening meeting would be scheduled, and both parties would sit down and work out the details of the compromise or settlement. As a team, two mediators work with both parties at once, establishing initial ground rules. Both parties detail their arguments and talk about how they would like the dispute resolved and what they would be willing to do to resolve it. Subsequent outcomes include mutually signed agreements, impasses, or refusals to continue the process. In any case, the program generated a 90 percent success rate during the years investigated (Morrill and McKee, 1993:490–491).

Removing criminal cases from the jurisdiction of criminal courts is not favorably viewed by everyone (Harrington and Merry, 1988). Those insisting that criminals receive their just deserts are dissatisfied with the ADR option. But logistically, ADR is a major court time-saver. Between 1984–1985, for example, 43 New York counties operated community ADR centers. These centers handled 56,002 cases satisfactorily, cases that otherwise would have to be processed by criminal courts. The average trial takes about 15 days, while the average time per dispute resolution through arbitration is 1 hour and 20 minutes, although in some jurisdictions the dispute resolution period may be much longer (Doherty, 1986:56).

North Carolina has at least 19 mediation programs (Clarke, Valente, and Mace, 1992). Most often targeted for ADR are misdemeanor cases involving interpersonal disputes referred to these programs by district courts. How effective are the mediation programs in North Carolina? An evaluation study was conducted comparing several counties with programs with several counties without programs. A sample of 1,421 clusters of cases filed in 1990 that matched eligibility criteria was followed in records of courts and mediation programs. Furthermore, interview data were collected from complainants and defendants. Of those cases referred, about 59 percent were actually mediated, with nearly all (92 percent) resulting in mediated agreements. Complainants were generally satisfied with the results of such mediation (Clarke et al., 1992).

Victim-Offender Reconciliation Projects

Another version of alternative dispute resolution is victim-offender reconciliation. According to Roy and Brown (1992), **victim-offender reconciliation** is a specific form of conflict resolution between the victim and the offender. Face-to-face encounter is the essence of this process. Elkhart County, Indiana, has been the site of the **Victim-Offender Reconciliation Project (VORP)** since 1987. The primary aims of VORP are to (1) make offenders accountable for their wrongs against victims,

(2) reduce recidivism among participating offenders, and (3) heighten responsibility of offenders through victim compensation and repayment for damages inflicted (Roy and Brown, 1992; Umbreit, 1986).

Officially, VORP was established in Kitchener, Ontario, in 1974 and was subsequently replicated as PACT, or Prisoner and Community Together, in northern Indiana near Elkhart. Subsequent replications in various jurisdictions have created different varieties of ADR, each variety spawning embellishments, additions, or program deletions deemed more or less important by the particular jurisdiction (Umbreit, 1986:53). The Genessee County (Batavia), New York, Sheriff's Department established a VORP in 1983, followed by programs in Valparaiso, Indiana; Quincy, Massachusetts; and Minneapolis, Minnesota, in 1985. In Quincy, for instance, the program was named EARN-IT and was operated through the Probation Department (Umbreit, 1986:55). More than 25 different states have one or another version of VORP (Umbreit, 1986). One of these sites involved a study of offender recidivism and ADR. During the years between 1987 and 1991, an investigation of ADR and its effectiveness was undertaken and the results evaluated (Roy and Brown, 1992). The VORP significantly reduced recidivism among offenders. Both juvenile and adult offenders have been involved in this project over the years. Results suggest that it will be continued.

Cross-site analyses of ADR programs in other jurisdictions suggest results comparable to those in Indiana. Victim-offender mediation programs have been evaluated in Albuquerque, New Mexico; Austin, Texas; Minneapolis, Minnesota; and Oakland, California. Over a thousand interviews were conducted in both premediation and postmediation periods, as well as with persons in several groups not participating in ADR. Most victims and offenders reported greater satisfaction and perceptions of fairness for victims, as well as a much higher rate of restitution completion by offenders (Umbreit and Coates, 1993).

PRETRIAL DIVERSION

Pretrial diversion is a procedure whereby criminal defendants are diverted to either a community-based agency for treatment or assigned to a counselor for social and/or psychiatric assistance (President's Commission on Law Enforcement and the Administration of Justice, 1967). Pretrial diversion may involve education, job training, counseling, or some type of psychological or physical therapy (Nardulli, Flemming, and Eisenstein, 1985). It is important that pretrial diversion not be confused with pretrial detention or preventive detention. There is absolutely no relationship between these concepts.

Generally, diversion is the official halting or suspension of legal proceedings against a criminal defendant or juvenile after a recorded justice system entry, and possible referral of that person to a treatment or care program administered by a nonjustice agency or private agency (Allen et al., 1985:287). Technically, diversion is not true probation, in that the alleged offender has not been convicted of a crime. The thrust of diversion is toward an informal administrative effort to determine (1) whether nonjudicial processing is warranted, (2) whether treatment is warranted, (3) if treatment is warranted, which one to use, and (4) whether charges against the defendant should be dropped or reinstated (McCarthy and McCarthy, 1984:23).

Diversion is used primarily for first offenders who have not committed serious crimes. It is like probation in that offenders must comply with specific conditions established by the court for a fixed period. Successful completion of those conditions usually leads to a dismissal of charges against the defendant. A **totality of circumstances** assessment of each offender's crime is made by the prosecutor and the court, and a decision about diversion follows. Each case is considered on its own merits. Those charged with driving while intoxicated may be diverted to attend Alcoholics Anonymous meetings or special classes for drunk drivers as a part of their diversion. Often, diverted defendants must pay monthly fees or **user fees** during the diversion period to help defray expenses incurred by the public or private agencies that monitor them.

Virginia established a diversion program in 1981, for example, which was designed to divert prison-bound offenders to intensive probation supervision. The **Community Diversion Incentive Program (CDI)** was created whereby offenders would be obligated to perform specified unpaid community services and make financial restitution to their victims (Virginia Joint Legislative Audit and Review Commission, 1985). Technically, the CDI program is not a true diversion program, because it involves only those prison-bound offenders who have already been convicted of one or more crimes. A similar program for convicted, prison-bound offenders has also been described by Latessa (1987b). He has discussed the success of the Incarceration Diversion Unit of the Lucas County, Ohio, Adult Probation Department. Again, the term *diversion* has been used, but we must be careful to clarify the meaning of the term in different studies and the population of offenders to whom it is applied. Divertees are not *prison-bound*. Rather, they are *prosecution-bound*, with their prosecutions deferred and even withdrawn if they complete their diversion programs successfully.

Unconditional and Conditional Diversion

Although a majority of diversion programs in the United States include one or more behavioral conditions and prescribe involvement in treatment programs such as Alcoholics Anonymous, driver's training schools, and/or individual or group psychological counseling, some programs are unconditional. Unconditional diversion programs place no restrictions on a divertee's behavior, and there are no formal controls operating through which divertee behaviors can be monitored (McCarthy and McCarthy, 1984:22–23).

Conditional diversion programs involve some degree of behavioral monitoring by probation officers or personnel affiliated with local probation departments in cities or counties. The degree of monitoring depends on the conditions of the diversion program and the special needs of divertees. For the least-monitored divertees, monthly contact with the probation department by letter or telephone may be all that is required, together with the payment of a monthly maintenance fee, which may range from $10 to $100 or more. Divertees are often required to submit a statement regularly (usually monthly or weekly) indicating their present successful employment, family support, and other pertinent data.

The History and Philosophy of Diversion

Some authorities believe that in addition to the innovation of probation, John Augustus introduced diversion in the United States through his intervention on behalf of drunkards and low-risk misdemeanants in Boston courts in 1841 (Doeren and Hageman, 1982:23). Augustus sought to help convicted offenders avoid the criminogenic, debilitating, and vile atmosphere of Boston jails. It is questionable whether Augustus truly originated this correctional alternative, since he dealt exclusively with convicted offenders. However, he did "stand bail" for more than a few defendants who were awaiting adjudication in Boston courts. In this sense, a function similar to diversion was served, because defendants were later able to demonstrate to the judge that they had behaved well while under Augustus's supervision.

The more likely account is that diversion originated in the United States through the early juvenile courts in Chicago and New York in the late 1800s. There were concerted efforts by religious groups and reformers to keep children from imprisonment of any kind, since children over eight years of age were considered eligible for adult court processing. Cook County, Illinois, implemented a diversion program for youthful offenders in 1899 (Doeren and Hageman, 1982:23).

Diversion for adults became increasingly popular during the 1960s and coincided with the rise of the rehabilitation model of corrections. The Law Enforcement Assistance Administration funded several experimental programs designed to keep offenders out of prisons and jails during the early 1970s. One type of program heavily funded by the LEAA was pretrial diversion. By 1975, over half the states operated pretrial diversion programs (Law Enforcement Assistance Administration, 1977).

The underlying philosophy of diversion is **community reintegration** and rehabilitation, such that offenders avoid the stigma of incarceration and the public notoriety accompanying appearances and trials. In most state courts where diversion is condoned, diversion does not entirely remove offenders from court processing, since the court usually must approve prosecutorial recommendations for diversion in each case. Since these approvals are often conducted in less publicized hearings, a divertee's crimes are less likely to be scrutinized publicly. In the federal system, prosecutors have considerable power to divert offenders on their own authority without judicial approval under Department of Justice Guidelines. When the LEAA was dissolved and funds for diversion programs significantly curtailed, many jurisdictions continued these programs fully under their own sponsorship. This is because the programs not only helped to alleviate prison and jail overcrowding, but there were indications that the philosophy of diversion was being realized as well.

Functions of Diversion

When the LEAA sponsored diversion programs in the early 1970s, it had several functions and objectives in mind. These were summarized in a 1977 evaluative report (Law Enforcement Assistance Administration, 1977). Some of the more important functions are

1. To permit divertees the opportunity of remaining in their communities where they can receive needed assistance or treatment, depending upon the nature of the crimes charged.
2. To permit divertees the opportunity to make restitution to their victims where monetary damages were suffered and property destroyed.
3. To permit divertees the opportunity of remaining free in their communities to support themselves and their families, and to avoid the stigma of incarceration.
4. To help divertees avoid the stigma of a criminal conviction.
5. To assist corrections officials in reducing prison and jail overcrowding by diverting less serious cases to nonincarcerative alternatives.
6. To save the courts the time, trouble, and expense of formally processing less serious cases and streamlining case dispositions through informal case handling.
7. To make it possible for divertees to participate in self-help, educational, or vocational programs.
8. To preserve the dignity and integrity of divertees by helping them avoid further contact with the criminal justice system and assisting them to be more responsible adults capable of managing their own lives.
9. To preserve the family unit and enhance family solidarity and continuity.

Whereas this list is not exhaustive, it does serve to highlight the rehabilitative nature of diversion, regardless of its particular form as practiced in any given jurisdiction. At present, it is unknown precisely how much diversion affects the court system and the degree to which court caseloads are alleviated among jurisdictions. And, it is difficult to formulate accurate estimates about how much of the prison and jail overcrowding problem is lessened by diversion programs. This is so, in part, because diversion records are difficult to obtain. Once offenders have successfully completed their diversion, their arrest records are usually rendered inaccessible to public examination either through expungement orders from judges or through limited access by other means.

Factors Influencing Pretrial Diversion

One way of determining the prime candidates for diversion is to examine those ordinarily not considered for it. In California, for example, the following kinds of offenders are usually excluded from diversion consideration:

1. Those with prior drug offense convictions, former drug offense divertees, and/or who traffic in drugs.
2. Those convicted of a felony within the previous five-year period.
3. Those whose current offense involves violence.
4. Those who are past or present probation or parole violators. (Galvin et al., 1977)

Given these restrictive criteria, diversion is most likely granted for low-risk, first-time, property offenders. Although recidivism rates among property offenders are not particularly different from those of violent offenders and drug traffickers, property offenders pose little public risk and are less dangerous compared with these other types of criminals. Also, one objective of diversion is to minimize offender contact with the criminal justice system and help them avoid the criminal label. Those designated by California officials as undeserving of diversion have already acquired the criminal label.

Relevant criteria operating in most jurisdictions where diversion exists as an option include the following:

1. The age of the offender
2. The residency, employment and familial status of the offender
3. The prior record of the offender
4. The seriousness of the offense
5. Aggravating or mitigating circumstances associated with the commission of the offense

The general residency, employment, and familial status of the offender are important considerations because they are indicators of future stability if diversion is granted. Most diversion programs require at least some regular contact with probation agencies operated by state or local authorities. Unemployed and transient offenders are more likely to flee from the jurisdiction contrasted with those offenders who are gainfully employed and have families in the area.

Also, it is difficult to categorize offenders easily for diversion on the basis of the crimes they have committed. Certain aggravating or mitigating circumstances may exist that explain more fully the offenders' motives. While knowingly violating the law is wrong, there are circumstances under which an offender's behavior may be at least mitigated, though not necessarily excused entirely. Prosecutors and probation officers often examine the circumstances under which offenses were committed, and if they determine that mitigating factors that sufficiently outweigh the aggravating ones are present, then diversion may be recommended.

Criticisms of Diversion

1. *Diversion is "soft" on criminals.* Critics of diversion generally target the nonpunitive nature of the conditions associated with diversion programs. Many of the same reasons are cited for not viewing probation favorably. Probation is considered as "going soft" on crime. Diversion is similarly viewed. A segment of criminal justice scholars, corrections officials, and the general public believes that offenders should receive their "just deserts" and be punished for their crimes. Incarceration is the most visible form of punishment, and it is difficult to convince people that other types of punishment may be imposed that are not only punitive but more productive.

2. *Diversion is the "wrong" punishment for criminals.* Another criticism is that diversion does not deal effectively with offenders. Recidivism occurs among divertees, and thus, diversion programs are seen as failures. No nonincarcerative option is perfect, and recidivism occurs with or without incarceration. Those favoring diversion counter by arguing that diversion enables divertees to avoid the stigma and criminogenic atmosphere of prisons and jails.

3. *Diversion leads to net widening.* A third criticism of diversion is that it may widen the net by increasing the numbers of offenders handled by the probation department and other agencies. For instance, police officers may pursue arrests of suspects if they believe those suspects will eventually be granted diversion. Otherwise, the officers would be inclined to warn suspects and not arrest them. Prosecutors also may participate in net widening by recommending diversion for some alleged offenders whose cases ordinarily would be dropped from formal processing.

4. *Diversion excludes female offenders.* A fourth criticism seems selectively applicable to those jurisdictions where few options exist or are recommended for the processing of alleged female offenders. Immarigeon (1987b) suggests that currently there is a scarcity of programs for diverting or displacing female offenders from imprisonment. Some of the few programs that do exist in various jurisdictions are the Women's Self-Help Center Outreach Program in St. Louis, the Community Services for Women in Boston, and the Elizabeth Fry Center in San Francisco.

5. *Diversion ignores "due process."* A fifth criticism is that diversion is a resolution of an offender's case without benefit of due process. A prosecutor examines the case, the evidence against the defendant, and other pertinent circumstances. An offer is extended to the defendant to participate in diversion. If the offer is rejected, formal proceedings against the defendant are implied if not actually carried out. Thus, there is an implicit threat of prosecution from district attorneys and others if certain offenders elect not to enter a diversion program and subject themselves to the jurisdiction of the court.

6. *Diversion assumes guilt without a trial.* This action assumes the defendant's guilt prior to any formal adjudication of the matter (Mullen, 1974). However, most, if not all, defendants enter diversion programs knowingly and voluntarily, because such programs have much to offer. The major benefit for defendants is the potential expungement of their criminal records. Since their participation in diversion is knowing and voluntary and they agree to comply with the conditions of diversion, this overcomes any constitutionally objectionable feature of diversion programs.

BOX 4.1

The Case of Jimenez

Should Divertees Have Their Programs Terminated When They Are Indigent and Cannot Make Full Restitution to One or More Victims?

The Case of Jimenez

It happened in New Mexico. A young man was working for the Little League baseball organization. Money was tight. He didn't think the organization would miss it. He embezzled almost $3,000 from the Little League over a period of a few months. He got caught. He was arrested by police and charged for stealing the money. His name was Jimenez.

The judge in Jimenez's case noted that Jimenez had no prior criminal record. Circumstances were such that there was pressure on Jimenez to acquire the money to provide for some minimal necessities. After consultation with the Little League officials, the victims, the case against Jimenez was deferred by the judge in favor of alternative dispute resolution. The case was diverted from the criminal justice system through an agreement whereby Jimenez would pay back the full amount embezzled of $2,854 by paying monthly installments of $200. According to the agreement, Jimenez would not be prosecuted for embezzlement for two years, contingent upon his action of making full restitution of the money stolen.

However, Jimenez was indigent. He couldn't afford the $200 monthly payments. He managed to make a few of them but quickly fell behind. The New Mexico district attorney sought to terminate the agreement and prosecute him. Jimenez's court-appointed attorney appealed, arguing that the diversion program depended on Jimenez's ability to pay the full restitution amount. It was significant that Jimenez didn't refuse to pay; he couldn't pay. The New Mexico Supreme Court heard the case and determined that Jimenez was not at fault because of his inability to pay back the embezzled money. The Court said that in this case, Jimenez should have been allowed to make either a partial or complete substitution of a cash payment to the victims through some form of public or community service. Almost every jurisdiction follows this practice today when indigent divertees are unable to make restitution to their victims.

Is alternative dispute resolution fair? Should those who have committed crimes be allowed to escape prosecution by doing community service or compensating their victims for losses resulting from theft or injuries?

Source: Adapted from "Indigent Can't Be Kicked Out of Diversion Program." *Corrections Compendium,* **16,** June, 1991. (*State v. Jimenez,* 49 CrL 1140 [NM SupCt], 1991).

STANDARD PROBATION

Standard probation in more than a few jurisdictions amounts to no supervision at all. When offenders are convicted of one or more crimes, sentencing judges place these convicted offenders into a probation program in lieu of incarceration. These programs may or may not have conditions. Probationers may be obligated to sign a form outlining the conditions of their probation. Compliance with these conditions is monitored by probation officers. These officers are often so overworked and understaffed that they cannot possibly oversee the activities of their probationers. The caseloads or numbers of offenders probation officers are assigned to supervise vary among jurisdictions. Offender caseloads may be as high as 2,000 in some cities or counties, whereas in others, the caseloads may be 30 or fewer. Caseloads vary according to the type of program, the number of offenders, and the number of probation officers who are available.

Standard probation is considered by many critics to be the most ineffective probationary form. Often, probationers may contact their probation officers by telephone and avoid face-to-face visits. Additionally, the requirements of their probationary programs are often less stringent compared with more intensive probation programs. The caseloads of probation officers in some jurisdictions are so high that officers cannot devote special attention to those offenders in the greatest need of special attention. This is the great failing of standard probation. There are no easy answers to the problem. The probation department can only do so much in view of its staffing problems and varying clientele. And there is no relief in sight. The chances are that this probation form is growing rather than declining, despite high recidivism rates among standard probationers.

Another problem with probation is that often, those in administrative positions in probation departments attach greater importance to those activities that enhance paper-processing, office efficiency, and career development rather than to those that directly affect probationers. For instance, a study of the Massachusetts probation system involved a mail survey that yielded 500 responses. These responses were supplemented with interviews and field efforts involving 60 different criminal courts and more than 400 individuals. The resulting report addressed at least 60 different improvements in Massachusetts probation programs. But a more selective list of those improvements receiving the greatest priority and attention is significant, not because of what is included, but rather, what is excluded. The list of 11 priority concerns is as follows:

1. The review and redefinition of the overall mission of probation
2. Career advancement opportunities for all personnel
3. Greater emphasis on affirmative action
4. Adjustments in the staffing level in some courts
5. Increased training opportunities
6. Substantially improved physical facilities
7. Immediate attention to computerizing the central file
8. Formation of citizen advisory groups
9. Substantially improved social services for offenders
10. Specific attention to the unique needs of the various trial court departments
11. An immediate and forceful public education campaign to enlist support for improved social services from all branches of government and the general public (Spangenberg et al., 1987)

All but one of these improvement recommendations has to do with office policy, office efficiency, office work, office environment, public relations with the community, and office relations with courts. It is unclear about what is meant by "improved social services for offenders." Ideally, probation offices exist to supervise offenders. Many probation departments act as brokers between the agency and various community businesses, to identify potential workplaces where probationer-clients might find and maintain employment. Probationer assistance has always been a mission of probation departments. However, most of these key priorities are unrelated to assisting probationers directly, except for improving their "social" activities, whatever they may be. This may be one reason why some experts have declared that probation is in trouble (Fitzharris, 1984).

In order to improve the image of probation departments and reduce probationer recidivism, various experiments have been conducted with probationers to see if closer supervision and other monitoring mechanisms might be helpful. Thus, several different types of intensive supervised probation programs have been devised over the years with respectable outcomes.

INTENSIVE SUPERVISED PROBATION (ISP)

Intensive supervised probation (**ISP**) is an increasingly common probationary form (Petersilia and Turner, 1990a, 1990c; Travis, 1984). Also known as *traditional probation,* ISP is a type of **intermediate punishment,** since it is somewhere between standard probation and incarceration (Byrne, 1992a, 1992b; Harland, 1992; Petersilia and Turner, 1993:1; U.S. Office of Justice Programs, 1990b). One short-range goal of intermediate punishments is to reduce prison and jail overcrowding (Petersilia and Turner, 1990d). There is government endorsement of this ISP program goal as well as support within the professional community (Thornburgh, 1990). Other types of intermediate punishments include electronic monitoring, home incarceration, and community-based corrections (Gowdy, 1993). These programs will be examined at length in subsequent chapters. Offenders are assigned probation officers who arrange frequent contacts with their clients on a face-to-face basis (Rhine, 1993; Taxman and Guynes, 1992). These contacts may be weekly, a few times per week, or daily. ISP is a special form of traditional probation with which the intensity of offender monitoring is greatly increased and the conditions of probation are considerably more stringent. The logic is that the greater the amount of contact between the probationer and PO, the more this contact will function as an incentive for greater offender compliance with program requirements. Known in some circles as *smart sentencing,* ISP often involves greater client-officer contact, which may mean that POs are more frequently accessible to clients who are experiencing personal or financial difficulties, social stresses, or other problems (Byrne, Lurigio, and Petersilia, 1992; Greenwood et al., 1989).

There is considerable variation in ISP programs among jurisdictions, since probation officer caseloads vary (Petersilia and Turner, 1990b, 1990c). These caseloads depend on the financial resources of the jurisdiction and local definitions of the maximum number of clients probation officers must supervise. ISP in many jurisdictions limits the number of offender-clients to 30 per probation officer. In some jurisdictions, the maximum number of offenders supervised may be limited to 15 or 20 (Clear and Latessa, 1993; U.S. General Accounting Office, 1993a).

Intensive supervised probation programs have received mixed reactions among the public. One problem is that many of these programs, their objectives, and the ways they are being implemented are misunderstood by community residents and interpreted in the most unfavorable light (Byrne, 1992a, 1992b; Turner, 1992). Despite the fact that these programs monitor probationers more closely than standard probation supervision and are tougher on offenders by comparison, many citizens believe that offender freedom in the community is not an acceptable punishment.

Recidivism rates of probationers, especially when serious crimes are involved, do little or nothing to show the public that probation programs work. In fact, corrections experts view the effectiveness or success of probation quite differently from the public impression. An analysis of 10 recidivism studies of probationers shows as a general "rule of thumb" that probation programs are "successful" if recidivism rates among probationers are below 30 percent, but programs with recidivism rates higher than 30 percent are considered "unsuccessful" (Allen et al., 1985:260; Vito, 1986a, 1986b:17). For many citizens, any recidivism among probationers and parolees is evidence of program failure (Turner, 1992).

The subject of much debate and controversy, ISP has been an integral feature of corrections since its creation by John Augustus in 1841 (Latessa, 1987a:1; Lipchitz, 1986:78; Van Ness, 1992). Currently, 80 percent of those offenders convicted of misdemeanors and 60 percent of those convicted of felonies are placed on probation (Petersilia, 1985c). Primarily because of prison overcrowding and fiscal constraints (e.g., in 1985, 31 states were either under court order or consent decrees to reduce their prison populations and improve inmate living conditions), the only option most states currently have to reduce prisoner intake is probation of some form (Petersilia, Turner, and Peterson, 1986:64–65).

There is no standard definition for ISP, although all ISP programs feature small offender caseload sizes (Agopian, 1990; Pearson and Bibel, 1986:25; Petersilia and Turner, 1991). *Intensive* is a relative term, but the basic idea is to "increase the heat" on probationers in order to satisfy public demand for "just" punishment (Erwin, 1986:17). Some persons distinguish between standard probation and intensive surveillance coupled with substantial community service and/or restitution (Petersilia et al., 1985:64–65). But probably the best way of conceptualizing what ISP means is to identify ISP program components that have been operationalized in several states.

Perhaps Joan Petersilia and Susan Turner (1993:1) describe the general features of ISP best by noting the following definition and characteristics: Intensive supervision probation/parole is a form of release into the community that emphasizes close monitoring of convicted offenders and imposes rigorous conditions on that release. Most ISPs call for

> Some combination of multiple weekly contacts with a supervising officer.
> Random and unannounced drug testing.
> Stringent enforcement of probation and parole conditions.

A requirement to participate in relevant treatment, hold a job, and perhaps perform community service.

The Georgia Intensive Supervised Probation Program

In the 1970s, Georgia had the highest per capita incarceration rate in the United States (Erwin, 1986:17, 1987; Erwin and Bennett, 1987). Because of prison over-crowding and the spillover effect into Georgia's jails to house their prison overflow, Georgia was desperate to devise a workable probation program. After spending much money on feasibility studies and considering alternatives to incarceration, Georgia's ISP was put into effect in 1982.

Georgia Program Elements. Being a conservative state, Georgia established several punitive intensive probation conditions that parallel the justice model. This program has been labeled by some experts as the "strictest probation program for adults in the United States" (Petersilia et al., 1985:70). Three phases of the program were outlined according to the level of control, Phase I being the most intensive supervision and Phase III being the least intensive. These standards include:

1. Five face-to-face contacts per week in Phase I (decreasing to two face-to-face contacts per week in Phase III).
2. 132 hours of mandatory community service.
3. Mandatory curfew.
4. Mandatory employment.
5. Weekly check of local arrest records.
6. Automatic notification of arrest elsewhere via State Crime Information Network listings.
7. Routine alcohol and drug screens.
8. Assignment of one probation officer and one surveillance officer to 25 probationers or one probation officer and two surveillance officers to 40 probationers (surveillance officers have corrections backgrounds or law enforcement training and make home visits, check arrest records, and perform drug/alcohol tests among other duties).
9. Probation officer determines individualized treatment (e.g., counseling, vocational/educational training) for offender.
10. Probation officer is liaison between court and offender and reports to court regularly on offender's progress from personal and surveillance observations and records. (Erwin, 1986:17–19).

Georgia had 45 judicial circuits, and by 1985, 33 of these circuits were involved in the ISP program. Between 1982 and 1985, the ISP program had supervised 2,322 probationers (Erwin, 1986:18). Offenders spend from 6 to 12 months under ISP and must pay from $10 to $50 per month as a probation supervision fee (Petersilia, 1987a:18).

The Success of the Georgia ISP Program. The success of Georgia's ISP program thus far has been demonstrated by low recidivism rates among offenders under ISP (recidivism rates are almost always used as measures of probation program effectiveness). Compared with paroled offenders and others supervised by standard probation practices, the ISP participants had systematically lower recidivism rates, depending on their risk classification. Classifications of risk were low risk, medium risk, high risk, and maximum risk. Reconvictions for these groups were 25 percent, 16 percent, 28 percent, and 26 percent respectively, compared with parolees who had considerably higher reconviction rates for all risk groupings (Erwin, 1986:20). Table 4.1 shows various outcomes after 18 months of tracking offenders in different risk levels or categories.

The New Jersey Intensive Supervised Probation Program

The **New Jersey ISP** began in June 1983 and is technically a form of parole, since only offenders currently incarcerated are eligible to participate. Perhaps the ISP is most closely related to shock probation in this regard. Also, the program has been influenced by the traditional, treatment-oriented rehabilitation model and is tar

TABLE 4.1 Outcomes After Tracking Offenders for Eighteen Months

	Number of Cases	Number and Percentage Rearrested	Number and Percentage Reconvicted	Number and Percentage Sentenced to Jail or Prison	Number and Percentage Incarcerated in State Prison
Low-Risk Classification					
Intensive supervision group	12	5 (41.6%)	3 (25.0%)	3 (25.0%)	2 (16.7%)
Regular probation group	11	3 (27.0%)	0 (0.0%)	1 (9.1%)	1 (9.1%)
Incarcerated group	13	6 (46.2%)	5 (38.5%)	4 (30.8%)	3 (23.1%)
Medium-Risk Classification					
Intensive supervision group	62	21 (33.9%)	10 (16.1%)	10 (16.1%)	9 (14.5%)
Regular probation group	58	20 (34.5%)	14 (24.1%)	9 (15.5%)	6 (10.3%)
Incarcerated group	12	7 (58.3%)	6 (50.0%)	4 (33.3%)	2 (16.7%)
High-Risk Classification					
Intensive supervision group	69	24 (34.5%)	19 (27.5%)	14 (20.3%)	11 (15.9%)
Regular probation group	73	22 (30.1%)	18 (24.7%)	3 (17.8%)	10 (13.7%)
Incarcerated group	47	27 (57.4%)	21 (44.7%)	10 (21.3%)	6 (12.8%)
Maximum-Risk Classification					
Intensive supervision group	57	25 (43.6%)	15 (26.3%)	12 (21.1%)	11 (19.3%)
Regular probation group	58	26 (44.8%)	16 (27.6%)	11 (19.0%)	8 (13.8%)
Incarcerated group	25	16 (64.0%)	9 (36.0%)	7 (36.0%)	6 (24.0%)

Source: Billie S. Erwin, "Turning up the Heat on Probation in Georgia," *Federal Probation,* **50** (1986),17–24.

geted to serve certain less serious incarcerated offenders (Pearson and Bibel, 1986:25).

New Jersey ISP Program Elements. Although New Jersey's prison overcrowding problem was not as severe as Georgia's, it was nevertheless an important factor leading to the creation of the ISP. Between June 1983 and December 1985, the ISP served nearly 600 offenders (Pearson and Bibel, 1986:25). The program's features include

1. Offender participation in the ISP for a term of 18 months.
2. Probation officer contacts with offenders 20 times per month during the first 14 months.
3. During the first six months of the program, at least 12 visits are face-to-face between offender and probation officer.
4. Between months 15 through 18, the remaining contacts shall be conducted by telephone.
5. Four out of 20 checks per month will be curfew checks (offenders must be home from 10:00 P.M. to 6:00 A.M. every night).
6. Offenders must be regularly employed during the program.
7. Offenders must pay all fines, victim compensation, or restitution, and other miscellaneous fees associated with program maintenance.
8. Random checks are made for drug use (through random urinalysis tests).
9. A probation officer caseload of 25.
10. Community service work is expected, although this is variable according to the seriousness of the offender's conviction offense and individual situation. Current standards call for 16 hours of community service per month, if available.
11. A daily diary must be maintained by the probationer to show accomplishments.

Selection and Participation in the New Jersey Program. An offender's entry into New Jersey's ISP is strictly voluntary. Not all applicants are selected. In fact, of 2,400 applications from incarcerated offenders, fewer than 25 percent were accepted into the program between 1983 and 1985 (Pearson and Bibel, 1986:26). Applicants originally had to serve a minimum of 30 days in prison to be considered for program participation, and full-time employment had to be arranged within 30 days of acceptance into the program (Pearson and Bibel, 1986:26). Although the 30-day minimum incarceration provision has been eliminated, almost all participants have served an average of four months in prison (Pearson and Bibel, 1986:26).

New Jersey Program Effectiveness. The selection process consists of seven screening stages. Final decisions on which applicants will be accepted are made by a resentencing panel of Superior Court judges. Reasons for rejecting applicants include first- and second-degree felonies, too many prior felony convictions, prior crimes of violence, and applicant reluctance to comply with ISP provisions (Pearson and Bibel, 1986:26). Thus, the New Jersey program is targeted for low-risk offenders with the least likelihood of recidivating. As of early 1986, over 80 percent of the offenders had made it through the first six months of the program, and those who failed did so primarily because of program rule violations rather than committing new crimes (Clear, Flynn, and Shapiro, 1987:38). Furthermore, nearly 100 offenders had been unconditionally released from supervision, and 185 offenders had completed at least one year successfully (Pearson and Bibel, 1986:28–29).

The Idaho Intensive Supervised Probation Program

The **Idaho ISP** was launched as a pilot project in 1982 (Brown, 1992:7). Initially, a team consisting of one PO and two surveillance officers closely supervised a small group of low-risk offenders who normally would have been sent to prison. The program was quite successful. In October 1984, Idaho established a statewide ISP program with legislative approval. This step was seen as a major element in the "get tough on crime" posture taken by the state.

Elements of the ISP Program.   When implemented in 1984, the ISP program operated in teams, consisting of two POs and a section supervisor responsible for supervising a maximum of 25 high-risk clients. This team was required to work evenings and in shifts. POs carried firearms while performing their duties. The court-referred clientele for these POs and supervisors consisted of felony probationers or parolees who were classified at a maximum level of supervision. All clients had lengthy criminal records of violent crimes and were in need of intensive supervision. Clients were obligated to stay in their programs for four to six months and had to complete two major phases of supervision.

The first phase consisted of seven face-to-face visits per week, four of which occurred in the clients' homes. Phase II reduced the number of face-to-face contacts with clients per week to four. Both phases included random, day or night checks for possible curfew violations, drug and/or alcohol abuse, and any other possible program violation. Probationers who violated one or more program conditions received either verbal warnings or informal staff hearings that might result in imposing several additional program conditions, including community service. Perhaps those probationers in Phase II would be returned to Phase I.

Idaho ISP Program Effectiveness.   Between 1984 and 1992, the Idaho Department of Corrections processed 2,487 clients. About 63 percent of these probationers completed the program successfully. During 1992, 179 clients were under ISP of one form or another. The overall rate of technical violations (e.g., curfew violations, drinking, unauthorized travel) was only about 28 percent, while the rate of new felonies charged was only 1.3 percent (Brown, 1992:7–8). During 1990, a survey of participating probationers showed an increase in technical violations accompanied by a slight decrease in new felony charges. Brown suggests that the rise in the rate of technical violations is due to the fact that offenders are supervised more closely under ISP and that technical violations are easier to detect. However, the major result of this ISP program has been a drastic reduction in new convictions for felonies among successful program participants.

The South Carolina Intensive Supervised Probation Program

In order to ease prison overcrowding in South Carolina, a legislative mandate was given in 1984 to establish an ISP program for statewide use. The South Carolina Department of Probation, Parole, and Pardon Services (DPPPS) was responsible for the **South Carolina ISP** implementation. The primary aims of the ISP program were to heighten surveillance of participants, increase PO-client contact, and increase offender accountability. Like Idaho, South Carolina started its ISP program as a pilot or experimental project. Its program goal was to involve 336 probationers during the first year of operation. By 1991, 13,356 offenders had been processed through the ISP program. During that year, South Carolina was supervising 1,589 probationers and 480 parolees (Cavanaugh, 1992:1,5).

South Carolina ISP Program Elements.   Offenders placed in South Carolina ISP programs must pay a $10 per week supervision fee. Supervision fees are not particularly unusual in many ISP programs. Clients are supervised by specialized POs known as *intensive agents* with caseloads of no more than 35 offenders at any given time. Weekly face-to-face contacts with offenders are mandatory, together with visits to neighbors, friends, employers and service providers of probationers. POs in the South Carolina program act as liaisons between the private sector and their clients, lining up job possibilities. Thus, POs do some employment counseling when necessary.

Offender Classification for Participation.   Each offender is classified according to risk and needs. Then POs tailor individual program requirements to fit these offender needs. The level of supervision over particular offenders is influenced by their particular risk level determined through risk assessment. The goal of DPPPS POs is to provide offenders with the proper balance of control and assistance. Thus, the ISP program is also supplemented with curfews, electronic monitoring, and house arrest or home incarceration elements for certain high-risk offenders. Offenders sentenced to home incarceration are in a program known as ISP Home Detention and confined to their homes from 10:00 P.M. to 6:00 A.M. except for authorized leaves from home by their supervising POs. Offenders are subject to random visits from POs, day or night. Clients must work or seek employment, undergo medical, psychiatric or mental health counseling or other rehabilitative treatment, attend religious services, or perform community service work (Cavanaugh, 1992:5–6).

The length of their stay in this ISP program varies from three to six months. Electronic monitoring is used to supplement this program. Offenders are placed on electronic monitoring and must wear an electronic wristlet or anklet for the first 30 days. After successfully completing the first 30-day period of ISP, they are taken off electronic monitoring and subject to a 60-day period of simple voice verification. Such verification occurs by telephone means, where POs call offenders at particular times to verify their whereabouts. Offenders give requested information over the telephone, and electronic devices verify whether the voice pattern transmitted matches that of the offender being called. Figure 4.1 shows the South Carolina Risk Management Flow Chart for participating probationer-clients.

Like POs in the Idaho program, POs in the DPPPS work in shifts so that offenders can be checked day and night. Thus, there are First- and Second-Shift Surveillance Teams. The DPPPS also uses paraprofessionals in Operation Specialist capacities. These persons assist POs in performing surveillance work, particularly in the larger counties throughout the state (Cavanaugh, 1992:6).

Effectiveness of the South Carolina ISP Program.   The ISP program in South Carolina appears successful. Only 13 percent of the 2,000 probationers during 1991

FIGURE 4.1 Flow chart. (*Source:* Michael J. Cavanough, "Intensive in South Carolina: Accountability and Assistance." *Corrections Compendium*, 17:6.)

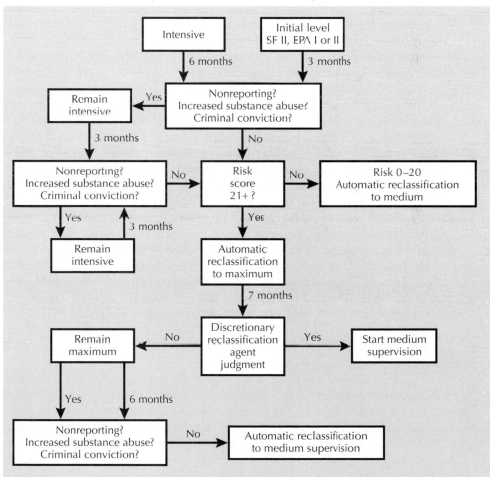

had their programs revoked (see Chapter 7 for an extensive discussion of probation and parole revocation). Two percent of the probationers had their programs revoked because of new offenses rather than for technical program violations. Of the participating parolees in 1991, 8 percent were revoked for program violations generally, and about 2 percent were revoked because of new law violations (Cavanaugh, 1992:6). Using the arbitrary 30 percent recidivism standard for determining whether a program is or is not successful, we would have to conclude that the South Carolina ISP program is successful for *both* its probationers as well as its parolees.

Criticisms of the Georgia, New Jersey, Idaho, and South Carolina ISP Programs

A general criticism leveled at any ISP program is that it does not achieve its stated goals (Beck, 1990; Fallin, 1989; Fulton and Stone, 1993:43). Some say that victims are ignored in probation decision making (Heisel, 1992:38). Yet others say that ISP programs contribute to net widening by bringing certain offenders under the ISP program umbrella who really do not need to be intensively supervised (Palumbo and Snyder-Joy, 1990). Simultaneously, an equally vocal aggregate of critics praises ISP for alleviating prison inmate overcrowding and providing a meaningful option to incarceration (Lemov, 1992:134; Oregon Crime Analysis Center, 1991; U.S. General Accounting Office, 1990). Among the ISP program components in certain jurisdictions that have drawn criticism have been supervision fees (Mills, 1992:10). These costs are normally incurred by probationer-clients. But even this particular issue is hotly debated (Duffie and Hughes, 1989:24–26). The controversy over ISP programs will likely remain unresolved for many years (DeJong and Franzeen, 1993).

In any case, the different ISP programs described earlier have been used by other states as models for their own ISP program development. For example, several elements of the Georgia model have been adopted by Arizona, Colorado, Illinois, Indiana, Louisiana, Nevada, and North Carolina. The New Jersey model has been partially implemented by Iowa and Kentucky for managing both probationers and parolees. These states have not copied Georgia or New Jersey precisely in their probation guidelines, but their newly developed programs resemble the Georgia and New Jersey Programs to a high degree. In Kentucky, for example, ISP is used exclusively with parolees as a condition of their supervision. Both programs have their supporters and critics, however.

The Georgia program has been both praised and criticized. First, it has demonstrated low rates of recidivism. Convicted criminals who participate in the program do not commit new offenses (or at least are not apprehended if they do). It has alleviated the prison overcrowding situation in Georgia by diverting a fairly large number of offenders to probationary status rather than incarceration. The most damaging aspects of Georgia's program credibility pertain to those selected to participate in it. Only 29 percent of the offenders placed on ISP consisted of "maximum risk" cases. Thus, most ISP probationers were those unlikely to recidivate anyway (Byrne, 1986:9). Also, the division of labor between probation officers and surveillance officers has not been as clear as originally intended. Surveillance officers wind up performing many of the expected functions of probation officers. Therefore, it is difficult to formulate a clear caseload picture for regular Georgia probation officer functions.

Another criticism is that Georgia handpicks its clients for ISP involvement. Closely related to the subject of risk, the selection process deliberately focuses on and emphasizes the inclusion of low- to medium-risk offenders with the greatest potential to succeed. In fact, some researchers have said the current composition of ISP clients consists of persons who would have been diverted from prison anyway (Clear, Flynn, and Shapiro, 1987:35). This is known as **creaming,** a practice in which only the most eligible low-risk offenders are selected for program participation. These are persons who would probably succeed on standard probation. Some experts believe that high-risk offenders ought to be targeted for ISP participation instead of those most likely to succeed (Dickey and Wagner, 1990). However, the client-staff ratio of 12.5:1 is considerably better than the regular 120:1 level for standard probationers (Clear et al., 1987:35). There is no question, however, that the ISP probation in Georgia is succeeding in minimizing recidivism rates, even among high-risk offenders.

New Jersey's ISP program is similarly flawed, although it has several strengths compared with the Georgia model. First, offenders must volunteer. And volunteers are not automatically included in the program. In fact, only 25 percent of all applicants are accepted. The most serious felons are excluded, thus creating a "bias" toward lower recidivism among those served by the program. Furthermore, the fact that participants must be incarcerated for a short time is tantamount to shock probation or shock parole. Therefore, space in prison is consumed at least temporarily by persons eventually selected for ISP.

The New Jersey ISP program follows traditional rehabilitative philosophy, with some modifications, which also contributes to its credibility. However, individualized counseling, sponsorship, and assistance provided by probation officers and private citizens seem to make a difference in recidivism rates contrasted with those not participating in the program and released from incarceration under other sentencing patterns. Limiting a probation officer's caseload to 25 helps as well (Clear et al., 1987:37–39).

New Jersey's screening process is considered stringent by some observers. Some experts contend that regular parolees have less "standard" supervision compared with ISP participants. Judges apparently contribute to the ISP problem by "backdooring" cases (i.e., sentencing borderline offenders to incarceration with the admonishment that an application for intensive supervision will be welcomed (Byrne, 1986; Clear et al., 1987:38).

Both the Georgia and New Jersey programs alleviate prison overcrowding to a degree, and viewed in this context, both programs are successful. This seems to be the "bottom line" politically and economically (Clear et al., 1987:36–37; Erwin, 1986; Pearson and Bibel, 1986). Of course, programs developed or being developed in other states serve similar ends and stand a good chance of being successful according to the same evaluative criteria associated with Georgia's and New Jersey's procedures.

The Idaho and South Carolina ISP programs exhibit relatively low rates of recidivism for their participating offenders. Compared with the Georgia and New Jersey programs, these programs rely fairly heavily on the use of risk assessment instruments for recruiting clients and determining their level of intensive supervision. The South Carolina program element involving the payment of a $10 per week supervision fee is only a token amount, but it nevertheless is regarded by staff as heightening offender accountability and serves as a reminder that they are paying for their crimes, even if the payment is hardly excessive. POs in both Idaho and South Carolina perform functions as liaisons when they unite their clients with receptive employers. Further, the integrated use of home confinement and electronic monitoring, together with frequent face-to-face visits and checks by supervising POs, means that offender control is heightened.

By 1992, Su Perk Davis (1992a:9) reported that over 48,000 offenders were under some form of ISP in the United States throughout 41 state jurisdictions. This represents a 48 percent increase in the number of ISP clients compared with a similar survey conducted in 1988 (Davis, 1992a:9). Table 4.2 summarizes the states using ISP programs in 1992. This table includes information about average caseloads for individual state ISP programs, the numbers of probationers, and the numbers of clients under ISP. Davis observes that the most frequent criticisms of these programs are lack of funding and misclassifications of participating offenders. Almost without exception, participating jurisdictions reported that ISP was keeping prison inmate populations down (Davis, 1992a:13–15).

It is interesting to note from Table 4.2 that with only a few exceptions, the number of offenders supervised under ISP averages about 25. Illinois, Montana, and South Dakota have the smallest ISP PO caseloads of 10 to 12 clients. South Carolina has the largest ISP caseloads at 61 per PO. Although ratios were not computed, it is clear that considerable variation exists among the states concerning the proportion of probationers who are in ISP programs compared with the total number of state probationers. Two states with similar total probationers, Georgia (132,000) and New York (139,132), have markedly different numbers of clients on ISP. Georgia has about 2,800 clients, while New York has 4,800 of them. Probation department resources are no doubt a factor influencing the actual numbers of probationers who become a part of ISP programs.

Another observation is that the normal PO caseloads in these states range from a low of 40 clients per PO in Texas to 202 clients per PO in Connecticut. Thus, even under standard probation supervision, some states have PO caseloads that are well within the ISP caseload range. It is easy to see from these figures how caseload discussions for either standard or intensive supervised probation and recidivism rates may be subject to widely different interpretations by experts. For instance, if we are discussing standard probation caseloads in Kentucky, someone from South Carolina may think we are referring to ISP PO caseloads, since the normal or standard probation caseload in Kentucky is 60 and the ISP caseload in South Carolina

TABLE 4.2 Summary of State ISP Probationers and Caseloads

State	No. of Probationers[a]	No. of ISP Probationers[b]	Normal Caseloads	ISP Caseloads
Alabama	24,200	180	147	25
Arizona	32,300	2,100	80	25
Colorado	28,700	479	160	20
Connecticut	47,629	160	202	40
Florida	88,640	12,431	120	25
Georgia	132,000	2,795	150	50
Hawaii	3,900	83	160–180	35–40
Idaho	3,194	110	75	25
Illinois	79,411	871	95	10
Iowa	13,580	271	—	20–25
Kansas	15,284	2,342	74	25
Kentucky	9,897	684	60	27
Maryland	88,289	—	142	47
Michigan	46,396	240	110	30
Mississippi	8,139	273	104	28
Missouri	31,319	771	75	20
Montana	625	—	88	10
Nebraska	18,793	318	109	21.5
Nevada	7,561	788	65–75	25–35
New Hampshire	4,100	70	85–95	25–30
New York	139,132	4,800	—	21
North Carolina	86,591	3,033	108	24
North Dakota	1,750	New ISP Program 6/1/92		—
Ohio	55,000	3,968	90–120	35–40
Oklahoma	24,871	139	85	—
Oregon	30,000	1,400	85	35–50
South Carolina	30,583	1,804	160	61
South Dakota	3,800	50	75	12.5
Tennessee	20,052	1,119	80	28
Texas	343,382	6,000	40–100	40
Utah	6,542	161	57	15–20
Vermont	6,007	265	97	44
Virginia	22,000	450	70	24
Wyoming	3,500	12	100	25

[a]Numbers of probationers
[b]Numbers of ISP probationer-clients

Source: Adapted from Su Perk Davis, "Survey: Number of Offenders under Intensive Probation Increases." *Corrections Compendium,* 17.9–17, 1992a.

is 61. There are obvious semantic problems here. In fact, there is such variability in PO caseloads among the states that we have to be careful when discussing recidivism rates or evaluating the success of different probation supervision programs.

ISP Program Components. Several program components are shared among states. These components include electronic surveillance, community sponsorship, payment of probation fees, and split-sentencing respectively (Wiebush, 1991).

However, it is likely that electronic monitoring offers an increasingly popular, inexpensive method of intensively supervising offenders (Lilly and Ball, 1987; Lilly, Ball, and Lotz, 1986; Lilly, Ball, and Wright, 1987). Electronic monitoring will be examined at length in Chapter 9.

SHOCK PROBATION AND SPLIT SENTENCING

Shock probation, also referred to as **split sentencing,** first appeared as a federal split sentencing provision in 1958, although the California legislature had authorized a bill permitting judges to impose a combination of incarceration and probation for the same offender in the early 1920s (Parisi, 1980:5). The term *shock probation* was later coined by Ohio in 1964 (MacKenzie, Shaw, and Gowdy, 1993; Vito, 1984:22). Ohio was the first state to use shock probation. It has been characterized as follows: "A brief application of the rigors of imprisonment (in Ohio, 90–130 days served) will deter criminal behavior and not impede the readjustment of the individual upon release" (Vito, 1984:22). Shock probation has been used increasingly in other states in recent years. In more than a few jurisdictions, problem drinkers, DWI cases, and drug abusers have been targeted for shock probation programs (MacKenzie, Shaw, and Souryal, 1992; Shaw and MacKenzie, 1991, 1992).

Shock probation is really a misnomer, because offenders are incarcerated in a jail or prison for a short period for shock value. Shock probation derives from the fact that judges initially sentence offenders to terms of incarceration, usually in a jail. After offenders have been in jail for a brief period (e.g., 30, 60, 90, or 120 days), they are brought back to reappear before their original sentencing judges. These judges reconsider the original sentences they imposed on these offenders. Provided that these offenders behaved well while incarcerated, judges resentence them to probation for specified terms. This is shock probation, and offenders who have been resentenced under these circumstances are **shock probationers** (Bennett, 1989; Osler, 1991).

Split Sentencing Distinguished from Shock Probation

There is a distinction between split sentencing and shock probation. *Split sentencing* means that the judge imposes a **combination sentence,** a portion of which includes incarceration and a portion of which includes probation. Thus, the judge may sentence the offender up to one year, with a maximum incarceration of six months. The remainder of the sentence is to be served on probation. Violating one or more conditions of probation may result in reincarceration, however.

Most states have authorized the use of one of three general types of either split sentencing or shock probation by judges in the sentencing of low-risk offenders (Parent, 1989b). These types include (1) the California scheme, whereby jail is attached as a condition of probation, (2) the federal scheme under the 1987 sentencing guidelines, whereby supervised release of up to five years may follow sentences of imprisonment of more than one year (the length of supervised release varies according to the crime classification and ranges from one year for misdemeanors to five years) (U.S. Sentencing Commission, 1987:5.15), and (3) the Ohio scheme, whereby a judge resentences offenders within a 130-day incarcerative period to a probationary sentence (Parisi, 1980:5–6). Other states, including Texas, have similar systems, although incarcerative periods are often longer than 130 days before resentencing to probation is considered.

Other terms used to describe these phenomena are *mixed sentence, intermittent confinement,* and *jail as a condition of probation* (Parisi, 1980:5). Although some critics regard them as synonymous, there are technical distinctions that can be made between these terms. A **mixed sentence** occurs when an offender has committed two or more offenses. The judge imposes a separate sentence for each offense. One sentence may involve probation, while the other may involve incarceration. The judge decides whether the two sentences are to be served concurrently or consecutively. An **intermittent sentence** occurs when the offender is sentenced to a term requiring partial confinement. Perhaps the offender must serve weekends in jail. A curfew may also be imposed. In all other respects, the nature of intermittent sentencing is much like probation. Finally, **jail as a condition of probation** is an option whereby the judge imposes a fixed jail term to be served prior to the offender's completion of a sentence of probation (Parisi, 1980:8).

Parisi (1980:6–7) notes that mixed sentences of any kind are problematic and sometimes pose dilemmas for both corrections officials and sentencing authorities. Four problems cited by Parisi include the fact that true mixed sentences as defined above can only be imposed if two or more convictions are obtained against the defendant simultaneously; offenders may be released on parole prior to probation, thus frustrating the original assumed plan of the judge; some jurisdictions have mandatory minimums that limit judicial flexibility in sentences imposed; and, if the conviction of the offender is reversed (in the mixed sentencing situation) on the offense that carried the incarceration penalty, the judge's plan is again frustrated. Despite these potential problems, split sentencing and shock probation appear to be increasing in popularity (Latessa and Vito, 1988; Shaw and MacKenzie, 1992; South Carolina State Reorganization Commission, 1992). Shock probation programs currently exist in Ohio, Kentucky, Maine, Indiana, Idaho, and various other states (MacKenzie, 1993; Parent, 1988a, 1988b, 1989a, 1989b).

The Philosophy and Objectives of Shock Probation

Shock Probation and Crime Deterrence. Deterrence is one of shock probation's dominant themes. Another prominent philosophical objective is reintegration. Confining offenders to jail for brief periods and obligating them to serve their remaining months on probationary status enables them to be employed, support themselves and their families, and otherwise be productive citizens in their communities. The freedom shock probation allows permits offenders to receive specialized attention and to participate in programs designed to deal with their problems.

Theoretically, exposure to jail conditions should be sufficiently traumatic to cause offenders to want to avoid further involvement with crime (Vito, 1984:22). Deterrence is seemingly fostered by placing offenders in jail for a short period. It doesn't always work, however, since there is always some degree of recidivism among a portion of those who have received shock probation in various jurisdictions.

Shock Probation and Rehabilitation.   Consistent with the philosophy of shock probation and split sentencing generally are community reintegration and rehabilitation. It is conceded by most authorities that confinement in prisons and jails fails to rehabilitate offenders or "correct" their behaviors. A brief exposure to incarceration followed by release into the community permits offenders to hold jobs, support themselves and their families, pay restitution to victims, perform various public services, and/or participate in therapeutic or educational programs designed to help them with their special problems.

Shock Probation and Creative Sentencing.   Another objective of shock probation is to permit judges and others greater flexibility in their sentencing of low-risk offenders. Jail and prison overcrowding is of great concern in most jurisdictions, and, although shock probation means that some valuable jail space will be used to house these offenders, the terms of confinement are usually short. This allows for greater numbers of convictions without having to build additional facilities to accommodate new offenders. However, it does not necessarily alleviate jail overcrowding.

Shock Probation as a Punishment.   The confinement phase of shock probation also functions as a punishment for offenders who otherwise would not know the true meaning of incarceration. This satisfies some critics since offenders are receiving a portion of their "just deserts" despite the fact that they will eventually be released to serve out the rest of their sentences on probation in their communities.

Shock Probation and Offender Needs.   One benefit accruing to officials through incarcerating offenders for a brief period is that a more thorough investigation may be conducted of offender needs. Therefore, when offenders come before judges for their second sentence, the judge may prescribe specific programs or treatments in accordance with those recommended by jail or prison officials (Friday, Petersen, and Allen, 1973). States such as Kansas, California, North Dakota, and Pennsylvania use shock probation in this fashion for the purpose of preparing more in-depth evaluative summaries of offenders so that judges may make more informed decisions in subsequent sentencing. This rationale is not always popular among corrections personnel, and some experts believe nothing more is learned about the offender beyond the information normally provided in a thorough presentence investigation report (Rosecrance, 1988b).

Shock Probation and Offender Accountability.   An additional objective of shock probation is that offenders may be made more aware of the seriousness of their crimes without resorting to a long and potentially damaging prison sentence (Vito,

1984:22). There are those who claim that incarceration, even for brief periods, is psychologically and socially damaging to offenders. One adverse effect of incarceration, even short-term incarceration, is the propensity of certain offenders to commit suicide (Anson, 1983; Kennedy, 1984; Burks and DeHeer, 1986; Library Information Specialists, Inc., 1983b). Several investigations of jail suicides show that initial incarceration stimulates a crisis reaction of depression and anxiety that cannot be tolerated by some offenders. Thus, suicides or suicide attempts often result within the first few days of confinement. If some shock probationers are suicide-prone or have psychological problems that have not been previously diagnosed, then unfortunate consequences may result for certain inmates. Although jail suicides are quite low proportionately compared with the number of offenders given shock probation, this is a disturbing implication to consider (Kennedy, 1984).

Shock Probation and Community Safety.   It has also been argued that shock probation protects society by placing offenders in jails for short periods. This appears to be an indirect consequence of the potential deterrent value shock probation has for first-offenders and low-risk criminals (Vito, 1984:22).

The Effectiveness of Shock Probation

Is shock probation effective? This is a relative question, since we must contrast the effectiveness of shock probation with other programs. Generally, shock probation has some potential for reducing recidivism rates among participating offenders (Vito, 1984:26). This conclusion has been reached through an analysis of the success of shock probation experiments conducted in various jurisdictions by several independent investigators. It has been demonstrated, for example, that reincareration rates among shock probationers have never exceeded 26 percent (Vito, 1984:26). Compared with other probation programs, this figure is commendable. However, some experts urge caution when interpreting both the short-term and long-term results of shock probation (Acorn, 1989).

An examination of the effectiveness of shock probation in the state that pioneered it was conducted by Vito (1978), who studied 1,508 Ohio offenders released on shock probation in 1975. He divided his sample according to the length of incarceration each offender received. This division yielded three categories of offenders: those who were incarcerated from 1 to 30 days, those incarcerated from 31 to 130 days, and those incarcerated for longer than 130 days.

Vito studied recidivism among these three categories of offenders and found no significant differences between them. He concluded that the length of incarceration mattered little, if at all, in affecting these offenders' recidivism rates. One of his conclusions was that the length of incarceration for shock probationers could be shortened drastically without seriously affecting their reincarceration rates. This is important because it means that more jail space can be made available to more serious offenders during any given time period. Subsequent investigations conducted by Vito and others (Vito and Allen, 1981) have tended to support Vito's original observations.

Bennett (1989) counters these positive results with evidence that suggests that, compared with straight probation, shock probation may *contribute* to being rearrested. Bennett examined two samples of convicted offenders in California. One sample had been sentenced to jail as a condition of probation, while the other sample was sentenced to straight probation. Those who served some jail time in addition to their probation sentences had a recidivism rate of 51 percent compared with a 26 percent recidivism rate for straight probationers. Since efforts were made to control for intergroup similarities and prior offense patterns, these findings fail to support the deterrent value that proponents of shock probation suggest. Bennett suggests, however, that although his findings are not consistent with expected shock probation outcomes, factors beyond his control, such as judicial political considerations, may have inadvertently been responsible for these unexpected differences. Thus, Bennett regards the research as "highly tentative" (Bennett, 1989:20).

The general conclusion reached by those who have studied shock probation and split sentencing programs intensively is that these options should be extended to those offenders who otherwise would not be particularly good candidates for standard probation (Latessa and Vito, 1988; Parisi, 1980; Vito, 1984:26). Latessa and Vito note that while shock probation may not necessarily be the best deterrent to further criminality to those who are given it, this alternative does have merit on the basis of the low recidivism rates reported. There is every indication to believe that shock probation has the potential to alleviate correctional institutional overcrowding to a degree. Another application of shock probation is the disposition of juvenile cases. Sometimes, juveniles are placed in detention for a brief period for its shock value.

BOOT CAMPS

Closely related to shock probation is **shock incarceration,** or boot camp. In the case of shock incarceration or boot camp, convicted offenders are jailed or otherwise confined, but their confinement resembles something like military boot-camp training. As we saw earlier, shock probation merely involved sentencing offenders to a straight jail term, with no participation in any military-like programs. In contrast, shock incarceration or boot camp programs do provide military-like regimentation and regulation of inmate behaviors.

Boot Camp Defined

Boot camps are highly regimented, military-like, short-term correctional programs (90 to 180 days in duration) in which offenders are provided with strict discipline, physical training, and hard labor resembling some aspects of military basic training. When successfully completed, boot camps provide for transfers of participants to community-based facilities for nonsecure supervision. By 1993, boot camps had been formally established in over half of the states (Anderson and Carson, 1991; Knight and Shively, 1991; U.S. General Accounting Office, 1993b). The present number of informally and locally operated boot camps in different city and county jurisdictions is presently unknown (Parent, 1989b). Some experts regard boot camps as the latest correctional reform (Coyle, 1990; Morash and Rucker, 1990). Other professionals are skeptical about their success potential (Salerno, 1991:28).

While boot camps were officially established in 1983 by the Georgia Department of Corrections Special Alternative Incarceration (SAI), the general idea for boot camps originated some time earlier in the late 1970s, also in Georgia (Parent, 1989b). The usual length of incarceration in boot camps varies from three to six months. During this period, boot camp participants engage in marching, work, and classes that are believed useful in rehabilitation (Osler, 1991:34). Usually, youthful offenders are targeted by these programs (Jones and Cuvelier, 1992). In 1993, there were 28 state prison systems operating 43 boot camp programs, with more states planning to establish similar programs (Austin, Jones, and Bolyard, 1993:1).

The Rationale for Boot Camps.   Boot camps have been established as an alternative to long-term traditional incarceration. Austin et al. (1993:1) outline a brief rationale for boot camps:

1. A substantial number of youthful first-time offenders now incarcerated will respond to a short but intensive period of confinement followed by a longer period of intensive community supervision.
2. These youthful offenders will benefit from a military-type atmosphere that instills a sense of self-discipline and physical conditioning that was lacking in their lives.
3. These same youths need exposure to relevant educational, vocational training, drug treatment, and general counseling services to develop more positive and law-abiding values and become better prepared to secure legitimate future employment.
4. The costs involved will be less than a traditional criminal justice sanction that imprisons the offender for a substantially longer period of time.

Goals of Boot Camps

Boot camps have several general goals, including (1) rehabilitation/reintegration, (2) discipline, (3) deterrence, (4) easing of prison/jail overcrowding, and (5) vocational, educational, and rehabilitative services.

Rehabilitation and Reintegration.   In 1986, the Orleans (Louisiana) Parish Prison System established a boot camp program called *About Face* (Caldas, 1990). This program sought to improve participants' sense of purpose, self-discipline, self-control, and self-confidence through physical conditioning, educational programs, and social skills training, all within the framework of strict military discipline (Caldas, 1990). One early criticism of this Louisiana program was the amount of inexperience among boot camp staff. Over time, however, this criticism was minimized (Caldas, 1990; MacKenzie, 1990, MacKenzie and Shaw, 1993:463–466).

Boot camps instill discipline in youthful offenders through adherence to a strict regimen of exercise and education for periods of six months or more. (The Image Works)

Discipline.   Boot camps are definitely aimed at improving discipline (Coyle, 1990; Taylor, 1992). Certain boot camps, especially those aimed at younger offenders, must deal with adjudicated juvenile offenders who usually resist authority and refuse to listen or learn in traditional classroom or treatment environments (Taylor, 1992:122). Physical conditioning and structure are most frequently stressed in these programs. But most boot camp programs also include educational elements pertaining to literacy, academic and vocational education, intensive value clarification, and resocialization (MacKenzie and Shaw, 1993; Taylor, 1992:124).

Deterrence.   The sudden immersion of convicted offenders into a military-like atmosphere is a frightening experience for many participants. The rigorous approach to formal rules and authority is a challenging dimension of boot camp programs for most participants (Shaw and MacKenzie, 1991). Latessa and Vito (1988) observe that offenders who are released early from prisons or jails will be deterred from returning to crime. They cite low recidivism rates among clients as evidence of the deterrent value of such programs. Other experts concur that boot camps and shock incarceration have positive impacts on crime deterrence as well (Mack, 1992; Marlette, 1991). Mack (1992:63–65) reports that of the many clients who have participated in the *Rikers Boot Camp High Impact Incarceration Program* (*HIIP*), only 23 percent have recidivated compared with 28 percent of those released from traditional incarceration. Even though these recidivism rate differences are not substantial, the direction of the difference says something about the potential deterrent value of boot camp programs. More dramatic results have been reported among boot camp programs in various state jurisdictions (Austin et al., 1993; Parent, 1989b).

Easing of Prison and Jail Overcrowding.   Boot camps are believed to have a long-term impact on jail and prison overcrowding (Warnock and Hunzeker, 1991). Theoretically, this is possible because of the low recidivism rates among boot camp participants (MacKenzie and Souryal, 1991; Mathias and Madhouse, 1991). The short-term nature of confinement in boot camp programs with the participant's subsequent return to the community helps to ease the overcrowding problem in correctional settings (Florida Department of Corrections, 1990; Klein-Saffran and Lutze, 1991). It is believed that boot camp experiences are significant in creating more positive attitudes among participants (Hunter et al., 1992; MacKenzie et al., 1988).

Vocational and Rehabilitative Services.   An integral feature of most boot camp programs is the inclusion of some form of educational and/or vocational training (MacKenzie and Ballow, 1989; MacKenzie, Shaw, and Gowdy, 1993; Parent, 1989b; Ward, 1991). A New York Shock Incarceration program makes it possible for participants to work on GED diplomas and provides elementary educational instruction (Aziz, 1988; New York State Department of Correctional Services, 1989, 1990, 1991). Educational training is also a key feature of *IMPACT,* or *Intensive Motivational Program of Alternative Correctional Treatment* in Louisiana jurisdictions (MacKenzie et al., 1988; Piquero and MacKenzie, 1993; Riechers, 1988). As an alternative to traditional incarceration, boot camps do much to promote greater social and educational adjustment for clients reentering their communities (Klein, 1988; Osler, 1991).

A Profile of Boot Camp Clientele

Who can participate in boot camps or shock incarceration programs? Participants may or may not be able to enter or withdraw from boot camps voluntarily. It depends on the particular program. Most boot camp participants are prison-bound youthful offenders convicted of less serious, nonviolent crimes who have not been previously incarcerated (Parent, 1988a, 1988b; 1989b). Depending on the program, there are some exceptions (MacKenzie, Shaw, and Gowdy, 1993:1–3). Participants may either be referred to these programs by judges or corrections departments or they may volunteer. They may or may not be accepted, and if they complete their programs successfully, they may or may not be released under supervision into their communities.

Boot Camp Programs

In this section, several boot camp programs are described. While the programs share certain features, there are obviously different program components among these boot camps to make them fairly distinctive from the others. It is interesting to note which features are included or excluded from one program to the next.

BOX 4.2
Six Boot Camps Compared

The Harris County (Texas) Courts Regimented Intensive Probation Program (CRIPP)

In Harris County, Texas, the CRIPP program has the following features:

a. Military model, militaristic chain of command;

b. Staff consists of volunteers from deputies of Harris County Sheriff's Department;

c. Handles convicted criminal offenders under probation supervision;

d. Probationers supervised for 90-day period by drill instructors;

e. Program accommodates 48 probationers as a "group" who begin and end as a group;

f. Regimen: breakfast at 4:00 A.M.; physical training; lunch at 11:00 A.M.; more physical training, barracks clean-up; general orders; dinner at 3:00 P.M.; more physical training; day ends with lights out at 10:00 P.M.; participants wear uniforms and combat boots, and different types of uniforms distinguish between different levels of probationers;

g. Services provided include medical, vocational, physical, social (drug and alcohol counseling); coping and life skills programs;

h. Participants required to practice good grooming and personal hygiene habits; structured activities designed to prepare them for successful reintegration into society; and

i. Program activities are mandatory.

The Camp Monterey Shock Incarceration Facility (New York State Department of Correctional Services)

New York State has a major boot camp project with the following features:

a. Accommodates 250 participants in minimum-security institution;

b. Has 131 staff (83 custody positions);

c. Participants are screened and must meet statutory criteria; three-fourths volunteer; one-third of applicants rejected;

d. Inmates form platoons and live in open dormitories;

e. Successful program completion leads to parole board releases to an intensive probation supervision program called *aftershock;*

f. Physical training, drill, eight hours daily of hard labor;

g. Inmates must participate in therapeutic community meetings, compulsory adult basic education courses, mandatory individual counseling, and mandatory recreation;

h. All must attend Alcohol and Substance Abuse Treatment; and

i. Job seeking skills training and reentry planning.

The Oklahoma Regimented Inmate Discipline Program (RID)

Oklahoma has a RID program with the following features:

a. 145-bed facility at the Lexington Assessment and Reception Center; also houses 600 long-term general population inmates as medium security;

b. Offenders screened according to statutory criteria and may volunteer;

c. Inmates live in single or double-bunk cells;

d. Strict discipline, drill, physical training; housekeeping and institutional maintenance;

e. Six hours daily of educational-vocational programs;

f. Drug abuse programs, individual and group counseling; and

g. Subsequently, participants are resentenced

by judges to intensive supervised probation or "community custody," perhaps commencing at a halfway house.

The Mississippi Regimented Inmate Discipline (RID) Program

The RID program established in Mississippi has the following program features:

a. 140 inmates in minimum-security camp;

b. Judges control inmate selection process, according to broad statutory criteria;

c. Program features physical training, drill and ceremony, hard labor, and treatment;

d. No vocational or educational program; and

e. Released inmates live in halfway houses, perform community service; subsequently released to regular probation supervision.

The Georgia Special Alternative Incarceration Program (SAI)

This program includes the following characteristics:

a. Program for male offenders;

b. Judges control selection process, and SAI is a "condition of probation"; if successful, boot camp graduates are released, since judges do not ordinarily resentence them to probation;

c. Program includes physical training, drill, hard work; two exercise and drill periods daily, with eight-hour hard labor periods in between;

d. Participants perform limited community services;

e. Little emphasis on counseling or treatment;

f. Inmates do receive drug abuse education and information about sexually transmitted diseases; and

g. Inmates are double-bunked in two 25-cell units at Dodge, and at Burris, 100 inmates are single-bunked in four 25-cell units.

The Louisiana Intensive Motivational Program of Alternative Correctional Treatment (IMPACT)

Louisiana's IMPACT program has the following characteristics:

a. Two-phase program, in which offenders spend 90 to 180 days in a medium-security prison participating in a rigorous boot camp program;

b. Carefully supervised daily activities, including work, physical exercise, and drills; group counseling, drug education, and other educational activities;

c. Offenders in second stage are paroled to intensive supervised parole programs in communities where they have four contacts per week with POs, strict 8:00 P.M. to 6:00 A.M. curfews; and

d. Must perform community service, and work; screened for alcohol and drug use.

The goals of the Louisiana shock incarceration program are to (1) provide a satisfactory alternative to the long-term incarceration of primarily youthful first-offenders, thereby helping to relieve crowded conditions that exist in prisons in Louisiana; (2) promote a positive image of corrections; and in general, (3) enhance public relations.

Source: MacKenzie, Shaw, and Gowdy, 1993:1.

Jail Boot Camps

A 1993 survey disclosed that there were 10 jurisdictions operating boot camps through city or county jails (Austin, Jones, and Bolyard, 1993:2). Thirteen other jurisdictions were contemplating establishing boot camps through their jails during the next several years. These **jail boot camps** are short-term programs for offenders in a wide age range. For example, jail boot camps in New York and New Orleans have age limits of 39 years and 45 years, respectively. Many of the existing jail boot camps target probation or parole violators who may face revocation and imprisonment. If the jail boot camp experience can deter some of these offenders from future offending, then some scarce prison space can be saved for more serious offenders.

One unique feature of four of these jail boot camps is that women are included in special programs. New York City and Santa Clara, California, operate jail boot camps designed for women, for example. While the number of women participants is small, the inclusion of women is highly innovative. In some of these programs for women, the military component is relaxed. At least one site with a program for women reports that it may be discontinued in the future (Austin, Jones, and Bolyard, 1993:4–5).

The Effectiveness of Boot Camps

Are boot camps or shock incarceration programs successful? As we have seen, programs of any kind with recidivism rates of 30 percent or less are considered successful by many criminal justice professionals. If we use this standard as a measure of boot camp effectiveness, there seems to be considerable support in the literature for their effectiveness. For instance, the Louisiana IMPACT program reported that during the first six months of community supervision following boot camp participation, between 7 to 14 percent of the boot camp clients recidivated, compared with from 12 to 23 percent of the boot camp dropouts or those who failed to complete the program (MacKenzie, Shaw, and Gowdy, 1993:4). The New York Rikers Boot Camp has reported recidivism rates of 23 percent among its graduates (Mack, 1992:65). However, 38 percent of the Georgia shock incarceration graduates recidivated over a three-year follow-up period. Younger Georgia shock incarceration graduates, those in their teens when commencing boot camp programs, had a higher recidivism rate of 47 percent (Parent, 1989b:4–5). Thus, Parent questions whether some boot camps actually reduce recidivism rates significantly.

Another large boot camp operation in South Carolina reported that of the 723 offenders who were admitted to the boot camp program from June 1990 through October 1991, only 67 participants, or about 9 percent, recidivated (South

Carolina State Reorganization Commission, 1992). This 91 percent success rate is impressive. We must remember, however, that the follow-up interval in South Carolina was substantially shorter than in Georgia (one year compared with three years). Nevertheless, the short-term recidivism rate is low enough to regard the South Carolina program as successful compared with traditional prison incarceration. Similarly, the Herman L. Toulson Boot Camp in Jessup, Maryland, a six-month program begun in 1990 for first-time and nonviolent male offenders aged 17 to 32, has reported only five new arrests among the first 300 offenders graduating in the first year (MacKenzie and Souryal, 1991). This is a recidivism rate of less than 2 percent. And, in Florida, the Department of Corrections Basic Training Program or Boot Camp has reported a recidivism rate among its graduates of 28 percent (Florida Department of Corrections, 1990).

Because many of these boot camp programs have been established since the late 1980s and early 1990s, extensive evaluation research about general boot camp program effectiveness has not been abundant. However, indications from available research are that boot camps are generally effective at reducing recidivism among participants. Currently, some states, such as Georgia, report relatively high rates of recidivism among boot camp clientele, whereas New York and South Carolina have much lower recidivism rates. Besides reducing recidivism, boot camps might also be effective at saving taxpayers money over time. For various states, operating boot camps is considerably cheaper than using traditional incarceration for particular offenders. In some instances, the cost savings is considerable.

Boot Camp Costs Compared with Traditional Incarceration

Evaluating boot camp programs according to their operating costs compared with the cost of incarcerating offenders for minimum jail or prison terms is illuminating. For instance, New York reports that its boot camp program has saved the state $2.7 million in per-diem housing costs between 1988 and 1989 (New York State Department of Correctional Services, 1989). A more recent survey of 18 different state shock incarceration programs report average daily operating costs of $39 per inmate per day compared with an average of $46 per inmate per day maintained under traditional prison incarceration (MacKenzie, 1993:8). The savings to various states is highly variable, since the shock incarceration costs per day vary from $9 in Mississippi to $66 in Michigan (MacKenzie, 1993:8). Table 4.3 shows a state-by-state comparison of the operating costs of shock incarceration or boot camps compared with prison incarceration. It is clear from Table 4.3 that for the most part, boot camp costs are lower compared with traditional incarceration. Thus, in addition to reducing rates of recidivism among boot camp clientele, shock incarceration programs are also economical compared with traditional prison housing.

TABLE 4.3 Shock Incarceration: Costs by Location

System	Has Shock or Boot Camp Program(s)	Current Budget	Change in Budget	Per Diem Cost of: Shock/Boot Camp	Per Diem Cost of: Prison	Length of Program
Alabama	Yes	$2M	More funding is requested	$29.90	$27	3 months (min. security); 6 months (max. security)
Alaska	No program currently; however, legislation has been passed to begin one					
Arizona	Yes	$1,129,310	Decrease from last year's budget	$23.24	$43.78	120 days
Arkansas	Yes	$1.4M	None	$27.00	$27.00	105 days
California	Yes	$1.5M	Decrease from last year's budget	Unknown	Unknown	3 months prison; 2 months work training; 4 months parole
Colorado	Yes	$1,462,419	Increase over last year's budget	$37.45	$52.68	3 months
Connecticut	No program					
Delaware	No program					
District of Columbia	No program					
Florida	Yes	Unavailable	More money is being proposed for next year's budget	$43.00	$43.00	3 months
Georgia	Yes	Unknown		$30.50	$45.00	3 months for probation facilities, 4 months for inmate
Hawaii						
Idaho						
Illinois	Yes	$5,404,900	Increase over last year's budget; more money is being proposed for next year	$42.67	$43.06	120 days
Indiana	No program					

State	Program?	Budget	Notes			Program length
Iowa	No program					
Kansas	Yes	$1,412,114	Increase over last year's budget; more money is being proposed for next year	$45.00	$56.50	180 days
Kentucky	Yes	$1.2M (for 18 months)	More money is being proposed for next year	Unavailable	$37.78	120 days plus a 6-day zero week that does not count on the program time length
Louisiana	Yes	Unavailable		$33.60	$29.96	90–180 days
Maine	No program					
Maryland						
Massachusetts	Yes	$4 million	None	Unavailable	Unavailable	4 months
Michigan	Yes	Unavailable	Increase over last year's budget	$66.00	$14,000–23,000 per yr.	3 months
Minnesota	Yes	$3.1 million	An increase is proposed from partial funding as it was not initially funded for a full year	Unavailable (program being phased in over time)	$56.00	6 months (Phase I—incarceration & Phase II—community); remainder of sentence (Phase III—supervised release)
Mississippi	Yes	Unavailable		$9.00	$27.00	4 months
Missouri	No program currently; however, there are plans to begin one					
Montana	New program began 7/12/93					
Nebraska	No program currently; however, planning to start 7/1/96 per legislation					
Nevada	Yes	$6,375 per trainee per 150-day program	None	$42.50	$40.80	150 days
New Hampshire	Yes	Unavailable		$47.05	$47.05	4 months
New Jersey	No program					
New Mexico	No program					
New York	Yes	Unavailable		$69.23	$52.06	6 months
North Carolina	Yes	$1.3M	More money is being proposed for next year	$49.00		3 months

(continued)

TABLE 4.3 (continued)

System	Has Shock or Boot Camp Program(s)	Current Budget	Change in Budget	Per Diem Cost of: Shock/Boot Camp	Per Diem Cost of: Prison	Length of Program
North Dakota						
Ohio	No program					
Oklahoma	Yes	Unavailable	More money is being proposed for next year	Unavailable	$34.02	45 days–5 months
Oregon	Scheduled to begin 10/1/93					
Pennsylvania	Yes	$3.8M	Increase over last year's budget; more money is being proposed for next year	$14,000 per year	$28,000 per year	6 months
Rhode Island	No program					
South Carolina	No program					
South Dakota						
Tennessee	Yes	$2,848,000	Increase over last year's budget	$50.76	$62.00	3 months
Texas	Yes	Unavailable		$45.70	$41.48	3 months
Utah	No program					
Vermont	No program					
Virginia	Yes	$2,620,274	Increase over last year's budget	$31.82	$45.24	3 months
Washington	Scheduled to begin 11/1/93					
West Virginia	No program					
Wisconsin	Yes	$1,233,900	Increase over last year's budget due to expansion	$50.41	$55.62	6 months
Wyoming						

Federal Bureau of Prisons	Yes	Unavailable	$45.41–$48.00	$56.84	6 months

Canadian Systems

Alberta	No response
British Columbia	No program
Manitoba	No program
New Brunswick	No response
Newfoundland	No program
Northwest Territory	No response
Nova Scotia	No program
Ontario	No program
Prince Edward Island	No response
Quebec	No program
Saskatchewan	No program
Yukon Territory	No program
Correctional Service of Canada	No program

Source: Corrections Compendium, September 1993.

KEY TERMS

Alternative dispute resolution (ADR)

Boot camp

Combination sentence

Community Diversion Incentive
  Program (CDI)

Community reintegration

Creaming

Georgia Intensive Supervised Probation
  Program

Idaho Intensive Supervised Probation
  Program

Intensive supervised probation (ISP)

Intensive supervised probation program

Intermediate punishments

Intermittent confinement

Intermittent sentence

Jail as a condition of probation

Jail boot camps

Limited-risk control model

Mixed sentence

New Jersey Intensive Supervised
  Probation Program

Restorative justice

Shock incarceration

Shock probation

Shock probationers

South Carolina Intensive Supervised
  Probation Program

Split sentencing

Tort

Totality of circumstances

Traditional, treatment-oriented model

User fees

Victim-Offender reconciliation

Victim-Offender Reconciliation Project
  (VORP)

QUESTIONS FOR REVIEW

1. What is meant by intensive supervised probation? How does it differ from "standard probation"?

2. What is community-based supervision? What are some general features of community-based supervision programs?

3. What is alternative dispute resolution? How does it avoid the stigma of a criminal prosecution? Explain.

4. Differentiate between the Georgia and New Jersey intensive supervised probation models. How are participants selected for each program?

5. What are three correctional models that have influenced intensive supervised probation programs in recent years? How does each model modify or shape existing probation programs?

6. What are some general criticisms of the New Jersey Intensive Supervised Probation program?

7. What is meant by an intermediate punishment? Is intensive supervised probation an intermediate punishment? Why or why not?

8. What are some principal program components of the South Carolina and Idaho ISP programs?

9. What is the relation between prosecutors and judges regarding diversion and who is recommended for a diversion program? What happens to divertees who unsuccessfully complete their diversion programs?

10. What kinds of offenders are prohibited by statute from participating in a diversion program in California?

5

Jails and Prisons
Inmate Profiles and Contemporary Issues

Introduction

Jails and Jail Characteristics

The Functions of Jails

A Profile of Jail Inmates

Prisons and Prison Characteristics

The Functions of Prisons

Inmate Classification Systems

A Profile of Prisoners in U.S. Prisons

Some Jail and Prison Contrasts

Selected Jail and Prison Issues

The Role of Jails and Prisons in Probation
   and Parole Decision Making

Key Terms

Questions for Review

INTRODUCTION

This chapter is about jails and prisons. Jails in the United States are one of the most maligned and forgotten components of the criminal justice system (Stone, 1984:84). In the first section, a brief history of jails in the United States is presented. Jail inmates are also profiled. Typically, *jails* are city- or county-funded facilities operated to confine offenders serving short sentences as well as those awaiting trial. Jails are an integral feature of U.S. corrections.

In contrast, *prisons* are intended as long-term custodial facilities for more serious offenders. The second section of this chapter presents a brief history of prisons in the United States and discusses their characteristics and functions. In past years, we could distinguish clearly between prisons and jails in terms of whether convicted offenders had committed felonies or misdemeanors. Misdemeanants were usually sent to jails, while convicted felons were sent to prisons. This is no longer the case, since overcrowding of prisons has caused prison officials to negotiate with smaller jails to accommodate some of their inmate overflow. Both state and federal governments have contracted with many local jails as a means of housing a certain proportion of their offender populations. This contracting has directly aggravated existing jail overcrowding. Prison inmates will be profiled and compared with jail inmates.

The last section of the chapter discusses several important issues relevant to both jails and prisons. These issues include the overcrowding problem, the problem of inmate violence and discipline, the design and control of jails and prisons, vocational and educational programs for inmates, and privatization. It is important to understand some of the functions and the culture of jails and prisons, since inmate conduct is one determinant of early release decisions by parole boards. Also, inmate conduct is important for those offenders experiencing shock probation. As we saw in Chapter 4, shock probation prescribes one to four months of incarceration, whereupon judges remove offenders from jails and resentence them to probation. However, inmates who behave poorly while confined for these short terms may not be resentenced to probation. Judges exercise discretion and are influenced by inmate conduct. They must decide whether to continue incarcerating offenders or resentence them to probation after one or more months of confinement. Thus, jails and prisons play an important role in probation and parole programs (South Carolina State Reorganization Commission, 1991).

JAILS AND JAIL CHARACTERISTICS

In 1991, there were 10.3 million admissions to and 9.9 million releases from U.S. jails, with an average daily jail population of 422,609 (Beck, Bonczar, and Gilliard, 1993:2). One year later in 1992, the daily jail population had grown to 444,584. Between 1970 and 1992, the nation's population grew by 25 percent, compared with a corresponding 176 percent increase in the U.S. jail inmate population. In fact, between 1991 and 1992, the U.S. population grew by about 1 percent, while the jail population grew by 4 percent (Beck et al., 1993:2–3). This jail population increase has created serious overcrowding problems in city and county jails in most jurisdictions (Klofas, Stojkovic, and Kalinich, 1992). In turn, jail overcrowding has been directly or indirectly responsible for numerous inmate deaths and extensive violence; much offender litigation challenging, among other things, the constitutionality of the nature of their confinement and treatment; and administrative and/or supervisory problems of immense proportions (Adwell, 1991; Cole and Call, 1992). How did jails reach this stage and acquire these problems? A brief history of jails in the United States tells us much about contemporary jail problems.

The term *jail* is derived from the old English term, **gaol** (also pronounced "jail"), which originated in A.D. 1166 through a declaration by Henry II of England. Henry II established gaols as a part of the Assize or Constitution of Clarendon (American Correctional Association, 1983:3). Gaols were locally administered and operated, and they housed many of society's misfits. Paupers or vagrants, drunkards, thieves, murderers, debtors, highwaymen, trespassers, orphan children, prostitutes, and others made up early gaol populations. Since the Church of England was powerful and influential, many religious dissidents were housed in these gaols as a punishment for their dissent. This practice continued for several centuries.

Local control over the administration and operation of jails by shire-reeves in England was a practice continued by the American colonists in later years. Most jails in the United States today are locally controlled and operated in a manner similar to that of their English predecessors. Thus, political influence on jails and jail conditions is strong. In fact, changing jail conditions from one year to the next are often linked to local political shifts through elections and new administrative appointments. And, the fact that local officials controlled jails and jail operations meant that no single administrative style typified these facilities. Each locality (shire) was responsible for establishing jails and managing them according to their individual discretion. Current U.S. jail operations in most jurisdictions are characterized by this same individuality of style.

Originally, jails were designed as holding facilities for persons accused of crimes. Alleged law violators were held until court convened, when their guilt or innocence could be determined. Today, **pretrial detainees** make up a significant proportion of the U.S. jail population. Shire-reeves made their living through reimbursements from taxes collected in the form of fees for each inmate housed on a daily basis. For instance, the reeve would receive a fixed fee, perhaps 50 or 75 cents per day, for each inmate held in the jail. Therefore, more prisoners meant more money for reeves and their assistants. Such a reimbursement scheme was easily susceptible to corruption, and much of the money intended for inmate food and shelter was pocketed by selfish reeves. It followed that the quality of inmate food and shelter was quite substandard, and jails became notorious because of widespread malnutrition, disease, and death among prisoners.

Workhouses

Deplorable jail conditions continued into the sixteenth century, when **workhouses** were established, largely in response to mercantile demands for cheap labor. A typical workhouse in the mid-sixteenth century was the **Bridewell workhouse,** created in 1557. This London facility housed many of the city's vagrants and general "riffraff" (American Correctional Association, 1983). Jail and workhouse sheriffs and administrators quickly capitalized on the cheap labor these facilities generated, and additional profits were envisioned. Thus, it became commonplace for sheriffs and other officials to "hire out" their inmates to perform skilled and semiskilled tasks for various merchants. The manifest functions of workhouses and prisoner labor were to improve the moral and social fiber of prisoners and train them to perform useful skills when they were eventually released, but profits from inmate labor were often pocketed by corrupt jail and workhouse officials.

Jails were commonplace throughout the colonies. Sheriffs were appointed to supervise jail inmates, and the fee system continued to be used to finance these facilities. All types of people were confined together in jails, regardless of their gender or age. Orphans, prostitutes, drunkards, thieves, and robbers were often contained in large, dormitory-style rooms with hay and blankets for beds. Jails were great melting pots of humanity, with little or no regard for inmate treatment, health, or rehabilitation. Even today, jails are characterized similarly (Friday and Brown, 1988; Irwin, 1985; Shelden and Brown, 1991).

The Walnut Street Jail

In 1790, the Pennsylvania legislature authorized the renovation of a facility originally constructed on Walnut Street in 1776, a two-acre structure initially designed to house the overflow resulting from overcrowding of the High Street Jail. The **Walnut Street Jail** was both a workhouse and a place of incarceration for all types of offenders. But the 1790 renovation was the first of several innovations in U.S. corrections. Specifically, the Walnut Street Jail was innovative because (1) it separated the most serious prisoners from others in 16 large solitary cells; (2) it separated other prisoners according to their offense seriousness; and (3) it separated prisoners according to gender. Besides these innovations, the Walnut Street Jail assigned inmates to different types of productive labor according to their gender and conviction offense. Women made clothing and performed washing and mending chores. Skilled inmates worked in carpentry, shoemaking, and other crafts. Unskilled prisoners beat hemp or jute for ship caulking. With the exception of women, prisoners received a daily wage for their labor, which was applied to defray the cost of their maintenance. The Quakers and other religious groups provided regular instruction for most offenders. The Walnut Street Jail concept was widely imitated by officials from other states during the next several decades. Many prisons were modeled after the Walnut Street Jail for housing and managing long-term prisoners.

The Quakers in Pennsylvania were a strong influence in jail reforms. In 1787, they established the Philadelphia Society for Alleviating the Miseries of Public Prisons. This society was made up of many prominent Philadelphia citizens, philanthropists, and religious reformers who believed prison and jail conditions ought to be changed and replaced with a more humane environment. Members of this Society visited each jail and prison daily, bringing food, clothing, and religious instruction to inmates. Some of these members were educators who sought to assist prisoners in acquiring basic skills such as reading and writing. Although their intrusion into prison and jail life was frequently resented and opposed by local authorities and sheriffs, their presence was significant and brought the deplorable conditions of confinement to the attention of politicians.

Subsequent Jail Developments

Information about the early growth of jails in the United States is sketchy. One reason is that there were many inmate facilities established during the 1800s and early 1900s serving many functions and operating under different labels. Sheriffs' homes were used as jails in some jurisdictions, while workhouses, farms, barns, small houses, and other types of facilities served similar purposes in others. Thus, depending on who did the counting, some facilities would be labeled as jails and some would not. Limiting jail definitions only to "locally operated" short-term facilities for inmates excluded those state-operated jails in jurisdictions such as Alaska, Delaware, and Rhode Island. Another reason for inadequate jail statistics and information was that there was little interest in jail populations. Another problem was that it was difficult to transmit information from jails and jail inmates to any central location during that period of time. Often, local records were not maintained, and many sheriff's departments were not inclined to share information about their prisoners with others. Streamlined communications systems did not exist, and information was compiled very slowly, if at all. State governments expressed little or no interest in the affairs of jails within their borders, since these were largely local enterprises funded with local funds. Even if there had been a strong interest in jail information among corrections professionals and others, it would have been quite difficult to acquire.

The U.S. Census Bureau began to compile information about jails in 1880 (Cahalan, 1986:73). At 10-year intervals following 1880, general jail information was systematically obtained about race, nativity, gender, and age. Originally, the U.S. Census Bureau presented data separately for county jails, city prisons, workhouses, houses of correction, and leased county prisoners (Cahalan, 1986:73). But in 1923, these figures were combined to reflect more accurately what we now describe as *jail statistics*. A special report was prepared by the U.S. Census Bureau entitled *Prisoners, 1923*. And, in that same year, Joseph Fishman, a federal prison inspector, published a book, *Crucible of Crime,* which described the living conditions of many U.S. jails (Cahalan, 1986:73; Reid, 1987:404). Comparisons with 1880 base figures show that the jail population of the United States was 18,686 in 1880, which then almost doubled to 33,093 by 1890.

Most reports about jail conditions in the United States have been largely unfavorable. The 1923 report by Fishman was based on his visits to and observations of 1,500 jails, describing the conditions he saw as "horrible" (Reid, 1987:404). More recent reports suggest these conditions have not changed dramatically since Fishman made his early observations (Thomas, 1988). Of course, there are exceptions, but these are few and far between. It was not until 1972 that national survey data about jails became available. Exceptions include the years 1910, 1923, and 1933, when jail inmate characteristics were listed according to several offense categories.

A majority of jail inmates each of those years had committed petty offenses such as vagrancy, public drunkenness, and minor property crimes (Cahalan, 1986:86). Even since 1972, jail data have not been regularly and consistently compiled.

There are several reasons for many of the continuing jail problems in the United States. While some of these persistent problems will be examined in depth later in this chapter, it is sufficient for the present to understand that (1) most of the U.S. jails today were built before 1970, and many were built five decades or more before that; (2) local control of jails often results in erratic policies that shift with each political election, thus forcing jail guards and other personnel to adapt to constantly changing conditions and jail operations; and (3) jail funding is a low-priority budget item in most jurisdictions, and, with limited operating funds, the quality of services and personnel jails provide and attract is considerably lower compared with state and federal prison standards and personnel (Wooldredge, 1991b).

The Number of Jails in the United States

No one knows the exact number of jails in the United States at any given time. One reason is that experts disagree about how jails ought to be defined. Some people count only locally operated and funded, short-term incarceration facilities as jails, while other people include state-operated jails in their figures. In remote territories such as Alaska, World War II Quonset huts may be used to house offenders on a short-term basis. Work-release centers, farms for low-risk inmates, and other facilities may be included or excluded from the jail definition. Sometimes, **lock-ups** (drunk tanks, holding tanks) are counted as jails, although these facilities exist primarily to hold those charged with public drunkenness or other minor offenses for up to 48 hours. These are not jails in the formal sense, but rather, they are simply holding tanks or facilities. The American Jail Association suggests that to qualify as a bona fide jail, the facility must hold inmates for 72 hours or longer, not 48 hours.

This uncertainty is underscored by Cahalan (1986:92–94), who shows that different federal agencies report vastly different numbers of jails for the same year observed. For instance, in 1970, the Census of Institutional Population estimated there were 2,317 jails in the United States, while the Law Enforcement Assistance Administration reported 4,037 U.S. jails operating that same year. Furthermore, the 1923 study conducted by the U.S. Census Bureau reported there were 3,469 U.S. jails in operation. And, in 1984, the Advisory Commission on Intergovernmental Relations reported there were 3,493 jails in the United States (Advisory Commission on Intergovernmental Relations, 1984:2). Perhaps the most accurate figure is from a report by the American Jail Association (1992) reporting that the number of jails in the United States in 1991 was 3,353. The fluctuating numbers of jails from year to year indicate new jail construction and old jail demolition or conversion. A study of 3,338 U.S. jails in 1983 by the National Institute of Justice (NIJ) showed that 2,111 or 63 percent had fewer than 50 beds, while another 1,013 (30 percent) had between 50 and 249 beds (Kiekbusch, 1987:14). In short, more than 80 percent of the jails studied by NIJ were considered small jails.

THE FUNCTIONS OF JAILS

John Irwin (1985) has said that jails are more likely to receive, process, and confine mostly detached and disreputable persons rather than true criminals. He says that many noncriminals are arrested simply because they are offensive and not because they have committed crimes. Irwin worked as a caseworker in several county jails in San Francisco, California, during the early 1980s, and he based his conclusions on personal observations as well as conversations and interviews with county pretrial release and public defender personnel.

Jails were originally conceived as short-term holding facilities for inmates serving short sentences as well as for those awaiting trial. Barry (1987:16) has observed that the general and most basic function of jails is security (Barry, 1987:16). In the last 20 years, however, jails have changed considerably in response to public policy and practicality (Pennsylvania Commission on Crime and Delinquency, 1990). At present, jails perform a myriad of functions, some of which are unrelated to their original historical purpose (Leone et al., 1991). The following functions characterize a majority of jails in the United States:

1. *Jails hold indigents, vagrants, and the mentally ill.* Jails are generally ill-equipped to handle those with mental or physical disorders. Often, physicians are available only on an "on-call" basis from local clinics in communities, and no rehabilitative programs or activities exist. Mentally ill jail inmates present several problems to jail officials. In Virginia, for instance, the 12,000 mentally ill persons who enter the state's jails each year present serious management problems as well as security risks (Virginia Department of Mental Health and Retardation, 1984). It is conceivable that they may be sources of civil liability for sheriffs and other administrators, because they may inadvertently harm themselves or others with whom they share cells. Virginia authorities recommend diverting these types of inmates back to mental health systems where they can be treated adequately for their particular mental disorders. When known mentally ill offenders are confined in jails, even for brief periods, there is the chance that sheriffs, jail administrators, and even diagnosing psychiatrists will be liable for physical harm to others through third-party liability actions (Beck, 1987). Another problem with mentally ill or retarded offenders is that they are often not aware of their rights under the law. They may remain in jails for prolonged periods without attempting to make contact with an attorney or a bail bondsperson. They are lost in the system, at least temporarily, until jail authorities decide what should be done with them. Because of the multiple labels applied to mental retardation and mental disorders generally throughout the various jail systems, scant information is available about the true magnitude of this problem on a national scale (Rockowitz, 1986a, 1986b).

2. *Jails hold pretrial detainees.* Offenders arrested for various crimes who cannot afford or are denied bail are housed in jails until a trial. For most defendants awaiting trial, their period of **pretrial detention** is fairly short (Friday and Brown, 1988). Under the Speedy Trial Act of 1974, charges against defendants must be

Jails contain pretrial detainees, misdemeanants, state and federal prisoners serving long-term sentences, and a wide assortment of what some writers term "rabble." (Peter Southwick/Stock Boston)

filed within 30 days of their arrest. The standards for speedy trials vary among state and local jurisdictions. In some local jurisdictions, minor misdemeanor cases prescribe that trials will be held within 60 days from the time of the defendant's arrest. In other jurisdictions, the time is shortened to 30 days between arrest and trial especially for petty offenses. In the event defendants are caused undue delay between their arrest and trial, they may challenge their detention on Sixth Amendment grounds (*Strunk v. United States,* 1973).

The Bail Reform Act of 1984 has contributed significantly to growing numbers of federal pretrial detainees. This Act was designed, in part, to "toughen up" the old Bail Reform Act of 1966, which permitted judges to authorize bail for all defendants other than those charged with capital crimes. The 1966 Act emphasized bail as a means of assuring only that the defendant would appear later in court. The 1984 Act specifically authorized judges to order the pretrial detention, without bail, of defendants charged with crimes of violence, offenses with possible life (or death) penalties, major drug offenses, and felonies when the defendant has a specified serious criminal record. Thus, the 1984 Act focused on the safety of individuals in the community (Kennedy and Carlson, 1988:2).

3. *Jails house witnesses in protective custody prior to their trials.* Material witnesses to crimes in key cases may be housed in jails until trials can be held, if it appears that their lives are in danger or their safety is threatened. Some witnesses may be reluctant to testify, and thus prosecutors may wish to guarantee their subsequent appearance by placing them in protective custody. Often, jails are designed so that special accommodations are provided these witnesses, and they do not ordinarily associate with offenders.

4. *Jails hold convicted offenders awaiting sentencing.* Convicted offenders awaiting sentencing are usually held in local jail facilities. These offenders may be federal, state, or local prisoners. When these offenders are housed in local jails, the jurisdiction is ordinarily reimbursed for offender expenses from state or federal funds.

5. *Jails house inmates who are serving short-term sentences.* Jails were never designed to accommodate offenders for lengthy incarcerative periods beyond one year. Prisons were constructed and intended for that type of long-term inmate confinement. Many offenders still serve relatively short terms in jails, but increasing numbers of inmates are incarcerated for periods exceeding the one-year standard.

6. *Some jails house juvenile offenders.* Because of the Jail Removal Initiative, most juveniles have been diverted from jails for processing. However, each year some juveniles are incarcerated in jails for short periods, until their identity can be verified. Many juveniles have fake IDs and lie to police about whom they are and where they live. Some juveniles appear to be much older than they really are. Thus, jail authorities may not know that they are incarcerating juveniles if their fake IDs say otherwise and they appear to be adults. In those cases where juveniles *are* held in jails for brief periods, they are usually segregated from adult offenders, unless jail conditions do not permit such segregation. A survey of local jail populations for 1986 indicated that about 1 percent or 1,404 jail inmates were juveniles (persons under a specific age indicated by state statutes, usually 18). About 93,000 admissions to jails in 1986 were juveniles, while juveniles accounted for about 92,000 releases. In 1984, the U.S. Supreme Court ruled in the case of *Schall v. Martin* (1984) that juveniles may be subject to the same pretrial detention as adults, especially if it is the opinion of the court that the juvenile would otherwise pose a risk or danger to society if released. This is called **preventive detention,** and it is designed to control offenders, adult or juvenile, who are high escape risks or who might pose a danger to themselves or others if released from jail prior to trial.

7. *Jails hold prisoners wanted by other states on detainer warrants.* Jails must often accommodate prisoners wanted by other jurisdictions in other states. **Detainer warrants** are notices of criminal charges or unserved sentences pending against prisoners (McShane, 1985). Even though these types of prisoners will eventually be moved to other jurisdictions when authorities from those jurisdictions take them into custody, detainees take up space and time when initially booked and processed.

8. *Jails hold probation and parole violators.* If probationers or parolees violate one or more of their program conditions, they are subject to arrest and incarceration until authorities can determine what to do about their program violations. Under the law, *all* probationers and parolees are entitled to a hearing regarding whether their probation or parole conditions have actually been violated. Furthermore, they are entitled to a hearing to determine whether their probation or parole programs should be revoked (*Morrissey v. Brewer,* 1972; *Gagnon v. Scarpelli,* 1973). Also, it is not necessarily the case that a program violation will automatically result in imprisonment. Sometimes, probation and parole violators are sentenced to a more intensive type of probation similar to programs described in Chapter 4. Often, these hearings take considerable time to arrange, and in the interim, these prisoners often remain jailed (Wood, Verber, and Reddin, 1985). Placements of probation and parole violators in prison have systematically increased between 1977 and 1991 (Gilliard, 1993:7). In 1977, for instance, probation or parole violators accounted for about 14.5 percent of all state prisoners. By 1991, probation or parole violators accounted for 30.5 percent of all state prison inmates (Gilliard, 1993:7). (See Chapter 7 for a more in-depth discussion of the parole revocation process.)

9. *Jails enter into agreements with state and federal prisons to house some of their inmate overflow through contracting.* In jurisdictions such as Louisiana, Maryland, and Tennessee, state and federal prison authorities enter into contracts or leasing arrangements with local city or county jails to accommodate excessive numbers of state or federal prisoners (Cole and Call, 1992; Contact Center, Inc., 1987a; Rich, Davis, and Larson, 1984). Thus, the Knox County Jail in Knoxville, Tennessee, has separate wings where state, federal, and local prisoners are housed. The Tennessee State Prison system was under a federal court order in 1983 to reduce the size of its prison population. Between 1983 and 1984, the Tennessee parolee population increased by 84 percent as a result of this court order. One alternative Tennessee officials exercised was to divert a portion of their prisoners to jails in local jurisdictions within the state. This poses several problems that will be examined later in this chapter. Among other things, some of these state and federal prisoners are serving long-term sentences. In many instances, state or federal prisoners assigned to jails instead of prisons are deprived of prison privileges and services otherwise available in prison settings.

A PROFILE OF JAIL INMATES

Drunks, Vagrants, and Juveniles.   All kinds of people are processed through jails every day. A hitchhiker may be picked up by a state trooper and taken to the nearest jail for a brief investigation. The hitchhiker is warned about local ordinances prohibiting hitchhiking; his or her name, address (if any), and other information may be recorded for future reference; and the person is soon released. These types of arrests and jail bookings account for a portion of the millions of annual jail admissions. If juveniles are taken to jail because of suspicious behavior, their brief stay before being turned over to parents is counted as a jail admission. Neighbors

BOX 5.1
Jail Overcrowding

The Case of Sheriff Michael Ashe

Michael Ashe had been the sheriff of Hampden County, Massachusetts, for about 15 years. His jail was built in 1887 and was originally designed to hold 279 inmates. At the time, over 450 prisoners were being housed there. Sheriff Ashe got angry and acted. He begged and pleaded with county authorities to give him more space. "No more space was available," they said. Judges were convicting and sentencing offenders at such a rate that a new phrase was created for the occasion: "convicted without correctional space." Indeed, many offenders were having their sentences deferred until such time as space was available for them.

Sheriff Ashe decided to "attack" the nearby National Guard Armory in Springfield. With a posse of 17 deputies, he commandeered the building, declaring "As of this moment, I'm seizing this building as a temporary correctional facility. We want to coexist with you here." On-duty National Guardsmen were shocked but nevertheless complied. Trucks and jeeps were cleared from a huge drill hall and soon replaced with 10 double-deck steel beds. Two television sets and a ping pong table were set up as well. After securing the hall, the sheriff posted deputies as "guards" and transferred 15 inmates from the Hampden County Jail to Springfield. The inmates would use the National Guard cafeteria for their meals as well as a reception area for meeting with visitors and family.

The federal government will probably have something to say about Sheriff Ashe's methods, but he left no doubt about his sincerity in attacking his jail overcrowding problem. At present, many states have arrangements or agreements with local jails to house prison inmate overflow. Most states are currently under court order to reduce drastically their inmate populations so that prison conditions will be constitutional. Usually, this alternative exacerbates the problems of jail overcrowding. In the Hampden County Jail case, however, the jurisdiction is having considerable difficulty keeping up with its own jail inmate population, let alone aggravating it by adding state and federal prisoners from Massachusetts prison overflows.

What should be done about jail overcrowding? Will the construction of newer and larger jails correct existing problems? What appear to be some short-range and long-range problems associated with correcting jail overcrowding? What role should sheriffs play in changing jail conditions? Is it a sheriff's responsibility to oversee jail conditions and inmate treatment?

Source: Adapted from Robert Ajemian, "The Sheriff Strikes Back: Instead of Freeing Dangerous Prisoners to Ease Overcrowding, a Massachusetts Lawman Seizes a National Guard Armory." *Time,* March 5, 1990:18.

may complain about loiterers in their neighborhoods. Persons wandering about in high-crime areas of cities are prime targets for arrest by police, especially if they are vagrants or indigents. Those sleeping in alleyways at night or in unoccupied buildings or dwellings are also subject to arrest and detention for violating city or county ordinances. Police officers may bring loiterers and vagrants to jail and hold them temporarily until they can establish their identity and account for their conduct (Shelden and Brown, 1991). These arrests and detentions most often result in releases several hours later. Drunk drivers are taken to jails by police officers every evening, and they are released in the morning, after they have sobered up.

Pretrial Detainees and Petty Offenders.   In 1986, 53 percent of all adults being held in jails were pretrial detainees awaiting trial (Kline, 1987:1). In 1992, pretrial detainees continued to account for about half of all jail inmates (Beck, Bonczar, and Gilliard, 1993:9). Most local jurisdictions have established policies governing how long these persons will be detained. Much depends on the seriousness of the offense and court efficiency. Sometimes, court calendars are clogged and inmates must be held beyond periods outlined in city or county policy. In some jurisdictions, a 30-day period is the maximum interval between one's arrest and trial for petty offending and city or county ordinance violations. Inmates may be held for longer periods if sufficient justification exists.

Shock Probationers and Prison Inmate Overflow.   As we have seen from Chapter 4, shock probationers and some of those participating in boot camp programs may be housed temporarily in jails for periods up to three or four months. Because these programs vary in their usage among jurisdictions and the number of program participants is highly variable, it is not known at any given time how many jail inmates are shock probationers. We do have figures about the numbers of convicted offenders housed in jails, and shock probationers would be lumped together with these other offenders. The impact of shock probationers on jail overcrowding is not substantial, however. But other types of prisoners are often held in jails. We know that some state prison systems as well as the Federal Bureau of Prisons contract with individual jails in cities and counties to house some of their state or federal prisoners. This practice helps the state and federal prison systems remain within constitutional guidelines by keeping their inmate populations at reasonable levels. In 1992, there were 18,191 state prisoners housed in U.S. jails (Gilliard, 1993:5). Jails in Louisiana, New Jersey, Tennessee, and Virginia held over half of these state and federal prisoners. Overall, about 2.1 percent of all state prisoners were housed in local jails in 1992 because of prison overcrowding.

What do jails get out of it? Usually, jail expenditures per inmate are not substantial. State and federal prison systems will provide contracting jails with subsidies according to how many state or federal prisoners are housed in these jails. These subsidies, or a fixed amount of money per prisoner per day, often are two or three times the amount allocated by cities or counties per inmate per day. For example, it may cost Jail X about $15 per day to maintain one inmate. State and federal governments may pay the county where Jail X is located $45 or $60 per day per inmate that Jail X can accommodate. Thus, it is profitable for jails to house state and federal prisoners. Cities and counties pocket these profits and may or may not allocate all funds received for jail improvements. Often, some of the money received from state and federal prisons goes to purchase new cruisers or equipment for county law enforcement officers. Local jurisdictions may be able to hire new school teachers with some of this state or federal money. Actually, only a small portion of these funds are eventually dispersed for city or county jail facility improvements. Table 5.1 shows the number of jurisdictions with large jail populations where courts have ordered these jails to either reduce their populations or improve the conditions of inmate confinement. Table 5.1 also shows the reasons for these court orders.

About one-fourth (26 percent) of the total number of inmates in large jails are state or federal prisoners. This figure is gradually rising annually. About 21 per-

TABLE 5.1 Jurisdictions with Large Jail Populations: Number of Jurisdictions under Court Order to Reduce Population or to Improve Conditions of Confinement, 1991–1992

	Number of Jurisdictions with Large Jail Populations					
	Total		Ordered to Limit Population		Not Ordered to Limit Population	
	1991	1992	1991	1992	1991	1992
Total	503	503	135	131	368	372
Jurisdictions under court order citing specific conditions of confinement	148	134	122	108	26	26
Subject of court order:						
Crowded living units	118	118	111	107	7	11
Recreation facilities	65	62	54	50	11	12
Medical facilities or services	58	57	45	41	13	16
Visitation practices or policies	35	37	30	29	5	8
Disciplinary procedures or policies	34	37	26	27	8	10
Food service	33	29	30	25	3	4
Administrative segregation procedures or policies	27	21	22	16	5	5
Staffing patterns	45	53	39	46	6	7
Grievance procedures or policies	29	38	24	29	5	9
Education or training programs	22	25	19	21	3	4
Fire hazards	17	22	17	19	0	3
Counseling programs	18	18	14	14	4	4
Inmate classification	37	40	34	32	3	8
Library services	50	49	38	36	12	13
Other	15	14	8	9	7	5
Totality of conditions	40	41	34	34	6	7

Note: Detail adds to more than the total number of jurisdictions under court order for specific conditions, because some jurisdictions were under judicial mandate for more than one reason.

Source: Beck, Bonczar, and Gilliard, 1993:5.

cent of the total jail inmate population in 1983 consisted of state and federal prisoners, whereas in 1985, this figure rose to 22 percent (Kline, 1987:3). While accommodating state and federal prison overflows generates greater jail revenues in these jurisdictions, such contracting frequently serves to aggravate existing jail overcrowding problems in these same jurisdictions. In 1992, 503 jurisdictions with large jail populations were under court order to reduce their inmate populations and improve the conditions of their confinement (Beck, Bonczar, and Gilliard, 1993:5).

Work Releasees and the Mentally Ill.   Jail services also include managing a certain portion of offenders on work release programs in those jurisdictions that have them. Jail inmates sentenced to work release programs are low risk, and some experts question whether such offenders should be jailed at all. One opinion is that work releasees should be diverted to halfway houses or community-based programs, so that scarce jail space may be utilized more productively for more serious offenders (Connecticut Prison and Jail Overcrowding Commission, 1985). And, many jail inmates are mentally ill or retarded (Rockowitz, 1986a, 1986b). Psychologically disturbed inmates may prove bothersome or disruptive to other inmates (Guy et al., 1985; Sechrest, 1991). These people pose additional problems to jail staff, because in especially small jail facilities, there are no separate facilities for segregating them from serious offenders. Often, local jail facilities are ill-equipped to meet the special needs of mentally ill offenders or those who may be retarded. As we have seen, large numbers of jail inmates have histories of mental illness or are psychologically disturbed and result in so-called *mercy bookings,* where jail confinement is the only alternative to sleeping in alleyways or on the streets (French, 1986). The homeless are especially susceptible to these mercy bookings (Adams, 1983b; Guy et al., 1985).

Probationers and Parolees.   A small proportion of jail inmates consists of probationers and parolees who have violated one or more conditions of their programs and are awaiting hearings to determine their dispositions and whether their programs should be revoked. These do not represent significant numbers of detainees. However, evidence suggests that their numbers are increasing. For instance, in 1983, about 4.3 percent of all jail detainees were probation and parole violators. By 1989, probation and parole violators accounted for about 6.6 percent of the jail detainees (Maguire, Pastore, and Flanagan, 1993:597).

A profile of jail inmates appears in Table 5.2. Nearly 91 percent of all jail inmates are men, and white non-Hispanics make up about 40 percent of the jail population (Beck, Bonczar, and Gilliard, 1993:2). Hispanic inmates account for about 14 percent of all jail prisoners, while blacks account for 44 percent. Convicted offenders make up about 50 percent of all jail inmates, while women account for about 10 percent of these. While juveniles account for less than 1 percent of all jail inmates, it is surprising that between 1991 and 1992, juvenile jail detainees increased by nearly 20 percent.

TABLE 5.2 Demographic Characteristics of Jail Inmates, 1992

Characteristic	Percent	Number
Gender		
Adult Men	90.8	401,106
Adult Women	9.1	40,674
Juveniles	.1	2,804
Race/Hispanic Origin		
White non-Hispanic	40.1	
Black non-Hispanic	44.1	
Hispanic	14.5	
Other	1.3	
Convicted	49.3	217,940
Men	90.2	196,656
Women	9.8	21,284
Unconvicted	50.7	223,840
Men	91.3	204,450
Women	8.7	19,390

Source: Beck, Bonczar, and Gilliard, 1993:2–3.

PRISONS AND PRISON CHARACTERISTICS

Prisons Defined. *Prisons* are state or federally funded and operated institutions to house convicted offenders under continuous custody on a long-term basis. Compared with jails, prisons are completely self-contained and self-sufficient. In 1990, there were 580,362 state and federal prison bed spaces available for over 715,649 state prisoners (Maguire, Pastore, and Flanagan, 1993:617). This means that prisoners occupied 123 percent of the available bedspace, indicative of serious overcrowding. Erving Goffman (1961) has described prisons as **total institutions,** because they are an environmental reality of absolute dominance over prisoners' lives. These self-contained facilities have recreational yards, workout rooms, auditoriums for viewing feature films, and small stores for purchases of toiletries and other goods.

The Development and Growth of U.S. Prisons. Early English and Scottish penal methods were influential on the subsequent growth and development of U.S. prisons (American Correctional Association, 1983; Hughes, 1987). Most English and Scottish prisons that existed to house criminals and others often had operational policies that were influenced by economic or mercantile interests as well as those of the Church. **John Howard** (1726–1790), an influential English prison reformer, criticized the manner and circumstances under which prisoners were administered and housed. Howard had been a county squire and later, in 1773, he was the sheriff of Bedfordshire. He conducted regular inspections of gaol facilities and found that prisoners were routinely exploited by gaolers, since gaolers had no regular income other than that extracted from prisoners through their labor.

Howard visited other countries to inspect their prison systems. He was impressed with the *Maison de Force* (House of Enforcement) of Ghent, where prisoners were treated humanely. They were clothed, lodged separately from others during evening hours, and well fed. He thought that these ideas could be used as models for British prisons and gaols. He succeeded in convincing British authorities that certain reforms should be undertaken. In 1779, the Penitentiary Act was passed.

The Penitentiary Act provided that new facilities should be created, where prisoners could work productively at hard labor rather than suffer the usual punishment of banishment. Prisoners were to be well fed, clothed, and housed in isolated sanitary cells. They were to be given opportunities to learn useful skills and trades. Fees for their maintenance were abolished, rigorous inspections were conducted regularly, and balanced diets and improved hygiene were to be strictly observed. Howard believed that prisoners should be given a hearty work regimen. Through hard work, prisoners would realize the seriousness and consequences of their crimes. Thus, work was a type of penance. The new word, *penitentiary,* was originated and was synonymous with reform and punishment. Presently, penitentiaries in the United States are regarded as punishment-centered rather than reform-oriented, as significant philosophical shifts have occurred in American corrections (American Correctional Association, 1983:15).

State Prisons.   The first state prison was established in Simsbury, Connecticut, in 1773. This prison was actually an underground copper mine that was converted into a confinement facility for convicted felons (American Correctional Association, 1983:26–27). It was eventually made into a permanent prison in 1790. Prisoners were shackled about the ankles, worked long hours, and received particularly harsh sentences for minor offenses. Burglary and counterfeiting were punishable in Simsbury by imprisonment not exceeding 10 years, while a second offense meant life imprisonment (American Correctional Association, 1983:26).

Actually, the Walnut Street Jail was the first true American prison that attempted to correct offenders. Compared with the Simsbury, Connecticut, underground prison, a strictly punishment-centered facility, the Walnut Street Jail operated according to rehabilitation model. A signer of the Declaration of Independence, Dr. Benjamin Rush (1745–1813), was both a physician and a humanitarian. He believed that punishment should reform offenders and prevent them from committing future crimes. He also believed that they should be removed temporarily from society until they became remorseful. Rush believed that prisoners should exercise regularly and eat wholesome foods. Thus, he encouraged prisoners to grow gardens where they could produce their own goods. Prisoner-produced goods were so successful at one point that produce and other materials manufactured or grown by inmates were marketed to the general public. Therefore, he pioneered the first prison industry in which prisoners could market goods for profit and use some of this income to defray prison operating expenses. Some of Rush's ideas were incorporated into the operation of the Walnut Street Jail, and, eventually, the pattern of discipline and offender treatment practiced there became known popularly as the *Pennsylvania System.* The Walnut Street Jail Pennsylvania

System became a model used by many other jurisdictions (American Correctional Association, 1983:31).

Auburn State Penitentiary.   New York correctional authorities developed a new type of prison in 1816, the **Auburn State Penitentiary,** which was designed according to a **tier system** by which inmates were housed on several different levels. The tier system became a common feature of subsequent U.S. prison construction, and today most prisons are architecturally structured according to tiers. The term **penitentiary** is used to designate an institution that not only segregates offenders from society but also from each other. The original connotation of penitentiary was a place where prisoners could think, reflect, and repent of their misdeeds and possibly undergo reformation (Allen et al., 1985). Presently, the words *prison* and *penitentiary* are often used interchangeably, since virtually every prison has facilities for isolating prisoners from one another according to various levels of custody and control. Thus, each state has devised different names for facilities designed to house its most dangerous offenders. Examples include Kentucky State Penitentiary, California State Prison at San Quentin, New Jersey State Prison, North Dakota Penitentiary, and Maine State Prison.

At the Auburn State Penitentiary, prisoners were housed in solitary cells during evening hours. This was the beginning of what is presently known as **solitary confinement.** Another innovation at Auburn was that inmates were allowed to work together and eat their meals with one another during daylight hours. This was known as the **congregate system** (American Correctional Association, 1983). Auburn State Penitentiary also provided for divisions among prisoners according to the nature of their offenses. The different tiers conveniently housed inmates in different offense categories, with more serious offenders housed on one tier and less serious offenders housed on another. Certain tiers were reserved for the most unruly offenders who could not conform their conduct to prison policies. The most dangerous inmates were kept in solitary confinement for long periods as punishment. These periods ranged from a few days to a few months, depending on the prison rule violated. Therefore, Auburn State Penitentiary is significant historically because it provided the minimum-, medium-, and maximum-security designations by which modern penitentiaries are known.

Prisoners were provided with different uniforms as well, to set them apart from one another. The stereotypical "striped" uniform of prison inmates was a novelty at Auburn that was widely copied as well. Over half of all state prisons patterned their structures after the Auburn system during the next half-century, including the style of prison dress and manner of separating offenders according to the seriousness of their crime (American Correctional Association, 1983:49–54). Striped prison uniforms for prisoners continued until the 1950s, when they became outmoded (American Correctional Association, 1983:54). Auburn inmates helped to defray a portion of their housing and food costs through their labor. Contracts were made with various manufacturers and retailers for purchases of prison goods. Thus, prison industry was gradually recognized as mutually beneficial for prisoners and for private business.

Other Prison Developments. Between 1816 and 1900, many state prisons were established. One of the first successful prisons was constructed in Cherry Hill, Pennsylvania, in the early 1830s. This prison was considered successful because it was the first to offer a continuing internal program of treatment and other forms of assistance to inmates (Johnston, 1973). The first state penitentiary in Ohio was opened in Columbus in 1834. The largest state prison of that time period was established in Jackson, Michigan, in 1839. By 1987, this State Prison of Southern Michigan contained 4,729 inmates, making it one of the largest and oldest state prisons in the United States. However, the original building constructed in 1839 had been rebuilt to accommodate larger numbers of inmates in 1926 (American Correctional Association, 1988:203). Another large state prison was built in Parchman, Mississippi, in 1900. In 1987, it housed 4,716 inmates. Louisiana claims one of the largest and oldest state prisons, however, built in 1866 with a capacity of 4,747 inmates. In 1987, the Louisiana State Penitentiary in Angola housed 4,646 men (American Correctional Association, 1988:203).

The Creation of the American Correctional Association and Elmira Reformatory. In 1870 the **American Correctional Association (ACA)** was established and Rutherford B. Hayes, a future U.S. president, was selected to head that organization. The goals of the ACA were to formulate a national correctional philosophy, to develop sound correctional policies and standards, to offer expertise to all interested jurisdictions in the design and operation of correctional facilities, and to assist in the training of correctional officers. The ACA was originally called the National Prison Association, then the American Prison Association, and, finally and more generally, the American Correctional Association.

The United States was entering a new era of correctional reform with the establishment of the ACA. Six years later, the **Elmira Reformatory** in Elmira, New York, was constructed. Elmira Reformatory experimented with certain new rehabilitative philosophies espoused by various penologists including its first superintendent, Zebulon Brockway (1827–1920). Brockway was critical of the harsh methods employed by the establishments he headed, and he envisioned better and more effective treatments for prisoners. He had his chance in 1876 when he was selected to head Elmira Reformatory. Elmira was considered the *new penology* and used the latest scientific information in its correctional methods. Penologists from Scotland and Ireland, **Captain Alexander Maconochie** and **Sir Walter Crofton,** were instrumental in bringing about changes in European correctional methods during the period when Elmira was established in the early 1870s. These men influenced American corrections by introducing the "mark system," whereby prisoners could accumulate good time credits applied against their original sentences. Through hard work and industry, prisoners could shorten their original sentences, which earlier had to be served in their entirety (American Correctional Association, 1983:67).

Elmira was truly a reformatory and used a military model comparable to contemporary boot camps. Prisoners performed useful labor and participated in educational or vocational activities through which their productivity and good conduct could earn them shorter sentences. Elmira inmates were trained in close-order drill, wore military uniforms, and paraded about with wooden rifles. Authorities regarded this as a way of instilling discipline in inmates and reforming them. Historians credit Elmira with individualizing prisoner treatment and the use of indeterminate sentencing directly suited for parole actions. Elmira was subsequently widely imitated by other state prison systems.

Rehabilitation remains as one of correction's continuing goals. However, prison overcrowding stimulates significant changes in prison operating policies, and criminal justice procedures are changed to accommodate growing numbers of inmates (*Corrections Compendium*, 1984). Many prisons report greater inmate idleness and violence as a result of greater overcrowding in recent years (Johnson, 1984). Also, many prisons are experiencing lower staff-to-prisoner ratios. Thus, the quality of programs offered to inmates suffers as prison capacities are exceeded through higher conviction rates and changes in sentencing and parole policies. Although the link between prison population growth and program quality is unclear, overcrowding does seem to adversely influence prison practices and policies (Zimmerman, 1986).

THE FUNCTIONS OF PRISONS

The functions served by prisons are closely connected with the overall goals of corrections. Broadly stated, correctional goals include deterrence, rehabilitation, societal protection, offender reintegration, "just-deserts," justice and due process, and retribution or punishment. The goals of prisons are noted below.

1. *Prisons provide societal protection.* Locking up dangerous offenders or those who are persistent nonviolent offenders means that society will be protected from them for variable time periods. It is not possible at present to lock up all offenders who deserve to be incarcerated. Space limitations are such that we would require at least four or five times the number of existing prisons to incarcerate all convicted felons and misdemeanants. Thus, the criminal justice system attempts to incarcerate those most in need of incarceration. Obviously, this goal is not realized, since many dangerous offenders are placed on probation annually and many nonviolent offenders are incarcerated. Varying state and federal statutes and prosecutorial practices contribute to sentencing inconsistencies and peculiar incarceration policies and patterns.

2. *Prisons punish offenders.* Restricting one's freedoms, confining inmates in cells, and obligating them to follow rigid behavioral codes while confined is regarded as punishment for criminal conduct. The fact of incarceration is a punishment compared with the greater freedoms enjoyed by probationers and parolees.

3. *Prisons rehabilitate offenders.* Few criminal justice scholars would agree that prisons are in the prisoner rehabilitation business. There is little support for the view that imprisonment does much of a rehabilitative nature for anyone confined. Nevertheless, many prisons have vocational and educational programs, psychological counselors, and an array of services available to inmates in order that they might improve their skills, education, and self-concept (Johnson, 1987). Prisons also have libraries for inmate self-improvement. However, more often than not, prisons also socialize inmates in adverse ways, having the effect that they might emerge from prisons later as "better criminals" who have, unfortunately, learned ways of avoiding detection when committing future crimes.

4. *Prisons reintegrate offenders.* It might be argued that moving offenders from higher security levels, where they are more closely supervised, to lower security levels, where they are less closely supervised, helps them understand that conformity with institutional rules is rewarded. As prisoners near their release dates, they may be permitted unescorted leaves, known as *furloughs* or *work release* (see Chapters 10 and 7, respectively), during which they may participate in work or educational programs and visit with their families during the week or on weekends. These experiences are considered reintegrative. Most prisons have such programs, but they are presumably aimed at certain offenders who are believed to no longer pose a threat to society. Occasionally, officials wrongly estimate the nondangerousness of certain furloughees and work releasees. In any case, the intent of reintegrative prison programs is to provide those wanting such programs the opportunity of having them. At least some inmates derive value from such programs, although some experts believe the costs of operating them are far outweighed by the lack of rehabilitation and reintegration that actually occurs.

INMATE CLASSIFICATION SYSTEMS

Religious movements are credited with establishing early **inmate classification** systems in the eighteenth century (American Correctional Association, 1983:194). The Walnut Street Jail in 1790 in Philadelphia attempted to segregate prisoners according to age, gender, and offense seriousness. Subsequent efforts were made by penal authorities to classify and separate inmates according to various criteria in many state and federal prison facilities. Adequate classification schemes for prisoners have yet to be devised (Austin, 1986; Austin and Pannell, 1986; Craddock, 1987; Wright, 1986b). Classification schemes are based largely on psychological, behavioral, and sociodemographic criteria. The use of psychological characteristics as predictors of risk or dangerousness and subsequent custody assignments for prisoners was stimulated by research during the period between 1910 and 1920 (American Correctional Association, 1983:196).

No single scheme for classifying offenders is foolproof, although several instruments have been used more frequently than others for inmate classification and placement. The Megargee Inmate Typology presumes to measure "inmate adjustment to prison life" (Megargee and Carbonell, 1985). Several items were selected from the Minnesota Multiphasic Personality Inventory (MMPI), a psychological assessment device, to define 10 prisoner types and to predict an inmate's inclination to violate prison rules or act aggressively against others. Basically a psychological tool, the Megargee Inmate Typology has been adopted by various state prison systems for purposes of classifying prisoners into different custody levels. The predictive utility of this instrument is questionable, however. One problem Megargee himself detected was that prisoner classification types based on his index scores change drastically during a one-year period. For some experts, this finding has caused serious questions about the reliability of Megargee's scale. For other experts, however, inmate score changes on Megargee's scale indicate behavioral change, possibly improvement. Thus, reclassifications are conducted of most prison inmates at regular intervals to chart their behavioral progress.

Besides Megargee, other professionals have devised useful inmate classification criteria (Gottfredson and Gottfredson, 1988). For example, Goetting and Howsen (1986) found that inmate misconduct is correlated with being young, black, and male; having a relatively high number of prior convictions; having been unemployed prior to incarceration; and having been imprisoned for a long period. But descriptions of those who engage in prison misconduct are difficult to apply in screening stages to decide the level of custody to which inmates should be assigned. Should all young, unemployed, black men with prior records and long sentences be placed in a high level of custody? Undoubtedly, classifications made according to such criteria would be discriminatory and violative of the equal protection clause of the Fourteenth Amendment.

One thing is certain about risk instruments and inmate classifications resulting from applications of these instruments: *how* prison inmates are initially classified and housed will directly influence their parole chances (Gottfredson and Gottfredson, 1988; Hoffman, 1983). Inmates classified as *maximum security* may not deserve this classification, since it means that the inmate is considered dangerous. Inmate opportunities for personal development and rehabilitation are limited by these classifications. However, inmates who are classified as *minimum security* have a wide variety of prison benefits and programs. They are neither supervised as closely nor considered as dangerous. When *minimum security* inmates face parole boards, their custody levels are assets. When *maximum security* inmates face parole boards, their classification is a liability. An example of a prison risk-assessment instrument to determine inmate placement or security level is one used by the Alaska Department of Corrections illustrated in Figure 5.1.

All prisons in the United States have classifications that differentiate between prisoners and cause them to be placed under various levels of custody or security. One of the main purposes for the initial inmate classification is to identify those likely to engage in assaultive or aggressive disciplinary infractions (Wright, 1986a, 1986b). Prisoners are eventually channeled into one of several fixed custody levels known as (1) minimum-, (2) medium-, and (3) maximum-security.

Minimum-Security Classification. **Minimum-security prisons** are facilities designed to house low-risk, nonviolent first-offenders. These institutions are also established to accommodate those serving short-term sentences. Sometimes, minimum-security institutions function as intermediate housing for those prisoners leaving more heavily monitored facilities on their way toward parole or eventual freedom. Minimum-security housing is often of a dormitory-like quality, with grounds and physical plant features resembling a university campus rather than a prison. Those assigned to minimum-security facilities are trusted to comply with whatever rules are in force.

Administrators place greater trust in inmates in minimum-security institutions, and these sites are believed to be most likely to promote greater self-confidence and self-esteem among prisoners. The rehabilitative value of minimum-security inmates is high. And, family visits are less restricted. The emphasis of minimum-security classification is definitely on prisoner reintegration into society.

Medium-Security Classification.   Sixty percent of all state and federal prisons in the United States are **medium-security prisons** and minimum-security institutions (Carney, 1979). The American Correctional Association (1988) says that a majority of state and federal prison facilities are designed to accommodate medium- and minimum-security inmates. As of 1987, of the six U.S. penitentiaries, all but the one in Atlanta, Georgia, were classified as maximum-security (American Correctional Association, 1988). Medium-security facilities at both state and federal levels offer inmates opportunities for work release, furloughs, and other types of programs.

Maximum-Security Classification.   Forty percent of all U.S. prisons are **maximum-security prisons.** Ordinarily, those sentenced to serve time in maximum-security facilities are considered among the most dangerous, high-risk offenders. Maximum-security prisons are characterized by many stringent rules and restrictions, and inmates are isolated from one another for long periods in single-cell accommodations. Closed-circuit television monitors often permit correctional officers to observe prisoners in their cells or in work areas that are limited. Visitation privileges are minimal. Most often, no efforts are made by officials to rehabilitate inmates (Israel, 1983).

An example of one of the most memorable maximum-security penitentiaries ever constructed was the federal prison at Alcatraz in San Francisco Bay. Alcatraz was constructed in 1934 but closed in 1963 because of poor sanitation and the great expense of prisoner maintenance. During the period Alcatraz was operated, Alcatraz held over 1,500 prisoners, including Al Capone and Robert "Birdman" Stroud. In maximum-security prisons, inmate isolation and control are stressed, and close monitoring by guards either directly or through closed-circuit television reduces prisoner misconduct significantly.

Maxi-Maxi Prisons.   Supposedly for the "baddest of the bad," there are prisons such as the Marion, Illinois, Federal Penitentiary. This **maxi-maxi prison** is the federal prison known as *Marion,* constructed in 1963. It accommodates only 574 inmates, and those incarcerated at Marion are considered the very worst prisoners. Marion inmates are the most violence prone, inclined to escape whenever the opportunity arises, and extremely dangerous. Two correctional officers were killed by prisoners in a riot in the Control Unit (Mauer, 1985). When the riot was contained, Marion officials ordered a **lockdown,** whereby all prisoners were placed in solitary

STATE OF ALASKA
DEPARTMENT OF CORRECTIONS

Security Designation Form for Long-Term Sentenced Prisoners

(1) _____ _____ (3) _____

    Institution
Staff Member   Designation

(2) _____ _____ (4) _____

    Date
(exception case only)

SECTION A	IDENTIFYING DATA

(1) ___ _____ _____

  Prisoner's Name   Last   First   Middle Initial

(2) _____

                                                Date of Birth

(3) Type of Case: Regular _____ Exception _ _____ (4) OBSCIS _____
(5) Separatees: _____

SECTION B	SECURITY SCORING

1. Type of Detainer:
   0 = None   3 = Class C Felony   7 = Unclassified or
   1 = Misdeameanor   5 = Class B Felony   Class A Felony [   ]   1
2. Severity of Current Offense:
   1 = Misdemeanor   3 = Class C Felony   7 = Unclassified or
                     5 = Class B Felony   Class A Felony [   ]   2
3. Time to Firm Release Date:
   0 = 0-12 months   3 = 60-83 months
   1 = 13-59 months   5 = 84 + months   _____ [   ]   3
                                                Firm Release Date
4. Type of Prior Convictions:
   0 = None   1 = Misdemeanor   3 = Felony   [   ]   4
5. History of Escapes or Attempted Escapes:

	None	+15 Years	10-15 Years	5-10 Years	<5 Years		
Minor	0	1	1	2	3		
Serious	0	4	5	6	7	[ ]	5

6. History of Violent Behavior:

	None	+15 Years	10-15 Years	5-10 Years	<5 Years		
Minor	0	1	1	2	3		
Serious	0	4	5	6	7	[ ]	6

7. SECURITY TOTAL   [   ]
8. Security Level:
     Minimum = 0-6 points   Medium = 7-13 points   Maximum = 14-36 points
9. Designated Custody Level:

Community/Minimum	Medium	Close	Maximum
0-6	7-13	14-25	26-36

FIGURE 5.1 State of Alaska long-term prisoner classification form.

(figure continues)

10. <u>Designation Staff Comments:</u>

_____

_____

_____

_____

SECTION C	MANAGEMENT CONSIDERATION	
1. Release Plans	5. Special Treatment	9. Residence
2. Medical	6. Ethnic/Cultural	10. Restitution Center
3. Psychiatric	Consideration	11. Contract Misdemeanant
	7. Overcrowding	Housing
	8. Judicial Recommen-	
	dation	

FIGURE 5.1 (continued)

confinement and severe restrictions were imposed. For Marion inmates, lockdown meant confinement in isolation for 23-1/2 hours per day, with 1/2 hour for exercise. Privileges were extremely limited.

A PROFILE OF PRISONERS IN U.S. PRISONS

Considerable diversity exists among prisoners in state and federal institutions. These differences involve the nature and seriousness of their conviction offenses, age, and psychological or medical problems. In order to cope more effectively with meeting the needs of such diverse offenders, prisons have established different confinement facilities and levels of custody, depending upon how each prisoner is classified.

Between 1980 and 1992, a majority of states more than doubled their number of sentenced prisoners (Gilliard, 1993:1). Overall, state and federal prisoner populations increased by 168 percent between 1980 and 1992. Generally, a 6.7 percent increase occurred in the national prison population between 1991 and 1992 (Gilliard, 1993:1). Table 5.3 shows federal and state prison population growth between 1980 and 1992.

A survey of state prison inmates was conducted in 1986 by the U.S. Bureau of Justice Statistics. This survey was contrasted with a state prisoner profile compiled in 1979 (Innes, 1986). The comparison revealed few significant differences in prisoner characteristics during the interval between 1979 and 1986. Despite vast sentencing reforms and policy changes in all states during the 1970s and 1980s, the aggregate state prison inmate profile remained fairly constant. Table 5.4 shows a subsequent comparison of 1977 and 1990 prison inmates according to their conviction offense.

An inspection of Table 5.4 shows a gradually changing profile of offenders committed to state prisons between 1977 and 1990. In 1977, for instance, drug offenders accounted for only 11.5 percent of all prison inmates. In 1990, drug offenders made up 32.1 percent of the prison inmate population. Public order offenders made up another 8.1 percent of the 1990 inmate population compared with only 4.4

TABLE 5.3 Change in the State and Federal Prison Populations, 1980–1992

Year	No. of Inmates	Annual Percentage Change	Total Percentage Change Since 1980
1980	329,821	—	—
1981	369,930	12.2	12.2
1982	413,606	11.9	25.5
1983	436,855	5.6	32.5
1984	482,002	5.8	40.1
1985	502,752	8.8	52.4
1986	546,378	8.5	65.4
1987	585,292	7.3	77.5
1988	631,990	8.0	91.6
1989	712,967	12.8	116.2
1990	773,124	8.4	134.4
1991	824,133	6.6	149.9
1992	883,593	7.2	167.9

Source: Gilliard, 1993:1.

percent of the same population in 1977. In contrast, *both* violent and property offenders decreased proportionately across these years. The proportion of violent offenders decreased from 41.6 percent in 1977 to 27 percent of the inmate population in 1990, while property offenders decreased proportionately from 42.9 percent in 1977 to 31.7 percent in 1990 (Gilliard, 1993:10).

Table 5.5 shows some demographic information about prison inmates in 35 states in 1990 (U.S. Department of Justice, 1993a:9). Most admissions in these states during 1990 were men (92.3 percent). Over 53 percent were black, and the largest age category of inmates was 25 to 29 years of age. The median educational level was the eleventh grade (U.S. Department of Justice, 1993a:9). For federal prisoners during the same year, 1990, the gender distribution was identical. Male prisoners accounted for 92.3 percent of all inmates in federal facilities. However, white offenders accounted for 66.1 percent of all federal inmates, compared with 46 percent of the state inmate population, as shown in Table 5.5.

More than a little evidence exists to suggest that both the state and federal inmate population in the United States is comprised of increasing numbers of older offenders. Some experts have suggested that prison systems will have to make certain adjustments in the variety of services provided in order to accommodate those older offenders with special needs (Dugger, 1988; Kelsey, 1986). For instance, older inmates may require ground-level accommodations with no stairs because of pulmonary diseases, arthritis, and other physical problems, as well as quick access to the medical department (Kelsey, 1986:56). One solution is to design and construct special prisons to meet the needs of particular offender groups such as the elderly, the mentally ill or retarded, or the drug- and alcohol-dependent. Most state prison systems either have internal facilities in their penitentiaries for addressing special offender needs or separate institutions that provide these services. In Lexington, Oklahoma, for example, the Joseph Harp Correctional Center is a mental health facility that can accommodate up to 714 prisoners with emotional or psychological

TABLE 5.4 New Court Commitments to State Prisons, by Type of Offense, 1977–1990

Most Serious Offense	Percent Admitted to State Prison													
	1977	1978	1979	1980	1981	1982	1983	1984	1985	1986	1987	1988	1989	1990
Violent offenses	41.6	40.7	43.6	48.2	38.5	39.0	36.8	36.4	35.1	33.5	31.7	29.9	27.6	27.0
Murder[a]	6.2	6.6	7.2	8.6	5.1	6.9	5.1	3.6	4.5	4.3	4.0	3.5	3.0	2.8
Sexual assault	4.0	4.5	5.2	6.3	4.3	4.3	6.0	6.0	7.4	6.9	7.0	6.2	5.5	5.6
Robbery	21.5	18.8	19.2	19.1	18.9	16.8	14.7	15.9	13.3	12.5	11.3	10.7	10.0	9.2
Aggravated assault	6.0	7.5	7.7	8.1	6.9	7.2	7.1	6.9	6.8	6.7	6.6	6.7	6.4	7.1
Property offenses	42.9	44.7	43.3	40.1	48.0	47.4	47.4	44.0	42.4	41.0	39.6	37.1	33.5	31.7
Burglary	25.0	23.7	23.0	23.0	27.2	26.1	26.1	22.2	21.2	20.3	18.5	17.5	15.6	14.4
Drug offenses	11.5	9.4	7.9	6.8	7.7	7.7	9.0	11.2	13.2	16.3	20.4	25.1	30.5	32.1
Public-order offenses	4.4	5.2	5.1	4.0	4.5	5.1	5.7	6.3	7.9	7.8	7.0	6.9	7.3	8.1
Other	0.1	—	—	—	1.3	1.0	1.1	2.1	1.4	1.4	1.6	1.0	1.0	1.1

[a]Includes nonnegligent manslaughter. The number of nonnegligent manslaughters was estimated for 1977–1984.

— = Data not available.

Source: Gilliard, 1993:10, and U. S. Department of Justice, 1993a and 1993b.

TABLE 5.5 Demographic and Social Characteristics of Prison Admissions in 35 States, 1990

Characteristics	All Admissions	New Court Commitments
Number of Admissions	390,087	268,330
Total	100%	100%
Sex		
Male	92.3	91.6
Female	7.7	8.4
Race		
White	46.0	45.3
Black	53.2	53.9
Other	0.7	0.6
Hispanic Origin		
Hispanic	19.5	18.3
Non-Hispanic	80.5	81.7
Age at Admission		
Under 18 years	1.2	1.7
18 to 24 years	29.6	34.0
25 to 29 years	25.0	23.5
30 to 34 years	20.0	18.3
35 to 44 years	18.7	17.0
45 to 54 years	4.2	4.1
55 years and older	1.3	1.5
Median Age	28 years	27 years
Education		
8th grade or less	16.9%	16.1%
9th to 11th grade	45.6	45.5
High school graduate	29.2	29.6
Some college	8.0	8.4
Other	0.4	0.4
Median Education	11th grade	11th grade

Source: U.S. Department of Justice. *National Corrections Reporting Program, 1990.* Washington, DC: U.S. Department of Justice, NCJ-141879, 1993:9.

problems. The Minnesota Correctional Facility at Oak Park Heights includes medical and psychiatric units in addition to solitary confinement units for dangerous offenders. These are only a few of the growing units and services catering to the elderly behind bars.

SOME JAIL AND PRISON CONTRASTS

Below are some of the contrasts between prisons and jails. Compared with prisons,

1. The physical plant of jails is poorer, with many jails under court order to improve their physical facilities to comply with minimum health and safety standards.

2. Jails usually do not have programs or facilities associated with long-term incarceration such as vocational, technical, or educational courses to be taken by inmates, jail industries, recreation yards, or psychological or social counseling or therapy.
3. Jails have a greater diversity of inmates, including witnesses for trials, suspects or detainees, defendants awaiting trial unable to post bail or whose bail was denied, juveniles awaiting transfer to juvenile facilities or detention, those serving short-term sentences for public drunkenness, driving while intoxicated, or city ordinance violations, mentally ill or disturbed persons awaiting hospitalization, and overflow from state and federal prison populations.
4. Jail inmate culture is less pronounced and persistent. There is a high inmate turnover in jails, with the exception of the state and federal convict population.
5. The quality of jail personnel is lower, with many jail personnel untrained, undertrained, or otherwise less qualified to guard prisoners compared with their counterparts, prison correctional officers.
6. Jails are not usually partitioned into minimum- , medium- , or maximum-security areas. Control towers from which armed correctional officers patrol regularly, do not exist. Jails are not surrounded by several perimeters, with barbed wire areas, sound-detection equipment, and other exotic electronic devices.

SELECTED JAIL AND PRISON ISSUES

In 1992, 503 jails in jurisdictions with large jail populations were under a court order to either reduce their inmate populations to constitutionally safe limits or to improve various confinement conditions (Beck, Bonczar, and Gilliard, 1993:5). This suggests that improvements have occurred since 1986, when 612 jail facilities were ordered to reduce their inmate populations (Kline, 1987:4). The major reason for these court-ordered inmate population reductions or jail improvements was jail or **prison overcrowding.** Any time jail populations exceed their rated or design capacity, overcrowding exists. Sometimes the overcrowding is only short term. In other cases, it is chronic. Most jails in the United States have serious overcrowding problems (Friday and Brown, 1988; Leone et al., 1991).

This section examines briefly five major issues representing problems for both jails and prisons. These issues include: (1) jail and prison overcrowding; (2) violence and inmate discipline; (3) jail and prison design and control; (4) vocational-technical and educational programs in jails and prisons; and (5) jail and prison privatization.

Jail and Prison Overcrowding

Jails are expected to accommodate almost everyone brought to them for booking or processing. Murder suspects as well as public intoxication cases may be housed temporarily in the same tank or detention area to await further processing. The millions of admissions to and releases from jails annually only aggravate persistent jail overcrowding problems, despite the fact that most of those admitted to jails are not confined for lengthy periods. The volume of admissions and releases is severe enough and persistent enough to cause continuing jail overcrowding problems

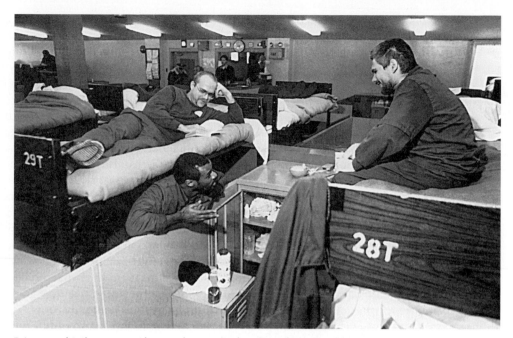

Prison and jail overcrowding is chronic in the United States, although the
U.S. Supreme Court has approved the constitutionality of overcrowding in
view of the "totality of circumstances." (The Image Works)

(Harris, 1992; Welsh and Smith, 1992). Law enforcement arrest policies in many ju
risdictions seriously aggravate jail overcrowding as well, as millions of arrestees occupy valuable jail space during booking and other perfunctory jail processing
(Welsh, 1993).

The fact that numerous state and federal prisons contract with local jail authorities to house some of the prison inmate overflow suggests serious prison overcrowding as well (Cole and Call, 1992; South Carolina State Reorganization Commission, 1991). Violent deaths, suicides, psychiatric commitments, and disciplinary
infractions have been linked to jail and prison overcrowding (Champion, 1988c;
Goetting and Howsen, 1986; Maier and Miller, 1987; Ruback and Carr, 1993;
Sechrest, 1991). Clarke and Coleman (1993) indicate that for the county jail population alone, the number of North Carolina jail inmates increased from 2,032 in
1976 to 8,760 in 1992. Three-fourths of these inmates were pretrial detainees. In
1992, North Carolina jails officially were not overcrowded, since the rated capacity
of the state's jails was 10,146. But North Carolina has had to engage in costly jail
construction, with the average cost of each new jail bed being $56,547. There is
likely to be a breaking point in county building construction budgets, since the cost
of new prison beds in North Carolina is less than half those of jails, at $25,000 per
bed (Clarke and Coleman, 1993).

An endless string of solutions has been suggested to ease jail and prison overcrowding. Some of these solutions are labeled as *front-door solutions* because they pertain to policies and practices by criminal justice officials who deal with offenders before and during sentencing. Other solutions are *back-door solutions,* in which strategies are suggested to reduce existing prison populations through early release or parole, furlough, administrative release, and several other options (Oklahoma State Board of Corrections, 1984).

Typically, front-door solutions to prison overcrowding are frequently directed at prosecutors and judges, and the way they handle offenders. Some experts suggest greater use of diversion and/or assignment to community service agencies, whereby offenders bypass the criminal justice system altogether and remain free within their communities (Martinez and Fabelo, 1985). Greater use of probation by judges and recommendations of leniency from prosecutors have also been suggested, with an emphasis upon some form of restitution, community service, victim compensation, and/or fine as the primary punishment (Hall, 1987). Other solutions include greater plea bargaining where probation is included (Maryland Committee on Prison Overcrowding, 1984), selective incapacitation, where those offenders deemed most dangerous are considered for incarceration (Brennan, 1985), assigning judges a fixed number of prison spaces so that they might rearrange their sentencing priorities and incarcerate only the most serious offenders (South Carolina State Reorganization Commission, 1991), and decriminalization of offenses to narrow the range of crimes for which offenders can be incarcerated (Gottfredson, 1984; Kapsch and Luther, 1985).

Some of the back-door proposals by experts include easing the eligibility criteria for early release or parole (Austin, 1986; Semanchik, 1990), the administrative reduction of prison terms, whereby the governor or others shorten originally imposed sentences for certain offenders (Finn, 1984b; North Carolina Governor's Advisory Board on Prisons and Punishment, 1990), modifying parole revocation criteria so as to encourage fewer parole violations (Finn, 1984b), and expanding the number of community programs, including the use of intensive supervised parole for more serious offender groups (Skovron and Simms, 1990; South Carolina Reorganization Commission, 1991).

Violence and Inmate Discipline

Because of the diversity of races, ethnicities, and ages of jail and prison inmates, coupled with chronic overcrowding, inmate violence is not an unusual occurrence (Goetting and Howsen, 1986; Ruback and Carr, 1993; Wolfe, Vega, and Blount, 1992). The existence of gangs is conducive to inmate violence and is something officials cannot eliminate (Buentello et al., 1992; Peat and Winfree, 1992). Interestingly, gang membership in many state prisons accounts for a small proportion of prisoners. But inmate gangs in prison systems such as in Texas account for most of the inmate violence. For example, inmate gang members in Texas make up less than 3 percent of all inmates, but they are responsible for the majority of violence that occurs (Ralph and Marquart, 1992). Every prison has screening mechanisms for new inmates according to standard criteria, but misclassifications frequently occur. Dangerous offenders and the mentally retarded or ill often commit aggressive acts against other inmates (Toch and Adams, 1986). Short of using solitary confinement, most prisons lack policy provisions for segregating different classes of offenders. Correctional standards are being formulated continuously for improving the quality of life for inmates and treating those who need counseling or special services (McGee, Warner, and Harlow, 1985). But policy provisions for ensuring inmate safety from other violent inmates are almost nonexistent. Often, prisoners themselves must be creative and establish their own means of self-protection within prison walls (McCorkle, 1992; Peat and Winfree, 1992).

A national study of state prison inmates indicates that prison rules exist to regulate inmate conduct to assure orderly operation of the institution and to protect inmates and staff (Stephan, 1989:1). However, as Stephen reports, in 1986, a national survey of prisoners showed that 53 percent of them had violated one or more prison rules while confined. This study suggests that rule violation is pervasive throughout all prison systems. Generally, only the most visible inmate violence is recognized by prison officials. Many prisoners suffer physical injuries, and these incidents are frequently unreported or unrecorded. Even when correctional officers suspect or observe rule breaking and certain forms of inmate violence, this behavior is frequently ignored. Some researchers indicate that correctional officers often ignore this misconduct in order to obtain inmate cooperation and compliance with prison rules (Hewitt, Poole, and Regoli, 1984). This fact gives prisoners some degree of psychological control or power over those correctional officers who look the other way when they observe rule infractions.

Increasingly common are sexual assaults and psychological harassment in jails and prisons (Cotton and Groth, 1984), although the extent of sexual attacks in prisons may be exaggerated. A study of sexual violence in the United States Penitentiary at Lewisburg, Pennsylvania, disclosed that only 9 percent of all inmates were actual victims of sexual attacks. Although 29 percent of the inmates reported sexual propositions from other inmates, a majority had not been involved with any kind of inmate sexual misconduct (Nacci and Kane, 1983). But a growing problem for prison administrators is the rapid spread of Acquired Immune Deficiency Syndrome, or AIDS. In the Maryland State Prison System, for instance, AIDS is currently the leading cause of inmate deaths (Salive, Smith, and Brewer, 1990).

Solutions to the AIDS problem in prisons have included physical isolation of any prisoner testing positive for the AIDS virus, the distribution of condoms to prisoners who wish to engage in sexual relations with other inmates, and hospitalizing any AIDS carrier. But isolating prisoners with AIDS in special cells is cost-prohibitive. Solitary confinement for affected prisoners is a luxury most prisons cannot afford. Condom distribution is less expensive. But prison officials oppose condom distribution among inmates because of their potential use as weapons. Prisoners can fill them with acid or other caustic substances and throw them in other inmates' faces or at correctional officers. Condoms can also be used for strangulation. Since sodomy is prohibited by law in jurisdictions such as Florida, some officials believe that distributing condoms to prisoners would be interpreted as condoning sodomy and encouraging its occurrence (Williams, 1987:6–7). Some officials oppose AIDS testing because of the prohibitive costs of such tests. For example, Sheriff Jim Gondles of the Arlington, Virginia, County Jail says that the cost of testing every inmate for AIDS would double the county's annual medical budget (Williams, 1987:8).

Prison violence has been mitigated successfully in at least some state prisons. In one South Carolina prison, for example, the rate of violent assaults has been reduced by 18 percent since using the Adult Inmate Management System (AIMS), whereby weaker prisoners are segregated from more violent and sexually aggressive prisoners during evening hours. Even though 70 percent of the prisoners in that South Carolina facility have violent offense records, AIMS has the lowest protective custody rate among its inmates in the entire state. Leeke and Mohn (1986) believe that this is because there is greater prisoner participation in special programs as well as greater accessibility of prisoners to security and human services. And, in the Washington State Penitentiary at Walla Walla, administrators have trained staff to cope with inmate violence through an approach known as *prevention and reaction* (Buentello et al., 1992). With appropriate staff training, Washington correctional officers are learning to prevent new prisoners from joining prison gangs through various intervention activities.

An important tool used by prison officials to manipulate prisoners and control their violent conduct to a degree is through staff reports and recommendations. These reports and recommendations directly influence an inmate's good-time credit, earned by an inmate who obeys the prison rules. However, if there is an absence of incentives, such as early-release recommendations by correctional officers or officials based on a prisoner's good conduct, an important incentive for inmates to comply with prison rules is destroyed (Stojkovic, 1986).

In recent years, prisoners themselves have formed inmate disciplinary councils. These disciplinary councils exist apart from administrative sanctioning mechanisms. They are mechanisms whereby many inmate complaints against other inmates and even correctional officers can be resolved to the satisfaction of most parties (Kane, 1987; Schafer, 1986). All prisons at the state and federal levels currently have formal grievance procedures. These councils consist of inmates and one or two prison correctional officers. Prisoners regard the addition of the corrections officer as providing these councils with some objectivity when processing inmate grievances. These councils are similar to civil alternative **dispute resolution** scenarios, in which two grieving parties have their grievances settled by an impartial third party or arbiter. However, some experts see a direct connection between new jail and prison design and a reduction in inmate violence (Cronin, 1992).

Jail and Prison Design and Control

Some proposals for resolving jail and prison problems are (1) to create new jails and prisons constructed in ways that will conserve scarce space and require fewer correctional officers and (2) to reconstruct existing facilities to minimize prison violence and house more inmates. Recent prison construction has included increasingly popular modular designs (Sechrest, Pappas, and Price, 1987). New modular designs also permit layouts and arrangements of cell blocks to enhance officer monitoring of inmates. But new prison construction is expensive, and many jurisdictions are either unwilling or unable to undertake new prison construction projects (California Legislative Analyst, 1986; DeWitt, 1987). One idea is to expand existing facilities to accommodate larger numbers of prisoners.

The cost of new prison construction can be gauged according to the cost of each new unit or cell per inmate. On the average, unit costs of new prison construction in New York may run between $50,000 and $80,000 per inmate (Contact Center, Inc., 1987a). In Oklahoma, existing facilities were used to establish **modular jail designs** using prefabricated units at a cost of only $17,000 per inmate. Furthermore, with prefabricated designs, prison completion time was shortened considerably. The facility was completed in only nine months, since components could be previously assembled in other locations and transported to the building site without considering the variable of weather (DeWitt and Unger, 1987:4).

New jail and prison construction, the renovation or expansion of existing facilities, or the conversion of existing buildings previously used for other purposes take into account the matter of security and safety for both staff and inmates. Stairwells and areas otherwise hidden from the view of correctional officers encourage inmate sexual or other physical assaults (Fehr, 1983; Sechrest and Price, 1985). These areas can either be reduced or eliminated entirely with new architectural designs (DeWitt, 1986c). It is generally conceded that reducing blind spots or areas not directly visible to officers and other corrections officials helps to reduce the incidence of inmate assaults.

Vocational-Technical and Educational Programs in Jails and Prisons

Most jails are not equipped to provide inmates with any vocational-technical and educational programs. In fact, many prisons lack a broad variety of programs geared to enhance inmate skills and education (Schlossman and Spillane, 1992). This state of affairs seems consistent with the view that the rehabilitation orientation in American prisons is on the decline (Shichor, 1992). For instance, it has been found that for at least some of the major state prison systems, the influence of higher education programs on graduating inmates and their subsequent rates of recidivism has been ineffective (Lockwood, 1989). However, certain programs designed to rehabilitate sex offenders have had positive effects on decreasing offender recidivism (Sapp and Vaughn, 1989). For drug offenders in the U.S. Bureau of Prison's *Choice* program, the plan of drug treatment and intervention has been regarded as successful. Inmates with drug dependencies are subjected to a 10-month program, including the phases of intake, evaluation, and follow-up; drug education; exposure to the concepts of skills development, lifestyle modification, wellness, and responsibility; and individualized counseling and case supervision

BOX 5.2
Direct Supervision Jails

Many of the nation's jails were built prior to 1970, and many are 50 years old or more (Senese et al., 1992). These jails are not only architecturally unsound and unsafe, they also are designed so that jail officers cannot always monitor inmate behaviors. One answer to escalating inmate violence is the establishment of jail and prison facilities that permit greater inmate monitoring. A new innovation in inmate management, a hybrid of architectural design and inmate management principles, is the **direct supervision jail,** sometimes called *new generation jails* (Zupan, 1993:21). Direct supervision jails are constructed so as to provide officers with 180-degree lines of sight to monitor inmates (Turturici and Sheehy, 1993). Direct supervision jails employ a podular design and combine closed-circuit cameras to continuously observe inmates when celled (Stohr-Gillmore, Stohr-Gillmore, and Lovrich, 1990:29–30). Correctional officers are in the same "pod" as inmates. These pods consist of secure dormitory-like areas housing approximately 40 inmates. Inmates are monitored 24 hours a day. The first podular, direct supervision jail was constructed in Contra Costa, California, in 1981 (Hutchinson, 1993:132). Coercion and threats by inmates against others are minimized and all but eliminated through the direct supervision concept (Stohr-Gillmore et al., 1990:30). This is because all inmate behavior is subject to correctional officer scrutiny. Also, inmates have fairly direct access to correctional officers in their central work locations. In 1993, there were about 150 direct supervision jails in the United States, with plans in many jurisdictions for building more of them (Zupan, 1993:21).

Many jail administrators believe that a "competent, well-managed staff working in an inadequate, antiquated building is far preferable to a mediocre staff working in a modern, state-of-the-art facility" (Kiekbusch, 1985:134–135). The major recruitment problem is an insufficient quantity of quality personnel to perform correctional officer functions (Huggins, 1986:118). Jails are regarded by many people as the social dumping ground for misfits, misdemeanants, and others (Huggins, 1986:116–118; Zupan, 1993:21). Jails are usually among the lowest funding priorities. This often results in the recruitment of poorly qualified and trained staff. However, the advent of direct supervision jails is a stimulating innovation capable of attracting more competent officers.

Source: Adapted from Turturici and Sheehy, 1993:106.

(Walters et al., 1992). The emphasis in the *Choice* program is on education and the development of cognitive skills rather than on treatment and insight-oriented therapy.

In jails in which educational programs are offered, no guarantees exist that all jail inmates with educational deficiencies will enroll in such programs. In a suburban Texas county, for instance, courses were offered to jail inmates pertaining to counseling, stress management, and education. High school dropouts and high school graduates were identified and targeted for these different programs. A disappointing 26.7 percent of the high school dropouts enrolled in self-enriching courses or utilized counseling services. Even the participation rates of high school graduates were low. Only 14 percent of them took advantage of the offered programs (Tobolowsky, Quinn, and Holman, 1991).

Participation in jail or prison educational programs is mandatory in only 13 states (DiVito, 1991). Of those states, the primary inmate targets are those with obvious educational deficiencies who do not meet minimum educational criteria. Reduced sentence lengths are offered as incentives to participate in educational programs. The measure of success of such programs is whether inmates continue their education in jail or prison beyond the mandatory minimum (DiVito, 1991). One of the more innovative inmate literacy programs is operated by the Virginia Department of Corrections. Since September 1986, the "no read, no release" program has emphasized literacy achievement at no lower than the sixth-grade level and has made such an achievement part of the parole decision-making process (Oberst, 1988). Results have been favorably viewed by various states. However, compulsory educational programs in jails and prisons have been subjected to constitutional challenges in recent years (DiVito, 1991).

There is some unsettling information to suggest that those acquiring greater education while in prison have higher percentages of new convictions (Knepper, 1989). A study of 526 inmates who enrolled in prison college, vocational, secondary, and elementary programs examined their postrelease success experiences. While those who had taken college coursework and other skills courses exhibited fewer problems adjusting to life outside of prison, the more educated group had somewhat higher rates of recidivism attributable to new criminal convictions (Knepper, 1989). Admittedly, it is difficult to predict precisely which inmates will be more amenable to treatment than others, although attempts have frequently been made to do so (Armor et al., 1989). Older and better-educated inmates generally benefit more from prison educational programs compared with those younger offenders who perhaps are most in need of such education (Armor et al., 1989).

We must not be too hasty to cast aside the importance of intervention and educational or vocational training programs for youthful offenders, however. For instance, the Sandhills (North Carolina) Vocational Delivery System (VDS) is a vocational rehabilitation program offered to offenders aged 18 to 22 (Lattimore, Witt, and Baker, 1990). An experiment was conducted involving 295 youths in an experimental group of 295 inmates who participated in the VDS program and 296 youths in a control who did not participate. A postrelease analysis of the arrest records of both experimental and control group offenders showed that the experimental group had a significantly lower arrest record. Researchers attributed this success to participation in the VDS program, although further research was recommended to improve the reliability of these findings.

Parolees often benefit from the array of services extended to them in prison settings. Participating in educational programs, Alcoholics Anonymous, or some other educational or counseling is viewed as a desire to better oneself and indicative that rehabilitation may have occurred. As we have seen, rehabilitation may or may not occur for particular inmates, depending on whether they manipulate the system or use it for true self-improvement. In any case, parole boards seem impressed with whatever progress inmates manifest, regardless of an inmate's motives.

Jail and Prison Privatization

A proposal that has received mixed reactions in recent years is the **privatization** of jail and prison management (Mayer, 1986). Few proposals in corrections have ever stimulated as sharply divided opinions as the prospect of privately operated jails (Mullen, 1985:1). Legally, there is nothing to prevent private enterprises from operating prisons and jails as extensions of state and local governments and law enforcement agencies (Fenton, 1985). Few states have legislation on the subject (Hackett et al., 1987:2). It is imperative that if private enterprises ensure minimal standards currently guaranteed by the law and comply with basic constitutional guarantees, the private operation of incarcerative facilities appears feasible. In fact, the U.S. Marshal's Service awarded a large contract to two private firms to design, build, and operate a 440-bed detention facility for federal inmates at Leavenworth, Kansas, in 1990 (*Corrections Compendium,* 1990a:21). The contracts were awarded to Nashville-based Corrections Corporation of America (CCA) and the St. Louis-based Correctional Development Corporation (CDC). The detention site was to be operated for an initial one-year period as a maximum-security facility, with the contracts renewable for another four years. The new facility is believed by the U.S. Marshal's Office to save the government considerable money during its operation. Furthermore, it will ease the severe jail overcrowding and free up valuable jail space for federal prisoners awaiting trial, sentencing, or hearings in the greater Kansas City area. It is intended to house both medium- and maximum-security prisoners. The $71 per day per inmate cost is expected to include medical and dental services, food services, and security. CCA and CDC officials believe revenues will exceed $10 million annually. Despite the built-in profit margin, this cost is well below what the government would have spent to accommodate these prisoners in standard government facilities.

Privatization has been most noticeable in the juvenile justice system (McDonald, 1993; U.S. Office of Juvenile Justice and Delinquency Prevention, 1988). In fact, in 1989, over 40 percent of all incarcerated juveniles were being held in facilities owned and operated by private interests (McDonald, 1993). Private interests argue that they can manage and operate jails and prisons more effectively and economically than many government agencies. At present, this issue remains unresolved. However, there is no debating the fact that private sector proposals for the management of jails and other facilities have been increasing in recent years and result in considerable savings for the contracting local and state governments (Hackett et al., 1987).

A significant hurdle is the political control issue. Who has control over offenders housed in and managed by persons in the private sector? Another issue is an administrative one. Should private enterprises be allowed to sanction convicted offenders? Will the current level of quality of inmate care be maintained when operated by private interests? Many government facilities are currently under court order to improve their living conditions for inmates. It is unlikely that the private sector would do a poorer managerial task relating to inmate management. But the accountability issue persists. How can private jail officials be held accountable when inmate problems arise? In a legal analysis of this issue, Hackett et al. (1987:4–5) indicate that there are similar liabilities for private owners and operators, compared with sheriffs and other administrators, including correctional officers.

Privatization has also spread to probation and parole program operations (Bowman, Hakim, and Seidenstat, 1992). We have seen that private corporations can prepare presentence investigation reports, or PSIs. They can also assist probation and parole departments in supervising probationer- or parolee-clients. In fact, guidelines are presently available to local and state governments about how private interests can interface with their own program operations and organization (U.S. Office of Juvenile Justice and Delinquency Prevention, 1988). In fact, the privatization phenomenon in corrections is not unique to the United States. Many other countries are currently experimenting with it (McDonald, 1993).

A positive way to think of privatization in corrections is to view this phenomenon as an extension and a complement to existing public correctional programs (Feeley, 1991). Private interests have been instrumental in devising many correctional innovations, including electronic monitoring and new technology for surveillance, control, and drug testing (Feeley, 1991). Feeley's arguments are persuasive. Private innovators in corrections have made it possible for many convicted offenders to become enrolled in intermediate punishment programs and endure many sanctions imposed in lieu of traditional incarceration in a jail or prison. Charles Logan (1993) also is convincing when he notes that private prisons tend to outperform public ones on numerous salient dimensions. He compared a private, a state, and a federal women's prison in New Mexico. He defined quality according to 333 indicators. The state prison consisted of 132 inmates and 112 staff members, while the private facility had 134 inmates and 76 staff members. The federal facility had 78 staff members and comparable numbers of inmates. By quite substantial margins, the private facility was superior on almost every dimension, including security, safety, order, activity, and conditions of confinement (Logan, 1993).

THE ROLE OF JAILS AND PRISONS IN PROBATION AND PAROLE DECISION MAKING

Whether inmates are in jails or prisons, they are obligated to comply with specific behavioral guidelines that will permit jail and prison officials to maintain order and discipline. Besides these requirements, many prisons and some jails have programs designed to assist inmates in different ways. Educational or vocational training are more readily available in prison settings, although some of the larger jails offer similar programs for long-term offenders. Remember that many jails have contracts with state and federal prison systems to house some of their inmate overflow. Thus, not every jail inmate is incarcerated for shorter intervals of a year or less. Counseling and other forms of assistance are available to inmates if they want such services. As we have seen, in some states, such as Virginia, a minimum amount of education is required as a release condition. Therefore, Virginia inmates are compelled to participate in educational programs since this participation will favorably influence their early release.

Jail and prison officers and administrators are in positions of submitting written reports about inmate conduct while confined. These reports may contain favorable or unfavorable information. Ultimately, this information is made available to paroling authorities so that a more informed parole decision can be made. If inmates cannot conduct themselves in a setting with explicit rules and regulations, then it is presumed that they cannot function well in their communities if released short of serving their full prison terms.

The federal government has experimented with various predictive classification systems used for pretrial detainees (Garner, 1991). Therefore, even in instances in which one's guilt or innocence has not yet been established through trial, some preliminary screening mechanisms have already been implemented that may impact either favorably or unfavorably on a judge's sentencing decision later. In the Federal Bureau of Prisons, for instance, pretrial detainees have been screened by various instruments and according to different predictive criteria to determine which alleged offenders would be good candidates for pretrial release. The results of such experimentation have been thus far inconclusive.

Attempts have also been made to forecast the successfulness of probationers based, in part, on their incarcerative experiences. In Eastern Pasco County, Florida, for example, a sample of 427 probationers sentenced to community supervision was examined between 1980 and 1982, with a follow-up investigation in 1987 (Liberton, Silverman, and Blount, 1992). Some of the probationers had been held in jails in pretrial detention until their trials. Others had been released on their own recognizance (ROR). Interestingly, researchers found that those offenders who had been incarcerated for periods exceeding two days had a much higher rate of recidivism compared with those offenders who were ROR. Specifically, the researchers found an inverse relationship between the length of pretrial commitment and the successful completion of probation. Factors relating to successful probation completion included being older, employed, and married and having some previous military service. We might speculate here that those offenders who were held in pretrial detention may have been more serious offenders compared with the ROR sample. Obviously, there were reasons for not allowing them to remain free in their communities pending their trial.

Some jails and most prisons attempt to screen incoming inmates according to their risk or dangerousness as well as their special needs (Krauth, 1991:131). Screening is also conducted to evaluate offenders and determine the most suitable level of custody for them (Alexander and Austin, 1992). Since it becomes increasingly expensive to monitor offenders as the level of custody increases (e.g., from minimum-security to medium-security, from medium-security to maximum-security), it is in an institution's best interests economically to maintain prisoners at the least intense custody level while they are confined. This is why most prisons have reassessments of inmates periodically (e.g., every six months or one year) to determine whether their present level of custody should be increased or decreased. And, this thinking is not particularly new. In 1981, for instance, Holt, Ducat, and Eakles (1981:24) advocated four conceptual goals pertaining to prisoner classification systems:

1. All inmates should be placed in the lowest custody level consistent with public safety.
2. Inmates should be classified on the basis of objective information and objective criteria.
3. The process must be applied uniformly, so that similarly situated inmates receive similar custody assignments.
4. The system must provide for centralized control over the process.

A major problem in most institutions today is overcrowding. This is especially true of our nation's jails, where chronic jail overcrowding has been characterized as having reached epidemic proportions (Moore and Ford, 1993:16). One direct solution to jail overcrowding is to release certain offenders. Decisions by jail administrators to grant early release to certain offenders is similar to parole by parole boards. Some experts have proposed to reduce jail overcrowding by expanding furloughs and transitional community correctional programs by increasing an inmate's eligibility for such programs (Moore and Ford, 1993:17). Indeed, jail officials must balance their concern for public safety with their general responsibility to inmates to provide access to rehabilitation programs and place deserving inmates in minimum-custody status (Brennan and Wells, 1992:51).

Of course, other actors in the criminal justice system, such as prosecutors and judges, can affect reductions in jail overcrowding if they ease up on excessive bail bonds for nonserious offenders or if they speed up their case processing and trial dates. Pretrial detainees account for a substantial portion of those incarcerated, as we have seen. Expanding programs of pretrial diversion have also been advocated (Moore and Ford, 1993:22). Jails can be quite influential in determining which offenders should have their incarcerative stays shortened (Ayres, 1988).

For inmates in various state and federal prison systems, inmate classifications are very important in several respects. Imposing more stringent monitoring and closer custody on those prisoners who are considered most aggressive and violent will serve to protect less serious and nonviolent inmates. Beyond this, the lower the classification level, the more the trust accorded that inmate. Parole boards consider the present level of custody and the behavior at that particular custody level. Again, it is in a prisoner's best interests to be confined at the lowest security level possible. Therefore, periodic reclassifications of offenders that tend to downgrade their present levels of custody are positive moves that influence parole chances accordingly. The prison system itself plays a crucial role in determining whether parole will be granted. Other relevant factors are the seriousness of the conviction offense, length of the original sentence, and the amount of time served in relation to that sentence length.

Good-time credits are applied toward the original sentence in most jurisdictions. Good-time credits are days deducted from the total sentence length. Good-time credits vary widely from state to state. The federal system grants federal prisoners 54 days per year as good-time credit against their original sentence lengths.

Oklahoma gives its prisoners 45 days of credit for every 30 days served. Most other jurisdictions are somewhere in between these ranges. But good behavior, involvement in prison educational and vocational programs, and individual or group therapy and counseling may be insufficient in certain prospective parolee cases.

For example, Patricia Krenwinkle and Leslie Van Houten, two women who were members of Charles Manson's "family" and convicted of the murders of several persons in the late 1960s, including actress Sharon Tate, appeared before the California Parole Board in 1993 for parole consideration. Despite impeccable and noteworthy behavior and accomplishments while confined, these women were rejected by the parole board as continuing public safety risks. These are special-circumstances cases involving a highly publicized event. Other offenders in California who have been convicted of equally heinous crimes, but with little or no prior publicity, have been paroled during the same time interval while these women have remained incarcerated.

In sum, jails and prisons are playing increasingly important roles in probation and parole decision making. Jails are devising more sophisticated classification procedures commensurate with those used in most prison systems. These classification systems are helpful in separating offenders according to several criteria that optimize their safety and needs. As jails become more like prisons by establishing a broader array of inmate programs of an educational and vocational nature, inmates themselves will be able to do more to influence their chances of more favorable treatment. They can take affirmative steps to ensure their involvement in community correctional programs where fewer restrictions exist. In the following two chapters, the parole decision-making process is examined. We will obtain a clearer picture of how an inmate's institutional behaviors relate to parole board early-release decision making.

KEY TERMS

American Correctional Association (ACA)
Auburn State Penitentiary
Bridewell workhouse
Burnout
Congregate system
Sir Walter Crofton
Detainer warrant
Direct supervision jail
Dispute resolution
Elmira Reformatory
Gaols
John Howard
Inmate classification
Lockdown
Lock-up
Captain Alexander Maconochie

Maxi-maxi prisons
Maximum-security prisons
Medium-security prisons
Minimum-security prisons
Modular jail designs
Penitentiary
Pretrial detainees
Pretrial detention
Preventive detention
Privatization
Solitary confinement
Tier system
Total institutions
Walnut Street Jail
Workhouse

QUESTIONS FOR REVIEW

1. What are some important events in the evolution of jails in the United States?
2. What are some general functions of jails? How do these contrast with the functions of prisons?
3. What are some of the major sociodemographic characteristics of prison inmates? Do prison inmates differ markedly from jail inmates? In what ways?
4. In what ways are jails becoming more like prisons? Explain.
5. What is privatization? How does privatization impact upon prison and jail overcrowding?
6. What is meant by jail and prison overcrowding? What strategies have been suggested to alleviate jail and prison overcrowding?
7. What problems do mentally ill and retarded inmates pose to institutional officials? Why should these persons be problematic for jail officials?
8. What are some recent developments in jail and prison architecture that have become a part of the new generation of jails and prisons?
9. What were some of the innovations introduced by the Auburn State Penitentiary? Are any of these innovations still in evidence in modern-day prisons?
10. How do jails differ from lock-ups and drunk tanks?

6

Parole and Parolees
History, Philosophy, Goals, and Functions

Introduction

Parole Defined

The Historical Context of Parole

Parole and Alternative Sentencing Systems

The Philosophy of Parole

The Functions of Parole

A Profile of Parolees in the United States

Parole Trends

Key Terms

Questions for Review

INTRODUCTION

In 1795, Jonathan Doe of Boston, Massachusetts, committed a crime and was sentenced to 10 years in prison at hard labor. Mr. Doe served the entire 10 years. Mr. Doe was a model prisoner. He did as he was told when he was told to do it. Prison officials kept no records and made no evaluations of Mr. Doe's progress while in prison. Mr. Doe broke rocks, cleared brush, and performed many other duties for 10 years. He was fed three times per day, and he was confined to a cell with others during the evening hours. Mr. Doe's life in prison was highly predictable. And, it was highly predictable for 10 years.

Two hundred years later in 1995, Jonathan Doe VI, one of Mr. Doe's descendants, was also living in Boston, Massachusetts, and committed a similar crime. When Mr. Doe VI was convicted, the judge ordered a presentence investigation, and, based on that information, sentenced Mr. Doe VI to 10 years in prison. Mr. Doe VI was a model prisoner. After Mr. Doe VI had served 18 months, a parole board convened and considered his good behavior and good-time credits. Their decision was to parole Mr. Doe VI into the custody of a parole officer. Now, Mr. Doe VI is under minimal supervision by a Massachusetts parole officer, lives at home in his community, is married and has children, is employed with a good company, and enjoys most of the freedoms that other citizens do.

This chapter is about what has happened in the last 200 years, especially during the 1980s and 1990s, to cause differences in the treatment of Mr. Doe VI and his ancestor. A brief history of parole in the United States is provided. Also included is a discussion of the philosophy of parole, some of the more important functions served by parole, and a general profile of parolees.

PAROLE DEFINED

Parole is the conditional release of a prisoner from incarceration (either from prison or jail) under supervision after a portion of the sentence has been served (Clear and Cole, 1986:539). Thus, the major distinguishing feature between probation and parole is that parolees have served some time incarcerated in either jail or prison, while probationers have avoided incarceration, with limited exceptions [see *shock probation*, Chapter 1]. Some common characteristics shared by both parolees and probationers are that (1) they have committed crimes, (2) they have been convicted of crimes, (3) they are under the supervision or control of probation or parole officers, and (4) they are subject to one or more similar conditions accompanying their probation or parole programs. Some general differences are that generally, parolees have committed more serious offenses, compared with probationers. And, parolees have been incarcerated for a portion of their sentences, whereas probationers are not generally incarcerated following their convictions for crimes. Furthermore, parolees may have more stringent conditions (e.g., curfew, participation in drug or alcohol rehabilitation, counseling, halfway house participation, more face-to-face contacts with their POs) accompanying their parole programs, compared with probationers.

THE HISTORICAL CONTEXT OF PAROLE

Experts differ about the origins of parole in the United States. However, it is generally agreed that parole, or at least an early version of it, existed in eighteenth-century Spain, France, England, and Wales (Bottomley, 1984; Hughes, 1987). British convicts under sentence of death or convicted of other serious offenses created for England a problem that the United States currently confronts: prison overcrowding. In the eighteenth century, Britain had no penitentiaries (Hughes, 1987; Evans, 1982). But one option available was to export excess prisoners to the American colonies. After the Revolutionary War, this option no longer existed.

Seeking new locations for isolating its criminals from the rest of society, England selected Australia, one of several remote English colonies that had accommodated small numbers of offenders during the American colonial period when prisoner exportation was popular (Fogel, 1979:4–5). The first large group of convicts from England came to Australia in 1788 (Hughes, 1987). Many of these transportees were convicted of minor theft, and the English government intended that they become builders and farmers. However, these were trades at which they were highly unsuccessful (Hughes, 1987). It became apparent that officials needed to establish prisons to house some of their prisoner-transportees. One such outpost 1,000 miles off the coast of Australia was **Norfolk Island,** where a penal colony was established. Another was **Van Dieman's Land.**

The private secretary to the lieutenant governor of Van Diemen's Land in 1836 was a former Royal Navy officer and social reformer, Alexander Maconochie (1787–1860). In 1840, Maconochie was appointed superintendent of the penal colony at Norfolk Island. When he arrived to assume his new duties, he was appalled by what he found. Prisoners were lashed repeatedly and tortured frequently by other means.

Because of Maconochie's personal views and penchant for humanitarianism, his lenient administrative style toward prisoners was unpopular with his superiors as well as other penal officials. For instance, Maconochie believed that confinement ought to be rehabilitative, not punitive. And, he believed that prisoners ought to be granted early release from custody if they behaved well and did good work while confined. Thus, he gave prisoners **marks of commendation** and authorized early release of some inmates who demonstrated a willingness and ability to behave well in society on the outside. This action was an early manifestation of indeterminate sentencing that was subsequently practiced in the United States. Maconochie's downfall at Norfolk Island occurred largely because of a report he filed condemning the English penal system generally and disciplinary measures used by the island penal colony specifically. He was relieved of his superintendent duties and sent back to England in 1844.

During the next five years, Maconochie was transferred from one desk job to another, although he continued to press for penal reforms. Eventually he was reassigned, probably as a probationary move by his superiors, to the governorship of the new Birmingham Borough Prison. His position there lasted less than two years. His superiors dismissed him for being too lenient with prisoners.

Maconochie's prison reform work did not end with this dismissal. In 1853, he successfully lobbied for the passage of the English Penal Servitude Act that established several rehabilitation programs for inmates and abolished transporting prisoners to Australia. Because of these significant improvements in British penal policy and the institutionalization of early-release provisions throughout England's prison system, Maconochie is credited as being the father of parole.

Impressed with Maconochie's work, Sir Walter Crofton, a prison reformer and director of Ireland's prison system during the 1850s, copied Maconochie's three-stage intermediate system whereby Irish prisoners could earn their early conditional release. Crofton, also known as another father of parole in various European countries, modified Maconochie's plan in such a way that prisoners would be subject to (1) strict imprisonment for a time; (2) transfer to an "intermediate" prison for a short period, where they could participate in educational programs and perform useful and responsible tasks to earn **good marks;** and (3) given **tickets-of-leave** and released from prison on license under the limited supervision of local police.

Under this third ticket-of-leave stage, released prisoners were required to submit monthly reports of their progress to police who assisted them in finding work. A study of 557 prisoners during that period showed only 17 had their tickets-of-leave revoked for various infractions (Clear and Cole, 1986:372). Thus, Walter Crofton pioneered what later came to be known as several major functions of parole officers: employment assistance to released prisoners, regular visits by officers to parolees, and the general supervision of their activities (Cole, 1986:595).

The U.S. connection with the European use of parole allegedly occurred in 1863 when Gaylord Hubbell, the warden at Sing Sing Prison, New York, visited Ireland and conferred with Crofton about his penal innovations and parole system (Clear and Cole, 1986:372). Subsequently, the National Prison Association convened in Cincinnati, Ohio, in 1870 and considered the Irish parole system as a primary portion of its agenda. Attending that meeting were Crofton, Hubbell, and other reformers and penologists. The meeting resulted in the establishment of a Declaration of Principles, which promoted an "indeterminate sentence" and a classification system based largely on Crofton's work (Clear and Cole, 1986:372-373).

Zebulon Brockway became the new superintendent of the New York State Reformatory at Elmira in 1876 and was instrumental in the passage of the first indeterminate sentencing law in the United States (Smykla, 1981:139–140). He is also credited with introducing the first **good-time system,** whereby an inmate's sentence to be served is reduced by the number of good marks earned. Once this system was in operation and shown to be moderately effective, several other states patterned their own early-release standards after it in later years.

Zebulon Brockway and Elmira Reformatory are important, in part, because they are credited with originating the good-time release system for prisoners in 1876. The practice of using early release for inmates occurred in the United States much earlier, although authorities dispute its true origin. Dressler (1969) claims parole was officially established in Boston by Samuel G. Howe in 1847. From 1790 to 1817, convicts were obligated to serve their entire sentences in prison.

In 1817, New York adopted a form of commutation or lessening of sentence that became known as *good time.* Through the accumulation of sufficient good time, an inmate could be granted early release through his good behavior (Levine, Musheno, and Palumbo, 1986:551; Smykla, 1981:139–140). This good-time early release was essentially a **pardon,** an executive device designed to absolve offenders of their crimes committed and release them, thus reducing the prison overcrowding. The unofficial practice of parole, therefore, preceded the unofficial practice of probation by several decades. Officially, however, true parole resulted from the ticket-of-leave practice and was first adopted by Massachusetts in 1884, also the state first officially implementing the practice of probation in 1878 (Shane-DuBow, Brown, and Olsen, 1985:4–5).

PAROLE AND ALTERNATIVE SENTENCING SYSTEMS

Indeterminate Sentencing and Parole

A general relation exists between *indeterminate sentencing* and *parole* (Clear and Cole, 1986:372–373). However, when jurisdictions adopt indeterminate sentencing schemes, this does not mean that either parole or parole boards are automatically established. As we saw in Chapter 1, indeterminate sentencing indicates a minimum and a maximum term of years or months inmates may serve. Ordinarily, inmates must serve the minimum amount of time specified, but they may be released in different ways short of serving their full terms. Ordinarily, parole boards determine early-release dates for inmates under this type of sentencing system. But there are other early-release options besides parole board actions. For example, by 1911, 9 states were using indeterminate sentencing (Shane-DuBow, Brown, and Olsen, 1985:6). However, 11 years earlier in 1900, 20 states had established parole plans to effect the early release of prison inmates (Clear and Cole, 1986:373). Some of these jurisdictions had *mandatory* sentencing provisions, while others had *determinate* sentencing schemes. Early release short of serving one's full term could be administratively granted, from prison officials or the governor, or through the accumulation of good-time credits applied against the maximum time to be served. In short, it is not the case that indeterminate sentencing and parole boards must coexist in any jurisdiction simultaneously.

Usually, a parole system in any state prison consisted of the warden and other local authorities including the prison physician, the superintendent of prisons, and certain community officials (Clear and Cole, 1986:373). The federal prison system had no formal parole board until 1910, and it was similarly comprised of officials making up state parole boards. Prior to the establishment of these boards and within the context of indeterminate sentencing, the discretion to release a prisoner short of serving his or her full term rested with the prison warden, superintendent, or state governor.

By 1944, all states had parole systems. The U.S. Congress formally established a United States Board of Parole in 1930 (Clear and Cole, 1986:373). And by the 1960s, all states had some form of indeterminate sentencing. Apart from the obvious benefits of reducing prison overcrowding, parole and indeterminate sentencing were perceived for nearly a century as panaceas for reforming criminals. The rehabilitative ideal dominated the structure and process of all phases of corrections as well as most corrections programs.

Not all states used parole for rehabilitative purposes, however. In 1893, California adopted parole as a way of minimizing the use of clemency by governors and to correct and/or modify excessive prison sentences in relation to certain crimes committed (Messinger et al., 1985). In fact, officials who favored parole in California were skeptical about its rehabilitative value. Parole was seen primarily as a period during which the end of a determinate sentence that was originally imposed by the court would occur (Messinger et al, 1985).

But a majority of the states stressed the rehabilitative value of indeterminate sentencing and parole generally. While the principle of *deterrence* dominated corrections philosophy for most of the period between 1820 and 1900, from 1900 to 1960, the principle of *rehabilitation* was of primary importance (Rothman, 1983). Indeterminate sentencing was largely in the hands of corrections "experts" such as social workers, wardens, and probation and parole officers (Rothman, 1983).

One early criticism of parole was contained in a series of reports issued in 1931 by the **Wickersham Commission,** a National Commission on Law Observance and Enforcement (National Commission on Law Observance and Enforcement, 1931). The Wickersham Commission derived its name from its chairman, George W. Wickersham, a former U.S. attorney general. Prepared shortly after the Prohibition era and the Great Depression, the Wickersham reports were very critical of most criminal justice agencies and how they dealt with crime and criminals.

Although parole was not the sole target of criticism by the Wickersham Commission, it did receive more than its fair share of complaints. Among the criticisms was that parole caused the release of many dangerous criminals into society, unrehabilitated and inadequately supervised. Also, Wickersham Commission members did not believe that a suitable system existed for determining which prisoners should be eligible for parole. While these reports resulted in much debate among corrections professionals for the next decade or so, nothing was accomplished that significantly altered the operations of state or federal parole systems. The rehabilitation or medical model became increasingly popular, together with social work and psychiatry, as members of these helping professions attempted to treat prisoner adjustment problems through therapy, medicine, and counseling.

Pros and Cons of Indeterminate Sentencing in Relation to Parole

Fogel and Hudson (1981:72–74) have effectively summarized the major positive and negative aspects of indeterminate sentencing in their work, *Justice as Fairness.* The positive aspects of indeterminate sentencing are that it

1. Allows for full implementation of rehabilitative ideal.
2. Offers the best means of motivating involuntarily committed inmates to work for rehabilitation.
3. Offers maximum protection to society from hard-core recidivists and mentally defective offenders.
4. Helps maintain an orderly environment within the institution.
5. Prevents unnecessary incarceration of an offender and thus helps to prevent the correctional system from becoming a factory from which offenders emerge as hardened criminals.
6. Offers a feasible alternative to capital punishment.

7. Removes judgment as to length of incarceration from the trial court and puts it in the hands of a qualified panel of behavioral experts who make their final decision based on considerably more evidence than is available at the postconviction stage of the trial.
8. Decision as to length of incarceration reflects the needs of the offender and not the gravity of the crime, in the best interests of both society and offender.
9. Prevents correctional authorities from being forced to release from custody an offender who is clearly not ready to rejoin society.
10. Prevents a problem offender from retreating into a "sick" role during rehabilitation.
11. Acts as a deterrent to crime.

Among the negative features of indeterminate sentences are

1. Treatment is a myth, and vocational training is a fraud; inmates are neither treated, trained, nor rehabilitated.
2. Even if treatment were honestly attempted by staffs, psychotherapy with involuntarily committed patients is generally considered difficult; indeterminate sentencing supplies only negative motivation which will be insufficient for long-range results.
3. Even if effective therapy were plausible for some offenders, it is neither justified nor proper for all offenders, and there should be a right not to receive unwanted therapy.
4. Treatment is tokenism and rehabilitation is almost nonexistent; therefore, the indeterminate sentence is a device to hide society's dehumanizing treatment of criminals, particularly those who are poor or members of minority groups.
5. While taking criminals off the street, indeterminate sentencing makes it easy for society to ignore the underlying causes of crime.
6. The indeterminate sentence is most often used as an instrument of inmate control.
7. Psychiatrists become more jailers than healers; they know they will have to testify later in court about the patient and recommend or not recommend a prisoner's release.
8. Designation of some offenders as mentally ill is extremely arbitrary; therefore, single treatment approaches are impossible to devise.
9. There is great danger that indeterminate sentencing will be used to punish persons for unpopular political beliefs and views; religious and political nonconformists are the ones most likely to rebel against the therapeutic system.
10. Indeterminate sentence encourages the smart or cunning offender and is more favorable to him [or her] than to the less intelligent offender.
11. Despite the fact that courts are supposed to retain some measure of control, there is no adequate protection from life imprisonment under the guise of indeterminate sentencing. (Fogel and Hudson, 1981:72–75)

Because of rising crime rates, unacceptable levels of recidivism among parolees, and general dissension among the ranks of corrections professionals about the most effective ways of dealing with offenders, the 1970s reflected a gradual decline in the significance and influence of the rehabilitation model (Jacks and Cox, 1984). However, selected jurisdictions have reported success with parole programs in which effective community supervision and offender management have been provided, or where POs have performed their supervisory roles properly (Atkinson, 1986; Byrne and Brewster, 1993; Dickey, 1989). Whether parole rehabilitates is arguable. In any case, the rehabilitation model has been largely replaced by the justice model (Fogel, 1979).

The mission of the justice model or perspective is *fairness*, whereby prison is regarded as the instrument whereby sentences are implemented and is not to be held accountable for rehabilitating offenders. Fogel (1979:202) says that

> The period of incarceration can be conceptualized as a time in which we try to reorient a prisoner to the lawful use of power. One of the more fruitful ways the prison can teach non-lawabiders to be law-abiding is to treat them in a lawful manner. The entire effort of the prison should be seen as an influence attempt based upon operationalizing justice. This is called the justice model.

In turn, the justice model has assisted greatly in prompting most states as well as the federal government to undertake extensive revisions of their sentencing guidelines. The general thrust of these revisions is toward a "get tough on crime" crusade that is replacing reform with retribution (Cullen and Travis, 1984; Fogel and Hudson, 1981:14).

Another goal of the justice model is to minimize if not eliminate entirely any sentencing disparities often associated with indeterminate sentencing schemes and the arbitrariness of parole board decisions (Goodstein and Hepburn, 1985:16–22). It is questionable, however, whether any sentencing scheme will achieve such desirable results. Some authorities suggest that there is every reason to believe that judges will continue to impose sentences according to previous discriminatory patterns where extra-legal factors are influential. These extra-legal factors include race, ethnicity, gender, age (in some cases), and socioeconomic status (Holmes et al., 1993; Steffensmeier, Kramer, and Streifel, 1993).

The Shift to Determinate Sentencing

Determinate Sentencing.   Nearly one third of all states had shifted from indeterminate to determinate sentencing by 1985 (Shane-DuBow, Brown, and Olsen, 1985). These sentencing shifts have resulted in the abolition of paroling authority in a few states for making early prisoner release decisions. An additional consequence has been to limit the discretionary sentencing power of judges. The remaining states and the District of Columbia have also instituted numerous sentencing reforms calculated to deal more harshly with offenders; to reduce or eliminate sentencing disparities attributable to race, ethnicity, or socioeconomic status; to increase prisoner release predictability as well as the certainty of incarceration; and/or to deter or control crime (Abt Associates, Inc., 1987; Goodstein, Kramer, and Nuss, 1984). In many of these states, the authority of parole boards to grant early release as well as the calculation of good-time credits has been restricted to varying degrees.

Sentencing Guidelines.   On November 1, 1987, the United States Sentencing Commission revamped entirely existing sentencing guidelines for federal district judges (Broderick et al., 1993; Champion, 1989). The long-range implications of these changes are unknown. However, some preliminary estimates have been projected. For instance, the average time served prior to November 1, 1987, for kidnapping was from 7.2 to 9 years. The new guidelines provide an incarceration period for offenders of from 4.2 to 5.2 years. However, for first-degree murder convictions, the new guidelines prescribe 30 years to life for all offenders, compared with 10 to 12.5 years time served, on the average, under old sentencing practices by federal judges. Therefore, in some cases more convicted felons will go to prison, but many of these offenses will carry shorter incarceration terms.

While these sentencing guidelines are applicable only to United States district courts and federal judges and magistrates, some states have similar guidelines-based or presumptive sentencing schemes (Burke, 1987:76). Other states such as California, Minnesota, Pennsylvania, and Washington already have existing penalties for certain offenses that are similar in severity to those prescribed for the same offenses by the U.S. sentencing guidelines. By 1991, at least 17 states had established sentencing guidelines for their prison inmates (*Corrections Compendium,* 1991b:10). There are various implications for offenders who are sentenced according to the guidelines. For instance, under existing California sentencing guidelines that became effective in 1977, Judge Robert Altman sentenced Los Angeles gang member Michael Hagan, 23, to the maximum term of 27 years to life in 1987 for the first-degree murder of 17-year old Kellie Mosier. Although the California parole board has been replaced by the Board of Prison Terms, it is doubtful that Hagan will serve the maximum term for his offense. First, one of the responsibilities of the Board of Prison Terms is to meet periodically and consider parole for offenders such as Hagan who are sentenced to life (American Correctional Association, 1994:40). And, the California guidelines did not abolish good-time credit, which can reduce time served by at least one-half (Shane-DuBow, Brown, and Olsen, 1985:35). Some authorities have suggested that it may be necessary to revive some version of a parole board in California in future years to overcome current legislative inflexibility in dealing with the problem of growing prison overcrowding (Casper, Brereton, and Neal, 1981). The creation of the California Board of Prison Terms has only partly remedied this problem, since its primary focus is on those serving life sentences (American Correctional Association, 1994:40).

In Pennsylvania, sentencing guidelines were introduced in the early 1980s (*Corrections Compendium,* 1992d:18). Compared with an indeterminate sentencing scheme used prior to these guidelines, actual sentences imposed have become more severe for violent offenders. But sentencing severity has also increased for many nonviolent property offenders as well. It is unclear whether this outcome was contemplated by the Pennsylvania State Legislature when the guidelines were determined. At least one objective of Pennsylvania's guidelines was to remedy sentencing disparities. Some evidence suggests that this outcome has been realized in part. But the Pennsylvania state prison population growth occurred at the rate of 171 percent during the 1980s, so that by 1990, the prison system accommodated more than 24,000 inmates in space actually designed for 16,000 inmates. At the time of this writing, Pennsylvania authorities were constructing new prison space to house

10,000 additional offenders at a cost of $1.3 billion (*Corrections Compendium,* 1992d:18).

Critics have said that although determinate sentencing may provide prisoners with release certainty and possibly result in more fairness in the sentencing process, there are several discretionary decisions at various stages in the adjudication and postadjudication period uncontrolled by this sentencing form (Goodstein, Kramer, and Nuss, 1984). Six decision-making stages and/or factors have been identified as critical to sentencing equity and predictability:

1. The decision to incarcerate.
2. The characteristics of the penalty scaling system, including the numbers of penalty ranges and offense categories.
3. Presence or absence of aggravating or mitigating circumstances.
4. The parole review process.
5. The use of good time in calculating early release.
6. Revocation from supervised release. (Goodstein, Kramer, and Nuss, 1984)

In addition, prosecutorial discretion about which cases to drop or pursue, reports of arresting officers and circumstances surrounding arrests, evidentiary factors, and judicial idiosyncrasies figure prominently in many sentencing decisions at state and federal levels (Champion, 1987a; 1987b). Thus, regardless of the nature and scope of existing sentencing provisions, the prospects for the effective control over all of the relevant discretionary decisions that influence sentencing are not overwhelmingly favorable (Goodstein, Kramer, and Nuss, 1984). Although parole boards in 36 states have continued to exercise discretion over the early release of prisoners, parole continues to draw criticism from both the public and corrections professionals (Corrothers, 1986:26; Metchik, 1992a, 1992b). Many people believe parole ought to be abolished. Determinate sentencing is believed to be a major cure to many of corrections' ills.

However, there is ample evidence to suggest that determinate sentencing in various states is not achieving results as originally predicted. For example, Minnesota implemented one of the most comprehensive and rigorous sets of sentencing guidelines in the United States in 1980. Researchers who compared preguideline data (1978) with data from three postguideline periods (1981, 1982, and 1984) concluded that while sentencing uniformity, neutrality, and proportionality were achieved in the early years of these reforms, these gains had diminished by 1984 (Moore and Miethe, 1987). And, in Indiana, the third state to adopt determinate sentencing in 1977, determinate sentencing has been found to have questionable legitimacy among lawmakers and corrections professionals (Hamm, 1987). In fact, Hamm (1987) concludes that the justice model as applied in Indiana is only a myth that obscures the true roles of correctional officials and their policies and leads to legislative misunderstandings.

The list of determinate sentencing critics is seemingly endless. In Colorado, no significant differences have been found between pre- and postdeterminate sentencing groups of offenders concerning either their likelihood of being convicted or going to prison (Covey and Mande, 1985). And a survey in 1984–1985 of sentencing reforms in 44 states designed to result in longer terms of incarceration for a special class of offenders, drug traffickers, disclosed no significant differences between those traffickers sentenced in pre- and postreform periods (Wakefield, 1985). In fact, as the result of these recent sentencing reforms, drug traffickers have tended to receive shorter sentences in those states surveyed!

Sensing a growing public distrust of parole and how offenders are punished, the American Correctional Association established a Task Force on Parole to carefully scrutinize how states have evolved their present parole policies and guidelines (Jackson, 1986:28). This Task Force has already found that parole is undergoing alteration in various jurisdictions because of both political and public pressures. States such as Pennsylvania have established guidelines for their parole boards to follow for making their early release decisions about offenders. These guidelines are similar to the ones created in these same states for judicial sentencing decisions.

One proponent of perpetuating parole boards says that abolishing parole has not led to fairer, more predictable, or less confusing sentencing (Breed, 1984). The fairest approach to managing the convicted offender in a fair and humane manner is to retain parole boards. However, objective parole guidelines coupled with court intervention and voluntary reforms should be introduced. A real need exists for rewarding "superior prisoner efforts" beyond passive avoidance of rule infractions (Breed, 1984). Parole also is viewed as a continuation of punishment in a rehabilitative context. Thus, parolees who are supervised effectively in their communities stand a much better chance of becoming rehabilitated and law abiding than they would if confined for their full terms (Atkinson, 1986). Atkinson (1986:54) says that strong parole systems do not release inmates who pose an undue risk to public safety or who would unlikely benefit from rehabilitative services in their communities.

Good-Time Credits and Early Release. Su Davis (1990a:1) says that good-time credits may be called *gain time, earned time, statutory time, meritorious time, commutation time, provisional credits, good conduct credits,* or *disciplinary credits.* Regardless of the term, good time is correction's carrot for good behavior and a management tool of long standing in U.S. prisons. Thus, when a convicted offender is sentenced to 10 years in an Arkansas State Prison, the offender knows that for every month served behind bars, 30 days will be deducted from the 10-year maximum term. Serving 6 years in an Iowa prison, therefore, will mean that 3 years of one's sentence is deducted from the original 10-year term. It doesn't take a mathematical genius to determine that an inmate can be released automatically by the Arkansas prison system if about 6 years, 8 months are served. Three years, 4 months will be deducted from the 10-year maximum, entitling the Arkansas inmate to either *conditional* or *unconditional* early release. This is not the same thing as being *paroled.* In this case, the Arkansas prisoner has done the time, paid the price, and is free to leave prison without having to adhere to any parole conditions. However, in most jurisdictions, inmates released as the result of good-time credits applied against their original sentences must serve either some or all of their remain-

Determinate sentencing means that states must free offenders after they have served their sentences less good-time credits. (Gary Wagner/Stock Boston)

ing time on **supervised mandatory release** (Jankowski, 1991:5). This is the functional equivalent of parole, since these supervised releasees must adhere to similar conditions associated with parole (e.g., curfew, random alcohol and drug checks, and other behavioral requirements). Failure to adhere to one or more of these conditions may result in their supervised mandatory releases being canceled, and they will be returned to prison, often having to serve the remainder of their sentences in their entirety.

Good-time credits are not equally allocated among the different state prison systems. Table 6.1 shows the amount of good-time credit applied against one's original maximum sentence for the various states. The most generous state prison system is Alabama, in which inmates can earn 75 days per month of good-time credit for each 30 days served. Yes, that's right. Alabama inmates can earn 2.5 months of good-time credit against their maximum sentences for every 30 days they serve behind bars. For those Alabama offenders sentenced to 30 years, they can be released, unconditionally, after serving *less than 9 years.* (For example, if they serve 9 years, they have 21 years left to serve. But in the meantime, they have accrued 2.5 times 9 years, or 9 + 9 + 4.5 = 22.5 years of good-time credit. In this instance, the actual amount of time they would have to serve would lie somewhere between 8 and 9 years.)

Prior to November 1988, Oklahoma was the most generous good-time provider, allowing inmates to accrue good-time days at the rate of 137 per month served. Therefore, prisoners sentenced to 30 years would actually serve less than 5 years, with good-time credits applied at 61/2 times the number of days served. However, Oklahoma reduced good-time days earned per month from 137 to 44.

TABLE 6.1 Good-Time Credits for Different State Jurisdictions

More than 30 days per month
  Alabama, Colorado, Illinois, Mississippi, North Carolina, Oklahoma, South Carolina, Texas
30 days per month
  Arkansas, California, Florida, Indiana, Louisiana, Montana, New Mexico, Virginia, West Virginia
20 days per month
  Iowa, Massachusetts, Nevada, New Jersey, Ohio
15 days per month
  Arizona, Connecticut, Delaware, District of Columbia, Kentucky, Maine, Minnesota, Nebraska, Rhode Island, South Dakota, Vermont, Washington, Wyoming
Less than 15 days per month
  Alaska, Federal Bureau of Prisons (54 days per year), Michigan (disciplinary credits), Missouri, New Hampshire, New York, North Dakota, Oregon
No good-time given
  Georgia, Hawaii, Idaho, Pennsylvania, Utah, Wisconsin

Adapted from Su Perk Davis, "Good Time." *Corrections Compendium,* **15**:5, 1990.

Now, Oklahoma prisoners sentenced to 30 years can get out automatically after serving 12 years, when 1.5 times their time served is deducted from their original maximum sentence.

A majority of states permit the accumulation of good-time credit at the rate of 15 days or more per month served. The Federal Bureau of Prisons permits 54 days per year as good-time credit to be earned by federal prisoners. Some states permit additional good-time credits to be accumulated for participation in vocational or educational programs. States such as New Hampshire have an interesting variation on this theme. Instead of rewarding prisoners with good-time credits, New Hampshire authorities *add* 150 days to the *minimum sentences* imposed. These 150 days can be reduced at the rate of 12.5 days per month of good behavior or *exemplary conduct,* according to the New Hampshire prison system (Davis, 1990a:5).

There are various motives behind different state provisions for good time. Prison overcrowding is perhaps the most frequently cited reason. However, good-time credit allowances can also encourage inmates to participate in useful vocational and educational programs. More than a few inmates abuse the good-time system by enrolling in these programs in a token fashion. But many inmates derive good benefits from them as well. And, good-time credits influence one's security placement while institutionalized. Those inmates who behave well may be moved from maximum- to medium-, or from medium- to minimum-security custody levels over time. And we know that an inmate's immediate classification level preceding a parole board hearing is taken into account as a factor influencing parole chances. Another reason for good-time allowances or credits is to maintain and improve inmate management by prison administrative staff. Well-behaved inmates make it easier for officials to administer prison affairs. Those who do not obey prison rules are subject to good-time credit deductions and are "written-up" by correctional officers for their misconduct. If inmates accumulate enough of these paper infractions, they may lose good-time credits or, as in New Hampshire, they may fail to reduce the extra time imposed above their minimum sentences.

THE PHILOSOPHY OF PAROLE

Like probation, parole has been established for the purpose of rehabilitating offenders and reintegrating them into society. Parole is a continuation of a parolee's punishment, under varying degrees of supervision by parole officers, ending when the originally imposed sentence has been served. Officials have noted that parole is earned rather than automatically granted after serving a fixed amount of a sentence (Dietz, 1985:32). The punitive nature of parole is inherent in the conditions and restrictions accompanying it, which other community residents are not obligated to follow.

Parole's eighteenth-century origins suggest no philosophical foundation. In the 1700s, penological pragmatism permitted correctional officials to use parole to reduce prison overcrowding. Roughly between 1850 and 1970, the influence of social reformers, religious leaders, and humanitarians on parole as a rehabilitative medium was quite apparent (Bottomley, 1984). But as has been seen, the pendulum has shifted away from rehabilitation (but not entirely) and toward societal retribution. The early California experience with parole was anything but rehabilitative. Rather, it was a bureaucratic tool to assist gubernatorial decision making in clemency cases involving excessively long sentences (Messinger et al., 1985).

THE FUNCTIONS OF PAROLE

The functions of parole are probably best understood when couched in terms of manifest and latent functions. *Manifest functions* are intended or recognized, apparent to all. *Latent functions* are also important, but they are hidden and less transparent. Two important manifest functions of parole are to reintegrate parolees into society and to control and/or deter crime. Three latent functions of parole are to ease prison and jail overcrowding, to remedy sentencing disparities, and to protect the public.

Offender Reintegration

Incarcerated offenders, especially those who have been incarcerated for long periods, often find it difficult to readjust to life in the community. Inmate idleness and a unique prison subculture, regimentation and strict conformity to numerous rules, and continuous exposure to a population of criminals who have committed every offense imaginable simply fail to prepare prisoners adequately for noncustodial living (Israel, 1983; Steelman, 1984; Webb, 1984). Parole provides a means whereby an offender may make a smooth transition from prison life to living in a community with some degree of freedom under supervision (Atkinson, 1986:56). (Chapters 8–11 examine several parole options and programs.)

Crime Deterrence and Control

Some correctional authorities believe that rewarding an inmate for good behavior while in prison through an early conditional release under supervision will promote respect for the law. Some people believe that keeping an offender imprisoned "too long" will increase the offender's bitterness toward society and result in the commission of new and more serious offenses (Travis, 1985:130). Early release from prison, under appropriate supervision, implies an agreement of trust between the state and offender. In many instances, this trust instills a degree of self-confidence in the offender that yields the desired law-abiding results (Dietz, 1985:32). Then again, there are those who claim parole is a failure, although they cannot say for certain whether the problem rests with parole itself or with the abuse of discretion on the part of parole-granting bodies (Alpert, 1985:135).

Decreasing Prison and Jail Overcrowding

Some authorities may disagree that the "safety-valve" function of parole as a means of alleviating prison overcrowding is a latent function. But it is undisputed that parole originated precisely to accomplish this objective. Critical of the use of parole as a means of alleviating space problems of prisons are Martinson (1974), Martinson and Wilks (1977), and von Hirsch (1976). These experts argue that prisoners should receive their just deserts for the crimes committed and that they should serve time proportionate to fit the crimes. Furthermore, existing methods for determining early release are considered unreliable and unscientific (Travis, 1985:130).

But prison overcrowding is an age-old problem that will not go away. It has existed for centuries and continues to influence decisions by police officers, prosecutors, judges, and parole boards. This is a dilemma that has major implications for public policy (Austin, 1986). Parole is seen by several authorities as a temporary solution to a growing problem that confronts the criminal justice system as a whole (Barclay, 1985; Lane, 1986; Lombardi and Lombardi, 1986:86–87).

At the federal level, J. Michael Quinlan, director of the Federal Prison System in 1987, said that the number of incarcerated inmates grew from 1981 to 1987 by 85 percent. During the same period, bed space increased only by 20 percent. The difference resulted in a system-wide crowding rate of 58 percent that continues to rise (Quinlan, 1987:17). Quinlan anticipates the eventual dissolution of the United States Parole Board, but in the meantime he "does not want to close the door to increased use of community resources, halfway houses, and house arrest" (Quinlan, 1987:17). It is likely that for the next several years at least, parole will remain a viable option to alleviate federal prison overcrowding (Hammrock, 1981:5). By 1994, the U.S. Parole Commission exercised discretion over the early release of federal offenders. Federal parolees and mandatory releasees are currently supervised by federal probation officers who are attached to each U.S. District Court. The term *parole* is no longer fashionable in the federal system; instead, federal "parolees" are now managed under *supervised release* (American Correctional Association, 1994:491).

Compensating for Sentencing Disparities

Sentencing reforms in various states have been enacted to eliminate or at least minimize sentencing disparities associated with race or socioeconomic status. Evidence exists to suggest that some disparities in sentencing have been minimized through determinate sentencing in selected jurisdictions (Holmes et al., 1993; Pommersheim and Wise, 1989; Steffensmeier, Kramer, and Streifel, 1993).

Among the states to implement wholesale changes in their sentencing practices is Minnesota. Putting a set of new guidelines into effect May 1, 1980, Minnesota officials observed substantial decreases in sentencing disparities. Sentences were more uniform as to who goes to prison and how long they serve. Furthermore, less racial disparity occurred during the first three years the new guidelines were in operation (Minnesota Sentencing Guidelines Commission, 1984). Similar results have been found as the result of sentencing reforms in North Carolina (Clarke, 1984). However, a disturbingly large number of states with new sentencing guidelines have reported little, if any, impact on reducing sentencing disparities (Eskridge, 1986). Even subsequent follow-up studies of the Minnesota sentencing guidelines and major guidelines changes and modifications in 1989 suggest uneven results, particularly relative to violent offender sentencing patterns (Frase, 1993).

A properly operated and fully informed parole board is often capable of making decisions about early releases of inmates that are more fair than otherwise calculated through determinate sentencing provisions. In New Jersey, parole boards permit victims of crimes, the sentencing judge, prosecutor, and the media to be notified of and attend parole hearings, and they actively solicit essential documentation to support their subsequent parole decision (Dietz, 1985:32). Inmates have an opportunity to present evidence of their progress while in prison as well as their constructive parole plans. If granted early release, they must sign an agreement to abide by the conditions required for successful parole supervision, and they are ultimately responsible for their own conduct while completing the term of their parole (Dietz, 1985:32). New Jersey officials, at least, are convinced that parole is a crucial component of the criminal justice system and can assist greatly in reducing the disparity of excessive sentences.

Public Safety and Protection

According to some parole authorities, the most important topic of public interest is *risk* (Burke, 1987:76). Are there foolproof ways of identifying high-risk parole applicants? No. In fact, predicting future dangerousness is one of the most difficult

BOX 6.1
Are Nonviolent Parolees Likely to Commit Violent Crimes While on Parole?
Sometimes Some of the Most Violent Acts Are Committed by Nonviolent Parolees

The Case of Carl Buntion

Carl Buntion was a young man convicted of child sexual abuse in April 1989. Carl's offense was reprehensible, but it was not considered violent. Buntion had fondled several children in Houston, Texas, and was subsequently apprehended. He had not physically injured any of his victims. Ordinarily, Buntion would be placed in a sex offender program and counseled at length. Buntion did receive counseling, but he also received a 15-year prison sentence in the Texas Department of Corrections. Because his crime was not considered particularly violent, and because he was considered a reasonably safe risk within his community if released, and because the Texas Department of Corrections was incredibly overcrowded, Buntion was paroled conditionally after serving only 13 months of the 15-year sentence, and the Houston, Texas, parole authorities became responsible for his supervision.

Among other things, Buntion was to report to a halfway house within 24 hours following his prison release and commence participation in a counseling program for sex offenders. Buntion ignored the halfway house order and went about his life in Houston, despite his parolee obligations and conditions. Six weeks after being pa-

roled, Buntion was driving down a Houston city street when he was stopped by a motorcycle patrolman for a routine traffic violation. As Officer Irby, 29, approached Buntion's car, Buntion pulled a gun and shot and killed the officer. Left behind was an angry widow, Maura Irby, and two fatherless children. If you ask Mrs. Irby what she thinks about parole and potentially dangerous parolees, she will tell you, "Our prison system was overcrowded and there were some problems, but I truly believe the pendulum has swung too far. Now we have what many people are terming a country club prison system. The message is being put across to all criminals that in Texas crime pays... It's hard. It's real hard. But a complete overhaul of our parole system is absolutely necessary. I think a lot of Texas citizens are as responsible as our legislators. I think it's the private citizens that can change it now."

Who was to blame? The Houston parole agency? The parole officer assigned to Buntion? The Texas Department of Corrections? The Texas Board of Criminal Justice? Mrs. Irby doesn't care at this point. She wants the problem corrected before it can happen again to someone else. Is this a solvable problem? How can we solve it?

Source: Adapted from Julie Morris, "System Blamed for Recidivist's Mistakes." *USA Today,* December 14, 1990:8A.

decisions to make in the criminal justice system (Champion, 1994; Gottfredson and Gottfredson, 1988:251–252). Among the earliest attempts to predict a prospective parolee's risk to the public if paroled occurred in the late 1920s (Bruce, Burgess, and Harno, 1928).

A PROFILE OF PAROLEES IN THE UNITED STATES

Numbers of Parolees Under Supervision. By 1991, 4.3 million persons were under some form of correctional supervision in the United States. Of these, 531,407 or about 11.3 percent were on parole (Jankowski, 1991:1). This represents a 77 percent increase in the parolee population between 1985 and 1991. About 4 percent of these were federal parolees, while the remainder were from state prisons. The parole population grew in the United States by 16.3 percent during 1990 (Jankowski, 1991:3). Five states reported parolee increases greater than 30 percent: Oklahoma (62.4 percent), Oregon (38.5 percent), Vermont (36.4 percent), Arizona (32.4 percent), and North Carolina (30.7 percent) (Jankowski, 1991:3). Table 6.2 shows the number of state and federal offenders on parole, according to both state and U.S. region.

TABLE 6.2 Adults on Parole, 1990

Region and Jurisdiction	Parole Population, 1/1/90	1990 Entries	1990 Exits	Parole Population, 12/31/90	Percent Change in Parole Population during 1990	Number on Parole on 12/31/90 Per 100,000 Adult Residents
U.S. total	456,803	358,820	284,216	531,407	16.3%	287
Federal	21,422	9,790	9,519	21,693	1.3%	12
State	435,381	349,030	274,697	509,714	17.1%	275
Northeast	110,749	71,214	53,017	128,946	16.4%	332
Connecticut	322	49	80	291	−9.6	11
Massachusetts	4,688	5,774	5,742	4,720	.7	101
New Hampshire	477	408	363	522	9.4	63
New Jersey	20,062	13,019	9,783	23,298	16.1	393
New York	36,885	23,273	17,321	42,837	16.1	312
Pennsylvania	47,702	28,225	19,270	56,657	18.8	623
Rhode Island	393	276	348	321	−18.3	41
Vermont	220	190	110	300	36.4	71
Midwest	55,773	50,053	40,133	65,693	17.8%	149
Illinois	14,550	16,349	13,228	17,671	21.5	208
Indiana	3,456	2,965	2,643	3,778	9.3	92
Iowa	1,900	1,572	1,361	2,111	11.1	103
Kansas	5,089	3,107	2,445	5,751	13.0	317

(table continues)

TABLE 6.2 (continued)

Region and Jurisdiction	Parole Population, 1/1/90	1990 Entries	Exits	Parole Population, 12/31/90	Percent Change in Parole Population during 1990	Number on Parole on 12/31/90 Per 100,000 Adult Residents
Michigan	9,890	8,994	6,983	11,901	20.3	174
Minnesota	1,699	2,249	2,075	1,873	10.2	58
Missouri	7,545	4,746	3,095	9,196	21.9	242
Nebraska	490	840	698	632	29.0	55
North Dakota	138	136	158	116	−15.9	25
Ohio	6,464	5,788	4,307	7,945	22.9	99
South Dakota	510	571	461	620	21.6	124
Wisconsin	4,042	2,736	2,679	4,099	1.4	114
South	183,715	117,556	85,498	215,773	17.4%	340
Alabama	5,724	2,225	1,979	5,970	4.3	200
Arkansas	3,657	2,402	2,088	3,971	8.6	230
Delaware	1,013	676	406	1,283	26.7	255
District of Columbia	4,915	3,268	2,837	5,346	8.8	1,091
Florida	2,318	645	899	2,064	−11.0	20
Georgia	17,437	16,611	11,402	22,646	29.9	477
Kentucky	3,133	2,210	2,160	3,183	1.6	117
Louisiana	9,177	6,220	6,520	8,877	−3.3	297
Maryland	9,862	7,715	6,385	11,192	13.5	309
Mississippi	3,349	1,657	1,528	3,478	3.9	190
North Carolina	7,559	9,148	6,824	9,883	30.7	197
Oklahoma	1,993	1,990	747	3,236	62.4	140
South Carolina	3,386	1,129	972	3,543	4.6	138
Tennessee	10,511	5,914	5,098	11,327	7.8	309
Texas	91,294	46,476	28,044	109,726	20.2	903
Virginia	7,444	8,790	7,186	9,048	21.5	193
West Virginia	943	480	423	1,000	6.0	74
West	85,144	110,207	96,049	99,302	16.6%	256
Alaska	533	542	507	568	6.6	150
Arizona	2,048	4,087	3,424	2,711	32.4	101
California	57,515	91,379	81,332	67,562	17.5	307
Colorado	1,974	2,149	1,727	2,396	21.4	98
Hawaii	1,287	527	389	1,425	10.7	172
Idaho	238	275	270	243	2.1	35
Montana	752	406	347	811	7.8	141
Nevada	2,417	1,620	1,187	2,850	17.9	315
New Mexico	1,151	1,277	1,204	1,224	6.3	115
Oregon	5,794	5,805	3,576	8,023	38.5	379
Utah	1,277	1,244	960	1,561	22.2	143
Washington	9,832	741	958	9,615	−2.2	267
Wyoming	326	155	168	313	−4.0	98

Note: Five states estimated numbers in one or more categories. Maine eliminated parole in 1976.

Source: Jankowski, 1991:3.

Methods of Release from Prison.   Releases of large numbers of inmates on parole are the result of many factors. Some of these factors are prison overcrowding and good behavior of prisoners while confined. Also, prisons are attempting to manage their scarce space in order to accommodate the most dangerous offenders. Another major contributing factor is court-ordered prison population reductions because of health and safety regulations and "cruel and unusual punishment" conditions associated with some prison facilities that have been unable to comply with federally mandated guidelines under which inmates may be confined. No court has ever declared that prison must be "comfortable." However, some prisons are notoriously ill-equipped to house their inmates in safe quarters. Some of the older prisons in the United States are rat-infested, roach-ridden structures without proper heat or ventilation in winter or summer months. Coupled with chronic overcrowding, some of these institutions are simply inhumane. This is where courts draw the line and require minimal conditions under which human beings can be held in confinement.

These release-through-parole figures are somewhat misleading, however. They suggest that granting parole under the discretionary authority of parole boards is increasing while just the opposite is true. As has been seen in this and previous chapters, sentencing reforms have modified greatly the methods of releasing state and federal prisoners in recent years. New presumptive sentencing guidelines and determinate sentencing schemes will probably modify inmate release profiles over the coming years. Table 6.3 shows state prison releases by various methods for the years 1977 through 1990.

State prison releases by discretionary parole board decisions in 1977 accounted for 72 percent of all releases. By 1990, this figure had dropped to 40.5 percent, reflecting the diminished role of parole boards through sentencing reforms (Jankowski, 1991:5). However, during the same period between 1977 and 1990, the number of supervised mandatory releases rose from 5.9 percent to 29.6 percent (Jankowski, 1991:5).

Profiling Parolees.   Some government information exists profiling the entire population of U.S. state and federal parolees. There are some limitations associated with these data, however. Although the number of persons sentenced to state and federal prisons and other facilities has been recorded annually since January 1, 1926, figures on the race and ethnicity of inmates, for example, were not compiled until 1978 (Minor-Harper, 1986:4). And, in several jurisdictions, inmate ethnicity has been difficult to determine, according to reporting officials. Table 6.4 shows selected characteristics of adults on parole for the years 1986, 1987, and 1989.

Perhaps the most interesting feature of Table 6.4 is that other than the increasing numbers of parolees from 1986 through 1989, the general characteristics of these parolees have not changed much. For instance, the amount of discretionary parole has fluctuated across these years about 3 percent, from 54 percent in 1986, to 55 percent in 1987, and to 57 percent in 1989. Even though this might be regarded as a "trend," it isn't much of one. Mandatory parole variation across these same years has varied by only about 4 percent. However, the percentage of successful pa-

TABLE 6.3 State Prison Releases, By Method, 1977–1990

			Percentage of Prison Releases						
			Conditional Releases				Unconditional Releases		
Year	Total Releases From Prison	All	Discretionary Parole	Supervised Mandatory Release	Probation	Other[a]	Expiration of Sentence	Commutation	Other
1977	115,213	100	71.9	5.9	3.6	1.0	16.1	1.1	.4
1978	119,796	100	70.4	5.8	3.3	2.3	17.0	.7	.5
1979	128,954	100	60.2	16.9	3.3	2.4	16.3	.4	.6
1980	136,968	100	57.4	19.5	3.6	3.2	14.9	.5	.8
1981	142,489	100	54.6	21.4	3.7	3.1	13.9	2.4	1.0
1982	157,144	100	51.9	24.4	4.8	3.6	14.4	.3	.6
1983	191,237	100	48.1	26.9	5.2	2.5	16.1	.5	.6
1984	191,499	100	46.0	28.7	4.9	2.7	16.3	.5	.9
1985	203,895	100	43.2	30.8	4.5	3.0	16.9	.4	1.2
1986	230,672	100	43.2	31.1	4.5	4.6	14.8	.3	1.4
1987	270,506	100	40.6	31.2	4.4	5.7	16.2	1.0	.9
1988	301,378	100	40.3	30.6	4.1	6.0	16.8	1.0	1.2
1989	364,434	100	39.1	30.5	4.4	8.9	16.0	.2	.9
1990	394,682	100	40.5	29.6	5.3	10.6	13.1	.1	.9

Note: The data are from the National Prisoner Statistics reporting program. The total releases from state prison are those for which the method of release was reported. Deaths, unspecified releases, transfers, and escapes were not included. Altogether, 419,783 persons were released or removed from state prison in 1990.

[a]Other conditional releases include prisoners discharged under special procedures that included early release because of crowding, supervised work furloughs, release to home detention, release to community residence, release to special programs with required supervision, supervised reprieves, and emergency releases. Approximately 93% of the 41,837 "other conditional releases" in 1990 occurred in five states: Arizona, Connecticut, Florida, Georgia, and Oregon.

Source: Jankowski, 1991:5.

TABLE 6.4 Selected Characteristics of Parolees for the Years 1986, 1987, and 1989

Characteristic	No. of Adults on Parole from State or Federal Prisons (000s)			Percentage of Persons with a Known Status		
	1986	1987	1989	1986	1987	1989
Status of supervision	322.8	355.4	456.7	100	100	100
Active	257.9	286.2	440.1	80	80	79
Inactive	19.9	27.0	32.4	6	8	8
Absconded	24.6	21.8	31.1	8	6	7
Supervised out-of-state	20.3	20.3	26.2	6	6	8
Adults entering parole	202.7	213.9	270.4	100	100	100
Discretionary parole	110.3	118.4	155.2	54	55	57
Mandatory parole	82.9	95.4	115.8	41	45	43
Reinstatement to parole	9.6	—	—	5	—	—
Adults leaving parole	183.9	182.1	229.6	100	100	100
Successful completions	104.6	104.9	112.7	57	58	49
Discharged absconders	3.2	2.7	2.3	2	2	1
Discharged to detainers/warrants	3.1	2.1	3.1	2	1	1
Returned to prison	—	—	105.9	—	—	46
With new sentence	20.9	16.1	35.9	11	9	34
With parole revoked	34.3	29.7	39.4	19	16	37
With revocation pending	9.7	19.8	29.6	5	11	28
With charges pending	2.1	0.9	0.7	1	1	1
Transferred to other state	3.8	3.7	2.9	2	2	1
Death	1.8	1.9	2.6	1	1	1
Sex of adults on parole	301.6	345.9	419.4	100	100	100
Male	281.2	321.8	387.3	93	93	92
Female	20.3	24.1	32.1	7	7	8
Race of adults on parole	298.8	305.6	381.7	100	100	100
White	165.9	158.0	201.7	55	52	53
Black	130.7	144.8	178.6	44	47	46
Other	2.1	2.8	3.4	1	1	1
Hispanic origin of adults on parole	199.1	213.4	291.0	100	100	100
Hispanic	38.3	44.5	59.5	18	21	20
Non-Hispanic	162.8	168.9	231.5	82	79	80

Sources: Besette, 1989a, 1989b; Dillingham, 1991

role completions has decreased substantially from 57 percent in 1986 to 49 percent in 1989. As far as gender, race, and Hispanic–non-Hispanic origins of adult parolees across these years, the figures have remained almost the same. About 93 percent of all adult parolees are men. About 53 percent of all adult parolees are white. And, about 20 percent of all adult parolees are of Hispanic origin.

    What about the types of crimes these parolees have committed? We have little data relating to the types of conviction offenses typifying them. Lacking direct information, we can rely to some extent on information about the types of crimes that were committed by those admitted to prison initially. Table 6.5 shows the most serious offenses by state prison inmates, by age, for 1991.

TABLE 6.5 Most Serious Offense of State Prison Inmates, by Age, 1991

Most Serious Offense	Total[a]	Age of State Prison Inmates					55 or Older
		18–24	25–29	30–34	35–44	45–54	
Violent offenses	46.6%	39.6%	44.1%	47.1%	48.9%	58.4%	66.6%
Murder	10.6	5.9	8.7	10.8	13.3	17.8	22.2
Negligent manslaughter	1.8	1.3	2.1	1.6	1.9	2.5	3.3
Kidnapping	1.2	0.9	1.1	1.6	1.2	1.5	1.0
Rape	3.5	1.2	3.2	3.8	4.3	6.0	9.4
Other sexual assault	5.9	3.2	4.2	5.0	7.7	12.7	17.2
Robbery	14.8	17.2	16.9	16.1	11.8	8.6	3.8
Assault	8.2	9.2	7.5	7.6	8.2	8.5	8.9
Other violent	0.6	0.7	0.5	0.5	0.4	0.7	0.8
Property offenses	24.8%	31.1%	26.2%	25.6%	21.6%	13.7%	10.5%
Burglary	12.4	16.1	13.4	13.4	10.1	5.8	2.9
Larceny/theft	4.9	5.5	4.7	5.0	5.1	3.5	2.6
Motor vehicle theft	2.2	4.4	2.2	1.4	1.4	0.5	0.5
Arson	0.7	0.7	0.8	0.8	0.5	0.5	0.5
Fraud	2.8	2.6	3.0	2.8	3.1	2.4	2.9
Stolen property	1.4	1.5	1.4	1.9	1.1	0.5	1.1
Other property	0.4	0.4	0.6	0.4	0.4	0.5	0
Drug offenses	21.3%	22.8%	22.4%	20.9%	21.6%	17.7%	14.3%
Possession	7.6	8.0	7.7	7.7	7.8	6.3	4.3
Trafficking	13.3	14.4	14.4	12.7	13.2	11.1	9.5
Other/ unspecified	0.5	0.5	0.4	0.5	0.6	0.3	0.4
Public-order offenses	6.9%	6.1%	6.8%	6.1%	7.5%	10.0%	7.9%
Weapons	1.8	2.3	1.7	1.6	1.9	1.2	1.4
Other public-order	5.1	3.8	5.1	4.5	5.6	8.8	6.5
Other offenses	0.4%	0.4%	0.4%	0.3%	0.5%	0.3%	0.8%
Number of inmates	704,181	150,378	170,783	150,936	159,797	45,894	21,839

Note: Excludes an estimated 7,462 prison inmates whose offense was unknown.

[a]Total includes inmates who were age 17 or younger.

Source: Snell, 1993:28.

Nearly 47 percent of the state prison inmates for 1991 were imprisoned for violent offenses, while about 25 percent were property offenders. Drug offenders accounted for another 21 percent, while public order and "other" accounted for another 7 percent of them. Violent offenders typically serve longer sentences compared with property offenders. This is supported by the age/crime figures shown in Table 6.5.

Table 6.6 shows the median sentence lengths and special conditions for these

TABLE 6.6 Sentence Length and Special Sentencing Conditions of State Prison Inmates, by Most Serious Offense, 1991

Most Serious Offense	Number of Inmates	Maximum Sentence Length		Special Conditions of Sentence							
		Median	Mean	Fines	Court Costs	Victim Restitution	Community Service	Drug Treatment	Drug Testing	Alcohol Treatment	Psychiatric/ Psychological Counseling[a]
All offenses	690,721	108 mos.	150 mos.	10.6%	12.1%	10.5%	1.0%	6.2%	5.2%	3.2%	2.5%
Violent offenses	323,064	180 mos.	216 mos.	7.5%	10.0%	9.7%	0.7%	3.7%	2.6%	2.6%	4.1%
Murder	73,838	Life	381	4.7	6.9	4.7	0.2	1.9	1.0	1.4	1.3
Negligent manslaughter	12,642	156	185	8.2	8.4	9.1	2.4	4.0	2.3	5.3	1.0
Kidnapping	8,092	360	293	12.7	11.1	11.5	0	3.3	4.1	2.6	3.2
Rape	24,477	240	277	6.1	11.0	10.3	0.5	3.0	2.0	3.9	12.6
Other sexual assault	41,352	120	175	11.4	12.0	6.7	0.9	3.8	1.5	3.7	14.8
Robbery	102,642	144	200	6.8	10.1	13.2	0.7	4.8	3.7	2.1	1.4
Assault	56,313	114	158	9.8	11.8	11.8	0.9	4.4	3.5	3.1	1.9
Other violent	3,708	72	103	2.1	18.4	9.7	2.0	1.7	5.5	6.1	2.0
Property offenses	171,446	60 mos.	114 mos.	10.7%	14.3%	18.7%	1.5%	6.6%	5.3%	4.0%	1.2%
Burglary	86,237	96	140	10.8	12.9	17.6	1.4	6.7	5.5	3.9	1.5
Larceny/theft	33,265	48	72	9.2	16.3	17.5	0.4	6.3	5.1	3.1	0.5
Motor vehicle theft	15,217	54	80	9.2	10.5	12.6	1.5	4.0	5.1	5.3	1.2
Arson	4,652	120	197	11.7	10.6	22.0	1.3	4.4	3.7	5.2	8.0
Fraud	19,496	60	98	11.1	18.5	28.6	3.9	8.7	4.6	3.2	0.4
Stolen property	9,554	60	79	16.5	19.6	21.4	1.2	5.6	8.0	4.8	0
Other property	3,025	48	76	11.6	14.4	17.5	0.6	10.9	1.7	9.0	0
Drug offenses	146,803	60 mos.	95 mos.	15.8%	13.2%	4.1%	1.2%	11.2%	10.6%	2.2%	0.5%
Possession	51,925	54	81	12.1	11.9	3.5	1.1	10.4	11.9	2.4	0.4
Trafficking	91,690	72	104	18.1	13.8	4.3	1.4	11.4	9.9	2.1	0.5
Other/Unspecified	3,188	48	70	12.7	17.2	6.6	0	15.9	10.3	2.3	1.9
Public-order offenses	46,590	48 mos.	82 mos.	14.7%	13.2%	6.0%	1.2%	6.3%	5.8%	7.2%	2.8%
Weapons	12,595	54	74	9.2	11.5	3.9	0.5	4.4	4.9	1.4	1.8
DWI[b]	9,985	30	40	26.4	14.9	7.2	1.9	3.2	7.1	15.5	0.6
Other public-order	24,010	60	104	12.8	13.1	6.6	1.2	8.5	5.7	6.8	4.1

Note: Excludes an estimated 20,922 inmates for whom current offense and sentencing information were unknown. Detail may add to more than total because inmates may have been given more than one special sentencing condition.

[a]Includes participation in sex offender treatment programs.

[b]Includes driving while intoxicated and driving under the influence of drugs or alcohol.

Source: Snell, 1993:29.

same state prison inmates. Both the mean and median sentence lengths for different offense categories are depicted. Thus, even for those offenders serving time for murder, their mean sentence lengths are 381 months, or nearly 32 years. At some point, however, even these persons are paroled short of serving their full terms. Few "lifers" are actually in either state or federal prisons, where their terms are under conditions of "life-without-parole" (Snell, 1993:29).

Some additional information is available, based on information reported from 34 states about their 186,465 parolees and conviction offenses. Table 6.7 shows entries to parole supervision for parolees in 34 states in 1990, according to their most serious conviction offense, and by gender and race. From Table 6.7, we can see that there were more male parolees for violent offenses (26 percent) compared with female parolees (16 percent). However, more females were paroled for property crimes (40.3 percent) compared with their male parolee counterparts (36.9 percent). Considerably larger proportions of females are paroled for drug offenses (37.1 percent) compared with parolees who had prior convictions for drug offenses (27.4 percent). Proportionately fewer white males were paroled who had previous violent offense records (23 percent) compared with black parolees with previous violent offense convictions (27 percent). However, substantially more white offenders were paroled for property offenses (nearly 42 percent) compared with black property offenders (34.5 percent) (U.S. Department of Justice, 1993).

Finally, Table 6.8 shows the various outcomes of 157,815 parole discharges reported by 27 states. Parole discharges are indicative of the various dispositions of those paroled. Thus, some offenders will successfully complete their parole terms, while others will commit new offenses and/or have their parole programs revoked. Some parolees may abscond from their jurisdictions, and some may die from natural causes.

It is interesting to note that for the data shown in Table 6.8 that of the 157,615 parolees discharged in 1990, about 36 percent of them successfully completed their parole programs (U.S. Department of Justice, 1993). But the failure rate, or those whose programs were either revoked or pending revocation, or who had been sentenced for new offenses, was over 63 percent. For those interested in the types of parolees who "fail" or "succeed" the most, the table contents may be inspected. Actually, violent offenders had higher success rates (40.7 percent) than property offenders (33.9 percent). But readers must be cautioned that these figures reflect statistics based on information from only 27 states and in only one year, 1990.

PAROLE TRENDS

It is evident from the information examined in this chapter that the number of people on parole in the United States is increasing annually. This does not mean that the success of parole is increasing to an equivalent degree. Rather, it would seem that much depends on the nature of particular parole programs and the intensity of supervised release relating to how parolees are managed. Thus, in subsequent chapters, different types of parole programs will be examined regarding their rela-

TABLE 6.7 Entries to Parole Supervision from Prisons in 34 States, by Offense, Sex, Race, and Hispanic Origin, United States, 1990

Most Serious Offense	All Entries	Sex		Race[a]			
		Male	Female	White	Black	Other[b]	Hispanic[c]
Number of entries	186,465	170,941	15,505	76,196	90,777	1,171	27,631
All offenses	100%	100%	100%	100%	100%	100%	100%
Violent offenses	25.2	26.0	16.1	23.0	27.1	34.1	22.2
Homicide	3.0	2.9	3.8	3.0	2.9	5.0	2.7
Murder and nonnegligent manslaughter	2.0	1.9	2.2	1.7	2.0	3.1	2.0
Murder	1.5	1.5	1.5	1.4	1.5	2.1	1.3
Nonegligent manslaughter	0.5	0.5	0.8	0.3	0.5	0.9	0.7
Negligent manslaughter	1.0	1.0	1.5	1.2	0.9	1.8	0.7
Unspecified homicide	d	d	0.1	0.1	d	0.1	d
Kidnapping	0.4	0.5	0.2	0.6	0.3	1.0	0.4
Rape	1.9	2.0	0.2	2.1	1.6	3.2	1.6
Other sexual assault	2.3	2.5	0.3	3.8	1.3	3.6	1.9
Robbery	11.2	11.6	6.8	7.2	14.4	10.0	9.9
Assault	5.8	6.0	4.3	5.6	6.2	10.0	5.3
Other violent	0.5	0.5	0.6	0.6	0.4	1.3	0.3
Property offenses	37.2	36.9	40.3	41.8	34.5	39.8	28.3
Burglary	17.5	18.5	6.4	20.0	15.2	19.0	16.4
Larceny-theft	9.6	8.9	16.6	9.9	10.1	8.4	5.9
Motor vehicle theft	2.7	2.8	1.0	2.9	2.4	4.5	2.7
Arson	0.7	0.6	0.7	0.9	0.5	0.9	0.4
Fraud	4.6	3.7	14.3	5.8	4.1	3.8	1.6
Stolen property	1.6	1.6	1.0	1.4	1.7	2.6	1.1
Other property	0.6	0.6	0.3	0.8	0.5	0.6	0.3
Drug offenses	28.2	27.4	37.1	22.2	31.4	15.7	40.6
Possession	8.6	8.4	11.4	6.0	10.6	3.3	7.8
Trafficking	15.6	15.3	19.3	11.7	16.8	10.1	27.5
Other drug	4.0	3.8	6.4	4.5	4.1	2.3	5.2
Public-order offenses	8.1	8.4	5.0	11.0	6.0	9.5	7.4
Weapons	1.8	1.9	0.5	1.3	2.1	1.5	2.0
Driving while intoxicated	3.0	3.2	1.1	5.6	1.0	4.9	4.6
Other public-order	3.2	3.2	3.3	4.2	2.9	3.2	0.8
Other offenses	1.4	1.4	1.4	2.0	0.9	0.9	1.6

Note: Data on offense distribution were reported for 99.8 percent of the 186,904 state parole entries who entered prison with a sentence of more than a year.

[a]Includes persons of Hispanic origin.

[b]Includes American Indians, Alaska Natives, Asians, and Pacific Islanders.

[c]Includes persons of all races.

[d]Less than 0.05 percent.

Source: U.S. Department of Justice, Bureau of Justice Statistics. *National Corrections Reporting Program, 1990,* NCJ-141879 (Washington, DC: U.S. Department of Justice, 1993), p. 35, cited in Maguire, Pastore, and Flanagan, 1993:661.

TABLE 6.8 Parole Discharges in 27 States, by Offense and Type of Discharge, United States, 1990

Most Serious Offense	Number	Total	Successful Completion of Term	Absconder	Return to Prison With:				Death	Other
					New Sentence	Parole Revocation	Revocation Pending	Transfer		
All offenses	157,815	100%	36.4%	0.5%	12.6%	27.4%	21.7%	0.2%	0.8%	0.4%
Violent offenses	42,401	100	40.7	0.7	10.0	27.9	18.8	0.2	1.2	0.5
Homicide	4,179	100	50.6	0.6	7.5	25.1	13.6	0.5	1.9	0.2
Murder and nonnegligent manslaughter	2,734	100	44.6	0.4	9.0	28.7	14.7	0.4	1.9	0.2
Murder	2,001	100	42.2	0.5	7.3	30.6	16.9	0.4	1.6	0.3
Nonnegligent manslaughter	733	100	51.0	0.3	13.6	23.5	8.6	0.3	2.7	0.0
Negligent manslaughter	1,346	100	63.1	1.0	3.6	18.1	12.3	0.1	1.6	0.2
Unspecified homicide	99	100	47.5	1.0	16.2	21.2	0.0	6.1	7.1	1.0
Kidnapping	780	100	38.3	0.3	10.3	23.1	26.0	0.5	1.0	0.5
Rape	2,935	100	47.9	0.7	5.6	28.5	15.2	0.3	1.1	0.7
Other sexual assault	3,141	100	57.0	0.2	5.1	19.5	17.0	a	1.1	0.1
Robbery	21,452	100	34.2	0.7	12.2	32.1	18.8	0.2	1.2	0.5
Assault	9,226	100	42.5	0.8	9.5	23.1	22.6	0.2	0.9	0.5
Other violent	688	100	53.9	0.9	6.1	22.2	15.7	0.1	0.9	0.1

Property offenses	65,359	100	33.9	0.4	12.2	32.2	19.9	0.3	0.6	0.4
Burglary	32,355	100	32.2	0.5	11.3	33.7	20.9	0.3	0.7	0.4
Larceny-theft	17,749	100	32.9	0.4	15.1	29.4	21.1	0.2	0.5	0.4
Motor vehicle theft	5,504	100	25.2	0.3	16.2	34.4	22.9	0.3	0.3	0.4
Arson	936	100	49.5	0.4	4.8	26.1	17.7	0.1	1.0	0.4
Fraud	6,236	100	44.4	0.4	6.9	32.0	14.8	0.3	0.7	0.5
Stolen property	1,877	100	43.8	0.2	12.8	33.5	2.5	1.0	0.9	0.3
Other property	702	100	54.0	0.4	6.6	28.2	9.3	0.0	1.4	0.1
Drug offenses	36,892	100	34.6	0.4	15.1	20.9	27.9	0.2	0.7	0.3
Possession	7,689	100	42.5	0.5	8.1	34.3	13.3	0.1	0.9	0.2
Trafficking	19,366	100	36.8	0.3	16.1	19.7	25.8	0.1	0.9	0.3
Other drug	9,837	100	24.0	0.3	18.6	12.6	43.5	0.5	0.4	0.2
Public-order offenses	9,329	100	45.5	1.4	13.9	21.4	16.1	0.2	1.0	0.5
Weapons	3,722	100	38.4	0.6	18.3	20.7	20.2	0.1	1.2	0.5
Driving while intoxicated	1,947	100	46.4	0.5	16.4	21.5	14.0	0.2	1.0	0.1
Other public-order	3,660	100	52.1	2.8	8.1	22.1	13.1	0.2	0.7	0.9
Other offenses	3,834	100	27.3	0.2	18.0	15.3	37.8	0.2	0.7	0.5

Note: Data on type of parole discharge and most serious offense were reported for 96.8 percent of the 162,959 state parole discharges who entered prison with a sentence of more than a year.

[a]Less than 0.05 percent.

Source: U. S. Department of Justice, Bureau of Justice Statistics, National Corrections Reporting Program, 1990, NCJ-141879 (Washington, DC: U.S. Department of Justice, 1993), p. 43, cited in Maguire, Pastore, and Flanagan. 1993:563.

tive effectiveness in parolee management and recidivism. Part III of this book, including Chapters 8 through 11, focuses on specific programs that are offered to both probationers and parolees. These programs are linked closely with community corrections, a widely used and increasingly popular client management tool that stresses either maintaining one's integration with families and communities (in the case of probationers) and enabling reintegration to occur for those deprived for lengthy periods from community interactions (e.g., inmates serving long prison terms).

The federal government has replaced parole with supervised release. Parole has already been abolished in Maine, and several other states have given serious consideration to proposals for its elimination. At one extreme, the just-deserts philosophy is that offenders should be punished for their crimes in accordance with whatever the law prescribes. However, the laws are not formulated with the right degree of precision. For example, most offenses prescribe a term of incarceration up to X years or months and/or a fine of not more than X dollars. Thus, important decisions must be made by prosecutors, judges, and other officials that attempt to match the severity of the punishment imposed with the seriousness of the crime committed. This is far from an exact science, although for centuries social scientists and others have wrestled with the problems of defining appropriate punishments that fit each crime. Scientific investigations have attempted to evolve ideal models or schemes that might fit neatly into a sentencing scheme that states or the federal

Group counseling while confined is an indicator to parole boards that parole-eligible inmates are taking important steps to deal with their problems in positive ways. (The Image Works)

government might adopt. In fact, there is little or nothing scientific about state and federal statutes and their accompanying sentencing patterns in any jurisdiction.

At the other extreme are those who are best labeled rehabilitation oriented and/or who promote or endorse nonincarcerative, reintegrative programs or the early release of offenders so as to minimize the criminogenic influence of prison or jail. Two general theoretical camps of criminologists are identified, those who advocate very conservative or very liberal correctional viewpoints. It is unlikely that parole will be abolished on a national scale, at least for the next several decades. Methods for controlling or monitoring offenders while on probation or parole are constantly being improved, and new and better devices are being developed to ensure greater supervisory effectiveness. Thus, better control of persons currently under PO supervision appears to be the most logical solution to present problems.

Prison overcrowding enters the picture as an extremely important intervening variable. Many state prison systems have contracts with local city or county jails to house some of their inmate overflow. Several state prison systems are currently under zero population growth court orders, where maximum prison capacities cannot be exceeded. A general shift in sentencing from indeterminate to determinate has eroded or eliminated parole board authority to grant prisoners early release. However, under determinate sentencing, considerable latitude in sentencing decisions and charging decisions exists for judges and prosecutors (Gottfredson and Gottfredson, 1988). One result of these sentencing reforms has been to increase the likelihood of being incarcerated for various offenses, although the length of incarceration has been significantly shortened.

The just deserts and rehabilitative philosophies present corrections officials with an unresolvable dilemma. Standing on the sidelines of the great debate are experts who claim that "nothing works" (Martinson, 1974). But while it is true that no offender rehabilitation program is 100 percent recidivism free, this does not mean that the program ought to be scrapped. When particular parole programs have recidivism rates of 30 percent or less, they also have success rates of 70 percent or higher. Some offenders appear to be benefiting from program participation.

A costly solution is to construct and staff more prisons to house more prisoners. But can the states and the federal government afford to do this? Consider California's dilemma. In 1984, California placed approximately 70 percent of its convicted felons on probation (Petersilia, 1985c). More recent information suggests that these figures have remained fairly constant over the intervening years (Jankowski, 1991; Maguire, Pastore, and Flanagan, 1993). What if these felons had been sentenced to incarceration, even for short terms? Where would California prison officials put them? Furthermore, it is difficult and costly to attract and hire educated and competent persons to work in correctional officer and PO positions to supervise and manage offenders in or out of prison (see Chapter 12 for an extensive discussion of recruitment problems involving POs).

However, communities are playing an increasingly important role in offender management. In fact, many organizations are being established in the private sector to assume roles and offender management functions originally performed by understaffed and underpaid government bureaucracies. Parolees are becoming in-

---

BOX 6.2

If Convicted Offenders Receive Longer Prison Sentences, Will These Longer Sentences Deter Them From Committing New Crimes When They Are Subsequently Paroled?

Sometimes, Sentence Length Is Unrelated to One's Potential for Violence

The Case of Arthur Shawcross

In 1972, Arthur Shawcross, 26, of Watertown, New York, was convicted of first degree manslaughter in the death of eight-year-old Karen Ann Hill. Hill was sexually molested and strangled while visiting her family in Watertown. When Shawcross was subsequently identified, charged, and convicted of her murder, he also confessed to strangling to death 10-year-old John Blake of Watertown, although he was not officially charged or convicted in that separate offense. Shawcross was sentenced to 25 years in prison. He was paroled in 1987 and became a food services worker in Rochester, New York.

During the next 22 months, the bodies of at least 14 slain women were discovered in different Rochester neighborhoods. Police believe that as many as 17 slain women may have been killed by the same serial killer. Almost every woman was strangled.

Shawcross, 44, was arrested during the first week of January 1990, after officers in a helicopter saw him speeding away from a culvert where another woman's body was found in Sweden, a community about 12 miles west of Rochester. When arrested, Shawcross was interrogated by police.

Shawcross admitted the crime and confessed to numerous other slayings. He told reporters that the women were killed for various reasons. He said several were killed for mocking him when he was unable to engage in sex with them. One was killed when she accidentally broke the gear shift knob on his girlfriend's car. Another was killed because she told him she was a virgin and he thought otherwise. Yet another woman was killed because she pushed him in the Genessee River while they were swimming.

Should Shawcross have been required to serve the entire 25-year sentence originally imposed? Do you think it would have made a difference if he had been released at age 52 instead of at age 42? Is the New York Parole Board to blame for Shawcross's violence? What about the Rochester, New York, parole officers who supervised Shawcross? Was his subsequent behavior in any way predictable? What could authorities do differently to prevent Shawcross from committing new murders? What does this story say, if anything, about adopting a general policy about *all* violent offenders such as Shawcross?

Source: Adapted from Associated Press, *Knoxville News-Sentinel*, January 6, 1990:A5.

volved in new and innovative community programs featuring useful activities, such as employment assistance, individual and group counseling, educational training, literacy services, and valuable networking with other community agencies and businesses. More dangerous offenders who are released on parole are often placed in electronic monitoring programs and/or subject to house arrest or home confinement. Some of these programs are featured in Chapter 9.

KEY TERMS

Zebulon Brockway
Good marks
Good-time system
Marks of commendation
Norfolk Island

Pardon
Tickets-of-leave
Van Dieman's Land
Wickersham Commission

QUESTIONS FOR REVIEW

1. What is parole? What are some manifest and latent functions of parole?
2. What are some of the goals of parole? Do corrections professionals agree on these goals and the extent to which they are being achieved?
3. What contributions have the following persons made to the use of parole in the United States?
   a. Alexander Maconochie
   b. Walter Crofton
   c. Gaylord Hubbell
4. What is the relation between indeterminate sentencing and parole?
5. How does determinate sentencing modify parole?
6. What was the Wickersham Commission, and what were some of its functions?
7. What are some of the pro's and con's of indeterminate sentencing in relation to parole?
8. Contrast the rehabilitative and justice models with parole.
9. What are some of the characteristics of parolees in the United States?
10. Do you think parole deters crime? Why or why not?

7

Judges and Parole Boards

Probation and Parole Revocation Actions

Introduction

Judicial Discretion in Granting Probation

Parole Boards and Early-Release Decision Making

Types of Parole and an Overview of Parole Programs

Probation and Parole Revocation: Some Common Elements and Landmark Cases

Cataloging the Rights of Probationers and Parolees

Key Terms

Questions for Review

INTRODUCTION

- *The Case of Samuel Lee Page Jr.* By definition, Samuel Lee Page Jr. is notorious! Why? Because Page is the first convicted offender to be sentenced to life-without-parole under a new law that went into effect in early 1994 under President Bill Clinton's anticrime proposals. Basically, this is how the "three-strikes-and-you're-out" flaw (that is, *law*) works. First, you must be convicted of a felony. Second, you must get convicted for another felony, preferably in the same state or federal jurisdiction (e.g., California, Oregon, Washington, or anywhere). Third, you must commit a third felony and be convicted of it. This qualifies you for the "three-strikes-and-you're-out" law. Prior juvenile records don't count, no matter how violent or lengthy they may be.

What did Samuel Lee Page Jr. do to qualify? Page was born in September 1948 and grew up in Seattle, Washington. In 1967, when Page was 19, he stole a car and was convicted of "joy-riding" in a stolen car. He received three years in prison for this conviction. During the next 27 years, he obtained three more convictions for various crimes, including bank robbery. Page never left home much, according to his sister. The fact is that all of his offenses occurred within three miles of his home. But on March 3, 1994, Page pleaded guilty to two additional felonies—attempted kidnapping and stealing $40 from a victim at knifepoint. This gave him six convictions, not just three. But our "three-strikes-and-you're-out" law wasn't in effect then, at least not in Seattle. In early 1994, the state of Washington enacted the "three-strikes" law. Samuel Lee Page Jr. was the first offender to be convicted under this law.

One of the interesting things about Page is that he is a very nice person, according to his lawyer—except when he is holding someone at knifepoint and attempting to kidnap them. Washington has mandated that not just any felony will qualify. According to their new three-strikes law, the felonies must be serious, the kind that engenders fear in the community. Another interesting thing about Page is that he entered the guilty plea voluntarily. He could have gone to trial, presented evidence, cross-examined witnesses against him, begged for jury mercy and sympathy—but he chose none of these options. Now, at age 45, this 5'7", balding, 175-pound man will occupy one of Washington State's prison cells for the rest of his life. There will be no possibility for parole. Nobody likes bank robbers, muggers, or thieves. Sure, Page is now out of the way, out of sight, out of mind. He will not be bothering any more Seattle residents within a three-mile radius of his former home. It is only a matter of time before we see the long-term impact of these life-without-parole cases under this "three-strikes-and-you're-out" law. In 1992, the Washington prison system was only at 128 percent of its rated capacity. That means that they were only holding 28 percent more inmates than their existing facilities were originally designed to accommodate. But no matter. Washingtonians will just build more prisons as the need for them arises, at the cost of approximately $50,000 per inmate per year. Do you suppose Washington taxpayers will mind seeing their property and personal income taxes rise substantially and predictably in response to predictably higher prison inmate populations? If you think Samuel Lee Page Jr.'s case is intriguing, wait until you read *The Case of Russell Obremski* (portions adapted from Tim Klass, *Associated Press* and *Minot Daily News,* March 21, 1994:A1, A6).

• *The Case of Russell Obremski.* It happened in the state of Washington in the 1950s. Russell Obremski, a man in his late teens, committed the statutory rape of a 14-year-old girl. He was sentenced to 20 years for his crime. After serving several years in a Washington prison, he was paroled in 1969. Obremski was supposed to report to his parole officer regularly, refrain from using drugs and alcohol, and comply with other standard parole conditions. Despite his conviction offense of statutory rape, Obremski was only loosely supervised. What happened later is almost too violent to contemplate. Obremski strayed south to Oregon, probably violating one of his Washington parole conditions. It is unusual for parolees to leave the jurisdictions where they are currently serving their parole terms. Washington paroling authorities probably didn't know Obremski was out of the state. However, it didn't take long for Obremski to make new headlines.

In February 1969, he murdered LaVerna May Lowe and Betty Ann Ritchie during his Oregon visit. He was quickly apprehended, charged with these crimes, and convicted of two murders. The Oregon court sentenced Russell Obremski to two life prison terms. He first became eligible for parole in August 1983. However, relatives of his murder victims kept him behind bars by delaying his parole on five separate occasions during the next 10 years. But Obremski was finally paroled on November 8, 1993, by the Oregon Board of Parole and Post-Prison Supervision. Daniel P. Santos, the Board of Parole chairperson, Jim Eckland, the Executive Assistant, and Parole Board members Lee Coleman and Marva Fabien considered Obremski a good risk for an Oregon parole program. Yes, you guessed it. It took Obremski less than five months to add sodomy, sexual abuse, and sexual molestation of a four-year-old girl to his list of previous offenses. He was arraigned March 21, 1994, on these charges. What ever happened to his parole violations from the State of Washington? Did someone forget about his statutory rape conviction and his murders of two other women there? If Russell Obremski is subsequently convicted of sodomizing a four-year-old girl in Oregon, there is absolutely no doubt that he will be paroled again. Oregon has no life-without-parole sanction for sodomy, not even for sexually abusing a four-year-old. Even President Bill Clinton's "three-strikes-and-you're-out" program won't apply to Obremski. If he is convicted of the child sexual abuse charge, that will only be his second offense in Oregon. Russell Obremski has a chance of being paroled in some future year. This possibility doesn't exist for Samuel Lee Page Jr. Something is very wrong with this picture, both in Oregon and in Washington (portions adapted from Associated Press and *Minot Daily News,* March 24, 1993:A-2).

This chapter is about judicial probation granting and parole board early-release decision making. It examines the options and alternatives available to probationers and parolees if either probation or parole is granted. Conditions of probation and parole are examined. The first part of this chapter distinguishes between the jurisdictional boundaries between probation granting and parole granting. Thus, judicial decision making relative to granting probation is discussed. And, parole board conduct is also examined as it relates to early-release decision making for eligible jail or prison inmates.

The second part of this chapter describes parole board composition and diversity. Parole boards exist in most states, although as we have seen, numerous modifications in sentencing strategies among the states and federal government have caused paroling authorities to modify their own parole-granting practices. In some cases, parole has been eliminated entirely as an early-release option for inmates. Parole boards orient themselves in various ways toward inmates. Some of these parole board orientations are described. Depending on a particular parole board orientation, different implications exist for affected parole-eligible inmates. Parole boards also attempt to employ objective criteria when making parole decisions. Some of these criteria are presented and critically examined. Risk-assessment instruments also function to furnish parole boards in different jurisdictions with vital data about the potential future conduct of inmates if they were to be granted early release through parole. As we have already seen from the two scenarios presented at the beginning of this chapter, parole boards are fallible and their decision making is far from perfect. Nevertheless, this fact does not deter them from seeking workable prediction tools that enable them to make more accurate forecasts of parolee conduct.

A third part of this chapter provides an overview of the types of parole programs available to inmates who are parole eligible. Many of these programs are also available to probationers. Furthermore, numerous parole options are community-driven. That is, community-based corrections agencies are often in the position of managing or supervising offenders who have recently been paroled or sentenced to a probation term. The final section of this chapter describes the landmark cases involving revoking both probation and parole. The reason for combining these cases is that the U.S. Supreme Court has already done so. In effect, the Court has declared that probationers and parolees are entitled to similar revocation circumstances and legal entitlements prior to having their respective probation or parole programs revoked, either by judges or parole boards. The chapter concludes by cataloging some of the legal rights of probationers and parolees and presents various scenarios involving legal challenges to the different conditions of their respective programs of supervision.

JUDICIAL DISCRETION IN GRANTING PROBATION

The primary distinguishing feature between probation and parole is that probation is granted or imposed as a sentence by a judge. Parole is administered and granted by parole-granting bodies in various states. These bodies are known as **parole boards.** When judges sentence offenders, unless they are compelled to sentence convicts to specific prison or jail terms, they have some latitude or discretionary authority to grant probation in lieu of incarceration. We have already addressed various arguments for and against probation in Chapters 2 and 4. Probation may be *conditional* or *unconditional.*

As the distinction was made in Chapter 4, all probation is conditional, although it is common to regard *standard probation* as relatively condition free. Many standard probationers mail in monthly reports. In some states, probationers might "check in" weekly or monthly much as one might make a deposit at a drive-through window at a local bank. Standard probation conditions are not easily enforceable. *Probation with special conditions,* such as home confinement, electronic monitoring, victim compensation, community service, restitution, or attendance at individual or group counseling sessions can be verified more easily. But the type of verification under probation with special conditions requires more personnel. This means more probation department resources must be allocated to intensify an offender's management or monitoring. And, as we have seen, corrections generally is the last component of the criminal justice system in line for funding.

Many probationers recidivate and commit new offenses. They may or may not come to the judge's attention again. If probationers commit new offenses out of their original sentencing jurisdiction, the sentencing judge may not be aware of the new offense. In many cases, however, probationers are brought back before the same judge to be reevaluated. Actually, judges must consider whether to revoke probation and impose harsher penalties or more stringent supervision conditions. Sometimes, revocation may mean a new sentence of actual incarceration in either a jail or prison. Revoking probation and parole are examined in detail in the last section of this chapter.

PAROLE BOARDS AND EARLY-RELEASE DECISION MAKING

Cases That Parole Boards Must Review.   The two cases selected to begin this chapter are both atypical and typical. One is atypical because it was targeted for extensive media coverage and had high visibility in publications such as *USA Today.* When Samuel Lee Page Jr. was convicted and sentenced to life without possibility of parole, the media highlighted the case as the first to be disposed under President Bill Clinton's anticrime "three-strikes" legislation. The case of Russell Obremski is typical largely because it received sparse coverage compared with Page's case. There is no question that Russell Obremski is the greater public risk. He always has been and there is no reason to believe that he will change his behavior in the future. In contrast, although Page is considered a violent offender, the fact is that he has never murdered or raped anyone, including four-year-olds. Yet Page is destined for a life-without-parole prison term, whereas Obremski will eventually be paroled again. Arguably, Page is a less serious offender compared with Obremski. Maybe both of these offenders should receive life-without-parole terms. But the system is virtually blind to the fact that Obremski has a prior record of violence in Washington. His recidivism in Oregon consists of only two offenses, thus far. He will eventually be released again through parole or the accumulation of good time, and there is little doubt that he will eventually qualify for the three-strikes law, provided that he stays in Oregon when he decides to reoffend.

In another sense, these cases are typical because parole boards regularly deal with all types of offenders and must make important decisions about whether they should be granted early release. In fact, the cases of Page and Obremski are relatively mild compared with other, less well-known criminals who have committed atrocities within the rubric of Nazi violence against the Jews during World War II. The 1993 Academy Award–winning movie *Schindler's List* depicted some of these Nazi atrocities and the officers who committed them, a situation where millions of people were killed, not just one or two.

A majority of parole board decisions, however, involve property offenders, although persons convicted of murder, robbery, assault, rape, and other violent crimes face parole boards regularly as well: Sirhan Sirhan, convicted killer of Robert Kennedy; Charles Manson, Patricia Krenwinkle, and Leslie Van Houten, convicted murderers of several persons, including heiress Abigail Folger and actress Sharon Tate; convicted murderer, James Richardson, who murdered his seven children by using a poison insecticide in Arcadia, Florida, on October 25, 1967; and confessed serial killer Joel Rifkin, who murdered at least 13 prostitutes on Long Island and in upstate New York between 1990 and 1993.

Parole boards hear bizarre stories from various parole-eligible inmates. Not all parole-eligible inmates are celebrities. Some have achieved no notoriety at all. In some cases, the interval between the commission of a crime and conviction for it may span several decades. In November 1990, for instance, Francis Malinosky, 45, entered into a plea agreement with city prosecutors about a murder committed 11 years earlier, as described earlier in the book.

Cases That Parole Boards Do Not Have to Review.   Sometimes, parole boards don't have to make difficult early-release decisions. They narrowly missed having to make a decision in the case of Dalton Prejean, however. Dalton Prejean was only 17 when he murdered a Louisiana state trooper in 1977. He was convicted for shooting Louisiana trooper Donald Cleveland who had stopped Prejean and his brother for a routine traffic violation. Prejean fired two shots through Cleveland's head, killing him outright. Oh, yes. There is more. Three years earlier when Prejean was only 14, he shot and killed a cab driver during an aborted robbery attempt. Subsequently, he was sentenced to the death penalty for the state trooper murder. After exhausting almost every appeal, his execution in the electric chair was scheduled for mid-May 1990.

Amnesty International and other capital punishment opponents appealed to the governor of Louisiana, Buddy Roemer, to commute Prejean's sentence to life through executive clemency. Prejean was black, convicted by an all-white jury, suffered from partial brain damage, claimed he was remorseful, and had a history of abuse as a child. But Candy Cleveland, the widow of the murdered state trooper, made a judgment of her own: "There is always the possibility of good time, good behavior . . . who knows, in 20 or 30 years, Prejean could be back on the street [to kill again]" (Shapiro, 1990:23). Governor Roemer denied Prejean's request for clemency, and Prejean was electrocuted on schedule at Angola Prison. If Prejean's death sentence had been commuted to life, it is possible that Candy Cleveland's prediction would have come true.

Another case parole boards will not review is Danny Harold Rolling, a drifter

Sirhan Sirhan, convincted assassin of Robert Kennedy, is unlikely to ever be paroled. (AP/Wide World Photos)

who killed five University of Florida students in Gainesville in 1990. Rolling was convicted of their murders in early 1994. They were numerous aggravating circumstances and only a few questionable mitigating ones. Rolling had stabbed his victims repeatedly, bound them with duct tape, raped and mutilated them, and decapitated one victim. Persuasive evidence indicates that he brutally tortured his victims prior to killing them. Is there any way to murder victims kindly? In March 1994, a second-phase jury decision recommended the death penalty for Rolling. Barring any compelling appeals, which are unlikely, Rolling will eventually be executed by Florida authorities. Daniel Harold Rolling will never kill any other community residents.

Parole Boards, Sentencing Alternatives, and the "Get-Tough" Movement.   By 1988, most states had changed their sentencing provisions (Champion, 1994). In many instances, these changes in sentencing provisions significantly limited the discretionary authority of parole boards to grant prisoners early release. This was part of the "get-tough-on-crime" movement in several states (Martin, 1983). Martin (1983) reports that among the states severely curtailing sentence commutation are Colorado (1982), Illinois (1980), and Oklahoma (1982). An example of the effects of the get-tough policy occurred in Pennsylvania, where reductions in sentence commutations dropped from 128 in 1977 to 2 in 1981. More recent examples are

President Clinton's "three-strikes-and-you're-out" anticrime legislation, stiffer penalties for more serious offenses, and greater certainty of punishment through mandatory prison terms for particular crimes. Habitual offender statutes are also evidence of the get-tough movement. These statutes carry life-without-parole terms. However, few states currently use their habitual offender statutes on any consistent basis (Contact Center, Inc., 1985:1).

In 1976, Maine became the first state to abolish parole supervision outright, although it retained the state parole board to make early-release decisions for those prisoners sentenced prior to that date. Connecticut abolished parole supervision in 1981 (Greenfeld, 1987a:3). However, by 1983, the Maine legislature enacted certain good-time provisions for the prison population. These liberal good-time provisions resulted in reductions of *total time served by inmates of 15 to 20 percent* and saved the state $48 million compared with previous policy (Ehrenkrantz Group, 1984). Obviously, reducing the amount of time served in prison is not consistent with the objective of getting tough on crime. More than a few state legislators are considering whether parole board discretion was abused in those jurisdictions where it has been abolished or diminished, particularly in view of the unintended consequences of certain new sentencing reforms (Barkdull, 1988; Dietz, 1985:30).

Metchik (1992a:1) says that given today's era of judicial decision-making guidelines and determinate sentencing systems, the future prospects for parole at the federal and state levels are increasingly unclear. In fact, says Metchik, many empirical studies of the importance of severity instrumentation on which parole boards rely in making their early-release decisions show that offense severity evaluations and other retributive judgments are often negatively correlated with risk assessment. This means that relying on risk-assessment scores that indicate certain offenders pose greater risk than others may generate just the opposite outcomes. Metchik doesn't advocate utilizing these risk-assessment instruments as negative predictors, but he does raise an important issue about the reliability of these instruments and perhaps how we ought to consider their value conservatively. Other researchers have found a variety of factors that relate to a parolee's chances for success (Bodapati and Marquart, 1992). Many of these factors are not included on risk-assessment instruments or available to parole boards on any consistent basis.

Furthermore, increasing numbers of parole-eligible inmates are elderly. There appears to be an inverse relation between age and criminality, although we can certainly find adequate numbers of dangerous elderly offenders today. Considered as an aggregate, however, the growing population of parole-eligible elderly offenders is such that risk-needs assessment instruments may be very misleading regarding whether certain of these offenders ought to be supervised intensively while on parole. Better client-management methods are recommended by various researchers, so that the elderly offenders on parole are not unduly sanctioned and unreasonably supervised to the extent that such supervision is cost-ineffective (Hall, 1992).

The question of abolishing parole boards in any jurisdiction is a hotly contested issue and one not likely resolvable in the near future. Cases such as Obremski's don't help those favoring the continuation of parole board authority. And, when persons currently on parole commit new offenses, angry community residents want to know why they were released short of serving their full terms in the first place. Malcolm MacDonald (1986:6) suggests that one reason communities may be upset with parole board decision making is that community residents do not fully comprehend the punitive dimensions of community corrections alternatives. "Community-based correctional programs are more than a slap on the wrist," says MacDonald.

> When properly funded and implemented, a comprehensive community correctional system could include pretrial diversion, unsupervised probation, traditional and intensive supervision, supervision of a specialized caseload, short-term placement in a residential facility, and electronic surveillance. All these strategies, effective in rehabilitating offenders, are less costly than prison. In addition, they assist in alleviating prison overcrowding problems while ensuring public safety. (MacDonald, 1986:6)

Other evidence suggests that community corrections programs can greatly enhance a parolee's success chances by providing valuable employment assistance, food, clothing, counseling, and a host of other services (Bosoni, 1992).

If parolees are released to some type of intensive parole supervision (ISP) program within their communities, it is not always the case that the ISP program will be beneficial to certain clients. For instance, a Texas study compared a sample of parolees released according to standard parole release criteria, similar to standard probation. Another sample of Texas parolees were subject to ISP by their parole officers. A total of 679 parolees were involved, 221 from Dallas and 458 from Houston (Petersilia and Turner, 1992). They were tracked by researchers from August 1987 through July 1988. The overall intent of these early-release decisions was to alleviate Texas prison overcrowding. Interestingly, the ISP sample had a higher recidivism rate of 30 percent compared with a recidivism rate of only 18 percent among those on standard parole. Petersilia and Turner concluded that the ISP program attracted more attention to parolee program violations because they involved more face-to-face contact with their POs. As a result of this greater contact, more technical program violations were detected by POs and parole was revoked in more of these types of intensively supervised cases. Petersilia and Turner indicate that if jurisdictions are primarily interested in providing flexibility in sentencing decisions by imposing ISP that more closely fits the crimes of offenders, then ISP will likely be fruitful. But if jurisdictions are mainly concerned with reducing recidivism and system costs, then ISP programs, as they are currently structured, will focus more on surveillance as opposed to treatment, and thus they will have a greater failure rate, where failure is defined as greater parolee-client recidivism (Petersilia and Turner, 1992).

Subtleties in Parole Name Changing: Politically Correct and Client-Friendly Labels.   In many jurisdictions, parole is a bad word. Simply using the word *parole* draws much criticism. But parole is indispensable. Without it, we would have to construct at least four, perhaps five times as many prisons and jails than presently exist, in order to accommodate all of those not granted this "bad word." One way of living with this word without using it is to use a "good word" instead. This is like changing the name of *insane asylum* to *mental hospital* to the *institute for the psychologically challenged*. Actually, this name changing toward greater social acceptance or acceptability can be traced to Niccolo Machiavelli (1469–1527), who served the infamous Borgia family in Florence in the early 1500s. Name changing was regarded by Machiavelli as an important strategy by which the Borgias could rule more effectively. Thus, he advised them to dole out empty or meaningless titles to powerful landowners in and around Florence to keep them contented. Actually, Machiavelli intended that everyone in Florence should be aware of how they were being manipulated by the Borgias, since he published his writings for all to see. Unfortunately, the illiteracy rate in Florence was high, and many interpreted his advice to the Borgias as nefarious. Essentially, he got a bad rap for trying to do something useful to counteract the controlling and manipulative Borgia family.

In any case, how does this apply to parole? For one thing, Maine abolished it. In subsequent years, however, Maine has been reconsidering it. Maine also continues to have a parole board that convenes to hear parole-eligible cases of those convicted before 1976, when parole was formally abandoned. The federal government has established an alternative program for its prior parolees. Although there is still a U.S. Parole Commission, the U.S. Probation Office of each U.S. District Court is responsible for supervising federal releasees.

Parole Board Composition and Diversity

There is as much diversity among parole boards in the United States as there is associated with sentencing systems. There are no graduate schools in the United States offering degrees leading to parole board membership. Furthermore, the diversity of legal structures among jurisdictions and the complex interaction of legislative, judicial, and administrative decisions that ultimately determine the time served in prison by inmates add to the already complicated tasks of parole boards (Gottfredson and Gottfredson, 1988:234; Winfree et al., 1988). Thus, it is difficult if not impossible to generalize about all parole boards, the decisions they make, and the reasons for those decisions.

Compared with other jurisdictions, Massachusetts probably has the most stringent criteria for parole board membership compared with other jurisdictions. Members of the Massachusetts Parole Board must possess a bachelor's degree and have five or more years of experience in corrections, law enforcement, social work, or other related field. One parole board member must be an attorney, while another must be a physician. States such as Texas, Oregon, and North Dakota do not prescribe special qualifications. Governors make parole board appointments in most jurisdictions. Thus, membership on these boards is highly politicized.

Functions of Parole Boards

Factors Influencing Parole Philosophy.   The functions of parole in a majority of jurisdictions are influenced by a philosophy promoting accountability, punishment, reintegration, and rehabilitation. Below are several general parole aims that reflect its philosophy:

1. Parole is a reintegrative mechanism for easing inmates back into their communities. The prison experience is highly regimented and far different from routine community life. Inmates who have served long prison terms frequently find it difficult to make the transition to community life.

2. Parole provides inmates with an incentive to obey prison rules. Failure to behave well while incarcerated will definitely jeopardize parole chances. As we have previously seen in at least one state, good-time credits may be earned and counted against extra time to be served, which is added on to an incoming inmate's sentence. If inmates earn good-time credit by obeying prison rules, then they can reduce or even eliminate this extra time to be served. In most states with good-time provisions, however, inmates may shorten their original sentences by exhibiting good or conforming behavior. This is a strong incentive to do well and does much to foster orderliness in prisons.

3. Prison overcrowding is eased through parole. It functions as an administrative safety valve to control overcrowding. However, some jurisdictions have restricted or eliminated entirely conditions under which parole may be granted (U.S. Sentencing Commission, 1987).

4. Parole deters criminal conduct, since parolees require some degree of supervision by parole officers. Those programs with greater intensity of supervision tend to have lower rates of recidivism. And, electronic monitoring programs have enhanced parole officer abilities to monitor client whereabouts and verify their presence at home or work.

5. Parole protects the public by controlling parolee conduct through supervised release. Parole officers visit parolee residences and workplaces and verify their whereabouts, attitude, and general conduct. The greater the supervision by parole officers, the less likelihood of committing new offenses.

6. Parole minimizes sentencing disparities that are often attributable to race or ethnicity, gender, and socioeconomic status. Early release decisions are calculated, in part, to remedy earlier sentencing disparities. This does not excuse parole board decisions that are not equitable, however.

7. Parole promotes rehabilitation. Few experts believe that inmates are rehabilitated by strict confinement. Inmates involved in prison vocational programs often fail to remain employed when released. At the very least, parole gives ex-convicts opportunities to support their families and participate in counseling.

Some Major Parole Board Functions.   Not every parole board in the United States has identical functions. However, a *synthesis* of functions is possible by comparing the goals and philosophical statements of various boards. A result of this synthesis includes the following major functions of parole boards:

1. To evaluate prison inmates who are eligible for parole and act on their application to approve or deny parole;
2. To convene to determine whether parole should be revoked on the basis of alleged parole violations.
3. To evaluate juveniles to determine their eligibility for release from detention;
4. To grant pardons or commutations of sentences to prisoners, where mitigating circumstances or new information is presented that was not considered at trial;
5. To make provisions for the supervision of adult offenders placed on parole; to establish supervisory agencies and select parole officers to monitor offender behavior;
6. To provide investigative and supervisory services to smaller jurisdictions within the state;
7. To grant reprieves in death sentence cases and to commute death penalties;
8. To restore full civil and political rights to parolees and others on conditional release, including probationers;
9. To review disparate sentences and make recommendations to the governor for clemency; and
10. To review the pardons and executive clemency decisions made by the governor.

Most parole boards make parole decisions exclusively. In a limited number of jurisdictions, these additional functions are performed, either according to statute or at the pleasure of the governor. In a limited number of jurisdictions, the paroling authority is vested in agencies independent of the governor.

Parole boards may evolve their own standards, subject to legislative approval. For instance, the Connecticut Parole Board has several standards that govern each early-release decision, including

1. Nature and circumstances of inmate offenses and their current attitudes toward them.
2. Inmate's prior record and parole adjustment if paroled previously.
3. Inmate's attitude toward family members, the victim, and authority in general.
4. Institutional adjustment of inmates, including their participation in vocational-educational programs while incarcerated.
5. Inmate's employment history and work skills.
6. Inmate's physical, mental, and emotional condition as determined from interviews and other diagnostic information available.
7. Inmate's insight into the causes of his or her own criminal behavior in the past.
8. Inmate's personal efforts to find solutions to personal problems such as alcoholism, drug dependency, and need for educational training or developing special skills.
9. Adequacy of the inmate's parole plan, including planned place of residence, social acquaintances, and employment program (Connecticut Board of Parole, 1974).

All parole boards establish criteria to govern their parole decisions similar to those developed by Connecticut. Occasionally, psychiatric reports or examinations are prepared at the time of an inmate's sentencing. Another document is the PSI. This report is often consulted in order to assist board members in making the best early-release decisions. Finally, parole boards may sometimes rely on victim testimony at parole hearings. Several states currently permit victim participation in parole board consideration for specific inmates. Victims may offer either written or oral testimony at these parole hearings, and parole boards weigh such written or oral testimony accordingly (Parsonage, 1992).

Parole Board Decision Making and Inmate Control

A major factor influencing parole board decision making is prison overcrowding. It is exerting a tremendous impact on how corrections professionals do their jobs. Dramatic increases in parole supervision have been observed, and the number of parole release and revocation hearings has grown markedly over the years (Burke, 1987:74). The aims of parole boards are similar to those of sentencing: treatment, incapacitation, deterrence, and desert (Gottfredson and Gottfredson, 1988:230). However, parole boards appear to receive more criticism from the public about the decisions they make compared with earlier similar judicial decisions. The significant question for parole boards is when to release inmates rather than whether to release them (Gottfredson, Wilkins, and Hoffman, 1978). Some states have attempted to adopt parole guidelines as a means of objectifying early-release decision making. However, parole boards in these jurisdictions have been hesitant, if not resistant, to adopting paroling guidelines. One reason given is parole board fears about losing control over the frequency of inmate releases (Martinez, 1988). Also, parole boards do not know for sure which variables are most crucial in making these early-release decisions for particular parole-eligible inmates (Bonham, Janeksela, and Bardo, 1986). The use of risk-screening instruments for determining which offenders should be paroled have exhibited results that are unimpressive (Austin and Litsky, 1985; Champion, 1994).

The National Institute of Corrections has received requests for and provided technical assistance to parole boards in making early release decisions (Burke, 1987:74). One result of these and other similar consultations has been the formulation of explicit guidelines and policies to govern individual release or revocation decisions (Burke, 1987:76). It has been suggested by some corrections experts that parole boards should focus on at least five major areas. These include

1. *Policy Making.* How does policy making differ from individual decision making? How does it relate to individual discretion? What steps are involved? Who must participate? How can policy be made operational?
2. *Management.* What management needs exist? How can board and staff roles for management be clarified?

3. *Roles of Research.* How can research be used to inform policy making and decision making? What role must policy makers play in developing risk instruments? How can parole decision makers communicate effectively with technical staff?

4. *Criminal Justice System Issues.* How can the critical overlap between parole and other agencies be identified? What are viable mechanisms for cooperation? How do other agencies' policies and practices influence workload?

5. *Strategies.* What are effective strategies for handling and building effective working relationships with the various public interests that are of importance to parole? (Burke, 1987:78)

Parole boards are faced with a difficult dilemma: They must balance carefully the decision to release an inmate who might be truly rehabilitated and reintegrated into his or her community through such a release with the decision to release an offender who might inflict further harm upon the community through the commission of future violent acts. They must resolve, or attempt to resolve, this dilemma in the context of satisfying consistent and impartial standards expected by both prisoners and public alike. If two persons in the same jurisdiction are convicted of identical crimes under similar circumstances and sentenced by the same judge to identical terms, and if a parole board decides to grant early release to one prisoner before the other, a disparity exists that ought to be explained. In California, for example, many citizens have strong antiparole attitudes (Barkdull, 1988). It is recommended by some experts, therefore, that paroling authorities spend some time acquainting and educating the citizenry about the various benefits of parole and how their objectives include public safety and protection as a primary consideration (Library Information Specialists, Inc., 1985a). However, when high-profile parolee cases occur or whenever halfway houses and other parolee services are placed in neighborhoods where they are immediately recognizable as havens for ex-convicts, public fears are heightened. Barkdull argues for a strong public relations program to involve the public to a greater degree in early-release decision making and parole board rationales for their decisions (Barkdull, 1988).

When offenders become eligible for parole, this does not mean parole will automatically be granted by the parole board. Parole boards have considerable discretionary power, and in many jurisdictions, they have absolute discretion over an inmate's early release potential. In fact, when federal courts have been petitioned to intervene and challenge parole board actions, the decisions of parole boards have prevailed (*Tarlton v. Clark*, 1971). Although we have already examined parole boards, their composition, and their functions, it is helpful to review briefly some of the more important factors influencing parole board decision making. In deciding whether or not to grant parole for given inmates, the following factors are considered:

1. The commission of serious disciplinary infractions while confined;
2. The nature and pattern of previous convictions;
3. The adjustment to previous probation, parole, and/or incarceration;
4. The facts and circumstances of the offense;

BOX 7.1
Deciding Not to Parole Dangerous Persons

The Case of Richard Speck

A parole board's evaluation of a prisoner's potential risk to society is believed by many to be a key function of parole (Rhine et al., 1989:78). Considering all other decisions made prior to an offender's incarceration, however, this particular parole function misleads the public (Dietz, 1985:32). Of course, there are exceptions. In 1987, Richard Speck, 45, became eligible for parole consideration for the fifth time. In July 1966, he was convicted of murdering eight student nurses in their Chicago townhouse. Originally sentenced to death, Speck was resentenced to serve from 400 to 1,200 years in prison when the constitutionality of the death penalty was questioned in the early 1970s. At the time of the murders, Speck was a 24-year-old high school dropout who drifted from job to job before moving to Chicago three weeks prior to the crime spree. According to Illinois statutes, however, Speck became eligible for parole after serving a minimum number of years of his original sentence.

Relatives and friends of the murdered student nurses attended the meeting of the Illinois Prisoner Review Board considering Speck's application for parole on September 2, 1987. They urged the parole board members not to grant Speck parole because they feared he would kill again. Would Speck kill again if released? No parole board can answer this question. No device exists at present that would allow any parole-granting body to make a decision such as this with any degree of certainty. At the same time, it is evident from prison reports that Speck has exhibited proper inmate behavior. Is parole under intensive supervision or is electronic monitoring a possible solution concerning Speck's parole chances? Obviously, relatives of Speck's victims are quite concerned about the particular function parole is intended to serve. But despite Speck's earlier atrocities, certain legal and ethical issues are raised involving Speck's own constitutional rights and the extent to which predictions of his dangerousness should influence his continued confinement. Subsequently, Richard Speck died in prison of natural causes in 1993.

Source: Gottfredson and Torry, 1987: 376–377.

5. The aggravating and mitigating factors surrounding the offense;
6. Participation in institutional programs that might have led to the improvement of problems diagnosed at admission or during incarceration;
7. Documented changes in attitude toward self or others;
8. Documentation of personal goals and strengths or motivation for law-abiding behavior;
9. Parole plans;
10. Inmate statements suggesting the likelihood that the inmate will not commit future offenses; and

11. Court statements about the reasons for the sentence (e.g., the presentence investigation report). (Dietz, 1985:32)

If the parole board reacts favorably and grants an inmate parole, it is usually conditional and subject to compliance with various rules and regulations. If the parole board reacts unfavorably and denies the inmate parole, usually one or more reasons are provided by the board for the action taken. Most jurisdictions obligate their parole boards to outline the reasons for their actions or at least make their reasons for denial of early release known to the inmate. This provides the inmate with an opportunity to improve in those areas cited by the board as unsatisfactory or unfavorable. Rehearings in some jurisdictions are conducted at regular intervals, usually annually (American Correctional Association, 1988:128).

Parole boards often rely on the idea that if inmates have behaved well while confined, they might behave well if paroled. Parole-release policies that utilize an inmate's good behavior while confined as a crucial factor in determining early release are in for a rude awakening. Evidence suggests that good behavior while incarcerated does not necessarily mean that an inmate will successfully adapt to the community and be law abiding following a favorable early-release decision (Emshoff and Davidson, 1987; Gottfredson and Gottfredson, 1988:251; Haesler, 1992; Metchik, 1992a, 1992b). In fact, many criminal justice professionals believe that a prisoner's behavior, either before or during prison confinement, does not correlate highly with recidivism (Gottfredson and Adams, 1982).

It is often the case that factors outside the prison setting are better predictors of parolee success. For instance, do parolees have favorable job prospects? Can they obtain jobs and retain them? Are they married? Are they participating in academic or vocational training programs while on parole? Have they had prior problems with drug or alcohol abuse? Are they taking steps to see that these particular addiction or dependency problems will not reoccur? One study reporting largely favorable results about parolee success examined 760 adult releasees from a midwestern prison. It was found that of these 760 releasees, only 177 became parole violators. Factors such as those listed above appeared crucial in determining their success chances. Most parole violators had no job services contacts following their release. Drug-dependent or alcohol-dependent releasees who did not seek treatment for their dependencies were more likely to recidivate while on parole. However, those who had good job contacts, manifested marital stability, and participated in constructive educational, vocational, or counseling programs were more apt to be successful while on parole (Anderson, Schumacker, and Anderson, 1991).

At the same time, there are community pressures exerted on known releasees. Sometimes, these pressures create obstacles to effective parolee reintegration, particularly if community residents actively reject them socially. Ex-offenders sometimes have great difficulty finding jobs and housing if it is known to employers and rental agencies that these persons have prior records. Thus, through no particular fault of their own (short of having a prior record), parolees who make an honest effort to become reintegrated into their communities are frustrated by community residents unwilling to accept them (Barkdull, 1988; Haesler, 1992, Milkman, 1985).

Parole Board Orientations

Decisions made by parole boards can be classified into six general categories, each manifesting a particular value system: (1) the jurist, (2) the sanctioner, (3) the treater, (4) the controller, (5) the citizen, and (6) the regulator (These types and their descriptions are derived largely from the work of O'Leary and Hall [1976] and presented in Gottfredson and Gottfredson, 1988:231–233.) The **jurist value system** sees parole decisions as a natural part of criminal justice where fairness and equity predominate. Emphasized are an inmate's rights, and parole board members strive to be sensitive to due process. The **sanctioner value system** equates the seriousness of the offense with the amount of time served. In some respects, this is closely connected with the just-deserts philosophy.

The **treater value system** is rehabilitative in orientation, and decisions are made in the context of what might most benefit the offender if parole is granted. Thus, participation in various educational or vocational programs, therapy or encounter groups, restitution, and other types of conditions might accompany one's early release. The **controller value system** emphasizes the functions of parole supervision and monitoring. Conditions that increase the degree of control over the offender are established. Perhaps electronic monitoring or house arrest might be part of the parole program. In any case, the controller value system sees offender incapacitation or severe restrictions of freedom while on parole as desirable. It is most concerned with the risk posed to the public by an offender's early release.

The **citizen value system** is concerned with appealing to public interests and seeing that community expectations are met by making appropriate early-release decisions. How will the public react to releasing certain offenders short of serving their full terms? Will public good be served by such decisions? Community harmony and social order should be preserved, and parole board decisions should be made that promote community harmony and order. In view of mixed public sentiment and current dissatisfaction with parole board decision making generally, this is seemingly an impossible task. Finally, the **regulator value system** is directed toward inmate reactions to parole board decisions. How will current inmates react to those decisions in view of their own circumstances? Will the parole supervision system be undermined or enhanced as the result of parole board decision making (Langston, 1988a, 1988b)? Inmate reaction is of paramount concern to parole board authorities who seek to maintain their credibility among the very persons their decisions directly affect (Gottfredson and Gottfredson, 1988:231–232; O'Leary and Hall, 1976).

When parole board decision making is considered in these diverse and sometimes conflicting contexts, it is easier to understand why extensive variability exists among parole boards in different jurisdictions. Each parole board member possesses one or another of these value systems. It is not likely that an entire parole board is closely connected with one view exclusively. Rather, these different values explain in part why apparently inconsistent decisions about the early release of similar inmates are made, even by the same parole boards, at different points in time.

Developing and Implementing Objective Parole Criteria

With such diversity among parole board members and the values they espouse, is it possible to establish objective parole criteria to govern all parole board decision making? Theoretically, objective parole criteria would immunize parole board members from accusations of racism as the result of releasing disproportionately large numbers of offenders of particular races or ethnic backgrounds. Parole board member liability would be limited in instances in which offenders are granted early release and who are especially dangerous and pose substantial danger to the community.

Objective parole criteria have been compared with determinate sentencing policies, whereas traditional parole criteria have been equated with indeterminate sentencing systems (Lombardi and Lombardi, 1986:86). Among the advantages of objective parole criteria are

1. Inmates know their presumptive release dates within several months of their incarceration.
2. The paroling authority is bound or obligated to meet the presumptive release date.
3. The paroling authority uses scores consisting of an inmate's criminal history and offense severity to determine time ranges for parole release.
4. The paroling authority uses a composite group score representing criminal histories of similar offenders to predict parole success. (Lombardi and Lombardi, 1986:86–87)

Ironically, these objective parole criteria function to restrict the discretionary power and flexibility of parole boards. Therefore, whereas fairness to offenders and parole board accountability are increased by making the parole release decision-making process more explicit and consistent, there are some undesirable, unanticipated consequences (Lombardi and Lombardi, 1986:8). For example, the Florida Parole Commission implemented new objective parole criteria in 1980 (Lombardi, 1981). Prior to 1980, adult inmates of Florida's prisons had filed an average of 400 civil lawsuits annually. After the objective criteria went into effect, the number of lawsuits increased to more than 1,800 per year. The Florida Parole Commission's legal department had to increase its staff of attorneys from two to seven (Lombardi and Lombardi, 1986:87).

Florida inmate lawsuits involved primarily four issues directly related to the new objective parole criteria. First, inmates alleged that objective scoring system errors led to unfavorable classifications and unjustifiably longer incarceration terms. Second, inmates claimed they originally had been placed in the wrong level of **offense severity,** often stemming from an erroneous interpretation of their plea agreements. Third, the inmates claimed parole board members inconsistently extended or shortened their incarceration length by either considering or failing to consider certain aggravating circumstances such as using a weapon during the commission of the crime or causing serious injury to victims. The fourth issue alleged parole board failure to consider mitigating circumstances that would lessen the length of incarceration (Lombardi, 1981). All of these issues seemingly could be remedied by close monitoring of all parole board decision making and insistence on consistency in the application of standards.

Actually, interest in devising consistent and objective early-release criteria is probably as old as parole itself. Most of the popular and more scientific methods for devising predictive criteria have been developed since the late 1960s, however. In 1972, the U.S. Parole Commission started to use an actuarial device in predicting parole success of federal prisoners (Hoffman, 1983). By the early 1980s, every state had either devised a system or was using one originated by another jurisdiction whereby parole decision making could be objectified (Gottfredson and Tonry, 1987).

Corrections experts currently contend that the technology exists that can classify offenders accurately on the basis of their potential risk to public safety, social service, educational and vocational needs, and individual behavioral profiles. However, these experts also charge that many paroling bodies have not as yet fully exploited this technology in a cooperative and systematic manner (Atkinson, 1986:56). At the same time, other experts caution that the current state-of-the-art in statistical risk prediction is such that many developed models are unstable when applied to various prisoner populations from one state to the next (Wright, Clear and Dickson, 1984). Furthermore, insufficient validation of prediction instruments has occurred. When a parole risk-assessment device was developed by Wisconsin officials for parole board decision making, for example, the device became popularly applied in several other states, especially after being recognized as a useful instrument by the National Institute of Corrections. However, the Wisconsin instrument appeared to lack validity when applied to a sample of New York parolees (Wright, Clear, and Dickson, 1984). This strongly suggests the need to devise measures that are applicable for selected inmate populations on a state-by-state basis.

For example, the Ohio Parole Board uses the following criteria as guidelines:

1. Current offense and details of the crime;
2. Prior record: felonies-misdemeanors-juvenile;
3. Supervision experiences: parole-furlough-probation;
4. Institution adjustment: job assignment–work-evaluation rule infractions;
5. Substance abuse program participation;
6. Vocational or academic training;
7. Personality evaluation: I.Q.–highest grade completed;
8. Psychological reports;
9. Psychiatric reports;
10. Personal history factors: marital status, employment history, work skills, special problems;
11. Parole plan: living arrangements, employment plans;
12. Community attitude: prosecutor's recommendation, judge's recommendation, police or sheriff's recommendation, victim's statement;
13. Detainers;
14. Type and number of prior hearings; and

15. Results of prehearing conference with Case Manager or Unit Manager. (Ohio Department of Rehabilitation and Correction, 1989:4)

These criteria are only guidelines, as noted by the Ohio Parole Board. Therefore, there may be departures, more or less punitive, considering the degree of aggravation or mitigation—accompanying any eligible inmate's early-release request. It is Ohio's experience that using these criteria in conjunction with several other measures will increase parole board effectiveness to about 75 percent. In short, Ohio authorities believe that 75 percent of their early-release decision making with these guidelines will result in successful decision making. Viewed another way, Ohio authorities expect no more than a 25 percent degree of recidivism among those paroled. Ohio bases its guidelines system on five major components:

1. *Risk Instrument:* The risk instrument is critical to the guidelines system. It looks at several factors dealing with an inmate's prior criminal history, including the number of probations, paroles, and revocations. Age at first felony conviction and substance abuse history are also related to risk-assessed points. The risk level totals equal 1, 2, or 3. The higher the number, the higher is the risk.
2. *Offense Score:* Included in the guideline system are several offenses designated as Endangering Offenses. If an inmate has ever been convicted of an Endangering Offense, either as a juvenile or adult, one point is assessed toward the total score.
3. *Institutional Score:* The Parole Board will make a determination of the inmate's institutional adjustment at the time of the hearing. If the inmate is now serving or has recently served time in Disciplinary Control, Local Control, or Administrative Control, one (1) point will be assessed toward the total score.
4. *Aggregate Score:* The sum total of the Risk Score, the Offense Score, and the Institution Score equals the Aggregate Score.
5. *Matrix:* The Matrix is a grid containing 24 cell divisions. Each cell contains the guidelines procedure into which an inmate is placed and a continuance range if the decision is not to release. The horizontal axis of the grid is the "Aggregate Score" 1–5. The vertical axis is the felony level reflecting the inmate's sentence. Sentences range from fourth degree to Life. (Ohio Department of Rehabilitation and Correction, 1989:6–7)

Age, prior record, and *drug and alcohol dependencies* are obviously considered significant risk factors, at least for these instruments developed in these particular jurisdictions. In fact, these are critical components of most scales examined. Many jurisdictions believe that one's employment history and attitude (measured in different ways) are also crucial to good parole decision making. The rationale for including these different components is grounded in considerable empirical research. We have already seen that many studies have focused on recidivism and the characteristics of recidivists. Most of these studies have provided the bases for making actuarial predictions for various offender aggregates. Thus, younger offenders have higher recidivism rates than older offenders (Baird et al., 1987; Bonham et al., 1984; Decker and Salert, 1986). The age at which the onset of criminal behavior occurs is an important predictor. The earlier the onset of criminal conduct, the more likely recidivism will occur (Murphy, 1980:14).

Those with poor previous employment histories have greater recidivism com-

When parolees are released from confinement conditionally, they must submit a parole plan indicating the nature of the future employment, residence, and social support. (Strickler/Monkmeyer Press)

pared with those with good previous employment histories. Alcohol and/or drug dependencies seem highly correlated with program failure. Unstable community and family life (indicated, in part, by frequent changes of address and evidence of family instability) are also associated with higher recidivism rates. Likewise, poor attitudes toward accepting responsibility for one's actions seem indicative of higher recidivism than good attitudes in this regard. Independent investigations of each of these factors as predictors have confirmed their utility for accurate parole forecasting (Gottfredson and Gottfredson, 1990; Haapanen, 1988; Hiday, 1990; Hughes, 1985; Kalichman, 1988; Komala and Shepperd, 1990; Mair, 1989; McGrath, 1991; Towberman, 1992; Valenzuela, Vallaneuva, and Aguilera, 1991; Zimmerman and Cohen, 1990). Some investigators have also noted that gender is a distinguishing variable in some parole decision making. Therefore, it may make a difference if the inmate's male or female (Erez, 1992).

The Nevada Department of Corrections attempts to assess parole success with a risk/needs instrument. This instrument contains Parole Success Likelihood Factors, including age, prior convictions, incarcerations since age 17, history of drug abuse, employment history, use of a weapon in the instant offense, and prison programming. On the basis of the score on this instrument, a prospective parolee will be placed into one severity level or another. These inmate placements significantly influence parole likelihood and subsequent parole board action.

The Massachusetts Parole Board uses a Release Risk Classification Instrument shown later in Figure 7.2. This is a relatively simple instrument and is based largely on Peter Hoffman's Salient Factor Score Index (SFS 81) (Hoffman, 1983). A somewhat more elaborate initial client assessment form is used by North Carolina. This form solicits and uses information about financial situation, employment or student status, marital status, educational attainment, general attitude, and prior history of alcohol or drug dependencies. The risk-needs assessment instrument used by Pennsylvania is one of the most elaborate parole instruments currently used by various state parole boards. This instrument contains extensive information about institutional conduct, specific program guidelines, stipulations, and special parole conditions, and a concurrence statement completed by parole board members. Again, however, we must be aware of the fact that simply because instruments are more or less complex, this does not mean they are more or less reliable when compared with one another. The particular length and complexity of risk-needs assessment inventories are unrelated to accurate prediction of future parole program behavior.

Similar to initial classifications conducted by prison officials and subsequent reassessments of inmates, parole boards also utilize reassessments of client risk after parolees have functioned for several months in their respective parole programs. Some jurisdictions have established rather specific prediction schemes based on some or all of these criteria. For example, Michigan has created five risk groupings based primarily on age, marital status, and previous institutional conduct, as follows:

Risk Group

Very High Risk: Instant offense of rape, robbery, or homicide and serious misconduct or security segregation and first arrest before fifteenth birthday.

High Risk: Instant offense of rape, robbery, or homicide and serious misconduct and age of first arrest was 15 or over.

Middle Risk: Instant offense of either rape, robbery, or homicide and no serious misconduct; or instant offense not rape, robbery, or homicide (may be other assaultive crime) and no reported felony while juvenile and never been married at time of instant offense.

Very Low Risk: Instant offense, not rape, robbery, nor homicide and no reported felony while juvenile and not serving on other assaultive crime and has been married. (Murphy, 1980:3)

Some criteria, such as a detainer, previous institutional misconduct, and a personality profile, all seem to indicate whether would-be parolees would be successful if released short of serving their full sentences. A *detainer warrant* means that another jurisdiction wants the inmate on other charges. Thus, if detainer warrants are outstanding, a parolee might be more likely to flee the jurisdiction to escape prosecution from other jurisdictions. Institutional misconduct suggests an inability or unwillingness to comply with existing institutional rules. How will the offender react to a different set of rules if released on parole in the community? Does one type of behavior, nonconformist conduct, while incarcerated indicate similar behavior, nonconformist conduct, in a new situation? The chances are that if inmates are unruly while confined, they will be poor parole risks later. Finally, personality assessments are helpful to determine the potential for adjusting to community life. Personality disturbances or personal problems may interfere with normal functioning. If these problems can be detected in advance of parole, then affected inmates might benefit from specific treatment plans.

Ohio has one of the most comprehensive early-release schemes compared with other jurisdictions. The Ohio Parole Board incorporates all or most criteria used by other states. In addition, information is obtained relating to personality through psychiatric reports. Parolees must also file a parole plan, indicating their stability in the community if paroled. The Board also obtains input from victims, if any. Almost every salient dimension of social and psychological life is profiled by the Board to render the most objective parole decisions. Despite this extensive personal and social information, however, the Board does not expect perfection in prediction. It anticipates an accuracy factor of about 75 percent.

The National Council on Crime and Delinquency (1990a, 1990b) has examined risk prediction extensively and has constructed risk-assessment devices for various states, including California, South Carolina, Oregon, Alaska, Illinois, Louisiana, and Tennessee (National Council on Crime and Delinquency, 1990b). The Council's survey of existing or currently used instruments indicates the following factors that most often appear as risk predictors:

1. Number of prior convictions;
2. Number of prior incarcerations;
3. Age at first commitment, conviction, or arrest;
4. Drug abuse history;
5. Convictions for burglary, forgery, theft;
6. Alcohol abuse history;
7. Employment history;
8. School adjustment;
9. Probation and/or parole history; and
10. Peer involvement. (1990b:5)

Regardless of the predictive utility of these items, the Council has exhibited a failure rate for various sample predictions of about 30 percent. According to the Council, its primary problem is that accurate data concerning prospective parolees are often difficult to obtain. Therefore, predictions of success for different offender aggregates are always tainted by the unknown influence of extraneous variables (National Council on Crime and Delinquency, 1990b:6–7).

Another important factor is the extent to which offenders will be supervised when released. The closer the supervision, the greater is the compliance with program requirements. Intensive supervised parole, with more face-to-face visits and drug or alcohol testing, seems to have a lower amount of recidivism compared with more standardized parole programs. Some programs for prospective parolees are most helpful in making the transition to community living, however. For instance, work and study release and furlough programs enable many program participants to gradually accept community responsibilities and prove themselves for full parole later. The rates of recidivism associated with these programs are considerably lower than rates of recidivism associated with standard parole.

Salient Factor Scores

Although a weighting system for parole prognosis was developed by Ernest W. Burgess of the University of Chicago in 1928 (Glaser, 1987:256), the development of currently applicable objective parole decision-making guidelines can be traced to the pioneering work of Don Gottfredson and Leslie Wilkins, leaders of the Parole Decision-Making Project in the early 1970s (Goldkamp, 1987:106). At that time, the National Council on Crime and Delinquency and the U.S. Parole Commission (originally the U.S. Board of Parole) were interested in parole decision making and solicited the assistance of social scientists to examine various criteria involved in early-release decisions (Goldkamp, 1987:106).

The Parole Decision-Making Project led to the adoption of a preliminary set of guidelines that provided parole board members with specific criteria to assess the success of granting parole to various offenders. Categories of offenders were established by these guidelines and based, in part, on a ranking of offense severity as well as a salient factor score (Gottfredson, Wilkins, and Hoffman, 1978). A **salient factor score (SFS)** is a numerical classification that supposedly predicts the probability of a parolee's success if parole is granted.

Ideally, the salient factor score was designed to assist parole board members to make fair, objective, and just parole decisions. Unusual departures from these guidelines by parole boards were to be accompanied by written rationales outlining the reasons for such departures. In 1973, the U.S. Parole Commission formally adopted these parole decision guidelines and SFSs were used in all federal parole hearings (Goldkamp, 1987:106). This was largely the result of a federal court order for the U.S. Board of Parole to articulate specifically its policies for granting parole (*Childs v. United States Board of Parole,* 1973). Several states were encouraged by the use of SFSs and either adopted the federal format or adopted their own systems.

At the federal level, the salient factor score was made up of seven criteria and was refined in 1976. This was referred to as **SFS 76.** In August 1981, the salient factor scoring instrument underwent further revision, and a new, six-factor predictive device, **SFS 81,** was constructed (Hoffman, 1983). A comparison of the revised SFS 81 with its previous counterpart (SFS 76) was made according to validity, stability, simplicity, scoring reliability, and certain ethical concerns. Both instruments appeared to have similar predictive characteristics, although the revised device possesses greater scoring reliability (Hoffman, 1983). Of even greater significance is that SFS 81 places considerable weight on the extent and recency of an offender's criminal history (Hoffman, 1983). Up to seven points can be earned by having no prior convictions or adjudications (adult or juvenile), no prior commitments of more than 30 days, and being 26 years of age or older at the time of the current offense (with certain exceptions). Figure 7.1 shows the six-item federal Salient Factor Score instrument, SFS 81.

Classification systems, such as the SFS 81 instrument, are simply models. These models are assigned names such as the National Institute of Corrections Prison Classification Model or the Iowa Risk Assessment Model (Rans, 1984:50). Another parole instrument is shown in Figure 7.2. Some authorities have outlined some important and desirable characteristics of such predictive models. These include

1. The model should be predictively valid.
2. The model should reflect reality.
3. The model should be designed for a dynamic system and not remain fixed over time.
4. The model should serve practical purposes.
5. The model should not be a substitute for good thinking and responsible judgment.
6. The model should be both qualitative and quantitative. (Rans, 1984:50)

Scores on the SFS 81 can range from 0 to 10. The following evaluative designations accompany various score ranges:

Raw Score	Parole Prognosis
0–3	Poor
4–5	Fair
6–7	Good
8–10	Very Good

The paroling authority next consults a table of offense characteristics that consists of categories varying in offense severity. Adult ranges in numbers of months served are provided for each category and are cross-tabulated with the four-category parole prognosis above. Thus, a parole board can theoretically apply a consistent set of standards to prisoners who commit similar offenses. When the board departs from these standards, especially when parole is possible for an offender but denied, a written rationale is provided for both the prisoner and appellate authorities.

Salient Factor Score Index

1. Prior convictions/adjudications (adult or juvenile):
   None (3 points)
   One (2 points)
   Two or three (1 point)
   Four or more (0 points)

2. Prior commitments of more than 30 days (adult or juvenile):
   None (2 points)
   One or two (1 point)
   Three or more (0 points)

3. Age at current offense/prior commitments:
   25 years of age or older (2 points)
   20–25 years of age (1 point)
   19 years of age or younger (0 points)

4. Recent commitment free period (three years):
   No prior commitment of more than 30 days (adult or juvenile) or released to the community from last such commitment at least three years prior to the commencement of the current offense (1 point)
   Otherwise (0 points)

5. Probation/parole/confinement/escape status violator this time:
   Neither on probation, parole, confinement, or escape status at the time of the current offense, nor committed as a probation, parole, confinement, or escape status violator this time (1 point)
   Otherwise (0 points)

6. Heroin or opiate dependence:
   No history of heroin or opiate dependence (1 point)
   Otherwise (0 points)
   Total score = _____

FIGURE 7.1 Salient Factor Score Index, SFS 81. (*Source:* U.S. Parole Commission *Rules and Procedures Manual.* Washington, DC: U.S. Parole Commission, 1985.)

The 1985 guidelines are somewhat less severe compared with those established in 1981. Comparing figures pertaining to time served before parole eligibility occurs shows many similarities, although in several instances, fewer months must be served for different offense severity levels. In any case, a parole board may depart from these guidelines and either shorten or lengthen the amount of time to be served (*Yamamoto v. U.S. Parole Commission,* 1986; *Lynch v. U.S. Parole Commission,* 1985; *Robinson v. Hadden,* 1983; *Stroud v. U.S. Parole Commission,* 1982). But written justification must be provided (*Myrick v. Gunnell,* 1983). And, an inmate has the right to appeal the decision of the parole board to a higher authority such as the National Appeals Board (18 U.S.C. Sec. 4215, 1995).

Consistency is highly desirable in the application of any parole criteria (Gabor, 1986:19). Many inmate lawsuits involve allegations of inconsistent application of parole eligibility guidelines. The U.S. Parole Commission has stressed consistency in the application of its own standards. In 1982, a sample of 100 initial pa-

MASSACHUSETTS PAROLE BOARD

Release Risk Classification Instrument

Name: _____ MCI-Number: _____

SID: _____ Actual Release Date: _____

Hearing Location: _____ Hearing Date: _____

Completed By: _____ Completion Date: _____

Controlling Effective Date of Commitment: _____

```
1. Number of returns to higher custody since      0 = 0 points
   the Controlling Effective Date of             1 = 2 points
   Commitment: (Count all revocations, returns   2, 3 = 4 points
   from escape and probation surrenders)     4 or more = 6 points  [  ]

2. Custody standing prior to the       Not under custody = 0 points
   Controlling Effective Date of   On street supervision = 1 point
   Commitment:                           Incarceration = 2 points  [  ]

3. Total number of parole revocations on prior     None = 0 points
   state sentences:                          1 or more = 1 point   [  ]

4. Number of adult convictions for property        None = 0 points
   offenses prior to the Controlling        1 or more = 1 point    [  ]
   Effective Date of Commitment:

5. Number of charges for a person offense          None = 0 points
   as a juvenile:                           1 or more = 1 point    [  ]

6. Age at release hearing:               34 or older = 0 points
                                               28-33 = 2 points
                                               24-27 = 4 points
                                     23 or younger = 6 points      [  ]

7. Evidence of heroin, cocaine, or crack cocaine    No = 0 points
   use:                                      Yes = 2 points        [  ]
   Notes (verbal admission): _____
   _____

8. SCORE: Add the numerical scores of questions 1 through 7
          and enter the total score in this box.              [  ]

SCORING: A score between 0-4 = Low Risk; 5-10 = Moderate Risk, 11 or
         more = High Risk
```

FIGURE 7.2 Massachusetts Parole Board Release Risk Classification Instrument.

role hearings was selected, 20 from each of five U.S. Parole Commission regions. Hearing examiners and various panels of research experts agreed on the appropriate guideline range in 86 percent of the cases. Disagreements were attributable to lack of guideline clarity, inadequate file information, or plain error within the hearing panel itself (Beck and Hoffman, 1985).

Regardless of their individual motives, parole board members face another persistent problem. No matter how carefully they make decisions about parole-eligible offenders, a majority of these offenders will offend again when released. A New Jersey study of 3,634 parolees from a New Jersey state prison in 1984 showed that within a three-year follow-up, 62 percent of all parolees were rearrested (Corbo, 1992). Even among those offenders who were released because they had completed all of their time to be served, rearrests were relatively high. Compared with parolees, 57 percent of those who had served all of their prison time were rearrested and convicted for new offenses. At least for the New Jersey study, approximately 60 percent of all released offenders (either through parole or through completing their original sentences) were convicted for new offenses (Corbo, 1992).

The parole agreement is a contract between the offender and the state. The parole officer is usually responsible for ensuring offender compliance with the conditions set forth in the contract. In the event one or more conditions of the agreement are not complied with by the parolee, the discretionary power of the parole officer is invoked. The parole officer may choose to overlook the violation, depending on its seriousness. Or the officer may decide under the circumstances to recommend parole revocation. In some jurisdictions, the discretionary power of these officers is severely limited by judges, by parole boards, or by statute.

One continuing issue often contingent on parole officer action is recidivism. If the officer reports parole violators for violating curfew (e.g., not being on their premises by 9:00 P.M. each evening), the violators stand a good chance of being returned to prison. Some persons consider this action an indication that the parole program has somehow failed. This is a "technical violation," however, and it is not evidence of new criminal activity. Circumstances beyond a parolee's control may prevent the parolee from complying with parole requirements. On the other hand, a technical violation may be deliberate. And, some technical violations are common occurrences for anyone else other than parolees. The use of alcohol and firearms possession are taken for granted by most citizens. But for parolees, these technical violations may result in parole revocation. Random drug and alcohol tests may disclose that parolees have done something prohibited by the rules governing their parole. Complying with the rules of parole is an indication that parolees can comply with societal rules when they are completely free from the correctional system. Thus, minor infractions are indicators of future deviant behavior and criminality for some authorities. Some parole board members may regard rule infractions as sufficient to deny a parolee continuation of parole.

Others say that the program fails only when parolees commit new crimes of which they are convicted. In any case, there is an important discretionary function to be performed by the parole officer whenever parole violations are apparent. The decision made affects the life of the parolee as well as the life or lives of others de-

BOX 7.2
Are Persons Who Are Convicted of Violent Crimes Likely to Commit New Violent Crimes if Subsequently Paroled from Prison?
Some Violence Is Random and Unpredictable

The Case of Ronald Cobb

Ask Sgt. Jim Ramsey, a Houston homicide detective. He'll tell you. Most adult arrestees in Houston have prior criminal records. Ramsey says, "It's so common it would be very unusual if we did a criminal history check and didn't find . . . a suspect . . . was out on parole or had a criminal history." In 1990, Texas led the nation in the numbers of parolees, with 91,294. One-third of these parolees were in Houston. One of these parolees was Ronald Cobb, convicted in May 1988 of robbery. Cobb was originally sentenced to eight years in the Texas Department of Corrections. After serving only 18 months, Cobb was paroled.

It didn't take long for Cobb. Within a few months, he began using crack cocaine. While driving with a companion one evening, he pulled out a gun and shot and killed a panhandler. His friend began to complain. Cobb turned in the car and shot his friend. He kicked his wounded friend from the car and drove off. About 5:30 A.M. he rammed his car into the home of Richard Martini. Cobb didn't know Martini. Martini awakened and grabbed a nearby rifle, training it on Cobb. One way or another, Cobb got the rifle away from Martini. Cobb savagely assaulted Martini, blackening his eye and leaving him badly bruised. After giving Martini a sound beat-

ing, Cobb walked to Martini's back bedroom and killed himself with Martini's rifle. At least Martini's life was somehow spared.

In 1990, the Texas Department of Corrections was a system in crisis. Its prisons were quite overcrowded. In fact, a prisoner lawsuit was settled in 1985 whereby Texas agreed to eliminate the crowding problem. This meant that thousands of inmates would be released before serving their normal sentences. At that time, Texas inmates were serving about 35 percent of their originally imposed sentences. But after the 1985 agreement, the actual average amount of time served was about 20 percent of the original sentences imposed. Ronald Cobb was one of the inmates released as the result of this 1985 agreement to end prison overcrowding.

Who is to blame for Cobb's behavior? Is the state of Texas responsible? What about the Texas Board of Criminal Justice? How about Cobb's parole officer? What about the parole agency in Houston, Texas, where Cobb was supposedly supervised? Did anyone conduct random drug or alcohol checks on Cobb as a part of his conditional parole program? Should correctional systems be permitted to discharge inmates who don't serve all of their sentence time?

Source: Adapted from Julie Morris, *USA Today,* December 14, 1990:8A.

pendent on the parolee (e.g., supported children, spouse, and victim, in the case of restitution forthcoming from monies earned through offender employment).

TYPES OF PAROLE AND AN OVERVIEW OF PAROLE PROGRAMS

The programs available to parolees parallel those available to probationers. In most states and in the federal system, parolees and probationers report regularly to the same persons. Parolees are granted early release from incarceration by parole boards or some other paroling authority. This does not mean that they will be removed entirely from custody, however. There are several different kinds of programs catering to particular types of parolees and requiring varying levels of parolee custody. This section examines seven of these programs. These include (1) prerelease, (2) standard parole with conditions, (3) intensive supervised parole, (4) furloughs, (5) shock parole and shock probation, (6) work release and study release and, (7) halfway houses. Several alternative parole programs are also described briefly for overview purposes. Each of these programs is treated more extensively in Chapters 8 through 11. Several of these programs are closely associated with community-based services extended to probationers. Sometimes in some jurisdictions, both parolees and probationers will share these same services.

Prerelease

Two general types of prerelease are conditional and unconditional. **Conditional releases** are further subdivided into (1) parole board release, (2) mandatory parole, and (3) other conditional. **Unconditional releases** are divided according to (1) expiration, (2) **commutation** or pardon, and (3) other conditional (Minor-Harper and Innes, 1987). The greatest number of conditional releases are through parole board action, where early-release decisions are made according to parole board discretion. Mandatory parole releases involve those inmates who have served their sentences less the good-time credits they have accumulated. Thus, these releases are determined by calculating the original sentence less any good-behavior credits inmates acquired while in prison. These **mandatory releases** accounted for about one-third of all conditional releases. The remainder, other conditional, are probation and court-ordered releases. Some of these include inmates in overcrowded prisons, in which court-ordered prison population reductions are implemented.

Unconditional releases comprise those whose prison terms have expired. These are *statutory releases,* since the maximum time prescribed by law for the offense has been served in its entirety. A small portion of these offenders have their sentences commuted through pardons or other administrative action. Again, some of the unconditional releases in the "other unconditional" category result from court-ordered prison population reductions. Overall, about 75 percent of all those paroled complete their parole terms successfully (Minor-Harper and Innes, 1987).

Standard Parole with Conditions

Little has changed between 1984 and 1993 regarding parole program lengths of offenders previously convicted of different crimes. A comparison shows that for all offense categories, convicts spend an average of 46 months under correctional supervision, either in prison or on parole. On the average, parole accounts for about 41 percent of all time served for all offender categories. The average length of time spent on parole is 19 months. Those offenses drawing the longest parole lengths include murder (38 months), kidnapping (26 months), rape (26 months), and robbery (25 months). Those offenses drawing the shortest parole lengths pertain to public order (13 percent), stolen property (15 percent), and larceny or theft (15 percent) (Maguire, Pastore, and Flanagan, 1993).

Intensive Supervised Parole

Parolees are often subject to precisely the same kinds of behavioral requirements as probationers who are involved in intensive supervision programs. The New Jersey Intensive Supervision Program is made up of inmates who have served at least three or four months of their prison terms (Pearson, 1987:86). In fact, the term **shock parole** has been applied to this and similar programs, because an inmate is "shocked" with what it is like to be incarcerated.

The use of house arrest, electronic monitoring, and a host of other programs may be part of conditional early release from prison. The level of monitoring will vary according to the risk posed by the offender. But as has been seen time and time again, it is very difficult to predict accurately an offender's risk to the public or general dangerousness.

Most parolees are standard parolees, in the sense that they are obligated to adhere to certain standard early release agreements formulated by paroling authorities. In 1987, the U.S. Sentencing Commission implemented new guidelines, which included the following policy statement of recommended conditions of probation and supervised release:

1. The defendant shall not leave the judicial district or other specified geographical area without the permission of the court or PO.
2. The defendant shall report to the PO as directed by the court or PO and shall submit a truthful and complete written report within the first five days of each month.
3. The defendant shall answer truthfully all inquiries by the PO and follow the instructions of the PO.
4. The defendant shall support his dependents and meet other family responsibilities.
5. The defendant shall work regularly at a lawful occupation unless excused by the PO for schooling, training, or other acceptable reasons.
6. The defendant shall notify the PO within 72 hours of any change in residence or employment.
7. The defendant shall refrain from excessive use of alcohol and shall not purchase, pos-

sess, use, distribute, or administer any narcotic or other controlled substance, or any paraphernalia related to such substances, except as prescribed by a physician.

8. The defendant shall not frequent places where controlled substances are illegally sold, used, distributed, or administered, or other places specified by the court.

9. The defendant shall not associate with any persons engaged in criminal activity, and shall not associate with any person convicted of a felony, unless granted permission to do so by the PO.

10. The defendant shall permit a PO to visit him at any time at home or elsewhere and shall permit confiscation of any contraband observed in plain view by the PO.

11. The defendant shall notify the PO within 72 hours of being arrested or questioned by a law enforcement officer.

12. The defendant shall not enter into any agreement to act as an informer or a special agent of a law enforcement agency without the permission of the court.

13. As directed by the PO, the defendant shall notify third parties of risks that may be occasioned by the defendant's criminal record or personal history or characteristics, and shall permit the probation officer to make such notifications and to confirm the defendant's compliance with such notification requirement.

Additional special provisions pertain to possession of weapons, restitution, fines, debt obligations, access to financial information, community confinement, home detention, community service, occupational restrictions, substance abuse program participation, and mental health program participation (U.S. Sentencing Commission, 1987:5.7–5.10).

Furloughs

Furloughs are authorized, unescorted leaves from confinement granted for specific purposes and for designated time periods, usually from 24 to 72 hours, although they may be as long as several weeks or as short as a few hours (McCarthy and McCarthy, 1984:163). The overall aim of furlough programs as a form of temporary release is to assist the offender in becoming reintegrated into society.

Work Release and Study Release

Another type of temporary release program is work release. *Work release* (also called work furlough, day parole, day pass, and community work) refers to any program that provides for the labor of jail or prison inmates in the community under limited supervision, and where inmates are paid the prevailing wage (McCarthy and McCarthy, 1984:159–160). Sometimes, the terms *work release* and *furlough* are used interchangeably, referring to similar activities such as an inmate's participation in an educational program not ordinarily available to prison inmates while in prison. These are study release programs and are directly connected to an inmate's improvement and plans for employment when paroled.

Shock Probation and Shock Parole

Shock probation or *shock parole* refer to planned sentences for which judges order offenders imprisoned for statutory incarceration periods related to their conviction offenses. However, after 30, 60, 90, or even 120 days of incarceration, offenders are taken out of jail or prison and "resentenced" to probation, provided they behaved well while incarcerated. The "shock" factor relates to the shock of being imprisoned initially. Theoretically, this trauma will be so profound that inmates will not want to return to prison later. Therefore, a strong deterrent factor is associated with these terms. Ohio introduced the first shock probation law in 1965. Several other states have adopted similar laws in recent years (Friday and Peterson, 1972; Vito, 1978, 1984). In 1988, 1,056 offenders participated in nine shock incarceration programs throughout the country (Yurkanin, 1988:87).

Halfway Houses

One of the most important components of community-based corrections is the halfway house. Halfway houses are either publicly or privately operated facilities staffed by professionals, paraprofessionals, and volunteers. They are designed to assist parolees to make the transition from prison to the community. They provide food, clothing, temporary living quarters, employment assistance, and limited counseling. Again, if the parolee has been confined for a long period, the transition can be difficult, possibly even traumatic (Donnelly and Forschner, 1984).

PROBATION AND PAROLE REVOCATION: SOME COMMON ELEMENTS AND LANDMARK CASES

In 1871, a Virginia judge wrote explicitly in *Ruffin v. Commonwealth* (1871) that prisoners have no more rights than slaves (Bronstein, 1980:20). This pronouncement was most harsh and led to a milder expression to the extent that "conditions in prisons were off-limits to judicial scrutiny." In short, prisoners were left to the mercy of their keepers (Bronstein, 1980:20). Subsequently, inmate rights have changed substantially, although until the late 1960s, due process under the Fourteenth Amendment was not extended by the United States Supreme Court to include parolees or probationers concerning revocations of their respective statuses.

The first major prisoners' rights decision by the United States Supreme Court occurred in the case of *Johnson v. Avery* (1969) (Singer, 1980:67). This was a **jailhouse lawyer's** case in which one inmate would lend some legal assistance to other inmates, regardless of the quality of such assistance. Some inmates were illiterate or otherwise ignorant of their rights under the law. Formerly, *writ writers,* or inmate preparers of legal complaints against the prison administration on behalf of other inmates, were punished in various ways. In *Johnson v. Avery* (1969), the

Court held that prisons could not punish writ writers for lending assistance to other inmates unless the prison provided other means for assuring full access to the courts (Singer, 1980:67).

Parolees are technically inmates who have been granted early release subject to several conditions. In effect, this is a form of continued imprisonment or "constructive custody," implying that while offenders remain free, they are accountable to authorities and must adhere to a rigid set of restrictive behavioral criteria accompanying their parole (Bronstein, 1980:38; Burke, 1994; Burke, Bellassai, and Toborg, 1992). Whether due process under the Fourteenth Amendment extends to inmates (either inside or outside of penal facilities) has been challenged in the last several decades. But the issue was finally decided in the case of *Greenholtz v. Inmates of Nebraska* (1979) (Bronstein, 1980:38). While the Court said that the due process clause itself does not in and of itself create any special liberty interest in parole, the significance assigned it by any state (such as Nebraska) entitles prisoners affected to "minimum due process." Thus, the Court held that Nebraska had created such an interest in its parole statutory scheme and that therefore, prisoners were entitled to minimum due process (Bronstein, 1980:39).

An earlier case dealing with the revocation of probation was *Mempa v. Rhay* (1967). This case involved due process under the Fourteenth Amendment and involved a probationer who violated the terms of his probation. The matter was referred back to the original sentencing judge in a combined sentencing-revocation hearing. The U.S. Supreme Court ruled that this is a critical stage in which substantial rights of an accused are affected, and, therefore, the probationer is permitted to have court-appointed counsel at such a hearing.

The most significant cases influencing probation or parole revocation or any probation or **parole revocation hearing** occurred in the early 1970s. These were *Morrissey v. Brewer* (1972) and *Gagnon v. Scarpelli* (1973). *Morrissey v. Brewer* is considered the landmark case of parolee rights in revocation proceedings. Morrissey was a parolee who allegedly violated several parole conditions. The paroling authority summarily revoked his parole and he was returned to prison. The violations included (1) failing to report his place of residence to his parole officer, (2) buying an automobile under an assumed name and operating it without parole officer permission, (3) obtaining credit under an assumed name, and (4) giving false statements to police after a minor traffic accident. Morrissey appealed the summary revocation and the U.S. Supreme Court heard his case.

Among other things, the U.S. Supreme Court said in *Morrissey v. Brewer* that the minimum due process requirements for **parole revocation** are:

1. Two hearings are required: (a) the first is a preliminary hearing to determine whether probable cause exists that a parolee has violated any specific parole condition, and (b) a general revocation proceeding.
2. Written notice must be given to the parolee prior to the general revocation proceeding.
3. Disclosure must be made to the parolee concerning the nature of parole violation(s) and evidence obtained.

4. Parolees must be given the right to confront and cross-examine their accusers unless adequate cause can be given for prohibiting such a cross-examination.
5. A written statement must be provided containing the reasons for revoking the parole and the evidence used in making that decision.
6. The parolee is entitled to have the facts judged by a detached and neutral hearing committee.

One year after *Morrissey* was decided in 1973, the case of *Gagnon v. Scarpelli* extended similar rights to probationers who face the possibility of having their probation revoked. They may be represented by counsel during any probation revocation proceeding, but only if the case is particularly complex or if the probationer has communication difficulty. This is a discretionary matter within the purview of the probation authority. The guiding principle in this case was to ensure fundamental fairness. Otherwise, the probationer is not constitutionally entitled to counsel at such hearings. Each case is considered on its own merits.

Each state has established specific procedures for dealing with parole or probation revocations (Burke, Adams, and Ney, 1990; Parent et al., 1992). In 1988, the federal government established guidelines for the U.S. Parole Commission to follow in all revocation proceedings. These are set forth in 18 U.S.C. Sec. 4214 (1995). Essentially, they are the same provisions elaborated in the case of *Morrissey* with a few exceptions. There are two hearings, one to determine probable cause that a parole violation occurred, and the other to determine whether parole should be revoked or continued. Any conviction for a new offense while on parole is sufficient to establish probable cause. In any case, if a second proceeding is warranted, the U.S. Parole Commission will give the parolee notice of the conditions of parole violated; the time, place, and purposes of the hearing; the opportunity for the parolee to have counsel (either privately obtained or appointed at government expense); an opportunity for parolees to testify in their own behalf and present witnesses; and the opportunity to cross-examine witnesses unless there is a good reason to prohibit such cross-examination.

Mempa v. Rhay (1967)

This case involved a probation revocation rather than a parole revocation, although the decision eventually influenced parole proceedings significantly. Jerry Mempa was convicted of "joyriding" in a stolen vehicle on June 17, 1959. He was placed on probation for two years by a Spokane, Washington, judge. Several months later, on September 15, 1959, Mempa was involved in a burglary. The county prosecutor in Spokane moved to have Mempa's probation revoked. Mempa admitted participating in the burglary. At his probation revocation hearing, the sole testimony about his involvement in the burglary came from his probation officer. Mempa was not represented by counsel, was not asked if he wanted counsel, and was not given an opportunity to offer statements in his own behalf. Furthermore, there was no cross-examination of the probation officer about his statements. The court revoked Mempa's probation and sentenced him to 10 years in the Washington State Penitentiary.

Six years later in 1965, Mempa filed a writ of **habeas corpus,** alleging that he had been denied a right to counsel at the revocation hearing. The Washington Supreme Court denied his petition, but the U.S. Supreme Court elected to hear it on appeal. The Supreme Court overturned the Washington decision and ruled in Mempa's favor. Specifically, the Court said Mempa was entitled to an attorney but was denied one. While the Court did not question Washington authority to defer sentencing in the probation matter, it said that any indigent (including Mempa) is entitled at every stage of a criminal proceeding to be represented by court-appointed counsel, when "substantial rights of a criminal accused may be affected." Thus, the Supreme Court considered a probation revocation hearing to be a "critical stage" that falls within the due process provisions of the Fourteenth Amendment. In subsequent years, several courts applied this decision to parole revocation hearings.

Morrissey v. Brewer (1972)

The first landmark case involving the constitutional rights of parolees was *Morrissey v. Brewer* (1972). In 1967, John Morrissey was convicted by an Iowa court for "falsely drawing checks" and sentenced to not more than seven years in the Iowa State Prison. He was eventually paroled from prison in June 1968. However, seven months later, his parole officer learned that while on parole, Morrissey bought a car under an assumed name and operated it without permission, obtained credit cards under a false name, and gave false information to an insurance company when he was involved in a minor automobile accident. And, Morrissey had given his parole officer a false address for his residence.

The parole officer interviewed Morrissey and filed a report recommending that parole be revoked. The reasons given by the officer were that Morrissey admitted buying the car and obtaining false I.D., obtaining credit under false pretenses, and being involved in the auto accident. Morrissey claimed he "was sick" and that this condition prevented him from maintaining continuous contact with his parole officer. The parole officer claimed that Morrissey's parole should be revoked because Morrissey had a habit of "continually violating the rules." The parole board revoked Morrissey's parole and he was returned to the Iowa State Prison to serve the remainder of his sentence. Morrissey was not represented by counsel at the revocation proceeding. Furthermore, he was not given the opportunity to cross-examine witnesses against him, he was not advised in writing of the charges against him, no disclosure of the evidence against him was provided, and reasons for the revocation were not given. Morrissey also was not permitted to offer evidence in his own behalf or give personal testimony.

Morrissey's appeal to the Iowa Supreme Court was rejected, but the U.S.

Supreme Court heard his appeal. While the Court did not directly address the question of whether Morrissey should have had court-appointed counsel, it did make a landmark decision in his case. It overturned the Iowa Parole Board action and established a two-stage proceeding for determining whether parole ought to be revoked. The first or preliminary hearing is held at the time of arrest and detention, when it is determined whether probable cause exists that the parolee actually committed the alleged parole violation. The second hearing is more involved and establishes the guilt and punishment of the parolee relating to the violations. This proceeding must extend to the parolee certain minimum due process rights. These rights are

1. The right to have written notice of the alleged violations of parole conditions;
2. The right to have disclosed to the parolee any evidence of the alleged violation;
3. The right of the parolee to be heard in person and to present exculpatory evidence as well as witnesses in his behalf;
4. The right to confront and cross-examine adverse witnesses, unless cause exists why they should not be cross-examined;
5. The right to a judgment by a neutral and detached body, such as the parole board itself; and
6. The right to a written statement of the reasons for the parole revocation.

Thus, the significance of the *Morrissey* case is that it set forth **minimum due process** rights for all parolees, creating a two-stage proceeding whereby the alleged infractions of parole conditions could be examined and a full hearing conducted to determine the most appropriate disposition of the offender.

Gagnon v. Scarpelli (1973)

Since the matter of representation by counsel was not addressed directly in *Morrissey,* and since it had been the subject of previous U.S. Supreme Court action in *Mempa,* it was only a matter of time until the Supreme Court made a decision about a parolee's right to court-appointed counsel in a parole revocation proceeding. This decision was rendered by the Court in the case of *Gagnon v. Scarpelli* (1973), a year following the *Morrissey* ruling.

Gerald Scarpelli pled guilty to a charge of robbery in July 1965 in a Wisconsin court. He was sentenced to 15 years in prison. But the judge suspended this sentence on August 5, 1965, and placed Scarpelli on probation for a period of 7 years. The next day, August 6, Scarpelli was arrested and charged with burglary. His probation was revoked without a hearing and he was placed in the Wisconsin State Reformatory to serve his 15-year term. About three years later, Scarpelli was paroled. Shortly before his parole, he filed a *habeas corpus* petition, alleging that his probation revocation was invoked without a hearing and without benefit of counsel, constituting a denial of due process. Following his parole, the Supreme Court acted on his original *habeas corpus* petition and ruled in his favor. Specifically, the Court said that Scarpelli was denied his right to due process because no revocation hearing was held and he was not represented by court-appointed counsel within the indigent claim. In effect, the Court, referring to *Morrissey v. Brewer* (1972), said that "a probation revocation, like parole revocation, is not a stage of a criminal prosecution, but does result in loss of liberty. . . . We hold that a probationer, like a parolee, is entitled to a preliminary hearing and a final revocation hearing in the conditions specified in *Morrissey v. Brewer*."

The significance of this case is that it equated probation with parole as well as the respective revocation proceedings. While the Court did not say that all parolees and probationers have a right to representation by counsel in all probation and parole revocation proceedings, it did say that counsel should be provided in cases where the probationer or parolee makes a timely claim contesting the allegations. While no constitutional basis exists for providing counsel in all probation or parole revocation proceedings, subsequent probation and parole revocation hearings usually involve defense counsel if legitimately requested. The Supreme Court declaration has been liberally interpreted in subsequent cases.

Bearden v. Georgia (1983)

Other more recent cases of interest involving parolees and probationers and whether to revoke their respective programs are *Bearden v. Georgia* (1983) and *Black v. Romano* (1985). In *Bearden*, Bearden's probation was revoked by Georgia authorities because he failed to pay a fine and make restitution to his victim as required by the court. He claimed he was indigent, but the court rejected his claim as a valid explanation for his conduct. The U.S. Supreme Court disagreed. It ruled that probation may not be revoked in the case of indigent probationers who have failed to pay their fines or make restitution. The Court further suggested alternatives for restitution and punishments that were more compatible with the abilities and economic resources of indigent probationers, such as community service. In short, the probationer should not be penalized when a reasonable effort has been made to pay court-ordered fines and restitution.

It should be noted, however, that offender indigence does not automatically lead to immunity from restitution orders. In *United States v. Bachsian* (1993), Bachsian was convicted of theft. He was required to pay restitution for the merchandise still in his possession under the Victim Witness Protection Act. Bachsian claimed, however, that he was indigent and unable to make restitution. The 9th Circuit Court of Appeals declared in Bachsian's case that it was *not* improper to impose restitution orders on an offender at the time of sentencing, even if the offender was unable to pay restitution then. In this instance, records indicated that Bachsian was considered by the court as having a future ability to pay, based on a presentence investigation report. Eventually, Bachsian would become financially able and in a position to make restitution to his victim. His restitution orders were upheld. And, bankruptcy does not discharge an offenders obligation to make restitution, although the amount and rate of restitution payments may be affected (*Baker v. State*, 1993; *State v. Hayes*, 1993).

Black v. Romano (1985)

In this case, a probationer had his probation revoked by the sentencing judge because of alleged program violations. The defendant had left the scene of an automobile accident, a felony in the jurisdiction where the alleged offense occurred. The judge gave reasons for the revocation decision but did not indicate that he had considered any option other than incarceration. The Supreme Court ruled that judges are not generally obligated to consider alternatives to incarceration before they revoke an offender's probation and place him in jail or prison. Clearly, probationers and parolees have obtained substantial rights in recent years. Supreme Court decisions have provided them with several important constitutional rights that invalidate the arbitrary and capricious revocation of their probation or parole programs by judges or parole boards. The two-stage hearing is extremely important to probationers and parolees, in that it permits ample airing of the allegations against the offender, cross-examinations by counsel, and testimony from individual offenders.

CATALOGING THE RIGHTS OF PROBATIONERS AND PAROLEES

For several decades, interest in the rights of probationers and parolees has increased considerably (del Carmen and Louis, 1988; Florida Department of Corrections, 1988; Guglielmelli, 1980; Robbins, 1985, 1987; South Carolina Department of Probation, Parole and Pardon Services, 1993). Not only has more attention been devoted to this subject in the professional literature, but various courts in different jurisdictions, including the U.S. Supreme Court, have set forth landmark decisions that influence either positively or negatively the lives of those in probation or parole programs (Bodapati and Marquart, 1992; Petersilia and Turner, 1992; Vigdal and Stadler, 1994:44). Below are listed a variety of cases dealing with numerous issues. Some of these issues may appear trivial, although their significance to affected probationers or parolees is profound.

Probationer and Parolee Rights Generally

Pardons.   When the U.S. president or a state governor pardons someone who may or may not be on probation or parole, the effect of these pardons is different, depending on the jurisdiction. Generally, a pardon is tantamount to absolution for a crime previously committed. Someone has been convicted of the crime, and the intent of a pardon is to terminate whatever punishment has been imposed. In *United States v. Noonan* (1990), for instance, Gregory Noonan was convicted and sentenced in 1969 for "failing to submit to induction into the armed forces." President Jimmy Carter granted a pardon to Noonan on January 21, 1977, wherein Carter declared a "full, complete and unconditional pardon" to persons convicted during the Vietnam War for refusing induction. Noonan sought to have his record of the original conviction expunged. An expungement order has the effect of wiping one's slate clean, as though the crime and the conviction had never occurred. Noonan believed that his conviction, which remained on his record, adversely affected his employment chances. Thus, he sought to expunge his record because of the pardon he had received from Carter. However, the Third Circuit Court of Appeals, a federal appellate court, refused to grant him this request. The court declared that "a pardon does not blot out guilt nor does it restore the offender to a state of innocence in the eye of the law." In short, at least in Noonan's case, the presidential pardon was effective in removing the punishment but not the criminal record.

Not all courts agree with the Third Circuit Court of Appeals. In some state appellate courts, a different position has been taken regarding the influence of a pardon on a criminal record. Following the lead of a Pennsylvania court of appeals, the Indiana Court of Appeals declared in *State v. Bergman* (1990) that a pardon does expunge a criminal record. The governor of Indiana had pardoned a convict, Bergman, for a crime he had previously committed. Bergman sought to have his record expunged, in much the same way as Noonan. The Indiana Court of Appeals declared that pardons "block out the very existence of the offender's guilt, so that, in the eye(s) of the law, he is thereafter as innocent as if he had never committed the offense." Subsequent state court decisions have concurred with both Pennsylvania and Indiana.

In Florida, for instance, an appellant was convicted of being an accessory to robbery in 1976. In 1986, after completing his full sentence, he was granted a full and unconditional pardon for his offense. He sought to expunge his record, and at first, Florida authorities acceded to his request for expungement. However, Florida subsequently objected to this expungement order and sought to have it set aside. Eventually, the case reached the Florida Court of Appeals, which held that "when the pardon is full, it remits the punishment and blots out the existence of guilt, so that in the eyes of the law the offender is as innocent as if he had never committed the crime. After a full pardon, the person who has been granted the pardon is no longer considered 'convicted' or 'adjudicated guilty' of that crime" (*Doe v. State,* 1992).

There are exceptions. In Rhode Island, for instance, in *State v. Gervais* (1992), the appellant, Gervais, had been convicted of a crime after entering a plea of *nolo contendere.* This is equivalent to a guilty plea. The conviction was suspended pending the satisfactory completion of a term of probation. When the probation was completed, Gervais's conviction was dismissed. Gervais subsequently sought to expunge his record of the original charges. The holding in Gervais's case turned on a technicality. The Rhode Island Court of Appeals declared that "expungements of records can occur within forty-five days only when a person is acquitted or exonerated from the offense with which he or she is charged. A plea of *nolo contendere* and a successfully served term of probation, while not constituting a conviction, remains as a record and does not constitute exoneration of that charge." In effect, if Gervais had served a probationary term of fewer than 45 days, he could have had his criminal record expunged. However, his term of probation went well beyond 45 days. Thus, a denial of his request for expungement was based on this technicality. Another technicality interfered with an Oregon resident's claim for a certification of rehabilitation and pardon in a California Court. In *People v. Matthews* (1993), Matthews completed a term of probation relative to a crime committed in California. He applied for a pardon and certification of rehabilitation from California and was denied this request. The denial was based on the fact that in order to qualify for the pardon and certification of rehabilitation, the applicant had to be a California resident for at least three years. Matthews didn't qualify.

Probationer or Parolee Program Conditions.   When probationers or parolees are subject to having their programs revoked by respective authorities, what is the nature of evidence that can be used against them to support their program revocation? What are their rights concerning PO searches of their premises? What about the program conditions they have been obligated to follow? What about parole board recognition of and obligation to follow minimum-sentence provisions from sentencing judges? These issues and several others are discussed briefly now.

   Statements made to a PO while being interrogated, not in custody, are admissible in court for the purpose of supporting new criminal charges. In *Minnesota v. Murphy* (1984), Murphy, a probationer, was serving a three-year probation term for criminal sexual conduct. One of Murphy's probation conditions was that he was to report regularly to his PO and answer all questions truthfully. Another condition was that he seek sex therapy and counseling. During one of these counseling sessions, Murphy confessed to one of his counselors that he had committed a rape and murder in 1974. The counselor told his probation officer, who, in turn, interrogated Murphy at his residence. Murphy admitted the crime (responding truthfully) after extensive interviewing and interrogation by the PO. The PO gave this incriminating information to police who arrested Murphy later and charged him with the 1974 rape and murder. Murphy claimed later that the PO had not advised him of his *Miranda* rights (e.g., right to an attorney, right to terminate questioning at any point, right against making self-incriminating statements), and, thus, his confession should not be admitted later in court against him. As a general rule, criminal suspects who are the targets of a police investigation must be advised of their *Miranda* rights if undergoing an interrogation, whether or not they are in custody. A similar rule pertains to probationers. It might be argued, for instance, that the fact of their probation is a form of "custody." Thus, all probationers (and parolees) might be considered "in custody" during the their program terms. However, "custody" implies being unable to leave the presence of the interrogator. When suspects conclude their interrogation, they may or may not be permitted to leave. If they leave, they are not considered to be in custody. Otherwise, they are in custody. Murphy was not in custody, however. Also, he was not compelled to answer the PO's questions. Obviously, this is a complex case involving seemingly conflicting obligations and constitutional rights.

   Search and seizure grounds are less stringent for POs who intend to search their client's homes for illegal contraband. In *Griffin v. Wisconsin* (1987), Griffin was placed on probation after being convicted of resisting arrest, disorderly conduct, and obstructing a Wisconsin police officer in 1980. One condition of Griffin's probation was that he not possess a firearm. An informant advised Griffin's PO that Griffin had a weapon on his premises. Based on previous reliable information provided by the informant, the PO believed that reasonable grounds existed to conduct a warrantless search. The PO went to Griffin's home, searched it without a warrant, and discovered a gun. Griffin was subsequently arrested, prosecuted, and convicted for being a convicted felon in possession of a firearm. He was sentenced to two years. He appealed on the grounds that the POs search of his premises should have been conducted with a properly issued warrant and based on **probable cause.** The U.S. Supreme Court declared in *Griffin,* that POs are entitled to *special consideration* because of their demanding jobs. They should not be held to the more stringent standard of probable cause, since they must often take immediate action to detect crimes or seize illegal contraband relating to their probationer or parolee clients. The "reasonable grounds" standard, a lesser standard than probable cause, is upheld to the extent that probation or parole agency policies make provisions for such warrantless searches of offender premises in their jurisdictions. The ruling is not intended as a blanket right to violate Fourth Amendment rights on a whim.

An even broader "search and seizure" case was upheld in *Crooker v. Metallo* (1993). POs conducted a "sweep" of a parolee's premises on the basis of a search incident to an arrest for alleged parole violations. The sweep included a quick search between the parolee's box springs and mattress of his bed, where illegal contraband was found. The First Circuit Court of Appeals held for the POs and indicated that they possessed qualified immunity while conducting the search, and that their search was objectively reasonable.

However, an interesting case, *Davis v. State* (1992), provides an exception for POs and police relative to warrantless searches of probationer's premises. Davis, a probationer convicted of a controlled substance charge, was away from his home one evening when his 10-year-old son dialed 911 and summoned police to the home. The boy had found drugs in the house and called police. These drugs were later used as evidence against Davis to revoke his probation. A Georgia Court of Appeals, however, threw out this evidence, concluding that a 10-year-old, regardless of his motives, has no authority to give police permission to enter his father's home and search his bedroom for illegal contraband. Police would have to find some other means to use the illegally seized evidence. In this instance, the police intrusion into Davis's home constituted *unlawful entry,* and no basis could be shown on which to issue a warrant on probable cause, using a telephone call from a 10-year-old to support such an action. The case against Davis was thrown out and his probation was reinstated.

Conditions of probation/parole, including victim restitution payments, are legitimate; however, there are situations when offenders may or may not be able to pay restitution declared by the court. In *Bearden v. Georgia* (1983), we saw that an inability to pay restitution cannot entitle judges to automatically revoke a probation program. In *Bearden,* the judge had not examined other options in lieu of the restitution order. More recent cases have upheld *Bearden,* and some interesting spins have been added. For instance, a Florida man, Moore, was convicted of purchasing a stolen truck (*Moore v. State,* 1993). The original truck's owner, the victim, claimed that there were tools worth $500 in the truck when it was stolen initially by the one who sold the truck to Moore. Nevertheless, the judge imposed a sentence of probation, with a restitution condition that Moore repay the victim $500 for the loss of the tools. A Florida Court of Appeals set aside this condition, since it did not show that the loss was caused by Moore's action and that there was a significant relation between the loss and the crime of purchasing a stolen vehicle.

In a federal case, Lombardi was convicted of mail fraud involving over $190,000 of unaccounted-for funds (*United States v. Lombardi,* 1993). Lombardi was fined $60,000 as a part of his sentence and obligated to make restitution in the sum of $190,000. Lombardi protested, claiming that he was unable to pay these amounts. The First Circuit Court of Appeals disagreed, however, indicating that Lombardi had never accounted for the whereabouts of these illegally obtained funds. His restitution order remained effective. Failure to make restitution, in Lombardi's case, would result in incarceration.

Judicial Actions and Rights.   Judges often impose various sentences that differ from those provided or recommended by statute. Sometimes these sentences contain special conditions of probation, involving victim compensation, community service, or participation in group or individual therapy. Below are some of the liberties taken by judges in sentencing decisions and/or departures, and a discussion about whether these liberties are valid.

Judges who impose probation in lieu of mandatory sentences for particular offenses may have their probation judgments declared invalid. In a New York case, a plea bargain was worked out between the state and a defendant, Hipp (*People v. Hipp,* 1993). Hipp was determined by the court to be addicted to gambling. The nature of the conviction offense and the gambling addiction compelled the court under mandatory sentencing to prescribe a jail term as well as accompanying therapy for the addiction. In this instance, the judge simply accepted a plea agreement, accepting the defendant's guilty plea in exchange for a term of probation. The New York Court of Appeals overruled the judge in this case, indicating that New York statutes do not authorize a trial court to ignore clearly expressed and unequivocal mandatory sentencing provisions of the New York Penal Law. However, in Florida, a judge imposed probation on an offender convicted under a habitual offender statute (*McKnight v. State,* 1993). McKnight was convicted of being a habitual felony offender. Ordinarily, this conviction carries a mandatory life-without-parole penalty. However, the judge in McKnight's case imposed probation. Even though the Florida Court of Appeals did not like the judge's decision, it upheld it, supporting the general principle of *judicial discretion.*

Defendants can refuse probation if the court imposes probation as a sentence. In a rather unique case, the defendant, Cannon, was convicted of criminally negligent homicide after entering a guilty plea (*Cannon v. State,* 1993). However, in open court, after probation was imposed, Cannon refused the probation and demanded to be incarcerated instead. The judge insisted that the probation sentence be accepted by Cannon. Cannon appealed. In an Alabama Court of Appeals decision, the court upheld Cannon's right to refuse probation, and he was remanded to prison instead. This is not as bad as it sounds, however. Cannon had been incarcerated for some time prior to his criminally negligent homicide conviction. By accepting probation, Cannon would have been obligated to adhere to certain restrictive conditions for a period of time far in excess of the time remaining to be served. In effect, he had only a few more months to serve of his original sentence, counting the many months he had been behind bars before his trial and conviction. Thus, a probation sentence in Cannon's case would have involved a longer term of conditional freedom than the number of months remaining before his unconditional release from prison. The court said that "Our holding merely recognizes a convict's right to reject the trial court's offer of probation if he or she deems it to be more onerous than a prison sentence."

Judges may revoke one's probation program or supervised release and impose a new sentence that the offender must serve the remainder of the term in confinement. A federal probationer, Levi, was under supervised release (*United States v. Levi*, 1993). During his first 11 months of supervised release, Levi committed one or more probation violations. The Judge revoked his probation and declared that he must spend the remaining 13 months incarcerated. The Eighth Circuit Court of Appeals upheld the judge's action, since the 13-month imprisonment was within the two-year sentence of probation originally imposed by the same judge.

Sometimes POs obligate their probationer-clients to conform to rules outside of those specified in probation orders. In the eyes of Texas law, at least, such orders or conditions are unconstitutional. In *Lemon v. State* (1993), Lemon, a probationer convicted of misappropriation of property, was required by a judge to perform community service at the orders or discretion of his probation officer. The Texas Court of Appeals reversed this condition of his probation, since the nature of community service had not been articulated by the judge. It is improper for POs to determine the nature of one's community service to be performed under a sentence of probation with conditions.

Ordinarily, sentences of probation cannot be served simultaneously with sentences of incarceration. If a judge imposes incarceration for an offender for Offense A, and if that same judge imposes probation for the same offender for Offense B, both the incarcerative sentence and the probationary sentence cannot be served concurrently, at least in Florida courts. In *Hill v. State* (1993), Hill, a convicted Florida offender, was sentenced to probation and to incarceration for different offenses. He wanted to serve both sentences concurrently. The Florida Court of Appeals denied his request, particularly in view of a prior case that was decided on the same issue (*Nobles v. State*, 1992).

When probationers admit to probation violations and waive direct appeal actions, this does not prevent them from being entitled to a transcript of the proceedings in order to appeal the revocation proceeding itself. In an Arizona case, *Wilson v. Ellis* (1993), an indigent defendant had his probation revoked after admitting to a probation violation. When he asked for a transcript of his revocation proceedings, he was denied access to this document. The Arizona Court of Appeals rejected this lower court denial and declared that the offender did have a right to pursue a challenge of the revocation proceeding itself, despite his waiver of appeal rights, in the context of a postconviction remedy.

Probationers are obligated to pay certain supervision fees to defray some of their program expenses, if they are financially able to do so. Failure to pay one's supervisory costs may be grounds for a probation revocation action. In a Florida case, *Anderson v. State* (1993), Anderson, the probationer, failed to pay his supervisory fees imposed by the court. These fees were due and payable on the fifth of each month. Anderson was employed and able to pay these fees. He simply elected not to pay them. In this case, based on his ability to pay, his probation was revoked by the judge. A higher court declared that the judge was justified in this probation revocation.

Parole Board Actions and Rights.   Parole boards have considerable discretionary powers. They may deny parole or grant it. They may revoke parole and return the offender to prison, or they may continue the offender's parole program, with additional supervision and other conditions. Below are some of the actions parole boards may take and how parolees are impacted.

Inmates who become eligible for parole are not automatically entitled to parole. Parole boards have considerable discretion whether to grant or deny parole to any inmate. Short of serving their full sentences or completing a portion of their term less any applicable good-time credit, inmates are not automatically entitled to be paroled. In *Williams v. Puckett* (1993), a Mississippi man convicted of armed robbery and forgery was sentenced to a mandatory sentence of 10 years plus a 5-year term for the forgery conviction. In Mississippi, inmates become eligible for parole after serving 10 years of terms imposed in excess of 10 years, by statute. However, since the armed robbery conviction involved a mandatory prison term of 10 years, this meant that the entire sentence of 10 years had to be served. Thus, according to Mississippi law, the inmate must serve at least one-fourth of the 5-year term for the forgery conviction before actual parole eligibility occurred. Even then, the Mississippi Parole Board would not be obligated to automatically grant his early release.

Parole boards do not have to recognize minimum-sentence provisions from sentencing judges when considering an inmate's parole eligibility. In another case, this time in Oregon, an inmate became eligible for parole after serving his minimum sentence, under a determined minimum-maximum sentence originally imposed by a judge (*Carroll v. Board of Parole,* 1993). The Oregon Parole Board is vested with the power to override any minimum-sentence provision that might otherwise provide a means whereby an offender might be paroled automatically. In this case, the inmate had been convicted of murder and had served the minimum sentence prescribed by law. However, the Parole Board voted to override the minimum sentence and continue the inmate's incarceration, considering the seriousness of the crime and other factors. The inmate contested this Parole Board action, but the Oregon Court of Appeals upheld the Parole Board action as legitimate, since a unanimous vote was required to override the minimum sentence and the Parole Board had voted unanimously.

Inmates who have been paroled and who subsequently commit a new violent act while on parole may have their parole programs revoked and be returned to prison to serve the remaining sentence in its entirety. In New York, a parolee, Richardson, committed a new violent felony while on parole. The Parole Board revoked his parole and returned him to prison without further parole consideration, despite the fact that he had not, as yet, been tried and convicted on the new violent offense charge (*Richardson v. New York State Executive Department,* 1993).

If a paroling authority imposes a special condition of parole, such as submitting to penile plethysmography, this is not considered an unusual and unconstitutional parole condition. Penile plethysmography is a test administered to convicted sex offenders. The test involves attaching devices to a prospective parolee's penis in order to determine the parolee's subsequent reaction to various forms of sexual stimuli. An erection response to various stimuli is incriminating in this instance, and the offender may be denied parole. The test is also used to determine whether a sex offender continues to pose a threat to society. In an Illinois federal action, a convicted sex offender, Walrath, was required to submit to a penile plethysmograph test as one condition preceding his parole by the Illinois Parole Board (*Walrath v. United States,* 1993). Walrath claimed that such a test would violate his Fifth Amendment right against self-incrimination. The U.S. District Court in Illinois upheld the U.S. Parole Commission's administration of the test to Walrath, holding that "there is no indication that any results from Walrath's plethysmograph could be used to prosecute him criminally for other acts. Instead, the results, like the treatment, might legitimately be used to assess the threat Walrath poses to society."

Other interesting decisions include the legitimizing life sentences of probation (*People v. Shafer,* 1992); consecutive probation sentences for two or more offenses (*Menifee v. State,* 1992); prisoners who complete their sentences less "gain" time have served their "full" sentences (*State v. Green,* 1989); admissions about probation violations must be entered by probationers themselves, not their attorneys (*State v. Lavoy,* 1992); conditionally dismissed criminal charges can be reinstated if a divertee violates one or more terms of his diversion (*Wallace v. State,* 1992); urinalyses are improper if not made conditions of a probation program, especially where drugs and/or alcohol were not involved (*Patterson v. State,* 1993); new programs for offenders cannot be imposed as parole-eligibility criteria after offenders have been convicted and sentenced under earlier laws (*Pareton v. Armontrout,* 1993); *ex post facto* laws for parolees and probationers are unconstitutional (*Roller v. Cavanaugh,* 1993); credit for the amount of time served on probation or parole may not be credited against incarcerative sentences if revocation of one's program occurs for one or more program violations (*State v. Oquendo,* 1993); probationers cannot have their probation revoked for violating a probation condition that is not in their probation orders or if they have not received a copy of such probation orders (*State v. Alves,* 1992); and judges have no authority to set parole conditions (*State v. Beauchamp,* 1993).

KEY TERMS

Citizen value system
Commutation
Conditional release
Controller value system
Gagnon v. Scarpelli (1973)
Habeas corpus
Jailhouse lawyer
Jurist value system
Mandatory release
Mempa v. Rhay (1967)
Minimum due process
Morrissey v. Brewer (1972)
Objective parole criteria

Offense severity
Parole board
Parole revocation
Parole revocation hearing
Probable cause
Regulator value system
Salient Factor Score (SFS), SFS 81
Sanctioner value system
Shock parole
Supervised release
Treater value system
Unconditional release

QUESTIONS FOR REVIEW

1. What is the nature of control parole exerts over inmates in prison?
2. Differentiate between conditional and unconditional release for inmates. What are some significant variations of conditional release?
3. What are some important functions performed by parole boards? What criteria do they usually employ when reaching decisions about individual inmates?
4. What is the Salient Factor Score index? Is there any apparent bias associated with this index?
5. Identify some of the major problems associated with trying to predict an offender's future dangerousness, and then making a decision about whether to parole the offender.
6. Is parole effective? How does parole compare with other programs designed to manage the nonincarcerated offender population?
7. What rights do offenders have before officials can revoke their parole? Cite four cases that are important in the matter of parole revocation.
8. Identify three important cases associated with probationer and parolee rights. What is the significance of the cases you have cited?
9. Who makes up a parole board? Are these persons corrections experts? Why or why not?
10. Why were the cases of Page and Obremski at the beginning of this chapter called both typical and atypical?

8

An Overview of Community Corrections

Types, Goals and Functions

Introduction

What Is Community Corrections?

The Community Corrections Act

The Philosophy of Community Corrections

The History of Community Corrections

Characteristics of Community Corrections
  Programs

Goals of Community Corrections

Functions of Community Corrections

Selected Issues in Community Corrections

Key Terms

Questions for Review

INTRODUCTION

Jail and prison overcrowding have reached critical levels. At present, we cannot afford to lock up all convicted offenders, despite public clamor for such action. The impossibility of it all is underscored by the fact that it would require at least a 500 percent increase in existing jail and prison space to accommodate our current population of convicted offenders. And, this does not address the room necessarily required for those subsequently convicted for new crimes.

Corrections is attacked from many sides, with critics contending that "nothing works." One of the most outspoken and visible critics was the late Robert Martinson. Martinson criticized probation, parole, and incarceration generally by concluding that none of them worked for rehabilitating criminals. Even though he believed that these supervisory and incarcerative strategies might be workable if properly implemented, he also believed that many of these programs were improperly administered, that POs had excessive caseloads that diminished their effectiveness in offender counseling and supervision, and that our prisons and jails were nothing more than warehouses for offenders rather than rehabilitative mediums (Walker, 1989). Other professionals have been similarly critical of the success of the rehabilitative ideal espoused by corrections in general.

When Martinson wrote these criticisms about corrections, there was considerable public discontent with the correctional product. For instance, probationers were committing new crimes while on probation; parolees were committing new crimes within months, weeks, and even days of their parole; and ex-inmates of prisons and jails who were released after serving their full sentences were committing large numbers of new offenses. Those experimenting with various intervention programs in prisons and jails were not realizing the low recidivism rates that were originally predicted. Some critics have blamed *prisonization,* or simple interaction among inmates and prisoner socialization that results in perpetuating criminal conduct (Biles, 1988; Poklewski-Koziel, 1988). Some experts are also critical of the various prison rehabilitation programs accessible to inmates. Often, these experts say, inmates will enroll in vocational or technical education courses or engage in individual or group therapy with the primary aim of earning early release. Thus, inmates may become involved in rehabilitative programs, but they are becoming involved in them for the wrong reasons (Marlin, 1988). Also, the wrong clients may be targeted for eligibility to participate (Jones, 1990). In short, prison rehabilitative programs do not work as they are supposed to work for all inmates participating in them. Whatever the causes of these program failures, the fact is that many probationers, inmates, and parolees were exhibiting high rates of reoffending contrary to the aims of reforms and rehabilitation.

Despite these program failures, the pace of innovation and experimentation has not decreased (Zoet, 1990). Rather, a broad array of correctional programs has been established at the community level that offer a less expensive alternative to incarceration (Winterfield, 1990). Especially during the 1980s, numerous programs were established and experiments conducted that were designed to gain greater nonincarcerative control over the growing offender population. The result has been the establishment of *community corrections,* broadly defined as community-based supervision and intervention programs that continue punishment, but in the context of the community (McCarthy, 1987a:1). Another term that encompasses community corrections is *intermediate punishments.* McCarthy (1987a:1) defines intermediate punishments as sanctions that lie somewhere between standard probation and incarceration.

This chapter is organized as follows: First, the general concept of community corrections is defined. A history of the development of community corrections and its general philosophy are also provided. Following this is a listing of characteristics that typify community corrections programs. The next part of the chapter outlines various goals and functions of community corrections programs and profiles community corrections clients. Next, an overview of different types of community corrections programs is presented, followed by a discussion of selected community corrections issues. Some of these issues relate to public opposition to the establishment of community corrections programs. Some people are critical of the nonincarcerative aspects of community corrections, and the idea of punishment associated with such programs is challenged. Other critics suggest that because of community corrections, some net widening has occurred, and certain clients have become involved in corrections simply because this alternative has been established. Yet other criticisms target the growing interest of private corporations in community corrections management and operations, the quality of services delivery, and staff training and education.

WHAT IS COMMUNITY CORRECTIONS?

Siedschlaw (1990) says that community corrections is difficult to define. One reason is that the concept is viewed differently from various positions in our society. Generally, however, *community corrections* refers to any **community-based corrections program** designed to supervise convicted offenders in lieu of incarceration, either by city, county, state, or federal authority; that provides various services to client-offenders; that monitors and furthers client/offender behaviors related to sentencing conditions; that heightens client/offender responsibility regarding payment of fines, victim compensation, community service, and restitution orders; and that provides for a continuation of punishment through more controlled supervision and greater accountability (adapted in part from Biles, 1988; Duffee and McGarrell, 1990; Reeves, 1992).

Nidorf (1989) indicates that various community corrections alternatives include intensive probation or parole supervision, home confinement, electronic surveillance or monitoring, narcotics and drug deterrence, work furlough programs or work release, study release, **day reporting centers,** and probationer violation and restitution residential centers. Also included under the community corrections umbrella are programs such as diversion, pretrial release, and preparole (Duffee and McGarrell, 1990; Lauen, 1990a; Way, 1992). Duffee and McGarrell (1990) note that community corrections programs can also be distinguished according to the controlling authority. They categorize such programs as *community-run* (locally operated, but lacking state funding and other external support); *community-placed* (programs that are located in communities but do not network with any community agency); and *community-based* (programs that are locally operated but are also financially supplemented from outside sources; programs that network with other community agencies and the criminal justice system). There is considerable interstate variation in community-based corrections programs (Harris, Jones, and Funke, 1990). However, there have been efforts in recent years among different jurisdictions to network with one another as a means of information dissemination and sharing regarding particular community corrections programs (Faulkner, 1994:23).

The term *community corrections* is often used in a general way to refer to a range of punishments known as *intermediate punishments.* As has been indicated, intermediate punishments are sanctions ranging between incarceration and standard probation on the continuum of criminal penalties (McCarthy, 1987a). The term may refer to any of several different programs designed to closely control or monitor offender behaviors. Since there are several possible meanings of intermediate punishments, the term is widely applied, correctly or incorrectly, to a variety of community-based offender programs involving nonincarcerative sanctions.

Major distinguishing features of intermediate punishments include the high degree of offender monitoring and control of offender behaviors by program staff. Other characteristics include curfews that require offenders to observe time guidelines and be at particular places at particular times, and frequent monitoring and contact with program officials (Reeves, 1992). The amount and type of frequent monitoring or contact varies with the program, although daily visits by probation officers at an offender's workplace or home are not unusual. One semantic problem is that the "intensive" supervision refers to different levels of monitoring or officer-offender contact, depending on the jurisdiction. Intermediate punishments are intended for prison- or jail-bound offenders. Offenders who are probably going to receive probation anyway are the least likely candidates for these more intensively supervised programs. However, judges often assign such low-risk probation-bound offenders to these programs anyway. This tends to defeat the goals of such programs, because they are intended for offenders who would otherwise occupy valuable prison or jail space unnecessarily. Cluttering these intensive supervision programs with offenders who don't need close supervision is a waste of money, time, and personnel. When this occurs, it is referred to as *net widening* (Jones, 1990). Offenders are given considerable freedom of movement within their communities, although it is believed that such intensive monitoring and control fosters a high degree of compliance with program requirements. It is also suspected that this intensive supervision deters offenders from committing new crimes.

THE COMMUNITY CORRECTIONS ACT

A **community corrections act** is the enabling medium by which jurisdictions establish local community corrections agencies, facilities, and programs. A generic definition of a community corrections act is a statewide mechanism through which funds are granted to local units of government to plan, develop, and deliver correctional sanctions and services at the local level. The overall purpose of this mechanism is to provide local sentencing options in lieu of imprisonment in state institutions (McManus and Barclay, 1994:12).

The aim of community corrections acts in various states is to make it possible to divert certain prison-bound offenders into local, city- or county-level programs where they can receive treatment and assistance rather than imprisonment. Usually, those offenders who are eligible or otherwise qualify for community corrections programs are low-risk, nonviolent, and nondangerous offenders (*Corrections Compendium,* 1991c:15). Community corrections acts also target those incarcerated offenders who pose little or no risk to the public if released into the community under close parole supervision. Thus, community corrections acts function to alleviate prison and jail overcrowding by diverting certain jail- or prison-bound offenders to community programs. The aims of several state community corrections acts help us to see what these acts encompass.

For instance, Kansas implemented a community corrections act in 1978. This act was designed to provide alternatives to both incarceration and new prison construction by encouraging local communities to provide appropriate community sanctions for adult and juvenile offenders. Kansas community corrections currently utilizes a variety of programs as a part of its community corrections, including home confinement, day reporting centers, halfway houses, electronic monitoring, and intensive supervised probation and parole (Townsend, 1991:26–27).

In 1993, there were over 20,000 offenders in Ohio community corrections programs (Ortega and Hardin, 1993:15). Targeted offenders include nonviolent clients who participate in both residential and nonresidential placement options. Ortega and Hardin note that these placement options include work release and halfway house programs, intensive supervised probation, day reporting centers, home confinement, community service, and standard probation. Personnel conduct urinalyses of clients as well as other forms of behavioral monitoring. Ortega and Hardin (1993:15) say that Ohio programming staff members look for the following resident-client traits:

1. A demonstrated willingness to comply with program rules and regulations.
2. A motivation to work on individual treatment plans as described by program staff.
3. A target population pool that consists primarily of nonviolent offenders, including but not limited to, misdemeanants, probation eligible felony offenders, and parolees who are amenable to community sanctions.

Finally, Virginia has a **Community Diversion Incentive Act.** This Act targets prison- or jail-bound offenders, including those convicted of nonviolent felonies and misdemeanors who have been sentenced to the Department of Corrections or local jails (McManus and Barclay, 1994:15). Virginia officials include those offenders who would have otherwise been incarcerated in prison or jail and whose treatment needs can better be met in the community. Statutory behavioral contracts guide client program participation. If offenders successfully complete these programs, their original imposed sentences may be suspended (McManus and Barclay, 1994:15).

THE PHILOSOPHY OF COMMUNITY CORRECTIONS

As outlined by many missions statements of community corrections programs throughout the United States, the philosophy of community corrections is to provide certain types of offenders with a rehabilitative and reintegrative milieu, in which their personal abilities and skills are improved and their chances for recidivism are minimized (Markley, 1994). Community-based programs established through community corrections acts include halfway houses, outreach centers, furlough-monitoring facilities for parolees, and halfway houses (McCarthy and McCarthy, 1984). The primary purpose of community-based correctional programs is to assist probationers in becoming reintegrated into their communities, although parolees are assisted by such programs as well (Racine, Vittitow, and Riggs, 1984). It is not so much the case that probationers (in contrast with parolees) have lost touch with their communities through incarceration, but rather that they have the opportunity of avoiding confinement and remaining within their communities to perform productive work to support themselves and others and to repay victims for losses suffered.

A secondary purpose of community-based programs is to help alleviate prison and jail overcrowding by accepting those offenders who are not dangerous and pose the least risk to society (Travis, 1985). Of course, the difficulty here is attempting to sort those most dangerous offenders from those least dangerous. Our measures of predicted risk or dangerousness are not infallible, and often, persons predicted to be dangerous may never commit future violent offenses or harm others. By the same token, those same instruments may forecast an offender to be nonviolent and not dangerous, and the offender may turn out to be quite dangerous. Respectively, these types of offenders are labeled *false positives* and *false negatives* by authorities. False positives are those considered dangerous on the basis of their risk scores from prediction instruments, but they are really not dangerous to others. False negatives are those forecasted to be nonviolent and posing the least public risk, but who nevertheless turn out to be dangerous by harming others and committing violent offenses.

Huskey (1984:5) says that community corrections acts recognize that

1. States should continue to house violent offenders in secure facilities;
2. Judges and prosecutors need a variety of punishments; and
3. Local communities cannot develop these programs without additional funding from such legislatures.

She adds that there are eight common elements essential to community corrections acts' success:

1. Prison- or jail-bound offenders are targeted, rather than adding additional punishments to those who would have otherwise remained in the community.
2. Financial subsidies are provided to local government and community agencies.
3. A performance factor is implemented to ensure funds are used for the act's specific goals.
4. Local advisory boards in each local community assess local needs, propose improvements in the local criminal justice system, and educate the general public about the benefits of alternative punishments.
5. Advisory boards submit annual criminal justice plans to the local government.
6. A specific formula is used for allocating funds.

Community-based corrections agencies include a wide array of programs designed to assist offenders while they reside within their communities. (Spencer Grant/Stock Boston)

7. Local communities participate voluntarily and may withdraw at any time.
8. There are restrictions on funding high-cost capital projects as well as straight probation services.

Huskey believes that community corrections acts appear to be working because they offer a mechanism to provide safe and cost-effective community-based programs. It has been amply demonstrated that these community-based programs are safer and less costly than incarceration, especially when the right, eligible nonviolent clients are targeted. Other professionals share Huskey's optimism about the effectiveness of community corrections (English and Mande, 1991; Eynon, 1989; Hughes, 1990; Tilow, 1989).

THE HISTORY OF COMMUNITY CORRECTIONS

Lawrence (1985:108) notes that California was one of the first states to implement a community corrections program. California's **Probation Subsidy Program** was implemented in 1965. This program provided local communities with supplemental resources to manage larger numbers of probationers more closely. A part of this subsidization provided for community residential centers where probationers could "check in" and receive counseling, employment assistance, and other forms of guidance or supervision. Soon, other states, such as Colorado and Oregon, established their own community-based programs to assist probationers and others (Huskey, 1984; Lauen, 1984). However, it took at least another decade for large-scale philosophical shifts to occur among different U.S. jurisdictions so that community corrections could be implemented more widely. Hughes (1990:37) adds that the Safe Streets Act of 1968 and the emergence of the **Law Enforcement Assistance Administration (LEAA)** provided the bases for developing more community-based corrections programs.

Community corrections acts involve the legislative appropriation of funds to local government units and community agencies to divert offenders from incarceration in jail or prison. Community-based programs are geared to assist offenders by providing nonsecure lodging, vocational and educational training, job assistance, and a limited amount of psychological counseling. Such programs perform rehabilitative and reintegrative functions. One of the first official acknowledgments of the need for community-based programs as a possible front-end solution to prison and jail overcrowding was the 1967 President's Commission on Law Enforcement and Administration of Justice (Lawrence, 1985). Subsequently, the National Advisory Commission on Criminal Justice Standards and Goals as well as the Law Enforcement Assistance Administration encouraged the establishment of community-based programs as alternatives to incarceration in 1973 and provided extensive financial sponsorship for such programs.

The growing use of community-based programs has occurred for at least three reasons. First, the 1967 President's Commission on Law Enforcement and Administration of Justice indicated that community-based monitoring of offenders is much less expensive than incarceration. The LEAA provided extensive funding for experiments in community-based programming. Second, since incarceration has been unable to offer the public any convincing evidence that large numbers of inmates emerge rehabilitated, community corrections programs will not be any worse. This is an indirect way of saying that community programs will at least be as effective as incarceration as rehabilitative agents (Travis, Schwartz, and Clear, 1983:112). Clear (1987) concludes that community-based correctional programs are perhaps the major form of offender management today. Offender management, control, and punishment are key functions of community corrections.

The destructiveness of prisons for both offenders and society is another important reason for community-based correctional programs (Travis et al., 1983:113). Many inmates who are confined in prisons for several years become accustomed to an alien lifestyle unlike anything occurring within their communities. There is physical separation from an offender's family unit and friends. Inmates are subject to demeaning experiences and treatment not designed to equip offenders with the necessary skills to cope with life "on the outside" when they are eventually released.

CHARACTERISTICS OF COMMUNITY CORRECTIONS PROGRAMS

Community-based programs vary in size and scope among communities. However, they share certain essential characteristics:

1. Community-based program administrators have the authority to oversee offender behaviors and enforce compliance with their probation conditions.
2. These programs have job referral and placement services with paraprofessionals or others acting as liaisons with various community agencies and organizations to facilitate offender job placement.
3. Administrators of these programs are available on premises on a 24-hour basis for emergency situations and spontaneous assistance for offenders who may need help.
4. One or more large homes or buildings located within the residential section of the community with space to accommodate between 20 and 30 residents are provided within walking distance of work settings and social services.
5. A professional and paraprofessional staff is "on call" for medical, social, or psychological emergencies.
6. A system is in place for heightening staff accountability to the court concerning offender progress.

In 1984, the American Correctional Association issued a policy statement about correctional staff and recruitment that underscored the need of these programs for qualified personnel either as professionals, paraprofessionals, or volunteers. Through the acquisition of a highly trained staff, community-based correctional programs can best serve the needs of client-offenders.

Community corrections is not interested in putting thousands of violent felons into communities. Rather, these programs advocate the continued use of incarceration for violent offenders (Huskey, 1984:45). However, it is its intent to accommodate exclusively jail- or prison-bound offenders rather than to service those criminals who would receive standard or intensive supervised probation anyway (Huskey, 1984). Some estimate of the savings accruing to states through community corrections is provided by the Tennessee Corrections Act established in July 1986. Officials estimate that it costs about $22,000 annually to house offenders in Tennessee prisons, but that through community corrections, this cost per offender drops to only $9,500 (*Corrections Today*, 1986:127).

GOALS OF COMMUNITY CORRECTIONS

Any program that seeks to preserve offender attachments with their communities by diverting them from incarceration and housing them in local neighborhoods will draw criticisms from community residents. Two primary objections are that freeing dangerous felons poses some risk to public safety and that offenders who remain free also remain unpunished. However, nonincarcerative alternatives are designed as and considered to be continuations of punishments for offenders, even if some citizens don't perceive them that way (Edna McConnell Clark Foundation, 1982). Paying restitution to victims, performing public service, paying fines, adhering to stringent rules, and complying with seemingly unreasonable behavioral restrictions and limitations are punishments, although more than a few citizens believe offenders should be incarcerated to reflect visibly total control by authorities and true societal retribution.

One important reason for public opposition to community corrections programs is that many community residents do not know or understand the goals sought by such programs (Reeves, 1992). The goals of community corrections programs include (1) facilitating offender reintegration, (2) fostering offender rehabilitation, (3) providing an alternative range of offender punishments, and (4) heightening offender accountability.

Facilitating Offender Reintegration

Lawrence (1990) observes that although the major aims of community corrections have been strongly linked with diversion, advocacy, and reintegration, the emphasis on reintegration has been replaced in recent years by an emphasis on offender control, surveillance, and monitoring. Benekos (1990) concurs with Lawrence, although Benekos says that the new emphasis is on punitive-restrictive restraint rather than therapeutic-integrative considerations.

Fostering Offender Rehabilitation

A key goal of any offender treatment program, whether it is institutional or community-based, is rehabilitation. Thus, community corrections programs are designed, in part, to rehabilitate offenders. Rehabilitation occurs when community correctional clients, offenders, participate in vocational, educational, and/or counseling programs that are intended to improve their coping skills (Camp, 1990; Corrigan, 1990).

Community-based corrections programs are particularly beneficial for first-time nonviolent offenders. Through probation, diversion, halfway houses, and parole, community-based programs are thought to have considerable success in rehabilitating offenders (Murty et al., 1987). In Fulton County, Georgia, for instance, **Project Re-Direction** is a program designed to reduce overcrowding in the Fulton County Jail as well as provide assistance in terms of counseling, job finding, and vocational and educational training for the individual before sentencing. Thus, reintegrating ties are established between offenders and their community and family links are restored. Such links help offenders to obtain employment and further their education. They also permit the development of a sense of place and pride in daily life (Murty et al., 1987).

Schumacher et al. (1991) suggest also the important role of employment in offender rehabilitation and reintegration. Unemployment is a major factor in most instances of offender recidivism. Thus, any community corrections agency assistance to offenders enabling them to find and retain jobs is a worthwhile enterprise. Dickey's (1989) evaluation of community corrections in various Wisconsin counties indicates that agency and program successes are attributable to those staff who provide offender-clients with high-quality job assistance services on an individualized basis. Dickey cites various economic and social stresses that impact unfavorably on offender-clients. Job assistance and counseling often deal effectively with these stresses and permit these offenders to improve their coping skills.

English and Mande (1991) have extensively investigated the development and operation of community corrections programs in Colorado. Their work and findings are consistent with other researchers concerning the importance of job development and assistance in job placement. Those without jobs or are underemployed tend to recidivate and cause programs to be less effective. Between July 1, 1988, and June 30, 1989, for example, they studied a sample of 1,796 male and female offenders who were terminated from the residential component of community corrections programs. They found that about half of all community corrections clients studied were returned to prison within a few months. These cases were classified as "failures." A follow-up study of those who failed in their community programs disclosed that most clients were younger, non–high school graduates with extensive criminal histories and employment problems. English and Mande recommend that high priority be given to job development assistance and job placement, substance abuse treatment, and the manner in which prison policies relate to community corrections.

Providing an Alternative Range of Offender Punishments

Intermediate punishments manifested by various community corrections agencies are diverse. Some of these programs include boot-camp–like atmospheres such as the **Georgia Special Alternative Incarceration Program (SAI).** The SAI program is a special condition of probation. Judges sentence offenders to 90 days in prison in a regimen of manual labor, rigorous physical conditioning, and military-like discipline. The second phase consists of less structured, postconfinement community supervision. An examination of participants between 1983 and 1990 showed that clients had a recidivism rate of about 41 percent (Flowers, Carr, and Ruback, 1991). This compares favorably with higher recidivism rates of 50 percent and 62 percent for standard probationers and traditional incarcerated inmates. While 41 percent recidivism is not particularly noteworthy nationally, at least it is a better recidivism rate compared with other more standard Georgia offender programs. More recently, Georgia officials have moved this program into traditional boot-camp status with the establishment of the Comprehensive Correctional Boot Camp Program.

For more youthful offenders, special programs such as the Hope Center Wilderness Camp in Apple Springs, Texas, equips offender-clients with various survival and coping skills. One goal of this program is to build self-respect and confidence. The program contains a psychoeducational component and various forms of counseling and social therapy (Claggett et al., 1992). And, for drug abusers or those offenders with special substance dependencies, the San Diego, California, Association of Governments has investigated an intensive supervision program for drug-dependent clients (Curtis, 1992). The results of the San Diego recovery program have been especially promising for those with poor self-concepts. Positive attitudinal changes have been a part of the recovery model used for rehabilitative purposes.

Heightening Offender Accountability

Often, sentencing offenders to community corrections programs involves compliance with one or more program conditions (e.g., victim compensation, community service, restitution). Often, these additional conditions are unmonitored to ensure offender compliance. Therefore, one reason for program failures is this lack of attention to whether these special conditions are met. Rehabilitation is enhanced to the extent that offenders learn to be accountable for the crimes they committed as well as to victims for any injuries or monetary losses sustained.

The private sector has joined with public community corrections agencies to provide alternative sanctions for low-risk offenders. A national survey of privately operated community corrections agencies conducted by the International Association of Residential and Community Alternatives (IARCA) found that the following programs are currently offered to offender-clients: intensive supervision, house arrest, electronic monitoring, day fines, community services, day and evening reporting, drug testing, boot camps, and community residential centers (Huskey and Lurigio, 1992). Four general observations have been made about such programs:

1. Privately operated community programs appear to be serving a significant number and range of offenders and are doing so with a wide variety of intermediate sanctions.
2. The community-based programs operated by these agencies seem responsive to contemporary correctional concerns; many offer substance abuse and employment services that address the major causes of crime, while others provide alternatives to incarceration.
3. Privately operated intermediate sanctions are generating considerable cost savings to the taxpayer as evidenced by offender wages, fines, restitution, taxes, and room and board, and by the number of offenders diverted from jails and prisons.
4. The low rearrest rate for offenders who participate in these sanctions suggests a minimal threat to public safety.

FUNCTIONS OF COMMUNITY CORRECTIONS

Community corrections performs the following functions: (1) client monitoring and supervision to ensure program compliance; (2) ensuring public safety; (3) employment assistance; (4) individual and group counseling; (5) educational training and literacy services; (6) networking with other community agencies and businesses; and (7) reducing jail and prison overcrowding.

Client Monitoring and Supervision to Ensure Program Compliance

When offenders are sentenced to a community corrections program, it is expected that they will comply with all program conditions. The nature of their supervision is more or less intense in order to ensure program compliance. Victim compensation, restitution, and/or community service are often crucial program components geared to heighten offender accountability and program effectiveness. For instance, the Washington County, Oregon, Community Corrections Restitution Center located at Hillsboro was established in 1979 to provide a structured residential setting where offenders could receive employment assistance and counseling. Mechanisms were also established to ensure that each offender was able to meet financial obligations associated with restitution and other forms of victim compensation. Oregon offender-clients served by this center have been able to perform required community services and otherwise participate in an organization in which their chances for success are maximized (Washington County Community Corrections, 1992).

The **Florida Community Control Program (FCCP)** also seeks to provide a milieu of accountability for offender-clients. Established in 1983, the FCCP has served more than 40,000 clients (Wagner and Baird, 1993:1). Supervision of Florida offenders placed in this program is intense. Offenders must have a minimum of 28 supervisory contacts per month. Supervising officers have caseloads of between 20 and 25 offenders. These caseloads are very low compared with standard probation or parole supervision. Besides close offender supervision, the FCCP utilizes home confinement. Offenders are regularly screened for drug and alcohol use, and offenders are monitored to ensure their payment of victim compensation, restitution, and/or community service. Offenders also pay supervision fees to offset some of the program costs. Recidivism is less than 20 percent for FCCP clients (Wagner and Baird, 1993:4). There is little question that the program is inexpensive. For instance, FCCP costs per day average $6.49, while jail and prison costs per day per offender are $19.52 and $39.05 respectively.

Ensuring Public Safety

An obvious concern of community residents is for their safety in view of the fact that recently convicted felons are roaming their neighborhoods more or less freely and in relatively large numbers (Eynon, 1989; Tilow, 1989). But most, if not all, community corrections agencies can cite substantial evidence that for the most part, their offender clients pose little or no risk to community residents. The supervisory safeguards, curfew, and drug and alcohol abuse checks are fairly intense. Offender-clients are usually selected on the basis of their low-risk profile and prospects for completing their programs successfully.

The public safety factor was the subject of a study of community corrections in Kansas. Harris, Jones, and Funke (1990) investigated various participating Kansas counties over time during the 1980s. They compared incarcerated felons with community corrections clients and those placed on standard probation. Interestingly, these researchers found few significant differences in recidivism rates of inmates and program clients. In fact, they indicate that at least a 50 percent false-positive rate would have been incurred had these offenders been incarcerated initially. In short, at least 50 percent of the prison-bound offenders did not recidivate after placement in community corrections programs. Further, the offenses committed by community corrections clients tended to be less serious than their conviction offenses. Thus, these researchers concluded that community corrections has not posed a serious public risk, at least in Kansas.

Other researchers have emphasized particular types of community corrections programs, such as home confinement and electronic monitoring, as particularly conducive to low recidivism rates. Schumacher et al. (1991) indicate that electronic monitoring has been especially helpful at reducing revocation rates of probationers and parolees in two metropolitan areas of a southwestern state. Researchers have reported similar success experiences in Washington and other states (Savage and Dumovich, 1991). Programs that incorporate substance abuse counseling together with job placement assistance seem especially effective. Haddock (1990) says that community corrections agencies can provide a variety of outpatient therapies, including self-help methods, skills training, coping skills training, stress reduction training, counseling, and marital and family therapy. Agencies can help to ensure continued abstinence from substance abuse by frequent monitoring and regular counseling.

Public safety is a key community corrections program feature in both Oklahoma and Kansas. In Oklahoma, for instance, an assessment was made of Oklahoma's Community Treatment Program during the years 1970 through 1977 (White, 1992). Oklahoma corrections officials released various inmates who were within one year of their probable release. These offenders were designated as "trustees" and placed in the Community Treatment Program. Once in this program, offenders were assigned to work release or study release. They received employment assistance, financial planning and budgeting assistance, and group/individual counseling. They participated in educational programs and received other forms of vocational and educational training from nearby schools. The program was regarded as highly successful, in large part because of the careful screening process used to include these offenders initially.

In Kansas, offenders were assigned to various community services available through community corrections programs. They were intensively supervised, made regular restitution payments to crime victims, and performed different types of community service. While participating in these community corrections programs, all clients were subject to regular and random drug and alcohol abuse checks. Those who manifested drug or alcohol problems were assigned to receive substance abuse counseling and treatment referrals (Townsend, 1991).

Victims are also increasingly involved in an effort to ensure public safety. Many offenders receive sentences that provide for their early release. For instance, in South Carolina, a Victim/Witness Bill of Rights was passed in 1984 by the state legislature. Under this Bill of Rights, victims are advised of the following: (1) notifi-

BOX 8.1
Should Community Corrections Supervise Elderly Inmates Who Are No Longer Dangerous?

The Case of Quenton Brown

In June 1973, 50-year-old Quenton Brown was out of work and a drifter. Needing food, Brown decided to rob a bread store in Morgan City, Louisiana. He got $117 and a 15-cent piece of cherry pie. After robbing the store, he walked across the street, where he sat near a house and ate his pie. Police showed up soon thereafter and arrested Brown. Brown offered no resistance and surrendered his .38 caliber revolver and the stolen money. In Brown's trial later, a court-appointed attorney entered a "guilty by reason of insanity" plea for Brown, whose IQ was about 51. The jury didn't believe his plea and convicted him of armed robbery. The judge sentenced Quenton Brown to 30 years without parole.

In 1994, Quenton Brown turned 71 years old. He will be released from prison in the year 2003. Five years earlier, Ginny Carroll of *Newsweek* did an article about Brown. At the time, Brown was 67, feeble, and suffering from emphysema, a crushed esophagus, and bleeding ulcers. His prison record is without blemish. He has never been in a fight or been involved with drugs, sex, or violence of any kind. He is a Class-A trustee, meaning that he has the best inmate security rating. At present, Quenton Brown is being held in the Louisiana State Prison at Angola. Over the years, he has watched many convicted murderers come and go, paroled by the Lousiana Board of Paroles. Being much older than many of the other inmates at Angola, Brown is frequently victimized. He says that younger inmates call him names and steal his personal effects when he walks to and from the prison store. He says it is like living in a jungle with savages.

The state of Louisiana spends about $69,000 per year maintaining Quenton Brown, including both his housing and medical costs. With changing sentencing schemes in various states, it is becoming more and more difficult for state penal systems to release prisoners such as Quenton Brown. It is fairly certain that Brown poses no threat to anyone if released. Despite a unanimous recommendation from the Lousiana Board of Paroles that the Governor of Louisiana should commute Brown's sentence, then-Governor Buddy Roemer denied this recommendation. Statisticians with the Bureau of Justice Statistics say that the older prisoners are when they are eventually released, the less likely they are to commit new crimes. But there is a "down" side. Older inmates often lack essential job skills to "make it" on the outside. Ex-cons most often have no savings or medical insurance, and many do not know how to access welfare programs to take advantage of them. About half of all long-term prisoners in U.S. prisons are age 55 or over, and many of these inmates are harmless.

What should be done about inmates like Quenton Brown? Should state and federal governments exact every single incarcerative day from all inmates as retribution for their crimes? Should older offenders be segregated somehow from younger offenders, in order to prevent their exploitation? Is community corrections the answer?

Source: Adapted from Ginny Carroll, "Growing Old Behind Bars: Some Cellblocks Are More Nursing Home than Jail." *Newsweek,* November 20, 1989:70.

cation of conviction and sentencing of the offender; (2) education regarding special programs administered by the department; (3) tracking of restitution payments; (4) notification of violation hearings and their dispositions; (5) education regarding availability of community resources offering assistance and support to crime victims; (6) victim/witness protection; and (7) liaison activities with other agencies of the criminal justice system and with victim advocacy groups (Moore, 1993:16).

Employment Assistance

An important objective of community corrections is to provide offender-clients with job assistance. Many of these clients do not know how to fill out job application forms. Other clients do not know how to interview properly with prospective employers. Minimal assistance from staff of community-based corrections agencies can do much to aid offenders in securing employment and avoiding further trouble with the law (Dickey, 1989; Musheno et al., 1989).

A successful employment assistance program tailored for female offenders was established in Pennsylvania in 1974 (Arnold, 1992). Known as the **Program for Female Offenders, Inc.,** it was guided by two goals: reforming female offenders and creating economically independent women. The program started with a job placement service. Training centers were eventually created and operated by different counties on a nonprofit basis. Training center offerings have included remedial math instruction, English instruction, and clerical classes such as word processing, data entry, and telecommunications skill training. Counseling has also been provided for those women with social and psychological problems. The importance of job training cannot be overstated. Currently, the program serves 300 women per year, and the community facilities have a low recidivism rate of only 3.5 percent (Arnold, 1992). During the 1980s, Pennsylvania officials expanded the program to assist male offenders in similar ways. Preliminary indications are that the program is also working successfully for male offenders.

Individual and Group Counseling

Many offender-clients who become involved in community corrections programs have drug or alcohol dependencies (Huskey, 1992:70). Many of these persons are maladjusted in the sense that they have difficulty getting along with others or coping with life's everyday problems. Therefore, these offenders have certain social, psychological, and physical needs that must be treated, either through individual or group counseling. Many community corrections agencies have established such counseling programs for these offenders. For example, Kansas enacted a community corrections act in 1978. By 1991, 105 Kansas counties had community services available that provided alcohol and drug testing, substance abuse counseling and treatment referrals, employment and education, budgeting methods, and evaluation (Townsend, 1991). The intent of such programs in Kansas is to motivate clients

Educating low-risk offenders in community corrections programs is fundamental to their community reintegration and rehabilitation. (Gary Wagner/Stock Boston)

to engage in activities and treatment programs that promote the development and maintenance of productive lifestyles within the community. Kansas probation officers also use telemonitoring devices to supervise at-risk offenders with various psychological and social adjustment problems.

Educational Training and Literacy Services

Many of these agencies provide education services for offenders with language deficiencies or who have dropped out of school previously. Many offenders do not know how to fill out job placement forms or applications. Community corrections staff offer assistance in this regard. In addition, offender-clients may participate in study release through local schools.

In Arizona, for instance, a task force investigated the literacy level of Arizonans and found that over 400,000 of them were functionally illiterate. Another 500,000 did not have a high school diploma. About 60 percent of Arizona's prison inmates had a reading level at about the sixth grade (O'Connell and Power, 1992). Seeking to remedy this situation, Arizona implemented L.E.A.R.N. labs, or Literacy, Education, and Reading Network, to remedy learning and educational deficiencies among its probationers and inmates. One purpose of this program is to raise the educational and reading level of offender-clients so that they will be more competitive in the workplace. Recent evidence suggests the L.E.A.R.N. program is successful (O'Connell and Power, 1992:7).

Networking with Other Community Agencies and Businesses

An important function of community corrections is to network with various community agencies and businesses to match offender-clients with needed treatments and services. Community corrections agencies may not have a full range of offender services (Taxman, 1994). Cooperative endeavors are necessary if certain offenders are to receive the type of treatment they need most. Sometimes, the networking performed by community corrections enables offender-clients to obtain vocational and educational training, or perhaps group or individual counseling. Networking with businesses enables community corrections personnel to determine job availability. Thus, community corrections offers a valuable job placement service for those offenders who have difficulty finding work.

Corbett (1993:11) regards community corrections as customer-driven enterprises, in which the needs of offender-clients are paramount. The activities of community corrections agencies are intended to accommodate and serve offender-clients in diverse ways. Corbett notes that community corrections is also mission-driven and results-oriented (Corbett, 1993:11). He sees community corrections as satisfying the functions of offender management and monitoring, helping to ensure public safety and provide community protection. Offender assistance is also directed toward helping clients achieve and maintain law-abiding lifestyles.

Reducing Jail and Prison Overcrowding

There is certainly no shortage of literature to document the fact that community-based corrections functions in large part to reduce jail and prison populations (*Corrections Compendium*, 1990b; Corrigan, 1990; English and Mande, 1991; Medler, 1985). In New York, for instance, it costs about $30,000 per prisoner per year for prison housing. In contrast, a Community Protective Program (COPP), which offers more intensive offender monitoring than ISP but less than full incarceration, costs the state about $3,500 per prisoner (*Corrections Compendium*, 1990b).

There are both short- and long-term benefits that accrue to various jurisdictions as the result of establishing community corrections programs (Cohen, 1994). A short-term benefit is reducing jail and prison populations by diverting a substantial number of offenders to community-based supervision. A long-term benefit is that offenders in community-based programs tend to have lower rates of recidivism compared with paroled offenders who have served some prison time. It may be that "creaming" or selecting the most eligible and least dangerous offenders for community-based correctional programs accounts for these recidivism differences. In any case, community-based programs have an ameliorative effect on offender-clients generally (Czajkowski, 1985a).

SELECTED ISSUES IN COMMUNITY CORRECTIONS

These issues include (1) the need for offender rehabilitation versus the amount of public risk created by permitting criminals the freedom of movement in their communities; (2) the amount of societal reintegration that actually occurs through these programs; (3) the use of volunteers and paraprofessionals and their legal liabilities and responsibilities; and (4) the extent to which privatization of these programs subverts accountability, societal authority, and offender control.

Public Resistance to Locating Community Programs in Communities (The NIMBY Syndrome: "Not in My Back Yard")

When community corrections agencies are proposed for different communities, the problem of where to locate these facilities arises. Community officials may desire community corrections programs in theory, anticipating that the community will acquire additional external resources from state or federal funding agencies. Community corrections organizations will provide new jobs for the community. Certain community businesses will anticipate additional revenue from these corrections agencies. However, the matter of locating these facilities becomes a sensitive one. This has become a major issue in many communities and persists today as the **NIMBY Syndrome:** "Not in My Back Yard." No one wants a halfway house or community corrections agency next door or across the street. The idea of felons living next door disturbs more than a few residents (Schiff, 1990). The NIMBY Syndrome has been investigated in various locations, including Canada.

Benzvy-Miller (1990) says that communities tend to manifest the NIMBY Syndrome for at least three reasons: (1) They fear crime and expect that close proximity to offenders will expose them to greater risk; (2) they have attitudes and perceptions about offenders that have little to do with reality; and (3) they are afraid that a group home will somehow taint the neighborhood and cause property values to decline. These attitudes and the problems they generate can be overcome by educating the public and increasing their awareness of what these programs are all about and how offenders are supervised or monitored. However, Benzvy-Miller says that educating the public is a long and sometimes difficult process.

Tilow (1989) agrees with Benzvy-Miller and describes similar community resistance to community corrections facilities being established in Cincinnati, Ohio. Cincinnati is the home of Talbert House, opened as a halfway house in 1965. The annual budget was originally $60,000, and the facility was designed to accommodate and counsel 16 parolees. Over the years, Talbert House has expanded its facilities to include 12 programs, including 5 community residential centers for correctional clients, 2 programs for individuals convicted of drunk driving, 2 other substance abuse programs, a crisis counseling and suicide intervention center, a victims-of-crime assistance program, and an employment placement project. There were 185 programs and a $4.2 million operating budget in 1989 (Tilow, 1989:88). Despite the success of Talbert House, the Cincinnati public has been slow to accept these facilities as nonthreatening. Tilow notes that developing such facilities has been as difficult as opening new jails. The public has strong fears about Talbert House clients.

Town meetings are often called in anticipation of community resistance to new Talbert House projects. The agency establishment process is quite lengthy. For instance, in 1984, Talbert House officials decided to establish a new facility for offender housing and counseling. A site was located in early 1985, a six-family, partially gutted apartment building. Renovations were planned and it was determined that the facility could accommodate 35 residents. Bank loans for construction and remodeling were acquired, and, in June 1986, a meeting was held with a dozen community leaders. A zoning permit was required and construction began in August 1987. Immediately, there was a flurry of community opposition, with telephone calls to the police, building and safety officials, and members of the city council. At least two city council members became involved in representing citizen interests opposing the facility construction. Further informative meetings were held with Talbert House officials and community residents. It was eventually agreed that Talbert House would exclude murderers and sex offenders from their facilities and operate on a 15:1 supervisory ratio. Despite these agreements and concessions, a neighborhood community group persisted in its opposition. After several more months of negotiation, most citizen fears and concerns were satisfactorily answered. In February 1988, this facility was officially opened. For most citizens and Talbert House officials, the long process was worth it.

Punishment versus Rehabilitation and Reintegration

Not everyone agrees about the true aims of community-based correctional programs (Schiff, 1990). The financial savings associated with their operation is certainly a strong argument favoring their continued use, however. This argument is especially strengthened with evidence showing that some offenders do not need to be incarcerated and prove of greater value free in society rather than in prison where they remain unhelped and relatively unproductive (Coffey, 1986). Petersilia (1990c) observes that the public often remains unconvinced that community corrections is imposing punishments that fit offender crimes. Petersilia argues that offender sanctions should be tailored in such a way that offenders themselves will regard such sanctions as at least as punitive as incarceration. Thus, the chances of persuading policymakers to accept community corrections as a legitimate sanctioning medium are increased substantially.

Admittedly, it is unsettling for some citizens to know that 1 percent of California's population is on probation and that one's next door neighbor might be a convicted felon involved in a community-based probation program, for example (Petersilia, 1985b). But the advantages and strengths of community-based programs need to be considered together with their disadvantages and weaknesses.

Thus, one issue arises about the risk to society posed by programs that grant substantial freedoms to convicted felons.

Does diverting convicted felons to probation or any other nonincarcerative alternative necessarily and seriously jeopardize public safety? Some researchers believe it is possible to not only reduce the use of incarceration but to maintain public safety in the process (Vito, 1983:70). For instance, a shock probation program was implemented in Ohio during the 1970s. Shock probation involves incarcerating convicted offenders for periods ranging from 90 to 130 days and then releasing them on probation by the sentencing judge (Vito, 1983:69). The "shock" of incarceration was deemed sufficiently important to make most offenders want to avoid future imprisonment through the commission of new offenses.

Vito and Allen (1981) reported substantial differences in the reincarceration rates of regular probationers and shock probationers in Ohio in 1975, for example. Over 40 percent of the regular probationers were reincarcerated for various new crimes, whereas only about 15 percent of the shock probationers were reincarcerated. Although these findings in and of themselves are not conclusive evidence of the effectiveness of shock probation on minimizing the risks to public safety through particular types of probation, the implication is that the type of offender experiences and supervision while on probation can make an important difference and function as a general deterrent to new crimes. Other researchers have found similarly low reincarceration rates with these types of programs (Kozuh et al., 1980).

It is evident that some offenders derive rehabilitative value from community-based programs. The question then becomes, "what proportion of those offenders served are unaffected and recidivate?" Reactions by professionals have been both optimistic and pessimistic. Some experts claim that these programs have done little to improve offenders (Austin and Krisberg, 1982; Scull, 1977; Travis, 1985). Others say these programs, if operated effectively, have made substantial offender improvements (Edna McConnell Clark Foundation, 1982; Coffey, 1986; Huskey, 1984). Vito (1983:66–67) argues, however, that when recidivism rates of those offenders who do not participate in these programs are compared with those who do, the programs do appear to be of value in deterring crime and reducing recidivism. No program is going to function perfectly as a crime deterrent or a rehabilitative tool. Much depends on how effectively the offender is controlled and monitored while free in the community (Clear and O'Leary, 1983).

Societal reintegration is one of community-based corrections' manifest goals (Lauen, 1984), although some critics say we are moving toward operations that have deterrence and control as priorities (Holman and Quinn, 1989). Some researchers have examined regular U.S. population growth and compared these figures with the concurrent growth of prison populations. Between 1970 and 1985, the U.S. prison population grew by over 60 percent, while the U.S. population increased about 10 percent during the same period (Lawrence, 1985:108). Thus, some persons have concluded erroneously that the impact of community corrections on prison populations has been negligible (Martinson, 1974). However, it is possible that prison populations would have grown even more without the increased use of community alternatives (Lawrence, 1985:108).

If community-based corrections fail to reintegrate offenders into their communities, is it the fault of the programs themselves or the way the programs are operated? One observer has suggested that community-based programs often include the same restrictive conditions as regular correctional institutions. Residents are locked up at night, required to have a pass before leaving, and prohibited from driving. Curfews are strictly enforced. Thus, true deinstitutionalization does not occur, but, rather, one institution is substituted for another (Greenberg, 1975; Lawrence, 1985:109).

Evidence of community-based program successes is more plentiful than evidence of program failures (Harris, 1984). The state of Wisconsin has operated Community Residential Centers in Milwaukee and other cities for several years with success rates among clientele of 83 percent (Wisconsin Department of Health and Social Services, 1982). Wisconsin officials have concluded overwhelmingly that their program has had a positive impact on offender community reintegration. Community correctional centers operating in southeast Washington, D.C. have reported similar success experiences with offender reintegration (Czajkowski, 1985). Where programs have evidenced high failure rates, limited funding, inadequate staffing, and unclear program goals have been cited as the major problems rather than the effectiveness of the programs themselves (Medler, 1985; Thomas, 1986). One reason for these funding inadequacies was the eventual elimination of the LEAA in the late 1970s and the withdrawal of its financial support. However, the National Institute of Justice and other government programs have continued to provide limited funding for certain programs, although this funding is only a fraction of what the LEAA provided.

Offender Needs and Public Safety

Public safety is a perennial issue whenever community corrections seeks to establish agencies within neighborhoods. Residents are repelled by the idea that they will have convicted felons roaming freely among them. We have already seen that the NIMBY Syndrome acts to inhibit community acceptance of community corrections, often on nonrational grounds (Benzvy-Miller, 1990). At the same time, corrections officials cite the need to place certain rehabilitation-friendly offenders into communities where they can learn to function normally and in law-abiding ways. Offenders need community experience, while community residents need to feel safe. Thus, public safety is often at odds with the rehabilitative ideal of community corrections programs. Is there common ground, on which both the public and corrections can function in mutually beneficial ways?

Oklahoma officials think they have an answer to this question. In the late 1980s, the Oklahoma Department of Corrections created several county-level **community work centers (CWCs).** These CWCs provide for inmates to live in residences located in various neighborhoods and to do work benefiting counties and cities. Oklahoma officials label these CWCs *constituency-based corrections* because the centers reduce prison overcrowding and the expense of incarceration. Furthermore, the CWCs give inmates positive work and personal growth experiences, such

BOX 8.2
Some Offenders May Be Beyond Rehabilitation

The Case of Willie Bosket Jr.

Willie Bosket Jr. is the son of Willie Bosket Sr. Willie Bosket Sr. had a third-grade education, was sentenced to reform school at age nine, and went on to commit double murders. Imprisoned for these crimes, Willie Bosket Sr. was subsequently paroled. He worked at a university as a teaching assistant for a year or so. Eventually, he was arrested again, this time for allegedly molesting a six-year-old child. Shortly after his arrest, he took a gun and killed his girlfriend. He followed this act by blowing his brains out.

Willie Bosket Jr. is a self-described homicidal maniac. In 1989, Willie Bosket Jr. was 26 years old. He was in the Woodbourne Correctional Facility in solitary confinement for life because of two murders he committed when he was 15. He shot to death two subway riders in New York City. Since then, during a brief respite from prison, he tried to rob and knife a 72-year-old half-blind man. He has also stabbed a prison officer, smashed the skull of another officer with a lead pipe, set fire to his cell seven times, choked a secretary, sodomized various inmates, beat up a psychiatrist, mailed a death threat to then-President Ronald Reagan, battered a reformatory teacher with a nail-studded club, and tried to blow up a truck. Willie Bosket Jr. spends his time throwing his feces and food from his cell at passersby.

Like his father, Willie Bosket Sr., Willie Bosket Jr. has an exceptionally high IQ, although you wouldn't think this from his behavior. He is extremely well read and knowledgeable. Now he is monitored constantly by three video cameras behind Plexiglas. It was rumored to Willie Bosket Jr. that New York might bring back the death penalty someday. Willie Bosket Jr. replied, "When that day comes, I won't kill people; I'll just maim them. I want to live every day so that I can just make *them* regret what they've done to me." Precisely to whom "*them*" refers is unknown to everyone. According to death penalty supporters, Willie Bosket Jr. is a living example of the need for the death penalty in New York.

Does the death penalty deter crime? Is deterrence a chief reason for applying the death penalty, or is it more realistic to view the death penalty purely as punishment? If we are going to use the death penalty, do some offenders deserve it more than others? What would you do to correct a problem inmate like Willie Bosket Jr.? Is it reasonable to assume that his problems can ever be corrected?

Source: Adapted from Richard Behar, "I Won't Kill, I'll Just Maim." *Time,* May 29, 1989:30–31.

as shopping, eating, and attending religious services in the community; visiting friends and relatives in noninstitutional settings; and receiving job training (Lawrence, 1992:130).

Selected low-security inmates placed in CWCs perform various work assignments, such as state park renovation. In January 1989, inmate work crews were put to the task of renovating Lake Murray State Park in Ardmore, Oklahoma. Ten inmates lived, ate, and slept in buildings on the park grounds. They were supervised by five correctional officers from the Lexington Assessment and Reception Center, about 75 miles south of Ardmore. Subsequent inmate work crews expanded the scope of their original renovation activities by doing additional building renovation, trail and bridge construction and improvement, and picnic table fabrication and placement. Some inmates performed routine maintenance functions. The general public soon learned about what the inmates had accomplished. This helped to increase their general acceptance of CWCs, since they were direct beneficiaries of inmate work. At the same time, the work performed by inmates was rehabilitative and provided them with skills that could be applied in various construction businesses throughout their communities (Lawrence, 1992). Subsequently, various communities throughout Oklahoma have solicited the state to establish CWCs in their locales.

Net Widening

Community corrections agencies have not been established so that offenders who would ordinarily receive a nonincarcerative sentence can be placed in them. For community corrections to maximize its functions and perform the services it was originally intended to perform, offender-clients need to be drawn from either prison- or jail-bound offenders who pose low risk of reoffending or from inmates who have demonstrated that they are low risk, can be trusted, and are likely to succeed in a nonincarcerative setting (Larivee et al., 1990).

While net widening is always a possible consequence of the establishment or implementation of new community programs, corrections experts seem in agreement that net widening has not been particularly troublesome for community corrections programs (Harris, Jones, and Funke, 1990). In order to continue successfully avoiding the inclusion of the wrong types of offenders for community corrections programs, experts suggest that community corrections programs should be expanded to include more serious cases from among those ordinarily placed on felony probation (Austin, Quigley, and Cuvelier, 1989).

Privatization

Jail and prison overcrowding problems have often been accompanied by the intrusion of private entrepreneurs into the corrections sector (Bowditch and Everett, 1987:441). The prevailing belief is that private enterprises, specifically for-profit industries, can provide private financing, delivery, and management of prison and community corrections services better than publicly operated institutions can (Logan and Rausch, 1985). Since one source of resistance to community-based correctional programs seems to be a general lack of citizen understanding of what these programs are, how they operate, and their community impact, one strategy by corrections officials has been the increased use of community residents as board members and volunteers in these community-based projects. This move theoretically facilitates citizen understanding of these programs and lessens resistance to their establishment in the community (Huskey, 1987:38). Thus, it is often necessary to "sell" corrections programs operating within the community to an unwilling and resistant public.

The privatization of corrections, or the intrusion of private industry into community programs and the administration of prison systems, is succeeding in furthering the public relations image of corrections generally in the community by suggesting greater control of prisons and offender programs by the private sector (Bowditch and Everett, 1987:442). Thus, when the public is better educated about corrections, it is more likely to respond favorably (Huskey, 1987:40).

Frank Cullen (1986:13–15) lists five reasons why privately run treatment programs would serve as a progressively oriented reform resulting in more effective inmate growth. These reasons include:

1. Privatization would break the traditional treatment-custody link and the resulting corruption from overconcern with custody and control. There would be a much greater incentive to make rehabilitation work if the profit motive were present, since profits are frequently connected with effectiveness.
2. Privatization would result in more, not less, accountability if program rehabilitation objectives fail. Systems linking payment or contract renewal to the quality and effectiveness of services provided would make private vendors more accountable and responsive.
3. The infusion of private interests into corrections would promote experimentation with new ideas and strategies for offender treatment and rehabilitation. Under existing management schemes, the routinization of policy is commonplace, with little or no innovativeness (Van Voorhis, 1987:56).
4. The introduction of business into offender rehabilitation may enhance the political acceptability of correctional treatment. In short, the public relations dimension of corrections would be enhanced and greater community acceptance would ensue, as Huskey (1987) suggests.
5. Privatization is consistent with capitalist philosophy, and this basic compatibility would "make sense" since it offers businesses the chance to make money from corrections.

However, one continuing criticism of privatization is that it removes control of offenders from professional corrections personnel and jeopardizes accountability to the courts and other officials. However, it is quite likely that those promoting privatization would hire corrections professionals. In short, the physical trappings of prisons and community-based programs would not change as the result of privatization. The most significant changes would be subtle administrative rearrangements and authority shifts resulting in more efficient operations. Private entrepreneurs do not appear interested in wrestling control of prisoners from the courts. In this respect, Cullen's reasons for the logical growth of privatization are more persuasive.

Several direct benefits accrue to the state from the privatization of corrections. First, private enterprises already operating in certain spheres of corrections appear to be more cost-effective and have a high performance level (Bowditch and Everett, 1987:444). And, private enterprise can respond more quickly to problems of financing than can legislatures and political agencies. A third benefit is that private enterprise can make initial capital investments in facility construction, thus saving the state millions of dollars. Privatization may also result in decreased government liability from lawsuits brought by clients against program administrators and staff (Robbins, 1986). Finally, private enterprises charge the state less than publicly funded community-based operations (Bowditch and Everett, 1987:444–445).

Major objections to privatization are closely linked with policy issues. Should private interests be assigned the responsibility for disciplining and rehabilitating offenders who have committed crimes against society? What type of regulation could be maintained by public agencies over privately established and operated corrections programs? What offender rights might be jeopardized or violated because of the involvement of private interests in discipline (probation revocation) and the provision of certain kinds of services and not others? Community corrections is highly susceptible to privatization, because a large segment of the public is already involved in community-based programs as either volunteers or paraprofessionals. And, some programs, especially those that provide various kinds of juvenile services, are already privately operated and appear to be effective in their performance and operations (Bendick, 1985; Greenwood, 1981).

While some public and expert opinion about community corrections is negative, community-based correctional programs do appear to accomplish the following:

1. They help to relieve institutional crowding and save beds.
2. They punish nonviolent offenders through strict supervision while ensuring the safety of the public.
3. They serve as a cost-effective and efficient correctional tool.
4. They demonstrate a high success rate for completion of offender programs (Huskey, 1987:40).

Huskey and Lurigio (1992) conducted an extensive survey of private community corrections organizations throughout the United States. They made four general observations: (1) Privately operated community programs appear to be serving a significant number and range of offenders and are doing so with a wide variety of community sanctions; (2) the community-based programs operated by these agencies seem responsive to contemporary correctional concerns; many offer substance abuse and employment services that address the major causes and correlates of crime, while others provide alternatives to incarceration; (3) privately operated intermediate sanctions are generating considerable cost savings to the taxpayer, as evidenced by offender wages, fines, restitution, taxes, and room and board, and by the number of offenders diverted from jails and prisons; and (4) the low rearrest rate for offenders participating in these sanctions suggests a minimal threat to public safety.

Services Delivery

Delivering the right services to the right types of offenders is sometimes a difficult task for community corrections agencies to accomplish. Assessments of offender-clients are often cursory, largely because of inadequate staffing and/or funding. If appropriate diagnoses of offender problems are made, available services may not be found. Sometimes, offenders have several problems related in complex ways. A single diagnosis and solution may not address other more deep-seated problems affecting these clients. Few studies have investigated the services provision process of community-based corrections (Gottschalk and Duffee, 1992; Lauen, 1990a, 1990b, 1990c). Historically, service delivery has been deficient in many community corrections programs in which supervisory chores and offender accountability have been regarded as primary goals (Benekos, 1990; Conrad, 1984).

One frequently leveled charge is that those most in need of community corrections resources and program components are least likely to receive such treatments. Often, multiple-conviction felons or high-risk misdemeanants are excluded from community corrections programs because of their great potential for reoffending. Yet, the principles espoused by community corrections are such that these offenders are likely to profit from participation (Racine, Vittitow, and Riggs, 1984). Failure or success rates of community-based offender-clients seem linked closely to one's age, employment history, criminal history, and treatment (Schumacher et al., 1991).

One way of ensuring that service delivery is of high quality and offender relevant is to individualize the goals of specific offenders (Dickey, 1989). For instance, in Grant County, Wisconsin, parole officers identify through interviews various offender needs, such as economic and/or social stresses in coping with life. Parole officers in this jurisdiction say that they often must wait "for the right time" before they can make a significant difference in helping certain offenders they supervise. Whenever offenders violate one or more program conditions, parole officers use these violation instances as opportunities for making changes in their clients' lives. Some offender-clients have family problems or difficulties living in their communities. Certain problems can be targeted for treatment with proper parole officer-client interactions (Dickey, 1989). Certain innovative programs in other states are responsive to particular community resources that exist. POs can take advantage of these resources in order to benefit their offender-clients in particular ways (Musheno et al., 1989).

Education and Training of Staff

Community corrections agencies have not been recognized for their consistency of staff quality. During the 1980s, many community-based facilities were established and staffed by persons with minimal training. When we consider the array of services provided by a majority of community corrections agencies today, it is becoming increasingly important to ensure that the staff are trained in subject areas and have expertise that will benefit the diverse population of offender-clients. Staff members for community-based corrections agencies are recruited from many different areas, including law enforcement and education.

Many former jail officers are currently performing community corrections functions (Cornelius, 1990). One problem encountered in training such persons for community corrections work is the former custody orientation they possess. Offenders in community corrections programs have to be monitored, but not nearly to the degree of supervision required for jail inmates. Thus, one important training feature is to help former jail officers learn how their former and current jobs differ in custody orientation. And, the techniques of offender control are different. The American Correctional Association and other interested organizations have established guidelines for training community corrections personnel. The ACA has indicated that community corrections staff should have training in human relations, communications skills, problem solving, guidance, group dynamics, crisis intervention, and special needs of residents.

Special education and training may be required if certain types of offender-clients are being supervised. If sex offenders are being managed by some community corrections agency, it may be important to provide HIV-relevant education for them through an AIDS education program (Florida Department of Corrections, 1992a). Florida officials who manage community-based corrections often network with existing health agencies to provide special educational seminars for offenders who have histories as sex offenders or who may be substance abusers. Substance abuse education programs are also provided.

As the clientele for community-based corrections becomes increasingly diversified, the staff component must be increasingly skilled in various ways to provide the best counseling and guidance. Another dimension is vocational training and job placement assistance. Staff members must acquire more expertise to assist offender-clients in budget management or financial planning, computer usage, and other forms of training and development (Florida Department of Corrections, 1992b).

The growing use of citizens as volunteers means additional training for those attempting to assist offender-clients in meeting their needs (New York State Department of Correctional Services, 1992). Citizen-volunteers can do much to promote agency recognition throughout the community. Public relations assistance, media support, and one-on-one offender guidance and counseling require that volunteers have some working knowledge of existing community resources and how to access such services (Shields, 1980). In some instances, former inmates themselves can work in these agencies on a volunteer basis to help other offenders adapt and adjust to community life.

The American Correctional Association offers accreditation programs to improve the overall quality of community-based corrections personnel. These accreditation programs do not necessarily guarantee high staff quality, but they do serve to promote the idea of professionalism to a greater degree than if accreditation were not available (McManus and Barclay, 1994). Some of the kinds of training received by staff include understanding punishable violations, problem identification, conflict resolution, and crisis intervention. In New Hampshire, for instance, correctional officers involved in community-based correctional programs learn about their custody obligations, security management policies, substance abuse monitoring, and conditions under which offender-clients are returned to correctional facilities (New Hampshire State Prison, 1992).

Coping with Special Needs Offenders

Any correctional program, whether it is institutional corrections or community-based corrections, will inevitably have to deal with and make provisions for special needs offenders. *Special needs offenders* include physically, mentally, psychologically, or socially impaired or handicapped offenders who require extraordinary care and supervision. Sometimes, elderly offenders are classified as special needs offenders to the extent that they might require special diets, medicines, or environments. Mental retardation, illiteracy, and physical disabilities are some of the many kinds of problems associated with special needs offenders (DeSilva, 1980). Operators of community-based correctional facilities face continual dilemmas over the need to accommodate these offenders in special facilities and the need to move offender-clients generally into mainstream society and assist them to live independently (Breed, 1982; Soskin, 1982).

Regarding the provisions for special needs offenders in many community corrections programs, major problems have been identified, including lack of access to adequate mental health services, inadequate information and training among court and corrections personnel, and insufficient interagency coordination and cooperation (Illinois Office of the Governor, 1988). Some community corrections facilities are linked closely with other close-custody prisons, such as the Massachusetts Correctional Institution (MCI) for women at Framingham (Massachusetts Department of Corrections, 1988). The Framingham institution, which houses 530 female convicts, offers assistance in the following areas: (1) mental health counseling; (2) substance abuse treatment; (3) parenting and family services; (4) employment planning, education, and vocational counseling; and (5) health screenings, treatment and referrals (American Correctional Association, 1994; Massachusetts Department of Corrections, 1988). These services seem offender-relevant, since a lack of education and drug abuse are two of the major obstacles to finding employment (Poethig, 1989).

Community corrections may not provide the degree of protection that might need to be extended to persons with one or more disabilities or handicaps. Those who are mentally ill may not be able to function normally in their communities.

Some offenders who are mentally impaired may require constant monitoring and supervision, primarily for their own protection (Illinois Department of Mental Health and Developmental Disabilities, 1988). Some experts believe that it will be necessary for entire Departments of Correction in each state to address the problems of special-needs offenders from a total systems approach. A comprehensive corrections plan can be effective at maximizing the cost-efficiency of correctional construction (Williams and Bissell, 1990). The growing number of special needs populations will require new thinking by architects and administrators to meet inmates' and clients' special health, program, and management needs (Williams and Bissell, 1990).

Sex offenders often pose special problems for community corrections staff. Sex offenders may have committed rape, incest, voyeurism, or any of several other sexual behaviors and/or perversions. Treatments of sex offenders sometimes involve the hormonal drug Depo-Provera, and some patients may be monitored by a penile plethysmograph, a device that measures the significance of various sexual stimuli relating to arousal (Knopp, Rosenberg, and Stevenson, 1986).

Many offenders involved in community-based corrections programs have learning disabilities. Special education courses and services are needed to meet their needs more effectively (Rutherford, Nelson, and Wolford, 1985). Several components of successful correctional special educational programs have been identified. These include functional assessments of the skills and learning needs of handicapped offenders, a curriculum that teaches functional academic and living skills, vocational special education, and transitional programs that facilitate moving from correctional systems to community living. Simultaneously, correctional educators should have some in-service and preservice training in special education to enhance their own effectiveness in relation to offender-clients (Rutherford, Nelson, and Wolford, 1985).

American Correctional Association policy guidelines have been formulated to outline the types of services and staff training considered as standards for future community-based correctional program development (American Correctional Association, 1986c).

KEY TERMS

Community-based corrections program
Community Diversion Incentive Act
Community work centers (CWCs)
Day reporting centers
Florida Community Control Program (FCCP)
Georgia Special Alternative Incarceration Program (SAI)

Law Enforcement Assistance Administration (LEAA)
NIMBY Syndrome
Probation Subsidy Program
Program for Female Offenders, Inc.
Project Re-Direction

QUESTIONS FOR REVIEW

1. What is meant by community-based corrections?
2. What are the major functions of community corrections programs?
3. In what sense is there a conflict between ensuring public safety and providing a community environment to promote offender therapy and reintegration? Discuss.
4. What is the general philosophy of community corrections? Based on what you have read up to now, is this philosophy consistent with the "get-tough" movement? Why or why not? Explain.
5. What fears do citizens have about locating community corrections agencies in their neighborhoods? Based upon some of the evidence that has been presented, are these fears justified? Why or why not? Explain.
6. How can community corrections personnel establish community corrections programs in given neighborhoods or communities with a minimum of resistance from residents?
7. Who are special needs offenders? What kinds of problems do they pose for the staff of community-based corrections?
8. Discuss the privatization of community-based correctional programs. What are some of the positive and negative aspects of privatization?
9. What is the current state of training of community-based correctional staff?
10. What is meant by accreditation? How is the American Correctional Association attempting to professionalize the staffs of community corrections facilities?

9

Home Confinement and Electronic Monitoring

Introduction

About Intermediate Punishments

Home Confinement Programs

The Goals of Home Confinement Programs

A Profile of Home Confinement Clients

Selected Issues Related to Home Confinement

Electronic Monitoring

Early Uses of Electronic Monitoring

Types of Electronic Monitoring Systems

Electronic Monitoring with Home Confinement

A Profile of Electronic Monitoring Clients

Selected Issues in Electronic Monitoring

The Success of Home Confinement and Electronic Monitoring Programs

Key Terms

Questions for Review

INTRODUCTION

- One day at the probation department, a staff member was overseeing the electronic verification device that kept track of various offenders sentenced to probation. In this probation department, some probationers sentenced to house arrest and electronic monitoring were equipped with electronic anklets or wristlets that emitted user-specific signals. These signals were relayed to the probation office through a central transmission device located on the probationer's premises. If the probationer were to leave the home or stray too far from the transmission device, a signal would be activated at the probation office, and the staff member would know that the offender had left the premises.

  As the staff member watched the monitor, a signal was suddenly activated, meaning that a probationer was not in close proximity to the transmission device located in the home. The staff member quickly alerted a probation officer and advised that a visit should be made to that offender's home. Just as the probation officer started out the door, another signal sounded, indicating that the probationer was back on premises. A few seconds later, another signal was sounded, indicating that the same probationer was off the premises again. And again, the probation officer headed out the door for a home visit. Just as suddenly, another alarm sounded, indicating that the offender was again off premises. In frustration, a home check was ordered. This time, regardless of the transmitted signal, the probation officer visited the probationer. When the probation officer arrived, she discovered that the probationer was cutting his large lawn with a riding lawn mower. As the probationer reached the edge of the lawn during cutting, the distance from the home transmitter was such that it caused a signal to be sent to the probation office, indicating that the probationer had "left the premises."

- In another probation department, probation and police officers were positioned on a stakeout of a probationer's premises. The probationer was under house arrest and electronic monitoring. The probationer had been convicted of drug trafficking, and there was evidence to indicate that the probationer was continuing this illicit activity. An informant indicated that the probationer was dealing drugs out of the rear entrance to the premises. As the probation officers and police watched, various persons would approach the rear door of the residence and pass money to the probationer in exchange for a white substance in plastic envelopes. The police moved in and made an arrest. A search of the probationer's premises disclosed several kilos of heroin, a large quantity of cocaine, several weapons, and a large stash of cash.

- In yet another probation department, a staff member watched a television monitor as she spoke with and observed a male probationer in the probationer's residence. The probationer had been sentenced to home confinement and electronic monitoring. The probationer's residence had been equipped with a video camera and other devices to detect possible program violations. The probationer was ordered to blow into a device near the transmitter. The probationer's breath was registered and analyzed electronically. The results disclosed that the probationer had recently used cocaine and alcohol. The probationer was subsequently apprehended for various program violations and his probation program was revoked.

- Finally, in another probation department, a monitor showed that a woman who had been convicted of fraud was at her residence for the first eight weeks of her sentence. She had been sentenced to six months of home confinement and electronic monitoring. A probation officer subsequently went to her residence for the first of several face-to-face visits. What she found was a grisly crime scene. The woman was found dead, with a self-inflicted gunshot wound to the head. Her husband and four children were also found shot to death in their beds. A suicide note was found near her body. It seems that her guilt and shame overcame her and she believed it would be best for all concerned if they were dead.

What is the point being made by these scenarios? First, home confinement and electronic monitoring can verify an offender's whereabouts and detect possible program violations, such as drug or alcohol abuse, or violation of curfew. Second, an offender's behavior cannot be controlled while on home confinement and/or electronic monitoring.

This chapter is about home confinement and electronic monitoring, two key programs used by community-based corrections. The first part describes the history, goals, and functions of home confinement. Several issues about home confinement as a punishment are raised and discussed. Home confinement clients are profiled.

The second part of the chapter investigates electronic monitoring, what it is, how it functions, and its goals. Described are different types of electronic monitoring systems. Also discussed are various issues about electronic monitoring, including the ethics and constitutionality of such monitoring, and whether it functions as a deterrent and preserves public safety. The chapter concludes with an examination of both home confinement and electronic monitoring and their effectiveness relative to offender supervision. The future of these offender supervision methods is discussed, together with the recent shift toward privatization of corrections.

ABOUT INTERMEDIATE PUNISHMENTS

Home confinement and electronic monitoring are two of several different kinds of intermediate punishments. As we have seen, intermediate punishments include any sanction that falls between standard probation and full incarceration. Besides home confinement and electronic monitoring, other kinds of intermediate punishments include intensive supervised probation, halfway houses, furloughs, work and study release, community service orders, and day reporting programs to monitor offender conduct, restitution provisions, and other program requirements.

HOME CONFINEMENT PROGRAMS

Home Confinement Defined

House arrest, home incarceration, home confinement, and home detention programs proliferated during the late 1980s, primarily because of jail and prison crowding and the increasing availability of reliable electronic monitoring equipment (Huff, 1990). **House arrest, home confinement,** or **home incarceration** are terms for a type of intermediate punishment consisting of confining offenders to their residences for mandatory incarceration during evening hours, curfews, and/or on weekends (Ball and Lilly, 1987; Corbett and Fersch, 1985). Petersilia (1988a:1) adds that house arrest is a sentence imposed by the court in which offenders are legally ordered to remain confined in their own residences; they are usually allowed to leave their residences for medical reasons or employment; they may also be required to perform community service or to pay victim restitution or probation supervision fees. Home confinement is not new. It has been said that St. Paul the Apostle was detained under house arrest in biblical times; and, in the 1600s, Galileo, the astronomer, was forced to live out the last eight years of his life under house arrest. In 1917, Czar Nicholas II of Russia was detained under house arrest until his death. And, during Czar Nicholas II's reign, Lenin was placed under house arrest for a limited period (Meachum, 1986:102).

The first U.S. city to use house arrest was St. Louis in 1971. Although St. Louis officials originally limited its use to juvenile offenders, house arrest became widespread during the next 15 years as an alternative to incarceration for adults as well as for juveniles in many jurisdictions, including Washington, D.C., Baltimore, Newport News, San Jose, and Louisville (Ball, Huff, and Lilly, 1988:34).

The Early Uses of Home Confinement

The first state to adopt home confinement as a statewide intermediate punishment was Florida, through its Correctional Reform Act of 1983 (Flynn, 1986:64). As originally conceived by this Act, Florida's community control house arrest is not an intensive supervision program. Offenders are confined to their own homes, instead of prison, where they are allowed to serve their sentences (Flynn, 1986:64). The cost of home confinement is only $2.86 per day, compared with nearly $30 per day in operating costs for imprisonment. Florida statutes define *community control* as "a form of intensive supervised custody in the community, including surveillance on weekends and holidays, administered by officers with restricted caseloads . . . an individualized program in which the freedom of an offender is restricted within the community, home, or noninstitutional residential placement and specific sanctions imposed and enforced." Community control officers work irregular hours and at nights to help ensure that offenders stay in their homes, except while working at paid employment to support themselves and dependents (Flynn, 1986:64–66).

In Florida, community controllees or offenders eligible for the house arrest program include low-risk, prison-bound criminals. They are expected to comply with the following program requirements:

1. Contribute from 150 to 200 hours of free labor to various public service projects during periods ranging from six months to one year.
2. Pay a monthly maintenance fee of $30 to $50 to help defray program operating costs and officer salaries.
3. Compile and maintain daily logs accounting for their activities; these logs are reviewed regularly by officers for accuracy and honesty.
4. Pay restitution to crime victims from a portion of salaries earned through employment.
5. Remain gainfully employed to support themselves and their dependents.
6. Participate in vocational, technical, or other educational courses or seminars that are individualized according to each offender's needs.
7. Observe a nightly curfew and remain confined to their premises during late evening hours and on weekends, with the exception of court-approved absences for health-related reasons or other purposes.
8. Submit to monitoring by officials 28 times per month either at home or at work.
9. Maintain court-required contacts with neighbors, friends, landlords, spouses, teachers, police, and/or creditors. (Flynn, 1986:66–68)

The record of successes through home incarceration in Florida has been impressive. By January 31, 1986, 5,066 offenders were under house arrest and supervision by probation officers. Since its inception in 1983, the program has served the needs of over 9,300 offenders, with only a 16.2 percent failure rate. Many of these failures included technical program violations such as failing to observe curfew, rather than revocations because of new crime convictions. For instance, by 1986, 889 offenders had had their privileges revoked for technical violations such as failure to pay the monthly maintenance fee on time. Only 619 had allegedly committed new misdemeanor or felony offenses. The Florida house arrest program takes in an average of 300 offenders each month. In view of the number of offenders who succeed while under home confinement, the low failure rate has been deemed respectable by state officials (Florida Department of Corrections, 1986; Flynn, 1986:68).

A similar house arrest program has been implemented in Oklahoma through the Extended Limits of Confinement Act of 1980. Because of administrative delays, the program was not underway until 1984. By April 1985, 963 Oklahoma offenders were under house arrest (Meachum, 1986:106). The eligibility requirements for Oklahoma offenders are different from Florida's. Oklahoma offenders must have served 15 percent of their maximum sentences, and no more than 15 percent of the total offender population can be on house arrest at any given time (1,300 criminals). In order for violent offenders to participate, they must be within six months of discharge from prison. Sex offenders and persons denied parole within the past six months are not considered eligible for the program. On the average, 850 offenders are under house arrest in Oklahoma at any given time at an annual per-offender cost of $1,410. Between October 1984 and October 1985, 2,404 offenders were released from house arrest supervision. The failure rate attributable to the commission of new offenses was only 5 percent. Another 21 percent had "failed" because of technical program violations, and another 7 percent had either absconded or failed to maintain a satisfactory residence or job plan (Meachum, 1986:110).

Oklahoma officials believe that their program is successful, although there was significant public opposition when it was first introduced. Much of the opposition to home confinement was attributed to public failure to understand the nature of this alternative as a punishment. Oklahoma officials decided that one way to improve the public impression of home confinement would be to avoid using program labels such as *alternatives to incarceration,* clarifying the intentions of the program and their expectations of offender-participants, conveying these same clarifications to staff, and making the public more aware of program goals and client behaviors through frequent public meetings with administrators of these programs. Program setbacks in Oklahoma are rare, although an isolated case of a previous sex offender raping and sodomizing a young couple while on house arrest did little, if anything, to further the public image of the concept. However, a study of 2,700 Oklahoma offenders in 1985 showed less than a 4 percent recidivism rate among offenders who had successfully completed their house arrest programs (Davis, 1986).

By 1977, home confinement programs had been implemented in many cities, including Baltimore, Maryland; Louisville, Kentucky; and Panama City, Florida (Lilly and Ball, 1987:360). Considered by many criminal justice professionals to be one of several variations of community-based correctional programs, home confinement varies in its sophistication and definition among jurisdictions. All house arrest programs are aimed at low-risk, prison-bound offenders, and most programs stress surveillance, employment, community service, victim restitution, and a monthly fee to offset some of the additional monitoring expenses (ranging from $15 to $200) (Petersilia, 1986a:50–51). Home confinement may consist of a curfew added on to an offender's probation conditions. Or, it may include restriction to one's residence during all hours except for court-approved limited activities. Or, it may even involve the use of electronic equipment and the requirement that the offender wear an electronic transmitter for the purpose of monitoring compliance (Petersilia, 1986a:50–51).

Under Florida's home confinement program, **community control house arrest,** offenders eligible for home confinement fall into three categories: (1) those found guilty of nonforcible felonies; (2) probationers charged with technical or misdemeanor violations; and (3) parolees charged with technical or misdemeanor violations (Blomberg, Waldo, and Burcoff, 1987:172). The basic requirements that offenders under home confinement must fulfill include the following:

1. They must report to a home confinement officer at least four times a week, or if employed part-time, report daily.
2. They must perform at least 140 hours of public service work, without pay, as directed by the home confinement officer.

3. They must remain confined to residence except for approved employment, public service work, or other special activities approved by the home confinement officer.
4. They must make monthly restitution payments for a specified total amount.
5. They must submit to and pay for urinalysis, breathalyzer, or blood specimen tests at any time as requested by the home confinement officer or other professional staff to determine possible use of alcohol, drugs, or other controlled substances.
6. They must maintain an hourly account of all activities in a daily log to be submitted to the home confinement officer upon request.
7. They must participate in self-improvement programs as determined by the court or home confinement officer.
8. They must promptly and truthfully answer all inquiries of the court or home confinement officer, and allow the officer to visit the home, employer, or elsewhere.
9. As a special condition of home confinement, the court requires the release of treatment information about sex offenders to the home confinement officer or the court (Blomberg, Waldo, and Burcroff, 1987:171–172).

This program may be terminated at any time by court order, with a maximum of two years in the program. If offenders complete the program satisfactorily, then they may be ordered transferred to a standard probation program (Blomberg et al., 1987:172–173). Between October 1983 and January 1986, 9,300 offenders were placed in community control. Of these, only 1,508 had their home confinement revoked, with a majority of these attributable to technical program violations (Flynn, 1986:68). The failure rate of 16.2 percent during that time (including both technical violators and persons committing new misdemeanors and felonies) has been considered respectable (Flynn, 1986:6).

The cost-effectiveness of the Florida program is impressive. For instance, it costs $2.86 per day to supervise a community controlee under house arrest, compared with $27.64 per day in operating costs for imprisonment (Flynn, 1986:68). A report issued by the Palm Beach, Florida, Sheriff's Department in 1986 showed that much of the additional expense of monitoring offenders was offset by payback fees charged to program participants (Palm Beach County, Florida, Sheriff's Department, 1987:185–187).

House arrest programs such as Florida's are increasingly common, especially in those states with prison overcrowding problems. For example, Oklahoma's prison population doubled from 1980 to 1985. During the 1984 legislative session, Oklahoma officials entertained the passage of a home incarceration bill. However, it was soon discovered that such a provision already existed in the earlier Extended Limits of Confinement Act of 1980 (Meachum, 1986:106).

By April 1985, 963 offenders were under house arrest and/or electronic monitoring. In June 1989, 2,300 offenders were involved in such programs (Silvia, 1989:130). By June 1993, this figure had risen to 19,969 (American Correctional Association, 1994:xxviii–xxix). This is an increase of 950 percent in less than eight years. Terms of supervision included random field contacts, substance abuse testing, employer contacts, curfew, and a $45 per month supervision-restitution fee required by the state (Meachum, 1986:108). Oklahoma officials extended their program to include all classes of offenders, probationers as well as persons soon-to-be paroled. Failure to comply with any program condition would be grounds to revoke

---

BOX 9.1
Does Home Confinement Deter Violent Crime?

The Case of Samuel Santiago

Samuel Santiago, 18, was convicted of auto theft in 1990. He had no prior record and the conviction offense was a nonviolent one. He was subsequently sentenced to probation and placed on home confinement and electronic monitoring. The court required him to wear an electronic ankle bracelet that emitted a signal. This signal was received by a telephone device located in Santiago's Illinois apartment. If Santiago were to stray beyond 100 feet from his apartment, an alarm would be activated that would alert probation officials that Santiago was gone from the premises. Santiago's anklet never activated the telephonic alarm, because Santiago never strayed more than 100 feet from his apartment.

One evening the police were alerted when Santiago's neighbors reported hearing gunfire from his apartment. When police arrived, they found that Santiago had

shot and robbed a man in his apartment in a drug deal gone bad. Santiago had killed the man. He was arrested and charged with armed robbery and murder. In a few short months, Santiago had become Illinois' first electronically monitored home confinement offender-client to commit a violent act since the electronic monitoring–house arrest program was established in June 1989.

Illinois officials responsible for operating the home confinement–electronic monitoring program were quick to note that they monitor program participants closely. "We do a lot of watching of these guys . . . This one incident should not bear on the rest of the program," said Mr. Howell, a spokesman for the Illinois Department of Corrections. Howell also said that Santiago is the first offender—out of 1,800 offenders assigned to home monitoring since its inception—to commit a serious crime while under home monitoring.

Source: Adapted from *News Reports,* "Home-Monitored Prisoner Charged with Murder. *Corrections Compendium,* **16:**14, 1991.

---

program participation as well as the automatic loss of good-time credits inmates may have earned prior to entering the program (Meachum, 1986:108). The success of Oklahoma's program is such that from October 1984 to October 1985, 2,404 offenders were released from house arrest supervision. The failure rate was 21 percent (again, including technical program violators and those committing new crimes). Oklahoma estimates that the annual cost of the program per offender is $1,410, and the program is designed to serve 850 offenders at any given time (Meachum, 1986:110).

The federal government has also experimented with home confinement. In 1988, the U.S. Parole Commission experimented with a Community Control Project (Baer and Klein-Saffran, 1990). This was a joint venture with the federal probation system and the U.S. Bureau of Prisons. Under this experimental program, certain federal prison inmates were selected for participation on the basis of their being nonviolent and within 180 days of their release dates. At year end, 1988, 169 parolees entered the project in the Central District of California and the Southern District of Florida. All participants were male, and about 80 percent were 30 years of age or older when they became offender-clients. Two-thirds of the sample were designated as "good risks" according to Hoffman's Salient Factor 81 Scale, although all risk levels were subsequently involved in the research. Each offender was placed in a residence under home confinement with electronic monitoring. Rigid curfews were imposed.

Preliminary study results indicated that overall, the home confinement with electronic monitoring program was successful. Only 31 offenders had their programs revoked because of program violations. Most of these offenders had high risk scores, and, thus, they were those most likely to fail anyway. Baer and Klein-Saffran (1990:30) indicate that

> the results of this project have major policy implications for low-risk offenders who are currently in prison. The consequences of prison crowding are well-documented; a rational, systematic approach is to punish many offenders using community corrections programs. As long as the public can be protected at least as well under strict curfew enforcement, programs within the community can be an appropriate equivalent to incarceration. The results of this project have been encouraging, and broader application of the technology and procedures appears to be feasible.

THE GOALS OF HOME CONFINEMENT PROGRAMS

The goals of home confinement programs include the following:

1. To continue one's punishment while permitting offenders to be confined to their personal residences (Walker and Hough, 1988).
2. To enable offenders freedom to hold jobs and earn a living while caring for their families and/or making restitution to victims (Wood, 1982).
3. To reduce jail and prison overcrowding (Onondaga County Probation Department, 1992; Robinson and Lurigio, 1990; Rosenthal, 1989).
4. To provide a means for ostracism while ensuring public safety (Brillon, 1988; Walker and Hough, 1988).
5. To reduce the costs of offender supervision (Hurwitz, 1987; Jolin and Stipak, 1992).
6. To foster rehabilitation and reintegration by maintaining one's controlled presence within the community (Flicker, 1983; Rush, 1989).

Petersilia (1988b:2–4) has described several advantages and disadvantages of home confinement or house arrest. Among the advantages she notes are that (1) it is cost-effective; (2) it has social benefits; (3) it is responsive to local citizen and offender needs; and (4) it is easily implemented and is timely in view of jail and prison overcrowding. Some of the more important disadvantages of home confinement are that (1) house arrest may actually widen the net of social control; (2) it may narrow the net of social control by not being a sufficiently severe sentence; (3)

House arrest as a sanction fails to deter family violence or other crimes for some offenders. (Mike Mazzaschi/Stock Boston)

it focuses primarily on offender surveillance; (4) it is intrusive and possibly illegal; (5) race and class bias may enter into participant selection; and (6) it may compromise public safety. Some of these advantages and disadvantages will be addressed at length below as issues concerning home confinement when electronic monitoring is also used.

A PROFILE OF HOME CONFINEMENT CLIENTS

No detailed figures exist to depict the present population of home confinement clients. However, a good idea of their characteristics may be gleaned from published research about the types of offenders who are deemed eligible for home confinement participation. Actually, two types of offender aggregates should be included in this description. One consists of probationers sentenced to home confinement, while the other consists of inmates who are released into home confinement programs.

For the probationer aggregate, the following characteristics have been identified:

1. Clients tend to be first-offenders (Beck and Klein-Saffran, 1991; Huff, 1990; Maxfield and Baumer, 1990).
2. Clients tend to be nonviolent and/or have been convicted of nonviolent property offenses (Beck and Klein-Saffran, 1991; Palm Beach County, Florida, Sheriff's Department, 1987; Rush, 1989).
3. Clients tend to be those who have fairly strong family ties, are married, and live with their spouses in structured living arrangements (*Corrections Compendium,* 1992e, 1992f; Petersilia, 1986b).
4. Clients do not have drug or alcohol dependencies (Somers, Jacobs, and Koehler, 1990.
5. Clients have jobs or good prospects of becoming employed and maintaining their employment over time (Davis, 1986; Florida Department of Corrections, 1986; Hurwitz, 1987; Klein-Saffran, 1990; Scott, 1991).
6. Clients tend to have higher amounts of education and vocational skills (Somers, Jacobs, and Koehler, 1990; Wood, 1982).
7. Clients tend to be older (age 30 and over) (Davis, 1986).

For prospective parolees, the following characteristics have been identified:

1. Clients tend to be older (age 30 and over) (Baer and Klein-Saffran, 1990).
2. Offenders have low risk scores indicating nonviolence and low public risk (Baer and Klein-Saffran, 1990; Beck, Klein-Saffran, and Wooten, 1990; Nevada Legislative Council, 1987).
3. Clients have jobs or arrangements for full-time employment (Baer and Klein-Saffran, 1990).
4. Clients have relative brief prior records, if any (Hofer and Meierhoefer, 1987).
5. Clients have stable home environments (Beck and Klein-Saffran, 1991).
6. Clients do not have drug or alcohol dependencies (Boudouris, 1985).
7. Clients have clean records relating to institutional behavior (Pallone, 1993).

SELECTED ISSUES IN HOME CONFINEMENT

Below are various issues that have been identified since home confinement became a relatively popular community corrections option. These issues include, but are not limited to (1) home confinement as insufficient punishment; (2) the constitutionality of home confinement; (3) public safety versus offender needs for community reintegration; and (4) home confinement as an insufficient crime deterrent.

Home Confinement May Not Be Much of a Punishment

One of the most frequently leveled criticisms of home confinement is that it does not appear to be much of a punishment. The public sees offenders confined to their homes and considers this "incarceration" more of a luxury rather than just deserts.

However, some of the experiences of those who have been sentenced to home confinement for a period of weeks or months, either involuntarily or voluntarily, suggest that home confinement is very much a punishment (see the box later in this chapter).

One reason for regarding home confinement as something less than a true punishment compared with institutional incarceration is that the courts do not often equate time served at home with time served in prison. In 1990, an Illinois defendant, Ramos, was placed at his parent's home for a period of weeks under house arrest while awaiting trial for an alleged crime. He was not permitted to leave the premises except for work or medical care. Subsequently, he was convicted of the crime and requested the court to apply the time he spent at home toward the time he would have to serve in prison. The court denied his request, holding that his confinement at home did not amount to custody (*People v. Ramos,* 1990). Subsequent court decisions have been consistent with the *Ramos* ruling. Several federal cases have held that the amount of time offenders spend in house arrest cannot be counted against jail or prison time to be served (*U.S. v. Zackular,* 1991; *U.S. v. Insley,* 1991; *U.S. v. Arch John Drummond,* 1992; *U.S. v. Edwards,* 1992; and *U.S. v. Wickman,* 1992).

And, when offenders leave their residences without permission while under house arrest, they are not guilty of escape from prison; rather, they are guilty of a technical program violation. Lubus, a convicted Connecticut offender, was sentenced to house arrest. At some point, he failed to report to his supervising probation officer. The officer claimed this was the equivalent of an "escape" and sought to have him prosecuted as an escapee. The Connecticut Supreme Court disagreed, indicating that unauthorized departures from community residences are not the same as unauthorized departures from halfway houses, mental health facilities, and hospitals and failures to return from furloughs or work release (*State v. Lubus,* 1990).

These two cases are only a few of the many cases in state courts that place community residences outside of the "time spent in custody" definition. Thus, if the courts do not recognize the home as a suitable site of "custody," why should the public be expected to define such house arrest differently? Despite these court distinctions and definitions, there is sufficient compelling evidence to indicate house arrest is very much a punishment.

The Constitutionality of Home Confinement

The claim that home confinement is unconstitutional is without legal merit. More than a few criminal justice scholars have sought to create an issue, however. Actually, the fact of using the home as a site where offenders can be monitored by their POs is not far removed from placing offenders in a semirestrictive halfway house setting, where a high degree of offender monitoring also occurs. The courts declare what is or is not unconstitutional. Thus far, house arrest has not been declared unconstitutional by the U.S. Supreme Court. But beyond the simple absence of a U.S. Supreme Court decision on the subject, home confinement or house arrest is one of several approved community corrections alternatives that are specified under probably every state community corrections act. The intent of the act is to provide alternative community punishments in lieu of incarceration in jails or prisons. Obviously, the idea is to reduce jail and prison overcrowding and divert the least serious offenders to some form of community corrections punishment. Offenders diverted to community corrections programs should be those who are determined to be in need of more restrictive monitoring or supervision compared with standard probationers or standard parolees. Thus, those with substance abuse histories or alcohol/drug dependencies might be targeted for house arrest, perhaps also with electronic monitoring (Rackmill, 1994).

Another persuasive argument negating the constitutionality issue is that sentences of house arrest are almost always voluntary. Thus, offenders are most often given a choice—either go to jail or prison for a period of months or accept house arrest with its restrictive conditions of curfew and limited freedoms. Specifically, certain rights under the First, Fourth, Fifth, Eighth, and Fourteenth Amendments have been questioned as the result of an offender submitting to house arrest. The First Amendment right-to-privacy issue occurs because some offenders believe that they are unduly restricted to their homes and are subject to unwanted intrusions from their POs. The fact is that officers could observe them under other sentencing conditions, and the home is not an unreasonable place for an offender to be supervised.

The Fourth Amendment issue of illegal search and seizure has been raised as well. Some offenders believe that the home is a sacred place and that curfew checks and travel restrictions are unreasonable sentencing conditions. Further, POs may visit a home at random times and collect evidence through searches of the premises. Such evidence may later be used against offenders as the basis for program revocations. However, such searches and evidence gathering are consensual, since house arrestees have entered into agreements with the court to permit such intrusions if the house arrest option is offered. Thus, Fourth Amendment violation allegations are groundless.

The Fifth Amendment provision cited by some house arrestees has to do with the fact that an offender's own actions, such as violation of curfew, can be a form of self-incrimination. Again, because of the consensual nature of house arrest per se, the allegations of Fifth Amendment violations are without merit.

The Eighth Amendment violations alleged by some house arrestees are that the use of the home as a site for incarceration is unduly restrictive and thus cruel and unusual. However, house arrest pales in comparison with confinement to a jail or prison cell. Quite simply, no evidence exists to suggest that the use of one's home as a place of confinement is cruel and unusual. It may appear unusual to some critics, and there may be seemingly cruel aspects, such as not being able to accompany one's family to the grocery store or buy one's child an ice cream cone from the corner store. But the fact of house arrest is not cruel and unusual per se.

Finally, the Fourteenth Amendment issue is raised because the use of house arrest appears to be discriminatory. Namely, certain protected classes of people are granted house arrest, whereas other unprotected classes of people—the poor—are unable to participate in such a community corrections program. The fact that home incarceration is often used in tandem with electronic monitoring makes it necessary that electronically monitored clients have telephones from which to operate the electronic monitoring equipment. The poor may not be able to afford such telephones or the maintenance fees and defrayments of costs associated with electronic monitoring. This constitutional argument is perhaps the strongest that can be employed against the use of electronic monitoring. However, many electronic monitoring devices are simply attached to the ankles or wrists of offenders and telephonic equipment is unnecessary. POs can simply drive by one's residence or apartment building and determine whether or not they are on the premises. Electronic signals emitted by these anklets or wristlets are received by equipment in the PO's vehicle. Thus, the equal protection clause of the Fourteenth Amendment would not be violated in these instances. Indications are that technology is making it such that future electronic monitoring programs will not require offenders to have telephones (McShane and Krause, 1993:127–128).

Public Safety versus Offender Needs for Community Reintegration

In any community corrections program, corrections staff consider the need for public safety to be of paramount importance. This is why great care is taken to restrict the eligibility requirements of those who become involved in home confinement programs. If offenders are first-timers without prior records and if their conviction offenses are nonviolent, they are considered for inclusion. An absence of a prior record is no guarantee that an offender will automatically qualify, however. Predictions are made, usually on the basis of sound criteria, about one's chances for success. Actually, the fact that program staff are so selective has drawn criticisms from criminal justice critics that officials are either creaming or net widening. That is, they are deliberately involving the best offenders and/or are extending house arrest to those who otherwise would be given standard probation if a house arrest program did not exist. Certainly officials engage in creaming. They want to accommodate the best offenders who are most likely to succeed. Some critics say that only jail- or prison-bound offenders should be included. But for most house arrest programs, this is one of the selection criteria. The net-widening charge applies only to the extent that certain offenders are included in house arrest programs who are not jail- or prison-bound. Again, house arrest selection criteria ordinarily exclude non-jail- or non-prison-bound offenders.

There are obvious problems with placing convicted felons under house arrest. Recall that we cannot control their behaviors. They may leave their homes at their discretion, despite the fact that it is a program violation if they do so during curfew periods or for the wrong reasons. But it is also true that because they are at home, they are not prevented from committing crimes or causing serious injury or death to victims (see earlier box). The therapeutic value and the absence of labeling are considered substantial and necessary in an offender's rehabilitation and reintegration. If proper steps and selection procedures are followed, the best and most eligible offenders are included. Jail and prison overcrowding are alleviated to the extent that some of these persons are diverted to the home as the principal place of confinement. And public safety is enhanced through the application of such selection criteria. But no selection criteria are foolproof. There are numerous false negatives out there, or cases in which offenders are predicted to be nondangerous but turn out to be dangerous anyway. These cases are in the minority, however. Many criminal justice scholars and community corrections practitioners believe that house arrest is worth it, despite the occasional house arrestee "failures" (Baer and Klein-Saffran, 1990; Quinn and Holman, 1990).

Home Confinement May Not Be Much of a Crime Deterrent

Does home confinement function as a crime deterrent? No. It isn't supposed to function as a crime deterrent (Florida Department of Corrections, 1987; Maxfield and Baumer, 1990; Palm Beach County, Florida, Sheriff's Department, 1987). Being confined in a prison or jail does not deter some incarcerated offenders from exploiting and victimizing other inmates. Why should we regard home confinement differently? The primary function of house arrest is to enable POs to maintain a high degree of supervisory control over an offender's whereabouts. No house arrest program can claim that house arrest deters crime from occurring. However, there are controls that deter house arrestees from violating program requirements, such as avoiding drugs or alcohol and observing curfew.

ELECTRONIC MONITORING

As mentioned previously, frequently accompanying home confinement are **electronic monitoring devices** (Mendelsohn and Baumer, 1990; Schmidt, 1989a, 1989b). Several manufacturers, such as GOSSlink, BI Incorporated, and Controlec, Inc., produce tamper-resistant wrist and ankle bracelets that emit electronic signals that are often connected to telephone devices and are relayed to central computers in police stations or probation departments. Offenders must not remove the devices during the course of their sentence. The sanction for tampering with an offender's telemetry device is strong, often revocation of privileges and return to prison or jail (Bellassai and Torborg, 1990; McCarthy, 1987a). In 1987, only 800 offenders were under some type of electronic monitoring program in the United States. By 1992, that figure had greatly increased and was estimated to be approximately 70,000 (Lilly, 1992:500).

EARLY USES OF ELECTRONIC MONITORING

The first commercial use of electronic monitoring devices occurred in 1964 as an alternative to incarcerating mental patients and certain parolees (Gable, 1986). In subsequent years, electronic monitoring was extended to include monitoring office work, employee testing for security clearances, and many other applications (U.S. Congress Office of Technology Assessment, 1987a, 1987b). The feasibility of using electronic devices to monitor probationers was investigated by various researchers during the 1960s and 1970s, and New Mexico officially sanctioned its use for criminal offenders in 1983 (Houk, 1984; Schmidt, 1986).

New Mexico Second Judicial District Judge Jack Love implemented a pilot project in 1983 to electronically monitor persons convicted of drunk driving and various white-collar offenses. The New Mexico Supreme Court examined the program and approved it subject to the voluntary consent and participation of offenders as a condition of their probation and as long as their privacy, dignity, and families were protected (Houk, 1984). Offenders were required to wear anklets or wristlets that emitted electronic signals that could be intercepted by probation officers conducting surveillance operations.

Following the New Mexico experiment, other jurisdictions commenced using a variety of electronic monitoring systems for supervising parolees, probationers, inmates of jails and prisons, and pretrial releasees (Cooprider and Kerby, 1990; Putnam, 1990; Rohn and Ostroski, 1991; Schmidt, 1986:56). Both praised and condemned by criminal justice practitioners, electronic monitoring seems to be the most promising cost-effective solution to the problems of prison overcrowding and the management of probation officer caseloads (Corbett and Marx, 1991; Quinn and Holman, 1991). Until the advent of electronic monitoring devices, the idea of confining convicted offenders to their homes as a punishment was simply unworkable, unless a jurisdiction was willing to pay for the continuous monitoring services of a probation officer. In 1983, an electronic device was used to monitor low-risk offenders in New Mexico (Schmidt and Curtis, 1987). In the next few years, experiments with electronic monitoring devices were tried in Florida, California, and Kentucky (Lilly, Ball, and Wright, 1987).

TYPES OF ELECTRONIC MONITORING SYSTEMS

There are four general categories of electronic monitoring equipment. Two include devices that use telephones at the monitoring location, whereas the remaining two categories include radio signal–emitting systems in which radio signals are received by either portable or stationary units.

Continuous Signaling Devices

Continuous signaling devices use a miniature transmitter strapped to the offender. The transmitter broadcasts an encoded signal that is picked up by a receiver-dialer in the offender's home. The signal is relayed to a central receiver over telephone lines. Although the uses of these monitoring devices are potentially unlimited and are obviously not restricted to probationers, thus far, probationers have been most likely to participate in electronic monitoring programs. In most cases, electronic monitoring systems are combined with home confinement programs. By 1987, the following states were using a combination of home confinement and electronic monitoring for supervising many of their probationers: California, Colorado, Idaho, Illinois, Kentucky, Michigan, New Jersey, New Mexico, New York, Oklahoma, Oregon, Utah, and Virginia (Blomberg, Waldo, and Burcroff, 1987:170).

Programmed Contact Devices

Programmed contact devices are similar to the continuous signaling units, except that a central computer calls at random hours to verify that offenders are where they are supposed to be. Offenders answer the telephone, and their voices are verified by computer. Some offenders have attempted to outwit this system by using call forwarding and personally tape-recorded messages. In some instances, these efforts have successfully deceived the machines.

Cellular Telephone Devices

Cellular telephone devices are also transmitters worn by offenders. These emit a radio signal that is received by a local area monitor. Such systems can monitor as many as 25 offenders simultaneously.

Continuous Signaling Transmitters

Finally, the **continuous signaling transmitter,** also worn by the offender, sends out a continuous signal. Portable receiver units are used by probation officers so that they may drive by an offender's home and verify the offender's presence. All of these devices are tamper-resistant (some claim tamper-proof), and there are usually stiff penalties imposed when offenders have been determined to have tampered with their electronic anklets or wristlets.

ELECTRONIC MONITORING WITH HOME CONFINEMENT

An example of home incarceration with electronic monitoring is a program conducted in Kenton County, Kentucky, from May 1, 1985, through mid-December 1986 (Lilly, Ball, and Wright, 1987:189–203). Influenced significantly by the Palm Beach County Sheriff's Department's use of house arrest, officials in Kenton County, Kentucky, decided to experiment with a similar program in their own jurisdiction in an effort to reduce jail overcrowding. In late 1984, the county jail was under court order to reduce overcrowding, and electronic monitoring coupled with house arrest offered one feasible solution to the overcrowding problem.

Offender participation in the program was strictly voluntary, and it was aimed especially at certain misdemeanants posing little risk to the community (Lilly, Ball, and Wright, 1987:190). However, a substantial number of offenders selected to participate had prior records including some serious offenses. Subsequently, 35 offenders became program participants. According to Lilly (1985), the Kentucky Department of Corrections had three objectives for its home incarceration program: (1) to protect the citizenry with minimal expense, (2) to assist in jail depopulation, and (3) to help offenders reintegrate into their communities through job training, employment, and restitution.

Some evidence has been presented by Lilly et al. (1987:191–192) of the cost-effectiveness of electronic monitoring programs. With the costs of hardware, computer training, salaries for monitoring personnel, and other expenditures, the total expense for the duration of the project was $42,568. The program served 35 offenders and amounted to 1,720 person-days of home incarceration with electronic monitoring. The cost of maintaining 35 offenders in the Kenton County Jail during this same period at the rate of $26 per day would have been $44,720, or over $2,100 more than home incarceration. These researchers caution that the operational figures are misleading, because additional funds were not required for salaries for the program's administrative assistant and the probation or parole officers involved. Furthermore, new offenders involved in the program would lead to more significant savings, since the direct costs of monitoring equipment and operator training had already been defrayed by the first wave of participants.

One concern of both officials and researchers was that home incarceration with electronic monitoring might serve to widen the net by imposing the program on offenders who might otherwise receive standard probation (Petersilia, 1986b:53–54). Although the sample of offenders was small, it was determined that 96 percent of these participants had prior Kentucky convictions, whereas 80 per cent had prior jail time. Most offenders involved probably would not have received standard probation, according to officials interviewed. Thus, net widening did not occur as some critics expected (Lilly et al., 1987:196).

Although the study was of relatively short duration, recidivism was extremely low. Only two offenders participating in the program were subsequently convicted of new offenses, for a recidivism rate of 5.7 percent (Lilly et al., 1987:196). Again, the small sample suggests cautious interpretation of percentages and/or trends. These researchers concluded that the Kenton County project was quite economical and that no additional financial burden was placed on Kentucky taxpayers. Nearly 65 percent of the participants maintained their jobs and supported their families, thus eliminating potential nonsupport problems that might otherwise arise. Equipment improvements and greater familiarity with some of the electronic problems encountered in the first phase of the program led these researchers to believe that on a long-range basis, home incarceration with electronic monitoring is an economical and practical alternative to incarceration (Lilly et al., 1987:201–202).

Another example of the use of electronic monitoring with home confinement occurred in Virginia. In 1989, Chesterfield County, Virginia, received a $34,470 state grant to investigate the feasibility of home confinement as an alternative to imprisonment. The Chesterfield County Jail was suffering from chronic overcrowding with 156 inmates, nearly twice its rated capacity (*Richmond Times-Dispatch,*

BOX 9.2
Is Electronic Monitoring Really a Punishment?

The Case of Judge David Ryan

So you're a judge named David Ryan in La Mesa, California. So you think that electronic monitoring sentences mean "going easy" on offenders. So you are challenged to find out what it is *really* like. You accept the challenge.

Judge David Ryan decided to see what it was like to be confined to his home under conditions of electronic monitoring, just for a weekend. His wife, Martha, and son, Travis, were skeptical. "What is that?" they asked. "Just electronic monitoring equipment," Ryan said. "How long do you have to wear that?" Martha asked. "During the entire weekend," he replied. On Friday evening, Martha asked David to return a videotape to a rental store. "Sorry, Martha, I'm under house arrest." Ryan pointed at his electronic anklet. "Listen, Travis, you can't use the cordless telephone this weekend, since the signal interferes with my electronic monitoring receptor." A neighbor called out to Ryan. "How about coming over for a while and watch the big game on TV?" "Sorry," said Ryan, "I can't. I'm under house arrest . . . I'll explain it to you later."

Judge Ryan spent the entire weekend adhering to the electronic monitoring and home confinement program. Twice, he violated his house arrest by being gone when he was supposed to be home. Trying to fool the computer, perhaps? When Ryan checked his equipment in on Monday morning, those monitoring his program said, "You were gone from your home twice." That made Ryan a believer in the system. "I would certainly use it again," said Ryan.

Ryan was equipped with an electronic anklet about the size of a cigarette package. It fit around his ankle comfortably, but it could not be removed without cutting it. The band sends signals to a black box that hooks into a telephone. The bracelet has wires in it, and, if it's cut, the box senses the loss of signal and dials a computer, which can spit out a report for court or probation staff. If the band goes beyond 150 feet from the telephone, it senses that, too, and the call immediately goes in to the computer. Ryan's first day on electronic monitoring involved a work schedule that included a judge's meeting at 6:00 P.M. He didn't get home from the meeting until 9:00 P.M. When he arrived home, the telephone immediately rang and someone asked "Where have you been for the last three hours?" In Judge Ryan's county, it costs about $47 per day per inmate housed in the county jail. In contrast, the electronic monitoring costs are from $10 to $15 per day. Judge Ryan's monitoring cost about $12. Offenders normally pay for this expense as a condition of their probation.

Source: Adapted from Alan Abrahamson, "Home Unpleasant During House Arrest, Judge Learns." *Corrections Today,* **53:**76, 1991.

1990). The county acquired 30 watch-size monitoring transmitters, activator devices, and computer equipment for a one-year trial period of an electronic monitoring home incarceration program. In this case, selected inmates were fitted with a black monitoring transmitter, which was attached to their wrists with a black plastic wristband. The wristband is waterproof and the only way it can be removed is by cutting it off. The transmitter fits into a second piece of equipment called the verifier that also goes home with the inmate. The verifier device plugs into a telephonic device. The verifier is then called at random times during the day by a computer located in the county jail offices. The inmate has 10 seconds to answer the telephone and state his name and time on the receiver. Then he inserts the wrist transmitter into a slot on the verifier. The transmitter sends an electronic tone back to the computer, verifying that the correct monitor has responded to the telephone call. The entire system is fully automated, with the offender's voice recorded and the results of the electronic signal printed out at the jail.

If the wrist monitor fails to activate the verifier or if the inmate doesn't answer the telephone, the computer redials the home in two minutes. If there is no answer, a third call is made. If there is still no answer, a sheriff's deputy visits the offender's home directly to verify his whereabouts. Violating home confinement or removing the electronic device are program violations that can result in probation or parole revocation. Further, offenders pay $5.50 daily to offset the electronic monitoring costs. Since Chesterfield County uses the devices for jail-bound offenders, there is some relief from jail overcrowding (*Richmond Times-Dispatch,* 1990:100).

Evaluating the success of electronic monitoring is difficult at present, because it is a relatively new technological phenomenon. However, considerable evidence about current programs shows potential long-range success relative to reducing prison and jail overcrowding and increasing probation officer efficiency in monitoring all types of offenders (Berry, 1985; Friel and Vaughn, 1986; Gable, 1986; Houk, 1984). Of course, electronic surveillance of probationers raises issues similar to those associated with home confinement. The right-to-privacy issue is especially apparent with the use of electronic monitoring systems for some probationers (del Carmen and Vaughn, 1986:65). However, probationers who participate in home confinement programs usually do so voluntarily, and, thus, they waive certain of their rights in the process. In the meantime, researchers caution that court decisions about the validity of waivers of rights in probation and parole cases are mixed (del Carmen and Vaughn, 1986:68).

Despite their advantages and successes at reducing jail and prison overcrowding and controlling offender behaviors, home confinement and electronic monitoring have stimulated criticisms from virtually every sector including academia, law, and even corrections (Ball, Huff, and Lilly, 1988:36). Many of these criticisms are rooted in basic public misunderstandings about how these sanctions are imposed and how offender compliance is obtained. Some experts see potential abuse of electronic monitoring, and they speculate that one logical extension of the monitoring of criminals is the monitoring of everyone, including innocent persons (Alexander and Alexander, 1985). In fact, the state-of-the-art technological capabilities are such that electronic devices may be surgically implanted in the bodies of offenders, and that offenders in future years may have the option of being incarcerated or electronically monitored in their communities (Alexander and Alexander, 1985).

Some of the pros and cons of electronic monitoring are summarized as follows:

Pros

1. Assists offenders in avoiding criminogenic atmosphere of prisons or jails and helps them reintegrate into their communities (e.g., avoids labeling as criminals) (Walker, 1990).
2. Permits offenders to retain jobs and support families.
3. Assists probation officers in their monitoring activities and has potential for easing their caseload responsibilities (Archambeault and Gould, 1992; Baumer and Maxfield, 1992; Frost and Stephenson, 1989; Rush, 1987; Watts and Glaser, 1990).
4. Gives judges and other officials considerable flexibility in sentencing offenders (e.g., persons in halfway houses or on work release) (Berry and Matthews, 1989; Goss, 1990; Maxfield and Baumer, 1992).
5. Has potential of reducing recidivism rate more than existing probationary alternatives (Hatchett, 1987; Jolin and Rogers, 1990; Rogers and Jolin, 1989; Rush, 1987).
6. Potentially useful for decreasing jail and prison populations (Goss, 1989, 1990).
7. More cost-effective in relation to incarceration (Corbett, 1989; Goss, 1989, 1990; Loveless, 1994; Petersilia, 1988a, 1990; Quinn and Holman, 1991).
8. Allows for pretrial release monitoring as well as for special treatment cases such as substance abusers, the mentally retarded, women who are pregnant, and juveniles (Charles, 1989a, 1989b; Goss, 1989; Jolin and Stipak, 1992; Lilly et al., 1992; New Orleans Office of the Criminal Justice Coordinator, 1991; Walker, 1990; Williams, Shichor, and Wiggenhorn, 1989).

Cons

1. Some potential exists for race, ethnic, or socioeconomic bias by requiring offenders to have telephones or to pay for expensive monitoring equipment and/or fees (Baumer and Maxfield, 1992; Schlatter, 1989; South Carolina State Reorganization Commission, 1990; Walker, 1990).
2. Public safety may be compromised through the failure of these programs to guarantee that offenders will go straight and not endanger citizens by committing new offenses while free in the community (Rogers and Jolin, 1989).
3. Electronic monitoring may be too coercive, and it may be unrealistic for officials to expect full offender compliance with such a stringent system (Burns, 1992; Mendelsohn and Baumer, 1990).
4. Little consistent information exists about the impact of electronic monitoring on recidivism rates compared with other probationary alternatives (Baumer, Maxfield, and Mendelsohn, 1993; Schmidt, 1989a, 1989b).
5. Persons frequently selected for participation are persons who probably don't need to be monitored anyway (Curtis and Pennell, 1990).
6. Technological problems exist making electronic monitoring somewhat unreliable (Baumer and Maxfield, 1992; Corbett and Marx, 1991; Marx and Corbett, 1990; South Carolina State Reorganization Commission, 1990).

7. Electronic monitoring may result in widening the net by being prescribed for offenders who otherwise would receive less costly standard probation (Baumer, Maxfield, and Mendelsohn, 1993; Mainprize, 1992).

8. Raises right to privacy, civil liberties, and other constitutional issues such as Fourth Amendment search and seizure concerns (Burns, 1992; del Carmen and Vaughn, 1986; Loveless, 1994).

9. Much of the public interprets this option as going easy on offenders and perceives electronic monitoring as a nonpunitive alternative (Loveless, 1994).

10. The costs of electronic monitoring may be more than published estimates (Loveless, 1994; Schlattcr, 1989).

A PROFILE OF ELECTRONIC MONITORING CLIENTS

It is difficult to articulate specific criteria that are applicable to all electronically monitored clients. Some clients are juveniles, while others are adults awaiting trial. Many are probationers for whom electronic monitoring has been specified as a condition of their probation. Others are parolees who are placed under an electronic monitoring program for short periods following their early release.

However, electronic monitoring isn't for all offenders. A 1988 survey of those being monitored electronically indicated that 33 percent of them were convicted of major traffic offenses and drunk driving, whereas about 20 percent were property offenders. Less than 6 percent of all monitorees were sex offenders or violent person offenders (Schmidt, 1991).

Sometimes, offenders who are likely to reoffend may be placed in electronic monitoring programs as a last resort before being sentenced to incarceration. In Knoxville, Tennessee, for instance, juvenile services personnel use electronic monitoring in selected instances for certain offenders who are unresponsive to other types of interventions or therapies. If certain juvenile offenders have continued to recidivate and show little hope for improvement, juvenile authorities may choose to give them one last chance to see if they can "make it" on the electronic monitoring program. If the youths are successful during the 30- or 60-day period of electronic monitoring, their cases are reopened by the juvenile court judge and a nonincarcerative disposition is imposed. In the early 1990s, Knoxville and Knox County operated an electronic monitoring program for about 25 juvenile offenders. Generally, the program was rated as successful, since most youths were compliant and law-abiding while being electronically monitored.

In Lake County, Illinois, experiments with electronic monitoring were conducted for various samples of pretrial releasees from February 1986 to mid-1989 (Cooprider and Kerby, 1990). One manifest function of electronic monitoring was to reduce jail overcrowding caused, in part, by accommodating large numbers of pretrial detainees. Many of these pretrial detainees were deemed nonthreatening or nonviolent, and, thus, it seemed unnecessary to confine them during intervals preceding their trials. Eligible clients for the electronic monitoring program, the **Bond Supervision Program,** were defined according to components that would make them ineligible: (1) The defendant poses a threat to the safety and welfare of

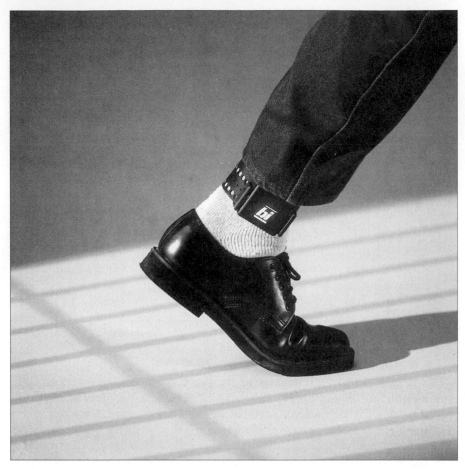

Electronic monitoring devices such as the anklet shown here are used to verify one's whereabouts; such devices are not intended to control behavior.

the community and/or to himself/herself; (2) the seriousness of the crime restricts the use of release on recognizance; and (3) the likelihood of the defendant's nonappearance in court is substantial. Therefore, anyone *not* fitting these characteristics might be eligible for electronic monitoring. Pretrial Services in Lake County placed 659 defendants on electronic monitoring between 1986 and 1989; the average program length was 90 days.

Defendants were visited by probation officers three times per week during the first three weeks of their programs. The number of face-to-face contacts was reduced to two times per week if clients were complying with program requirements. Over the three years, only 19 percent of the 659 clients violated program regulations. Violations included a new arrest, a failure to appear, and technical violations (e.g., tampering with the anklet or wristlet device). The electronically monitored clients were compared with sample defendants during the same time period who were not electronically monitored. For the electronically monitored clients who violated one or more program requirements, the most frequent violations were technical. Researchers explained this as the result of more intensive face-to-face monitoring. In short, because these clients were supervised so closely, it was easier for POs to detect any program violations when they occurred. Generally, the results of the study were positive. Cooprider and Kerby (1990:35) said that "in essence, electronic monitoring, as a component of bond supervision, enhances ability to supervise defendants in the community. It cannot, in total, replace officer surveillance or casework (the 'human' element) but it does change the nature of community supervision."

Each case considered for electronic monitoring must be considered on its own merits. Not all burglars or thieves are particularly nonviolent. By the same token, there are some armed robbers who are not violent, although they have been classified as violent offenders. Program mistakes are often the result of unwise decision making, such as when clearly violence-prone individuals have been released into electronic monitoring and home confinement when they should have been barred from such participation. At the same time, false negatives clutter this picture, in that some persons designated as nondangerous actually turn out to be dangerous. No paper-and-pencil or judgmental criteria are absolutely foolproof (Champion, 1994; Goss, 1989; Quinn and Holman, 1991; Walker, 1990).

SELECTED ISSUES IN ELECTRONIC MONITORING

Invariably, electronic monitoring has generated considerable controversy since its inception in the 1960s. Any attempt to employ electronic means in offender supervision is going to raise one or more issues about the suitability and/or legality of these devices. Electronic monitoring is no exception. Some of the more important issues are described here. The following list is fairly thorough although not comprehensive: (1) the ethics of electronic monitoring; (2) the constitutionality of electronic monitoring and client rights; (3) punishment versus rehabilitation and reintegration; (4) the public safety issue; (5) the deterrence issue; (6) the privatization issue; and (7) the net-widening issue.

The Ethics of Electronic Monitoring

One criticism of electronic monitoring is the potential for the ultimate political control of the public. Is electronic monitoring ethical? At present, the Internal Revenue Service, the FBI, and other agencies maintain electronic files and other information about millions of citizens. The use of electronic monitoring conjures up frightening images of George Orwell's *1984* and "Big Brother." If criminal offenders are electronically tracked in their own homes, what is in store for the law-abiding public-at-large from an inventive government? Ball, Huff, and Lilly (1988:39) have asked

> Does house arrest represent 'progress' as a genuine alternative to the harsh conditions of jail and prison? Is it a promising policy that must be given careful scrutiny because of certain latent dangers of going awry? Or are we witnessing a general decline of privacy and personal autonomy and a movement toward a society characterized by a passive and docile citizenry and devoted to maximum security through technological power?

One response to these questions is to address the fundamental purpose or intent of electronic monitoring. Is electronic monitoring intentionally designed to snoop on private citizens? No. Is electronic monitoring intentionally designed to invade one's privacy? No. Is electronic monitoring intentionally designed to assist POs in verifying an offender's whereabouts? Yes. Is electronic monitoring capable of detecting program violations in lieu of direct PO supervision? Yes.

Perhaps the ethical issue becomes more relevant or focused if we theoretically project what the limits of electronic monitoring might be in some future context. Some critics might be justified, therefore, in contending that if we use electronic monitoring for a limited purpose today (e.g., to verify an offender's whereabouts), what other uses might be made of electronic monitoring in future years (e.g., intruding into bedrooms to detect criminal sexual acts or other possible criminal behaviors)? At present, electronic monitoring equipment is placed in convenient areas, such as kitchens or living rooms. Video-capable electronic monitoring equipment is also presently limited to verifying identity and determining whether drug or alcohol program violations have occurred. No one has suggested that cameras be placed in a bedroom or bathroom to be activated at the whim of an equipment operator. If there is an issue to be raised here, then it would be the reasonableness issue.

One social issue raised by some observers pertains to the potential threat an offender poses to family members in the home where incarceration is ordered (Ball, Huff, and Lilly, 1988:122–123). Accounts of spousal or child abuse by offenders under home confinement programs have been reported, although not with great frequency. However, the risks of familial abuses that are associated with parole board decision making also pertain to those sentenced to electronic monitoring and/or home confinement. Of course, parole boards, judges, and probation officers must generally acknowledge the tort criterion of "reasonably foreseeable risk" when restoring offender freedoms (Ball et al., 1988:122).

Whether or not house arrest and electronic monitoring are intended to represent "progress" as an alternative to jail or prison may be an irrelevant question. A more fundamental question might be, is electronic monitoring with home confinement a suitable alternative to jail or prison, for certain types of offenders? The principal use of electronic monitoring presently is to verify offender presence at a particular time and in a particular place (Schmidt and Curtis, 1987). Intrusions by cameras and other devices into offender homes have occurred, although the nature of these intrusions is to verify one's presence and/or detect certain program violations, such as drug or alcohol abuse. Thus, electronic monitoring is used strictly to monitor an offender's presence or absence through the emission and detection of electronic beeps with appropriate devices. It would seem that Fourth and Eighth Amendment criticisms are premature, and that they reflect what the public believes may eventually occur rather than what has actually transpired thus far. No greater invasion of one's privacy occurs through house arrest and electronic monitoring compared with the invasion of privacy experienced in prisons and jails. In fact, there is considerably less privacy in prisons and jails compared with home incarceration.

It is difficult to separate the emotional issues associated with home confinement and electronic monitoring from the true legal and social issues. The manifest intent of every home confinement and electronic monitoring program is to save taxpayers money by offering an inexpensive method of maintaining offenders who otherwise would take up valuable prison and jail space. Diverting some low-risk and nonviolent offenders to home incarceration and electronic monitoring frees otherwise occupied prison space for more serious offenders who should be separated from the public for particular periods of confinement. An obvious gain is the reduction of some prison and jail overcrowding, although we are not certain about to what degree electronic monitoring and/or home confinement actually fulfills this objective.

The Constitutionality of Electronic Monitoring and Client Rights

Certain legal issues about electronic monitoring are presently unresolved to everyone's satisfaction, although the constitutionality of electronic monitoring has never been successfully challenged (Blomberg, Waldo, and Burcroff, 1987:169). Many of the same legal arguments that are raised to question the constitutionality of home confinement also are raised regarding current applications of electronic monitoring. However, most, if not all, offenders who are placed in electronic monitoring programs agree to abide by all electronic monitoring program conditions. The consensual nature of offender participation in such programs undermines virtually all challenges they may raise about whether such program conditions are constitutional. If we consider the restrictive nature of jail or prison confinement and the high degree of control exerted over offenders by jail and prison officers, by comparison, electronic monitoring actually imposes fewer restrictive conditions. Nevertheless, reasonable searches and seizures of one's residence without warrant are permitted by POs in much the same way that correctional officers might conduct warrantless searches of one's cell in a jail or prison setting.

Civil liabilities accrue to program authorities, officers, volunteers, and paraprofessionals whenever their clients commit new crimes and injure others. All decisions about offenders that result in their community freedom, no matter how restricted, are calculated in terms of the potential dangerousness of the offender and the amount of risk the offender poses to the public. And, this raises the false positives–false negatives issue, such that decisions about offenders are made according to their expected future conduct and despite the punishments they have already undergone for past crimes (Gottfredson and Gottfredson, 1988).

One of the better discussions of the constitutional issues raised in conjunction with electronic monitoring programs is by del Carmen and Vaughn (1986:62–63). These authors describe the landmark case *Olmstead v. United States* (1928), which held that a wiretap executed without an accompanying trespass into a person's home was not a Fourth Amendment violation. Two subsequent cases upheld the use of "bugging" devices by police officers to eavesdrop on conversations of crime suspects. In *Goldman v. United States* (1942), police officers eavesdropped with a bugging device through an adjoining wall of the offices of suspected criminals. In *On Lee v. United States* (1952), a government informant entered the subject's laundry and wore a concealed microphone to record their subsequent conversation. In this instance, however, On Lee gave the informant permission to enter the premises, and, thus, the trespass was lawful. The issue of trespass was rendered irrelevant in *Katz v. United States* (1967), however. In that case, a public telephone booth was wired with a microphone by police officers so that they could monitor conversations of a criminal suspect, Katz. The U.S. Supreme Court excluded the conversations by Katz recorded by police, since they violated the defendant's reasonable expectation of privacy. Further, no warrant had ever been issued to authorize the surveillance.

Del Carmen and Vaughn (1986:64–65) observe that regarding current interpretations of possible Fourth Amendment violations and electronic monitoring, the concept of *reasonableness* is very important. Thus, if conditions set forth by electronic monitoring are reasonable and relate logically to one's rehabilitation needs and/or public safety, they are constitutionally valid conditions. Electronic monitoring is considered an electronic enhancement to assist POs in the supervision of their offender-clients. POs theoretically can watch the behaviors of their clients directly. The use of electronic surveillance equipment merely enhances their supervisory ability. Courts generally have refused to hold that such scientific enhancements create a constitutional issue (del Carmen and Vaughn, 1986:65).

Another constitutional issue raised pertains to the Fifth Amendment right against self-incrimination. Some offender-clients have alleged that the fact of electronic monitoring is self-incriminating, since clients must disclose to POs information about themselves at random times. This information may be adverse for these clients, in that their probation programs may be revoked. The courts have held, however, that technical program violations that result in probation revocation do not fall within the Fifth Amendment self-incrimination provision. The nature of incrimination must be considered. Electronic monitoring cases involve *physical incrimination* rather than *testimonial incrimination* (del Carmen and Vaughn, 1986:66). Physical incrimination is not protected as a Fifth Amendment right.

Some offender-clients have alleged Eighth Amendment violations because they regard electronic monitoring as cruel and unusual punishment. The rationale is that being compelled to wear an electronic wristlet or anklet is humiliating and degrading. This argument has been unconvincing, at least according to the U.S. Supreme Court. Del Carmen and Vaughn (1986:66) indicate that compared with incarceration, electronic monitoring is certainly less restrictive and much more humane.

Finally, the equal protection clause of the Fourteenth Amendment has been used by some offender-clients to challenge electronic monitoring's constitutionality. Many jurisdictions using electronic monitoring require their probationers to defray a portion of their monitoring costs. Offender-clients who are not indigent have to pay these fees and don't like to do so. But these claims have failed to persuade the U.S. Supreme Court that the Fourteenth Amendment has been violated by requiring such fee payments. A more convincing argument has been raised alleging inequity in the selection of eligible electronic monitoring clients. These cases involve some offenders who have been offered the choice of electronic monitoring and accompanying payment of supervisory fees. The alternative is imprisonment. The argument is that one's ability to pay determines whether one is placed on electronic monitoring. This is unfair to persons who are not financially able to pay supervision fees (del Carmen and Vaughn, 1986:67).

Most, if not all, of these constitutional questions are undermined by the fact that one's participation in either electronic monitoring or home confinement is voluntary. Offenders are not forced into home confinement, and they are not compelled to wear anklets or wristlets if there are other sentencing options that may be exercised. In view of this voluntariness, therefore, it is peculiar that some of these program volunteers have sought relief in court for alleged infringements of their constitutional rights. Supposedly, these offender-clients sign rights waivers, submitting themselves to random visits and searches of their premises by their supervising POs. Del Carmen and Vaughn (1986:69) suggest that the constitutionality of electronic monitoring will likely be upheld in future legal cases involving probationers or parolees, primarily based on the concept of *diminished rights.*

Punishment versus Rehabilitation and Reintegration

Another criticism is that home confinement and electronic monitoring are not really punishments at all, because offenders are not assigned "hard time" behind jail or prison walls. However, scattered personalized reports from offenders themselves suggest that home confinement and/or electronic monitoring are possibly more intimidating and restrictive than any jail or prison. One offender sentenced to house arrest reported the intense frustration experienced by not being able to do something as simple as taking his child for a walk (Petersilia, 1986c).

The average length of time offenders are placed on electronic monitoring is about 80 days, according to the *NIJ Reports* (*Corrections Compendium,* 1991a:14). Thus, critics might claim that less than three months is insufficient time to accomplish any significant reintegration or rehabilitation.

The Public Safety Issue

Arguably, if offenders are placed on electronic monitoring and/or under house arrest, they are relatively free to commit new crimes of their own volition. They are not incapacitated; therefore, they pose possible risks to public safety. However, the criteria used for including offenders in electronic monitoring programs are rather restrictive. For example, the Nevada County Probation Department uses electronic monitoring with home confinement as a means of providing an alternative incarceration site besides jail. Participants are eligible for electronic monitoring if they meet the following criteria:

1. Participants must be assessed as low-risk offenders.
2. Participants must exhibit good conduct while in jail.
3. They must be physically and mentally capable of caring for themselves or be in circumstances where another person can provide their needed care.
4. Participants must have a verifiable local address as well as a telephone and electricity at their home location.
5. They must have no less than 10 days and no more than 90 days to serve in jail.
6. Participants must pay an administrative fee of $10 per day while being monitored.
7. Participants cannot have any holds or warrants from other jurisdictions while on the program.
8. Participants must wear an electronic anklet and have a field monitoring device placed in their home.
9. Participants must have the support and cooperation of family members.
10. Participants must seek and maintain employment while on the program.
11. Participants must participate in any specified rehabilitative programs while on the program.
12. Participant *must volunteer to participate in the program* (italics added). (Lattimer, Curran, and Tepper, 1992)

The Deterrence Issue

Despite these technological innovations, however, technology can be beaten. POs have found that some offenders have installed call forwarding systems so that when the computers dial their telephone numbers, they may seem to be in the required location when, in fact, they are in another location several miles from their residences. And, some offenders have devised tape-recorded messages so that electronic voice verifications are deceived about their actual whereabouts. Some offenders convert their homes into a criminal base of operations, conducting fencing operations, fraud, illegal drug exchanges, and other criminal activity without attracting suspicion from the POs who supervise them.

In Houston, Texas, for instance, a 17-year-old was placed on electronic monitoring while on pretrial release on a robbery charge. The youth thereby remained free from a juvenile detention center. While on electronic monitoring, the youth allegedly "slipped free" from an electronic ankle bracelet and killed a restaurant employee during another robbery. The Harris County Juvenile Detention Center personnel responsible for placing the youth on electronic monitoring stated that they did not view this killing as a "failure" of electronic monitoring. Journalists misinterpreted the electronic monitoring as some sort of behavior control device, which it isn't. Whether the youth did or did not slip free of the device would not affect the commission of the murder in any case, since electronic monitoring does not control behavior to that degree (*Associated Press*, 1993:A2). Perhaps the Houston officials in charge of the electronic monitoring program could have exercised better judgment in allowing a teenage robbery suspect and potentially dangerous felon to be eligible for the electronic monitoring program initially.

One dimension of electronic monitoring that seems effective is the impact of social stigma on those wearing electronic devices. A large sample of electronically monitored offenders was interviewed by Glaser and Watts (1993). Many of the offender-clients reported that there was considerable social stigma attached to wearing electronic wristlets or anklets. Some of those who have been electronically monitored in other programs say that the wristlets and anklets function to prevent them from becoming involved in any possible criminal activity when they are in the company of other criminals (Petersilia, 1986a). Thus, the wristlet or anklet can inadvertently be one's "excuse" for *not* participating in a burglary or robbery.

Privatization

Electronic monitoring is susceptible to privatization by outside interests. Companies that manufacture electronic monitoring equipment and the wristlets and anklets worn by offenders already are involved to a degree in the implementation and operation of home confinement programs in various jurisdictions. They train probation officers and others in the use of monitoring equipment, and they offer instruction to police departments and probation agencies on related matters of offender control. Thus, it is conceivably a short step to complete involvement by private interests in this growing nonincarcerative alternative.

Net Widening

One additional concern is the potential home confinement and electronic monitoring have for net widening (Mainprize, 1992). Some officials have said that judges and others may use these options increasingly for larger numbers of offenders who would otherwise be diverted to standard probation involving minimal contact with probation officers. In order for home confinement and electronic monitoring to be effective in reducing jail and prison overcrowding and not result in the feared net widening, only jail- or prison-bound offenders should be considered for participation in these programs (Rogers and Jolin, 1989).

THE FUTURE OF HOME CONFINEMENT
AND ELECTRONIC MONITORING

Most experts are optimistic about the future of home confinement and electronic monitoring as useful criminal sanctions and alternatives to incarceration despite certain risks that have already been noted (Ball, Huff, and Lilly, 1988; Burns, 1992; Byrne, 1990a, 1990b; Jolin and Stipak, 1992; McCarthy, 1987a). Jail and prison overcrowding is the number-one correctional problem faced by U.S. corrections officials and legislatures. The prospects for seriously decreasing jail and prison overcrowding in the near future are bleak, as crime continues to increase and jails and prisons fill to capacity as fast as they are constructed (Cooprider and Kerby, 1990; Rush, 1987; South Carolina State Reorganization Commission, 1990).

There are limited options available to corrections officials for managing a growing offender population. The promising option of home confinement with electronic monitoring is considered by at least some observers to be crucial to the long-term survival and success of middle-range probation programs (Petersilia, 1986a). The flexibility of home confinement as a sentencing alternative is apparent, and the electronic monitoring of the location of offenders offers potentially unlimited applications both inside and outside prison or jail walls. Something needs to be done to deal effectively with the overcrowding problem most states are currently experiencing. House arrest and electronic monitoring offer the greatest degree of offender control proposed thus far. The tremendous savings to local, state, and federal officials and agencies have been amply demonstrated, where electronic monitoring cuts to a fraction the original costs of offender maintenance while incarcerated. The public remains to be convinced, however, that these options are really punishments, although, as we have seen here, many participating offenders regard them as such.

Since electronic monitoring is relatively new, few studies have been conducted that assess the cost of implementing electronic monitoring systems. Lilly, Ball, and Wright (1987) have reported the costs of experimenting with electronic monitoring in a Kentucky county, however. They believe these costs would be comparable to the costs incurred by other jurisdictions, were electronic monitoring installed similar to theirs. The total cost of establishing and operating the program of home confinement with electronic monitoring, including hardware, software, postage, telephone, computer training, probation officer salaries, and travel reimbursement was $42,568. This is significant since the comparable cost of maintaining the 35 offender/clients in the Kenton County Jail during the 1985–1986 study period would have been $44,720. Therefore, within eighteen months, the program had paid for itself. Continuing to operate the program for new offenders beyond December 1986 would mean even greater savings for jail officials and county residents, since the initial equipment expenditures and investments had already been made and defrayed. Thus, by the end of 1987, Kenton County savings would increase to over $30,000 compared with the costs of jailing the same offenders placed on electronic monitoring during the same time period. These figures are based on an average daily incarceration fee per inmate of $26 contrasted with $3 or $4 per day per offender using the electronic monitoring system.

KEY TERMS

Bond Supervision Program
Cellular telephone device
Community control house arrest
Continuous signaling device
Continuous signaling transmitter

Electronic monitoring device
Home confinement
Home incarceration
House arrest
Programmed contact device

QUESTIONS FOR REVIEW

1. What is meant by home confinement? What are some of the more important characteristics of home confinement programs?
2. How do the costs of home confinement compare with the costs of incarceration in any particular jurisdiction?
3. What are some of the constitutional challenges that have been leveled against home confinement as an intermediate punishment?
4. What are some of the critical elements of Florida's community control house arrest program? What are some of the behavioral requirements of offender-clients who are sentenced to the Florida program?
5. What are the goals of home confinement? In what respects are these goals realized?
6. What are some of the general characteristics of home confinement offender clients?
7. What is meant by electronic monitoring? What are some of the types of electronic monitoring systems?
8. What are some of the major criticisms of electronic monitoring?
9. How is it possible for net widening to occur under electronic monitoring? Explain.
10. What are the major constitutional issues raised about the use of electronic monitoring? How does one's voluntariness to become involved in electronic monitoring programs influence the credibility of these constitutional issues?

10

Work or Study Release and Furlough Programs

Introduction
Prerelease Programs
Work Release
Study Release Programs
Furlough Programs

Preparole Release Programs and Day
  Reporting Centers
Key Terms
Questions for Review

INTRODUCTION

With the exception of life imprisonment and death penalty cases, most offenders sentenced to incarceration are eventually released back into their communities, either through the natural conclusion of their original sentences or through some alternative early-release scheme, such as parole. As a conditional type of early release, parole may include several behavioral conditions such as filing regular reports with parole agencies, observance of curfew, restitution, community service, individual or group counseling, or participation in an educational or vocational training program. Each parolee's case is different, and what might be prescribed as

338

a behavioral model for one parolee may be quite different from the program prescribed for another.

In several respects, there is diversity among programs for parolees as there is among programs for probationers. Some parolees may need to be supervised intensively, while others may simply be required to report in a manner similar to standard probation. Many parolees and probationers may be required only to make contact by letter or telephone with their POs, while others must make themselves accessible to random face-to-face visits at home or in the workplace.

Some programs devised by corrections personnel for those sentenced to probation or who have been incarcerated for a period and granted early release are used by both parolees and probationers alike. But because parolees differ from probationers in a few very important respects, several programs for parolees have been developed that are designed to deal with their specific needs. For one thing, parolees have been confined in state or federal prisons, often for many years. They are accustomed to observing a way of life that is alien to living unrestricted in a community where citizen freedoms are taken for granted. Although some experts may disagree, parolees are also generally considered more serious offenders by the public when contrasted with probationers. Those sentenced to probation are often, though not always, low-risk, property offenders who have committed nonviolent crimes. Many are first-offenders, although there are more than a few exceptions.

This chapter examines more closely several programs for parolees. Compared with programs designed for probationers such as pretrial diversion, shock probation, split sentencing, and various forms of intensive probation supervision, programs for parolees are unique in that they are, for the most part, transitional programs. Transitional programs are designed to assist imprisoned offenders in making any necessary psychological and social adjustments to reintegrate into their communities. Those parolees with special problems (e.g., mental illness, mental retardation, alcohol or drug dependencies) may be required to participate regularly in centers or agencies that deal directly with these special problems. Sometimes parolees will be expected to make restitution to their victims or perform a limited amount of community service for the duration of their original sentences. These are additional conditions that parole boards may see fit to make a part of an offender's parole program.

This chapter looks at the parole alternatives of work and study release and furloughs. The first section describes several prerelease programs. These involve releases of inmates for limited purposes, such as short-term work assignments and/or time allocated to take courses at nearby schools. Some inmates take courses in order to complete their G.E.D. degrees. Others take courses or participate in group or individual therapy not ordinarily offered in prison settings. Work and study release are defined and their advantages and disadvantages for participating offenders are described. Work and study releasees are also profiled.

The second part of the chapter examines furlough programs. Furloughs are generally limited to weekends and involve visits with family members. Some furloughs may serve other purposes, such as to perform work or community service or to make restitution to victims. The general nature of furlough programs is described, together with a description of the functions, goals, and advantages and disadvantages of furlough programs. Furloughees are also profiled.

PRERELEASE PROGRAMS

Transitional programs for parole-eligible inmates are generally termed **prerelease programs**. In Oklahoma, for instance, the state operates a Preparole Conditional Supervision Program, or PPCS (*Corrections Compendium,* 1991a:1–4). Oklahoma officials say that preparole release is a "traditional exit from the prison system for many inmates" (*Corrections Compendium,* 1991a:1). In the Oklahoma case, many prisoners who are about to be paroled are released under close supervision for limited periods. The program has a powerful incentive for complying with program rules—if you violate the rules of the program, you are placed back into prison, you cannot be paroled, and you can never re-enter the preparole program.

The PPCS program began in Oklahoma in September 1988. Initially, about 800 inmates became involved in the program. Eventually, this figure grew to 4,000. When inmates are placed in the preparole program, they must submit a weekly parole plan to their POs, submit to drug and/or alcohol checks, observe curfew, maintain employment, and pay off their court costs (*Corrections Compendium,* 1991c:5). If prospective program applicants do not have a job, they must obtain one within 30 days following their preparole release. Over 80 percent of all preparole releasees have some sort of job lined up before being released.

Eligibility requirements for the program are that inmates must have served at least 15 percent of their time and are within one year of their scheduled parole eligibility date. Any parole-eligible inmate is also eligible for the preparole program. Usually, institutional infractions may delay an inmate's acceptance into the preparole program. But in these instances, the Oklahoma Department of Corrections Pardon and Parole Board hears an inmate's request after a one-month period following the infraction date. From money earned, offender-clients pay a $20 monthly supervision fee, restitution, court costs, and child support. Since the program was established in 1988, about 26 percent of the first 5,000 releasees "failed" by violating one or more program conditions. In view of the conventional standards used to assess program success, the 26 percent failure rate is below the arbitrary 30 percent standard (*Corrections Compendium,* 1991c:7).

Three other types of preparole release programs are (1) work release, (2) study release, and (3) furloughs. These are described below.

WORK RELEASE

Work release is any program in which inmates in jails or prisons are permitted to work in their communities with minimal restrictions and supervision, are compensated at the prevailing minimum wage, and must serve their nonworking hours housed in a secure facility (adapted from McCarthy and McCarthy, 1984:159–160).

The growth of work release among state correctional departments has been substantial. For instance, in 1986, Florida led all states with 2,873, or about 10 percent of its total inmate population, involved in work release programs. Other states with large numbers of work releasees include North Carolina (1,852), California (1,254), Alabama (1,179), and New York (1,086). There were about 17,000 work releasees at that time. By 1994, there were 24,492 work releasees in the United States. This represents an increase of 44 percent. Of the states and Federal Bureau of Prisons, 43 correctional systems had work release programs and 31 had educational release programs (American Correctional Association, 1994:xxviii–xxix). In 1994, New York had the largest number of work releasees, with 5,500. Florida had about 2,100 work releasees, followed by Alabama (1,800), California (1,300), and South Carolina (1,025).

The first use of work release in the United States was in Vermont in 1906, where sheriffs, acting on their own authority, assigned inmates to work outside jail walls in the community (Busher, 1973). Legislation-authorized work release was first introduced in Wisconsin in 1913, and, by 1975, all states and the federal system had initiated some form of work release program (Rosenblum and Whitcomb, 1978). At that time, county sheriffs issued passes to certain low-risk inmates to work in the community during daytime hours, but they were obligated to return to jail at particular curfew periods. Work release is also known as **day pass, day parole, temporary release,** or work or education furlough (Busher, 1973; Fitzharris, 1971).

Work release was not formally adopted on a statewide basis until 1913, when Senator Huber of Wisconsin successfully secured the passage of a bill that permitted Wisconsin correctional institutions to grant temporary releases to low-risk misdemeanants (Johnson and Kotch, 1973). Like the furlough system, work release was not popular and only sluggishly adopted on a large scale as an alternative to incarceration in the 1960s and 1970s. By the early 1980s, almost all states had work release programs. An inspection of professional literature cataloged by the National Institute of Justice shows early descriptive and investigative articles about work release in the mid-1960s. The frequency of such articles increased gradually throughout the 1970s and 1980s. If the accumulation of research and investigations of work release programs in the justice literature is any indication of the growing popularity of this type of preparole program, then it is quite popular.

Although work release programs are beneficial to offenders, in part, because they permit participation in various educational and vocational-technical programs, some observers claim that inmates may not be receiving the type of training best suited for community reintegration. One expert says that of the technologies currently in place today, 50 percent of these will change completely in the next few years (Nelson, 1985:70). High technology is the primary reason for this change. Therefore, it is imperative that vocational programs that emphasize traditional trades of woodworking, metalworking, and other familiar shop skills will also have to make available to offenders more broadly based technical skills suitable for work in a high-tech environment (Nelson, 1985:70). One criticism generally made of parole is that it has failed to prepare parolees to perform relevant jobs on the outside.

Most preparole release programs, including work release, can be faulted because of the degree of recidivism among the various inmate-clients. However, recidivism figures for work releasees are no better or no worse on the average than many other nonincarcerative programs. Some community residents have complained that inmates pose competition for scarce community jobs. At the same time, some employers claim that work releasees don't have the right kinds of skills for contemporary work activity. This sounds much like a *Catch-22* claim, however, inasmuch as one important function fulfilled by work release is to enable releasees to acquire valuable work skills. (In the film, *Catch-22,* some World War II combat pilots did not want to fly over enemy territory and possibly be killed. In order to avoid flying duties, they had to be certified as "crazy." However, by merely asking to be relieved of flight duty because it was dangerous, the pilots were declared "sane" by examining psychiatrists, since any "sane" person doesn't want to be subjected to hazards, such as piloting warplanes over enemy territory. This was the "catch" in *Catch-22.*)

As we have seen, work release programs are increasing in many jurisdictions. An examination of recidivism of 179 work releasees was conducted between 1979 and 1983 for the Fishkill, New York, Correctional Facility (MacDonald and Bala, 1983). Using an actuarial method of forecasting recidivism, researchers predicted a 30 percent failure rate. However, only 15.6 percent of the inmates who had successfully completed their work release programs had recidivated by the end of 1983. Researchers concluded that work release participation is positively related to successful postrelease adjustment (MacDonald and Bala, 1983). Similarly successful results have been reported in Massachusetts and Minnesota as well (Miller, 1984b; Minnesota Department of Corrections, 1984).

The Goals of Work Release Programs

The goals of work release programs are

1. To reintegrate the offender into the community.
2. To give the offender an opportunity to learn and/or practice new skills.
3. To provide offenders with the means to make restitution to victims of crimes.
4. To give offenders a chance to assist in supporting themselves and their families.
5. To help authorities to more effectively predict the likelihood of offender success if paroled.
6. To foster improvements in self-images or self-concepts through working in a nonincarcerative environment and assuming full responsibility for one's conduct.

Specific benefits accruing to offenders and the community are that prisoners are not idle and not exposed to continuous moral decay associated with incarceration; prisoners pay confinement costs and can support their families; and prisoners can receive rehabilitative treatment and possibly work to pay back victims (Fitzharris, 1971).

Prison labor often fails to prepare inmates for routine employment in their communities. (The Image Works)

The Functions of Work Release

The primary functions of work release for parolees are (1) community reintegration, (2) participation in educational or vocational training, (3) promotion of inmate self-respect, (4) repayment of debts to victims and society, and (5) provision of support for self and dependents.

Community Reintegration.   First and foremost, work release enables the parolee to become reintegrated into the community (National Office for Social Responsibility, 1987). Even though parolees must return to their prisons or other places of confinement during nonworking hours, they enjoy temporary freedoms while performing useful work. Thus, when it comes time for them to be officially released through either a parole board decision, administrative action, or the normal com-

BOX 10.1
Are Work Releasees Dangerous?

The Case of Charles Rodman Campbell

It happened in 1974. Charles Rodman Campbell, 19, was a drifter who came through Clearview in Snohomish County near Seattle, Washington. He encountered and savagely raped Renae Wicklund, 23, a resident of Clearview. Subsequently, he was identified by Wicklund and her family friend, Barbara Hendrickson, 43. Eyewitness testimony from Wicklund and Hendrickson at Campbell's trial resulted in his conviction for rape. He was sentenced to 15 years in Washington State Penitentiary.

During Campbell's incarceration, he conformed to prison rules and policies. In 1982, he became eligible for work release. While on work release, Campbell sought out Wicklund and Hendrickson for revenge. He had murder on his mind. He found Wicklund with her 8-year-old daughter, and in the company of Barbara Hendrickson. He bludgeoned each of the women to death and slit their throats. He almost beheaded Wicklund's daughter, Shannah. Another trial for these crimes resulted in a death sentence for Campbell.

On May 27, 1994, Campbell was scheduled for execution. Mrs. Iverson, Wicklund's sister, wanted to watch. "It will be an emotion of foreclosure. The fear of him getting out hangs on us very heavily. As victims of a vicious murder, we comfort each other in full awareness that along with those who were murdered, we, too, have become victims who have had to endure endless pain and suffering."

Campbell was belligerent up to the very end. When given a choice between hanging or lethal injection as his preferred execution method, Campbell said some censored things to prison officials, essentially stating that he was *not* going to be a party to helping Washington administer a death penalty that he, Campbell, finds objectionable and unconstitutional. This is curious, since Campbell himself administered the death penalty to three innocent people in 1982. In any event, Washington officials hanged Campbell, on schedule, Friday, May 27, 1994. Campbell is no more, and family members of his victims can take some solace in the fact that although Campbell's death cannot bring back their own loved ones, he will never be around in future years to rape and kill others.

Because of this case and others like it, Washington has enacted laws to protect victims of violent crimes, especially victims who eventually give incriminating testimony against their attachers. Victims now have the right to be notified when these inmates are released and to be told the outcome of cases.

Yes, some work releasees are dangerous. Is Charles Campbell the sort of inmate who should have been granted work release? Do you think he would have eventually killed these women if he had served his full incarcerative term?

Source: Adapted from *Associated Press,* "Triple Murderer Faces Hanging: N.D. Relatives of Victims Say They'll Be Glad When Case Is Over." *Minot (N.D.) Daily News,* Thursday, May 26, 1994:A5.

pletion of their sentences, the adjustment to community life will not be abrupt and potentially upsetting psychologically or socially.

A study of postrelease employment, known as the Postrelease Employment Project, investigated the pre- and postrelease behaviors of a large sample of federal inmates who were placed in work release programs before their paroles were granted (Saylor and Gaes, 1992). Researchers report that inmates who receive training and work experience during their incarceration tend to have more favorable conduct reports in prison, are likely to be employed during their halfway house stay and after release, and are less likely to recidivate than similar inmates who are not trained or who are unemployed during their imprisonment. Thus, the work release experience of these federal releasees proved valuable to their subsequent community reintegration.

In a study of another sample of federal releasees, researchers also found that work release experiences were helpful in promoting better institutional as well as community adjustments (U.S. Bureau of Prisons, 1991). This particular sample consisted of inmates who were study releasees taking courses at nearby schools. The study group participants demonstrated better institutional adjustment, in that they were less likely to have misconduct reports and were rated as more responsible by supervising correctional officers. Study group inmates also had better work records, in that they secured and maintained full-time employment for longer periods compared with standard parolees who did not participate in either work or study release.

Participation in Educational or Vocational Training.   An additional advantage of work release is that parolees can learn useful occupations and professional skills of value to them when they are eventually released. The standard work routines of inmates in many state prisons are associated with making license plates or other products which require little, if any, skilled or even semiskilled labor. And, when the inmates are released from incarceration, their acquired skills do not enable them to obtain new jobs easily.

However, it would be misleading to contend that no prison or jail job performed by inmates is helpful in securing employment in the private sector when prisoners are released. For example, the Stateville Correctional Center in Joliet, Illinois, operates a barber school for interested inmates. Furthermore, the Hennepin County Adult Correctional Facility Industrial Program in Plymouth, Minnesota, employs inmates for toy assembly and packaging, and the Ohio Department of Rehabilitation and Correction operates an employment service to further inmate job placements in their communities when eventually paroled. Several prisons and penal institutions in California have successful programs in which inmates are trained for work on oil rigs, deep-water diving, welding, and other skills.

Promotion of Inmate Self-Respect.   Plans for inmate labor in some jurisdictions are designed with rehabilitation in mind. The Hennepin County, Minnesota, program mentioned earlier attempts to instill self-esteem within those inmates originally untrained and incapable of performing even menial labor in the private sector. These work experiences are designed to equip inmates with skills useful to employers. Furthermore, inmates can earn sufficient income to offset some of their own housing expenses while in prison and provide supplementary amounts to their families.

In Philadelphia, Pennsylvania, a prison prerelease program was established in 1990 (Philadelphia Prison System, 1990). This program, which includes a prerelease center, includes work, educational, and medical release components. The program encourages inmates to work, study, or obtain medical assistance outside the prisons while they are still serving their sentences. It aims to ease the transition from institutional to community life. Offender-clients receive room and board at a modest cost, as well as assistance and counseling in the management of their financial affairs. Social awareness groups provide new participants with instruction in communication and problem-solving skills, financial management, legal procedures, and other topics necessary for successful social integration (Philadelphia Prison System, 1990).

Repayment of Debts to Victims and Society.   On October 12, 1984, President Reagan signed Public Law 98-473, which established the Comprehensive Crime Control Act. Chapter 14 of this Act is known as the **Victims of Crime Act of 1984** (Peak, 1986:39–40). Currently, all states and the federal government have **victim compensation** programs. As a part of offender work release requirements, a certain amount of their earned wages may be allocated to restitution and to a general victim compensation fund. In fact, in the federal system, the Federal Victim/Witness Protection Act of 1982 created a statute whereby federal judges should order restitution to the victim in all cases in which the victim has suffered a financial loss, unless there is a compelling reason for a contrary ruling on the record (Herrington, 1986:160). Thus, fines, restitution, and some form of community service have become common features of federal sentencing (18 U.S.C. Sec. 3563[a][2], 1995).

A survey was conducted by the National Institute of Justice of 28 restitution programs in 1985. It was found that the restitution range varied per case from $158 to $1,000, with an average restitution of $250 (McGillis, 1986). Through victim-offender reconciliation programs, prisoners on work release were able to make full payment in 71 percent of the cases in which victims had medical bills, lost wages, and property damage resulting from the crimes committed (Herrington, 1986:158). In Quincy, Massachusetts, a restitution and employment program was created that assists offenders in finding jobs to meet their obligations. More than 40 businesses in the area have consented to employ offenders up to 100 hours at minimum wage; two-thirds of their earnings go to victims (Herrington, 1986:160).

Among the states, Virginia has reported favorable results with its work release program. In 1982, Virginia was operating six work release centers—small, community-based units for minimum security prisoners. There were 314 inmate-participants who represented about 30 percent of the eligible population of prisoners (Jones, 1982). In fiscal 1981, prisoners earned $1,123,611 and contributed $65,580 for family support as well as $307,995 to Virginia (representing a defrayment of 14 percent of the total cost of the program) (Jones, 1982).

Some researchers claim that work release doesn't work for every offender. Many work release programs are simply not designed for inmates who desire to raise their standard of living but who possess poor work skills and poor work habits (Orsagh and Marsden, 1987:174). In a study of over 2,700 North Carolina inmates participating in various types of programs in 1980 including work release, study release, vocational training, GED study, and prison work, Orsagh and Marsden (1987) found that those inmates most responsive to work release were those with good prior work histories and short criminal careers. And, those offenders with poor prior work histories who obtained the GED tended to have lower recidivism rates than those in the GED program who did not complete it. In short, the Orsagh-Marsden study found strong support for matching types of offenders with specific kinds of educational and vocational programs and work release as a means of reducing recidivism.

Provision of Support for Self and Dependents. Those prisoners with wives and/or children ordinarily do not earn enough on work release to support their dependents totally. However, their income from work performed is helpful in providing for a portion of their dependents' necessities.

It is also apparent that the potential for becoming involved in a work release program can function as an incentive for prisoners to comply with prison rules. Thus, prison officials sometimes reveal that one means of eliciting prisoner compliance with prison rules is to hold out to them the prospect of work release or a denial of such participation, depending on inmate behavior while in custody (Witte, 1973).

A Profile of Work Releasees

Ordinarily, those considered for work release are nonviolent, property offenders who pose the least risk to community residents. It is likely that this profile will change dramatically by the year 2000, however, as prison and jail overcrowding force paroling authorities to consider more serious offenders each year as parole candidates.

North Carolina provides an example of the criteria used for work release consideration. All prisoners who are serving sentences of fewer than five years are considered eligible by statute for work release. While a few inmates serving longer terms are sometimes considered for this program, they must first secure administrative approval. Before offenders can be eligible for work release, they must meet the following criteria statutorily imposed by the state (McCarthy and McCarthy, 1984:173):

1. Inmates must have served a minimum of 10 percent of their sentences.
2. Inmates must have attained minimum custody by the date they are to begin participating in work release.
3. Inmates must not have had an escape within six months of the approval.

4. Inmates must not have had a major infraction of prison rules within three months of approval.
5. If inmates are serving a sentence for a serious sexual or assaultive crime or have such a history, the approving authority for minimum custody is the director's review committee.

Determining Inmate Eligibility for Work Release Programs

Not all inmates in prisons and jails are eligible for work release programs. Before inmates are eligible for such programs in some jurisdictions, they must serve a minimum portion of their originally prescribed sentences. Long-term inmates who have committed serious crimes are often automatically excluded from participation in work release because of their projected public risk if loosed in their communities. Statutory provisions in several states specify the minimum amount of time that must be served before inmates may make application to participate in work release. Of course, an advantage of being able to participate in work release is that it weighs heavily and favorably when inmates are eventually considered for parole. Those inmates who have completed work release programs successfully stand a much better chance of being paroled than those who have not been selected for participation. In short, they have proven themselves capable of living and working with others "on the outside" and are not considered potentially troublesome.

Parole boards in most jurisdictions are increasingly sensitive about their parole decision making, since there have been successfully litigated lawsuits against parole boards that have made decisions regarding the release of dangerous offenders who have subsequently injured community residents (Benson, 1988; *Division of Corrections v. Neakok,* 1986). An Alaska court held that parolees and the state have a special relationship that requires the state to control any parolee with dangerous propensities and to protect anyone foreseeably endangered by the parolee. The significance of this decision is that the court extended the state's liability to anyone in the community, thus rejecting a line of national cases that requires the threat of harm to be directed at specifically identifiable persons before liability for negligent supervision attaches for parole authorities (Benson, 1988). This same concern applies to work releasees (see box in this chapter).

Also, some prisoners find it difficult to enter parole programs because of the notoriety they achieved through the serious offenses they committed. For example, a convicted rapist, Larry Singleton, was released after fulfilling his determinate sentence in San Francisco, California. Although Singleton was not a parolee because he had otherwise served the required time for his crime under California's determinate sentencing law, community residents in San Francisco and scores of other towns and cities in California rejected Singleton's entry into their communities. This was because Singleton's crime was especially heinous—he had cut the arms off of a young female hitchhiker he had raped and left her for dead in a roadside ditch. Later, she was found and recovered from her wounds. Singleton was identified, arrested, and convicted. Authorities eventually had to place Singleton in quarters outside of San Quentin prison for his own safety (Klein and Rogers, 1988).

Weaknesses and Strengths of Work Release Programs

Whether work release is successful may be gauged according to individual parolee successes such as low recidivism rates and parole revocations. Or, the successfulness of work release may be couched in the context of how much people benefit from inmate labor. Are victims compensated for their financial losses? Are the families of work releasees recipients of supporting funds? Does inmate participation in work release foster self-esteem and help prisoners become reintegrated into their communities?

Generally, work release programs have been successful when one or more of these standards have been applied. These programs tend to have low recidivism rates compared with standard parole recidivism figures (McCarthy and McCarthy, 1984:182–183). However, some programs such as those operated in North Carolina and Florida have found little difference, if any, in recidivism among work releasees and other parolees (Waldo and Chiricos, 1977; Witte, 1973).

Because prison labor is used in many private-sector organizations, the wages paid inmates are not particularly high. Prisoners participating in work release programs in Massachusetts in 1982 worked in outside jobs an average of 95 days, earning an average of $2,145. While these figures are averages and susceptible to skewness from extremely low- or extremely high-paying jobs, estimated total per prisoner earnings were such that prisoners appeared to earn an average of $23 per day (Miller, 1984b). However, hourly wage figures suggest that prisoner payments were in line with those payments received by nonprisoners performing unskilled or semiskilled work in the community. Thus, some prisoners work relatively few hours per week, while others work well beyond the 40-hour standard. This may be inferred on the basis of the average number of hours worked per week by prisoners, or 38 hours (Miller, 1984b).

Some participating inmates do not believe that work release is beneficial to the extent that the jobs available to them on work release are useful. A large sample of work releasees was interviewed by researchers in conjunction with **Project Recidivism and Alcohol-Related Crimes of Aggression** (MacGrady, Bemister, and Fontaine, 1991). Of those interviewed, it was found that 61 percent of these offenders had been drinking at the time their conviction offenses were committed, and 56 percent of those were drunk at the time. Only 10 percent actually thought about committing the offense before committing it. After placement in work release, 53 percent were dissatisfied with the education and training required to get the job they wanted. Researchers recommended that subsequent programming for work release should (1) incorporate treatment elements related to drug and/or alcohol abuse and (2) make provisions for acquiring requisite skills and education to secure and maintain particular types of employment.

One way states can incorporate more inmates into continuous work projects and programs is to sponsor such work programs themselves. In Minnesota there is a project known as State Use Industries (SUI). State Use Industries is an organization authorized under Minnesota statutes to use inmate labor for the manufacture of goods, services, and merchandise to be sold to the state and to public agencies or private charitable or educational organizations. The SUI program provides work experiences that replicate nonprison work environments as well as job training and apprenticeship programs. A placement service under the auspices of SUI is available to all former inmates employed by SUI (St. Paul Police Department, 1991). In the St. Paul SUI program, postrelease employment was obtained by 58 of 65 inmates. During the period of the study, 75 percent worked at least half the time, while former inmates were employed in a variety of semiskilled, service, and white-collar occupations and professions. Their pay averaged $5.95 per hour. Another project, Project CARE (Cooperative Assistance and Resources for Employment), provides for job skills training and placement services to ex-offenders. During the report period, 707 offenders were referred to Project CARE. Of these, 328 requested services from the organization and 177 were placed in jobs. Many of these Project CARE clients were placed in lower-skill occupations, while some were placed in skilled or white-collar jobs. Their pay averaged $4.39 per hour. Many of the other offenders secured and maintained jobs through self-placement (St. Paul Police Department, 1991).

STUDY RELEASE PROGRAMS

Study release programs are essentially the same as work release programs but for the express purpose of securing educational goals. Several types of study release have been identified: adult basic education, high school, or high school equivalency (G.E.D.), technical or vocational education, and college (McCarthy and McCarthy, 1983; Siegel, 1994). Researchers report that absconder rates for these educational or study release programs have been very low. In 1977, for instance, absconder rates were only 1 percent.

In 1993, there were 31 jurisdictions with educational release programs. About 750 inmates were participating in study release nationwide (*Corrections Compendium,* 1993b:5). Study release figures have not been compiled by the American Correctional Association. This form of release is grouped under supervised release, and, thus, study release figures for 1994 are not available.

Determining Inmate Eligibility for Study Release

An inmate's eligibility for study release involves several factors. First, inmates must be within a short time of being released anyway. Study release may be granted to those within a year or less of being paroled. A second criterion is whether inmates have behaved well while institutionalized. Good behavior on the "inside" does not necessarily mean that inmates will behave well when on study release. However, compliance with institutional rules is generally a good indicator of compliance with program rules for study release. Few offenders wish to jeopardize their parole chances by violating program rules while on study release. Absconding or escaping while on work or study release will result in additional time to be served when these inmates are eventually apprehended. Usually, the time to be served becomes "flat time" that *must* be served if an inmate has previously absconded. Study release involves an element of trust on the part of the releasing institution. Violations of this trust by inmates are not favorably viewed by paroling authorities.

Inmates must also file a plan indicating the reasons for acquiring additional education and where their educational goals will lead them when released into the community. Educational training enhances an inmate's eligibility for particular kinds of work when parole is granted or whenever the offender is released from the system. Inmates who are more highly educated are more employable. If restitution is a part of one's parole program, then acquiring greater amounts of education can assist in making restitution payments later.

Advantages and Disadvantages of Study Release Programs

Study release programs—in fact, any program designed to permit inmates to leave prisons or jails temporarily and unsupervised—create fears among community residents that somehow, study releasees and other types of releasees will harm them or pose various threats to community safety. In view of some of the more publicized releasee "failures," it would seem that their fears are justified (Duff and Hong, 1977). However, the "failure rate" of study releasees is so low that program advantages far outweigh any of these "disadvantages" (Mason, 1977; Stiles, 1994; U.S. Department of Justice, 1991).

Study release helps to prepare inmates for different types of occupations or professions. The Tennessee Department of Corrections, for instance, has a study release program in which selected inmates can learn data entry, building construction, welding, food services, industrial maintenance, surveying, and drafting. They become certified upon completing their study release programs. Many of their educational credits are transferrable to colleges and universities where they can undertake advanced graduate study, if interested (Tennessee Department of Corrections, 1994). However, some jurisdictions have reported inmate discontent with the types of jobs their education has qualified them to perform (MacGrady, Bemister, and Fontaine, 1991).

Some inmates do not actually utilize these work and study release programs for anything other than their cosmetic value for parole board appearances. For instance, a study of work and study release programs in two states, Oregon and California, has shown that many prisoners believe that they are "under pressure" to participate in these types of prison programs and that such participation would "look good" to their parole boards (U.S. Department of Justice, 1989). However, there are other jurisdictions, such as Tennessee, in which inmates show remarkable progress related to greater knowledge about the harmful effects of drug abuse, greater discipline, and improved development in self-awareness and self-concept (Tennessee Department of Corrections, 1994).

Work release and furlough programs are intended to gradually reintegrate offenders into community life and away from the strict regimentation of prison living. (Gary Wagner/Stock Boston)

FURLOUGH PROGRAMS

Furloughs are authorized, unescorted leaves from confinement granted for specific purposes and for designated time periods (Marlette, 1988; McCarthy and McCarthy, 1984:163). Nationwide, more than 230,960 furloughs were granted in 1990 from 40 U.S. prison systems. This was an increase of 15 percent over the estimated 200,000 furloughs granted in 1987 and 35 percent more than the 170,000 granted in 1988 for all systems (Davis, 1991:10). Abscondence rates are quite low, about one-half of 1 percent (Smith and Sabatino, 1989, 1990). Furloughs may be granted to prisoners for periods ranging from 24 hours to several weeks and are similar to leaves enjoyed by military personnel. In 1986, those states granting the largest numbers of furloughs were North Carolina and Oklahoma (American Correctional Association, 1987:xvi–xvii). By 1994, the number of furloughees had increased to 16,201 (American Correctional Association, 1994:xxviii–xxix). This is an increase of 131 percent during the period between 1986 and 1994. Florida and Rhode Island became the largest grantors of furloughs, with 7,729 and 5,705 respectively. [*Note:* The furloughs reported by Davis (1991) are instances of *multiple furloughs* granted to the same offenders during the course of their final months of incarceration in different state and federal facilities—the later figures reported by the ACA are the numbers of the same individuals granted multiple furloughs by any given state or federal system.]

Furloughs originated in 1918 in Mississippi. By 1970, about half the states had furlough programs (Marley, 1973). In those days, prisoners who had completed two or more years of their original sentences were considered eligible for furloughs. These furloughs usually involved conjugal visits with families or Christmas holiday activities for brief, 10-day periods. These furloughs were believed valuable for preparing offenders for permanent reentry into their respective communities once parole had been granted. In 1990, 46 states and the federal government had furlough programs (Davis, 1991:10).

Furloughs are an outgrowth of work release programs, for which select inmates are chosen, usually through application, for participation. Typically, inmates have served a significant portion of their originally prescribed sentences and are eligible for parole consideration. The success of inmate furlough experiences figures prominently in early release decisions by parole boards. Thus, offenders who are granted furloughs and who successfully comply with furlough requirements have an advantage over those not otherwise considered for such special consideration.

Furloughs have many of the same characteristics as work release programs. Furloughs are used only about one-third of the time compared with work release, however. The length of the temporary release varies according to the jurisdiction. Most furlough programs tend to range from 24 to 72 hours throughout the United States, although some programs may provide inmates with two weeks or more of freedom for special activities (McCarthy and McCarthy, 1984:163).

Some of the information compiled by authorities in jurisdictions in which furlough programs have been established and are operated show numerous details. For instance, selected California counties maintain the following information relating to furloughs: the minimum time of the furlough; number of beds; acceptance of misdemeanants or felons; fee amount; process time; processed presentence or postsentence; waiting period; fee per day; fee collection; minimum and maximum number of work hours; whether or not two jobs are allowed; worker's compensation; car registration and insurance on file; reciprocal agreement; number of reciprocals; reciprocal program transfer; program transfer interval; application fee; excused absences allowed and defined; collection; mandatory appearance for first weekend; booking and release location; appeal process for entry denial and termination; number of writs filed; notification; and the officer providing supervision (Nevada County Probation Department, 1990).

The Goals of Furlough Programs

The purposes of a **furlough program** are several. Offenders are given a high degree of trust by prison officials and are permitted leaves to visit their homes and families. Interestingly, such furloughs are beneficial to both prisoners and to their families, because they permit family members to get used to the presence of the offender after a long incarcerative absence. Sometimes, prisoners may participate in educational programs, such as study release, outside prison. They can arrange for employment once paroled, or they can participate in vocational training for short periods. In Illinois, for instance, furloughs may be granted to eligible inmates for the following reasons: to make contacts for employment; to visit close relatives; to obtain medical or psychiatric services; to visit seriously ill relatives or attend the funerals of close relatives; to appear before study groups; to make contacts for discharge; and to secure a residence on release on parole or discharge (Illinois Department of Corrections, 1971).

Furloughs also provide officials with an opportunity to evaluate offenders and determine how they adapt to living with others in their community. Thus, the furlough is a type of test to determine, with some predictability, the likelihood that inmates will conform to society's rules if they are eventually released through parole. For some prisoners, furloughs function as incentives to conform to prison rules and regulations, because only prisoners who have demonstrated they can control their behaviors in prison will be considered by officials for temporary releases. Usually, although not always, prisoners selected for participation in furlough programs are nearing the end of their sentences and will eventually be paroled or released anyway. They are good risks because the likelihood they will abscond while on a furlough is quite remote.

The "Willie Horton Incident."   The intent of furlough programs is to give offenders a chance to become reintegrated into their communities; but, sometimes, there are bizarre twists. In 1985, a liberal furlough program in Massachusetts granted a furlough to Willie Horton, an inmate convicted of the murder of a gas station attendant. Horton had been sentenced to life without possibility of parole. However, under Massachusetts's lenient furlough program, Horton was permitted weekend freedoms on nine occasions after serving 10 years of his original sentence. On the tenth trip, Horton failed to return. He was apprehended in Washington, D.C., nearly a year later, after he had terrorized a young couple, Clifford and Angela Barnes. When Michael Dukakis, then governor of Massachusetts, ran for the U.S. presidency in 1988, much was made by the opposing political party about Dukakis's furlough policy and the leniency of Massachusetts programs. These incidents, though factually accurate, are rare. Unlike Massachusetts, most furlough programs permit unsupervised weekend releases only for those offenders who are nearing their paroles or mandatory releases. In Massachusetts, however, the furlough program permitted those serving life-without-parole sentences weekend passes from prison. Therefore, it may be unfair to judge the furlough programs of other states by citing violence resulting from the release of offenders from the state with the most liberal furlough policies.

The Functions of Furlough Programs

Furloughs are intended to accomplish certain functions. These include (1) offender rehabilitation and reintegration; (2) the development of self-esteem and self-worth; (3) opportunities to pursue vocational and educational programs; and (4) aiding parole boards in determining when inmates are ready to be released.

Offender Rehabilitation and Reintegration. As has been observed with other temporary release programs such as work release, the manifest intent of furloughs is to provide offenders with outside experiences to enable them to become accustomed to living with others in the community apart from the highly regulated life in prison or jail settings. Indications are that furloughs fulfill this objective in most instances.

A study of a furlough program established by the Oahu Community Correctional Center, Corrections Division, Department of Social Services and Housing, showed, for example, that from 1977 to 1983, 98 inmates were granted furloughs before their eventual releases or paroles. Of these, 68 percent were successful, whereas the remainder were considered failures. In this situation, failures were either returned to prison because of new criminal convictions or terminated from the program because of technical program violations (Uriell, 1984).

This raises an interesting point. Of those who failed, was the failure due to new criminal convictions or to technical program violations, such as curfew violation or drug testing failure? In the Oahu furlough program, a program violation might be violation of curfew or testing positive for drugs or alcohol. Of course, a new criminal conviction would also be an indication of program failure. Obviously, the more serious program violation would be a new criminal conviction. But only a small number of those granted furloughs were reconvicted. In the opinion of authorities in charge of the Oahu furlough program, the program was successful. Thus, caution must be exercised before deciding whether a program accomplishes or fails to accomplish its manifest objectives. In this instance, most program participants remained "clean" and were not convicted of new crimes (Uriell, 1984).

The Development of Self-Esteem and Self-Worth. In addition, furloughs seem to instill within inmates feelings of self-esteem and self-worth. Again, the element of trust plays an important role in enabling those granted furloughs to acquire trust for those who place trust in them. The development of self-esteem and self-worth are unmeasurable. Yet, many of those granted furloughs report that they believe they have benefited from their temporary release experiences.

Opportunities to Pursue Vocational and Educational Programs. Another benefit of furlough programs is that inmates can participate in programs not available to them in prisons or jails. Thus, if inmates wish to take courses in typing, art, automobile repair, or philosophically oriented offerings in social science or related areas, furloughs permit them the time to pursue such courses. Sometimes, these furloughs are labeled as study release because they involve a program of study designed for the offender's specific needs.

Aiding Parole Boards in Determining When Inmates Ought to Be Released. A key function of furloughs as tests of inmate behavior is to alert parole boards to which inmates are most eligible to be released and who will likely be successful while on parole (Milling, 1978). Connecticut, for instance, has an 80 percent success rate with its furlough program as used for parole board decision making. In that jurisdiction, inmates are granted furloughs if they are within 60 days of being paroled. They are limited to three-day furloughs, during which they can make home visits, obtain required medical treatment or psychological counseling, participate in special training courses, and perform work or other duties (Milling, 1978).

Determining Inmate Eligibility for Furlough Program Involvement

Incidents such as the Willie Horton episode in Massachusetts are relatively rare for furlough programs. As a general rule, those serving life sentences are ineligible for furlough participation. There are some exceptions, however. In Hawaii and Oregon, some "lifers" or those serving life imprisonment are granted permission to become involved in furlough programs (Marlette, 1988). Life imprisonment doesn't always mean *life imprisonment.* Often, it means only seven years, or some other fixed figure. After a lifer serves this minimum time, parole eligibility is activated. In recent years, however, increasing numbers of offenders have been sentenced to *life without parole (LWOP)*. These LWOP sentences are generally "flat time" sentences from which parole relief is not available.

For most furloughees, however, program participation is restricted to the following types of inmates: those who have minimum-custody status, have served a fixed amount of their sentences, and are within some fixed time of release; have been approved by a committee that reviews all furlough applications; and have a clean institutional record, a stable home situation, and a past criminal history of nonviolent conduct. Those who are excluded from program participation commonly include those who have committed notorious or heinous crimes, crimes of violence, or sex offenses (Smith and Milan, 1973).

Weaknesses and Strengths of Furlough Programs

Not all states have furlough programs. One reason is that under certain types of sentencing systems, any sort of temporary release is not permitted. Those offenders sentenced to mandatory prison terms cannot be released before they have served their entire sentences, less the good-time credits they may have acquired during the initial incarceration period. Under an indeterminate sentencing scheme, there is considerable latitude for paroling authorities to grant furloughs or work releases to those inmates who have shown they can conform their conduct to the institutional rules (Harer and Eichenlaub, 1992).

In recent years, however, sentencing reforms have been undertaken at the federal level and in virtually every state (Shane-DuBow, Brown, and Olsen, 1985). A general shift has been observed toward determinate and presumptive sentencing schemes, which permit little variation from whatever sentences have been imposed by judges. Thus, in some jurisdictions, it is difficult, if not impossible, to operate furlough or work release programs because of statutory prohibitions (California

Board of Prison Terms, 1984; *Corrections Compendium,* 1993b; Davis, 1991; Goodstein, Kramer, and Nuss, 1984).

One possible consequence of the reduction of furlough and work release programs nationally is that inmates of prisons and jails have less incentive to abide by institutional rules. In some jurisdictions that have abolished parole, furloughs, and work release were deemed incentives to comply with prison and jail regulations, since parole boards viewed favorably any offender who completed these programs successfully. But despite the curtailment of these programs, incentives to conform continue to exist in the form of good-time credits that may be applied against an offender's original sentence.

Another consideration is the unavailability of funds to operate programs such as work release and furloughs. When the Law Enforcement Assistance Administration (LEAA) was in operation during the 1970s, large sums of money were allocated to different jurisdictions for experimental purposes. New programs were undertaken as a means of determining their long-range effect on offender recidivism or rehabilitation. When the LEAA was terminated, these funds diminished significantly. Of course, other agencies took up the slack, in part, by making grants available to applicants in various jurisdictions.

In view of diminished resources and unenthusiastic response from the public and corrections officials to furlough programs and other temporary release options, these alternatives are less prevalent compared with past years. States such as Arkansas and North Carolina continue to offer furloughs in relatively large numbers to deserving inmates, but the administrative costs have surpassed the general benefits derived from such programs.

The successfulness of furlough programs is demonstrated by the relatively low recidivism rates in certain jurisdictions using such programs on a limited basis. In 1977, for example, the Oahu Community Correctional Center, Corrections Division, Department of Social Services and Housing, implemented a furlough program for selected offenders. Officials kept track of offender progress while on furloughs during a six-year period. By December 1983, they had permitted 98 inmates to participate in the furlough program. Of these, nearly 70 percent successfully complied with furlough rules and completed their program. These authorities regard their success rate of 68 percent as highly favorable for future adult correctional programs, despite the fact that most of the failures were convicted of new offenses while on furloughs (Uriell, 1984).

PREPAROLE RELEASE PROGRAMS AND DAY REPORTING CENTERS

For many furloughees and work/study releasees, community residences or centers are established to facilitate their work or educational placement and assist them in other needs they might have. These are known as *day reporting centers* (Diggs and Pieper, 1994:9; Williams, 1990). Known in some circles as "invisible jails," day reporting centers are a hybrid of intensive probation supervision, house arrest, and early release. In these programs, participants serve their last weeks or months of jail or prison still in the government's custody but technically on their own—living at home, perhaps working at a regular job in the community. Meanwhile, by presenting themselves daily to the program's offices after work or after school, they still benefit from traditional in-jail services ranging from Alcoholics Anonymous to financial planning to GED classes to "group" (Williams, 1990:4). Another view is that day reporting is a highly structured nonresidential program utilizing supervision, sanctions, and services coordinated from a central focus (Curtin, 1990:8; Diggs and Pieper, 1994:9).

Day reporting centers are conveniently located in the midst of various prepa-role releasees living within the community (Parent, 1990a). Day reporting centers originated in Great Britain during the 1970s as an alternative to incarceration for older petty criminals who were chronic offenders (Larivee, 1990). Subsequently, in the United States, they were funded by the German Marshall Fund and the Boston-based Crime and Justice Foundation. The funding organizations secured the cooperation of Sheriff Michael Ashe of Hampden County, Massachusetts, to start a center (Curtin, 1990; Williams, 1990:5).

Today, day reporting centers handle the daily activities and provide minimum supervision for participating work and study releasees and furloughees. Many of these offender-clients have special conditions associated with their work or study release or furlough programs, such as restitution to victims, payment of program costs, and supervisory fees. Clients must be checked to determine if they are involved in drug or alcohol abuse. Day reporting centers assist authorities in providing these services and offender monitoring. Another function of day reporting centers is assisting clients in job placement and completing job applications. In some instances, these programs provide some educational and vocational opportunities to prepare them for better-paying jobs.

Diggs and Pieper (1994:9) say that

> offenders committed to day reporting centers live at home and report to the center regularly, often daily. While at [these centers, participants] submit an itinerary that details [their] travels, destinations, and purposes. This schedule allows the supervision staff to monitor and control the client's behavior and is also a valuable tool for teaching responsibilities to offenders. [They] are normally required to call in several times a day, and center staff also call the clients to verify their whereabouts. While at the center, participants may be required to submit to drug testing and participate in counseling, education, and vocational placement assistance. Offenders are normally required to be employed in the community or be full-time students. (quoted from Larivee, 1990)

These centers are often operated in the midst of a work release program or halfway house. Parent (1990a) says that these day reporting centers (1) provide enhanced supervision and decreased liberty of offenders, (3) enable them to have treatment for their diverse problems; and (3) provide a means of reducing crowding of incarcerative facilities.

Certain guidelines for operating day reporting centers have been established.

BOX 10.2
The Other Side of Prerelease Centers

**The Case of Park Drive
Pre-Release Center**

Prerelease centers house convicted felons, don't they? Neighborhoods ought to reject them, shouldn't they? Maybe not.

In Boston, Massachusetts, the Park Drive Pre-Release Center was established in 1977. It was designed to house 50 inmates who were within 18 months of regular parole. The Park Drive Pre-Release Center is located near Fenway Park in Boston. The facility is a five-story brick and stone townhome at the end of a row of respectable, well-kept stone structures in Boston's Back Bay. When it first opened, neighbors picketed. They didn't want prisoners in their neighborhood. Who does?

Several years later, a new view of Park Drive Pre-Release Center was acquired by area residents. It became a 24-hour safe-house for persons in trouble. One evening, a woman with blood streaming down her face fled a night attacker and ran into the building, into the arms of a convicted murderer. The man held her in his arms to comfort her, got her clothing and shoes to wear, and alerted the police. Other victims of muggings, burglaries, and assaults have found their way to Park Drive Pre-Release Center for safety from criminals lurking on the streets. It is ironic that a facility that was originally picketed is now viewed as a community asset in a high-crime area. Some convict residents of Park Drive have been offered positions as members of the Fenway Garden Club.

Are all prerelease centers designed to house violent felons? What about Park Drive? Do you think the area residents have a different perspective of Park Drive from the one they had when it was first constructed?

Adapted from Randy Welch, "Back to the Community . . . Pre-Release in Massachusetts." *Corrections Compendium,* **14:**1–8, 1989.

An editorial in the *Corrections Compendium* (1990b:14) indicates the following day reporting program suggestions:

1. Sign a contract with participants spelling out expectations about home, work, schooling, financial matters, drug tests, counseling, community service, and restitution.
2. Notify the police department in the offender's hometown.
3. Set a curfew; 9:00 P.M. is frequent.
4. Require an advance copy of the participant's daily itinerary points.
5. Perform spot-checks of the participant's home, job, other itinerary points.
6. Institute proper urinalysis procedures—this is crucial; twice a week is typical.
7. Schedule telephone checks more heavily on Thursday, Friday, and Saturday nights.
8. Establish services—addiction education, parenting, and transition skills are popular topics.

Participants should include the following:

1. Those convicted of drug offenses, larceny, driving while intoxicated, breaking and entering of commercial buildings, and similar charges; Massachusetts excludes sex offenders and, for the most part, violent offenders.
2. Offenders without an identified victim.
3. Those with a home to go to (check).
4. Inmates within six months of release. (Williams, 1990:7)

Generally, eligibility variables include the instant offense for which offenders are responsible, gender, legal status, treatment needs, prior record, and residential stability (Diggs and Pieper (1994:10). Excluded offenders are those considered dangerous to the community or who are otherwise unresponsive to day reporting center therapy programs.

KEY TERMS

Day parole	Study release
Day pass	Temporary release
Furlough program	Victim compensation
Furlough	Victims of Crime Act of 1984
Project Recidivism and Alcohol-Related Crimes of Aggression	Work Release

QUESTIONS FOR REVIEW

1. What is work release? What are some potential benefits for inmates who participate in work release?
2. What are furloughs? Are furloughs the same as work release? What are some advantages of furloughs for prisoners?
3. How does the community benefit from work release and furlough programs?
4. When and where was work release first established as an option in the United States? How prevalent is work release among the states today?
5. What are the functions of work release and furloughs? From your reading, what assessment can you make of the effectiveness of these programs?
6. What is study release? Which types of inmates are usually eligible for study release?
7. In what respects was Willie Horton not eligible for a furlough? What safeguards would you employ to keep incidents from happening such as the one involving Willie Horton?
8. What is a day reporting center? What are some of its functions?
9. What types of offender-clients use day reporting centers?

11

Halfway Houses and Community Residential Centers

Introduction
Halfway Houses
Community Residential Centers and Day
    Reporting/Treatment Programs

Other Programs and Sanctions
Key Terms
Questions for Review

INTRODUCTION

- In October 1993, a man was finally brought to justice and sentenced on charges that he strangled his five-month-old poodle for defecating on his rug in 1988. Originally charged with "malicious intent to kill an animal" (a felony), Todd Burwell, 29, of Gardner, Massachusetts, entered a guilty plea to the lesser charge of "cruelty to an animal." A spokeswoman for the Society for the Prevention of Cruelty to Animals in Boston said that the dog was not Burwell's. Rather, it belonged to Burwell's landlord, Mal McCunney. Aggravating circumstances associated with the offense included the fact that after strangling the puppy, Burwell disposed of the animal in his trash compactor.

All facts considered, the judge sentenced Burwell to a one-year-in-jail suspended sentence and to complete 100 hours of community service as a part of the plea bargain agreement (*Associated Press,* reported in *Minot Daily News,* October 31, 1993:A-2).

- Father Bruce Ritter, a Franciscan priest, founder and president of Covenant House, resigned in October 1989 after a halfway house resident alleged that Ritter had committed a sexual act with him. Covenant House, a very successful halfway house, is internationally known. Run principally as a charitable organization to accommodate runaway youths and others exploited on city streets, Covenant House serves 20,000 homeless teens annually. Father Ritter's resignation was also triggered, in part, by an internal investigation of the distribution of agency funds, some of which were diverted to family members for construction contracts, gifts, and other favors. Others in the business of halfway house operation were quick to point out that Covenant House is, for the most part, an honest, well-meaning organization that performs a valuable service. The actions of a few persons in the upper echelons of organizational management, however, have created a scandal that has tended to taint not only Covenant House, but other halfway houses as well. (Frank Washington, Tony Clifton, and Lauren Picker, "Sex, Cash and Family Favors: New Allegations Rock Covenant House, *Newsweek,* March 26, 1990:21).

This chapter is about halfway houses and community residential centers. The first part of the chapter defines halfway houses and examines their philosophy and functions. Halfway house clients are profiled. And, certain weaknesses and strengths of halfway houses are identified.

In the second part of the chapter, community residential centers are described. The philosophy, goals, and functions of such centers are presented and their clients are profiled. Finally, the chapter concludes with an examination of community service orders and other restitution programs, including a discussion of victim compensation.

HALFWAY HOUSES

Halfway houses are transitional residences for inmates who are released from prison (G. Wilson, 1985:152). Ordinarily, these homes offer temporary housing, food, and clothing for parolees recently released from prison. Their assignment to one of these homes may be mandatory for a short period. In many jurisdictions, these homes offer services to offenders on a voluntary basis. They assist greatly in helping former inmates make the transition from rigid prison life to community living (Miller, 1977).

Halfway House Origins.   The halfway house concept probably originated in England during the early 1800s. But the first formal recommendation for the creation of a halfway house in the United States was made in 1817 in Pennsylvania (Chamberlain, 1977; McCarthy and McCarthy, 1984:204). A Pennsylvania prison riot had stirred the legislature to think of various prison reforms, including housing provisions for ex-convicts who were often poor and could not find employment or adequate housing. But these proposals were never implemented, because the public feared **criminal contamination**—if ex-offenders lived together, they would spread their criminality like a disease (McCarthy and McCarthy, 1984:204).

Sponsorship of halfway houses for the next 150 years stemmed primarily from private and/or religious sources. In 1845, the Quakers opened the **Isaac T. Hopper Home** in New York City, followed by the Temporary Asylum for Disadvantaged Female Prisoners established in Boston in 1864 by a reformist group (G. Wilson, 1985:153). In 1889, the House of Industry was opened in Philadelphia, and, in 1896, **Hope House** was established in New York City by Maud and Ballington Booth. Receiving considerable financial support from a missionary religious society called the Volunteers of America, the Booths were able to open additional Hope Houses or **Hope Halls** in future years in Chicago, San Francisco, and New Orleans (G. Wilson, 1985:153).

State and federal governments during the 1800s and early 1900s continued to work toward the creation of halfway houses apart from those established in the private sector, however. In 1917, the Massachusetts Prison Commission recommended the establishment of houses to accommodate recently released offenders who were indigent (G. Wilson, 1985:152). But this plan was rejected. Eventually in the 1960s, Attorney General Robert F. Kennedy recommended government sponsorship and funding for halfway house programs. In 1965, the Prisoner Rehabilitation Act was passed, authorizing the establishment of community-based residential centers for both juvenile and adult prerelease offenders (G. Wilson, 1985:154).

One of the most significant events to spark the growth of state-operated halfway houses was the creation of the **International Halfway House Association (IHHA)** in Chicago in 1964. Although many of the halfway house programs continued to be privately operated after the formation of the IHHA, the growth in the numbers of halfway houses was phenomenal during the next decade. For instance, from 1966 to 1982, the number of halfway houses operating in the United States and Canada rose from 40 to 1,800 (G. Wilson, 1985:154). These figures are probably lower than the actual number of halfway houses in existence during those time periods, since these numbers were based on affiliation with the IHHA and the American Correctional Association through a directory. Other researchers have reported as many as 2,300 halfway house facilities with over 100,000 beds existing in 1981 (Gatz and Murray, 1981).

Halfway House Variations.   Because there are so many different government-sponsored and private agencies claiming to be halfway houses, it is impossible to devise a consistent definition that fits all jurisdictions. Extensive variations in the level of custody for clients range from providing simple shelter on a voluntary basis to mandatory confinement with curfew. There are also many different services provided by halfway houses. These might include alcohol or drug-related rehabilita-

tion facilities with some hospitalization on premises, minimal or extensive counseling services, and/or employment assistance (McCarthy and McCarthy, 1984:201; Latessa and Allen, 1982a). And, halfway house programs are designed for offenders ranging from probationers and prereleasees to parolees and others assigned to community service with special conditions (Miller and Montilla, 1977).

Some idea of the variation among halfway houses can be gleaned by the following. Brooke House, established in 1965 in Massachusetts, accepts prerelease-status placements from federal institutions and state prison parolees. It employs reality therapy and emphasizes job placement, improved work habits, and sound financial planning (Beha, 1977). This is generally the case with other Massachusetts-based halfway houses under the auspices of Massachusetts Halfway Houses, Inc., or MHHI (Massachusetts Halfway Houses, Inc., 1980). Under the MHHI concept, reality therapy and mutual agreement programming are the primary treatment modes as services offered since 1968. These services are supplemented with newsletters, workshops, training advice, conferences, and technical assistance for staff.

In 1973, Dreyfous House in New Orleans was established for emotionally disturbed youths. Strong community opposition to Dreyfous House resulted in its termination in 1975, however (Slotnick, 1976). In San Mateo, California, the El Camino House was established for ex-mental patients (Richmond, 1970). The El Camino House has a twofold program thrust: (1) a performance-oriented culture for residents within the halfway house and (2) the utilization of existing housing in the community to create post–halfway house living accommodations with built-in provisions for follow-up. These programs serve the overall program goal of assisting severely disturbed psychiatric patients in their adjustment to the community by preparing them socially and emotionally for more independent living (Richmond, 1970). Other halfway houses include the Ralph W. Alvis House; the Bridge Home for Young Men; the Denton House; Fellowship House; Fresh Start, Inc.; the Helping Hand Halfway Home, Inc.; Talbert House; and Vander Meulen House. All of these latter houses are located in Ohio (Seiter, Petersilia, and Allen, 1974).

Halfway-Out and Halfway-In Houses.   The concept of a halfway house is closely connected with the reintegrative aim of corrections. In recent years, at least two hyphenated versions of the term have emerged (Travis, 1985). First, **halfway-out houses** have been mentioned in the correctional literature to distinguish facilities designed to serve the immediate needs of parolees from those established to accommodate probationers in the community. Second, **halfway-in houses** provide services catering to those probationers in need of limited or somewhat restricted confinement apart from complete freedom of movement in the community (McCarthy and McCarthy, 1984:154–155).

Travis (1985) adds that halfway-in houses, designed for probationers, are deliberately intended to create uncomfortable atmospheres for them. Halfway-in houses structure the lives of probationers in various ways, mostly by making them comply with various program requirements (e.g., curfew, random drug and alcohol checks, and other technical details). This is because probation is actually a punishment and must necessarily contain certain elements of punishment. In contrast, halfway-out houses, for parolees, are designed to provide homelike and supportive environments aimed at aiding the offender's readjustment to society. Like halfway-in houses, these homes also continue punishment through the high degree of supervision or offender control exerted by halfway-out house staff. But because their clientele are parolees and have served substantial time behind bars, their functions are more therapeutic, rehabilitative, and reintegrative rather than punishment-centered.

The Philosophy and Characteristics of Halfway Houses

Halfway houses are transitional residences for inmates about to be released from prisons and jails (G. Wilson, 1985:152). The concept of the halfway house was initiated by the **Massachusetts Prison Commission** in 1817 and was initially designed to serve the needs of "destitute released offenders" who had no money, food, or living accommodations. The original concept of halfway houses envisioned providing temporary shelter, food, limited assistance in gaining employment, and decompression from institutions to the free community, although more contemporary goals attempt to meet the needs of special client groups, such as divertees, prereleasees, postreleasees, drug addicts, and alcoholics (Riley, 1974). By 1981, there were nearly 2,300 halfway houses, both public and private, serving the needs of over 100,000 offenders (Gatz and Murray, 1981). Many of these facilities serve the needs of both male and female offenders (Donnelly and Forschner, 1987).

More than any other parole program, the halfway house typifies the transition prisoners must make from the unique custodial world of prisons and jails to the outside community. Today, halfway houses furnish not only living accommodations and food but also job placement services for parolees, group and/or individual counseling, medical assistance, placement assistance in vocational and technical training programs, as well as numerous other opportunities for self-development (Donnelly and Forschner, 1987; National Office for Social Responsibility, 1987).

Before the federal maximum-security prison Alcatraz was closed in 1964, federal prisoners scheduled for early release within six months were sometimes housed in large, secure homes in and around San Francisco. Life in Alcatraz was totally regulated. Head counts by guards and bed checks were made 8 or 10 times daily, and "shakedowns" of prisoner cells to detect contraband or devices that might be in violation of prison regulations were regularly conducted. Although escapes from Alcatraz were few, several were nevertheless attempted. Rules prohibiting inmate conversations and interactions were rigidly enforced, with the exception of exercise periods in the main recreational yard.

When prisoners were eventually paroled from Alcatraz, authorities considered it helpful to provide some inmates with accommodations at halfway houses for brief periods before permitting them nearly total community freedom (parole conditions usually include regular reports to POs, behavioral requirements, observance of curfews, avoidance of contact with other criminals, and occasional participation in groups such as AA, depending on offender needs). Their strict regimentation while in prison had to be overcome, and living in a comparatively spacious homelike dwelling—in contrast with an 8'-by-6' prison cell for nearly 24 hours a day—provided them with the opportunity to make a smoother transition from prison to the community. California and most other states currently operate halfway houses in many cities and towns to serve the needs of parolees and others.

The Functions of Halfway Houses

The major functions of halfway houses overlap some of those associated with other programs for parolees. These include (1) parolee rehabilitation and reintegration into the community; (2) provisions for food and shelter; (3) job placement, vocational guidance, and employment assistance; (4) client-specific treatments; (5) reducing jail and prison overcrowding; (6) supplementing supervisory functions of probation and parole agencies; and (7) monitoring probationers, work and study releasees, and others with special program conditions.

Parolee Rehabilitation and Reintegration into the Community.   The major function of halfway houses is to facilitate offender reintegration into the community (Sinnett, 1970). This is accomplished, in part, by providing necessities and making various services accessible to offenders. The administrative personnel of halfway houses as well as the professional and paraprofessional staff members assist in helping offenders with specific problems such as alcohol or drug dependencies. Often, parolees have worked out a plan for themselves in advance of their parole date. This plan is subjected to scrutiny by parole board members, and the parolee often has the assistance of a PO in its preparation.

Provisions for Food and Shelter.   Some parolees have acquired savings from their work in prison industries, while other parolees have no operating capital. Thus, halfway houses furnish offenders with a place to stay and regular meals while they hunt for new occupations and participate in self-help programs. Furthermore, halfway house personnel help offenders locate apartments or more permanent private housing for themselves and their families (Donnelly and Forschner, 1984, 1987).

Job Placement, Vocational Guidance, and Employment Assistance.   Almost every halfway house assists offenders by furnishing them job leads and negotiating contacts between them and prospective employers (Gotwalt, 1984; National Alliance of Business, 1983). Some halfway houses provide offenders with financial subsidization that must be repaid when the offender has successfully acquired employment and is relatively stable. However, programs such as the Transitional Aid Research Project (TARP) in Georgia and Texas found that such subsidization sometimes led to offenders squandering their money on drugs or alcohol and/or drinking more frequently (Curtis and Schulman, 1984).

Although women make up only about 4 percent of the entire inmate population of prisons and jails, some halfway houses are exclusively operated for female offenders. In Long Beach, California, sixty female federal offenders in a halfway house for women were studied between 1972 and 1977. It was found that their reentry into society was made considerably smoother through their affiliation with the Long Beach halfway house. Many female ex-offenders disclosed that the halfway house gave them an "edge" over other female parolees in returning to society and obtaining employment.

Client-Specific Treatments. Those offenders with special needs or problems (e.g., ex–sex offenders, drug addicts or alcoholics, or mentally retarded clients) benefit from halfway houses by being permitted the freedom to take advantage of special treatment programs. They may receive counseling, medical treatment, or other services custom-designed for their particular needs. If these offenders were to be placed on the street on parole directly from a prison or jail, the transition for some would be too traumatic, and it is likely that they would revert to old habits or dependencies.

Of course, not all halfway houses are equally effective in the treatments and services provided. In Texas, for instance, it is significant that recidivism among halfway house clients varies according to the particular halfway house selected (Eisenberg, 1985a). Thus, Eisenberg recommends that careful selection of a halfway house can result in substantially improved outcomes, especially where alcohol and drug abuse cases are involved or when clients have an assaultive history. This is due, in large part, to the greater closeness of supervision of clients by halfway house personnel in those offender-client cases requiring more intensive monitoring throughout the transition period.

Some halfway houses are designed to accommodate those offenders who are mentally ill or developmentally disabled (Lippold, 1985:46). In Washington State, the Department of Corrections began compiling records of mentally retarded inmates of prisons in 1977. As one result of this activity, special offender needs were targeted and authorities planned to establish several residential placement programs in various communities (Lippold, 1985:46). Two halfway houses were opened in 1980 and 1981 in the Tacoma area. These were called the Rap House and the Lincoln Park House and were large, older homes in a residential neighborhood (Lippold, 1985:82).

Lippold (1985:82) indicates that the staff of both Rap House and Lincoln Park House, includes a state supervisor, three parole officers who provide ongoing program supervision, a developmental disabilities specialist, therapists, cooks, a consulting psychiatrist, and a nurse. Parole officer caseloads that include parolees from these homes are deliberately small, usually less than 15. The homes are designed to help parolees with goal setting, skills training, and individual program planning. Each participant is screened by a community screening committee composed of area neighbors and corrections professionals. Entry into the program begins with a referral from either institutional staff, field probation or parole officers, or other agencies that deal with developmentally disabled or mentally ill prisoners.

Mental retardation, indicated by an IQ of 69 or lower, qualifies a person for place-ment in Rap House, and evaluations and diagnoses are made by psychiatrists or clinical psychologists. Persons suffering from cerebral palsy, epilepsy, dyslexia, autism, auditory impairment, or other visual handicap may be referred (Lippold, 1985:82).

The resident at Rap House or Lincoln Park House moves through four phases of increasingly expanded privileges, with the eventual goal of complete re-lease into the community. Rules are tight and inappropriate behavior may result in termination from the program and return to a state institution or county jail (Lip-pold, 1985:82). Inmates with personality or severe behavioral disorders cannot par-ticipate in the program. People who are selected to participate must be medication compliant at all times.

Lippold (1985:112) says that between 1980 and 1983, 22 residents successfully completed their programs. However, 35 clients were terminated. Of those 35 termi-nations, 18 were readmitted to the program and have either completed it success-fully or were still there at the time the study was conducted in 1984. Lippold says that "the Rap House and Lincoln Park experiences clearly have demonstrated their value in dealing with this population. They also have clearly identified the ne-cessity of program flexibility, specialized staff training, systemwide cooperation, and the intraagency support needed for successful management of the mentally and developmentally disabled offender" (1985:112).

Some halfway houses are designated *co-correctional* and serve the needs of both male and female adult offenders. One of these projects is the Cope House, a nonprofit, community-based correctional agency that attempts to rehabilitate and reintegrate adult offenders (Donnelly and Forschner, 1987:7). It was founded in 1975 in Cincinnati, Ohio. Between January 1980 and December 1982, researchers studied the characteristics of 417 Cope House clients as well as factors seemingly associated with their success or failure in the program (Donnelly and Forschner, 1987:10). Donnelly and Forschner (1987) note that Cope House has four or five full-time professional staff and seven part-time employees. It has a 22-bed capacity. The clientele consist primarily of federal, state, and county prereleasees. Chronic and violent offenders, rapists, psychotics, the severely retarded, arsonists, and se-vere drug and alcohol abusers are not admitted.

When clients enter Cope House, they are interviewed by an examiner who administers a standard intake questionnaire. The Cope House programming cen-ters around a behavioral contract called a Mutual Agreement Plan (MAP) mod-eled after the Massachusetts Halfway House Association. This contract is client oriented and focuses on employment, educational training, housing, and social ser-vices (Donnelly and Forschner, 1987:8). Most of the women in Cope House during the study period were misdemeanants, whereas the male offenders were convicted primarily of felony offenses. This could likely account for the fact that 82 percent of the women and 58 percent of the men successfully completed the program.

Reducing Jail and Prison Overcrowding. Any program that provides a safety valve for prison or jail populations contributes to reducing overcrowding. Thus, halfway houses alleviate jail and prison overcrowding in that some probationers are "diverted" to them, whereas certain inmates may be paroled to them for brief periods as transitional phases. Probably the major function of halfway houses is to assist offenders in becoming reintegrated into society after long periods in secure confinement. But as we have seen, the functions of such houses have become diversified over the years. In any case, the existence of halfway houses has contributed to some reduction in jail and prison overcrowding as both a front-end and back-end solution (Curtis and Schulman, 1984; Dowell, Klein, and Krichmar, 1985; Hicks, 1987; Petersilia, 1987c).

Supplementing Supervisory Functions of Probation and Parole Agencies.   One latent function of halfway houses is to exercise some degree of supervision and control over both probationers and parolees. These supervisory functions are ordinarily performed by probation or parole officers. However, when some inmates are released to halfway houses, halfway house staff assume a high degree of responsibility for client conduct (Donnelly and Forschner, 1987). Some experts believe that the dual responsibilities of supervising and controlling clients and simultaneously providing them with counseling services are in direct conflict. Halfway house staff should counsel clients, not control their behavior, according to this argument (Ruygrok, 1988).

Monitoring Probationers, Work or Study Releasees, and Others with Special Program Conditions.   For paroles, halfway houses are intended to serve as transitional residences, located within the community, a home where these former prison inmates can adjust to life outside prison. Occasionally, a requirement or condition associated with parole is to reside in a halfway house for a predetermined period. The offender benefits by being provided basic necessities such as food, clothing, and shelter, as well as employment opportunities that serve to defray the costs of maintaining these homes (McCarthy and McCarthy, 1984:202).

Halfway houses also accommodate those probationers who require more supervision than they would otherwise receive under standard probation. When these offenders stay in halfway houses, they may be required to observe several rules. They may be required to observe curfew during the evening hours. During the daytime, they perform their jobs in the community. In Minnesota, for example, the **P.O.R.T. (Probationable Offenders Rehabilitation and Training) Program** is operated to serve the needs of both adults and juveniles (McCarthy and McCarthy, 1984:120–121). Such facilities are especially workable for juveniles without families or with parents declared unfit and irresponsible by the court. The duration of an offender's stay in these halfway houses is about 18 months (McCarthy and McCarthy, 1984:121).

The program's purposes are to

1. Reintegrate ex-convicts into their communities by providing a temporary shelter and limited monitoring.
2. Provide counseling, if needed.
3. Provide job placement or employment assistance, and/or to function as an ex-inmate's spokesperson if problems on the job should arise.

4. Provide medical treatment, if needed, in the case of alcohol abuse or drug dependency.
5. Provide emergency aid or paralegal assistance if an ex-offender is rearrested or becomes involved in a police matter.
6. Provide skill or vocational training, or assistance in locating where such training can be obtained.
7. Provide crisis management services when needed.
8. Provide pre- and postnatal care for pregnant ex-offenders.
9. Provide temporary foster care for youthful offenders.
10. Monitor offenders who are expected to perform some public service/restitution to/for community/victims.
11. Assist ex-offenders with rehabilitative plans. (Dowell, Klein, and Krichmar, 1985; National Alliance of Business, 1983; Orsagh and Marsden, 1985).

Nearly 20,000 parolees were assigned to community homes, either state operated or under private contract, or to some other comparable program in 1994 (American Correctional Association, 1994:xxviii–xxix). Costs of operating a majority of these halfway houses range from $15 to $25 per day per resident, with the state accounting for about 75 percent of the funding and city and county monies providing the remainder (G. Wilson, 1985:158–159).

A Profile of Halfway House Clients

A profile of halfway house clients is difficult to present here because of the current diversity of halfway houses throughout the United States. Some are designed for juveniles, while others are designed for adults. Among adult offenders who might be eligible for halfway house assignments, certain halfway houses may be more appropriate, such as those catering to offenders with former or present drug or alcohol abuse problems, or those who may be mentally ill. Furthermore, the profile of halfway house clientele changes annually. Indeed, Bonta and Motiuk (1990: 498–499) underscore this problem by noting that correctional personnel are often frustrated because it is difficult to identify low-risk inmates suitable for halfway house placement. Even clinical assessments of various inmates are unreliable and have unacceptably high error rates (Alexander and Austin, 1992; Bonta and Motiuk, 1990:498). Despite these chronic classification problems, correctional staff frequently make arbitrary decisions and place a variety of offenders into halfway houses for societal reintegration purposes (Bonta and Motiuk, 1990:498). In some instances, prison administrators exercise considerable discretion by placing some of their inmates into halfway houses while these offenders are serving sentences of imprisonment (Beha, 1975; Bonta and Motiuk, 1987).

Some idea of the nature of halfway house clientele might be gleaned from an inspection of various studies of halfway house residents. For example, Latessa and Travis (1991) conducted a quasi-experimental study of 132 probationers who resided in two halfway houses in 1983. Using Travis's (1985) previous designation, these probationers could be classified as halfway-in clients. These probationers exhibited the characteristics shown in Table 11.1.

TABLE 11.1 Characteristics of Halfway-In Clients

Characteristic	Halfway House		Probation	
	N	Percentage	N	Percentage
Gender				
Male	78	59.1%	80	57.1%
Female	54	40.9	60	42.9
Race				
White	83	65.4%	77	55.8%
Black	44	34.6	61	44.2
Age				
18–21	55	43.3%	35	25.1%
22–30	41	32.2	67	48.2
31–40	20	15.7	28	20.1
41+	11	8.6	9	6.4
Education				
8 years of less	38	28.8%	18	12.9%
9–11 years	45	34.1	59	42.1
High school graduate	34	25.8	41	29.3
Postgraduate	15	11.4	22	15.7
Marital Status				
Married	39	29.8%	60	43.5%
Never married	84	64.1	65	47.1
Other	8	6.2	13	9.4

Source: Edward J. Latessa and Lawrence F. Travis III, "Halfway House or Probation. A Comparison of Alternative Dispositions." *Journal of Crime and Justice,* **14:**53–75, 1991. Reprinted with permission.

In the Latessa-Travis study, 59 percent of the halfway house residents were males, 65 percent were white, 75 percent were 30 or younger, and over half had less than a high school education. About 30 percent were married. These clients consisted of parolees, pretrial detainees, and furloughees (1991:57). Most had histories of alcohol and drug abuse, employment problems, and large numbers of prior arrests.

In an independent study of 417 halfway house clients in Cincinnati, Ohio, conducted by Donnelly and Forschner (1987), the sample consisted of a mixture of prereleasees, probationers, and parolees, including those with social and/or psychological problems. About 70 percent of these clients were male, over half had less than a high school education, 80 percent were 30 or younger, and about 20 percent were married. Thus, when we match the figures from the Latessa-Travis study and those of the Donnelly-Forschner study, there are some differences, but there are also several similarities.

When we attempt to examine the nature of offending that typifies either one or both of these samples studied, no clear-cut characteristics are found. In the Latessa-Travis study, for instance, felony property offending was the most frequent prior-record client characteristic (49 percent), followed by violent offending (26 percent), and drug offending (12 percent). The Donnelly-Forschner study noted that 91 percent of all halfway house clients had prior felony convictions. It is probably the case that general parolee information would describe the majority of halfway house residents, absent any specific survey documentation.

Weaknesses and Strengths of Halfway House Programs

Blanket generalizations about halfway house effectiveness are difficult because there is so much diversity among halfway house programs. Furthermore, these programs have been established on widely different philosophical bases or rehabilitative models (G. Wilson, 1985:160). But several attempts to measure halfway house effectiveness have been observed. Such effectiveness has been measured primarily in one of three ways. First, are halfway houses more cost-effective compared with incarceration? Second, do halfway houses actually assist in reintegrating offenders into society? And, third, do halfway houses reduce recidivism to a greater degree among parolees compared with other programs such as standard parole (G. Wilson, 1985:160–161)?

The cost-effectiveness of halfway houses is undisputed when contrasted with the cost of maintaining inmates in prisons or jails. Halfway houses are able to service ex-offenders at a fraction of the cost required to incarcerate them (Gotwalt, 1984; G. Wilson, 1985). Also, even though halfway houses are not necessarily useful for every parolee assigned to them, they do appear to function to the benefit of most clients (G. Wilson, 1985:161). And, there is also "fairly conclusive evidence" (G. Wilson, 1985:162) that halfway houses compared with traditional prison-parole cycle programs curb recidivism among parolees to a greater degree (Carlson and Seiter, 1977).

Some of the major strengths and weaknesses of halfway house programs have been summarized by Carlson et al. (1977):

1. Halfway houses are effective in preventing criminal behavior in the community as alternatives that involve community release.
2. The placement of halfway houses in communities neither increases nor decreases property values.
3. Halfway houses assist their clients in locating employment but not necessarily in maintaining it.
4. Halfway houses are able to provide for the basic needs of their clients as well as other forms of release.
5. At full capacity, halfway houses cost no more, and probably less, than incarceration, although they cost more than straight parole or outright release from correctional systems.

Donnelly and Forschner (1987:12) indicate that often, program failure is measured three ways: if the client absconded, committed a new criminal offense, or failed to obey house rules. Although these researchers found it difficult to identify any specific predictor variable associated highly with failure, they concluded that Cope House can be successful for certain groups of politically and sexually diversified offenders. But predictions of risk, of the likelihood to abscond, or of dangerousness are presently unreliable (Champion, 1994). The success of a halfway house or any other prerelease program designed to assist in the rehabilitation or reintegration of offenders into their communities is frequently measured by recidivism. Recidivism is often interpreted as program failure. But this is not necessarily the case.

Measures of recidivism vary considerably among studies (Melnicoe, 1990). For example, recidivism might be a simple re-arrest. Does re-arrest necessarily mean that the offender committed a new crime? What about a subsequent conviction? Or what if the offender is released without charges being filed? Some studies use rule violations as indicators of recidivism (Donnelly and Forschner, 1984). The offender failed to observe curfew and reported at 10:18 P.M. instead of 10:00 P.M. Or, the offender may fail a urinalysis test to detect drugs. Some medications legitimately prescribed for an ex-offender may cause positive results and provide misleading evidence about an ex-offender's suspected drug use.

Of course, the most serious measure of recidivism is a conviction for a new criminal offense while the offender is involved in a particular parole program. A newspaper headline such as "Man from Halfway House Kills Three at Local Restaurant" does little to enhance the public image of halfway houses and their usefulness (Walsh and Beck, 1990).

One of the more favorable studies of halfway houses and their rehabilitative effectiveness was conducted in Texas between 1983 and 1984. The Texas Department of Corrections (TDOC) tracked the progress of 2,072 prisoners who were paroled between January and June 1983 (Eisenberg, 1985a). Of these, about 25 percent or 536 were assigned to halfway houses. About 15 percent of all parolees had their parole revoked over the next one-year period. The TDOC study showed halfway house resident revocations were slightly lower compared with those parolees involved in other parole programs. For those halfway house cases with a history of alcohol abuse, only 7 percent had their parole revoked compared with 15 percent of the non–halfway house cases. And when salient factor scores were examined, those parolees with poor risk salient factor scores who were assigned to halfway houses did significantly better than similar non–halfway house cases (Eisenberg, 1985b). The TDOC concluded that halfway houses, at least in their jurisdictions, appeared to influence parolee outcomes favorably.

At the federal level, a study investigated the client success of adult male and female federal parolees assigned to Cope House, a halfway house located in Dayton, Ohio, between 1980 and 1982 (Donnelly and Forschner, 1984). Program failure was measured by either being removed from the house for violating house rules and regulations or for committing a new offense. Of the 409 residents examined during the two-year period, 35 percent failed and had their paroles revoked. Those most likely to fail were younger males with less education, while the most successful program participants were older, more educated females. Race and drinking history were unrelated to one's success at the halfway house. However, persons

BOX 11.1
Does House Arrest and Electronic Monitoring Prevent Crime and Control Criminal Behavior?

The Case of the 16-Year-Old Harris County, Texas, Juvenile

It wasn't supposed to work like this. The number of offenders supervised by electronic monitoring programs throughout the nation has grown rapidly during the 1980s and early 1990s. Many experts envision this supervisory method as the future of American corrections. Fewer than 100 electronic monitoring programs were in effect in 1986, but by 1989, there were 6,490 of them. A majority of those offenders on electronic monitoring are probationers, but increasing numbers of offenders are parolees. Parolees are ordinarily ex-cons who have been convicted of more serious felonies. The average duration of placing someone on electronic monitoring is about 80 days (*Corrections Compendium,* **16,** March 1991, and *NIJ Reports,* No. 222, Washington, DC: Department of Justice, 1991).

Another characteristic of electronic monitoring is that low-risk offenders are targeted for these programs. Ideally, electronic monitoring is supposed to heighten offender accountability and help probation and parole officers verify a client's whereabouts at any particular time, night or day. In Harris County (Houston), Texas, a program of electronic monitoring was established in April 1993. By December 1993, 43 clients had been outfitted with electronic anklets or bracelets. One of these was a 16-year-old youth who was awaiting trial on robbery charges. On Sunday evening, December 5, 1993, the youth removed the electronic bracelet, armed himself with a pistol, and robbed a fast-food restaurant. During the robbery, he shot and killed a 17-year-old youth working at the restaurant.

The media were quick to make a judgment. The electronic monitoring program *failed.* "No, it didn't fail," said Carole Allen, a spokeswoman for the Harris County Juvenile Detention Center. "The kid failed," she added. Allen is right. The program didn't fail. Electronic monitoring programs are designed to verify one's whereabouts, not inhibit or control their behavior. The bracelets or anklets are not tamper-proof and are easily removed. They are slightly more durable than plastic hospital identification bracelets used to identify patients. "Authorities" said that somehow, the teenager was able to remove the device and shoot the restaurant worker, strongly suggesting that the bracelet was some type of behavior control apparatus. This misconception of electronic monitoring and its objectives is hardly helpful to those wishing to promote such programs.

Who should be at fault when electronic monitoring devices fail? Can electronic monitoring programs fail? What criteria should be used to determine whether certain offenders should be fitted with such devices? How closely should they be supervised? Who should supervise them? Should they be subject to other controls and checks by the probation department and courts?

Source: Adapted from *Associated Press,* "Houston Police: Teen Discarded Ankle Monitor, Then Killed Restaurant Worker." *Minot (ND) Daily News,* December 10, 1993:A-2.

with prior records and those who started their criminal careers at earlier ages were also those most likely to fail (Donnelly and Forschner, 1984).

Finally, an examination of 493 prisoners assigned to the Savannah, Georgia, Transitional Center for male offenders, a halfway house for offenders prior to their discharge from imprisonment, showed that between January 1977 and March 1983, only 24.7 percent were returned to prison (Gotwalt, 1984).

One interesting aspect of each of the three studies reported is that emphasis was placed on program failure rather than program success. The Texas parolees had a success rate of 85 percent, whereas the Georgia sample exhibited a 75 percent success rate. Accordingly, 65 percent of the Cope House clients in Dayton, Ohio, were successful during the study period. Viewed in this fashion, the studies are impressive. Thus, statements such as "nothing works" as applied to halfway houses or any other type of offender rehabilitation program are only defensible to the extent that we have not, as yet, devised perfect programs that have 0 percent recidivism among program participants. No program currently established is that good. Some experts stress that the nothing-works philosophy overstates the case against offender rehabilitation and that if specific offender populations are dealt with through the application of rational choices in view of offender needs, program failures can be significantly reduced. For instance, an economically motivated offender could be treated fairly effectively through income-enhancing activities such as skills or vocational training or educational improvement (Orsagh and Marsden, 1985).

There is no question that halfway houses provide substantial support for parolees in making the transition from prison life to community living. Even poor risks (identified as such by their salient factor scores) are reasonably successful when assigned to halfway houses as a part of their transition to normal life on the outside. Many halfway houses are poorly or inadequately operated, however, and this undermines public confidence in the ability of such a program to assure public safety.

Community acceptance of halfway houses is fraught with many fears, however (Hecht, 1970). Many citizens believe crime rates are higher in those neighborhoods with halfway houses, although no evidence exists to support such beliefs (McCarthy and McCarthy, 1984:232–233). Also, some citizens believe that ex-offenders serviced by halfway houses are a risk to or endanger the public. Again, no direct evidence exists to show that community violence is any greater in those communities with halfway houses compared with those without them (Hecht, 1970). Another criticism is that it is difficult to assess the long-term effects of halfway house programs on clientele (Calathes, 1990; Wiederanders, 1990).

Some experts say public support can be obtained through effective public relations and public education programs. In Tennessee, after the enactment of a community corrections law, Tennessee officials implemented an aggressive public education program (Huskey, 1987:40). Most of Tennessee's newspapers, television stations, and radio networks featured interviews with corrections spokespersons, with a total audience reached in Tennessee and neighboring states of over 10 million. After the campaign, the Tennessee Department of Corrections received 18 applications for community corrections funds, nearly double the number of programs projected for funding for the first year. This represented 38 out of the state's 95 counties or about 40 percent (Huskey, 1987:40). It seems important that the negative media image of community corrections generally needs to be overcome in order for many of these programs including halfway houses to succeed.

In the meantime, the halfway house is a viable alternative for parolees, a significant support facility for making the transition from prison to living once again in the community. Certainly the management of some halfway houses could be improved, and staffing needs could be addressed more effectively through greater community–halfway house cooperation. There are no easy solutions, however.

COMMUNITY RESIDENTIAL CENTERS AND DAY REPORTING/TREATMENT PROGRAMS

Community Residential Centers

Closely related to halfway houses are community residential centers and day reporting/treatment programs. **Community residential centers** are transitional agencies located in neighborhoods where offenders may obtain employment counseling, food and shelter, and limited supervision pertaining to one or more conditions of probation or parole. Day reporting/treatment programs are an integral part of community residential centers. The Alaska Department of Corrections, for instance, operates several community residential centers as relatively open facilities located in neighborhoods. These centers rely heavily on community resources to provide most of the services required by offenders, including offender detention and/or supervision on behalf of the Department of Corrections (Alaska Department of Corrections, 1990). Alaska centers are designed to provide individuality for a variety of offender needs, including employment, housing, and counseling services. The diversity of clientele served by Alaska community residential centers includes furloughees, parolees, probationers, misdemeanants, and offenders who are under court orders to pay restitution or victim compensation. Citizen involvement is solicited through volunteer work.

Community residential centers have played a transitional role in corrections for many decades. In 1966, for instance, community residential treatment centers existed as transitions from prison to community life. They provided educational, vocational, and recreational activities for parolees and others. They were deliberately located in neighborhoods to facilitate the reintegration of parolees back into community life (Alper, 1966).

The Philosophy and Goals of Community Residential Centers

The philosophy of community residential treatment centers is reintegrative and rehabilitative. It was and continues to be the philosophy of community centers to vest clients with self-sufficiency and independence through appropriate counseling, employment assistance, and limited supervision (Collins and Richmond, 1971). Many residential treatment centers have emergency on-call services and 24-hour access by clients in need of special treatment or assistance (Mawhiney and Bassis, 1992).

A good example of a community residential treatment center is the one established in King County, Washington, in 1975 (Johnson, 1978). The Women's Community Center (WCC) started as a nonprofit facility in April 1975. It was originally designed to hold 22 women. Eligibility for admission to WCC was limited to convicted female felons who face commitment to prison, cannot be currently dependent on methadone maintenance, and cannot have a history of violent behavior. Selection of nonviolent clientele is a fairly consistent characteristic of such centers throughout the United States (Evatt and Brown, 1991; Murphy, 1983). Furthermore, prospective clients must agree to employment in a vocational training or academic program structured to encourage self-sufficiency and responsible behavior.

Between 1975 and 1978, 86 women had successfully completed the program, while 28 clients were returned to jail. At least 81 percent of the women served by the WCC would have been incarcerated anyway if WCC hadn't existed. Thus, net widening was not a consideration in this case. The cost of operating WCC then was about $28 per client per day. This is about one-fourth the cost of daily incarceration in Washington's prison system (Johnson, 1978). One important reason for the success of WCC was the support women received from WCC staff while housed there.

Day Reporting Centers

Day treatment centers are operated primarily during daytime hours for the purpose of providing diverse services to offenders and their families. A **day reporting center** is defined as a highly structured, nonresidential program utilizing supervision, sanctions, and services coordinated from a central focus (Curtin, 1990:8; Diggs and Pieper, 1994:9). Offenders live at home and report to these centers daily (Diggs and Pieper, 1994:9). As a part of community residential treatment centers, day treatment programs provide services according to offender needs (Parent, 1990a, 1990b). These services might include employment assistance, family counseling, and educational/vocational training. Day treatment centers can also be used for supervisory and/or monitoring purposes. Client behavior modification is a key goal of such centers (Bowling and Hobbs, 1990). Limited supervisory functions can be performed by day treatment centers as well, such as employment verification and evidence of law-abiding conduct for probationers and parolees. These centers are also operated for the purpose of providing family counseling in juvenile delinquency cases through parent education and support groups (Wolford and Miller, 1990).

Williams (1990:4) says that day reporting centers are like "invisible jails," or halfway houses without the houses. In a way, they are jails on an "out-patient" basis. Actually, they are a hybrid of intensive probation supervision, house arrest, and early release. Many participants serve out their last few weeks or months of jail still in the government's custody, but technically on their own—living at home, perhaps working at a regular job in the community (Williams, 1990:4).

Day reporting centers, such as those operating in Hampden County, Massachusetts, select clients who are considered "good clients" (Williams, 1990:7). These include those convicted of drug offenses, larceny, driving while intoxicated, breaking and entering of commercial buildings, and similar charges. Sex offenders and violent offenders are for the most part excluded. Typically, those offenders without an identified victim (e.g., property offenders), those with a home to go to, and those within six months of release from prison or jail are considered eligible. They must sign a contract about program expectations concerning home, work, schooling, financial matters, drug tests, counseling, community service, restitution, and sliding-scale payments and observe curfew, submit an intinerary about their day-to-day (and even hour-by-hour) activities, submit to urinalyses and drug checks, submit to frequent telephone checks, and participate in relevant programs, given the problems they may have (Williams, 1990:7).

OTHER PROGRAMS AND SANCTIONS

Fines

Fines and Criminal Statutes.   An integral part of sentencing in an increasing number of cases is the use of **fines** (Gordon and Glaser, 1991; Wheeler et al., 1990; Zamist, 1986). The use of fines as sanctions can be traced to preindustrialized and non-Western societies (Davis and Lurigio, 1992:25; Winterfield and Hillsman, 1993:1). Estimates suggest that over 14 million persons are arrested each year in the United States, and that a significant portion of these receive fines upon conviction (McDonald, Greene, and Worzella, 1992:1). Ordinarily, state and federal criminal statutes provide for various incarcerative lengths upon conviction. Additionally, various fines are imposed as "and/or" conditions exercised at the discretion of sentencing judges. For instance, if law enforcement officers were to violate one's civil rights by the unlawful use of physical force or excessive force in making an arrest, they might be subject to penalties, including confinement in a state penitentiary up to five years and a fine of "not more than" $10,000. This means that if these law enforcement officers are convicted of violating one's civil rights, the judge can sentence them to prison for up to five years and impose a fine of $10,000. This would be within the judge's discretionary powers (Cole, 1989).

Another example pertains to "driving-while-intoxicated" (DWI) or DUI (driving under the influence) cases. First offenders might be required to pay a fine of $250, $500, or more, including court costs. In Santa Ana, California, for instance, court costs are $1,100 or more. In addition, these offenders driver's licenses would be suspended for a period of months or years, and offenders might be required to attend victim impact panels, driving schools, M.A.D.D. meetings, Alcoholics Anonymous meetings, and/or submit to random alcohol checks. They might even be required to pay the costs of attending some of these required schools and meetings.

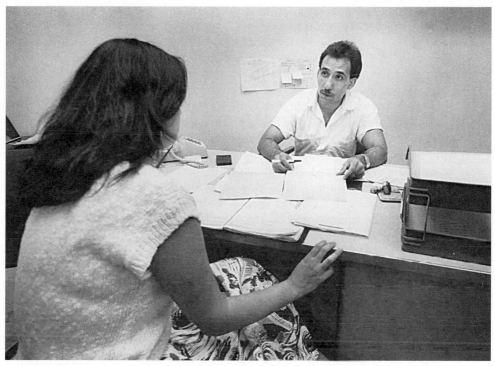

Payments of fines and restitution to victims are normally supervised by probation or court officers. (The Image Works)

Types of Fines and Fine Collection Problems.   Different types of fine scenarios have been described: (1) fines plus jail or prison terms; (2) fines plus probation; (3) fines plus suspended jail or prison terms; (4) fines or jail alternatives ($30 or 30 days); (5) fines alone, partially suspended; and (6) fines alone (Hillsman, Sichel, and Mahoney, 1984:12). The arguments for and against the use of fines as sanctions have also been clearly delineated. For instance, McDonald, Greene, and Worzella (1992:1) say that (1) fines are logically suited for punishment because they are unambiguously punitive; (2) many offenders are poor and cannot afford fines; (3) because the poor cannot afford fines as easily as the rich, there is obvious discrimination in fine imposition; (4) someone else may pay the fine other than the offender; (5) often, fine payments are unenforceable because of offender absconding; (6) courts lack sufficient enforcement capability; and (7) fines may actually increase crime so that the poor can get enough money to pay previously imposed fines. The problems of fine collection are such that less than half of the fines imposed are ever collected in most U.S. courts (Davis and Lurigio, 1992:26; Finn and Parent, 1992a, 1992b; McDonald et al., 1992). Billions of dollars are involved in fine nonpayment (Wheeler et al., 1990; Zamist, 1986). In New York City, for instance, a sampled jurisdiction disclosed that the fine payment rate upon conviction was 19 percent. In another nearby jurisdiction, the fine payment rate at conviction was only 14 percent (McDonald et al., 1992:33).

Suspending Fines.   In many criminal cases, however, fines are suspended. This is because indigent or poor offenders cannot pay these fines or would have great difficulty paying them and supporting their families or fulfilling any of their other financial obligations. From our examination of probation and parole revocation, we know that a probation or parole program cannot be revoked simply because of inability to pay program fees or fines. Thus, many judges do not impose fines because they will be uncollectible (Wheeler, Rudolph, and Hissong, 1989). Also, fines are not imposed in many cases because of certain jurisdictional precedents (Cole, 1989). In other instances, fines may be imposed but those obligated to pay fines will abscond. Even if those assessed fines do not abscond, the collection procedures in different jurisdictions are lax or unenforced. Many of these problems have been outlined in the literature (Finn and Parent, 1992a, 1992b; Hillsman, Sichel, and Mahoney, 1984; McDonald, Greene, and Worzella, 1992; Wheeler, Rudolph, and Hissong, 1989).

Day Fines

Until recently, the fine was not a prominent intermediate penalty in the United States because of deep skepticism among American criminal justice professionals (Winterfield and Hillsman, 1993:1). During the late 1970s and early 1980s, considerable effort was expended investigating alternative sentencing for offenders different from traditional indeterminate sentencing. Some experts have attributed this shift to heightened interest in just deserts and away from the rehabilitative model (Gordon and Glaser, 1991:651). Besides attempting to devise more equitable sentencing schemes through guidelines-based sentencing, determinate sentencing, and mandatory sentencing, offender accountability was heightened various ways. Some of these ways involved restitution, victim compensation, and fines, with some or all of these fine payments being used to restore damaged victim property or pay for the costs of law enforcement necessary to apprehend offenders. However, a key issue continued to haunt sentencing courts: How much should fines be in relation to an offender's ability to pay?

One answer to this dilemma has been the *day fine,* an early European invention. **Day fines** are a two-step process whereby courts (1) use a unit scale or benchmark to sentence offenders to certain numbers of day-fine units (e.g., 15, 30, 120) according to offense severity and without regard to income; and (2) determine the value of each unit according to a percentage of the offender's daily income; total fine amounts are determined by multiplying this unit value by the number of units accompanying the offense (Winterfield and Hillsman, 1993:2). For instance, if Offender X were convicted of simple assault, this might have a unit value of 30. The offender may have a net daily income of $50. Suppose the percentage of the net daily income to be assessed as a fine is 10 percent. This means that the total fine would be $50 × 10% × 30 units (for simple assault), or $5 × 30 = $150. This $150 fine would be assessed an offender at the time of sentencing, and the method of fine payment would be determined as well. Fine payments may be in installments, usually over no longer than a three-month period (McDonald, Greene, and Worzella, 1992:35–37).

The Staten Island Day-Fine Experiment.   In August 1988, judges in the New York City borough of Staten Island established a day-fine system similar to that developed earlier in Europe. This experiment was conducted because this jurisdiction and others like it in New York had considerable trouble collecting fines imposed when offenders were convicted of crimes. It was believed by Staten Island officials that day fines would actually increase the rate of fine payments, since day fines were determined in accordance with ability to pay. The project's planners had several goals in mind:

1. A system of sentencing benchmarks proposing a specific number of day-fine units for each criminal offense.
2. A system for collecting necessary information about offenders concerning their ability to pay.
3. Policy guidelines and easy-to-use methods for establishing the value of each day-fine unit imposed for each offender.
4. Strategic improvements in the court's collection and enforcement mechanisms.
5. A microcomputer-based information system that automates and records collection and enforcement activities (McDonald, Greene, and Worzella, 1992:19–22).

Establishing the amount of a day-fine unit involved determining net daily income expected as well as the number of dependents. Day-fine unit amounts would be scaled down according to increased numbers of dependants. Thus, every effort was made to distribute day fines equitably, according to ability to pay. This is in stark contrast with the idea of a fixed-fine system imposed on offenders, regardless of their earnings or numbers of dependents.

The Staten Island experiment wanted to determine several things. First, were day fines higher or lower than fines previously assessed for similar offenses? Second, would the burden of calculating day-fine amount deter fine collection? And, third, would the new collection techniques used with day fines have any favorable impact on collection outcomes? The results were favorable.

In a pilot study involving the use of day fines in Staten Island between April 1987 and March 1988, the total fine amounts imposed by the courts increased by 14 percent, while fines for average penal law offenses increased by 25 percent. Further, judges' sentencing decisions were generally unaffected by day fines. And most important, collection rates under the new day-fine system rose to 85 percent.

Table 11.2 shows a comparison of fine amounts levied during the pilot year in the Staten Island experiment. Capped collection amounts were those governed by statute. Thus, day-fine payments could not exceed statutory maximum fines for specific offenses, despite the fact that a day-fine amount may be generated in excess of this statutory maximum. A theoretical projection was made to determine the fine amounts collected under the day-fine scenario and pre-day-fine collection methods.

TABLE 11.2 Comparison of Fine Amounts Levied in Pilot Year, Capped by Statutory Maximums and Uncapped

| | Pre-Day-Fines Pilot | | Capped | | | | | | Uncapped | | | | | |
| | | | Day Fines and Flat Fines | | Day Fines Only | | % of Total[a] | Day Fines and Flat Fines | | Day Fines Only | | % of Total[a]* |
	n	%	n	%	n	%		n	%	n	%	
$1–24	1	0.3	1	0.3	1	0.4	100.0	1	0.3	1	0.4	100.0
$25	33	8.3	4	1.1	3	1.3	75.0	4	1.1	3	1.3	75.0
$26–49	—	—	4	1.1	4	1.7	100.0	4	1.1	4	1.7	100.0
$50	69	17.3	29	8.0	12	5.0	41.4	29	8.0	12	5.0	41.4
$51–74	2	0.5	6	1.6	4	1.7	66.7	6	1.6	4	1.7	66.7
$75	34	8.5	15	4.1	10	4.2	66.7	15	4.1	10	4.2	66.7
$76–99	—	—	9	2.5	8	3.3	88.9	9	2.5	8	3.3	88.9
$100	78	19.5	38	10.4	22	9.2	57.9	38	10.4	22	9.2	57.9
$101–149	1	0.3	15	4.1	14	5.8	93.3	15	4.1	14	5.8	93.3
$150	14	3.5	18	4.9	11	4.6	61.1	18	4.9	11	4.6	61.1
$151–199	3	0.8	11	3.0	10	4.2	90.9	11	3.0	10	4.2	90.9
$200	22	5.5	18	4.9	11	4.6	61.1	18	4.9	11	4.6	61.1
$201–249	8	2.0	9	2.5	6	2.5	66.7	9	2.5	6	2.5	66.7
$250	79	19.8	124	34.0	84	35.0	67.7	56	15.4	16	6.7	28.6
$251–499	8	2.0	12	3.3	8	3.3	66.7	37	10.2	33	13.8	89.2
$500	22	5.5	22	6.0	12	5.0	54.5	17	4.7	7	2.9	41.2
$501–999	4	1.0	7	1.9	6	2.5	85.7	37	10.2	36	15.0	97.3
$1,000	21	5.3	22	6.0	14	5.8	63.6	16	4.4	8	3.3	50.0
$1,001+	—	—	—	—	—	0.0	—	24	6.6	24	10.0	100.0
Total	399	100.0	364	100.0	240	100.0	65.9	364	100.0	240	100.0	65.9
Total fines ordered	$82,060.55		$93,856.00		$61,994.00			$137,660.00		$105,798.00		
Average	$205.66		$257.85		$258.31			$378.19		$440.83		

[a]This percentage was calculated, for each fine amount, by dividing the number of day fines of that amount by the total number of fines of that amount, to determine what percentage were day fines.

Source: Winterfield and Williams, 1993:4.

Table 11.2 shows that an average of $440.83 would have been collected using uncapped day fines compared with $205.66 collected under pre–day-fine traditional fine methods (Winterfield and Hillsman, 1993:3–5).

Winterfield and Hillsman (1993:5–6) say that the new collection techniques established by the Staten Island project has had the following advantages over traditional or more routine court procedures related to fine assessments and payment:

1. More extended terms for payment of the larger day fines;
2. Fewer costly court appearances; and
3. Fewer warrants for nonappearance at postsentence hearings.

Considered significant in the Staten Island experiments was the individualized nature of fine assessments and collection. Clearly, determining one's fine according to their ability to pay and arranging for installment payments of these fines is a more profitable way of court operation as well as a means of enhancing offender accountability. Similar experiments have been conducted in Milwaukee with consonant results.

Outreach Centers. Outreach centers are substations or satellite offices of regular probation and parole agencies. These are usually located in the neighborhoods of offenders and are open on weekends and evenings to assist with offender emergencies or special problems (McCarthy and McCarthy, 1984:121). Often, these centers are staffed by paraprofessionals and volunteers who help offenders work out personal problems, find jobs, and adjust to community life. Outreach programs are operated in cities such as Denver and Philadelphia (McCarthy and McCarthy, 1984:121).

Parolees are served by outreach centers in many ways. It is worth noting that a list of outreach centers and modes of treatment for outreach clients would be a monumental task to accomplish (G. Wilson, 1985:155). Only a few of these have been listed below and are often equated with the functions such facilities serve.

Community Service Orders and Options

Increasingly, conditions are imposed on parolees and probationers that provide for fines, some amount of community service, and restitution to crime victims (Hudson and Galaway, 1990). Travis (1985) says that community service sentencing is one of the best examples of the use of probation as a means of achieving offender accountability (Allen and Treger, 1990). Although judges may impose fines as a part of an offender's sentence for almost any crime, in many jurisdictions, fines are imposed about a third of the time (Zamist, 1986). Furthermore, when fines are imposed, not all offenders pay them. In New York State, for example, 74 percent of all fines imposed were collected from offenders within one year of their sentences. Some were indigent and unable to pay any portion of their fines.

Under the Victim and Witness Protection Act of 1982 (18 U.S.C. Sec. 3579-

---

BOX 11.2
Collecting in Staten Island

The Day-Fine Program in Action

Actual collection methods used by the Staten Island experiment are illustrated in two different scenarios below.

Joseph Burke

Joseph Burke was prosecuted for stealing a car. He was arraigned for grand larceny (a class E felony); possession of stolen property (a class E felony); and unauthorized use of an auto (a class A misdemeanor). He pleaded guilty to attempted unauthorized use of an auto (a class B misdemeanor). Mr. Burke is 21 years old. He is single and lives with his mother, to whom he contributes support. He works at a restaurant and reports take-home pay of $180 per week. He was sentenced to pay a 10-unit day fine, and his unit value was set at $11.78. His fine totals $115. He was given an installment schedule for payment

and has paid his fine in five payments over three months.

Robert Silver

Robert Silver was prosecuted for trying to prevent the arrest of his brother and for possession of a pellet gun. He was arraigned for obstructing governmental administration (a class A misdemeanor) and a related administrative code violation. He pleaded guilty to disorderly conduct (a violation). Mr. Silver is 23 years old. He lives with his brother. When he was arrested, he was working as a stock clerk in a store, but at sentencing he said he was unemployed and living on savings. The judge assumed he could easily find another job and estimated his potential income at about $6 an hour. Mr. Silver was sentenced to pay a five-unit day fine with a unit value set at $19.64—for a total amount of $100. He paid the day fine in two installments over a period of one month.

Source: Adapted from McDonald, Greene, and Worzella, 1992:36–37.

3580, 1995), restitution to victims was incorporated as an option in addition to incarceration at the federal level. One flaw of the Act was that it left unspecified when restitution orders were to be imposed. Thus, judges could impose restitution orders at the time of sentencing, or parole boards could make restitution a provisional requirement for an inmate's early release (Fletcher, 1984). Victim advocates strongly urge that restitution to victims be an integral feature of the sentencing process (Carrington and Nicholson, 1984). Although federal judges now have such restitution options at their disposal, not all states have adopted similar options (Merritt, 1984).

Also, restitution to victims is often a victim-initiated action. Therefore, if the victim fails to notify the court of financial losses or medical expenses, the restitution order may be neglected. Currently, there are no reliable statistics concerning

Parole-eligible female inmates receive advance employment and parental assistance from outreach centers and other community agencies.
(Gary Wagner/Stock Boston)

the proportion of convictions for which restitution orders are imposed, nor are there statistics showing the extent to which probationers and parolees must make restitution as a part of their probation or parole programs (Fletcher, 1984).

Community service is different from restitution in that usually, although not always, offenders perform services for the state or community. The nature of community service to be performed is discretionary with the sentencing judge or paroling authority (Maher and Dufour, 1987). In some jurisdictions, prisoners must perform a specified number of hours of community service such as lawn maintenance, plumbing and other similar repairs, or services that fit their particular skills (Carter, Cocks, and Glaser, 1987). The philosophy underlying community service is more aligned with retribution than rehabilitation. Few judges in any jurisdiction offer community service sentences as alternatives to imprisonment, however (Immarigeon, 1986a, 1986b).

Forms of Community Service and Restitution

Community service is considered a punishment and is court-imposed (Galaway, 1988; Maher and Dufour, 1987; Williams, 1986). Many types of projects are undertaken by offenders as community service. Usually, these projects are supervised by POs or other officials, although reports are sometimes solicited from private individuals such as company managers or supervisors (U.S. National Highway Traffic Safety Administration, 1985). A portion of offender earnings is allocated to victims as well as to the state or local public or private agencies overseeing the community services provided (Florida Department of Corrections, 1986).

Restitution to victims may be through periodic payments from offender earnings while on work release, probation, or parole. Sometimes, restitution takes non-monetary forms; for example, offenders rebuild or restore property destroyed earlier by their crimes. But often, the restitution ordered by the court or specified by parole boards only partially covers the losses suffered by crime victims.

The Effectiveness of Community Service and Restitution

Serious questions are raised by authorities about the effectiveness of community service and restitution as sentencing options or parole program requirements. The fact that offenders are released into their communities for the purpose of performing community service raises a public risk issue for some people, although those offenders ordinarily selected for community service are low-risk and nonviolent (Mathias, 1986). Other questions relate to the personal philosophies of judicial and correctional authorities, the offender eligibility and selection criteria used among jurisdictions, organizational arrangements, the nature of supervision over offenders performing community services, and how such services are evaluated (Carter, Cocks, and Glaser, 1987).

Perhaps the best view of community service and restitution is that they are just and fitting accompaniments to whatever sentence is imposed by judges or whatever conditions are established by paroling authorities when considering inmates for early release. The element of retribution is strong, and it is believed by some experts that offenders are better able to understand the significance of the harm they inflicted on others by their criminal acts (U.S. National Highway Traffic Safety Administration, 1985; Young, 1984). Some experts have suggested that if properly implemented, community service can function effectively as an alternative to imprisonment (Immarigeon, 1986a, 1986b). However, there are those who oppose these programs as sanctions in much the same way as they oppose intensive supervised probation in lieu of incarceration (U.S. Probation Division, 1989).

Restitution Programs

An increasingly important feature of probation programs is restitution (Rubin, 1986; Staples, 1986). *Restitution* is the practice of requiring offenders to compensate crime victims for damages offenders may have inflicted (adapted from Davis and Lurigio, 1992:25). Several models of restitution have been described.

The Financial–Community Service Model. This model stresses the offender's financial accountability and community service to pay for damages inflicted upon victims and to defray a portion of the expenses of court prosecutions. It is becoming more commonplace for probationers and divertees to be ordered to pay some restitution to victims and to perform some type of community service. Community service may involve clean-up activities in municipal parks, painting projects involving graffiti removal, cutting courthouse lawns, or any other constructive project that can benefit the community (McDonald, 1986). These community service sentences are imposed by judges. Probation officers are largely responsible for overseeing the efforts of convicted offenders in fulfilling their community service obligations. These sentencing provisions are commonly called *community service orders.*

Community service orders are symbolic restitution, involving redress for victims, less severe sanctions for offenders, offender rehabilitation, reduction of demands on the criminal justice system, and a reduction of the need for vengeance in a society, or a combination of these factors (Donnelly, 1980; U.S. National Highway Traffic Safety Administration, 1985). Community service orders are found in many different countries and benefit the community directly (Lutz, 1990; Sapers, 1990). Further, where convicted offenders are indigent or unemployed, community service is a way of paying their fines and court costs. Donnelly (1980) summarizes some of the chief benefits of community service: (1) The community benefits because some form of restitution is paid; (2) offenders benefit because they are given an opportunity to rejoin their communities in law-abiding responsible roles; and (3) the courts benefit because sentencing alternatives are provided. Typically, offenders sentenced to community service should be individually placed where their skills and interests can be maximized for community benefit. Usually, between 50 and 200 hours of community service might be required for any particular convicted offender (Byrne, Lurigio, and Petersilia, 1992; Donnelly, 1980).

The Victim-Offender Mediation Model.   This model focuses on victim-offender reconciliation. Alternative dispute resolution is used as a mediating ground for resolving differences or disputes between victims and perpetrators (Patel and Soderlund, 1994). Usually, third-party arbiters, such as judges, lawyers, or public appointees, can meet with offenders and their victims and work out mutually satisfactory arrangements whereby victims can be compensated for their losses or injuries. (See the discussion of alternative dispute resolution in Chapter 4 for a more extended discussion of this process.)

The Victim Reparations Model.   This model stresses that offenders should compensate their victims directly for their offenses (Schneider and Schneider, 1985). Many states have provisions that provide *reparations,* or financial payments, to victims under a Crime Victims Reparations Act. The Act establishes a state-financed program of reparations to persons who suffer personal injury and to dependents of persons killed as the result of certain criminal conduct. In many jurisdictions, a specially constituted board determines, independent of court adjudication, the existence of a crime, the damages caused, and other elements necessary for reparation. Reparations cover such economic losses as medical expenses, rehabilitative and occupational retraining expenses, loss of earnings, and the cost of actual substitute services (Rothstein, 1974).

Restitution can heighten accountability and result in a reduction in recidivism among offenders. In Atlanta, Georgia, for example, 258 offenders participated in several experimental treatment programs; one of the programs included restitution. The restitution offender group had a 26 percent reduction in recidivism compared with other offenders where restitution was not included as a condition (Schneider and Schneider, 1985). But other experts caution that if restitution is not properly implemented by the court or carefully supervised, it serves little deterrent purpose (Staples, 1986).

KEY TERMS

Community residential center
Community service orders
Criminal contamination
Day fine
Day reporting center
Fine
Halfway house
Halfway-in house
Halfway-out house

Hope Hall
Hope House
International Halfway House Association (IHHA)
Isaac T. Hopper Home
Massachusetts Prison Commission
P.O.R.T. Program (Probationable Offenders Rehabilitation and Training)

QUESTIONS FOR REVIEW

1. What is a halfway house? Are there halfway houses for women? What are some of the functions of halfway houses?
2. Why are halfway houses important to inmates who have been imprisoned for many years?
3. What are some of the services provided to offenders by halfway house personnel?
4. Are prisoners in all states denied the right to vote in state elections?
5. What is the nature of community opposition to furlough and work release programs?
6. What is community service? Is it an effective deterrent to crime?
7. What is meant by restitution? What are some forms of restitution?
8. What is a day fine? What is the origin of the day fine?
9. What are some of the goals of the Staten Island experiments?
10. How are day-fine units calculated? What are the factors considered in these calculations?

12

Probation and Parole Officer Training, Retention, and Caseloads

Rewards and Hazards of PO Work

Introduction

Probation, Parole, and Corrections Officers: A Distinction

The Organization and Operation of Probation and Parole Programs

Selection Requirements, Education, and Training for POs

Probation and Parole Officer Caseloads

Officer-Client Interactions

The Changing Probation and Parole Officer Role

Probation and Parole Officer Labor Turnover

Stress and Burnout in Probation and Parole Officer Role Performance

Key Terms

Questions for Review

INTRODUCTION

In 1967, the President's Commission on Law Enforcement and Administration of Justice recommended that the training and educational standards of all law enforcement personnel should be upgraded (Zevitz, 1987a:89). This recommendation extended not only to front-line law enforcement officers who make arrests and investigate crimes, but also to all personnel who work with offenders in corrections. Between 1966 and 1985, the number of postsecondary institutions offering crime-related degree programs grew from 39 to 985 (Nemeth, 1986). Although estimates vary, there were over 1,500 degree-granting programs in criminal justice and other crime-related fields by 1994.

This chapter is about the recruitment, selection, and training of probation and parole officers. In the course of implementing the mandate of the 1967 President's Commission, significant developments have occurred in corrections generally and probation/parole specifically pertaining to improvements in programs, personnel, and policies in almost every local, state, and federal jurisdiction. We look at the state of probation and parole services today as well as in previous years. Even though considerable improvements have been made in efforts to recruit and retain quality personnel and upgrade the nature of services provided offenders, much more needs to be done. This chapter assesses the progress made as well as highlighting those areas in need of improvement.

PROBATION, PAROLE, AND CORRECTIONS OFFICERS: A DISTINCTION

Some confusion exists among the general public about what to call probation and parole officers. In a technical sense, probation and parole officers are also **corrections officers,** because part of their responsibilities include the rehabilitation and reintegration of offenders. This is generally considered an integral part of **corrections.** The *corrections officer* label also makes sense because most probation and parole departments in the United States come under the general administrative rubric, *Department of Corrections.* And, it has been increasingly customary to refer to *guards* in prisons and jails as *correctional officers* (Philliber, 1987:9–10). Both the American Jail Association and the American Correctional Association have made official statements to the effect that the term *guard* is outmoded, since it no longer reflects the skills and training required to perform correctional officer work. Furthermore, this labeling Tower of Babel is complicated and perpetuated by official state and federal reports lumping all correctional personnel (probation officers, parole officers, jail officers, prison officers, correctional officers, secretaries, jail and prison administrators, paralegals who work in jails and prisons, volunteers, and paraprofessionals who work in community corrections) into one general category (National Manpower Survey, 1978:8).

For clarity, *correctional officers* are prison or jail staff and their supervisors who manage inmates, while probation and parole officers supervise and manage probationers and parolees in a variety of offender aftercare programs (American Correctional Association, 1994:xlii–xlvi). Since the Departments of Correction in many states select POs as well as prison staff and conduct training programs for all of their correctional personnel, similar criteria are often used for selecting correctional officers as for POs. Thus, some useful information may be gleaned from the general correctional literature that may be applicable to POs as well as prison and jail personnel. This does not mean that prison and jail correctional officers necessarily share the same characteristics with POs. One major difference is that correctional officers manage and interact with incarcerated offenders, whereas POs manage and interact with nonincarcerated criminals. There are also differing pay scales, work requirements, and other important characteristics that serve to distinguish between these two officer populations that deal with offenders at different points in time.

A substantial and continuing increase in the number of personnel working in the area of adult and juvenile corrections has occurred since 1986. In 1994, there were over 370,900 personnel in corrections for both adults and juveniles. This represents an increase of 20 percent over the 309,361 personnel reported in 1992, a 30 percent increase over the 285,000 personnel in 1988, and a 73 percent increase over the 214,000 personnel in 1986 (American Correctional Association, 1994:xlii–xliii; *Corrections Compendium,* 1990b:14; *Corrections Compendium,* 1993a:4). These figures include probation and parole officers as well as their administrative staffs. These officers make up about 20 percent of all correctional personnel.

Probation officers are hired to manage probationers exclusively in many jurisdictions, whereas parole officers deal only with parolees. An argument may be made that probation officers deal with low-risk and less dangerous offenders compared with parole officers. Parole officers are assigned ex-convicts who have already served a portion of their sentences in prisons or jails, usually because of felony convictions. Confinement implies a greater level of dangerousness compared with those who are selected to participate in probation programs. Evidence suggests that probation officers are receiving more dangerous offenders into their charge annually through felony probation, as prison and jail overcrowding makes it impossible to incarcerate all criminals who should be incarcerated (Champion, 1988c; Petersilia, 1986a).

In many jurisdictions, probation and parole officers supervise both types of offenders interchangeably (American Correctional Association, 1994:xii–xiii). In many states, probation and parole officers are combined in official reports of statistical information to organizations such as the American Correctional Association. Within the adult category, states such as Alabama, Florida, Virginia, Washington, and Wyoming report total numbers of probation and parole aftercare personnel rather than separating them. Separate probation and parole officer designations are used in some states, including Arizona, North Carolina, Ohio, and Texas. In this and other chapters, probation and parole officers will be treated as a single category—as POs—while continuing to recognize that some jurisdictions make sharp distinctions between these officers according to the types of offender clientele supervised.

THE ORGANIZATION AND OPERATION OF PROBATION AND PAROLE PROGRAMS

Organizationally, probation and parole departments in various states are administered by different agencies. Although most states have departments of corrections that supervise both incarcerated and nonincarcerated offenders, these tasks are sometimes overseen in other jurisdictions by departments of human services, departments of youth services, or some other umbrella agency that may or may not have the expertise to service these clients adequately.

During the 1980s and 1990s, a growing concern has been the **professionalization of corrections** (Jurik and Musheno, 1986; Philliber, 1987; Sieh, 1990). When the **President's Commission on Law Enforcement and Administration of Justice** made its recommendations in 1967, few standards were in place in most jurisdictions to guide administrators in their selection of new recruits. Thus, it was not unusual for critics of corrections to frequently make unfavorable remarks about and unflattering characterizations of those who manage criminals and oversee their behaviors.

Some observers noted that correctional officers collectively were "a residue of the dark ages, but because of the complexity of contemporary correctional roles, new pools from which to recruit, and social science training, a new breed of correctional officer may emerge" (Pelfrey, 1986:65; Toch, 1978:20). The most unkind remarks were often directed at officers who were projected as less than quick-witted, too young, less than the highest level of intelligence, experience, and education, and sadistic (Davidson, 1974). Also, some correctional officer jobs were seen as requiring only "20/20 vision, the IQ of an imbecile, a high threshold for boredom and a basement position in Maslow's hierarchy" (Philliber, 1987:9; Toch, 1978). Although these criticisms and depictions were not specifically directed at probation and parole officers, they are nevertheless included within the same correctional rubric. Thus, unwarranted generalizations are made about those who are involved with corrections in any capacity, regardless of the different roles they perform and other important differences, including professional training, educational background, and human relations skills.

Despite considerable money invested in corrections generally by the Law Enforcement Assistance Administration and National Institute of Justice, critics continue to hold the view of the field as one in search of a focus (Watson, 1981). One expert has said that

> the field of corrections is likely to continue to flounder in the abyss of inefficiency unless major emphasis is placed on the selection and promotion of good managers. Private corrections is prospering because its agencies and corporations recognize the need for managerial talent and, generally, outclass public corrections in attracting and rewarding good managers while discarding poor or ill-suited ones. The time has come for state and local correctional agencies, including probation, parole, and institutional corrections, to awaken to better ways to identify good managers. (Pelfrey, 1986:65)

In recent years, administrators of corrections programs have done much to overcome these negative stereotypes. In a later section of this chapter, important changes in the upgrading and improvement of PO selections are described.

Selected Criticisms of Probation and Parole Programs

Why has corrections been viewed so unfavorably over the years? And, why have state and federal policymakers targeted probation, parole, and the field of corrections generally for massive institutional changes and reforms? Although no single answer adequately satisfies these and related questions, the most obvious explanation is that the public is dissatisfied with the correctional product. A great anomaly is that *corrections doesn't correct.* This statement applies to jails, prisons, and programs of probation and parole.

In the early years of correctional reforms, officials believed that the treatment or medical model was sound, and that rehabilitation on a large scale was possible for both incarcerated and nonincarcerated offenders. Of course, rehabilitation was projected as the direct result of proper therapeutic programs and treatments. Educational and vocational-technical programs were coupled with group and individual counseling in prisons and jails. Offenders sentenced to probation were slotted for involvement in various training courses and assigned to programs designed to improve their self-concept, skills, and marketability as job-holders and breadwinners.

The rehabilitative aim of corrections was not entirely abandoned, but, over the years, an increasingly skeptical public became disenchanted with what corrections officials espoused and how they sought to rehabilitate offenders. Too many ex-convicts were committing new crimes and subject to rearrests. Former clients of probation or parole programs were also apprehended for new law violations. To make matters worse, rearrests of offenders frequently occurred during the course of a criminal's participation in a probation or parole program.

Robert Martinson (1974), a criminologist, asked a crucial question, "What works?," concerning the criminal justice system. His response to his own question was, "Nothing works." This answer has become a widely used cliché, but, at the time, it had an immediate influence on both popular and professional thinking about rehabilitation as a correctional aim in all criminal justice system components (Walker, 1985:168). Martinson's proclamation was seriously received by the criminal justice community. In effect, Martinson had issued a challenge to corrections and to the general field of criminal justice to show precisely what had been accomplished as the result of a massive infusion of funds by the federal government and private resources since the original President's Commission recommendations in 1967 and the establishment of the **Law Enforcement Assistance Administration (LEAA).**

Martinson's own research critically evaluated studies of correctional programs between 1945 and 1967. He found only 231 studies during that period worthy of scientific merit. And, even these were beset with methodological and theoretical faults that seriously questioned the findings each deduced. Martinson concluded that both corrections officials and the academic community-at-large were grossly negligent by failing to provide a means whereby self-assessments and effectiveness evaluations of programs could be conducted. Thus, it was impossible to determine any particular program's effectiveness and whether Law Enforcement Assistance Administration monies had been wisely invested. Martinson believed the case to be largely one of massive professional irresponsibility (Walker, 1985:169). In fairness to him as well as to the field of corrections, Martinson did not reject all correctional programs outright. Elements of success were associated with many of the programs studied, although frequently the level of success was not as high as Martinson and others desired.

In the aftermath of Martinson's criticisms, the New York Governor's Special

Committee on Criminal Offenders, the committee that originally sponsored Martinson's research, sought to suppress his report from public disclosure. It was well known that fairly large sums of money were being extended to this and other committees from the Law Enforcement Assistance Administration and other government sources during that period, and the release of such unfavorable information about corrections might cause the curtailment of these monies. Martinson's work was eventually published despite committee objections and legal problems, and a special National Academy of Sciences Panel on Research on Rehabilitative Techniques later supported Martinson by affirming that his findings were essentially correct (Walker, 1985:169).

During the same period when Martinson criticized and questioned the rehabilitative value of corrections, other sectors of the criminal justice system were undergoing scathing criticism from both the public and private researchers. For example, the **Kansas City Preventive Patrol Experiments** had recently been concluded. These experiments were also funded by a grant from the LEAA, and the intent was to show the effect on crime of more intensive police patrolling of certain sectors of Kansas City compared with less intensive police patrols (Kelling, Pate, Dieckman, and Brown, 1974). Kansas City police patrols were tripled in some sections of the city, while no patrols were assigned to other sections, and police officers responded to calls for assistance on an as-needed basis. The findings revealed no significant differences in crime rates regardless of the presence or absence of police patrols. This finding shocked the law enforcement community and undermined efforts by police chiefs and mayors in different jurisdictions to obtain more funds to hire more officers to reduce crime. If hiring more police officers doesn't reduce crime, why hire more police officers? The Kansas City Preventive Patrol Experiments were controversial, and they occurred during a period when monies for law enforcement studies were abundant from various federal agencies. Increasing or decreasing police visibility in various sections of Kansas City had no effect on crime in those city sections. Spending more money to fight crime did not result in less crime.

The Law Enforcement Assistance Administration was terminated in 1984. One reason for the organization's demise was the lack of successful results associated with the studies it funded. Since a large portion of funds was allocated to corrections, corrections was adversely affected when these funds were withdrawn. But the lack of success of various corrections experiments and programs, many couched in the context of rehabilitation, contributed to the Administration's termination in ways similar to the law enforcement experiments in Kansas City and other jurisdictions.

Efforts have been made to link the failure of rehabilitation in corrections with specific programs and personnel. The most common criticisms of rehabilitation programs are that they are disorganized as well as inadequately funded and staffed. It should be noted that few programs dependent on public funds for their operation and continuation will admit to adequate staffing and funding. Thus, most programs are in a perpetual state of need, with requests made annually for larger portions of public resources and budgets stretched to justify greater allocations for agency funding.

If more police patrols in Kansas City were unable to secure a commensurate drop in crime in the affected areas, what evidence is there to suggest that enlarging correctional staffs and spending more money on correctional programs will necessarily result in lower recidivism rates? Interestingly, the enlargement of correctional staffs, especially in probation and parole, has made it possible in some jurisdictions for officers to supervise their clients more closely through lower offender caseloads. However, greater supervision of offenders has resulted occasionally in an increase in the number of reported technical violations of an offender's probation or parole program (Walker, 1985:188). Technical violations do not mean that crimes among probationers and parolees have increased, only that they are now more frequently observed and recorded. These offenders stand a good chance of having their probation or parole revoked because of such violations, thus giving the public the impression that their criminal activity is increasing.

Criticisms of correctional personnel generally have centered on the inadequacy of their training, lack of experience, and poor educational background. For example, studies of prison correctional officers have shown that they are typically white, come from rural areas, are politically conservative, have mixed job histories, have entered corrections work at a turning point or after failure in another career, or are merely holding their present job while anticipating a career move to a more promising alternative (Philliber, 1987:10–11; Sieh, 1992).

The location of correctional facilities influences the quality of the employment pool from which recruits are selected. Those facilities located in remote rural areas may not attract those who are highly educated and have had previous experience working closely with others under conditions of stress. Much of the training they receive is on-the-job training, or learning by watching their work associates. Educational requirements for these positions are not particularly stringent in many jurisdictions. If many of these officers consider their work temporary, it is difficult for them to achieve the personal level of commitment required to do a good job in the supervision of dangerous offenders (Nau, 1987:28–31).

To the extent that probation and parole officers are similar in their backgrounds and training compared with corrections officers who perform inmate management chores, then these characteristics have implications for the quality of services delivered by probation and parole agencies. If it is true that a majority of probation and parole officers enter this work with little or no training, that they lack the enthusiasm and energy to perform their jobs efficiently and effectively, and that they lack basic educational skills for dealing with offender clients, then it may be that these factors significantly influence the quality of services delivered to offenders (Bishop, 1993:13–14). If probation and parole officers cannot cope effectively with the demands of their jobs because of their own limited resources and experiences, then suggested reforms involving their professionalization would be justified.

All too often, **professionalization** is equated with the acquisition of more formal education rather than with the acquisition of practical skills that involve one-to-one human relationships with different types of offender-clients. Probation officers frequently hear the phrase, "That may be what they taught you at the academy, but here's the way we do it here," whenever they are given their initial probation or parole assignments (Cheatwood and Hayeslip, 1986:15). Educational programs for officers often overemphasize the laws and rules of institutions and the mechanics of enforcement. Often underemphasized are "people skills" and the ability to cope with human problems (e.g., physically or mentally impaired clients), those abilities required if the quality of officers is to be raised (*Georgia Parole Review*, 1990:174–176).

Although the following list is not exhaustive, it contains some of the more prevalent reasons for criticisms of probation and parole programs and personnel:

1. *Probation and parole programs have historically been fragmented and independent of other criminal justice organizations and agencies.* Without any centralized planning and coordinating, probation and parole programs have developed haphazardly in response to varying jurisdictional needs. Furthermore, developing programs have not instituted regular self-assessments of agency or personnel effectiveness (Watson, 1981:26–27).

2. *The general field of corrections has lacked professionalization associated with established fields with specialized bodies of knowledge* (Whitehead and Lindquist, 1992:13–15). Often, corrections officers have secured their training through affiliation with an academic program in sociology, criminal justice, or political science. While these programs offer much relating to the correctional field, they are not designed to give corrections career-oriented students the practical exposure to real problems faced by officers on duty and dealing with real offenders.

3. *Most jurisdictions have lacked licensing mechanisms whereby officers can become certified through proper in-service training and education.* In 1985, training was provided for probation and parole officers in central academies in only 18 states and at decentralized academies in only 6 states (Dare, 1992; Library Information Specialists, Inc., 1985a, 1985b).

4. *Until the early 1980s, only one state required a college education of probation or parole officer applicants, and some states had as their only prerequisite the ability to read and write, presumably for the purpose of completing PSIs* (Snarr and Wolford, 1985). Despite the fact that the relation between a college education and probation or parole officer effectiveness has not been demonstrated conclusively, some evidence suggests that college training is particularly helpful in the preparation of presentence investigations and understanding criminal law and potential legal issues and liabilities that might arise in the officer-client relationship (Library Information Specialists, Inc., 1985a, 1985b; Maine Criminal Justice Academy, 1986; Philliber, 1987).

5. *Past selection procedures for probation and parole officers have focused on physical attributes and security considerations* (Wahler and Gendreau, 1985). An emphasis in recruitment on physical attributes has historically operated to exclude women from probation and parole work, although there is evidence showing a greater infusion of women into correctional roles in recent years (Carlen and Davis, 1987). For example, in 1986 only 12 percent of 88,492 corrections officers in the United States were women (Hunter, 1986). By 1994, the number of corrections officers had more than doubled to 179,958. Of these, 36,500, or 20.3 percent, were women (American Correctional Association, 1994:xliv–xlv). In recent years, screening mechanisms have changed to include psychological interviews and personality assessment inventories for the purpose of identifying those most able to handle the stresses and psychological challenges of probation and parole work, with less emphasis on physical abilities. Several studies have found that PO work generally is more enriching and complicated, in the sense that personal problem-solving skills are becoming more important compared with past

years, when learned "standard" solutions were applied consistently to similar situations (Leonardi and Frew, 1991; Whitehead, 1986b). Thus, PO work has become more of an art than the application of a limited range of standard strategies for diverse client problems, regardless of whether those strategies are applicable or inappropriate.

6. *Probation and parole officer training has often been based on the military model used for police training* (Cheatwood and Hayeslip, 1986:15). In those states with centralized corrections officer training and in-service programs for those preparing for careers in probation and parole work, a fundamental program flaw has been overreliance on police training models whose relevance is frequently questioned by new recruits. Highly structured training programs frequently fail to provide prospective probation and parole officers with the sorts of practical experiences they will encounter face-to-face with offender-clients. In the 1980s some in-service training of up to so many hours annually is required for probation and parole officers in 44 states, and slightly more than half of these jurisdictions use private trainers as part of their programs (Library Information Specialists, Inc., 1985b).

In view of a number of continuing problems confronting those entering probation and parole service as a career, it is understandable why there is a high degree of labor turnover among POs (Jacobs and Retsky, 1975; Whitehead and Lindquist, 1985). Although POs account for only about 10 to 15 percent of the corrections personnel component, they make up the largest single correctional service in terms of numbers of offenders served (U.S. Bureau of Justice Statistics, 1983). For example, the probation and parole populations in 1984 grew by 9 percent, with three times as many offenders being supervised in the community on probation or parole as there are incarcerated in prisons or jails (Greenfeld, 1987a).

The rapid increase in the offender population managed by POs has created significant logistical problems. Some observers have indicated that POs must continue to maintain their current level of activity in an environment in which the public demands greater punishment, incarceration, and a decrease in public expenditures (Callanan, 1986:18). Furthermore, there is a lack of consensus among POs about their goals and professional objectives, as well as how these goals ought to be realized. Some POs see themselves as brokers who provide referral services to their offender-clients or arrange offender contacts with community agencies that provide special services, including counseling and training. Other POs see themselves as **caseworkers** who attempt to change offender behavior through educating, enabling, or mediating whenever offender problems occur. Many POs have asked whether the public has come to expect too much from them, particularly in view of financial cutbacks and greatly increased offender caseloads (Callanan, 1986:18).

Probation and Parole Officers: A Profile

Interacting with ex-offenders, visiting their homes or workplaces, and generally overseeing their behavior while on probation or parole is a stressful experience. The danger associated with PO work is well documented, and each day exposes most POs to risks similar to those encountered by police officers (American Correctional Association, 1985; Cullen et al., 1985; Whitehead, 1985a, 1985b, 1986b, 1987). Of course, offenders are obliged to comply with probation or parole program requirements, whatever they might be, and to be responsive and accessible whenever POs wish to contact them.

The primary control mechanism operating to moderate offender behavior is the probation or parole revocation power possessed by POs. Although their recommendations for a parole or probation revocation are not binding on any body convened to hear allegations of violations against an offender, it is their report that initially triggers a revocation proceeding. An unfavorable report about an offender may involve a technical violation or a serious crime allegation. POs often overlook minor supervision violations, in part because they judge such violations not to be serious and also because they do not wish to prepare the extensive paperwork that is a preliminary requirement for a formal probation or parole revocation hearing. Despite the leverage POs have over their offender-clients, the possibility of violent confrontation with injury or death and hostility from the public-at-large make PO work increasingly stressful and demanding.

Characteristics of Probation and Parole Officers. Who are probation and parole officers? What are their characteristics? Although little comprehensive information about POs exists, surveys have been conducted in recent years that depict the characteristics of those performing various correctional roles. These surveys indicate a gradual move toward greater corrections officer professionalization. One indication of this greater professionalization has been the movement toward accreditation and the establishment of accreditation programs through the American Correctional Association (ACA) and the American Probation and Parole Association (APPA).

The ACA was established in 1870 with Rutherford B. Hayes as its first president. Since its inception, the ACA has advocated general improvements and reforms throughout all phases of corrections, including the professionalization of POs. The ACA sponsors training seminars and educational programs throughout the United States. Those who belong to the ACA or to a similar organization, such as the APPA, receive current information about parole and probation innovations and programs. Many officers attend annual meetings of the associations and learn much from other POs and corrections professionals. Being up-to-date in the correctional field is not contingent on memberships in these or any other similar organizations; nevertheless, membership at least evidences support for these organizations and their goals. One goal is upgrading the selection and training requirements of correctional officers, including POs.

The *Corrections Compendium* (1990) conducted a survey of parole officers in 1990, while the American Correctional Association solicited information from its probation and parole officer membership in 1994. Even though the responses may not necessarily be typical of all correctional personnel in the United States, the ACA boasts a membership of about a third of all correctional personnel nationwide. Over 10,000 ACA members responded and provided information about their age, educational level, and other pertinent information concerning the positions held. Table 12.1 summarizes selected socioeconomic and job-related characteristics for these responding POs.

TABLE 12.1 Summary Characteristics for Probation and Parole Officers in the United States

Characteristic	Percentage/Median	
	ACA[a]	CC[b]
Age	34	36
Gender		
Male	64.4%	74.6%
Female	35.6%	25.4%
Educational Level	B.S.	B.S.
Length of experience	9–11 yrs.	11–12 yrs.
Salary (average annual) (ACA)	$16,135–$41,215	
(CC)	$12,768–$34,560	
Cultural background		
Caucasian	82.4%	80.2%
Black	9.6%	12.3%
Hispanic	4.1%	5.0%
Other	3.9%	2.5%

Source: [a]*Corrections Today,* "Survey" 1994; [b]"Survey I: Fourteen State Systems Reduce Correctional Officer Positions." *Corrections Compendium,* **17**:7–20, 1990.

A majority of POs are male and white, possess bachelor's degrees, and have 9 to 12 years experience. The length of employment for these POs is longer than the period suggested by others who note a high amount of turnover among POs. One reason for this apparent discrepancy may be that those belonging to the American Correctional Association (ACA) are perhaps more committed to their work as evidenced through their membership in this voluntary professional association. Average PO annual salaries in 1994 ranged from $12,768 to $41,215. These salaries are slightly higher than those reported by Shirley Davis (1990) for POs surveyed in 1990 ($12,768–$34,560).

The larger proportion of women in the *Corrections Compendium* survey is actually larger than the proportion of women in corrections generally. As we have seen, about 21 percent of all corrections officers were women, according to ACA 1994 figures (American Correctional Association, 1994:xliv–xlv). However, those women pursuing PO careers believe that they must constantly prove themselves to their male co-workers (Hunter, 1986). This greater aggressiveness among female POs may manifest itself in part through more frequent professional memberships in ACA or APPA.

Most POs in the sample studied have a bachelor's degree as the median educational level attained. However, a majority of state systems (29) require the bachelor's degree as the minimum educational level for entry-level parole officer positions. In many states, however, the general entry-level requirements for PO positions are less stringent. In 1990, 16 jurisdictions required a bachelor's degree or "equivalent experience" (Su Davis, 1990b:7). Davis (1990b:7) notes, however, that in at least 42 systems surveyed, the minimum entry-level requirements for PO work were exceeded by applicants.

Considering the relatively low salaries of POs compared with those in other correctional positions and in the private sector, their higher median ages, and their comparatively lower educational levels, it is understandable that probation and parole have drawn criticism in the last few decades concerning the lack of professionalism POs seem to exhibit (Lawrence, 1984). This problem is explained, in part, by the lack of professional identity characterizing PO work, the fact that there is no recognized professional school to prepare leaders for probation, and no nationally recognized scholars or administrators who can be called eminent leaders in probation or parole (Lawrence, 1984; Thomas, 1986).

What Do POs Do?   Most studies of correctional personnel have focused on prison and jail correctional officers, their behaviors and backgrounds, and work orientations (Brown-Young, 1987; Camp, 1985; Jurik, 1986; Parisi, 1984; Poole and Regoli, 1983). When POs were investigated in later years, the findings were consistent with the results of earlier investigations, suggesting that POs continue to have negative self-images (Lawrence, 1984). This means that although there have been definite gains in the selection, recruitment, and professionalization of POs, little has occurred simultaneously to cause them to change their attitudes about their work roles and relationships with offender-clients. The highest labor turnover among POs usually occurs during the early years of their employment (Brown, 1987; Maryland Department of Budget and Fiscal Planning, 1986). Those anticipating changing careers will probably avoid professional memberships, because they may perceive the programs as offering little or nothing of value for their advancement in other professions. Even though these organizations have modest membership fees, those electing not to join may believe that their money is best spent elsewhere.

The duties of POs are diverse (Ring, 1989:43–48). Burton, Latessa, and Barker (1992:277–280) have listed 23 different legally prescribed functions performed by POs. These include supervision, surveillance, investigation of cases, assistance in rehabilitation, development and discussion of probation conditions, counseling, visiting homes and working with clients, making arrests and referrals, writing PSIs, keeping records, performing court duties, collecting fines, supervising restitution, serving warrants, maintaining contracts with courts, recommending sentences, developing community service programs, assisting law enforcement officers and agencies, assisting courts in transferring cases, enforcing criminal laws, locating employment for clients, and initiating program revocations.

As Lawrence (1984) and others have indicated, there is a direct relation between professionalism and the nature and quality of work performed in the organization. Where POs lack self-esteem and are often scorned by others because of their apparent leniency with the offenders they manage, they have sometimes acquired counterproductive definitions of their work roles and functions. An element of cynicism has been detected by Blumberg (1979) and others who have investigated POs and their work attitudes, although some investigators have found low levels of cynicism in selected jurisdictions (Rush, 1992:13). Some of the major orientations manifested by POs are summarized as follows:

1. Probation officers are "mere instruments to be utilized for larger organizational ends . . . their body of professional skills cannot be autonomously employed but must be exercised within the framework of precise organizational limits and objectives."
2. Probation officers' "lack of genuine professional status in the court" is a constant source of personal anxiety, work alienation, and general dissatisfaction.
3. "The pre-sentence investigation document is often cynically employed to validate judicial behavior or is otherwise used to reinforce administrative action already taken . . . the circumstances under which probation reports are prepared cast serious doubts as to their objectivity, validity and integrity."
4. "Frustrated as professionals, stripped of real decision-making power, lacking a genuine career motif, and assigned relatively low status by the community, it is not surprising that probation workers often develop a high degree of cynicism."
5. Probation officers "come to view their administrators as frightened, insecure, petty officials who will respond to any organization need at the expense of workers and clients. There is a constant undercurrent of antagonism between probation workers and their supervisors." (Blumberg, 1979:198–285; Lawrence, 1984:15)

While POs themselves may be at fault directly or indirectly by being ill-prepared or undereducated for the roles they perform, probation and parole agencies must absorb some of the blame (Jurik and Musheno, 1986:473–475). It has been suggested by more than one critic that probation and parole organizations and agencies often fail to clarify their own goals and objectives for the staff to achieve (Barkdull, 1987). If the goals of the organization itself are diffuse, it is difficult for agency members to adhere to particular policies or move in constructive directions when helping their offender-clients.

True fragmentation of effort exists among many POs who have their own ideas about how their jobs ought to be performed and what correctional philosophies should guide their own thinking about themselves and what they do (Spica, 1993:24–25). Increasing PO accountability through more effective leadership from administrators is one possible solution. Agency management must be willing to establish reasonable standards of performance for both staff and clients. They must then follow through by monitoring and assessing performance objectively (Cohn, 1987:42).

Frequently, organizational constraints inhibit the development of professional orientations toward probation and parole work. Although more educated POs are sought by probation and parole agencies, their beginning PO duties remain perfunctory or routine and custodial (Jurik and Musheno, 1986:474–475). In short, more educated POs are not permitted the latitude to adapt their skill and education to their supervisory tasks and dealings with offender-clients. Many PO training programs, where they exist, simply fail to train new POs to deal effectively with the practical problems they will encounter on the job. It also seems that new POs are neither allowed nor encouraged to utilize the skills they have developed.

Tenured POs feel threatened by what they perceive as greater emphasis on education, which operates to the exclusion of prior experience. These feelings foster interpersonal strains between senior, more experienced POs and newer POs with vastly different educational backgrounds and experiences. The importance of dealing effectively with the offender-client is shifted to a lower priority, as POs spend more time dealing with conflicting role and training expectations and less time helping offenders. Accordingly, more highly educated POs reflect greater disappointment with their work, when they were promised more challenging tasks but must often perform routine and menial ones.

Experts have concluded that POs experience much frustration in the performance of their work roles and associations with colleagues, and that much of this frustration is organizationally induced. Greater professionalization is called for, and it has been suggested that such professionalization can be engendered through greater participation in decision making by the POs themselves (Jurik and Musheno, 1986:476–477). Standard business practices desperately need to be applied to this field.

POs must prepare reports or PSIs for convicted offenders at the request of judges. They must maintain contact with all offenders assigned to their supervision. They must be aware of community agencies and employment opportunities so that their function as resource staff may be maximized. They must perform informal psychological counseling. They must enforce the laws and ensure offender compliance with the requirements of the particular probation or parole program. When faced with dangerous or life-threatening situations in their contacts with offenders, they must be able to make decisions about how best to handle these situations. They must be familiar with their legal rights, the rights of offenders, and their own legal liabilities in relation to clients. POs must be flexible enough to supervise a wide variety of offender-clients.

For example, the Medal of Valor award was presented to a PO by the American Correctional Association in 1989 for saving a client's life. Charles Smith, an Oklahoma probation and parole officer, exhibited extraordinary bravery when he encountered one of his clients who had just doused himself and his home with gasoline and threatened suicide. Smith's on-the-job training and experience were significant in enabling him to eventually talk his client out of committing suicide. Not only was the client's life saved, but the lives of neighbors as well. Not many POs have to face this kind of situation, but Charles Smith did and applied his skills and training appropriately (*Corrections Compendium,* 1989). In another suicide-attempt case involving a parole officer, Jerry Smith of Halifax, Canada, saved a woman from jumping off of a bridge. His counseling experience did much to convince the woman through a three-hour dialogue that suicide was not the answer to her problems (Mardon, 1992:26). And, in a third case involving a parole officer, Barry Bolthouse, with the Michigan Department of Corrections, received the American Correctional Association's 1992 Medal of Valor for convincing a gunman, one of his parolee-clients, to surrender a hostage and give himself up to authorities. The rapport Bolthouse had developed with his client was most valuable in defusing this potentially lethal situation (*Corrections Compendium,* 1992a:13).

SELECTION REQUIREMENTS, EDUCATION, AND TRAINING FOR POS

When POs are recruited, what type of training should they receive? How much education should be required, and what educational subjects have the greatest relevance for correctional careers? No immediate answers are available for these questions. While most of us would agree that Ph.D. degrees are not essential for the effective performance of PO work, some educational training is desirable. Currently, experts disagree about how much education should be officially required as part of the recruitment process.

The selection requirements and recruitment procedures included in this section are not exhaustive. But they serve as a set of standards against which PO recruitment, selection, and training programs may be evaluated. Traditional PO selection procedures have tended to focus on weeding out those unfit for PO work rather than on selecting those possessing the skills needed for successful job performance (Stinchcomb, 1985:120). PO training in most states includes several weeks of class time (e.g., social sciences, humanities, and/or police sciences) and two or more weeks of in-service training (American Correctional Association, 1991). However, some states have no in-service or course requirements in place for those aspiring to PO roles. Tables 12.2 and 12.3 show the salaries, qualifications, and responsibilities of parole officers in most U.S. jurisdictions for 1990.

In 1991, minimum educational requirements of those entering the correctional field continued to be fairly low. For example, 78 percent of the jurisdictions required the G.E.D. or a high school diploma for an entry-level PO position, whereas 4 percent required either a community college (two years) diploma or 15 credit hours of college work. Because of the emphasis on professionalization, it is surprising that 12 percent of the jurisdictions had no educational requirements as the minimum for entry-level PO positions (American Correctional Association, 1986b:38; 1991).

The PO examination processes used in most jurisdictions for 1991 have been described by the American Correctional Association. Over 80 percent of the programs required a written examination, only about 20 percent subjected recruits to psychological screening. A breakdown of various psychological assessment inventories used by different programs is provided. The Minnesota Multiphasic Personality Inventory and Inwald Personality Inventory appear to be those most popularly applied, when any are used. Very few programs included physical examinations, medical checks, or FBI inquiries. Several programs had no formal testing or examination procedures as a means of screening correctional officer candidates (American Correctional Association, 1991).

In 1981 the National Institute of Corrections (NIC) responded to the need for greater professionalization and training among POs by sponsoring a series of training programs in various jurisdictions. The American Correctional Association (ACA) was selected to administer some of these programs and eventually developed the Development of Correctional Staff Trainers program, which provided comprehensive, experience-based training for more than 1,000 trainers and other

TABLE 12.2 Survey of Parole Officers—Salaries, Qualifications

System	Total Number of Officers	Salary Starting; Average	Qualifications for Job
Alabama	215 (also supervise probation)	$18,699.20; $32,730.46	No age requirement; bachelor's degree in criminal justice or a related field.
Alaska	64	$2,205; $3,336 (monthly)	Baccalaureate in related field or experience substituted on a year for year basis.
Arizona	62	$21,200; $25,403	Age 21; education-high school graduate; previous experience as correctional program officer with department.
Arkansas	60	$18,200	Applicants must have a bachelor's degree in sociology, psychology or related field.
California	1,279 (as of 7/1/89)	$2,880–$3,678; $3,279 est. (monthly)	Age 21, U.S. citizen or permanent resident alien who has applied for citizenship, felony disqualification, degree plus 1 yr. experience of 2 yrs. of college and 4 yrs. experience.
Colorado	38	$26,656–$38,724 max. range pay scale; $35,000 (approx. avg.)	Age 21, B.A. from accredited college or university with a major in corrections, criminal justice, helping services or other human or behavioral sciences; ability to qualify with an approved firearm, suitable experience may substitute for required education on a year-for-year basis.
Connecticut	60	$22,400; $27,250	Age 21, bachelor's degree, no experience for entry level position.
Delaware	No response		
District of Columbia	37	$21,225; $34,006	Successfully completed a course of study in an accredited college or university leading to a bachelor's degree, including 24 hrs. in a social science with 1 yr. of related experience.

Qualifications Exceeded?	At Start of Employment	During Employment	Turnover	Expect to Add Officers in 1990?
Yes, many officers have prior experience in law enforcement or counseling and social work.	40 hrs. in service; 280 hrs. min. STDS training	40 hrs. inservice and firearms qualification	Slight	No
Yes, we have a well-trained, highly qualified staff.	Mostly on-the-job training		10%	Yes, 12
State personnel system does not currently allow us to do so.	40 hrs.	40 hrs.	5%	No
Whenever possible officers are hired who exceed the qualifications, but when none are available we will hire those with minimum qualifications.	2 weeks training, 1 at academy and 1 in the field	Seminars and training workshops	12%	No
Yes. Most new parole agents have degrees and several yrs. of prior criminal justice experience.	4 wks. academy training	84 hrs.	1%	Yes, 165 new positions
Applicants and appointees frequently exceed education/experience requirements.	18 working days	40 hrs. min.	1 2 officers per year	Yes, anticipating 40 new parole officer positions Jan. 1990
Yes, very few are hired directly out of college. There are varying degrees of experience, some of which may have been in another area of corrections.	6 wks. department of correction orientation, 2 wks. division of parole orientation followed by 4 wks. of intensive supervision	40 hrs.	4 positions, FY 1988–89	Yes, 15
No	Close supervision for 6 mos.	Not systematic	3%, approx.	Yes, 14

(table continues)

TABLE 12.2 (continued)

System	Total Number of Officers	Salary Starting; Average	Qualifications for Job
Florida	1,794 (also supervise probation)	$20,120.76; average not available	4 yr. college degree and 1 yr. experience in the care and custody of offenders, completion of the Florida Corrections Academy, drug screening.
Georgia	352	$20,310; $24,870	4 yr. degree, 21 years of age.
Hawaii	21	$26,700; $30,000	Bachelor's degree in social science, 1 yr. experience in corrections, 21 yrs. of age.
Idaho	54 (also supervise probation)	$19,200; $23,005	
Illinois	125 (9/30/89) 104 (supervising parole cases)	$23,792; $28,500	Requires knowledge, skills and mental development equivalent to 4 yrs. of college with a bachelor's degree in the behavioral or social science or law enforcement; knowledge of laws, rules and regulations of the department and of problems of adult and juvenile offenders.
Indiana	75	$18,070; $21,000	High school diploma, 5 yrs. correctional experience, 2 yrs. of college.
Iowa	208.45	$22,214–$32,864	Associate of arts degree in social sciences and 2 yrs. experience in human services, criminal justice, or corrections or bachelor's degree with major work in social sciences or equivalent combination of education and experience to equal 4 yrs.
Kansas	73	$22,644; $24,372	Graduation from a 4 yr. college in corrections, criminal administration or behavioral sciences, substitution of up to 2 yrs. of experience in corrections.
Kentucky	234	$15,100; $21,300	21 yrs., bachelor's degree, no experience required for entry level.
Louisiana	273 (also supervises probation)	$16,216; $20,500 (field agents)	College degree, can substitute similar work experience for each missing year of college, preference is college degree.

Qualifications Exceeded?	At Start of Employment	During Employment	Turnover	Expect to Add Officers in 1990?
	320 hrs. at Florida Corrections Academy	40 hrs. per yr. of ongoing training	13%	Yes
Generally yes, competitive interviewing	6 mos.	20 hrs. minimum	10%	Yes, 186
Prefer	40 hrs.	40 hrs.	1%	Yes, 12
	200 hrs.	40 hrs.	18%	Yes
Individuals are hired from the certified eligibility lists sent to the agency by Central Management Services.	40 hrs. orientation and 40 hrs. firearms qualifications	40 hrs. in-service, including first aid, CPR, and firearms requalification (semiannual)	7.3%	Yes, 39 total staff for Electronic Detention
Yes, many parole agents have college degrees or above.	Supervisor provides job orientation training	18 hrs.		Yes, 7
	80 hrs. preservice training at Training Academy	40 hrs.		Yes, dependent upon action in 1990 Legislative session
Officers are hired from eligible registers maintained by Department of Administration, Division of Personnel, and from within Department of Corrections. Majority hired meet or exceed requirements.	200 hrs.	40 hrs.	Approximately 14% during calendar year 1989	Yes, 8 positions requested in 1991 budget
	40 hrs. with corrections training and OJT packet	40 hrs. in-service	Not available	No
	40 hrs.+	20 hrs.+	30%	Yes

(*table continues*)

TABLE 12.2 (continued)

System	Total Number of Officers	Salary Starting; Average	Qualifications for Job
Maine	Eliminated parole in 1976. The few people still under pre-1976 sentencing status is now statistically insignificant.		
Maryland	619 (also supervise probation)	$17,261; $27,500	21 yrs., bachelor's degree with no less than 30 credits in a social or behavioral science, no experience.
Massachusetts	94	$27,261; $36,000–$38,000	2 yrs. experience in probation/parole work, criminal justice, social work, psychology, vocational or rehabilitative counseling or a combination, or an undergraduate degree may substitute for a portion of the required experience.
Michigan	79	$23,000; $34,000	21 yrs., bachelor's degree in criminal justice, or related political science or human services degree.
Minnesota	54	$23,364; $28,000 (approx.)	Must pass a test on English, writing; some psychological and human behavior knowledge.
Mississippi	112 (also supervise probation)	$15,695.20; $18,712.20	Master's degree in related field or bachelor's degree with 1 yr. experience or high school diploma with related experience substituting for education.
Missouri	572 (also supervise probation)	$1,460; $1,700 (monthly)	College degree in criminal justice, social or behavioral sciences, no age requirements, experience as a probation and parole officer not required, but related experience is preferred over none.
Montana	47 (also supervise probation)	$18,673; $21,300	Bachelor's degree with 2 yrs. of related experience.
Nebraska	12 (adult parole officers)	$24,036; $24,378	Bachelor's in criminal justice, sociology or related field or equivalent or 2 yrs. experience working with individuals on parole.

Qualifications Exceeded?	At Start of Employment	During Employment	Turnover	Expect to Add Officers in 1990?
No.	Completion of 6 1/2 wks. at training academy	20 hrs.		
Try to get candidates with master's degree.	Yes	40 hrs.	2%	Yes, 100
No.	120 hrs. classroom and 8 wks. OJT	40 hrs.	5–10%	No
Yes, all have a B.A. degree and a growing number have other advanced training and/or education.	80 hrs. preservice	40 hrs. annually		Yes, 3 (added 10 in 1989)
	2 wks. basic field officer training, 3 1/2 days firearms training	varies year to year	Informa- not compiled	No
Probation and parole officers are hired from the top 10 scorers on the merit registers which ranks those meeting the min. requirements according to a combined score of education and experience.	The division provides 4 wks. of training in the area of report writing, client supervision, special problems, criminal justice, etc.	Specific training courses are offered routinely in the areas of sex offender, holistic counseling, family dysfunctioning, mental health, substance abuse, etc.		Yes, 67 positions have been requested
Yes, the majority of newly hired officers have well over 2 yrs. of previous experience and some have advanced degrees.	40 hrs. of orientation training	By statute, all officers must receive a min. of 16 hrs. of annual training	4%	No, recently filled 8 new parole/probation positions
Numerous applications are received for correction's parole officers with qualifications that exceed the stated requirements.	80 hrs. classroom, 80 hrs. on-the-job training	40 hrs., including classroom and OJT	13.5% (FY 1988/1989)	No

(table continues)

TABLE 12.2 (continued)

System	Total Number of Officers	Salary Starting; Average	Qualifications for Job
Nevada	234 officers, 311 total staff (also supervise probation)	$22,000; $25,000	Bachelor's degree preferred, but law enforcement experience can be substituted, 21 yrs. of age.
New Hampshire	49 (also supervise probation)	$28,853–$31,399 (depending on experience); $34–37,000 (approx.)	No age requirement, B.A. in criminal justice, corrections, law enforcement or related area; experience in parole, probation, law enforcement, corrections, counseling, etc.
New Jersey	177	$22,505; $25,800	No age requirement, valid NJ drivers license, bachelor's degree, 1 yr. experience in related social casework field, experience may be substituted for education on year for year basis, master's degree may be substituted for year's experience in related field when not utilizing experience in lieu of education.
New Mexico	125 (also supervise probation)	$18,000 (approx.); $22,000 (approx.)	Bachelor's degree with course work in sociology, psychology, corrections, guidance and counseling, social work or police science, plus combination of further education and/or experience in these fields totaling 18 mos., 12 mos. of which must have been as a probation/parole officer.
New York	985 parole officers and 176 senior parole officers employed by the division as of 9/89	$33,994; $33,994–$42,048 (parole officer) $39,813–$48,887 (senior parole officer)	Bachelor's degree, 3 yrs. experience as a social caseworker or group worker in a recognized social services, corrections, criminal justice or human welfare agency. A law degree or master's degree in social work, probation and parole, sociology, criminal justice, psychology, or in black or hispanic cultural studies may be substituted for up to one year of the required experience.
North Carolina	92	$18,994 (hiring rate); $26,916	Trainee-graduation from an accredited 4 yr. college or university, preferably with a major in criminal justice, correctional services, psychology, social work, or other related human services or criminal justice field.

Qualifications Exceeded?	At Start of Employment	During Employment	Turnover	Expect to Add Officers in 1990?
	11 wks. basic training	40 hrs. annually	10%	Yes
	DOC has unique 286 hr. Parole/ Probation Officer Certificate Program		Less than 5%	Yes
Hiring is generally at the B.A. level.		Mandated 40 hrs. per officer, including various supervision-related topics		No
	Orientation and OJT, 40 hrs. basic PPO course first year.	40 hrs. in-service training	About 15%	Yes
Yes, most new employees exceed the experience qualification and many have already obtained an M.A. in a job-related field.	All new recruits attend a seven-week basic training course which covers every aspect of a parole officer's duties and responsibilities.	Every officer receives an update on the use of deadly physical force, street survival training, and 40 hrs. of in-service training on issues related to AIDS, domestic violence, and other areas.	Less than 5%	Yes, approximately 100
No	160 hrs. basic training	40 hrs. per year	10%	Yes, 26

(table continues)

TABLE 12.2 (continued)

System	Total Number of Officers	Salary Starting; Average	Qualifications for Job
North Dakota	19	$17,688-agent I, $20,496-agent II; $24,096	21 yrs., B.A. or B.S. degree, 2 yrs. experience in related field for agent II position.
Ohio	173 (including 22 first line supervisors)	$19,698; $24,500	Age 21, completion of undergraduate major program core course work in behavioral or social science, law enforcement, corrections, criminal justice, or related field, or 2 yrs. training/experience in probation or parole field services involving writing, treatment, referrals, case service delivery and contact with other criminal justice agencies or equivalent.
Oklahoma	291 (also supervise probation)	$18,504; $20,597	No age requirement, 4 yr. degree in any subject as long as there is 24 hrs. in a social or behavioral science, education, or correction. No experience required.
Oregon	376 (state and option I counties)	$22,524; $26,064	Age 21 at time of appointment, must be certifiable by the Board of Police Standards and Training (BPST), 2 yrs. counseling experience and a bachelor's degree in a behavioral or related field (with copy of transcripts), or a master's degree may be substituted for 1 yr. of required experience.
Pennsylvania	248	$22,742; $31,686	Bachelor's degree or any equivalent combination of experience and training
Rhode Island	8	$27,000; $36,000	Age 21, bachelor's degree, with experience in counseling
South Carolina	454 (also supervise probation)	$18,533; $18,533	Age 21, bachelor's degree, no required experience.

Qualifications Exceeded?	At Start of Employment	During Employment	Turnover	Expect to Add Officers in 1990?
Just in age	9 wks. if they do not have law enforcement license	32 hrs.	Less than 5%	No
Yes, all have either a B.A. and/ or much more experience than just the required 2 yrs., some have M.A. in related field.	3 wks. preservice, 40 hrs. of on-the-job training, 40 hrs. basic firearms, 24 hrs. in-service training, sex offender training and field confrontation tactics.		7%	Yes
	4 wks. preservice, 300 hrs. of class to obtain Peace Officer Certificate	40 hrs. per year	8.9%	Yes
	Field training officer-160 hrs. at BPST within 1 yr. of hire date.	40 hrs. of annual in-service training beginning in 1990	6.7%	Yes, number unknown at this time.
Yes, candidates generally come to us with some experience in criminal justice field or social services field in addition to having a bachelor's degree		40 hrs. required annually to be selected from in-service curriculum, out-service training or a combination of both	4.24	Yes
	2 mos. OJT and orientation	Training sessions on an issue need basis	2%	No
	4 weeks classroom, 2 mos. on-the-job training	40 hrs. in-service training.	10–12%	Yes

(table continues)

TABLE 12.2 (continued)

System	Total Number of Officers	Salary Starting; Average	Qualifications for Job
South Dakota	23	$17,472; $19,193	No age requirements, graduation from college or university with a bachelor's degree in social or behavioral science with course work in criminal justice or a related field. No experience required.
Tennessee	196 (positions)	$13,752; $15,000	21 yrs., bachelor's degree, pass civil service exam.
Texas	1,103	$1,731; $1,975 (monthly)	Bachelor's degree, no required age.
Utah	27	$10.80; $13.00 (hourly)	21 years of age or above, bachelor's degree in psychology, sociology, criminology or related field, must meet basic physical requirements for peace officer status.
Vermont	60 (also supervise probation)	$19,000; $25,000	21 years of age, B.A. or B.S. or 2 yrs. experience.
Virginia	401.5	$20,461	No age requirement; degree in a social science related field or have comparable experience of a nature indicating they possess the skills and abilities, necessary to do the job.
Washington	328 (also supervise probation)	$24,372; $1,937–$2,596 per month	Age 21, 2 yrs. as a community corrections officer or a bachelor's degree and 3 yrs. of professional experience in adult or juvenile corrections or closely related field, or a master's degree, also a valid driver's license.
West Virginia	22	$12,768; $16,910	21 years old, college degree in social sciences, under civil service system guidelines, no experience required
Wisconsin	441.5 (12/1/89)	$20,000; $28,000 est.	Education or life experience equivalent to bachelor's degree, qualify on state civil service exam.

Qualifications Exceeded?	At Start of Employment	During Employment	Turnover	Expect to Add Officers in 1990?
Yes, officers generally have work experience in a related field.	Review police manual and time spent with other agent.	3 in-house staff meetings, various work-shops at South Dakota Correctional Association	10%	No
Generally hire officers who meet min. qualifications.	40 hrs. preservice	40 hrs. in-service	8% (approx.)	No
Yes, most have hours past a B.A. and are overly qualified.	2 wks. academy training	Both internal and external training is available	Less than 10%	No
No, on the average applicants are well qualified within the defined parameters.	560 hrs. Pre-Service Academy	Average of 40 hrs. in-service, additional 40 hrs. each year of specialized or elective training	15% (approx.)	Yes, 10–15 (approx.)
Yes, usually exceed experience.	Yes	Yes	2–3 (annually)	No
Yes, a large percentage of the officers hired possess degrees and/or study beyond the B.A. level and prior correctional experience.	120 hrs. basic officer training, DOC orientation.	40 hrs. per year for the first 6 yrs., then 30 hrs. for years 6–8 and 20 hrs. thereafter	14%	Yes, 27
	Adult services academy	Arrest, search and seizure, personal safety, training, fire-arms familiarization training, AIDS, CPR/first aid training.	8%	Yes
No	40 hrs. with regional supervisor	40 hrs. in-service training	5%	No
Generally.	Basic training for Milwaukee based agents, OJT elsewhere	Training for reclassification.		Yes, 15.5

(table continues)

TABLE 12.2 (continued)

System	Total Number of Officers	Salary Starting; Average	Qualifications for Job
Wyoming	48 (also supervise probation)	$18,060–$21,564; $20,800	21 year of age, bachelor's degree in related field. Officer II also needs 2 yrs. of related experience in counseling or rehabilitative work.

Canadian Systems

System	Total Number of Officers	Salary Starting; Average	Qualifications for Job
Correctional Service of Canada	388, supervision of conditionally released offenders across Canada	$38,801; $42,716 (top salary)	No age requirement, min. of a bachelor's degree in the social services or have some experience in the field and has successfully passed an equivalance exam.

professionals between 1981 and 1985 (Taylor, 1985:24). In turn, by 1985, over 6,000 individuals had enrolled in ACA correspondence courses and participated in related programs, seminars, and workshops on a variety of correctional topics. These training programs are being continued, and enrollments have escalated considerably (American Correctional Association, 1989a, 1992).

Stressed in these programs and workshops have been legal liabilities of POs and other types of corrections officers, as well as the cultivation of skills in the management and supervision of offender-clients. Additionally, programs and coursework are offered for managing stress, crisis intervention and hostage negotiations, proposal and report writing, legal issues training, managing community corrections facilities, dealing with the mentally ill offender, and suicide prevention. By 1985, more than 600 agencies and institutions were seeking accreditation or reaccreditation so that greater professionalization could occur for prospective PO recruits.

Today, most jurisdictions currently require bachelor's degrees or equivalent experience, with an emphasis on a social science major. Nevada and Minnesota appeared to have the least strenuous entry requirements. For example, Minnesota requires applicants to pass a basic reading comprehension examination and a structured oral interview. In Nevada, POs must possess a high school diploma and have

Qualifications Exceeded?	At Start of Employment	During Employment	Turnover	Expect to Add Officers in 1990?
	Brief orientation training and 24 hrs. of an in-service basic training course.	40 hrs. per year in-service training.	22% professional; 19% support	Asking legislature for 4 positions.
No. If the person has more than a master's degree, we try to direct to other areas.	1 yr. probationary period with on-site training by supervisor or senior parole officer	Opportunity to attend at least 1 conference per yr. and has received at least 2 hrs. of training per month, usually case conferences with supervisor. A national training program is being developed.	Not available	No

Source: Corrections Compendium (March 1990).

four years' experience, although the type of experience is unspecified. Nevada offers prospective recruits the option of possessing a bachelor's degree in lieu of four years' experience, however. Various skills useful in PO work are transmitted by various programs offered by the American Correctional Association as well as private agencies.

Besides providing training seminars and other programs for prospective corrections employees, the ACA has established a feedback mechanism for evaluating the effectiveness of training delivery thus far. Although certification for correctional trainers is purely voluntary at present, the ACA together with the American Association of Correctional Training Personnel is suggesting strongly that all trainers voluntarily undergo recertification every three years as a means of possessing the most current skills and knowledge about legal and correctional developments (Taylor, 1985:25).

One way of gauging the nature and quantity of education that should logically be expected of potential POs is to examine the situations they would ordinarily encounter. The fact that POs interact with violent and nonviolent offenders requires more than one approach or solution to any situation. Certain types of offenders on probation or parole are dangerous, and incarceration has not necessarily made

TABLE 12.3 Survey of Parole Officers—Responsibilities

System	Caseload per Officer	Number of Officers	Caseload	Population
Alabama	118	6	30	
Alaska	90	2	18	
Arizona	55+			Sex offenders Home arrest
Arkansas	62	4	15	
California	53.2	269	35.3	Sex Offenders Drug/alcohol dependent offenders
Colorado	70	2	30	Sex offenders Drug/alcohol dependent offenders Gang members Community Corrections Liaison duties
Connecticut	79	No specialized caseloads at this time		
Delaware	No response			
District of Columbia	125	4	60	None
Florida	101 (adult offender caseload)	No		Sex offenders Drug/alcohol dependent offenders
Georgia	54	20	25	
Hawaii	70	4	35	Sex offenders
Idaho	77	14	25 for a team of 2	
Illinois	120 (9/30/89)	No		
Indiana	45	No		Sex Offenders Drug/alcohol dependent offenders
Iowa	74–120 depending upon area	9	25	Sex offenders Drug/alcohol dependent offenders
Kansas	57	In urban areas, some parole officers have a specialized caseload to some extent, however, because of numbers, a caseload is not made up of a specific type of client.		
Kentucky	60	52	25	Advanced supervision
Louisiana	150	14	2 (supervise 25 cases)	
Maine	Eliminated parole in 1976.			

Number of Officers	Caseload	Counseling	Enforcement-Supervision
		Yes	Yes
		Yes	Yes
5	35	Yes	Yes
		Yes	Yes
2	35.3	Yes	Yes
55	53		
4 specially trained	Also supervises other high risk offenders	Yes	Yes
2 officers in Denver designated for liaison duties with Denver TASC Program	No specialized caseload		
Several officers provide liaison with law enforcement units and details that deal with gangs.			
8.5 (equivalent of 1.0 officer assigned to providing liaison with institution case managers and the parole board	No specialized caseloads		
		Yes	
Unknown	Varies	Yes	Yes
Unknown	Varies		
		Yes	Yes
1	20	Yes	Yes
		Yes	Yes
		Yes	Yes
1	35	Yes	Yes
1	50		
2 (1 officer is surveillance)	28	Yes	Yes
2 (1 officer is surveillance)	38	Yes	
		Yes	
		Yes	
20	50	Yes	Yes
		Yes	Yes

(*table continues*)

TABLE 12.3 (continued)

System	Caseload per Officer	Number of Officers	Caseload	Population
Maryland	196 (including probation cases)	No		Sex offenders
Massachusetts	78–80	4	45	Part of their position duties
Michigan	134.2 work units	No		
Minnesota	90	Not at this time		
Mississippi	94 (if not handling specialized caseloads	No		Drug/alcohol dependent offenders Diversion program
Missouri	86			
Montana	86	4 (also supervises intensive probation)	15	
Nebraska	50	4	20 on intensive parole; supervise some not on intensive parole	
Nevada	75 (parolees and probationers)	15	30	Gang members
New Hampshire	25 (average)		28	
New Jersey	73	Yes		
New Mexico	55–60	7	20	
New York	38 newly released parolees for first 15 mos., 97 regular caseloads	451	38	Gang members Adolescent offenders unit Shock parole Medical
North Carolina	76	None		Drug/alcohol dependent offenders
North Dakota	79	None		None
Ohio	55 (approx.)	No		Sex offenders
Oklahoma	95	20	45	Presentence investigation Sex offenders PPCS

Number of Officers	Caseload	Counseling	Enforcement-Supervision
1		Yes	Yes
		50%	50%
		Limited	Yes
		Limited	Yes
12	20	Yes	Yes
2	37		
		Yes. Referrals also made to appropriate treatment centers as needed	No
		Yes	Yes
		Yes	Yes
2	30		
		Yes	Yes
		Yes	Yes
		Yes	Yes
6	20	Yes	Yes
8	30		
44	30		
4	20		
3	33	Yes	Yes
		Yes	Yes
150–175 (trained to supervise)	35 (caseload of officers supervising only sex offenders)	Yes	Yes
5	20	Yes	Yes
11	55		
20	45		

(table continues)

TABLE 12.3 (continued)

System	Caseload per Officer	Number of Officers	Caseload	Population
Oregon	71	12.75 (probation)	31.5 (average)	Sex offenders Drug/alcohol dependent offenders
Pennsylvania	84	5	Mixed caseload	Drug/alcohol dependent offenders
Rhode Island	57	No		None
South Carolina	108 (regular agents), 34 (intensive agents)	40	34	
South Dakota	30	8	15	None
Tennessee	59	30	15	Substance abuse Institutional Employment
Texas	75 (without special programs), 25 (with special programs)	73	25	Sex offenders Drug/alcohol dependent offenders Mental retardation
Utah	15–70 (based upon workload formula)	11	Average 15–20	Sex offenders Mentally ill offenders
Vermont	100	10 (also supervises probation)	5	
Virginia	64.4	22	24	Sex offenders Drug/alcohol dependent offenders
Washington	70 (approx.)	None		
West Virginia	55	No		Drug/alcohol dependent offenders
Wisconsin	Does not reflect caseload but workload points	22		Sex offenders Drug/alcohol offenders Spanish speaking Developmentally disabled Mental health
Wyoming	5 (parolees) (probationers)	2	Share 15 clients	
Canadian Systems				
Correctional Services of Canada	23	4 (pilot project in Toronto, area)	16	None of the parole officers handle specialized supervision, however all officers have a mix of caseloads.

Number of Officers	Caseload	Counseling	Enforcement-Supervision
12.8	6.3 (average)	Yes	Yes
21.5	30 (average)		
10	38	Yes	Yes
		Yes	Yes
		Yes	Yes
		Yes	Yes
5		Yes	Yes
14			
5			
32	25	Yes	Yes
11	25		(supervision)
5	25		
1	50	No, refer to	Yes
2	35–50	outside agencies	
		Yes	Yes
39	Unreported	Yes	Yes
39	Unreported		
			Yes
1	55	Yes	Yes
10		Yes	Yes
16			
		Yes	Yes
		Yes	Yes

Source: Corrections Compendium (March 1990).

them less dangerous than they were when they originally committed serious crimes. For example, female POs risk sexual assault if they are assigned especially violent sex offenders with one or more previous rape convictions. Both male and female POs risk injury through assault if they make decisions that affect offender freedoms such as recommendations for parole or probation revocations because of program violations they detect.

One interesting "hands-on" program for parole officer training occurred in California as part of the California Department of Corrections' Parole and Community Services Division (Smith, 1993b:24). One requirement of the training program was that all prospective parole officer applicants had to engage in role reversal, thereby placing themselves in the roles of parolees for a 26-hour period. During this period, "parolees" were expected to survive in a strange city with little or no money, one piece of real identification, and the assumed identity of a parolee just released from prison. When these "parolees" finished the experiment, most had acquired an empathy for offenders that they otherwise would not have obtained. Many interviewed afterward believed that the training was of great value in heightening their awareness of parolee problems and gave them insight into how to be more effective in their actual PO work. Unfortunately, California discontinued this role-reversal program after a few short experimental years (Smith, 1993b:24–27).

In Georgia, state, county, and city correctional officers as well as all youth development workers have undergone a needs assessment. Officials subsequently determined that three different kinds of curricula were in order depending on the nature of correctional duties performed. State institutional officers and guards are currently required to undergo a 160-hour training program. An 88-hour course has been mandated for county correctional officers including POs, and a 36-hour program has been instituted for city and county jailers who perform primarily custodial functions (Camp, 1985). Georgia officials have measured the amount of training officers should receive on the basis of the danger and potential risks and liabilities associated with the positions they perform.

Offenders on probation or parole as well as those incarcerated are frequently adept at manipulating those supervising them. Thus, in some jurisdictions, POs receive training for resisting group pressure, acquiring self-control, and making less risky decisions (McGuire and Priestley, 1985). In addition, they receive offensive and defensive training for self-protection as well as their own manipulative skills for eliciting and altering offenders' values and beliefs about themselves in both formal and informal counseling (McGuire and Priestley, 1985).

Increasing the amount of training considered relevant by prospective POs through simulated situations of officer-offender interactions is one means of increasing the professionalism of officers generally (Cheatwood and Hayeslip, 1986:16). Many POs believe they need more practical training as part of their training programs, rather than mere attendance in awareness or other related educational courses. One reason for a more practical training emphasis is that the kinds of persons traditionally attracted to corrections positions have not been particularly excited about or motivated to participate in academic programs. Thus, topics such as when to use deadly force and spotting those situations likely to create legal liability are directly relevant to the future tasks performed by POs. Those officers most likely to leave the correctional field often lack the motivation, education, and commitment, but a more relevant curriculum could function to reduce labor turnover significantly in various training programs (Cheatwood and Hayeslip, 1986:16).

Some colleges and universities are currently offering internships for those interested in careers as POs. These internships are combined with their program of formal study and include assisting POs in their work roles on an internship basis. Thus, prospective POs have an opportunity of experiencing directly what it will be like when they enter these positions as professionals later.

Recruiting Women and Minorities

Although women comprise only 5.9 percent of the incarcerated offender population and 18 percent of the probation/parole population, women in various correctional fields are currently underrepresented proportionately (American Correctional Association, 1994:xxvi). Only about 21 percent of the correctional officers in the United States are women (American Correctional Association, 1994). Many of the women employed in correctional positions perform clerical and staff roles and/or deal primarily with female or juvenile offenders (Holeman and Krepps-Hess, 1983).

Most studies of women in all types of corrections work have focused on the role of women as prison or jail matrons (Carlen and Davis, 1987; Hunter, 1986; Kerle, 1985; Zupan, 1986). Although the greatest opposition to the idea of women entering the correctional field has been found among male officers, few significant differences have actually been observed when comparisons of male and female correctional officer effectiveness have been made (Chapman, et al., 1983).

One barrier to the recruitment of women into corrections, especially as correctional officers, is the legal obstacle of offender privacy (Jurik, 1985). The privacy issue is moot for the most part in PO work. Nevertheless, women must contend with their male PO counterparts as they seek to perform similar work roles. Evidence suggests larger numbers of women are being recruited into correctional work annually and that greater numbers are being represented in PO and other mainline correctional activity (Shawver, 1987).

Assessment Centers and Staff Effectiveness

The focus on behaviorally based methods for selecting and evaluating POs not only results in the hiring of better line personnel, but it also functions to identify those most able to perform managerial tasks (Murphy, 1987:20–21; Pelfrey, 1986:65). It is clear that a key element in the success of any probation program is the quality of line staff (Ciuros, 1986:24). A key element in maintaining line staff quality is managerial adequacy (Maine Criminal Justice Academy, 1986; Morgenbesser, 1987; Ryan, 1987; Wahler and Gendreau, 1985).

Assessment centers, such as the one established in Dade County, Florida, are useful for identifying potential chief probation officers and administrators for probation and parole programs (Pelfrey, 1986:65–67). These assessment centers are often patterned after those used in the selection of law enforcement officers (Whitehead and Lindquist, 1987). One fairly popular assessment center format used by various jurisdictions was established by the New York City Police Department during the 1970s. This assessment center concept sought to identify the following skills areas:

1. *Problem-solving dimensions* (problem analysis—ability to grasp the source, nature, and key dimensions of a problem; judgment—recognition of the significant factors to arrive at sound and practical decisions).
2. *Communication dimensions* (dialogue skills—effectiveness of discussion in person-to-person or small group interactions; writing skills—expression of ideas in writing with facility).
3. *Emotional and motivational dimensions* (reactions to reassure—functioning in a controlled, effective manner under stress; keeping one's head; drive—amount of directed and sustained energy brought to bear in accomplishing objectives).
4. *Interpersonal dimensions* (insight into others—the ability to proceed giving due consideration to the needs and feelings of others; leadership—the direction of behavior of others toward the achievement of common goals by charisma, insights, or the assertion of will).
5. *Administrative dimensions* (planning—forward thinking, anticipating situations and problems, and preparation in advance to cope with these problems; commitment to excellence—determination that the task will be well done, the achievement of high standards). (Pelfrey, 1986:67)

If the right kinds of managers can be selected and promoted, line staff can be molded into productive work units to better serve offender-clients. Managers can assist their probation and parole organizations to devise more clearly defined mission statements of goals and objectives and to establish greater uniformity of quality of performance among staff members (Brown, 1987; Ciuros, 1986:24–25). While assessment centers are not foolproof and should not be considered as cookbook methods for selecting "good managers," they are helpful by providing for specific tests and assessments of those desirable qualities of leadership and managerial effectiveness that should be seriously considered by administrators. Criminal justice generally has had a continuing need for better managers, and thus criminal justice professionals including corrections personnel should explore every management evaluation tool available, including assessment centers (Pelfrey, 1986:68).

The Florida Assessment Center

The Dade County, Florida, Department of Corrections and Rehabilitation was one of the first state corrections agencies to establish an assessment center for the selection of entry-level officers (Stinchcomb, 1985:120). Although using assessment centers to screen personnel for organizational positions is not a new concept, especially in private industry, the use of such centers in corrections recruitment and training is innovative. Currently, a large number of law enforcement agencies employ assessment centers or other pivotal screening facilities to separate the fit from the unfit among applicants for law enforcement positions.

The **Florida Assessment Center** moves beyond traditional selection mechanisms such as the use of paper-and-pencil measures and standard personality, interests, and aptitude and IQ tests or inventories by examining a candidate's potential on the basis of the full scope of the job (Stinchcomb, 1985:122). This is accomplished by a previously established job task analysis made of the different correctional chores to be performed by prospective applicants. The Dade County Assessment Center has identified the following skills associated with corrections work of any kind:

1. The ability to understand and implement policies and procedures;
2. The ability to be aware of all elements in a given situation, and to use sensitivity to others and good judgment in dealing with the situation (Brennan et al., 1987); and
3. The ability to communicate effectively (Davis, 1984).

On the basis of various measures designed to tap into each of these personal and social skills, the most qualified candidates are targeted for further testing and interviews. These tests include preparations of written reports, role playing and acting out problem situations, and videotaped situational exercises. The Center strives to provide candidates with as much realism as possible concerning the kinds of situations they will encounter in dealing with criminals either inside or outside prison. Also emphasized is an awareness of race, gender, and ethnicity in the social dimension of relating to offenders.

Three-person teams of evaluators screen applicants on the basis of their objectivity and manner in responding to various job-related simulated challenges. A key objective is to assist prospective corrections personnel to avoid legal challenges and suits by clients and/or prisoners. Thus, when subsequent decisions are made by corrections officers and others and challenged in court, the basis for the challenges will be unlikely attributable to faults associated with the selection process (Stinchcomb, 1985:122).

The evaluators in the Florida Assessment Center are themselves trained by other assessors or correctional officers so that they may more readily determine those most appropriate candidates for correctional posts. Observing, categorizing, and evaluating candidate skills are procedures requiring extensive training, and the Center continually subjects its own selection process to both internal and external scrutiny and evaluation (Stinchcomb, 1985:124). The cost for processing each candidate was $75 in 1985; this fee does not cover administrative costs and the expenses of role players and other professionals involved in candidate training. Dade County officials consider the money well spent, since it costs $20,000 per candidate to train and equip all prospective officers during the one-year probationary period (Stinchcomb, 1985:124). Additionally, the reduced costs resulting from fewer legal challenges by offenders on probation or parole or who are incarcerated more than justify the expense of the Center.

The Use of Firearms in Probation and Parole Work

Because the idea of POs carrying firearms is fairly new, not a great deal has been written about it. And, it is too early to evaluate the long-range implications of PO firearms use in the field (Brown, 1989:194, 1990:21; Velt and Smith, 1993:17–20). More probation and parole officer training programs are featuring topics related to PO safety, especially in view of the shift from the medical model toward more proactive, client-control officer orientations (Smith, 1991b:38–39). Few professionals in criminology and criminal justice question that each generation of probationers and parolees includes more dangerous offenders (Lindner, 1992a). Largely because it is impossible at present to incarcerate everyone convicted of crimes, the use of probation and parole as front-end and back-end solutions to jail and prison overcrowding is increasing. Also increasing are reports of victimization from POs working with probationers and parolees in dangerous neighborhoods (Blauner and Migliore, 1992:21–23). It is not necessarily the case that probationer-clients or parolee-clients are becoming more aggressive or violent toward their PO supervisors, although there have been reports of escalating client violence against their supervising POs. The fact is that POs are obligated to conduct face-to-face visits with their clients, and in many instances, these visits involve potentially dangerous situations and/or scenarios (Lindner, 1992c). However, some evidence suggests a decline in the future of home visits as a standard PO function (Lindner, 1991:115).

Life-Threatening Situations and Assaults against POs by Their Clients. Anonymous interviews with POs supervising both adults and juveniles give us some insight as to the potential hazards of PO work. One PO supervising juvenile offenders in Cincinnati, Ohio, reported that she was assaulted and physically beaten by youthful gang members associated with one of her juvenile clients. The juvenile client himself was apologetic and promised to advise his gang members to "leave her alone" the next time she appeared in his neighborhood. However, her broken arm, jaw, and lost teeth will be reminders of her neighborhood visit. In another situation, a male PO visited a parolee in a run-down section of Los Angeles. The parolee had been drinking excessively. When the PO entered the client's apartment, the parolee held a rifle to his own chin, threatening suicide. At one point, as the parolee continued to drink, he pointed the rifle at the PO and said, "You're the reason it's come to this . . . I might as well blow your f____ head off too." After three hours of talking, the parolee was coaxed into surrendering his weapon with a promise from the PO "not to do anything." The PO left and never said a word about the incident. Within a month, the PO had resigned and became a postal worker. Increasingly, PO training involves understanding how to deal with drug- or alcohol-dependent clients in productive ways (Read, 1988, 1992).

The hazards of PO work are clearly portrayed in the results of a nationwide survey conducted by the Federal Probation and Pretrial Officers Association in

1993 (Bigger, 1993:14–15). This study disclosed the following assaults or attempted assaults against officers nationwide since 1980 (Bigger, 1993:15):

Murders or attempted murders	16
Rapes or attempted rapes	7
Other sexual assaults or attempted sexual assaults	100
Shot and wounded or attempted shot and wounded	32
Uses or attempted use of blunt instrument or projectile	60
Slashed or stabbed or attempted slashed or stabbed	28
Car used as weapon or attempted use of car as weapon	12
Punched, kicked, choked, or other use of body/attempted	1,396
Use or attempted use of caustic substance	3
Use or attempted use of incendiary device	9
Abducted or attempted abduction and held hostage	3
Attempted or actual unspecified assaults	944
Total	2,610

Several states and territories did not respond to this national survey. We do not know how these numbers would have changed had other figures been added. The fact is that between 1980 and 1993, at least, over 2,600 victimizations or attempted victimizations of POs had occurred, based on the majority of reporting jurisdictions. Any assault or attempted assault of a PO is one too many. Seemingly, there are no justifiable reasons for these assaults or attempted assaults, since all of these clients, whether they are probationers or parolees, are released subject to various program conditions. Clearly, abusing their supervising officers places these clients in the position of having their probation or parole programs revoked. Although it does not excuse such conduct, many of these clients are drug- or alcohol-dependent. In an effort to cut down on the frequency of such assaults, some practitioners have proposed more frequent drug/alcohol testing among clientele (Tedder, 1993:28–29).

Self-Protection or Provocation? Whether POs should arm themselves during their visits to clients is often a moot question, since they arm themselves anyway, regardless of probation/parole office policy. When POs are put to a vote, however, the results are often divided 50–50. For instance, a study of 159 POs attending an in-service training session during 1990 at a state probation training academy investigated these POs' opinions about their right to carry firearms while on the job. A carefully worded question, "Should POs be given the legal option to carry a firearm while working?" was asked. Responses indicated that 59 percent of the officers believed that they should have the legal option to carry a firearm. This doesn't mean that 59 percent of these officers would carry firearms on the job; rather, they supported the idea of a choice to carry a firearm while working if such a choice were made available (Sluder, Shearer, and Potts, 1991). In the same study, POs were asked whether they would endorse a requirement to carry a firearm as a part of one's PO work. Over 80 percent of the female POs interviewed opposed such a requirement, while about 69 percent of the male POs responded similarly. However,

---

BOX 12.1
Should Probation and Parole Officers Arm Themselves Against Increasingly Violent Generations of Probationers and Parolees?

The Case of the Florida Department of Corrections

What is the world coming to? Since when should probation and parole officers have to go armed when visiting their clients, who are, by definition, supposed to be on good behavior? Since a growing number of probation and parole officers have been getting either wounded or killed while visiting their clients, that's why! Probation and parole officer work is increasingly risky business.

Art Meyer, a former probation officer, is a correctional training instructor for the Lively Criminal Justice Academy near Quincy, Florida. Meyer knows that probation and parole officers are taking greater risks each year by entering dangerous neighborhoods merely to meet briefly with their probationer or parolee-clients. In many cases, it is not a matter of being threatened or assaulted by the clients. Rather, neighborhood toughs take it upon themselves to harm officers if they believe the officers are "cops." Some clients are violent and may inflict serious injuries on the very officers attempting to help them. It is Meyer's hope that none of his officers will ever have to draw a weapon and use it. But at least they will have some protection when entering dangerous premises.

The state of Florida presently does not require its probation and parole officers to arm themselves. Carrying firearms is strictly voluntary, at least for now. Besides permitting officers to carry firearms, Florida is providing extensive firearms training for those officers who plan to use them. In fact, Henry K. Singletary Jr., head of the Florida prison system, says that this is an idea whose time has come: "The environment in which these officers work is becoming more hostile and volatile, and their safety must be ensured." Some states, such as California, have conducted firearms training and certification courses for its probation and parole officers since the 1970s. The vote is still out on whether these officers in all jurisdictions throughout the United States should carry firearms while performing their tasks. The controversy continues.

Source: Adapted from *Corrections Compendium*, "Florida's P & P Officers Train for Concealed Weapons." *Corrections Compendium*, **17,** December 1992; and Edward Velt and Albert G. Smith, "The Arming of Probation and Parole Officers." *APPA Perspectives*, **17:**17–20.

---

80 percent of all officers interviewed said that they would carry a firearm if required to do so.

Different jurisdictions have varied opinions about firearms use during PO work. The California Parole Division adopted a firearms policy in 1979 (Sluder, Shearer, and Potts, 1991:3–5; Smith, 1991a, 1991b, 1991c). Coincidentally, there was a dramatic shift in PO philosophy toward clients from rehabilitation to control and enforcement during that same period. Many officers as well as the public believed that PO firearms possession and display during PO-client confrontations would lead to numerous shooting incidents, even deaths, of officers and/or clients. During the next 12 years, however, seven unholsterings per month among California POs were reported, and only one incident of a gun being fired was reported. No agents were killed or seriously injured during this period. The California Parole Division averaged 800 armed agents during this period, ranging from 250 in 1979 to 1,500 in 1990, with an average of 7,000 arrests per year (Smith, 1991a, 1991b, 1991c). This is a remarkable record, considering the public clamor and debate preceding PO arming. One reason for such an excellent record of few or no injuries caused by firearms acquisition by officers is that they are simultaneously taught to deal with increasingly dangerous offenders and to exercise behavior modification concepts to defuse potentially hazardous or lethal encounters (Remington and Remington, 1987; Smith, 1991a).

Some of those opposed to POs carrying firearms contend that this shifts POs into a law enforcement function (Jones and Robinson, 1989:88; Schuman and Holden, 1989:6). Furthermore, if it becomes generally known that POs carry firearms, this may escalate a situation between a PO and an armed client to the point that injuries or deaths could occur. In contrast, other professionals argue that changing offender populations have transformed into successive generations of more dangerous, violent clientele (Schuman and Holden, 1989:7–8). A fundamental issue at the center of this controversy is the amount and type of training POs who will carry these firearms receive (Nowell and Stinchcomb, 1988:160; Paparozzi and Bass, 1990:8–9). Some states, such as Florida, have authorized their POs to use firearms as of July 1992. However, these POs have received extensive firearms training as well as psychological training so that the necessity of using a firearm will be for self-protection and as a last resort (*Corrections Compendium*, 1992b, 1992c).

Establishing Negligence in Training, Job Performance, and Retention

Not only is PO work increasingly hazardous, but POs are become increasingly liable for their actions taken in relation to the clients they supervise. Lawsuits against POs are becoming more commonplace. Many of these lawsuits are frivolous, but they consume much time and cause many job prospects to turn away from PO work (Jones and del Carmen, 1992). There are three basic forms of immunity: (1) absolute immunity, meaning that those acting on behalf of the state can suffer no liability from their actions taken while performing their state tasks (e.g., judges, prosecutors, and legislators); (2) qualified immunity, such as that enjoyed by probation officers if they are performing their tasks in good faith; and (3) quasi-judicial immunity, which generally refers to PO preparation of PSIs at judicial request (Jones and del Carmen, 1992:36–37). In the general case, POs enjoy only qualified immunity, meaning that they are immune only when their actions were taken in good faith. However, there is some evidence that the rules are changing related to the types of defenses available to POs, although the limits of immunity continue to be vague and undefined. Jones and del Carmen (1992) have clarified at least two different conditions that seem to favor POs in the performance of their tasks and the immunity they derive from such conditions:

1. Probation officers are considered officers of the court and perform a valuable court function, namely the preparation of PSIs.
2. Probation officers perform work intimately associated with court process, such as sentencing offenders.

Despite these conditions, Jones and del Carmen (1992) believe that it is unlikely that POs will ever be extended absolute immunity to all of their work functions (see Box 12.2). In some later and related research, del Carmen and Pilant (1994:14–15) described judicial immunity and qualified immunity as two types of immunity that are generally available to public officials including POs. Judicial liability is like absolute immunity described earlier. Judges must perform their functions and make decisions that may be favorable or unfavorable to defendants. Lawsuits filed against judges are almost always routinely dismissed without trial on the merits. Parole boards also possess such judicial immunity in most cases. In contrast, qualified immunity ensues only if officials, including POs, did not violate some client's constitutional rights according to what a reasonable person would have known (del Carmen and Pilant, 1994:14).

One of the ambiguities of PO work is the fact that the letter of the law is often replaced by the spirit of the law. POs simply create their own informal rule for dealing with their clients. Annual regional and national conferences of probation and parole officers, such as those sponsored by the American Correctional Association, the American Jail Association, and the American Probation and Parole Association, optimize conditions in which officers from different jurisdictions can exchange information with one another about how their work is performed. Much of this informal dialogue is casual conversation, but in many instances, POs glean from their counterparts in other jurisdictions certain ideas about rule bending. Not all of this dialogue is nefarious, however. Often, a PO in South Carolina will tell another PO from California that South Carolina POs have a right to take one or more actions that affect client programs. The California PO may be surprised, because in California, PO interference with or modification of client programs may be prohibited.

For example, Matthews (1993:31) reports that in South Carolina, POs may place clients in halfway houses for up to 75 days; they may place offenders in residential or nonresidential treatment; they may restructure the supervision of a client's plan of action; they may increase the numbers of supervisory contacts; and they may order up to 40 hours of community service. But in Florida, some or all of these actions by POs are strictly prohibited. For instance, in *Reynard v. State* (1993), a PO had ordered a client to perform so many hours of community service. A Florida appellate court struck down the community service orders because the sentencing judge had not included such community service orders as one of the probation conditions.

Liability Issues Associated with PO Work.   A summary of some of the key liability issues related to PO work follows.

1. *Only some information about a PO's clients is subject to public disclosure.* Del Carmen (1990:34) says that POs must constantly reassess their working materials about specific clients and decide which information is relevant under certain circumstances. It would be advisable, for instance, to inform prospective employers of certain probationers or parolees if the work involves custodial services in a large apartment complex and the particular probationers or parolees are convicted voyeurs, rapists, exhibitionists, or burglars. POs might also inform banks that particular probationers or parolees have been convicted of embezzlement if these clients are seeking work in a bank setting or any other business where they will be working around and handling money. But it may not be appropriate to advise an employer that the probationer or parolee is a convicted drug dealer if the client is seeking to become a car salesperson or factory worker. And, in most states, if POs know that their clients have AIDS, it is improper for POs to report this fact to a client's employer. This is because there are statutory prohibitions against such disclosures except under certain circumstances. These circumstances vary considerably among state jurisdictions. Some states have no policy on this issue. Thus, it is up to individual agencies to adopt their own policies (del Carmen, 1990:38–40). Del Carmen says that the general rule throughout most PO agencies is that "if a probationer or parolee obtains a job on his or her own, there is no officer or agency liability because reliance is absent. However, an agency's rules may require disclosure by the officer when he or she learns of the probationer or parolee's job, even if the job was obtained by the offender" (del Carmen, 1990:36).

2. *POs have a duty to protect the public; their work in this regard may subject them to lawsuits.* This issue relates closely to the first. If particular probationers or parolees have made threats to seek revenge against particular persons or organizations, it would be advisable for POs to report that these clients are in the community and may pose a risk to one or more former victims. There are some notable distinctions in degrees of liability, however. Del Carmen (1990:36) indicates that if a probationer says he is going to kill his wife and the PO does nothing about it, liability may attach and the PO may be liable for not warning the wife or notifying authorities. But if a parolee tells his PO that he feels like going out to commit armed robbery and actually carries it out, the liability of the PO is questionable, since it is unreasonable for us to assume that the PO knew where and when the client would commit the robbery. Furthermore, saying one may go out and commit armed robbery and actually committing the robbery are two different matters. The PO may conclude that her client is simply "blowing off steam," "getting emotions out in the open where they can be dealt with productively," or some other such similar interpretation.

3. *PO use of firearms may create hazards for both POs and their clients.* POs are increasingly carrying firearms for their personal protection when entering dan-

BOX 12.2
Can POs Be Sued by Their Clients?

The Case of Vincent Shelton

One of the thankless chores heaped on POs is the preparation of presentence investigation reports. As we have seen in Chapter 3, PSIs include much factual information about events surrounding arrest, statements from victims and/or witnesses, and other pertinent background information and details. Although POs attempt to be as objective as possible when gathering PSI information, some of this information may be inaccurate. Those interviewed may give deliberately false or unintentionally inaccurate information when interviewed. School records may contain errors of fact, where inaccurate information may have been entered or where some important information may have been omitted. Victim impact statements appended to these PSIs may be exaggerated or deliberately slanted so as to portray offenders in the worst ways. What can happen to a PO when a PSI is submitted that contains false or inaccurate information?

In Monroe County, New York, in 1988, a convicted felon, Vincent Shelton, had a PSI prepared for him by Probation Officer McCarthy and another PO. The factual contents of the report contained information that resulted in Shelton's detention for a prolonged period at the Great Meadow Correctional Facility, in Comstock, New York. This facility is a maximum-security institution constructed in 1911 and designed to house 1,610 inmates. According to the American Correctional Association *Directory* (1994:293), the facility "receives by transfer young male of-

fenders, usually those with quite serious backgrounds, personality problems, and fairly long minimum sentences." The facility is consistently overcrowded, usually exceeding the 1,610 rated capacity by 50 or more inmates. It was in this facility that Vincent Shelton resided for a prolonged period (according to Shelton) "before being transferred to his final destination" (*Corrections Compendium,* **14:**16, 1989).

Shelton filed suit against these POs, alleging that they violated his constitutional rights when they submitted a PSI on him that was false and inaccurate. He claimed these alleged falsifications caused him to be held in the Great Meadow Correctional Facility longer than he should have before being transferred to his final destination. Furthermore, Shelton alleged, this delay caused him "mental stress, loss of valuable program time and loss of the opportunity to have an operation."

The New York courts were unsympathetic. In accordance with federal and state holdings in other jurisdictions about similar allegations against POs, the New York court held that POs who prepare and submit PSIs are entitled to absolute immunity. The court argument continued: "Absolute immunity is rarely granted and is limited to functions integrally related to the judicial process. Because presentence reports are such an important facet of sentencing, probation officers while preparing reports are clearly acting as arms of the court and are entitled to absolute immunity."

Answer: Yes, POs can be sued. But these suits are often frivolous. Even if they are not frivolous, an important presumption is made by the courts that POs are acting in good faith in the performance of their court-ordered duties and are most likely entitled to absolute immunity in their PSI preparation.

Source: Adapted from "Probation Officers Entitled to Absolute Immunity." *Corrections Compendium,* **14:**17, 1989.

gerous neighborhoods or housing projects where their clients reside. If they use their firearms, there is some likelihood that someone, possibly the probationer or parolee, the PO, or an innocent bystander or relative may be seriously or fatally injured. Liability of this sort is always possible. One way of minimizing such liability, according to del Carmen (1990.38) is to provide POs with proper firearms training prior to authorizing them to carry dangerous weapons. Even though this doesn't guarantee that they will avoid lawsuits and liability, it does minimize the risk of such legal actions by others. Often, when POs are sued by their clients or others, U.S. Code, Title 42 Section 1983 civil rights actions are involved. These are usually tort actions and settled in civil courts rather than criminal courts (del Carmen, 1985; Jones and del Carmen, 1992:36).

4. *POs may supervise their clients in a negligent manner.* Watkins (1989:30–31) describes an Arizona case in which several POs were sued because of victim injuries sustained as the result of a failure to properly supervise a dangerous client. In the Arizona case (*Acevedo v. Pima County Adult Probation Department,* 1984), a convicted felon, a child sexual abuser, was placed on probation and subsequently sexually molested several children of the plaintiff. The POs supervising this offender knew of his sexual deviance and propensities. However, they allowed him to rent a room on premises where the plaintiff and her five children resided. The Arizona Supreme Court observed that although POs perform many diverse tasks and have demanding responsibilities, they must not knowingly place clients in situations in which their former conduct might create a hazard to the public. In this case, the lawsuit against the POs was successfully pursued. It may also be argued that these POs failed to warn the plaintiff of their client's sexual propensities. This, too, could have warranted a lawsuit against these POs.

5. *PO PSI report preparation may result in liability.* One of the more important PO functions is the preparation of PSIs at the request of judges prior to offender sentencing. Much information is contained in these PSIs, some of which may not be directly relevant to sentencing. Thus, it may not be necessary to disclose the entire contents of PSIs at any particular time. Del Carmen (1986:69) indicates that at the federal level, at least, federal judges may disclose the contents of PSIs except where (1) disclosure might disrupt rehabilitation of the defendant; (2) the information was obtained on a promise of confidentiality; and (3) harm may result to the defendant or to any other person. Subsequently, when inmates are about to be paroled, the PSI may again be consulted. Obviously, the long-term impact of a PSI is substantial. Errors of fact, unintentional or otherwise, may cause grievous harm to inmates and jeopardize seriously their chances for early release. If the information barring them from early release is contained in the PSI document, and if the parole board relies heavily on this information in its denial of parole to particular offenders, and if the information contained therein is inaccurate or false, a cause of action or lawsuit may be lodged against the original PO who prepared the PSI.

6. *Liabilities against POs and/or their agencies may ensue for negligent training, negligent retention, and deliberate indifference to client needs.* POs may not have particular counseling skills when dealing with certain offenders who have psychological problems. They may give poor advice. Such advice may cause offenders to behave in ways that harm others. And, POs may not be adequately prepared or trained to carry firearms. They may discharge their firearms under certain circumstances that can cause serious injury or death. These are examples of negligent training. Negligent retention might be a situation where certain POs are maintained by a probation agency after they have exhibited certain conduct or training deficiencies which they have failed to remedy. Failing to rid an organization of incompetent employees is negligent retention. Finally, when POs meet with their probationer-parolee-clients, they may believe particular offenders need certain community services or assistance. However, these POs may deliberately refrain from providing such assistance or making it possible for their clients to receive such aid. If certain clients are drug-dependent and obviously in need of medical services, deliberate indifference on the part of the PO would be exhibited if the PO did nothing to assist the client in receiving the needed medical treatment. This would be an example of deliberate indifference. Deliberate indifference may be a vengeful act on the part of the PO, an omission, or simple failure to act promptly.

Although the above listing of potential legal liabilities of POs is by no means exhaustive, it does represent the major types of situations in which POs incur potential problems from lawsuits. Jones and del Carmen (1992:36) and Sluder and del Carmen (1990:3–4) suggest at least three different types of defenses used by POs when performing their work. These defenses are not perfect, but they do make it difficult for plaintiffs to prevail under a variety of scenarios. These defenses include the following:

1. POs were acting in good faith while performing the PO role.
2. POs have official immunity, since they are working for and on behalf of the state, which enjoys sovereign immunity.
3. POs may not have a "special relationship" with their clients, thus absolving them of possible liability if their clients commit future offenses that result in injuries or deaths to themselves or others.

The idea of a special relationship is vague, according to Sluder and del Carmen (1990:3–4). It is usually created, they say, whenever one takes charge of a third person who the PO knows or should know is likely to cause bodily harm to others if not controlled. Thus, POs are under a duty to exercise reasonable care to control client behavior. Because there is so much variation among states about what constitutes a special relationship, there is considerable subjectivity associated with the term. Often, it becomes a matter to be decided by a jury rather than a judge, since the prevailing rules governing special relationships are either nonexistent or ambiguous.

PROBATION AND PAROLE OFFICER CASELOADS

The caseload of a probation or parole officer is considered by many authorities to be significant in affecting the quality of supervision POs can provide their clients. Caseloads refer to the number of offender-clients supervised by POs. **Caseloads** are the numbers of offenders supervised by POs, and they vary among jurisdictions (Su Davis, 1990b:16). Theoretically, the larger the caseload, the poorer the quality of supervision and other services. As we have seen in Chapter 4, intensive probation supervision (IPS) is based on the premise that low offender caseloads maximize the attention POs can give their clients, including counseling, employment options, and social and psychological assistance. The success of such IPS programs suggests that lower caseloads contribute to lower recidivism rates among parolees and probationers. It is conceded that other program components such as fines, curfews, and community service may have some influence on the overall reduction of these rates.

Ideal Caseloads

The earliest work outlining optimum caseloads for professionals was done by Chute (1922). Chute advocated caseloads for POs no larger than 50. Similar endorsements of a 50-caseload limit were made by Edwin Sutherland in 1934, the American Prison Association in 1946, the Manual of Correctional Standards in 1954, and the National Council of Crime and Delinquency in 1962 (Gottfredson and Gottfredson, 1988:182). The 1967 President's Commission on Law Enforcement and Administration of Justice lowered the optimum caseload figure to 35.

Actual caseloads of POs vary greatly, ranging from a low of 5 or 10 clients to a high of 200 clients (Su Davis, 1990b:7). The IPS programs described in Chapter 4 tended to have caseloads in the 20-to-30 range, and these varied according to the jurisdiction and available funding for the particular program. Some jurisdictions consider a caseload of 40 to be intensive (Wisconsin Department of Health and Social Services, 1985). Although the figures are somewhat dated, the Task Force on Corrections appointed by the 1967 President's Commission reported that in 1965, for instance, 75 percent of all probation officers had caseloads of 90 or higher, whereas over 50 percent of the parole officers had caseloads in excess of 60 (Cahalan, 1986:185). Growing numbers of parolees and probationers in recent years in relation to a fairly constant number of POs suggest that little change in PO caseloads has occurred since 1965. These caseloads will probably continue to increase, given current attitudes and philosophies (e.g., using probation and parole as strategies for prison and jail overcrowding).

Currently there is no agreement among professionals as to what is an ideal PO caseload. On the basis of evaluating caseloads of POs in a variety of jurisdictions, Gottfredson and Gottfredson (1988:182) have concluded that "it may be said with assurance . . . that (1) no optimal caseload size has been demonstrated, and (2) no clear evidence of reduced recidivism, simply by reduced caseload size, has been found." This declaration applies mainly to standard probation/parole supervision, and it is not intended to reflect on the quality of recent ISP programs established in many jurisdictions. Because the composition of parolees and probationers varies considerably among jurisdictions, it is difficult to develop clear-cut conclusions about the influence of supervision on recidivism and the delivery of other program services. An arbitrary caseload figure based on current caseload sizes among state jurisdictions would be about 30 clients per PO. This is perhaps closest to an ideal caseload size.

Changing Caseloads and Officer Effectiveness

Do Smaller PO Caseloads Mean Greater Effectiveness and Quality of Services Provided Clients by Their Supervising POs? ISP programs such as those developed in Oregon, Massachusetts, Alabama, and New Jersey have demonstrable effectiveness compared with standard probation/parole practices in decreasing recidivism among offender-participants (McCarthy, 1987a; Pearson, 1985). However, a project conducted in Fort Worth, Texas, in 1985 showed that although POs were able to make significantly more contacts per month with their clients, little relationship was found between new arrests of clients and the level of contacts, even when the risk level was held constant (Eisenberg, 1986a, 1986b). Frequency of contacts between POs and their clients has been speculated to be less important than the quality of these contacts. Thus, frequently stopping by an offender's residence to see whether the offender is on the premises and abiding by a curfew is less important than infrequent visits when such visits are accompanied by informative inquiries from officers about offender progress and problems. Genuine offers of assistance and follow-throughs by providing that assistance seem to personalize the officer-client relation.

Earlier research investigating changing caseloads and client recidivism has been equally disappointing. A classic study of the effectiveness of probation was the San Francisco Project, an investigation of the federal probation system, in the 1960s (Banks et al., 1977). Probationers were assigned to POs with varying caseloads. Some POs had caseloads of 20 offenders, while other POs had caseloads of 40 offenders. The ideal level of supervision was considered 40 clients, while 20 probationers as a caseload was considered "intensive." No significant differences in recidivism rates among the various groups of probationers were observed. However, those POs with offender caseloads of 20 reported significantly more technical violations such as curfew, use of alcohol or drugs, and traveling restrictions. If we were to use these technical violations of an offender's probation program as our measure of recidivism, it would appear that more intensive supervision was counterproductive compared with less intensive supervision. Obviously, technical violations are not new crimes. When rearrests for new crimes were contrasted for probationers under ideal and intensive supervision, no significant differences were reported, however.

The importance of the San Francisco Project is that it showed no differences in probation supervision effectiveness as the result of increasing the intensity of supervision. Greater offender monitoring through the lower caseload assignments merely made it possible for officers to spot more technical violations committed by probationers. Of course, it is impossible to calculate the value of greater contact with probationers and parolees insofar as it concerns their greater access to POs as resource persons for personalized counseling and assistance where required. No doubt some offenders are helped immeasurably by POs who are able to spend more time with them. Some POs are good listeners and function as emotional outlets for offenders with special problems. The primary fringe benefit accruing to probationers from greater contact with their POs is the more personalized attention POs can provide. However, no direct evidence shows that varying caseloads under standard probation supervision has a deterrent effect regarding new crimes.

One possible explanation for these findings from the San Francisco Project might be that when POs had lighter caseloads, they could spend a greater portion of their time citing offenders for minor technical violations, such as not observing curfew or abusing alcohol or drugs. With higher caseloads, POs might be inclined to overlook minor rule violations, simply because there would be little or no time available to prepare lengthy reports and subject offenders to parole or probation revocation hearings. Thus, caseload reductions may be ineffective if not accompanied by improvements in officer-client interactions. POs must enforce rules, but at the same time, they must provide their clients with adequate resources and assistance. Using their greater time with clients to enforce rules seems inconsistent with the original intent of intensive supervision and reduced caseloads.

Caseload Assignment and Management Models

The court sentences offenders to probation, while parole boards release many prisoners short of serving their full terms. POs must reckon with fluctuating numbers of offenders monthly, as new assignments are given them and some offenders complete their programs successfully (Baird, 1992a). No particular caseload assignment method has been universally adopted by all jurisdictions. Rather, depending on the numbers of offenders assigned to probation and parole agencies, PO caseload assignment practices vary (Cushman and Sechrest, 1992:19–20; Shapiro and Flynn, 1989:13–15). Some states are cutting back the actual numbers of offenders to be supervised. In Oregon, for instance, state officials are projecting a significant reduction in the numbers of parole and probation officers as approximately 17,000 offenders are redefined as *not* in need of PO supervision (*Corrections Compendium,* 1993a:17).

Carlson and Parks (1979) have studied various caseload assignment schemes.

Their investigation has led to the identification of four popular varieties of assignment methods. These include (1) the conventional model, (2) the numbers game model, (3) the conventional model with geographic considerations, and (4) specialized caseloads.

1. The Conventional Model. The **conventional model** involves the random assignment of probationers or parolees to POs. Thus, any PO must be prepared to cope with extremely dangerous offenders released early from prison on parole, those with drug or alcohol dependencies or in need of special treatment programs, and those requiring little, if any, supervision. However, those convicted of violent offenses may no longer be violent. Spouses may kill in the heat of passion, but it is highly unlikely that they will kill again. By the same token, it is possible that low-risk, less dangerous property offenders may become violent through offense escalation. Research suggests there is no pattern among recidivists to indicate that they progress to more serious offenses, however (Maltz, 1984; Willstadter, 1984).

The conventional model is probably used most frequently in probation and parole agencies throughout the United States. There are no specific logistical problems that need to be dealt with, and POs can be assigned offender-clients on an "as needed" basis. The major drawback is that POs must be extremely flexible in their management options, because of the diversity of clientele they must supervise.

2. The Numbers Game Model. The **numbers game model** is similar to the conventional model. In order to apply this model, the total number of clients is divided by the number of POs, and POs are randomly given the designated number. For instance, if there are 500 offenders and 10 POs, 500 divided by 10 equals 50 offenders per PO. Another version of the numbers game model is to define an optimum caseload such as 40 and determine how many POs are required to supervise 40 offenders each. Thus, PO hiring is influenced directly by the numbers of offenders assigned to the jurisdiction and whatever is considered the optimum caseload.

3. The Conventional Model with Geographic Considerations. The **conventional model with geographic considerations** is applied on the basis of the travel time required for POs to meet with their offender-clients regularly. Those POs who supervise offenders in predominantly rural regions are given lighter caseloads so that they may have the time to make reasonable numbers of contacts with offenders on a monthly or weekly basis. Those POs who supervise urban offenders are given heavier caseloads because less travel time between clients is required.

4. The Specialized Caseloads Model. Sometimes caseload assignments are made on the basis of PO specialties, according to the **specialized caseloads model.** Some POs have unique skills and knowledge relative to drug or alcohol dependencies. Often, these POs have developed liaisons with Alcoholics Anonymous or other organizations so that their service to clients can be enhanced (Pierson et al., 1992). Perhaps certain POs have had extensive training and education in particular problem areas to better serve certain offender-clients who may be retarded or mentally ill. Some POs by virtue of their training may be assigned more dangerous offenders. Those POs with greater work experience and legal training can manage dangerous offenders more effectively compared with fresh new PO recruits. In some respects, this is close to client-specific planning, where individualization of cases is stressed (Robertson and Blackburn, 1984; Yeager, 1992:537–544).

Some experts are downright bitter about the current importance given to caseloads and caseload management. For instance, Andrew R. Klein, Chief Probation Officer in Quincy, Massachusetts, says that "case management is ruining probation. Developed as a tool to help probation officers manage escalating caseloads, case management has become an end in itself. The goal of probation is no longer crime control, retribution, rehabilitation, or anything else; it is the management of cases. Let a probation officer exercise some creativity, even common sense in dealing with criminals, and the wrath of middle management will strike as surely as a multiple offender drunk driver will deny he has a drinking problem" (Klein, 1989:27). Klein objects to the idea that X number of cases can be pigeon-holed into some common aggregate and then divided by the number of POs in a given agency. This is "by-the-numbers" caseload assignments, whether certain probationers need or do not need supervision. He also believes that POs should attack the sources of the problems that get offenders, such as drunk drivers, into trouble. For instance, he suggests visiting bars drunk drivers are known to frequent. He would order a round of softdrinks for everyone and say, "What are we doing here, anyway?" (Klein, 1989:28).

Some experts, such as Ferns (1994), believe that caseloads ought to be refocused to heighten offender accountability through cognitive restructuring and restorative case management. Traditional caseloads are oriented largely toward offender monitoring and control. Ferns suggests that offenders need to experience some actual change in their behavior while on probation or parole. They need to learn about the adverse impact they had on possible victims of their crimes. Their accountability should be heightened and their self-awareness in this regard sharpened. Basically, Ferns says that the intent of restorative case management is to provide an ethical foundation and specific direction for the function of offender case management (Ferns, 1994:38). Attention of supervising POs is shifted toward the offender's level of cognitive distortion and skill defects, the level of antisocial behaviors, and the ability of offenders to provide restoration to communties and victims. The emphasis of restorative case management is on the victims of offenders, although offenders themselves should acquire a greater degree of empathy toward their victims. This program, as Ferns notes, is similar to the balanced approach described by Maloney, Romig, and Armstrong, 1988). The balanced approach, devised originally for juvenile offenders, stresses heightening offender accountability, individualizing sanctions or punishments, and promoting community safety as critical program components. Ferns' restorative case management synthesizes these elements and blends them with heightened offender awareness through cognitive restructuring.

OFFICER-CLIENT INTERACTIONS

Although recruitment for POs is designed to identify and select those most capable of performing increasingly demanding PO tasks, little uniformity exists among jurisdictions regarding the types of POs ultimately recruited. Each PO brings to the job a philosophy of supervision based, in part, on agency expectations. Furthermore, each PO has individual differences and attitudes toward work that influence their supervisory style. Some POs are more punitive than others, while some see themselves as rehabilitators or therapists.

In the course of interacting with different kinds of offenders, it is not unusual for POs to acquire a certain amount of cynicism about their jobs and those they supervise. If an offender recidivates by committing a new offense, some POs may take this new offense personally and consider it an indication of their failure at helping certain offender-clients. Strong (1981) and others have examined the multifaceted nature of PO work and identified a variety of roles performed by POs. Sometimes, these work roles come into conflict with one another.

These work roles include but are not limited to the following: (1) the **detector** role, in which the PO attempts to identify troublesome clients or those who have one or more problems that could present the community with some risk; (2) the **broker** role, in which the PO functions as a referral service and supplies the offender-client with contacts with agencies that provide needed services; (3) the **educator, enabler,** and **mediator** roles, in which the PO seeks to instruct and assist offenders to deal with problems as they arise in the community; and (4) the **enforcer** role, in which POs perceive themselves as enforcement officers charged with regulating client behaviors (Strong, 1981).

Since POs are obligated to check on their clients, they are often viewed with suspicion and apprehension by probationers and parolees. According to the rules and terms of probation or parole, infractions of any kind are to be reported to agency authorities and dealt with accordingly. However, if every single infraction observed by POs was reported and acted on officially, there would be an endless series of hearings about whether probation or parole should be revoked in each reported case. The required attendance and participation of POs at such hearings would consume virtually every minute of their time, and little or no time would be left to supervise and help other offenders.

Therefore, the PO–offender-client relationship often becomes one of negotiation, in which the PO conveniently overlooks certain rule infractions, particularly minor ones, and in which the offender-client conscientiously attempts to adhere to the more important probation or parole provisions. This means that an unwritten relationship is often established in which the PO and offender can help each other in complementary ways.

Role conflict is inherent in the PO-offender relationship. The PO desires a successful outcome for the client, in which the terms of the probation or parole are fulfilled and the client emerges from the program to lead a productive life. But often, the circumstances leading to an offender's original arrest and conviction continue to exist and influence offender behaviors. Old acquaintances, family circumstances, and the added pressures of maintaining a job and complying with stringent probation or parole program conditions cause problems for more than a few offenders. Many revert to their old ways by committing new crimes and/or violating one or more program requirements.

If a PO reports a parolee or probationer for violating a program rule, there is a possibility that the offender will eventually retaliate by either threatening the PO or carrying out aggressive acts (Parsonage and Bushey, 1988). At the same time, the PO has considerable power and can influence significantly the life chances of those supervised. An unfavorable report may mean prison for probationers or a longer term in prison for parolees. Objectivity is required of all POs, although achieving objectivity and detachment in performing the PO role is difficult. Many POs take it personally whenever one of their offenders fails or is returned to prison. They regard offender failure as their own failure. After all, some of these POs entered their profession originally to help others. When their strategies for helping others are apparently ineffective, this failure reflects adversely on their own job performance. Seasoned POs recommend to those entering the field initially that they should not get too friendly with their offender-clients. They must constantly divorce their emotions from their work roles. There is some evidence, however, that POs find this difficult to do. POs attempt to perform helping functions while they must be enforcers of legal conditions at the same time (Silverman, 1993).

Special offenders pose special problems for POs as well. In recent years, sex offenders in some jurisdictions have been treated with Depo-Provera, a drug that reduces the production of the sex hormone, testosterone, and, thus, reduces sexual interest (Knopp, Rosenberg, and Stevenson, 1986). For POs managing sex offenders, more elaborate evaluations are required of an offender's cognitive, emotional, and behavioral state in addition to ensuring that regular Depo-Provera treatments are administered. Sex offenders may commit new sex offenses despite these drug treatments. Thus, POs have considerable responsibility for assessing several complex dimensions of their clients' lives. More effective counseling methods are being incorporated into PO training programs annually, but no counseling program prepares an officer for every eventuality (Dierna, 1987:4–7). Errors in such assessments can be costly and are an additional source of stress for POs (Romero and Williams, 1983).

Many POs consider women on probation or parole troublesome (Norland and Mann, 1984). Some POs believe women take up too much of their time with a variety of what agents consider minor problems. Additionally, female clients evidence problems of adjustment related to family, children, and employment. For these and related reasons, women are less likely than men to be reported for anything but the most serious kinds of rule infractions. Researchers suggest that POs treat female probationers and parolees differently because of their paternalistic beliefs that women's family-based obligations are more important than men's (Norland and Mann, 1984).

Many POs are frustrated because they lack the time and resources to do the kind of job they believe is maximally helpful to their clients. Because of their increasing caseload responsibilities, POs cannot possibly devote the proper amount of time to any given offender without interfering with their time allocations to other clients. The immense paperwork associated with the PO role has caused more than a few POs to opt for alternative professions. The progress of offenders must be reported regularly to the courts, parole boards, and various agencies. These reports are tedious to complete. For example, an investigation of the time allocations of a sample of Missouri POs in 1980 showed that paperwork tasks and travel consumed over 50 percent of their monthly work activities (Hartke, 1984:66–68). Increased caseloads and work pressures are not only stressful; they also lead to a reduction in the quality of general services and supervision extended to offender-clients.

One important implication for POs of the reduction of the quality of client supervision is the increased potential for lawsuits arising from their "negligent supervision of clients" (Benson, 1988). POs cannot guarantee public safety completely by their supervision of offenders; however, it is generally believed that the more intense the supervision, the less likely offenders will commit dangerous offenses. Where supervision by POs is less intense, the risk to the public posed by the offender theoretically increases. In a 1986 case, the Alaska Supreme Court ruled that state agencies and their officers may be held liable for negligence when probationers and parolees under their supervision commit violent offenses (*Division of Corrections v. Neakok,* 1986). Thus, POs are increasingly at risk through tort actions filed by victims harmed by the crimes committed by their offender-clients (Jones, Ascolillo, and Hanrahan, 1988). The American Correction Association currently conducts seminars and other types of training to make POs more knowledgeable about their personal liabilities, especially if one or more of their clients harm victims while under PO supervision.

THE CHANGING PROBATION AND PAROLE OFFICER ROLE

There is every indication to believe that the quality of PO personnel is increasing, compared with past years (Davis, 1990b:7; Van Ness, 1988). The American Correctional Association and several other agencies are expanding their training options and arrangements to permit larger numbers of prospective corrections recruits to acquire skills and training. "Beefing up" the minimum standards and qualifications associated with corrections positions generally and PO work specifically will eventually spawn new generations of better trained officers to managing growing offender populations (Camp, 1985). New generations of POs are also having to familiarize themselves with computers and computer software programs designed for offender control and surveillance (Dean, 1989:61–67).

Theoretically, more educated POs may be able to manage better the stress associated with PO work. But at the same time, there are indications that more educated POs and other corrections officers have higher levels of dissatisfaction with their work compared with less educated officers (Cohn, 1987; Cullen et al., 1985).

Personality factors appear crucial for making successful adaptations to PO work (Sluder and Shearer, 1992:29–30). And, there is high labor turnover among corrections personnel. This means that comparatively few officers remain in PO work long enough to acquire useful skills and abilities to assist their clients effectively.

While the composition of the PO work force is changing gradually each year, technological developments and changes in the laws governing PO–offender-client interactions and the rights of offenders are also occurring (Bahn and Davis, 1991:17; Brown, 1990:66; Pierson et al., 1992:18; Sluder and del Carmen, 1990:3). For instance, the use of electronic monitoring of offenders is making it possible to increase officer caseloads dramatically without affecting seriously the amount of time officers spend monitoring offender whereabouts. This is especially applicable in the case of low-risk offenders sentenced to probation or paroled property offenders.

But electronic monitoring, together with home incarceration, is inadvertently changing the qualifications of those who supervise offenders with these electronic devices. Private enterprises are entering the correctional field in increasing numbers, and their involvement in probation or parole programs in which electronic monitoring and house arrest are used as sanctions is apparent. What kinds of POs will be needed in future years to read computer printouts, drive by offender homes with electronic receiving devices, and conduct telephonic checks of offenders?

Not all clients on probation or parole are nonviolent, low-risk offenders. Increasing numbers are dangerous felons who have committed violent crimes (Petersilia, 1987b). Therefore, POs are required who possess more than minimal qualifications in order to adequately supervise those uncharacteristic of the average probationer or parolee. While in-service training is desirable, not all states include it in their recruitment process (Library Information Specialists, Inc., 1985b). Unless there are drastic changes in both the image and rewards associated with PO work in the near future, more offenders will receive increasingly inadequate services from probation and parole professionals as caseloads are enlarged. This circumstance will only serve to increase recidivism rates associated with various probation and parole programs.

PROBATION AND PAROLE OFFICER LABOR TURNOVER

Labor turnover is a major problem among POs (Philliber, 1987:9). As we have seen, low pay, low self-esteem, a poor public image, and increasingly difficult work responsibilities make PO positions less attractive (Crouch, 1983). High turnover among POs occurs not only during the first few years of an employee's service, but high turnover rates are also observed among recruits during the initial phases of their training.

Many recruits say that PO work is not what they had originally envisioned. There may be an ideal-real discrepancy here. Ideally, PO work involves fruitful interactions with offenders who want to be helped. POs are on the scene to provide counsel and assistance to offenders when needed. They supervise offender progress and influence the course of an offender's program. They have minimal paperwork and spend most of their time in helping capacities. In reality, they spend a great deal of their time preparing PSIs, performing routine checks of their clients' premises and workplaces, and furnishing courts with periodic up-dated information about offender progress. This lackluster work role is sometimes disenchanting for POs. It is perfunctory, especially when writing skills are more highly valued than the assistance POs provide to help their clients adopt or continue noncriminal behavior patterns.

A large portion of those who leave PO positions during their first few years report that they considered the work temporary, as a position to be held while they sought better-paying jobs in the private sector (Philliber, 1987). Since the educational requirements are not particularly demanding, probation and parole work is fairly easy to obtain. Holding a job with some degree of responsibility is considered an asset on one's vita or resume, especially for those looking forward to working in other professions.

Closely related to high employee turnover in corrections officer positions is the absence of challenging work. Many POs claim that the only thing going for them in their work is job security (Thomas, 1988). Others say that corrections work generally is like being on a treadmill, where no matter how hard one tries, one feels no sense of accomplishment. The major implication is that job impoverishment results, and few self-rewards are forthcoming from good work effort (Ellsworth, 1990b; Smith, 1993a:80–87; Whitehead and Lindquist, 1992).

Some indication of the willingness of POs to switch professions if better job opportunities arise is a study of officers conducted in an Eastern state in 1980 (Toch and Klofas, 1982:36–38). On the basis of 832 responses to a questionnaire about various aspects of correctional work, Toch and Klofas found that 75 percent of all respondents would change professions if they had a chance. Only 25 percent said they get recognition for good work, while 75 percent disagreed with this statement. These results are not unlike other research conducted in previous years (Jacobs, 1978; Teake and Williamson, 1979).

The American Correctional Association, the American Probation and Parole Association, and various training agencies are sensitive to the problem of high labor turnover in corrections. Organizational responses have been geared to provide more meaningful and relevant training for new recruits and to socialize them to the realities of PO work (Crouch, 1983; Miller and Adwell, 1984). Some training programs are designed to provide new recruits with coping strategies to combat stress and burnout (Cullen et al., 1985; Stinchcomb, 1986:22).

STRESS AND BURNOUT IN PROBATION AND PAROLE OFFICER ROLE PERFORMANCE

The selection and recruitment of the right kinds of personnel to perform PO work roles is designed to identify those most able to handle the stresses and strains accompanying the job. The concern about occupational stress has been rising steadily

Neighborhoods where parolees live are often
dangerous places for parole officers who must make
periodic face-to-face visits with their clients. (Paul
Conklin/Monkmeyer Press)

in recent years (Olekalns, 1985). Virtually all occupations and professions have
varying degrees of stress associated with them. Probation and parole work is not
immune from stress and burnout. Whitehead and Gunn (1988:143) studied 400 probation and parole officers in various states and found that they tended to offer
more negative than positive comments about their work. In fact, these researchers
reported that the POs studied had stress levels comparable to police officers as well
as significant job burnout, stress levels, and job dissatisfaction (Whitehead, 1989).

***Possible Gender and Age Differences in Stress and Burnout Associated with PO
Work.***   Do female POs have more or less stress and burnout compared with their
male PO counterparts? Another study by Whitehead (1986a:51–52) showed that
when 700 male and female POs were studied in New York and Indiana, there were

no significant stress or burnout differences. Whitehead concluded that "the clearest implication [for these null findings] of little or no differences [between male and female POs] is that specific attention to the needs of women officers is not important either for researchers or for policy makers. Apparently, the problems of women officers are the problems of male officers, so that neither gender requires special attention." However, an anonymous reviewer of Whitehead's research suggested that this nondifference may be attributable to a self-selection function, whereby male POs are attracted to PO work, which is more nurturant and people-oriented rather than profit, authority, and control. Thus, both males and females who pursue PO careers may have similar personality backgrounds, and these similar characteristics might possibly account for the lack of gender differences found by Whitehead's study. This is pure speculation, however, and the premise of personality as a determinant has not been systematically studied thus far. Some more recent research suggests that PO attitudes may be changing more toward behavior control interests and away from objectives of treatment and assistance (Harris, Clear, and Baird, 1989:235).

Age also seems to be a contributing factor to burnout. We might simplify such thinking by stating that as POs get older, the more burnout they experience. This postulation has little consistent empirical support. For instance, one study has reported that older POs (age 51 or older) tend to experience more emotional exhaustion and low feelings of personal accomplishment. In turn, this sensed lack of accomplishment led to decreased client contact, which, in turn, decreased PO work effectiveness (Holgate and Clegg, 1991). In the same study, however, younger POs often exhibited greater role conflict and emotional exhaustion, accompanied by greater client contact. Apparently, in this study at least, younger officers are driven toward greater client contact to resolve role conflict situations and reduce emotional exhaustion, while older officers are driven away from clients because of feelings of depersonalization and a lack of accomplishment.

Stress

Stress is a nonspecific response to a perceived threat to an individual's well-being or self-esteem (Selye, 1974, 1976). It is important that we recognize that these stress responses are not specific, and that each person reacts differently to the same situation triggering stress. Some people react to stress with somatic complaints of aches and pains, while others may exhibit irritability, loss of attention span, or fatigue (Moracco, 1985:22). Furthermore, what is stressful for one person may not be stressful to another. Therefore, several factors including one's previous experiences with the event, constitutional factors, and personality may function to mediate the stress and one's reaction to the event (Moracco, 1985:22–23).

In-service training is regarded by many departments of correction as important, since the training exposes new recruits to different officer-offender relationships that generate stress. Becoming familiar with a variety of officer-offender interactions and recognizing potentially problematic interpersonal situations is one means of effectively combating stress or at least minimizing it. Although it is not known precisely how education relates to stress reduction, more educated POs probably are more aware of several behavioral or interactional options whenever problems arise between themselves and probationers or parolees (Brown, 1987; Stinchcomb, 1986:20–21).

Some stress is good. A moderate amount of stress enhances the learning and creative processes, while too little stress may induce boredom or apathy (Moracco, 1985:22). However, we don't know for sure how much stress is too much. We do know that correctional officers have twice the national average divorce rate. Also, they have the highest heart attack rates among all types of state employees, including police officers (Moracco, 1985:22). These statistics appear to result directly from the stressful aspects of corrections work. However, a study by Patterson (1992) of 4,500 police, correctional, and probation/parole officers showed that there was a curvilinear relation between perceived stress and time on the job. This might be interpreted as follows: there is considerable stress among many of these officers in their early years on the job, followed by a stress decline. In turn, this stress increases as on-the-job experience increases. Obviously, blanket generalizations about stress and the amount of one's job experience are difficult to formulate.

Burnout

Burnout is one result of stress. *Burnout* emerged as a popular term in the mid-1970s to describe work alienation, apathy, depersonalization, depression, and a host of other job-related complaints (Paine, 1982:29). Not everyone agrees about how burnout ought to be defined. Maslach (1982b:30–31) has identified at least 15 different connotations of the term. These are

1. A syndrome of emotional exhaustion, depersonalization, and reduced personal accomplishment that can occur among individuals who do "people work" of some kind.
2. A progressive loss of idealism, energy, and purpose experienced by people in the helping professions as a result of the conditions of their work.
3. A state of physical, emotional, and mental exhaustion marked by physical depletion and chronic fatigue, feelings of helplessness and hopelessness, and the development of a negative self-concept and negative attitudes toward work, life, and other people.
4. A syndrome of inappropriate attitudes toward clients and self, often associated with uncomfortable physical and emotional symptoms.
5. A state of exhaustion, irritability, and fatigue that markedly decreases the worker's effectiveness and capability.
6. To deplete oneself; to exhaust one's physical and mental resources; to wear oneself out by excessively striving to reach some unrealistic expectations imposed by oneself or by the values of society.
7. To wear oneself out doing what one has to do; an inability to cope adequately with the stresses of work or personal life.
8. A malaise of the spirit; a loss of will; an inability to mobilize interests and capabilities.
9. To become debilitated, weakened, because of extreme demands on physical and/or mental energy.
10. An accumulation of intense negative feelings that is so debilitating that a person withdraws from the situation in which those feelings are generated.

11. A pervasive mood of anxiety giving way to depression and despair.
12. A process in which a professional's attitudes and behavior change in negative ways in response to job strain.
13. An inadequate coping mechanism used consistently by an individual to reduce stress.
14. A condition produced by working too hard for too long in a high-pressure environment.
15. A debilitating psychological condition resulting from work-related frustrations, which results in lower employee productivity and morale.

The common elements of these definitions seem to be emotional, mental, and physical exhaustion that debilitates and weakens one's ability to cope with situations. Definitions 2, 3, and 4 are particularly crucial for PO work, since POs must maintain effective relations with their clients on a continuous basis and regularly evaluate their progress. When stress rises to the level that generates burnout, offender-clients experience corresponding decreases in the quality of services from probation/parole personnel (Stinchcomb, 1986:20). The importance of burnout is that it signifies a reduction in the quality or effectiveness of an officer's job performance (Brown, 1987:17). Such debilitating reductions in effectiveness are often accompanied by higher recidivism rates among probationers and parolees, more legal problems and case filings from officer-client interactions, and greater labor turnover among POs (Cheek and Miller, 1983a; Stinchcomb, 1986:22).

POs are subject to inputs from the work environment that can cause burnout. The work environment consists of *role senders* such as administrators, supervisors, and even the general public. As we have seen, the public seems dissatisfied with the apparent leniency of probation and parole and how these programs operate. The work structure is comprised of the inherent challenge of work tasks, duties or assignments (caseloads for POs), troublesome clients and incidents, and a degree of role conflict. The demands and expectations of others may conflict with the way in which POs perceive how their roles should be performed. The lack of a specific mission for probation and parole programs invites role ambiguity and conflicts between officers and administrators as well as the public-at-large.

Intervening variables consist of gender, age, amount and type of education, length of job-related experience, self-esteem, marital status, and the degree of autonomy and job satisfaction associated with PO chores (Rosecrance, 1985; Virginia Department of Corrections, 1987). The social support system is made up of others who perform similar tasks as well as the frequency of contact with these people for the purpose of sharing the frustrations of work. These factors form a mosaic from which stress stems. Stress is manifested by physiological, psychological, and/or emotional indicators. Burnout may result. One important consequence of burnout may be labor turnover. The PO may decide to follow a less stressful career alternative.

Sources of Stress

Stress among POs and other professionals emanates from several sources. Stress researchers have targeted the following as the chief sources of stress among POs: (1) job dissatisfaction, (2) role conflict, (3) role ambiguity, (4) officer-client interactions, (5) excessive paperwork and performance pressures, (6) low self-esteem and public image, and (7) high risks and liabilities.

Job Dissatisfaction.   **Job dissatisfaction** is somewhat unwieldy—it results from a variety of factors (Brown, 1987; Dierna, 1987; Gray and Wren, 1992). Some are similar to those cited earlier for generating work-related stress. Specific reasons for dissatisfaction among POs have been identified by Cheek and Nouri (1980) and include the following:

1. Lack of clear guidelines for job performance;
2. Institutional policies not being clearly communicated to all staff members;
3. Crisis situations;
4. Conflicting orders from supervisors;
5. Having to do things against your better judgment;
6. Having your supervisor give you things to do which conflict with other things you have to do;
7. Not being treated as a professional;
8. Low morale of other officers;
9. Lack of training;
10. Officers in the department not being quickly informed about policy changes;
11. Criticism from supervisor in front of clients;
12. Poor physical conditions and equipment;
13. Having too little authority to carry out assigned responsibilities;
14. Not being kept well informed by the immediate supervisor;
15. Not having adequate sharing of information among all officers;
16. Not receiving adequate pay;
17. Not having a chance to develop new talents;
18. Feelings of pressure from having to please too many bosses; and
19. Lack of opportunity to participate in decision making. (Bright, 1981:22).

Low pay, burgeoning caseloads, and unchallenging work figure prominently in an officer's decision to leave PO work for better employment opportunities elsewhere (Cushman and Sechrest, 1992; Silverman, 1993). Not being involved in decisions that affect work and being excluded from influencing agency policy are factors causing satisfaction with work to decrease (Cheek and Nouri, 1980).

Role Conflict.   **Role conflict** occurs as the result of having to adhere to conflicting expectations (Burton, Latessa, and Barker, 1992:274–275; Clear and Latessa, 1993; Ellsworth, 1990a, 1990b, 1990c). Collecting supervision fees from their indigent clients often creates a type of conflict for POs about their roles as rehabilitators and enforcers (Finn and Parent, 1992b; Wheeler and Rudolph, 1990). The expectations of the probation officer role are unusual and sometimes conflicting (Mills, 1990:3). These expectations may be those of supervisors, and they sometimes are in conflict with a PO's concept of how the job ought to be performed (Manning, 1983; McCabe, 1986). Sometimes role conflict occurs when the probation supervisor and administrator expect the PO to complete different tasks at the same time. The logistical complications are apparent, and role conflict ensues (Mills, 1990). Mills (1990:3–6) summarizes many of the feelings of POs who sense the frustrations of role conflict: "Nobody said it would be like this"; "Why do you think they call them [probationer/clients] cons?"; "If there is a problem, see the probation officer"; "How am I doing so far?"; "I never took this job to get rich"; and "Will this ever end?" Mills (1990:7) says that "for the probation officer, it is important to maintain a freshness and enthusiasm toward the career. In part this calls on the officer to establish and maintain a well-balanced life." Unfortunately, nobody ever explains to the average PO how all this can be accomplished.

Whitehead and Gunn (1988:155) report a comment from a Connecticut probation officer experiencing role conflict: "Sometimes you feel like the ancient Hebrews who, when they asked for time off, were told by the Pharaoh to make bricks without straw seeing they must have so much free time." Another probation officer from New York said, "I am asked to assume a tremendous responsibility: the control of another person's life, but I . . . am trained and paid subject to the whims of my particular county."

Role Ambiguity.   Closely related to role conflict is role ambiguity. **Role ambiguity** occurs whenever POs have inadequate or even conflicting information about their work roles, the scope and responsibilities of the job, and the ethics of certain unwritten practices that are commonplace among many POs (Brown, 1987:20; Wehmhoefer, 1993:8–9). Experts have long been critical of probation and parole agencies and organizations for failing to make explicit program goals and mission statements (Conrad, 1984; McAnany, Thomson, and Fogel, 1984). The fact that probation and parole program goals are often diffuse or unspecified makes it difficult for POs working with those programs to focus their energies in productive directions consistent with program objectives (McCabe, 1986; Poole and Regoli, 1983).

Whitehead and Gunn (1988:154–155) highlight this ambiguity by noting a comment by a female probation officer from Indiana:

> Basically, I feel probation is abused by the legal profession, judges, DAs, and attorneys who set themselves up as experts in probation and social work when it is to their convenience. I find it actually painful to see the inconsistencies in sentences that occur every day and know full well that one person goes to jail and another is placed on probation simply based on the mix of personalities involved. God help the person that gets into the system unprepared and naive.

Two other comments from probation officers in New York and Connecticut address certain role ambiguities seemingly inherent in PO work:

> [from New York] People who are in supervisory positions do not attempt to explain procedures or rules . . . until one "fouls up" or "makes a wrong move".
>
> [from Connecticut] Management and judicial authorities are not responsive to our problems. They say they are, but nothing ever seems to improve . . . I really think management and moreover legislators, in charge of the purse strings, see us as a necessary evil and don't really care if we are truly performing. Our statistics are much more important to them. Today a district supervisor called and said, "Our total restitution so far this month is $37,000—push for $40,000." That is demoralizing!

Sometimes, institutionalized procedures for conducting parole supervision activities may not be legal procedures. In essence, POs in certain agencies may adopt the policies and practices of other officers during their training, simply because "we have always done it this way." These traditional practices are not immune from constitutional challenges by clients. For instance, in a 1991 case, a Pennsylvania parolee's premises were searched incident to an arrest for his suspected cocaine dealing. The parolee, Michael Green, had previously missed appearing at his residence the night before in violation of curfew. An anonymous tip received by his supervising PO, James Hines, indicated Green's possible involvement in drug dealing. The following morning, Green appeared at Hines's office and was arrested for the curfew violation. Next, Hines and other officers transported Green to his home, where his rooms were searched without warrant. The search uncovered 29 grams of cocaine and other drug paraphernalia. The police received the drugs from Hines and charged Green with cocaine possession and distribution. Green objected, contending that the search of his premises was illegal. Was it? The Pennsylvania Superior Court determined that Pennsylvania parole officers always conducted such searches upon arrests of their parolees, especially when sufficient grounds existed to conduct such searches, even without warrants. Although there was no written policy authorizing such searches by Pennsylvania POs, the searches were legally conducted, said the court, since "reasonable grounds" existed to believe that additional violations of parole might be uncovered. No warrant was necessary because of Green's parole status, said the Court (*Commonwealth v. Green,* 1991).

Officer-Client Interactions.   A study of 108 Alabama PO officers surveyed in 1984 showed that over half suffered from stress and burnout (Whitehead and Lindquist, 1985). Specifically, work overload, inadequate agency resources, and problems related to client contact contributed to job stress. In some instances, officers believed that their efforts in relating to offender-clients were frequently misunderstood and they were perceived as antagonistic toward those they were supposed to help. Mismatching of officers and their clients also accounts for a certain proportion of interpersonal problems that arise in various agencies. Workload deployment systems based on a successful match between officer skills and clients to be supervised can make a significant difference in the day-to-day operation of probation and parole agencies (Burke, 1990:37–39).

Whitehead and Gunn (1988:156) report a view expressed by a New York probation officer that expresses some of the frustration of PO-client interactions: "The greatest understanding gap is why probationers commit new crimes. The burnout symptoms occur upon violation—where did I fail? Therein lies the explanation for the hardening of the attitudes. I cannot supervise them 24 hours a day, seven days per week—the assumption of probation is that with authoritative guidance, they can overcome their disabilities." Some experts say that failures are the result of expert client manipulation rather than anything helpful the officer attempts to do (Morrison, 1992:24).

The findings of Whitehead and Lindquist (1985) are consistent with those of Maslach (1982a, 1982b), who has also determined that the depersonalization of offender-clients is stress inducing. However, in a subsequent investigation that sought to test Maslach's theory of burnout resulting from depersonalizing officer-client interactions, Whitehead (1987) found that greater client contact led to more frequent feelings of accomplishment among POs. Perhaps these apparent inconsistencies in findings are explained by the relative lack of autonomy POs are given in relation to their offender-clients. More autonomous POs seem to have a better outlook toward their work as well as offender-clients, while those who must adhere to rigid behavioral guidelines established by their supervisors and agencies are generally discontent with their work roles (Brown, 1987; Pines and Aronson, 1981). In fact, Pines and Aronson (1981) have declared, "the more autonomy, the less burnout."

Excessive Paperwork and Performance Pressures.   The larger a PO's caseload, the more the paperwork associated with the clients supervised (Hartke, 1984). A growing problem is increased caseloads in many jurisdictions without an accompanying increase in the numbers of POs to perform the greater amount of work. Officers working under increased work pressure must produce more work in the same amount of time (Dierna, 1989:4–6; Hartke, 1984:67). The preparation of PSIs takes time. An investigation of the Missouri Division of Probation and Parole in 1980 disclosed that POs were allocating almost 12 hours per PSI. During any given period, the amount of time devoted to report preparation accounts for almost three-fourths of the PO's 40-hour workweek (Hartke, 1984:66–67). Over the years, these demands have only intensified in most jurisdictions (Smith, 1992:136–138).

Whitehead and Gunn (1988:152–154) show how excessive paperwork can exacerbate performance pressures with comments from two probation officers in different states:

> The emphasis is on turning out the paper in the name of "accountability" at the expense of serving the needs of the people we're responsible for (the probationers and community). I'm supposed to keep my desk neat, avoid any attention to detail, and pump out 30 quarterly reports a month. [This bureaucracy] has lost sight of its function and is concerned only with its maintenance needs. Hence, the emphasis is upon accountability.

Another officer said, "We're overloaded with paper and the philosophy is turning to law enforcement rather than helping others which makes things uncomfortable." A third officer from Connecticut says, "The caseload keeps going up, budgets are being cut back, no new help is hired, and people leave due to attrition—the expectation remains the same: to do everything required, no matter how much work comes in."

Closely related to excessive paperwork and performance pressures is the fact of bureaucratization. Bureaucratization stresses adherence to abstract rules, a hierarchy of authority, task specialization, explicit spheres of competence, emotional neutrality, and promotion on the basis of merit and expertise (Champion, 1975). Probation departments have been depicted by various investigators as more or less bureaucratic (Burton, Latessa, and Barker, 1992; Horn, 1992). As a result of these variable bureaucratic features either present or absent in probation and parole agencies, POs acquire different orientations toward their work. Some adapt well to

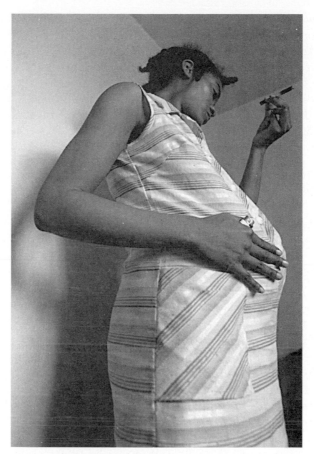

Parole violations, such as the use of crack cocaine or other illegal drugs, frequently result in parole revocations and return to prison. (Magnum Photos, Inc.)

bureaucratic organization, while others hate it. Indifferent and/or upwardly mobile probation officers in highly bureaucratized settings tend to experience greater challenge and job fulfillment compared with others who are intimidated by the competition bureaucratization inspires (Rosecrance, 1987b).

And, since PO work pays less than many other positions, it fails to attract highly educated recruits with a proficiency for writing. Thus, less competent and inadequately prepared POs find the pressures of report preparation even more demanding than more educated POs. This generates role conflict through one's inability to fulfill adequately the expectations of the position (Bright, 1981; Brown, 1986). Despite this potential role conflict, many recruits seek careers in PO work for reasons unrelated to income. PO work offers the opportunity to work with and assist others. Parolee or probationer successes are often perceived by POs as their own personal successes. And, PO work is flexible—officers often establish their own work schedules and hours when diverse duties are performed (Burton, Latessa, and Barker, 1992).

The importance of writing PSIs is one thing. Changing the nature of such report writing in mid-stream with the introduction of new sentencing guidelines, such as the U.S. Sentencing Guidelines, is something else. Preguidelines POs have had to modify significantly how their report writing is done. They have also had to learn many new tasks and develop new proficiencies. For instance, Denzlinger and Miller (1991:50–51) say that

> as a result of the implementation of guideline sentencing, wholly discretionary sentencing was abandoned for a determinate model, featuring fixed sentences without possibility of parole ... the author of the presentence report became not only a preliminary fact-finder but also was required to apply law—the guidelines—to those facts. Thus, the officer's required knowledge base increased significantly and became considerably different from that required in the prior system ... To effectively perform under the guideline system, it was necessary for the officer to assimilate a great deal of new information. More importantly, the new knowledge required included understanding abstract concepts and legal principles such as "relevant conduct," "reasonably foreseeable," and "level of proof" in order to conduct pertinent investigations, make decisions in applying the guidelines to specific facts, and come to correct conclusions.

Colley, Culbertson, and Latessa (1986) suggest that problems of adjusting to PO life may sometimes be attributable to whether an officer is employed by a rural PO agency or an urban one. Rural agencies tend to give their POs more to do. While there may be fewer offenders, there are also fewer POs, but these POs have the same kinds of responsibilities that typify urban POs. In their study of 240 Illinois probation officers, these researchers found that

> the variety of role expectations is greater for rural officers simply because the same number of tasks that are critical to successful performance of the respective probation agency are performed by fewer officers in their rural agency. The rural officer, then, must have a greater variety of skills, knowledge, and training than the urban officer, particularly in the area of supervision and presentence investigation ... Training the rural probation officer is similar to training the general practitioner in medicine who is responsible for providing a vast array of medical services to a generalized patient constituency. (Colley, Culbertson, and Latessa, 1986:71)

Low Self-Esteem and Public Image. The low self-esteem and public image of POs is well known, and it invariably influences the quality of work they perform (Cheek and Miller, 1983b; Miller and Adwell, 1984). POs can do little in the short range to modify significantly their low public image (Curan, 1989). However, as recruitment efforts are more successful in attracting better-qualified applicants for PO positions, it is likely that the quality of services delivered will improve (Matthewson, 1991). One result of improved delivery of services may be a better public image associated with PO work (Bright, 1981:22–23; Brown, 1986). Whitehead and Gunn (1988:157) sum up the low self-esteem and public image possessed by many POs by noting a comment from an Indiana PO: "I generally describe probation work as 'dealing in frustration.' We seldom see our successes; they just disappear into the community. It is our failures that we see all the time." Another New York officer says, "Probation officers seem to be considered as machines. Both the clients and our employers seem to think that we are not entitled to have our own feelings, and certainly personal problems are not allowed."

High Risks and Liabilities.   Those working with criminals incur several risks. Some risks may be associated with the type of offender clientele served (Brown, 1994; Harris and Watkins, 1987; Johnson and Jones, 1994; Parsonage, 1990). Parolees who have been formerly convicted of aggravated assault, murder, rape, or some other type of violent crime may pose a degree of risk to the personal safety of POs. There is also an element of risk incurred from a client's associates who may be violent criminals. These are unknown and incalculable hazards (Martin, 1991:160). In addition to these personal risks, however, are legal liabilities incurred by POs who must interact with their offender-clients. In the course of furnishing them with counseling, job assistance, and other services, POs risk giving them poor advice, violating their privacy, maligning them to others, and preventing them from participating in various programs (Drass and Spencer, 1987; Haddock and Beto, 1990). POs must be aware of their legal responsibilities. At the same time, they must be aware of those actions that may lead to lawsuits against them from dissatisfied offender clientele. Many POs say that their training may not be sufficient to equip them with the legal and practical expertise needed to do good jobs (Lindner, 1992b; Nowicki, 1993).

Mitigating Factors That Alleviate Stress and Burnout

Many authorities believe that probation and parole organizations and agencies are at fault in creating dangerously high stress and burnout levels among POs and other correctional officers (Stinchcomb, 1986; Whitehead, 1987). One theory is that organizational factors directly contribute to employee stress (Cherniss, 1980a, 1980b). When a calling becomes the job, one no longer lives to work but works to live. Thus, POs may lose enthusiasm, excitement, and a sense of mission about the work.

Some experts say that although it is virtually impossible to prevent burnout among POs, regardless of their coping strategies and mechanisms, it is possible for the organization to implement changes to minimize it (McCabe, 1986; Thomas, 1988). If organization heads will recognize what causes stress and burnout, they have a better than even chance of dealing with it effectively (Brown, 1986:5). One way of alleviating stress and burnout is to incorporate features into PO training programs to make POs more "streetwise" so as to be safer when conducting face-to-face visits with their clients (Morrison, 1992:20–22). This might encompass hand-to-hand combat training and other self-defense skills.

Participative Management.   Participative management is the philosophy of organizational administration in which substantial input is solicited from the work staff and used for decision-making purposes when the staff's work might be affected. Thus, subordinates' opinions become crucial to organizational decision making as lower-level participants are given a greater voice in how the organization is operated or administered (Champion, 1975; Shirley Davis, 1990).

Organizational solutions stress greater employee involvement in the decision-making process relating to offender treatment and supervision (Atkinson, 1989; Brown, 1986, 1987; Cushman and Sechrest, 1992; Honnold and Stinchcomb, 1985:50). Generally, a lack of participation in decision making is a key source of stress and burnout (Shirley Davis, 1990). Employee commitment to do better work can be enhanced through bringing a PO's goals into harmony with those of the organization (Rath, 1991). Management by Objectives or MBO has been suggested as one means of accomplishing participatory goal setting between organizational heads and agency personnel, although MBO has lost momentum as a goal-setting and motivating strategy in recent years.

POs often cite the fact that their supervisors focus only on the negative aspects of work performed. POs' interviews in 1984 showed that many officers believed they were either not recognized by their superiors or only given attention "when something goes wrong" (Stinchcomb, 1986:22). When supervisors provide only criticisms of work improperly done and leave unrewarded work of good quality, the morale of personnel suffers greatly (Brown, 1987; Cheek and Miller, 1983b). Furthermore, some administrators have failed to evaluate employees consistently and objectively in their performance appraisals (Bright, 1981:22). In many instances, POs actively participate in facilitating programs that do much valuable work to aid their clients. For instance, the Kalamazoo, Michigan, Probation Enhancement Program developed in 1981 utilized employment skills classes, a job club, peer support groups, basic life-skills classes, and general equivalency diploma preparation to assist probationers and parolees. POs involved in this Kalamazoo project derived considerable satisfaction from this activity. The evaluation of the program by Kalamazoo probation office officials focused primarily on the success rates of program participants rather than on the POs who worked closely with them to achieve those success rates. This is one indication of the failure of agency leaders to reward their staffs properly for work they are "expected" to do anyway (Minor and Hartmann, 1992).

Honnold and Stinchcomb (1985:50) suggest that organizations focus on team-building, problem-solving approaches to agency problems and providing mutual support among staff members. They suggest also that probation/parole programs seek to enlarge decision-making authority of POs and to create a more positive climate in which rewards can be administered more freely. The general upgrading of recruitment and selection procedures may then result in a better-prepared employee component that can handle stressful situations more effectively whenever they arise. Accreditation of probation agencies is also an important step toward greater professionalization and building staff competence (Dare, 1992:48–50; Whitehead and Lindquist, 1992).

KEY TERMS

Assessment center
Broker
Burnout
Caseload
Caseworker
Conventional model
Conventional model with geographic
　considerations
Corrections officer
Detector
Educator
Enabler
Enforcer
Florida Assessment Center
Job dissatisfaction

Labor turnover
Mediator
Numbers game model
Role ambiguity
Role conflict
Specialized caseloads model
Stress
Kansas City Preventive Patrol Experiments
Law Enforcement Assistance
　Administration (LEAA)
President's Commission on Law
　Enforcement and the Administration of
　Justice
Professionalization
Professionalization of corrections

QUESTIONS FOR REVIEW

1. What is stress? What are some manifestations of stress?
2. What is burnout? What are some common meanings of burnout? What causes burnout and how can it be dealt with effectively?
3. How does education relate to burnout and stress? What can organizational administrators do to alleviate the stresses and accompanying burnout associated with PO work?
4. What are various common sources of stress? What is it about the PO role that triggers unusually high stress levels?
5. What is the source and nature of role conflict associated with the officer-client relation?
6. What are some of the mitigating factors which can alleviate burnout and stress?
7. What seems to account for comparatively high levels of labor turnover in corrections work in relation to other occupations or professions? How do many POs perceive correctional work and what reasons do they cite for leaving it?
8. Is there an ideal caseload for a PO? How are caseloads determined?
9. Identify and describe four types of caseload assignment methods.
10. How does the size of caseload relate to a PO's effectiveness?

13

Utilizing Volunteers and Paraprofessionals in Intermediate Punishment Programs

Introduction
The Role of Volunteers in Corrections
Criticisms of Volunteers in Correctional
   Work

Paraprofessionals in Community Corrections
Key Terms
Questions for Review

INTRODUCTION

This chapter examines the use of volunteers and paraprofessionals in intermediate punishments and/or community-based correctional programs. For several centuries, volunteers have been involved in various ways with offender rehabilitation and reintegration. Since the 1940s, we have seen the gradual emergence of paraprofessionals who have limited training to deal with various types of criminal clients.

The first part of this chapter defines in a general way the special roles of volunteers in correctional work. This description is followed by several criticisms associated with utilizing volunteers. These criticisms pertain to certain ethical considerations, the economy and money saved through the use of volunteers, and the potential legal liabilities for using untrained personnel in helping capacities. The second part of this chapter looks at paraprofessionals, how they are educated and trained, and the various types of roles they perform in probation and parole and correctional work generally. Certain criticisms have arisen concerning the use of paraprofessionals in community-based correctional programs. Like volunteers, paraprofessionals may be liable legally for the quality of assistance they provide various offender-clients. The issue of confidentiality is also raised frequently in conjunction with both volunteers and paraprofessionals. The chapter concludes by considering the future of volunteers and paraprofessionals in probation, parole, and community corrections.

THE ROLE OF VOLUNTEERS IN CORRECTIONS

Who Are Volunteers?   An investigation of the professional literature relating to volunteers in correctional work yielded no clear definition of volunteers. Perhaps the most succinct definition of a volunteer is provided by Winter (1993:22). He says that volunteers are people helping people. Margaret A. Moore, deputy commissioner assigned to the Central Region of the Pennsylvania Department of Corrections, has given some breadth to Winter's definition by noting that "**volunteers** are integral to correctional programming . . . they are hardworking, dedicated individuals who fill in the gaps for correctional agencies and provide much-needed services that victims, inmates, parolees, probationers and their families might otherwise not receive because of limited funding for programs" (Moore, 1993:8; emphasis added).

For purposes of this chapter, our definition of a **corrections volunteer** is any unpaid person who performs auxiliary, supplemental, augmentative, or any other work or services for any law enforcement, court, or corrections agency. Corrections volunteers vary greatly in their characteristics and abilities, in their ages, and in their functions. For instance, Girl Scouts, aged 12 to 16, work closely with female inmates and their children at the Maryland Correctional Institution for Women in Jessup, Maryland (Moses, 1993:132). Girl Scouts play with the daughters of female inmates during twice-monthly Girl Scout troop meetings. Troop projects as well as future activities are planned. Female inmates and their daughters may become involved and experience more intimate bonding not ordinarily possible under penal conditions (Codelia and Willis, 1989:168–170).

What Do Corrections Volunteers Do?   Some volunteers are retired schoolteachers who work with jail and prison inmates in various kinds of literacy programs (Tracy, 1993:102). The Gray Panthers, an organization of senior citizen volunteers, provides various services and programs targeting older inmates (Lehman, 1993:84). Some volunteers, such as septuagenarian Brigitte Cooke in Huntington, Pennsylvania, work with death row inmates or those serving life sentences. Her services include spiritual guidance, support, and compassion (Love, 1993:76–78). Some volunteers are crime victims who confront criminals who have committed crimes

Volunteers often assist inmates by filling out job application forms and other types of services after these offenders are released from custody. (The Image Works)

suffered by victims (Costa and Seymour, 1993:110). Yet, other volunteers provide religious training and conduct services for inmates and others (Pace, 1993:114). Other types of volunteers work as day care service personnel to care for young children of female parolees and probationers who perform full-time work in connection with their probation or parole programs (Arnold, 1993:118).

Other types of volunteers perform work that frees up jail and/or prison officers to do more important crime control work within their communities. For instance, in Knoxville, Tennessee, the Knox County Sheriff's Department has used a corps of volunteers known as the Organized Reserve Officers. These officers are sworn deputies of Knox County. They carry weapons, may or may not be involved in cruiser work, and undergo extensive law enforcement training at their own expense. Mostly these officers perform "guard duty" at the Knox County Jail. Jail correctional officers, at least at the Knox County Jail, are mostly assigned monitoring tasks. Jail inmates are segregated according to gender. And, the Knox County Jail houses both federal and state prisoners as a way of accommodating a portion of state and federal prison overflow. These Organized Reserve Officers spend a great deal of time, without pay, monitoring visitors to the jail on weekends. Family members of jail inmates bring various kinds of toiletries and other articles, including clothing, newspapers, magazines, and other items. This material must be searched before inmates can receive it. Thus, reserve officers must screen packages and other gifts. Visitors have no direct contact with their inmate-friends. Rather, they may speak with one another by telephonic means while separated by clear glass partitions. Thus, there is no danger of direct transmission of contraband from visitors to inmates.

During the week, these officers may be assigned particular "watches" for specified periods. All of this work is strictly voluntary. The benefits accruing to Knox County are obvious. At least 40 regular deputies are freed to patrol remote neighborhoods of one of Tennessee's largest counties. If the Organized Reserve Officer corps did not exist, most of these regular deputies would have to perform jail duties. Jail duties are subordinate to regular sheriff's patrols, according to these officers. Having to perform jail duty is regarded as a "punishment" by many of these officers. They readily acknowledge the contribution made by volunteer officers, although some of them openly resent the fact that these volunteers are permitted to carry weapons and make arrests.

Various criminal justice programs are another source of volunteers. Many of these programs operate internship services, that enable undergraduate or graduate students to obtain valuable on-the-job work experience in law enforcement, the courts, and corrections. These internships are fairly prevalent in most undergraduate criminal justice programs throughout the United States (Charles, 1989c:79–83). When prospective interns wish to work for any law enforcement agency, they are usually screened and their backgrounds are carefully scrutinized for possible prior criminal records (Baysc, 1993:16). For instance, the Probation Department of the 46th District Court in Michigan advertises for volunteers regularly. Anyone interested in becoming a volunteer probation officer (VPO) must have good communication skills, enthusiasm, a desire to assist others, and a commitment to the community. Candidates are interviewed and routine background checks are conducted. In 1993, between 20 and 25 VPOs were being used in this Michigan jurisdiction (Brian Smith, 1993:80–81). In this Michigan probation program, volunteers attend an orientation and training session. Those volunteers who are selected are assigned an average of 10 low-risk, nonviolent first offenders. Some of the volunteers working with this probation department have worked in this capacity for five years or longer (Brian Smith, 1993:81). Similar probation programs in other jurisdictions have utilized volunteer services with juveniles as well as adults (Greenberg, 1988:39).

Criminal justice students may also function as volunteer security workers for different community events. Thus, they might supplement conventional law enforcement agencies by providing extra supervision over exhibits at state fairs or other functions. It is unusual for such students to carry weapons or make arrests, however. Usually, they observe and report any unlawful conduct. They also identify potential perpetrators of crimes after observing them.

Students are also used in conjunction with inmate programs in jails and prisons. For instance, volunteers at the Minnesota Correctional Facility in Shakopee, a women's facility, are divided into three types: (1) interns, (2) institutional volunteers, and (3) custody interns. Interns are unpaid students completing course requirements; institutional volunteers assist staff and help run various counseling groups; and custody volunteers provide custody of inmates in the community (Masin, 1993:128). Masin (1993:128) notes that some interns come from the nearby

Alfred Adler Institute, a graduate school in Minnesota. These interns help staff run discussion groups and also provide one-on-one counseling.

Peter Kratcoski (1982) has said that volunteer involvement in corrections historically, has increased whenever the public believed important corrections needs and concerns have been neglected. The use of volunteers rose dramatically during the 1950s and 1960s. The majority of volunteers during that period worked in jails, prisons, probation, parole, halfway houses, detoxification centers, refuges for runaways, and job training programs for ex-offenders. Independent evidence from other researchers confirms Kratcoski's observations (Bayse, 1993; *DOCS Today*, 1993; Lucas, 1987).

How Many Correctional Volunteers Are There? A 1989 Gallup Poll revealed that an estimated 98.4 million Americans volunteered an average of four hours per week. Between 1987 and 1989, the number of adult volunteers increased by 23 percent. The use of volunteers services in criminal justice settings is at best uneven (Winter, 1993:20). A 1987 estimate by Wayne Lucas suggests that between 300,000 and 500,000 citizen volunteers were involved in community corrections in approximately 2,000 to 3,000 jurisdictions (Lucas, 1987:63). In subsequent years, the literature suggests that the number of correctional volunteers has dramatically increased (American Correctional Association, 1992; Bayse, 1993; Hawk et al., 1993). For instance, in the Alston Wilkes Society, a nonprofit agency that assists offenders, former offenders, and their families in South Carolina, boasts a volunteer component of at least 5,000 persons (Walker, 1993:94). Approximately 3,000 volunteers work in various capacities with the Pennsylvania Department of Corrections (Lehman, 1993:84). The Federal Bureau of Prisons (BOP) uses at least 4,000 volunteers in different ways for institutional and community corrections services. In 1992, for instance, the BOP created the National Office of Citizen Participation (NOCP) in conjunction with the Bureau's chaplaincy and education departments. The NOCP creates and maintains partnerships with local colleges, national service organizations, schools, and community-based organizations. These contacts provide a means of attracting volunteers who offer a wide variety of services, skills, and expertise to federal inmates (Hawk, 1993:72).

Some Examples of Correctional Volunteer Work. At Fort Leavenworth, Kansas, there are four chaplains who attempt to meet the religious needs of 1,300 male and female inmates at the U.S. Disciplinary Barracks. About 70 volunteers representing 16 different religions conduct more than 30 weekly programs for inmates. These volunteers conduct worship services, religious studies, study classes, workshops, and retreats (Pace, 1993:114). These volunteers do much to improve inmate morale. In the Leavenworth program, volunteers must be at least 16 years of age and certified or ordained as chaplains or ministers. Volunteer candidates are carefully screened to determine why they wish to work with these inmates. Two background checks are conducted—one to determine whether any of their relatives are incarcerated at Leavenworth and the other to determine whether they have any felony convictions or arrest warrants. For this particular program, volunteers receive rather extensive training. They must attend training classes that instruct them

BOX 13.1
Focusing on Volunteer Work

The Case of Volunteers in Prison

Volunteers in Prison is part of the Voluntary Action Center of Centre County, Pennsylvania. Early members of this program received their training from the Society of Friends in 1979 in Baltimore, Maryland. At that time, volunteers received two weekend workshop training sessions to prepare them for their subsequent encounters with inmates. In 1988, the director of the Voluntary Action Center and coordinator of the Volunteers in Prison program, Marie Hamilton, began to conduct similar programs in other jurisdictions.

One of the functions of Volunteers in Prison is to conduct 10-week conflict resolution sessions at various Pennsylvania State Correctional Institutions (SCIs). Three or four volunteers work with 8 to 12 men for a period of one hour, and then an additional hour is reserved for socializing. Sessions have routinely been conducted in prerelease cellblocks of the SCI facility. Subsequently, the locations of these sessions have been changed to prison areas more conducive to serving inmates with physical handicaps or special needs. The purpose of the conflict resolution sessions is to give prisoners experience with problem-solving and listening skills through various group exercises and serious discussion. Games and other activities are used to build camaraderie among these inmates and volunteers. Self-concept introspection and positive image building are key goals of these conflict-resolution sessions.

One interesting session concerns a list of about 10 to 20 choices inmates are given by volunteers. One statement is, "If I heard someone coming in my window at night, I would 'shoot to kill.'" The inmates are then instructed that if they agree with that statement, they should walk to one side of the room. Those that disagree should walk to the other side of the room. At first when the sessions commenced, most prisoners walked to the "agree" side of the room. By the end of the sessions, however, most inmates walked to the "disagree" side of the room, indicating that they had learned various alternatives to lethal force in resolving that situation. Volunteer Alice Kountz says that "I think that over the years, I've made a difference in some small way. Sometimes in a particular session, an individual will talk with you and sometimes we feel that we help. Occasionally, a man says he feels better." Kountz recalls an incident when an inmate told her that he was in prison for becoming involved in a barroom brawl. He had also torn the door off of the bar. Later, he couldn't believe he had done that. He said that he seemed to have his head "on straight" now that he was about to be released. Kountz believes her services contributed to his readjustment.

Should volunteers be permitted to work with dangerous offenders in prison settings? Should they be required to have special training or insurance? Who should be held accountable if volunteers act in ways that cause inmates psychological harm?

Source: Adapted from Tracy Rose, "Volunteers in Prison: The Community Link." *Corrections Today,* **50:**216–218, 1988.

in proper dress and conduct. Potential pitfalls and inmate manipulation are explained. Volunteer services at Leavenworth are limited to three-year terms. This is probably because over time, interpersonal acquaintances with inmates may cloud a volunteer's judgment, and some volunteers may succumb to inmate manipulation and persuasion. In any case, all participating chaplain-volunteers give inmates the highest quality of voluntary service, and their assistance at Leavenworth is greatly appreciated (Pace, 1993:116).

An interesting volunteer program is presently underway in 19 Connecticut prison facilities. For instance, at the Brooklyn, Connecticut, Community Correctional Center, several female volunteers work daily with groups of 11 or 12 female inmates in producing quilts. Fabric is cut, and six sewing machines are used to produce brightly decorated quilts that are subsequently distributed to children and families of female inmates. The program is known as ABC, which stands for At-risk Babies Crib (Wheeler, 1993:136). This project started in August 1992. It was patterned after programs in 39 other states. In 1993, at least 39 states and seven countries had established such ABC programs, producing over 57,000 quilts for at-risk babies in hospitals, day-care centers, and foster homes (Wheeler, 1993:136). One of the principal advantages of having volunteers participate with inmates in custodial institutions with varying degrees of security is that they provide a humane quality that transcends the correctional officer-inmate relation (Lehman, 1993: 84–86).

Another volunteer program designed for working with female offenders in both prison and community-based programs is called The Program for Female Offenders. This program provides for volunteers who visit the Allegheny County, Pennsylvania, jail three times per week and the State Correctional Institution at Muncy on a less frequent but regular basis (Arnold, 1993:120). Incarcerated women are assisted by volunteers who help them adjust to prison life. Certain family and legal problems may be dealt with, using the volunteers as intermediaries. For those women who have been recently released, the agency operates a training center, two residential facilities, and a day treatment program. All of these facilities are located in Pittsburgh (Arnold, 1993:120). One facility, the Program Center, is a work release facility that serves 34 female prisoners. Volunteers provide these women with job assistance, GED preparation, and life skills. Parenting programs and day care services are also provided largely through the use of volunteer services.

This Pennsylvania program has outlined some valuable types of functions performed by these volunteers:

1. Serving as tutors at the skill training center and handling most GED preparation;
2. Providing transportation to parenting sessions at their residential centers;
3. Teaching women hobby skills such as knitting, sewing, and dressmaking;
4. Teaching computer and job search skills at the skill training center; and
5. Providing gifts for women and their children every Christmas.

Arnold (1993) says that these tasks often lead to friendships between volunteers and inmate-clients and that volunteers deserve special recognition for their unpaid services. Arnold also advises that it is important to place volunteers in positions where they will feel safe and comfortable. She suggests the following guidelines:

1. Don't take offenders home or lend them money.
2. Don't share your troubles with offenders.
3. Learn to listen effectively.
4. Don't try to solve offenders' problems.
5. Don't make judgments.
6. Report irregular behavior to the agency staff. This is not being disloyal.
7. Don't provide drugs or alcohol to offenders.
8. Don't always expect to be appreciated.
9. Do have empathy and patience.
10. Do care. (Arnold, 1993:122)

The Salvation Army has operated a volunteer program for inmates in various states since 1883. Over the years, at local, state, and federal levels, the Salvation Army has averaged supervising more than 13,000 people, visiting nearly 200,000 inmates, helping 27,000 offenders or their families, and assisting 72,000 court cases annually (Salvation Army, 1993:66). It is generally conceded that the Salvation Army has been instrumental in crime prevention and inmate rehabilitation. Actually, the Salvation Army works with corrections and law enforcement at virtually all justice stages—arrest, prosecution, incarceration, and rehabilitation. Salvation Army members work with judges, prison officials, and POs. One program worth noting was established in Florida, which represents a rather comprehensive approach to corrections. In Florida, the Salvation Army has established various Adult Rehabilitation Centers (ARCs), which are open to probationers and their families. Salvation Army volunteers provide employment counseling, referrals for alcohol treatment, and courses in AIDS awareness. Parolees can use these ARCs to facilitate their transition and reintegration into their communities. These centers are clean, well-maintained, and attractive, providing balanced meals for probationers and parolees. Clothing and other personal articles are provided, as well as limited medical, optical, and dental services (Salvation Army, 1993:66). The Salvation Army believes in rehabilitating the total person physically, spiritually, and psychologically. Evidence suggests that recidivism rates of Salvation Army clients are relatively low (Salvation Army, 1993:70).

Finally, many volunteer programs in community corrections are designed to assist with juvenile offenders. For instance, in Norristown, Pennsylvania, the Montgomery County Youth Center has established an interesting environment for treatment opportunities and relationship-building experiences for youths (Maniglia, 1993:146). Senior citizens and retirees volunteer as role models to work with youths at the Center. The Center has facilities to accommodate short-term juveniles held in detention as well as shelter housing for abused and neglected children placed there by the Office of Children and Youth and status offenders placed by Juvenile Probation (Maniglia, 1993:146). The senior citizens act as role models for these youths as well as teachers' aides for those housed at the secure detention center. A Foster Grandparent Program assigns a senior citizen to one of three classrooms located in the educational area of the Youth Center, where all residents must attend school daily, throughout the year. Conventional classroom teachers are responsible for overseeing the classes as a whole; the foster grandparent focuses on one-on-one activities with individual students (Maniglia, 1993:146). For instance, foster grandparents might provide individual tutoring, assist with student assignments, administer educational tests, or oversee a youth's involvement with computer software. Donald W. DeVore, the Center's executive director, says that "the program benefits both groups of people who are often isolated from the mainstream of society by their special circumstances. It emphasizes the natural pairing of the young and senior citizens by providing older adults and special needs children with the means to reach across the generations to give love and compassion to each other" (Maniglia, 1993:148).

CRITICISMS OF VOLUNTEERS IN CORRECTIONAL WORK

There Is Pervasive Volunteer Naiveté.   Not everyone is enthusiastic about volunteer involvement in law enforcement, the courts, or corrections. Unusual situations arise from time to time in which inmates and other types of offenders might harm volunteers or be harmed by the very volunteers trying to help them. One problem that is cited frequently by critics of correctional volunteerism is volunteer naiveté. John Kramer, a professor of sociology at Pennsylvania State University, says that sometimes, volunteers are asked to serve as mediators between inmates and their spouses or to contact inmate's attorneys. Whenever these volunteers attempt to do things that they are not trained to do (e.g., marriage counseling), their well-intentioned do-gooding may go awry and prison staff may regard them as a "pain" (Rose, 1988:218). Sometimes, the problems caused by well-intentioned volunteers may cause prison staff to spend more time remedying the problems than if volunteer assistance had never been rendered.

Volunteers Do Not Make Long-Term Commitments with Clients.   Because of the unpaid nature of volunteer work, many volunteers may be in correctional settings for brief periods, tire of their activities, and leave. For instance, Lucas (1987:72–73) investigated the roles of volunteers in the Missouri Division of Probation and Parole. This Division employs 300 probation and parole officers and uses the services of about 110 volunteers. Probation and parole officers were surveyed concerning their perceptions of volunteer effectiveness in dealing with probationers and parolees to whom they were assigned in order to reduce regular PO caseloads. While POs generally held positive attitudes about the influence of volunteers in assisting them in their regular duties, the most frequent criticism was that a significant proportion of volunteers do not stay with their clients for adequate time periods. Often, clients are shuffled back and forth between volunteers and regular POs. As a result, clients feel manipulated or "let down" by the particular volunteer absence.

Volunteers Often Do Not Want to Work Independently.   In the same study, Lucas (1987:72–73) found that some volunteers in the Missouri Division of Probation and Parole were reluctant to work independently with individual probationers and parolees. Thus, a regular PO would be required to monitor or supervise volunteer-client relations. This necessitated a considerable and unnecessary expenditure of valuable time on the part of the supervising PO, who was often overworked with heavy caseloads and numerous other required duties. Further, depending on the particular personalities of POs, some of them would not be as effective in working with volunteers. For instance, various POs might manifest personalities as law enforcers, social workers, sympathetic officers, or time servers in relation to their offender-clients. These different dispositions toward their work might carry over and influence their work relations with volunteers.

Volunteers Often Lack Expertise and Experience.   Again, Lucas (1987:72) found that the chief concern of POs employed by the Missouri Division of Probation and Parole was that volunteers lacked general knowledge about the specific rules and policies of the Division. This meant that volunteers did not know how to handle unusual developing scenarios between themselves and particularly troublesome clients. If offenders were violating program rules, volunteers experienced difficulty reporting them for these infractions. Volunteers were thus more easily manipulated compared with regular POs. This says much about the differential training of POs and volunteers, because POs saw their training as career-relevant and volunteers did not value their own training with the same importance or priority.

Law Enforcement Agencies and the Courts Are Reluctant to Share Information about Offenders with Volunteers Serving PO Functions.   It is probably natural for law enforcement organizations and the courts to take a dim view of disclosing confidential information about offender-clients to volunteers who are operating in unofficial capacities. Despite the fact that PO agencies authorize volunteers to do PO work for them, volunteers are not credentialed. Further, they do not carry badges and other formal documentation enabling them to inquire about and obtain confidential client information. Lucas (1987:72) cites this additional disadvantage accruing as the result of using volunteers in quasi-PO capacities.

Volunteers Threaten Job Security.   It seems to follow that if a department or agency utilizes the services of volunteers to supplement the work performed by full-time staff, then some of those full-time staff may not be needed in future months or years. Some employees of corrections agencies have expressed this particular fear, regardless of its foundation in truth (Winter, 1993:20).

Since Volunteers Are Not Paid, They Don't Respond to Orders Like Other Staff.
Unpaid personnel who work with corrections agencies on a voluntary basis are under no special obligation to adhere to specific working hours or schedules. Of course, most volunteers wish to comply with the requirements of the tasks they are assigned. But volunteers may have a totally different type of commitment to work

compared with paid staff members. It might be difficult for supervisors or administrators to sanction them with traditional threats of pay cuts, loss of seniority privileges, or extra work assignments. If volunteers don't like certain tasks they are assigned, they don't have to reappear at work in the future. Often, staff pay little or no attention to the opinions of volunteers and do not seek their suggestions regarding decision making. According to some experts, volunteers are tolerated but closely controlled (Winter, 1993).

Some Volunteers May Be Aiders and Abetters.   Bayse (1993:16) describes a situation that occurred at a prison when a local pastor regularly brought church members into the prison for worship services together with inmates. He allowed a woman from a nearby church to join the group one Sunday at the last moment. The pastor did not know that the woman was wearing two dresses and a wig. When she excused herself to go to the bathroom, an inmate discretely followed her and outfitted himself in her extra dress and wig. Dressed as a woman, he returned with her to the church group and left with them when they exited the prison. He was apprehended a few days later. But this story indicates some of the potential harm volunteers can cause to corrections officials if they develop close relationships with prisoners or if their backgrounds are not carefully screened.

On the Ethics of Using Volunteers

Because of the nonprofessional nature of volunteer work generally, questions often arise concerning the quality of work volunteers can perform. If volunteers are assigned case-sensitive work, such as working with probationers and/or parolees, they must necessarily become exposed to confidential materials or information about their clients. In fact, some volunteers in certain probation/parole agencies often act on instructions from these agencies to obtain such information from law enforcement sources or the courts. Should these volunteers be granted access to this information? Some experts think that volunteers should not have such access to this potentially sensitive information (del Carmen and Trook-White, 1986).

Some programs that utilize volunteers may attract persons who may endanger specific types of clientele, such as children. For instance, pedophiles and child sexual abusers may actively volunteer to work in community corrections programs where young children are involved. As we have seen, some of the services provided female inmates and their families are day care programming and child supervision. If unknown child molesters are allowed to work around children, especially in one-on-one situations in which their interactions with children might go unobserved, considerable harm might result to the children involved. Interviews with prospective volunteers who want to work with children are not foolproof. For example, McCormack and Selvaggio (1989) indicate that some organizations, such as the Big Brothers and Big Sisters of Greater Lowell, Massachusetts, conduct extensive screening interviews to select or reject prospective volunteers for work in youth-serving community agencies. These organizations wish to avoid legal liabilities possibly resulting from selecting the wrong volunteers for this type of work.

At this point, arguments about the ethics of using volunteers in correctional work are largely moot. This is because the use of volunteers in various capacities throughout all aspects of the criminal justice system is pervasive. Furthermore, the use of volunteers by almost every correctional agency is increasing annually. It is significant, therefore, to direct our attention to the steps taken by different programs to prepare volunteers adequately for the work they propose to undertake. The American Correctional Association has produced an insightful and instructive manual designed to provide correctional volunteers with skills and resources necessary for working with criminals in or out of prison settings (Bayse, 1993). Besides this resource, numerous guidelines have been generated by individual programs in most jurisdictions to focus volunteer work along specified lines.

For example, Ogburn (1993:66) provides the following admonitions to volunteers and others who are interested in establishing volunteer programs:

1. Evaluate the need.
2. Develop goals and job descriptions.
3. Involve staff.
4. Actively recruit volunteers.
5. Educate volunteers about inmates.
6. Explain security needs to volunteers.
7. Give volunteers the big picture.
8. Evaluate program effectiveness.
9. Recognize your volunteers' contributions.

Further, Bayse (1993:43–47) admonishes volunteers to be (1) ethical; (2) good listeners; (3) empathetic, but not gullible; (4) respectful; (5) genuine; (6) patient; (7) trustworthy; (8) confrontive; (9) objective—don't take sides; (10) nonhostile; and (11) nonexpectant of thanks.

Bayse (1993:48–50) also provides prospective volunteers with some suggestions and rules:

1. Use appropriate language. Don't pick up inmate slang or vulgarity. Using language that isn't a part of your style can label you a phoney.
2. Do not volunteer if you are a relative or visitor of an inmate in that institution.
3. Do not engage in political activities during the time voluntary services are being performed.
4. Do not bring contraband into prison. If you are not sure what is contraband, ask the staff. People who bring in contraband are subject to permanent expulsion and/or arrest.
5. Do not bring anything into or out of a facility for an inmate at any time, no matter how innocent or trivial it may seem, unless with the written permission of the superintendent. Volunteers should adopt a policy of saying no to any request by an inmate to bring in cigarettes, money, magazines, or letters. If in doubt, ask a staff member.
6. Keep everything in the open. Do not say or do anything with an inmate you would be embarrassed to share with your peers or supervisors.
7. Do not give up if you failed at your first try. Try again.

8. Don't overidentify. Be a friend, but let inmates carry their own problems. Be supportive without becoming like the inmates in viewpoint or attitude.

9. Do not take anything, including letters, in or out of a correctional facility without permission. Respect the confidentiality of records and other privileged information.

10. Do not bring unauthorized visitors or guests with you to the institution. They will be refused admission.

11. Do not give out your address or telephone number. If asked, you might say, "I'm sorry, but I was told that it was against the rules to do that."

12. Do not correspond with inmates in the facility in which you volunteer or accept collect telephone calls from them at your place of residence.

13. Be aware that the use of, or being under the influence of, alcohol or drugs while on institution grounds is prohibited.

14. Don't impose your values and beliefs on inmates. Do not let others impose a lower set of values on you.

15. Don't discuss the criminal justice system, the courts, inconsistency in sentencing, or related topics. Although everyone is entitled to his or her own opinion, what volunteers say can have serious repercussions in the dorms or with staff.

16. Ask for help. If you are uncertain about what to do or say, be honest. It is always best to tell the inmate that you will have to seek assistance from your supervisor. Inmates don't expect you to have all the answers.

17. Know your personal and professional goals. Be firm, fair, and consistent.

18. If you have done something inappropriate, tell your coordinator regardless of what happened. It is far better to be reprimanded than to become a criminal.

Economic Considerations versus Inadequate Training

We have already noted the fact that using volunteers can save local, state, and federal governments considerable money by freeing up staff to do more important work with offenders. For instance, if we consider the Knox County, Tennessee, jail's use of the Organized Reserve Officer corps, the savings to Knox County is considerable. Many regular sheriff's deputies are freed to engage in cruiser work for the purpose of crime prevention or crime control. Furthermore, since the work of these officers is free, the money saved over the many years this corps has existed has permitted Knox County to purchase additional cruisers, equipment, and jail furnishings that improve overall services delivery.

Almost every correctional agency using volunteer services will be able to demonstrate dollar savings in operating costs as one result (Burden, 1988). However, there is a down side to this picture. This is simply that volunteers are often ill-equipped to deal with offender problems and emergency situations that might arise in the course of their volunteer work. Prison settings are ideal places for volunteers to be manipulated by inmates. In attempting to assist in reintegrating offenders, volunteers must be empathetic to a degree. The danger is that once a relationship is established between an inmate and a volunteer, it is impossible to draw a line to determine where the intimacy of that relationship should be terminated (Bayse, 1993). This problem is closely linked with the confidentiality issue. Volunteers frequently have access to or learn about confidential information about offender-clients. Many volunteers may not know what to do with such confidential information. Sometimes, they may disclose it in ways that adversely impact these clients or their families. In short, volunteers may create problems where no problems existed previously (Berkeley Planning Associates, 1980).

Whereas the economic benefits of using volunteers are generally acknowledged, the adequacy of their training is variable from one agency or organization to the next. We have seen some programs that attempt to screen and train volunteers rather consistently. However, the training many volunteers receive is often superficial. A safe assumption is that whenever volunteers are working closely with offender-clients, they may not have all of the skills necessary to provide useful, meaningful advice or assistance (Hawk et al., 1993).

For example, some volunteers work with offenders in developing their parenting skills. Some volunteers may work with alcohol- or drug-dependent clients (Brooks, 1990). The advice volunteers give, or the models they suggest, or the assistance they provide, may not be appropriate under certain circumstances. Cultural differences among offenders and different types of familial relationships suggest that many volunteers do not have the necessary awareness to be effective in their "counseling" attempts. Hispanic, Asian American, and African American offenders often exhibit widely different parenting histories and cultural practices. Even educators have a difficult time relating to diverse cultures in formal classroom settings. If educators find these tasks difficult, what rationale exists to convince us that volunteers can do as well as or better than educators?

The more training volunteers receive, the more effective they will be in assisting their offender-clients. But training volunteers takes time. Also, training is not what most volunteers envision as the motivation for becoming involved in volunteer efforts initially. Some agencies report high turnover among volunteers (California Department of the Youth Authority, 1987). A survey of 49 California juvenile probation departments found that of these, about 75 to 80 percent use volunteers in juvenile halls and county camps. Although cost savings were substantial, many of these agencies reported that there simply was not enough time to spend training volunteers for their work with juvenile offenders. Thus, many of these untrained or undertrained volunteers would become easily frustrated and fail to reappear. In this study, a major organizational challenge was to develop truly innovative approaches for integrating volunteer services into the daily work of probation (California Department of the Youth Authority, 1987).

The Legal Liabilities of Volunteers and Agencies Using Them

In recent years, officials administering community-based programs have become increasingly aware of certain legal implications and liabilities stemming from the use of volunteers and paraprofessionals in working with various types of offenders (del Carmen and Trook-White, 1986; Pellicciotti, 1987). Since professionals are at risk from lawsuits filed by their clients for alleged misconduct of one type or another, paraprofessionals and volunteers are even more at risk.

The actions that are bases for lawsuits by clients against agencies and community-based program personnel are diverse, and they include negligence in training, hiring, assignment, supervision, entrustment, and retention (Williams, Callaghan, and Scheier, 1974). Officers may be liable to third parties for injuries caused by offenders or by program volunteers, and liability to offenders may occur because of unauthorized or inappropriate record disclosures, injuries in job performance, and offender physical injuries caused by volunteers (del Carmen and Trook-White, 1986). If a volunteer counsels an offender inappropriately, the psychological harm resulting from unprofessional counseling may be most devastating (del Carmen, 1985). If a volunteer unwittingly tells a third party about the criminal record of the offender and if such a disclosure is irrelevant to the job performed, liability is incurred. Of course, agency personnel are under a duty to disclose certain factual information about offenders to employers if such background information is relevant. For example, a convicted rapist would be an unlikely candidate as a security guard for an apartment complex housing large numbers of single women. It would be obligatory for agency representatives to advise apartment managers or owners that prospective employees with criminal records have prior rape convictions (Rada, 1978). A convicted embezzler would not be a good candidate as a bank employee or someone who would handle money or financial affairs for a small business. Disclosures of such information to prospective employers would be imperative. But it would be questionable whether agency representatives should go out of their way to report to a garbage-hauling company that a prospective employee has a prior conviction for vehicular theft or shoplifting.

Del Carmen and Trook-White (1986) say that volunteers may incur some liability as the result of (1) improper record disclosures; (2) injuries inflicted on clients in job performance; and (3) injuries sustained while on the job. Some volunteers obtain liability insurance as a hedge against potential lawsuits arising in the future for any wrongful acts they might commit. The Knox County, Tennessee, Organized Reserve Officer corps is required to secure a substantial bond while performing its volunteer services, for example. If one of these officers injures an inmate or arrestee at some future date, then the bond will likely cover a portion or all of the monetary damages sought by inmate-arrestee-plaintiffs.

The Case of Hyland v. Wonder *(1992).* One of the few higher-profile legal cases involving volunteers was *Hyland v. Wonder* (1992). This case involved a volunteer who had worked at a juvenile probation department for several years. The volunteer became critical of how the probation office was being managed. He wrote a letter to those overseeing the probation department where he was volunteering, outlining various complaints and asserting how certain improvements would benefit the office. His services as a volunteer were subsequently terminated. He sued, claiming that his criticisms of the probation department were protected by the free speech provision of the First Amendment. Furthermore, he contended that he had a protected liberty interest in his continued status as a volunteer, and that this liberty interest was protected by the due process clause of the Fourteenth Amendment. The federal Ninth Circuit Court of Appeals heard his appeal after his complaint was dismissed by a U.S. district court earlier. The appellate court determined that the agency could not deprive the defendant of a valuable government benefit as punishment for speaking out on a matter of public concern. The nature of his public concern was government inefficiency, incompetence, and waste. But the court declared that he was not vested with a property and liberty interest in his volunteer position. Thus, he was not in the position of being able to state or create a claim of entitlement for the purposes of the due process clause of the Fourteenth Amendment.

In *Hyland,* a volunteer had spent so much time in his volunteer work with the probation department that he came to regard his position and opinions as equivalent to those of regular full-time employees, or so it would appear. His lawsuit is evidence of his enthusiasm for the work and the seriousness he attached to it. However, the court was unsympathetic to the extent that his volunteer time accrued did not vest him with any real standing regarding office policies. This is a good example of how some volunteers can lose their perspective of who they are and why they are there. It is also a good example of one pitfall of volunteer work.

Many states currently have laws that protect volunteers from lawsuits filed by inmates (Bayse, 1993:66). Some states provide liability insurance for volunteers who work in state agencies with offender-clients. Worker's compensation insurance also provides limited coverage for injuries volunteers might sustain while working. Even a homeowner policy might provide limited coverage for such injuries while volunteering. Bayse (1993:67) recommends that volunteers should know whether they are covered for various types of liabilities before they commence their volunteer work for any organization.

PARAPROFESSIONALS IN COMMUNITY CORRECTIONS

Who Are Paraprofessionals? Paraprofessionals in virtually every field are salaried assistants who work with professionals. They have received some degree of training in their respective fields, although they do not have professional credentials, such as a Ph.D., M.D., J.D., or some other such credentialing entitling one to be considered **professional.** An inspection of at least 30 articles in the correctional literature about paraprofessionals in jails, prisons, community corrections, and probation/parole work yielded no definition of them. Rather, descriptions of the work of paraprofessionals are amply provided. The same is generally true regarding use of the term *professionalism.* Everyone seems to know intuitively what it means, but few if any are able to define it.

For purposes of this book, a **corrections paraprofessional** is a someone who possesses some formal training in a given correctional area, is salaried, works specified hours, has formal duties and responsibilities, is accountable to higher-level supervisors for work quality, and has limited immunity under the theory of agency. **Agency** is the special relation between an employer and an employee whereby the employee acts as an agent of the employer, able to make decisions and take actions on the employer's behalf (adapted from Black, 1990:62). Black (1990:1112) also defines a paraprofessional as "one who assists a professional person though not a member of the profession himself." Black cites a paralegal as a type of paraprofessional who would assist an attorney, for example. Black also notes that a professional is one who is a member of a learned profession or has achieved a high level of proficiency, competency, and training. Using an example from the previous section about volunteers, we might say that if the members of the Knox County, Tennessee, Organized Reserve Officers corps were salaried, they might constitute paraprofessionals, since they have received some training regarding inmate management, firearms use, and law enforcement communication.

The Education and Training of Paraprofessionals

Most researchers view favorably the work of paraprofessionals compared with professionals working in the same correctional endeavors (Coleman, 1988; Gaudin, 1993; Gordon and Arbuthnot, 1988; Latessa, Travis, and Allen, 1983; McCarthy and McCarthy, 1991). Paraprofessionals seem to operate optimally when working together with professionals in casework teams (Glaser, 1983). Evidence suggests that paraprofessional roles in probation and parole are increasing (Love, 1981, 1993).

It is impossible to profile the education and training of all paraprofessionals as an aggregate. Rather, specific categories of paraprofessionals are more easily described. Third-year law school students may "clerk" for attorneys as paraprofessionals, since they have acquired sufficient legal expertise to look up cases and brief them for use in courtroom arguments. Paralegals may offer gratis assistance to indigent defendants who are faced with minor court appearances. We know the general educational level of these types of paraprofessionals.

In many community colleges and universities, students may earn associate degrees for which they have taken a fixed number of courses in a given academic area; this qualifies them to work in certain related fields as assistants or aides. Senior criminal justice students often become involved through internship programs with various law enforcement organizations, including probation and parole departments. Students might be placed in the U.S. Probation Office or some comparable local or state probation/parole agency. These paraprofessionals might assist regular POs in the preparation of PSIs or in offender supervisory functions.

A home builder's program has been described by Glenwick (1988). Home-based family therapy is an increasingly useful intervention tool, and many paraprofessionals are becoming involved in this activity. Social workers and other professionals work with fractured families or families with various interpersonal problems. Parents may lack sufficient skills to manage their children, or the children may be completely unruly, disrespectful, and/or truant. Paraprofessionals might receive limited training in family problems and processes. Some psychology courses in small-group and adolescent behavior are helpful supplements, because they sensitize paraprofessionals to working with and understanding others. Working together with family interventionists and counselors, home-builder paraprofessionals may deliver home-based therapy to many juvenile delinquents or status offenders, assisting them in various ways to adjust and adapt to the school and community (Glenwick, 1988). Paraprofessionals have also been used to assist youthful offenders to develop better negotiation skills when dealing with juvenile courts, parents, and school officials (Carbone et al., 1983).

The Roles of Paraprofessionals

In some instances, particularly during the 1960s and 1970s, ex-offenders were used as paraprofessionals in conjunction with LEAA grant money in various jurisdictions such as Ohio (McCarthy and McCarthy, 1991; Scott, 1981). For example, Ohio initiated a Parole Officer Aide Program (POAP) as part of the Ohio Adult Parole Authority's plan to increase the effectiveness of parole programs throughout the state. Administrators believed that the use of ex-cons or ex-offenders working as a team with regular POs would be more effective at reducing recidivism rates among the Ohio parolee population. Although such recidivism rate reductions did not occur as anticipated, it was demonstrated that after three years of operation, ex-offenders as paraprofessionals could perform PO work about as well as regular POs (Scott, 1981). Furthermore, because ex-offenders were used in quasi-PO roles, the program was regarded as unique. Subsequently, Ohio terminated the POAP program, although the use of ex-offenders was not to blame. A new administration disagreed with previous administration decision making. And, LEAA funds were withdrawn. Third, many lower-level personnel did not support the general concept of using ex-offenders in PO roles.

In a subsequent study described by Latessa, Travis, and Allen (1983), paraprofessionals were used in a fashion similar to the one described by Scott (1981) above. Interested ex-offenders were given limited training and assisted POs as support staff and provided auxiliary work in direct caseload supervision. These researchers indicate that while the work of these paraprofessionals was satisfactory and comparable with the quality of work performed by regular POs, ex-offenders were decreasingly used over time. Reasons given were that there were attitudes of resistance among regular POs and other employees, fiscal constraints, and a loss of interest among the ex-offenders themselves.

The quality of paraprofessional work reflects the amount of training these personnel receive. For instance, in various prisons, paraprofessionals are used to assist mental health professionals and psychiatrists. Some correctional staff may have demonstrable abilities as mental health caregivers. In some jurisdictions, corrections personnel are given specialized mental health training and experience with mental health counseling. Although the primary professional goals of clinical and correctional staff may conflict from time to time, it is apparent that the two professions share common functions (Coleman, 1988). Actually, properly trained correctional staff as mental health paraprofessionals can supply quality mental health care compared with the work quality of many professionals who work with inmates.

Virginia's Department of Corrections has invested considerable time and effort to establish literacy programs for its prison inmates and community corrections clients (Traynelis-Yurek and Yurek, 1990). Paraprofessionals have been used extensively in several Virginia DOC projects. The Wechsler Adult Intelligence Scale was used by Virginia officials to define offenders with IQ levels ranging from 72 to 90. And, men aged 16 to 19 were chosen who had reading levels that were from 50 to 83 percent below normal grade level. Paraprofessionals were hired to read in unison with these offenders. Reading material would be chosen and read several times to establish a fluent, normal reading pattern. Through the use of paraprofessionals in these educational endeavors, Virginia officials estimate that they were able to raise the reading level of most offenders by more than four years (Traynelis-Yurek and Yurek, 1990).

The National Center for Missing and Exploited Children has reported increasing use of older paraprofessionals to assist with runaways (M. Forst, 1983). The major causes of runaway behavior are family difficulties and interpersonal conflicts. Runaways are in need of counseling. Often, jurisdictions provide team counseling, with a family therapist and a paraprofessional or volunteer. Paraprofessionals working with family therapists in this fashion learn about family and juvenile laws and how youths should be counseled and treated. In Seattle, Washington, for instance, paraprofessionals are used to counsel repeat runaway offenders through the Community Services Section of the Seattle Police Department (M. Forst, 1983; Gaudin, 1993; Wedlund, 1990).

Smykla and Selke (1982) have described the work of paraprofessionals who are responsible for maintaining surveillance with various juveniles involved in a home detention program in Tuscaloosa, Alabama, in 1977. Home detention authorizes youth workers to send juveniles directly to secure confinement when they fail to meet program requirements. Some of these rules include regular school attendance, curfew, restraint in the use of drugs or alcohol, avoidance of companions or places that might lead to trouble, and notification of parents or workers as to their whereabouts at all times when not in school, at home, or at work (Smykla and Selke, 1982). Responsibilities of paraprofessionals in this program included regular one-on-one, face-to-face visits with each juvenile daily, together with personal or telephonic contacts with parents, teachers, and/or employers. Each paraprofessional, known as an **outreach worker,** supervises about five juveniles at any given time. Paraprofessionals may serve as counselors or they may refer clients and/or their families to other agencies for specialized services (Smykla and Selke, 1982).

Paraprofessionals have also been used in mediation projects, such as alternative dispute resolution. As we have seen, alternative dispute resolution is a civil alternative to a criminal prosecution. Impartial arbiters reconcile differences between offenders and their victims and attempt to mediate these conflicts in an equitable manner. A study was conducted by the Institute for Mediation and Conflict Resolution in 1979 (Felstiner and Williams, 1979). The goals of the mediation project included (1) resolving disputes according to each disputant's sense of justice and (2) preventing recurrences of conflicts between the disputants by resolving the underlying causes of their conflicts (Felstiner and Williams, 1979). Designated paraprofessionals received some hands-on training from lawyers and judges. Sub-

BOX 13.2
On Careworkers

The Case for Good Juvenile Careworkers

Lloyd Mixdorf has furnished a detailed description of a juvenile careworker. According to Mixdorf, "the careworker's job is to be a role model, and it is important that the staff include a variety of positive personalities. All juvenile careworkers need to be decent, honest, moral, and trustworthy. They need to be drug-free and willing to submit to drug tests from time to time. Add to the list a little common sense and a genuine interest in the juveniles under their care, and you have a person with a great foundation for being a careworker."

Experience is a desirable qualification and is hard to top. Juvenile careworkers experienced in the system are valuable assets to juveniles and to other staff members as well. These paraprofessionals acquire day-to-day experiences that work to their advantage in crisis situations. New careworkers can learn much from experienced juvenile careworkers who have had extensive on-the-job training.

Counseling skills are also valuable attributes for juvenile careworkers. Many youths in the system have been counseled so extensively that they "know" the "right" answers when undergoing conventional interviews. Good careworkers know when to be observant and listen. Careworkers must establish a bond of trust between themselves and their youthful clients. They must be able to interpret sig-nals from youths that may be cries for help. Juveniles are a diverse population, and no single treatment strategy will work with all of them all of the time. Different social and cultural backgrounds account for this diversity. And, youths of different genders have different needs and strengths. Careworkers must be able to set good examples and be role models for youths of both genders.

Activity skill is another critical attribute for a good juvenile careworker. Careworkers must be able to interact with youths for a full eight-hour day. They cannot isolate themselves in offices. They should not limit their assistance to physical education or work details. These paraprofessionals should be able to generate the types of activities that will keep youths interested and involved.

Writing skill is also important. Good juvenile careworkers will need to describe day-to-day activities and behavior in a neat, coherent form. Daily logs must be maintained, and special incidents or discipline reports will have to be prepared and submitted. The ability to record such events accurately is critical to good work performance. In short, the juvenile careworker should be a caring, patient, experienced, honest, stable, literate, healthy, and drug-free person with varied interests and common sense.

Source: Adapted from: Lloyd Mixdorf, "Profile of a Good Juvenile Careworker." In *Vital Statistics in Corrections,* American Correctional Association, Laurel, MD, 1991:34.

sequently, these paraprofessionals intervened as mediation experts in numerous cases. Results of the study were largely positive, indicating that paraprofessionals were able to resolve disputes in most instances with agreements between offenders and their victims.

Legal Liabilities of Paraprofessionals

As employees of various helping agencies associated with law enforcement, the courts, and corrections, paraprofessionals enjoy immunity from prosecution similar to that of regular law enforcement officers, corrections officers, and POs. This immunity is not absolute, but rather, it is limited to acts within the scope of one's duties and responsibilities. Thus, paraprofessionals act on behalf of the agencies employing them. Under certain conditions, organizations that employ staff who injure or cause harm to others may be liable under the theory of **respondeat superior.** This doctrine is based on the principle of master and servant. If the servant does something to harm others while performing work for the master, then the master might be liable. An example might be if a Los Angeles County probation officer shot and wounded a probationer during a confrontation, the Los Angeles County Probation Department might be liable under certain conditions. However, public agencies, such as the Los Angeles County Probation Department, enjoy some qualified immunity from lawsuits, many of which are often frivolous.

In many respects, with the exception that paraprofessionals are hired employees of various corrections agencies, their liability coverage is similar to that of volunteers. Organizations using both volunteers and paraprofessionals are subject to lawsuits in the event an action by a paraprofessional or volunteer results in damages to inmates or offender-clients. These damages may be monetary, physical, or intangible, such as psychological harm. Title 42, Section 1983 of the U.S. Code (U.S. Code Annotated, 1995) outlines various types of civil rights violations that might be used as bases for lawsuits. Among the bases for different lawsuits by offender-clients are allegations of negligence. **Negligence** may be

1. Negligent hiring (e.g., organization failed to "weed out" unqualified employees who inflicted harm subsequently on an inmate or probationer/parolee).
2. Negligent assignment (e.g., armed employee without firearms training is assigned to guard prisoners; firearm discharges, wounding or killing an inmate).
3. Negligent retention (e.g., an employee with a known history of poor work and inefficiency is retained; subsequently, work of poor quality performed by that employee causes harm to an inmate or offender-client).
4. Negligent entrustment (e.g., employee may be given confidential records and may inadvertently furnish information to others that may be harmful to inmates or offender-clients).
5. Negligent direction (e.g., directions may be given to employees that are not consistent with their job description or work assignment; this may result in harm to inmates or offender-clients.
6. Negligent supervision (e.g., employee may supervise prisoners such that inmate problems are overlooked, causing serious harm and further injury or death to inmate or offender-client). (Barrineau, 1994:55–58)

Paraprofessionals may be educators who offer courses to inmates through work study programs; various skills imparted to inmates increase their employment chances. (AP/Wide World Photos)

One way of minimizing lawsuits against paraprofessionals and other employees of correctional agencies is to train them so that they can perform their jobs appropriately. Barrineau (1994:84) lists several criteria that are important to establish as part of a training program for paraprofessionals and others in the event subsequent lawsuits are filed:

1. The training was necessary as validated by a task analysis.
2. The persons conducting the training were, in fact, qualified to conduct such training.
3. The training did, in fact, take place and was properly conducted and documented.
4. The training was "state-of-the-art" and up-to-date.
5. Adequate measures of mastery of the subject matter can be documented.
6. Those who did not satisfactorily "learn" in the training session have received additional training and now have mastery of the subject matter.
7. Close supervision exists to monitor and continually evaluate the trainee's progress.

Barrineau notes that these criteria alone are insufficient to insulate an organization fully against lawsuits from offender-clients. Nevertheless, they provide some suitable criteria that can be cited in the event an organization or its employees are ever sued.

The rule recommended by Barrineau is to document that such training is provided and has occurred (*Whiteley v. Warden,* 1971). The theory is that if an event is not documented, it did not happen. The greater the documentation, the greater the chance of winning negligence suits.

KEY TERMS

Agency

Corrections volunteer

Corrections paraprofessional

Negligence

Outreach worker

Paraprofessional

Professional

Respondeat superior

Volunteer

QUESTIONS FOR REVIEW

1. What is a volunteer? Do we know how many volunteers there are in the U.S.? Why or why not?
2. What qualifications do you need to qualify as a corrections volunteer?
3. How do volunteers differ from paraprofessionals?
4. Volunteers differ in their degree of training. From this chapter, give examples of two different organizations using volunteers with different degrees of training.
5. What legal rights do volunteers have as far as having a "say" in how an agency is operated?
6. Where are volunteers recruited? Why are criminal justice internship programs good sources for volunteers?
7. Not everyone agrees that volunteers are good for community corrections. What are some disadvantages of using volunteers?
8. What is the Program for Female Offenders? What are some of the tasks performed by volunteers in this program?
9. How is the Salvation Army involved in correctional work as a voluntary agency?
10. What is the doctrine of *respondeat superior?* Do organizations have absolute immunity against lawsuits filed against them because of poor work done by their employees?

14

Supervising Women and Special Needs Offenders
Officer-Client Interactions

Introduction

Female Probationers and Parolees: A Profile

Special Programs and Services for Female
  Offenders

Other Special Needs Offenders

Community Programs for Special Needs
  Offenders

Key Terms

Questions for Review

INTRODUCTION

At any given time in most jurisdictions throughout the United States, women constitute no more than 20 percent of the probationer and parolee populations. Women also make up less than 10 percent of all jail and prison inmates. Because of these low percentages, women have seldom been targeted for services by different probation and parole agencies or community-based correctional organizations (Bloom, 1993; Mills and Barrett, 1992; Radosh, 1988). Looking at this matter a different way, most probation, parole, and community-based agencies have developed programs primarily for men. Female offenders have been systematically deprived of the same wide range of services and treatment programs that have favored the predominantly male population (Kizer, 1991; Williams and Bissell, 1990).

It is beyond the scope of this text to provide an in-depth discussion of the major social and political forces and events that have caused this state of affairs, as well as the various events that have prompted widespread changes during the last few decades. No doubt the women's movement, the Equal Rights Amendment, and other similar causes or organizations have heightened our awareness of the existence of women in jails, prisons, and community corrections programs. Women have a right to equal access to services provided incarcerated male inmates, and community corrections programs should extend their treatment programs to cater to the needs of female as well as male clientele. The factual basis to justify this priority shift is well-documented. There are growing numbers of female offenders. This means greater numbers of women in jails and prisons. In turn, this means that more women are becoming involved in probation, parole, and community-based corrections programs annually (Nesbitt, 1992:6). Between 1986 and 1991, for instance, the number of women in state prisons grew by 75 percent (Snell and Morton, 1994:1). Evidence also suggests that courts have frequently intervened to correct gender biases in correctional programming (Morash, Haarr, and Rucker, 1994).

Moyer and Giles (1993) note that there were 12,000 women in prison in 1979, 32,700 in 1988, and 43,000 in 1992. Most are single mothers who are the sole support of their dependent children (Bloom, 1993; Radosh, 1988). Thus, there are compelling needs to preserve the mother-child bonds while women are confined. The first part of this chapter examines female probationers and parolees and includes a description of the various kinds of programs established to meet the needs of female offenders, including women with dependent children.

Besides growing numbers of female offenders entering the criminal justice system and corrections, there has also been a growing presence of special needs offenders. These include offenders with drug or alcohol dependencies, mentally ill offenders, those with physical handicaps or disabilities, and those with AIDS and other communicable diseases. Many jails and prisons have had to redesign existing facilities to accommodate a greater variety of offenders. A more diverse array of services and treatment programs has been established in many jurisdictions to meet the needs of offenders with special problems. The second part of the chapter examines several types of special needs offenders and their impact on probation, parole, and community-based correctional programs. The chapter concludes with an examination of the various policy implications posed by women and special needs offenders in corrections generally.

FEMALE PROBATIONERS AND PAROLEES: A PROFILE

In 1992, females accounted for 15 percent of all probationers and 8.3 percent of all parolees (Maguire, Pastore, and Flanagan, 1993:570, 661). Table 14.1 shows the distribution of conviction offenses for women on probation for 1992, while Table 14.2

TABLE 14.1 Percentage of Female Offenders on Probation for Selected Offense Categories, 1992

Offense	Percentage of Female Offenders
All offenses	15
Violent offenses	9
Murder	15
Rape	3
Robbery	7
Assault	11
Property Offenses	18
Burglary	5
Larceny	21
Fraud	42
Drug Offenses	15
Other	14

Source: Maguire, Pastore, and Flanagan, 1993:570.

shows the percentage distribution of females, by conviction offense, paroled for the same year.

Table 14.1 shows that for 1992, 15 percent of all probationers in the United States were women. Women constituted 9 percent of all probationers convicted of violent offenses. It is clear from Table 14.1 that women were most represented proportionately in various property offense categories, such as fraud (42 percent) and larceny (21 percent). Overall, women made up 18 percent of all probationers convicted of property offenses. Reading between the lines, this figure suggests that on the average, women are sentenced to probation more often than men. But this is likely attributable to the fact that male and female offenders have different offending patterns. Males are involved to a greater degree in violent offending, while females are involved to a greater degree in property offending (see Chapter 1). Another explanation for these sentencing differences is that judges have tended to be more paternalistic toward female offenders in the past. In recent years, however, presumptive or guidelines-based sentencing schemes used by different states and the federal government have caused male-female sentencing differentials to narrow. Generally, the rate of female offending and incarceration has increased both dramatically and systematically since the early 1980s (Nesbitt, 1992:6). This does not necessarily mean that there is a "new breed" or a more dangerous female offender in society—rather, more women are being subject to less lenient treatment by a more equitable criminal justice system (Erez, 1988). Some experts have labeled this phenomenon *gender parity* (Steffensmeier and Streifel, 1989).

Regarding parole, women tended to be distributed in ways similar to their conviction patterns. For instance, only 8.3 percent of all parolees in 1992 were women. This proportion is similar to the proportionate distribution of women incarcerated in federal and state prisons. With a few exceptions, female parolee dis-

TABLE 14.2 Conviction Offenses for Women on Parole in 34 States, 1992

Offense	Percentage[a]
All Offenses	8.3
Violent Offenses	16.1
Murder	3.8
Rape	0.2
Robbery	6.8
Assault	4.3
Property Offenses	40.3
Burglary	6.4
Larceny	16.6
Fraud	14.3
Drug Offenses	37.1
Other	2.0

[a]Percentage does not equal 100% because of selected offenses; not all offenses included.
Source: Maguire, Pastore, and Flanagan, 1993:661.

tributions by conviction offense were similar to their original conviction offense patterns. For instance, 16.1 percent of all female parolees had been convicted for violent offenses. And, 40.3 percent of all female parolees were property offenders. This is approximately the same percentage for women convicted of property offenses. Over 37 percent of all female parolees had prior convictions for drug offenses. A similar figure accounts for the proportion of convictions for women involving drug offenses. Another interesting observation is that the female "failure rate" while on parole is approximately the same as it is for male parolees, about 61.5 percent (Maguire, Pastore, and Flanagan, 1993:662). Men have a slightly lower "success rate"—36.3 percent, compared with 37.3 percent for female parolees.

SPECIAL PROGRAMS AND SERVICES FOR FEMALE OFFENDERS

In 1992, the American Correctional Association formulated the following National Correctional Policy on Female Offender Services (Nesbitt, 1992:7):

INTRODUCTION: Correctional systems must develop service delivery systems for accused and adjudicated female offenders that are comparable to those provided to males. Additional services must also be provided to meet the unique needs of the female offender population.

STATEMENT: Correctional systems must be guided by the principle of parity. Female offenders must receive the equivalent range of services available to other offenders, including opportunities for individualized programming and services that recognize the unique needs of this population. The services should

A. Assure access to a range of alternatives to incarceration, including pretrial and posttrial diversion, probation, restitution, treatment for substance abuse, halfway houses, and parole services;

B. Provide acceptable conditions of confinement, including appropriately trained staff and sound operating procedures that address this population's needs in such areas as clothing, personal property, hygiene, exercise, recreation, and visitation with children and family;

C. Provide access to a full range of work and programs designed to expand economic and social roles of women, with emphasis on education; career counseling and exploration of nontraditional as well as traditional vocational training; relevant life skills, including parenting and social and economic assertiveness; and prerelease and work/education release programs;

D. Facilitate the maintenance and strengthening of family ties, particularly those between parent and child;

E. Deliver appropriate programs and services, including medical, dental, and mental health programs, services to pregnant women, substance abuse programs, child and family services, and provide access to legal services; and

F. Provide access to release programs that include aid in establishing homes, economic stability, and sound family relationships. (Nesbitt, 1992:7)

Criticisms of Women's Prisons and Community Programs.   A Minnesota study highlights some of the continuing problems associated with women's prisons and community-based treatment services. Hokanson (1986) gathered information about female inmates from 87 county correctional facilities and 31 jails. She found that the typical female offender was young, either single, divorced, or separated; educated at a level approximating the general population; lacking in work skills and dependent on public assistance; overrepresentative of minority groups; and having a high probability of physical and/or sexual abuse victimization; and a history of substance abuse. Similar observations have been made about women offenders by others (Carp and Schade, 1992:152).

It is generally acknowledged that women's prisons and programming for women in community-based correctional programs have not compared favorably with programs and facilities for men. For instance, programs for female offenders have been poorer in quality, quantity, variability, and availability in both the U.S. and Canada (Muraskin, 1990; Ross and Fabiano, 1985). Despite these inequities, courts generally declare that men and women in prisons do not have to be treated equally, and that separate can be equal when men's and women's prisons are compared (Knight, 1992). There are exceptions, however.

The case of *Glover v. Johnson* (1979) involved the Michigan Department of Corrections and the issue of equal programming for female inmates. A class-action suit was filed on behalf of all Michigan female prison inmates to the effect that their constitutional rights were violated because they were being denied educational and vocational rehabilitation opportunities that were then being provided male inmates only. Among other things, the Michigan Department of Corrections was ordered to provide the following to its incarcerated women: (1) two-year college programming; (2) paralegal training and access to attorneys to remedy past inadequacies in law library facilities; (3) an inmate wage policy to ensure that female

Compared with male inmates, female inmates are at a disadvantage, since there are fewer prison educational and vocational programs available to prepare them for life on the outside. (Paul Conklin/Monkmeyer Press)

inmates were provided equal wages; (4) access for female inmates to programming at camps previously available only to male inmates; (5) enhanced vocational offerings; (6) apprenticeship opportunities; and (7) prison industries that previously existed only at men's facilities (American Correctional Association, 1993c:32). Several similar cases in other jurisdictions (Connecticut, California, Wisconsin, and Idaho) have been settled without court action.

The *Glover* case is like the tip of an iceberg when it comes to disclosing various problems associated with women's prisons and other corrections institutions for women. The following are criticisms that have been leveled against women's correctional facilities in the last few decades. Some of these criticisms have been remedied in selected jurisdictions.

1. *No adequate classification system exists for female prisoners* (Culliver, 1993:407). Women from widely different backgrounds with diverse criminal histories are celled with one another in most women's prisons. This is conducive to greater criminalization during the incarceration period. Further, most women's prisons have only medium-security custody, rather than a wider variety of custody levels to accommodate more or less dangerous female offenders (Pollock-Byrne, 1990:84–85). Better classification methods should be devised.

2. *Most women's prisons are remotely located.* Thus, many female prisoners are deprived of immediate contact with out-of-prison educational or vocational services that might be available through study or work release.

3. *Women who give birth to babies while incarcerated are deprived of valuable parent-child contact.* Some experts contend this is a serious deprivation for newborn infants (Culliver, 1993:406; Pollock-Byrne, 1990:35; Ryan and Grassano, 1992:184).

4. *Women have less extensive vocational and educational programming in the prison setting.*

5. *Women have less access to legal services.* In the past, law libraries in women's facilities were lacking or nonexistent; recent remedies have included provisions for either legal services or more adequate libraries in women's institutions.

6. *Women have special medical needs, and women's prisons do not adequately provide for these needs* (Pollock-Byrne, 1990:35).

7. *Mental health treatment services and programs for women are inferior to those provided for men in men's facilities.*

8. *Training programs that are provided women do not permit them to live independently and earn decent livings when released on parole* (Culliver, 1993:407; Klausner, 1991).

Because of the rather unique role of women as caregivers for their children, many corrections professionals view the imprisonment of women differently from the imprisonment of men. For various reasons, female imprisonment is opposed on moral, ethical, and religious grounds. Legally, these arguments are often unconvincing. In an attempt to at least address some of the unique problems confronting female offenders when they are incarcerated or when they participate in community-based programs, some experts have advocated the following as recommendations:

1. Institute training programs that would enable imprisoned women to become literate.
2. Provide female offenders with programs that do not center on traditional gender roles—programs that will lead to more economic independence and self-sufficiency.
3. Establish programs that would engender more positive self-esteem for imprisoned women and enhance their assertiveness and communication and interpersonal skills.
4. Establish programs that would allow imprisoned mothers to interact more with their children and assist them in overcoming feelings of guilt and shame for having deserted their children. In addition, visitation areas for mothers and children should be altered to minimize the effect of a prison-type environment.
5. An alternative to mother-and-child interaction behind prison bars would be to allow imprisoned mothers to spend more time with their children outside the prison.
6. Provide imprisoned mothers with training to improve parenting skills.
7. Establish more programs to treat drug-addicted female offenders.
8. Establish a community partnership program to provide imprisoned women with employment opportunities.
9. Establish a better classification system for incarcerated women—one that would not permit the less hardened offender to be juxtaposed with the hardened female offender.
10. Provide in-service training (sensitivity awareness) to assist staff members (wardens, correctional officers) in understanding the nature and needs of incarcerated women (Culliver, 1993:409–410).

Other experts have recommended the establishment and provision for an environment that would allow all pregnant inmates the opportunity to rear their newborn infants for a period of one year and provide counseling regarding available parental services, foster care, guardianship, and other relevant activities pending their eventual release. Some women's facilities have cottages on prison grounds where inmates with infants can accomplish some of these objectives.

THE PROGRAM *for Female Offenders, Inc. (PFO).*   The PROGRAM for Female Offenders, Inc. was established in 1974 as the result of jail overcrowding in Allegheny County, Pennsylvania (Arnold, 1992:37). The PFO is a work-release facility operated as a nonprofit agency by the county. It is designed to accommodate up to 36 women with space for six preschool children. It was originally created to reduce jail overcrowding, but because of escalating rates of female offending and jail incarceration, the overcrowding problem persists.

When the PFO was established, the Allegheny County Jail was small. Only 12 women were housed there. Nevertheless, agency founders worked out an agreement with jail authorities so that female jail prisoners could be transferred to PFO by court order. Inmate-clients would be guilty of prison breach if they left PFO without permission. While at PFO, the women would participate in training, volunteering in the community, and learning how to spend their leisure time with the help of a role-modeling and parent-education program for mothers and children. The program is based on freedom reached by attaining levels of responsibility (Arnold, 1992:37–38). In 1984, a much larger work-release facility was constructed in Allegheny County. At present, over 300 women per year are served by PFO. PFO authorities reserve the right to screen potential candidates for work release. During 1992, the following companion projects were implemented in Allegheny County:

1. Good-time project at the county jail;
2. Male work-release center accommodating 60 beds;
3. Development of criminal justice division in county government;
4. Drug treatment and work-release facility at St. Francis Health Center's Chemical Dependency Department;
5. Development of a male job placement program;
6. Expansion of the existing THE PROGRAM Women's Center; and
7. Expansion of the retail theft project. (Arnold, 1992:38)

The success of THE PROGRAM is demonstrated by its low 3.5 percent recidivism rate in the community program and only a 17 percent recidivism rate at the residential facility. Over $88,000 has been collected in rent, $27,000 in fines, and $8,000 in restitution to victims of the female offenders. For the male offenders, $106,500 has been collected in rent and $107,400 in fines and restitution. Long-range plans for THE PROGRAM call for a crime prevention program, including a day care center, intervention therapy for drug-abusing families, intensive work with preschool children who are already giving evidence of impending delinquency, and a scholarship program (Arnold, 1992:40). Plans also include expanding THE PROGRAM's services to more areas throughout Pennsylvania.

The Women's Activities and Learning Center (WALC) Program.   The Kansas Department of Corrections has established a program for women with children that has been patterned after *PATCH (Parents and Their Children)* begun by the Missouri Department of Corrections and *MATCH (Mothers and Their Children)* operated by the California Department of Corrections. The Kansas program is known as the **Women's Activities and Learning Center, or WALC.** WALC was started with a grant from the U.S. Department of Education under the Women's Educational Opportunity Act and is based in Topeka (Logan, 1992:160).

The Topeka facility has a primary goal of developing and coordinating a broad range of programs, services, and classes and workshops that will increase women offender's chances for a positive reintegration with their families and society upon release (Logan, 1992:160). A visiting area at the center accommodates female inmates and their visiting children. Thus, women with children are given a chance to take an active part in caring for their children. Mothers acquire some measure of a mother-child relationship during incarceration. They are able to fix meals for their children and play with them in designated areas. Various civic and religious groups contribute their volunteer resources to assist these women. Both time and money are expended by outside agencies and personnel, such as the Kiwanis, the Kansas East Conference of the United Methodist Church, and the Fraternal Order of Police (Logan, 1992:161).

One advantage of WALC is that it provides various programs and courses in useful areas such as parenting, child development, prenatal care, self-esteem, anger management, nutrition, support groups, study groups, cardiopulmonary resuscitation, personal development, and crafts. The parenting program, for instance, is a 10-week course during which inmate-mothers meet once a week to discuss their various problems. In order to qualify for inclusion in this program, female inmates must be designated low risk and minimum security and have no disciplinary reports filed against them during the 90 days prior to program involvement. When the 10-week course is completed, the women are entitled to participate in a three-week retreat sponsored by the Methodist Church. The retreat includes transportation for inmates, with fishing, horse riding, hay rides, and game playing for mothers and their children. Volunteers and a correctional officer are present during the retreat experience. Since September 1991, more than 300 women and 500 children have participated in the WALC program with a low rate of recidivism (Logan, 1992:161).

New York's Prison Nursery/Children's Center.   At the Bedford Hills, New York, Correctional Facility, a 750-woman maximum-security prison constructed in 1933, the **New York Prison Nursery/Children's Center** was established in 1989–1990. Since 1930, New York legislation has provided for women in prison to keep their babies. At present, New York is the only state that maintains a prison nursery (Roulet, 1993:4).

Authorities at Bedford Hills believe that it is important for women to maintain strong ties with their families during incarceration. Further, they believe that women will have a greater chance at reintegration and lower recidivism as the op-

BOX 14.1
Services for Women

Project Green Hope: Services for Women, Inc.

A halfway house for women was opened in New York City in 1975. This became known as **Project Green Hope** and was originally designed to meet the needs of female parolees (Calathes, 1991:136). The goals of Project Green Hope are to assist female offenders toward living healthy, productive lives and to resolve some of the causative factors involved in their criminal conduct. Over 800 women have participated in Project Green Hope since it was established. These women have engaged in individual and group counseling, vocational services, and substance abuse work. Parolees are housed in an East Harlem facility that is a converted convent that houses 24 women. Most women served by Project Green Hope are black or Hispanic, poor, mothers without high school diplomas who have a history of recent substance abuse problems. The present transitional program accommodates women for periods of up to six months. Some women are sent to the facility for pretrial housing or as an alternative to incarceration. Thus, Project Green Hope functions as both a halfway-in house and a halfway-out house for women. Calathes (1991:136) indicates that Project Green Hope is often a woman's last resort. Most clients for Project Green Hope are referred by corrections or the courts.

Most of Project Green Hope's funding comes from the New York State Division of Parole, the New York State Division of Probation and Correctional Alternatives, and the New York State Division of Substance Abuse Services. Program costs average about $125 per day, or $46,000 per year, per offender-client. Clients participate in GED programs and have a fairly high completion rate. Women learn how to be self-sufficient and cope with everyday problems (Calathes, 1991:137).

When women come to Project Green Hope, they go through three residential phases: orientation, intermediate, and discharge. Vocational and social services counselors assist these women on an as-needed basis throughout the duration of their stay at the facility. Extensive substance abuse counseling and education courses are provided clientele, together with job placement assistance. Vocational counselors help these women determine suitable careers for which they are most qualified through a vocational rehabilitation program and needs-assessment process. Educational courses supplement counseling and other productive activities. These women open bank accounts and attempt to acquire some savings so that they can have a greater chance of reintegrating into mainstream society.

Calathes (1991:139) indicates that program success is defined as meeting the required criteria for the discharge phase, abiding by house rules and regulations, and not committing a criminal offense. Failure is removal from the halfway house for violating house rules and regulations (i.e., abusive behavior, drug usage, or absconding). When an evaluation study was conducted of this facility in 1988, 44 Project Green Hope clients were investigated over a two-year period. Unfortunately, only 16 percent of these persons successfully completed the program. The primary reason for program failure was drug abuse. Calathes (1991:139–141) has indicated that clients with a prior history of serious chemical dependency or drug addiction are not likely to succeed in Project Green Hope. Most arrests of unsuccessful program clientele involved crack cocaine usage or heroin addiction. A higher level of client supervision and monitoring is indicated (Calathes, 1991:141).

Interestingly, women who fail in the Project Green Hope program are subsequently sent to a female version of boot camp or a Shock Incarceration Program.

Although some Project Green Hope officials are not happy with the boot camp alternative for these young women who fail, evidence suggests that the boot camp experience is helpful by reducing subsequent recidivism, at least recidivism attributable to drug dependency. Each year, newer treatment methods and supervision strategies are being attempted to assist these women and future clientele in successfully completing their programs. Few programs such as Project Green Hope presently exist throughout the United States, and thus, this is a compelling reason to invest more time, effort, and money into this program so that greater success rates can be achieved.

portunity for familial interaction increases. Further, there is a positive impact on babies, since they can remain with and be nurtured by their mothers. In 1993, there were two state nurseries. Besides the one at Bedford Hills, another was opened at Taconic. This is a smaller facility, also located in Bedford Hills, housing about 400 female offenders.

Roulet (1993:4) says that not all women incarcerated at Bedford Hills are eligible to participate in the prison nursery program. A woman's criminal background, past parenting performance, disciplinary record, and educational needs are examined and assessed before they are accepted. Women who are selected are expected to make the best use of their time by developing their mothering skills and caring for their infants. They are also expected to participate in various self-help programs of a vocational and educational nature (Roulet, 1993:4). The center's main program goal is to help women preserve and strengthen family ties and receive visits from their children as often as possible in a warm, nurturing atmosphere. They are kept closely informed of their children's physical, educational, intellectual, and emotional well-being while they are separated. Through the various classes and programs offered at Bedford Hills, women acquire a better understanding of their roles as parents and are able to reinforce their feelings of self-worth (Roulet, 1993:5).

Inmates at Bedford Hills also participate in a Parent's Center. The primary concerns and components of the Parent's Center are

1. Bilingual parenting (allows women to learn English while exploring issues of mothers and children; provides a bilingual parenting class);

2. Child development associate course (the CDA is a national accreditation program that prepares candidates to teach in accredited nursery schools anywhere in the country);

3. Children's advocate office (trained advocates meet with inmate mothers individually to address all child-related problems);

4. Children's library (caregivers help mothers to select age-appropriate books; occasionally films and special storytime sessions are arranged);

5. Choices and changes courses (this class helps inmates develop self-awareness and learn the process of decision making and accountability to improve parenting);

6. Foster care committee (the committee helps women learn their legal rights and responsibilities as incarcerated women; the committee helps mothers with letter-writing, direct services, monthly group meetings; provides handbooks, support groups, and so on);

7. Holiday activities (the center provides holiday activities, as directed by inmate staff members);

8. Infant day care center (cares for the babies of nursery mothers who are programmed into school or work assignments; provides hands-on experience for CDA interns);

9. Mental hygiene program (inmate staff become "parents" for other less fortunate inmate parents; it is considered to be useful and relaxing therapy for these women);

10. Mother's group (a certified social worker conducts group sessions for women who have children and want an opportunity to discuss their relationships; it also provides the services of a family therapist);

11. Nursery aides (inmate staff member works with nursery coordinators; she sews clothes for nursery babies and helps with inventory and distribution of clothes);

12. The overnight program (volunteer host parents in the community take in nursery children for a day and overnight once a month);

13. Parenting program (covers parenting from the prenatal stages to adulthood through the use of educational classes and films);

14. Prenatal center (women receive parenting classes; address their drug problems; learn sewing, crocheting, and other handiwork);

15. Records and teaching material (inmate staff member collects information on the history of the nursery program, new materials or studies on children, education, imprisoned women, drugs and their effects on children; these archival resources are used by staff and facility college students);

16. Summer program (older children spend a week during the summer with volunteer host families who live near the nursery; each day the children are brought to visit their mothers for a few hours);

17. Study corner (mothers tape-record themselves reading a children's story, which is then sent to their child);

18. Sponsor a baby (churches, temples, and other groups provide necessities for inmate mothers and babies when they leave prison and the nursery and also for families of inmates not eligible for the nursery program who are unexpectedly burdened with an infant);

19. Transportation clinic (provides transportation for children of inmates to visit their mothers at the nursery and children's center); and

20. Toy library (mothers select games, crafts, and toys for their children's visit; some can be taken home; others are returned to the library) (Roulet, 1993:5–6).

Roulet (1993:6) says that women whose babies are born while incarcerated may keep them at Bedford for up to one year. Babies are delivered in a hospital outside of prison, and the mother and infant live in the nursery for as long as the child remains. If it is likely that the mother will be paroled by the time the infant is 18 months old, then the infant may remain with the mother with special permission until that date. It is important to keep mothers and children together as much as possible while at Bedford Hills. The child's welfare is of utmost concern to authorities (Roulet, 1993:6). Such bonding is considered significant at reducing rates of recidivism among paroled Bedford Hills women. Parenting programs for female inmates have been implemented in many other state jurisdictions, attesting to the importance of this theme for corrections officials throughout the United States and abroad (Mott, 1989; Stevens et al., 1993).

Changing Policies, Programs, and Services for Female Offenders.   In 1992, *Corrections Compendium* published the results of a survey of 85 state-operated women's facilities in 46 states (Su Davis, 1992b). Approximately 31,000 women were housed in these facilities at a cost of $1.5 million annually. Serious health problems were related to pregnancies, AIDS, substance abuse and mental health.

When this survey was conducted, all facilities had on-site medical staff available. Not all facilities had gynecological-obstetrical services, however. Only 68 percent of all facilities offered prenatal and postpartum services and none of the responding institutions allowed newborn infants to remain with their mothers. In the most recent 12-month period, 1,445 babies were born to inmates (Su Davis, 1992b:7).

Davis (Su 1992b:7) says that more women are being convicted of drug offenses annually. Three-fourths of all women inmates were in need of substance abuse treatment, although only 28 percent of all incarcerated women had conviction offenses involving drugs. Most offenders had dropped out of high school or had not received the GED. Most had been unable to hold a job for longer than six months. Presently, most of the surveyed institutions offer vocational and educational courses for these women. Two-thirds offer college courses and 70 have pre-release programs. Most facilities have institutional work assignments, and about half have parenting programs.

Between 1987 and 1992, policy changes have been implemented in over half of the facilities surveyed (Su Davis, 1992b:8). These policy changes involve increased opportunities for women to work and/or participate in vocational and educational programming originally available only to male inmates. Major changes have occurred in classification, visitation, and housing. Clothing policy changes have also been effected. Many of these changes have been occasioned by the parity issue, which has brought women's facilities more in line with men's. In most instances, this has meant improved services delivery to women's prisons. In some instances, however, deprivations have resulted. For instance, Su Davis (1992b:8) notes that at Pewee Valley, Kentucky, the personal property of female inmates was reduced to equal that of male inmates. And, in Portland, Oregon, female inmates can no longer wear earrings, since men are forbidden to wear them. Nevertheless, despite these limited deprivations, most policy changes have benefited women inmates generally. Each year, the conditions in women's facilities are being improved and services delivery to these institutions is being expanded.

OTHER SPECIAL NEEDS OFFENDERS

Correctional agencies must manage a wide range of offenders, including those with special problems. These offenders, or clients, present unusual challenges for probation and parole officers as well as program administrators who must adjust their supervisory methods and program components accordingly. Special types of offenders may have deep-seated psychological problems that are not immediately diagnosed. They may react in unpredictable ways to various types of treatments or therapy. Because their behaviors may be unexpected or unanticipated, they may become violent and harm themselves or others. Persons who are abnormal in some respects behave in abnormal ways. Probation and parole personnel are not always prepared for each and every contingency that may arise. It is a good idea to know about these special types of offenders, their needs, behavior patterns, and what, if anything, of an unusual nature might be expected from them. Special needs offenders have an array of problems beyond the scope of this book. Thus, the topics discussed in this section related to special needs offenders is not exhaustive. Rather it will be limited to (1) drug/alcohol-dependent offenders, (2) mentally ill offenders, (3) sex offenders and child sexual abusers, (4) physically handicapped or challenged offenders; and (5) offenders with AIDS or other communicable diseases and/or medical problems.

Drug- and Alcohol-Dependent Offenders

Drug and alcohol abuse are highly correlated with criminal conduct (Deschenes, Turner, and Clear, 1992; Speckart and Anglin, 1986; Wish, 1987; Wish, Brady, and Cuadrado, 1986). Large numbers of pretrial detainees are characterized as having drug and/or alcohol dependencies. For instance, between September and October 1986, 92 percent of all suspects arrested, booked, and charged with robbery and 81 percent of those charged with burglary in New York City tested positive for cocaine use (Wish, 1987). Additionally, officials in charge of the Hampden County (Springfield, Massachusetts) Pre-Release Center for parolees about to be released into the community indicate that 87 percent of their clients had significant prior drug or alcohol problems and that a large majority of them had committed crimes while under the influence of one or more of these substances (Atmore and Bauchiero, 1987:22). Furthermore, there is evidence that many offenders suffer from polysubstance abuse (Capodanno and Chavaria, 1991).

Offenders with drug or alcohol dependencies present several problems for correctional personnel (Kraus and Lazear, 1991). Often, jails are not equipped to handle their withdrawal symptoms, especially if they are confined for long periods. And, the symptoms themselves are frequently dealt with rather than the social and psychological causes for these dependencies. Thus, when offenders go through alcohol detoxification programs or are treated for drug addiction, they leave these programs and are placed back into the same circumstances that caused the drug or alcohol dependencies originally.

Prisons and jails do not always insulate inmates from continued drug or alcohol abuses. Illegal substance abuse is so prevalent within state and federal prisons that the Federal Bureau of Prisons has revised its regulations to require random urinalyses of high-risk inmates who are known to have been drug dependent prior to their incarceration (Federal Bureau of Prisons, 1985). The abuse of drugs is not strictly confined to inmates. Corrections employees are often about as likely as prisoners to abuse drugs, since the employees themselves are frequently the major conduits for smuggling drugs into prison settings (Ellsworth, 1985). Currently, many state, local, and federal agencies conduct routine urinalyses of their employees to detect and/or deter drug abuse among them as well as inmates (Ellsworth, 1985:13).

RORs have often been involved in additional criminality while awaiting trial. Even samples of RORs who were subjected to periodic drug tests as a specific deterrent were found to have high failure-to-appear rates and rearrests (Britt, Gottfredson, and Goldkamp, 1992). Drug dependencies also account for greater numbers of dropouts and failures among those involved in both juvenile and adult intervention programs (Dawson, 1992). For those on either probation or parole, drug and/or alcohol dependencies present various problems and account for program infractions, rearrests, and general adjustment and reintegration problems (Deschenes, Turner, and Clear, 1992; Haddock and Beto, 1988).

Those reentering the community on parole after years of incarceration are especially vulnerable to drug dependencies during the first six months following their release (Nurco, Hanlon, and Bateman, 1992). Individual or group counseling and other forms of therapy are recommended for drug- or alcohol-dependent clients, although many clients are considered as treatment resistant (Dawson, 1992). Since 1972, various community-based treatment programs have been implemented to treat and counsel drug-dependent clients. These community-based programs have been collectively labeled **Treatment Alternatives to Street Crime (TASC)** and currently are being operated in numerous jurisdictions throughout the United States to improve client abstinence from drugs, increase their employment potential, and improve their social/personal functioning (U.S. Bureau of Justice Assistance, 1988).

Mentally Ill Offenders

It was estimated in the early 1980s that the 3,493 local jails in cities and counties throughout the United States confined over 600,000 mentally ill inmates annually (Johnson, McKeown, and James, 1984). Another 12,600 inmates confined in all types of correctional institutions in the United States were classified as mentally retarded (Denkowski and Denkowski, 1985). Some experts consider these estimates too low. In Virginia, for example, a task force survey of jails showed that about 12,000 severely mentally ill persons enter the state's jails each year (Virginia Department of Mental Health and Retardation, 1984).

Mentally ill or retarded inmates present correctional officials with problems similar to those who have drug or alcohol dependencies. Frequently, inadequate staffing makes diagnoses of inmates and their problems difficult. Because of the short-term confinement purpose of jails, these facilities are not prepared to adequately treat those inmates with serious mental disturbances or deficiencies. Suicides in jails and prisons are frequently linked with the mental condition of inmates unable to cope with confinement (Winfree, 1987). Mentally ill inmates also exhibit a high degree of socially disruptive behavior. This disruptive behavior occurs not only during confinement but later, when these inmates are discharged. In many jurisdictions, treatment services for mentally retarded offenders receive a low budgetary and program priority.

Offenders who are mentally ill are incarcerated disproportionately in relation to other offenders (Ayres, 1988; Stern, 1990). Mentally ill inmates tend to mask their limitations and are highly susceptible to prison culture and inmate manipulation (Santamour, 1986). Also, these offenders are often unresponsive to traditional rehabilitation programs available to other inmates. They present correctional officers with unusual discipline problems unlike other inmates (Rockowitz, 1986a, 1986b). Corrections officers often are high school educated with little, if any, training in dealing with mentally ill individuals. Obviously, proper classification systems should be devised to identify different types of disabled inmates. Evidence indicates that such classification systems are currently being devised in many jail settings and that corrections generally is becoming more responsive to the needs of these types of offenders (Brennan and Wells, 1992; Schafer and Dellinger, 1993; U.S. Bureau of Prisons, 1989; Wells and Brennan, 1992).

The Texas Department of Corrections has established a Mentally Retarded Offender Program to identify offenders with psychological disorders as they enter the system. Those mentally retarded offenders are separated from the general prison population and placed in sheltered units where they receive appropriate medical care and fair discipline (Pugh and Kunkel, 1986). The U.S. Supreme Court has declared in *Estelle v. Gamble* (1976) that deliberate indifference by prison authorities to serious medical disorders of prisoners violates the Eighth Amendment as "cruel and unusual punishment." Thus, corrections administrators in Texas and other states have made significant efforts to provide for effective initial classifications of offenders and to deal with those diagnosed as mentally ill or retarded (Hall, 1986; Kramer, 1986; White and Wood, 1986).

A deinstitutionalization movement began in 1968 in the United States, and mentally ill offenders were increasingly shifted from institutional to community care (Steadman et al., 1984). This movement has not been uniform throughout all jurisdictions, however. One aim of deinstitutionalization has been to reduce jail and prison populations by diverting the mentally ill or retarded to nonincarcerative surroundings such as hospitals. However, deinstitutionalization has not been entirely successful in this respect (Johnson, McKeown, and James, 1984). One unintended consequence of deinstitutionalization has been to discharge large numbers of mentally disturbed offenders back into the community prematurely after a short hospitalization. Police once again encounter these offenders because of their inability to cope with the "rigors of the street" (French, 1986). In fact, the police bring these same individuals back into jails and prisons through "mercy bookings," when they mistakenly believe correctional personnel can take care of them more effectively. Thus, the cycle is repeated, and the stresses of jail or prison exacerbate latent psychotic, convulsive, and behavioral factors (French, 1986).

Of course, deinstitutionalization of mentally ill offenders does not significantly alleviate the burden on the probation and parole departments that must supervise these clients. POs and their agencies have had to make significant adjustments and programmatic changes to accommodate mentally ill offenders. One of the greatest areas of concern, from the standpoint of agency personnel, relates to supervising those who are learning disabled or mentally retarded (Wertleib and Greenberg, 1989). Often, because these offenders cannot express themselves or indicate their needs, it is difficult to identify the most appropriate services or legal assistance they might require. Many POs lack skills in dealing with these clients, although many agencies throughout the United States are improving their services delivery (Wertleib and Greenberg, 1989).

Sex Offenders and Child Sexual Abusers

Another category of offenders receiving special emphasis from corrections are **sex offenders,** including child sexual abusers. Sometimes these offenders are grouped with criminals who are mentally ill and deserve special services, while others believe they should not receive special consideration (Driggs and Zoet, 1987). Since many sex offenses are committed against victims known by the offender as a friend or family member, a large number of these incidents are not reported to the police. Thus, no one really knows how many sex offenders there are in the United States at any given time.

It has been estimated that convicted rapists make up about 2 percent of the prison population in the United States (Kuznestov, Pierson, and Harry, 1992; McCormack et al., 1992). In selected jurisdictions such as Minnesota, the general category *sex offenders* accounts for a much larger portion of inmates. In 1986, for example, the Minnesota Department of Corrections reported that 23 percent of all adult inmates were sex offenders (Driggs and Zoet, 1987:124). **Sex offenders** are persons who commit a sexual act prohibited by law. Fairly common types of sex offenders include rapists and prostitutes, although sex offenses may include voyeurism ("peeping toms"), exhibitionism, child sexual molestation, incest, date rape, and marital rape. This list is not exhaustive. Child sexual abusers are adults who involve minors in virtually any kind of sexual activity ranging from intercourse with children to photographing them in lewd poses. Although the exact figure is unknown, it is believed that approximately 2 million children are sexually victimized annually (Prentky et al., 1991a, 1991b). It is also estimated that 90 percent of all child sexual abuse cases are never prosecuted, although this situation appears to be changing (Champion, 1988c; Whitcomb, Shapiro, and Stellwagen, 1985).

Public interest in and awareness of sex offenders is based on the belief that most convicted sex offenders will commit new sex offenses when released (Clark, 1986). However, some studies of recidivism among sex offenders show relatively low recidivism rates of from 14 to 17 percent (Greenfeld, 1985:4). Regardless of the

BOX 14.2
Covenant House: A Place Where Youths May Be Exploited!

The Case of Father Bruce Ritter

It can happen even at Covenant House. Headquartered in New York with international branches, Covenant House has been operating for many years. It is a philanthropic enterprise with the primary objective of providing shelter for runaway youths who have no place to stay, no shelter, no food, no hope. Its annual $83 million budget annually shelters over 20,000 homeless teenagers. Many of the youths who seek refuge at Covenant House are male prostitutes and those with drug or alcohol dependencies. Covenant House counselors and staff assist these youths in linking up with the right agencies for treatment and therapy. There is no question that Covenant House does a lot of good work in many cities every day. So what is the problem?

In December 1989, several youths came forward to tell how they had been sexually exploited by Father Bruce Ritter, the founder and president of Covenant House. Ritter, 63, a Franciscan priest, denied the charges at first but subsequently resigned after numerous headlines indicated that a scandal was in the making. Far beyond sexual exploitation of some of Covenant House's youthful clients were additional charges of financial wrong-doing. Among other things discovered were a secret $1 million trust fund apparently managed and manipulated by Ritter. Ritter contended that this trust fund was originally established with part of his $98,000 annual salary, donations from others, and his personal investments. The purpose, he said, was to provide a "safe harbor" to support exploited youth. Instead, Ritter made loans to his sister, two board members, and a former Covenant House resident. A $350,000 fee was paid to Ritter's niece and her husband for contractual work on agency structures. Ritter himself took $140,000 from this fund to pay for his expenses and "conduct his ministry."

Covenant House auditors are in the process of cleaning up the place financially. The obvious nepotism is being minimized and eliminated. The Internal Revenue Service is also investigating. Despite these weak timbers, the original intent of Covenant House to function as a sound refuge to wayward or runaway youth remains a worthy goal that should not be compromised or abandoned because of the actions of Father Bruce Ritter and his relatives.

Source: Adapted from Frank Washington, Tony Clifton, and Lauren Picker, "Sex, Cash and Family Favors: New Allegations Rock Covenant House." *Newsweek,* March 26, 1990:21.

diverse motives of sex offenders, there is general agreement among professionals that these offenders usually need some form of counseling or therapy (Knopp, Rosenberg, and Stevenson, 1986; Matek, 1986; McGrath and Carey, 1987). Many jurisdictions currently operate sex therapy programs designed to rehabilitate sex offenders, depending on the nature of their sex crime.

Missouri operates the **Missouri Sexual Offender Program (MOSOP),** which is targeted to serve the needs of incarcerated, nonpsychotic sexual offenders. The program can supervise effectively over 700 offenders who are required to complete the program before becoming eligible for parole (Kuznestov, Pierson, and Harry, 1992). MOSOP approaches sex offenders on the assumption that their sex offenses resulted from learned patterns of behavior associated with anxious, angry, and impulsive individuals. The three-phase program obligates offenders to attend 10 weeks of courses in abnormal psychology and the psychology of sexual offending. In other phases, inmates meet in group therapy sessions to talk out their problems with counselors and other inmates. MOSOP officials believe that if the program can reduce sex offender recidivism by only 3 percent, it will pay for itself from the savings of court costs and inmate processing and confinement (Kuznestov, Pierson, and Harry, 1992).

The Minnesota Department of Corrections operates a project known as **180 Degrees, Inc.** This is similar to a halfway house for parolees, but it is designed for those who have received no previous treatment for their sex offenses (Driggs and Zoet, 1987). Participation in 180 Degrees, Inc., is limited to only those offenders willing to admit they have committed one or more sex offenses and who can function as group members. Offenders form men's sexuality groups that meet for 90-minute meetings over a 13-week period. All participants contract with officials to write an autobiography of their offense, a description of the victim, a listing of sexual abuse cues, the development of a control plan, and personal affirmations (Driggs and Zoet, 1987:126). Even though this program is not fully effective, it does seem to help some offenders understand their behavior.

Sex offenders, especially child sexual abusers, pose significant problems for both jail and prison authorities as well as community-based corrections personnel. Child sexual abusers are often abused themselves by other inmates when their crimes become known. Other sex offenders become the prey of stronger inmates who use these offenders for their own sexual gratification. Many sex offenders request that they be segregated from other prisoners because of danger to themselves. But because of limited resources and space, jail and prison officials cannot often segregate these offenders effectively from other inmates.

Within communities, many sex offenders and child sexual abusers are placed in community-based facilities for treatment and counseling. A survey of 2,961 juvenile and adult sex offender treatment programs has indicated an increase of 133 percent in the number of these providers between 1986 and 1990 (Knopp, Freeman-Longo, and Stevenson, 1992). The most frequently used treatment method in sex offender treatment agencies is peer group counseling. For example, the state of Washington operates the Special Sex Offender Sentencing Alternative (SSOSA), which permits community treatment in lieu of determinate sentences for adult, felony sex offenders (Washington State Department of Social and Mental Health Services, 1991). The Washington program has found that intensive counseling and therapy for many of these clients has substantially reduced their recidivism within the community.

Various models of PO training and caseload assignments have been described that include sex offender specialization. Some officers are specialists in that they have received unique training in counseling sex offenders. Some POs have acquired M.S.W. degrees and are certified counselors for those with sex or alcohol problems. One of these PO training models is the specialized caseloads model, in which clients are assigned according to their particular offenses and/or psychological problems. Sex offenders and child sexual abusers are among those clients receiving particular supervision from PO specialists, just as chemically dependent persons might be supervised by special POs who have acquired additional chemical dependency training (Anthony, 1988).

Offenders with Physical Handicaps and Disabilities

A growing but neglected population of offenders are those with physical handicaps. Some offenders are confined to wheelchairs, and therefore, special facilities must be constructed to accommodate their access to probation or parole offices or community-based sites. Other offenders have hearing or speech impairments that limit them in various ways. For instance, Counselor Kay McGill of the Rehabilitation Services Division of the Georgia Department of Human Resources has described her role in dealing with certain handicapped parolees (*Georgia Parole Review,* 1990). One of her parolee-clients was described as suffering from tinnitus, an inherited condition involving a constant roaring in one's head and amplified, unfiltered sound. The client had difficulty holding a job and suffered from depression and insecurity stemming from this condition. McGill arranged for her client to acquire a job involving work with an electronics program with low noise levels and some isolation. The Georgia Rehabilitation Services Division is an agency whose mission is to get its clients functioning at an optimal level so that they may adjust more normally within their communities (*Georgia Parole Review,* 1990:176).

Physically challenged offenders often require greater attention from their POs. Acquiring and maintaining employment is sometimes difficult for persons with different types of physical handicaps, such as the parolee-client managed by Kay McGill. Many POs become brokers between their own agencies and community businesses who are encouraged to employ certain of these clients with special problems. Community volunteers are increasingly helpful in assisting probation and parole agencies with physically handicapped clients. Chapter 13 examined the utilization of volunteers and paraprofessionals in community correctional work.

AIDS: A Growing Problem in Probation, Parole, and Community Corrections

A growing problem in corrections is AIDS, or Acquired Immune Deficiency Syndrome. Estimates are that by 1988, there were 1.5 million AIDS cases in the United States and that the number of AIDS cases was doubling about every 8 to 10 months (Lurigio, 1989:16; Lurigio, Bensinger, and Laszlo, 1990). AIDS is particularly prevalent among jail and prison inmates (Gostin, 1986; Hammett, 1992; Hammett and Moini, 1990; Martin and Zimmerman, 1992). Prisoners living in close quarters are highly susceptible to the AIDS virus because of the likelihood of anal-genital or oral-genital contact, although in 1986, AIDS in prisons had not yet reached epidemic proportions. An examination of 25 state and federal prison systems in January 1986 disclosed 455 confirmed AIDS cases, with 311 cases reported in 20 large city and county jail systems (Hammett and Sullivan, 1986). And in October 1987, 1,964 confirmed AIDS cases among inmates were reported in 70 federal, state, and local correctional systems according to a study conducted by the National Institute of Justice (Stewart, 1988:2). In subsequent years, AIDS education in incarcerative settings has been expanded to provide inmates with a greater understanding of the causes and spreading of this disease (Marcus, Amen, and Bibace, 1992).

It follows that if AIDS is prevalent and increasing among jail and prison inmates, then it is prevalent and increasing among probationers and parolees as well. Thus, AIDS has become a primary topic of concern among POs and their agencies (Lurigio, Bensinger, and Laszlo, 1990). In view of the various circumstances under which AIDS has been transmitted in recent years, from saliva or blood residue from dentists and others working in different health professions, POs have perceived that their risk of being infected with the AIDS virus has increased greatly. Many probationers and parolees are former drug offenders. Drug-dependent clients represent a special danger, since AIDS is known to be easily transmitted when drug addicts share the needles used to inject heroin and other substances. It is widely known from media reports that some crimes have been perpetrated by some offenders wielding needles and other objects they say have been infected with AIDS. In earlier chapters, we have seen that certain types of supervisory programs for probationers and parolees require more or less close interpersonal contact with their PO supervisors. In fact, most probation and parole agencies have established policies to both educate and prepare their officers for dealing with AIDS-infected clients.

The list of special offender categories can be extended to include many other kinds of criminals with unique problems. Only some of the more common special offender categories have been discussed here. With its limited budget and personnel, corrections must attempt to cope with each type of offender encountered. Obviously, there are insufficient resources and personnel to address adequately each and every inmate problem that arises. But at least we have become aware of some of the problems corrections officials are expected to deal with and solve daily. Classifying offenders properly and adequately meeting their individual needs are often beyond the scope of correctional resources.

COMMUNITY PROGRAMS FOR SPECIAL NEEDS OFFENDERS

Networking among Agencies to Maximize Services Delivery

As we have seen in previous chapters, POs and others involved in community-based corrections and intermediate punishments must often perform diverse functions for their offender-clients. POs must act as enforcers. They are also brokers, networking throughout their communities to connect their clients with needed services and treatments. POs and their affiliate agencies must maintain cooperative working relations between correctional agencies, community service agencies, and employers in local communities providing services to ex-offenders (National Alliance of Business, 1981). But networking among agencies is often difficult because of the diverse problems of offender-clientele (Frank and Atkins, 1981; National Alliance of Business, 1981; Treger, 1972).

Some offenders have psychological problems and are in need of individual or group counseling. POs often arrange for their clients to receive these services. This involves some networking among interested community agencies to maximize services delivery. Many parolees have been incarcerated for lengthy periods, and their readjustment and reintegration into communities is sometimes difficult. For some offenders, attempting to reestablish familial relations is traumatic. Thus, some amount of family counseling or therapy is recommended or required as a part of one's parole program. Clients under intensive supervised probation or parole may require emergency housing or crisis services. It is the PO's responsibility to make suitable arrangements for provision of these services (Tapper, 1980).

In many cases, probationers and parolees have families that need services or counseling. Battered women and abused children must be looked after by one or more community agencies while offender-clients participate in various probation/parole programming (Virginia Department of Corrections, 1988). The Virginia program attempts to enhance public safety while effectively addressing offender needs in the least restrictive settings. Provisions for such services have been a fundamental part of probation and parole programs for the last several decades. Jurisdictions, such as California, implemented a supervision subsidy program for probationers in the mid-1960s, and similar efforts have been subsequently undertaken in other jurisdictions (U.S. Youth Development and Delinquency Prevention Administration, 1971).

A program was implemented in Franklin County, Ohio, in January, 1975. This program was known as the **Services to Unruly Youth Program,** and it was designed to provide crisis intervention and counseling as well as other services to unruly youth (status offenders) and their families. Since 1975, the program has served over 19,000 youths and their families. A major component of the program is the **Community Services System,** which is a coordinated system of community-based social services integrating at least 70 agencies with varying funding sources, governing bodies, and philosophies (Services to Unruly Youth Program, 1979). Many children of probationers and parolees have been included in this program over the years.

Individualizing Offender Needs

Most POs recognize the importance of individualizing the treatment programs available to their offender-clients. Not all offenders should necessarily participate in the same programs or receive the same treatments or services. Some offenders have serious drug- or alcohol-dependency problems. Thus, they should receive special consideration and placement in the most relevant programs fitting their problems. For instance, some offender-clients and their families may exhibit substance abuse to varying degrees. A court-ordered treatment program may be effective in lessening the extent of substance abuse for them (Eddy, 1992). Probation departments can play a critical role in enhancing the system's overall response through the establishment of tracking systems to maintain close contact with offender-clients and their families (Hofford, 1991).

For drug- or alcohol-dependent offender-clients, several treatment modalities have been described. Drug-abuse treatment programs include outpatient methadone maintenance for narcotics addicts, detoxification, therapeutic communities, and out-patient drug-free programs. Civil commitments are also used for particularly severe cases (Anglin and Hser, 1990:393–404). A recognized relation exists between drug or alcohol abuse and problems such as domestic violence (Pepino et al., 1993, Reiss and Roth, 1993; Swain, 1986; Wisconsin Department of Health and Social Services, 1989).

Domestic Violence Prevention Programs

Family violence among probationers and parolees is fairly high. Often, familial disruptions are contributory to criminal acts originally committed. Family violence is not only high among offender-clients, but it has also received national recognition as a major social problem (Dickstein and Nadelson, 1989). A contemporary approach to family violence stresses prevention (Stratton, 1988).

In 1988, a consortium of U.S. federal agencies asked the National Academy of Sciences to assess the understanding of family violence and the implications of that understanding for developing preventive interventions (Reiss and Roth, 1993). **Violence** was defined as behaviors by individuals that intentionally threaten, attempt, or inflict physical harm on others. Four recommendations were forthcoming:

1. Sustained problem-solving initiatives should be undertaken on interventions related to biological and psychosocial development of individuals' propensity for violent behavior, modification of crime-prone settings and situations, and intervention to reduce public and domestic violence.
2. High priority should be given to modifying and expanding statistical information systems on violent behavior.
3. New research is needed on instrumental effects of weapons, risk factors, and comparative development sequences.
4. A new multicommunity program of developmental studies of aggressive, violent, and antisocial behaviors should be launched to improve both causal understanding and preventive interventions (Reiss and Roth, 1993).

One of the first problems for POs is to detect spouse abuse and family violence (Swain, 1986; U.S. Civil Rights Commission, 1981). This is often discovered during face-to-face visits with offender-clients and their families. However, many victims of family violence are unwilling to report such abuse to POs at any time.

Probation and parole programs are often individualized
to cater to an offender's specific needs and problems.
(Photo Researchers, Inc.)

This is a prevalent phenomenon observed by experts investigating family violence
(Saunders and Azar, 1989). Saunders and Azar (1989:486–491) indicate the following measures to be taken in many family violence cases:

1. Crisis lines are established for victims as well as offenders;
2. Shelters are provided for victims; and
3. Victims or offenders are removed from the family setting.

Family abuse victims often need legal aid, medical treatment, psychological
counseling, and job readiness preparation. For sexually abused women and children, several treatment models exist that emphasize or promote child advocacy.
These programs are also concerned with restructuring the legal system and developing procedures for reducing the trauma to young children, developing psychiatric and family systems orientation, and engaging in behavior modification designed to assist offenders. Some of these techniques are considered coercive, since

they force offenders to enter specific treatment programs (Saunders and Azar, 1993:502–504). One program is the **Child Sexual Abuse Treatment Program (CSATP).** This program involves individual counseling for all family members of offender-clients, including mother-daughter counseling, marital counseling, father-daughter counseling, and group counseling, where such counseling is based on the principles of humanistic psychotherapy; self-help groups are also provided (Saunders and Azar, 1993:504). Volunteer men's collectives, social services agencies, and women's shelters are also effective in changing offender behaviors. Because probationers and parolees are under the immediate jurisdiction of either the courts or parole boards, their participation in different kinds of intervention programs and therapies can be incorporated as part of their probation or parole programs as an important component and requirement. Continued familial abuses of any kind can be grounds for probation or parole revocation if detected.

Supervising Dangerous Offenders

Supervising dangerous offenders doesn't always mean supervising offenders who will endanger others. Sometimes offenders represent dangers to themselves. Some offenders who are mentally ill may pose threats to themselves as well as to others. Many of those released from jails and prisons exhibit signs or characteristics of mental illness and should receive needed treatment from one or more community agencies. However, not all communities have the capacity to deal with these offenders. Mentally ill offenders may engage in self-destructive acts. They may also be unwilling to be referred to a mental health agency for treatment. In Delaware County, Pennsylvania, for instance, a study was conducted to determine the extent to which mentally ill persons of all kinds come to the attention of police. Further, the study explored the response of interested community agencies in meeting these mentally ill offender needs (Bonovitz, 1980). Delaware police department information disclosed that the mentally ill pose a significant problem for police officers. Police officers are faced with having to classify mentally ill persons initially, and then they must determine where these offenders should be taken. It is not always the case that these persons are shuffled back to jails. Rather, community mental health agencies exist to treat these persons in limited ways. The study highlighted serious gaps in the community social services network, at least in Delaware County, Pennsylvania.

Supervising high-risk offenders may pose other risks. Some offender-clients are dangerous and/or have a high likelihood of program failure (Griffiths and Nance, 1980; Pepino et al., 1993). These persons need closer supervision or monitoring than other offenders on standard probation (Dickey and Wagner, 1990; Lawrence, 1991; Wisconsin Department of Health and Social Services, 1989). Some experts suggest high-risk offender intervention strategies that incorporate accountability and acceptance of responsibility with law internalization and community expectations (Lawrence, 1991).

Parent Education and Early Childhood Intervention Services

Parenting courses are being created in various jurisdictions throughout the United States to educate probationers and parolees and their families (Carmouche and Jones, 1989). These reflect the attempts of behavior therapists to influence the natural environment by engaging parents in behavior management roles at home (Frazier, Hawkins, and Howard, 1988). Trainers who conduct these parenting classes use lectures, reading assignments, and videotapes to provide instruction in skills, followed by demonstration, modeling, and supervised practice to ensure acquisition at the level of application. Frazier, Hawkins, and Howard (1988) argue that effective parent training can function as a good delinquency prevention strategy. The program they describe is targeted particularly at low-income families and those experiencing various forms of disruption, as in the case of parolees and probationers who are involved in community programs and who must adhere to stringent program requirements. Instruction in these parent education programs also includes exposure to various problems of drug and alcohol abuse and how to deal with these problems whenever they arise (Hawkins et al., 1987).

KEY TERMS

Child sexual abuser

Child Sexual Abuse Treatment Program (CSATP)

Community Services System

Estelle v. Gamble (1976)

Glover v. Johnson (1979)

Missouri Sexual Offender Program (MOSOP)

New York Prison Nursery/Children's Center

180 Degrees, Inc.

THE PROGRAM for Female Offenders, Inc.

Project Green Hope: Services for Women, Inc.

Services to Unruly Youth Program

Sex offenders

Treatment Alternatives to Street Crime (TASC)

Violence

Women's Activities and Learning Center Program (WALC)

QUESTIONS FOR REVIEW

1. What proportion of parolees and probationers are female? Why is female offending an important problem for community-based corrections?
2. Describe the criminal characteristics of female offenders in view of official statistical information.
3. What provisions for women are included in the American Correctional Association statement for female offender services?
4. What is the significance of *Glover v. Johnson?* Are all states compelled to follow the *Glover* case? Why or why not? Explain.

5. What was the significance of the case of *Estelle v. Gamble?* Discuss.

6. What are some of the more prevalent criticisms of facilities for women?

7. What is THE PROGRAM? What types of women are targeted for inclusion in this program? Can any female offender join? Why or why not? What were some of the companion projects established in Allegheny County to supplement this program?

8. What is the Women's Activities and Learning Center (WALC) Program?

9. What type of client is likely to fail at Project Green Hope? Describe the types of clients served by Project Green Hope.

10. What is significant about the women's facility in Bedford Hills, New York? Why do you think it is important for women's prisons to have nursery facilities? Do you think that men's prisons should be similarly equipped to allow fathers to bond with their children? Why or why not?

15

Probation and Parole in the Juvenile Justice System

Introduction
Juveniles and Juvenile Delinquency
An Overview of the Juvenile Justice System
Juvenile Rights
Offense Seriousness and Dispositions

Juvenile POs and Predispositional Reports
Juvenile Probation and Parole Programs
Revoking Juvenile Probation and Parole
Key Terms
Questions for Review

INTRODUCTION

This chapter is about juvenile probation and parole. There is little consistency among jurisdictions throughout the United States about how juvenile probation and parole are handled. No national policies exist that apply to every jurisdiction. Thus, it is impossible to make blanket generalizations about the juvenile probation and parole process, except in the broadest of terms.

The first section describes juveniles and juvenile delinquency. How are juvenile delinquents defined? How do they differ from the status offender? These differences are described. The deinstitutionalization of status offenders is a movement that began in the 1970s to remove status offenders from incarcerative settings normally used for more serious juveniles. Many states have implemented the deinstitutionalization of status offenders; other states are either undecided on the issue or are moving slowly toward such a policy. This policy is described and its significance for affected juveniles is explained.

The second section presents an overview of the juvenile justice system, describing briefly the origins and functions of juvenile courts. The doctrine of *parens patriae,* which has been inherited from England and has had a profound influence on juvenile courts in the United States, is described. The juvenile justice system or process, as some professionals prefer to label it, is presented from the point of juvenile arrests, intake, petitions and adjudicatory proceedings, and judicial dispositions. Various dispositional options available to juvenile court judges are listed and described. The next section of the chapter examines various juvenile probation and parole programs. It is not intended to be comprehensive, since juvenile justice textbooks cover this information in far greater detail. Nevertheless, several key programs that provide the reader with a broad perspective of available juvenile probation and parole programs are described.

The final section presents the juvenile probation and parole revocation process. Almost no U.S. Supreme Court action has been taken regarding revocations of juvenile probation and parole. Often, state and local jurisdictions have followed the guidelines of probation and parole revocations set forth by various precedent-setting landmark cases for adult criminals. These cases were described in detail in Chapter 7. They included *Mempa v. Rhay, Gagnon v. Scarpelli,* and *Morrissey v. Brewer.* The reader is referred to Chapter 7 for a brief review of these adult landmark probation and parole revocation cases. Juvenile courts and revocation proceedings are not bound by these adult cases, however. But the cases do serve as guidelines for juvenile courts to follow at their option. Several state cases involving juvenile probation and parole revocation are presented, however, in order to illustrate how different jurisdictions deal with juvenile probation or parole program violations.

JUVENILES AND JUVENILE DELINQUENCY

Juvenile Offenders. **Juvenile offenders** are classified and defined according to several different criteria. For instance, the 1899 Illinois Act that created juvenile courts determined that the jurisdiction of juvenile courts extended to all juveniles under the age of 16 who were found to be in violation of any state or local laws. About one-fifth of all states, including Illinois, currently place the upper age limit for juveniles at either 15 or 16. In the remaining states, the upper limit for juveniles is 17 (except for Wyoming, where it is 18). Ordinarily, the jurisdiction of juvenile courts includes all young persons who have not yet attained the age at which they should be treated as adults for purposes of criminal law (Black, 1990:867). At the federal level, **juveniles** are considered to be persons who have not yet attained their eighteenth birthday (18 U.S.C., Sec. 5031, 1995).

Upper and Lower Jurisdictional Age Limits.   Whereas fairly uniform upper age limits for juveniles have been established in all U.S. jurisdictions (either under 16, under 17, or under 18 years of age), there is no uniformity concerning applicable lower age limits. English common law placed juveniles under age seven beyond the reach of criminal courts, since it was believed that those under age seven were incapable of formulating criminal intent, or *mens rea.* However, many juvenile courts throughout the United States have no specified lower age limits for those juveniles within their purview. Few, if any, juvenile courts will process three-year-olds who kill others through the juvenile court, although these courts technically can do so in some jurisdictions.

Treatment and Punishment Functions of Juvenile Courts.   The idea that in order for juvenile courts to exercise jurisdiction over juveniles, these youths must be offenders and have committed criminal acts is misleading. Many youths who appear before juvenile court judges have not violated any criminal laws. Rather, their status as juveniles renders them subject to juvenile court control, provided certain circumstances exist. These circumstances may be the quality of their adult supervision, if any. Other circumstances may be that they ran away from home, are truant from school, or loiter on certain city streets during evening hours. Runaways, truants, or curfew violators are considered **status offenders,** since their actions would not be criminal ones if committed by adults. Additionally, children who are physically, psychologically, or sexually abused by parents or other adults in their homes are brought within the scope of juvenile court authority. Some of these children are *PINS,* or *persons in need of supervision.* These youths are often supervised and treated by community social welfare agencies.

Delinquency and Juvenile Delinquents

The majority of youthful offenders who appear before juvenile courts are those who have violated state or local laws or ordinances. The jurisdiction of juvenile courts depends on the established legislative definitions of juveniles among the different states. The federal government has no juvenile court. Rather, federal cases involving juveniles infrequently are heard in federal district courts, but adjudicated juveniles are housed in state or local facilities if the sentences involve commitment to secure youth facilities. Ordinarily, upper and lower age limits are prescribed. In reality, the most liberal definition of **juvenile delinquency** is whatever the juvenile court believes should be brought within its jurisdiction. This definition vests juvenile judges and other juvenile authorities with broad discretionary powers to define almost any juvenile conduct as delinquent conduct (Watkins, 1987). Today, the majority of U.S. jurisdictions restrict their definitions of *juvenile delinquency* to any act committed by a juvenile which, if committed by an adult, would be considered a crime (Rogers and Mays, 1987:566).

Status Offenders

Status offenses are any acts committed by juveniles which would (1) bring the juveniles to the attention of juvenile courts and (2) not be crimes if committed by adults. Common juvenile status offenses include running away from home, truancy, and curfew violations. Many of the youths who engage in this conduct are incorrigible, habitually disobedient, and beyond parental control. Truants and liquor law violators may be more inclined to become *chronic offenders* and to engage in more serious, possibly criminal, behaviors (Clarke, Ringwalt, and Ciminello, 1985; Shelden, Horvath, and Tracy, 1989). An influential factor contributing to juvenile offender chronicity and persistence is contact with juvenile courts. Such contact, especially if frequent, is believed by some researchers to "stigmatize" youths and cause them to either be labeled or acquire self-concepts as delinquents or deviants (Davidson et al., 1987; DeAngelo, 1988; Frazier and Cochran, 1986; Pratt, 1983). Therefore, diversion of certain types of juvenile offenders from the juvenile justice system has been advocated and recommended to minimize these potentially adverse consequences of systemic contact (Osgood, 1983; Polk, 1984).

AN OVERVIEW OF THE JUVENILE JUSTICE SYSTEM

The juvenile justice system consists of a more or less integrated network of agencies, institutions, organizations, and personnel that process juvenile offenders. This network is made up of law enforcement agencies, prosecutors, and courts; corrections, probation, and parole services; and public and private community-based treatment programs that provide youths with diverse services. The definition is intentionally qualified by the phrase "more or less integrated" because the concept of juvenile justice means different things for the states and to the federal government. Also, in some jurisdictions, the diverse components of the juvenile justice system are closely coordinated, while in other jurisdictions, these components are at best loosely coordinated, if they are coordinated at all.

The Origins and Purposes of Juvenile Courts

Juvenile Courts as an American Creation.   Juvenile courts are a relatively recent American creation. However, modern American juvenile courts have various less formal European antecedents. Although the origin of this cutting point is unknown, the age of seven was used in Roman times to separate infants from those older children who were accountable to the law for their actions. During the Middle Ages, English common law established under the monarchy adhered to the same standard. In the United States, several state jurisdictions currently apply this distinction and consider all children below the age of seven not accountable for any criminal acts they may commit.

A frequent reason for police-juvenile contact is violating curfew, where officers stop youths and question them concerning their identity and reasons for being on the street during late evening hours. (The Image Works)

Early Juvenile Reforms.   Reforms in the American colonies relating to the treatment and/or punishment of juvenile offenders occurred slowly. Shortly after the Revolutionary War, religious interests in the United States moved forward with various proposals designed to improve the plight of the oppressed, particularly those who were incarcerated in prisons and jails. In 1787, the Quakers in Pennsylvania established the **Philadelphia Society for Alleviating the Miseries of Public Prisons.** This largely philanthropic society comprised of prominent citizens, religious leaders, and philanthropists was appalled by existing prison and jail conditions. Male, female, and juvenile offenders alike were housed in common quarters and treated poorly. In 1790, the Society's efforts were rewarded. The Philadelphia Walnut Street Jail described in Chapter 5 had considerable historical significance for corrections as well as for juvenile offenders. One of its major innovations was that women and children were maintained in separate rooms apart from adult male offenders during evening hours.

The **New York House of Refuge** was established in New York City in 1825 by the Society for the Prevention of Pauperism (Cahalan, 1986:101). This was an institution largely devoted to managing status offenders, such as runaways or incorrigible children. Compulsory education and other forms of training and assistance were provided to these children. However, the strict, prison-like regimen of this organization was not entirely therapeutic for its clientele.

The Case of* Ex parte Crouse**.   Until the late 1830s, little consistency was apparent related to the division of labor between parental, religious, and state authority over juveniles. In 1838, a decision in a state case invested juvenile authorities with considerable parental power. The case of ***Ex parte Crouse (1838) involved a father who sought custody of his daughter from the Philadelphia House of Refuge. The girl had been committed to that facility by the court because she was declared unmanageable. She was not given a jury trial. Rather, the judge arbitrarily committed her. A higher court rejected the father's claim that parental control of children is exclusive, natural, and proper. It upheld the power of the state to exercise necessary reforms and restraints to protect children from themselves and their environments. While this decision was applicable only to Pennsylvania citizens and their children, other states took note of it and sought to invoke similar controls over errant children in their jurisdictions. In effect, children (at least in Pennsylvania) were temporarily deprived of any legal standing to challenge decisions made by the state in their behalf. This was the general state of juvenile affairs until the post–Civil War period known as Reconstruction.

Extensive family migration toward large cities occurred after the Civil War. New York, Philadelphia, Boston, and Chicago were centers where fragmented families attempted to find work. Often, both parents had to work, and such work involved extended working hours (e.g., 16-hour work periods). This meant that while parents worked, increasing numbers of children roamed city streets unsupervised. Religious organizations subsequently intervened as a way of protecting unsupervised youths from the perils of life in the streets. Believing that these youths would subsequently turn to lives of crime as adults, many reformers and philanthropists sought to "save" them from their plight. Thus, in different cities throughout the United States, various groups were formed to find and control these youths by offering them constructive work programs, healthful living conditions, and above all, adult supervision. Collectively, these efforts became widely known as the **child-saver movement.** Child-savers came largely from the middle and upper classes, and their assistance to youths took many forms. Food and shelter were provided to children who were in trouble with the law or who were simply idle. Private homes were converted into settlements where social, educational, and other important activities could be provided for needy youths.

Reform Schools.   In a period prior to the Civil War, **reform schools** were established and proliferated. One of the first state-operated reform schools was established in Westboro, Massachusetts, in 1848 (U.S. Department of Justice, 1976). By the end of the century, all states had reform schools. All of these institutions were characterized by strict discipline, absolute control over juvenile behavior, and compulsory work at various trades. Another common feature was that they were controversial.

Children's Tribunals.   Even though Illinois is credited with establishing the first juvenile court system in the United States, an earlier juvenile justice apparatus was created in Massachusetts in 1874. This was known as the **children's tribunal,** and it was used exclusively as a mechanism for dealing with children charged with crimes; it was kept separate from the system of criminal courts for adults (Hahn, 1984:5). Some years later, Colorado implemented an education law in 1899 known as the Compulsory School Act.

Dependent and Neglected Children.   Few legal challenges of state authority over juveniles were lodged by parents during the 1800s. But in 1870, an Illinois case made it possible for special courts to be established to dispose of juvenile matters and represented an early recognition of certain minimal rights they might have. Daniel O'Connell, a youth who was declared vagrant and in need of supervision, was committed to the Chicago Reform School for an unspecified period. O'Connell's parents challenged this court action, claiming that his confinement for vagrancy was unjust and untenable. Existing Illinois law vested state authorities with the power to commit any juvenile to a state reform school as long as a "reasonable justification" could be provided. In this instance, vagrancy was a reasonable justification. The Illinois Supreme Court distinguished between misfortune (vagrancy) and criminal acts in arriving at its decision to reverse Daniel O'Connell's commitment. In effect, the court nullified the law by declaring that reform school commitments of youths could not be made by the state if the "offense" was simple misfortune. They reasoned that state's interests would be better served if commitments of juveniles to reform schools were limited to those committing more serious criminal offenses rather than those who were victims of misfortune.

The First Juvenile Court.   Three decades later, the Illinois legislature established the first juvenile court on July 1, 1899, by passing the Act to Regulate the Treatment and Control of Dependent, Neglected, and Delinquent Children, or the **Juvenile Court Act.** This Act provided for limited courts of record, where notes might be taken by judges or their assistants, to reflect judicial actions against juveniles. The jurisdiction of these courts, subsequently designated as "juvenile courts," would include all juveniles under the age of 16 who were found in violation of any state or local law or ordinance. And, provision was made for the care of dependent and/or neglected children who had been abandoned or who otherwise lacked proper parental care, support, or guardianship. No minimum age was specified that would limit the jurisdiction of juvenile court judges. However, the Act provided that judges could impose secure confinement on juveniles 10 years of age or over by placing them in state-regulated juvenile facilities such as the state reformatory or the State Home for Juvenile Female Offenders. Judges were expressly prohibited from confining any juvenile under 12 years of age in a jail or police station. Extremely young juveniles would be assigned POs who would look after their needs and placement on a temporary basis. Between 1900 and 1920, 20 states passed similar acts to establish juvenile courts. By the end of World War II, all states had created juvenile court systems. However, considerable variation existed among these court systems, depending on the jurisdiction.

Major Differences between Criminal and Juvenile Courts

The intent of this section is not to describe either criminal or juvenile courts in depth, but, rather, to show several major similarities and differences between them. Also, the diversity among juvenile courts in every jurisdiction is such that it precludes blanket generalizations about them. Generally, the following statements about these different courts are accurate:

1. Juvenile courts are civil proceedings exclusively designed for juveniles, whereas criminal courts are proceedings designed for alleged violators of criminal laws. In criminal courts, alleged criminal law violators are primarily adults, although selected juveniles may be tried as adults in these same courts.
2. Juvenile proceedings are informal, whereas criminal proceedings are formal. Attempts are made in many juvenile courts to avoid the formal trappings that characterize criminal proceedings.
3. In most states, juveniles are not entitled to a trial by jury, unless the juvenile judge approves.
4. Both juvenile and criminal proceedings are adversarial. Juveniles may or may not wish to retain or be represented by counsel. Today, most states make provisions in their juvenile codes for public defenders for juveniles if they are indigent and cannot afford to hire private counsel.
5. Criminal courts are courts of record, whereas juvenile proceedings may or may not maintain a running transcript of proceedings.
6. The standard of proof used for determining one's guilt in criminal proceedings is **beyond a reasonable doubt.** In juvenile courts, judges use the same standard for juvenile delinquents who face possible commitment to secure juvenile facilities. In other court matters leading to noncommitment alternatives, the court uses the civil standard of "preponderance of the evidence." (Some states, particularly more rural ones such as North Dakota, continue to commit status offenders to secure youth facilities together with juvenile delinquents.)
7. The range of penalties juvenile judges may impose is more limited than in criminal courts. Both juvenile and criminal courts can impose fines, restitution, community service, probation, and other forms of conditional discharge. Juvenile courts can also impose residential secure or nonsecure placement, group homes, and camp/ranch experiences. Long terms of commitment to secure facilities are also within the purview of juvenile court judges. In most criminal courts, however, the range of penalties may include life imprisonment or the death penalty in those jurisdictions that impose the death penalty.

This comparison indicates that criminal court actions are more serious and have more significant long-term consequences for offenders compared with actions taken by juvenile courts. However, juvenile courts do have sanctioning power to place juveniles in secure confinement for lengthy periods, if circumstances warrant.

We should not discount this type of court power just because the court deals with juvenile matters and not criminal cases.

Juvenile courts are guided by strong rehabilitative orientations in most jurisdictions, despite a general "get-tough" movement that has occurred during the 1980s and 1990s, whereas criminal courts are seemingly adopting more punitive sanctions for adult offenders. While many critics see juvenile courts moving toward a "just-deserts" philosophy in the treatment and adjudication of juveniles, many youths are still subject to treatment-oriented nonsecure alternatives rather than custodial options. Furthermore, overcrowding is a chronic problem in many juvenile facilities. Thus, correctional agencies for juveniles mirror many of the same problems of adult corrections. It is in the best interests of the state to provide alternatives to incarceration for both adult and juvenile offenders. This "best interests" philosophy of juvenile courts is based on an early doctrine known as *parens patriae.*

Parens Patriae

Juvenile courts have always had considerable latitude in regulating the affairs of juveniles. This freedom to act in a child's behalf was rooted in the largely unchallenged doctrine of **parens patriae.** The *parens patriae* doctrine received formal recognition in U.S. courts in the case of *Ex parte Crouse* (1838). This case involved the commitment of an unruly and incorrigible female child to a state agency. When the parents of the child attempted to regain custody over her later, their request was denied. She remained a ward of the state by virtue of the power of the state agency charged with her supervision. This case set a precedent in that the state established almost absolute control over juvenile custody matters.

The primary elements of *parens patriae* that have contributed to its persistence as a dominant philosophical perspective in the juvenile justice system are summarized as follows:

1. It encourages informal handling of juvenile matters as opposed to more formal and criminalizing procedures.
2. It vests juvenile courts with absolute authority to provide what is best for youthful offenders (e.g., support services and other forms of care).
3. It strongly encourages benevolent and rehabilitative treatments to assist youths in overcoming their personal and social problems.
4. It avoids the adverse labeling effects that formal court proceedings might create.
5. It means state control over juvenile life chances.

One early example of *parens patriae* in action occured when police officers interacted with juveniles during the 1940s, 1950s, and 1960s. Whenever juveniles were apprehended by police officers for alleged infractions of the law, they were eventually turned over to juvenile authorities or taken to *juvenile halls* for further processing. Juveniles were not advised of their right to an attorney, to have an attorney present during any interrogation, and to remain silent. They were subject to lengthy interrogations by police, without parental notification and consent or legal counsel. Juveniles had virtually no protection against adult constitutional rights violations by law enforcement officers and/or juvenile court judges. Due process simply did not apply to juveniles.

Because of the informality of juvenile proceedings in most jurisdictions, there were frequent and obvious abuses of judicial discretion. These abuses occurred because of the absence of consistent guidelines whereby cases could be adjudicated. Juvenile POs might casually recommend to judges that particular juveniles "ought to do a few months" in an industrial school or other secure detention facility, and the judge might be persuaded to adjudicate these cases accordingly. However, several forces were at work simultaneously during the 1950s and 1960s that would eventually have the conjoint consequence of making juvenile courts more accountable for specific adjudications of youthful offenders. One of these forces was increased parental and general public recognition of and concern for the liberal license taken by juvenile courts in administering the affairs of juveniles. The abuse of judicial discretion was becoming increasingly apparent and widely known. Additionally, there was a growing disenchantment with and apathy for the rehabilitation ideal, although this disenchantment was not directed solely at juvenile courts. Rogers and Mays (1987:383) note that "disaffection during the 1960s and 1970s with the juvenile court was typical of the disenchantment then with many of society's institutions."

Feld (1988) says that the juvenile court as originally envisioned by Progressives was procedurally informal, characterized by individualized, offender-oriented dispositional practices. However, the contemporary juvenile court has departed markedly from this Progressive ideal. Today, juvenile courts are increasingly criminalized, featuring an adversarial system and greater procedural formality. This formality effectively inhibits any individualized treatment these courts might contemplate, and it has increased the perfunctory nature of sentencing juveniles adjudicated as delinquent.

The major shift from *parens patriae*, state-based interests to a due process, juvenile justice model gradually occurred during the 1970s. This shift signified a general abandonment of most of these *parens patriae* elements. Decision making relative to youthful offenders became more rationalized, and the philosophy of just deserts become more dominant as a way of disposing of juvenile cases. Thus, this shift meant less discretionary authority among juvenile judges, since they began to decide each case more on the basis of offense seriousness and prescribed punishments rather than on the basis of individual characteristics of youthful offenders.

Arrests and Other Options

Generally, police officers need little justification to apprehend juveniles or take them into custody. Little uniformity exists among jurisdictions about how an arrest is defined. There is even greater ambiguity about what constitutes a juvenile arrest. Technically, an *arrest* is the legal detainment of a person to answer for criminal charges or (infrequently at present) civil demands (Rush, 1990:16). By degree, ar-

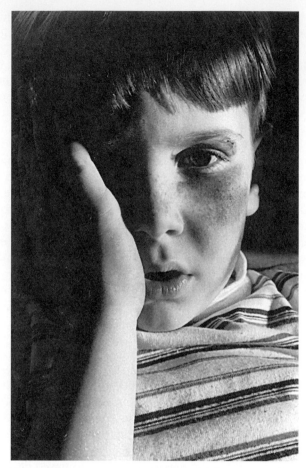

Through *parens patriae,* juvenile courts have jurisdiction over dependent and neglected children, although community agencies are assuming a greater role annually in these types of cases. (Monkmeyer Press)

rests of juveniles are more serious than taking them into custody. Since any juvenile may be taken into custody for suspicious behavior or on any other pretext, all types of juveniles may be detained at police headquarters or at a sheriff's station, department, or jail temporarily. Suspected runaways, truants, or curfew violators may be taken into custody for their own welfare or protection, not necessarily for the purpose of facing subsequent offenses. It is standard police policy in most jurisdictions, considering the sophistication of available social services, for officers and jailers to turn over juveniles to the appropriate agencies as soon as possible after these youths have been apprehended and taken into custody. The first screening of juveniles before further proceedings occur is *intake.*

Intake Screenings and Detention Hearings

Intake, or an **intake screening,** is the second major step in the juvenile justice process. It is a more or less informally conducted screening procedure whereby intake POs or other juvenile court functionaries decide whether detained juveniles should be (1) unconditionally released from the juvenile justice system, (2) released to parents or guardians subject to a subsequent juvenile court appearance, (3) released or referred to one or more community-based services or resources, (4) placed in secure detention subject to a subsequent juvenile court appearance, or (5) waived or transferred to the jurisdiction of criminal courts.

During intake hearings, intake POs have virtually unbridled discretion regarding a youth's chances in the system. Apart from certain state-mandated hearings that must precede formal adjudicatory proceedings by juvenile judges, no constitutional provisions require states to conduct such hearings (Wadlington et al., 1983). Intake officers seldom hear legal arguments or evaluate the sufficiency of evidence on behalf of or against youths sitting before them. These proceedings, which most often are informally conducted, usually result in *adjustments*—intake officers adjust the particular matter informally to most everyone's satisfaction. Dougherty (1988:78) notes that while intake officers may advise juveniles and their parents that they may have attorneys present during such proceedings, these officers also indicate that the presence of attorneys may jeopardize the informal nature of these proceedings and any possible informal resolution of the case that might be made. Thus, parents and youths are tacitly discouraged from having legal counsel to assist them at this critical screening stage (Guggenheim, 1985).

Petitions and Adjudicatory Proceedings

Jurisdictional Variations in Juvenile Processing. There is considerable variation in different jurisdictions about how juvenile courts are conducted. Increasingly, juvenile courts are emulating criminal courts in many respects (Krisberg, 1988). Most of the physical trappings are present, including the judge's bench, tables for the prosecution and defense, and a witness stand. In some jurisdictions such as Ocean County, New Jersey, however, these facilities are being redesigned to appear less courtlike and threatening (Kearney, 1989). Manuals are currently available that catalog various pleadings defense attorneys may enter in juvenile courtrooms, and there is growing interest in the rules of juvenile court procedure (Volenik, 1986). Further, there appears widespread interest in holding juveniles more accountable for their actions than was the case in past years (Feld, 1987).

Petitions. Prosecutors either file *petitions* or act on the petitions filed by others (Laub and MacMurray, 1987). **Petitions** are official documents filed in juvenile courts on the juvenile's behalf, specifying reasons for the youth's court appearance. These documents assert that juveniles fall within the categories of dependent or neglected, status offender, or delinquent, and the reasons for such assertions are usually provided (Rogers and Mays, 1987:571). Filing a petition formally places the juvenile before the juvenile judge in many jurisdictions. But juveniles may come before juvenile judges in less formal ways. Those able to file petitions against juveniles include their parents, school officials, neighbors, or any other interested party. The legitimacy and factual accuracy of petitions are evaluated by juvenile court judges.

Juvenile Court Judicial Discretion.   In most jurisdictions, juvenile judges have almost absolute discretion in how their courts are conducted. Juvenile defendants alleged to have committed various crimes may or may not be granted a trial by jury, if one is requested. Few states permit jury trials for juveniles in juvenile courts, according to legislative mandates. After hearing the evidence presented by both sides in any juvenile proceeding, the judge decides or *adjudicates* the matter. An **adjudication** is a judgment or action on the petition filed with the court by others. If the petition alleges delinquency on the part of certain juveniles, the judge determines whether the juveniles are delinquent or not delinquent. If the petition alleges that the juveniles involved are dependent, neglected, or otherwise in need of care by agencies or others, the judge decides the matter. If the **adjudicatory hearing** fails to support the facts alleged in the petition filed with the court, the case is dismissed and the youth is freed. If the adjudicatory proceeding supports the allegations, then the judge must adjudicate the youth as either a delinquent, a status offender, or a youth in need of special treatment or supervision. Then, the juvenile court judge must dispose of the case according to several options. The judge may order a predispositional report to be prepared by a juvenile probation officer. Another option is for the judge to declare the juvenile to be an adult and *transfer* or *waive* the youth to a criminal court for processing.

Transfers, Waivers, and Certifications

Waivers, also known in different jurisdictions as **transfers** and **certifications,** are transferrals or shifts of jurisdiction over certain types of cases from juvenile courts to criminal courts. These terms will be used interchangeably throughout this chapter. Youths who are subjected to waivers are not tried as juveniles in juvenile courts. Rather, they are redefined and classified as adults and eventually tried in criminal courts. Only a small proportion of juveniles are subject to criminal court transfers annually. Preliminary determinations are made of crime seriousness, the youth's characteristics, such as age and other factors associated with the type of crime committed, and the amount or degree of victim injuries inflicted.

Types of Waivers.   There are four types of waiver actions. These include (1) prosecutorial waivers, (2) judicial or discretionary waivers, (3) demand waivers, and (4) legislative or automatic waivers.

   1. *Prosecutorial Waivers.* Whenever offenders are screened at intake and referred to the juvenile court for possible prosecution, prosecutors in various jurisdictions will conduct further screenings of these youths. They determine which cases merit further action and formal adjudication by judges. Not all cases sent to prose-cutors by intake POs automatically result in subsequent formal juvenile court ac-tion. In an Oregon case, for instance, a juvenile was charged with armed robbery and had recently turned 18. The prosecutor in the case believed the charge was se-rious enough to warrant transfer of that juvenile to criminal court. Further, the youth had an extensive prior delinquency record. Although the youth appealed, the Oregon Court of Appeals rejected the appeal and the youth was tried as an adult in criminal court (*State ex rel. Juvenile Dept. v. George,* 1993).

2. *Judicial/Discretionary Waivers.* The largest numbers of waivers from juve-nile to criminal court annually come about as the result of direct judicial action. Ju-venile judges in most jurisdictions may take independent action and waive certain juveniles to criminal court jurisdiction. Judicial waivers are also known as **discre-tionary waivers,** since judges exercise their discretion when transferring jurisdiction over these juveniles to criminal court judges.

3. *Demand Waivers.* Under certain conditions and in selected jurisdictions, juveniles may submit motions for **demand waiver** actions. Demand waiver actions are demands by juveniles to have their cases transferred from juvenile courts and tried in criminal courts. Why would they want to do this? Most U.S. jurisdictions do not provide jury trials for juveniles in juvenile courts as a matter of right. However, about one-fifth of the states have legislatively provided for jury trials for juveniles at their request and depending on the nature of the charges against them. In the re-mainder of the states, jury trials for juveniles are granted only at the discretion of the juvenile judge. Most juvenile judges are not inclined to grant jury trials to juve-niles. Thus, if juveniles (1) are in a jurisdiction where they are not entitled to a jury trial even if they request one from the juvenile judge, (2) face serious charges, and (3) believe that their cases would receive greater impartiality from a jury in a crimi-nal courtroom, they may use a demand waiver in order to have their cases trans ferred to criminal court where they will be entitled to a jury trial. For example, Florida permits demand waivers as one of several waiver options (Carter, 1984). Nearly 40 states, including Oregon, do not permit juveniles to have jury trials in ju-venile courts according to their state constitutions (*State ex rel. Juvenile Dept. v. Jackson,* 1993).

4. *Legislative or Automatic Waivers. Legislative waivers* or *automatic transfers* are statutorily prescribed actions that provide for a specified list of crimes to be ex-cluded from the jurisdiction of juvenile courts, when offending juveniles are within a specified age range and the resulting action gives criminal courts immediate juris-diction over these juveniles. By the mid-1980s, 36 states excluded certain types of offenses from juvenile court jurisdiction. These excluded offenses were either very minor or very serious, ranging from traffic or fishing violations to rape or murder (U.S. Department of Justice, 1988:79). Also, many state jurisdictions have made provisions for automatic transfers of juveniles to criminal court. Among those states with automatic transfer provisions are Washington, New York, and Illinois (Sagatun, McCollum, and Edwards, 1985).

Waiver Hearings.   All juveniles are entitled to waiver hearings prior to being transferred to criminal court (*Kent v. United States,* 1966). Waiver hearings are normally conducted before the juvenile judge. These hearings are to some extent evidentiary, since a case must be made for why criminal courts should have jurisdiction in any specific instance. Usually, juveniles with lengthy prior records, several previous referrals, and/or one or more previous adjudications as delinquent are more susceptible to being transferred. Although the offenses alleged are most often crimes, it is not always the case that the crimes are the most serious ones. In some instances, chronic, persistent, or habitual status offenders have been transferred, particularly if they have violated specific court orders to attend school, participate in therapeutic programs, perform community service work, make restitution, or engage in some other constructive enterprise.

In those jurisdictions that use automatic or legislative waivers, **reverse waiver hearings** are conducted. These hearings seek to restore the original jurisdiction over the case to the juvenile court, if a juvenile defendant wishes to seek such jurisdiction. For both waiver and reverse waiver hearings, defense counsel and the prosecution attempt to make a case for their desired action. The results of waiver or reverse waiver hearings are that juveniles will have their cases decided in either criminal courts, in which criminal penalties can be imposed, or in juvenile court, in which judicial dispositional options are more restricted. In New York, for example, there are special sentencing guidelines to be followed by criminal court judges in cases in which juveniles have been transferred to criminal court and convicted of crimes. New York law provides that youths 13 to 16 years of age must be sentenced to particular ranges of years and months for specific crimes, such as murder, arson, kidnapping, burglary, rape, and robbery. These sentencing ranges are 3 to 15 years, depending on the conviction offense.

JUVENILE RIGHTS

During the mid-1960s and for the next 20 years, significant achievements were made in the area of juvenile rights. Although the *parens patriae* philosophy continues to be somewhat influential in juvenile proceedings, the U.S. Supreme Court has vested youths with certain constitutional rights. These rights do not encompass all of the rights extended to adults who are charged with crimes. But those rights conveyed to juveniles thus far have had far-reaching implications for how juveniles are processed from arrest through probation and parole.

Landmark Cases in Juvenile Justice

Kent v. United States (*1966*).   *Kent v. United States* (1966), the first major juvenile rights case to preface further juvenile court reforms, established the universal precedents of (1) requiring waiver hearings before juveniles can be transferred to the jurisdiction of a criminal court (excepting legislative or automatic waivers, although reverse waiver hearings must be conducted at the juvenile's request), and (2) entitling juveniles to consult with counsel before and during such hearings.

In 1959, Morris A. Kent Jr., a 14-year-old in the District of Columbia, was apprehended and charged with several housebreakings and attempted purse snatchings. He was adjudicated a delinquent and placed on probation. Subsequently in 1961, an intruder entered the apartment of a woman, took her wallet, and raped her. Fingerprints at the crime scene were later identified as those of Morris Kent, who had been fingerprinted in connection with his delinquency case in 1959. On September 5, 1961, Kent admitted the offense as well as other crimes, and the juvenile court judge advised of his intent to waive Kent to criminal court. Kent's mother had obtained an attorney in the meantime, and Kent's attorney advised the court that he intended to oppose the waiver. The judge ignored the attorney's motion and transferred Kent to the U.S. District Court for the District of Columbia where Kent was tried and convicted by a federal jury of six counts of housebreaking, although the jury found him "not guilty by reason of insanity" on the rape charge. Kent's conviction was reversed by the U.S. Supreme Court. The majority held that Kent's rights to due process and to the effective assistance of counsel were violated when he was denied a formal hearing on the waiver and his attorney's motions were ignored. The U.S. Supreme Court said that the matter of a waiver to criminal court was a "critical stage" and thus, attorney representation was fundamental to due process. In adult cases, for instance, critical stages are those that relate to the defendant's potential loss of freedoms (i.e., incarceration). Because of the *Kent* decision, waiver hearings are now considered *critical stages*.

In re Gault (1967). *In re Gault* is the most significant of all landmark juvenile rights cases. Certainly it is considered the most ambitious. In a 7-to-2 vote, the U.S. Supreme Court articulated the following rights for all juveniles: (1) the right to a notice of charges; (2) the right to counsel; (3) the right to confront and cross-examine witnesses; and (4) the right to invoke the privilege against self-incrimination. The petitioner, Gault, requested the Court to rule favorably on two additional rights sought: (1) the right to a transcript of proceedings; and (2) the right to an appellate review. The Court did not rule on either of these additional rights.

Briefly, the facts are that Gerald Francis Gault, a 15-year-old, and a friend, Ronald Lewis, were taken into custody by the sheriff of Gila County, Arizona, on the morning of June 8, 1964, for allegedly making an obscene telephone call to a female neighbor. At the time, Gault was on probation because of purse snatching. A verbal complaint was filed by the neighbor of Gault, Mrs. Cook, alleging that Gault had called her and made lewd and indecent remarks. When Gault was taken into custody by police, his mother and father were at work. Indeed, they did not learn where their son was until much later that evening. A subsequent informal adjudication hearing was held, at which a one-sided presentation was given about Gault's alleged obscene conduct. The witness against him, Mrs. Cook, did not appear or offer testimony. Thus, she was not available for cross-examination by Gault or his attorney. A court probation officer gave the basically one-sided account incriminating Gault. Subsequently, the judge ordered Gault to the Arizona State Industrial

School until he became 21. (If an adult had made an obscene telephone call, he would have received a $50 fine and no more than 60 days in jail. In Gerald Gault's case, he was facing nearly six years in a juvenile prison for the same offense.) After exhausting their appeals in Arizona state courts, the Gaults appealed to the U.S. Supreme Court. The U.S. Supreme Court reversed the Arizona Supreme Court, holding that Gault did, indeed, have the right to an attorney, the right to confront his accuser (Mrs. Cook) and to cross-examine her, the right against self-incrimination, and the right to have notice of the charges filed against him. All of these rights had been violated by the original juvenile court judge during the adjudicatory proceedings.

In re Winship *(1970).*   *In re Winship* established an important precedent in juvenile courts relating to the *standard of proof* used to establish defendant guilt. The U.S. Supreme Court held that "beyond a reasonable doubt," a standard ordinarily used in adult criminal courts, was henceforth to be used by juvenile court judges and others in establishing a youth's delinquency. Formerly, the standard used was the civil application of "preponderance of the evidence."

The facts in *Winship* are that Samuel Winship was a 12-year-old charged with larceny in New York City. He purportedly entered a locker and stole $112 from a woman's pocketbook. Under Section 712 of the New York Family Court Act, a juvenile delinquent was defined as "a person over seven and less than sixteen years of age who does any act, which, if done by an adult, would constitute a crime." Interestingly, the juvenile judge in the case acknowledged that the proof to be presented by the prosecution might be insufficient to establish the guilt of Winship beyond a reasonable doubt, although he did indicate that the New York Family Court Act provided that "any determination at the conclusion of [an adjudicatory hearing] that a [juvenile] did an act or acts must be based on a preponderance of the evidence" standard (397 U.S. at 360). Winship was adjudicated as a delinquent and ordered to a training school for 18 months, subject to annual extensions of his commitment until his eighteenth birthday. Appeals to New York courts were unsuccessful. The U.S. Supreme Court subsequently heard Winship's appeal and reversed the New York Family Court ruling because the "beyond a reasonable doubt" standard had not been used in a case where incarceration or loss of freedom was likely.

McKeiver v. Pennsylvania *(1971).*   *McKeiver v. Pennsylvania* was important because the U.S. Supreme Court held that juveniles are not entitled to a jury trial as a matter of right. The facts are that in May 1968, Joseph McKeiver, age 16, was charged with robbery, larceny, and receiving stolen goods. McKeiver was represented by counsel who asked the court for a jury trial "as a matter of right." This request was denied. McKeiver was subsequently adjudicated delinquent. On appeal to the U.S. Supreme Court later, McKeiver's adjudication was upheld. The U.S. Supreme Court said that jury trials for juveniles are not a matter of right but rather at the discretion of the juvenile court judge. In about one-fifth of the states today, jury trials for juveniles in juvenile courts are held under certain conditions.

Breed v. Jones *(1975).* *Breed v. Jones* raised the significant constitutional issue of "double jeopardy." The U.S. Supreme Court concluded that after a juvenile has been adjudicated as delinquent on specific charges, those same charges may not be alleged against those juveniles subsequently in criminal courts through transfers or waivers. The facts are that on February 8, 1971, in Los Angeles, California, Gary Steven Jones, then 17 years old, was armed with a deadly weapon and allegedly committed a robbery. Jones was subsequently apprehended and an adjudicatory hearing was held on March 1. Jones was adjudicated delinquent on these robbery charges. Following this delinquency adjudication, the juvenile court judge transferred Jones to criminal court to stand trial on these same charges. Jones was subsequently convicted of robbery. Jones appealed the decision and the U.S. Supreme Court reversed the robbery conviction, concluding that the robbery adjudication was considered the equivalent of a criminal trial on the same charges. This constituted double jeopardy. The juvenile court judge should have disposed Jones to secure confinement following his adjudication on the robbery charges or simply waived jurisdiction over Jones initially to criminal court. Dual court actions on the same charges were unconstitutional because they represented double jeopardy for Jones.

Schall v. Martin *(1984).* In *Schall v. Martin,* the U.S. Supreme Court issued juveniles a minor setback regarding the state's right to hold them in preventive detention pending a subsequent adjudication. The Court said that the preventive detention of juveniles by states is constitutional, if judges perceive these youths to pose a danger to the community or an otherwise serious risk if released short of an adjudicatory hearing. This decision was significant, in part, because many experts advocated the separation of juveniles and adults in jails, those facilities most often used for preventive detention. Also, the preventive detention of adults was not ordinarily practiced at that time. [Since then, the preventive detention of adults who are deemed to pose societal risks has been upheld by the U.S. Supreme Court (*United States v. Salerno,* 1987).]

The facts are that 14-year-old Gregory Martin was arrested at 11:30 P.M. on December 13, 1977, in New York City. He was charged with first-degree robbery, second-degree assault, and criminal possession of a weapon. Martin lied to police at the time, giving a false name and address. Between the time of his arrest and December 29 when a fact-finding hearing was held, Martin was detained (a total of 15 days). His detention was based largely on the false information he had supplied to police and the seriousness of the charges pending against him. Subsequently, he was adjudicated a delinquent and placed on two years' probation. Later, his attorney filed an appeal, contesting his preventive detention as violative of the Due Process Clause of the Fourteenth Amendment. The U.S. Supreme Court eventually heard the case and upheld the detention as constitutional.

OFFENSE SERIOUSNESS AND DISPOSITIONS: AGGRAVATING AND MITIGATING FACTORS

In 1990, an estimated 1,264,800 delinquency cases were disposed of in the juvenile justice system. This is about 46 delinquency cases per 1,000 juveniles. Only 230,000 of these cases involved some confinement between referral to court intake and disposition. About 39.2 percent of all final delinquency adjudications resulted in either nonsecure or secure detention (Maguire, Pastore, and Flanagan, 1993: 540–541). Serious older juvenile offenders are more likely to have their cases transferred to criminal courts for processing, depending on the jurisdiction (Fagan and Deschenes, 1990). About 34,150 delinquency cases were transferred to criminal courts in 1990 (Maguire et al., 1993:540–541).

Whether juveniles are first-offenders or have prior juvenile records is crucial to many prosecutorial decisions. The overwhelming tendency among prosecutors is to divert petty first-offenders to some conditional program. Influencing prosecutorial decision making is the presence of aggravating and/or mitigating factors.

Aggravating and Mitigating Factors.   *Aggravating factors* are those that enhance penalties imposed by juvenile court and criminal court judges. *Mitigating factors* are those that lessen penalties imposed by these respective courts.

Key aggravating factors include the following:

1. Death or serious bodily injury to one or more victims.
2. An offense committed while an offender is awaiting resolution of other delinquency charges.
3. An offense committed while the offender is on probation, parole, or work release.
4. Previous offenses for which the offender has been punished.
5. Leadership in the commission of a delinquent act involving two or more offenders.
6. A violent offense involving more than one victim.
7. Extreme cruelty during the commission of the offense.
8. The use of a dangerous weapon in the commission of the offense, with high risk to human life.

Key mitigating factors include the following:

1. No serious bodily injury resulting from the offense.
2. No attempt to inflict serious bodily injury on anyone.
3. Duress or extreme provocation.
4. Circumstances that justify the conduct.
5. Mental incapacitation or physical condition that significantly reduced the offender's culpability in the offense.
6. Cooperation with authorities in apprehending other participants, or making restitution to the victims for losses they suffered.
7. No previous record of delinquent activity.

Judicial Dispositional Options

Juvenile court judges may exercise several options when deciding specific cases. These judges may adjudicate youths as delinquent and do no more other than record the event. If the juvenile appears again before the same judge, harsher sentencing measures may be taken. The judge might divert juveniles to community-based services or agencies for special treatment. Those youths with psychological problems or who are emotionally disturbed or sex offenders or have drug and/or alcohol dependencies may be targeted for special community treatments. Various conditions as punishments such as fines, restitution, or some form of community service may also be imposed by judges. The more drastic alternatives are varying degrees of custodial sentences, ranging from the placement of juveniles in foster homes, camp ranches, reform schools, or industrial schools. These nonsecure and secure forms of placement and/or detention are usually reserved for the most serious offenders. Below is a summary of judicial options. One or more of the following 11 options may be exercised in any delinquency adjudication:

Nominal Sanctions

1. A stern reprimand may be given.
2. A verbal warning may be issued.

Conditional Sanctions

3. An order may be given to make restitution to victims.
4. An order may be given to pay a fine.
5. An order may be given to perform some public service.
6. An order may be given to submit to the supervisory control of some community-based corrections agency on a probationary basis.
7. A sentence may be imposed, but the sentence may be suspended for a fixed term of probation.

Custodial Sanctions (Nonsecure and Secure)

8. An order may be issued for the placement of the juvenile in a foster home.
9. An order may be issued for the placement of the juvenile in a residential center or group home.
10. An order may be given to participate under supervision at a camp ranch or special school (either nonsecure or secure detention).
11. An order may be given to be confined in a secure facility for a specified period.

Nominal and Conditional Sanctions

Nominal dispositions are verbal and/or written warnings issued to low-risk juvenile offenders, often first-offenders, for the purpose of alerting them to the seriousness of their acts and their potential for receiving severe conditional punishments if they ever should re-offend. These sanctions are the least punitive alternatives.

Youth Diversion and Community-Based Programs.   One of the earliest delinquency prevention strategies that can be implemented by juvenile court judges and
other actors throughout the juvenile justice system is diversion. *Diversion* is the
temporary directing of youths from the juvenile justice system, where they can remain with their families or guardians, attend school, and be subject to limited supervision on a regular basis by a juvenile PO.

Youth Service Bureaus.   Diversion programs have operated in the United States
for many years. In the early 1960s, **Youth Service Bureaus (YSBs)** were established
in numerous jurisdictions. Although we still cannot identify precisely those youths
considered delinquency prone or *youths at risk,* YSBs were created, in part, as
places within communities where "delinquent-prone" youths could be referred by
parents, schools, and law enforcement agencies (Norman, 1970). Actually, YSBs
were forerunners of our contemporary community-based correctional programs,
since they were intended to solicit volunteers from among community residents
and to mobilize a variety of resources that could assist in a youth's treatment. The
nature of treatments for youths, within the YSB concept, originally included referrals to a variety of community services, educational experiences, and individual or
group counseling. YSB organizers attempted to compile lists of existing community
services, agencies, organizations, and sponsors who could cooperatively coordinate
these resources in the most productive ways to benefit affected juveniles (Norman,
1970; Romig, 1978).

Diversion may be either *unconditional* or *conditional. Unconditional diversion* simply means that the divertee will attend school, behave, and not reappear
before the juvenile court for a specified period. *Conditional diversion* may require
juveniles to attend lectures, individual or group psychotherapy, drug or alcohol
treatment centers, police department–conducted DUI classes, and/or vocational or
educational classes or programs. Successful completion of the diversion program
likely means dismissal of the case. These programs are of variable lengths, but most
run for periods of six months to one year.

The Juvenile Diversion/Non-Custody Intake Program.   Officials in Orange
County, California, implemented in 1982 a diversionary program called the **Juvenile Diversion/Non-Custody Intake Program** (JD/NCI Program). Diversionary efforts in previous years by Orange County officials had been ineffective. The
JD/NCI Program was designed to target more serious juvenile offenders by giving
them more concentrated attention by police, probation, community agencies,
schools, and families (Binder et al., 1985). The JD/NCI Program was a type of conditional diversion, because juvenile clients were required to pay restitution to their
victims. Binder et al. reported that the program successfully diverted a large proportion of intake cases ordinarily referred to the district attorney for formal processing. Besides easing the juvenile court caseload, the JD/NCI Program clients
tended to have lower recidivism rates compared with those in more traditional programs, although these differences were not substantial.

The Juvenile Diversion Program (JDP).   Litton and Marye (1983) have described a reasonably successful diversion program. A **Juvenile Diversion Program (JDP)** was established in New Orleans, Louisiana, in 1981 by the District Attorney's Office whereby youths could receive diversion before being petitioned and adjudicated delinquent. During the period between 1981 and 1983, 233 juveniles were accepted into the program, although the program capacity was estimated at 400. The program consisted of intensive counseling and evaluative and social services. Other elements included family and individual counseling, parent involvement, restitution to victims, and utilization of various community services. After a one-year follow-up, results disclosed only a 20 percent recidivism rate among program participants. Although the researchers complained that the program was ineffective because it did not serve the full complement of 400 juveniles as it was originally conceived, there is certainly nothing wrong with a 20 percent recidivism rate. This is even more significant when those accepted into the program were first-offender felons (excluding murder, rape, and robbery) and serious misdemeanants.

The Youth at Risk Program.   Significant success rates (i.e., lower recidivism) have been reported by another California program known as the **Youth at Risk Program,** which was operated in Los Angeles and Contra Costa Counties between 1982 and 1984 for youths aged 13 to 19. The program consisted of a 10-day rural training course consisting of classes; outdoor sites for running and other physical activities; and emphasis on self-reliance, peer resistance, peer and staff support, and individual responsibility (MetaMetrics, Inc., 1984). A community follow-up program was implemented as a continuation of these experiences. Of the 155 youths participating in the program during the period 1982 to 1983, 49 were studied over a 15-month period and compared with a matched group of probationers with similar characteristics and delinquency histories. Youth at Risk Program participants had incident recidivism rates of 34.7 percent compared with 55.1 percent for the comparison group, and a serious offense recidivism rate of only 18.4 percent contrasted with 40.8 percent for the comparison group. These figures led program officials to conclude that their program had a profound positive impact on their juvenile clients (MetaMetrics, Inc., 1984).

The See Our Side Program (SOS).   In Prince George's County, Maryland, a program was established in 1983 called **See Our Side (SOS)** (Mitchell and Williams, 1986:70). SOS is referred to by its directors as a "juvenile aversion" program and dissociates itself from "scare" programs such as Scared Straight. Basically, SOS seeks to educate juveniles about the realities of life in prison through discussions and hands-on experience and attempts to show them the types of behaviors that can lead to incarceration (Mitchell and Williams, 1986:70). Clients coming to SOS are referrals from various sources, including juvenile court, public and private schools, churches, professional counseling agencies, and police and fire departments. Youths served by SOS range in age from 12 to 18, and they do not have be adjudicated as delinquent in order to be eligible for participation. SOS consists of four, three-hour phases:

Phase I: Staff orientation and group counseling session in which staff attempts to facilitate discussion and ease tension among the youthful clients; characteristics of jails are discussed, including age and gender breakdowns, race, and types of juvenile behavior that might result in jailing for short periods.

Phase II: A tour of a prison facility.

Phase III: Three inmates discuss with youths what life is like behind bars; inmates who assist in the program are selected on the basis of their emotional maturity, communications skills, and warden recommendations.

Phase IV: Two evaluations are made—the first is an evaluation of SOS sessions by the juveniles; a recidivism evaluation is also conducted for each youth after a one-year lapse from the time they participated in SOS; relative program successfulness can therefore be gauged.

SOS officials conducted an evaluation of the program in September 1985. It was found that SOS served 327 youths during the first year of operation and a total of 38 sessions were held. Recidivism of program participants was about 22 percent. Again, this low recidivism rate is favorable. Subsequent evaluations of the SOS program showed that the average rate of client recidivism dropped to only 16 percent. The cost of the program was negligible. During the first year, the cost was only $280, or about 86 cents per youth served.

Custodial Sanctions

The custodial options available to juvenile court judges are of two general types: (1) nonsecure facilities and (2) secure facilities. *Nonsecure custodial facilities* are those that permit youths freedom of movement within the community. Youths are generally free to leave the premises of their facilities, although they are compelled to observe various rules, such as curfew, avoidance of alcoholic beverages and drugs, and participation in specific programs that are tailored to their particular needs. These types of nonsecure facilities include foster homes, group homes and halfway houses, camps, ranches, experience programs, and wilderness projects.

Nonsecure Facilities

Foster Homes. If the juvenile's natural parents are considered unfit, or if the juvenile is abandoned or orphaned, **foster homes** are often used for temporary placement. Those youths placed in foster homes are not necessarily law violators. They may be children in need of supervision (CHINS) or persons in need of supervision (PINS) (*Matter of Zachary "I,"* 1993). Foster home placement provides youths with a substitute family. A stable family environment is believed by the courts to be beneficial when youths have no consistent adult supervision or are unmanageable or unruly in their own households. In 1990, approximately 4,000 youths were under the supervision of foster homes in state-operated public placement programs (American Correctional Association, 1991). Rogers and Mays (1987:429) indicate that many of those assigned to foster homes are dependent, neglected, or abused and typically are younger, in the 10-to-14 age range.

Foster home placements are useful when youths have been apprehended for status offenses. Most families who accept youths into their homes have been investigated by state or local authorities in advance to determine their fitness as foster parents. Socioeconomic factors and home stability are considered important for child placements. Foster parents are often middle-aged, middle-class citizens with above-average educational backgrounds. Despite these positive features, it is unlikely that foster homes are able to provide the high intensity of adult supervision required by more hard-core juvenile offenders. Further, it is unlikely that these parents can furnish the quality of special treatments that might prove effective in the youth's possible rehabilitation or societal reintegration. Most foster parents simply are not trained as counselors, social workers, or psychologists. For many nonserious youths, however, a home environment, particularly a stable one, has certain therapeutic benefits.

Group Homes.   Another nonsecure option for juvenile judges is the assignment of juveniles to **group homes.** Placing youths in group homes is considered an intermediate option available to juvenile court judges. Group homes are community-based operations that may be either publicly or privately administered (Simone, 1984:110).

Usually, group homes will have counselors or residents to act as parental figures for youths in groups of 10 to 20. Certain group homes, referred to as *family group homes,* are actually family-operated, and thus, they are in a sense an extension of foster homes for larger numbers of youths. In group homes, nonsecure supervision of juvenile clients is practiced. Nearly 4,000 youths were in state-sponsored group homes during 1990 (American Correctional Association, 1991).

Privately or publicly operated, group homes require juvenile clients to observe the rights of others, participate in various vocational or educational training programs, attend school, participate in therapy or receive prescribed medical treatment, and observe curfew. Urinalyses or other tests may be conducted randomly as checks to see whether juveniles are taking drugs or consuming alcohol contrary to group home policy. If one or more program violations occur, group home officials may report these infractions to juvenile judges who retain dispositional control over the youths. Assignment to a group home is usually for a determinate period.

Positively, group homes provide youths with the companionship of other juveniles. Problem-sharing often occurs through planned group discussions. Staff are available to assist youths to secure employment, work certain difficult school problems, and absorb emotional burdens arising from difficult interpersonal relationships. However, these homes are sometimes staffed by community volunteers with little training or experience with a youth's problems. There are certain risks and legal liabilities that may be incurred as the result of well-intentioned but bad advice or inadequate assistance. Currently, there are limited regulations among states for how group homes are established and operated. Training programs for group home staff are scarce in most jurisdictions, and few standards exist relating to staff preparation and qualifications. Therefore, considerable variation exists among group homes relating to the quality of services they can extend to the juveniles they serve.

Camps, Ranches, Experience Programs, and Wilderness Projects. **Camps, ranches,** or "camp ranches" are nonsecure facilities that are sometimes referred to as **wilderness programs** or **experience programs.** A less expensive alternative to the detention of juvenile offenders, even those considered chronic, is participation in experience programs. Experience programs include a wide array of outdoor programs designed to improve a juvenile's self-worth, self-concept, pride, and trust in others (McCarthy and McCarthy, 1984:318).

Hope Center Wilderness Camp.   An example of a fairly successful wilderness experiment is the **Hope Center Wilderness Camp** in Houston, Texas (Clagett, 1989). This camp has an organized network of four interdependent, small living groups of 12 teenagers each. The camp's goals are to provide quality care and treatment in a nonpunitive environment, with specific emphases on health, safety, education, and therapy. Emotionally disturbed youths whose offenses range from truancy to murder are selected for program participation. Informal techniques are used, including "aftertalk" (informal discussing during meals), "huddle up" (a group discussion technique), and "pow wow" (a nightly fire gathering). Special nondenominational religious services are conducted. Participants are involved in various special events and learn to cook meals outdoors, camp, and other survival skills. Follow-ups by camp officials show that camp participants exhibit recidivism rates of only about 15 percent (Clagett, 1989).

Project Outward Bound.   Another wilderness project, **Project Outward Bound** is one of more than 200 programs of its type in the United States today. Outward Bound was first introduced in Colorado in 1962 with objectives emphasizing personal survival in the wilderness. Youths participated in various outdoor activities including rock climbing, solo survival, camping, and long-range hiking during a three-week period (McCarthy and McCarthy, 1984:319). Program officials were not concerned with equipping these juveniles with survival skills per se, but rather, they wanted to instill within the participants a feeling of self-confidence and self-assurance to cope with other types of problems in their communities.

Homeward Bound.   A program known as **Homeward Bound** was established in Massachusetts in 1970. Homeward Bound was designed to provide juveniles with mature responsibilities through the acquisition of survival skills and wilderness experiences. A six-week training program subjected 32 youths to endurance training, physical fitness, and performing community service (McCarthy and McCarthy, 1984:318–319). Additionally, officials of the program worked with the boys to develop a release program when they completed the project requirements successfully. During the evenings, the juveniles were given instruction in ecology, search and rescue, and overnight treks.

Toward the end of the program, the boys were subjected to a test—surviving a three-day, three-night trip in the wilderness to prove that each boy had acquired the necessary survival skills. Recidivism rates among these boys were lower than for boys who had been institutionalized in industrial or reform schools (Willman and Chun, 1974). Although these programs serve limited numbers of juveniles and some authorities question their value in deterring further delinquency, some evidence suggests that these wilderness experiences generate less recidivism among participants compared with those youths who are institutionalized in industrial schools under conditions of close custody and monitoring (McCarthy and McCarthy, 1984:319).

Secure Facilities

Short-Term and Long-Term Facilities. Secure-custody juvenile facilities in the United States emulate adult prisons or penitentiaries in several of their characteristics. They are also either short term or long term. These terms are ambiguous as they pertain to juvenile secure custody facilities. Technically, *short-term confinement* facilities, sometimes referred to as *detention,* are designed to accommodate juveniles on a *temporary* basis. These juveniles are either awaiting a later juvenile court adjudication, subsequent foster home or group home placement, or a transfer to criminal court. Sometimes youths will be placed in short-term confinement because their identity is unknown, and it is desirable that they should not be confined in adult lock-ups or jails. When juveniles are placed in these short-term facilities, they are considered held in detention. Opposed to detention, juveniles placed in *long-term facilities* may be confined for several days or years, although the average duration of juvenile incarceration across all offender categories nationally is about six or seven months (U.S. Bureau of Justice Statistics, 1986a:391). The average short-term incarceration in public facilities for juveniles is about 30 days. Most juvenile court judges use incarceration as a last-resort disposition, if the circumstances merit incarceration. By far the most frequently used sanction against juveniles is probation.

JUVENILE POs AND PREDISPOSITIONAL REPORTS

Predispositional reports are completed for more serious juveniles and function like presentence investigation reports prepared by POs for adults. Juvenile court judges order these prepared in most cases, unless there are statutory provisions in certain jurisdictions that govern their automatic preparation. These predispositional reports contain much of the same information as PSIs. Sometimes, juveniles whose families can afford them have private predispositional reports prepared to influence judges to exert leniency on the juvenile offender (Greenwood and Turner, 1993:231). In fact, that is precisely what Greenwood and Turner found when they compared case dispositions of youths who had private predispositional reports prepared against those cases in which standard reports had been compiled by juvenile POs. Greenwood and Turner described client-specific planning as the name given by the National Center on Institutions and Alternatives to its process of developing alternative sentencing plans designed to minimize the incarceration of its clients (Greenwood and Turner, 1993:232).

JUVENILE PROBATION AND PAROLE PROGRAMS

Hurst (1990:16) says that at least 1.3 million cases annually are processed in juvenile courts. About 570,000 of these are assigned to POs for predispositional study, while 400,000 are assigned for supervision. The most common form of probation is standard probation. Standard juvenile probation is more or less elaborate, depending on the jurisdiction. Of all sentencing options available to juvenile court judges, standard probation is the most common. The first probation law was enacted in Massachusetts in 1878, although probation was used much earlier. John Augustus is credited with developing probation in Boston in 1841. **Standard probation** is either a conditional or unconditional nonincarcerative sentence of a specified period following an adjudication of delinquency.

Unconditional and Conditional Probation

Probation programs for juveniles are either *unconditional* or *conditional* and exhibit many similarities with adult probation programs. *Unconditional standard probation* basically involves complete freedom of movement within the juvenile's community, perhaps accompanied by periodic reports by telephone or mail with a PO or the probation department. Because a PO's caseload is often high, with several hundred juvenile clients who must be managed, individualized attention cannot be given to most juveniles on standard probation. The period of unsupervised probation varies among jurisdictions depending on offense seriousness and other circumstances.

Conditional probation programs may include optional conditions and program requirements, such as performing a certain number of hours of public or community service, providing restitution to victims, payment of fines, employment, and/or participation in specific vocational, educational, or therapeutic programs. It is crucial to any probation program that an effective classification system is in place so that juvenile judges can sentence offenders accordingly. Baird (1985:32–34) suggests that a variation of the National Institute of Corrections' (NIC) Model Classification Project scheme be used for juvenile classifications, in which both risk and needs are assessed.

General terms of standard probation usually include the following:

1. To obey one's parents or guardians;
2. To obey all laws of the community, including curfew and school laws;
3. To follow the school or work program approved by the PO;
4. To follow instructions of the PO;
5. To report in person to the PO or court at such times designated by the PO;
6. To comply with any special conditions of probation; and
7. To consult with the PO when in need of further advice.

Standard probation exhibits relatively high rates of recidivism, ranging from 40 to 75 percent. Even certain youth camps operated in various California counties have reported recidivism rates as high as 76 percent (Palmer and Wedge, 1989). Therefore, it is often difficult to forecast which juveniles will have the greatest likelihood of reoffending, regardless of the program we are examining.

According to Baird (1985:36), the following elements appear to be predictive of future criminal activity and reoffending by juveniles: (1) age at first adjudication; (2) a prior criminal record (a combined measure of the number and severity of priors); (3) the number of prior commitments to juvenile facilities; (4) drug/chemical abuse; (5) alcohol abuse; (6) family relationships (parental control); (7) school problems; and (8) peer relationships. An additional factor not cited by Baird that may have significant predictive value is whether youths who are currently on probation violate one or more conditions of their probation programs.

Needs assessments should be individualized, based on the juvenile's past record and other pertinent characteristics, including the present adjudication offense (Baird, 1985:36). The level of supervision should vary according to the degree of risk posed to the public by the juvenile. Baird does not provide a weighting procedure for the different risk factors listed above, but he does describe a supervisory scheme that acts as a guide for juvenile probation and aftercare. This scheme would be applied based on the perceived risk of each juvenile offender. His scheme would include the following:

Regular or Differential Supervision

1. Four face-to-face contacts per month with youth
2. Two face-to-face contacts per month with parents
3. One face-to-face contact per month with placement staff
4. One contact with school officials

Intensive Supervision

1. Six face-to-face contacts per month with youth
2. Three face-to-face contacts per month with parents
3. One face-to-face contact per month with placement staff
4. Two contacts with school officials

Alternative Care Cases

1. One face-to-face contact per month with youth
2. Four contacts with agency staff (one must be face-to-face)
3. One contact every two months with parents

Just Because You're a Juvenile, It Doesn't Mean You Can Avoid Serious Probation Conditions and Time.   Not all probation orders involving juveniles are lenient. In the *Matter of Jessie GG* (1993), for instance, a New York high school student was placed on a two-year probationary term and ordered to pay $1,500 restitution for damages to a victim's property. The two-year probationary period coincided with his ability to pay. Further, it was the harshest disposition the juvenile court judge could impose.

Juvenile probationers do not have the same rights as adult probationers. For instance, a California juvenile probationer, Michael T., was placed on probation with the provision that supervising POs and police could conduct warrantless searches of his premises at any time (*In re Michael T.,* 1993). A similar provision for warrantless searches and seizures on a juvenile probationer's premises was made in the case of *In re Bounmy V.* (1993), in which the offender was a known cocaine dealer and was suspected of secreting cocaine on his premises at different times.

Intensive Supervised Probation (ISP) Programs

Intensive supervised probation (ISP) programs, alternatively known as intensive probation supervision (IPS) programs, have become increasingly popular for managing nonincarcerated offender populations (Snyder and Marshall, 1990). Since the mid-1960s, these programs have been aimed primarily at supervising adult offenders closely, and in recent years, ISP programs have been designed for juvenile offenders as well (Armstrong, 1988:342). *Intensive supervised probation* is a highly structured and conditional supervision program for either adult or juvenile offenders that serves as an alternative to incarceration and provides for an acceptable level of public safety (adapted from a definition by Armstrong, 1988:343). Some researchers argue that the effectiveness of ISP is how well certain risk control factors are managed by supervising POs rather than the sheer intensity of their supervision over clients (Sontheimer and Goodstein, 1993:197–198, 222–225).

Characteristics of ISP Programs.   ISP programs for juveniles have been developed and are currently operating in about one-third to one-half of all U.S. jurisdictions (Armstrong, 1988; Weibush, 1990). Similar to their adult ISP program counterparts, juvenile ISP (JISP) programs are ideally designed for secure detention-bound youths and are considered as acceptable alternatives to incarceration. According to Armstrong (1988:342), this is what JISP programs were always meant to be. Armstrong differentiates JISP programs from other forms of standard probation by citing obvious differences in the amount of officer/client contact during the course of the probationary period. For example, standard probation is considered no more than two face-to-face officer/client contacts per month. Armstrong says that JISP programs might differ from standard probation according to the following face-to-face criteria: (1) two or three times per week versus once per month; (2) once per week versus twice per month; or (3) four times per week versus once per week (the latter figure being unusually high for standard probation contact) (Armstrong, 1988:346).

Different types of PO dispositions toward their work are evident in descriptions of the various services provided by the different JISP programs investigated by Armstrong. For example, of the 55 programs he examined (92 percent of his total program sample), he found that the following range of services, skills, and resources were mentioned as being brokered by POs in different jurisdictions:

1. Mental health counseling
2. Drug and alcohol counseling
3. Academic achievement and aptitude testing
4. Vocational and employment training
5. Individual, group, and family counseling
6. Job search and placement programs
7. Alternative education programs
8. Foster grandparents programs
9. Big Brother and Big Sister programs

Not all ISP programs are alike, however (Wiebush, 1990:26). Nevertheless, many juvenile ISP programs share similarities, including the following:

1. Recognition of the shortcomings of traditional responses to serious and/or chronic offenders (e.g., incarceration or out-of-home placement);
2. Severe resource constraints within jurisdictions that compel many probation departments to adopt agency-wide classification and workload deployment systems for targeting a disproportionate share of resources for the most problematic juvenile offenders;
3. Program hopes to reduce the incidence of incarceration in juvenile secure detention facilities and reduce overcrowding;
4. Programs tend to include aggressive supervision and control elements as a part of the "get-tough" movement; and
5. All programs have a vested interest in rehabilitation of youthful offenders.

From these analyses of ISP program content generally, we can glean the following as basic characteristics of ISP programs:

1. Low officer/client caseloads (i.e., 30 or fewer probationers);
2. High levels of offender accountability (e.g., victim restitution, community service, payment of fines, partial defrayment of program expenses);
3. High levels of offender responsibility;
4. High levels of offender control (home confinement, electronic monitoring, frequent face-to-face visits by POs); and
5. Frequent checks for arrests, drug and/or alcohol use, and employment/school attendance (drug/alcohol screening, coordination with police departments and juvenile halls, teachers, family) (Armstrong, 1988:342–343; Wiebush, 1990).

The Ohio Experience

The value of JISP can be appreciated by what Wiebush described as the **Ohio Experience.** Wiebush compared three different Ohio counties that used different ISP programs for their juvenile offenders, as well as the Ohio Department of Youth Services (ODYS). The different counties include Delaware County (predominantly rural), Lucas County (Toledo), and Cuyahoga County (Cleveland). The ODYS is state operated and manages the most serious offenders—felony offenders on parole from secure detention. In each of the county jurisdictions, most of the offenders are detention bound, with the exception of the Lucas County juveniles who are sentenced to ISP after having their original sentences of detention reversed by juvenile court judges.

Targeted by the Delaware JISP program are those juveniles with a high propensity to recidivate as well as more serious felony offenders who are detention bound. Youths begin the program with a five-day detention, followed by two weeks of house arrest. Later, they must observe curfews, attend school and complete schoolwork satisfactorily, report daily to the probation office, and submit to periodic urinalysis. Each youth's progress is monitored by intensive counselors and surveillance staff 16 hours per day, seven days per week. Wiebush says that although the Delaware program has a rather strict approach, it embodies rehabilitation as a primary program objective. The Delaware program has about a 40 percent recidivism rate, which is high, although it is better than the 75 percent rate of recidivism among the general juvenile court population of high-risk offenders elsewhere in Ohio jurisdictions.

Lucas County program officials select clients from those already serving sentences of detention and who are considered high-risk offenders. Lucas County officials wished to use this particular selection method, since they wanted to avoid any appearance of net widening that their JISP program might reflect. Drawing from those already incarcerated seemed the best strategy in this case. The Lucas program is similar to the Delaware program in its treatment and control approaches. However, the Lucas program obligates offenders to perform up to 100 hours of community service as a program condition. House arrest, curfew, and other Delaware program requirements are also found in the Lucas program. The successfulness of the Lucas program has not been evaluated fully, although it does appear to have reduced institutional commitments by about 10 percent between 1986 and 1987.

The Cuyahoga County program (Cleveland) was one of the first of several ISP programs in Ohio's metropolitan jurisdictions. It is perhaps the largest county program, with 1,500 clients at any given time, as well as 6 juvenile court judges and 72 supervisory personnel. One innovation of the Cuyahoga program was the development of a team approach to client surveillance and management. This program, like the other county programs, performs certain broker functions by referring its clients to an assortment of community-based services and treatments during the program duration. Currently, there are six teams of surveillance officers, each serving about 60 youths. These teams are comprised of a team leader, two counselors, and three surveillance staff. In 1989, an interim evaluation of the Cuyahoga program made by Hamparian and Sametz (1989) showed that the rate of recidivism among Cuyahoga clients was about 31 percent during a nine-month follow-up. Additional evaluations of the program were being made at the time of this writing.

The ODYS program operates the state's nine training schools in addition to supervising the 3,000 youths each year who are released on parole. The ODYS has 93 youth counselors to staff seven regional offices. The ODYS commenced JISP in February 1988 and supervised those high-risk offenders with a predicted future recidivism rate of 75 percent or higher. Since these clients were all prior felony of-fenders with lengthy adjudication records, they were considered the most serious group to be supervised compared with the other programs. Accordingly, the ODYS supervision and surveillance structure exhibited the greatest degree of of-fender monitoring. The team approach has been used by the ODYS, with teams consisting of three youth counselors and two surveillance staff.

Since its creation, the JISP program operated by the ODYS has exhibited a drop in its recidivism rate. On the basis of a comparison of the first year of its oper-ation with recidivism figures for its clients from the previous year, the ODYS pro-gram had a 34 percent reduction in its rate of recidivism. Further, a 39 percent re-duction in parole revocations occurred. This is significant, considering the high-risk nature of the offender population being managed.

All of these programs have required enormous investments of time and en-ergy by high-quality staff, according to Wiebush. Further, each program has illus-trated how best to utilize existing community resources to further its objectives and best serve juvenile clients in need. However, Wiebush says that what is good for Ohio probationers and parolees may not necessarily be suitable for those offenders of other jurisdictions. Nevertheless, these programs function as potential models after which programs in other jurisdictions may be patterned.

The Allegheny Academy

In February 1982, the **Allegheny Academy** in Pennsylvania was opened and oper-ated by the Community Specialists Corporation, a private, nonprofit corporation headquartered in Pittsburgh and specializing in the community-based treatment of young offenders (Costanzo, 1990:114). The program's general aim is to change the negative behavior of offenders. The targets of the Allegheny Academy are those juvenile offenders who have failed in other, traditional probation programs in the state. Thus, the youthful clients are recidivists who, Allegheny officials believe, would not particularly benefit from further institutionalization through secure de-tention.

The Allegheny Academy was originally designed as a facility that could pro-vide meaningful aftercare to adjudicated offenders. Clients are referred to the Academy by juvenile court judges in lieu of incarceration. The program may be completed by clients in about six months. Youths live at home, but they must at-tend the Academy each day after school and also on weekends. They receive two full-course meals a day and arrive at their homes around 8:00 or 9:00 P.M. each evening. Follow-up calls are made to these youths' homes by supervisors who mon-itor the program-imposed curfew of 10:30 P.M. The Academy offers instruction and other forms of assistance that enable participants to acquire greater responsibili-ties. Buses carrying 15 passengers each pick clients up daily and return them to their homes in the evenings. After they have successfully complied with program requirements for 28 days in a row, they are gradually allowed community days at home on weekends. Student failure to attend classes or observe curfews may result in placement in the county juvenile detention facility for 2 to 14 days (Costanzo, 1990:116).

The Allegheny Academy includes in its program various student activities, such as woodworking, carpentry, masonry, painting, electrical and structural repair, food services, vehicle maintenance, graphic arts, and computer skills. Clients also receive individual or group counseling as well as some family counseling. Clients are encouraged to learn about substance abuse and behaving well in their schools and homes. Between 1982 and 1990, the cost of operating Allegheny Academy has been only a fraction of what it would have required to impose long-term detention on all of the juveniles served. Further, clients have paid out over $100,000 in restitution to various victims through earnings from summer work programs.

Boston Offender Project (BOP)

Sometimes, a compromise relating to the custody imposed in various juvenile probation programs is preferred, involving some degree of secure custody over youths for a short time, but nonsecure supervision would also be permitted and desirable. One of the most frustrating aggregates of juvenile offenders is that only a small minority commit violent offenses (Murphy, 1985:26). Judges and POs are often at a loss for strategies to deal effectively with such offenders. Often, the options are secure custody in a reform school or a waiver to criminal courts, presumably for more stringent punishments and longer sentences of confinement. Some professionals in juvenile corrections continue to believe, however, that other options are available, provided that the time and resources could be allocated properly.

In 1981, an experimental program began in Boston to give some of these professionals their chance to put into practice what they believed could be done in theory. The Massachusetts Department of Youth Services was awarded a grant to implement what eventually became known as the Boston Offender Project (BOP). BOP was one of five demonstration sites selected. Its target was violent juveniles, and the program goals included reducing recidivism among them, enhancing public protection by increasing accountability for major violators, and improving the likelihood of successful reintegration of juveniles into society by focusing on these offenders' academic and vocational skills (Murphy, 1985:26).

BOP sought to improve the typical handling of a violent juvenile case in the following ways:

1. By developing three coordinated phases of treatment that include initial placement in a small, locked, secure-treatment program, followed by planned transition into a halfway house; and finally, a gradual return to the juvenile's home community;
2. By assuring the delivery of comprehensive services by assigning particularly experienced caseworkers responsible for working intensively with a caseload of not more than eight violent offenders and their families; and
3. By providing services focused on increasing the educational level of offenders and tying educational programs to the marketplace, significantly increasing the prospects of meaningful employment. (Murphy, 1985:26)

BOP was similar to shock probation, in that violent juvenile offenders would experience some confinement in a secure facility, but after a short time, they would be released to less secure surroundings.

The BOP has several important features compared with the treatment received by those juveniles in the control group. First, diagnostic assessments of juveniles in BOP went well beyond standard psychological assessments, and these measures were administered on an ongoing basis to chart developments in psychological, vocational, and medical areas. Second, caseworkers in the BOP program were three times more experienced (in numbers of years) compared with standard program caseworkers. A third important difference was that BOP caseworker loads were limited to 7, while caseloads for workers in the standard program were as high as 25.

A fourth feature was that BOP caseworkers were actively involved in the treatment phase, while the standard program caseworker involvement was passive. A fifth feature of BOP was that caseworker visits to juveniles were eight times as frequent per month compared with standard program visits. A sixth BOP feature was an automatic assignment to nonsecure residential facilities once the first secure phase of the program was completed. For standard program participants, this was not necessarily an option. Furthermore, in the BOP program, continued violence would subject a participant to regression, so that the offender could be placed back in secure confinement. In the standard program, there was only limited flexibility to make this program shift. Finally, the standard program was terminated for youths when they reached 18 years of age, while the BOP could be discontinued or continued before or after age 18, depending on caseworker judgment.

Some important differences between the two groups emerged over the next several years. For instance, 79 percent of BOP clients found unsubsidized employment compared with only 29 percent of the control group. Also, only about one-third of the BOP clients had been rearrested. This was about half the rearrest rate exhibited by the control group. Thus, while the BOP may not be the perfect solution to the problem of violent juvenile offenders, it does offer a viable, middle-ground alternative that has demonstrable success, at least with some offenders. For the chronic, hard-core, and most dangerous offenders, detention is one of the last resorts as a judicial option.

Other Juvenile Probation and Parole Programs

Electronic Monitoring for Juvenile Offenders.   Charles (1989a) describes the implementation of an electronic monitoring program for juvenile offenders in Allen County, Indiana. Known as the Allen County, Indiana Juvenile Electronic Monitoring Program Pilot Project or EMP, this program began as an experimental study in October 1987 and was conducted for nine months through May 1988. At the time the study started, the probation department had 25 POs who were appointed by the court and certified by the Indiana Judicial Conference. During 1987, 2,404 juveniles were referred to the probation department by the court. About 34 per-

BOX 15.1
Alternatives to Secure Confinement for Juveniles

The Cases of Project New Pride and Visionquest

Project New Pride

One of the most popular probation programs is **Project New Pride,** which was established in Denver, Colorado, in 1973. It has been widely used as a model for probation programs in other jurisdictions in subsequent years (Laurence and West, 1985). New Pride is a blend of education, counseling, employment, and cultural education directed at those more serious offenders between the ages of 14 and 17. Juveniles eligible for the New Pride program must have at least two prior convictions for serious misdemeanors and/or felonies, and they must be formally charged or adjudicated for another offense when referred to New Pride. There are very few women in New Pride, only about 10 or 15 percent. This is not deliberate exclusion, but women tend to have lower rates of recidivism and commit less serious offenses compared with their male delinquent counterparts. Those who are deliberately excluded are offenders previously diagnosed as severely psychotic or who have committed forcible rape.

Project New Pride's goals include (1) reintegrating participants into their communities through school participation or employment and (2) reducing recidivism rates among offenders. The project emphasizes schooling, employment, and closeness with families. It is a community-based project and utilizes professional POs as well as volunteers. The project staff offer employment counseling services and job placement, tutoring for school assign-

ments and projects, and vocational training. Project New Pride personnel will help juveniles fill out job application forms and answer other questions relevant for effective job hunting and success in school.

Some of the areas in which New Pride programs have been established have led to juveniles developing small businesses such as bakeries, janitorial services, and lawn and gardening services to help defray the costs of their program expenses. Taxpayer dollars finance New Pride projects in various jurisdictions. It is estimated that the cost for each juvenile serviced by Project New Pride is $4,500, compared with $28,000, the cost of incarcerating the same offender in a reform or industrial school (Project New Pride, 1985). The goals of Project New Pride seem obtainable. Over the years, recidivism rates have been low, less than 20 percent. Furthermore, nearly half the juveniles who have participated in various New Pride projects through the United States have returned to finish their high school education or have completed the GED. Almost three-fourths of all participants hold full-time jobs successfully (McCarthy and McCarthy, 1984:312; Pacific Institute for Research and Evaluation, 1985).

Community-based programs are particularly advantageous for youths because they provide opportunities for them to remain integrated in their communities. At the same time, youths receive assistance from agency referrals to available services and treatments. Altschuler and Armstrong (1990:170) suggest that community-based correctional programs and other intensive probation supervision programs can maximize their effectiveness and assistance to youthful clients if they attempt to realize five important principles:

1. Preparing youths for gradually increased responsibility and freedom in the community;
2. Helping youths become involved in the community and getting the community to interact with them;
3. Working with youths and their families, peers, schools and employers to identify the qualities necessary for success;
4. Developing new resources and supports where needed; and
5. Monitoring and testing youths and the community on their abilities to interact.

VisionQuest

VisionQuest is another wilderness program. It is a private, for-profit enterprise operated from Tucson, Arizona. At present, Vision-Quest operates in about 15 states, serves about 500 juveniles annually, and is about half of the cost of secure institutionalization (Gavzer, 1986.10). Among the various juris dictions that have used VisionQuest for its juvenile probationers is San Diego County, California (Greenwood and Turner, 1987). Clients selected for participation in the VisionQuest program in San Diego were secure detention-bound offenders with several prior arrests and placements with the California Youth Authority. VisionQuest staff members conducted interviews with certain juveniles who were tentatively selected for inclusion in the program. On the basis of VisionQuest staff recommendations, juvenile court judges would assign these juveniles to VisionQuest, where they would be under an indeterminate sentence of from six months to one year or more (Greenwood, 1990).

VisionQuest experiences of youths have been described by Greenwood (1990:20)

as follows. They immediately find themselves in a rustic type of boot camp environment, where they live in an Indian tepee with 6 to 10 other youths and two junior staff. They sleep on the ground and engage in a strenuous physical fitness program. They complete regular schoolwork. Failure to perform their daily chores adequately results in an immediate confrontation between them and senior staff. They participate in an orientation and outdoor training program, which takes several months to complete. Eventually, they take a wagon train on the back roads of the Western states to Canada, averaging about 24 miles a day, for four to six months. All the while, they are given increased responsibilities, including breaking horses that VisionQuest acquires annually. Eventually, they attend the VisionQuest group home in Arizona where it is determined whether they can be reintegrated into their communities (Greenwood, 1990:20–21).

Greenwood and Turner (1987) have evaluated the effectiveness of VisionQuest by comparing a sample of 89 male juvenile offenders with a sample of 177 juveniles assigned to San Diego County Probation. Both the San Diego County probationers and the VisionQuest youths were tracked for one year following the completion of their respective programs. VisionQuest participants had a recidivism rate of 55 percent compared with 71 percent for the regular probationers. Although this rate of recidivism is high compared with many other intensive supervision probation programs, the sizable difference in recidivism for both groups is viewed as moderately successful. Other researchers in different jurisdictions where VisionQuest has been used report that average recidivism figures are about 33 percent for VisionQuest participants (Gavzer, 1986).

cent of these were female offenders. During that same year, 167 youths were incarcerated in secure facilities for delinquents at a total cost of $1.5 million.

Charles (1989b:152–153) indicates that because of fiscal constraints, Allen County agreed to place only six juveniles in the electronic monitoring program. However, two of these youths recidivated and were dropped from it shortly after it started. The remaining four youths remained in the program. The juvenile judge in these cases sentenced each youth to a six-month probationary period with electronic monitoring. Each youth wore a conspicuous wristlet, which eventually became a symbol of court sanctions. Like the proverbial string tied around one's finger, the wristlet was a constant reminder that these juveniles were on probation. Further, others who became aware of these electronic devices helped these youths to avoid activities that might be considered in violation of probation program conditions.

Despite the small number of participants in Charles's research, his findings are of interest and suggest similar successful applications on larger offender aggregates. All juveniles were interviewed at the conclusion of the program. They reported that their wristlets were continuous reminders of their involvement in the probation program. However, they didn't feel as though program officials were spying on them. In fact, one of the youths compared his experience with electronic monitoring with his previous experience of being supervised by a PO. He remarked that whenever he was under the supervision of the PO, he could do whatever he wished, and there was little likelihood that his PO would ever find out about it. However, he was always under the threat of being discovered by the computer or by the surveillance officer.

Another interesting phenomenon was the fact that the wristlet enabled certain offenders to avoid peer pressure and "hanging out" with their friends. Since they had wristlets, they had good excuses to return home and not violate their curfews. And, the families of these juveniles took a greater interest in them and their program. In short, at least for these four youths, the program was viewed very favorably and considered successful. Parents who were also interviewed at the conclusion of the program agreed that the program and monitoring system had been quite beneficial for their sons. While electronic monitoring for juveniles is still in its early stages of experimentation in various jurisdictions, Charles (1989b) believes that it is a cost-effective alternative to incarceration.

Home Confinement for Juvenile Offenders.   In many jurisdictions, home confinement is supplemented with electronic monitoring (Schlatter, 1989). Relatively little is known about the extent to which home confinement is used as a sentencing alternative for juvenile offenders. Since probation is so widely used as the sanction of choice except for the most chronic recidivists, home confinement is most often applied as an accompanying condition of electronic monitoring. However, this type of sentencing may be redundant, since curfew for juvenile offenders means home confinement anyway, especially during evening hours. As a day sentence, home confinement for juveniles would probably be counterproductive, since juveniles are often obligated to finish their schooling as a probation program condition. Again, since school hours are during the daytime, it would not make sense to deprive juveniles of school opportunities through some type of home detention.

Shock Probation and Boot Camps.   Shock probation has sometimes been compared erroneously with Scared Straight, a New Jersey program implemented in the late 1970s. Scared Straight sought to frighten samples of hard-core delinquent youths by having them confront inmates in a Rahway, New Jersey, prison. Inmates would yell at and belittle them, calling them names, cursing, and yelling. Inmates would tell them about sexual assaults and other prison unpleasantries in an attempt to get them to refrain from reoffending. However, the program was unsuccessful. Despite early favorable reports of recidivism rates of less than 20 percent, the actual rate of recidivism among these participating youths was considerably higher. Furthermore, another control group not exposed to Scared Straight had a lower recidivism rate (Lundman, 1984). The Scared Straight program is perhaps closer in principle to the SHAPE-UP program implemented in Colorado and discussed as a diversionary measure earlier. However, SHAPE-UP program authorities deny any program similarities other than prisoner-client interaction for brief periods (Mitchell and Shiller, 1988).

The juvenile version of shock probation or shock incarceration is perhaps best exemplified by juvenile boot camps. Also known as the *army model,* boot camp programs are patterned after basic training for new military recruits. Juvenile offenders are given a taste of hard military life, and such regimented activities and structure for up to 180 days are often sufficient to "shock" them into giving up their lives of delinquency or crime and staying out of jail (Ratliff, 1988:98). Boot camp programs in various states have been established, including the Regimented Inmate Discipline program in Mississippi, the About Face program in Louisiana, and the shock incarceration program in Georgia. These are paramilitary-type programs that emphasize strict military discipline and physical training (Ratliff, 1988:98).

Two good examples of boot camp programs are the U.S. Army Correctional Activity (USACA) in Fort Riley, Kansas, established in 1968 (Ratliff, 1988), and the Butler (New York) Shock Incarceration Correctional Facility (Waldron, 1990). In both programs, inmates wear army uniforms, learn basic army drills, salute, and participate in a rigorous correctional treatment program. Ordinarily, youthful first-offender felons are targeted for involvement in these programs. The Butler Shock program, for instance, involves young offenders ranging in age from 16 to 29. They must stay in the camp for six months and comply with all program rules. About 88 percent of all boot camp trainees are successful and win a parole later. The Butler facility has inmates who have been heavily involved in drug dealing. About 90 percent of all participants have been convicted of drug offenses. They have rigorous work details and must complete schoolwork and adhere to a highly disciplined regimen. They are given eight minutes for meals, and they must carry their leftovers in their pockets.

Their days begin at 5:30 A.M., with reveille blaring over the intercom. Immediately, drill instructors start screaming at them. Besides military drilling, all inmates must experience drug counseling and study. At the Fort Riley facility, inmates may learn vocational skills and crafts. They also receive counseling and other therapy and treatment. At both camps, physicians and other support staff are ready to furnish any needed medical treatment. When they eventually leave the facility, most have changed their outlook on life and have acquired new lifestyles not associated with crime. Again, recidivism rates among these inmates are under 30 percent, which is considered an indication of program success.

REVOKING JUVENILE PROBATION AND PAROLE

Parole for juveniles is similar to parole for adult offenders. Those juveniles who have been detained in various institutions for long periods may be released prior to serving their full sentences. Generally, *parole* is a conditional supervised release from incarceration granted to youths who have served a portion of their original sentences (Altschuler and Armstrong, 1993).

Purposes of Parole.   The general purposes of parole are to

1. Reward good behavior while youths have been detained;
2. Alleviate overcrowding;
3. Permit youths to become reintegrated back into their communities and enhance their rehabilitation potential; and
4. Deter youths from future offending by ensuring their continued supervision under juvenile parole officers.

Some authorities also believe that the prospect of earning parole might induce greater compliance to institutional rules among incarcerated youths. Also, parole is seen by some experts as a continuation of the juvenile's punishment, since parole programs are most often conditional in nature (e.g., observance of curfew, school attendance, staying out of trouble, periodic drug and alcohol urinalyses, participation in counseling programs, and vocational and educational training).

How Many Juveniles Are on Parole?   Estimates vary about how many juvenile offenders are on parole at any given time. The present lack of coordination among jurisdictions relating to juvenile offender record-keeping makes it difficult to determine actual numbers of juvenile parolees or probationers at any given time. Further, some jurisdictions continue to prevent public scrutiny of juvenile court adjudicatory proceedings or their results. Since a juvenile record is expunged or sealed on reaching adulthood, even historical research on this subject is limited by various systemic constraints. Attesting to the dearth of information about juvenile parole is the work of Knepper and Cavender (1990). They underscore the fact that juvenile parole is one of the most underresearched topics within the juvenile justice system. Nevertheless, apart from intermediate punishment programs and secure-detention facilities, the American Correctional Association (1994:xxxvi–xxxvii) has reported that over 11,700 juveniles were in nonsecure, state-operated halfway houses and other community-based facilities in 1994 and that about another 15,000 youths were under other forms of state-controlled supervision as parolees.

Characteristics of Juvenile Parolees.   Selected studies of juvenile parolees indicate that a majority are male, black, and between 17 and 19 years of age (Chambers, 1983). Some jurisdictions, such as New York, have Juvenile Offender Laws. These laws define 13-, 14-, 15-, and 16-year-olds as adults whenever they are charged with committing specified felonies. They may be tried as adults and convicted. When they are subsequently released from institutionalization, they are placed under adult parole supervision. Many other jurisdictions do not have such Juvenile Offender Laws but have waiver or transfer provisions for particularly serious juvenile offenders.

Wylen (1984) describes the characteristics of 464 juvenile offenders who were paroled to the New York State Division of Parole from 1978 through 1983. She says that 96 percent were male, 93 percent were minorities, 60 percent came from families receiving some form of public assistance, 43 percent abused drugs such as marijuana, 18 percent abused alcohol, and about 10 percent had been hospitalized for psychiatric problems. More than 75 percent of these offenders had prior records and had acted in concert with at least one other juvenile in the commission of their adjudication offenses. About 65 percent of these youths were considered supervision "successes," although one-third had previously been under the supervision of the Division of Parole. It should be noted that juveniles who are held in secure facilities in New York are often transferred to state adult institutions when they reach the age of 21.

Juvenile parolees share many of the same programs used to supervise youthful probationers, such as intensive supervised probation programs. Further, juvenile POs often perform dual roles as juvenile parole officers as they supervise both types of offenders. Some jurisdictions, such as New York State, have established specialized supervision units to work with juvenile parolees, who tend to be older than probationers. In New York, probation is a judicial function operated by counties. Parole is under the Executive Department and operated by the state. In a pilot project of parole work with juvenile offenders called PARJO, for instance, juvenile parole officers were especially effective as brokers in directing parolees to vocational training agencies where they could learn useful skills and become employed (New York State Division of Parole, 1985). PARJO coupled intensive supervision through reduced caseloads with highly motivated officers who worked on the youths' behalf to match them with prospective employers. The PARJO project reported significant reductions in recidivism among those youthful clients who participated.

Studies of juvenile parolees tend to show that the greater the intensity of parole, the lower the recidivism (New York State Division of Parole, 1985; Wiederanders, 1983). Influencing the success of juvenile parole is whether juveniles are successfully employed or actively involved in development or counseling programs (Chambers, 1983; Wylen, 1984). For most juveniles who spend time behind bars or reform school walls, this experience is traumatic. About 65 percent of the juveniles on parole refrain from committing new offenses (Wylen, 1984).

In 1990, the Office of Juvenile Justice and Delinquency Prevention (OJJDP) was conducting a research project designed to formulate guidelines for and identify favorable features of successful intensive parole supervision programs for juveniles (Altschuler and Armstrong, 1990). Their research interests were targeted at identifying those youths who might benefit the most from a parole program, as well as the most useful methods for supervising offenders. Among their chief concerns was the reduction and potential elimination of recidivism among youthful parolees. It is unrealistic to expect that any program will ever eliminate recidivism; nevertheless, it is possible to target certain program features that might serve to reduce it among specific populations, including juvenile parolees. It is hoped that the efforts of the OJJDP will eventually yield more successful strategies for managing an especially troublesome offender aggregate.

Juvenile Parole Decision Making.   The decision to parole particular juveniles is left to different agencies and bodies, depending on the jurisdiction. Studies of imposing secure confinement upon juvenile delinquents indicate that in 45 state jurisdictions, the lengths of secure confinement are indeterminate (Frost, Fisher, and Coates, 1985). In 32 states, early-release decisions are left up to the particular juvenile correction agency, whereas six states use parole boards exclusively, and five other states depend on the original juvenile court judge's decision. Only a few states had determinate schemes for youthful offenders, and therefore, their early release from secure custody would be established by statute in much the same way as it is for adult offenders.

A seven-member parole board in New Jersey is appointed by the governor and grants early release to both adult and juvenile inmates. Utah uses a Youth Parole Authority, a part-time board consisting of three citizens and four staff members from the Utah Division of Youth Corrections (Norman, 1986). This board employs objective, decision-making criteria to determine which juveniles should be paroled. Norman (1986) says, however, that discrepancies often exist between what the Authority actually does and what it is supposed to do. Some criticisms have been that the primary parole criteria are related to former institutional behavior rather than other factors, such as prospects for successful adaptation to community life, employment, and participation in educational or vocational programs. Norman investigated 300 juvenile parole hearings over 37 days as the basis for his observations.

Similar criticisms have been made about youth parole boards in other states. Many of these juvenile parole boards consist of persons who make subjective judgments about youths on the basis of extralegal and subjective criteria. Predispositional reports prepared by juvenile POs, records of institutional behavior, a youth's appearance and demeanor during the parole hearing, and the presence of witnesses or victims have unknown effects on individual parole board members. Parole decision making is not an exact science. Subjectivity is endemic to this process. When subjective criteria impact this decision-making process, a juvenile's parole chances are significantly subverted. Thus, parole board decision making profiles in various jurisdictions may show evidence of early-release disparities attributable to racial, ethnic, gender, or socioeconomic factors.

A Survey of Juvenile Parole Policy.   Between November 1987 and November 1988, Ashford and LeCroy (1993:186) undertook an investigation of the various state juvenile parole programs and provisions. They sent letters and questionnaires to all state juvenile jurisdictions, soliciting any available information on their juvenile paroling policies. Their response rate was 94 percent, with 47 of the 50 states responding. One interesting result of their survey was the development of a typology of juvenile parole. Ashford and LeCroy discovered eight different kinds of juvenile parole used more or less frequently among the states. These were listed as follows:

1. *Determinate parole* (length of parole is linked closely with the period of commitment specified by the court; paroling authorities cannot extend confinement period of juvenile beyond original commitment length prescribed by judge; juvenile can be released short of serving the full sentence).

2. *Determinate parole set by administrative agency* (parole release date is set immediately following youth's arrival at secure facility).

3. *Presumptive minimum with limits on the extension of the supervision period for a fixed or determinate length of time* (minimum confinement period is specified, and youth must be paroled after that date unless there is a showing of bad conduct).

4. *Presumptive minimum with limits on the extension of supervision for an indeterminate period* (parole should terminate after fixed period of time; parole period is indeterminate, where PO has discretion to extend parole period with justification; parole length can extend until youth reaches age of majority and leaves juvenile court jurisdiction).

5. *Presumptive minimum with discretionary extension of supervision for an indeterminate period* (same as #4 except PO has discretion to extend parole length of juvenile with no explicit upper age limit; lacks explicit standards limiting the extension of parole).

6. *Indeterminate parole with a specified maximum and a discretionary minimum length of supervision* (follows Model Juvenile Court Act of 1968, providing limits for confinement but allows parole board authority to specify length of confinement and period of supervised release within these limits).

7. *Indeterminate parole with legal minimum and maximum periods of supervision* (parole board is vested with vast power to parole youths at any time with minimum and maximum confinement periods; more liberal than #1 and #2 above).

8. *Indeterminate or purely discretionary parole* (length of parole unspecified; may maintain youths on parole until youths reach the age of majority; at this time, parole is discontinued; may release youths from parole at any time during this period) (Ashford and LeCroy, 1993:187–191).

The most popular parole type is #8; the least popular is #1.

Recidivism and Probation or Parole Revocation

Juvenile Probation and Parole Revocations.   Probation and parole revocations are the termination of one's *probation or parole program (PPP),* usually for one or more program violations. When one's PPP is terminated, regardless of who does the terminating, there are several possible outcomes. One is that the offender will be returned to secure detention. This is the most severe result. A less harsh alternative is that the offender will be shifted to a different kind of PPP. For instance, if a juvenile is assigned to a halfway house as a part of a parole program, the rules of the halfway house must be observed. If one or more rules are violated, such as failing to observe curfew, failing drug or alcohol urinalyses, or committing new offenses, a report is filed with the court or the juvenile corrections authority for possible revocation action. If it is decided later that one's PPP should be terminated, the result may be to place the offender under house arrest or home confinement, coupled with electronic monitoring. Thus, the juvenile would be required to wear an electronic wristlet or anklet and remain on the premises for specified periods. Other program conditions would be applied as well. The fact is that one is not automatically returned to detention following a parole revocation.

Usually, if a return to incarceration or detention is not indicated, the options available to judges, parole boards, or others are limited only by the array of supervisory resources in the given jurisdiction. These options ordinarily involve more intensive supervision or monitoring of offender behaviors. Severe overcrowding in many juvenile detention facilities discourages revocation action that would return large numbers of offenders to industrial schools or youth centers. Intermediate punishments, therefore, function well to accommodate larger numbers of serious offenders, including those who have their parole revoked.

The process of PPP revocation for juveniles is not as clear-cut as it is for adult offenders. The U.S. Supreme Court has not ruled decisively thus far about how juvenile PPP revocation actions should be handled. Prior to several significant U.S. Supreme Court decisions, PPP revocation could be accomplished for adult offenders on the basis of reports filed by POs that offenders were in violation of one or more conditions of their PPPs. Criminal court judges, those ordinarily in charge of determining whether to terminate probationary status, could decide this issue on the basis of available evidence against offenders. For adult parolees, former decision making relative to terminating their parole could be made by parole boards without much fanfare from offenders. In short, parole officers and others might simply present evidence that one or more infractions or violations of PPP conditions had been committed. These infractions, then, could form the basis for revoking PPPs as well as a justification for these decisions.

Juvenile Case Law on Probation Revocations

When youths are placed on probation, the most frequently used dispositional option by juvenile court judges, they are subject to having their program revoked for one or more violations of program conditions. Several cases are presented below to show how different juvenile courts handle probation revocations.

In re Kazuo G. *(1994).*   A California youth, Kazuo G., was charged with various offenses and the court imposed a term of commitment to a secure facility for six months. But this commitment was suspended and probation was ordered instead. Shortly thereafter, the youth was adjudicated delinquent for misdemeanor battery. The juvenile court judge ordered him committed to a boy's ranch for six months, but again suspended this order and placed him on probation. Two more misdemeanor charges were filed against Kazuo G. within a few weeks and he was adjudi-

BOX 15.2
Should Probationers Be Compelled to Submit to Random Drug and Alcohol Testing, Even if the Offense Is Not Drug Related?

The Case of Ricky Morris

Ricky Morris, a resident of Hawaii, is a probationer. He was convicted of a non-drug-related offense, burglary. Furthermore, there was no indication that he committed burglary for any purpose related to drug use. Nevertheless, when he was placed on probation by the judge, among his probation conditions was that he must submit to random drug and alcohol testing. The court also declared as a part of his probation conditions that he must refrain from any drug or alcohol use while on probation.

During a surprise visit from Ricky's probation officer, Ricky submitted to a urinalysis. His urine tested positive for cocaine. When questioned by his probation officer, Ricky admitted that he had been using cocaine. The probation officer was a nice guy. Instead of running to the judge with a negative probation report about Ricky, the PO told him to quit using cocaine and seek drug treatment and/or rehabilitation. Ricky agreed to do this. However, a month later, another surprise visit by Ricky's PO disclosed additional cocaine use. This time, the PO reported his findings to the court, whereupon the judge revoked Ricky's probation.

Ricky and his attorneys objected to the revocation on the grounds that the PO lacked reasonable suspicion that Ricky was using drugs or that a urinalysis ought to be conducted. The lawyers further argued that the urinalyses violated Ricky's right to privacy. On appeal, the Hawaii Supreme Court ruled that the sentencing judge was within his authority to impose any reasonable condition of probation relative to Ricky Morris's rehabilitation. The drug and alcohol checks administered on a random basis would not be considered violative of Morris's right to privacy. The judge said that "while probationers have a right to enjoy a significant degree of privacy and liberty, there is limited freedom afforded someone who but for the grace of the sentencing court would be imprisoned."

Should random drug and alcohol checks be required of all probationers? Should probation officers be allowed to make random, unscheduled visits with their clients? When, if ever, would such visits constitute a violation of one's right to privacy?

Source: Adapted from *Corrections Compendium,* "Random Probation Drug Testing Upheld." *Corrections Compendium,* **16,** April, 1991. (*State v. Morris,* 48 CrL 1498 [Ha. SupCt.], 1991.)

cated delinquent on one of these charges. This time the judge ordered Kazuo G. to the boy's ranch. The youth contested this decision, arguing that he was not given a dispositional hearing. The California Court of Appeals rejected this appeal and Kazuo G. was finally placed in the boy's ranch for six months.

In re F. N. *(1993).* "F. N.," a juvenile, was adjudicated delinquent on an attempted murder charge in Illinois. He was placed on probation. Subsequently he was arrested on new charges involving criminal assault and a petition was filed to revoke his probation. He admitted the offense. In exchange for this admission (a form of plea bargaining), his original probation was continued. The judge also ordered him to a youth home for 30 days, with credit for time served while in custody earlier. Another court disagreed, noting that F. N. had participated in a gang-related shooting and was belligerent toward officers seeking to search his home with a warrant. Numerous probation program violations were noted by authorities and F. N. was subsequently placed in the Kane County, Illinois, Youth Home for 30 days. That the trial court was justifiably concerned with F. N.'s activities, which indicated an "aggressive nature," is an understatement!

Matter of Tammy JJ *(1993).*   Tammy JJ was a New York juvenile who was adjudicated as a status offender and placed on probation. However, she violated several probation conditions, including running away from home, not attending school, and failing to keep her appointments with her PO. The court ordered her probation revoked after a showing of the factual accuracy of these allegations, and Tammy JJ was placed in the custody of the Department of Social Services.

J. G. v. State *(1992).*   J. G. was a Florida juvenile who was adjudicated delinquent and placed in a community control program. Subsequently, he violated several program rules and requirements. Florida authorities held him in contempt of court for these program violations and placed him in a secure facility for a period of months. He appealed, in this case successfully. The Florida District Court of Appeals held that his punishment should have been more intensive supervised probation rather than confinement in a secure facility.

State v. H. B. *(1992).*   A New Jersey juvenile was placed on probation. Two of several probation conditions were that he (1) remain in school and get a C+ grade average or better and (2) not go out after dark unless accompanied by a parent. Subsequently, he was apprehended by police late at night and charged with possession of a stolen automobile. The juvenile court judge revoked his probation and he was committed to a one-year term in a New Jersey youth center. H. B. appealed, claiming that the one-year term was "not rehabilitative" consistent with the Family Court policies of New Jersey. The court declared, however, that although rehabilitation is desirable, a breach of probation conditions is serious and may lead to the imposition of more coercive penalties. That the judge could impose such an incarcerative penalty was viewed as a proper means to encourage compliance with probationary conditions. Otherwise, the whole process would be farcical and ineffective.

Avery v. State *(1993).*   This is a peculiar case, since it involves an Arkansas juvenile who was placed on probation; subsequently a motion was filed to revoke his probation, but the motion was denied. Instead, the court lengthened the term of his probation. A few months later, the court found that the juvenile was not in compliance with certain probation program requirements, revoked the probation, and fined the juvenile. An appeals court held that while the original trial court had the right to deny the revocation motion and extend a probationary term, it could wait several months, then change its mind, and grant the original motion to revoke probation. This raised a double jeopardy issue (*Breed v. Jones,* 1975).

Matter of J.K.A. *(1993).* It is not always necessary for the court to adjudicate juveniles for new offenses if they are currently on probation and probation revocation is a consideration. In the Texas case of *Matter of J.K.A.* (1993), J.K.A. was charged with violating his probation by possessing an illegal weapon. J.K.A. was not adjudicated delinquent on the new charge, although he could have been. However, the court revoked his probation simply because of a valid probation program condition that he not "violate the law." Possessing an illegal firearm violated the law, and hence, his probation was revoked.

Juvenile Case Law on Parole Revocations

There is very little current information about juvenile parole revocation. A few of the more recent cases involving parole eligibility and/or revocation involving juveniles are reported here.

Patuxent Institution Board of Review v. Hancock *(1993).* A juvenile, Hancock, was found to be a "defective delinquent," and he was ordered committed to Patuxent Institution in Jessup, Maryland. Patuxent Institution holds 750 males and 50 females and provides various services for offenders of diverse ages. Hancock served several months in Patuxent and sought parole. His parole application was denied. On appeal, the Institutional Board of Review found that Hancock had been wrongfully denied parole and ordered Patuxent authorities to release him. These institutional paroling authorities cited numerous institutional infractions committed by Hancock and revoked his parole again. Because of a procedural technicality, Hancock was subsequently paroled. Essentially, he was denied the basic due process right to advance notice of the conditions he allegedly violated and no hearing was held at which he could contest these charges. The order of parole revocation in Hancock's case was reversed, and Hancock was finally paroled (*Patuxent Institution Board of Review v. Hancock,* 1993).

C.D.R. v. State *(1992).* A Texas juvenile was adjudicated delinquent after being charged with aggravated sexual assault. He was placed in a facility under the direction of the Texas Youth Commission. One month before his eighteenth birthday, he petitioned for parole. His parole was denied and he was subsequently transferred to the adult Texas Department of Corrections to serve more time. The Texas Court of Appeals upheld these proceedings.

Prospective juvenile parolees are entitled to certain minimum due process rights in various states. In 1972, for instance, New York mandated juvenile parole revocation hearings similar to those held for adults (Goddard, 1977). In the New York case, this was largely because youths were being tried as adults in criminal courts and subsequently placed under adult parole supervision. Similar procedures are followed in several other states (Silbert and Sussman, 1974). Despite these procedural safeguards, parole revocation hearings for juveniles are often scripted in advance. For instance, Cavender and Knepper (1992) investigated 114 parole revocation hearings in a western U.S. state. They found that revocation decisions were most frequently made "backstage" in prehearing conferences among parole board members. Thus, informal conferences were held among these members, juveniles to be considered for parole were typed, and a script to be performed was agreed upon before the actual proceedings began. The hearings, therefore, were primarily shams with decision making about parole chances concluded much earlier.

Because the literature on juvenile parole violators is scant, it is difficult to profile them. Early research has shown, however, that those parolees who have had the longest institutional commitment lengths are also the more likely to have their parole revoked (Wheeler and Nichols, 1974). However, this may be a somewhat self-fulfilling observation, since the most serious offenders are given the longest sentences anyway, and they are more likely to recidivate.

A study of some magnitude was conducted by Visher, Lattimore, and Linster (1991). This study involved 1,949 juveniles paroled from the California Youth Authority between July 1, 1981, and June 30, 1982. An 88 percent failure rate was reported by these researchers. This is somewhat misleading, however, since a "failure" was any rearrest or parole revocation following parole. Only 14 percent failed because of a parole revocation. This means that there were many rearrests, but apparently these rearrests were unsubstantiated subsequently and these parolees were released or had their cases dismissed if charges had been filed against them. The 14 percent failure figure is impressive. At least for this sample of juvenile offenders, parole seemed to work for 86 percent of them, despite the failures observed by these researchers. The average length of time between parole and rearrest was 10 months. Considering what we know about juvenile offending, most juvenile delinquents eventually grow out of delinquent conduct anyway as they mature. This is also known as the *aging out process.*

KEY TERMS

Adjudication
Adjudicatory hearing
Allegheny Academy
Automatic waivers (also legislative waivers)
Beyond a Reasonable Doubt
Boston Offender Project (BOP)
Breed v. Jones
Camp

Certification
Children's tribunal
Child-saver movement
Demand waiver
Dependent and Neglected Children
Discretionary Waiver
Ex parte Crouse
Experience program
Foster home

Group home
Homeward Bound
Hope Center Wilderness Program
Intake screening
In re Gault
In re Winship
Judicial waiver (also discretionary waiver)
Juvenile
Juvenile Court Act
Juvenile Diversion/Non-Custody Intake Program (JD/NCI Program)
Juvenile Diversion Program (JDP)
Juvenile Justice and Delinquency Prevention Act of 1974
Juvenile delinquency
Juvenile offenders
Kent v. United States
McKeiver v. Pennsylvania
New York House of Refuge
Nominal disposition
Ohio Experience

Parens Patriae
Petition
Philadelphia Society for Alleviating the Miseries of Public Prisons
Predispositional report
Project New Pride
Project Outward Bound
Ranch
Reform school
Reverse waiver hearing
Schall v. Martin
See Our Side Program (SOS)
Standard probation
Status offender
Transfer
Transfer hearing
VisionQuest
Waiver
Wilderness program
Youth at Risk Program
Youth service bureau (YSB)

QUESTIONS FOR REVIEW

1. Distinguish between delinquents and status offenders. What are several "official" definitions of delinquency? What seem to be the major criteria used in these different definitions?

2. Do status offenders tend to escalate to delinquency? Why or why not? What is the general sentiment among different juvenile jurisdictions for placing status offenders in jails or prisons?

3. Describe briefly the historical growth of juvenile courts. Include in your discussion the doctrine of *parens patriae.*

4. What was the significance of the New York House of Refuge? How do status offenders relate to such institutions as the New York House of Refuge?

5. What was the significance of the following cases: (a) *Schall v. Martin;* (b) *Ex parte Crouse;* (c) *In re Gault;* (d) *In re Winship.*

6. Who were the child-savers? What were children's tribunals? Why are they significant for the subsequent emergence of juvenile courts?

7. Describe some of the major differences between criminal and juvenile courts.

8. Describe nonsecure and secure custodial sanctions. Give some examples of programs or circumstances that might portray these types of sanctions.

9. What is a predispositional report? Does it bear some resemblance to a PSI?

10. What is the Ohio Experience? How does it differ from the Boston Offender Project?

16

Evaluating Programs
Balancing Service Delivery and Recidivism Considerations

Introduction

Program Evaluation: How Do We Know Programs Are Effective?

Balancing Program Objectives and Offender Needs

Recidivism Defined

Recidivist Offenders and Their Characteristics

Probationers, Parolees, and Recidivism

A View from Probationers and Parolees

Key Terms

Questions for Review

INTRODUCTION

How do we know if community-based correctional programs for probationers and parolees work? There are so many programs out there. Which ones are most effective? Do these programs achieve their objectives, and to what degree?

This chapter is about program evaluation and recidivism. Every intervention program applied to both juveniles and adults is subject to evaluation at one time or another. Investigators want to know whether a particular program is cost-effective and whether it accomplishes its stated goals. Programs are either successful or unsuccessful. Offender-clients either fail or succeed. How is the success or failure of programs and offender-clients measured? The first part of this chapter examines the criteria conventionally used to evaluate program effectiveness. Both objective and subjective criteria are considered in this discussion.

Because there are so many different kinds of offenders of various ages, there are numerous intervention, rehabilitation, and reintegration programs designed to assist them in meeting their diverse needs. We find that program success is subject to widely different interpretations, and many professionals use diffuse and even inconsistent criteria to evaluate whether a program's goals are attained. Because the success of programs often depends on the nature of the program clientele, some attention will be given to how clients are selected for inclusion in particular programs. Some programs engage in *creaming,* a process in which only the most low-risk and eligible offenders are included. Thus, some bias exists at the outset favoring program success. If only the most desirable clients are included, more favorable results will be expected, compared with those programs that include more dangerous and higher risk clientele.

Recidivism is an important measure of program success or failure. Therefore, considerable attention is devoted to describing recidivism and its many varieties. Recidivism is examined in the context of both juvenile and adult probationers and parolees. Probationer recidivism is compared with parolee recidivism to determine any significant differences. What kinds of offenders are more likely to recidivate, and under what types of conditions? What factors are useful in decreasing recidivism? Recidivism seems to fluctuate among probationers and parolees according to various program conditions. Which program conditions seem most likely to reduce recidivism? The chapter concludes with an examination of attitudes expressed by probationers and parolees themselves about their reasons for recidivating.

PROGRAM EVALUATION: HOW DO WE KNOW PROGRAMS ARE EFFECTIVE?

Program evaluation is the process of assessing any corrections intervention or program for the purpose of determining its effectiveness in achieving manifest goals. Program evaluation investigates the nature of organizational intervention strategies, counseling, interpersonal interactions, staff quality, expertise, and education, and the success or failure experiences of clients served by any program. Several examples illustrate what is meant by program evaluation.

Example 1. Corrections officials might say that one reason criminals get into trouble initially is that they lack social skills and abilities enabling them to have normal human relationships. Whether we agree or disagree with this statement is irrelevant. The fact is, some researchers believe it. In fact, some researchers engage in experiments to determine whether improving the level of social skill development and interpersonal abilities will modify behaviors to the extent that the offenders will be less likely to engage in criminal behavior in the future. Sue McCulloch (1993) studied the impact of a Social Skills and Human Relationships Training Program for sex offenders in Queensland, Australia. A Self-Evaluation Scale and a Social Reinforcement Survey Schedule were administered to six sex offenders who participated in the project. A personal history interview was conducted with each.

The program consisted of several small-group sessions with a counselor and interventionist. The program's subject matter consisted of short-term courses on interpersonal behaviors as well as educational information. Measures were taken for all six offenders at the beginning and end of the program, and the scores on these different instruments were compared. Results showed marked improvement in the level of offender social skills and human relations development as well as more favorable self-images and self-evaluations. Some questions arose concerning the applicability of this experience to subsequent reintegration of these offenders into their communities and whether they would refrain from future sex offending. Even though this was a small sample, McCulloch (1993) was impressed with the intervention strategy enough to recommend it for more general application to Australia's sex offender population. *The program evaluation consisted of comparing scores before and after the intervention (coursework and small-group sessions) had occurred. Score differences in favorable directions indicated program promise for reducing recidivism among sex offenders.*

Example 2.   Some juvenile corrections officials may think that youths with severe psychological dysfunction and behavioral problems and aggressiveness are more violence prone and tend to become violent offenders. If this aggressiveness can be curbed, and if these behavior problems and severe psychological impairments can be remedied some way, then it follows that perhaps these youths' propensity toward violent conduct can be controlled or decreased. Again, whatever we believe is irrelevant. Hagan and King (1992) studied 55 youths classified as suffering from severe psychological dysfunction, various behavioral problems, and extraordinary aggressiveness. These youths had been incarcerated in the Intensive Treatment Unit of Ethan Allen School, a state juvenile correctional facility in Wales.

The intervention program utilized a positively based behavior modification strategy that included family and group therapy and instruction in independent living skills. A two-year follow-up was used to determine whether any change in these youths' behavior had occurred. Hagan and King found that one-third of the youths received future state correctional placement (failed), one-third had no further convictions (a high success level), and one-third had further convictions but their offending was nonviolent and less severe, and they were not incarcerated in state facilities (moderately successful). *The program evaluation consisted of contrasting the behaviors of these youths during the two-year follow-up period and determining whether there were any behavioral changes as indicated by rearrests or reincarcerations.* Hagan and King (1992) believed that their findings that two-thirds of the youths either engaged in no further violent offending or engaged in less violent conduct supported the therapeutic efficacy of the Intensive Treatment Unit Experiment.

Example 3. Investigators interested in electronic monitoring and home confinement as sound reintegrative strategies designed to deter criminal conduct may believe that clients who experience home confinement will be less likely to reoffend. Again, whether we agree with this point of view or argument is irrelevant. Maxfield and Baumer (1992) studied the effectiveness of electronically monitored home detention in Indianapolis, Indiana for 224 defendants between 1988 and 1989. One of their aims was to determine whether this electronic monitoring with home confinement acted as a sufficient deterrent to further criminal conduct. These 224 defendants were carefully screened, low-risk, relatively stable property offenders. Most offenders completed the program without incurring any program infractions or new arrests. Maxfield and Baumer believed that successful completion of monitored detention was more likely if these persons had suitable living arrangements, including parents or a spouse, and possessed a criminal record consisting of only minor offenses. *The program evaluation consisted of monitoring the behaviors of these 224 clients during the period of monitored detention and determining the incidence of new offending. An absence of new offending was indicative of program success in this instance.* These researchers were careful to indicate that program effectiveness in their study depended heavily on careful defendant screening, organization, and effective management of the monitoring and close coordination between judges, prosecutors, and probation personnel.

Example 4. Some researchers think that if juveniles are subjected to positive peer experiences while incarcerated in state industrial schools, they will have a greater chance at reintegrating into mainstream society when paroled. Whether we believe this view is irrelevant. The Minnesota Corrections Department (1972) conducted a study of 242 boys who were transferred from the Minnesota State Training School for Boys in 1969 and placed in a Positive Peer Culture, guided-group interaction program. The program attempts to reverse the effects of the delinquent subculture by substituting positive sets of values and goals through peer pressure and staff guidance. The method is the basic treatment modality for the institution and consists of group meetings five nights per week, 90 minutes in length. During these meetings, group leaders serve to redirect, guide, and bring into focus problem areas that might be contributing to a juvenile's difficulties and then allows the group to work on the problem.

During 1969, 219 boys were paroled. A follow-up disclosed that 51 percent (111 boys) had their parole programs revoked because of one or more program violations. But the 49 percent success rate was regarded as positive by these researchers. Although no official standards presently exist to define good or bad recidivism rates, informal standards suggest that recidivism of 30 percent or higher among any given sample is considered high recidivism. However, recidivism rates of two-thirds or 65 percent or higher are commonly observed for both juvenile and adult parolees 12 months or more following their initial release. Thus, the 49 percent success rate was considered good by investigators, because it is substantially lower than 65 percent. *The program evaluation consisted of comparing the recidivism rates of these juvenile parolees with the standards observed in other comparable jurisdictions. Since all youths in the Minnesota facility received the Positive Peer Culture program, no control groups were available with which to compare these parolees. In the present case, the researchers compared their parolee successes with a comparable program in California, the James Marshall Treatment Program, a 90-day intervention program, and their results were similar.*

Some Recommended Outcome Measures

The American Probation and Parole Association (APPA) has been involved in a longitudinal investigation and survey to determine various alternative outcome measures for assessing intermediate punishment program effectiveness. The APPA Board of Directors consists of probation and parole administrators, probation and parole line staff, and representatives from various affiliate organizations (American Correctional Association, American Jail Association) throughout the United States and Canada. The APPA distributed a survey instrument to all APPA board members and prefaced their questionnaire with the following:

> Assume that your department is going to be evaluated by an outside evaluator. The results of the evaluation will determine the level of funding for the next fiscal year. What outcome measure(s) would you want the evaluator to use in "measuring" the success of your program(s)? What outcome measure(s) would you not want the evaluator to use in the evaluation?

The survey yielded a response from 30 different board members. This was a response rate of 31 percent, since survey instruments were originally sent to over 90 persons. Table 16.1 shows the relative rankings and ratings of the top 23 criteria cited by these board members as alternative outcome measures they would like to see used.

An inspection of Table 16.1 shows that the amount of restitution collected tops the list of criteria preferred by these board members. Logically, this would be a direct empirical and tangible indicator of agency effectiveness. As we have seen in previous chapters, community-based programs are increasingly incorporating elements that heighten offender accountability. Making restitution to victims or to the community is an increasingly common program element. Employment is also a key agency goal of many community-based agencies. Thus, many board members selected "number of offenders employed" as another preferred indicator of agency effectiveness. Other criteria in the top five included technical violations, alcohol/drug test results, and new arrests. Possibly because agencies have more effective monitoring mechanisms in place and improved supervision styles, it is less likely for program clients to engage in technical program violations, fail in drug/alcohol test results, and be rearrested for new offenses.

When asked which measures were *not* preferred for program evaluation, the responding board members cited 12 program components. These are shown in Table 16.2.

Table 16.2 shows that board members at least would downplay recidivism rates, revocation rates, technical violations, and new arrests as outcome measures

**TABLE 16.1 Alternative Outcome Measures from APPA Board
of Director Survey: Top 23**

Measure	No. of Board Members Selecting Measure
Amount of restitution collected	10
Number of offenders employed	10
Technical violations	9
Alcohol and drug test results	9
New arrests	8
Fines and fees collected	7
Number completed supervision	6
Hours community service	6
Number sessions of treatment	5
Number and ratio revocations	5
Percent financial obligations collected	5
Employment stability/days employed	5
New arrests: crime type/seriousness	4
Meeting needs of offenders	4
Family stability	4
Education attainment	4
Costs/benefits/services/savings	4
Days alcohol/drug free	4
Number of treatment referrals	3
Time between technical violations	3
Marital stability	3
Wages/taxes paid	3
Compliance with court orders	3

Source: Harry N. Boone, Jr. (1994b). "Recommended Outcome Measures for
Program Evaluation: APPA's Board of Directors Survey Results." *APPA Perspectives,*
18:19.

of program effectiveness. Boone (1994b:20) said that "there was considerable confusion among the 30 respondents as to exactly what outcome measures should or should not be used to evaluate their respective programs." Interestingly, the top four outcome measures cited by board members in Table 16.2 are either direct or indirect recidivism measures. Ideally, more effective programs have lower recidivism rates than less effective programs. All agencies want to exhibit low rates of recidivism among their clientele. Any agency disclosing a recidivism rate of 10 percent or less would most certainly be considered for federal or private funding, since the program would be demonstrably successful. But such low recidivism rates are hard to obtain in most agencies. Again, an informal standard of 30 percent has existed for several decades. This 30 percent standard suggests that programs with recidivism rates of 30 percent or less are successful programs, while those with rates above 30 percent are not successful. Some observers use the word *failure* to describe such programs.

TABLE 16.2 Outcome Measures Not to Use to Measure Program Success

Measure	No. of Board Members Selecting Measure
Recidivism	8
Revocation rates	6
Technical violations	5
New arrests	4
Single measure	2
Public/media perception	2
New conviction	2
Number of positive drug tests	2
Cost of services/efficiency	2
Number of contacts	2
Number of clients	2
Client evaluation	2

Source: Harry N. Boone, Jr. (1994b). "Recommended Outcome Measures for Program Evaluation: APPA's Board of Directors Survey Results." *APPA Perspectives,* **18**:20.

In many respects, it is unfair to label any particular program as a "failure" or a "success" on the basis of demonstrated client recidivism rates (Matthews, Boone, and Fogg, 1994). Every agency deals with a different kind of offender—sex offenders, property offenders, chronic delinquents, persistent property offenders, shoplifters, robbers, and thieves. For instance, Wilson and Vito (1990) describe samples of persistent felony offenders they investigated in Kentucky. Designing intervention programs that will decrease the chronicity of such offenders is probably an impossible task, since these offenders persist in their offending, no matter what types of intervention strategies are applied. Also, different time periods are used to gauge recidivism. Some standards are a year following program commencement, while other standards are two or three years. Some standards are even shorter, as short as three or six months. With such different time dimensions over which to determine recidivism of clientele, a meaningful discussion of recidivism in any general sense is of little or no consequence when assessing the merits and weaknesses of particular programs.

Another factor is that many program and agency personnel wish to include those offenders most likely to succeed in those programs. However, these clientele may not be the ones who need the particular program intervention. Ideally, if jail- or prison-bound offenders, and both high- and low-risk types, are program targets, then any program that reduces recidivism among these offenders will deserve more careful consideration and should be given greater funding priority. But many community-based intervention programs are designed to work with low-risk offenders as a means of keeping them integrated in their communities. These persons are usually first-offenders with little likelihood of reoffending. Unfortunately, there is a net-widening effect that occurs with the establishment of such programs. This ef-

About 65 percent of all probationers and parolees will be rearrested for new offenses within a 36-month period following their probation or parole programs. (Photo Researchers, Inc.)

fect is that many persons who often would be placed on standard probation or whose cases might otherwise be dismissed as a matter of prosecutorial priority might find their way into community programs designed to keep them from reentering the criminal justice system. Thus, some persons are served by programs when these persons do not need to be in these programs. And, those programs that select only those offenders most likely to succeed—offenders with jobs, stable families, good education, middle-class social standing, first-offenders, low-risk offenders—actually create a clientele milieu with a predictably low "failure rate." This is called *creaming.*

BALANCING PROGRAM OBJECTIVES AND OFFENDER NEEDS

The major objectives of community-based probation and parole programs for juveniles and adults are summarized as follows:

1. Facilitating offender reintegration.
2. Continuing offender punishment.
3. Heightening offender accountability.

4. Ensuring community protection or safety.
5. Promoting offender rehabilitation.
6. Improving offender skills and coping mechanisms.
7. Resolving offender social and psychological problems.
8. Alleviating jail and prison overcrowding.
9. Monitoring offender behaviors.
10. Reducing offender chemical dependencies.
11. Collecting fines, restitution payments, and other fees.
12. Enforcing the law, including community service orders.
13. Employing support personnel, corrections workers, and professionals and paraprofessionals.
14. Producing low rates of recidivism among agency clientele.
15. Coordinating and networking agency tasks and functions with other community agencies.
16. Justifying agency budget.

This list is by no means exhaustive. Many functions or objectives above overlap. The fact is that agencies are multifaceted, striving to achieve diverse goals or aims. Many of these organizational aims are mentioned by Petersilia and Turner (1993). She notes the following agency goals with accompanying performance indicators:

1. *Assessing offender's suitability for placement* (performance indicators = accuracy and completeness of PSIs; timeliness of revocation and termination hearings; validity of classification/prediction instrument; percent of offenders receiving recommended sentence or violation action; and percent of offenders recommended for community who violate).

2. *Enforcing court-ordered sanctions* (performance indicators = number of arrests and technical violations during supervision; percentage of ordered payments collected; number of hours/days community service performed; number of favorable discharges; numbers of days employed in vocational education or school; and drug-free and/or alcohol-free days during supervision).

3. *Protecting the community* (performance indicators = number and type of supervision contacts; number and type of arrests during supervision; number and type of technical violations during supervision; number of absconders during supervision).

4. *Assisting offenders to change* (performance indicators = number of times attending treatment/work programming; employment during supervision; number of arrests and/or technical violations during supervision; number drug-free and/or alcohol-free days during supervision; and attitude change).

5. *Restoring crime victims* (performance indicators = payment of restitution; extent of victim satisfaction with service and department).

Thus, these programs exist for a variety of reasons. Some of these reasons are totally unrelated to offender needs, such as employment of agency personnel and justifying the agency budget. It is important to coordinate agency processes with offender needs as a way of demonstrating program effectiveness. Petersilia and Turner (1993) have reduced almost all of these agency functions to items that can be counted. We can count the amount of collected fine payments and restitution.

We can count numbers of days alcohol free or drug free. We can count numbers of rearrests, numbers of favorable discharges, numbers of days employed. There are many intangibles, however, that cannot be counted. We do not know, for instance, whether offender familial relations are actually improving. We might count the number of 911 calls, however, for reports of spousal abuse or other forms of familial conflict for various offender-clients. This might be a negative gauge of positive family functioning. Also, we do not know whether true psychological changes are occurring within any particular offender-client. We only know that these offender-clients have been provided with the means for change. We don't know for sure whether changes actually occur in designated or targeted program areas.

When PSIs are prepared for any offender, POs make a point of identifying problem areas that could or should be addressed by subsequent programming. These are identified as offender needs. We have an array of risk-needs instruments that assess both offenders' degree of dangerousness and any special needs they might exhibit. When inmates are classified upon entry into jails or prisons, they are usually assessed with either self-administered or other types of paper-and-pencil tests or devices that seek to determine their most appropriate placement, whether it is a particular custody level or rehabilitation/educational/vocational/counseling program. In Virginia, for instance, inmates with low reading levels are tracked to special educational classes designed to improve their literacy levels (Hawk et al., 1993). It is logical to assume that if the literacy levels of inmates can be improved, then their chances for employment are also improved. Completing job application forms requires a minimum amount of literacy, for example. Offenders with psychological or social adjustment problems may benefit from individual or group therapy or various forms of sensitivity training.

What about alcohol or drug usage? In prison, there is a low likelihood that alcoholism or drug dependency will continue to be problematic for inmates. We know that inmates have access to drugs in most prisons or jails. But what can we do now that will help offenders cope with their community environment when they are subsequently released from prison? If alcohol or drug dependencies contributed to their crimes, then what coping mechanisms can be provided these offenders while they are institutionalized? Drug and alcohol dependency classes are provided. But do these classes prevent subsequent recurrences of alcohol and drug dependency? Parole boards in most jurisdictions face offenders every day who are chronic recidivists with drug and alcohol dependencies. They ask prospective parolees, "Did you participate in Alcoholics Anonymous while in prison?" Prospective parolee: "Yes." Parole board: "But you have been convicted of a new crime, and when you were caught, you were drunk. What happened?" Prospective parolee: "I got in with the wrong crowd," or "I had a setback," or "I had some personal problems," or "I just couldn't pass up a drink," or "I went along with the crowd for old time's sake." Some offenders never escape the problems that contributed to their criminal activity, no matter how much training, coursework, therapy, or counseling they receive.

Any community-based corrections program attempts to provide useful interventions that will assist offender-clients in various ways. Volunteers and paraprofessionals assist offender-clients in filling out job application forms, in reading programs, or in other reintegrative or rehabilitative activities. Meeting diverse offender needs is viewed as a primary way of reducing or eliminating recidivism. And recidivism is probably the most direct way of measuring program effectiveness, despite other program components, aims, or alternative outcome measures.

RECIDIVISM DEFINED

A conceptual Tower of Babel exists regarding recidivism. Numerous investigations of this phenomenon have been conducted, although no consensus exists about the meaning of the term. Criminologists and other experts can recite lengthy lists of characteristics that describe recidivists. But describing recidivists and using those characteristics as effective predictors of recidivism are two different matters. For example, if a parole board uses a salient factor score to predict an offender's degree of success on parole, some inmates will be refused parole because their scores suggest they are "poor risks." At the same time, other inmate scores may indicate they are "good risks." The poor risks are denied parole, while the good risks are granted it. However, among the poor risks are inmates who will never recidivate, while among the good risks (who eventually become parolees) are serious recidivists. These have been labeled respectively as false positives and false negatives, discussed at length in Chapter 3. Parole boards are interested in minimizing the frequency of both false positives and false negatives.

When a false positive is denied parole, certain moral, ethical, and legal issues are raised about continuing to confine otherwise harmless people. When a false negative is granted parole and commits a new, serious offense, the public is outraged, the parole board is embarrassed, and the integrity of test developers and the validity of prediction instruments are called into question. Judges who impose probation instead of incarceration or incarceration instead of probation are subject to similar attacks on similar grounds. Numerical scales are often used as more objective criteria for probation or parole decision making. It is not necessarily the case that these scales are superior to personal judgments by judges or parole boards. But references to numbers seem to objectify early release or probation-granting decisions compared with visual appraisals of offenders and subjective interpretations of their backgrounds contained in PSIs.

Several problems have been identified relating to recidivism and its measurement. A brief listing of some of the more common problems follows:

1. The time interval between commencing a probation or parole program and recidivating is different from one study to the next. Some studies use six months, while others use a year, two years, or five years (Boone, 1994a:13; Langan and Cunniff, 1992; Smith and Akers, 1993).
2. There are at least 14 different meanings of recidivism (Maltz, 1984). Comparing one definition of recidivism with another is like comparing apples with oranges.
3. Recidivism is often dichotomized rather than gradated. Thus, people either recidivate

or they don't recidivate. No variation exists to allow for *degrees of seriousness of reoffending of any type* (Boone, 1994a:13).

4. Recidivism rates are influenced by multiple factors, such as the intensity of supervised probation or parole, the numbers of face-to-face visits between POs and their clients, and even the rate of prison construction (Ekland-Olson and Kelly, 1993; Kelly and Ekland-Olson, 1991).

5. Recidivism rates may be indicative of program failures rather than client failures (Waldo and Griswold, 1979).

6. Recidivism accounts only for *official* rule or law violations; self-reported information indicates that higher rates of recidivism may actually exist compared with those that are subsequently reported and recorded (Waldo and Griswold, 1979).

7. Considerable client variation exists, as well as numerous programmatic variations. Depending on the client population under investigation, recidivism is more or less significant.

8. Policy shifts in local and state governments may change how recidivism is used or defined as well as the amount of recidivism observed in given jurisdictions (Maltz and McCleary, 1977).

A word of caution is in order regarding the seemingly contradictory study findings cited in Box 16.1. In all fairness to the authors of those studies, almost all concluded by saying that additional research is needed and/or implied that their studies are not to be taken as absolute proof of recidivism. Most, if not all, of these authors cited their own methodological and theoretical weaknesses or highlighted other study deficiencies. But despite these standard research precautions and safeguards, some corrections officials, parole boards, and judges are influenced by the kinds of things these findings suggest. Improper policy decisions are sometimes based on a study that uses an unusual methodological strategy or definition (Maltz, 1984). Regardless of the variation among studies regarding characteristics associated with recidivism, how useful are these characteristics in predicting recidivism? Can a profile of the typical recidivist be drawn? Can parole boards see potential recidivists in their interview proceedings?

We know, or at least we think we know, that recidivists tend to be male, black, younger, less educated, and have lengthy prior records. In fact, having a lengthy prior record appears to be most consistently related to recidivism. Therefore, should we make it official judicial or parole board policy *not* to grant probation or parole to younger, less educated, black males with lengthy prior records? No. These are aggregate characteristics and do not easily lend themselves to individualized probation or parole decision making.

One continuing problem is that while these and other characteristics describe the general category of recidivists (whomever they may be), these characteristics are also found among many nonrecidivists. Thus, based on relevant information about offenders, prediction measures must be devised and tested to improve their validity (Gottfredson and Gottfredson, 1988:200). A related problem is determining whether recidivism has occurred. This means some degree of agreement needs to be established concerning what recidivism does and does not mean.

Existing measures of recidivism complicate rather than simplify its definition. It is important to pay attention to how recidivism is conceptualized in the research

---

BOX 16.1
A Focus on Recidivism

A Recidivist is a Recidivist is a Recidivist . . .

Below is a list of recidivist characteristics. Each has some support from the research literature. Yet each characteristic, considered singly or in combination with some of the others, lacks predictive utility.

1. Men are more likely than females to recidivate (Delaware Executive Department, 1984; Greenfeld, 1985; Grenier and Roundtree, 1987; McReynolds, 1987; Deborah Wilson, 1985).

2. Younger felons are more likely to recidivate than older felons (Chown and Davis, 1986; Clarke, Lin, and Wallace, 1988; Clayton and Carr, 1987; Delaware Executive Department, 1984; Linster, Lattimore, and Visher, 1990; McCord and Tremblay, 1992; Rutherford, 1992; White, 1992; Deborah Wilson, 1985).

3. Recidivism declines with advancing age (Clarke and Crum, 1985; Delaware Executive Department, 1984; Shover and Thompson, 1992; Tunnell, 1992).

4. Higher recidivism rates occur among those with less formal education compared with those with more formal education (Fabelo, 1992; Jordan and Jones, 1988; McReynolds, 1987; Roundtree, Edwards, and Parker, 1984; Shover and Thompson, 1992; Stevens, 1986; White, 1992).

5. The longer the time served in prison, the more likely a person will be to recidivate when released (Clarke and Harrison, 1992; Delaware Executive Department, 1984; U.S. Sentencing Commission, 1990; White, 1992).

6. Most recidivism occurs within the first three years of release from prison or placement on probation (Beck and Shipley, 1987; Petersilia, 1985a; U.S. Sentencing Commission, 1990).

7. The greater the number of prior arrests, the more likely the recidivism (Broadhurst and Maller, 1991; Ely, 1989; Florida Department of Corrections, 1992b; Roundtree, Edwards, and Parker, 1984; U.S. Sentencing Commission, 1990).

8. Violent offenders on parole are rearrested more often than nonviolent offenders on parole (Chown and Davis, 1986; Visher, Lattimore, and Linster, 1991).

9. Blacks tend to recidivate at a higher rate compared with whites and others (Beck and Shipley, 1987; Delaware Executive Department, 1984; Florida Department of Corrections, 1992; McReynolds, 1987; Minnesota Corrections Department, 1972).

10. The earlier offenders begin their criminal careers, the more likely the recidivism (Deborah Wilson, 1985).

11. Felony probationers are more likely than parolees to recidivate because they usually have longer probationary periods to serve compared with parole lengths (Roundtree, Edwards, and Parker, 1984).

12. Recidivism decreases as participation in furloughs, work study, and other prerelease activities increase (Bank et al., 1991; Claggett et al., 1992; Eckert et al., 1987; LeClair, 1985, 1990; Liu, 1993; Segall, Wilson, and Allen, 1991; Van Stelle, Mauser, and Moberg, 1994; Vito, 1989).

13. Property offenders are more likely to recidivate compared with violent offenders (Wallerstedt, 1984).

14. Those offenders with previous stable employment records recidivate less frequently compared with offenders with less stable employment records (Bahn and Davis, 1991; Eisenberg, 1985b; Finn, 1992a; Genevie et al., 1983; Jurik, 1983).

15. Prisoners with more disciplinary reports while incarcerated recidivate more than those paroled who have fewer or no disciplinary reports filed against them (U.S. Bureau of Justice Statistics, 1992; Eisenberg, 1985b).

16. Releasees who have a record of one or more juvenile arrests or convictions will re-

cidivate more than those releasees without juvenile arrests or convictions (Eisenberg, 1985b; Wallerstedt, 1984; Boudouris, 1983).

17. The younger the age when a person is released, the more likely the recidivism (Wallerstedt, 1984; White, 1992).

18. Parolees who recidivate do so for similar crimes for which they were originally imprisoned (Oregon Crime Analysis Center, 1984; Troia, 1990).

19. Substance and alcohol abusers have higher rates of recidivism compared with those who do not use drugs or alcohol (Clarke, Lin, and Wallace, 1988; Eisenberg, 1985b; Lockhart, 1990; Los Angeles County Countrywide Criminal Justice Coordination Committee, 1992; McReynolds, 1987; Smith and Polsenberg, 1992).

20. Religious experiences lower recidivism rates of parolees (*Prison Fellowship,* 1991).

21. Offenders with mental illnesses are more likely to recidivate (Gee et al., 1993; Harris, Rice, and Quinsey, 1993).

22. The more the probation supervision, the less the recidivism (Program Resources Center, 1988).

23. Psychopaths have higher recidivism rates than nonpsychopaths (Chown and Davis, 1986; Harris, Rice, and Cormier, 1991).

24. Parolees and probationers have similar recidivism rates (Wilson, Denton, and Williams, 1987).

BUT,

1. Recidivism is not related to age when paroled (Beck and Shipley, 1987; Blumstein, Cohen, and Farrington, 1988; Klein, 1987).

2. Persons paroled for violent crimes are less likely to recidivate compared with persons paroled for property crimes (Beck and Shipley, 1987; Boudouris, 1983; Clarke and Harrison, 1992; Wallerstedt, 1984).

3. The longer the time served in prison has no effect on recidivism ((Beck and Shipley, 1987; Lattimore and Baker, 1992).

4. Race and recidivism are not related (Roundtree, Edwards, and Parker, 1984; Boudouris, 1983).

5. Men do not recidivate any more frequently than women (Roundtree, Edwards, and Parker, 1984).

6. Participation or nonparticipation in prison rehabilitative or vocational/technical programs has no influence on recidivism (Bleick and Abrams, 1987; Clarke and Harrison, 1992; Eisenberg, 1985b; EMT Group Inc., 1990; Gottfredson and Taylor, 1985; New Jersey Juvenile Delinquency Commission, 1991; Troia, 1991).

7. An inmate's good time credits earned in prison are not related to recidivism (Delaware Executive Department, 1984).

8. Drug abuse and recidivism are not related (Beto, 1990; University of Hawaii at Manoa, 1984).

9. Employment record is unrelated to recidivism (Rauma and Berk, 1987; Roundtree, Edwards, and Parker, 1984).

10. Parolees who recidivate commit offenses different from the ones they originally committed (Tunnell, 1992; Wallerstedt, 1984).

11. The intensity of program supervision does not necessarily reduce recidivism rates (Clear, Harris, and Baird, 1992; Petersilia and Turner, 1990b; 1991).

12. The nature of the punishment and recidivism are not necessarily related (Clear, Harris, and Baird, 1992; Dubber, 1990; Stewart, Gruenewald, and Parker, 1992).

13. Schizophrenics are less likely to reoffend than nonschizophrenics (Rice and Harris, 1992).

14. Mentally ill offenders are no more likely to recidivate than those not having mental illness (Cooke, 1992; Teplin, 1992).

15. Community corrections clients do not differ in recidivism rates compared with prison inmates who have been paroled (Jones, 1991).

16. Felons are about as likely to recidivate as misdemeanants (van Alstyne, 1991).

17. The longer the period of confinement, the less likely the recidivism (Steiger and Dizon, 1991).

18. Age at first involvement with the criminal

justice system is unrelated to recidivism (Benda, 1987; Wooldredge, 1991a).

19. First-offenders tend to commit more violent crimes than persistent or chronic offenders (Wilson and Vito, 1986, 1990).

20. Probationers and parolees tend to have similar recidivism rates (Genevie et al., 1983; Neithercutt, 1987).

21. Shock incarceration has no influence on recidivism (Latessa and Vito, 1988; MacKenzie, 1991a, 1991b; Noonan and Latessa, 1987).

Reading these statements gives the impression that studies of recidivism are mixed and inconsistent in their conclusions. They *are* mixed and inconsistent. But there are several logical reasons for

this. First, each study examines a particular offender aggregate. The sample may consist of first-offender probationers, low-risk parolees who participate in GED programs, traffic or DUI offenders, former alcohol/drug abusers who have been paroled from a federal penitentiary, state correctional center inmates, work releasees, and released inmates with histories of mental illness. Furthermore, these studies are conducted using diverse methodologies. Sample sizes vary from less than 5 or 6 to 100,000 or more. Adding to the diversity of samples and databases is the fact that definitions of recidivism vary among studies.

literature, since probation or parole program failures or successes are measured by **recidivism rates** (Deborah Wilson, 1985:160–161; McCarthy and McCarthy, 1984:116–118; Petersilia, 1987a:89). And, a general standard has emerged among professionals that a failure rate above 30 percent means that a probation or parole program is ineffective (Allen et al., 1985:260–261; Vito, 1986a, 1986b:17). Ineffective in what sense? Reducing crime? Rehabilitating offenders? Both?

Recidivism means program failure. Or does it? As earlier chapters have indicated, a wide variety of probation and parole programs are available to the courts and corrections officials for many different kinds of offenders. One common problem faced by all programs is that experts have trouble matching the right programs with the right clientele. We have much descriptive information about recidivists. Numerous evaluation studies are conducted annually of various offender programs and virtually all strategies for dealing with offenders are examined and reexamined. No matter the cure proposed, the illness remains. Treatments are rarely pure, however, and therefore, their evaluations are necessarily complicated (Gottfredson and Gottfredson, 1988:197). Probationers or parolees who violate one or more terms of their probation or parole, regardless of the type of program examined, are considered recidivists. This chapter is about recidivism among probationers and parolees. Recidivism in the general case is examined, and recidivists are described. Also examined here are some of the factors contributing to recidivism and strategies officials use to combat it.

Barry Nidorf, chief probation officer for Los Angeles County, takes issue with using recidivism as a measure of program failure (Petersilia, 1987a:89). He says that if rehabilitation is the probation or parole program goal, then recidivism rates seem appropriate measures of program success or failure.

However, if control and community protection are [program] goals, then a "success" might be viewed as the identification and quick revocation of persons who are committing crimes. After all, the police are in the business of surveillance and control, and they judge an "arrest" a success, whereas we deem it a "failure." If community safety is the primary goal, then perhaps an arrest and revocation should be seen as a success and not a failure. (Petersilia, 1987a:89).

Nidorf's argument is persuasive, in that persons should consider how they wish program success or failure to be evaluated. Recidivism seems relevant when we are interested in the rehabilitative value of programs, but many programs involving intensive supervision of parolees and probationers seem focused primarily on crime control (Petersilia, 1987a:89).

Some of the different ways of operationalizing recidivism are

1. Rearrest;
2. Parole or probation revocation or unsatisfactory termination;
3. Technical parole or probation rule violations;
4. Conviction for a new offense while on parole or probation;
5. Return to prison;
6. Having a prior record and being rearrested for a new offense;
7. Having a prior record and being convicted for a new offense;
8. Any new commitment to a jail or prison for 60 days or more;
9. Presence of a new sentence exceeding one year for any offense committed during a five-year parole follow-up;
10. Return of released offenders to custody of state correctional authorities;
11. Return to jail;
12. Reincarceration;
13. The use of drugs or alcohol by former drug or alcohol abusers; and
14. Failure to complete educational or vocational/technical course or courses in or out of prison or jail custody. (Maltz, 1984)

The most commonly used conceptualizations include *rearrests, reconvictions, revocations of parole or probation, reincarcerations,* and *technical program violations.*

Rearrests

As a measure of recidivism, **rearrest** is frequently used in evaluation studies of parole/probation program effectiveness, although rearrests are highly misleading (Cadigan, 1991; Chavaria, 1992; Jones, 1991; Los Angeles County Countrywide Criminal Justice Coordination Committee, 1992; Petersilia and Turner, 1993; Smith and Akers, 1993). The most obvious flaw is that it is uncertain whether offenders have actually committed new offenses. Sometimes, if a crime has been committed in the neighborhood in which particular clients are residing in a halfway house, *and* if the crime is similar in nature to the crime(s) for which the ex-offenders were previously convicted, detectives and police may look up the offenders and interview them. Since offender associations with police authorities are inherently strained anyway, it is likely that police would interpret an offender's nervousness as a sign of guilt. Thus, the offender might be subject to rearrest based on the suspicions of officers. The crucial element is whether the officers have probable cause to justify the client's arrest. The **totality of circumstances** may be such that officers may in good faith believe they have reasonable suspicion that the client has committed a crime or has guilty knowledge. They have wide discretion to question ex-offenders in an effort to learn more about the crime and the potential culpability of those they interview (Abrahamse et al., 1991:142–143). In New York, for instance, whenever an inmate is granted parole, the supervising PO brings the parolee's fingerprints and criminal record to the local police precinct where the offender resides. Thus, police are notified of the parolee's return to their community. Constitutional safeguards exist, of course, to protect all citizens from unreasonable arrests by police. However, law enforcement officers find it relatively easy to justify their actions to the court when dealing with former offenders and parolees, even when the constitutional rights of ex-offenders have been infringed.

Another flaw associated with using rearrests to measure recidivism is that ex-offenders may be released after police determine that they are not likely suspects. However, a rearrest is interpreted as recidivism by some researchers, and this means program failure. Rearrested offenders are not necessarily taken to jail or returned to prison; they may continue in their present probation or parole programs. Of course, it is also possible that the ex-offender did, indeed, commit a new crime. But this must be proved, beyond a reasonable doubt, in a court of law. Some jurisdictions use the **preponderance of evidence** standard for probation/parole revocations. This standard is less stringent than "beyond a reasonable doubt."

In New York, for instance, many probationers/parolees adjourn their revocation hearings pending the outcome of their court cases. If they are acquitted of criminal charges, this obviously impacts their probation/parole revocation process favorably. If the result of a trial is a conviction for the probationer/parolee, then a revocation hearing on the violation will not be conducted. A certificate of disposition would suffice as evidence of a conviction and sentence. However, not all parolees or probationers who are rearrested for new crimes are prosecuted for those crimes. They may instead be sent to prison (Megargee and Bohn, 1979:151). Because of the *Morrissey v. Brewer* (1972) decision, however, two hearings (i.e., one to determine probable cause and the other an actual revocation proceeding) are required before the paroling authority can summarily revoke parole.

There is a vast discrepancy between the number of arrests by police and the number of convictions. The *Uniform Crime Reports (UCR),* compiled by the Federal Bureau of Investigation, annually presents much statistical material about the prevalence of crime in the United States. One statistic involves those **cleared by arrest,** meaning that someone has been arrested for the reported crime. This does not mean that any given arrest will be followed by a conviction, however. For instance, it has been reported that the FBI clearance rate for crimes is about 26 percent, taking into account the fact that unreported crime probably cuts this figure in half (Walker, 1989). The conviction figures are even lower, with about one-fifth of all arrests resulting in convictions (Walker, 1989). It is apparent, then, that rearrest figures should be viewed with caution when evaluating the effectiveness of probation or parole programs and/or assessing offender rehabilitation. Hearings such as those provided under *Morrissey v. Brewer* (1972) should do much to objectify offender treatment and classification in matters of probation or parole revocation.

Reconvictions

Reconviction for a new offense is probably the most reliable indicator of recidivism as well as the most valid definition of it (Commonwealth of Virginia, 1991; Hairston, 1988; Jones, 1991). This represents that at least one new crime has been committed by an offender while on probation or parole, and the court has determined offender guilt beyond a reasonable doubt. Arguably, some experts may counter by saying that any failure to observe probation or parole conditions or placing oneself in a position of increasing the likelihood of arrest (e.g., violating curfew or associating with other offenders) is evidence that offender rehabilitation has not occurred. However, if crime control is of primary importance to those involved with probationers and parolees, then this argument fails to hold.

In a well-publicized study conducted by the **Rand Corporation,** approximately 16,500 men in 17 of California's largest counties were sentenced to either prison or probation (Petersilia et al., 1985:vi). Of these 16,500 men, a subsample of 1,672 felony probationers sentenced in Los Angeles and Alameda counties were tracked by researchers for 40 months, with recordings made of arrests, filings, convictions, and incarcerations. During the 40-month follow-up period, these researchers found that 65 percent of the probationers (1,087) were rearrested, and 51 percent (853) were reconvicted for one or more new offenses. Using the violent-nonviolent crime distinction, however, most (82 percent) of these new convictions involved nonviolent crimes (e.g., burglary and larceny). Rand researchers also found that 34 percent (568) were reincarcerated. Interestingly, 285 reconvictions (17 percent) resulted in a continuation of probation. Many of the reconvictions were for misdemeanor offenses, and PSI recommendations favored continuing probation.

In a study of recidivism that partially replicated the methodology of the Rand researchers, 317 felony probationers were studied from three Kentucky judicial districts in 1982 (Vito, 1986b:18). A 36-month follow-up disclosed that 22.1 percent (70) probationers were rearrested, 56 (17.7 percent) were reconvicted, and 37 were reincarcerated. About 7 percent (22) were reincarcerated as probation violators. Thus, the reincarceration figures in the Kentucky study were similar to those described by Rand.

In both studies, the issue of representativeness was raised by the researchers themselves. To what extent do these felons compare with those in other jurisdictions? And, did the 40-month follow-up in the Rand research make a significant difference in recidivism figures compared with the 36-month follow-up used by Kentucky investigators? Both Kentucky and California have implemented inten-

Probation or parole revocation doesn't always mean offenders will be jailed or imprisoned; in many jurisdictions, supervision by POs is intensified as a punishment. (Bernard Wolf/Monkmeyer Press)

sive supervision programs in response to prison overcrowding, and according to the 30 percent recidivism standard, both studies are well within the effective program range (Vito, 1986b:24).

Revocations of Parole or Probation

A **revocation action** relating to parole or probation is a decision to revoke a program because a parolee or probationer has violated one or more of the conditions associated with his or her supervision status. These conditions may be as harmless as missing a 10:00 P.M. curfew by five minutes or as serious as committing and being convicted of a new felony. Parole and probation officers have some discretionary authority when technical program violations are involved. They may overlook these incidents or report them. If the incident is a rearrest, the discretion passes to others such as arresting officers and prosecutors or is at least shared. If interpersonal relations between clients and POs have become strained, the PO may exaggerate the violation, regardless of how minor it may be.

Many factors influence a parole or probation revocation decision. Prison or jail overcrowding is one of them. The seriousness of the violation is also considered. A third factor is the recommendation of the PO. The main problem with a technical violation of parole or probation, however, is that often it is not related to crime of any kind. Therefore, a revocation based solely on technical criteria is irrelevant as a crime control strategy, unless it can be demonstrated empirically that failure to revoke would have resulted in a new crime being committed. And most, if not all, experts are not prepared to make such assertions at present. A revocation of probation or parole does not necessarily mean a return to prison or jail, however. Depending on the grounds for the revocation and other factors, an offender may be placed on probation or parole program with a higher control level. This is one reason why revocations of probation and parole cannot be equated directly with reincarceration.

Reincarcerations

The use of **reincarceration** as a measure of recidivism is as misleading as counting the numbers of rearrests and revocations among probationers and parolees. Reincarceration does not specify the type of incarceration. After probation is revoked, a probationer may be placed in a state or federal prison. After a federal parolee's status has been revoked, the parolee may be placed in a city or county jail for a short period rather than returned to the original federal prison.

A study of 9,549 offenders released from North Carolina state prisons in 1979 to 1980 showed that 32.7 percent (3,123) were returned to prison within 36 months of their release. However, 6.5 percent or 620 of these offenders were technical parole violators (Clarke and Crum, 1985). This figure is similar to the Kentucky study reported earlier, in which 6.9 percent of the reincarcerations were due to technical parole violations (Vito, 1986b).

The most frequent usages of recidivism include rearrests, reconvictions, and reincarcerations, although many other meanings have been given it. Arguably, it seems that the most relevant connotation applied to recidivism is a new conviction for a criminal offense as opposed to a simple rearrest or parole revocation for a technical program violation, both of which might be grounds for reincarceration. Reincarceration as a measure of recidivism is unreliable as well because it fails to distinguish between the true law breaker and the technical rule violator.

Technical Program Violations

Technical program violations might include curfew violation, failing a drug or alcohol urinalysis, failing to report employment or unemployment, failing to "check in" with the PO, failing to file a monthly status report in a timely way, or missing a group therapy meeting. Technical program violations are not crimes. However, they are legitimate conditions of probation or parole that are enforceable. Failure to comply with any one more of these program requirements (e.g., making restitution to victims, performing so many hours of community service) may be the basis for a possible probation or parole revocation action. Technical program violations have been used in more than a few studies as a measure of recidivism (Commonwealth of Virginia, 1991; Petersilia and Turner, 1993; Vito, 1986a, 1986b, 1987).

Although technical program violations have been used as recidivism measures, they are not particularly the best indicators. Prioritizing the most frequently used measures of recidivism, we might list reconvictions, reincarcerations, rearrests, and probation and parole revocations, in that order. Boone (1994a:17) has offered some suggestions to clarify the use of recidivism in program evaluation and research. He says that we ought to

1. Standardize the definition of recidivism;
2. Discourage the use of recidivism as the only outcome measure for community corrections programs;
3. Define alternative outcome measures for the evaluation of community corrections programs;
4. Educate interested stakeholders, including the general public, on the alternative measures; and
5. Encourage researchers, evaluators, and agency personnel to use appropriate outcome measures to evaluate program success/failure.

It is unlikely that Boone's first two suggestions will ever be implemented. There is simply too much variety among community corrections programs presently. Too many different vested interests have a stake in seeing recidivism conceptualized in different ways to fit neatly into particular funding priorities by showing program "successes." The public as well as stakeholders definitely need to be educated concerning various ways of measuring agency success or effectiveness. True, recidivism is not the only way successfulness or effectiveness should be measured. The last three of Boone's suggestions suggest both short- and long-range planning to allow for testing alternative outcome measures of program accomplishments.

RECIDIVIST OFFENDERS AND THEIR CHARACTERISTICS

A nationwide survey of 153,465 male felony offenders admitted to state prisons in 1979 was conducted and sponsored by the Bureau of Justice Statistics (Greenfeld, 1985). Of these, 94,134 or 61.3 percent had been incarcerated previously in either a state prison (58.7 percent), jail (28.4 percent), juvenile detention (9.5 percent), or federal and military facilities (3.4 percent). First offenders accounted for 38.7 percent or 59,331 new prison admissions.

Avertable and Nonavertable Recidivists

One of most innovative aspects of the study was the classification of recidivists with prior records of incarceration into avertable recidivists and nonavertable recidivists. **Avertable recidivists** are those offenders who would have still been in prison serving their original sentences in full at the time they were confined in 1979 for committing new offenses. **Nonavertable recidivists** are those offenders whose prior sentences would not have affected the commission of new crimes.

Examples of avertable and nonavertable recidivists using more recent sentencing periods are as follows. Suppose John Doe is a new 1989 prison admission. Doe was previously incarcerated in 1985 for armed robbery and given a 2-to-15 year sentence in a state prison. The parole board released Doe in 1988 whereupon Doe committed several burglaries. He was apprehended by police and eventually convicted of burglary in 1989. Had he still been in prison serving his entire 15-year sentence, those burglaries he committed never would have occurred. Doe is called an *avertable recidivist* because his crimes occurred within the maximum range of his original sentence (i.e., 1985–2000).

John Doe's sister, Jane, was convicted in 1981 of vehicular theft. Jane was sentenced to three years. Jane served her time and was eventually released. Jane obeyed the law for several years, but, in 1989, she was arrested for and convicted of stealing another automobile. Since she had already served the maximum sentence of three years for vehicular theft from 1981 to 1984, the maximum range of her original sentence no longer applied. Jane is classified as a *nonavertable recidivist.* Both she and her brother John are recidivists, because they are criminal offenders who have been convicted of previous crimes. But John's new crimes may have been averted had John been forced to serve his maximum sentence. This doesn't rule out the possibility that when John finally served the maximum 15-year sentence for armed robbery, he could commit new crimes and therefore be classified as a nonavertable recidivist like his sister.

The U.S. Department of Justice reported on a total of 200,189 criminal offenses. There were 50,899 nonavertable recidivists, 43,235 avertable recidivists, and 59,331 first-timers. The nonavertable recidivists accounted for 34.8 percent of the 200,189 crimes, avertable recidivists accounted for 24.4 percent of them, and first-offenders made up the remaining 40.8 percent. The significance of these data is twofold. First, nonavertable recidivists accounted for substantially higher percentages of crimes compared with avertable recidivists in virtually every crime category. Second, nonavertable recidivists compared with first-timers accounted for substantially smaller percentages of violent crimes and drug offenses but somewhat higher percentages of property crimes (with few exceptions). The percentage of offenses under the avertable recidivists category theoretically represents the proportion of crimes that would not have been committed by these offenders had they been obligated to serve out their entire sentences. This is somewhat misleading, however, because it ignores the fact that when many of these crimes were committed, other criminals were involved. Thus, the potential absence of the conspiratorial involvement of these avertable recidivists may or may not have prevented these crimes.

In the same study of 1979 state prisoners, selected characteristics of offenders were presented. Fifty percent or more of all 1979 admissions, regardless of admission type, were 26 years of age or less. Again, by age category, 1979 prison admissions decline with advancing age, with an average of 91 percent of all admissions being 40 or less. Two-thirds of all admissions had not completed high school, while about half had never married. Contrary to what might be expected, 63.2 percent of all 1979 admissions were employed full-time prior to their arrest. About one-third had one or more family members who had been previously incarcerated, and about the same proportion were under the influence of drugs when the offense occurred. About half of these admissions had been drinking at the time of the crime, and one-third were drunk.

At the time these offenders committed the crimes leading to their 1979 incarceration, about two-thirds of the avertable recidivists were on parole, while about one-fourth of the first-timers and nonavertable recidivists were on probation. An important point emphasized by these researchers is that nearly half of the recidivists who entered prison in 1979 were avertable, and they would have still been in prison during 1979 and unable to commit those new crimes if they had fully served the maximum term of their last confinement sentence (Greenfeld, 1985:6). While we don't know for sure, it is likely that had the avertable recidivists never been paroled, the prison inmate population would have risen to constitutionally unsafe limits. Overcrowding would be an even greater problem than it is presently. Thus, a trade-off of sorts occurs, in which the early release of future recidivists triggers more crime, but continuing their incarceration aggravates prison overcrowding. Little is known about how many inmates would not have been recidivists had they been paroled. Incapacitation is a feasible strategy for those who will become recidivists, but we have not devised measures as yet that will predict recidivism among prospective parolees with any acceptable degree of accuracy.

A more recent investigation of this issue is the work of Miranne and Geerken (1991). These investigators tested a seven-item scale devised by Peter Greenwood at the Rand Corporation (Chaiken and Chaiken, 1982; Greenwood, 1982). This scale purportedly differentiated between high- and low-rate offenders on the basis of their responses to seven items on a self-report instrument. The Miranne-Geerken study utilized a similar, but more elaborate, form of the original Greenwood instrument and obtained self-reports from 200 convicted inmates at facilities operated by the Orleans (Louisiana) Parish Criminal Sheriff in New Orleans. Essentially, their findings were similar to those of the Greenwood study. High-rate and low-rate offenders could be identified, although the findings were inconclusive to the extent that a change in public policy about selective incapacitation could not be substantiated. Miranne and Geerken (1991:514) do highlight an important consideration, however: "If high-rate offenders could be accurately identified and distinguished from low-rate offenders, sentencing the former to a longer period of incarceration than the latter could possibly increase cost-effectiveness" (and conceivably lower the crime rate by incarcerating the high-rate offenders for longer periods).

Public Policy and Recidivism

State legislators and policymakers have seized results such as these as foundations for arguments that mandatory and/or determinate sentencing and more rigorous parole criteria ought to be employed. In view of the sentencing reforms enacted by various states and current trends, these figures have apparently been persuasive or at least influential in changing sentencing policies and parole criteria.

The study conducted by the *Bureau of Justice Statistics (BJS)* is one of the larger surveys of recidivists and their characteristics. But each year, new waves of offenders enter jails and prisons. The profile changes, probably daily. But there are some general patterns that emerge, not only from this analysis but from other research as well. According to the *BJS* survey, using reconviction as an indicator of an adult recidivist, recidivists tend

1. To be male.
2. To be younger (under 30), and recidivism declines with advancing age.
3. To have an educational level equivalent to high school or less.
4. To have lengthy records of arrests and/or convictions.
5. To be under no correctional supervision when committing new offenses.
6. To have a record of juvenile offenses.
7. To commit crimes similar to those for which they were convicted previously.
8. To have alcohol or drug dependency problems associated with the commission of new offenses.
9. Not to commit progressively serious offenses compared with their prior records.
10. To be unmarried, widowed, or divorced.
11. To be employed, either full-time or part-time, when committing new offenses.

Again, these characteristics considered singly or in any combination make predictions of dangerousness or public risk difficult at best. Parole boards might use such information as supplemental when interviewing prospective parolees. Judges might consider such information when deciding the appropriate sentence for a convicted offender. The odds favor future offender behaviors consistent with previous offender behaviors. The odds increase as the number of characteristics associated with recidivists increases. But the certainty of recidivism for any specific offender can never be predicted in any absolute sense. Prediction schemes seem more effective when large numbers of offenders sharing similar characteristics are aggregated, but parole boards and judges make decisions about individual offenders, not groups of them (Morris and Miller, 1987:4).

PROBATIONERS, PAROLEES, AND RECIDIVISM

The immense interest of states in sentencing reforms directed away from rehabilitation and toward justice with greater certainty of punishment stems, in part, from public dissatisfaction with how the courts and corrections have dealt with offenders in recent decades. Recidivism spells failure to many citizens, and judicial leniency in sentencing, real or imagined, has contributed to a backlash of sorts. This backlash is similar to the public reaction to John Hinckley's acquittal on charges that he attempted to assassinate President Reagan, on the grounds that he was insane at the time the offense was committed. The insanity defense was quickly abolished in several states and vastly overhauled in others. This occurred despite the fact that the insanity defense is used in fewer than 1 percent of all criminal prosecutions and is successfully used in only a small fraction of those cases.

Alarming statistics stimulate public concern about parole and probation programs. The U.S. Department of Justice says that 65 percent of released prisoners will return to prison within two years, and most often within one year of release. Parole may hold down prison populations, but there may be a trade-off through increased street crime (Petersilia, 1987a:vi). Greater certainty of incarceration coupled with longer terms of confinement for law violators are advanced by reformers as solutions for reducing and controlling crime. However, research has never demonstrated conclusively that longer prison sentences make ex-offenders less likely to commit new crimes (Petersilia, 1987a:vi). In view of public sentiment favoring longer prison sentences for offenders, we may conclude that the primary goal achieved by longer incarcerative sentences is incapacitation and control rather than deterrence. "Getting tough" on crime is best illustrated to the public by imposing harsher and longer sentences on convicted offenders. Again, the deterrent value of lengthy incarceration is questionable.

Probationers and Parolees Compared

Few studies have actually compared probationers with parolees directly regarding their recidivism. As has been seen, there is an abundance of research about recidivists and their characteristics, but few investigators have focused on probationers and parolees simultaneously to see whether two reasonably matched sets of offenders differ in their recidivism rates and other related characteristics. However, Rand Corporation researchers utilized an existing database of 16,500 men convicted of felonies in several California counties in 1980 in order to compare probationers and parolees regarding their recidivism (Petersilia, Turner, and Peterson, 1986).

The Rand offender database consisted of persons convicted of robbery, assault, burglary, larceny-theft, forgery, and drug sale/possession. These crimes were selected because offenders convicted of them may be sentenced to either prison or probation (Petersilia et al., 1986:9). Offenders were compared according to characteristics including age, race, gender, employment, juvenile/adult criminal history, and several other salient factors. Eventually, 511 probationers and 511 parolees were roughly matched according to several criteria. The probationers tended to be more serious probationers than probationers in general, while the parolees were among the least serious offenders imprisoned. In short, Rand researchers selected the least serious offenders from the more serious offending group, while they selected the most serious offenders from the less serious offending group. On this basis, Rand researchers argued that the two offender samples were generally comparable in terms of their offense seriousness (Petersilia et al., 1986:12). For example, they were fairly evenly matched according to number of prior adult convictions, prior prison terms, number of conviction counts, and the percentage under the influence of drugs when crime was committed. A higher proportion of parolees compared with probationers had been on adult or juvenile parole, were armed with a gun during the crime, and were classified as drug addicts. However, a higher proportion of probationers knew their victims, caused serious injury during the crime, and used a weapon. Both samples were about the same age when they started serving their sentences (Petersilia et al., 1986:15).

The Petersilia, Turner, and Peterson study examined more dimensions of offender behaviors than are reported here. Also, the Rand researchers found that parolees recidivated more quickly compared with probationers. These investigators used rearrests, charges filed, reconvictions, and reincarceration as various recidivism dimensions. In virtually every category, parolees had higher recidivism scores compared with probationers, although these differences were not that dramatic for all categories. For example, 19 percent of the probationer sample was incarcerated in prison, compared with 26 percent of the parolees. Another comparison showed 72 percent of the parolees were rearrested compared with 63 percent of the probationers.

Rand concluded that at least for their sample, parolees had higher recidivism rates than probationers, although their new crimes were not more serious (Petersilia et al., 1986:21). These investigators also found little influence of incarceration on recidivism. Interestingly, incarceration tended to increase recidivism rates slightly, especially for property offenders who historically have higher recidivism rates anyway (Petersilia et al., 1986:24). Finally, serving longer prison terms did not influence significantly the rate of recidivism for most offense categories, although a slight decrease in recidivism occurred with longer prison terms.

This is consistent with a study sponsored by the U.S. Department of Justice. Although between 1979 and 1986, average lengths of regular prison sentences increased by 32 percent, the rate of parole revocations for both technical violations and major crimes doubled for parolees during the same period (Abt Associates, Inc., 1987:2). And, of more than 20,000 federal offenders leaving probation and parole between July 1, 1985, and June 30, 1986, more than one in five had committed a new crime or violated the technical conditions of their release (Abt Associates, Inc., 1987:2). Again, incarceration seemed to make little difference. When it did make a difference, it seemed only to increase recidivism rates.

Prison versus Probation

The question was raised in the Rand study about whether the greater cost of confinement in jail or prison was worth the small differences in recidivism rates observed between prisoners and probationers. The researchers demonstrated that probation/parole programs are about half the cost of incarceration. For example, average costs per offender on probation in California for the samples they studied were $11,600 compared with $23,400 for incarcerated offenders (Petersilia et al., 1986:34). They concluded that

1. Public safety would clearly benefit from somehow incapacitating a larger proportion of the felons represented in the study's matched sample of prisoners and felony probationers.
2. Building more prisons can move toward accomplishing this goal, but cannot fully realize it.

3. Relying on only one form of incapacitation necessarily limits society's ability to respond to the overall crime problem. In addition to imprisonment, other means of incapacitating felony offenders may be necessary to control the threat of serious crimes from felony offenders released to the community from prison and on probation.

4. Intensive probation supervision, electronic monitoring, house arrest, and other intermediate sanctions are untested, but promising new ways to ease prison overcrowding while better incapacitating felony offenders who now receive traditional probation sentences. (Petersilia et al., 1986:37).

Curbing Recidivism

Strategies for decreasing recidivism rates include incarceration, intensive supervised probation or parole, and a wide range of intermediate punishments already discussed including electronic monitoring, house arrest, and community-based treatment programs. The more intensive monitoring an offender receives, the less the recidivism, although some intensively supervised offenders recidivate.

The treatment or rehabilitation orientation is not a bad one, although many experts believe that many established treatment programs do not fulfill their stated goals. The fact that 50 percent or more of all offenders, incarcerated or on probation, will recidivate in the future at some unspecified time is evidence of the rehabilitative failure of any program, including incarceration. However, one influential but conservative voice favoring incapacitation is James Q. Wilson, who argues that while imprisonment may not rehabilitate offenders, it does keep them off the streets away from the general public. And, this may be the most effective means of crime control (James Q. Wilson, 1985). Another controversial solution recommended by some experts is selective incapacitation (Struckhoff, 1987:30; also see Chapter 1).

A report prepared by the National Council on Crime and Delinquency (NCCD) has examined parolee recidivism in California and has found that parolee failures have increased from 23 percent in 1975 to 53 percent in 1983 (Austin, 1987). This report yields findings similar to those presented by Rand researchers. Administrative parole revocations have jumped from 5 to 35 percent since 1975, but the proportion of parolees being returned for new felonies committed while on parole increased by only 5 percent. Parolee failures do not seem related to program failures, however. Rather, external and administrative factors appear largely to blame for many of these. The NCCD cites the following as contributing significantly to the growing numbers of administrative parole revocations:

1. Declining levels of financial assistance and narcotic treatment resources for parolees;
2. Increases in parole supervision caseloads;
3. A shift in public and law enforcement attitudes regarding parolees and law violators in general;
4. Jail overcrowding; and
5. A more efficient law enforcement/parole supervision system. (Austin, 1987:i)

Thus, curbing recidivism rates might be achieved by more effective implementation of probation/parole program goals, smaller caseloads for POs (probably resulting in more frequent contact with probationer or parolee clients), and increasing the capacity of delivery systems (i.e., greater funding) to meet the specialized needs of offenders such as those with drug-dependency problems or alcoholism. The NCCD findings and corresponding recommendations are shared by other researchers as well (Blumstein, 1983; Petersilia, 1987a). Paradoxically, more frequent contact between POs and their clients may make POs more aware of client technical violations of their program requirements. This doesn't mean that PO clients are committing more program violations, but, rather, that POs are in the position of observing their clients more frequently and that the likelihood of observing program infractions is increased.

A VIEW FROM PROBATIONERS AND PAROLEES

Recidivism research almost exclusively is conducted from the standpoint of the practitioner. Seldom are the targets of this research considered, the offenders themselves. Investigators describe various programs, their costs and benefits, successes, and offender characteristics. But what do offenders themselves think about the programs imposed on them? Do offenders view programs the way administrators of those programs intend for them to be viewed?

An investigation was conducted in 1983 involving 106 federal probationers selected from the U.S. Probation and Parole Office in Chicago, Illinois (Allen 1985:69). Probationers were asked by researchers to indicate what the probationers believed to be the purpose in placing them on probation. They were also asked about the probation officer's role in relation to them. Included in this inquiry were requests for opinions about how the probation system could be improved, what services could be provided, and who should provide these services (Allen, 1985:67).

Personal, semistructured interviews were conducted with each probationer shortly after each completed his or her probation term. Among other things, ex probationers were presented with four models of probation practice and asked to react to them. The four models are presented in Table 16.3.

These four models of probation practice include the traditional rehabilitation model, the deterrence model, the desert (just-deserts) model, and the justice model. Respondents were asked to react to each of these models as possible goals of probation. Considering the recent emphasis given just deserts and justice in sentencing reforms, the study results were somewhat surprising. Ex-probationers believed that rehabilitation was the primary aim of their probation programs. However, they also believed that deterrence was ideally the ultimate objective of their probation. The rehabilitative goal of probation was reinforced by program emphases on education and employment assistance, and plea bargaining efforts prior to sentencing. A majority of probationers believed that probation officers sincerely wished to assist them, but these offenders were split concerning the value of probation officers in providing assistance in working out personal problems (Allen, 1985:72).

Although the sample of ex-probationers was small, it nevertheless highlighted certain weaknesses of existing delivery systems. Generally, these offenders were

Table 16.3 Four Models of Probation Practice

	Rehabilitation Model	Deterrence Model	Desert Model	Justice Model
Goal	Utilitarian: community protection via treatment of the offender.	Utilitarian: crime reduction via threat of punishment.	Nonutilitarian: penal sanction is deserved for deviant behavior.	Nonutilitarian: just and fair penal sanction for deviant behavior.
Assumption concerning cause of deviance	Social pathology, disorganization, differential association, opportunity, labeling, etc.	Economic model—risk-reward decision by offender.	Multiple social factors. Risk-reward decision by responsible offender.	Rejects "theories" of causation. Offender responsible actor capable of responsible choice.
Theoretical concerns	Psychodynamic Treatment-motivated.	Punitively motivated.	Punitively motivated.	Punitively motivated.
Basic change strategy	Care and control.	Threats.	Surveillance.	Surveillance.
Salient role of probation officer	Ego-strengthening via identification and relationship.	Nontreatment role. Surveillance.	Enforcement of probation rules.	Policing activities. Helper as per request. (Advocate for offender)
Policy implication	Decriminalization, deinstitutionalization, community reorganization, psychosocial-oriented programs.	Mandated sentences Reduced discretion of judges.	Mandated ranges of sentences.	Concept of fairness and equality. Proportional sentencing based on seriousness of offense. Scaling down the levels of punishment. Limited discretion. Deference to individual's rights.

Source: G. Frederick Allen, 1985, p. 68.

satisfied with their programs, although several believed that certain logistical and administrative changes were in order. For instance, they suggested that probation officers should strive to be more client centered. This could be achieved through lower caseloads and closer contact with probationers. Also, they believed probation officers should be permitted more authority to act on their own, to increase their contact level. More home visits by POs were suggested as well.

These ex-probationers believed that probation programs should incorporate certain incentives or rewards for compliance such as early termination of probation for good behavior. Probationers seemed inclined to agree that their probation should benefit the community directly. Of additional interest was the fact that their view of the program influenced directly their view of the PO role. Rehabilitation-oriented probationers saw their POs in a support role, while deterrence-oriented probationers saw their POs as serving a monitoring function (Allen, 1985:73).

Allen (1985:74) says that the real value of his study is demonstrating that offenders are willing to provide input and they have something to say. Each program for probationers and parolees will vary in its effectiveness, and administrators and others will evaluate the successfulness of these programs. But offenders may be an important source of feedback as well. Administrators may be able to remedy existing program defects (or at least some of them) by listening to those involved in these programs. In a sense, this is reminiscent of the participation hypothesis pertaining to employers and workers: employees will produce more and generally be more cooperative to the extent that they are involved in decisions affecting their work. This does not mean that offenders should be placed on parole boards or in advisory capacities to judges during the sentencing process. But it does suggest that corrections officials can learn much from offenders about how programs can be improved. And if the offender suggests certain improvements, there is the chance that other offenders will benefit from those improvements eventually. This may not eliminate recidivism, but it may function to limit it.

KEY TERMS

Avertable recidivist	Rearrest
Cleared by arrest	Recidivism rate
Nonavertable recidivist	Reconviction
Preponderance of evidence	Reincarceration
Program evaluation	Revocation action
Rand Corporation	Totality of circumstances

QUESTIONS FOR REVIEW

1. What is meant by creaming? How does creaming influence program effectiveness?
2. Differentiate between avertable recidivists and nonavertable recidivists. Give some examples.

3. Identify at least six different connotations of recidivism. Which recidivism measures are most popular?
4. Which recidivism measure seems most realistic and why?
5. What are some characteristics of recidivists? Are experts in agreement about these characteristics? Why or why not?
6. How well can recidivist characteristics be used to predict offender risk or dangerousness?
7. What kinds of changes do probationers feel ought to be made in probation programs?
8. Does the length of incarceration exert any impact on the likelihood of recidivism?
9. Some researchers believe that recidivists tend to commit more serious offenses. Is this true? Why or why not?
10. Which offenders tend to have higher recidivism rates: property or violent offenders? What differences in recidivism rates would you expect when comparing probationers with parolees? Cite a study where such a comparison was made.

Glossary

Acceptance of Responsibility
Acknowledgment by convicted offenders that they are responsible for their actions and have rendered themselves totally and absolutely accountable for the injuries or damages they may have caused; used by judges to mitigate sentences during sentencing hearings; an integral factor in U.S. sentencing guidelines offense severity calculations, influencing number of months of confinement offenders may receive.

Actuarial Prediction
Prediction of future inmate behavior based on a class of offenders similar to those considered for parole.

Adjudication
A decision by a juvenile court judge as to whether juvenile is delinquent, status offender, or dependent/neglected; finding may be "not delinquent."

Adjudicatory Hearing
A formal proceeding involving a prosecutor and defense attorney in which evidence is presented and the juvenile's guilt or innocence is determined by the juvenile court judge.

Aftercare
A general term to describe a wide variety of programs and services available to both adult and juvenile probationers and parolees; includes halfway houses, psychological counseling services, community-based correctional agencies, employment assistance, and medical treatment for offenders or ex-offenders.

Agency
The special relation between an employer and an employee whereby the employee acts as an agent of the employer, able to make decisions and take actions on the employer's behalf.

Aggravating Circumstances
Circumstances that enhance a sentence; includes whether serious bodily injury or death occurred to a victim during crime commission and whether offender was on parole at time of crime.

Alaska Judicial Council.
Public council that evaluates judicial sentencing practices and assesses all matters pertinent to the Alaska judiciary.

Allegheny Academy
In 1982, this Pennsylvania facility was opened and operated by the Community Specialists Corporation, a private, nonprofit corporation headquartered in Pittsburgh and specializing in the community-based treatment of young offenders; general aim is to change the negative behavior of offenders; targeted are juvenile offenders who have failed in other, traditional probation programs.

Alternative Dispute Resolution (ADR)
A procedure whereby a criminal case is redefined as a civil one and the case is decided by an impartial arbiter, and both parties agree to amicable settlement; criminal court is not used for resolving such matters; usually reserved for minor offenses.

Alternative Care Cases
Borderline cases in which judges may sentence offenders to either incarceration or probation subject to compliance with various conditions.

Alternative Sentencing
Also "creative sentencing," whereby judge imposes sentence other than incarceration; often involves good works such as community service, restitution to victims, and other public service activity.

American Correctional Association (ACA)
An association established in 1870 to disseminate information about correctional programs and correctional training; designed to foster professionalism throughout correctional community.

Anamnestic Prediction
Prediction of inmate behavior according to past circumstances.

Arraignment
Proceeding following an indictment by a grand jury or a finding of probable cause from a preliminary hearing; determines plea, specification of final charges against defendant(s), and trial date.

Arrest
Taking persons into custody and restraining them until they can be brought before court to answer the charges against them.

Assessment Center
A center for selecting entry-level officers for correctional work; an assessment center hires correctional officers and probation or parole officers.

Auburn State Penitentiary
A prison constructed in New York in 1816; known for its creation of tiers, or different levels of custody for different types of offenders; also known for use of striped clothing for prisoners to distinguish them from the general population if prisoners escape confinement; also known for the use of the congregate system, whereby offenders could dine in large eating areas; also used solitary confinement; custody levels are medium and maximum.

Augustus, John
A private citizen who is acknowledged as formulator of probation in the United States in Boston, Massachusetts, 1841.

Automatic Waiver (also Legislative Waiver)
An action initiated by a state legislature whereby certain juvenile offenders are sent to criminal courts for processing rather than to juvenile courts; usually requires a certain age range (16–17) and prescribed list of offenses (e.g., rape, homicide, armed robbery, arson); a type of certification or waiver or transfer.

Avertable Recidivist
An offender who would still have been in prison serving a sentence at a time when new offense was committed.

Backdooring Cases
The practice by judges of sentencing borderline (low-risk) offenders to incarceration with strong admonishment that they be encouraged to apply for intensive probation supervision programs.

Bail
A surety to procure the release of those under arrest and to assure that they will appear later to face criminal charges in court; also known as a *bailbond.*

Banishment
A punishment form used for many centuries as a sanction for violations of the law or religious beliefs; those found guilty of crimes or other infractions were ordered to leave their communities and never return; in many instances, this was the equivalent of the death penalty, since communi-

ties were often isolated and no food or water was available within distances of hundreds of miles from these communities (see also *Transport*).

Behavioral Reform
John Augustus's attempt to change behaviors of persons charged with crimes in the early 1840s; Augustus believed that changes in behavior could be influenced by periods of probation, contrition, and abstinence (e.g., from alcohol).

Beyond a Reasonable Doubt
A standard used in criminal courts to establish guilt or innocence of criminal defendant.

Bond Supervision Program
A Lake County, Illinois, experiment with electronic monitoring for clients who did not fit the following profile: (1) the defendant poses a threat to the safety and welfare of the community and/or to himself or herself; (2) the seriousness of the crime restricts the use of release on recognizance; and (3) the likelihood of the defendant's nonappearance in court is substantiated; anyone *not* fitting these characteristics might be eligible for electronic monitoring; pretrial services in Lake County placed 659 defendants on electronic monitoring between 1986 and 1989; average program length was 90 days.

Booking
An administrative procedure designed to furnish personal background information to a bonding company and law enforcement officials. Booking includes compiling a file for defendants, including their name, address, telephone number, age, place of work, relatives, and other personal data.

Boot Camp
A highly regimented, military like, short term correctional program (90–180 days) in which offenders are provided with strict discipline, physical training, and hard labor resembling some aspects of military basic training; when successfully completed, boot camps provide for transfers of participants to community-based facilities for nonsecure supervision.

Boston House of Corrections
A jail in which convicted offenders were confined for various offenses, including drunkenness and disorderly behavior; operated during 1830s and 1840s.

Boston Offender Project (BOP)
An experimental juvenile treatment program begun in 1981 through the Massachusetts Department of Youth Services; aimed at reducing recidivism, reintegrating youths, and increasing offender accountability.

Breed v. Jones (1975)
A landmark juvenile rights case that established right against double jeopardy; juveniles may not be adjudicated as delinquent in juvenile courts and then tried as adults in criminal courts later on the same charges.

Bridewell Workhouse
Established in 1557 in London, England; designed to house vagrants and general "riffraff"; noted for exploitation of inmate labor by private mercantile interests.

Brockway, Zebulon
First superintendent of New York State Reformatory at Elmira in 1876; arguably credited with introducing first "good-time" system whereby inmates could have their sentences reduced or shortened by the number of good marks earned through good behavior.

Broker
A PO work-role orientation in which the PO functions as a referral service and supplies offender-client with contacts with agencies that provide needed services.

Ernest W. Burgess
Collaborated with Robert Park to devise concentric zone hypothesis to explain crime in different Chicago city sectors.

Burnout
The psychological equivalent of physical stress, characterized by a loss of motivation and commitment related to task performance.

Camp
A nonsecure youth program, usually located in a rural setting, designed to instill self confidence and interpersonal skills for juvenile offenders; also known as a wilderness program.

Career Criminal
An offender who earns his or her living through crime; a career criminal goes about his or her criminal activity in much the same way workers or professional individuals engage in their daily work activities; a career criminal often considers his or her work as a "craft," since a career crimi-

nal acquires considerable technical skill and competence in the performance of crimes.

Career Escalation
The phenomenon of gradually progressing to more serious forms of offending; people who commit misdemeanors eventually commit felonies; over time, seriousness of offending intensifies.

Caseload
The number of clients or offenders probation or parole officers must supervise during any given time period, such as one week or one month.

Caseworker
Any probation or parole officer who works with probationers or parolees as clients; term originates from social work where caseworkers attempt to educate, train, or rehabilitate those without coping skills.

Cellular Telephone Device
Electronic monitoring device worn by offenders that emits a radio signal received by a local area monitor.

Certification (see Transfers)

Chancery Court
Court of equity rooted in early English common law in which civil disputes are resolved; also responsible for juvenile matters and adjudicating family matters such as divorce; has jurisdiction over contract disputes, property boundary claims, and exchanges of goods disputes.

Charge Reduction Bargaining
A type of plea bargaining whereby the inducement from the prosecutor is a reduction in the seriousness of charge or number of charges against a defendant in exchange for a guilty plea.

Children's Bureau
U.S. agency operated during 1912–1940 and charged with compiling statistical information about children and methods whereby delinquency could be prevented and treated.

Children's Tribunal
An early form of court dealing with juvenile offending; 1850s through 1890s; informal judicial mechanisms for evaluating seriousness of juvenile offenders and prescribing punishments for them.

Child-Saver Movement (also Child-Savers)
Largely religious in origin, loosely organized attempt to deal with unsupervised youth following the Civil War; child-savers were interested in the welfare of youths who roamed city streets unsupervised.

Child Sexual Abuse Treatment Program
Individual counseling for all family members of offender-clients, including mother-daughter counseling, marital counseling, father-daughter counseling, and group counseling based on the principles of humanistic psychotherapy; self-help groups are also provided; volunteer men's collectives, social services agencies, and women's shelters are often effective in changing behaviors of offender-abusers.

Child Sexual Abuser
An adult who involves minors in virtually any kind of sexual activity ranging from intercourse with children to photographing them in lewd poses.

Citizen Value System
A parole board decision-making model that appeals to public interests in seeing that community expectations are met by making appropriate early-release decisions.

Civil Rights Act
Title 42, Section 1983 of the U.S. Code permitting inmates of prisons and jails as well as probationers and parolees the right to sue their administrators and/or supervisors under the "due process" and "equal protection" clauses of the Fourteenth Amendment.

Clark, Benjamin C.
A philanthropist and "volunteer" probation officer who assisted courts with limited probation work during 1860s; carried on John Augustus's work commenced in early 1840s.

Classification
An attempt to categorize offenders according to type of offense, dangerousness, public risk, special needs, and other relevant criteria; used in institutional settings (prisons) for purposes of placing inmates in more or less close custody and supervision.

Classification System
The means used by prisons and probation/parole agencies to separate offenders according to offense seriousness, type of offense, and other criteria; no classification system has been demonstrably successful at effective prisoner or client placements.

Cleared by Arrest
The term used by the FBI in *Uniform Crime Reports* to indicate that someone has been arrested for a reported crime; does not necessarily mean that the crime has been solved or that the actual criminals who committed the crime have been apprehended or convicted.

Client Specific Plan
One alternative sentencing program involving selective tailoring of sentence (other than imprisonment) for each individual offender, depending on offense committed; requires judicial approval.

Clinical Prediction
Prediction of inmate behavior based on professional's expert training and working directly with offenders.

Combination Sentence (see Split Sentencing)

Community-Based Corrections
Several types of programs that manage offenders within the community instead of prison or jail; includes electronic monitoring, day fine programs, home confinement, and intensive supervised probation/parole.

Community-Based Corrections Program
A minimum-security prison facility designed to accommodate only low-risk offenders, nonviolent offenders, usually about to be paroled; funded by local government; and often affiliated with work release.

Community-Based Supervision
Reintegrative programs operated publicly or privately to assist offenders by providing therapeutic, support, and supervision programs for criminals; may include furloughs, probation, parole, community service, and restitution.

Community Control House Arrest
A Florida program in which offenders are confined to and allowed to serve their sentences in their own homes instead of prison.

Community Corrections (see Community-Based Corrections Program)

Community Corrections Act
A statewide mechanism included in legislation whereby funds are granted to local units of government and community agencies to develop and deliver "front-end" alternative sanctions in lieu of state incarceration.

Community Diversion Incentive Act
Targets prison- or jail-bound offenders, including those convicted of nonviolent felonies and misdemeanors who have been sentenced to the Department of Corrections or local jails; Virginia officials include those offenders who would have otherwise been incarcerated in prison or jail and whose treatment needs can better be met in the community; statutory behavioral contracts guide client program participation; if offenders successfully complete these programs, their original imposed sentences may be suspended.

Community Diversion Incentive (CDI)
Virginia diversion program established in 1981 for prison-bound offenders; participants were required to perform specified unpaid community services and make financial restitution to victims; clients were also subject to intensive supervised probation.

Community Diversion Incentive Program (CDI)
Any program established under the Community Diversion Incentive Act.

Community Model
New concept based on correctional goal of offender reintegration into the community.

Community Reintegration
The process whereby offender who has been incarcerated is able to live in community under some supervision and gradually adjust to life outside of prison or jail; theory is that transition to community life from regimentation of prison life can be eased through community-based correctional program and limited community supervision.

Community Residential Center
A transitional agency located in neighborhoods in which offenders may obtain employment counseling, food and shelter, and limited supervision pertaining to one or more conditions of probation or parole; an example might be a day reporting and treatment program.

Community Service
Sentence imposed by judges in lieu of incarceration whereby offenders are obligated to perform various tasks that assist the community and help to offset the losses suffered by victims or the community-at-large.

Community Service Orders
Symbolic restitution, involving redress for victims, less severe sanctions for offenders, offender rehabilitation, reduction of demands on the crim-

inal justice system, and a reduction of the need for vengeance in society, or a combination of these factors.

Community Services System
A coordinated system of community-based social services integrating at least 70 agencies with varying funding sources, governing bodies, and philosophies.

Community Protection Program
New York State county-based program as an alternative to prison whereby prison-bound offenders are diverted to intensive supervision and treatment.

Community Work Centers (CWCs)
An Oklahoma program that provides for inmates to live in residences located in various neighborhoods and to do work benefiting counties and cities; Oklahoma officials label these CWCs *constituency-based corrections,* because the centers reduce prison overcrowding and the expense of incarceration; the CWCs give inmates positive work and personal growth experiences, such as shopping, eating, and attending religious services in the community; visiting friends and relatives in noninstitutional settings; and receiving job training.

Commutation
Administratively authorized early release from custody (e.g., prisoners serving life terms may have their sentences commuted to 10 years).

Conditional Diversion Program
Program in which divertee is involved in some degree of local monitoring by probation officers or personnel affiliated with local probation departments.

Conditional Release
Any release of inmates from custody with various conditions or program requirements; parole is a conditional release; any release to a community-based corrections program is a conditional release.

Congregate System
A housing system by which inmates are allowed to work together and eat their meals with one another during daylight hours.

Continuous Signaling Device
An electronic monitoring device that broadcasts an encoded signal that is received by a receiver-dialer in the offender's home (see *Electronic Monitoring*).

Controller Value System
A parole board decision-making system that emphasizes the functions of parole supervision and management.

Conventional Model
A caseload assignment model in which probation or parole officers are assigned clients randomly.

Conventional Model with Geographic Considerations
Similar to the conventional model; caseload assignment model is based on the travel time required for POs to meet with offender-clients regularly.

Cook, Rufus R.
A philanthropist who continued John Augustus's work, particularly assisting juvenile offenders through the Boston Children's Aid Society in 1860.

Corrections
The aggregate of programs, services, facilities, and organizations responsible for the management of people who have been accused or convicted of criminal offenses.

Corrections Officer
A person who works in any correctional institution, such as a jail, prison, or penitentiary; formerly known as a *guard;* correction officer is current preferred term, as per American Correctional Association and American Jail Association resolutions.

Corrections Paraprofessional
Someone who possesses some formal training in a given correctional area, is salaried, works specified hours, has formal duties and responsibilities, is accountable to higher-level supervisors for work quality, and has limited immunity under the theory of agency.

Corrections Volunteer
Any unpaid person who performs auxiliary, supplemental, augmentative, or any other work or services for any law enforcement, court, or corrections agency.

Court
A public judiciary body that applies the law to controversies and oversees the administration of justice.

Creaming
A term to denote taking only the most qualified offenders for succeeding in a rehabilitative pro-

gram; these offenders are low risk, unlikely to re-offend.

Creative Sentencing
The name applied to a broad class of punishments that offer alternatives to incarceration and are designed to fit a particular crime.

Crime Classification Index
A selected list of offenses that are used to portray crime trends; index offenses are usually divided into Type I or more serious offenses, and Type II or less serious offenses; compiled by Federal Bureau of Investigation and Department of Justice.

Crime Control
A model of criminal justice that emphasizes containment of dangerous offenders and societal protection.

Crime against the Person
Any criminal act involving direct contact with another person and/or injury to that person (e.g., aggravated assault, rape, homicide, robbery; more recently designated as violent crime).

Crime against Property
Any criminal act not directly involving a victim [e.g., burglary, vehicular theft (not carjacking); larceny; arson (of an unoccupied dwelling); more recently designated as property crime].

Criminal Contamination
The belief that if ex-offenders live together or associate closely with one another, they would spread their criminality like a disease; fear originally aroused from construction of halfway houses for parolees.

Criminal Justice System
Integrated network of law enforcement, prosecution and courts, and corrections designed to process criminal offenders from detection to trial and punishment.

Criminal Trial
An adversarial proceeding within a particular jurisdiction, whereby a judicial determination of issues can be made, and a defendant's guilt or innocence can be decided impartially.

Criminogenic Environment
Typically, prisons are viewed as "colleges of crime" in which inmates are not rehabilitated but rather learn more effective criminal techniques; any interpersonal situation in which the likelihood of acquiring criminal behaviors is enhanced.

Crofton, Sir Walter
Director of Ireland's prison system during 1850s; considered "father of parole" in various European countries; established system of early release for prisoners; issued "tickets of leave" as an early version of parole.

Dangerousness
Defined differently in several jurisdictions; prior record of violent offenses; potential to commit future violent crimes if released; propensity to inflict injury.

Day Fine
A two-step process whereby courts (1) use a unit scale or benchmark to sentence offenders to certain numbers of day-fine units (e.g., 15, 30, 120) according to offense severity and without regard to income; and (2) determine the value of each unit according to a percentage of the offender's daily income; total fine amounts are determined by multiplying this unit value by the number of units accompanying the offense.

Day Parole (see Work Release)

Day Pass (see Work Release)

Day Reporting Center
Operated primarily during daytime hours for the purpose of providing diverse services to offenders and their families; defined as a highly structured nonresidential program utilizing supervision, sanctions, and services coordinated from a central focus; offenders live at home and report to these centers regularly; provides services according to offender needs; these services might include employment assistance, family counseling, and educational and vocational training; may be used for supervisory and/or monitoring purposes; client behavior modification is a key goal of such centers.

Decarceration
Removal of youths from secure-custody facilities; part of the deinstitutionalization of status offenders movement in late 1970s and 1980s; utilizing secure facilities to a lesser degree as punishment for minor offending.

Defendant
Any person who has been charged with one or more crimes.

Defendant's Sentencing Memorandum
Version of events leading to conviction offense in the words of the convicted offender; version may

be submitted together with Victim Impact Statement.

Deinstitutionalization of Status Offenses (DSO)
The process of removing status offenses from jurisdiction of juvenile court and secure-custody facilities.

Delinquent (see Juvenile Delinquent)

Delinquency (see Juvenile Delinquency)

Delinquency Petition
Any formal paper filed to have a juvenile adjudicated as a delinquent; may be filed by law enforcement officers, school officials, parents, neighbors, probation/parole personnel, or any interested party.

Demand Waiver
An action filed by juveniles and their attorneys to have a case in juvenile court transferred to the jurisdiction of criminal courts.

Department of Justice
Organization headed by attorney general of the United States; responsible for prosecuting federal law violators; oversees Federal Bureau of Investigation and the Drug Enforcement Administration.

Dependent and Neglected Children
The official category used by juvenile court judges to determine whether juveniles should be placed in foster homes and taken away from parents or guardians who may be deemed unfit; children who have no or little familial support or supervision.

Desert Model (see Justice Model)

Detainer Warrant
A notice of criminal charges or unserved sentences pending against a prisoner in the same or other jurisdictions.

Detector
A PO work-role orientation in which the PO attempts to identify troublesome clients or those who are most likely to pose high community risk.

Detention Hearing
A judicial or quasi-judicial proceeding held to determine whether it is appropriate to continue to hold or detain a juvenile in a shelter facility.

Determinate Sentencing
Sentences involving confinement for a fixed period of time that must be served in full and with-

out parole board intervention, less any "good time" earned in prison.

Deterrence
Actions that are designed to prevent crime before it occurs by threatening severe criminal penalties or sanctions; may include safety measures to discourage potential lawbreakers such as elaborate security systems, electronic monitoring, and greater police officer visibility.

Deterrence Model
A model of crime control based on the philosophy of deterrence (see also Deterrence).

Differential Association Theory
A theory of criminal behavior stressing the priority, duration, frequency, and intensity of interactions with other criminals.

Direct Supervision Jail
A jail constructed so as to provide officers with 180-degree lines of sight to monitor inmates; employs a podular design; modern facilities also combine closed-circuit cameras that continuously observe inmates while celled.

Discretionary Waiver (see Judicial Waiver)

Dispute Resolution (see Alternative Dispute Resolution)

Diversion
The official halting or suspension of legal proceedings against criminal defendants after a recorded justice system entry, and possible referral of those persons to treatment or care programs administered by a nonjustice or private agency (see also Pretrial Release).

Diversion Program (see also Diversion)
One of several programs preceding formal court adjudication of charges against defendants; defendants participate in therapeutic, educational, or other helping programs; may result in expungement of criminal charges originally filed against defendant; may include participation in Alcoholics Anonymous or driver's training programs.

Diversion to Civil Court (see also Alternative Dispute Resolution)
Procedure whereby a crime is reduced in seriousness to that of a tort action and placed for disposition in civil court rather than in criminal court.

Divertee
A person who participates in a diversion program or who is otherwise granted diversion.

Double Jeopardy
Fifth Amendment guarantee that protects against a second prosecution for the same offense following acquittal or conviction for the offense and against multiple punishments for the same offense.

Due Process
The right to a fair trial, presumption of innocence until guilt is proven, beyond a reasonable doubt, opportunity to be heard, to be aware of pending matter, and given choice to acquiesce or defend with reasons.

Due Process Model (see Justice Model)

Early Release (see Parole)

Economic Philosophy
A numbers-management scheme for probation and parole offices, in which the goal is to maximize probation officer caseloads or increase the numbers of those supervised while minimizing supervisory costs, time expenditures, and probationer-client criminality.

Educator (see Enabler)

Electronic Monitoring
Use of telemetry devices to verify that an offender is at a specified location at specified times.

Electronic Monitoring Device
A device worn about the wrist or leg that is designed to monitor an offender's presence in a given environment in which the offender is required to remain.

Elmira State Reformatory
An institution constructed in Elmira, New York, in 1876; experimented with certain new rehabilitative philosophies espoused by various penologists including its first superintendent, Zebulon Brockway (1827–1920); considered the *new penology* and used the latest scientific information in its correctional methods; used a military model comparable to contemporary boot camps; prisoners performed useful labor and participated in educational or vocational activities; their productivity and good conduct could earn them shorter sentences; inmates were trained in close-order drill, wore military uniforms, and paraded about with wooden rifles; authorities regarded this as a way of instilling discipline in inmates and reforming them; Elmira Reformatory credited with individualizing prisoner treatment and the use of indeterminate sentencing directly suited for parole actions; widely imitated by other state prison systems subsequently.

Enabler
A PO work-role orientation in which the PO seeks to instruct and assist offenders in dealing with problems as they arise.

Enforcer
A PO work-role orientation in which POs see themselves as enforcement officers charged with regulating client behaviors.

Entrapment
Illegal activity planned, suggested, or encouraged by police, whereby individual is aided in the commission of a specific crime in order to effect an arrest.

Estelle v. Gamble (1976)
Decision declared that deliberate indifference by prison authorities to serious medical disorders of prisoners violates the Eighth Amendment as "cruel and unusual punishment."

Exculpatory Evidence
Any evidence or material that shows or supports a defendant's innocence.

Ex Parte Crouse (1838)
Gives the state authority over families in deciding best interests of children.

Experience Program (see Wilderness Program)

Expungement Order (see also Sealing of Record)
The act of removing a juvenile's record from public view; issued by juvenile court judges, order instructs police and juvenile agencies to destroy any file material related to juvenile's conduct.

False Negative
An offender predicted not to be dangerous who turns out to be dangerous.

False Positive
An offender predicted to be dangerous who turns out not to be dangerous.

Federal Bureau of Investigation (FBI)
Investigative agency that is the enforcement arm of the Department of Justice; investigates over 200 different kinds of federal law violations; maintains extensive files on criminals; assists other law agencies.

Federal *Habeas Corpus* Statute
Title 28, Section 2241 of the U.S. Code permitting probationers, parolees, and inmates of prisons and jails to challenge the fact, length, and conditions of their confinement or placement in particular facilities or programs.

Federal Tort Claims Act of 1946
Title 28, Section 2674 of the U.S. Code permitting federal prisoners and those under federal probation or parole supervision the right to sue their supervisors and/or administrators for punitive damages arising from physical, personal, social, or psychological harm stemming from the PO-client, correctional officer–inmate relation.

Felony
Crime punishable by imprisonment for a term of one or more years; a major crime; an index crime.

Felony Probation
Procedure of granting convicted felons probation in lieu of incarceration, usually justified because of prison overcrowding; involves conditional sentence in lieu of incarceration.

Fine
A financial penalty imposed at time of sentencing convicted offenders; most criminal statutes contain provisions for the imposition of monetary penalties as sentencing options.

First-Offender (see First-Time Offender)

First-Time Offender
Criminals who have no previous criminal records; these persons may have committed crimes, but they have only been caught for the instant offense.

Florida Assessment Center
The Dade County, Florida, Department of Corrections and Rehabilitation was one of the first state corrections agencies to establish a center for the selection of entry-level correctional officers; the center uses intensive screening procedures for selecting applicants for officer positions.

Florida Community Control Program (FCCP)
A Florida program that seeks to provide a milieu of accountability for offender-clients; established in 1983, the FCCP has served more than 40,000 clients; supervision of Florida offenders placed in this program is intense; offenders must have a minimum of 28 supervisory contacts per month; supervising officers have caseloads of between 20 and 25 offenders; caseloads are very low compared with standard probation or parole supervision; utilizes home confinement; offenders are regularly screened for drug and alcohol use, and offenders are monitored to ensure their payment of victim compensation, restitution, and/or community service; offenders also pay supervision fees to offset some of the program costs; recidivism is less than 20 percent for FCCP clients.

Foster Home
Temporary placement in a home when family setting is regarded as vital; children in need of supervision targeted for out-of-own-home placement.

Freedom of Information Act (FOIA)
Makes it possible for private citizens to examine certain public documents containing information about them, including IRS information or information compiled by any other government agency, criminal or otherwise.

Front-End Solution
Any solution for jail and prison overcrowding prior to placement of convicted offenders in jail or prison settings; programs include diversion, probation, and any community-based correctional program.

Furlough
An authorized, unescorted leave from confinement granted for a specific purpose and for a designated time period.

Furlough Program
A program designed to permit incarcerated offenders the opportunity of leaving prison temporarily to visit their homes, with the promise to return to the facility at the expiration of furlough.

Gaol
Early English term for jail (pronounced "jail").

***Gagnon v. Scarpelli* (1973)**
Landmark probation revocation case declaring probation revocation to be a critical stage requiring notice of charges against probationer and a hearing to determine whether probation should be revoked; probationers may be represented by counsel, give testimony on their own behalf, and cross-examine accusers.

Georgia Intensive Supervision Probation Program

A program begun in 1982 that established three phases of punitive probation conditions for probationers; phases moved probationers through extensive monitoring and control to less extensive monitoring, ranging from 6 to 12 months; program has demonstrated low rates of recidivism among participants.

Georgia Special Alternative Incarceration Program (SAI)

This SAI program is a special condition of probation; judges sentence offenders to 90 days in prison in a regime of manual labor, rigorous physical conditioning, and military-like discipline; the second phase consists of less structured, postconfinement community supervision.

Glover v. Johnson (1979)

A landmark case involving the Michigan Department of Corrections and the issue of equal programming for female inmates; class-action suit filed on behalf of all Michigan female prison inmates to the effect that their constitutional rights were violated because they were being denied educational and vocational rehabilitation opportunities that were then being provided male inmates only; female inmates obtained desired concessions from prison administration.

Good Marks

Marks obtained by prisoners in nineteenth-century England that were given to prisoners as credit for participating in educational programs and other self-improvement activities.

"Good Time"

Credit applied to a convicted offender's sentence based on the amount of time served; states vary in allowable good time; average is 15 days off of maximum sentence for every 30 days served in prison or jail; incentive for good behavior.

Good-Time System

A system introduced by Elmira State Reformatory in 1876 whereby an inmate's sentence is reduced by the number of good marks earned; once this system was in operation and shown to be moderately effective, several other states patterned their own early-release standards after it in later years.

Grand Jury

Special jury convened in about one-half of all states; comprised of various citizens; numbers vary among states; purposes are to investigate criminal activity and/or determine probable cause that a crime has been committed and a designated suspect probably committed it; yields "true bill" or indictment or presentment, or "no true bill," finding insufficient probable cause to merit indictment.

Greenholtz v. Inmates of Nebraska (1979)

Case bestowing minimum due process rights on prisoners.

Group Home

Also known as a *group center* or *foster home,* a facility for juveniles that provides limited supervision and support; juveniles live in homelike environment with other juveniles and participate in therapeutic programs and counseling; considered nonsecure custodial.

Guidelines-Based Sentencing

Also known as *presumptive sentencing,* this form of sentencing specifies ranges of months or years for different degrees of offense seriousness or severity and record of prior offending; the greater the severity of conduct and the more prior offending, the more incarceration time is imposed; originally used to create objectivity in sentencing and reduce sentencing disparities attributable to gender, race, ethnicity, or socioeconomic status.

Habeas Corpus

A writ meaning *produce the body;* used by prisoners to challenge the nature and length of their confinement.

Habitual Offender Statute

A legislative provision that usually requires the mandatory imposition of a life sentence for offenders with prior records; three or more felony convictions might be used as a standard for applying these statutes; offenders may be prosecuted as "habitual offenders" and given life terms if convicted.

Halfway House

A nonconfining residential facility intended to provide alternative to incarceration as a period of readjustment of offenders to the community after confinement.

Halfway-In House

A house that provides services catering to those probationers in need of limited or somewhat restricted confinement apart from complete freedom of movement in the community.

Halfway-Out House
A facility designed to serve the immediate needs of parolees, as distinguished from those established to accommodate probationers in the community.

Home Confinement
Called *house arrest* or *home incarceration;* intended to house offenders in their own homes with or without electronic devices; reduces prison overcrowding and prisoner costs; intermediate punishment involving the use of offender residences for mandatory incarceration during evening hours after a curfew and on weekends.

Home Incarceration (see Home Confinement)

Homeward Bound
Established in Massachusetts in 1970; program designed to provide juveniles with mature responsibilities through the acquisition of survival skills and wilderness experiences; six-week training program subjected 32 youths to endurance training, physical fitness, and performing community service.

Hope Center Wilderness Program
Organized network of four interdependent, small living groups of 12 teenagers each; goals are to provide quality care and treatment in a nonpunitive environment, with specific emphases on health, safety, education, and therapy; emotionally disturbed youths whose offenses range from truancy to murder are selected for program participation; informal techniques used, including "aftertalk" (informal discussion during meals), "huddle up" (a group discussion technique), and "pow wow" (a nightly fire gathering); special nondenominational religious services are conducted; participants involved in various special events and learn to cook meals outdoors, camp, and other survival skills.

Hope Hall (see Hope House)

Hope House
In 1896, Hope House was established in New York City by Maud and Ballington Booth; receiving considerable financial support from a missionary religious society called the Volunteers of America, the Boothes were able to open additional Hope Houses or Hope Halls in future years in Chicago, San Francisco, and New Orleans.

House Arrest (see Home Confinement)

Howard, John (1726-1790)
English prison reformer who influenced upgrading prison conditions throughout England and the United States.

Idaho Intensive Supervised Probation Program
Launched as a pilot project in 1982; a team consisting of one PO and two surveillance officers closely supervised a small group of low-risk offenders who normally would have been sent to prison; the program was quite successful; in October 1984, Idaho established a statewide ISP program with legislative approval; this step was seen as a major element in the "get-tough-on-crime" posture taken by the state.

Implicit Plea Bargaining
Entry of guilty plea by defendant with the expectation of receiving a more lenient sentence from authorities.

Incident
A specific criminal act involving one or more victims.

Inculpatory Evidence
Any evidence that tends to show the guilt or culpability of a defendant charged with a crime.

Indeterminate Punishment (see Indeterminate Sentencing)

Indeterminate Sentencing
Sentences of imprisonment by the court for either specified or unspecified durations, with the final release date determined by a parole board.

Index Offense
Includes eight serious types of crimes used by the FBI to measure crime trends; information is also compiled about 21 less serious offenses ranging from forgery and counterfeiting to curfew violations and runaways; index offense information is presented in the *UCR* for each state, city, county, and township that had submitted crime information during the most recent year.

Indictment
A charge against a criminal defendant issued by a grand jury at the request of the prosecutor; the establishment of probable cause by a grand jury that a crime has been committed and a specific named individual committed it.

Infant
The legal term applicable to juveniles who have not attained the age of majority; in most states, age of majority is 18.

Information
Prosecutor-initiated charge against criminal defendant.

Initial Appearance
First formal appearance of criminal suspect before a judicial magistrate, usually for the purpose of determining the nature of criminal charges and whether bail should be set.

Inmate Classification
Classification schemes based largely on psychological, behavioral, and sociodemographic criteria; the use of psychological characteristics as predictors of risk or dangerousness and subsequent custody assignments for prisoners was stimulated by research during the period between 1910 and 1920.

In re Gault (1967)
A landmark juvenile rights case that established a juvenile's right to an attorney, adequate notice of charges, the right to confront and cross-examine witnesses, and the right to be warned of incriminating nature of statements made by the juvenile that might be used against him or her.

In re Winship (1970)
A landmark juvenile rights case that changed the evidentiary standard from "preponderance of the evidence" to "beyond a reasonable doubt."

Intake Screening
A critical phase during which determination is made by probation officer to release juvenile, to detain juvenile, or to release juvenile to parents pending subsequent court appearance.

Intensive Supervised Parole (ISP)
Intensified monitoring by POs in which more face-to-face visits and drug/alcohol testing are conducted; seems to have a lower amount of recidivism compared with more standardized parole programs.

Intensive Supervised Probation Programs (ISP)
Supervised probation under probation officer; involves close monitoring of offender activities by various means (also known as "Intensive Probation Supervision" or IPS).

Intermediate Punishment
A punishment involving sanctions existing somewhere between incarceration and probation on a continuum of criminal penalties; may include home incarceration and electronic monitoring.

Intermittent Confinement
A sentence a portion of which must be served in jail, perhaps on weekends or specific evenings; considered similar to probation with limited incarceration (see also Split Sentence).

Intermittent Sentence
Occurs when offenders are sentenced to a term requiring partial confinement; perhaps the offender must serve weekends in jail; a curfew may also be imposed; in all other respects, the nature of intermittent sentencing is much like probation.

International Halfway House Association (IHHA)
The number of state-operated halfway houses increased after the creation of the IHHA in Chicago, 1964; although many of the halfway house programs continued to be privately operated after the formation of the IHHA, the growth in the numbers of halfway houses was phenomenal during the next decade; for instance, from 1966 to 1982, the number of halfway houses operating in the United States and Canada rose from 40 to 1,800.

Investigatory Stage
That stage of a criminal investigation in which law enforcement officers are collecting information and evidence and no charges have been brought against any particular suspect.

Isaac T. Hopper Home
In 1845, the Quakers opened the Isaac T. Hopper Home in New York City, followed by the Temporary Asylum for Disadvantaged Female Prisoners established in Boston in 1864 by a reformist group.

Jail
A facility designed to house short-term offenders for terms less than one year; also a place for persons awaiting trial or on trial; funded and operated by city or county funds; American Jail Association defines jail as a facility that holds offenders for periods of 72 hours or longer.

Jail as a Condition of Probation
A sentence whereby the judge imposes limited jail time to be served before commencement of probation (see also Split Sentence).

Jail Boot Camp
A short-term program for offenders in a wide age range; those in New York and New Orleans have age limits of 39 years and 45 years respectively; many of the existing jail boot camps target probation or parole violators who may face revocation and imprisonment.

Jailhouse Lawyer
A prisoner who has become proficient in the law through self-teaching; a prisoner who represents others or explains the law to other inmates.

Job Dissatisfaction
Lack of interest in work performed by correctional officers; apathy or discontentment with tasks or assignments.

Job Impoverishment
Work condition resulting from few self-rewards as the result of good work effort; related to high correctional employee turnover.

Judicial Plea Bargaining
A type of plea bargaining whereby judge offers a specific sentence.

Judicial Reprieve
A temporary relief or postponement of the imposition of a sentence; begun during the Middle Ages at the discretion of judges to permit defendants more time to gather evidence of their innocence or to allow them to demonstrate that they had reformed their behavior.

Judicial Waiver (also Discretionary Waiver)
The transfer of jurisdiction over juvenile offenders to criminal court, where judges initiate such action.

Jurisdiction
The power of a court to hear and determine a particular case.

Jurist Value System
A category of decision making by parole boards in which parole decisions are regarded as a natural part of the criminal justice process and in which fairness and equity predominate.

Jury Trial
An entitlement of being charged with a crime carrying a penalty of incarceration of six months or more; an adversarial proceeding involving either a civil or criminal matter that is resolved by a vote of a designated number of one's peers, usually 12 members; as opposed to a "bench trial," in which a judge hears a case and decides guilt or innocence of defendants or whether plaintiffs have prevailed against defendants in civil cases.

"Just-Deserts" Model (see Justice Model)

Justice Model
Punishment orientation emphasizing fixed sentences, abolition of parole, and an abandonment of the rehabilitative ideal.

Justice Philosophy (see Justice Model)

Juvenile
Also known as an *infant* legally; a person who had not attained his or her eighteenth birthday.

Juvenile Court Act
Provided for limited courts of record in 1899 in Illinois, where notes might be taken by judges or their assistants, to reflect judicial actions against juveniles; the jurisdiction of these courts, subsequently designated as "juvenile courts," would include all juveniles under the age of 16 who were found in violation of any state or local law or ordinance; also, provision was made for the care of dependent and/or neglected children who had been abandoned or who otherwise lacked proper parental care, support, or guardianship.

Juvenile Delinquency
Violation of the law by a person prior to his or her eighteenth birthday; any illegal behavior committed by someone within a given age range punishable by juvenile court jurisdiction.

Juvenile Delinquent
Any minor who commits an act that would be a crime if committed by an adult.

Juvenile Diversion/Non-Custody Intake Program (JD/NCI Program)
A California juvenile program implemented in 1982 for more serious juvenile offenders; characterized by intensive supervised probation, required school attendance, employment, and counseling.

Juvenile Diversion Program (JDP)
Any program for juvenile offenders that temporarily suspends their processing by the juvenile justice system; similar to adult diversion programs (see Diversion); also program established in 1981 in New Orleans, Louisiana, by district attorney's office in which youths could receive

treatment before being petitioned and adjudicated delinquent.

Juvenile Justice and Delinquency Prevention Act of 1974 (see also Office of Juvenile Justice and Delinquency Prevention)
Act establishing many policies for juvenile courts, including separation of delinquent offenders from status offenders and the placement of status offenders beyond jurisdiction of juvenile courts (divestiture); also included recommendation to remove status offenders from institutions (deinstitutionalization of status offenders).

Juvenile Offender (see Juvenile Delinquent)

Kansas City Preventive Patrol Experiments
Experiments conducted to determine whether greater police officer visibility functioned as deterrent to crime; funded by grant from Law Enforcement Assistance Administration during early 1970s; revealed no significant differences in crime levels due to police visibility.

***Kent v. United States* (1966)**
A landmark juvenile case that led to the requirement of a hearing before juveniles could be transferred summarily to criminal court by juvenile court judges.

Labor Turnover
The degree to which new POs and correctional officers replace those who quit, die, or retire.

Latent Functions
Unrecognized, unintended functions; associated with probation or parole, latent functions might be to alleviate prison or jail overcrowding.

Law Enforcement
Action by any law enforcement agency to enforce all criminal laws.

Law Enforcement Assistance Administration (LEAA)
A program started in 1968 and terminated in 1984 that was designed to provide financial and technical assistance to local and state police agencies to combat crime in various ways.

Level of Custody
The degree of supervision and confinement for inmates, depending on the type of crime committed, whether they pose a danger to themselves or other prisoners, and their past institutional history; varies from minimum-security, medium-security, to maximum-security conditions.

Limited Risk Control Model
A model of supervising offenders based on anticipated future criminal conduct; uses risk assessment devices to place offenders in an effective control range.

Litigation Explosion
A phenomenon observed between 1970 and late 1980s of escalating numbers of lawsuits filed by inmates in jails and prisons against prison officials; a concomitant of greater prisoner rights through landmark Supreme Court cases involving inmates.

Lockdown
Security measure implemented in prisons that have experienced rioting; usually involves solitary confinement of prisoners for undetermined period and removal of amenities, such as televisions, store privileges.

Lock-Up
A short-term facility to hold minor offenders; includes drunk tanks, holding tanks; counted as jails but exist primarily to hold those charged with public drunkenness or other minor offenses for up to 48 hours; the American Jail Association suggests that to qualify as a bona fide jail, the facility must hold inmates for 72 hours or longer, not 48 hours.

Long-Term Facility
Any incarcerative institution for either juveniles or adults that is designed to provide prolonged treatment and confinement, usually for periods of one year or longer; prisons are considered long term.

Maconochie, Captain Alexander
A prison reformer and former superintendent of the British penal colony at Norfolk Island and governor of Birmingham Borough Prison; known for humanitarian treatment of prisoners and issuance of "marks of commendation" to prisoners that led to their early release; considered the forerunner of indeterminate sentencing in the United States.

Mandatory Release
A type of release from jail or prison whereby inmates have served their full terms or have fulfilled sentences specified according to particular sentencing scheme, such as guidelines-based sen-

tencing or determinate sentencing; mandatory releasees would be subject to automatic release upon serving some portion of their incarcerative terms less good-time credits applied for so many months or days served.

Mandatory Sentencing
The court is required to impose an incarcerative sentence of a specified length, without the option for probation, suspended sentence, or immediate parole eligibility.

Manifest Function
Intended or recognized function; associated with probation and parole, manifest functions are to permit offender reintegration into society.

Marks of Commendation
Points accrued by convicts for good behavior under Alexander Maconochie's (1840s) term of leadership at Norfolk Island; authorized early release of some inmates who demonstrated a willingness and ability to behave well in society on the outside; this action was forerunner of indeterminate sentencing subsequently practiced in the United States.

Mark System (see Tickets of Leave)

Massachusetts Prison Commission
An investigative body appointed by the Massachusetts governor in 1817 to examine prison conditions and prisoner early-release options and to make recommendations about policy issues; noted for originating concept of halfway house.

Maxi-Maxi Prison (see also Maximum-Security Prison)
Supposedly for the "baddest of the bad," these are prisons such as the Marion, Illinois, Federal Penitentiary constructed in 1963, accommodates 574 inmates who are considered the very worst prisoners; houses the most violence-prone, inclined to escape whenever the opportunity arises, and extremely dangerous; in many cases, maxi-maxi prison inmates are placed in solitary confinement and severe restrictions are imposed; confinement in isolation for 231/2 hours per day, with 1/2 hour for exercise is not uncommon; privileges are extremely limited.

Maximum-Security Prison
A prison that holds prisoners to a high standard of custody, including constant surveillance, often solitary confinement; limited privileges.

McKeiver v. Pennsylvania (1970)
A landmark juvenile rights case that established that juveniles are not entitled to a jury as a matter of right in a juvenile court proceeding; the right to a jury trial in juvenile court is discretionary with the juvenile judge.

Mediator (see Enabler)

Medical Model
Also known as the *treatment model,* this model considers criminal behavior as an illness to be treated.

Medium-Security Prison
In this type of prison, inmates are given more freedoms than in a maximum-security facility; their movements are monitored; often, these facilities are dormitory-like, and prisoners are eligible for privileges.

Mempa v. Rhay (1967)
A landmark probation revocation case involved due process under the Fourteenth Amendment and involved a probationer who violated the terms of his probation; matter referred back to the original sentencing judge in a combined sentencing-revocation hearing; U.S. Supreme Court ruled this to be a critical stage at which substantial rights of an accused are affected, and, therefore, the probationer is permitted to have court-appointed counsel at such a hearing.

Minimum Due Process (see Due Process)
Rights accorded parolees resulting from *Morrissey v. Brewer* (1972), a landmark case; two hearings are required: the first is a preliminary hearing to determine whether probable cause exists that a parolee has violated any specific parole condition. The second is a general revocation proceeding; written notice must be given to the parolee prior to the general revocation proceeding; disclosure must be made to the parolee concerning the nature of parole violation(s) and evidence obtained; parolees must be given the right to confront and cross-examine their accusers unless adequate cause can be given for prohibiting such a cross-examination; a written statement must be provided containing the reasons for revoking the parole and the evidence used in making that decision; the parolee is entitled to have the facts judged by a detached and neutral hearing committee.

Minimum-Security Prison
A prison designated for nonviolent, low-risk offenders; housed in efficiency apartments; inmates

permitted family visits, and considerable inmate privileges are granted.

Minnesota Sentencing Grid

Sentencing guidelines established by Minnesota legislature in 1980 and used by judges to sentence offenders; grid contains criminal history score, offense seriousness, and presumptive sentences to be imposed; judges may depart from guidelines upward or downward depending on aggravating or mitigating circumstances.

Misdemeanant

One who commits a misdemeanor.

Misdemeanor

A crime punishable by confinement in city or county jail for a period of less than one year; a lesser offense.

Missouri Sexual Offender Program (MOSOP)

A program targeted to serve the needs of incarcerated, nonpsychotic sexual offenders; the program can supervise effectively over 700 offenders who are required to complete the program before becoming eligible for parole; approach is that sex offenders' behavior resulted from learned patterns of behavior associated with anxious, angry, and impulsive individuals; the three-phase program obligates offenders to attend 10 weeks of courses in abnormal psychology and the psychology of sexual offending. In other phases, inmates meet in group therapy sessions to talk out their problems with counselors and other inmates.

Mitigating Circumstances

Factors that lessen the severity of the crime and/or sentence; such factors include old age, co-operation with police in apprehending other offenders, and lack of intent to inflict injury.

Mixed Sentence (see also Split Sentence)

Two or more separate sentences imposed where offenders have been convicted of two or more crimes in the same adjudication proceeding.

Modular Jail Designs

New prison construction arrangements based on self-contained, prefabricated structures that permit supervising officers to view prisoners in their cells and have direct viewing access to inmates at all times.

Morrissey v. Brewer (1972)

Landmark parole revocation case establishing two-stage proceeding to determine probable cause that a parole violation occurred and punishment.

Narrative

That portion of presentence investigation report prepared by probation officer or private agency in which a description of the offense and the offender is provided; culminates in and justifies a recommendation for a specific sentence to be imposed on the offender by judges.

National Crime Survey (NCS)

A random survey of approximately 60,000 dwellings, about 127,000 persons age 12 and over, and approximately 50,000 businesses; smaller samples of persons from these original figures form the database from which crime figures are compiled; carefully worded questions lead people to report incidents that can be classified as crimes. This material is statistically manipulated in such a way so as to make it comparable with *UCR* statistics; this material is usually referred to as *victimization data.*

National Institute of Corrections' Model Classification Project

Risk and needs assessment project established by the federal government to enable juvenile judges to make more informed sentencing decisions.

Needs-Assessment Instrument

Any questionnaire device designed to forecast an offender's problems and required community services (e.g., physical and/or mental health, education, counseling).

Negligence

Liability accruing to prison or correctional program administrators and POs as the result of a failure to perform a duty owed clients or inmates or the improper or inadequate performance of that duty; may include negligent entrustment, negligent training, negligent assignment, negligent retention, or negligent supervision (for example, providing POs with revolvers and not providing them with firearms training).

Net Widening

The process of pulling juveniles into the juvenile justice system who would not otherwise be involved in delinquent activity; applies to many status offenders (also known as *widening the net*).

New Jersey Intensive Supervision Probation Program

A program begun in 1983 to serve low-risk incarcerated offenders; draws clients from inmate volunteers; program selectivity limits participants through a seven-stage selection process; participants must serve at least four months in prison or jail before being admitted to program, which monitors their progress extensively; similar to Georgia Intensive Probation Supervision Program in success and low recidivism scores among participants.

New York House of Refuge
Established in New York City in 1825 by the Society for the Prevention of Pauperism; an institution largely devoted to managing status offenders, such as runaways or incorrigible children; compulsory education and other forms of training and assistance were provided to these children; the strict, prison-like regimen of this organization was not entirely therapeutic for its clientele.

New York Prison Nursery/Children's Center
A center established at the women's facility at Bedford Hills, New York, in 1989–1990; since 1930, New York legislation provided for women in prison to keep their babies; New York is the only state that maintains a prison nursery; function is to permit mothers to bond with infants in family-like setting on prison grounds.

NIMBY Syndrome
Meaning "Not in my back yard"; refers to attitudes of property owners who live near where community-based correctional facilities are planned for construction; property owners believe they will suffer declined property values and will be at risk because of felons roaming freely near their homes; opposition toward construction of community-based correctional facilities.

No True Bill
A finding by a grand jury that insufficient probable cause exists to proceed against one or more criminal defendants.

Nominal Disposition
A juvenile adjudicatory disposition resulting in lenient penalties such as warnings and/or probation.

Nonavertable Recidivist
An offender whose prior sentence would not have affected the commission of new crimes.

Norfolk Island
A penal colony established on this island in the 1840s; supervised by Alexander Maconochie;

noted for establishment of a mark system and marks of commendation, which led to contemporary use of good-time credits in U.S. prisons and jails.

Numbers Game Model
A caseload assignment model for probation or parole officers in which total number of offender-clients is divided by number of officers.

Objective Parole Criteria
General qualifying conditions that permit parole boards to make nonsubjective parole decisions without regard to an inmate's race, religion, gender, age, or socioeconomic status.

Offender-Based Transaction Statistics (OBTS)
Bureau of Justice Statistics program, originally included 14 states volunteering information about 648,453 incidents of felony arrests during 1988; program tracks arrestees from arrest to final disposition, describes sociodemographic characteristics and correlates different crimes with these characteristics; program includes adult felons and juveniles involved in very serious felonies and tried as adults in criminal courts; Honolulu Police Department also defines OBTS as a system developed to collect data elements on defendants as they flow through the criminal justice system and to present summarized data for intelligent decision making in the criminal justice system.

Offender Control
A philosophy that says if we can't rehabilitate offenders, we can control their behavior while on probation; a priority shift in probationer management toward greater use of intermediate punishments designed for better offender monitoring.

Offender Rehabilitation
Condition achieved when criminals are reintegrated into their communities and refrain from further criminal activity (see Rehabilitation).

Offense Escalation
The belief that less serious adult or juvenile offenders will eventually progress to more serious types of crimes.

Offense Seriousness Score
A score based on criminal offense severity; often used in guidelines-based sentencing schemes such as are used in Minnesota; U.S. Sentencing Guidelines uses offense seriousness scores, together with a criminal history score, to calculate

numbers of months of incarceration for convicted offenders.

Offense Severity
The seriousness of an offense, according to monetary amount involved in theft, embezzlement; degree of injury inflicted on one or more victims; amount of drugs involved in drug transactions; other alternative measures of crime seriousness.

Office of Juvenile Justice and Delinquency Prevention
Agency established by Congress under the Juvenile Justice and Delinquency Prevention Act of 1974; designed to remove status offenders from jurisdiction of juvenile courts and dispose of their cases less formally.

Ohio Experience
Several different types of programs established in Ohio during late 1980s for juvenile offenders; uses home confinement, electronic monitoring, intensive supervised probation; has three goals of heightening offender accountability, individualizing punishments, and promoting community safety.

180 Degrees, Inc.
A program similar to a halfway house for parolees but designed for those who have received no previous treatment for their sex offenses; participation is limited only to those offenders willing to admit they have committed one or more sex offenses and who can function as group members; offenders form men's sexuality groups that meet for 90-minute meetings over a 13-week period; all participants contract with officials to write an autobiography of their offense, a description of the victim, a listing of sexual abuse cues, the development of a control plan, and personal affirmations.

Outreach Centers
Substations or satellite offices of regular probation and parole agencies.

Outreach Worker
Paraprofessional who supervises juveniles on probation or parole; counsels and assists juveniles.

Overcharging
Action by prosecutors of charging a defendant with more crimes than are reasonable under the circumstances; raising the charge to a more serious level, expecting a conviction of lesser crime.

Pardon
An executive device designed to absolve offenders of their crimes committed and release them, thus reducing prison overcrowding.

Parens Patriae
Literally, "parent of the country"; refers to doctrine whereby state oversees the welfare of youth; originally established by King of England and administered through chancellors.

Parole
Status of offenders conditionally released from a confinement facility prior to expiration of their sentences, placed under supervision of a parole agency.

Parole Board
Body of governor-appointed or elected people who decide whether eligible inmates may be granted early release from incarceration.

Parolee
Offender who has served some time in jail or prison, but has been released prior to serving entire sentence imposed on conviction.

Parole Officers (POs)
Corrections officers who supervise and counsel parolees and perform numerous other duties associated with parolee management.

Parole Revocation
A two-stage proceeding that may result in a parolee's reincarceration in jail or prison; first stage is a preliminary hearing to determine whether parolee violated any specific parole condition; second stage determines whether parole should be cancelled and the offender reincarcerated.

Parole Revocation Hearing
Two-stage proceeding to determine (1) whether parolee has committed offense or offenses requiring revocation of parole and (2) what punishment should be imposed; a critical stage.

Penitentiary
A facility generally designed to be self-contained and to house large numbers of serious offenders for periods of one year or longer; characterized by manned perimeters, walls, electronic security devices, and high custody levels.

Petit Jury
Persons or peers of criminal defendants who are selected to render a judgment of guilty or not

guilty in a criminal prosecution; distinguished from grand jury, which convenes for probable cause purposes.

Petition
Official document filed in juvenile courts on the juvenile's behalf specifying reasons for court appearance.

Philadelphia Society for Alleviating the Miseries of Public Prisons
Established in 1787, Quaker society devoted to improving jail conditions in Philadelphia; consisted of philanthropists and religionists.

Plea Bargaining
A preconviction agreement between the defendant and the state whereby the defendant pleads guilty with the expectation of a reduction in the charges, a promise of sentencing leniency, or some other government concession short of the maximum penalties that could be imposed under the law.

Prediction
An assessment of some expected future behavior of a person including criminal acts, arrests, or convictions.

Predictions of Risk or Dangerousness
Any type of assessment made of future offender behavior, particularly behavior that might be threatening or harmful to others; often includes paper-and-pencil measures that yield score values; used to make parole and probation decisions by parole boards and judges; also used for inmate placements in different custody levels in prison institutions.

Predisposition Report
A report prepared by a juvenile intake officer for a juvenile judge; purpose of report is to furnish the judge with background about juveniles to make a more informed sentencing decision; similar to PSI.

Preliminary Hearing, Preliminary Examination
A hearing by magistrate or other judicial officer to determine if person charged with a crime should be held for trial; proceeding to establish probable cause; does not determine guilt or innocence.

Preponderance of Evidence
Standard used in civil courts to determine defendant or plaintiff liability.

Prerelease Program
Prior to granting parole, inmates may be placed on furloughs or work or study release to reintegrate them gradually back into their communities.

Presentence Investigation (PSI)
Conducted by either a probation officer or private organization to assist judges in sentencing convicted offenders; includes description of offense, work background and social history of offender, victim impact statement, educational attainment, work record, and other important details.

Presentence Investigation Report (PSI)
Report prepared as the result of a presentence investigation; a written record for judicial use in sentencing.

Presentment
A charge issued by a grand jury upon its own authority against a specific criminal defendant; a finding of probable cause against a criminal suspect that a crime has been committed and the named suspect committed it.

President's Commission on Law Enforcement and the Administration of Justice
A national commission established in 1967 to establish and promote standards for the selection of police officers and correctional employees; led to the establishment of the Law Enforcement Assistance Administration (LEAA) (see Law Enforcement Assistance Administration).

Presumptive Sentencing
A sentence prescribed by statute for each offense or class of offense; the sentence must be imposed in all unexceptional circumstances; when there are mitigating or aggravating circumstances, the judge is permitted some latitude in shortening or lengthening the sentence within specific boundaries, usually with written justification.

Pretrial Detainee
A person charged with a crime and placed in custody, usually a jail, prior to his or her trial.

Pretrial Detention
An order by a court for defendant (juvenile or adult) to be confined prior to adjudicatory proceeding; usually reserved for defendants consid-

ered dangerous or likely to flee the jurisdiction if released temporarily.

Pretrial Diversion
The act of deferring prosecution of a criminal case by permitting defendant to complete a specified period of months or years, usually with conditions; usually persons who comply with behavioral requirements of diversion may have their original charges dismissed, reduced, or expunged.

Pretrial Release
Freedom from incarceration prior to trial granted to defendants (see ROR).

Preventive Confinement
Placement of alleged offenders in custody, usually a city or county jail, prior to trial; also known as *preventive detention.*

Preventive Detention (see Preventive Confinement)

Prison
A facility designed to house long-term serious offenders; operated by state or federal government; houses inmates for terms longer than one year.

Prison Overcrowding
Condition resulting whenever inmate population exceeds rated or design capacity.

Privatization
A general movement in corrections and law enforcement to supplement existing law enforcement agencies and correctional facilities with privately owned and operated institutions, organizations, and personnel; the theory is that private management of such organizations can be more cost-effective and reduce capital outlays (taxation) associated with public expenditures for similar functions.

Probable Cause
Reasonable cause that a crime has been committed and a specific person or persons committed it; reasonable-person conclusion that crime has been committed and a suspect identified.

Probatio
A period of proving or trial or forgiveness (Latin).

Probation
Sentence not involving confinement that imposes conditions and retains authority in sentencing court to modify conditions of sentence or resentence offender for probation violations.

Probation Officer (PO)
A corrections official who functions to monitor convict's progress outside of prison.

Probation Officer Caseloads
The number of probationer/clients supervised by a probation officer; caseloads are determined in different ways, depending on particular probation agency policies.

Probationable Offenders Rehabilitation and Training Program (P.O.R.T.)
Halfway house operated to serve needs of juvenile and adult offenders; a reintegrative program providing counseling and job placement assistance.

Probationer
A person who does not go to jail or prison, but rather serves a term outside of prison subject to certain behavioral conditions.

Probation Subsidy Program
A California program implemented in 1965 and providing for local communities with supplemental resources to manage larger numbers of probationers more closely; a part of this subsidization provided for community residential centers where probationers could "check in" and receive counseling, employment assistance, and other forms of guidance or supervision.

Professional
One who is a member of a learned profession or has achieved a high level of proficiency, competency, and training.

Professionalization
Equated with the acquisition of more formal education rather than with the acquisition of practical skills that involve one-to-one human relationships with different types of offender-clients; more recently, associated with improvements in officer selection, training, and education; accreditation measures are implemented to standardize curricula and acquisition of skills that improve work proficiency.

Professionalization of Corrections
Efforts by American Correctional Association, American Probation and Parole Association, American Jail Association, and other interested organizations to establish accredited training programs for corrections officer selection and education; generally refers to upgrading selection and entry-level requirements for correctional officer work.

Program Evaluation
The process of assessing any corrections intervention or program for the purpose of determining its effectiveness in achieving manifest goals; investigates the nature of organizational intervention strategies, counseling, interpersonal interactions, staff quality, expertise, and education, and the success or failure experiences of clients served by any program.

Programmed Contact Device
An electronic monitoring device; similar to continuous signaling device, except that a central computer calls at random hours to verify that offenders are where they are supposed to be; offenders answer the telephone, and their voices are verified by computer.

PROGRAM for Female Offenders, Inc.
A Pennsylvania program begun in 1974 and guided by two goals: reforming female offenders and creating economically independent women; started with a job placement service; training centers were eventually created and operated by different counties on a nonprofit basis; center offerings have included remedial math instruction, English instruction, and clerical classes such as word processing, data entry, and telecommunications skill training; counseling has also been provided for those women with social and psychological problems; currently serves 300 women per year, and the community facilities have a low recidivism rate of only 3.5 percent.

Progressive Era
1960s and 1970s time period when liberals stressed rehabilitation for convicted offenders rather than lengthy prison sentences.

Project Green Hope: Services for Women, Inc.
A halfway house for women opened in New York City in 1975; originally designed to meet the needs of female parolees; goals are to assist female offenders toward living healthy, productive lives and to resolve some of the causative factors involved in their criminal conduct; more than 800 women have participated in Project Green Hope since it was established; the female clients have engaged in individual and group counseling, vocational service, and substance abuse work.

Project New Pride
A program established in Denver, Colorado, in 1973 that blends education, counseling, employment, and cultural education for children aged 14 through 17; eligible juveniles include those with two prior adjudications for serious misdemeanors and/or felonies; goals are to reintegrate juveniles into their communities through school participation and employment and reduce recidivism rates of juveniles.

Project Outward Bound
First introduced in Colorado in 1962 with objectives emphasizing personal survival in the wilderness; youths participated in various outdoor activities including rock climbing, solo survival, camping, and long-range hiking during a three-week period; program officials were not concerned with equipping these juveniles with survival skills, but rather, they wanted to instill within the participants a feeling of self-confidence and self-assurance to cope with other types of problems in their communities.

Project Re-Direction
A Fulton County, Georgia, program designed to reduce overcrowding in the Fulton County Jail as well as provide assistance in terms of counseling, job finding, and vocational and educational training for the individual prior to sentencing; thus, reintegrating ties are established between offenders and their community and family links are restored; these links help offenders to obtain employment and further their education; also permit the development of a sense of place and pride in daily life.

Project Recidivism and Alcohol-Related Crimes of Aggression
Work releasee program that incorporates treatment elements related to drug and/or alcohol abuse and makes provisions for inmates to acquire the requisite skills and education to secure and maintain particular types of employment.

Property Crime
A crime that does not involve direct contact with specific victims; examples include theft, burglary

of unoccupied dwellings, vehicular theft (not car-jacking), embezzlement; fraud.

Prosecution
One or more persons having the responsibility of pursuing criminal charges against defendants; a criminal action at law.

Prosecutor
A court official who commences civil and criminal proceedings against defendants; represents state interests or government interest; prosecutes defendants on behalf of state or government.

Public Defender
A court-appointed attorney for indigent defendants who cannot afford private counsel.

Public Risk
A subjective gauge of an offender's perceived dangerousness to the community if released, either on probation or parole; sometimes assessed through risk-assessment instruments.

Ranch (see also Wilderness Program)
A nonsecure facility for juvenile delinquents designed to promote self-confidence and self-reliance; located in a rural setting; involves camping out and other survival activities for confidence building.

Rand Corporation
A private institution that conducts investigations and surveys of criminals and examines a wide variety of social issues; located in Santa Monica, California; distributes literature to many criminal justice agencies; contracts with and conducts research for other institutions.

Rearrest
One indicator of recidivism; consists of taking parolee or probationer into custody for investigation in relation to crimes committed; not necessarily indicative of new crimes committed by probationers or parolees; may be the result of police officer suspicion.

Recidivism
New crime committed by an offender who has served time or was placed on probation for previous offense; tendency to repeat crimes.

Recidivism Rate
The proportion of offenders who, when released from probation or parole, commit further crimes.

Recidivist
An offender who has committed previous offenses.

Reconviction
A measure of recidivism; former convicted offenders are found guilty of new crimes by a judge or jury.

Reform Schools
An early establishment that provided secure confinement for more serious types of juvenile offenders; juvenile equivalent to prisons; taught youths various crafts and trade skills; intended to reform youth's behavior; unsuccessful at behavior modification.

Regimented Inmate Discipline Program (RID)
Oklahoma Department of Corrections program operated in Lexington, Oklahoma, for juveniles; program stresses military-type discipline and accountability; facilities are secure and privately operated.

Regulator Value System
A parole board orientation toward inmate reactions to parole board decisions; for example, how will current inmates react to those decisions in view of their own circumstances? Will the parole supervision system be undermined or enhanced as the result of parole board decision making?

Rehabilitation
Correcting criminal behavior through educational and other means, usually associated with prisons.

Rehabilitation Model
Orientation toward offenders that stresses reintegration into society through counseling, education, and learning new ways of relating to others.

Rehabilitative Ideal (see Rehabilitation)

Reincarceration
A return to prison or jail for one or more reasons including parole or probation violations and revocations, rearrests, and reconvictions.

Release on Own Recognizance (ROR)
Nonbail provision whereby a criminal defendant is released pending a subsequent trial; ROR means person is vested with responsibility to appear at trial later.

Respondeat Superior
A doctrine that holds a "master" (supervisor, administrator) liable for actions of a "servant" (employees).

Restitution
A stipulation by a court that offenders must compensate victims for their financial losses resulting from crime; compensation for psychological, physical, or financial loss by victim; may be imposed as part of an incarcerative sentence.

Restorative Justice

Reverse Waiver Hearing
A formal meeting with a juvenile court judge and criminal court to determine whether a youth who has been transferred to criminal court for processing as the result of an automatic waiver or legislative waiver can have this waiver set aside so that the case may be heard in juvenile court.

Revocation
Action taken by parole board or judge to revoke or rescind the parolee's or probationer's program because of one or more program violations.

Reynolds, James Bronson
An early prison reformer who established the University Settlement in 1893 in New York; settlement project ultimately abandoned after Reynolds and others could not demonstrate its effectiveness at reform to politicians and the public generally.

Risk
The danger or potential harm posed by an offender, convicted or otherwise; likelihood of being successful if placed in a probation or parole program intended to reintegrate or rehabilitate through community involvement.

Risk Assessment
Any attempt to characterize the future behaviors of persons charged with or convicted of crimes; involves behavioral forecasts of propensity to pose harm or danger to themselves or to others, usually paper-and-pencil devices that yield scores of potential dangerousness; used for probation and parole decision making.

Risk-Assessment Instrument
A predictive device intended to forecast offender propensity to commit new offenses or recidivate.

Risk-Needs Instrument
The same type of device as a risk-assessment instrument, with the exception that items are included that attempt to determine or define necessary services, counseling, education, or any other helpful strategy that will deter offenders from future offending.

Role Ambiguity
A lack of clarity about work expectations; unfamiliarity with correctional tasks.

Role Conflict
The clash between personal feelings and beliefs and job duties as probation, parole, or correctional officer.

Rules of Criminal Procedure
Formal rules followed by state and federal governments in processing defendants from arrest through trial; these vary from state to state.

Runaway
Any juvenile who leaves his or her home for long-term periods without parental consent or supervision; unruly youth who cannot be controlled or managed by parents or guardians.

Salient Factor Score (SFS), SFS 76, SFS 81
A score used by parole boards and agencies to forecast an offender's risk to the public and future dangerousness; numerical classification that predicts the probability of a parolee's success if parole is granted.

Sanctioner Value System
A system used by parole boards in early-release decision making in which the amount of time served is equated with the seriousness of conviction offense.

***Schall v. Martin* (1984)**
A landmark juvenile rights case that upheld a court's right to order the pretrial detention of juveniles deemed to be dangerous.

Screening
The procedure used by prosecutor to define which cases have prosecutive merit and which do not; some screening bureaus are made up of police and lawyers with trial experience.

Sealing Records
A juvenile court act of ordering juvenile records closed and unavailable to the public or police agencies; the equivalent of expungement orders.

Secure Confinement
The confinement of juvenile offender in facility that restricts movement in community; similar to adult penal facility involving total incarceration.

See Our Side Program (SOS)
Prince George's County, Maryland, program established in 1983; SOS is referred to by its directors as a "juvenile aversion" program, and disso-

ciates itself from "scare" programs such as Scared Straight; seeks to educate juveniles about the realities of life in prison through discussions and hands-on experience and attempts to show them the types of behaviors that can lead to incarceration; clients coming to SOS are referrals from various sources, including juvenile court, public and private schools, churches, professional counseling agencies, and police and fire departments; youths served by SOS range in age from 12 to 18, and they do not have to be adjudicated as delinquent in order to be eligible for participation. SOS consists of four 3-hour phases.

Selective Incapacitation
The process of selectively incarcerating individuals who show a high likelihood of repeating their previous offenses; based on forecasts of potential for recidivism; includes but not limited to dangerousness.

Sentence Recommendation Plea Bargaining
Plea bargaining in which prosecutor recommends a specific sentence to the judge in exchange for a defendant's guilty plea.

Sentencing
The phase of criminal justice process in which judge imposes a penalty for a criminal conviction; penalty may include a fine and/or incarceration in a jail or prison for a period of months or years; may also include numerous nonincarcerative punishments, such as community-based corrections.

Sentencing Disparity
Any sentencing that results in differential punishments for persons with similar criminal histories and who have committed similar offenses; usually based on gender, race, ethnicity, or socioeconomic factors.

Sentencing Hearing
A formal procedure following criminal conviction in which the judge hears evidence from convicted offender and others concerning crime seriousness and impact; PSI introduced as evidence to influence judicial decision making; additional testimony heard to either mitigate or aggravate sentence imposed.

Sentencing Memorandum
A court decision that furnishes ruling or finding and orders to be implemented relative to convicted offenders; does not necessarily include reasons or rationale for sentence imposed.

Sentencing Memorandum, Defendant's
The core element of presentence investigation report, in which offenders provide their version of the offense and the nature of their involvement in that offense; may include mitigating factors that might lessen sentencing severity.

Sentencing Reform Act of 1984
The Act that provided federal judges and others with considerable discretionary powers to provide alternative sentencing and other provisions in their sentencing of various offenders.

Services to Unruly Youth Program
Established in Franklin County, Ohio, in January 1975; designed to provide crisis intervention and counseling as well as other services to unruly youth (status offenders) and their families; has served over 19,000 youths and their families since its inception.

Sex Offender
A person who commits a sexual act prohibited by law; common types of sex offenders include rapists and prostitutes, although sex offenses may include voyeurism ("peeping toms"), exhibitionism, child sexual molestation, incest, date rape, and marital rape.

Shock Incarceration (see Shock Probation)

Shock Parole (see Shock Probation)

Shock Probation (see also Shock Probation Program)
The placement of an offender in prison for a brief period, primarily to give him or her a taste of prison life (for "shock value") and the subsequent release of the person into the custody of a probation or parole officer.

Shock Probationer
Any convicted offender sentenced to a shock probation program.

Shock Probation Program
Derives from the fact that judges initially sentence offenders to terms of incarceration, usually in a jail; after offenders have been in jail for a brief period (e.g., 30, 60, 90, or 120 days), they are brought back to reappear before their original sentencing judges; these judges reconsider the original sentences they imposed on these offenders; provided that these offenders behaved well while incarcerated, judges resentence them to probation for specified terms; first used in Ohio in 1964.

Short-Term Facility
Any incarcerative institution for either adults or juveniles in which confinement is for a period of less than one year; jails are considered short-term facilities.

Situational Offender
A first-offender who commits only the offense for which he or she was apprehended and prosecuted; a situational offender is unlikely to commit future crimes.

Solitary Confinement
A prison housing system that technically originated with the Walnut Street Jail; used subsequently and origin attributed to the Auburn (New York) State Penitentiary in 1820s, where prisoners were housed individually in separate cells during evening hours.

South Carolina Intensive Supervision Probation Program
A program that was implemented in 1984; primary aims of the ISP program were to heighten surveillance of participants, increase PO-client contact, and increase offender accountability; started ISP program as a pilot or experimental project.

Specialized Caseloads Model
A PO caseload model based on POs' unique skills and knowledge relative to offender drug or alcohol problems; some POs are assigned particular clients with unique problems that require greater-than-average PO expertise.

Specialized Offender Accountability Program (SOAP)
A program operated by the Lexington Correctional Center in Oklahoma for juveniles under 22 years of age; based on military disciplinary model, individualized treatment is provided, although a strict military regimen is observed.

Split Sentencing
A procedure whereby judge imposes a sentence of incarceration for a fixed period, followed by a probationary period for a fixed duration; similar to shock probation.

Standard Probation
In this program, probationers conform to all terms of their probation programs, but their contact with probation officers is minimal; often, their contact is by telephone or letter once or twice a month.

Status Offender
Any juvenile who commits an offense that would not be a crime if committed by adults (e.g., runaway behavior, truancy, curfew violation).

Status Offense
A violation of statute or ordinance by a minor, which, if committed by an adult, would not be considered either a felony or a misdemeanor.

Statutory Release
Release from prison after inmate has served full sentence or full sentence less "good-time" credit; state or federal government must release such inmates by statute.

Stigmatization
A social process in which offenders acquire undesirable characteristics as the result of imprisonment or court appearances; undesirable criminal or delinquent labels are assigned those who are processed through the criminal and juvenile justice systems.

Stress
Negative anxiety that is accompanied by an alarm reaction, resistance, and exhaustion; such anxiety contributes to heart disease, headaches, high blood pressure, and ulcers.

Structured Discretion
Term applied to judicial sentencing decisions where guidelines exist to limit the severity or leniency of sentences imposed; intention of structured discretion is to standardize sentences and create greater fairness in the courts; also applies to early release parole decisions by parole boards.

Study Release
Essentially the same as a work release program, but study release is for the express purpose of securing educational goals; several types of study release have been identified: adult basic education; high school, or high school equivalency (G.E.D.); technical or vocational education; and college.

Summary Offense
Any petty crime punishable by a fine only.

Supervised Release
Any type of offender management program in which clients must be supervised by probation/parole officers more or less intensively.

Temporary Release Program
Any type of program for jail or prison inmates designed to permit absence from confinement,

either escorted or unescorted, for short-term periods; work release, study release, and furloughs are most common types of temporary release.

Ticket-of-Leave

A document given to a prisoner as the result of accumulating good-time marks that obligates the prisoner to remain under limited jurisdiction and supervision of local police.

Tier System

An Auburn (New York) State Penitentiary innovation in 1820s designed to establish multiple levels of inmate housing, probably according to type of conviction offense and institutional conduct.

Tort

Civil wrong, omission in which plaintiff seeks monetary damages; as distinguished from crimes, for which incarceration and fines may be imposed.

Total Institution

Erving Goffman's term describing self-contained nature of prisons; depicts all community functions inside prison walls, including social exchange.

Totality of Circumstances

Sometimes used as the standard whereby offender guilt is determined or where search and seizure warrants may be obtained; officers consider entire set of circumstances surrounding apparently illegal event and act accordingly.

Traditional Rehabilitation Model (see Rehabilitation)

Traditional Treatment-Oriented Model

A model that stresses traditional rehabilitative measures that seek to reintegrate the offender into the community through extensive assistance; may include elements of the justice and limited risk control models, its primary aim is "long-term change in offender behavior"; includes strategies, such as (1) developing individual offender plans for life in the community such as work, study, or community service, (2) full-time employment and/or vocational training, and/or (3) using community sponsors or other support personnel to provide assistance and direction for offenders.

Transfer

A proceeding in which juveniles are remanded to the jurisdiction of criminal courts to be processed as though they were adults; also known as *certification* and *waiver*.

Transfer Hearing

Also known as *certification* or *waiver*, this is a proceeding to determine whether juveniles should be certified as adults for purposes of being subjected to jurisdiction of adult criminal courts where more severe penalties may be imposed.

Transport

Often referred to as *transportation*, this form of punishment was banishment to remote territories or islands where law violators would work at hard labor in penal colonies isolated from society.

Transportation (see Transport)

Treater Value System

A parole board decision-making system in which emphasis is on rehabilitation and early-release decisions made on the basis of what will best suit the offender.

Treatment Alternatives to Street Crime (TASC)

Since 1972, various community-based treatment programs have been implemented to treat and counsel drug-dependent clients; collectively labeled *Treatment Alternatives to Street Crime (TASC)* and currently operated in numerous jurisdictions throughout the United States to improve client abstinence from drugs, increase their employment potential, and improve their social and personal functioning.

Treatment Model (see Medical Model)

True Bill

Finding by grand jury that probable cause exists that a crime was committed and a specific person or persons committed it; an indictment; a presentment.

Unconditional Diversion Program

A program in which no restrictions are placed on offender's behavior; no formal controls operate to control or monitor divertee's behavior.

Unconditional Release

Any authorized release from custody, either as a defendant or convicted offender, without restriction; usually applicable to inmates who have served their statutory time in jail or prison; diversion or probation may be unconditional.

Uniform Crime Reports (UCR)

Published annually by the Federal Bureau of Investigation; includes statistics about the number and kinds of crimes reported in the United States annually by over 15,000 law enforcement agencies; the major sourcebook of crime statistics in the United States; compiled by gathering information on 29 types of crime from participating law enforcement agencies; crime information is requested from all rural and urban law enforcement agencies and reported in the FBI.

User Fees
Monthly fees paid by divertees or probationers during the diversion or probationary period to help defray expenses incurred by the public or private agencies that monitor them.

U.S. Bureau of Justice Statistics
Bureau created in 1979 to distribute statistical information concerning crime, criminals, and crime trends.

U.S. Code Annotated
Comprehensive compendium of federal laws and statutes, including landmark cases and discussions of law applications.

U.S. Sentencing Guidelines
Guidelines implemented by federal courts in November 1987 obligating federal judges to impose presumptive sentences on all convicted offenders; guidelines exist based on offense seriousness and offender characteristics; judges may depart from guidelines only by justifying their departures in writing.

University Settlement
A privately operated facility in New York begun in 1893 by James Bronson Reynolds to provide assistance and job referral services to community residents; settlement involved in probation work in 1901; eventually abandoned after considerable public skepticism, and when political opponents withdrew their support.

Van Dieman's land
A 1780s English island penal colony established off the coast of Australia; used to accommodate dangerous prisoners convicted of crimes in England.

Vicarious Liability
Indirect accountability of prison administrators who suffer the consequences of negligence of those they supervise (see also Respondeat Superior).

Victim and Witness Protection Act of 1982
A federal Act designed to require criminals to provide restitution to victims; provides a sentencing option that judges may impose.

Victim Compensation
Any financial restitution payable to victims by either the state or convicted offenders.

Victim Impact Statement
A statement filed voluntarily by a victim of crime, appended to the presentence investigation report as a supplement for judicial consideration in sentencing offender; describes injuries to victims resulting from convicted offender's actions.

Victimization Data
Carefully worded questions lead people to report incidents that can be classified as crimes; this material is statistically manipulated in such a way so as to make it comparable with *UCR* statistics.

Victimization
The basic measure of the occurrence of a crime and is a specific criminal act that affects a single victim.

Victim-Offender Reconciliation
Any mediated or arbitrated civil proceeding or meeting between offender and victim in which a mutually satisfactory solution is agreed on and criminal proceedings are avoided.

Victim-Offender Reconciliation Project (VORP)
Elkhart, Indiana–based program to heighten offender accountability to victims and reduce offender recidivism; face-to-face victim-perpetrator encounter contemplating mutually agreeable compensation and repayment.

Victims of Crime Act of 1984
Under Public Law 98-473, the Comprehensive Crime Control Act was established; Chapter 14 of this Act is known as the *Victims of Crime Act of 1984;* as part of all state and federal government victim compensation programs and work release requirements, a certain amount of earned wages of work releasees may be allocated to restitution and to a general victim compensation fund.

Violence
Behaviors and individuals that intentionally threaten, attempt, or inflict physical harm on others.

Violent crime
Any criminal act involving direct confrontation of one or more victims; may or may not involve injury or death; examples are aggravated assault, robbery, forcible rape, homicide.

VisionQuest
A type of wilderness program; a private, for-profit enterprise operated from Tucson, Arizona; program operates in about 15 states, serves about 500 juveniles annually, and is about one-half of the cost of secure institutionalization.

Volunteer
A hardworking, unpaid, dedicated individual who fills in the gaps for correctional agencies to provide much-needed services that victims, inmates, parolees, probationers, and their families might otherwise not receive because of limited funding for programs.

Waiver (see Transfer)

Waiver Motion or Hearing
A motion by a prosecutor to transfer a juvenile charged with various offenses to a criminal or adult court for prosecution; waiver motions make it possible to sustain adult criminal penalties.

Walnut Street Jail
In 1790, the Pennsylvania legislature authorized the renovation of a facility originally constructed on Walnut Street in 1776 to house the overflow resulting from overcrowding of the High Street Jail; used as both a workhouse and a place of incarceration for all types of offenders; the 1790 renovation was the first of several innovations in U.S. corrections, including (1) separating the most serious prisoners from others in 16 large solitary cells; (2) separating other prisoners according to their offense seriousness; and (3) separating prisoners according to gender.

Wickersham Commission
The National Commission on Law Observance and Enforcement established in 1931 and chaired by George W. Wickersham; evaluated and critiqued parole as well as the practices of various criminal justice agencies in managing the criminal population.

Wilderness Program
Any nonsecure outdoor program that enables juvenile delinquents to learn survival skills, self-con-

fidence, self-reliance, and self-esteem; used for secure-confinement bound offenders.

Women's Activities and Learning Center Program (WALC)
The Kansas Department of Corrections established a program for women with children that has been patterned after *PATCH (Parents and Their Children)* begun by the Missouri Department of Corrections and *MATCH (Mothers and Their Children)* operated by the California Department of Corrections; Topeka facility primary goal of developing and coordinating a broad range of programs, services, and classes and workshops that will increase women offender's chances for a positive reintegration with their families and society upon release.

Workhouse
An incarcerative facility in England in the 1700s where sheriffs and other officials "hired out" their inmates to perform skilled and semiskilled tasks for various merchants; the manifest functions of workhouses and prisoner labor were supposed to improve the moral and social fiber of prisoners and train them to perform useful skills when they were eventually released; however, profits from inmate labor were often pocketed by corrupt jail and workhouse officials.

Work Release
Any program in which inmates in jails or prisons are permitted to work in their communities with minimal restrictions and supervision, are compensated at the prevailing minimum wage, and must serve their nonworking hours housed in a secure facility.

Youth-At-Risk Program
Any juvenile program targeting youths considered "at risk" because of low socioeconomic status, poor family relationships, members of families with known criminal parents or siblings; any program designed to improve a youth's skills in various educational and social areas, where such immediate limitations make conditions favorable for acquiring delinquent characteristics and behaviors.

Youth Service Bureau (YSB)
Established in numerous jurisdictions in order to accomplish diversions several objectives; places within communities where "delinquent-prone" youths could be referred by parents, schools, and

law enforcement agencies; forerunners of contemporary community-based correctional programs, since they were intended to solicit volunteers from among community residents and to mobilize a variety of resources that could assist in a youth's treatment; the nature of treatments for youths, within the YSB concept, originally included referrals to a variety of community services, educational experiences, and individual or group counseling; original YSBs attempted to compile lists of existing community services, agencies, organizations, and sponsors who could cooperatively coordinate these resources in the most productive ways to benefit affected juveniles.

Bibliography

Abrahamse, Allan F. et al. 1991. "An Experimental Evaluation of the Phoenix Repeat Offender Program." *Justice Quarterly,* **8:**141–168.

Abrahamson, Alan. 1991. "Home Unpleasant During House Arrest, Judge Learns." *Corrections Today,* **53:**76.

Abt Associates, Inc. 1987. *Sentencing and Time Served.* Washington, DC: Bureau of Justice Statistics.

Acorn, Linda. 1989. "Study Urges Cautious Use of Shock Incarceration." *Corrections Today,* **51:**138.

Adams, Kenneth. 1983a. "The Effect of Evidentiary Factors on Charge Reductions." *Journal of Criminal Justice,* **11:**525–537.

Adams, Kenneth. 1983b. "Former Mental Patients in a Prison and Parole System: A Study of Socially Disruptive Behavior." *Criminal Justice and Behavior,* **10:**358–384.

Administrative Office of the U.S. Courts. 1984. *Presentence Investigation Report Guidelines.* Washington, DC: Administrative Office of the U.S. Courts.

Advisory Commission on Intergovernmental Relations. 1984. *Jails: Intergovernmental Dimensions of a Local Problem—A Commission Report.* Washington, DC: U.S. Government Printing Office.

Adwell, Steven T. 1991. "A Case for Single-Cell Occupancy in America's Prisons." *Federal Probation,* **55:**64–67.

Agopian, Michael W. 1990. "The Impact of Intensive Supervision Probation on Gang-Drug Offenders." *Criminal Justice Policy Review,* **4:**214–222.

Alaska Department of Corrections. 1990. *Community Residential Center Standards.* Juneau, AK: Alaska Department of Corrections.

Alaska Judicial Council. 1992. *Resolving Disputes Locally: Alternatives for Rural Alaska . . . Executive Summary.* Anchorage, AK: Alaska Judicial Council.

Alexander, E. and L. Alexander. 1985. "Electronic Monitoring of Felons by Computer: Threat or Boon to Civil Liberties?" *Social Theory and Practice,* **11:**89–95.

Alexander, Jack and James Austin. 1992. *Handbook for Evaluating Objective Prison Classification Systems.* Washington, DC: U.S. National Institute of Corrections.

Allen, G. Frederick. 1985. "The Probationers Speak: Analysis of the Probationers' Experiences and Attitudes." *Federal Probation,* **49:**67–75.

Allen, G. Frederick and H. Treger. 1990. "Community Service Orders in Federal Probation: Perceptions of

Probationers and Host Agencies." *Federal Probation,* **54:**8–14.

Allen, Harry E. et al. 1985. *Probation and Parole in America.* New York: Macmillan.

Alper, B. S. 1966. *Community Residential Treatment Centers.* Washington, DC: U.S. Department of Health, Education and Welfare, National Parole Institutes.

Alpert, Geoffrey P. 1985. *The American System of Justice.* Beverly Hills, CA: Sage.

Alschuler, Albert W. 1976. "The Trial Judge's Role in Plea Bargaining." *Columbia Law Review,* **76:** 1059–1154.

Alschuler, Albert W. 1979a. "Plea Bargaining and Its History." *Law and Society Review,* **13:**211–245.

Alschuler, Albert W. 1979b. "The Trial Judge's Role in Plea Bargaining." *Columbia Law Review,* **76:** 1059–1154.

Altschuler, David M. and Troy L. Armstrong. 1990. "Intensive Parole for High-Risk Juvenile Offenders: A Framework for Action." Unpublished paper presented at the American Society of Criminology meetings, Baltimore, MD (November).

Altschuler, David M. and Troy L. Armstrong. 1993. "Intensive Aftercare for High-Risk Juvenile Parolees: Program Development and Implementation in Eight Pilot Sites." Unpublished paper presented at the annual meeting of the American Society of Criminology, Phoenix, AZ (October).

Alvarez, W. C. and L. L. Stanley. 1930. "Blood Pressure in Six Thousand Prisoners and Four Hundred Prison Guards." *Archives of Internal Medicine,* **46:**17–39.

American Correctional Association. 1983. *The American Prison: From the Beginning . . . A Pictorial History.* College Park, MD: Author.

American Correctional Association. 1985. "Stress: Finding Light at the End of the Tunnel." *Corrections Today,* **47:**4–26.

American Correctional Association. 1986a. *The Drunk Driver and Jail: Alternatives to Jail.* Washington, DC: U.S. National Highway Traffic Safety Administration.

American Correctional Association. 1986b. "Probation and Parole: Today's Challenges: Future Directions." *Corrections Today,* **48:**4–87.

American Correctional Association. 1986c. *Public Policy for Corrections—A Handbook for Decision-Makers.* Laurel, MD: Author.

American Correctional Association. 1987. *Directory.* Laurel, MD: Author.

American Correctional Association. 1988. *Directory.* Laurel, MD: Author.

American Correctional Association. 1989a. *Correctional Officer Resource Guide.* Laurel, MD: Author.

American Correctional Association. 1989b. *Emerging Technologies and Community Corrections.* Laurel, MD: Author.

American Correctional Association. 1991. *Vital Statistics in Corrections.* College Park, MD: Author.

American Correctional Association. 1992. *Correctional and Juvenile Justice Training Directory–2nd Edition.* Laurel, MD: Author.

American Correctional Association. 1993a. *Classification: A Tool for Managing Today's Offenders.* Laurel, MD: Author.

American Correctional Association. 1993b. *Community Partnerships in Action.* Laurel, MD: Author.

American Correctional Association. 1993c. *Female Offenders: Meeting Needs of a Neglected Population.* Laurel, MD: Author.

American Correctional Association. 1994. *Directory: Juvenile and Adult Correctional Departments, Institutions, Agencies, and Paroling Authorities.* Laurel, MD: Author.

American Jail Association. 1992. *Who's Who in Jail Management.* Washington, DC: Author.

Andersen, Brian David and Kevon Andersen. 1984. *Prisoners of the Deep.* San Francisco, CA: Harper & Row.

Anderson, Dennis B., Randall E. Schumacker, and Sara L. Anderson. 1991. "Releasee Characteristics and Parole Success." *Journal of Offender Rehabilitation,* **17:**133–145.

Anderson, James and Gary Carson. 1991. "Alabama Boot Camps." Unpublished paper presented at the annual meeting of the American Society of Criminology, San Francisco, CA (November).

Anglin, M. Douglas and Yih-Ing Hser. 1990. "Treatment of Drug Abuse." In *Drugs and Crime,* Michael Tonry and James Q. Wilson (eds.). Chicago: University of Chicago Press.

Anson, Richard H. 1983. "Inmate Ethnicity and the Suicide Connection: A Note on Aggregate Trends." *The Prison Journal,* **58:**91–99.

Anthony, Lawrence M. 1988. "Supervising the Chemically Dependent Person." *Federal Probation,* **52:**7–10.

Archambeault, W. G. and L. A. Gould. 1992. "Measurement Issues in the Evaluation of Computer-Assisted Monitoring." *Journal of Offender Monitoring,* **5:**1–24.

Arizona Department of Corrections. 1991. *Offender Classification System (OCS): Classification Operating Manual.* Phoenix, AZ: Author.

Armor, Jerry C. et al. 1989. "Amenability to Rehabilitation among Prison Inmates." *Journal of Offender Counseling, Services & Rehabilitation,* **14:**137–142.

Armstrong, Troy L. 1988. "National Survey of Juvenile Intensive Probation Supervision, Part I." *Criminal Justice Abstracts,* **20:**342–348.

Arnold, Charlotte S. 1992. "The Program for Female Offenders, Inc.—A Community Corrections Answer to Jail Overcrowding." *American Jails,* **5:**36–40.

Arnold, Charlotte S. 1993. "Respect, Recognition are Keys to Effective Volunteer Programs." *Corrections Today,* **55:**118–122.

Ashford, Jose B. and Craig Winston LeCroy. 1993. "Juvenile Parole Policy in the United States: Determinate Versus Indeterminate Models." *Justice Quarterly,* **10:**179–195.

Associated Press. 1993. "Houston Police: Teen Discarded Ankle Monitor, Then Killed Restaurant Worker." *MINOT (N.D.) Daily News,* December 10:A2.

Atkinson, Donald. 1986. "Parole Can Work!" *Corrections Today,* **48:**54–56.

Atkinson, Donald. 1989. "In Maryland: Progressive Probation and Parole System Plays Important Role." *Corrections Today,* **51:**78–80.

Atmore, Toni and Edward J. Bauchiero. 1987. "Substance Abusers: Identification and Treatment." *Corrections Today,* **49:**25–36.

Augustus, John. 1852. *A Report of the Labors of John Augustus for the Last Ten Years: In Aid of the Unfortunate.* New York: Wright and Hasty.

Austin, James. 1986. "Using Early Release to Relieve Prison Crowding: A Dilemma for Public Policy." *Crime and Delinquency,* **32:**404–502.

Austin, James. 1987. *Success and Failure on Parole in California: A Preliminary Evaluation.* San Francisco, CA: National Council on Crime and Delinquency.

Austin, James and Luiza Chan. 1989. *Evaluation of the Nevada Department of Prisons Prisoner Classification System.* San Francisco, CA: National Council on Crime and Delinquency.

Austin, James, Michael Jones, and Melissa Bolyard. 1993. *The Growing Use of Jail Boot Camps: The Current State of the Art.* Washington, DC: U.S. Department of Justice, Office of Justice Programs.

Austin, James and B. Krisberg. 1982. "The Unmet Promise of Alternatives to Incarceration." *Crime and Delinquency,* **28:**374–409.

Austin, James and Paul Litsky. 1985. *Identifying Absconders from Parole and Probation Supervision: An Evaluation of Nevada's Risk Screening Instruments.* San Francisco, CA: National Council on Crime and Delinquency.

Austin, James and William Pannell. 1986. *The Growing Imprisonment of California.* San Francisco: National Council on Crime and Delinquency.

Austin, James, Peter Quigley, and Steve Cuvelier. 1989. *Evaluating the Impact of Ohio's Community Corrections Programs: Public Safety and Costs.* San Francisco: National Council on Crime and Delinquency.

Aylesworth, George N. 1991. *Forfeiture of Real Property: An Overview.* Washington, DC: U.S. Justice Department.

Ayres, Marilyn B. 1988. *Jail Classification and Discipline.* Alexandria, VA: National Sheriff's Association.

Aziz, David W. 1988. "The Research Component of Shock Incarceration." Unpublished paper presented at the annual meeting of the American Society of Criminology, Chicago, IL (November).

Baer, Benjamin F. and Jody Klein-Saffran. 1990. "Home Confinement Program: Keeping Parole Under Lock and Key." *Corrections Today,* **52:**17–18, 30.

Bahn, Charles and James R. Davis. 1991. "Social-Psychological Effects of the Status of Probationer." *Federal Probation,* **55:**17–25.

Baird, Christopher. 1985. "Classifying Juveniles: Making the Most of an Important Management Tool." *Corrections Today,* **47:**32–38.

Baird, Christopher. 1992a. "The Management of Probation Caseloads: A National Assessment." Unpublished paper presented at the annual meeting of the American Society of Criminology, New Orleans, LA (November).

Baird, Christopher. 1992b. *Validating Risk Assessment Instruments Used in Community Corrections.* Madison, WI: National Council on Crime and Delinquency.

Baird, S. Christopher and James Austin. 1986. *Current State of the Art in Prison Classification Models: A Literature Review for the California Department of Corrections.* Sacramento, CA: California Department of Corrections.

Baird, Christopher and Deborah Neuenfeldt. 1990. *Improving Correctional Performance through Better Classification: The Client Management Classification System.* San Francisco, CA: National Council on Crime and Delinquency.

Baird, Christopher et al. 1987. *Oregon Risk Assessment Project: Final Report.* Madison, WI: National Council on Crime and Delinquency.

Ball, Richard A., R. Huff, and J. Robert Lilly. 1988. *House Arrest and Correctional Policy: Doing Time at Home.* Beverly Hills, CA: Sage.

Ball, Richard A. and J. Robert Lilly. 1987. "The Phenomenology of Privacy and the Power of the State: Home Incarceration with Electronic Monitoring." In *Critical Issues in Criminology and Criminal Justice,* J. E. Scott and T. Hirschi (eds.). Beverly Hills, CA: Sage.

Bank, Lew et al. 1991. "A Comparative Evaluation of Parent-Training Interventions for Families of Chronic Delinquents." *Journal of Abnormal Child Psychology,* **19:**15–33.

Banks, Jerry et al. 1977. *Evaluation of Intensive Special Probation Projects National Evaluation Program, Phase I.* Washington, DC: U.S. Government Printing Office.

Banks, Jerry. 1984. *Validation of Risk and Needs Assessment Instruments.* Atlanta, GA: Georgia Department of Offender Rehabilitation.

Barclay, David Henry. 1985. *Controlling Prison Overcrowding: The Failure of Incremental Solutions.* Unpublished paper.

Barrineau, H. E. III. 1994. *Civil Liability in Criminal Justice,* 2nd ed. Cincinnati, OH: Anderson.

Barkdull, Walter L. 1987. "Probation: Call it Control— And Mean It." *Federal Probation,* **51:**50–55.

Barkdull, Walter L. 1988. "Parole and the Public: A Look at Attitudes in California." *Federal Probation,* **52:**15–20.

Barry, Thomas R. 1987. "Jail Security: A Unique Challenge." *Corrections Today*, **49:**16–18.

Bass, Chloe. 1987. "Adopting Alternative Dispute Resolution in the Field of Criminal Justice." Unpublished paper presented at the annual meetings of the Academy of Criminal Justice Sciences, St. Louis, MO (April).

Baumer, Terry L. and Michael G. Maxfield. 1992. "Electronic Monitoring: A Viable Sanction, Not a Magic Bullet." *Corrections Compendium*, **17:**1–8.

Baumer, Terry L., Michael G. Maxfield, and Robert I. Mendelsohn. 1993. "A Comparative Analysis of Three Electronically Monitored Home Detention Programs." *Justice Quarterly*, **10:**121–142.

Bayse, D. J. 1993. *Helping Hands: A Handbook for Volunteers in Prisons and Jails.* Laurel, MD: American Correctional Association.

Beck, Allen J. and Bernard E. Shipley. 1987. *Recidivism of Young Parolees.* Washington, DC: U.S. Bureau of Justice Statistics.

Beck, Allen J., Thomas P. Bonczar, and Darrell K. Gilliard. 1993. *Jail Inmates 1992.* Washington, DC: U.S. Department of Justice, Bureau of Justice Statistics.

Beck, James C. 1987. "The Psychotherapist's Duty to Protect Third Parties from Harm." *Mental and Physical Disability Law Reporter*, **11:**141–168.

Beck, James L. and Peter B. Hoffman. 1985. "Reliability in Guideline Application: Initial Hearings—1982." *Federal Probation*, **49:**33–41.

Beck, James L. and Jody Klein-Saffran. 1991. "Home Confinement: The Use of New Technology in the Federal Bureau of Prisons." *Federal Prisons Journal*, **2:**23–27.

Beck, James L., Jody Klein-Saffran, and Harold B. Wooten. 1990. "Home Confinement and the Use of Electronic Monitoring with Federal Parolees." *Federal Probation*, **54:**22–33.

Beck, Jim. 1990. "A Federal Perspective on Intermediate Sanctions." Unpublished paper presented at the annual meeting of the American Society of Criminology, Baltimore, MD (November).

Beha, James A. 1975. "Halfway Houses in Adult Corrections: The Law, Practice and Results." *Criminal Law Bulletin*, **11:**434–477.

Beha, James A. 1977. "Testing the Functions and Effects of the Parole Halfway House: One Case Study." *Journal of Criminal Law and Criminology*, **67:**335–350.

Bellassai, John P. and Mary A. Torborg. 1990. "Electronic Surveillance of Pretrial Releasees in Indianapolis." Unpublished paper presented at the annual meetings of the American Society of Criminology, Baltimore, MD (November).

Bench, Larry L. 1990. "Validating the National Institute of Corrections Objective Prison Classification Model." Unpublished paper presented at the annual meeting of the American Society of Criminology, Baltimore, MD (November).

Benda, Brent B. 1987. "Comparison Rates of Recidivism among Status Offenders and Delinquents." *Adolescence*, **22:**445–458.

Bendick, M. 1985. *Privatizing the Delivery of Social Welfare Services.* Washington, DC: National Conference on Social Welfare. Working Paper 6, Project on the Federal Social Role.

Benekos, Peter J. 1990. "Beyond Reintegration: Community Corrections in a Retributive Era." *Federal Probation*, **54:**52–56.

Benekos, Peter J. 1992. "Public Policy and Sentencing Reform: The Politics of Corrections." *Federal Probation*, **56:**4–10.

Bennett, Lawrence A. 1989. "Jail as a Part of Probation: What Price Punishment?" *APPA Perspectives*, **13:**18–21.

Benson, James. 1988. "Damage Suits by Crime Victims Against State Agencies Arising from the Negligent Supervision of Parolees." Unpublished paper presented at the Academy of Criminal Justice Science meetings, San Francisco, CA (April).

Benzvy-Miller, Shereen. 1990. "Community Corrections and the NIMBY Syndrome." *Forum on Corrections Research*, **2:**18–22.

Berecochea, John E. and Joel B. Gibbs. 1991. "Inmate Classification: A Correctional Program that Works." *Evaluation Review*, **15:**333–363.

Berkeley Planning Associates. 1980. *Client Impact Study Report: National Evaluation of the Runaway Youth Program.* Washington, DC: U.S. Youth Development Bureau.

Berry, Bonnie. 1985. "Electronic Jails: A New Criminal Justice Concern." *Justice Quarterly*, **2:**1–22.

Berry, Bonnie and R. Matthews. 1989. "Electronic Monitoring and House Arrest: Making the Right Connections." in *Privatizing Criminal Justice*, Roger Matthews (ed.). Beverly Hills, CA: Sage.

Besette, Joseph M. 1989a. *Correctional Populations in the United States, 1986.* Washington, DC: U.S. Department of Justice, Bureau of Justice Statistics.

Bessette, Joseph M. 1989b. *Correctional Populations in the United States, 1987.* Washington, DC: U.S. Department of Justice, Bureau of Justice Statistics.

Beto, Dan Richard. 1990. "Substance Abuse: Strategies for Community Corrections Agencies." *APPA Perspectives*, **14:**4–53.

Bigger, Phillip J. 1993. "Officers in Danger: Results of the Federal Probation and Pretrial Officers Association's National Study on Serious Assaults." *APPA Perspectives*, **17:**14–20.

Biles, David (ed.). 1988. *Current International Trends in Corrections.* Washington, DC: Department of Justice, Bureau of Justice Statistics.

Binder, Arnold et al. 1985. "A Diversionary Approach for the 1980s." *Federal Probation*, **49:**4–12.

Bishop, Bill. 1993. "New York's Crime War: The Empire Strikes Out!" *APPA Perspectives*, **17:**13–14.

Black, Henry Campbell. 1990. *Black's Law Dictionary*, 6th ed. St. Paul, MN: West Publishing Company.

Blackmore, John and Jane Welsh. 1983. "Selective Incapacitation: Sentencing According to Risk." *Crime and Delinquency,* **29:**504–528.

Blackmore, John, Marci Brown, and Barry Krisberg. 1988. *Juvenile Justice Reform: The Bellweather States.* Ann Arbor, MI: University of Michigan Press.

Blauner, Peter and Gerry Migliore. 1992. "Street Stories." *APPA Perspectives,* **16:**21–23.

Bleick, Catherine R. and Allan I. Abrams. 1987. "The Transcendental Meditation Program and Criminal Recidivism in California." *Journal of Criminal Justice,* **15:**211–230.

Blomberg, Thomas G., Gordon P. Waldo, and Lisa C. Burcroff. 1987. "Home Confinement and Electronic Surveillance." In *Intermediate Punishments: Intensive Supervision, Home Confinement, and Electronic Surveillance,* Belinda R. McCarthy (ed.). Monsey, NY: Criminal Justice Press.

Bloom, Barbara. 1993. "Female Offenders in the Community." *APPA Perspectives,* **17:**22–23.

Blumberg, Abraham. 1979. *Criminal Justice: Issues and Ironies,* 2nd ed. New York: New Viewpoints.

Blumstein, Alfred. 1983. "Selective Incapacitation as a Means of Crime Control." *American Behavioral Scientist,* **27:**87–108.

Blumstein, Alfred, Jacqueline Cohen, and David P. Farrington. 1988. "Criminal Career Research: Its Value for Criminology." *Criminology,* **26:**1–36.

Blumstein, Alfred, Jacqueline Cohen, and Richard Rosenfeld. 1991. "Trend and Deviation in Crime Rates: A Comparison of UCR and NCS Data for Burglary and Robbery." *Criminology,* **29:**237–263.

Bodapati, Madhava R. and James Marquart. 1992. "Analyzing Parole Decision Making in Texas, 1980–1990." Unpublished paper presented at the annual meetings of the American Society of Criminology, New Orleans, LA (November).

Bonham, Gene et al. 1984. "Predicting Parole Outcome Via Discriminant Analysis." *Justice Quarterly,* **1:**329–341.

Bonham, Gene, Galan Janckscla, and John Bardo. 1986. "Predicting Parole Decision in Kansas via Discriminant Analysis." *Journal of Criminal Justice,* **14:**123–133.

Bonovitz, Jennifer C. 1980. "Mental Health Procedures and the Criminal Justice System." Unpublished doctoral dissertation, Bryn Mawr College. Ann Arbor, MI: University Microfilms International.

Bonta, James and Laurence L. Motiuk. 1987. "The Diversion of Incarcerated Offenders to Correctional Halfway Houses." *Journal of Research in Crime and Delinquency,* **24:**302–333.

Bonta, James and Laurence L. Motiuk. 1990. "Classification to Halfway Houses: A Quasi-Experimental Evaluation." *Criminology,* **28:**497–506.

Boone, Harry N., Jr. 1994a. "An Examination of Recidivism and Other Outcome Measures: A Review of the Literature." *APPA Perspectives,* **18:**12–18.

Boone, Harry N., Jr. 1994b. "Recommended Outcome Measures for Program Evaluation: APPAs Board

of Directors Survey Results." *APPA Perspectives,* **18:**19–20.

Bosoni, Anthony J. 1992. *Post-Release Assistance Programs for Prisoners: A National Directory.* Jefferson, NC: McFarland.

Bottomley, A. Keith. 1984. "Dilemmas of Parole in a Penal Crisis." *The Howard Journal of Criminal Justice,* **23:**24–40.

Boudouris, James. 1983. *The Recidivism of Releasees from the Iowa State Penitentiary at Fort Madison.* Des Moines, IA: Iowa Division of Adult Corrections.

Boudouris, James. 1985. *The Revocation Process in Iowa.* Des Moines, IA: Iowa Department of Corrections, Bureau of Data, Research, and Planning.

Bowditch, Christine and Ronald S. Everett. 1987. "Private Prisons: Problems within the Solution." *Justice Quarterly,* **4:**441–453.

Bowker, Arthur and Robert E. Schweid. 1992. "Habilitation of the Retarded Offender in Cuyahoga County." *Federal Probation,* **56:**48–52.

Bowling, L. and L. Hobbs. 1990. "Day Treatment Services." In *Transitional Services for Troubled Youth,* Bruce Wolford and Cynthia J. Miller (eds.). Richmond, KY: Eastern Kentucky University Department of Correctional Services.

Bowman, Gary W., Simon Hakim, and Paul Seidenstat (eds.). 1992. *Privatizing the United States Justice System: Police, Adjudication, and Corrections Services from the Private Sector.* Jefferson, NC: McFarland.

Brantingham, Patricia L. 1985. "Sentencing Disparity: An Analysis of Judicial Consistency." *Journal of Quantitative Criminology,* **1:**281–305.

Breed, Allen F. 1982. "Corrections and the Alienated." *Corrections Today,* **44:**14–16, 20.

Breed, Allen F. 1984. "Don't Throw the Parole Baby Out With the Justice Bath Water." *Federal Probation,* **48:**11–15.

Brennan, Thomas P. et al. 1987. "A Vision for Probation and Court Services: Forensic Social Work: Practice and Vision." *Federal Probation,* **51:**63–70.

Brennan, Tim. 1985. *Offender Classification and Jail Crowding: Examining the Connection between Poor Classification and the Problem of Jail Crowding.* Boulder, CO: HSI, Inc.

Brennan, Tim. 1987a. "Classification: An Overview of Selected Methodological Issues." In *Prediction and Classification: Criminal Justice Decision Making,* Don M. Gottfredson and Michael Tonry (eds.). Chicago: University of Chicago Press.

Brennan, Tim. 1987b. "Classification for Control in Jails and Prisons." In *Prediction and Classification: Criminal Justice Decision Making,* Don M. Gottfredson and Michael Tonry (eds.). Chicago: University of Chicago Press.

Brennan, Tim and David Wells. 1992. "The Importance of Inmate Classification in Small Jails." *American Jails,* **6:**49–52.

Bright, Frank. 1981. "Increasing Probation and Parole

Officer Job Satisfaction Through Participatory Goal Setting." In *The Status of Probation and Parole?* College Park, MD: American Correctional Association.

Brillon, Y. 1988. "Punitiveness, Status and Ideology in Three Canadian Provinces." In *From Public Attitudes to Sentencing,* Nigel Walker and Mike Hough (eds.). Brookfield, VT: Gower.

Britt, Chester L., III, Michael R. Gottfredson, and John S. Goldkamp. 1992. "Drug Testing and Pretrial Misconduct: An Experiment on the Specific Deterrent Effects of Drug Monitoring Defendants on Pretrial Release." *Journal of Research in Crime and Delinquency,* **29:**62–78.

Broadhurst, R. G. and R. A. Maller. 1991. "Estimating the Numbers of Prison Terms in Criminal Careers from One-Step Probabilities of Recidivism." *Journal of Quantitative Criminology,* **7:**275–290.

Broderick, Vincent L. et al. 1993. "The Criminal Justice Challenge: An Overview." *Intergovernmental Perspectives,* **19:**7–40.

Bronstein, Alvin J. 1980. "Prisoners' Rights: A History." In *Legal Rights of Prisoners,* G. Alpert (ed.) Beverly Hills, CA: Sage.

Brooks, M. K. 1990. *Legal Issues for Alcohol and Other Drug Use Prevention and Treatment Programs Serving High-Risk Youth.* New York: Legal Action Center.

Brown, Marjorie E., and Donald Cochran. 1984. *Executive Summary of Research Findings from the Massachusetts Risk/Need Classification System, Report #5.* Boston, MA: Office of the Commissioner on Probation.

Brown, Paul W. 1986. "Probation Officer Burnout: An Organizational Disease/An Organizational Cure." *Federal Probation,* **50:**4–7.

Brown, Paul W. 1987. "Probation Officer Burnout: An Organizational Disease/An Organizational Cure, Part II." *Federal Probation,* **51:**17–21.

Brown, Paul W. 1989. "Probation and Parole Officers Up in Arms over the Gun Issue." *Corrections Today,* **57:**194–196.

Brown, Paul W. 1990. "Guns and Probation Officers: The Unspoken Reality." *Federal Probation,* **54:**21–26.

Brown, Paul W. 1994. "Mental Preparedness: Probation Officers Need to Rely on More Than Luck to Ensure Safety." *Corrections Today,* **56:**180–187.

Brown, Valerie. 1992. "Idaho's Intensive Supervision Program." *Corrections Compendium,* **17:**7–8.

Brown-Young, Cheryl. 1987. "Contextual Analysis of Correctional Programming: A Case Study in Multidimensional Meaning." Unpublished paper presented at the American Society of Criminology meetings, Montreal, CAN (November).

Bruce, A. A., E. W. Burgess, and A. J. Harno. 1928. *The Working of the Indeterminate Sentence Law and the Parole System in Illinois.* Springfield, IL: Illinois Parole Board.

Buchanan, R. A. 1986. *Evaluation of Objective Prison*

Classification Systems. Kansas City, MO: Correctional Services Group.

Buentello, Salvador et al. 1992. "Gangs: A Growing Menace on the Streets and in Our Prisons." *Corrections Today,* **54:**58–97.

Burden, O. P. 1988. "Volunteers: The Wave of the Future?" *Police Chief,* **55:**25–29.

Burke, Peggy B. 1987. "Parole Decision-Making: A Hard Job Just Got Harder." *Corrections Today,* **49:**76–78.

Burke, Peggy B. 1990. "Classification and Case Management for Probation and Parole: Don't Shoot the Messenger." *APPA Perspectives,* **14:**37–42.

Burke, Peggy B. 1994. "Probation Violation and Revocation Policy: Opportunities for Change." *APPA Perspectives,* **18:**24–31.

Burke, Peggy B., Linda Adams, and Becki Ney. 1990. *Policy for Parole Release and Revocation: The National Institute of Corrections 1988–1989 Technical Assistance Project.* Washington, DC: U.S. Department of Justice, National Institute of Corrections.

Burke, Peggy B., John Bellassai, and Mary Toborg. 1992. *Parole Violation and Revocation: Lessons for Policy Development.* Washington, DC: U.S. Department of Justice, National Institute of Corrections.

Burks, David N. and N. Dean DeHeer. 1986. "Jail Suicide Prevention." *Corrections Today,* **48:**52–88.

Burns, Mark E. 1992. "Electronic Home Detention: New Sentencing Alternative Demands Uniform Standards." *Journal of Contemporary Law,* **18:** 75–105.

Burton, Velmer S., Jr., Edward J. Latessa, and Troy Barker. 1992. "The Role of Probation Officers: An Examination of Statutory Requirements." *Journal of Contemporary Criminal Justice,* **8:**274–282.

Bush, Eleanor L. 1990. "Not Ordinarily Relevant? Considering the Defendants' Children at Sentencing." *Federal Probation,* **54:**15–21.

Bush, Robert A. Baruch. 1991. *Mediation Involving Juveniles: Ethical Dilemmas and Policy Questions.* Ann Arbor, MI: Center for the Study of Youth Policy, University of Michigan.

Busher, Walter. 1973. *Ordering Time to Serve Prisoners: A Manual for the Planning and Administering of Work Release.* Washington, DC: U.S. Government Printing Office.

Byrne, James M. 1986. "The Control Controversy: A Preliminary Examination of Intensive Probation Supervision Programs in the United States." *Federal Probation,* **50:**4–16.

Byrne, James M. 1990a. "Evaluating the Effectiveness of the 'New' Intermediate Sanctions: A Nationwide Review of Intensified Community Corrections Programs." Unpublished paper presented at the annual meetings of the American Society of Criminology, Baltimore, MD (November).

Byrne, James M. 1990b. "Intermediate Sanctions and the Search for a Theory of Community Control." Unpublished paper presented at the annual meeting of the American Society of Criminology, Baltimore, MD (November).

Byrne, James M. 1992a. "Treatment in the Intermediate Sanction Paradigm." Unpublished paper presented at the annual meeting of the American Society of Criminology, New Orleans, LA (November).

Byrne, James M. 1992b. "Two Models for Intensive Probation." Unpublished paper presented at the annual meeting of the American Society of Criminology, New Orleans, LA (November).

Byrne, James M. and Mary Brewster. 1993. "Crime Control Policy and Community Corrections Practice: An Assessment of Gender, Race, and Class Bias." Unpublished paper presented at the annual meetings of the American Society of Criminology, Phoenix, AZ (October).

Byrne, James M., Arthur J. Lurigio, and Joan M. Petersilia (eds.). 1992. *Smart Sentencing: The Emergence of Intermediate Sanctions.* Newbury Park, CA: Sage.

Cadigan, Timothy P. 1991. "Electronic Monitoring in Federal Pretrial Release." *Federal Probation,* **55:**26–33.

Cahalan, Margaret W. 1986. *Historical Corrections Statistics in the United States, 1850–1984.* Washington, DC: U.S. Department of Justice.

Calathes, William. 1990. "A Halfway House for Women Offenders: Construction of an Assessment Mechanism." Unpublished paper presented at the annual meetings of the American Society of Criminology, Baltimore, MD (November).

Calathes, William. 1991. "Project Green Hope, A Halfway House for Women Offenders: Where Do They Go From Here?" *Journal of Contemporary Criminal Justice,* **7:**135–145.

Caldas, Stephen J. 1990. "Intensive Incarceration Programs Offer Hope of Rehabilitation to a Fortunate Few: Orleans Parish Prison Does an 'About Face.'" *International Journal of Offender Therapy and Comparative Criminology,* **34:**67–76.

California Board of Prison Terms. 1984. *Sentencing Practices under the Determinate Sentencing Law.* Sacramento, CA: Youth and Adult Correctional Agency.

California Department of the Youth Authority. 1987. *Volunteers in Juvenile Probation 1987: A California Survey.* Sacramento, CA: California Department of the Youth Authority, Prevention and Community Corrections Branch.

California Legislative Analyst. 1986. *The New Prison Construction Program at Midstream.* Sacramento, CA: California Legislative Analyst.

Callanan, Thomas J. 1986. "Pointers for Probation and Parole Leadership." *Corrections Today,* **48:**76–81.

Callanan, Thomas J. 1987. "Probation and Parole: Meeting the Future Head-On." *Corrections Today,* **48:**16–20.

Camp, Damon D. 1985. "Mandated Correctional Training: A Task Analysis Approach to Curriculum Design." *Criminal Justice Review,* **10:**32–39.

Camp, Damon D. 1990. "Diversion Center Operations: A Case of Community." Unpublished paper presented at the annual meetings of the Academy of Criminal Justice Sciences, Denver, CO (April).

Capodanno, Daniel J. and Frederick R. Chavaria. 1991. "Polysubstance Abuse: The Interaction of Alcohol and Other Drugs." *Federal Probation,* **55:**24–27.

Carbone, Vincent J. et al. 1983. "Negotiation Skills Training with Juvenile Offenders." *Juvenile and Family Court Journal,* **34:**31–36.

Carlen, Pat and J. Nanette Davis. 1987. "Women in the Health, Welfare, and Criminal Justice Systems." *Contemporary Crises,* **10:**361–443.

Carlson, Eric W. et al. 1977. *Halfway Houses: National Evaluation Program: Phase 1 Summary Report.* Columbus, OH: Ohio State University Program for the Study of Crime and Delinquency.

Carney, Louis P. 1979. *Introduction to Correctional Science,* 2nd ed. New York: McGraw-Hill.

Carp, Scarlett V. and Linda S. Schade. 1992. "Tailoring Facility Programming to Suit Female Offenders' Needs." *Corrections Today,* **54:**152–159.

Carrington, Frank and George Nicholson. 1984. "The Victims' Movement: An Idea Whose Time Has Come." *Pepperdine Law Review,* **11:**1–13.

Carroll, Ginny. 1989. "Growing Old Behind Bars: Some Cellblocks Are More Nursing Home than Jail." *Newsweek,* November 20:70.

Carroll, John L. 1986. "The Defense Lawyer's Role in the Sentencing Process: You've Got to Accentuate the Positive and Eliminate the Negative." *Mercer Law Review,* **37:**981–1004.

Carter, Robert M., Jack Cocks, and Daniel Glaser. 1987. "Community Service: A Review of the Basic Issues." *Federal Probation,* **51:**4–10.

Casper, Jonathan D., David Brereton, and David Neal. 1981. *The Implementation of the California Determinate Sentencing Law.* Palo Alto, CA: Stanford University.

Cavanaugh, Michael J. 1992. "Intensive Supervision in South Carolina: Accountability and Assistance." *Corrections Compendium,* **17:**1–6.

Cavender, Gray. 1984. "A Critique of Sentencing Reform." *Justice Quarterly,* **1:**1–16.

Cavender, Gray and Paul Knepper. 1992. "Strange Interlude: An Analysis of Juvenile Parole Revocation Decision Making." *Social Problems,* **39:**387–399.

Chaiken, Jan M. and Marcia R. Chaiken. 1982. *Varieties of Criminal Behavior.* Santa Monica, CA: Rand.

Chamberlain, N. F. 1977. "Halfway Houses for Nondangerous Offenders: What Are They? What Part Do They Play in Crime Control and Correctional Management?" *Center for Information on America,* **26:**1–6.

Chambers, Ola R. 1983. *The Juvenile Offender: A Parole Profile.* Albany, NY: Evaluation and Planning Unit, New York State Division of Parole.

Champion, Dean J. 1975. *The Sociology of Organizations.* New York: McGraw-Hill.

Champion, Dean J. 1987a. "Criminal Defense Counsels, District Attorneys, and the Insanity Plea: A Modest Difference of Opinion." *American Journal of Criminal Justice,* **11:**165–179.

Champion, Dean J. 1987b. "District Attorneys and Plea Bargaining: An Analysis of the Prosecutorial Priorities Influencing Negotiated Guilty Pleas." *The Prosecutor,* **20:**25–32.

Champion, Dean J. 1987c. "Felony Offenders, Plea Bargaining, and Probation: A Case of Extra-Legal Exigencies in Sentencing Practices." *Justice Professional,* **2:**1–18.

Champion, Dean J. 1988a. "Felony Plea Bargaining and Probation: A Growing Judicial and Prosecutorial Dilemma." *Journal of Criminal Justice,* **16:**291–301.

Champion, Dean J. 1988b. *Felony Probation: Problems and Prospects.* New York: Praeger.

Champion, Dean J. 1989. "Private Counsels and Public Defenders: A Look At Weak Cases, Prior Records, and Leniency in Plea Bargaining." *Journal of Criminal Justice,* **17:**253–263.

Champion, Dean J. 1990. *Corrections in the United States: A Contemporary Perspective.* Englewood Cliffs, NJ: Prentice Hall.

Champion, Dean J. 1994. *Measuring Offender Risk: A Criminal Justice Sourcebook.* Westport, CT: Greenwood Press.

Chapman, Jane Roberts et al. 1983. *Women Employed in Corrections.* Washington, DC: U.S. Government Printing Office, Prepared for the U.S. National Institute of Justice, Center Women Policy Studies.

Charles, Michael T. 1989a. "The Development of a Juvenile Electronic Monitoring Program." *Federal Probation,* **53:**3–12.

Charles, Michael T. 1989b. "Electronic Monitoring for Juveniles." *Journal of Crime and Justice,* **12:** 147–169.

Charles, Michael T. 1989c. "Security Volunteers at the Tenth Pan American Games: The Coproduction of an Urban Enterprise." *Journal of Crime and Justice,* **12:**79–101.

Chavaria, F. R. 1992. "Successful Drug Treatment in a Criminal Justice Setting: A Case Study." *Federal Probation,* **56:**48–52.

Cheatwood, Derral and David W. Hayeslip Jr. 1986. "Reasonable Expectations in Correctional Officer Training: Matching Methods to Audience." In *Issues in Correctional Training and Casework,* B. I. Wolford and P. Lawrenz (eds.). College Park, MD: American Correctional Association.

Cheek, Frances E. and Marie D. Miller. 1983a. "The Experience of Stress for Correctional Officers: A Double-Bind Theory of Correctional Stress." *Journal of Criminal Justice,* **11:**105–120.

Cheek, Frances E. and Marie D. Miller. 1983b. "A New Look at Officers' Role Ambiguity." *Correctional Officers: Power, Pressure and Responsibility.* College Park, MD: American Correctional Association.

Cheek, Frances E. and G. M. Nouri. 1980. "Coping with Stress and Burnout for Members of the Caring Profession." 1980 Eastern Regional Conference on the Association for Humanistic Psychology, Philadelphia, PA.

Cherniss, C. 1980a. *Professional Burnout in Human Service Organizations.* New York: Praeger.

Cherniss, C. 1980b. *Staff Burnout: Job Stress in the Human Services.* Beverly Hills, CA: Sage.

Chown, Bill and Steven Davis. 1986. *Recidivism among Offenders Incarcerated by the Oklahoma Department of Corrections: A Survival Analysis.* Oklahoma City, OK: Oklahoma Department of Corrections.

Chute, C. L. 1922. "Probation and Suspended Sentence." *Journal of the American Institute of Criminal Law and Criminology,* **12:**558.

Ciuros, William, Jr. 1986. "Line Staff: They Make It Work!" *Corrections Today,* **48:**24–25.

Clagett, Arthur F. 1989. "Effective Therapeutic Wilderness Camp Programs for Rehabilitating Emotionally-Disturbed, Problem Teenagers and Delinquents." *Journal of Offender Counseling, Services, and Rehabilitation,* **14:**79–96.

Claggett, Arthur P. et al. 1992. "Corrections—Innovative Practices, Inmate Behavior Dynamics, Policy Analyses, and Personnel." *Journal of Offender Rehabilitation,* **17:**1–211.

Clark, Marie. 1986. "Missouri's Sexual Offender Program." *Corrections Today,* **48:**84–89.

Clarke, Stevens H. 1984. *North Carolina's Determinate Sentencing Legislation.* Chapel Hill, NC: Institute of Government, University of North Carolina.

Clarke, Stevens H. and Emily Coleman. 1993. "County Jail Population Trends, 1975–1992." *Popular Government,* **59:**10–15.

Clarke, Stevens H. and Larry Crum. 1985. *Returns to Prison in North Carolina.* Chapel Hill, NC: Institute of Government, University of North Carolina at Chapel Hill.

Clarke, Stevens H. and Anita L. Harrison. 1992. *Recidivism of Criminal Offenders Assigned to Community Correctional Programs or Released from Prison in North Carolina in 1989.* Chapel Hill, NC: Institute of Government, University of North Carolina.

Clarke, Stevens H., Y. H. W. Lin, and W. L. Wallace. 1988. *Probationer Recidivism in North Carolina: Measurement and the Classification of Risk.* Chapel Hill, NC: Institute of Government, University of North Carolina.

Clarke, Stevens H., Christopher Ringwalt, and Andrea Ciminello. 1985. *Perspectives on Juvenile Status Offenders: A Report to the North Carolina Governor's Crime Commission.* Chapel Hill, NC: Institute of Government, University of North Carolina.

Clarke, Stevens H., Ernest Valente Jr., and Robyn R. Mace. 1992. *Mediation of Interpersonal Disputes: An Evaluation of North Carolina's Programs.* Chapel Hill, NC: Institute of Government, University of North Carolina at Chapel Hill, Mediation Network of North Carolina.

Clayton, Obie, Jr. 1983. "Reconsideration of the Effects of Race in Criminal Sentencing." *Criminal Justice Review,* **8:**15–20.

Clayton, Obie, Jr. and Tim Carr. 1987. "An Empirical Assessment of the Effects of Prison Crowding upon Recidivism Utilizing Aggregate-Level Data." *Journal of Criminal Justice,* **15:**201–210.

Clear, Todd R. 1987. "Punishment and Control in Community Corrections." Unpublished paper presented at the annual meetings of the Academy of Criminal Justice Sciences, St. Louis, MO (April).

Clear, Todd R. 1993. "Thinking about Community Corrections." Unpublished paper presented at the annual meeting of the American Society of Criminology, Phoenix, AZ (October).

Clear, Todd R., Val B. Clear, and William D. Burrell. 1989. *Offender Assessment and Evaluation: The Presentence Investigation Report.* Cincinnati, OH: Anderson Publishing Company.

Clear, Todd R. and George F. Cole. 1986. *American Corrections.* Belmont, CA: Brooks/Cole.

Clear, Todd R., Suzanne Flynn, and Carol Shapiro. 1987. "Intensive Supervision in Probation: A Comparison of Three Projects." In *Intermediate Punishments: Intensive Supervision, Home Confinement, and Electronic Surveillance,* Belinda R. McCarthy (ed.). Monsey, NY: Criminal Justice Press.

Clear, Todd R. and Kenneth W. Gallagher. 1985. "Probation and Parole Supervision: A Review of Current Classification Practices." *Crime and Delinquency,* **31:**423–444.

Clear, Todd R., Patricia M. Harris, and Christopher S. Baird. 1992. "Probationer Violations and Officer Response." *Journal of Criminal Justice,* **20:**1–12.

Clear, Todd R. and Edward J. Latessa. 1993. "Probation Officers' Roles in Intensive Supervision: Surveillance Versus Treatment." *Justice Quarterly,* **10:**441–462.

Clear, Todd R. and Vincent O'Leary. 1983. *Controlling the Offender in the Community.* Lexington, MA: Lexington Books.

Codelia, Eddie and Jane Willis. 1989. "Volunteers: A Catalyst for Change." *Corrections Today,* **51:** 168–170.

Coffey, Alan et al. 1974. *An Introduction to the Criminal Justice System and Process.* Englewood Cliffs, NJ: Prentice Hall.

Coffey, Betsy B. 1986. "Community Corrections: An Equal Partner." *Corrections Today,* **48:**44–46.

Cohen, Fred. 1994. "Legal Issues and Community Corrections." *APPA Perspectives,* **18:**28–31.

Cohn, Alvin W. 1987. "Behavioral Objectives in Probation and Parole: A New Approach to Staff Accountability." *Federal Probation,* **51:**40–49.

Cole, George F. 1970. "The Decision to Prosecute." *Law and Society Review,* **4:**313–343.

Cole, George F. 1986. *The American System of Criminal Justice.* Belmont, CA: Wadsworth.

Cole, George F. 1989. *Innovations in Collecting and Enforcing Fines.* Washington, DC: National Institute of Justice.

Cole, Richard B. and Jack E. Call. 1992. "When Courts Find Jail and Prison Overcrowding Unconstitutional." *Federal Probation,* **56:**29–39.

Coleman, C. R. 1988. "Clinical Effectiveness of Correctional Staff in Prison Health Units." *Psychiatric Annals,* **18:**684–687.

Colley, Lori L., Robert G. Culbertson, and Edward Latessa. 1986. "Probation Officer Job Analysis: Rural-Urban Differences." *Federal Probation,* **50:**67–71.

Collins, G. A. and M. S. Richmond. 1971. *Residential Centers: Corrections in the Community.* Washington, DC: U.S. Department of Justice Federal Bureau of Prisons.

Commonwealth of Virginia. 1991. *Drugs in Virginia: A Criminal Justice Perspective.* Richmond, VA: Commonwealth of Virginia Department of Justice Services.

Connecticut Board of Parole. 1974. *Statement of Organization and Procedures.* Hartford, CT: Connecticut Board of Parole.

Connecticut Prison and Jail Overcrowding Commission. 1985. *Prison and Jail Overcrowding: A Report to the Governor and Legislature.* Hartford, CT: Office of Policy and Management.

Conrad, John P. 1981. "Where There's Hope, There's Life." In *Justice as Fairness: Perspectives on the Justice Model,* David Fogel and Joe Hudson (eds.). Cincinnati, OH: Anderson Publishing Company.

Conrad, John P. 1984. "The Redefinition of Probation: Drastic Proposals to Solve an Urgent Problem." In *Probation and Justice,* P. McAnany, D. Thomson, and D. Fogel (eds). Cambridge, MA: Oelgeschlager

Contact Center, Inc. 1985. "Survey: Habitual Offender Statutes." *Corrections Compendium,* **10:**1, 5, 10–14.

Cooke, D. J. 1992. "Reconviction Following Referral to a Forensic Clinic: The Criminal Justice Outcome of Diversion." *Medicine, Science and the Law,* **32:**325–330.

Cooper, Robert and Paul D. Werner. 1990. "Predicting Violence in Newly Admitted Inmates: A Lens Model Analysis of Staff Decision Making." *Criminal Justice and Behavior,* **17:**431–447.

Cooprider, Keith W. and Judith Kerby. 1990. "A Practical Application of Electronic Monitoring at the Pretrial Stage." *Federal Probation,* **54:**28–35.

Corbett, Ronald P., Jr. 1993. "Reinventing Community Corrections." *APPA Perspectives,* **17:**7–10.

Corbett, Ronald P., Jr. and Ellsworth A. L. Fersch. 1985. "Home as Prison: The Use of House Arrest." *Federal Probation,* **49:**13–17.

Corbett, Ronald P., Jr. and Gary T. Marx. 1991. "Critique: No Soul in the New Machine: Technofallacies in the Electronic Monitoring Movement." *Justice Quarterly,* **8:**399–414.

Corbo, Cynthia A. 1992. *Release Outcome—1984: A Follow-Up Study.* Trenton, NJ: New Jersey Department of Corrections.

Cornelius, G. F. 1990. "Training Officers from Jail to

Community Corrections: New Strategies for a New Era." *American Jails,* **4:**32–34.

Corrections Compendium. 1984. "Correctional Officers." *Corrections Compendium,* **8:**1–4.

Corrections Compendium. 1989. "Medal of Valor to Charles Smith." *Corrections Compendium,* **14:**14.

Corrections Compendium. 1990a. "Privatization Gains as Marshals Service Contracts for New Jail." *Corrections Compendium,* **15:**21.

Corrections Compendium. 1990b. "Use of Prison Alternatives Could Save New York Millions." *Corrections Compendium,* **15:**14.

Corrections Compendium. 1991a. "Electronic Monitoring Programs Grow Rapidly From 1986 to 1989." *NIJ Reports,* No. 222, *Corrections Compendium,* **16:**14.

Corrections Compendium. 1991b. "Survey: Sentencing Guidelines Determine Penalties in 17 Systems." *Corrections Compendium,* **16:**10–18.

Corrections Compendium. 1991c. "Survey Shows High Public Support for Community Programs." *Corrections Compendium,* **16:**15.

Corrections Compendium. 1992a. "ACA's Medal of Valor Goes to Michigan Parole Officer." *Corrections Compendium,* **17:**13–14.

Corrections Compendium. 1992b. "Florida Authorizes Probation, Parole Officers to Carry Firearms." *Corrections Compendium,* **17:**2.

Corrections Compendium. 1992c. "Florida's Officers Train for Concealed Weapons." *Corrections Compendium,* **17:**16.

Corrections Compendium. 1992d. "Greater Jail Terms Have Not Cut Crime Rates in Pennsylvania." *Corrections Compendium,* **17:**18.

Corrections Compendium. 1992e. "Home Confinement." *Corrections Compendium,* **17:**16.

Corrections Compendium. 1992f. "IPS Use of House Arrest and Electronic Monitoring." *Corrections Compendium,* **17:**13.

Corrections Compendium. 1993a. "Oregon to Reduce Parole Offices." *Corrections Compendium,* **18:**17.

Corrections Compendium. 1993b. "Work and Educational Release, 1993." *Corrections Compendium,* **18:**5–18.

Corrections Today. 1986. "Alternative Punishment." *Corrections Today,* **48:**127.

Corrigan, Mark. 1990. "The Use of Community-Based Sentencing Alternatives to Reduce Prison Overcrowding: An Assessment of Policy and Practice." Unpublished paper presented at the annual meetings of the American Society of Criminology, Baltimore, MD (November).

Corrothers, Helen G. 1986. "The Effects of Federal Sentencing Reform." *Corrections Today,* **48:**24–28.

Costa, Jeralita and Anne Seymour. 1993. "Experienced Volunteers: Crime Victims, Former Offenders Contribute a Unique Perspective." *Corrections Today,* **55:**110–111.

Costanzo, Samuel A. 1990. "Juvenile Academy Serves as Facility Without Walls." *Corrections Today,* **52:**112–126.

Cotton, Donald J. and Nicholas A. Groth. 1984. "Sexual Assault in Correctional Institutions: Prevention and Intervention." In *Victims of Sexual Aggression,* Irving R. Stuart and J. Greer (eds.). New York: Van Nostrand Reinhold.

Covey, Herbert C. and Mary Mande. 1985. "Determinate Sentencing in Colorado." *Justice Quarterly,* **2:**259–270.

Coyle, Edward J. 1990. *Boot Camp Prisons: A Survey of Early Programs and Some Preliminary Evaluation Evidence.* Newark, NJ: New Jersey Criminal Disposition Commission.

Craddock, Amy. 1987. "Classification and Correctional Policies: An Empirical Assessment." Unpublished paper presented at the annual meeting of the American Society of Criminology, Montreal, Canada (November).

Crew, B. Keith. 1991. "Sex Differences in Criminal Sentencing: Chivalry or Patriarchy?" *Justice Quarterly,* **8:**59–83.

Cronin, Mary. 1992. "Gilded Cages: New Designs for Jails and Prisons are Showing Positive Results: The Question Is, Can We Afford Them?" *Time,* May 1992:52–54.

Crouch, Ben M. 1983. "Maximizing the Effectiveness of Preservice Training." In *Correctional Officers: Power, Pressure, and Responsibility.* College Park, MD: American Correctional Association.

Cullen, Francis T. 1986. "The Privatization of Treatment: Prison Reform in the 1980's." *Federal Probation,* **50:**8–16.

Cullen, Francis T. et al. 1985. "The Impact of Social Supports on Police Stress." *Criminology,* **23:**503–522.

Cullen, Francis T. and K. E. Gilbert. 1982. *Reaffirming Rehabilitation.* Cincinnati, OH: Anderson Publishing Company.

Cullen, Francis T. and Lawrence F. Travis. 1984. "Work as an Avenue of Prison Reform." *New England Journal on Criminal and Civil Confinement,* **10:**45–64.

Cullen, Francis T., Gregory A. Clark, and John F. Wozniak. 1985. "Explaining the Get Tough Movement: Can the Public Be Blamed?" *Federal Probation,* **49:**16–24.

Culliver, Concetta C. 1993. *Female Criminality: The State of the Art.* New York: Garland Press.

Cunniff, Mark A. 1986. *A Sentencing Postscript: Felony Probationers under Supervision.* Washington, DC: National Association of Criminal Justice Planners.

Cunniff, Mark A., Dale K. Sechrest, and Robert C. Cushman. 1992. "Redefining Probation for the Coming Decade." *APPA Perspectives,* **16:**12–17.

Curan, John J., Jr. 1989. "A Priority for Parole: Agencies Must Reach Out to the Media and the Community." *Corrections Today,* **51:**30–34.

Curtin, E. L. 1990. "Day Reporting Centers, A Promising Alternative." *IARCA Journal,* **3:**8.

Curtis, Christine. 1992. "Effects of Intensive Supervision Probation on Attitudes of Drug Offenders." Unpublished paper presented at the annual meetings of the American Society of Criminology, New Orleans, LA (November).

Curtis, Christine and Susan Pennell. 1990. "Electronic Monitoring of Offenders: Methodological Considerations." Unpublished paper presented at the annual meetings of the American Society of Criminology, Baltimore, MD (November).

Curtis, Russell L. and Sam Schulman. 1984. "Ex-Offenders, Family Relations, and Economic Supports: The 'Significant Women' Study of the TARP Project." *Crime and Delinquency,* **30:**507–528.

Cushman, Robert C. and Dale Sechrest. 1992. "Variations in the Administration of Probation Supervision." *Federal Probation,* **56:**19–29.

Czajkoski, Eugene H. and Laurin A. Wollan Jr. 1985. *Alternatives to Incarceration: The Community Correctional Center.* Washington, DC: U.S. Bureau of Prisons.

Czajkoski, Eugene H. and Laurin A. Wollan Jr. 1986. "Creative Sentencing: A Critical Analysis." *Justice Quarterly,* **3:**215–229.

Czajkowski, Susan M. et al. 1985. "Responses to the Accreditation Program: What Correctional Staff Think about Accreditation." *Federal Probation,* **49:**42–49.

Dare, James E. 1992. "Accreditation in Probation Services: Looking Beyond the Basic Benefits." *Corrections Today,* **54:**48–50.

Davidson, R. Ted. 1974. *Chicano Prisoners: The Key to San Quentin.* New York. Holt, Rinehart and Winston.

Davidson, William S. et al. 1987. "Diversion of Juvenile Offenders: An Experimental Comparison." *Journal of Consulting and Clinical Psychology,* **55:**68–75.

Davis, Mark S. 1984. *Selected Issues in Adult Probation: The Officers and Their Work.* Columbus, OH: Governor's Office of Criminal Justice Services.

Davis, Robert C. and Arthur J. Lurigio. 1992. "Compliance with Court-Ordered Restitution: Who Pays?" *APPA Perspectives,* **16:**25–31.

Davis, Shirley. 1990. "Participatory Management: A Technique for Reducing Probation/Parole Officer Burnout." Unpublished paper presented at the annual meeting of the Academy of Criminal Justice Sciences, Denver, CO (April).

Davis, Steven. 1986. *Oklahoma Department of Corrections Evaluation of the First Year of Expanded House Arrest, October 1, 1984–September 30, 1985.* Oklahoma City, OK: Oklahoma Department of Corrections.

Davis, Su Perk. 1990. "Survey: Parole Officers' Roles Changing in Some States." *Corrections Compendium,* **15:**7–16.

Davis, Su Perk. 1991. "Number of Furloughs Increasing—Success Rates High." *Corrections Compendium,* **16:**10–22.

Davis, Su Perk. 1992a. "Survey: Number of Offenders Under Intensive Probation Increases." *Corrections Compendium,* **17:**9–17.

Davis, Su Perk. 1992b. "Survey: Programs and Services for the Female Offender." *Corrections Compendium,* **17:**7–20.

Dawson, Roger E. 1992. "Opponent Process Theory for Substance Abuse Treatment." *Juvenile and Family Court Journal,* **43:**51–59.

Dean, James M. 1989. "Computers Are Like Cars Are Like Computers Are Like Cars." *Federal Probation,* **53:**61–64.

DeAngelo, Andrew J. 1988. "Diversion Programs in the Juvenile Justice System: An Alternative Method of Treatment for Juvenile Offenders." *Juvenile and Family Court Journal,* **39:**21–28.

Decker, Scott H. and Barbara Salert. 1986. "Predicting the Career Criminal: An Empirical Test of the Greenwood Scale." *Journal of Criminal Law and Criminology,* **77:**215–236.

DeJong, William and Stan Franzeen. 1993. "On the Role of Intermediate Sanctions in Corrections Reform: The Views of Criminal Justice Professionals." *Journal of Crime and Justice,* **16:**47–73.

del Carmen, Rolando V. 1985. *Potential Liabilities of Probation and Parole Officers.* Washington, DC: U.S. National Institute of Corrections.

del Carmen, Rolando V. 1986. *Potential Liabilities of Probation and Parole Officers.* Cincinnati, OH: Anderson.

del Carmen, Rolando V. 1990. "Probation and Parole: Facing Today's Tough Liability Issues." *Corrections Today,* **52:**34–42.

del Carmen, R. V. and P. T. Louis. 1988. *Civil Liabilities of Parole Personnel for Release, Non-Release, Supervision, and Revocation.* Huntsville, TX: Sam Houston State University Criminal Justice Center.

del Carmen, Rolando V. and James Alan Pilant. 1994. "The Scope of Judicial Immunity for Probation and Parole Officers." *APPA Perspectives,* **18:**14–21.

del Carmen, R. V. and F. Trook-White. 1986. *Liability Issues in Community Service Sanctions.* Washington, DC: U.S. National Institute of Corrections.

del Carmen, Rolando V. and Joseph B. Vaughn. 1986. "Legal Issues in the Use of Electronic Surveillance in Probation." *Federal Probation,* **50:**60–69.

Delaware Executive Department. 1984. *Recidivism in Delaware: A Study of Rearrest after Release from Incarceration.* Dover, DE: Delaware Executive Department.

DeLuca, H. R., Thomas J. Miller, and Carl F. Wiedemann. 1991. "Punishment vs. Rehabilitation: A Proposal for Revising Sentencing Practices." *Federal Probation,* **55:**37–45.

Denkowski, George C. and Kathryn M. Denkowski. 1985. "The Mentally Retarded Offender in the State Prison System: Identification, Prevalence, Adjustment, and Rehabilitation." *Criminal Justice and Behavior,* **12:**55–69.

Denzlinger, Jerry D. and David E. Miller. 1991. "The Federal Probation Officer: Life Before and After

Guideline Sentencing." *Federal Probation,* **55:** 49–53.

Deschenes, Elizabeth, Susan Turner, and Todd Clear. 1992. "The Effectiveness of ISP for Different Types of Drug Offenders." Unpublished paper presented at the annual meetings of the American Society of Criminology. New Orleans, LA (November).

DeSilva, B. 1980. "Retarded Offender: A Problem without a Program." *Corrections Magazine,* **6:** 24–33.

DeWitt, Charles B. 1986b. *Ohio's New Approach to Prison and Jail Financing.* Washington, DC: U.S. Department of Justice, National Institute of Justice.

DeWitt, Charles B. 1987. *Building on Experience: A Case Study of Advanced Construction and Financing Methods for Corrections.* Washington, DC: U.S. National Institute of Corrections.

DeWitt, Charles B. and Cindie A. Unger. 1987. *Oklahoma Prison Expansion Saves Time and Money.* Washington, DC: National Institute of Justice.

Dickey, Walter J. 1989. *From the Bottom Up: Probation and Parole Supervision in Milwaukee.* Madison, WI: Continuing Education and Outreach, University of Wisconsin Law School.

Dickey, Walter J. and Dennis Wagner. 1990. *From the Bottom Up: The High Risk Offender Intensive Supervision Program.* Madison, WI: Continuing Education and Outreach, University of Wisconsin Law School.

Dickstein, L. J. and C. C. Nadelson. 1989. *Family Violence: Emerging Issues of a National Crisis.* Washington, DC: American Psychiatric Press.

Dierna, John S. 1987. "Counseling in Federal Probation: The Introduction of a Flowchart into the Counseling Process." *Federal Probation,* **51:**4–16.

Dierna, John S. 1989. "Guideline Sentencing: Probation Officer Responsibilities and Interagency Issues." *Federal Probation,* **53:**3–11.

Dietz, Christopher. 1985. "Parole: Crucial to Our Criminal Justice System." *Corrections Today,* **47:**30–32.

Diggs, David W. and Stephen L. Pieper. 1994. "Using Day Reporting Centers as an Alternative to Jail." *Federal Probation,* **58:**9–23.

DiVito, Robert J. 1991. "Survey of Mandatory Education Policies in State Penal Institutions." *Journal of Correctional Education,* **42:**126–132.

DOCS Today, New York. 1993. "Volunteers Cover all Bases." *Corrections Compendium,* **18:**16.

Doeren, Stephen E. and Mary J. Hageman. 1982. *Community Corrections.* Cincinnati, OH: Anderson.

Doherty, Donald P. 1986. "Effective Dispute Resolutions." *Corrections Today,* **48:**56, 60, 88.

Donnelly, Patrick G. and Brian E. Forschner. 1984. "Client Success or Failure in a Halfway House." *Federal Probation,* **48:**38–44.

Donnelly, Patrick G. and Brian E. Forschner. 1987. "Predictors of Success in a Co-Correctional Halfway House: A Discriminant Analysis." *Journal of Crime and Justice,* **10:**1–22.

Donnelly, S. M. 1980. *Community Service Orders in*

Federal Probation. Washington, DC: National Institute of Justice.

Dowell, David, Cecelia Klein, and Cheryl Krichmar. 1985. "Evaluation of a Halfway House for Women." *Journal of Criminal Justice,* **13:**217–226.

Drass, Kriss A. and J. William Spencer. 1987. "Accounting for Pre-Sentencing Recommendations: Typologies and Probation Officers' Theory of Office." *Social Problems,* **34:**277–293.

Dressler, David. 1962. *Practice and Theory of Probation and Parole.* New York: Columbia University Press.

Dressler, David. 1969. *Practice and Theory of Probation and Parole,* 2nd ed. New York: Columbia University Press.

Driggs, John and Thomas H. Zoet. 1987. "Breaking the Cycle: Sex Offenders on Parole." *Corrections Today,* **49:**124–129.

Dubber, Markus Dirk. 1990. "The Unprincipled Punishment of Repeat Offenders: A Critique of California's Habitual Offender Statute." *Stanford Law Review,* **43:**193–240.

Duff, R. W. and L. K. Hong. 1977. "Implementing Work Release: The Need for Neighborhood Impact Studies." *Lambda Alpha Epsilon Journal,* **40:**2–6.

Duffee, David E. and Edmund F. McGarrell (eds.). 1990. *Community Corrections: A Community Field Approach.* Washington, DC: Department of Justice, Bureau of Justice Statistics.

Duffie, Henry C. and Gail Hughes. 1989. "Point and Counterpoint: Fees for Supervision—Debating the Issues for Probation and Parole." *APPA Perspectives,* **13:**24–26.

Dugger, Richard L. 1988. "The Graying of America's Prisons: Special Care Considerations." *Corrections Today,* **50:**26–34.

Eckert, Mary A. et al. 1987. *An Evaluation of the Court Employment Project's FY84 Alternatives-to-Incarceration Program: Final Report.* New York: New York City Criminal Justice Agency.

Eddy, William A. 1992. "Motivating Substance Abusing Parents in Dependency Court." *Juvenile and Family Court Journal,* **43:**11–20.

Edna McConnell Clark Foundation. 1982. *Overcrowded Time: Why Prisons Are So Crowded and What Can Be Done.* New York: The Edna McConnell Clark Foundation.

Edwards, Harry T. 1986. "Alternative Dispute Resolution: Panacea or Anathema?" *Harvard Law Review,* **99:**668–684.

Ehrenkrantz Group. 1984. *State of Maine, Department of Corrections—Legislation Impact Study.* New York: Ehrenkrantz Group.

Eisenberg, Michael. 1985a. *Release Outcome Series: Halfway House Research.* Austin, TX: Texas Board of Pardons and Paroles.

Eisenberg, Michael. 1985b. *Factors Associated with Recidivism.* Austin, TX: Texas Board of Pardons and Paroles.

Eisenberg, Michael. 1986a. *Intensive Caseload Pilot*

Project: Research Report. Austin, TX: Texas Board of Pardons and Paroles.

Eisenberg, Michael. 1986b. *Parole Supervision: Administrative Time Study.* Austin, TX: Texas Board of Pardons and Paroles.

Ekland-Olson, Sheldon and William R. Kelly. 1993. *Justice Under Pressure: A Comparison of Recidivism Patterns among Four Successive Parolee Cohorts.* New York: Springer-Verlag.

Ellsworth, John. 1985. "Treating Substance Abuse: A Good Approach Is to Combine Urinalysis, Education, and Referral." *Corrections Today,* **47:**92–94.

Ellsworth, Thomas. 1990a. "The Actual and Preferred Goals of Adult Probation: A Study of Enforcement and Rehabilitation." Unpublished paper presented at the annual meetings of the Academy of Criminal Justice Sciences, Denver, CO (April).

Ellsworth, Thomas. 1990b. "The Goal Orientation of Adult Probation Professionals: A Study of Probation Systems." *Journal of Crime and Justice,* **12:**55–76.

Ellsworth, Thomas. 1990c. "Identifying the Actual and Preferred Goals of Adult Probation." *Federal Probation,* **54:**10–15.

Ely, Richard E. 1989. *Report on the Safety Concerns of Probation and Alternatives to Incarceration Staff in New York State.* Albany, NY: New York State Bureau of Policy, Planning, and Information.

Emshoff, James G. and William S. Davidson. 1987. "The Effect of 'Good Time' Credit on Inmate Behavior: A Quasi-Experiment." *Criminal Justice and Behavior,* **14:**335–351.

EMT Group Inc. 1990. *Evaluation of the California Ignition Interlock Pilot Program for DUI Offenders—Final Report.* Sacramento, CA: Office of Traffic Safety.

English, Kim and Mary J. Mande. 1991. *Community Corrections in Colorado: Why Do Some Clients Succeed and Others Fail?* Denver, CO: Department of Public Safety, Colorado Division of Criminal Justice.

Erez, Edna. 1988. "The Myth of the New Female Offender: Some Evidence from Attitudes toward Law Justice." *Journal of Criminal Justice,* **16:**499–509.

Erez, Edna. 1992. "Dangerous Men, Evil Women: Gender and Parole Decision-Making." *Justice Quarterly,* **9:**105–126.

Erez, Edna and Pamela Tontodonato. 1990. "The Effect of Victim Participation in Sentencing on Sentence Outcome." *Criminology,* **28:**451–474.

Erwin, Billie S. 1986. "Turning Up the Heat on Probationers in Georgia." *Federal Probation,* **50:**17–24.

Erwin, Billie S. and Lawrence A. Bennett. 1987. *New Dimensions in Probation: Georgia's Experience with Intensive Probation Supervision (IPS).* Washington, DC: U.S. Department of Justice, National Institute of Justice.

Eskridge, Chris W. 1986. "Sentencing Guidelines: To Be or Not To Be?" *Federal Probation,* **50:**70–76.

Evans, Donald G. 1993a. "Probation: The Adaptable Agency." *APPA Perspectives,* **17:**10–12.

Evans, Donald G. 1993b. "Putting 'Community' Back into Community Corrections." *Corrections Today,* **55:**152–154.

Evans, Robin. 1982. *The Fabrication of Virtue: English Prisons and Architecture, 1750–1840.* New York: Cambridge University Press.

Evatt, Parker and J. A. Brown. 1991. *Community Residential Treatment Centers: Facilities.* Washington, DC: U.S. Department of Justice.

Eynon, Thomas G. 1989. "Building Community Support." *Corrections Today,* **51:**148–152.

Fabelo, Tony. 1992. *The Reading to Reduce Recidivism Program: Development, Implementation, and Termination—Implications for Future Correctional Treatment.* Austin, TX: Texas Criminal Justice Policy Council.

Fallin, Vince. 1989. "Gaining Support for Sentencing Options." *Corrections Today,* **51:**66–72.

Faulkner, Rick. 1994. "Networking in Community Corrections." *APPA Perspectives,* **18:**23.

Fehr, Larry. 1983. *Rethinking Imprisonment in Washington State: Critical Public Policy Choices.* Seattle, WA: Washington Council on Crime and Delinquency.

Feeley, Malcolm M. 1991. "The Privatization of Prisons in Historical Perspective." *Criminal Justice Research Bulletin,* **6:**1–10.

Feld, Barry. 1987. "The Juvenile Court Meets the Principle of the Offense: Legislative Changes in Juvenile Waiver Statutes." *Journal of Criminal Law and Criminology,* **78:**471–533.

Feld, Barry. 1988. "The Right to Counsel in Juvenile Court: An Empirical Study of When Lawyers Appear and the Differences They Make." Unpublished paper presented at the American Society of Criminology meetings, Chicago (November).

Felstiner, William L. F. and Lynne A. Williams. 1979. "Mediation as an Alternative to Criminal Prosecution: Ideology and Limitations." *Law and Human Behavior New York,* **2:**223–244.

Ferns, Ray. 1994. "Restorative Case Management: The Evolution of Correctional Case Management." *APPA Perspectives,* **18:**36–41.

Fichter, Michael, Peter Hirschburg, and Johnny McGaha. 1986. *Felony Probation in Missouri: A Comparative Analysis to the California "Rand" Report.* Cape Girardeau, MO: Southeast Missouri State University.

Fichter, Michael, Peter Hirschburg, and Johnny McGaha. 1987. "Increased Felony Probation: Is It the Answer to Overcrowded Prisons?" Unpublished paper presented at the Academy of Criminal Justice Sciences meetings, St. Louis, Missouri (April).

Finkelman, Paul (ed.). 1992. *Race and Criminal Justice.* New York and London, UK: Garland Publishing Company.

Finn, Peter. 1984. "Judicial Responses to Prison Crowding." *Judicature,* **67:**318–326.

Finn, Peter and Dale Parent. 1992a. *Making the Offender Foot the Bill: A Texas Program.* Washington, DC: National Institute of Justice.

Finn, Peter and Dale Parent. 1992b. "Texas Collects Substantial Revenues From Probation Fees." *Federal Probation,* **57:**17–22.

Fitzharris, Timothy L. 1971. *Work Release in Perspective—An Exploratory Analysis of Extramural Correctional Employment.* Berkeley, CA: University of California.

Fitzharris, Timothy L. 1984. "The Federal Role in Probation Reform." In *Probation and Justice,* P. D. McAnany, D. Thomson, and D. Fogel (eds.). Cambridge, MA: Oelgeschlager, Gunn and Haig, Publishers.

Fletcher, Lawrence P. 1984. "Restitution in the Criminal Process: Procedures for Fixing the Offender's Liability." *Yale Law Journal,* **93:**505–522.

Flicker, B. 1983. *Reducing Overcrowding in Juvenile Institutions.* New York: Vincent Astor Foundation.

Florida Department of Corrections. 1986. *Implementation Manual for Community Control: A New Concept.* Tallahassee, FL: Probation and Parole Services Program Office.

Florida Department of Corrections. 1987. *Community Control "House Arrest": A Three-Year Longitudinal Report.* Tallahassee, FL: Author.

Florida Department of Corrections. 1988. *Adult Probation and Parole Revocation Process Research Report, Final Report.* Tallahassee, FL: Author.

Florida Department of Corrections. 1990. *Boot Camp: A Twenty-Five Month Review.* Tallahassee, FL: Author, Bureau of Planning, Research and Statistics.

Florida Department of Corrections. 1992a. *Florida Department of Corrections: Annual Report.* Tallahassee, FL: Author.

Florida Department of Corrections. 1992b. *Habitual Felony Offenders in Florida's Prisons: A Simulation of Early Release Eligibility Policy.* Tallahassee, FL: Author, Bureau of Planning, Research and Statistics.

Floud, Jean and Warren Young. 1981. *Dangerousness and Criminal Justice.* London, UK: Heinemann Educational Books.

Floud, Jean and Warren Young. 1982. *Dangerousness and Criminal Justice.* Totowa, NJ: Barnes and Noble.

Flowers, Gerald T., Timothy S. Carr, and Barry R. Ruback. 1991. *Special Alternative Incarceration Evaluation.* Atlanta, GA: Georgia Department of Corrections.

Flynn, Leonard E. 1986. "House Arrest: Florida's Alternative Eases Crowding and Tight Budgets." *Corrections Today,* **48:**64–68.

Fogel, David. 1975. *We Are the Living Proof.* Cincinnati, OH: Anderson Publishing Company.

Fogel, David. 1979. *We Are the Living Proof,* 2nd ed. Cincinnati, OH: Anderson Publishing Company.

Fogel, David and Joe Hudson. 1981. *Justice as Fairness: Perspectives on the Justice Model.* Cincinnati, OH: Anderson Publishing Company.

Forst, Brian. 1983. "Selective Incapacitation: An Idea Whose Time Has Come?" *Federal Probation,* **46:**19–22.

Fraboni, Maryann et al. 1990. "Offense Type and Two-Point MMPI Code Profiles: Discrimination between Violent and Nonviolent Offenders." *Journal of Clinical Psychology,* **66:**774–777.

Frank, Susan J. and Darlene M. Atkins. 1981. "Policy Is One Thing: Implementation Is Another: A Comparison of Agencies in a Juvenile Justice Referral Network." *American Journal of Community Psychology,* **9:**581–604.

Frase, Richard S. 1993. "Big-City Crime and 'Get-Tough' Politics Arrive in Minnesota: Changes in the States Sentencing Guidelines and Practices Since 1989." Unpublished paper presented at the annual meeting of the American Society of Criminology, Phoenix, AZ (October).

Frazier, Charles E. and John K. Cochran. 1986. "Official Intervention, Diversion from the Juvenile Justice System, and Dynamics of Human Services Work: Effects of a Reform Goal on Labeling Theory." *Crime and Delinquency,* **32:**157–176.

Frazier, Mark W., J. David Hawkins, and Matthew O. Howard. 1988. "Parent Training for Delinquency Prevention." *Child and Youth Services,* **11:**93–125.

Frederick, Bruce C., Edward T. Guider, and Vincent D. Monti. 1984. *The Effects of Limiting Discretion in Sentencing.* New York: New York State Division of Criminal Justice Services.

French, Laurence. 1986. "Treatment Considerations for the Mentally Retarded Inmates." *Corrective and Social Psychiatry and Journal of Behavior Technology and Therapy,* **32:**124–129.

Friday, Paul C. and Michael Brown. 1988. "Jail Overcrowding: It's Not Just a Corrections Problem." Unpublished paper presented at the annual meeting of the American Society of Criminology, Chicago, IL (November).

Friday, Paul C. and David M. Petersen. 1972. "Shock of Imprisonment: Comparative Analysis of Short-term Incarceration as a Treatment Technique." Paper presented at the annual meeting of the American Society of Criminology, Caracas, Venezuela.

Friday, Paul C., D. M. Petersen, and H. E. Allen. 1973. "Shock Probation: A New Approach to Crime Control." *Georgia Journal of Corrections,* **1:**1–13.

Friel, Charles M. and Joseph B. Vaughn. 1986. "A Consumer's Guide to the Electronic Monitoring of Probationers." *Federal Probation,* **50:**3–14.

Frost, Martin L., Bruce A. Fisher, and Robert B. Coates. 1985. "Indeterminate and Determinate Sentencing of Juvenile Delinquents: A National Survey of Approaches to Commitment and Release Decision-making." *Juvenile and Family Court Journal,* **36:**1–12.

Frost, Sally M. and Geoffrey M. Stephenson. 1989. "A Simulation of Electronic Tagging as a Sentencing Option." *Howard Journal of Criminal Justice,* **28:**91–104.

Fulton, Betsy and Susan Stone. 1993. "Achieving Public Safety Through the Provision of Intense Services: The Promise of a New ISP." *APPA Perspectives,* **17:**43–45.

Gable, Ralph K. 1986. "Application of Personal Telemonitoring to Current Problems in Corrections." *Journal of Criminal Justice,* **14:**167–176.

Galaway, Burt. 1988. "Restitution as Innovation or Unfilled Promise?" *Federal Probation,* **52:**3–14.

Galvin, John J. et al. 1977. *Alternatives to Prosecution: Instead of Jail.* Washington, DC: U.S. Government Printing Office.

Garner, Joel H. 1991. "The Feasibility of Predictive Classification for Inmates Held Pretrial in Federal BOP Facilities." Unpublished paper presented at the annual meeting of the American Society of Criminology, San Francisco, CA (November).

Gatz, Nick and Chris Murray. 1981. "An Administrative Overview of Halfway Houses." *Corrections Today,* **43:**52–54.

Gaudin, J. M., Jr. 1993. "Effective Intervention with Neglectful Families." *Criminal Justice and Behavior,* **20:**66–89.

Gavzer, B. 1986. "Must Kids be Bad?" *Parade,* March 9:8–10.

Gee, Travis et al. 1993. "Recidivism." *Focus on Corrections Research,* **5:**3–38.

Genevie, L. et al. 1983. *Trends in the Effectiveness of Correctional Intervention.* Washington, DC: U.S. National Institute of Justice.

Georgia Parole Review. 1990. "Georgia Rehabilitation Program Helps Disabled Parolees." *Corrections Today,* **52:**174–176.

Gibbs, John J. 1991. "Environmental Congruence and Symptoms of Psychopathology: A Further Exploration of the Effects of Exposure to the Jail Environment." *Criminal Justice and Behavior,* **18:**351–374.

Gilliard, Darrell K. 1993. *Prisoners in 1992.* Washington, DC: U.S. Department of Justice, Bureau of Justice Statistics.

Glaser, Daniel. 1983. "Supervising Offenders Outside of Prison." In *Crime and Public Policy,* James Q. Wilson (ed.). San Francisco. Institute for Contemporary Studies.

Glaser, Daniel. 1987. "Classification for Risk." In *Prediction and Classification: Criminal Justice Decision Making,* Don M. Gottfredson and Michael Tonry (eds.). Chicago: University of Chicago Press.

Glaser, Daniel F. and R. Watts. 1993. "Electronic Monitoring of Drug Offenders on Probation." *Journal of Offender Monitoring,* **6:**1–10, 14.

Glenwick, David S. (ed.). 1988. "Community Psychology Perspectives on Delinquency." *Criminal Justice and Behavior,* **15:**275–393.

Goddard, Malcolm S. 1977. "Juvenile Parole Revocation Hearings: The New York State Experience." *Criminal Law Bulletin,* **13:**552–573.

Goetting, Ann and R. M. Howsen. 1986. "Correlations of Prisoner Misconduct." *Journal of Quantitative Criminology,* **2:**49–67.

Goffman, Erving. 1961. *Asylums.* Garden City, NY: Anchor Press.

Goldkamp, John S. 1987. "Prediction in Criminal Justice Policy Development." In *Prediction and Classification: Criminal Justice Decision Making,* Don M. Gottfredson and Michael Tonry (eds.). Chicago, IL: University of Chicago Press.

Goodstein and Hepburn. 1985. *Determinate Sentencing and Imprisonment: A Failure of Reform.* Cincinnati, OH: Anderson.

Goodstein, Lynne, John Kramer, and Laura Nuss. 1984. "Defining Determinacy: Components of the Sentencing Process Ensuring Equity and Release Certainty." *Justice Quarterly,* **1:**47–73.

Gordon, D. A. and J. Arbuthnot. 1988. "Use of Paraprofessionals to Deliver Home-Based Family Therapy to Juvenile Delinquents." *Criminal Justice and Behavior: An International Journal,* **15:**364–378.

Gordon, Margaret A. and Daniel Glaser. 1991. "The Use and Effects of Financial Penalties in Municipal Courts." *Criminology,* **29:**651–676.

Goss, Mike. 1989. "Electronic Monitoring: The Missing Link for Successful House Arrest." *Corrections Today,* **51:**106–108.

Goss, Mike. 1990. "Serving Time Behind the Front Door: Electronic Monitoring Programs Provide Prison Alternatives." *Corrections Today,* **52:**80–84.

Gostin, Larry. 1986. "AIDS Policies Raise Civil Liberties Concerns." *Journal of the National Prison Project,* **10:**10–11.

Gottfredson, Don M. and Michael Tonry. 1987. *Prediction and Classification: Criminal Justice Decision Making.* Chicago, IL: University of Chicago Press.

Gottfredson, Don M., Leslie T. Wilkins, and Peter B. Hoffman. 1978. *Guidelines for Parole and Sentencing.* Lexington, MA: Heath.

Gottfredson, Michael R. and K. Adams. 1982. "Prison Behavior and Release Performance: Empirical Reality and Public Policy." *Law and Policy Quarterly,* **4:**373.

Gottfredson, Michael R. and Don M. Gottfredson. 1988. *Decision Making in Criminal Justice: Toward the Rational Exercise of Discretion,* 2nd ed. New York: Plenum Press.

Gottfredson, Stephen D. 1984. "Institutional Responses to Prison Overcrowding." *New York University Review of Law and Social Change,* **12:**259–273.

Gottfredson, Stephen D. and Don M. Gottfredson. 1990. *Classification, Prediction, and Criminal Justice Policy: Final Report to the National Institute of Justice.* Washington, DC: U.S. National Institute of Justice.

Gottfredson, Stephen D. and Ralph B. Taylor. 1985. *Prediction of Recidivism: Neighborhood Effects.* Washington, DC: U.S. National Institute of Justice.

Gottlieb, Barbara and Phillip Rosen. 1984. *Public Danger as a Factor in Pretrial Release: Summaries of*

State Danger Laws. Washington, DC: Toborg Associates.

Gottschalk, Martin and David Duffee. 1992. "The Effect of Offender Characteristics and Problems on the Service Provision Process." Unpublished paper presented at the annual meetings of the American Society of Criminology, New Orleans, LA (November).

Gotwalt, Deborah A. 1984. *Evaluation of Savannah Transitional Centers.* Atlanta, GA: Georgia Department of Offender Rehabilitation.

Gowdy, Voncile B. 1993. *Intermediate Sanctions.* Washington, DC: U.S. Department of Justice, National Institute of Justice.

Grande, Carolyn Gerlock and Andrew Oseroff. 1991. "Special Education Planning in Jails?" *Journal of Offender Rehabilitation,* **16:**103–111.

Gray, Doug and Greg Wren. 1992. *Pre-Release at South Idaho Correctional Institute: "Something Works."* Boise, ID: South Idaho Correctional Institution.

Gray, Richard. 1986. "Probation: An Exploration in Meaning." *Federal Probation,* **50:**26–31.

Gray, Tara et al. 1991. "Using Cost-Benefit Analysis to Evaluate Correctional Sentences." *Evaluation Review,* **15:**471–481.

Green, Gary S. 1993. "The Study of 'White Collar Criminal' Careers." Unpublished paper presented at the annual meeting of the American Society of Criminology. Phoenix, AZ (October).

Greenberg, David F. 1975. "The Incapacitative Effect of Imprisonment: Some Estimates." *Law and Society,* **2:**541–580.

Greenberg, David F. 1991. "Modeling Criminal Careers." *Criminology,* **29:**17–46.

Greenberg, Norman. 1988. "The Discovery Program: A Way to Use Volunteers in the Treatment Process." *Federal Probation,* **52:**39–45.

Greenfeld, Lawrence A. 1985. *Examining Recidivism.* Washington, DC: Bureau of Justice Statistics.

Greenfeld, Lawrence A. 1987. *Probation and Parole 1985.* Washington, DC: U.S. Department of Justice, Bureau of Justice Statistics.

Greenwood, Peter. 1981. *Private Enterprise Prisons? Why Not? The Job Would Be Done Better at Less Cost.* Santa Monica, CA: Rand.

Greenwood, Peter W. 1982. *Selective Incapacitation.* Santa Monica, CA: Rand Corporation.

Greenwood, Peter W. 1990. "Reflections on Three Promising Programs." *APPA Perspectives,* **14:**20–24.

Greenwood, Peter W. and Susan Turner. 1987. *The VisionQuest Program: An Evaluation.* R-3445-OJJDP. Santa Monica, CA: Rand.

Greenwood, Peter W. and Susan Turner. 1993. "Private Presentence Reports for Serious Juvenile Offenders: Implementation Issues and Impacts." *Justice Quarterly,* **10:**229–243.

Greenwood, Peter W. et al. 1989. *The RAND Intermediate-Sanction Cost Estimation Model.* Santa Monica, CA: RAND, prepared for the Edna McConnell Clark Foundation.

Grenier, Charles E. and George A. Roundtree. 1987. "Predicting Recidivism among Adjudicated Delinquents: A Model to Identify High-Risk Offenders." *Journal of Offender Counseling, Services and Rehabilitation,* **12:**101–112.

Griffiths, Curt T. and Margit Nance. 1980. *The Female Offender: Selected Papers from an International Symposium.* Vancouver, BC: Simon Fraser University, Criminology Research Center.

Grimes, Ruth-Ellen M. 1992. "The Relevance of Term Sentence Disparities in Measuring Discrimination." Unpublished paper presented at the annual meetings of the American Society of Criminology, New Orleans, LA (November).

Guggenheim, Martin. 1985. *The Rights of Young People.* New York: Bantam Books.

Guglielmelli, J. 1980. "Due Process behind Bars: The Intrinsic Approach." *Fordham Law Review,* **48:**1067–1109.

Guy, Edward et al. 1985. "Mental Health Status of Prisoners in an Urban Jail." *Criminal Justice and Behavior,* **12:**29–53.

Haapanen, Rudy A. 1988. *Selective Incapacitation and the Serious Offender: A Longitudinal Study of Criminal Career Patterns.* Sacramento, CA: California Department of the Youth Authority.

Hackett, Judith C. et al. 1987. *Contracting for the Operation of Prisons and Jails.* Washington, DC: National Institute of Justice.

Haddock, Billy D. and Dan Richard Beto. 1990. "An Evolutionary Model for Probation." *APPA Perspectives,* **14:**16–20.

Haesler, Walter T. 1992. "The Released Prisoner and His Difficulties to Be Accepted Again as a 'Normal' Citizen." *Euro-Criminology,* **4:**61–68.

Hagan, Michael and Robert P. King. 1992. "Recidivism Rates of Youth Completing an Intensive Treatment Program in a Juvenile Correctional Facility." *International Journal of Offender Therapy and Comparative Criminology,* **36:**349–358.

Hahn, Paul H. 1984. *The Juvenile Offender and the Law.* Cincinnati, OH: Anderson.

Hairston, C. F. 1988. "Family Ties During Imprisonment: Do They Influence Criminal Activity?" *Federal Probation,* **52:**48–52.

Hall, Andy. 1987. *Systemwide Strategies to Alleviate Jail Overcrowding.* Washington, DC: National Institute of Justice.

Hall, Jane N. 1986. "Identifying and Serving Mentally Retarded Inmates." *Journal of Prison Jail Health,* **5:**29–38.

Hall, Julia. 1992. "Parole Agents: Casemakers for Elderly Clients: A New Role." Unpublished paper presented at the annual meeting of the American Society of Criminology, New Orleans, LA (November).

Hamm, Mark S. 1987. "Determinate Sentencing in Indiana: An Analysis of the Impact of the Justice Model." Unpublished paper presented at the annual meeting of the American Society of Criminology, Montreal, Canada (November).

Hammett, Theodore M. 1992. "HIV/AIDS in Correctional Institutions: Legal Issues." Unpublished paper presented at the annual meetings of the American Society of Criminology, New Orleans, LA (November).

Hammett, Theodore M. and Saira Moini. 1990. *Update on AIDS in Prisons and Jails.* Washington, DC: U.S. Department of Justice.

Hammett, Theodore M. and Monique Sullivan. 1986. *AIDS in Correctional Facilities: Issues and Options.* Washington, DC: U.S. Government Printing Office.

Hammrock, Edward R. 1981. "Prison Overcrowding: Should the Parole Board Be the Safety Valve?" In *The Status of Probation and Parole?* College Park, MD: American Correctional Association.

Hamparian, Donna M. and Lynn Sametz. 1989. *Cuyahoga County Juvenile Court Intensive Probation Supervision: Interim Report.* Cleveland, OH: Federation for Community Planning.

Hanson, Richard W. et al. 1983. "Predicting Inmate Penitentiary Adjustment: An Assessment of Four Classificatory Methods." *Criminal Justice and Behavior,* **10:**293–309.

Harer, Miles D. and Christopher Eichenlaub. 1992. "Prison Furloughs and Recidivism." Unpublished paper presented at the annual meeting of the American Society of Criminology, Pittsburgh, PA (November).

Harland, Alan T. 1993. "Structuring Judicial Discretion in Community Corrections." Unpublished paper presented at the annual meetings of the American Society of Criminology, Phoenix, AZ (October).

Harland, Alan T. 1992. "The Intermediate Sanction Decision Tree." Unpublished paper presented at the annual meeting of the American Society of Criminology, New Orleans, LA (November).

Harlow, Nora. 1984. "Implementing the Justice Model in Probation." In *Probation and Justice,* P. D. McAnany, D. Thomson, and D. Fogel (eds.). Cambridge, MA: Oelgeschlager, Gunn and Hain.

Harrington, Christine B. and Sally Engle Merry. 1988. "Ideological Production: The Making of Community Mediation." *Law and Society Review,* **22:**709–735.

Harris, George A. and David Watkins. 1987. *Counseling the Involuntary and Resistant Client.* College Park, MD: American Correctional Association.

Harris, Grant T., Marnie E. Rice, and Catherine A. Cormier. 1991. "Psychopathy and Violent Recidivism." *Law and Human Behavior,* **15:**625–637.

Harris, Grant T., Marnie E. Rice, and Vernon L. Quinsey. 1993. "Violent Recidivism of Mentally Disordered Offenders: The Development of a Statistical Prediction Instrument." *Criminal Justice and Behavior,* **20:**315–335.

Harris, M. Kay. 1984. "Rethinking Probation in the Context of the Justice Model." In *Probation and Justice: Reconsideration of a Mission,* P. McAnany, D. Thomson, and D. Fogel (eds.). Cambridge, MA: Oelgeschlager, Gunn, and Hain.

Harris, M. Kay. 1992. "Reducing Jail Overcrowding: What Can Be Done after Fifteen Years with a Court-Ordered Population Cap?" Unpublished paper presented at the annual meeting of the American Society of Criminology, New Orleans, LA (November).

Harris, M. Kay, Peter R. Jones, and Gail S. Funke. 1990. *The Kansas Community Corrections Act: An Assessment of a Public Policy Initiative.* Philadelphia, PA: Prepared for the Edna McConnell Clark Foundation.

Harris, Patricia, Todd R. Clear, and S. Christopher Baird. 1989. "Have Community Supervision Officers Changed Their Attitudes Toward Their Work?" *Justice Quarterly,* **6:**233–246.

Hartke, Kenneth L. 1984. "Work Units in Theory and Practice." *Corrections Today,* **46:**66–68.

Haskell, Martin R. and Lewis Yablonsky. 1974. *Criminology: Crime and Criminality.* Chicago: Rand-McNally.

Hatchett, Paulette. 1987. *The Home Confinement Program: An Appraisal of the Electronic Monitoring of Offenders in Washtenaw County, Michigan.* Lansing, MI: Michigan Department of Corrections.

Hawk, Kathleen M. 1993. "4,000 BOP Volunteers Are Committed to Working within the Federal System." *Corrections Today,* **55:**72–75.

Hawk, Kathleen et al. 1993. "Volunteers: Corrections' Unsung Heroes." *Corrections Today,* **55:**63–139.

Hawkins, J. David et al. 1987. "Delinquency Prevention Through Parent Training: Results and Issues from Work in Progress." In *Delinquency Prevention,* James Q. Wilson and Glenn C. Loury (eds.). New York: Springer-Verlag.

Hecht, J. A. 1970. *Effects of Halfway Houses on Neighborhood Crime Rates and Property Values: A Preliminary Survey.* Washington, DC: District of Columbia Department of Corrections.

Heisel, Christine. 1992. "APPA Training Seminar Brings Victim Issues to the Forefront in Nebraska State Probation System." *APPA Perspectives,* **16:**38–39.

Herrington, Lois Haight. 1986. "Dollars and Sense: The Value of Victim Restitution." *Corrections Today,* **48:**156–160.

Hester, Thomas. 1988. *Probation and Parole 1987.* Washington, DC: Bureau of Justice Statistics.

Hewitt, John D., Eric D. Poole, and Robert M. Regoli. 1984. "Self-Reported and Observed Rule-Breaking in Prison: A Look at Disciplinary Justice." *Justice Quarterly,* **1:**437–447.

Hicks, N. 1987. "New Relationship: Halfway Houses and Corrections." *Corrections Compendium,* **12:**5–8.

Hiday, Virginia Aldige. 1990. "Dangerousness of Civil Commitment Candidates: A Six-Month Follow-up." *Law and Human Behavior,* **14:**551–567.

Hillsman, Sally T., Joyce L. Sichel, and Barry Mahoney. 1984. *Fines in Sentencing: A Study of the Use of the Fine as a Criminal Sanction.* Washington, DC:

National Institute of Justice, Vera Institute of Justice and Court Management.

Hofer, Paul J. and Barbara S. Meierhoefer. 1987. *Home Confinement: An Evolving Sanction in the Federal Criminal Justice System.* Washington, DC: U.S. Federal Judicial Center.

Hoffman, Peter B. 1983. "Screening for Risk: A Revised Salient Factor Score, (SFS 81)." *Journal of Criminal Justice,* **11:**539–547.

Hoffman, Peter B. and James L. Beck. 1985. "Recidivism among Released Federal Prisoners: Salient Factor Score and Five-Year Follow-Up." *Criminal Justice and Behavior,* **12:**501–507.

Hofford, Meredith. 1991. "Family Violence: Challenging Cases for Probation Officers." *Federal Probation,* **55:**12–17.

Hokanson, Shirley. 1986. *The Woman Offender in Minnesota: Profile, Needs and Future Directions.* St. Paul, MN: Minnesota Department of Corrections.

Holeman, Herbert and B. J. Krepps-Hess. 1983. *Women Correctional Officers in the California Department of Corrections.* Sacramento, CA: Research Unit, California Department of Corrections.

Holgate, Alina M. and Ian J. Clegg. 1991. "The Path to Probation Officer Burnout: New Dogs, Old Tricks." *Journal of Criminal Justice,* **19:**325–337.

Holman, John E. and James F. Quinn. 1989. "Latent Functions of Therapeutic and Punitive Approaches to Community Corrections: A Theoretical Comparison." Unpublished paper presented at the annual meetings of the American Society of Criminology, Reno, NV (November).

Holmes, Malcolm D. et al. 1993. "Judges' Ethnicity and Minority Sentencing: Evidence Concerning Hispanics." *Social Science Quarterly,* **74:**496–506.

Holt, Norman, Gary Ducat, and H. Gene Eakles. 1981. "California's New Inmate Classification System." *Corrections Today,* **43:**24–30.

Honnold, Julie A. and Jeanne B. Stinchcomb. 1985. "Officer Stress: Costs, Causes, and Cures." *Corrections Today,* **47:**46–51.

Honolulu Police Department. 1982. *Socio-Economic and Demographic Characteristics of Offender Population.* Honolulu, HI: Author.

Horn, Jim. 1992. "Kentucky Officers Get Involved: Political Arena." *APPA Perspectives,* **16:**27–28.

Houk, Julie M. 1984. "Electronic Monitoring of Probationers: A Step Toward Big Brother?" *Golden Gate University Law Review,* **14:**431–446.

Hudson, Joe and Burt Galaway. 1990. "Community Service: Toward Program Definition." *Federal Probation,* **54:**3–9.

Huff, C. Ronald. 1990. "The Impact of a House Arrest Program on the Offenders, the Community, and the System." Unpublished paper presented at the annual meetings of the American Society of Criminology, Baltimore, MD (November).

Huggins, M. Wayne. 1986. "Urban Jails: Facing the Future." *Corrections Today,* **48:**114–120.

Hughes, Gail D. 1990. "The 90's: A Great Time for Community Corrections?" *APPA Perspectives,* **14:**37–38.

Hughes, Graham. 1985. "Legal Aspects of Predicting Dangerousness." In *Critical Issues in American Psychiatry and the Law,* Richard Rosner (ed.). New York: Plenum.

Hughes, Robert. 1987. *The Fatal Shore.* New York: Alfred Knopf.

Humphries, Drew. 1984. "Reconsidering the Justice Model." *Contemporary Crises,* **8:**167–173.

Hunter, Robert J. et al. 1992. "Measuring Attitudinal Change of Boot Camp Participants." *Journal of Contemporary Criminal Justice,* **8:**283–298.

Hunter, Susan M. 1986. "On the Line: Working Hard with Dignity." *Corrections Today,* **48:**12–13.

Hunzeker, Donna and Cindy Conger (eds.). 1985. *Inmate Lawsuits: A Report on Inmate Lawsuits against State and Federal Correctional Systems Resulting in Monetary Damages and Settlements.* Lincoln, NE: Contact Center.

Hurst, Hunter. 1990. "Juvenile Probation in Retrospect." *APPA Perspectives,* **14:**16–20.

Hurwitz, Jeffrey N. 1987. "House Arrest: A Critical Analysis of an Intermediate-Level Penal Sanction." *University of Pennsylvania Law Review,* **135:** 771–811.

Huskey, Bobbie L. 1984. "Community Corrections Acts Help Promote Community-Based Programming." *Corrections Today,* **46:**45.

Huskey, Bobbie L. 1987. "Public Relations Beyond Marketing." *Corrections Today,* **49:**38–40.

Huskey, Bobbie L. 1992. "The Expanding Use of CRCs." *Corrections Today,* **54:**70–73.

Huskey, Bobbie L. and Arthur J. Lurigio. 1992. "An Examination of Privately-Operated Intermediate Sanctions with the U.S." *Corrections Compendium,* **17:**1–3, 5.

Hutchinson, Virginia. 1993. "NIC Update." *Corrections Today,* **55:**132–133.

Illinois Department of Corrections. 1971. *Facts About Furloughs.* Springfield, IL: Author.

Illinois Department of Corrections. 1988. *Female Classification, Report 5, Assessment Instrument.* Springfield, IL: Author.

Illinois Department of Mental Health and Developmental Disabilities. 1988. *Mentally Retarded and Mentally Ill Task Force Report.* Springfield, IL: Author.

Illinois Office of the Governor. 1988. *Mentally Retarded and Mentally Ill Offender Task Force Report.* Springfield, IL: Author.

Immarigeon, Russ. 1985a. "Private Prisons, Private Programs, and Their Implications for Reducing Reliance on Imprisonment in the United States." *The Prison Journal,* **65:**60–74.

Immarigeon, Russ. 1985b. *Probation at the Crossroads: Innovative Programs in Massachusetts.* Boston, MA: Massachusetts Council for Public Justice, Inc.

Immarigeon, Russ. 1986a. "Community Service Sentences Pose Problems, Show Potential." *Journal of the National Prison Project,* **10:**13–15.

Immarigeon, Russ. 1986b. "Surveys Reveal Broad Support for Alternative Sentencing." *Journal of the National Prison Project,* **9:**1–4.

Immarigeon, Russ. 1987. "Few Diversion Programs Are Offered Female Offenders." *Journal of the National Prison Project,* **12:**9–11.

Innes, Christopher A. 1986. *Population Density in State Prisons.* Washington, DC: Bureau of Justice Statistics.

Iowa Department of Correctional Services. 1992. *Iowa Classification System: Assessment & Reassessment of Client Risk Instructions & Scoring Guide.* Davenport, IA: Author.

Irwin, John. 1985. *The Jail: Managing the Underclass in American Society.* Berkeley, CA: University of California Press.

Israel, Michael. 1983. "Jack Henry Abbott, American Prison Writing, and the Experience of Punishment." *Criminal Justice and Behavior,* **10:**441–460.

Ivanoff, Andre. 1992. "Background Risk Factors Associated with Parasuicide among Male Prison Inmates." *Criminal Justice and Behavior,* **19:**426–436.

Jacks, Irving and Steven G. Cox (eds.). 1984. *Psychological Approaches to Crime and Its Correction: Theory, Research and Practice.* Chicago, IL: Nelson-Hall.

Jackson, Ronald W. 1986. "ACA Task Force on Parole: Planning Strategies." *Corrections Today,* **48:**28.

Jacobs, James B. 1978. "What Prison Guards Think: A Profile of the Illinois Force." *Crime and Delinquency,* **26:**185–196.

Jacobs, James B. and Harold G. Retsky. 1975. "Prison Guard." *Urban Life,* **4:**5–29.

Jaffe, Harry Joe. 1989. "The Presentence Report, Probation Officer Accountability, and Recruitment Practices." *Federal Probation,* **53:**12–14.

Jankowski, Louis. 1991. *Probation and Parole 1990.* Washington, DC: U.S. Department of Justice, Bureau of Justice Statistics.

Jensen, Magdeline et al. 1991. "The Sentencing Reform Act of 1984 and Sentencing Guidelines." *Federal Probation,* **55:**4–57.

Johnson, Dennis L., James G. Simmons, and B. Carl Gordon. 1983. "Temporal Consistency of the Meyer-Megargee Inmate Typology." *Criminal Justice and Behavior,* **10:**263–268.

Johnson, Elmer H. and Kenneth E. Kotch. 1973. "Two Factors in Development of Work Release: Size and Location of Prisons." *Journal of Criminal Justice,* **1:**44–45.

Johnson, Jan. 1984. *The Context for Crisis: Background Report on the Kansas Corrections System.* Topeka, KS: Division of the Budget, Kansas Department of Administration.

Johnson, Judith, Keith McKeown, and Roberta James. 1984. *Removing the Chronically Mentally Ill from Jail: Case Studies of Collaboration between Local Criminal Justice and Mental Health Systems.* Washington, DC: National Coalition for Jail Reform.

Johnson, R. L. 1978. *Women's Community Center—Project Evaluation.* Olympia, WA: Washington Law and Justice Planning Office.

Johnson, W. Wesley. 1992. "Racial Distributions and Punishment: An Analysis of State-Level Data in the 1980s." Unpublished paper presented at the annual meetings of the American Society of Criminology, New Orleans, LA (November).

Johnson, W. Wesley and Mark Jones. 1994. "The Increased Felonization of Probation and Its Impact on the Function of Probation: A Descriptive Look at County Level Data from the 1980s and 1990s." *APPA Perspectives,* **18:**42–46.

Jolin, Annette and Robert Rogers. 1990. "The Impact of Electronic Surveillance on Recidivism Rates: An Empirical Study." Unpublished paper presented at the annual meetings of the American Society of Criminology, Baltimore, MD (November).

Jolin, Annette and B. Stipak. 1992. "Drug Treatment and Electronically Monitored Home Confinement: An Evaluation of a Community-Based Sentencing Option." *Crime and Delinquency,* **38:**158–170.

Jones, John, Victor Ascolillo, and Joseph Hanrahan. 1988. "*Griffith v. Wisconsin:* Special Needs Versus Probable Cause: An Emerging Standard." Unpublished paper presented at Academy of Criminal Justice Sciences meetings, San Francisco, CA (April).

Jones, Justin and Carol Robinson. 1989. "Keeping the Piece: Probation and Parole Officers' Right to Bear Arms." *Corrections Today,* **51:**88–90.

Jones, Mark and Steven Cuvelier. 1992. "Are Boot Camp Graduates Better Probation Risks?" Unpublished paper presented at the annual meeting of the American Society of Criminology, Baltimore, MD (November).

Jones, Mark and Rolando V. del Carmen. 1992. "When Do Probation and Parole Officers Enjoy the Same Immunity as Judges?" *Federal Probation,* **56:**36–41.

Jones, Michael. 1982. *A Report on the Virginia Work Release Program.* Research and Reporting Unit, Division of Program Development and Evaluation, Virginia Department of Corrections.

Jones, Peter R. 1990. "Community Corrections in Kansas: Extending Community Based Corrections or Widening the Net?" *Journal of Research in Crime and Delinquency,* **27:**79–101.

Jones, Peter R. 1991. "The Risk of Recidivism: Evaluating the Public Safety Implications of a Community Corrections Program." *Journal of Criminal Justice,* **19:**49–66.

Jordan, Bill and Marlyn Jones. 1988. "Poverty, the Upper Class, and Probation Practice." *Probation Journal,* **35:**123–127.

Joyce, Nola M. 1985. "Classification Research: Facing the Challenge." *Corrections Today,* **47:**78–86.

Jurik, Nancy C. 1983. "The Economics of Female Recidivism: A Study of TARP Women Ex-Offenders." *Criminology,* **21:**603–622.

Jurik, Nancy C. 1985. "An Officer and a Lady: Organizational Barriers to Women Working as Correctional Officers in Men's Prisons." *Social Problems,* **32:**375–388.

Jurik, Nancy C. 1986. "Individual and Organizational Determinants of Correctional Officer Attitudes Toward Inmates." *Criminology,* **23:**523–529.

Jurik, Nancy C. and Michael C. Musheno. 1986. "The Internal Crisis of Corrections: Professionalization and the Work Environment." *Justice Quarterly,* **3:**457–480.

Kalichman, Seth C. 1988. "Empirically Derived MMPI Profile Subgroups of Incarcerated Homicide Offenders." *Journal of Clinical Psychology,* **44:** 733–738.

Kane, Thomas R. 1987. "Inmates' Perceptions of Justice in Prison Disciplinary Sanctions." Unpublished paper presented at the American Society of Criminology meetings, Montreal, Canada (November).

Kaplan, John and Jerome H. Skolnick. 1987. *Criminal Justice: Introductory Cases and Materials.* Mineola, NY: The Foundation Press, Inc.

Kaplan, Lisa et al. 1989. "Runaway, Homeless, and Shut-Out Children and Youth in Canada, Europe, and the United States." *Children and Youth Services,* **11:**1–108.

Kapsch, Stefan J. and Diane M. Luther. 1985. *Punishment and Risk Management as an Oregon Sanctioning Model.* Portland, OR: Oregon Prison Overcrowding Project.

Kaufman, Irving R. 1990. "Reform for a System in Crisis: Alternative Dispute Resolution in the Federal Courts." *Fordham Law Review,* **49:**1–38.

Kearney, William J. 1989. "Form Follows Function—And Function Follows Philosophy: An Architectural Response." *Juvenile and Family Court Journal,* **40:**27–34.

Keckeisen, George L. 1993. *Retail Security versus the Shoplifter: Confronting the Shoplifter While Protecting the Merchant.* Springfield, IL: Charles C. Thomas.

Kelly, William R. and Sheldon Ekland-Olson. 1991. "The Response of the Criminal Justice System to Prison Overcrowding: Recidivism Patterns among Four Successive Parolee Cohorts." *Law and Society,* **25:**601–620.

Kelsey, O. W. 1986. "Elderly Inmates: Providing Safe and Humane Care." *Corrections Today,* **48:**56–58.

Kempf, K. L. and R. L. Austin. 1986. "Older and More Recent Evidence on Racial Discrimination in Sentencing." *Journal of Quantitative Criminology,* **2:**29–48.

Kennedy, Daniel B. 1984. "A Theory of Suicide while in Police Custody." *Journal of Police Science and Administration,* **12:**191–200.

Kennedy, Stephen and Kenneth Carlson. 1988. *Pretrial Release and Detention: The Bail Reform Act of 1984.* Washington, DC: U.S. Department of Justice, Bureau of Justice Statistics.

Kerle, Kenneth E. 1985. "The American Woman County Jail Officer." In *The Changing Roles of Women in the Criminal Justice System,* Imogene L. Moyer (ed.). Prospect Heights, IL: Waveland Press.

Kiekbusch, Richard G. 1985. "Management: One Jail's Experience." *Corrections Today,* **47:**134–138.

Kiekbusch, Richard G. 1987. "Small Jails: Ignored and Misunderstood?" *Corrections Today,* **49:**14–18.

Kizer, George C. 1991. "Female Inmates and Their Families." *Federal Probation,* **55:**56–63.

Klausner, Marian L. 1991. *Opening Doors for Change: Alternatives to Incarceration—A Report on Alternative Sentencing for Women.* Boston: Social Justice for Women.

Klein, Andrew R. 1988. *Alternative Sentencing: A Practitioner's Guide.* Cincinnati, OH: Anderson Publishing Company.

Klein, Andrew R. 1989. "The Curse of Caseload Management." *APPA Perspectives,* **13:**27–28.

Klein, Lloyd and Susan Rogers. 1988. "On the Road Again: The Development of Organized Sentiment Against Parolee Placement." Paper presented at the Academy of Criminal Justice Sciences, San Francisco, CA (April).

Klein, Stephen P. 1987. "Predicting Recidivism." Unpublished paper presented at the annual meeting of the American Society of Criminology, Montreal, Canada (November).

Klein-Saffran, Jody. 1990. "Electronic Monitoring vs. Halfway Houses: Measures in Post-Release Outcome." Unpublished paper presented at the annual meetings of the American Society of Criminology, Baltimore, MD (November).

Klein-Saffran, Jody and Faith Lutze. 1991. "The Effect of Shock Incarceration of Federal Offenders: Community Corrections and Post-Release Follow-Up." Unpublished paper presented at the annual meeting of the American Society of Criminology, San Francisco, CA (November).

Kline, Susan. 1987. *Jail Inmates 1986.* Washington, DC: Bureau of Justice Statistics.

Klofas, John M., Stan Stojkovic, and David A. Kalinich. 1992. "The Meaning of Correctional Crowding: Steps Toward an Index of Severity." *Crime & Delinquency,* **38:**171–188.

Knepper, Paul. 1989. "Selective Participation, Effectiveness, and Prison College Programs." *Journal of Offender Counseling, Services, and Rehabilitation,* **14:**106–135.

Knepper, Paul and Gray Cavender. 1990. "Decision-Making and the Typification of Juveniles on Parole." Unpublished paper presented at the Academy of Criminal Justice Science meetings, Denver, CO (April).

Knight, Barbara B. 1992. "Women in Prison as Litigants: Prospects for Post-Prison Futures." *Women and Criminal Justice,* **4:**91–116.

Knight, Janet and Michael Shively. 1991. "Assessing Inmate Receptivity to a Voluntary Shock Incarceration Program." Unpublished paper presented at the annual meeting of the American Society of Criminology, San Francisco, CA (November).

Knopp, Fay H., Jean Rosenberg, and William Stevenson. 1986. *Report on Nationwide Survey of Juvenile and Adult Sex-Offender Treatment Programs.* Syracuse, NY: Safer Society Press.

Knopp, Fay H., Robert Freeman-Longo, and William Ferree Stevenson. 1992. *Nationwide Survey of Juvenile and Adult Sex-Offender Treatment Programs and Models.* Orwell, VT: Safer Society Program.

Komala, Merly and Val Shepperd. 1990. "The Development of Texas Felony Offender Risk Assessment." Unpublished paper presented at the annual meeting of the American Society of Criminology, Baltimore, MD (November).

Koppel, Herbert. 1984. *Sentencing Practices in 13 States.* Washington, DC: Bureau of Justice Statistics.

Kozuh, J. R. et al. 1980. *1980 TAPC Shock Probation Survey.* Austin, TX: Texas Department of Corrections.

Krajick, Kevin. 1980. "Probation: The Original Community Program." *Corrections Magazine,* **6:**7–15.

Kramer, Norm. 1986. "A Treatment Program for the Developmentally Disabled and Mentally Retarded Offender." *Prison Journal,* **66:**85–92.

Kratcoski, Peter C. 1982. "Volunteers in Corrections: Do They Make a Meaningful Contribution?" *Federal Probation,* **46:**30–35.

Kraus, Melvyn B. and Edward P. Lazear (eds.). 1991. *Searching for Alternatives: Drug-Control Policy in the United States.* Stanford, CA: Hoover Institution Press.

Krisberg, Barry. 1988. *The Juvenile Court: Reclaiming the Vision.* San Francisco: National Council on Crime and Delinquency.

Kulis, Chester J. 1983. "Profit in the Private Presentence Report." *Federal Probation,* **47:**11–16.

Kuznestov, Andrei, Timothy A. Pierson, and Bruce Harry. 1992. "Victim Age Basis for Profiling Sex Offenders." *Federal Probation,* **56:**34–38.

Lane, Michael P. 1986. "A Case for Early Release." *Crime and Delinquency,* **32:**399–403.

Langan, Patrick A. and Mark A. Cunniff. 1992. *Recidivism of Felons on Probation, 1986–1989.* Washington, DC: Department of Justice, Bureau of Justice Statistics.

Langan, Patrick A. and John M. Dawson. 1993. *Felony Sentences in State Courts, 1990.* Washington, DC: U.S. Department of Justice, Bureau of Justice Statistics.

Langan, Patrick A., Craig A. Perkins, and Jan M. Chaiken. 1994. *Felony Sentences in the United States, 1990.* Washington, DC: U.S. Department of Justice, Bureau of Justice Programs.

Langston, Denny. 1988a. "The Economic Impact of Probation and Parole Supervision." Unpublished paper presented at the Academy of Criminal Justice Sciences meetings, San Francisco, CA (April).

Langston, Denny. 1988b. "Probation and Parole: No More Free Rides." *Corrections Today,* **50:**92–93.

Larivee, John et al. 1990. "On the Outside: Corrections in the Community." *Corrections Today,* **52:**84–106.

Latessa, Edward J. 1983. *The Fifth Evaluation of the Lucas County Adult Probation Department's Incarceration Diversion Unit.* Cincinnati, OH: University of Cincinnati Criminal Justice Program.

Latessa, Edward J. 1986. "The Cost Effectiveness of Intensive Supervision." *Federal Probation,* **50:**70–74.

Latessa, Edward J. 1987a. "Intensive Supervision: An Eight Year Follow-Up Evaluation." Paper presented at the annual meeting of the Academy of Criminal Justice Sciences, St. Louis, MO (April).

Latessa, Edward J. 1987b. *The Incarceration Diversion Unit of the Lucas County Adult Probation Department.* Cincinnati, OH: University of Cincinnati.

Latessa, Edward J. and Harry E. Allen. 1982a. "Halfway Houses and Parole: A National Assessment." *Journal of Criminal Justice,* **10:**153–163.

Latessa, Edward J. and Harry E. Allen. 1982b. *Management Issues in Parole.* San Jose, CA: San Jose State University Foundation.

Latessa, Edward J. and Lawrence F. Travis. 1991. "Halfway House or Probation: A Comparison of Alternative Dispositions." *Journal of Crime and Justice,* **14:**53–75.

Latessa, Edward J., Lawrence F. Travis, and Harry E. Allen. 1983. "Volunteers and Paraprofessionals in Parole: Current Practices." *Journal of Offender Counseling, Services, and Rehabilitation,* **8:**91–106.

Latessa, Edward J. and Gennaro F. Vito. 1988. "The Effects of Intensive Supervision on Shock Probationers." *Journal of Criminal Justice,* **16:**319–330.

Latimer, H. D., J. C. Curran, and B. D. Tepper. 1992. *Home Detention Electronic Monitoring Program.* Nevada City, NV: Nevada County Probation Department Second Floor Courthouse.

Lattimore, Pamela K. and Joanna R. Baker. 1992. "The Impact of Recidivism on Prison Populations." *Journal of Quantitative Criminology,* **8:**189–215.

Lattimore, Pamela K., Ann Dryden Witt, and Joanna R. Baker. 1990. "Experimental Assessment of the Effect of Vocational Training on Youthful Property Offenders." *Evaluation Review,* **14:**115–133.

Lauen, Roger J. 1984. "Community Corrections? Not in My Neighborhood!—Developing Legitimacy." *Corrections Today,* **46:**117–130.

Lauen, Roger J. 1990a. "Community Corrections: Getting Involved." *Proceedings of the American Correctional Association Annual Conference.* Laurel, MD: American Correctional Association.

Lauen, Roger J. 1990b. *Community-Managed Corrections: And Other Solutions to America's Prison Costs.* Washington, DC: St. Mary's Press and the American Correctional Association.

Lauen, Roger J. 1990c. "Community-Managed Corrections." Unpublished paper presented at the annual meeting of the Academy of Criminal Justice Sciences, Denver, CO (April).

Laurence, S. E. and B. R. West. 1985. *National Evaluation of the New Pride Replication Program: Final Report, Volume I.* Lafayette, CA: Pacific Institute for Research and Evaluation.

Law Enforcement Assistance Administration. 1977. *Instead of Jail: Pre- and Post-Trial Alternatives to Jail Incarceration.* Washington, DC: Author.

Lawrence, Daniel W. 1992. "Constituency-Based Corrections: Oklahoma's Community Work Centers Benefit Both Inmates and the Public." *Corrections Today,* **54:**130–134.

Lawrence, Richard A. 1984. "Professionals or Judicial Civil Servants? An Examination of the Probation Officer's Role." *Federal Probation,* **48:**14–21.

Lawrence, Richard A. 1985. "Community-Based Corrections: Are They Effective?" *Corrections Today,* **47:**108–112.

Lawrence, Richard A. 1990. "Re-Examining Community Corrections Models." Unpublished paper presented at the annual meetings of the Academy of Criminal Justice Sciences, Denver, CO (April).

Lawrence, Richard A. 1991. "Reexamining Community Corrections Models." *Crime and Delinquency,* **37:**449–464.

LeClair, Daniel P. 1985. *The Effect of Community Reintegration on Rates of Recidivism: A Statistical Overview of Data for the Years 1971–1982.* Boston, MA: Massachusetts Department of Corrections.

Leeke, William D. and Heidi Mohn. 1986. "Violent Offenders: AIMS and Unit Management Maintain Control." *Corrections Today,* **48:**22–24.

Lehman, Joseph D. 1993. "A Commissioner's Appreciation: Pennsylvania Volunteers Build Bridges Between Our Prisons and the Community." *Corrections Today,* **55:**84–86.

Lemov, Penelope. 1992. "The Next Best Thing to Prison." *Corrections Today,* **54:**134–136.

Leonardi, Thomas J. and David R. Frew. 1991. "Applying Job Characteristics Theory to Adult Probation." *Criminal Justice Policy Review,* **5:**17–28.

Leone, Michael C. et al. 1991. "Nowhere to Hide: Local Police and Crowded Jails." *Police Studies,* **14:**166–175.

Lester, David and Bruce L. Danto. 1993. *Suicide Behind Bars: Prediction and Prevention.* Philadelphia, PA: Charles Press.

Levine, James P., Michael C. Musheno, and Dennis J. Palumbo. 1986. *Criminal Justice in America: Law in Action.* New York: Wiley.

Liberton, Michael, Mitchell Silverman, and William R. Blount. 1992. "Predicting Probation Success for the First-Time Offender." *International Journal of Offender Therapy and Comparative Criminology,* **36:**335–347.

Library Information Specialists, Inc. 1983b. *Suicide in Jails.* Boulder, CO: Information Center, U.S. National Institute of Corrections.

Library Information Specialists, Inc. 1985a. *Parole in the United States, 1985.* Boulder, CO: U.S. National Institute of Corrections, Information Center.

Library Information Specialists, Inc. 1985b. *State Training Requirements for Probation and Parole Officers.* Boulder, CO: U.S. National Institute of Corrections.

Lieberman, Jethro K. and James F. Henry. 1986. "Lessons from the Alternative Dispute Resolution Movement." *University of Chicago Law Review,* **53:**424–439.

Lilly, J. Robert. 1985. "A Proposal for Evaluating Home Incarceration in Kenton County, Kentucky." Submitted to the Kentucky Department of Corrections.

Lilly, J. Robert. 1992. "Review Essay: Selling Justice: Electronic Monitoring and the Security Industry." *Justice Quarterly,* **9:**493–503.

Lilly, J. Robert and Richard A. Ball. 1987. "A Brief History of House Arrest and Electronic Monitoring." *Northern Kentucky Law Review,* **13:**343–374.

Lilly, J. Robert, Richard A. Ball, and W. Robert Lotz Jr. 1986. "Electronic Jail Revisited." *Justice Quarterly,* **3:**353–361.

Lilly, J. Robert, Richard A. Ball, and Jennifer Wright. 1987. "Home Incarceration with Electronic Monitoring in Kenton County Kentucky: An Evaluation." In *Intermediate Punishments: Intensive Supervision, Home Confinement, and Electronic Surveillance.* Belinda McCarthy (ed.). Monsey, NY: Criminal Justice Press.

Lilly, J. Robert et al. 1992. "The Pride, Inc., Program: An Evaluation of 5 Years of Electronic Monitoring." *Federal Probation,* **56:**42–47.

Lindner, Charles. 1991. "The Refocused Probation Home Visit: A Subtle But Revolutionary Change." *Journal of Contemporary Criminal Justice,* **7:**115–127.

Lindner, Charles. 1992a. "The Probation Field Visit and Office Report in New York State: Yesterday, Today, and Tomorrow." *Criminal Justice Review,* **17:**44–60.

Lindner, Charles. 1992b. "Probation Officer Victimization: An Emerging Concern." *Journal of Criminal Justice,* **20:**53–62.

Lindner, Charles. 1992c. "The Refocused Probation Home Visit: A Subtle But Revolutionary Change." *Federal Probation,* **56:**16–21.

Lindner, Charles and Margaret R. Savarese. 1984. "The Evolution of Probation: University Settlement and the Beginning of Statutory Probation in New York City." *Federal Probation,* **48:**3–12.

Linster, Richard L., Pamela K. Lattimore, and Christy A. Visher. 1990. *Predicting the Recidivism of Serious Adult Offenders.* Washington, DC: U.S. National Institute of Justice.

Lipchitz, Joseph W. 1986. "Back to the Future: A Historical View of Intensive Probation Supervision." *Federal Probation,* **50:**78–81.

Lippold, Robert A. 1985. "Halfway Houses: Meeting Special Needs." *Corrections Today,* **47:**46, 82, 112.

Litton, Gilbert and Linda Marye. 1983. *An Evaluation of the Juvenile Diversion Program in the Orleans*

Parish District Attorney's Office. New Orleans, LA: Mayor's Justice Coordinating Council, City of New Orleans.

Liu, Liang Y. 1993. *DWI Recidivism in Texas, 1987–1990.* Austin, TX: Texas Commission on Alcohol and Drug Abuse.

Lockhart, Paula K. 1990. *Results of DPCA Drug Survey.* Albany, NY: New York State Division of Probation and Correctional Alternatives.

Lockwood, Dan. 1989. "Prison Higher Education and Recidivism: A Review of the Literature." Unpublished paper presented at the annual meeting of the American Society of Criminology, Reno, NV (November).

Logan, Charles H. 1993. "Well Kept: Comparing Quality of Confinement in Private and Public Prisons." *Journal of Criminal Law and Criminology,* **83:** 577–613.

Logan, Charles H. and Sharla P. Rausch. 1985. "Why Deinstitutionalizing Status Offenders is Pointless." *Crime and Delinquency,* **31:**501–517.

Logan, Gloria. 1992. "In Topeka: Family Ties Take Top Priority in Women's Visiting Program." *Corrections Today,* **54:**160–161.

Lombardi, John H. 1981. "Florida's Objective Parole Guidelines: Analysis of the First Year's Implementation. Ph.D. Dissertation, Florida State University, Tallahassee, FL.

Lombardi, John H. and Donna M. Lombardi. 1986. "Objective Parole Criteria: More Harm than Good?" *Corrections Today,* **48:**86–87.

Los Angeles County Countywide Criminal Justice Coordination Committee. 1992. *Impact of Repeat Arrests of Deportable Criminal Aliens in Los Angeles County: Final Report.* Los Angeles: Author.

Love, Bill. 1993. "Volunteers Make a Big Difference Inside a Maximum Security Prison." *Corrections Today,* **55:**76–78.

Love, Kevin G. 1981. "Paraprofessionals in Parole and Probation Services: Selection, Training, and Program Evaluation." *Journal of Criminal Justice,* **9:**367–374.

Loveless, Patricia. 1994. "Home Incarceration with Electronic Monitoring: Myths and Realities." *American Jails,* **7:**35–40.

Lovell, David G. 1985. *Sentencing Reform and the Treatment of Offenders.* Olympia, WA: Washington Council on Crime and Delinquency.

Lucas, Wayne L. 1987. "Staff Perceptions of Volunteers in a Correctional Program." *Journal of Crime and Justice,* **10:**63–78.

Lucas, Wayne L. 1988. "Cost Savings from Volunteer Services: A Research Note." *Journal of Offender Counseling and Rehabilitation,* **12:**203–207.

Lundman, Richard J. 1984. *Prevention and Control of Juvenile Delinquency.* New York: Oxford University Press.

Lurigio, Arthur J. 1989. "Practitioners' Views on AIDS in Probation and Detention." *Federal Probation,* **53:**16–24.

Lurigio, Arthur J., Gad J. Bensinger, and Anna T. Laszlo (eds.). 1990. *AIDS and Community Corrections: The Development of Effective Policies.* Chicago, IL: Loyola University Chicago.

Lutz, Gene M. 1990. "Danish Community Service Orders: Implementing an Experiment." Unpublished paper presented at the annual meeting of the American Society of Criminology, Baltimore, MD (November).

MacDonald, Malcolm. 1986. "Probation and Parole: Sanctions That Work." *Corrections Today,* **48:**6.

MacGrady, J., W. Bemister, and B. Fontaine. 1991. *Project R.E.I.D.I.D. (Recidivism and Alcohol-Related Crimes of Aggression.* Rockville, MD: National Institute of Justice, National Criminal Justice Reference Service Microfiche Program.

Mack, Dennis E. 1992. "High Impact Incarceration Program: Rikers Boot Camp." *American Jails,* **6:**63–65.

MacKenzie, Doris Layton. 1990. "Boot Camp Prisons: Components, Evaluations, and Empirical Issues." *Federal Probation,* **54:**44–52.

MacKenzie, Doris Layton. 1991a. "The Effect of Shock Incarceration Programs in Eight Different States." Unpublished paper presented at the annual meeting of the American Society of Criminology, San Francisco, CA (November).

MacKenzie, Doris Layton. 1991b. "The Parole Performance of Offenders Released from Shock Incarceration (Boot Camp Prisons): A Survival Time Analysis." *Journal of Quantitative Criminology,* **7:**213–236.

MacKenzie, Doris Layton. 1993. "NIJ Sponsored Studies Ask: Does Shock Incarceration Work?" *Corrections Compendium,* **18:**5–12.

MacKenzie, Doris Layton and DeAnna Ballow. 1989. *Shock Incarceration Programs in State Correctional Jurisdictions—An Update.* Washington, DC: U.S. Department of Justice, Office of Justice Programs.

MacKenzie, Doris Layton and Robert A. Buchanan. 1990. "The Process of Classification in Prisons: A Descriptive Study of Staff Use of the System." *Journal of Crime and Justice,* **13:**1–26.

MacKenzie, Doris Layton and James W. Shaw. 1993. "The Impact of Shock Incarceration on Technical Violations and New Criminal Activities." *Justice Quarterly,* **10:**463–487.

MacKenzie, Doris Layton, James W. Shaw, and Voncile B. Gowdy. 1993. *An Evaluation of Shock Incarceration in Louisiana.* Washington, DC: U.S. Department of Justice, Office of Justice Programs.

MacKenzie, Doris Layton, James W. Shaw, and Claire Souryal. 1992. "Characteristics Associated with Successful Adjustment to Supervision: A Comparison of Parolees, Probationers, Shock Participants, and Shock Dropouts." *Criminal Justice and Behavior,* **19:**437–454.

MacKenzie, Doris Layton and Claire C. Souryal. 1991. "Boot Camps." *Corrections Today,* **53:**90–115.

MacKenzie, Doris Layton et al. 1988. *Evaluating Shock*

Incarceration in Louisiana: A Review of the First Year. Baton Rouge, LA: Louisiana State University.

Maguire, Kathleen, Ann L. Pastore, and Timothy J. Flanagan (eds.). 1993. *Sourcebook of Criminal Justice Statistics, 1992.* Washington, DC: U.S. Department of Justice, Bureau of Justice Statistics.

Maher, Richard J. and Henry Dufour. 1987. "Experimenting with Community Service: A Punitive Alternative to Imprisonment." *Federal Probation,* **51:**22–28.

Maier, Gary J. and Robert D. Miller. 1987. "Models of Mental Health Service Delivery to Corrections Institutions." *Journal of Forensic Sciences,* **32:**225–232.

Maine Criminal Justice Academy. 1986. *Entry-Level Corrections Officer Task Analysis and Training Standards Validation.* Waterville, ME: Maine Department of Public Safety.

Mainprize, Stephen. 1992. "Electronic Monitoring in Corrections: Assessing Cost Effectiveness and the Potential for Widening the Net of Social Control." *Canadian Journal of Criminology,* **34:**161–180.

Mair, George (ed.). 1989. *Risk Prediction and Probation: Papers from a Research and Planning Unit Workshop.* London, UK: UK Home Office.

Maloney, D., D. Romig, and T. Armstrong. 1988. "Juvenile Probation: The Balanced Approach." *Juvenile and Family Court Journal,* **38:**1–63.

Maltz, Michael D. 1984. *Recidivism.* Orlando, FL: Academic Press.

Maltz, Michael D. and R. McCleary. 1977. "The Mathematics of Behavioral Change—Recidivism and Construct Validity." *Evaluation Quarterly,* **1:** 421–438.

Maniglia, Rebecca. 1993. "Experience and Innocence: Pennsylvania Youth Center Program Reaches across Generational Lines." *Corrections Today,* **55:**146–148.

Mann, Cora Mae. 1993. *Unequal Justice: A Question of Color.* Indianapolis, IN: Indiana University Press.

Manning, W. 1983. "An Underlying Cause of Burnout." *Corrections Today,* **45:**20–22.

Marcus, David K., Theodore M. Amen, and Roger Bibace. 1992. "A Developmental Analysis of Prisoners' Conceptions of AIDS." *Criminal Justice and Behavior,* **19:**174–188.

Mardon, Steven. 1992. "Jerry Smith: Parole Officer's Experiences Helped Prevent Woman's Suicide." *Corrections Today,* **54:**26.

Markley, Greg. 1994. "The Role of Mission Statements in Community Corrections." *APPA Perspectives,* **18:**47–50.

Marlette, Marjorie. 1988. "Furloughs for Lifers Successful." *Corrections Compendium,* **13:**11–20.

Marlette, Marjorie. 1990. "Furloughs Tightened— Success Rates High." *Corrections Compendium,* **15:**6–21.

Marlette, Marjorie. 1991. "Boot Camp Prisons Thrive." *Corrections Compendium,* **16:**1–10.

Marley, C. W. 1973. "Furlough Programs and Conjugal Visiting in Adult Correctional Institutions." *Federal Probation,* **37:**19–25.

Marlin, D. 1988. "Reading and Rehabilitation: Literacy Volunteers of America in Corrections." *Journal of Correctional Education,* **39:**135–136.

Marshall, Franklin H. 1989. "Diversion and Probation." In *The U.S. Sentencing Guidelines: Implications for Criminal Justice,* Dean J. Champion (ed.). New York: Praeger.

Marshall, Tony F. et al. 1985. *Alternatives to Criminal Courts: The Potential for Non-Judicial Dispute Settlement.* Brookfield, VT: Gower.

Martin, Dennis R. 1991. "Survey on Probation, Parole Officer Safety Details the Dangers of Community Contact." *Corrections Today,* **53:**160–164.

Martin, Randy and Sherwood Zimmerman. 1992. "Aids Education in U.S. Prisons." Unpublished paper presented at the annual meetings of the American Society of Criminology, New Orleans, LA (November).

Martin, Susan E. 1983. "Commutation of Prison Sentences." *Crime and Delinquency,* **29:**593–612.

Martinez, Pablo E. 1988. "The Parole Score: A Non-Matrix System for Parole Guidelines." Unpublished paper presented at the annual meetings of the American Society of Criminology, Chicago, IL (November).

Martinez, Pablo E. and Antonio Fabelo. 1985. *Texas Correctional System: Growth and Policy Alternatives.* Austin, TX: Texas Criminal Justice Policy Council.

Martinson, Robert. 1974. "What Works? Questions and Answers about Prison Reform." *The Public Interest,* **35:**22–54.

Martinson, Robert and J. Wilks. 1977. "Save Parole Supervision." *Federal Probation,* **41:**23–27.

Marx, Gary and Ronald Corbett. 1990. "Electronic Monitoring and Community Protection: A Consideration of Political and Social Realities." Unpublished paper presented at the annual meetings of the American Society of Criminology, Baltimore, MD (November).

Maryland Committee on Prison Overcrowding. 1984. *Report.* Towson, MD: Maryland Criminal Justice Coordinating Council, Committee on Prison Overcrowding.

Maryland Department of Budget and Fiscal Planning. 1986. *Review of the Maryland Parole Commission.* Annapolis, MD: Division of Management Analysis and Audits.

Masin, Sandra. 1993. "Shakopee Volunteers Help Inmates and Offenders in the Community." *Corrections Today,* **55:**128–130.

Maslach, Christina. 1982a. "Understanding Burnout: Definitional Issues in Analyzing a Complex Phenomenon." In *Job Stress and Burnout,* W. S. Paine (ed.). Beverly Hills, CA: Sage.

Maslach, Christina. 1982b. *Burnout: The Cost of Caring.* Englewood Cliffs, NJ: Prentice Hall.

Mason, K. W. 1977. *Montgomery County (MD) Work Release/Pre-Release Program—Review and Performance Evaluation: Summary Report August, 1972–August, 1975.* Rockville, MD: Montgomery County Department of Correction and Rehabilitation.

Massachusetts Department of Corrections. 1988. *Services for Female Offenders in Massachusetts: Executive Summary.* Boston, MA: Massachusetts Department of Corrections Advisory Group on Female Offenders.

Massachusetts Halfway Houses, Inc. 1980. *MHHI (Massachusetts Halfway Houses Incorporated) Annual Report, 1980.* Boston, MA: Massachusetts Halfway Houses, Inc.

Matek, Ord. 1986. "The Use of Fantasy Training as a Therapeutic Process in Working with Sexual Offenders." *Journal of Social Work and Human Sexuality,* **4:**109–123.

Mathias, Robert A. 1986. *The Road Not Taken: Cost-Effective Alternatives for Non-Violent Felony Offenders in New York State.* New York: Correctional Association of New York.

Mathias, Robert A., Paul DeMuro, and Richard S. Allinson. 1984. *Violent Juvenile Offenders: An Anthology.* San Francisco, CA: National Council on Crime and Delinquency.

Mathias, Rudolf E. S. and James W. Madhouse. 1991. "The Boot Camp Program for Offenders: Does the Shoe Fit?" *International Journal of Offender Therapy and Comparative Criminology,* **35:** 322–327.

Matthews, Tim. 1993. "Pros and Cons of Increasing Officer Authority to Impose or Remove Conditions of Supervision." *APPA Perspectives,* **17:**31.

Matthews, Timothy, Harry N. Boone Jr., and Vernon Fogg. 1994. "Evaluation of Probation and Parole Programs: The Development of Alternative Outcome Measures." *APPA Perspectives,* **18:**10–12.

Matthewson, Terry L. 1991. "I.D. Entity." *American Jails,* **5:**64–68.

Mauer, Marc. 1985. *The Lessons of Marion: The Failure of a Maximum Security Prison: A History and Analysis, with Voices of Prisoners.* Philadelphia: American Friends Services Committee.

Mawhiney, A. M. and E. Bassis. 1992. "Community-Based Approach for Rural Residential Treatment Services." *Community Alternatives International Journal of Family Care,* **4:**33–48.

Maxfield, Michael G. and Terry L. Baumer. 1990. "Home Detention with Electronic Monitoring: Comparing Pretrial and Postconviction Programs." *Crime and Delinquency,* **36:**521–536.

Maxfield, Michael G. and Terry L. Baumer. 1992. "Pretrial Home Detention with Electronic Monitoring: A Nonexperimental Salvage Evaluation." *Evaluation Review,* **16:**315–332.

Mayer, Connie. 1986. "Legal Issues Surrounding Private Operation of Prisons." *Criminal Law Bulletin,* **22:**309–325.

Maynard, Douglas W. 1984. *Inside Plea Bargaining: The Language of Negotiation.* New York: Plenum.

McAnany, Patrick D. 1984. "Mission and Justice: Clarifying Probation's Legal Context." In *Probation and Justice,* P. McAnany, D. Thomson, and D. Fogel (eds.). Cambridge, MA: Oelgeschlager.

McAnany, Patrick D. and Doug Thomson. 1982. *Equitable Responses to Probation Violations: A Guide for Managers.* Chicago, IL: Center for Research in Law and Justice, University of Illinois at Chicago.

McAnany, Patrick D., Doug Thomson, and David Fogel (eds.). 1984. *Probation and Justice: Reconsideration of a Mission.* Cambridge, MA: Oelgeschlager, Gunn and Hain.

McCabe, J. M. 1986. *The Relationship of Burnout, Coping Methods, and Locus of Control among Probation and Parole Officers.* Unpublished doctoral dissertation, University Missouri, Kansas City.

McCarthy, Belinda R. 1987. *Intermediate Punishments: Intensive Supervision, Home Confinement, and Electronic Surveillance.* Monsey, NY: Willow Tree Press.

McCarthy, Belinda R. and Bernard J. McCarthy. 1983. "Are Study Release Programs Making the Grade?" In *Correctional Education: A Focus on Success,* Helen E. Pecht (ed.). Huntsville, TX: Correctional Education Association.

McCarthy, Belinda R. and Bernard J. McCarthy. 1984. *Community-Based Corrections.* Monterey, CA: Brooks/Cole.

McCarthy, Belinda R. and Bernard J. McCarthy. 1991. *Community-Based Corrections,* 2nd ed. Monterey, CA: Brooks/Cole.

McCleod, Maureen. 1986. "Victim Participation at Sentencing." *Criminal Law Bulletin,* **22:**501–517.

McCord, Joan and Richard E. Trembley (eds.). 1992. *Preventing Antisocial Behavior: Interventions from Birth Through Adolescence.* New York and London: Concord Press.

McCorkle, Richard C. 1992. "Personal Precautions to Violence in Prison." *Criminal Justice and Behavior,* **19:**160–173.

McCormack, Arlene, Mark-David Janus, and Ann W. Burgess. 1986. "Runaway Youths and Sexual Victimization: Gender Differences in an Adolescent Runaway Population." *Child Abuse and Neglect,* **10:**387–395.

McCormack, Arlene and Marialena Selvaggio. 1989. "Screening for Pedophiles in Youth-Oriented Community Agencies." *Social Casework,* **70:**37–42.

McCormack, Arlene et al. 1992. "An Exploration of Incest in the Childhood Development of Serial Rapists." *Journal of Family Violence,* **7:**219–228.

McCulloch, Sue. 1993. "Social Skills and Human Relationships: Training for Sex Offenders." *Australian and New Zealand Journal of Criminology,* **26:**47–58.

MacDonald, Donald and Gerald Bala. 1983. *Follow-Up Study Sample of Rochester Work Release Participants.* Albany, NY: Division of Program Planning,

Research, and Evaluation, NY Department of Correctional Services.

McDonald, Douglas C. 1986. *Punishment without Walls: Community Service Sanctions in New York City.* New Brunswick, NJ: Rutgers University Press.

McDonald, Douglas C. 1993. "Private Penal Institutions." In *Crime and Justice: A Review of Research, Volume 16,* Michael Tonry (ed.). Chicago and London: University of Chicago Press.

McDonald, Douglas C. and Kenneth E. Carlson. 1992. *Federal Sentencing in Transition, 1990–96.* Washington, DC: U.S. Bureau of Justice Statistics, BJS Special Report.

McDonald, Douglas C., Judith Greene, and Charles Worzella. 1992. *Day Fines in American Courts: The Staten Island and Milwaukee Experiments.* Washington, DC: U.S. Department of Justice, Office of Justice Programs.

McDonald, William F. 1985. *Plea Bargaining: Critical Issues and Common Practices.* Washington, DC: U.S. Department of Justice, National Institute of Justice.

McDowall, David and Colin Loftin. 1992. "Comparing the UCR and NCS Over Time." *Criminology,* **30:**125–132.

McGaha, Johnny E. 1991. "Probationers at Risk: Parental Alcoholism." *APPA Perspectives,* **15:** 14–18.

McGee, Richard A., George Warner, and Nora Harlow. 1985. *The Special Management Inmate.* Washington, DC: U.S. National Institute of Justice.

McGrath, Robert J. 1991. "Sex-Offender Risk Assessment and Disposition Planning: A Review of Empirical and Clinical Findings." *International Journal of Offender Therapy and Comparative Criminology,* **35:**328–350.

McGrath, Robert J. and Carolyn H. Carey. 1987. "Treatment of Men Who Molest Children: A Program Description." *Journal of Offender Counseling,* **7:**23–33.

McGuire, James and Philip Priestley. 1985. *Offending Behavior: Skills and Strategems for Going Straight.* New York: St. Martin's Press.

McManus, Patrick D. and Lynn Zeller Barclay. 1994. *Community Corrections Act: Technical Assistance Manual.* College Park, MD: American Correctional Association.

McReynolds, Veon. 1987. *Variables Related to Predicting Absconding Probationers.* Ann Arbor, MI: University Microfilms International.

McShane, Frank J. and Barrie A. Noonan. 1993. "Classification of Shoplifters by Cluster Analysis." *International Journal of Offender Therapy and Comparative Criminology,* **37:**29–40.

McShane, Marilyn. 1985. *The Effect of Detainer on Prison Overcrowding.* Huntsville, TX: Criminal Justice Center, Sam Houston State University.

McShane, Marilyn and Wesley Krause. 1993. *Community Corrections.* New York: Macmillan.

Meachum, Larry R. 1986. "House Arrest: The Oklahoma Experience." *Corrections Today,* **48:**102–110.

Medler, Jerry F. 1985. *Oregon Community Corrections: 1977–1984: An Evaluation.* Salem, OR: Oregon Department of Human Resources.

Meeker, James W., Paul Jesilow, and Joseph Aranda. 1992. "Bias in Sentencing: A Preliminary Analysis of Community Service Sentences." *Behavioral Sciences & the Law,* **10:**197–206.

Megargee, Edwin I. and Martin J. Bohn Jr. 1979. *Classifying Criminal Offenders: A New System Based on the MMPI.* Beverly Hills, CA: Sage.

Megargee, Edwin I. and Joyce Carbonell. 1985. "Predicting Prison Adjustment with MMPI Correctional Scales." *Journal of Consulting and Clinical Psychology,* **53:**874–883.

Melnicoe, Shirley. 1990. "Employment of Ex-Offenders and Recidivism." Unpublished paper presented at the annual meeting of the American Society of Criminology, Baltimore, MD (November).

Mendelsohn, Robert I. and Terry L. Baumer. 1990. "A Comparative Assessment of Three Approaches to Home Detention." Unpublished paper presented at the annual meetings of the American Society of Criminology, Baltimore, MD (November).

Merritt, Frank S. 1984. "Restitution under the Victim and Witness Protection Act of 1982." *Criminal Law Bulletin,* **20:**44–48.

Messinger, Sheldon L. et al. 1985. "The Foundations of Parole in California." *Law and Society Review,* **19:**69–106.

MetaMetrics, Inc. 1984. *Evaluation of the Breakthrough Foundation Youth at Risk Program: The 10-Day Course and Follow-Up Program: Final Report.* Washington, DC: MetaMetrics, Inc.

Metchik, Eric. 1992a. "Judicial Views of Parole Decision Processes: A Social Science Perspective." *Journal of Offender Rehabilitation,* **18:**135–157.

Metchik, Eric. 1992b. "Legal Views of Parole Decision Making: A Social Science Perspective." Unpublished paper presented at the annual meeting of the American Society of Criminology, New Orleans, LA (November).

Miethe, Terance D. and Charles A. Moore. 1985. "Socioeconomic Disparities under Determinate Sentencing Systems: A Comparison of Preguideline and Postguideline Practices in Minnesota." *Criminology,* **23:**337–363.

Milkman, R. H. 1985. *Employment Services for Ex-Offenders Field Test: A Summary Report.* Washington, DC: National Institute of Justice.

Miller, Dallas H. 1984b. *A Description of Work Release Job Placements from Massachusetts State Correctional Facilities During 1982.* Boston, MA: Massachusetts Department of Corrections.

Miller, E. Eugene. 1977. "Halfway House: Correctional Decompression of the Offender." In *Corrections in the Community: Success Models in Correctional Reform,* E. Eugene Miller and M. Robert Montilla (eds.). Reston, VA: Reston.

Miller, E. Eugene and M. Robert Montilla (eds.). 1977. *Corrections in the Community: Success Models in Correctional Reform.* Reston, VA: Reston.

Miller, L. E. and S. T. Adwell. 1984. "Purpose in Life: A Concept for Understanding and Combating Stress and Burnout among Correctional Employees." *Correctional Monograph.* Lexington, KY: Eastern Kentucky University.

Milling, L. 1978. *Home Furlough Functions and Characteristics.* Hartford, CT: Connecticut Department of Corrections.

Mills, Darrell K. 1990. "Career Issues for Probation Officers." *Federal Probation,* **54:**3–7.

Mills, Jim. 1992. "Supervision Fees: APPA Issues Committee Report." *APPA Perspectives,* **16:**10–12.

Mills, William Reginald and Heather Barrett. 1992. "Meeting the Special Challenge of Providing Health Care to Women Inmates in the '90s." *American Jails,* **4:**55–57.

Minnesota Corrections Department. 1972. *A Follow-Up Study of Boys Participating in the Positive Peer Culture Program at the Minnesota State Training School for Boys: An Analysis of 242 Boys Released During 1969.* Minneapolis, MN: Minnesota Corrections Department Research Information and Data Systems Division.

Minnesota Department of Corrections. 1984. *Work/Study Release Report to the Commissioner of Corrections.* St. Paul, MN: Work/Study Release Committee of the Advisory Task Force on the Woman Offender in Corrections.

Minnesota Sentencing Guidelines Commission. 1984. *The Impact of the Minnesota Sentencing Guidelines: Three Year Evaluation.* St. Paul, MN: Author.

Minnesota Sentencing Guidelines Commission. 1991. *Report to the Legislature on the Mandatory Minimum Law for Weapons Offenses.* St. Paul, MN: Author.

Minor, Kevin I. and David J. Hartmann. 1992. "An Evaluation of the Kalamazoo Probation Enhancement Program." *Federal Probation,* **56:**30–41.

Minor-Harper, Stephanie. 1986. *State and Federal Prisoners, 1925–1985.* Washington, DC: U.S. Department of Justice.

Minor-Harper, Stephanie and Christopher A. Innes. 1987. *Time Served in Prison and on Parole, 1984.* Washington, DC: U.S. Department of Justice.

Miranne, Alfred C. and Michael R. Geerken. 1991. "The New Orleans Inmate Survey: A Test of Greenwood's Predictive Scale." *Criminology,* **29:**497–518.

Mitchell, Bill and Gene Shiller. 1988. "Colorado's Shape-Up Program Gives Youth a Taste of the Inside." *Corrections Today,* **50:**76–87.

Mitchell, John J., Jr. and Sharon A. Williams. 1986. "SOS: Reducing Juvenile Recidivism." *Corrections Today,* **48:**70–71.

Mixdorf, Lloyd. 1991. "Profile of a Good Juvenile Careworker." In *Vital Statistics in Corrections.* Laurel, MD: American Correctional Association.

Monahan, John. 1984. "The Prediction of Violent Behavior: Toward a Second Generation of Theory and Policy." *American Journal of Psychiatry,* **141:**10–15.

Moore, Charles A. and Terance D. Miethe. 1987. "Can Sentencing Reform Work? A Four-Year Evaluation of Determinate Sentencing in Minnesota." Unpublished paper presented at American Society of Criminology meetings, Montreal, Canada (November).

Moore, Francis T. and Marilyn Chandler Ford. 1993. "A Model to Reduce Jail Overcrowding." *American Jails,* **3:**16–22.

Moore, James R. 1993. "The South Carolina Experience: Victim Services in Community Corrections." *APPA Perspectives,* **17:**16–20.

Moracco, John C. 1985. "Stress: How Corrections Personnel Can Anticipate, Manage, and Reduce Stress on the Job." *Corrections Today,* **47:**22–26.

Moran, John S. et al. 1989. "Prison Sexuality, Part II: AIDS, Sexual Victimization, Sexual Adaptation among Male Prisoners, Affirmative Action, and Sex Offender Treatment." *Prison Journal,* **69:**3–89.

Morash, Merry, Robin N. Haarr, and Lila Rucker. 1994. "A Comparison of Programming for Women and Men in U.S. Prisons in the 1980s." *Crime and Delinquency,* **40:**197–221.

Morash, Merry and Lila Rucker. 1990. "A Critical Look at the Idea of Boot Camp as a Correctional Reform." *Crime & Delinquency,* **36:**204–222.

Morgenbesser, Leonard I. 1987. "Work-Related Attitudes of Sergeants in a State Correctional System." Unpublished paper presented at the American Society of Criminology meetings, Montreal, Canada (November).

Morrill, Calvin and Cindy McKee. 1993. "Institutional Isomorphism and Informal Social Control: Evidence from a Community Mediation Center." *Social Problems,* **40:**445–463.

Morris, Norval. 1984. "On Dangerousness in the Judicial Process." *The Record of the Association of the Bar of the City of New York,* **39:**102–128.

Morris, Norval and Marc Miller. 1985. "Predictions of Dangerousness." In *Crime and Justice: An Annual Review of Research,* M. Tonry and N. Morris (eds.). Chicago, IL: University of Chicago Press.

Morris, Norval and Marc Miller. 1987. *Predictions of Dangerousness in the Criminal Law.* Washington, DC: National Institute of Justice.

Morris, Richard M. 1986. "Burnout: Avoiding the Consequences of On-the-Job Stress." *Corrections Today,* **48:**122–126.

Morrisson, Richard D. 1992. "Spotting and Handling the Manipulators in Your Parole and Probation Caseload." *Corrections Today,* **54:**22–24.

Moses, Marilyn C. 1993. "Girl Scouts Behind Bars: New Program at Women's Prisons Benefits Mothers and Children." *Corrections Today,* **55:**132–134.

Mott, Joy. 1989. "Is Criminology Any Use?" *Home Office Research and Planning Unit Research Bulletin,* **26:**1–48.

Moyer, Imogene L. and Susan E. Giles. 1993. "Mothers in Prison: Supporting the Parent-Child Bond." Unpublished paper presented at the annual meeting of the American Society of Criminology, Phoenix, AZ (October).

Mullen, Joan. 1974. *The Dilemma of Diversion.* Washington, DC: U.S. Government Printing Office.

Mullen, Joan. 1985. *Corrections and the Private Sector.* Washington, DC: National Institute of Justice.

Muraskiun, Roslyn. 1990. "Females in Correctional Facilities: Separate But Equal?" Unpublished paper presented at the annual meeting of the American Society of Criminology, Baltimore, MD (November).

Murphy, Edward M. 1985. "Handling Violent Juveniles." *Corrections Today,* **47:**26–30.

Murphy, Joseph P. 1987. "Some Axioms for Probation Officers." *Federal Probation,* **51:**20–23.

Murphy, T. H. 1983. *Community Residential Programs and the Issue of Threat.* Lansing, MI: Michigan Department of Corrections.

Murphy, Terrence H. 1980. *Final Report (#AP-O) Michigan Risk Prediction: A Replication Study.* Lansing, MI: Program Bureau, Michigan Department of Corrections.

Murty, K. S. et al. 1987. "Community-Based Programs as an Alternative to Incarceration: The Case of Fulton County, Project Re-Direction." Unpublished paper presented at the annual meeting of the Academy of Criminal Justice Sciences, St. Louis, MO (April).

Musheno, Michael C. et al. 1989. "Community Corrections as an Organizational Innovation: What Works and Why?" *Journal of Research in Crime and Delinquency,* **26:**136–167.

Nacci, Peter and Thomas R. Kane. 1983. "Incidence of Sex and Sexual Aggression in Federal Prisons." *Federal Probation,* **47:**31–36.

Nardulli, Peter F., Roy B. Flemming, and James Eisenstein. 1985. "Criminal Courts and Bureaucratic Justice: Concessions and Consensus in the Guilty Plea Process." *Journal of Criminal Law and Criminology,* **76:**1123–1131.

National Alliance of Business. 1981. *Community Alliance Program for Ex-Offenders.* Washington, DC: Author.

National Alliance of Business. 1983. *Employment Training of Ex-Offenders: A Community Program Approach.* Washington, DC: Author.

National Commission on Law Observance and Enforcement. 1931. *Wickersham Commission Reports,* 14 Volumes. Washington, DC: U.S. Government Printing Office.

National Council on Crime and Delinquency. 1990b. *Tennessee Board of Paroles Risk Assessment Report.* San Francisco, CA: Author.

National Council on Crime and Delinquency. 1992. *Criminal Justice Sentencing Policy Statement.* San Francisco, CA: Author.

National Manpower Survey. 1978. *The National Manpower Survey of the Criminal Justice System: Corrections.* Washington, DC: U.S. Government Printing Office.

National Office for Social Responsibility. 1987. *Reparative Work, Phase II: A Feasibility Study of an Alternative Punishment.* Alexandria, VA: National Office for Social Responsibility.

Nau, William C. 1987. "A Day in the Life of a Federal Probation Officer." *Federal Probation,* **51:**28–32.

Neithercutt, M. G., B. G. Carmichael, and Kenneth Mullen. 1990. "A Perspective on Determinate Sentencing." *Criminal Justice Policy Review,* **4:**201–213.

Nelson, Paul L. 1985. "Marketable Skills." *Corrections Today,* **47:**70.

Nemeth, Charles P. 1986. *Dictionary of Criminal Justice Education.* Cincinnati, OH: Anderson Publishing Company.

Nesbitt, Charlotte A. 1992. "The Female Offender: Overview of Facility Planning and Design Issues and Considerations." *Corrections Compendium,* **17:**1–7.

Neuhoff, Elizabeth. 1987. "The Indeterminate Sentence vs. the Determinate Sentence." Unpublished paper presented at the Academy of Criminal Justice Sciences meetings, St. Louis, MO (April).

Nevada County Probation Department. 1990. *Alternative Program Profiles of California Counties.* Nevada City, CA: Author.

Nevada Legislative Council. 1987. *Sentencing Reform and Alternatives to Incarceration.* Carson City, NV: Nevada Legislative Council Bureau of Research Division.

New Hampshire State Prison. 1992. *Community Correction Centers Handbook of Rules and Regulations: New Hampshire State Prison.* Concord, NH: Author.

New Jersey Juvenile Delinquency Commission. 1991. *The Chronic Juvenile Offender: A Challenge to New Jersey's Juvenile Justice System.* Trenton, NJ: Author.

New Orleans Office of the Criminal Justice Coordinator. 1991. *Electronic Monitoring at the Youth Study Center: An Evaluation.* New Orleans, LA: Author.

New York State Department of Correctional Services. 1989. *Follow-Up Study of First Six Platoons of Shock Graduates.* Albany, NY: Author, Division of Program Planning.

New York State Department of Correctional Services. 1990. *The Second Annual Report to the Legislature: Shock Incarceration in New York.* Albany, NY: Author, Division of Parole.

New York State Department of Correctional Services. 1991. *The Third Annual Report to the Legislature: Shock Incarceration in New York.* Albany, NY: Author, Division of Program Planning.

New York State Department of Correctional Services. 1992. *Guidelines for Volunteer Services.* Albany, NY: Author.

New York State Division of Parole. 1985. *PARJO III: Final Evaluation of the PARJO Pilot Supervision*

Program. Albany, NY: Division of Parole, Evaluation and Planning Unit.

New York State Unified Court System. 1985. *The Community Dispute Resolution Centers Program: A Progress Report.* New York: Author.

Nidorf, Barry J. 1989. "Community Corrections: Turning the Crowding Crisis into Opportunities." *Corrections Today,* **51:**86–88.

Noonan, Susan B. and Edward J. Latessa. 1987. "Intensive Probation: An Examination of Recidivism and Social Adjustment for an Intensive Supervision Program." *American Journal of Criminal Justice,* **12:**45–61.

Norland, Stephen and Priscilla J. Mann. 1984. "Being Troublesome: Women on Probation." *Criminal Justice and Behavior,* **11:**115–135.

Norman, Michael D. 1986. "Discretionary Justice: Decision-Making in a State Juvenile Parole Board." *Juvenile and Family Court Journal,* **37:**19–25.

Norman, Sherwood. 1970. *The Youth Service Bureau—A Key to Delinquency Prevention.* Hackensack, NJ: National Council on Crime and Delinquency.

North Carolina Administrative Office of the Courts. 1988. *Presentence Reports to Judges.* Raleigh, NC: Author.

North Carolina Governor's Advisory Board on Prisons and Punishment. 1990. *A Report to the Governor: North Carolina's Prison Crisis.* Raleigh, NC: Author.

Nowell, Carl and Joanne B. Stinchomb. 1988. "Firearms Training: Targeting Effective Programs." *Corrections Today,* **50:**160–161.

Nowicki, Ed (ed.). 1993. *Total Survival: A Comprehensive Guide for the Physical, Psychological, Emotional and Professional Survival of Law Enforcement Officers.* Powers Lake, WI: Performance Dimensions Publishing.

Oberst, Margaret. 1988. *Inmate Literacy Programs: Virginia's 'No Read, No Release' Program.* Lexington, KY: Council of State Governments.

O'Connell, Paul and Jacquelyn M. Power. 1992. "The Power of Partnerships: Establishing Literacy Programs in Community Corrections." *APPA Perspectives,* **16:**6–8.

Ogburn, Kevin R. 1993. "Volunteer Program Guide." *Corrections Today,* **55:**66–70.

Ohio Department of Rehabilitation and Correction. 1989. *The Ohio Parole Board.* Columbus, OH: Author.

Ohio Parole Board. 1992. *The Parole Board Guidelines.* Columbus, OH: Author.

Oklahoma State Board of Corrections. 1984. *Recommendations for Controlling Prison Population Growth: A Response to HB 1483.* Oklahoma City, OK: Author.

O'Leary, Vincent and J. Hall. 1976. *Frames of Reference in Parole.* Hackensack, NJ: National Council on Crime and Delinquency Training Center, National Parole Institute Training Document.

Olivero, J. Michael. 1990. "The Treatment of AIDS behind the Walls of Correctional Facilities." *Social Justice,* **17:**113–125.

O'Neil, Marion. 1990. "Correctional Higher Education: Reduced Recidivism?" *Journal of Correctional Education,* **41:**28–31.

Onondaga County Probation Department. 1992. *Onondaga County Probation Department Annual Report.* Syracuse, NY: Author.

Oregon Crime Analysis Center. 1984. *Recidivism of Releasees from Oregon Corrections Institutions.* Salem, OR: Author.

Oregon Crime Analysis Center. 1991. *Intermediate Sanctions.* Salem, OR: Author.

Orsagh, Thomas and Mary Ellen Marsden. 1985. "What Works When: Rational-Choice Theory and Offender Rehabilitation." *Journal of Criminal Justice,* **13:**269–277.

Orsagh, Thomas and Mary Ellen Marsden. 1987. "Inmates + Appropriate Programs = Effective Rehabilitation." *Corrections Today,* **49:**174–180.

Ortega, Sandra and Carolyn Hardin. 1993. "Community Corrections Programs Promoting Safety through Screening and Structure." *Corrections Compendium,* **18:**15–16.

Osgood, D. Wayne. 1983. "Offense History and Juvenile Diversion." *Evaluation Review,* **7:**793–806.

Osler, Mark W. 1991. "Shock Incarceration: Hard Realities and Real Possibilities." *Federal Probation,* **55:**34–42.

Pace, Chaplain Arthur C. 1993. "Religious Volunteers Form Partnership with the Military's Chaplaincy Program." *Corrections Today,* **55:**114–116.

Pacific Institute for Research and Evaluation. 1985. *National Evaluation of the New Pride Replication Program: Final Report.* Lafayette, CA: U.S. Office of Juvenile Justice and Delinquency Prevention.

Padgett, John F. 1985. "The Emergent Organization of Plea Bargaining." *American Journal of Sociology,* **90:**753–800.

Paine, Whiton Stewart (ed.). 1982. *Job Stress and Burnout: Research, Theory, and Intervention Perspectives.* Beverly Hills, CA: Sage.

Palenski, Joseph E. 1984. *Kids Who Run Away.* Saratoga, CA: R & E Publishers.

Palermo, George B., Frank J. Liska, and Maurice B. Smith. 1991. "Jails versus Mental Hospitals: A Social Dilemma." *International Journal of Offender Therapy and Comparative Criminology,* **35:**97–106.

Palm Beach County, Florida, Sheriff's Department. 1987. "Palm Beach County's In-House Arrest Work Release Program." In *Intermediate Punishments: Intensive Supervision, Home Confinement, and Electronic Surveillance,* Belinda McCarthy (ed.). Monsey, NY: Willow Tree Press.

Palmer, Ted and Robert Wedge. 1989. "California's Juvenile Probation Camps: Findings and Implications." *Crime and Delinquency,* **35:**234–253.

Palone, N. J. 1993. "Inmate Behavior Dynamics." *Journal of Offender Rehabilitation,* **19:**96–104.

Palumbo, Dennis J. and Zoann Snyder-Joy. 1990.

"From Net-Widening to Intermediate Sanctions: The Transformation of Alternatives to Incarceration from Malevolence to Benevolence." Unpublished paper presented at the annual meeting of the American Society of Criminology, Baltimore, MD (November).

Paparozzi, Mario A. and Barry B. Bass. 1990. "Firearms—Debating the Issues for Probation and Parole." *APPA Perspectives,* **14:**8–9.

Papy, Joseph F. and Richard Nimer. 1991. "Electronic Monitoring in Florida." *Federal Probation,* **55:** 31–33.

Parent, Dale G. 1988a. "Shock Incarceration Programs." *APPA Perspectives,* **12:**9–15.

Parent, Dale G. 1988b. "Sentencing Purpose, Design and Operation of Shock Incarceration Program." Unpublished paper presented at the annual meeting of the American Society of Criminology, Chicago, IL (November).

Parent, Dale G. 1989a. "Probation Supervision Fee Collection in Texas." *APPA Perspectives,* **13:**9–12.

Parent, Dale G. 1989b. *Shock Incarceration: An Overview of Existing Programs.* Washington, DC: U.S. Department of Justice, Office of Justice Programs.

Parent, Dale G. 1990a. *Day Reporting Centers for Criminal Offenders: A Descriptive Analysis of Existing Programs.* Washington, DC: U.S. Department of Justice, Office of Justice Programs, National Institute of Justice.

Parent, Dale G. 1990b. *Recovering Correctional Costs Through Offender Fees.* Washington, DC: U.S. National Institute of Justice.

Parent, Dale G. et al. 1992. *Responding to Probation and Parole Violation.* Washington, DC: U.S. Department of Justice, National Institute of Justice, Unpublished report.

Parisi, N. 1980. "Combining Incarceration and Probation." *Federal Probation,* **44:**3–12.

Parisi, Nicolette. 1984. "The Female Correctional Officer: Her Progress toward and Prospects for Equality." *The Prison Journal,* **64:**92–109.

Parsonage, William H. 1990. *Worker Safety in Probation and Parole.* Washington, DC: U.S. National Institute of Corrections.

Parsonage, William H. 1992. "The Impact of Victim Testimony on Parole Decision Making." Unpublished paper presented at the annual meeting of the American Society of Criminology, New Orleans, LA (November).

Parsonage, William and W. Conway Bushey. 1988. "The Victimization of Probation/Parole Officers: An Occupational Health Problem." Unpublished paper presented at the Academy of Criminal Justice Sciences meetings, San Francisco, CA (April).

Patel, Jody and Curt Soderlund. 1994. "Getting a Piece of the Pie: Revenue Sharing with Crime Victims Compensation Programs." *APPA Perspectives,* **18:**22–27.

Patterson, Bernie L. 1992. "Job Experience and Perceived Stress among Police, Correctional, and Probation/Parole Officers." *Criminal Justice and Behavior,* **19:**260–285.

Peak, Ken. 1986. "Crime Victim Reparation: Legislative Revival of the Offended Ones." *Federal Probation,* **50:**36–41.

Pearson, Frank S. 1985. "New Jersey's Intensive Supervision Program: A Progress Report." *Crime and Delinquency,* **31:**393–410.

Pearson, Frank S. 1987. "Taking Quality into Account: Assessing the Benefits and Costs of New Jersey's Intensive Supervision Program." In *Intermediate Punishments: Intensive Supervision, Home Confinement, and Electronic Surveillance,* Belinda R. McCarthy (ed.). Monsey, NY: Criminal Justice Press.

Pearson, Frank S. and Daniel B. Bibel. 1986. "New Jersey's Intensive Supervision Program: What Is It Like? How Is It Working?" *Federal Probation,* **50:**25–31.

Peat, Barbara J. and L. Thomas Winfree Jr. 1992. "Reducing the Intra-Institutional Effects of 'Prisonization': A Study of the Therapeutic Community for Drug-Using Inmates." *Criminal Justice and Behavior,* **19:**206–225.

Pelfrey, William V. 1986. "Assessment Centers as a Management Promotion Tool." *Federal Probation,* **50:**65–69.

Pelicciotti, Joseph M. 1987. "42 U.S. C. Sec. 1983 & Correctional Officials Liability: A Look to the New Century." *Journal of Contemporary Criminal Justice,* **3:**1–9.

Pennsylvania Commission on Crime and Delinquency. 1990. *Containing Pennsylvania Offenders: The Final Report of the Pennsylvania Commission on Crime and Delinquency Corrections Overcrowding Committee.* Harrisburg, PA: Author.

Pepino, Jane N. et al. 1993. "Managing Risk in Corrections." *Forum on Corrections Research,* **5:**12–38.

Petersilia, Joan M. 1983. *Racial Disparities in the Criminal Justice System.* Washington, DC: U.S. Department of Justice, National Institute of Corrections.

Petersilia, Joan M. 1985a. "Rand's Research: A Closer Look." *Corrections Today,* **47:**37–40.

Petersilia, Joan M. 1985b. "Community Supervision: Trends and Critical Issues." *Crime and Delinquency,* **31:**18–22.

Petersilia, Joan M. 1985c. *Probation and Felony Offenders.* Washington, DC: Bureau of Justice Statistics.

Petersilia, Joan M. 1986a. *Exploring the Option of House Arrest.* Santa Monica, CA: Rand Corporation.

Petersilia, Joan M. 1986b. "Exploring the Option of House Arrest." *Federal Probation,* **50:**50–55.

Petersilia, Joan M. 1986c. *Taking Stock of Probation Reform.* Santa Monica, CA: Rand Corporation.

Petersilia, Joan M. 1987a. *Expanding Options for Criminal Sentencing.* Santa Monica, CA: Rand Corporation.

Petersilia, Joan M. 1987b. "Los Angeles Experiments with House Arrest." *Corrections Today,* **49:**132–134.

Petersilia, Joan M. 1987c. "Prisoners without Prisons." *State Legislatures,* August:22–25.

Petersilia, Joan M. 1988a. *House Arrest.* Washington, DC: U.S. Department of Justice, National Institute of Justice.

Petersilia, Joan M. 1988b. "Probation Reform." In *Controversial Issues in Crime and Justice,* Joseph E. Scott and Travis Hirschi (eds.). Beverly Hills, CA: Sage.

Petersilia, Joan M. 1990. "Expanding Sentencing Options Through Electronically Monitored Home Detention." Unpublished paper presented at the annual meetings of the American Society of Criminology, Baltimore, MD (November).

Petersilia, Joan M. and Susan Turner. 1987. "Guideline-Based Justice: Prediction and Racial Minorities." In *Prediction and Classification,* D. M. Gottfredson and M. Tonry (eds.). Chicago, IL: University of Chicago Press.

Petersilia, Joan M. and Susan Turner. 1990. "Evaluating Intensive Supervision Probation (ISP) in California." Unpublished paper presented at the annual meeting of the American Society of Criminology, New Orleans, LA (November).

Petersilia, Joan M. and Susan Turner. 1990c. *Intensive Supervision for High-Risk Probationers: Findings from Three California Experiments.* Santa Monica, CA: Rand Corporation.

Petersilia, Joan M. and Susan Turner. 1990d. "Reducing Prison Admissions: The Potential of Intermediate Sanctions." *APPA Perspectives,* **14:**32–36.

Petersilia, Joan M. and Susan Turner. 1991. "An Evaluation of Intensive Probation in California." *Journal of Criminal Law & Criminology,* **82:**610–658.

Petersilia, Joan M. and Susan Turner. 1992. "Focusing on High-Risk Parolees: An Experiment to Reduce Commitments to the Texas Department of Corrections." *Journal of Research in Crime and Delinquency,* **29:**34–61.

Petersilia, Joan M. and Susan Turner. 1993. *Evaluating Intensive Supervision Probation/Parole: Results of a Nationwide Experiment.* Washington, DC: U.S. Department of Justice, Office of Justice Programs.

Petersilia, Joan M., Susan Turner, and Joyce Peterson. 1986. *Prison Versus Probation in California: Implications for Crime and Offender Recidivism.* Santa Monica, CA: Rand Corporation.

Petersilia, Joan M. et al. 1985. *Granting Felons Probation in California: Implications for Crime and Offender Recidivism.* Santa Monica, CA: Rand Corporation.

Philadelphia Prison System. 1990. *Philadelphia Prisons Pre-Release Program—Policy and Operations Manual.* Philadelphia, PA: Author.

Philliber, Susan. 1987. "Thy Brother's Keeper: A Review of the Literature on Corrections Officers." *Justice Quarterly,* **4:**9–37.

Pierson, E. Jane et al. 1992. "A Day in the Life of a Federal Probation Officer—Revisited." *Federal Probation,* **56:**18–28.

Pines, Ayala M. and E. Aronson. 1981. *Burnout.* New York: The Free Press.

Pingree, David H. 1984. "Florida Youth Services." *Corrections Today,* **46:**60–62.

Piquero, Alex and Doris Layton MacKenzie. 1993. "The Impact of an Alternative Program on Bedspace." Unpublished paper presented at the annual meeting of the American Society of Criminology, Phoenix, AZ (October).

Poethig, M. 1989. "Trying to Halt the Cycle." *State Peace Officers Journal,* **38:**69–71.

Poklewski-Koziel, C. 1988. "Community Participation in Corrections." In *Current International Trends in Corrections,* David Biles (ed.). Washington, DC: Department of Justice, Bureau of Justice Statistics.

Polk, Kenneth. 1984. "Juvenile Diversion: A Look at the Record." *Crime and Delinquency,* **30:**648–659.

Pollock-Byrne, Joycelyn M. 1990. *Women, Prison & Crime.* Pacific Grove, CA: Brooks/Cole Publishing Company.

Pommersheim, Frank and Steve Wise. 1989. "Going to the Penitentiary: A Study of Disparate Sentencing in South Dakota." *Criminal Justice and Behavior,* **16:**155–165.

Poole, E. D. and R. M. Regoli. 1983. "Professionalism, Role Conflict, Work Alienation and Anomia: A Look at Prison Management." *Social Science Journal,* **20:**63–70.

Powers, Kevin. 1992. *Intensive Supervision in the Northern District of Ohio.* Washington, DC: U.S. Parole Commission.

Pratt, John D. 1983. "Law and Social Control: A Study of Truancy and School." *Journal of Law and Society,* **10.**223–240.

Prentky, Robert A. et al. 1991a. *Classification of Rapists: Implementation and Validation.* Bridgewater, MA: Research Department, Massachusetts Treatment Center.

Prentky, Robert A. et al. 1991b. "Child Molesters Who Abduct." *Violence and Victims,* **6:**213–224.

President's Commission on Law Enforcement and Administration of Justice. 1967. *Task Force Report: Corrections.* Washington, DC: U.S. Government Printing Office.

Prison Fellowship. 1991. "Study Finds Religious Experience Lowers Inmate Recidivism." *Corrections Compendium,* **16:**14.

Probation Association. 1939. *John Augustus: The First Probation Officer.* New York: Author.

Program Resources Center. 1988. *The Probation Development Project: Successes, Failures and Question Marks.* Newark, NJ: Author, Rutgers University School of Criminal Justice.

Project New Pride. 1985. *Project New Pride.* Washington, DC: U.S. Government Printing Office.

Pugh, Michael and Mark Kunkel. 1986. "The Mentally

Retarded Offenders Program of the Texas Department of Corrections." *The Prison Journal,* **66:**39–51.

Putnam, Jim. 1990. "Electronic Monitoring: From Innovation to Acceptance in Five Years." *Corrections Today,* **52:**96–98.

Quay, Herbert C. 1984. *Managing Adult Inmates.* College Park, MD: American Correctional Association.

Quay, Herbert C. and L. B. Parsons. 1971. *The Differential Behavioral Classification of the Adult Male Offender.* Philadelphia, PA: Temple University [Technical report prepared for the U.S. Department of Justice Bureau of Prisons, Contract J-1C-22, 253].

Quinlan, J. Michael. 1987. "The New Man at the Top." *Corrections Today,* **49:**16–20.

Quinn, James F. and John E. Holman. 1990. "Purpose Versus Practice in the Use of Electronically Monitored Home Confinement." *American Journal of Crime and Justice,* **15:**157–170.

Quinn, James F. and John E. Holman. 1991. "The Efficacy of Electronically Monitored Home Confinement As a Case Management Device." *Journal of Contemporary Criminal Justice,* **7:**128–134.

Racine, Trudy, Tom Vittitow, and Rick Riggs. 1984. *Examining Potential Duplication between Community Corrections Programs and District Court Probation Services.* Topeka, KS: Kansas Legislative Post Audit Committee.

Rackmill, Stephen J. 1994. "An Analysis of Home Confinement as a Sanction." *Federal Probation,* **58:**45–56.

Rada, R. T. 1978. *Legal Aspects in Treating Rapists.* Marysville, OH: American Association of Correctional Psychologists.

Radosh, Polly F. 1988. "Inmate Mothers: Legislative Solutions to a Difficult Problem." *Journal of Crime and Justice,* **11:**61–76.

Ralph, H. Paige and James W. Marquart. 1992. "Correlates of Gang-Related Homicides in Prison." Unpublished paper presented at the annual meetings of the American Society of Criminology, New Orleans, LA (November).

Ranish, Donald R. and David Shichor. 1985. "The Victim's Role in the Penal Process: Recent Developments from California." *Federal Probation,* **49:**50–57.

Rans, Laurel L. 1984. "The Validity of Models to Predict Violence in Community and Prison Settings." *Corrections Today,* **46:**50–63.

Rath, Quentin C. 1991. "Minnesota Corrections: Perspectives from Probation and Parole Officers." *Corrections Today,* **53:**228–230.

Ratliff, Bascom W. 1988. "The Army Model: Boot Camp for Youthful Offenders." *Corrections Today,* **50:**90–102.

Rauma, David and Richard A. Berk. 1987. "Remuneration and Recidivism: The Long-Term Impact of Unemployment Compensation on Ex-Offenders." *Journal of Quantitative Criminology,* **3:**3–27.

Read, Edward M. 1988. "Identifying the Alcoholic: A Practical Guide for the Probation Officer." *Federal Probation,* **52:**59–65.

Read, Edward M. 1992. "Euphoria on the Rocks: Understanding Crack Addiction." *Federal Probation,* **56:**3–11.

Reckless, Walter C. 1961. *The Crime Problem.* New York: Appleton-Century-Crofts.

Reeves, R. 1992. "Approaching 2000: Finding Solutions to the Most Pressing Issues Facing the Corrections Community." *Corrections Today,* **54:**74, 76–79.

Reid, Sue Titus. 1987. *Criminal Justice: Procedures and Issues.* St. Paul, MN: West.

Reiss, Albert J., Jr. and Jeffrey A. Roth (eds.). 1993. *Understanding and Preventing Violence.* Washington, DC: National Academy Press.

Remington, Bob and Marina Remington. 1987. "Behavior Modification in Probation Work: A Review and Evaluation." *Criminal Justice and Behavior,* **14:**156–174.

Rhine, Edward E. et al. 1989. "Parole: Issues and Prospects for the 1990s." *Corrections Today,* **51:**78–147.

Rhine, Edward E. (ed.). 1993. *Reclaiming Offender Accountability: Intermediate Sanctions for Probation and Parole Violators.* Laurel, MD: American Correctional Association.

Rice, Marnie E. and Grant T. Harris. 1992. "A Comparison of Criminal Recidivism among Schizophrenic and Nonschizophrenic Offenders." *International Journal of Law and Psychiatry,* **15:**397–408.

Richmond, C. 1970. "Expanding the Concepts of the Halfway House: A Satellite Housing Program." *International Journal of Social Psychiatry,* **16:**986–1102.

Richmond Times-Dispatch. 1990. "Virginia County Tries Home Incarceration Program." *Corrections Today,* **52:**100.

Riechers, Lisa M. 1988. "The Effect of Shock Incarceration on the Mastery and Control Expectations of Inmates." Unpublished paper presented at the annual meeting of the American Society of Criminology, Chicago, IL (November).

Riley, J. B. 1974. *Halfway Houses: A Key to Citizen Acceptance.* Rockville, MD: National Institute of Justice, National Criminal Justice Reference Service Microfiche Program.

Ring, Charles R. 1989. "Probation Supervision Fees: Shifting Costs to the Offender." *Federal Probation,* **53:**43–46.

Robbins, Ira P. 1985. "Rights of Parolees." In *Prisoners and the Law,* Ira P. Robbins (ed.). New York: Clark Boardman.

Robbins, Ira P. 1986. "Privatization of Corrections: Defining the Issues." *Federal Probation,* **50:**24–30.

Robbins, Ira P. 1987. *Prisoners and the Law,* 2nd ed. New York: Clark Boardman.

Robertson, James M. and J. Vernon Blackburn. 1984. "An Assessment of Treatment Effectiveness by Case Classification." *Federal Probation,* **48:**34–38.

Robins, Arthur J. et al. 1986. "The Missouri Classification System Applied to Female Offenders: Reliability and Validity." *Corrective and Social Psychiatry and Journal of Behavior Technology Methods and Therapy,* **32:**21–30.

Robinson, J. J. and A. J. Lurigio. 1990. "Responding to Overcrowding and Offender Drug Use: How About Community Corrections Approach?" *APPA Perspectives,* **14:**22–27.

Rockowitz, Ruth J. 1986a. "Developmentally Disabled Offenders: Issues in Developing and Maintaining Services." *The Prison Journal,* **66:**19–23.

Rockowitz, Ruth J. (ed.). 1986b. "The Developmentally Disabled Offender." *The Prison Journal,* **66:**1–92.

Rogers, Joseph W. and G. Larry Mays. 1987. *Juvenile Delinquency and Juvenile Justice.* New York: Wiley.

Rogers, Robert and Annette Jolin. 1989. "Electronic Monitoring: A Review of the Empirical Literature." *Journal of Contemporary Criminal Justice,* **5:**141–152.

Rohn, Warren and Trish Ostroski. 1991. "Checking IDs: Advances in Technology Make It Easier to Monitor Inmates." *Corrections Today,* **53:**142–145.

Romero, Joseph and Linda M. Williams. 1983. "Group Psychotherapy and Intensive Probation Supervision: A Comparative Study." *Federal Probation,* **47:**36–42.

Romig, Dennis A. 1978. *Justice for Our Children.* Lexington, MA: Lexington Books.

Rose, Tracy. 1988. "Volunteers in Prison: The Community Link." *Corrections Today,* **50:**216–218.

Rosecrance, John. 1985. "The Probation Officer's Search for Credibility: Ball Park Recommendations." *Crime and Delinquency,* **31:**539–554.

Rosecrance, John. 1986. "Probation Supervision: Mission Impossible." *Federal Probation,* **50:**25–34.

Rosecrance, John. 1987a. "Extralegal Factors and Probation Presentence Reports." *Journal of Contemporary Criminal Justice,* **3:**38–56.

Rosecrance, John. 1987b. "Getting Rid of the Prima Donnas: The Bureaucratization of a Probation Department." *Criminal Justice and Behavior,* **14:**138–155.

Rosecrance, John. 1988a. "Maintaining the Myth of Individualized Justice: Probation Presentence Reports." *Justice Quarterly,* **5:**235–256.

Rosecrance, John. 1988b. "The Presentence Probation Report: No Longer Relevant?" Unpublished paper presented at the Academy of Criminal Justice Sciences meetings, San Francisco, CA (April).

Rosenblum, Robert and Debra Whitcomb. 1978. *Montgomery County Work Release/Pre-Release Program, Montgomery County, Maryland.* Washington, DC: U.S. Government Printing Office.

Rosenthal, C. S. 1989. *Opportunities in Community Corrections.* Denver, CO: National Conference of State Legislatures.

Ross, Robert R. and Elizabeth A. Fabiano. 1985. *Correctional Afterthoughts: Programs for Female Of-*

fenders. Ottawa, Canada: Ministry of the Solicitor General of Canada.

Rothman, David J. 1983. "Sentencing Reforms in Historical Perspective." *Crime and Delinquency,* **29:**631–647.

Rothstein, P. F. 1974. *How the Uniform Crime Victims Reparations Act Works.* Washington, DC: American Bar Association.

Roulet, Sister Elaine. 1993. "New York's Prison Nursery/Children's Center." *Corrections Compendium,* **18:**4–6.

Roundtree, George A., Dan W. Edwards, and Jack B. Parker. 1984. "A Study of the Personal Characteristics of Probationers as Related to Recidivism." *Journal of Offender Counseling,* **8:**53–61.

Roy, Sudipto and Michael Brown. 1992. "Victim-Offender Reconciliation Project for Adults and Juveniles: A Comparative Study in Elkhart County, Indiana." Unpublished paper presented at the annual meetings of the American Society of Criminology, San Francisco, CA (November).

Royse, David and Steven A. Buck. 1991. "Evaluating a Diversion Program for First-Time Shoplifters." *Journal of Offender Rehabilitation,* **17:**147–158.

Ruback, R. Barry and Timothy S. Carr. 1993. "Prison Crowding over Time: The Relationship of Density and Changes in Density to Infraction Rules." *Criminal Justice and Behavior,* **20:**130–148.

Rubel, Howard C. 1986. "Victim Participation in Sentencing Proceedings." *Criminal Law Quarterly,* **28:**226–250.

Rubin, H. Ted. 1985a. *Behind the Black Robes: Juvenile Court Judges and the Court.* Beverly Hills, CA: Sage.

Rubin, H. Ted. 1985b. *Juvenile Justice: Policy, Practice, and the Law,* 2nd ed. New York: Random House.

Rush, Fred L., Jr. 1987. "Deinstitutional Incapacitation: Home Detention in Pre-Trial and Post-Conviction Contexts." *Northern Kentucky Law Review,* **13:**375–408.

Rush, George E. 1989. "Electronic Surveillance: An Alternative to Incarceration: An Overview of the San Diego County Program." *American Journal of Criminal Justice,* **12:**219–242.

Rush, George E. 1990. *The Dictionary of Criminal Justice,* 3rd ed. Guilford, CT: The Dushkin Publishing Group.

Rush, Jeffrey P. 1992. "Juvenile Probation Officer Cynicism." *American Journal of Criminal Justice,* **16:**1–16.

Rutherford, Andrew. 1986. *Growing Out of Crime.* New York: Penguin Books.

Rutherford, Andrew. 1992. "Adolescents and the Penal System: Hopeful Results in the Wind." *Criminal Behaviour and Mental Health,* **2:**15–23.

Rutherford, R. B., C. M. Nelson, and B. I. Wolford. 1985. "Special Education in the Most Restrictive Environment: Correctional/Special Education." *Journal of Special Education,* **19:**59–71.

Ryan, Patrick J. 1987. "Police Professionalism and the

First-Line Supervisor." Unpublished paper presented at the American Society of Criminology meetings, Montreal, Canada (November).

Ryan, T. A. and James B. Grassano. 1992. "Taking a Progressive Approach to Treating Pregnant Offenders." *Corrections Today,* **54:**184–186.

Sagatun, Inger, Loretta L. McCollum and Leonard P. Edwards. 1985. "The Effect of Transfers from Juvenile to Criminal Court: A Loglinear Analysis." *Journal of Crime and Justice,* **8:**65–92.

Salerno, Anthony W. 1991. "Let's Give Shock Incarceration the Boot." *Corrections Today,* **53:**28–32.

Salive, Marcel, E. Gordon, B. Smith, and T. Fordham Brewer. 1990. "Death in Prison: Changing Mortality Patterns among Male Prisoners in Maryland, 1979–1987." *American Journal of Public Health,* **80:**1479–1480.

Salvation Army. 1993. "The Salvation Army: Offering Support to Corrections for More than a Century." *Corrections Today,* **53:**66–70.

Samaha, Joel. 1988. *Criminal Justice.* St. Paul, MN: West.

Santamour, Miles. 1986. "The Offender with Mental Retardation." *The Prison Journal,* **66:**3–18.

Sapers, Howard. 1990. "The Fine Options Program in Alberta." Unpublished paper presented at the annual meeting of the American Society of Criminology, Baltimore, MD (November).

Sapp, Allen D. and Michael Vaughn. 1989. "Sex Offender Treatment Programs: An Evaluation." Unpublished paper presented at the annual meeting of the American Society of Criminology, Reno, NV (November).

Saunders, Daniel G. and Sandra T. Azar. 1989. "Treatment Programs for Family Violence." In *Family Violence,* Lloyd Ohlin and Michael Tonry (eds.). Chicago: University of Chicago Press.

Savage, David A. and Michael Dumovich. 1991. "Community Residential Programs." *Community Corrections Quarterly,* **5:**1–16.

Saylor, W. G. and G. G. Gaes. 1992. "Post-Release Employment Project: Prison Work Has Measurable Effects on Post-Release Success." *Federal Prison Journal,* **2:**32–36.

Schafer, N. E. 1986. "Discretion, Due Process, and the Prison Discipline Committee." *Criminal Justice Review,* **11:**37–46.

Schafer, N. E. and A. B. Dellinger. 1993. "Is It Time to Include Women?" *American Jails,* **7:**33–38.

Schiff, Martha F. 1990. "Shifting Paradigms from a Presumption of Incarceration to Community Based Supervision and Sanctioning." Unpublished paper presented at the annual meetings of the American Society of Criminology, Baltimore, MD (November).

Schlatter, Gary. 1989. "Electronic Monitoring: Hidden Costs of Home Arrest Programs." *Corrections Today,* **51:**94–96.

Schlossman, Steven and Joseph Spillane. 1992. *Bright Hopes, Dim Realities: Vocational Innovation in American Correctional Education.* Santa Monica, CA: Rand Corporation.

Schmidt, Annesley K. 1986. "Electronic Monitors." *Federal Probation,* **50:**56–59.

Schmidt, Annesley K. 1989a. "Electronic Monitoring." *Journal of Contemporary Criminal Justice,* **5:** 133–140.

Schmidt, Annesley K. 1989b. *Electronic Monitoring of Offenders Increases.* Washington, DC: U.S. Department of Justice, Office of Justice Programs.

Schmidt, Annesley K. 1991. "Electronic Monitors: Realistically, What Can Be Expected?" *Federal Probation,* **55:**47–53.

Schmidt, Annesley K. and Christine E. Curtis. 1987. "Electronic Monitors." In *Intermediate Punishments: Intensive Supervision, Home Confinement, and Electronic Surveillance,* Belinda R. McCarthy (ed.). Monsey, NY: Criminal Justice Press.

Schneider, Anne L. (ed.). 1985. *Guide to Juvenile Restitution.* Washington, DC: U.S. National Institute of Justice.

Schneider, Anne L. and Peter R. Schneider. 1985. "The Impact of Restitution on Recidivism of Juvenile Offenders: An Experiment in Clayton County, Georgia." *Criminal Justice Review,* **10:**1–10.

Schumacher, Michael A. et al. 1991. "Community Corrections." *Journal of Contemporary Criminal Justice,* **7:**iii–145.

Schumacker, Randall E., Dennis B. Anderson, and Sara L. Anderson. 1990. "Vocational and Academic Indicators of Parole Success." *Journal of Correctional Education,* **41:**8–13.

Schuman, Alan M. and Tamara Holden. 1989. "Point and Counterpoint: Firearms—Debating the Issues for Probation and Parole." *APPA Perspectives,* **13:**6–8.

Scott, J. E. 1981. "Dismantling of an LEAA Exemplary Project—the Parole Officer Aide Program of Ohio." In *Mad, the Bad, and the Different,* Israel L. Barak-Glantz et al. (eds.). Washington, DC: National Institute of Justice.

Scott, John F. 1991. "Managing a Home Detention Program." *Journal of Offender Monitoring,* **4:**1, 3.

Scull, Andrew. 1977. *Decarceration: Community Treatment and the Deviant—A Radical Overview.* New York: Spectrum.

Sechrest, Dale K. 1991. "The Effects of Density on Jail Assaults." *Journal of Criminal Justice,* **19:**211–223.

Sechrest, Dale K., Nick Pappas, and Shelley J. Price. 1987. "Building Prisons: Pre-Manufactured, Prefabricated, and Prototype." *Federal Probation,* **51:** 35–41.

Sechrest, Dale K. and Shelley J. Price. 1985. *Correctional Facility Design and Construction Management.* Washington, DC: U.S. National Institute of Justice.

Sechrest, Lee. 1987. "Classification for Treatment." In *Prediction and Classification: Criminal Justice Deci-*

sion Making, Don M. Gottfredson and Michael Tonry (eds.). Chicago: University of Chicago Press.

Sechrest, Lee, Susan O. White, and Elizabeth Brown. 1979. *The Rehabilitation of Criminal Offenders: Problems and Prospects.* Washington, DC: National Academy of Sciences.

Segall, William E., Anna V. Wilson, and Harry E. Allen. 1991. "A Working Paper on the Study of Recidivism and Literacy in Oklahoma." Unpublished paper presented at the annual meeting of the American Society of Criminology, San Francisco, CA (November).

Seiter, R. P., J. R. Petersilia, and H. E. Allen. 1974. *Evaluation of Halfway Houses in Ohio.* Columbus, OH: Ohio State University Program for the Study of Crime and Delinquency.

Selva, Lance H. and Robert M. Bohm. 1987. "A Critical Examination of the Information Experiment in the Administration of Justice." *Crime and Social Justice,* **29:**43–57.

Selye, Hans. 1974. *Stress without Distress.* Philadelphia, PA: Lippincott.

Selye, Hans. 1976. *The Stress of Life,* 2nd ed. New York: McGraw-Hill.

Semanchik, David A. 1990. "Prison Overcrowding in the United States: Judicial and Legislative Remedies." *New England Journal on Criminal and Civil Confinement,* **16:**67–88.

Services to Unruly Youth Program. 1979. *Services to Unruly Youth Program.* Columbus, OH: Franklin County Children Services.

Shane-DuBow, Sandra, Alice P. Brown, and Eric Olsen. 1985. *Sentencing Reform in the United States. History, Content, and Effect.* Washington, DC: U.S. Department of Justice.

Shapiro, C. 1982. "Creative Supervision: An Underutilized Antidote." In *Job Stress and Burnout: Research, Theory, and Intervention Perspectives,* W. Paine (ed.). Beverly Hills, CA: Sage.

Shapiro, Carol and Suzanne Flynn. 1989. "Linking Policy Reform to Supervision: A Look at the Probation Development Project in Multnomah County, Oregon." *APPA Perspectives,* **13:**13–17.

Shapiro, Walter. 1990. "A Life in His Hands." *Time,* May 28:23–24.

Shaw, James W. and Doris Layton MacKenzie. 1991. "Shock Incarceration and Its Impact on the Lives of Problem Drinkers." *American Journal of Criminal Justice,* **16:**63–96.

Shaw, James W. and Doris Layton MacKenzie. 1992. "The One-Year Community Supervision Performance of Drug Offenders and Louisiana DOC-Identified Substance Abusers Graduating from Shock Incarceration." *Journal of Criminal Justice,* **20:**501–516.

Shawver, Lois. 1987. "On the Question of Having Women Guards in Male Prisons." *Corrective and Social Psychiatry and Journal of Behavior Methods and Therapy,* **38:**154–159.

Shelden, Randall G. and William B. Brown. 1991. "Correlates of Jail Overcrowding: A Case Study of a County Detention Center." *Crime & Delinquency,* **37:**347–362.

Shelden, Randall G., John A. Horvath, and Sharon Tracy. 1989. "Do Status Offenders Get Worse? Some Clarifications on the Question of Escalation." *Crime and Delinquency,* **35:**202–216.

Shichor, David. 1985. "Male-Female Differences in Elderly Arrests: An Exploratory Analysis." *Justice Quarterly,* **2:**399–414.

Shichor, David. 1992. "Following the Penological Pendulum: The Survival of Rehabilitation." *Federal Probation,* **56:**19–25.

Shields, L. F. 1980. *Citizen Involvement.* Lincoln, NE: Contact, Inc.

Shilton, Mary K. 1992. *Community Corrections Acts for State and Local Partnerships.* American Correctional Association.

Shockley, Carol. 1988. "The Federal Presentence Investigation Report: Postsentence Disclosure under the Freedom of Information Act." *Administrative Law Review,* **40:**79–119.

Shover, Neal and Carol Y. Thompson. 1992. "Age, Differential Expectations, and Crime Desistance." *Criminology,* **30:**89–104.

Siegel, Gayle R. 1994. "Making a Difference: The Effect of Literacy and General Education Development Programs on Adult Offenders on Probation." *APPA Perspectives,* **18:**38–43.

Sieh, Edward W. 1990. "Role Perception among Probation Officers." Unpublished paper presented at the annual meeting of the Academy of Criminal Justice Sciences, Denver, CO (April).

Sieh, Edward W. 1992. "Probation Work: Mendacity and the Favorite Client." Unpublished paper presented at the annual meetings of the American Society of Criminology, New Orleans, LA (November).

Silverman, Mitchell. 1993. "Ethical Issues in the Field of Probation." *International Journal of Offender Therapy and Comparative Criminology,* **37:**85–94.

Silvia, Jerry. 1989. "Home Detention: New Technology Enhances Program." *Corrections Today,* **51:**130–132.

Simone, Margaret V. 1984. "Group Homes: Succeeding by Really Trying." *Corrections Today,* **46:**110–119.

Singer, Richard G. 1980. "The *Wolfish* Case: Has the *Bell* Tolled for Prisoner Litigation in the Federal Courts?" In *Legal Rights of Prisoners,* Geoffrey Alpert (ed.). Beverly Hills, CA: Sage.

Skovron, Sandra Evans and Brian Simms. 1990. "The Use of Task Forces to Develop Strategies to Alleviate Prison Crowding: An Analysis of Their Recommendations and . . . a Typology . . . of Activities." *Journal of Crime and Justice,* **12:**1–28.

Slotnick, M. 1976. *Evaluating Demonstration Programs: Two Case Studies (Drug Treatment in a Parish Prison and a Community-Based Residential*

Facility. New Orleans, LA: New Orleans Mayor's Criminal Justice Coordinating Council.

Sluder, Richard D. and Rolando V. del Carmen. 1990. "Are Probation and Parole Officers Liable for Injuries Caused by Probationers and Parolees?" *Federal Probation,* **54:**3–12.

Sluder, Richard D. and Robert A. Shearer. 1992. "Personality Types of Probation Officers." *Federal Probation,* **56:**29–35.

Sluder, Richard D., Robert A. Shearer, and Dennis W. Potts. 1991. "Probation Officers' Role Perceptions and Attitudes toward Firearms." *Federal Probation,* **55:**3–12.

Smith, Albert G. 1991a. "Arming Officers Doesn't Have to Change an Agency's Mission." *Corrections Today,* **53:**114–124.

Smith, Albert G. 1991b. "The California Model: Probation and Parole Safety Training." *APPA Perspectives,* **15:**38–41.

Smith, Albert G. 1991c. "Probation and Parole Agents: Arming Officers Doesn't Have to Change an Agency's Mission." *Corrections Today,* **53:** 114–124.

Smith, Albert G. 1992. "Proper Planning: Organizational Skills for Managing Your Probation and Parole Workload." *Corrections Today,* **54:**136–142.

Smith, Albert G. 1993a. "Practical Advice on Designing Probation and Parole Offices." *Corrections Today,* **55:**80–87.

Smith, Albert G. 1993b. "A Training Program in Probation and Parole Whose Time Has Come and Gone: Role Reversals." *APPA Perspectives,* **17:**24–27.

Smith, Brian M. 1993. "VPO Program: Probation Department in Michigan Finds Volunteers Make Fine Officers." *Corrections Today,* **55:**80–82.

Smith, Douglas A. and Christina Polsenberg. 1992. "Specifying the Relationship between Arrestee Drug Test Results and Recidivism." *Journal of Criminal Law and Criminology,* **83:**364–377.

Smith, Freddie V. 1984. "Alabama SIR Program." *Corrections Today,* **46:**129–132.

Smith, Linda G. and Ronald L. Akers. 1993. "A Comparison of Recidivism of Florida's Community Control and Prison: A Five-Year Survival Analysis." *Journal of Research in Crime and Delinquency,* **30:**267–292.

Smith, Robert R. and M. A. Milan. 1973. "Survey of the Home Furlough Policies of American Correctional Agencies." *Criminology,* **11:**95–104.

Smith, Robert R. and D. A. Sabatino. 1989. *American Prisoner Home Furloughs.* Unpublished manuscript.

Smykla, John O. 1981. *Community-Based Corrections: Principles and Practices.* New York: Macmillan.

Smykla, John O. and William Selke. 1982. "The Impact of Home Detention: A Less Restrictive Alternative to the Detention of Juveniles." *Juvenile and Family Court Journal,* **33:**3–9.

Snarr, Richard W. and Bruce I. Wolford. 1985. *Intro-duction to Corrections.* Dubuque, IA: Wm. C. Brown.

Snell, Tracy L. 1993. *Correctional Populations in the United States, 1991.* Washington, DC: U.S. Department of Justice, Bureau of Justice Statistics.

Snell, Tracy L. and Danielle C. Morton. 1994. *Women in Prison.* Washington, DC: U.S. Department of Justice, Office of Justice Programs.

Snyder, Keith B. and Cecil Marshall. 1990. "Pennsylvania's Juvenile Intensive Probation and Aftercare Programs." Unpublished paper presented at the American Society of Criminology meetings. Baltimore, MD (November).

Somers, Ira, Nancy F. Jacobs, and Richard Koehler. 1990. "Community-Based Supervision Detention." Unpublished paper presented at the annual meetings of the American Society of Criminology, Baltimore, MD (November).

Sontheimer, Henry and Lynne Goodstein. 1993. "An Evaluation of Juvenile Intensive Aftercare Probation: Aftercare Versus System Response Effects." *Justice Quarterly,* **10:**197–227.

Soskin, R. M. 1982. *Mentally Retarded Offender—Competence, Culpability, and Sentencing.* New York: Praeger.

South Carolina Department of Probation, Parole, and Pardon Services. 1993. *Violations Guidelines and Administrative Hearings.* Columbia, SC: Author, Unpublished report.

South Carolina State Reorganization Commission. 1990. *Evaluation of the Electronic Monitoring Pilot Program 1988–1989.* Columbia, SC: Author, A Jail and Prison Overcrowding Project Report.

South Carolina State Reorganization Commission. 1991. *Prison Crowding in South Carolina: Is There a Solution?* Columbia, SC: Author.

South Carolina State Reorganization Commission. 1992. *An Evaluation of the Implementation of the South Carolina Department of Corrections.* Columbia, SC: Author, A Jail and Prison Overcrowding Project Report.

Spangenberg, Robert L. et al. 1987. *Assessment of the Massachusetts Probation System.* West Newton, MA: Spangenberg Group.

Speckart, George and M. Douglas Anglin. 1986. "Narcotics Use and Crime: An Overview of Recent Research Advances." *Contemporary Drug Problems,* **13:**741–769.

Spica, Arthur R., Jr. 1987. "Presentence Reports: The Key to Probation Strategy." *Corrections Today,* **49:**192–196.

Spica, Arthur R., Jr. 1993. "The Resource Referral Process: What Is Between Human Services and Offender Adjustment?" *APPA Perspectives,* **17:**24–26.

Spieker, Diane J. and Timothy A. Pierson. 1989. *Adult Internal Management System (AIMS): Implementation Manual.* Washington, DC: U.S. Department of Justice, National Institute of Corrections (National Institute of Corrections Grant #87-N081).

Spohn, Cassia and Jerry Cederblom. 1991. "Race and

Disparities in Sentencing: A Test of the Liberation Hypothesis." *Justice Quarterly,* **8:**325–327.

Staples, William G. 1986. "Restitution as a Sanction in Juvenile Court." *Crime and Delinquency,* **32:** 177–185.

Starr, Mark. 1988. "The Ballot Box Goes to Prison." *Newsweek,* January 25:65.

Steadman, Henry J. et al. 1984. "The Impact of State Mental Hospital Deinstitutionalization on United States Prison Populations, 1968–1978." *Journal of Criminal Law and Criminology,* **75:**474–490.

Steelman, Diane. 1984. *Doing Idle Time: An Investigation of Inmate Idleness in New York's Prisons and Recommendations for Change.* New York: Correctional Association of New York.

Steffensmeier, Darrell and Miles D. Harer. 1991. "Did Crime Rise or Fall During the Reagan Presidency? The Effects of an 'Aging' U.S. Population on the Nation's Crime Rate." *Journal of Research in Crime and Delinquency,* **28:**330–359.

Steffensmeier, Darrell J., John Kramer, and Cathy Streifel. 1993. "Gender and Imprisonment Decisions." *Criminology,* **31:**411–446.

Steffensmeier, Darrell J. and Cathy Streifel. 1989. "Indicators of Female Status and Trends in Female Crime 1960–1980." Unpublished paper presented at the annual meeting of the American Society of Criminology, Reno, NV (November).

Steiger, John C. and Cary Dizon. 1991. *Rehabilitation, Release and Reoffending: A Report on the Criminal Careers of the Division of Juvenile Rehabilitation "Class of 1982."* Olympia, WA: Juvenile Offender Research Unit, Washington Department of Social and Health Services.

Stephan, James. 1989. *Prison Rule Violators.* Washington, DC: U.S. Department of Justice, Bureau of Justice Statistics.

Stephens, Gene. 1986. "Participatory Justice: The Politics of the Future." *Justice Quarterly,* **3:**67–82.

Steppe, Cecil H. 1986. "Public Support: Probation's Backbone." *Corrections Today,* **48:**12–16.

Stern, Barry J. 1990. *Baseline Study: Education in County Jails.* Sacramento, CA: California Department of Education.

Steury, Ellen Hochstedler. 1989. "Prosecutorial and Judicial Discretion." In *The U.S. Sentencing Guidelines: Implications for Criminal Justice,* Dean J. Champion (ed.). New York: Praeger.

Stevens, Gail Flint et al. 1993. "Inmate Behavior Dynamics." *Journal of Offender Rehabilitation,* **19:** 1–192.

Stevens, Reid D. 1986. "The Effect on Recidivism of Attaining the General Educational Development Diploma." *Journal of Offender Counseling,* **7:**3–9.

Stewart, James K. 1988. *NIJ AIDS Clearinghouse Helps You Respond to the AIDS Challenge.* Washington, DC: National Institute of Justice.

Stewart, Kathryn, Paul J. Gruenewald, and Robert Nash Parker. 1992. "Assessing Legal Change: Re-

cidivism and Administrative Per Se Laws." *Journal of Quantitative Criminology,* **8:**375–394.

Stiles, Don R. 1994. "A Partnership for Safe Communities: Courts, Education and Literacy." *APPA Perspectives,* **18:**8–9.

Stinchcomb, Jeanne B. 1985. "Why Not the Best? Using Assessment Centers for Officer Selection." *Corrections Today,* **47:**120–124.

Stinchcomb, Jeanne B. 1986. "Correctional Officer Stress: Is Training Missing the Target?" In *Issues in Correctional Training and Casework.* College Park, MD: American Correctional Association.

Stohr-Gillmore, Mary K., Michael W. Stohr-Gillmore, and Nicholas P. Lovrich. 1990. "Sifting the Gold from the Pebbles: Using Situational Interviews to Select Correctional Officers for Direct Supervision Jails." *American Jails,* **3:**29–34.

Stojkovic, Stan. 1986. "Social Bases of Power and Control Mechanisms among Correctional Administrators in a Prison Organization." *Journal of Criminal Justice,* **14:**157–166.

St. Paul Police Department. 1991. *Placement of Released Inmates in Private Employment: Executive Summary.* St. Paul, MN: St. Paul Police Department.

Stratton, Neil R. M. 1988. *How Will California Handle Spousal Abuse Incidents by the Year 2000?* Walnut Creek, CA: California Commission on Peace Officer Standards and Training.

Strong, Ann. 1981. *Case Classification Manual, Module One: Technical Aspects of Interviewing.* Austin, TX: Texas Adult Probation Commission.

Struckhoff, David R. 1987. "Selective Incapacitation." *Corrections Today,* **49:**30–34

Sullivan, C., M. Q. Grant, and J. D. Grant. 1957. "The Development of Interpersonal Maturity: Applications to Delinquency." *Psychiatry,* **23:**373–385.

Sutherland, Edwin H. 1972. *The Professional Thief.* Chicago: University of Chicago Press.

Swain, Kay. 1986. "Probation Attitudes toward Battered Women: Apathy, Error and Avoidance?" *Probation Journal,* **33:**132–134.

Sweeney, Laura T. and Craig Haney. 1992. "The Influence of Race on Sentencing: A Meta-Analytic Review of Experimental Studies." *Behavioral Sciences & the Law,* **10:**179–195.

Tapper, Donna M. 1980. *Research on Services Delivery: Services for Battered Women in New York City and Crime Victim Services.* New York: Community Council of Greater New York.

Task Force on Corrections. 1966. *Task Force Report: Corrections.* Washington, DC: U.S. Government Printing Office.

Taxman, Faye S. 1994. "Correctional Options and Implementation Issues: Results from a Survey of Corrections Professionals." *APPA Perspectives,* **18:** 32–37.

Taxman, Faye S. and Randall Guynes. 1992. "The Multi-Dimensional Approach to Intermediate Sanctions." Unpublished paper presented at the annual meeting of the American Society of Criminology, New Orleans, LA (November).

Taylor, William J. 1985. "Training: ACA Priority." *Corrections Today,* **47:**24–29.

Taylor, William J. 1992. "Tailoring Boot Camps to Juveniles." *Corrections Today,* **54:**122–124.

Teake, R. and H. Williamson. 1979. "Correctional Officers' Attitudes toward Selected Treatment Programs." *Criminal Justice and Behavior,* **6:**64–72.

Tennessee Department of Corrections. 1994. *Tennessee Project CERCE (Comprehensive Education and Rehabilitation in a Correctional Environment) Resident Manual.* Nashville, TN: Author.

Teplin, Linda A. 1992. "Are Mentally Ill Criminals the Most Violent Criminals? A Six-Year Follow-Up." Unpublished paper presented at the annual meetings of the American Society of Criminology, New Orleans, LA (November).

Thomas, Charles W. 1986. "Corrections in America: Its Ambiguous Role and Future Prospects." In *The Dilemmas of Punishment: Readings in Contemporary Corrections,* K. C. Haas and G. P. Alpert (eds.). Chicago, IL: Waveland Press.

Thomas, Fate. 1988. "The Crisis in Our Jails: Overcrowded Beds or Underused Resources?" *American Jails,* **2:**60–62.

Thomas, Robert L. 1988. "Stress Perception among Select Federal Probation and Pretrial Services Officers and Their Supervisors." *Federal Probation,* **52:**48–58.

Thomson, Doug and David Fogel. 1980. *Probation Work in Small Agencies: A National Study of Training Provisions and Needs.* Chicago, IL: Center for Research in Law and Justice, University of Illinois at Chicago.

Thornburgh, Richard. 1990. "U.S. Attorney General Thornburgh Urges Incarceration Alternatives." *Corrections Compendium,* **52:**132–134.

Tilow, Neil F. 1989. "Community Facilities: Overcoming Obstacles and Opposition." *Corrections Today,* **51:**88–94.

Timasheff, Nicholas S. 1941. *One Hundred Years of Probation, 1841–1941.* New York: Fordham University Press.

Tobin, Patricia. 1983. *1982 Yearly Statistical Report of the Furlough Program.* Boston, MA: Massachusetts Department of Corrections.

Tobolowsky, Peggy M., James F. Quinn, and John E. Holman. 1991. "Participation of Incarcerated High School Dropouts in County Jail Programs." *Journal of Correctional Education,* **42:**142–145.

Toch, Hans. 1978. "Is a 'Correctional Officer' by Any Other Name a 'Screw'?" *Criminal Justice Review,* **3:**19–35.

Toch, Hans and Kenneth Adams. 1986. "Pathology and Disruptiveness among Prison Inmates." *Journal of Research in Crime and Delinquency,* **23:**7–21.

Toch, Hans and John Klofas. 1982. "Alienation and Desire for Job Enrichment among Corrections Officers." *Federal Probation,* **46:**35–44.

Tonry, Michael H. 1993. "Mandatory Penalties." In *Crime and Justice: A Review of Research, Volume 16,* Michael Tonry (ed.). Chicago and London: University of Chicago Press.

Tonry, Michael H. and Franklin Zimring. 1983. *Reform and Punishment: Essays on Criminal Sentencing.* Chicago, IL: University of Chicago Press.

Towberman, Donna B. 1992. "A National Survey of Juvenile Risk Assessment." *Juvenile & Family Court Journal,* **43:**61–67.

Townsend, Gail. 1991. "Kansas Community Corrections Programs." *American Jails,* **5:**26–30.

Tracy, Alice. 1993. "Literacy Volunteers Share a Belief in Rehabilitative Effect of Education." *Corrections Today,* **55:**102–112.

Travis, Lawrence F., III. 1984. "Intensive Supervision in Probation and Parole." *Corrections Today,* **46:**34–40.

Travis, Lawrence F., III. 1985. *Probation, Parole, and Community Corrections.* Prospect Heights, IL: Waveland Press.

Travis, Lawrence F., III, Edward J. Latessa, and Gennaro F. Vito. 1987. "Felony Probation: An Examination of the Research." Unpublished paper presented at the Midwestern Criminal Justice Association, Chicago, IL (October).

Travis, Lawrence F., III, Martin D. Schwartz, and Todd R. Clear. 1983. *Corrections: An Issues Approach,* 2nd ed. Cincinnati, OH: Anderson.

Travisano, Anthony P. et al. 1986. "Special Needs Offenders: Handle with Care." *Corrections Today,* **48:**4–80.

Traynelis-Yurek, E. and F. G. Yurek. 1990. "Increased Literacy through Unison Reading." *Journal of Correctional Education,* **41:**110–114.

Treger, Harvey. 1972. "A Breakthrough in Preventive Corrections." Urbana, IL: University of Illinois, Unpublished paper.

Troia, Nina. 1990. *Analysis of Juvenile Arrest Rates and Recidivism among Youth Released from Wisconsin Juvenile Institutions.* Madison, WI: Department of Health and Human Services.

Troia, Nina. 1991. *An Evaluation of the SPRITE Program.* Madison, WI: Wisconsin Department of Health and Social Services.

Tunnell, Kenneth D. 1992. *Choosing Crime: The Criminal Calculus of Property Offenders.* Chicago, IL: Nelson-Hall.

Turner, Susan. 1992. "Intensive Supervision in the Community." Unpublished paper presented at the annual meeting of the American Society of Criminology, New Orleans, LA (November).

Turturici, Jack and Gregory Sheehy. 1993. "How Direct Supervision Jail Design Affects Inmate Behavior Management." *Corrections Today,* **55:**102–106.

Umbreit, Mark S. 1986. "Victim/Offender Mediation: A National Survey." *Federal Probation,* **50:**53–56.

Umbreit, Mark S. 1991. "Restorative Justice: Having Offenders Meet with Their Victims Offers Benefits for Both Parties." *Corrections Today,* **53:**164–165.

Umbreit, Mark S. and Robert B. Coates. 1993. "Cross-Site Analysis of Victim-Offender Mediation in Four States." *Crime and Delinquency,* **39:**565–585.

University of Hawaii at Manoa. 1984. *Recidivism of 1979 Adult Probation, Third Circuit Court Hawaii.* Honolulu, HI: University of Hawaii, Manoa Youth Development and Research Center.

Uriell, Patricia. 1984. *The Furlough Program: An Evaluation.* Manoa, HI: Youth Development and Research Center, School of Social Work, University of Hawaii, Manoa.

U.S. Bureau of Justice Statistics. 1983. *Setting Prison Terms.* Washington, DC: Author.

U.S. Bureau of Justice Statistics. 1986a. *Children in Custody.* Washington, DC: Author.

U.S. Bureau of Justice Statistics. 1986b. *Crime and Justice Facts, 1985.* Washington, DC: U.S. Government Printing Office.

U.S. Bureau of Justice Statistics. 1986c. *Setting Prison Terms.* Washington, DC: Author.

U.S. Bureau of Justice Assistance. 1988. *Guidelines for Implementing and Operating Treatment Alternatives to Street Crime (TASC) Programs.* Washington, DC: Author.

U.S. Bureau of Justice Statistics. 1992. *Recidivism of Felons on Probation.* Washington, DC: Bureau of Justice Statistics.

U.S. Bureau of Prisons. 1989. *The December 1, 1989 Conference on Issues in Corrections: A Record and Proceedings on "Medical Issues."* Washington, DC: Author.

U.S. Bureau of Prisons. 1991. *Post-Release Employment Project: Summary of Preliminary Findings.* Washington, DC: U.S. Department of Justice, Federal Bureau of Prisons Office of Research.

U.S. Bureau of the Census. 1994. *Vital Statistics.* Washington, DC: U.S. Government Printing Office.

U.S. Civil Rights Commission. 1981. *Battered Women in New Jersey.* Washington, DC: Author.

U.S. Code. 1995. *The U.S. Code Annotated.* St. Paul, MN: West Publishing Company.

U.S. Congress Office of Technology Assessment. 1987a. *The Electronic Supervisor: New Technology, New Tensions.* Washington, DC: U.S. Government Printing Office.

U.S. Congress Office of Technology Assessment. 1987b. *Defending Secrets, Sharing Data: New Locks and Keys for Electronic Information.* Washington, DC. U.S. Government Printing Office.

U.S. Department of Justice. 1976. *Two Hundred Years of American Criminal Justice: An LEAA Bicentennial Study.* Washington, DC: Law Enforcement Assistance Administration.

U.S. Department of Justice. 1988. *Report to the Nation on Crime and Justice.* Washington, DC: Author, Bureau of Justice Statistics.

U.S. Department of Justice. 1989. *Report on Strategies of Determinate Sentencing.* Washington, DC: Author, National Institute of Justice.

U.S. Department of Justice. 1990. *Report to the Nation on Crime and Justice.* Washington, DC: Author, Bureau of Justice Statistics.

U.S. Department of Justice. 1991. *Post-Release Employment Project: Summary of Preliminary Findings.* Washington, DC: U.S. Department of Justice Federal Bureau of Prisons Office of Research.

U.S. Department of Justice. 1993. *Prisoners in the United States.* Washington, DC: Author.

U.S. General Accounting Office. 1986. *Bank Robbery: Sentences Imposed/Time Served for Offenders Convicted of Bank Robbery.* Washington, DC: U.S. Government Printing Office.

U.S. General Accounting Office. 1990. *Intermediate Sanctions: Their Impacts on Prison Crowding, Costs, and Recidivism are Still Unclear.* Washington, DC: Author.

U.S. General Accounting Office. 1993a. *Intensive Probation Supervision: Crime-Control and Cost-Saving Effectiveness.* Washington, DC: Author.

U.S. General Accounting Office. 1993b. *Prison Boot Camps: Short-Term Prison Costs Reduced, But Long-Term Impact Uncertain.* Washington, DC: U.S. Department of Justice, Office of Justice Programs.

U.S. National Highway Traffic Safety Administration. 1985. *Community Service Restitution Programs for Alcohol Related Traffic Offenders.* Washington, DC: U.S. Government Printing Office.

U.S. Office of Justice Programs. 1990. *Survey of Intermediate Sanctions.* Washington, DC: Author.

U.S. Office of Juvenile Justice and Delinquency Prevention. 1988. *Involving the Private Sector in Public Policy and Program Development: A Resource Manual for Administrators of Juvenile and Criminal Justice Agencies.* Washington, DC: Author.

U.S. Probation Division. 1989. "Implementing Community Service: The Referral Process." *Federal Probation,* **53:**3–9.

U.S. Sentencing Commission. 1987. *United States Sentencing Commission Guidelines Manual.* Washington, DC: Author.

U.S. Sentencing Commission. 1990. *Recidivism of Incarcerated Federal Offenders.* Washington, DC: Author.

U.S. Sentencing Commission. 1991. *The Federal Sentencing Guidelines: A Report on the Operation of the Guidelines System and Short-Term Impacts.* Washington, DC: Author.

U.S. Youth Development and Delinquency Prevention Administration. 1971. *A Quiet Revolution: Probation Subsidy.* Washington, DC: Author.

Valenzuela, Aurora, Enrique Vallaneuva, and Jose Aguilera. 1991. "Importance of Criminal Behavior Related Variables in Criminal Prognosis." *American Journal of Forensic Psychology,* **9:**31–42.

van Alstyne, David J. 1991. *Trends in Recidivism among Misdemeanants Sentenced to Probation.* Albany, NY: New York State Division of Criminal Justice Services.

Van Ness, Shela R. 1988. "Correctional Treatment:

Values in Transition." Unpublished paper presented at the Academy of Criminal Justice Sciences meetings, San Francisco, CA.

Van Ness, Shela R. 1992. "Intensive Probation versus Prison Outcomes in Indiana: Who Could Benefit?" *Journal of Contemporary Criminal Justice,* **8:** 351–364.

Van Stelle, Kit R., Elizabeth Mauser, and D. Paul Moberg. 1994. "Recidivism to the Criminal Justice System of Substance-Abusing Offenders Diverted into Treatment." *Crime and Delinquency,* **40:** 175–196.

Van Voorhis, Patricia. 1987. "Correctional Effectiveness: The High Cost of Ignoring Success." *Federal Probation,* **51:**56–62.

Velt, Edward and Albert G. Smith. 1993. "A Primer: The Arming of Probation and Parole Officers." *APPA Perspectives,* **17:**17–20.

Vigdal, Gerald L. and Donald W. Stadler. 1994. "Alternative to Revocation Program Offers Offenders a Second Chance." *Corrections Today,* **56:**44–47.

Virginia Department of Corrections. 1987. *Adult Probation and Parole Services: Workload Measurement Study.* Richmond, VA: Division of Adult Community Corrections.

Virginia Department of Corrections. 1988. *Intensive Supervision Program: Client Characteristics and Supervision Outcomes: A Caseload Comparison.* Richmond, VA: Author.

Virginia Department of Mental Health and Retardation. 1984. *Mentally Ill in Virginia's Jails: Final Report of the Joint Task Force.* Richmond, VA: Virginia Department of Corrections.

Virginia Joint Legislative Audit and Review Commission. 1985. *The Community Diversion Incentive Program of the Virginia Department of Corrections.* Richmond, VA: Virginia Joint Legislative Audit and Review Commission.

Visher, Christy A., Pamela K. Lattimore, and Richard L. Linster. 1991. "Predicting the Recidivism of Serious Youthful Offenders Using Survival Models." *Criminology,* **29:**329–366.

Vito, Gennaro F. 1978. "Shock Probation in Ohio: A Re-Examination of the Factors Influencing the Use of an Early Release Program." *Journal of Offender Rehabilitation,* **3:**123–132.

Vito, Gennaro F. 1983. "Reducing the Use of Imprisonment." In *Corrections: An Issues Approach,* 2nd ed., L. Travis, M. Schwartz, and T. Clear (eds.). Cincinnati, OH: Anderson.

Vito, Gennaro F. 1984. "Developments in Shock Probation: A Review of Research Findings and Policy Implications." *Federal Probation,* **48:**22–27.

Vito, Gennaro F. 1986a. *Felony Probation and Recidivism in Kentucky.* Frankfort, KY: Kentucky Criminal Justice Statistical Analysis Center (NCJRS Document No. 112566).

Vito, Gennaro F. 1986b. "Felony Probation and Recidivism: Replication and Response." *Federal Probation,* **50:**17–25.

Vito, Gennaro F. 1987. *First Year Evaluation: Kentucky Substance Abuse Program—July 1986–July 1987.* Unpublished manuscript, University of Louisville.

Vito, Gennaro F. 1989. "The Kentucky Substance Abuse Program: A Private Program to Treat Probationers and Parolees." *Federal Probation,* **53:**65–72.

Vito, Gennaro F. and H. E. Allen. 1981. "Shock Probation in Ohio: A Comparison of Outcomes." *International Journal of Offender Therapy,* **25:**70–76.

Von Cleve, Elizabeth, Ron Jemelka, and Eric Trupin. 1991. "Reliability of Psychological Test Scores for Offenders Entering a State Prison System." *Criminal Justice and Behavior,* **18:**159–165.

von Hirsch, Andrew. 1976. *Doing Justice.* New York: Hill and Wang.

von Hirsch, Andrew. 1983. "Recent Trends in American Criminal Sentencing Theory." *Maryland Law Review,* **42:**6–36.

von Hirsch, Andrew. 1984. "The Ethics of Selective Incapacitation: Observations on the Contemporary Debate." *Crime and Delinquency,* **30:**175–194.

von Hirsch, Andrew. 1992. "Proportionality in the Philosophy of Punishment." In *Crime and Justice: A Review of Research, Volume 16,* Michael Tonry (ed.). Chicago and London: University of Chicago Press.

Wagner, Dennis and Christopher Baird. 1993. *Evaluation of the Florida Community Control Program.* Washington, DC: U.S. Department of Justice, Office of Justice Programs.

Wahler, Cindy and Paul Gendreau. 1985. "Assessing Correctional Officers." *Federal Probation,* **49:**70–74.

Wakefield, Penny. 1985. "The Sentencing Process: Redefining Objectives." In *State Laws and Procedures Affecting Drug Trafficking Control,* J. Bentivoglio et al. (eds.). Washington, DC: National Governor's Association.

Waldo, Gordon P. and Theodore G. Chiricos. 1977. "Work Release and Recidivism: An Empirical Evaluation of a Social Policy." *Evaluation Quarterly,* **1:**87–108.

Waldo, Gordon P. and D. Griswold. 1979. "Issues in the Measurement of Recidivism." In *The Rehabilitation of Criminal Offenders: Problems and Prospects,* Lee Sechrest, S. O. White, and E. D. Brown (eds.). Washington, DC: National Academy of Sciences.

Walker, James L. 1990. "Sharing the Credit, Sharing the Blame: Managing Political Risks in Electronically Monitored House Arrest." *Federal Probation,* **54:**16–20.

Walker, Mickie C. 1992. "Co-Dependency and Probation." *Federal Probation,* **56:**16–18.

Walker, Nigel and Mike Hough (eds.). 1988. *Punitiveness, Status, and Ideology in Three Canadian Provinces: From Public Attitudes to Sentencing.* Brookfield, VT: Gower.

Walker, S. Anne. 1993. "Alston Wilkes Society: South Carolina Volunteer Agency Plays Vital Role in Corrections." *Corrections Today,* **55:**94–100.

Walker, Samuel. 1985. *Sense and Nonsense about Crime: A Policy Guide.* Monterey, CA: Brooks/Cole.

Walker, Samuel. 1989. *Sense and Nonsense about Crime: A Policy Guide,* 2nd ed. Monterey, CA: Brooks/Cole.

Wallace, W. LeAnn and Stevens H. Clarke. 1986. "The Sentencing Alternatives Center in Greensboro, NC: An Evaluation of Its Effects on Prison Sentences." Unpublished paper presented at American Society of Criminology, Atlanta, GA.

Wallerstedt, John F. 1984. *Returning to Prison.* Washington, DC: Bureau of Justice Statistics.

Walsh, Charles L. and Scott H. Beck. 1990. "Predictors of Recidivism among Halfway House Residents." *American Journal of Criminal Justice,* **15:**137–152.

Walters, Glenn D. et al. 1992. "The Choice Program: A Comprehensive Residential Treatment Program for Drug Involved Offenders." *International Journal of Offender Therapy and Comparative Criminology,* **36:**21–29.

Ward, Richard J. 1991. "Boot Camps." *American Jails,* **5:**107–111.

Warnock, Kae M. and Dona Hunzeker. 1991. "Prison Boot Camps: Policy Considerations and Options." *State Legislative Report,* **16:**1–10.

Washington, Frank, Tony Clifton, and Lauren Picker. 1990. "Sex, Cash and Family Favors: New Allegations Rock Covenant House." *Newsweek,* March 26:21.

Washington, Jeffrey. 1987. "ACA Reevaluates Small Jail Standards." *Corrections Today,* **49:**15.

Washington County Community Corrections. 1992. *Washington County Restitution Center.* Hillsboro, OR: Author.

Washington State Department of Social and Mental Health Services. 1991. *SSOSA Blue Ribbon Panel Final Report to the Legislature.* Olympia, WA: Author.

Washington State Sentencing Guidelines Commission. 1985. *Sentencing Practices under the Sentencing Reform Act: A Preliminary Report.* Olympia, WA: Author.

Watkins, John C., Jr. 1987. "The Convolution of Ideology: American Juvenile Justice from a Critical Legal Studies Perspective." Paper presented at American Society of Criminology meetings, Montreal, Canada (November).

Watkins, John C., Jr. 1989. "Probation and Parole Malpractice in a Noninstitutional Setting: A Contemporary Analysis." *Federal Probation,* **53:**29–34.

Watson, Robert J. 1981. "Long-Range Planning for Corrections." In *The Status of Probation and Parole.* College Park, MD: American Correctional Association.

Watts, Ronald and Daniel Glaser. 1990. "Strains and Gains of Case-Flow Randomization for Evaluating Electronic Monitoring Probationers in a Large Metropolis." Unpublished paper presented at the an-

nual meetings of the American Society of Criminology, Baltimore, MD (November).

Way, C. T. 1992. "Innovative Incarceration: Community Corrections in the Federal Bureau of Prisons." *Federal Prisons Journal,* **2:**20–28.

Webb, Gary L. 1984. *The Prison Ordeal.* Fayetteville, GA: Coker.

Wedlund, R. B. 1990. "The Use of Paraprofessionals in Missing Children and Juvenile Runaway Follow-Up Investigations." In *Missing Children: The Law Enforcement Response,* Martin L. Forst (ed.). Springfield, IL: Charles C Thomas.

Wehmhoefer, Richard A. 1993. "Ethics in the Probation and Parole Profession: A Vision for the Future." *APPA Perspectives,* **17:**8–9.

Weintraub, Benson B. 1987. "The Role of Defense Counsel at Sentencing." *Federal Probation,* **51:**25–29.

Welch, Randy. 1989. "Back to the Community . . . Pre-Release in Massachusetts." *Corrections Compendium,* **14:**1–8.

Wells, Dave and Tim Brennan. 1992. "The Michigan Classification Project." *American Jails,* **6:**59–62.

Welsh, Wayne N. 1993. "Changes in Arrest Policies as a Result of Court Orders against County Jails." *Justice Quarterly,* **10:**89–120.

Welsh, Wayne N. and Stephen H. Smith. 1992. "The Impact of Court Orders against County Jails: A National University." Unpublished paper presented at the annual meetings of the American Society of Criminology, New Orleans, LA (November).

Wenck, Ernst A., James O. Robison, and Gerald W. Smith. 1972. "Can Violence Be Predicted?" *Crime and Delinquency,* **18:**393–402.

Wertleib, Ellen C. and Martin A. Greenberg. 1989. "Strategies for Working with Special-Needs Probationers." *Federal Probation,* **53:**10–17.

Wheeler, Gerald R. and D. Keith Nichols. 1974. *A Statistical Inquiry into Length of Stay and the Revolving Door: The Case for a Modified Fixed Sentence for the Juvenile Offender.* Columbus, OH: Ohio Youth Commission.

Wheeler, Gerald R. and Amy S. Rudolph. 1990. "New Strategies to Improve Probation Officer's Fee Collection Rates: A Field Study in Performance Feedback." *Justice System Journal,* **14:**78–94.

Wheeler, Gerald R., Amy S. Rudolph, and Rodney V. Hissong. 1989. "Economic Sanctions in Perspective: Do Probationers' Characteristics Affect Fee Assessment, Payment and Outcome?" *APPA Perspectives,* **13:**12–17.

Wheeler, Gerald R. et al. 1990. "Economic Sanctions in Criminal Justice: Dilemma for Human Service?" *Justice System Journal,* **14:**63–77.

Wheeler, William L. 1993. "Gentle Gestures: Inmates in Connecticut Comfort At-Risk Babies Through Quilting Program." *Corrections Today,* **55:**138–139.

Whitcomb, Debra, Elizabeth R. Shapiro, and Lindsey D. Stellwagen (eds.). 1985. *When the Victim Is a*

Child: Issues for Judge and Prosecutors. Washington, DC: National Institute of Justice.

White, David and Hubert Wood. 1986. "The Lancaster County, Pennsylvania Mentally Retarded Offenders Program." *Prison Journal,* **66:**77–84.

White, H. P. 1992. *Community Treatment Centers Corrections Evaluation Report.* Oklahoma City, OK: Oklahoma Crime Commission.

White, Michael. 1992. "Identifying Characteristics That Distinguish Recidivists and Non-Recidivists: An Application of Discriminant Analysis." Unpublished paper presented at the annual meetings of the American Society of Criminology, New Orleans, LA (November).

Whitehead, John T. 1985. "Job Burnout in Probation and Parole: Its Extent and Intervention Implications." *Criminal Justice and Behavior,* **12:**91–110.

Whitehead, John T. 1986a. "Gender Differences in Probation: A Case of No Differences." *Justice Quarterly,* **3:**51–65.

Whitehead, John T. 1986b. "Job Burnout and Job Satisfaction among Probation Managers." *Journal of Criminal Justice,* **14:**25–35.

Whitehead, John T. 1987. "Probation Officer Burnout: A Test of Two Theories." *Journal of Criminal Justice,* **15:**1–16.

Whitehead, John T. 1989. *Burnout in Probation and Parole.* New York: Praeger.

Whitehead, John T. 1991. "The Effectiveness of Felony Probation: Results from an Eastern State." *Justice Quarterly,* **8:**525–543.

Whitehead, John T. and Susan Gunn. 1988. "Probation Employee Job Attitudes: A Qualitative Analysis." *Journal of Crime and Justice,* **11:**143–164.

Whitehead, John T. and Charles A. Lindquist. 1985. "Job Stress and Burnout among Probation/Parole Officers Perceptions and Causal Factors." *International Journal of Offender Therapy and Comparative Criminology,* **29:**109–119.

Whitehead, John T. and Charles A. Lindquist. 1987. "Determinants of Correctional Officer Professional Orientation." Paper presented at the American Society of Criminology meetings, Montreal, Canada.

Whitehead, John T. and Charles A. Lindquist. 1992. "Determinants of Probation and Parole Officer Professional Orientation." *Journal of Criminal Justice,* **20:**13–24.

Wiebush, Richard G. 1990. "The Ohio Experience: Programmatic Variations in Intensive Supervision for Juveniles." *Perspectives,* **14:**26–35.

Wiebush, Richard G. 1991. *Evaluation of the Lucas County Intensive Supervision Unit: Diversionary Impact and Youth Outcomes.* Columbus, OH: Governor's Office of Criminal Justice Services.

Wiederanders, Mark R. 1983. *Success on Parole: The Influence of Self-Reported Attitudes and Experiences on the Parole Behaviors of Youthful Offenders.* Sacramento, CA: Department of Youth Authority.

Wiederanders, Mark R. 1990. "Effects of Intensive Community Supervision on the Community Performances of Mentally Disordered Offenders." Unpublished paper presented at the annual meeting of the American Society of Criminology, Baltimore, MD (November).

Wilber, Lalena N. 1992. "AIDS in the Prison." Unpublished paper presented at the annual meetings of the American Society of Criminology, New Orleans, LA (November).

Wilcenski, Gregory B., Elizabeth D. Disney, and Edward Miklosey. 1993. "Just the Facts . . . Probation." *APPA Perspectives,* **17:**16–17.

Williams, D. R., D. P. Callaghan, and I. H. Scheier. 1974. *Volunteers in the Criminal Justice System: Rights and Legal Liability.* Washington, DC: American Bar Association.

Williams, Frank P., III, David Shichor, and Allan H. Wiggenborn. 1989. "Fine Tuning Social Control: Electronic Monitoring and Surrogate Homes for Drug Using Parolees." *Journal of Contemporary Criminal Justice,* **5:**173–179.

Williams, Jay R. 1986. *Community Penalties in North Carolina: An Examination of Programs Established by N.C.G.S. 143B-500.* Raleigh, NC: Division of Victim Justice Services, North Carolina Department of Crime Control and Public Safety.

Williams, Sharon and Cheryll Bissell. 1990. "Total Systems Approach: Using the Past to Push Forward." *Corrections Today,* **44:**44–46.

Williams, Susan Darst. 1987. "Corrections New Balancing Act: AIDS." *Corrections Compendium,* **11:**1–9.

Williams, Susan Darst. 1990. "The Invisible Jail: Day Reporting Centers." *Corrections Compendium,* **15:**1–7.

Willman, Herb C., Jr. and Ron Y. Chun. 1974. "Homeward Bound: An Alternative to the Institutionalization of Adjudicated Juvenile Offenders." In *Alternatives to Imprisonment: Corrections and the Community,* George C. Killinger and Paul F. Cromwell Jr. (eds.). St. Paul, MN: West Publishing Company.

Willstadter, R. 1984. *Time Served: Does It Relate to Patterns of Criminal Recidivism? Final Report No. 1.* Seattle, WA: Spectrum Analysis.

Wilson, Deborah G. 1985. *Persistent Felony Offenders in Kentucky: A Profile of the Institutional Population.* Louisville, KY: Kentucky Criminal Justice Statistical Analysis Center.

Wilson, Deborah G., Judith L. Denton, and Coleen E. Williams. 1987. *Intensive Supervision Program Evaluation.* Frankfort, KY: Planning and Evaluation Branch, Kentucky Corrections Center.

Wilson, Deborah G. and Gennaro F. Vito. 1986. *Persistent Felony Offenders in Kentucky: A Comparison of Incarcerated Felons.* Louisville, KY: Urban Studies Center, University of Louisville.

Wilson, Deborah G. and Gennaro F. Vito. 1990. "Persistent Felony Offenders in Kentucky: A Comparison of Incarcerated Felons." *Journal of Contemporary Criminal Justice,* **6:**237–253.

Wilson, George P. 1985. "Halfway House Programs for Offenders." In *Probation, Parole, and Community Corrections,* Lawrence Travis III (ed.). Prospect Heights, IL: Waveland Press.

Wilson, James Q. 1985. *Thinking About Crime.* New York: Basic Books.

Winfree, L. Thomas. 1987. "Toward Understanding State-Level Jail Mortality: Correlates of Death by Suicide and by Natural Causes, 1977 and 1982." *Justice Quarterly,* **4:**51–71.

Winfree, L. Thomas et al. 1988. "Parole Survival and Legislated Change: A Before/After Study of Parole Waivers and Parole Hearings." Unpublished paper presented at the annual meetings of the American Society of Criminology, Chicago, IL (November).

Winter, Bill. 1993. "Does Corrections Need Volunteers?" *Corrections Today,* **55:**20–22.

Winterfield, Laura A. and Sally T. Hillsman. 1993. *The Staten Island Day-Fine Project.* Washington, DC: U.S. Department of Justice.

Wisconsin Department of Health and Social Services. 1982. *An Evaluation of the Milwaukee Community Corrections Residential Centers.* Madison, WI: Bureau of Evaluation, Division of Policy and Budget.

Wisconsin Department of Health and Social Services. 1985. *Alternative to Prison Revocation Study.* Madison, WI: Author.

Wisconsin Department of Health and Social Services. 1989. *Reducing Criminal Risk: An Evaluation of the High Risk Offender Intensive Supervision Project.* Madison, WI: Author, Office of Policy and Budget.

Wish, Eric D. 1987. *Drug Use in Arrestees in Manhattan: The Dramatic Increase in Cocaine from 1984 to 1986.* New York: Narcotic and Drug Research.

Wish, Eric D., E. Brady, and M. Cuadrado. 1986. *Urine Testing of Arrestees: Findings from Manhattan.* New York: Narcotic and Drug Research.

Witte, Ann D. 1973. *Work Release in North Carolina: The Program and the Process.* Chapel Hill, NC: Institute of Government.

Wolfe, Manuel, Manuel Vega, and William R. Blount. 1992. "The Relationship between Education and Degree of Racial-Ethnic Bias in Inmates." Unpublished paper presented at the annual meetings of the American Society of Criminology, New Orleans, LA (November).

Wolford, Bruce and Cynthia J. Miller. 1990. *Transitional Services for Troubled Youth.* Richmond, KY: Eastern Kentucky University Department of Correctional Services.

Wood, D. 1982. *Women in Jail.* Milwaukee, WI: Benedict Center for Criminal Behavior.

Wood, Dorothy, Jean Verber, and Mary Reddin. 1985. *A Study of the Inmate Population of the Milwaukee County Jail.* Milwaukee, WI: Wisconsin Correctional Service and Benedict Center for Criminal Justice.

Wooldredge, John D. 1991. "Age at First Court Intervention and the Likelihood of Recidivism among Less Serious Juveniles." *Journal of Criminal Justice,* **19:**515–523.

Wright, Kevin N. 1986a. "An Exploratory Study of Transactional Classification." *Journal of Research in Crime and Delinquency,* **23:**326–348.

Wright, Kevin N. 1986b. *Improving Correctional Classification through a Study of the Placement of Inmates in Environmental Settings.* Binghamton, NY: Center for Social Analysis, SUNY.

Wright, Kevin N., Todd R. Clear, and Paul Dickson. 1984. "Universal Applicability of Probation Risk-Assessment Instruments: A Critique." *Criminology,* **22:**113–134.

Wylen, Jane. 1984. *A Descriptive Study of Juvenile Offenders Released to State Parole Supervision.* Albany, NY: New York State Division of Parole.

Yeager, Matthew G. 1992. "Client-Specific Planning: A Status Report." *Criminal Justice Abstracts,* September:537–549.

Young, Marlene A. 1987. "A Constitutional Amendment for Victims of Crime: The Victim's Perspective." *Wayne Law Review,* **34:**51–68.

Young, Malcolm C. 1984. *The Defense Attorney and Alternative Sentencing: Fourteen Sentencing Programs.* Washington, DC: National Council on Crime and Delinquency.

Yurkanin, Ann. 1988. "Trend Toward Shock Incarceration Increasing Among States." *Corrections Today,* **50:**87.

Zamist, Ida. 1986. *Fines in Sentencing: An Empirical Study of Fine Use, Collection, and Enforcement in New York City Courts.* New York: Vera Institute of Justice.

Zatz, Marjorie S. 1987. "The Changing Forms of Racial/Ethnic Biases in Sentencing." *Journal of Research in Crime and Delinquency,* **24:**69–92.

Zevitz, Richard G. 1987. "Criminal Justice Education: Toward a Law Studies Model." *The Justice Professional,* **2:**89–110.

Zimmerman, Sherwood E. 1986. "Planning for Growth." *Corrections Today,* **48:**60–66.

Zimmerman, Sherwood E. and Jacqueline Cohen. 1990. "Criminal Justice Prediction Instruments." Unpublished paper presented at the annual meetings of the American Society of Criminology, Baltimore, MD (November).

Zoet, T. H. 1990. "Community Based Correctional Facilities as EM Service Providers: A New Option for Criminal Justice Administrators." *Journal of Offender Monitoring,* **3:**8–10.

Zupan, Linda L. 1986. "Gender-Related Differences in Correctional Officers' Perceptions and Attitudes." *Journal of Criminal Justice,* **14:**349–361.

Zupan, Linda L. 1993. "Direct Inmate Supervision." *American Jails,* **7:**21–22.

Cases Cited

Acevedo v. Pima County Adult Probation Department, 690 P.2d 38 (1984), 435

Anderson v. State, 624 So.2d 362 (1993), 272

Applewhite v. United States, 614 A.2d 888 [D.C.App.], 1992, 46

Avery v. State, 844 S.W.2d 364 (1993), 554–555

Baker v. State, 616 So.2d 571 (1993), 265

Bearden v. Georgia, 461 U.S. 660 (1983), 265, 268–270

Black v. Romano, 471 U.S. 606 (1985), 265–266

Booth v. Maryland, 107 S. Ct. 2529 (1987), 76

Breed v. Jones, 421 U.S. 519 (1975), 527, 555

Cannon v. State, 624 So.2d 238 (1993), 270–271

Carroll v. Board of Parole, 859 P.2d 1203 (1993), 272

C.D.R. v. State, 827 S.W.2d 589 (1992), 555

Childs v. United States Board of Parole, 371 F. Supp. 1246 (1973), 251

Commonwealth v. Green, 49 CrL 1222 (PA SupCt) (1991), 453

Crooker v. Metallo, 5 F.3d 583 (1993), 269

Davis v. State, 422 S.E.2d 546 (1992), 269

Division of Corrections v. Neakok, 721 P. 2d 1121 (1986), 348, 444

Doe v. State, 595 So.2d 212 (1992), 267

Estelle v. Gamble, 429 U.S. 97 (1976), 498

Ex parte Crouse, (1838), 515, 518

Gagnon v. Scarpelli, 411 U.S. 778 (1973), 164, 261, 264–265, 511

Glover v. Johnson, 478 F.Supp. 1075 (1979), 487–488

Goldman v. United States, 316 U.S. 129 (1942), 332

Grady v. State, 604 So.2d 1255 [Fla.Dist.App.], 1992, 46

Griffin v. Wisconsin, 483 U.S. 868 (1987), 268–269

Hill v. State, 624 So.2d 417 (1993), 271

Hyland v. Wonder, 972 F.2d 1129 (1992), 474–475

In re Bounmy V., 17 Cal.Rptr.2d 557 (1993), 538

In re F. N., 624 N.E.2d 853 (1993), 554

In re Gault, 387 U.S. 1 (1967), 525–526

In re Kazuo G., 27 Cal.Rptr.2d 155 (1994), 552–553

In re Michael T., 17 Cal.Rptr.2d 923 (1993), 538

In re Winship, 397 U.S. 358 (1970), 526

J.G. v. State, 604 So.2d 1255 (1992), 554

Johnson v. Avery, 393 U.S. 483 (1969), 260

Katz v. United States, 389 U.S. 347 (1967), 332

Kent v. United States, 383 U.S. 541 (1966), 524–525

Kriner v. State, 798 P.2d 359 (1990), 1–2

Lanford v. State, 800 S.W.2d 434 (1990), 2

Lemon v. State, 861S.W.2d 248 (1993), 271

Lynch v. United States Parole Commission, 768 F. 2d 491 (1985), 253

Mace v. Amestoy, 49 CrL 1254 [DCVt], 1991, 45

Matter of Jessie GG, 593 N.Y.S.2d 375 (1993), 537

Matter of J.K.A., 855 S.W.2d 58 (1993), 555

Matter of Tammy JJ, 47 CrL 1891 [NY.SupCt.], 1993, 554

Matter of Zachary "I", 604 N.Y.S.2d 628 (1993), 532

McKeiver v. Pennsylvania, 403 U.S. 528 (1971), 526–527

McKnight v. State, 616 So.2d 31 (1993), 270

Mempa v. Rhay, 389 U.S. 128 (1967), 261–263, 511

Menifee v. State, 601 N.E.2d 359 (1992), 273

Minnesota v. Murphy, 465 U.S. 420 (1984), 24, 268

Moore v. State, 623 So.2d 842 (1993), 270

Morrissey v. Brewer, 408 U.S. 471 (1972), 164, 261–265, 511, 574–575

Myrick v. Gunnell, 563 F. Supp. 51 (1983), 253

Nobles v. State, 605 So.2d 996 (1992), 271

Olmstead v. United States, 227 U.S. 438 (1928), 332

On Lee v. United States, 343 U.S. 747 (1952), 332

Pareton v. Armontrout, 983 F.2d 881 (1993), 273

Patterson v. State, 612 So.2d 692 (1992), 273

Patuxent Institution Board of Review v. Hancock, 620 A.2d 917 (1993), 555

People v. Hipp, 861 S.W.2d 377 (1993), 270

People v. Matthews, 23 Cal.Rptr.2d 434 (Cal.App. Sept.) (1993), 268

People v. Ramos, 48 CrL 1057 (Ill. S.Ct.) 1990, 317

People v. Shafer, 491 N.W.2d 266 (1992), 273

Reynard v. State, 622 So.2d 1026 (Fla.Dist.App., 1993), 432

Richardson v. New York State Executive Department, 602 N.Y.S.2d 443 (1993), 273

Robinson v. Hadden, 723 F. 2d 59 (1983), 253

Roller v. Cavanaugh, 984 F.2d 120 (1993), 273

Ruffin v. Commonwealth, 62 Va. (21 Gratt) 790 (1871), 260

Schall v. Martin, 104 S. Ct. 2403 (1984), 163, 527

State ex rel. Juvenile Dept. v. George, 862 P.2d 531 (1993), 523

State ex rel. Juvenile Dept. v. Jackson, 858 P.2d 158 (1993), 523

State v. Alves, 851 P.2d 129 (1992), 273

State v. Beauchamp, 621 A.2d 516 (1993), 273

State v. Bergman, 147 CrL 1475 (Ind.Ct.App., 2nd District) (1990), 267

State v. Friberg, 44 CrL 2391 [Minn.SupCt.], 1989, 45

State v. Gervais, 6087 A.2d 881 (R.I.Sup. May) (1992), 267

State v. Green, 547 So.2d 925 (1989), 273

State v. H. B., 614 A.2d 1081 (1992), 554

State v. Jimenez, 49 CrL 1140 (NM SupCt) (1991), 124

State v. Lavoy, 614 A.2d 1077 (1992), 273

State v. Lubus, 48 CrL 1173 (Conn. SupCt.) (1990), 317

State v. Mosburg, 44 CrL 2391 [Kan.SupCt.], (1989), 46

State v. Oquendo, 612 A.2d 24 (1993), 273

Stroud v. United States Parole Commission, 668 F. 2d 843 (1982), 253

Strunk v. United States, 412 U.S. 434 (1973), 162

Tarlton v. Clark, 441 F. 2d. 384 (1971), 241

Turner v. U.S. Parole Commission, 934 F.2d 254 (1991), 2

United States v. Arch John Drummond, 967 F.2d 593 (1992), 317

United States v. Bachsian, 4 F.3rd 288 (1993), 265

United States v. Edwards, 960 F.2d 278 (1992), 317

United States v. Insley, 927 F.2d 185 (1991), 317

United States v. Levi, 2 F.2d 842 (1993), 271

United States v. Lombardi, 5 F.3rd 568 (1993), 271

United States v. Mills, 51 CrL 1146 [5th Cir.], (1992), 41

United States v. Noonan, 47 CrL 1287 (3rd Cir.) (1990), 266

United States v. Salerno, 107 S. Ct. 2095 (1987), 527

United States v. Wickman, 955 F.2d 828 (1992), 317

United States v. Williams, 919 F.2d 266 (1990), 2–3

United States v. Zackular, 945 F.2d 23 (1991), 317

Wallace v. State, 607 So.2d 1184 (1992), 273

Walrath v. United States, 830 F. Supp. 444 (1993), 273

Whiteley v. Warden, 401 U.S. 560 (1971), 481

Williams v. Puckett, 624 So.2d 496 (1993), 272

Wilson v. Ellis, 859 P.2d 744 (1993), 271

Yamamoto v. United States Parole Commission, 794 F. 2d 1295 (1986), 253

Author Index

A

Abrahamse, Allan F., 574
Abrams, Allan I., 571
Abt Associates, Inc., 98, 203
Acorn, Linda, 141
Adams, K., 243
Adams, Kenneth, 168, 185
Adams, Linda, 261
Advisory Commission on Intergovernmental Relations, 160
Adwell, Steven T., 156, 446
Agopian, Michael W., 127
Aguilera, Jose, 248
Akers, Ronald L., 568, 573
Alaska Department of Corrections, 376
Alaska Judicial Council, 115
Alexander, E., 326
Alexander, Jack, 10, 192, 370
Alexander, L., 326
Allen, G. Frederick, 383, 585–587
Allen, Harry E., 32–33, 118, 127, 140, 142, 171, 295, 364, 476–477, 570, 572
Alper, B. S., 376
Alpert, Geoffrey P., 210
Alschuler, Albert W., 15
Altschuler, David M., 548, 550
Amen, Theodore M., 503
American Correctional Association, 7, 34, 47, 50, 82, 157, 169–172, 174, 204, 211, 243, 303–304, 312, 341, 352, 370, 390–391, 396–399, 403, 415–417, 425, 464, 488, 532–533, 548
American Jail Association, 160
Anderson, Dennis B., 243
Anderson, James, 143
Anderson, Sara L., 243
Anglin, M. Douglas, 496, 505
Anson, Richard H., 141
Anthony, Lawrence M., 502
Aranda, Joseph, 26
Arbuthnot, J., 476
Archambeault, W. G., 326
Arizona Department of Corrections, 84
Armor, Jerry C., 189
Armstrong, Troy L., 441, 538–539, 548, 550

Arnold, Charlotte S., 290, 462, 466–467, 490
Aronson, E., 454
Ascolillo, Victor, 444
Ashford, Jose B., 551
Associated Press, 335, 362
Atkins, Darlene M., 504
Atkinson, Donald, 202, 206, 210, 246, 458
Atmore, Toni, 496
Augustus, John, 34–35
Austin, James, 10, 143, 145, 148, 174, 184, 192, 210, 240, 295, 298, 370, 584
Austin, R. L., 26
Ayres, Marilyn B., 193, 498
Azar, Sandra T., 506–507
Aziz, David W., 145

B

Baer, Benjamin F., 313–314, 316, 320
Bahn, Charles, 445, 570
Baird, S. Christopher, 10, 247, 287, 439, 448, 536–537, 571
Baker, Joanna R., 189, 571
Bala, Gerald, 342
Ball, Richard A., 138, 309, 311, 321–322, 325, 330, 336
Ballow, DeAnna, 145
Bank, Lew, 570
Banks, Jerry, 438
Barclay, David Henry, 210
Barclay, Lynn Zeller, 279, 303
Bardo, John, 240
Barkdull, Walter L., 97, 235, 241, 243, 401
Barker, Troy, 400, 451, 454, 456
Barrett, Heather, 483
Barrineau, H. E., III, 479, 481
Barry, Thomas R., 161
Bass, Barry B., 431
Bass, Chloe, 115
Bassis, E., 377
Bateman, Richard W., 497
Bauchiero, Edward J., 496
Baumer, Terry L., 316, 320, 326–327, 561
Bayse, D. J., 463–464, 470–472, 475
Beck, Allen J., 17, 156, 161, 166, 168, 182, 570–571

Beck, James L., 255, 316
Beck, Jim, 134
Beck, Scott, 373
Beha, James A., 364, 351
Bellassai, John P., 261, 320
Bemister, W., 349, 351
Benda, Brent B., 572
Bendick, M., 300
Benekos, Peter J., 4, 284, 301
Bennett, Lawrence A., 128, 138, 142
Bensinger, Gad J., 502–503
Benson, James, 348, 444
Benzvy-Miller, Shereen, 293, 296
Berk, Richard A., 571
Berkeley Planning Associates, 473
Berry, Bonnie, 325–326
Beto, Dan Richard, 43, 457, 497, 571
Bibace, Roger, 503
Bibel, Daniel B., 127, 130–131, 135
Bigger, Phillip J., 429
Biles, David, 276–277
Binder, Arnold, 530
Bishop, Bill, 394
Bissell, Cheryll, 304, 484
Black, Henry Campbell, 7, 32–33, 60, 69, 475–476, 511
Blackburn, J. Vernon, 441
Blauner, Peter, 36, 428
Bleick, Catherine R., 571
Blomberg, Thomas G., 311–312, 322, 331
Bloom, Barbara, 483–484
Blount, William R., 184, 192
Blumberg, Abraham, 400–401
Blumstein, Alfred, 10, 94, 571, 585
Bodapati, Madhave R., 235, 266
Bohm, Robert M., 115
Bohn, Martin J., Jr., 574
Bolyard, Melissa, 143, 148
Bonczar, Thomas P., 127, 156, 166, 168, 182, 247
Bonham, Gene, 240
Bonovitz, Jennifer C., 507
Bonta, James, 370
Boone, Harry N., Jr., 563–564, 568–569, 578
Bosoni, Anthony J., 236
Bottomley, A. Keith, 36, 197, 209
Boudouris, James, 316, 571
Bowditch, Christine, 298–300
Bowker, Arthur, 11
Bowling, Linda R., 377
Bowman, Gary W., 191
Brady, E., 496
Brantingham, Patricia L., 72
Breed, Allen F., 206, 303
Brennan, Thomas P., 427
Brennan, Tim, 184, 193, 498
Brereton, David, 204
Brewer, T. Fordham, 47, 185
Brewster, Mary, 50, 202
Bright, Frank, 451, 455–456, 458
Brillon, Y., 314
Britt, Chester L., III, 497

Broadhurst, R. G., 570
Broderick, Vincent L., 203
Bronstein, Alvin J., 260–261
Brooks, M. K., 473
Brown, Alice P., 44, 200, 203–204, 356
Brown, Charles E., 394
Brown, Elizabeth, 42
Brown, J. A., 377
Brown, Marjorie E., 91
Brown, Melvin, Jr., 445
Brown, Michael, 117–118, 158, 161, 182
Brown, Paul W., 400, 426, 428, 449–452, 454–458
Brown, Valerie, 131
Brown, William B., 158, 166
Brown-Young, Cheryl, 400
Bruce, A. A., 213
Buchanan, Robert A., 10
Buck, Steven A., 115
Buentello, Salvador, 184, 186
Burcroff, Lisa C., 311–312, 322, 331
Burden, O. P., 472
Bureau of Justice Statistics, 57
Burgess, E. W., 213
Burke, Peggy B., 204, 211, 240–241, 261–262, 453
Burks, David N., 141
Burns, Mark E., 326–327, 336
Burrell, William D., 66, 68, 71
Burton, Velmer S., 400, 451, 454, 456
Bush, Robert A. Baruch, 116
Busher, Walter, 341
Bushey, W. Conway, 443
Byrne, James M., 47, 50, 126–127, 135, 202, 336, 387

C

Cadigan, Timothy P., 573
Cahalan, Margaret Werner, 159–160, 437
Calathes, William, 375, 492–493
Caldas, Stephen J., 143
California Board of Prison Terms, 356–357
California Department of the Youth Authority, 473
California Legislative Analyst, 187
Call, Jack E., 156, 164, 183
Callaghan, D. P., 474
Callanan, Thomas J., 51, 72, 397
Camp, Damon D., 284, 400, 424, 444
Capodanno, Daniel J., 496
Carbonell, Joyce, 82, 174
Carey, Carolyn H., 500
Carlen, Pat, 396, 425
Carlson, Eric W., 372, 439, 477
Carlson, Kenneth E., 4, 162
Carmichael, R. G., 22
Carmouche, Joyce, 508
Carp, Robert A., 487
Carr, Timothy S., 183–184, 285, 570
Carrington, Frank, 385
Carroll, John L., 78
Carson, Gary, 143

Carter, Robert M., 385–386, 523
Casper, Jonathan D., 204
Cavanaugh, Michael J., 132, 134
Cavender, Gray, 22, 548, 556
Cedarblom, Jerry, 42
Chaiken, Jan M., 27, 580
Chaiken, Marcia R., 27, 580
Chambers, Ola R., 549
Champion, Dean J., 15, 19, 40, 44, 50, 52, 61, 63, 81,
    84, 183, 203, 205, 213, 234, 240, 329, 391, 439, 454,
    458, 499
Chan, Luiza, 10
Chapman, Jane Roberts, 425
Charles, Michael T., 326, 463, 543
Chavaria, F. R., 496, 573
Cheatwood, Derral, 396–397, 424–425
Cheek, Frances E., 450–451, 456, 458
Cherniss, G., 457
Chiricos, Theodore G., 349
Chown, Bill, 570–571
Chun, Ron Y., 534–535
Chute, C. L., 437
Ciminello, Andrea, 513
Ciuros, William, Jr., 425–426
Clagett, Arthur P., 286, 534, 570
Clark, Gregory A., 61
Clark, Marie, 499
Clarke, Stevens H., 20, 60, 117, 183, 211, 513,
    570–571, 577
Clayton, Obie, Jr., 570
Clear, Todd R., 7, 47, 50, 63, 66, 68, 71, 91, 127, 131,
    135, 197, 199–200, 246, 282, 295, 373, 448, 451,
    496–497, 571
Clear, Val B., 66, 68, 71
Clegg, Ian J., 448
Coates, B. R., 550
Coates, Robert B., 118
Cochran, Donald, 91
Cochran, John K., 513
Cocks, Jack, 385–386
Codelia, Eddie, 461
Coffey, Alan, 38
Coffey, Betsy B., 294–295
Cohen, Fred, 292
Cohen, Jacqueline, 10, 248, 571
Cohn, Alvin W., 401, 444
Cole, George F., 7, 13, 197, 199–200, 378, 380
Cole, Richard B., 156, 164, 183
Coleman, C. R., 183, 476–477
Colley, Lori L., 456
Collins, G. A., 377
Commonwealth of Virginia, 575, 578
Connecticut Board of Parole, 239
Connecticut Prison and Jail Overcrowding
    Commission, 168
Conrad, John P., 42, 63, 301, 452
Contact Center, Inc., 164, 235
Cooke, D. J., 571
Cooper, Robert, 10
Cooprider, Keith W., 321, 327, 329, 336

Corbett, Ronald P., Jr., 292, 309, 321, 326
Corbo, Cynthia A., 255
Cormier, Catherine A., 571
Cornelius, G. F., 302
Corrections Compendium, 4, 49, 173, 190, 204–205,
    279, 292, 316, 333, 340, 350, 357, 359, 391, 398, 402,
    431
Corrections Today, 283
Corrigan, Mark, 284, 292
Corrothers, Helen G., 205
Costa, Jeralita, 462
Costanzo, Samuel A., 541–542
Cotton, Donald J., 185
Covey, Herbert C., 206
Cox, Steven G., 202
Coyle, Edward J., 143–144
Craddock, Amy, 174
Crew, B. Keith, 42
Cronin, Mary, 186
Crouch, Ben M., 445–446
Crum, Larry, 60, 570, 577
Cuadrado, M., 496
Culbertson, Robert G., 456
Cullen, Francis T., 43, 61, 203, 299, 397, 444, 446
Culliver, Concetta C., 488–489
Cunniff, Mark A., 38, 43, 48, 568
Curan, John J., Jr., 456
Curran, J. C., 34
Curtin, E. L., 358, 377
Curtis, Christine E., 286, 321, 326, 330
Curtis, Russell L., 366, 369
Cushman, Robert C., 43, 48, 439, 451, 458
Cuvelier, Steve, 143, 298
Czajkoski, Eugene H., 20
Czajkowski, Susan M., 292, 296

D

Danto, Bruce L., 10
Dare, James E., 396, 458
Davidson, R. Ted, 392
Davidson, William S., 243, 513
Davis, J. Nanette, 396, 425
Davis, James R., 445, 570 571
Davis, Mark S., 63, 427
Davis, Robert C., 378–379, 386
Davis, S. T., 164
Davis, Shirley, 399, 458
Davis, Steven, 311, 316, 570
Davis, Su Perk, 136, 206, 208, 352–353, 357, 400, 437,
    444, 495
Dawson, John M., 53–54, 58
Dawson, Roger E., 497
Dean, James M., 444
DeAngelo, Andrew J., 513
Decker, Scott H., 247
DeHeer, N. Dean, 141
DeJong, William, 134
Delaware Executive Department, 60, 570–571

del Carmen, Rolando V., 266, 325, 327, 332–333, 431–433, 435–436, 445, 470, 473–474
Dellinger, A. B., 498
DeLuca, H. R., 22
Denkowski, George C., 497
Denkowski, Kathryn M., 497
Denton, Judith L., 571
Denzlinger, Jerry D., 456
Deschenes, Elizabeth Piper, 496–497, 528
DeSilva, B., 303
DeWitt, Charles B., 187
Dickey, Walter J., 50, 135, 202, 285, 290, 301, 507
Dickson, Paul, 91, 246
Dickstein, L. J., 505
Dieckman, Duane, 394
Dierna, John S., 443, 451, 454
Dietz, Christopher, 209–211, 242–243
Diggs, David W., 357–358, 360, 377
Disney, Elizabeth D., 38
DiVito, Robert J., 189
Dizon, Cary, 571
DOCS Today, New York, 464
Doeren, Stephen E., 120
Doherty, Donald P., 117
Donnelly, Patrick G., 260, 365–366, 368–369, 371–373, 375, 387
Dougherty, Joyce, 521
Dowell, David, 369–370
Drass, Kriss A., 68, 72–73, 457
Dressler, David, 199
Driggs, John, 499, 501
Dubber, Markus Dirk, 571
Ducat, Gary, 193
Duff, R. W., 351
Duffee, David E., 277, 301
Duffie, Henry C., 134
Dufour, Henry, 385
Dugger, Richard L., 179
Dumovich, Michael, 288

E

Eakles, Gene, 193
Eckert, Mary A., 570
Eddy, William A., 505
Edna McConnell Clark Foundation, 284, 295
Edwards, Dan W., 570–571
Edwards, Harry T., 116
Edwards, Leonard P., 523
Ehrenkrantz Group, 235
Eichenlaub, Christopher, 356
Eisenberg, Michael, 367, 373, 438, 570–571
Eisenstein, James, 118
Ekland-Olsen, Sheldon, 569
Ellsworth, John, 497
Ellsworth, Thomas, 43, 50, 446, 451
Ely, Richard E., 570
Emshoff, James G., 243
EMT Group Inc., 571

English, Kim, 281, 285, 292
Erez, Edna, 74, 76, 249, 485
Erwin, Billie S., 127–129, 135
Eskridge, Chris W., 211
Evans, Donald G., 38, 47
Evans, Robin, 34, 198
Evatt, Parker, 377
Everett, Ronald S., 298–300
Eynon, Thomas G., 281, 287

F

Fabelo, Tony, 184, 570
Fabiano, Elizabeth A., 487
Fagan, Jeffrey A., 528
Fallin, Vince, 134
Farrington, David P., 571
Faulkner, Rick, 278
Federal Bureau of Prisons, 497
Feeley, Malcolm M., 191
Fehr, Larry, 187
Feld, Barry C., 519
Felstiner, William L. F., 478
Ferns, Ray, 441
Fersch, Ellsworth A. L., 309
Fichter, Michael, 401
Finkelman, Paul, 42
Finn, Peter, 27, 184, 379–380, 451, 570
Fisher, Bruce A., 550
Fitzharris, Timothy L., 96–97, 126, 341–342
Flanagan, Timothy J., 61, 168–169, 225, 258, 484, 486, 528
Fleming, Roy B., 188
Fletcher, Lawrence P., 384–385
Flicker, B., 314
Florida Department of Corrections, 145, 149, 266, 302, 310, 316, 320, 386, 570
Floud, Jean, 89
Flowers, Gerald T., 285
Flynn, Leonard E., 309–310, 312
Flynn, Suzanne, 131, 135, 439
Fogel, David, 38, 43–44, 46–47, 97, 198, 201–203, 452
Fogg, Vernon, 564
Fontaine, B., 349, 351
Ford, Marilyn Chandler, 193
Forschner, Brian E., 260, 365–366, 368–369, 371–373, 375
Forst, M., 478
Fraboni, Maryann, 10
Frank, Susan J., 504
Franzeen, Stan, 134
Frase, Richard S., 211
Frazier, Charles E., 508, 513
Frederick, Bruce C., 22
Freeman-Longo, Robert E., 501
French, Laurence, 168, 498–499
Frew, David R., 397
Friday, Paul C., 140, 158, 161, 182, 260
Friel, Charles M., 325

Frost, Martin L., 550
Frost, Sally M., 326
Fulton, Betsy, 134
Funke, Gail S., 277, 287, 298

G

Gable, Ralph K., 320, 325
Gabor, Thomas, 253
Gaes, Gerald G., 345
Galaway, Burt, 383, 385
Gallagher, Kenneth W., 63
Galvin, John J., 122
Garner, Joel H., 192
Gatz, Nick, 363, 365
Gaudin, J. M., Jr., 476, 478
Gavzer, B., 545
Gee, Travis, 571
Geerken, Michael R., 580
Gendreau, Paul, 396, 425
Genevie, L., 570, 572
Georgia Parole Review, 396, 502
Gibbs, John J., 10
Gilbert, Karen E., 43, 61
Giles, Susan E., 484
Gilliard, Darrell K., 17, 156, 164, 166, 168, 178–179, 182
Glaser, Daniel, 251, 326, 335, 378, 380, 385–386, 476
Glenwick, David S., 476–477
Goddard, Malcolm S., 556
Goetting, Ann, 175, 183–184
Goffman, Erving, 169
Goldkamp, John S., 251, 497
Goodstein, Lynne, 203, 205, 357, 538
Gordon, B. Carl, 82
Gordon, D. A., 476
Gordon, Margaret A., 378, 380
Goss, Mike, 326, 329
Gostin, Larry, 502
Gottfredson, Don M., 52, 89, 91–92, 175, 184, 213, 225, 237, 240, 242–244, 246, 248, 251, 332, 437–438, 569, 572
Gottfredson, Michael R., 52, 175, 213, 225, 237, 240, 243–244, 332, 437–438, 497, 569, 572
Gottfredson, Stephen D., 92, 248, 571
Gottschalk, Martin, 301
Gotwalt, Deborah A., 366, 375
Gould, L. A., 326
Gowdy, Voncile B., 126, 138, 145, 148
Grande, Carolyn Gerlock, 10
Grant, J. D., 82
Grant, M. Q., 82
Grassano, James B., 489
Gray, Doug, 451
Gray, Richard, 32
Gray, Tara, 41–42
Green, Gary S., 12
Greenberg, David F., 12, 296
Greenberg, Martin A., 11, 499

Greenberg, Norman, 463
Greene, Judith, 378–381
Greenfeld, Lawrence A., 20, 235, 397, 499, 570, 578, 580
Greenwood, Peter, 126, 300, 535, 545, 580
Grenier, Charles E., 570
Griffiths, Curt T., 507
Grimes, Ruth-Ellen M., 4
Griswold, David B., 569
Groth, Nicholas A., 185
Gruenewald, Paul J., 571
Guggenheim, Martin, 521
Guglielmelli, J., 266
Guider, Edward T., 22
Gunn, Susan, 447–448, 452–454, 456
Guy, Edward, 168
Guynes, Randall, 126

H

Haapanen, Rudy A., 248
Hackett, Judith C., 190–191
Haddock, Billy D., 43, 288, 457, 497
Haesler, Walter T., 243
Hagan, Michael, 560
Hageman, Mary J., 120
Hahn, Paul H., 316
Hakim, Simon, 191
Hall, Andy, 184
Hall, J., 244
Hall, Jane N., 498
Hall, Julia, 235
Hamm, Mark S., 205
Hammett, Theodore M., 502–503
Hammrock, Edward R., 210
Hamparian, Donna, 540
Haney, Craig, 4
Hanlon, Thomas E., 497
Hanrahan, Joseph, 444
Hardin, Carolyn, 279
Harer, Miles D., 10, 356, 484
Harland, Alan T., 47, 126
Harlow, Nora, 43, 185
Harno, A. J., 213
Harrington, Christine B., 117
Harris, George A., 457
Harris, Grant T., 571
Harris, M. Kay, 42, 183, 277, 287, 296, 298
Harris, Patricia M., 448, 571
Harrison, Anita L., 570–571
Harry, Bruce, 499, 501
Hartke, Kenneth L., 444, 454
Hartmann, David J., 458
Haskell, Martin R., 11
Hatchett, Paulette, 326
Hawk, Kathleen M., 464, 473, 567
Hawkins, J. David, 508
Hayeslip, David W., Jr., 396–397, 424–425
Hecht, J. A., 375

Heisel, Christine, 134
Henry, James F., 115
Hepburn, John R., 203
Herrington, Lois Haight, 346
Hester, Thomas, 56
Hewitt, John D., 185
Hicks, N., 369
Hiday, Virginia Aldige, 185
Hillsman, Sally T., 378–380, 383
Hirschburg, Peter, 40
Hissong, Rodney V., 380
Hobbs, L., 379
Hofer, Paul J., 316
Hoffman, Peter B., 175, 240, 246, 249, 251–252, 255
Hofford, Meredith, 505
Hokanson, Shirley, 487
Holden, Tamara, 431
Holeman, Herbert, 425
Holgate, Alina M., 448
Holman, John E., 189, 295, 320–321, 326, 329
Holmes, Malcolm D., 203
Holt, Norman, 193
Hong, L. K., 351
Honnold, Julie A., 458
Honolulu Police Department, 58
Horn, Jim, 454
Horvath, John A., 513
Hough, Mike, 314
Houk, Julie M., 321, 325
Howard, Matthew W., 508
Howsen, R. M., 175, 183–184
Hser, Yah-Ing, 505
Hudson, Joe, 43, 201–203, 383
Huff, C. Ronald, 309, 316, 325, 330, 336
Huggins, M. Wayne, 188
Hughes, Gail D., 134, 281
Hughes, Graham, 248
Hughes, Robert, 169, 197–198
Humphries, Drew, 43
Hunter, Robert J., 145
Hunter, Susan M., 396, 399, 425
Hunzeker, Donna, 145
Hurst, Hunter, 536
Hurwitz, Jeffrey N., 316
Huskey, Bobbie L., 280–281, 283, 286, 290, 295, 299–300, 314, 375–376
Hutchinson, Virginia, 188

I

Illinois Department of Corrections, 83–85, 87, 354
Illinois Department of Mental Health and Developmental Disabilities, 304
Illinois Office of the Governor, 303
Immarigeon, Russ, 123, 385–386
Innes, Christopher A., 178, 257
Iowa Department of Correctional Services, 84, 93
Irwin, John, 158, 161
Israel, Michael, 209
Ivanoff, Andre, 10

J

Jacks, Irving, 202
Jacobs, James B., 397, 446
Jacobs, Nancy F., 316
Jaffe, Harry Joe, 77
Jamelka, Ron, 10
James, Roberta, 497–498
Janeksela, Galan, 240
Jankowski, Louis, 19, 56–57, 61, 207, 213, 215, 225
Jensen, Christy, 23
Jesilow, Paul, 26
Johnson, Dennis, 82
Johnson, Elmer H., 341
Johnson, Jan, 173
Johnson, Judith, 497–498
Johnson, Perry M., 4
Johnson, R. L., 377
Johnson, Robert, 174
Johnson, W. Wesley, 457
Johnston, Norman, 172
Jolin, Annette, 314, 326, 335–336
Jones, John, 444
Jones, Joretta, 508
Jones, Justin, 431
Jones, Mark, 143, 431–432, 436, 457
Jones, Michael, 143, 148, 346
Jones, Peter R., 276–278, 287, 570–571, 573, 575
Jordan, Bill, 570
Joyce, Nola M., 81
Jurik, Nancy C., 391–392, 400–402, 425, 570

K

Kalichman, Seth C., 248
Kalinich, David A., 156
Kane, Thomas R., 185–186
Kaplan, John, 15
Kapsch, Stefan J., 184
Kaufman, Irving R., 115
Kearney, William J., 521
Keckeisen, George L., 12
Kelling, George, 394
Kelly, William R., 569
Kelsey, O. W., 179
Kempf, K. L., 26
Kennedy, Daniel B., 141
Kennedy, Stephen, 162
Kerby, Judith, 321, 327–329, 336
Kerle, Kenneth E., 425
Kiekbusch, Richard G., 160, 188
King, Robert P., 560
Kizer, George C., 484
Klausner, Marian L., 489
Klein, Andrew R., 20, 22, 145, 441
Klein, Cecilia, 369–370
Klein, Lloyd, 349
Klein, Stephen P., 571
Klein-Saffran, Jody, 145, 313–314, 316, 320
Kline, Susan, 166, 168, 182

Klofas, John M., 156, 446
Knepper, Paul, 189, 548, 556
Knight, Barbara B., 487
Knight, Janet, 143
Knopp, Fay Honey, 304, 443, 500–501
Koehler, Richard, 316
Komala, Merly, 248
Koppel, Herbert, 22–23
Kotch, Kenneth E., 341
Kozuh, J. R., 295
Krajick, Kevin, 37
Kramer, John H., 203, 205, 357
Kramer, Norm, 498
Kratcoski, Peter C., 464
Kraus, Melvyn B., 496
Krause, Wesley, 319
Krauth, Barbara, 192
Krepps-Hess, B. J., 425
Krichmar, Cheryl, 369–370
Krisberg, Barry, 295, 521
Kulis, Chester J., 76–77
Kunkel, Mark, 498
Kuznestov, Andrei, 499, 501

L

Lane, Michael P., 210
Langan, Patrick A., 53–54, 58, 568
Langston, Denny, 244
Larivee, John, 47, 298, 358
Larson, R. C., 164
Laszlo, Anna T., 502–503
Latessa, Edward J., 63, 96, 119, 127, 139, 142, 144, 364, 371, 400, 451, 454, 456, 476–477, 572
Lattimore, Pamela K., 189, 334, 556, 570–571
Laub, John H., 521
Lauen, Roger J., 277, 282, 295, 301
Law Enforcement Assistance Administration, 120–121
Lawrence, Daniel W., 48, 298
Lawrence, Richard A., 282, 284, 295–296, 400–401, 507
Lazear, Edward P., 496
LeClair, Daniel P., 570
LeCroy, Craig Winston, 551
Leeke, William D., 186
Lehman, Joseph D., 461, 464, 466
Lemov, Penelope, 134
Leonardi, Thomas J., 397
Leone, Michael C., 161, 182
Lester, David, 10
Levine, James P., 199
Liberton, Michael, 192
Library Information Specialists, Inc., 141, 241, 396–397, 445
Lieberman, Jethro K., 115
Lilly, J. Robert, 138, 309, 311, 320–323, 325–326, 330, 326
Lin, Y. H. W., 570–571
Lindner, Charles, 37–38, 428, 457

Lindquist, Charles A., 396–397, 426, 446, 453, 458
Linster, Richard L., 556, 570
Lipchitz, Joseph W., 127
Lippold, Robert A., 367–368
Liska, Frank J., 10
Litsky, Paul, 240
Litton, Gilbert, 531
Liu, Liang Y., 570
Lockhart, Paula K., 571
Lockwood, Dan, 187
Loftin, Colin, 10
Logan, Charles H., 191, 299
Logan, Gloria, 491
Lombardi, Donna M., 210, 245
Lombardi, John H., 210, 245–246
Los Angeles County Countywide Criminal Justice Coordination Committee, 571, 573
Louis, P. T., 266
Love, Bill, 461, 476
Loveless, Patricia, 326–327
Lovell, David G., 50
Lovrich, Nicholas P., 188
Lucas, Wayne L., 464, 468–469
Lundman, Richard J., 547
Lurigio, Arthur J., 126, 286, 300, 314, 378–379, 386–387, 502–503
Luther, Diane M., 184
Lutz, Gene M., 387
Lutze, Faith, 145

M

MacDonald, Donald G., 342
MacDonald, Malcomb, 236
Mace, Robyn R., 117
MacGrady, J., 349, 351
Mack, Dennis E., 144, 148
MacKenzie, Doris Layton, 10, 138–139, 143–145, 148–149, 572
MacMurray, Bruce K., 521
Madhouse, James W., 145
Maguire, Kathleen, 61, 168–169, 225, 258, 484, 486, 528
Maher, Richard J., 385
Mahoney, Barry, 379–380
Maier, Gary J., 183
Maine Criminal Justice Academy, 396, 425
Mainprize, Stephen, 327, 335
Mair, George, 248
Maller, R. A., 570
Maloney, Dennis, 441
Maltz, Michael D., 12, 440, 568–569, 573
Mande, Mary J., 206, 281, 285, 292
Maniglia, Rebecca, 467–468
Mann, Cora Mae, 42
Mann, Priscilla J., 443
Manning, W., 451
Marcus, David K., 503
Mardon, Steven, 402
Markley, Greg, 280

Marlette, Marjorie, 144, 352, 356
Marley, C. W., 353
Marlin, D., 276
Marquart, James W., 184, 235, 266
Marsden, Mary Ellen, 347, 375
Marshall, Cecil, 538
Marshall, Franklin H., 81
Marshall, Tony F., 16, 115–116
Martin, Dennis R., 457
Martin, Randy, 502
Martin, Susan E., 234
Martinez, Pablo E., 184, 240
Martinson, Robert, 51, 210, 225, 295, 393
Marx, Gary T., 321, 326
Marye, Linda, 531
Maryland Committee on Prison Overcrowding, 184
Maryland Department of Budget and Fiscal
  Planning, 400
Masin, Sandra, 463
Maslach, Christina, 449–450, 453–454
Mason, K. W., 351
Massachusetts Department of Corrections, 303
Massachusetts Halfway Houses, Inc., 364
Matek, Ord, 500
Mathias, Robert A., 386
Mathias, Rudolf E. S., 145
Matthews, R., 326
Matthews, Timothy, 432, 564
Matthewson, Terry L., 456
Mauser, Elizabeth, 570
Mawhiney, A. M., 377
Maxfield, Michael G., 316, 320, 326–327, 561
Mayer, Connie, 190
Maynard, Douglas W., 15
Mays, G. Larry, 512, 519, 522, 532
McAnany, Patrick D., 38, 46, 97, 452
McCabe, J. M., 451–452, 457
McCarthy, Belinda R., 48, 119, 259, 276, 278, 280,
  320, 336, 340, 347, 349–350, 369, 375, 383, 438,
  476–477, 534–535, 544, 572
McCarthy, Bernard J., 48, 119, 259, 280, 340, 347,
  349–350, 352, 363–364, 369, 375, 383, 476–477,
  534–535, 544, 572
McCleary, R., 569
McCleod, Maureen, 74, 78
McCollum, Loretta L., 523
McCord, Joan, 570
McCorkle, Richard C., 185
McCormack, Arlene, 470, 499
McCulloch, Sue, 560
McDonald, Douglas C., 4, 20, 190, 378–381, 387
McDonald, William F., 15
McDowall, David, 10
McGaha, Johnny, 11, 40
McGarrell, Edmund F., 277
McGee, Richard A., 185
McGillis, Daniel, 346
McGrath, Robert J., 248, 500
McGuire, James, 424
McKee, Cindy, 116–117
McKeown, Keith, 497–498

McManus, Patrick D., 279, 303
McReynolds, Veon, 450–571
McShane, Frank J., 12
McShane, Marilyn, 319
Meachum, Larry R., 309–313
Medler, Jerry F., 292, 296
Meeker, James W., 26
Megargee, Edwin I., 82, 174, 574
Meierhoefer, Barbara S., 316
Melnicoe, Shirley, 373
Mendelsohn, Robert I., 320
Merritt, Frank S., 384
Merry, Sally Engle, 117
Messinger, Sheldon L., 201, 209
MetaMetrics, Inc., 531
Metchik, Eric, 205, 235
Miethe, Terance D., 205
Migliore, Gerry, 36, 428
Miklosey, Edward, 38
Milan, M. A., 356
Milkman, R. H., 243
Miller, Cynthia J., 377
Miller, Dallas H., 342, 349
Miller, David E., 456
Miller, E. Eugene, 362, 364
Miller, L. E., 446, 456, 458
Miller, Marc, 88–89, 581
Miller, Marie D., 450
Miller, Robert D., 183
Miller, Thomas J., 22
Milling, L., 355–356
Mills, Darrell K., 451–452, 456
Mills, Jim, 134
Mills, William Reginald, 483
Minnesota Corrections Department, 561, 570
Minnesota Department of Corrections, 342
Minnesota Sentencing Guidelines Commission, 4, 20,
  98, 211
Minor, Kevin I., 458
Minor-Harper, Stephanie, 215, 257
Miranne, Alfred C., 580
Mitchell, Bill, 547
Mitchell, John J., Jr., 531
Moberg, D. Paul, 570
Mohn, Heidi, 186
Moini, Saira, 502
Monahan, John, 94
Monti, Vincent D., 22
Montilla, M. Robert, 364
Moore, Charles A., 205
Moore, Francis T., 193
Moore, Margaret A., 290, 461
Moracco, John C., 448–449
Moran, John S., 10
Morash, Merry, 143, 484
Morgenbesser, Leonard I., 425
Morrill, Calvin, 116–117
Morris, Norval, 88–89, 96, 581
Morrison, Richard D., 453, 457
Morton, Danielle C., 484
Moses, Marilyn C., 461

Mott, Joy, 495
Motiuk, Laurence L., 470
Moyer, Imogene L., 484
Mullen, Joan, 22, 123, 190
Muraskiun, Roslyn, 487
Murphy, Edward M., 542
Murphy, Joseph P., 425
Murphy, Terrence H., 247, 249, 377
Murray, Chris, 363, 365
Murty, K. S., 284
Musheno, Michael C., 199, 290, 301, 391–392, 401–402

N

Nacci, Peter, 185
Nadelson, C. C., 505
Nance, Margit, 507
Nardulli, Peter F., 118
National Alliance of Business, 366, 504
National Commission on Law Observance and Enforcement, 201
National Council on Crime and Delinquency, 4, 250–251
National Manpower Survey, 390
National Office for Social Responsibility, 343, 365
Nau, William C., 394
Neal, David, 204
Neithercutt, M. G., 22, 572
Nelson, C. M., 304
Nelson, Paul L., 341
Nemeth, Charles P., 390
Nesbitt, Charlotte A., 484–487
Neuenfeldt, Deborah, 10
Neuhoff, Elizabeth, 22
Nevada County Probation Department, 353
Nevada Legislative Council, 316
New Hampshire State Prison, 303
New Jersey Juvenile Delinquency Commission, 571
New Orleans Office of the Criminal Justice Coordinator, 326
New York State Department of Correctional Services, 145, 149, 302
New York State Unified Court System, 549
Ney, Becki, 262
Nichols, D. Keith, 556
Nicholson, George, 385
Nidorf, Barry J., 277
Noonan, Barrie A., 12
Noonan, Susan B., 572
Norland, Stephen, 443
Norman, Michael D., 550
Norman, Sherwood, 530
North Carolina Administrative Office of the Courts, 71
North Carolina Governor's Advisory Board on Prisons and Punishment, 184
Nouri, G. M., 451
Nowell, Carl, 431
Nowicki, Ed, 457

Nurco, David, 497
Nuss, Laura, 203, 205, 357

O

Oberst, Margaret, 85, 189
O'Connell, Paul, 291
Ogburn, Kevin R., 471
Ohio Department of Rehabilitation and Correction, 247
Ohio Parole Board, 94
Oklahoma State Board of Corrections, 184
O'Leary, Vincent, 244, 295
Olekalns, M., 447
Olivero, J. Michael, 10
Olsen, Eric, 44, 200, 203–204, 356
Onondaga County Probation Department, 314
Oregon Crime Analysis Center, 60, 134, 571
Oretega, Sandra, 279
Orsagh, Thomas, 347, 375
Oseroff, Andrew, 10
Osgood, D. Wayne, 513
Osler, Mark W., 138, 143, 145
Ostling, Richard N., 24
Ostroski, Trish, 321

P

Pace, Chaplain Arthur C., 462, 464, 466
Pacific Institute for Research and Evaluation, 544
Padgett, John F., 15
Paine, Whiton Stewart, 449
Palermo, George B., 10
Palm Beach County Florida Sheriff's Department, 312, 316, 320
Palmer, Ted, 537
Palone, N. J., 316
Palumbo, Dennis J., 134, 199
Pannell, William, 174
Paparozzi, Mario A., 431
Pappas, Nick, 187
Parent, Dale G., 48, 138–139, 143, 145, 148, 262, 358, 377, 379–380, 451
Parisi, Nicolette, 138–139, 142, 400
Parker, Jack B., 570–571
Parker, Robert Nash, 571
Parks, Evalyn, 439
Parnas, Raymond I., 23
Parsonage, William H., 240, 443, 457
Parsons, L. B., 82
Pastore, Ann L., 61, 168–169, 225, 258, 484, 486, 528
Pate, Tony, 394
Patel, Jody, 387
Patterson, Bernie L., 449
Peak, Ken, 346
Pearson, Frank S., 50, 127, 130–131, 135, 258, 438
Peat, Barbara J., 184–185
Pelfrey, William V., 39, 392, 425–426
Pellicciotti, Joseph M., 473

Pennell, Susan, 326
Pennsylvania Commission on Crime and Deliquency, 161
Pepino, Jane N., 505, 507
Petersen, David M., 140, 260
Petersilia, Joan M., 11, 26, 38, 41, 44, 50, 57–58, 66, 91, 126–128, 225, 236, 266, 294, 309, 311, 314, 316, 323, 326, 333, 335–336, 364, 369, 387, 445, 566, 500–502, 575, 578, 582–585
Peterson, Joyce, 50, 127, 582, 584
Philadelphia Prison System, 346
Philiber, Susan, 390–392, 394–396, 445–446
Pieper, Stephen L., 357–358, 360, 377, 432
Pierson, E. Jane, 440
Pierson, Timothy A., 82–84, 445, 499, 501
Pines, Ayala M., 454
Piquero, Alex, 145
Poethig, M., 303
Poklewski-Koziel, C., 276
Polk, Kenneth, 513
Pollock-Byrne, Joycelyn M., 488–489
Polsenberg, Christina, 571
Poole, Eric D., 185, 400, 452
Potts, Dennis W., 429–430
Power, Jacquelyn M., 291
Pratt, John D., 513
Prentky, Robert A., 499
President's Commission on Law Enforcement and the Adminstration of Justice, 118
Price, Albert C., 27
Price, Shelley J., 187
Priestley, Phillip, 424
Prison Fellowship, 571
Probation Association, 37
Program Resources Center, 571
Project New Pride, 544–545
Pugh, Michael, 498
Putnam, Jim, 321

Q

Quay, Herbert C., 82
Quigley, Peter, 298
Quinlan, J. Michael, 210
Quinn, James F., 189, 320–321, 326, 329
Quinsey, Vernon L., 571
Quiring, John, 321

R

Raciune, Trudy, 280, 301
Rackmill, Stephen J., 318
Rada, R. T., 474
Radosh, Polly F., 483–484
Ralph, H. Paige, 184
Ramish, Donald R., 76
Rans, Laurel L., 252
Rath, Quentin C., 458
Ratliff, Bascom W., 547
Rauma, David, 571

Rausch, Sharla P., 299
Read, Edward M., 428
Reckless, Walter C., 12
Reddin, Mary, 164
Reeves, R., 277–278, 284
Regoli, Robert M., 185, 400, 452
Reid, Sus Titus, 159
Reiss, Albert J., Jr., 505
Remington, Bob, 431
Remington, Marina, 431
Retsky, Harold G., 397
Rice, Marnie E., 571
Rich, T. F., 164
Richmond, C., 364
Richmond, M. S., 377
Richmond Times-Dispatch, 323, 325
Riechers, Lisa M., 145
Riggs, Rick, 280, 301
Riley, J. B., 365
Ring, Charles R., 400
Ringwalt, Christopher, 513
Robbins, Ira P., 266, 300
Robertson, James M., 441
Robins, Arthur J., 85
Robinson, Carol, 431
Robinson, J. J., 314
Robison, James O., 90
Rockowitz, Ruth J., 161, 168, 498
Rogers, Joseph W., 512, 519, 522, 532
Rogers, Robert, 326
Rogers, Susan, 349
Rohn, Warren, 321
Romero, Joseph, 443
Romig, Dennis A., 441, 530
Rose, Tracy, 468
Rosecrance, John, 66–68, 74, 90, 96, 140, 450, 455
Rosenberg, Jean, 304, 443, 500
Rosenblum, Robert, 341
Rosenfeld, Richard, 10
Rosenthal, Marguerite G., 314
Ross, Robert R., 487
Roth, Jeffrey A., 505
Rothman, David J., 201
Rothstein, P. F., 387
Roulet, Sister Elaine, 491–495
Roundtree, George A., 570–571
Roy, Sudipto, 117–118
Royse, David, 115
Ruback, Barry R., 183–184, 285
Rubel, Howard C., 76
Rubin, H. Ted, 78, 386
Rucker, Lila, 143, 484
Rudolph, Amy S., 380, 451
Rush, Fred L., Jr., 326, 336
Rush, George E., 314, 316, 519
Rush, Jeffrey P., 401
Rutherford, Andrew, 570
Rutherford, R. B., 304
Ruygrok, G., 369
Ryan, Patrick J., 425
Ryan, T. A., 489

S

Sabatino, D. A., 352
Sagatun, Inger, 523
St. Paul Police Department, 350
Salerno, Anthony W., 143
Salert, Barbara, 247
Salive, Marcel, 175
Salvation Army, 467
Samaha, Joel, 3
Sametz, Lynn, 540
Santamour, Miles, 498
Sapers, Howard, 387
Sapp, Allen D., 187
Saunders, Daniel G., 506–507
Savage, David A., 288
Savarese, Margaret R., 37–38
Saylor, W. G., 345
Schade, Linda S., 487
Schafer, N. E., 186, 498
Scheier, I. H., 474
Schiff, Martha F., 293–294
Schlatter, Gary, 326–327, 545
Schlossman, Steven, 187
Schmidt, Annesley K., 320–321, 327, 330
Schneider, Anne L., 387–388
Schneider, Peter R., 387–388
Schulman, Sam, 366, 369
Schumacher, Michael A., 284, 288, 301
Schumacker, Randall E., 243
Schuman, Alan M., 431
Schweid, Robert E., 11
Scott, J. E., 477
Scull, Andrew, 295
Sechrest, Dale K., 48, 439, 451, 458
Sechrest, Lee, 42, 82, 168, 183, 187
Segall, William E., 570
Seidenstat, Paul, 191
Seiter, Richard P., 364, 372
Selke, William, 478
Selva, Lance H., 115
Selvaggio, Marialena, 470
Selye, Hans, 448
Semanchik, David A., 184
Senese, Jeffrey D., 188
Services to Unruly Youth Program, 504
Seymour, Anne, 462
Shane-DuBow, Sandra, 44, 200, 203–204, 356
Shapiro, Carol, 131, 135, 439
Shapiro, Elizabeth R., 499
Shapiro, Walter, 233
Shaw, James W., 138, 143–145, 148
Shawver, Lois, 425
Shearer, Robert A., 429–430, 445
Sheehy, Gregory, 188
Shelden, Randall G., 158, 166, 513
Shepperd, Val, 248
Shichor, David, 42, 76, 187, 326
Shields, L. F., 303
Shiller, Gene, 547
Shilton, Mary K., 48

Shipley, Bernard E., 570–571
Shively, Michael, 143
Shockley, Carol, 70
Shover, Neal, 570
Sichel, Joyce L., 379–380
Siedschlaw, Kurt, 277
Siegel, Gayle R., 350
Sieh, Edward W., 392, 395
Silbert, James D., 556
Silverman, Mitchell, 192, 443, 451
Silvia, Jerry, 312
Simmons, James G., 82
Simms, Brian, 184
Simone, Margaret V., 533
Singer, Richard G., 260–261
Sinnett, E. R., 366
Skolnick, Jerome H., 15
Skovron, Sandra Evans, 184
Sluder, Richard D., 429–430, 445
Smith, Albert G., 424, 428, 431, 436, 454
Smith, Brian M., 446, 463
Smith, Douglas A., 571
Smith, Freddie V., 63
Smith, Gerald W., 90
Smith, Gordon B., 185
Smith, Linda G., 568, 573
Smith, Maurice B., 10
Smith, Robert R., 352, 356
Smith, Stephen H., 183
Smykla, John O., 199, 478
Snarr, Richard W., 396
Snell, Tracy L., 220, 484
Snyder, Keith B., 538
Snyder-Joy, Zoann, 134
Soderlund, Curt, 387
Somers, Ira, 316
Sontheimer, Henry, 538
Soskin, R. M., 303
Souryal, Claire, 138, 145, 149
South Carolina Department of Probation, Parole, and Pardon Services, 266
South Carolina State Reorganization Commission, 148–149, 156, 183–184, 326, 336
Spangenberg, Robert L., 125
Speckart, George, 496
Spencer, J. William, 68, 72, 74, 457
Spica, Arthur R., Jr., 73, 401
Spieker, Diane J., 82–84
Spillane, Joseph, 187
Spohn, Cassia, 42
Stadler, Donald W., 266
Staples, William G., 386, 388
Steadman, Henry J., 498
Steelman, Diane, 209
Steffensmeier, Darrell, 10, 203, 485
Steiger, John, 571
Stellwagen, Lindsey D., 499
Stephan, James, 185
Stephens, Gene, 74
Stephenson, Geoffrey M., 326
Steppe, Cecil H., 63

Stern, Barry J., 498
Steury, Ellen Hochstedler, 80–81
Stevens, Gail Flint, 495, 570
Stevenson, William Ferree, 304, 443, 500–501
Stewart, James K., 185
Stewart, Katheryn, 571
Stiles, Don R., 351
Stinchcomb, Jeanne B., 403, 426–427, 431, 446, 449–450, 457–458
Stipak, B., 314, 326, 336
Stohr-Gillmore, Mary K., 188
Stohr-Gillmore, Michael W., 188
Stojkovic, Stan, 156, 186
Stone, Susan, 134
Stone, William E., 155
Stratton, Neil R. M., 505
Streifel, Cathy, 203, 485
Strong, Ann, 442
Struckhoff, David R., 584
Sullivan, C., 82
Sullivan, Monique, 503
Sussman, Alan, 556
Sutherland, Edwin H., 12
Swain, Kay, 505
Sweeney, Laura T., 4

T

Tapper, Donna M., 504
Task Force on Corrections, 37
Taxman, Faye S., 126, 292
Taylor, Ralph B., 571
Taylor, William J., 144, 416–417
Teake, R., 446
Tedder, Ed, 429
Tennessee Department of Corrections, 351
Teplin, Linda A., 571
Tepper, B. D., 334
Thomas, Charles W., 296, 400
Thomas, Fate, 457
Thomas, Robert L., 159, 446
Thompson, Carol Y., 570
Thomson, Doug, 38, 44, 46, 97, 452
Thornburgh, Richard, 126
Tilow, Neil F., 281, 287, 293–294
Timasheff, Nicholas S., 37–38
Tobolowsky, Peggy M., 189
Toborg, Mary, 261
Toch, Hans, 185, 391–392, 446
Tonry, Michael H., 23, 26, 44, 89, 91, 242, 246
Torborg, Mary A., 320
Tontodonato, Pamela, 74, 76
Towberman, Donna B., 248
Townsend, Gail, 279, 288
Tracy, Alice, 461, 512
Travis, Lawrence F., III, 61, 63, 126, 203, 210, 280, 282, 295, 364, 370–371, 383, 476–477
Travisano, Anthony P., 61
Traynelis-Yurek, E., 478

Treger, Harvey, 383, 504
Trembley, Richard E., 570
Troia, Nina, 571
Trook-White, F., 470, 473–474
Trupin, Eric, 10
Tunnell, Kenneth D., 570–571
Turner, Susan, 50, 66, 91, 126–128, 236, 266, 496–497, 535, 545, 566, 571, 573, 578, 582–584
Turturici, Jack, 188

U

Umbreit, Mark S., 115–116, 118
Unger, Cindie A., 187
U.S. Bureau of Census, 56, 159
U.S. Bureau of Justice Assistance, 10, 497
U.S. Bureau of Justice Statistics, 397, 570
U.S. Bureau of Prisons, 345, 498
U.S. Civil Rights Commission, 505
U.S. Department of Justice, 179, 220, 351, 515, 523
U.S. General Accounting Office, 127, 134
U.S. National Highway Traffic Safety Administration, 386–387
U.S. News & World Report, 31
U.S. Office of Justice Programs, 126
U.S. Office of Juvenile Justice and Delinquency Prevention, 190–191
U.S. Office of Technology Assessment, 321
U.S. Probation Division, 386
U.S. Sentencing Commission, 4, 19–20, 139, 238, 259, 570
U.S. Youth Development and Delinquency Prevention Administration, 504
University of Hawaii at Manoa, 571
Uriel, Patricia, 355, 357

V

Valenzuela, Aurora, 248
Valente Ernest, Jr., 117
Vallaneuva, Enrique, 248
van Alstyne, David J., 571
Van Ness, Shela R., 127, 444
Van Stelle, Kit R., 570
Van Voorhis, Patricia, 299
Vaughn, Joseph B., 325, 327, 332–333
Vaughn, Michael, 187
Vega, Manuel, 184
Velt, Edward, 428
Verber, Jean, 164
Vigdal, Gerald L., 266
Virginia Department of Corrections, 450, 504
Virginia Department of Mental Health and Retardation, 161, 497
Virginia Joint Legislative Audit and Review Commission, 119
Visher, Christy A., 555, 570

Vito, Gennaro F., 63, 138–142, 144, 260, 295, 564, 570, 572, 575–577
Vittitow, Tom, 280, 301
Volenik, Adrienne E., 521
Von Cleve, Elizabeth, 10
von Hirsch, Andrew, 23, 42–44, 89, 94, 210

W

Wadlington, W., 526
Wagner, Dennis, 50, 135, 287, 507
Wahler, Cindy, 396, 425
Wakefield, Penny, 206
Waldo, Gordon P., 311–312, 322, 331, 349, 569
Waldron, Thomas W., 547
Walker, James L., 326, 329
Walker, Mickie C., 11
Walker, Nigel, 314
Walker, Samuel, 39, 41, 43, 50–51, 90–91, 276, 393–395, 574–575
Wallace, W. LeAnn, 20
Wallace, William L., 570–571
Wallerstedt, John F., 570–571
Walters, Glenn D., 188
Ward, Richard H., 145
Warner, George, 185
Warnock, Kae M., 145
Washington County Community Corrections, 287
Washington State Department of Social and Mental Health, 501
Washington State Sentencing Guidelines Commission, 98
Watkins, David, 457
Watkins, John C., Jr., 435, 512
Watson, Robert J., 391–392, 396
Watts, Ronald, 326, 335
Way, Gary L., 277
Webb, Gary L., 209
Wedge, Robert, 537
Wedlund, R. B., 478
Wehmhoefer, Richard A., 452
Weintraub, Benson B., 72, 74, 77
Wells, David, 193, 498
Welsh, Wayne N., 183
Wenck, Ernst A., 90
Werner, Paul D., 10
Wertleib, Ellen C., 11, 499
Wheeler, Gerald R., 378–380, 451, 556
Wheeler, William L., 466
Whitcomb, Debra, 341, 499
White, David, 498
White, H. P., 288, 570–571
White, Susan O., 42
Whitehead, John T., 40, 396–397, 426, 446–448, 452–454, 456–458
Wiebush, Richard G., 137, 538–539
Wiedemann, Carl F., 22
Wiederanders, Mark R., 375, 549
Wiggenborn, Allan H., 326

Wilber, Lalena N., 10
Wilcenski, Gregory B., 38
Wilkins, Leslie T., 240, 251
Williams, Coleen, 571
Williams, D. R., 474
Williams, Frank P., III, 326
Williams, Linda M., 443
Williams, Lynne A., 478
Williams, Sharon A., 304, 484, 531
Williams, Susan Darst, 186, 357–358, 360, 377–378, 385
Williamson, H., 446
Willis, Jane, 461
Willman, Herb C., Jr., 534–535
Willstadter, R., 440
Wilson, Anna V., 570
Wilson, Deborah G., 564, 570–572, 584
Wilson, George P., 362–363, 365, 370, 372, 383
Wilson, James Q., 584
Winfree, L. Thomas, Jr., 184–185, 237, 498
Winter, Bill, 461, 464, 469–470
Winterfield, Laura A., 276, 378, 380, 383
Wisconsin Department of Health and Social Services, 296, 437, 505, 507
Wish, Eric D., 496
Witt, Anne Dryden, 189
Witte, Ann D., 347, 349
Wolfe, N. T., 184
Wolford, Bruce I., 304, 377, 396
Wollan, Laurin A., Jr., 20
Wood, D., 314, 316, 498
Wood, Dorothy, 164
Wooldredge, John D., 160, 572
Wooten, Harold, 316
Worzella, Charles, 378, 381
Wozniak, John F., 61
Wren, Greg, 451
Wright, Jennifer, 321–323, 336
Wright, Kevin N., 91, 174–175, 246
Wylen, Jane, 549

Y

Yablonsky, Lewis, 11
Yeager, Matthew G., 441
Young, Malcolm C., 386
Young, Marlene A., 76
Young, Warren, 89
Yurek, F. G., 478
Yurkanin, Ann, 260

Z

Zamist, Ida, 378–379, 383
Zatz, Marjorie S., 43
Zevitz, Richard G., 389
Zimmerman, Sherwood E., 173, 248, 502
Zimring, Franklin, 44
Zoet, Thomas H., 276, 499, 501
Zupan, Linda L., 188, 425

Subject Index

A

ABC, 466
About Face, 143, 547
Acceptance of responsibility, 69–70
Accreditation programs, 303
   community corrections, 303
ACLU, 24
Act to Regulate the Treatment and Control of
   Dependent, Neglected and Delinquent Children,
   516
Actuarial prediction, 88
Adjudications, 521
Adjudicatory hearings, 521
Administrative Office of the U.S. Courts, 69, 71–72
Adult Inmate Management System (AIMS), 186
Adult Rehabilitation Centers, 467
Aftercare, 5
Age, 247
   risk instruments, 247
Agency, theory of, 475
Aging-out process, 556
Aggravating circumstances, 60, 78–79, 528
   defined, itemized, 78
   juveniles, 528
AIDS, 10, 185–186, 302, 433, 467, 496, 502–503
   community corrections, 302
   jails and prisons, 185–186
   PO interactions with clients, 432
   special needs offenders, 496, 502–503
   volunteers, 467
AIMS (Adult Inmate Management System), 82
Alaska Department of Corrections, 376
Alaska Long-Term Classification Form, 177–178
Alaska needs scale, 87
Alcatraz, 176, 365
Alcoholics Anonymous, 189–190, 365–366, 440, 567
   specialized offender caseloads, 440
Allegheny Academy, 541–542
Allegheny County Jail, 490
Allen County, Indiana, Juvenile Electronic
   Monitoring Program Pilot Project (EMP), 543,
   546
Alston Wilkes Society, 464
Alternative dispute resolution (ADR), 115–117, 186
   centers, 117
   defined, 115
   jails and prisons, 186
Alternative sentencing, 19–20
Alternatives to incarceration, 311
American Correctional Association, 172, 283, 302,
   391, 398, 402–403, 432, 444–446, 486–487, 562
   female offender policy, 486–487
   founding, 398
   training seminars, 444–445
American Jail Association, 432, 562
American Prison Association, 172, 437
American Probation and Parole Association
   (APPA), 398, 432, 446, 562
Amnesty International, 233
Anamnestic prediction, 88
Army model, 547
Arraignments, 16
Arrest, 13
Ashe, Sheriff Michael, 165
Assessment centers, 426–428
Assessment instruments, 84–89
At-Risk Babies Crib, 466
Auburn State Penitentiary, 171
Augustus, John, 34–36, 40–41, 120
Automatic transfers, 523
Avertable recidivists, 578–579

B

Back-end solutions to overcrowding, 428
Bail, 13, 120
Bail Reform Act of 1966, 1984, 162
Balanced approach, 441
Battered spouses, 504
Bedford Hills, 491–495
Behavioral reform, 40
Big Brothers, 470, 539
Big Sisters, 470, 539
Bolthouse, Barry, 402
Bond Supervision Program, 327–328
Booking, 5, 13
Boot camps, 142–153, 172, 547–548
   costs, 148

defined, 142–143
effectiveness, 148–149
goals, 143–145
juvenile involvement, 547–548
prison overcrowding, 145
profile of clients, 145
rationale, 143
recidivism, 144–145
types of programs, 145–148
Boston Children's Aid Society, 37
Boston House of Corrections, 35, 37
Boston Municipal Court, 40
Boston Offender Project (BOP), 542–543
Bridewell Workhouse, 157–158
Bridge Home for Young Men, 364
Broadman, Judge Howard, 18
Brockway, Zebulon, 43, 172, 199
Brokers, 442
Brook House, 364
Brooklyn, Connecticut Community Correctional
        Center, 466
Brown, Quentin, 289
Bureaucratization, 454–455
Burke, Joseph, 384
Burnout, 446–458
    defined, 449
    gender differences, 447–448
    sources, 450–457
    ways of combatting, 457–458
Butler (New York) Shock Incarceration Correctional
        Facility, 547

C

California Board of Prison Terms, 204
California Department of Corrections' Parole and
        Community Services Division, 424
California Parole Board, 194
California Parole Division, 431
California Youth Authority, 556
Campbell, Charles Rodman, 344
Camp Monterey Shock Incarceration Facility, 146
Camp ranches, 534
Camps, 534
Capone, Al, 176
Career criminals, 12
Caseload assignment models, 439–441
Caseloads for POs, 437–441
    defined, 437
    ideal sizes, 437–438
Caseworkers, 397
Catch-22, 342
Cellular telephone devices, 322
Certifications, 522–523
Charge reduction bargaining, 15
Chesterfield County, Virginia Jail, 323–324
Children in need of supervision (CHINS), 532
Children's tribunals, 516

Child-saver movement, 515
Child Sexual Abuse Treatment Program (CSATP),
        507
Child sexual abusers, 499–502
Choice Program, 187
Chronic offenders, 513
Citizen-volunteers, 302
Citizen value system, 244
Civil procedure, 115–117
Clark, Benjamin C., 37
Classification instruments, 81–84
    female scales, 83–84
Classification, 4, 10, 174–178
    elements included, 92
    functions, 84
    inmate, 174–178
    offenders, 4, 10
"Cleared by arrest," 574
Clinical prediction, 88–89
Cobb, Ronald, 256
Combination sentence, 138
Community-based corrections, 47, 565–566
    objectives, 565–566
Community control, 309–311
Community control house arrest, 311–312
Community control programs, 313–314
Community correction act, 278–279
    client-resident traits, 279
    Kansas, 279
    Ohio, 279
    Virginia, 279
Community corrections, 5, 277–304
    characteristics, 283
    defined, 277–278
    functions, 280–281, 286–292
    goals, 283–286
    history, 282–283
    philosophy, 279–281
Community-based corrections program, 277–278
Community Diversion Incentive Act, 279
Community model, 47
Community Protective Program (COPP), 292
Community reintegration, 50, 120–121, 319–320
    home confinement, 319–320
Community Residential Centers, 296, 376
Community service, 385–386
Community service orders, 383–385, 387
Community Services System, 504
Community Specialists Corporation, 541
Community work centers (CWCs), 296–297
Commutation, 257
Conditional diversion, 119–120
Conditional release, 206, 231–232, 257
Conditional sanctions, 529
Confidentiality of PSIs, 70
Congregate system, 171
Continuous signaling devices, 321–322
Continuous signaling transmitters, 322
Controller value system, 244
Conventional model, 440

Conventional model with geographic considerations, 440
Cook, Rufus, 37
Cope House, 368, 373, 375
Correctional Reform Act of 1983, 309
Corrections, 4, 17–20, 425
Corrections officers, 390–391, 425
  distinguished from POs, 390–391
  recruitment of women, 425
Corrections paraprofessionals, 475
Corrections volunteers, 461
Court dockets, 16
Covenant House, 362, 500
Creaming, 135, 559, 565
Creative sentencing, 19–20, 140
  shock probation and, 140
Crime Classification Index, 9
Crime control, 48–50, 210
Crime deterrence, 210
Criminal contamination, 363
Criminal procedure, 115
Criminogenic environments, 50
Crofton, Sir Walter, 172, 198–199
Crucible of Crime, 159
Custodial sanctions, 529

D

Dangerousness, 28, 81–84
  predictions, 28
Day fine programs, 380–383
Day fines, 380–381
Day parole programs, 341
Day pass programs, 341
Day reporting centers, 277, 357–360, 377–378
  defined, 358, 377
Decriminalization, 116
Defendant, 15
Defendant's sentencing memorandum, 74
Deinstitutionalization, 296, 498–499
  community corrections, 296
  mentally ill offenders, 498–499
Deliberate indifference, 436
Demand waivers, 523
Denton House, 364
Depo-Provera treatments, 443
Detainer warrants, 163
Detectors, 442
Determinate sentencing, 22, 26, 203–206
  criticisms, 205
  states using, 26
Deterrence, 51
Differential association theory, 12
Diminished rights, 333
Direct supervision jails, 188
Discretion, judicial, 27
Discretionary waivers, 523
Dispute resolution, 186
Diversion, 5, 7, 119–124
  conditional, 119–120

  criticisms, 122–124
  defined, 14
  functions, 122–123
  history and philosophy, 120–121
  unconditional, 119–120
Double jeopardy, 16–17
Dreyfous House, 364
Drug and Alcohol-Dependent Offenders, 496–497
Due process model, 43–44
DWI, 378
  fine programs, 378

E

Early childhood intervention services, 508
Early release, 36, 206–209
EARN-IT, 118
Economic philosophy, 41
Educational training, 345
  work release, 345
Educators, 442
Eighth Amendment, 36, 318, 332–333
  electronic monitoring, 332–333
  home confinement, 318
El Camino House, 364
Electronic monitoring, 72, 320–337, 543–546
  client profile, 327–329
  constitutionality, 331–333
  costs, 323–324
  defined, 320
  deterrence, 334
  ethics, 329–330
  history and early uses, 320–321
  issues, 329–335
  juvenile probationers, 543–546
  probationers and, 72
  pros and cons, 326–327
  public safety, 334
  types, 321–322
Electronic monitoring devices, 320
Elizabeth Fry Center, 123
Elmira Reformatory, 43, 172, 199–200
Enablers, 442
Enforcers, 442
Experience programs, 534
Extralegal factors, 203–204

F

False negatives, 90–91, 568
False positives, 90–91, 568
Family group homes, 533
Family violence, 506–507
Federal Bureau of Prisons, 43, 166, 464
  volunteers used, 464
Federal Juvenile Delinquency Act, 38
Federal Prison System, 210
Federal Probation and Pretrial Officers Association, 428–429

Fellowship House, 364
Felonies, 7–8
Felony sentences, 59
Female probationers and parolees, 484–495
  criticisms of programs, 487–490
  numbers, 484–485
  special programs and services, 486–487, 490–495
Fifth Amendment, 17, 318
  home confinement, 318
Financial-community service model, 386–387
Fine programs, 278–383
  collection problems, 379–380
Firearms and PO work, 428–431
First Amendment, 474
First-offenders, 11, 60–61
Fishkill, New York, Correctional Facility, 342
Fishman, Joseph, 159
Florida Assessment Center, 426–428
Florida Community Control Program (FCCP), 287, 309–311
  profile of clients, 310
Folger, Abigail, 233
Foster Grandparent Program, 467–468
Foster homes, 532–533
Fourteenth Amendment, 44, 260, 318, 333, 474, 527
  electronic monitoring, 333
  home confinement, 318
  juveniles, 527
  volunteers, 474
Fourth Amendment, 318, 332
  electronic monitoring, 332
  home confinement, 318
Freedom of Information Act (FOIA), 70
Fresh Start, Inc., 364
Front-door solutions, 184
Front-end solution, 33, 41, 428
Furlough programs, 352–357
  criticisms, 356–357
  defined, 352
  functions, 354–356
  goals, 353–354
  history, 352–353
Furloughs, 174, 259

G

Gaols, 157, 169
GED programs, 347, 358, 466
Georgia Department of Corrections Special Alternatives Incarceration (SAI), 143, 147, 285–286
Georgia Intensive Supervised Probation Program, 128–129
  criticisms, 134–137
  program elements, 128
German Marshall Fund, 358
Get-tough movement, 36, 234–236, 518, 539, 582
Good marks, 199
Good-time credits, 22, 172–173, 193–194, 203–204, 206–209

prison crowding, 208
  state computations, 208
Good-time system, 199
Grand juries, 15
Gray Panthers, 461
Group homes, 533
Guidelines-based sentencing, 22

H

Habitual offender statutes, 21–22
Hagan, Michael, 204
Halfway house programs, 362–376
  criticisms, 372–376
  defined, 362
  functions, 366–370
  history, 362–363
  profile of clients, 370–372
  types, 363–364
Halfway houses, 260, 362–376
Halfway-in houses, 364–365
Halfway-out houses, 364–365
Harris County Courts Regimented Intensive Probation Program, 146
Harris County Juvenile Detention Center, 335
Hayes, Rutherford B., 172, 398
Helping Hand Halfway Home, Inc., 364
Hennepin County Adult Correctional Facility Industrial Program, 345
Hinckley, John, 581
Home confinement, 309
Home confinement programs, 309–320, 546–547
  constitutionality, 317–319
  defined, 309
  deterrent effect, 320
  early uses, 309–314
  goals, 314–315
  issues, 316–320
  juvenile participation, 546–547
  profile of clients, 315–316
Home incarceration, 132
Homeward Bound, 534–535
Hope Center Wilderness Camp, 534
Hope Hall, 363
Hope Houses, 363
House arrest, 309
House of Industry, 363
Howard, John, 169–170

I

Idaho Intensive Supervised Probation Program, 131
  criticisms, 134–137
I-Level classification, 82
Immunity, 431–432
  PO work, 431–432
IMPACT, 148
Implicit plea bargaining, 15
Indeterminate sentencing, 22, 26, 200–201

Indeterminate sentencing (*continued*)
   pros and cons, 201–202
   states using, 26
Indictments, 15
Informations, 15
Index offenses, 9
Initial appearance, 13
Inmate classification, 174
Inmate classification systems, 174–178
Inmate discipline, 184–185
Inmate violence, 184–185
Institute for Mediation and Conflict Resolution, 478
Institutional risk, 94
Intake screening, 521
Intensive supervised parole, 258–259
Intensive supervised probation (ISP), 126–138, 538–543
   characteristics, 127–128, 137–138, 538–539
   criticisms, 134–138
   defined, 126
   juvenile programs, 538–543
Intensive Treatment Unit Experiment, 560
Intermediate punishments, 276, 308–337
Intermittent sentences, 139
International Association of Residential and
   Community Alternatives (IARCA), 286
International Halfway House Association (IHHA),
   363
"Invisible jails," 358
Iowa Classification Risk-Assessment Scale, 93
Iowa Risk Assessment Model, 252
Isaac T. Hopper Home, 363

J

Jail as a condition of probation, 139
Jail bootcamps, 148
Jail design, 186–187
Jail overcrowding, 17–18, 27, 140, 193, 292
   community corrections, 292
Jail personnel, 182
Jail populations, 156–157
   compared with U.S. population, 156
Jail privatization, 190–191
Jail Removal Initiative, 163
Jail space, 183
Jailhouse lawyers, 260–261
Jails, 17, 156–169, 181–182
   characteristics, 156–157, 181–182
   compared with prisons, 156, 181–182
   defined, 17
   functions, 161–164
   history, 157–160
   inmate characteristics, 164–169
   juveniles, 163
   numbers, 160
   overcrowding, 17–18, 27, 140
James Marshall Treatment Program, 562
Job placement services, 366
   halfway houses, 366
Job satisfaction/dissatisfaction, 451

Joseph Harp Correctional Center, 179
Judicial discretion, 19, 27, 231–232
   probation, 231–232
   PSIs and, 71
Judicial dispositional options, 529–536
Judicial plea bargaining, 15
Judicial reprieves, 34
Judicial waivers, 522–523
Judicial workloads, 16
Jurist value system, 244
Jury trials, 16
Just-deserts philosophy, 26, 36, 47
Justice model, 21, 43–44, 203
Juvenile Court Act, 516
Juvenile courts, 513, 517–519
   compared with criminal courts, 517–519
   discretion, 522
   jurisdictional variations, 521–522
Juvenile delinquency, 511–512
Juvenile Diversion/Non-Custody Intake Program
   (JD/NCI), 530
Juvenile Diversion Program (JDP), 531
Juvenile halls, 518
Juvenile Intensive Supervision Programs (JISP),
   538–543
   characteristics, 539
   electronic monitoring, 543–544
Juvenile Offender Laws, 549
Juvenile offenders, 511–556
   defined, 511–512
   intensive supervised probation, 537–548
Juvenile parole, 548–550
   purposes, 548
Juvenile parole and probation revocation, 548–556
Juvenile parole policies, 551
Juvenile parolees, 548–549, 551–552
   recidivism, 551–552
Juvenile reforms, 514–417

K

Kalamazoo, Michigan, Probation Enhancement
   Program, 458
Kansas City Preventive Patrol Experiments, 394
Kennedy, Robert, 233
Kenton County, Kentucky, 322–323, 336–337
Knox County Jail, 164
Knox County Sheriff's Department Organized
   Reserve Officers, 462–463, 474
Krenwinkle, Patricia, 194, 233

L

Labor turnover among POs, 445–446
Latent functions, 209
Law enforcement, 12–13
   components, 12–20
Law Enforcement Assistance Administration
   (LEAA), 120–121, 160, 282, 357, 392–394, 477

Legislative waivers, 523
Liability issues, 431–437
Life imprisonment, 356
Life-without-parole sentences (LWOP), 356
Lincoln Park House, 367–368
Literacy, Education, and Reading Network
    (L.E.A.R.N.), 291
Literacy services, 291
Leo-Coneys, Judith, 75
Level of custody, 10
Lockdown, 176
Lock-ups, 160
Los Angeles County Probation Department, 480
Louisiana Intensive Motivational Program of
    Alternative Correctional Treatment (IMPACT),
    147
Louisiana State Penitentiary, Angola, 172
Love, Judge Jack, 321

M

Machiavellii, Niccolo, 237
Maconochie, Captain Alexander, 172, 198–199
Maison de Force, 170
Malinosky, Francis, 75
Management by objectives (MBO), 458
Mandatory releases, 257
Mandatory sentencing, 24, 97, 200–201
Manifest functions, 209
Manson, Charles, 194, 233
Manual of Correctional Standards, 437
MAP, 368
Marks of commendation, 198
Mark system, 172–173
Maryland Correctional Institution for Women, 461
Maslow's hierarchy of needs, 392
Massachusetts Department of Youth Services, 542
Massachusetts Halfway House Association, 368
Massachusetts Halfway Houses, Inc. (MHHI), 364
Massachusetts Parole Board, 249
Massachusetts Parole Board Release Risk
    Classification Instrument, 254
Massachusetts Prison Commission, 365
Maxi-maxi prisons, 176–178
Maximum-security classification, 175–176
Maximum-security custody, 10, 47
Maximum-security prisons, 176
Medical model, 42–43
Medium-security classification, 175–176
Medium-security custody, 10
Medium-security prisons, 176
Megargee Inmate Typology, 174–175
Mentally ill, 161, 168, 497–499
    and jails, 161, 168
Michigan Department of Corrections, 487–488
Minimum-security classification, 174–175
Minimum-security custody, 10
Minnesota assessment of client risk scale, 86
Minnesota Correctional Facility at Shakopee,
    463–464

Minnesota Corrections Department, 561
Minnesota Multiphasic Personality Inventory
    (MMPI), 82, 174–175
Minnesota Sentencing Guidelines Grid, 25
Misdemeanants, 8
Misdemeanors, 7–8
Mississippi Regimented Inmate Discipline Program
    (RID), 147
Missouri Division of Probation and Parole, 454,
    468–469
Missouri Sexual Offender Program (MOSOP),
    501–502
Mistretta, John, 24
Mitigating circumstances, 60, 69, 528–529
    defined, itemized, 69
    juveniles, 528–529
MMPI (Minnesota Multiphasic Personality
    Inventory), 82, 174–175
Mixed sentences, 139
Model Juvenile Court Act of 1968, 551
Modular jail designs, 187
Morris, Ricky, 553
Mosier, Kellie, 204
Mutual Agreement Plan (MAP), 368

N

Narratives in PSIs, 69
National Center for Missing and Exploited Children,
    478
National Correctional Policy on Female Offender
    Services, 486–487
National Council on Crime and Delinquency, 437
National Crime Survey, 4
    criticisms, 9–10
    defined, 9
National Institute of Corrections (NIC) Model
    Classification Project, 536–537
National Institute of Corrections Prison Classification
    Model, 252
National Office for Citizen Participation (NOCP),
    464
National Prison Association, 172, 199
Needs assessment, 85–88
Negligence, 431–437, 480
    paraprofessionals, 480
    PO work, 431–437
Net widening, 298, 335–336, 564–565
    electronic monitoring, 335–336
Nevada County Probation Department, 334
    eligibility criteria for electronic monitoring, 334
Nevada Department of Corrections, 249
New generation jails, 188
New Jersey Intensive Supervised Probation Program,
    50, 129–131
    criticisms, 134–137
    effectiveness, 130–131
    program elements, 130
    selection criteria, 130
New York City Probation Department, 49

New York Governor's Special Committee on
    Criminal Offenders, 393–394
New York House of Refuge, 514
New York's Prison Nursery/Children's Center,
    491–496
NIMBY syndrome, 293–294
Norfolk Island, 198
Nolo contendere pleas, 267
Nominal dispositions, 529–530
Nonavertable recidivists, 578–579
Norristown, Pennsylvania, Montgomery County
    Youth Center, 467
No true bills, 16
Numbers game model, 440

O

Oahu Community Correctional Center, 355
Objective parole criteria, 245–251
Obremski, Russell, 229–230, 232
Offender-Based Transaction Statistics (OBTS), 58
Offender-client ratios, 40
Offender-clients, 66
Offender control, 41
Offender reintegration, 209–210
Offense-seriousness scores, 80
    calculating, 80
    U.S. sentencing guidelines, 80–81
Offense severity, 245–246
Office of Children and Youth, 467
Office of Juvenile Justice and Delinquency
    Prevention (OJJDP), 550
Officer-client interactions, 442–444, 453–454
Ohio Adult Parole Authority, 477
Ohio Department of Rehabilitation and Correction,
    345
Ohio Department of Youth Services (ODYS),
    539–541
Ohio Experience, 539–541
Ohio Parole Board, 246–247, 250
Oklahoma Community Treatment Program, 288
Oklahoma Extended Limits of Confinement Act,
    310, 312–313
Oklahoma Regimented Inmate Discipline Program
    (RID), 146
Orientations toward PO roles, 442–444
Outreach centers, 383
Outreach workers, 478
Overcrowding, jail and prison, 145, 182–183, 193

P

Page, Samuel Lee, 228–229, 232
Palm Beach County Florida Sheriff's Department,
    312, 322
Paraprofessionals, 475–481
    defined, 475–476
    education and training, 476–477

legal liabilities, 480–481
work roles, 477–480
Pardons, 199–200
Parens patriae, 518–519
Parent education services, 508
PARJO, 549
Park Drive Pre-Release Center, 359
Parole, 3, 33, 197–227, 231–232
    conditional, 231
    contrasted with probation, 33
    defined, 33, 197
    functions, 209–213
    history, 197–200
    parole boards, 231–232
    philosophy, 209
    trends, 220–227
    unconditional, 231
Parole boards, 33, 231–273
    composition, 237
    decision making, 240–243
    early-release discretion, 231–232
    functions, 238–240
    get-tough movement, 234
    orientations, 244
    philosophy, 238
    programs, 257–260
Parolees, 168–169, 213–220, 429
    adults, 213–214
    assaults against POs, 429
    characteristics, 217
    jails, 168–169
    profiling, 213–220
    sentence lengths, 219
Parole Officer Aide Program (POAP), 477
Parole officers, 4, 390–458
    carrying firearms, 131
    caseloads, 418–423
    characteristics, 398–400
    duties, 400–402
    firearms use, 428–431
    liability issues, 431–437
    recruitment criteria, 404–418
    salaries, 399–400
Parole programs, 257–260, 392–397
    criticisms, 392–397
Parole revocation, 261–266
Parole revocation hearings, 262–266
Participative management, 458
Penitentiaries, 170
Penitentiary Act, 170
Pennsylvania Department of Corrections, 464
Pennsylvania system, 170
Perkins, Robert Lee, 83
Petit juries, 16
Petitions, 521–522
Philadelphia Society for Alleviating the Miseries of
    Public Prisons, 158, 514
Physically handicapped persons, 502
Plea bargaining, 15
    charge reduction, 15

implicit, 15
judicial, 15
sentence recommendation, 15
sitive Peer Culture, 561–562
edicting dangerousness, 81–82, 88–91
actuarial prediction, 88
anamnestic prediction, 88
clinical prediction, 88–89
ediction, 89
ediction instruments, 89–91, 192
prison uses, 192
edispositional reports, 535
ejean, Dalton, 233
eparole Conditional Supervision Program (PPCS), 340
eponderance of the evidence standard, 574
erelease, 257
erelease programs, 340, 357–360
esentence investigation reports (PSIs), 68–77, 89–90, 95, 191, 402, 434–435
confidentiality of, 70–71, 434–435
costs of preparation, 76
criticisms of, 732
defendant's sentencing memorandum, 74
defined, 68
errors, 434–435
functions and uses, 71–72, 95
narrative portion, 69
PO work, 402
preparation of, 71
presumptive sentencing, 77
privatizing, 76–77, 191
public safety, 211–212
recommendations, 96
sample report, 99–112
victim impact statements, 774–75
esentence investigations, 37, 40, 66–68
defined, 68
esentments, 15
esident's Commission on Law Enforcement and Administration of Justice, 392
esumptive sentencing, 23, 66, 77
probation officers and, 66
PSI preparation, 77
etrial detainees, 157, 166
etrial detention, 161
etrial diversion, 118–119
eventive confinement, 94–95
eventive detention, 163
ior records, 247
risk prediction, 247
ison admissions, 181
ison-bound offenders, 119
ison industry, 171
isoner and Community Together (PACT), 118
isoner classification systems, 193
isoners, 178–181
isonization, 276
ison overcrowding, 182–183, 208, 210–211, 225
good-time credits, 208

Prison privatization, 190–191
Prisons, 17, 169–194
characteristics, 169–173
compared with jails, 181–182
defined, 17, 169
functions, 173–174
overcrowding, 17–18, 27
prisoner classification, 174–178
Privatization, 190–191, 298–301
community corrections, 298–301
cost-effectiveness, 299
criticisms, 299–300
jail and prison, 190–191
services delivery, 301
Probable cause, 269
Probatio, 32
Probation, 5, 17, 32–63, 96–97, 231–232
defined, 17, 32–33
distinguished from parole, 33
functions, 48–51
history, 33–35
major events, 39
models, 42–48
philosophy, 38–42
trends, 61–63, 96–97
unconditional, 231–232
Probation and parole programs for juveniles (PPPs), 551–552
Probation programs, 392–397
criticisms, 392–397
Probationable Offenders Rehabilitation Training Program (P.O.R.T.), 369–370
Probationer-clients, 66, 429
Probationers, 52–61, 168–169, 429
assaults against POs, 429
demographic characteristics, 55
felony convictions and, 52
jails, 168–169
number on probation, 56
profiled, 52–59
Probation officers, 5, 41, 66–68, 136, 390–458
caseloads, 41, 136, 418–423
characteristics, 398–400
duties, 400–402
distinguished from corrections officers, 390–391
firearms use, 428–431
liability issues, 431–437
PSI preparation, 66–68
recruitment criteria, 403
role in sentencing, 66–68
salaries, 399
selection requirements, 403–418
women, 425
Probation Subsidy Program, 282
Professionalization, 392, 395–397
characteristics, 396–397
POs, 392, 395–397
Professionals, 475
Program evaluation, 559–587
defined, 559

Program for Female Offenders, Inc. (PFO), 290,
    466–467, 490
Programmed contact devices, 322
Progressive Era, 42
Project CARE, 350
Project Green Hope, 492
Project New Pride, 544–545
Project Outward Bound, 534
Project Recidivism and Alcohol-Related Crimes of
    Aggression, 349–350
Project Re-Direction, 284
Prosecution, 13
Prosecution-bound offenders, 119
Prosecutorial priorities, 14
Prosecutorial waivers, 522–523
Public risk, 94
Punishment, 51

Q

Qualified immunity and POs, 431–432

R

Ralph W. Alvis House, 364
Ranches, 534
Rand Corporation, 575
Rap House, 367–368
Reagan, President Ronald, 581
Rearrests, 573–575
Recidivism, 12, 51, 123, 136, 144–145, 243, 568–578
    boot camps, 144–145
    defined, 568
    divertees, 123
    ISP programs, 136
    parolees, 243, 581–584
    probationers, 51, 581–584
    public policy, 580–581
Recidivism rates, 572
Recidivists, 11–12, 60–61, 88–89, 578–580
    characteristics, 578–580
Reconvictions, 575–576
Reform schools, 515
Regimented Inmate Discipline Program (RID), 547
Regulator value system, 244
Rehabilitation, 27, 40–41, 50, 295–296, 366
    community corrections, 295–296
    halfway houses, 366
Rehabilitation model, 43
Reincarcerations, 577
Release on own recognizance (ROR), 13, 192, 497
Respondeat superior, 480
Restitution, 383–385
Restitution programs, 386–388
Restorative case management, 441
Restorative justice, 116
Reynolds, James Bronson, 37–38
Reverse waiver hearings, 524

Revocation actions, 576–577
Revoking parole and probation, 548–556, 57
Rifkin, Joel, 233
Rikers Boot Camp High Impact Incarceratic
    Program (HIIP), 144–145, 148
Risk assessment, 84–89, 211–212, 246–247
    defined, 84–85
    parole boards, 246–247
Risk assessment instruments, 84–89, 246–247
    effectiveness, 91–93
    reliability and validity, 89–90
Risk instruments, 81–84
Risk-needs assessment, 85–88
Risk/needs instruments, 93–94
    applications, 93
Ritter, Father Bruce, 362, 500
Role ambiguity, 452–453
Role conflict, 451–452
Role senders, 450
Rolling, Danny Harold, 233–234
ROR, 13
Runaways, 478
Rush, Dr. Benjamin, 170
Ryan, Judge David, 324

S

Salient Factor Scores, 249–253
    defined, 251
    scale illustrated, 253
Salvation Army, 467
Sanctioner value system, 244
Sand Hills Vocational Delivery System (VDS
San Francisco Project, 438–439
San Quentin, 7
Santiago, Samuel, 313
Scared Straight, 547
Screening cases, 14
Seattle Police Department Community Servi
    Section, 478
Secure facilities, 535
See Our Side Program (SOS), 531–532
Selective incapacitation, 94–95
Self-reports, 9
Sentence recommendation bargaining, 15
Sentencing, 16–17, 44, 200–201
    determinate, 22
    functions, 20–22
    guidelines-based, 22
    indeterminate, 22, 200–201
    issues, 26–28
    mandatory, 23–24, 200–201
    presumptive, 23
Sentencing disparities, 42, 44, 211
Sentencing hearings, 77–78
Sentencing memorandum, 74
Sentencing Reform Act of 1984, 19–20
Sentencing reforms, 44
Services delivery, 503–504

Services to Unruly Youth Program, 504
Settlements, 37
Sex offenders, 367–368, 499–502, 560
    halfway houses, 367–368
    programs, 560
SFS 76, SFS 81, 249, 251–253
Shakedowns, 365
SHAPE-UP Program, 547
Shawcross, Arthur, 226
Shelton, Vincent, 434
Shock incarceration, 142 (*see also* Boot camps)
Shock parole, 135, 258–260
Shock probation, 33, 135, 137–142, 260, 547–548
    community safety, 141
    defined, 138
    effectiveness, 141–142
    ISP programs, 135
    juvenile involvement, 547–548
    philosophy and objectives, 139–140
Shock probationers, 138–139, 166–167
    jails, 166–167
Short-term confinement, 535
Silver, Robert, 384
Singleton, Larry, 348–349
Sing Sing Prison, 199
Sirhan Sirhan, 233
Situational offenders, 11
Smart sentencing, 126
Smith, Charles, 402
Social Skills and Human Relationships Training
        Program, 560
Society for the Prevention of Pauperism, 514
Solitary confinement, 171
South Carolina Department of Probation, Parole and
        Pardon Services (DPPPS), 132–133
South Carolina Intensive Supervised Probation
        Program, 132–134
    classification of offenders, 132
    criticisms, 134–137
    effectiveness, 133–134
    program elements, 132
Specialized caseloads model, 440
Special needs offenders, 303–304, 496–508
    community corrections, 303–304
Speck, Richard, 242
Speedy Trial Act of 1974, 161–162
Speedy trials, 16
Split sentencing, 33, 137–142
Staff training, 302–303
    community corrections, 302–303
Standard parole, 258
Standard probation, 124–126
    criticisms, 125
    priorities, 125
Staten Island Day-Fine Experiment, 381–383
State Prison of Southern Michigan, 172
State Use Industries (SUI), 350
Stateville Correctional Center (Illinois), 345
Status offenders, 512
Status offenses, 513

Statutory releases, 257
Stress, 446–458
    defined, 448
    sources, 450–457
    ways of mitigating, 457–458
Stroud, Robert "Birdman," 176
Study release, 259–260, 350–351
Study release programs, 350–351
    defined, 350
    inmate eligibility requirements, 350–351
    pros and cons, 351
Summary offenses, 8
Sunshine Mediation Center, 116–117
Supervised mandatory release, 207
Supervision fees, 132, 136–137

T

Talbert House, 293–294, 364
Task Force on Corrections, 437
Task Force on Parole, 206
Tate, Sharon, 233
Technical program violations, 577–578
Temporary Asylum for Disadvantaged Female
        Prisoners, 363
Temporary release programs, 341
Tennessee Corrections Act, 283
Tennessee Department of Corrections, 375
Tennessee State Prison, 164
Texas Department of Corrections, 373
Thatcher, Judge Oxenbridge, 34
THE PROGRAM, 490
Three-strikes-and-you're-out legislation, 235
Tickets of leave, 199
Tier system, 171
Total institutions, 169
Totality of circumstances, 119, 574
Traditional probation, 126
Transfers, 522–523
Transitional Aid Research Project (TARP), 366
Transportation, 198
Treater value system, 244
Treatment Alternatives to Street Crime (TASC), 497
Treatment model, 42–43
True bills, 16

U

Unconditional diversion, 119–120
Unconditional release, 206, 231–232, 257
Uniform Crime Reports, 4, 574
    criticisms, 9
    defined, 8–9
U.S. Army Correctional Activity (USACA), 547
U.S. Parole Board, 210
U.S. Parole Commission, 246, 313–314
U.S. Sentencing Commission, 23–24, 258–259
U.S. sentencing guidelines, 69–70, 203–206, 456

University Settlement, 37–38
User fees, 119
Utah Division of Youth Corrections, 550

V

Vander Meulen House, 364
Van Dieman's Land, 198
Van Houten, Leslie, 194, 233
Victim and Witness Protection Act of 1982, 383–384
Victim compensation programs, 346
Victim impact statements, 74
Victim-offender mediation model, 387
Victim-offender reconciliation, 117–118
Victim-Offender Reconciliation Project (VORP), 117–118
Victim reparations model, 387
Victims of Crime Act of 1984, 346–347
Victim/Witness Bill of Rights, 288, 290
Violence, 505
Virginia Department of Corrections, 450, 504
VisionQuest, 545
Vocational-technical education programs, 187
Vocational training, 22, 345
    work release, 345
Volunteers, 461–475
    criticisms, 468–472
    defined, 461
    economical considerations, 472–473
    ethical problems using, 470–472
    examples, 464–468
    legal liabilities, 473–475
    numbers of, 464
    work duties, 461–464
Volunteers in Prison, 465

W

Waiver hearings, 523–524
Waivers, 522–623
Walnut Street Jail, 158, 170
Washington State Penitentiary, Walla Walla, 186
Wechsler Adult Intelligence Scale, 478
Wickersham Commission, 201
Wilderness experiences, 534
Willie Horton incident, 354
Women in corrections, 425
Women's Activities and Learning Center Program (WALC), 491
Women's Community Center (WCC), 377
Women's Educational Opportunity Act, 491
Women's prisons, 191
Women's Self-Help Center Outreach Program, 123
Work release programs, 174, 259–260, 340–350
    criticisms, 349–350
    defined, 340
    eligibility requirements, 348–349
    functions, 343–347
    goals, 342
Work releasees, 168, 347–348
    profiled, 347–348
Workhouses, 157–158
Workloads, judicial, 16

Y

Youth Center, 468
Youth Diversion, 530
Youths at risk, 530
Youth Service Bureaus (YSBs), 530

KALAMAZOO VALLEY
COMMUNITY COLLEGE

Presented By

Jeff Shouldice